THE WRITINGS OF THE
Ante-Nicene Fathers

VOLUME ONE:
Apostolic Father
Justin Martyr
Irenaeus

Edited by
THE REV. ALEXANDER ROBERTS, DD
JAMES DONALDSON, LLD

Chronologically arranged, with
brief notes and prefaces by
A. CLEVELAND COXE, DD

the apocryphile press
BERKELEY, CA
www.apocryphile.org

apocryphile press
BERKELEY, CA

Apocryphile Press
1700 Shattuck Ave #81
Berkeley, CA 94709
www.apocryphile.org

First published in Edinburgh in 1867. First American edition, 1885. Apocryphile Press edition, 2007.

Printed in the United States of America
ISBN 1-933993-44-8

PREFACE

This volume, containing the equivalent of three volumes of the Edinburgh series of the ANTE-NICENE FATHERS, will be found a library somewhat complete in itself. The Apostolic Fathers and those associated with them in the third generation, are here placed together in a handbook, which, with the inestimable Scriptures, supplies a succinct autobiography of the Spouse of Christ for the first two centuries. No Christian scholar has ever before possessed, in faithful versions of such compact form, a supplement so essential to the right understanding of the New Testament itself. It is a volume indispensable to all scholars, and to every library, private or public, in this country.

The American Editor has performed the humble task of ushering these works into American use, with scanty contributions of his own. Such was the understanding with the public: they were to be presented with the Edinburgh series, free from appreciable colour or alloy. His duty was (1) to give historic arrangement to the confused mass of the original series; (2) to supply, in continuity, such brief introductory notices as might slightly popularize what was apparently meant for scholars only, in the introductions of the translators; (3) to supply a few deficiencies by short notes and references; (4) to add such references to Scripture, or to authors of general repute, as might lend additional aid to students, without clogging or overlaying the comments of the translators; and (5) to note such corruptions or distortions of Patristic testimony as have been circulated, in the spirit of the forged Decretals, by those who carry on the old imposture by means essentially equivalent. Too long have they been allowed to speak to the popular mind as if the Fathers were their own; while, to every candid reader, it must be evident that, alike, the testimony, the arguments, and the silence of the Ante-Nicene writers confound all attempts to identify the ecclesiastical establishment of "the Holy Roman Empire," with "the Holy Catholic Church" of the ancient creeds.

In performing this task, under the pressure of a virtual obligation to issue the first volume in the first month of the new year, the Editor has relied upon the kindly aid of an able friend, as typographical corrector of the Edinburgh sheets. It is only necessary to add, that he has bracketed all his own notes, so as to assume the responsibility for them; but his introductions are so separated from those of the translators, that, after the first instance, he has not thought it requisite to suffix his initials to these brief contributions. He regrets that the most important volume of the series is necessarily the experimental one, and comes out under disadvantages from which it may be expected that succeeding issues will be free. May the Lord God of our Fathers bless the undertaking to all my fellow-Christians, and make good to them the promise which was once felicitously chosen for the motto of a similar series of publications: "Yet shall not thy teachers be removed into a corner any more, but thine eyes shall see thy teachers."

A. C. C.

JANUARY 6, 1885.

N.B. — The following advertisement of the original editors will be useful here: —

The Ante-Nicene Christian Library is meant to comprise translations into English of all the extant works of the Fathers down to the date of the first General Council held at Nice in A.D. 325. The sole provisional exception is that of the more bulky writings of Origen. It is intended at present only to embrace in the scheme the *Contra Celsum* and the *De Principiis* of that voluminous author; but the whole of his works will be included should the undertaking prove successful.

The present volume has been translated by the Editors.[1] Their object has been to place the English reader as nearly as possible on a footing of equality with those who are able to read the original. With this view they have for the most part leaned towards literal exactness; and wherever any considerable departure from this has been made, a *verbatim* rendering has been given at the foot of the page. Brief introductory notices have been prefixed, and short notes inserted, to indicate varieties of reading, specify references, or elucidate any obscurity which seemed to exist in the text.

Edinburgh, 1867.

---

[1] This refers to the first volume only of the original series.

INTRODUCTORY NOTICE.

[A.D. 100–200.] THE APOSTOLIC FATHERS are here understood as filling up the second century of our era. Irenæus, it is true, is rather of the sub-apostolic period; but, as the disciple of Polycarp, he ought not to be dissociated from that Father's company. We thus find ourselves conducted, by this goodly fellowship of witnesses, from the times of the apostles to those of Tertullian, from the martyrs of the second persecution to those of the sixth. Those were times of heroism, not of words; an age, not of writers, but of soldiers; not of talkers, but of sufferers. Curiosity is baffled, but faith and love are fed by these scanty relics of primitive antiquity. Yet may we well be grateful for what we have. These writings come down to us as the earliest response of converted nations to the testimony of Jesus. They are primary evidences of the Canon and the credibility of the New Testament. Disappointment may be the first emotion of the student who comes down from the mount where he has dwelt in the tabernacles of evangelists and apostles: for these disciples are confessedly inferior to the masters; they speak with the voices of infirm and fallible men, and not like the New-Testament writers, with the fiery tongues of the Holy Ghost. Yet the thoughtful and loving spirit soon learns their exceeding value. For who does not close the records of St. Luke with longings to get at least a glimpse of the further history of the progress of the Gospel? What of the Church when its founders were fallen asleep? Was the Good Shepherd "always" with His little flock, according to His promise? Was the Blessed Comforter felt in His presence amid the fires of persecution? Was the Spirit of Truth really able to guide the faithful into all truth, and to keep them in the truth?

And what had become of the disciples who were the first-fruits of the apostolic ministry? St. Paul had said, "The same commit thou to faithful men, who shall be *able to teach others also*." How was this injunction realized? St. Peter's touching words come to mind, "I will endeavour that ye may be able after my decease to have these things always in remembrance." Was this endeavour successfully carried out? To these natural and pious inquiries, the Apostolic Fathers, though we have a few specimens only of their fidelity, give an emphatic reply. If the cold-hearted and critical find no charm in the simple, childlike faith which they exhibit, ennobled though it be by heroic devotion to the Master, we need not marvel. Such would probably object: "They teach me nothing; I do not relish their multiplied citations from Scripture." The answer is, "If you are familiar with Scripture, you owe it largely to these primitive witnesses to its Canon and its spirit. By their testimony we detect what is spurious, and we identify what is real. Is it nothing to find that your Bible is their Bible, your faith their faith, your Saviour their Saviour, your God their God?" Let us reflect also, that, when copies of the entire Scriptures were rare and costly, these citations were "words fitly spoken, — apples of gold in pictures of silver." We are taught by them also that they obeyed the apostle's precept, "Let the word of Christ dwell in you richly in all wisdom; teaching and admonishing," etc. Thus they reflect the apostolic care that men should be raised up able to teach others also.

Their very mistakes enable us to attach a higher value to the superiority of inspired writers. They were not wiser than the naturalists of their day who taught them the history of the Phœnix and other fables; but nothing of this sort is found in Scripture. The Fathers are inferior in kind as well as in degree; yet their words are lingering echoes of those whose words were spoken "as the Spirit gave them utterance." They are monuments of the power of the Gospel. They were made out of such material as St. Paul describes when he says, "Such were some of you." But for Christ, they would have been worshippers of personified Lust and Hate, and of every crime. They would have lived for "bread and circus-shows." Yet to the contemporaries of a Juvenal they taught the Decalogue and the Sermon on the Mount. Among such beasts in human form they reared the sacred home; they created the Christian family; they gave new and holy meanings to the names of wife and mother; they imparted ideas unknown before of the dignity of man as man; they infused an atmosphere of benevolence and love; they bestowed the elements of liberty chastened by law; they sanctified human society by proclaiming the universal brotherhood of redeemed man. As we read the Apostolic Fathers, we comprehend, in short, the meaning of St. Paul when he said prophetically, what men were slow to believe, "The foolishness of God is wiser than men; and the weakness of God is stronger than men. . . . But God hath chosen the foolish things of the world to confound the wise; and God hath chosen the weak things of the world to confound the things which are mighty; and base things of the world, and things which are despised, hath God chosen, yea, and things which are not, to bring to nought things that are."

A. C. C.

DECEMBER, 1884.

Contents of Volume I

	PAGE
PREFACE	v
INTRODUCTORY NOTICE	vii
I. ST. CLEMENT. Epistle to the Corinthians	1
II. MATHETES. Epistle to Diognetus	23
III. POLYCARP. Epistle to the Philippians	31
Martyrdom	37
IV. IGNATIUS. Epistle to the Ephesians	45
Epistle to the Ephesians: Shorter and Longer Versions	49
Epistle to the Magnesians	59
Epistle to the Trallians	66
Epistle to the Romans	73
Epistle to the Philadelphians	79
Epistle to the Smyrnæans	86
Epistle to Polycarp	93
Appendix. Syriac Version	97
Spurious Epistles	105
Martyrdom	127
V. BARNABAS. Epistle	133
VI. PAPIAS. Fragments	151
VII. JUSTIN MARTYR. The First Apology	159
The Second Apology	188
Dialogue with Trypho, a Jew	194
The Discourse to the Greeks	271
Hortatory Address to the Greeks	273
On the Sole Government of God	290
On the Resurrection, Fragments	294
Other Fragments	300
Martyrdom	303
VIII. IRENÆUS. Against Heresies	309
Fragments	568

THE APOSTOLIC FATHERS

INTRODUCTORY NOTE

TO THE

FIRST EPISTLE OF CLEMENT TO THE CORINTHIANS

[A.D. 30–100.] CLEMENT was probably a Gentile and a Roman. He seems to have been at Philippi with St. Paul (A.D. 57) when that first-born of the Western churches was passing through great trials of faith. There, with holy women and others, he ministered to the apostle and to the saints. As this city was a Roman colony, we need not inquire how a Roman happened to be there. He was possibly in some public service, and it is not improbable that he had visited Corinth in those days. From the apostle, and his companion, St. Luke, he had no doubt learned the use of the Septuagint, in which his knowledge of the Greek tongue soon rendered him an adept. His copy of that version, however, does not always agree with the Received Text, as the reader will perceive.

A co-presbyter with Linus and Cletus, he succeeded them in the government of the Roman Church. I have reluctantly adopted the opinion that his Epistle was written near the close of his life, and not just after the persecution of Nero. It is not improbable that Linus and Cletus both perished in that fiery trial, and that Clement's immediate succession to their work and place occasions the chronological difficulties of the period. After the death of the apostles, for the Roman imprisonment and martyrdom of St. Peter seem historical, Clement was the natural representative of St. Paul, and even of his companion, the "apostle of the circumcision;" and naturally he wrote the Epistle in the name of the local church, when brethren looked to them for advice. St. John, no doubt, was still surviving at Patmos or in Ephesus; but the Philippians, whose intercourse with Rome is attested by the visit of Epaphroditus, looked naturally to the surviving friends of their great founder; nor was the aged apostle in the East equally accessible. All roads pointed towards the Imperial City, and started from its *Milliarium Aureum*. But, though Clement doubtless wrote the letter, he conceals his own name, and puts forth the brethren, who seem to have met in council, and sent a brotherly delegation (Chap. lix.). The entire absence of the spirit of Diotrephes (St. John, Ep. III. 9), and the close accordance of the Epistle, in humility and meekness, with that of St. Peter (Ep. I, v. 1–5), are noteworthy features. The whole will be found animated with the loving and faithful spirit of St. Paul's dear Philippians, among whom the writer had learned the Gospel.

Clement fell asleep, probably soon after he despatched his letter. It is the legacy of one who reflects the apostolic age in all the beauty and evangelical truth which were the first-fruits of the Spirit's presence with the Church. He shares with others the aureole of glory attributed by St. Paul (Phil. iv. 3), "His name is in the Book of Life."

The plan of this publication does not permit the restoration, in this volume, of the recently discovered portions of his work. It is the purpose of the editor to present this, however, with other recently discovered relics of primitive antiquity, in a supplementary volume, should the undertaking meet with sufficient encouragement. The so-called second Epistle of Clement is now known to be the work of another, and has been relegated to another place in this series.

The following is the INTRODUCTORY NOTICE of the original editors and translators, Drs. Roberts and Donaldson: —

THE first Epistle, bearing the name of Clement, has been preserved to us in a single manuscript only. Though very frequently referred to by ancient Christian writers, it remained unknown to the scholars of Western Europe until happily discovered in the Alexandrian manuscript. This MS. of the Sacred Scriptures (known and generally referred to as Codex A) was presented in 1628 by Cyril, Patriarch of Constantinople, to Charles I., and is now preserved in the British Museum. Subjoined to the books of the New Testament contained in it, there are two writings described as the Epistles of one Clement. Of these, that now before us is the first. It is tolerably perfect, but there are many slight *lacunæ*, or gaps, in the MS., and one whole leaf is supposed to have been lost towards the close. These *lacunæ*, however, so numerous in some chapters, do not generally extend beyond a word or syllable, and can for the most part be easily supplied.

Who the Clement was to whom these writings are ascribed, cannot with absolute certainty be determined. The general opinion is, that he is the same as the person of that name referred to by St. Paul (Phil. iv. 3). The writings themselves contain no statement as to their author. The first, and by far the longer of them, simply purports to have been written in the name of the Church at Rome to the Church at Corinth. But in the catalogue of contents prefixed to the MS. they are both plainly attributed to one Clement; and the judgment of most scholars is, that, in regard to the first Epistle at least, this statement is correct, and that it is to be regarded as an authentic production of the friend and fellow-worker of St. Paul. This belief may be traced to an early period in the history of the Church. It is found in the writings of Eusebius (*Hist. Eccl.*, iii. 15), of Origen (*Comm. in Joan.*, i. 29), and others. The internal evidence also tends to support this opinion. The doctrine, style, and manner of thought are all in accordance with it; so that, although, as has been said, positive certainty cannot be reached on the subject, we may with great probability conclude that we have in this Epistle a composition of that Clement who is known to us from Scripture as having been an associate of the great apostle.

The date of this Epistle has been the subject of considerable controversy. It is clear from the writing itself that it was composed soon after some persecution (chap. i.) which the Roman Church had endured; and the only question is, whether we are to fix upon the persecution under Nero or Domitian. If the former, the date will be about the year 68; if the latter, we must place it towards the close of the first century or the beginning of the second. We possess no external aid to the settlement of this question. The lists of early Roman bishops are in hopeless confusion, some making Clement the immediate successor of St. Peter, others placing Linus, and others still Linus and Anacletus, between him and the apostle. The internal evidence, again, leaves the matter doubtful, though it has been strongly pressed on both sides. The probability seems, on the whole, to be in favour of the Domitian period, so that the Epistle may be dated about A.D. 97.

This Epistle was held in very great esteem by the early Church. The account given of it by Eusebius (*Hist. Eccl.*, iii. 16) is as follows: "There is one acknowledged Epistle of this Clement (whom he has just identified with the friend of St. Paul), great and admirable, which he wrote in the name of the Church of Rome to the Church at Corinth, sedition having then arisen in the latter Church. We are aware that this Epistle has been publicly read in very many churches both in old times, and also in our own day." The Epistle before us thus appears to have been read in numerous churches, as being almost on a level with the canonical writings. And its place in the Alexandrian MS., immediately after the inspired books, is in harmony with the position thus assigned it in the primitive Church. There does indeed appear a great difference between it and the inspired writings in many respects, such as the fanciful use sometimes made of Old-Testament statements, the fabulous stories which are accepted by its author, and the general diffuseness and feebleness of style by which it is distinguished. But the high tone of evangelical truth which pervades it, the simple and earnest appeals which it makes to the heart and conscience, and the anxiety which its writer so constantly shows to promote the best interests of the Church of Christ, still impart an undying charm to this precious relic of later apostolic times.

[N.B. — A sufficient guide to the recent literature of the Clementine MSS. and discoveries may be found in *The Princeton Review*, 1877, p. 325, also in Bishop Wordsworth's succinct but learned *Church History to the Council of Nicæa*, p. 84. The invaluable edition of the *Patres Apostolici*, by Jacobson (Oxford, 1840), with a critical text and rich *prolegomena* and annotations, cannot be dispensed with by any Patristic inquirer. A. C. C.]

THE FIRST EPISTLE OF CLEMENT TO THE CORINTHIANS[1]

CHAP. I. — THE SALUTATION. PRAISE OF THE CORINTHIANS BEFORE THE BREAKING FORTH OF SCHISM AMONG THEM.

The Church of God which sojourns at Rome, to the Church of God sojourning at Corinth, to them that are called and sanctified by the will of God, through our Lord Jesus Christ: Grace unto you, and peace, from Almighty God through Jesus Christ, be multiplied.

Owing, dear brethren, to the sudden and successive calamitous events which have happened to ourselves, we feel that we have been somewhat tardy in turning our attention to the points respecting which you consulted us;[2] and especially to that shameful and detestable sedition, utterly abhorrent to the elect of God, which a few rash and self-confident persons have kindled to such a pitch of frenzy, that your venerable and illustrious name, worthy to be universally loved, has suffered grievous injury.[3] For who ever dwelt even for a short time among you, and did not find your faith to be as fruitful of virtue as it was firmly established?[4] Who did not admire the sobriety and moderation of your godliness in Christ? Who did not proclaim the magnificence of your habitual hospitality? And who did not rejoice over your perfect and well-grounded knowledge? For ye did all things without respect of persons, and walked in the commandments of God, being obedient to those who had the rule over you, and giving all fitting honour to the presbyters among you. Ye enjoined young men to be of a sober and serious mind; ye instructed your wives to do all things with a blameless, becoming, and pure conscience, loving their husbands as in duty bound; and ye taught them that, living in the rule of obedience, they should manage their household affairs becomingly, and be in every respect marked by discretion.

CHAP. II. — PRAISE OF THE CORINTHIANS CONTINUED.

Moreover, ye were all distinguished by humility, and were in no respect puffed up with pride, but yielded obedience rather than extorted it,[5] and were more willing to give than to receive.[6] Content with the provision which God had made for you, and carefully attending to His words, ye were inwardly filled[7] with His doctrine, and His sufferings were before your eyes. Thus a profound and abundant peace was given to you all, and ye had an insatiable desire for doing good, while a full outpouring of the Holy Spirit was upon you all. Full of holy designs, ye did, with true earnestness of mind and a godly confidence, stretch forth your hands to God Almighty, beseeching Him to be merciful unto you, if ye had been guilty of any involuntary transgression. Day and night ye were anxious for the whole brotherhood,[8] that the number of God's elect might be saved with mercy and a good conscience.[9] Ye were sincere and uncorrupted, and forgetful of injuries between one another. Every kind of faction and schism was abominable in your sight. Ye mourned over the transgressions of your neighbours: their deficiencies you deemed your own. Ye never grudged any act of kindness, being "ready to every good work."[10] Adorned by a thoroughly virtuous and religious life, ye did all things in the fear of God. The commandments and ordinances of the Lord were written upon the tablets of your hearts.[11]

CHAP. III. — THE SAD STATE OF THE CORINTHIAN CHURCH AFTER SEDITION AROSE IN IT FROM ENVY AND EMULATION.

Every kind of honour and happiness[12] was bestowed upon you, and then was fulfilled that which is written, "My beloved did eat and drink, and was enlarged and became fat, and kicked."[13] Hence flowed emulation and envy, strife and sedition, persecution and disorder, war and captivity. So the worthless rose up against the honoured, those of no reputation

---

[1] In the only known MS. of this Epistle, the title is thus given at the close.
[2] [Note the fact that the Corinthians *asked* this of their brethren, the personal friends of their apostle St. Paul. Clement's own name does not appear in this Epistle.]
[3] Literally, "is greatly blasphemed."
[4] Literally, "did not prove your all-virtuous and firm faith."
[5] Eph. v. 21; 1 Pet. v. 5.
[6] Acts xx. 35.
[7] Literally, "ye embraced it in your bowels." [Concerning the complaints of Photius (ninth century) against Clement, see Bull's *Defensio Fidei Nicænæ*, Works, vol. v. p. 132.]
[8] 1 Pet. ii. 17.
[9] So in the MS., but many have suspected that the text is here corrupt. Perhaps the best emendation is that which substitutes συναισθήσεως, "compassion," for συνειδήσεως, "conscience."
[10] Tit. iii. 1.
[11] Prov. vii. 3.
[12] Literally, "enlargement."
[13] Deut. xxxii. 15.

against such as were renowned, the foolish against the wise, the young against those advanced in years. For this reason righteousness and peace are now far departed from you, inasmuch as every one abandons the fear of God, and is become blind in His faith,[1] neither walks in the ordinances of His appointment, nor acts a part becoming a Christian,[2] but walks after his own wicked lusts, resuming the practice of an unrighteous and ungodly envy, by which death itself entered into the world.[3]

CHAP. IV. — MANY EVILS HAVE ALREADY FLOWED FROM THIS SOURCE IN ANCIENT TIMES.

For thus it is written: "And it came to pass after certain days, that Cain brought of the fruits of the earth a sacrifice unto God; and Abel also brought of the firstlings of his sheep, and of the fat thereof. And God had respect to Abel and to his offerings, but Cain and his sacrifices He did not regard. And Cain was deeply grieved, and his countenance fell. And God said to Cain, Why art thou grieved, and why is thy countenance fallen? If thou offerest rightly, but dost not divide rightly, hast thou not sinned? Be at peace: thine offering returns to thyself, and thou shalt again possess it. And Cain said to Abel his brother, Let us go into the field. And it came to pass, while they were in the field, that Cain rose up against Abel his brother, and slew him."[4] Ye see, brethren, how envy and jealousy led to the murder of a brother. Through envy, also, our father Jacob fled from the face of Esau his brother.[5] Envy made Joseph be persecuted unto death, and to come into bondage.[6] Envy compelled Moses to flee from the face of Pharaoh king of Egypt, when he heard these words from his fellow-countryman, "Who made thee a judge or a ruler over us? wilt thou kill me, as thou didst kill the Egyptian yesterday?"[7] On account of envy, Aaron and Miriam had to make their abode without the camp.[8] Envy brought down Dathan and Abiram alive to Hades, through the sedition which they excited against God's servant Moses.[9] Through envy, David underwent the hatred not only of foreigners, but was also persecuted by Saul king of Israel.[10]

CHAP. V. — NO LESS EVILS HAVE ARISEN FROM THE SAME SOURCE IN THE MOST RECENT TIMES. THE MARTYRDOM OF PETER AND PAUL.

But not to dwell upon ancient examples, let us come to the most recent spiritual heroes.[11] Let us take the noble examples furnished in our own generation. Through envy and jealousy, the greatest and most righteous pillars [of the Church] have been persecuted and put to death.[12] Let us set before our eyes the illustrious[13] apostles. Peter, through unrighteous envy, endured not one or two, but numerous labours; and when he had at length suffered martyrdom, departed to the place of glory due to him. Owing to envy, Paul also obtained the reward of patient endurance, after being seven times thrown into captivity,[14] compelled[15] to flee, and stoned. After preaching both in the east and west, he gained the illustrious reputation due to his faith, having taught righteousness to the whole world, and come to the extreme limit of the west,[16] and suffered martyrdom under the prefects.[17] Thus was he removed from the world, and went into the holy place, having proved himself a striking example of patience.

CHAP. VI. — CONTINUATION. SEVERAL OTHER MARTYRS.

To these men who spent their lives in the practice of holiness, there is to be added a great multitude of the elect, who, having through envy endured many indignities and tortures, furnished us with a most excellent example. Through envy, those women, the Danaids[18] and Dircæ, being persecuted, after they had suffered terrible and unspeakable torments, finished the course of their faith with stedfastness,[19] and though weak in body, received a noble reward. Envy has alienated wives from their husbands, and changed that saying of our father Adam, "This is now bone of my bones, and flesh of my flesh."[20] Envy and strife have overthrown great cities and rooted up mighty nations.

---

[1] It seems necessary to refer αὐτοῦ to *God*, in opposition to the translation given by Abp. Wake and others.
[2] Literally, "Christ;" comp. 2 Cor. i. 21, Eph. iv. 20.
[3] Wisd. ii. 24.
[4] Gen. iv. 3–8. The writer here, as always, follows the reading of the Septuagint, which in this passage both alters and adds to the Hebrew text. We have given the rendering approved by the best critics; but some prefer to translate, as in our English version, "unto thee shall be his desire, and thou shalt rule over him." See, for an ancient explanation of the passage, Irenæus, *Adv. Hær.*, iv. 18, 3.
[5] Gen. xxvii. 41, etc.
[6] Gen. xxxvii.
[7] Ex. ii. 14.
[8] Num. xii. 14, 15. [In our copies of the Septuagint this is not affirmed of Aaron.]
[9] Num. xvi. 33.
[10] 1 Kings xviii. 8, etc.
[11] Literally, "those who have been athletes."
[12] Some fill up the *lacuna* here found in the MS. so as to read, " have come to a grievous death."
[13] Literally, "good." [The martyrdom of St. Peter is all that is thus connected with his arrival in Rome. His numerous labours were restricted to the Circumcision.]
[14] *Seven* imprisonments of St. Paul are not referred to in Scripture.
[15] Archbishop Wake here reads "scourged." We have followed the most recent critics in filling up the numerous *lacunæ* in this chapter.
[16] Some think *Rome*, others *Spain*, and others even *Britain*, to be here referred to. [See note at end.]
[17] That is, under Tigellinus and Sabinus, in the last year of the Emperor Nero; but some think Helius and Polycletus referred to; and others, both here and in the preceding sentence, regard the words as denoting simply the *witness* borne by Peter and Paul to the truth of the gospel before the rulers of the earth.
[18] Some suppose these to have been the names of two eminent female martyrs under Nero; others regard the clause as an interpolation. [Many ingenious conjectures might be cited; but see Jacobson's valuable note, *Patres Apostol.*, vol. i. p. 30.]
[19] Literally, "have reached to the stedfast course of faith."
[20] Gen. ii. 23.

CHAP. VII. — AN EXHORTATION TO REPENTANCE.

These things, beloved, we write unto you, not merely to admonish you of your duty, but also to remind ourselves. For we are struggling on the same arena, and the same conflict is assigned to both of us. Wherefore let us give up vain and fruitless cares, and approach to the glorious and venerable rule of our holy calling. Let us attend to what is good, pleasing, and acceptable in the sight of Him who formed us. Let us look stedfastly to the blood of Christ, and see how precious that blood is to God,[1] which, having been shed for our salvation, has set the grace of repentance before the whole world. Let us turn to every age that has passed, and learn that, from generation to generation, the Lord has granted a place of repentance to all such as would be converted unto Him. Noah preached repentance, and as many as listened to him were saved.[2] Jonah proclaimed destruction to the Ninevites;[3] but they, repenting of their sins, propitiated God by prayer, and obtained salvation, although they were aliens [to the covenant] of God.

CHAP. VIII. — CONTINUATION RESPECTING REPENTANCE.

The ministers of the grace of God have, by the Holy Spirit, spoken of repentance; and the Lord of all things has himself declared with an oath regarding it, "As I live, saith the Lord, I desire not the death of the sinner, but rather his repentance;"[4] adding, moreover, this gracious declaration, "Repent, O house of Israel, of your iniquity.[5] Say to the children of My people, Though your sins reach from earth to heaven, and though they be redder[6] than scarlet, and blacker than sackcloth, yet if ye turn to Me with your whole heart, and say, Father! I will listen to you, as to a holy[7] people." And in another place He speaks thus: "Wash you, and become clean; put away the wickedness of your souls from before mine eyes; cease from your evil ways, and learn to do well; seek out judgment, deliver the oppressed, judge the fatherless, and see that justice is done to the widow; and come, and let us reason together. He declares, Though your sins be like crimson, I will make them white as snow; though they be like scarlet, I will whiten them like wool. And if ye be willing and obey Me, ye shall eat the good of the land; but if ye refuse, and will not hearken unto Me, the sword shall devour you, for the mouth of the Lord hath spoken these things."[8] Desiring, therefore, that all His beloved should be partakers of repentance, He has, by His almighty will, established [these declarations].

CHAP. IX. — EXAMPLES OF THE SAINTS.

Wherefore, let us yield obedience to His excellent and glorious will; and imploring His mercy and loving-kindness, while we forsake all fruitless labours,[9] and strife, and envy, which leads to death, let us turn and have recourse to His compassions. Let us stedfastly contemplate those who have perfectly ministered to His excellent glory. Let us take (for instance) Enoch, who, being found righteous in obedience, was translated, and death was never known to happen to him.[10] Noah, being found faithful, preached regeneration to the world through his ministry; and the Lord saved by him the animals which, with one accord, entered into the ark.

CHAP. X. — CONTINUATION OF THE ABOVE.

Abraham, styled "the friend,"[11] was found faithful, inasmuch as he rendered obedience to the words of God. He, in the exercise of obedience, went out from his own country, and from his kindred, and from his father's house, in order that, by forsaking a small territory, and a weak family, and an insignificant house, he might inherit the promises of God. For God said to him, "Get thee out from thy country, and from thy kindred, and from thy father's house, into the land which I shall show thee. And I will make thee a great nation, and will bless thee, and make thy name great, and thou shalt be blessed. And I will bless them that bless thee, and curse them that curse thee; and in thee shall all the families of the earth be blessed."[12] And again, on his departing from Lot, God said to him, "Lift up thine eyes, and look from the place where thou now art, northward, and southward, and eastward, and westward; for all the land which thou seest, to thee will I give it, and to thy seed for ever. And I will make thy seed as the dust of the earth, [so that] if a man can number the dust of the earth, then shall thy seed also be numbered."[13] And again [the Scripture] saith, "God brought forth Abram, and spake unto him, Look up now to heaven, and count the stars if thou be able to number them; so shall thy seed be. And Abram believed God, and it was counted to him for righteousness."[14] On account of his faith and hospitality, a son

---

[1] Some insert "Father."
[2] Gen. vii.; 1 Pet. iii. 20; 2 Pet. ii. 5.
[3] Jonah iii.
[4] Ezek. xxxiii. 11.
[5] Ezek. xviii. 30.
[6] Comp. Isa. i. 18.
[7] These words are not found in Scripture, though they are quoted again by Clem. Alex. (*Pædag.*, i. 10) as from Ezekiel.
[8] Isa. i. 16–20.
[9] Some read ματαιολογίαν, "vain talk."
[10] Gen. v. 24; Heb. xi. 5. Literally, "and his death was not found."
[11] Isa. xli. 8; 2 Chron. xx. 7; Judith viii. 19; James ii. 23.
[12] Gen. xii. 1–3.
[13] Gen. xiii. 14–16.
[14] Gen. xv. 5, 6; Rom. iv. 3.

was given him in his old age; and in the exercise of obedience, he offered him as a sacrifice to God on one of the mountains which He showed him.[1]

CHAP. XI. — CONTINUATION. LOT.

On account of his hospitality and godliness, Lot was saved out of Sodom when all the country round was punished by means of fire and brimstone, the Lord thus making it manifest that He does not forsake those that hope in Him, but gives up such as depart from Him to punishment and torture.[2] For Lot's wife, who went forth with him, being of a different mind from himself and not continuing in agreement with him [as to the command which had been given them], was made an example of, so as to be a pillar of salt unto this day.[3] This was done that all might know that those who are of a double mind, and who distrust the power of God, bring down judgment on themselves,[4] and become a sign to all succeeding generations.

CHAP. XII. — THE REWARDS OF FAITH AND HOSPITALITY. RAHAB.

On account of her faith and hospitality, Rahab the harlot was saved. For when spies were sent by Joshua, the son of Nun, to Jericho, the king of the country ascertained that they were come to spy out their land, and sent men to seize them, in order that, when taken, they might be put to death. But the hospitable Rahab receiving them, concealed them on the roof of her house under some stalks of flax. And when the men sent by the king arrived and said, "There came men unto thee who are to spy out our land; bring them forth, for so the king commands," she answered them, "The two men whom ye seek came unto me, but quickly departed again and are gone," thus not discovering the spies to them. Then she said to the men, "I know assuredly that the Lord your God hath given you this city, for the fear and dread of you have fallen on its inhabitants. When therefore ye shall have taken it, keep ye me and the house of my father in safety." And they said to her, "It shall be as thou hast spoken to us. As soon, therefore, as thou knowest that we are at hand, thou shalt gather all thy family under thy roof, and they shall be preserved, but all that are found outside of thy dwelling shall perish."[5] Moreover, they gave her a sign to this effect, that she should hang forth from her house a scarlet thread. And thus they made it manifest that redemption should flow through the blood of the Lord to all them that believe and hope in God.[6] Ye see, beloved, that there was not only faith, but prophecy, in this woman.

CHAP. XIII. — AN EXHORTATION TO HUMILITY.

Let us therefore, brethren, be of humble mind, laying aside all haughtiness, and pride, and foolishness, and angry feelings; and let us act according to that which is written (for the Holy Spirit saith, "Let not the wise man glory in his wisdom, neither let the mighty man glory in his might, neither let the rich man glory in his riches; but let him that glorieth glory in the Lord, in diligently seeking Him, and doing judgment and righteousness"[7]), being especially mindful of the words of the Lord Jesus which He spake, teaching us meekness and long-suffering. For thus He spoke: "Be ye merciful, that ye may obtain mercy; forgive, that it may be forgiven to you; as ye do, so shall it be done unto you; as ye judge, so shall ye be judged; as ye are kind, so shall kindness be shown to you; with what measure ye mete, with the same it shall be measured to you."[8] By this precept and by these rules let us stablish ourselves, that we walk with all humility in obedience to His holy words. For the holy word saith, "On whom shall I look, but on him that is meek and peaceable, and that trembleth at My words?"[9]

CHAP. XIV. — WE SHOULD OBEY GOD RATHER THAN THE AUTHORS OF SEDITION.

It is right and holy therefore, men and brethren, rather to obey God than to follow those who, through pride and sedition, have become the leaders of a detestable emulation. For we shall incur no slight injury, but rather great danger, if we rashly yield ourselves to the inclinations of men who aim at exciting strife and tumults, so as to draw us away from what is good. Let us be kind one to another after the pattern of the tender mercy and benignity of our Creator. For it is written, "The kind-hearted shall inhabit the land, and the guiltless shall be left upon it, but transgressors shall be destroyed from off the face of it."[10] And again [the Scripture] saith, "I saw the ungodly highly exalted, and lifted up like the cedars of Lebanon: I passed by, and, behold, he was not; and I diligently sought his place, and could not find it. Preserve innocence, and look on equity: for there shall be a remnant to the peaceful man."[11]

---

[1] Gen. xxi. 22; Heb. xi. 17.
[2] Gen. xix.; comp. 2 Pet. ii. 6–9.
[3] So Joseph., *Antiq.*, i. 11, 4; Irenæus, *Adv. Hær.*, iv. 31.
[4] Literally, "become a judgment and sign."
[5] Josh. ii.; Heb. xi. 31.
[6] Others of the Fathers adopt the same allegorical interpretation, e.g., Justin Mar., *Dial. c. Tryph.*, n. 111; Irenæus, *Adv. Hær.*, iv. 20. [The whole matter of symbolism under the law must be more thoroughly studied if we would account for such strong language as is here applied to a poetical or rhetorical figure.]
[7] Jer. ix. 23, 24; 1 Cor. i. 31; 2. Cor. x. 17.
[8] Comp. Matt. vi. 12–15, vii. 2; Luke vi. 36–38.
[9] Isa. lxvi. 2.
[10] Prov. ii. 21, 22.
[11] Ps. xxxvii. 35–37. "Remnant" probably refers either to the *memory* or *posterity* of the righteous.

CHAP. XV.—WE MUST ADHERE TO THOSE WHO CULTIVATE PEACE, NOT TO THOSE WHO MERELY PRETEND TO DO SO.

Let us cleave, therefore, to those who cultivate peace with godliness, and not to those who hypocritically profess to desire it. For [the Scripture] saith in a certain place, "This people honoureth Me with their lips, but their heart is far from Me."[1] And again: "They bless with their mouth, but curse with their heart."[2] And again it saith, "They loved Him with their mouth, and lied to Him with their tongue; but their heart was not right with Him, neither were they faithful in His covenant."[3] "Let the deceitful lips become silent,"[4] [and "let the Lord destroy all the lying lips,[5]] and the boastful tongue of those who have said, Let us magnify our tongue; our lips are our own; who is lord over us? For the oppression of the poor, and for the sighing of the needy, will I now arise, saith the Lord: I will place him in safety; I will deal confidently with him."[6]

CHAP. XVI.—CHRIST AS AN EXAMPLE OF HUMILITY.

For Christ is of those who are humble-minded, and not of those who exalt themselves over His flock. Our Lord Jesus Christ, the Sceptre of the majesty of God, did not come in the pomp of pride or arrogance, although He might have done so, but in a lowly condition, as the Holy Spirit had declared regarding Him. For He says, "Lord, who hath believed our report, and to whom is the arm of the Lord revealed? We have declared [our message] in His presence: He is, as it were, a child, and like a root in thirsty ground; He has no form nor glory, yea, we saw Him, and He had no form nor comeliness; but His form was without eminence, yea, deficient in comparison with the [ordinary] form of men. He is a man exposed to stripes and suffering, and acquainted with the endurance of grief: for His countenance was turned away; He was despised, and not esteemed. He bears our iniquities, and is in sorrow for our sakes; yet we supposed that [on His own account] He was exposed to labour, and stripes, and affliction. But He was wounded for our transgressions, and bruised for our iniquities. The chastisement of our peace was upon Him, and by His stripes we were healed. All we, like sheep, have gone astray; [every] man has wandered in his own way; and the Lord has delivered Him up for our sins, while He in the midst of His sufferings openeth not His mouth. He was brought as a sheep to the slaughter, and as a lamb before her shearer is dumb, so He openeth not His mouth. In His humiliation His judgment was taken away; who shall declare His generation? for His life is taken from the earth. For the transgressions of my people was He brought down to death. And I will give the wicked for His sepulchre, and the rich for His death,[7] because He did no iniquity, neither was guile found in His mouth. And the Lord is pleased to purify Him by stripes.[8] If ye make [9] an offering for sin, your soul shall see a long-lived seed. And the Lord is pleased to relieve Him of the affliction of His soul, to show Him light, and to form Him with understanding,[10] to justify the Just One who ministereth well to many; and He Himself shall carry their sins. On this account He shall inherit many, and shall divide the spoil of the strong; because His soul was delivered to death, and He was reckoned among the transgressors, and He bare the sins of many, and for their sins was He delivered."[11] And again He saith, "I am a worm, and no man; a reproach of men, and despised of the people. All that see Me have derided Me; they have spoken with their lips; they have wagged their head, [saying] He hoped in God, let Him deliver Him, let Him save Him, since He delighteth in Him."[12] Ye see, beloved, what is the example which has been given us; for if the Lord thus humbled Himself, what shall we do who have through Him come under the yoke of His grace?

CHAP. XVII.—THE SAINTS AS EXAMPLES OF HUMILITY.

Let us be imitators also of those who in goat-skins and sheep-skins[13] went about proclaiming the coming of Christ; I mean Elijah, Elisha, and Ezekiel among the prophets, with those others to whom a like testimony is borne [in Scripture]. Abraham was specially honoured, and was called the friend of God; yet he, earnestly regarding the glory of God, humbly declared, "I am but dust and ashes."[14] Moreover, it is thus written of Job, "Job was a righteous man, and blameless, truthful, God-fearing, and one that kept himself from all evil."[15] But bringing an accu-

---

[1] Isa. xxix. 13; Matt. xv. 8; Mark vii. 6.
[2] Ps. lxii. 4.
[3] Ps. lxxviii. 36, 37.
[4] Ps. xxxi. 18.
[5] These words within brackets are not found in the MS., but have been inserted from the Septuagint by most editors.
[6] Ps. xii. 3–5.
[7] The Latin of Cotelerius, adopted by Hefele and Dressel, translates this clause as follows: "I will set free the wicked on account of His sepulchre, and the rich on account of His death."
[8] The reading of the MS. is τῆς πληγῆς, "purify, or free, Him from stripes." We have adopted the emendation of Junius.
[9] Wotton reads, "If He make."
[10] Or, "fill Him with understanding," if πλῆσαι should be read instead of πλάσαι, as Grabe suggests.
[11] Isa. liii. The reader will observe how often the text of the Septuagint, here quoted, differs from the Hebrew as represented by our authorized English version.
[12] Ps. xxii. 6–8.
[13] Heb. xi. 37.
[14] Gen. xviii. 27.
[15] Job i. 1.

sation against himself, he said, "No man is free from defilement, even if his life be but of one day."[1] Moses was called faithful in all God's house;[2] and through his instrumentality, God punished Egypt[3] with plagues and tortures. Yet he, though thus greatly honoured, did not adopt lofty language, but said, when the divine oracle came to him out of the bush, "Who am I, that Thou sendest me? I am a man of a feeble voice and a slow tongue."[4] And again he said, "I am but as the smoke of a pot."[5]

CHAP. XVIII. — DAVID AS AN EXAMPLE OF HUMILITY.

But what shall we say concerning David, to whom such testimony was borne, and of whom[6] God said, "I have found a man after Mine own heart, David the son of Jesse; and in everlasting mercy have I anointed him?"[7] Yet this very man saith to God, "Have mercy on me, O Lord, according to Thy great mercy; and according to the multitude of Thy compassions, blot out my transgression. Wash me still more from mine iniquity, and cleanse me from my sin. For I acknowledge my iniquity, and my sin is ever before me. Against Thee only have I sinned, and done that which was evil in Thy sight; that Thou mayest be justified in Thy sayings, and mayest overcome when Thou[8] art judged. For, behold, I was conceived in transgressions, and in my sins did my mother conceive me. For, behold, Thou hast loved truth; the secret and hidden things of wisdom hast Thou shown me. Thou shalt sprinkle me with hyssop, and I shall be cleansed; Thou shalt wash me, and I shall be whiter than snow. Thou shalt make me to hear joy and gladness; my bones, which have been humbled, shall exult. Turn away Thy face from my sins, and blot out all mine iniquities. Create in me a clean heart, O God, and renew a right spirit within me.[9] Cast me not away from Thy presence, and take not Thy Holy Spirit from me. Restore to me the joy of Thy salvation, and establish me by Thy governing Spirit. I will teach transgressors Thy ways, and the ungodly shall be converted unto Thee. Deliver me from blood-guiltiness,[10] O God, the God of my salvation: my tongue shall exult in Thy righteousness. O Lord, Thou shalt open my mouth, and my lips shall show forth Thy praise. For if Thou hadst desired sacrifice, I would have given it; Thou wilt not delight in burnt-offerings. The sacrifice [acceptable] to God is a bruised spirit; a broken and a contrite heart God will not despise."[11]

CHAP. XIX. — IMITATING THESE EXAMPLES, LET US SEEK AFTER PEACE.

Thus the humility and godly submission of so great and illustrious men have rendered not only us, but also all the generations before us, better; even as many as have received His oracles in fear and truth. Wherefore, having so many great and glorious examples set before us, let us turn again to the practice of that peace which from the beginning was the mark set before us;[12] and let us look stedfastly to the Father and Creator of the universe, and cleave to His mighty and surpassingly great gifts and benefactions of peace. Let us contemplate Him with our understanding, and look with the eyes of our soul to His long-suffering will. Let us reflect how free from wrath He is towards all His creation.

CHAP. XX. — THE PEACE AND HARMONY OF THE UNIVERSE.

The heavens, revolving under His government, are subject to Him in peace. Day and night run the course appointed by Him, in no wise hindering each other. The sun and moon, with the companies of the stars, roll on in harmony according to His command, within their prescribed limits, and without any deviation. The fruitful earth, according to His will, brings forth food in abundance, at the proper seasons, for man and beast and all the living beings upon it, never hesitating, nor changing any of the ordinances which He has fixed. The unsearchable places of abysses, and the indescribable arrangements of the lower world, are restrained by the same laws. The vast unmeasurable sea, gathered together by His working into various basins,[13] never passes beyond the bounds placed around it, but does as He has commanded. For He said, "Thus far shalt thou come, and thy waves shall be broken within thee."[14] The ocean, impassable to man, and the worlds beyond it, are regulated by the same enactments of the Lord. The seasons of spring, summer, autumn, and winter, peacefully give place to one another. The winds in their several quarters[15] fulfil, at the proper time, their service without hindrance. The ever-flowing fountains, formed both for enjoyment and health, furnish without fail their breasts for the life of men. The very smallest

---

[1] Job xiv. 4, 5. [Septuagint].
[2] Num. xii. 7; Heb. iii. 2.
[3] Some fill up the *lacuna* which here occurs in the MS. by "Israel."
[4] Ex. iii. 11, iv. 10.
[5] This is not found in Scripture. [They were probably in Clement's version. Comp. Ps. cxix. 83.]
[6] Or, as some render, "to whom."
[7] Ps. lxxxix. 21.
[8] Or, "when Thou judgest."
[9] Literally, "in my inwards."
[10] Literally, "bloods."
[11] Ps. li. 1-17.
[12] Literally, "Becoming partakers of many great and glorious deeds, let us return to the aim of peace delivered to us from the beginning." Comp. Heb. xii. 1.
[13] Or, "collections."
[14] Job xxxviii. 11.
[15] Or, "stations."

of living beings meet together in peace and concord. All these the great Creator and Lord of all has appointed to exist in peace and harmony; while He does good to all, but most abundantly to us who have fled for refuge to His compassions through Jesus Christ our Lord, to whom be glory and majesty for ever and ever. Amen.

CHAP. XXI. — LET US OBEY GOD, AND NOT THE AUTHORS OF SEDITION.

Take heed, beloved, lest His many kindnesses lead to the condemnation of us all. [For thus it must be] unless we walk worthy of Him, and with one mind do those things which are good and well-pleasing in His sight. For [the Scripture] saith in a certain place, "The Spirit of the Lord is a candle searching the secret parts of the belly."[1] Let us reflect how near He is, and that none of the thoughts or reasonings in which we engage are hid from Him. It is right, therefore, that we should not leave the post which His will has assigned us. Let us rather offend those men who are foolish, and inconsiderate, and lifted up, and who glory in the pride of their speech, than [offend] God. Let us reverence the Lord Jesus Christ, whose blood was given for us; let us esteem those who have the rule over us;[2] let us honour the aged[3] among us; let us train up the young men in the fear of God; let us direct our wives to that which is good. Let them exhibit the lovely habit of purity [in all their conduct]; let them show forth the sincere disposition of meekness; let them make manifest the command which they have of their tongue, by their manner[4] of speaking; let them display their love, not by preferring[5] one to another, but by showing equal affection to all that piously fear God. Let your children be partakers of true Christian training; let them learn of how great avail humility is with God — how much the spirit of pure affection can prevail with Him — how excellent and great His fear is, and how it saves all those who walk in[6] it with a pure mind. For He is a Searcher of the thoughts and desires [of the heart]: His breath is in us; and when He pleases, He will take it away.

CHAP. XXII. — THESE EXHORTATIONS ARE CONFIRMED BY THE CHRISTIAN FAITH, WHICH PROCLAIMS THE MISERY OF SINFUL CONDUCT.

Now the faith which is in Christ confirms all these [admonitions]. For He Himself by the Holy Ghost thus addresses us: "Come, ye children, hearken unto Me; I will teach you the fear of the Lord. What man is he that desireth life, and loveth to see good days? Keep thy tongue from evil, and thy lips from speaking guile. Depart from evil, and do good; seek peace, and pursue it. The eyes of the Lord are upon the righteous, and His ears are [open] unto their prayers. The face of the Lord is against them that do evil, to cut off the remembrance of them from the earth. The righteous cried, and the Lord heard him, and delivered him out of all his troubles."[7] "Many are the stripes [appointed for] the wicked; but mercy shall compass those about who hope in the Lord."[8]

CHAP. XXIII. — BE HUMBLE, AND BELIEVE THAT CHRIST WILL COME AGAIN.

The all-merciful and beneficent Father has bowels [of compassion] towards those that fear Him, and kindly and lovingly bestows His favours upon those who come to Him with a simple mind. Wherefore let us not be double-minded; neither let our soul be lifted[9] up on account of His exceedingly great and glorious gifts. Far from us be that which is written, "Wretched are they who are of a double mind, and of a doubting heart; who say, These things we have heard even in the times of our fathers; but, behold, we have grown old, and none of them has happened unto us."[10] Ye foolish ones! compare yourselves to a tree: take [for instance] the vine. First of all, it sheds its leaves, then it buds, next it puts forth leaves, and then it flowers; after that comes the sour grape, and then follows the ripened fruit. Ye perceive how in a little time the fruit of a tree comes to maturity. Of a truth, soon and suddenly shall His will be accomplished, as the Scripture also bears witness, saying, "Speedily will He come, and will not tarry;"[11] and, "The Lord shall suddenly come to His temple, even the Holy One, for whom ye look."[12]

CHAP. XXIV. — GOD CONTINUALLY SHOWS US IN NATURE THAT THERE WILL BE A RESURRECTION.

Let us consider, beloved, how the Lord continually proves to us that there shall be a future resurrection, of which He has rendered the Lord Jesus Christ the first-fruits[13] by raising Him from the dead. Let us contemplate, beloved, the resurrection which is at all times taking place. Day and night declare to us a resurrection. The night sinks to sleep, and the day arises; the day [again] departs, and the night comes on.

---

[1] Prov. xx. 27.
[2] Comp. Heb. xiii. 17; 1 Thess. v. 12, 13.
[3] Or, "the presbyters."
[4] Some read, "by their silence."
[5] Comp. 1 Tim. v. 21.
[6] Some translate, "who turn to Him."
[7] Ps. xxxiv. 11–17.
[8] Ps. xxxii. 10.
[9] Or, as some render, "neither let us have any doubt of."
[10] Some regard these words as taken from an apocryphal book, others as derived from a fusion of James i. 8 and 2 Pet. iii. 3, 4.
[11] Hab. ii. 3; Heb. x. 37.
[12] Mal. iii. 1.
[13] Comp. 1 Cor. xv. 20; Col. i. 18.

Let us behold the fruits [of the earth], how the sowing of grain takes place. The sower[1] goes forth, and casts it into the ground; and the seed being thus scattered, though dry and naked when it fell upon the earth, is gradually dissolved. Then out of its dissolution the mighty power of the providence of the Lord raises it up again, and from one seed many arise and bring forth fruit.

CHAP. XXV. — THE PHŒNIX AN EMBLEM OF OUR RESURRECTION.

Let us consider that wonderful sign [of the resurrection] which takes place in Eastern lands, that is, in Arabia and the countries round about. There is a certain bird which is called a phœnix. This is the only one of its kind, and lives five hundred years. And when the time of its dissolution draws near that it must die, it builds itself a nest of frankincense, and myrrh, and other spices, into which, when the time is fulfilled, it enters and dies. But as the flesh decays a certain kind of worm is produced, which, being nourished by the juices of the dead bird, brings forth feathers. Then, when it has acquired strength, it takes up that nest in which are the bones of its parent, and bearing these it passes from the land of Arabia into Egypt, to the city called Heliopolis. And, in open day, flying in the sight of all men, it places them on the altar of the sun, and having done this, hastens back to its former abode. The priests then inspect the registers of the dates, and find that it has returned exactly as the five hundredth year was completed.[2]

CHAP. XXVI. — WE SHALL RISE AGAIN, THEN, AS THE SCRIPTURE ALSO TESTIFIES.

Do we then deem it any great and wonderful thing for the Maker of all things to raise up again those that have piously served Him in the assurance of a good faith, when even by a bird He shows us the mightiness of His power to fulfil His promise?[3] For [the Scripture] saith in a certain place, "Thou shalt raise me up, and I shall confess unto Thee;"[4] and again, "I laid me down, and slept; I awaked, because Thou art with me;"[5] and again, Job says, "Thou shalt raise up this flesh of mine, which has suffered all these things."[6]

CHAP. XXVII. — IN THE HOPE OF THE RESURRECTION, LET US CLEAVE TO THE OMNIPOTENT AND OMNISCIENT GOD.

Having then this hope, let our souls be bound to Him who is faithful in His promises, and just in His judgments. He who has commanded us not to lie, shall much more Himself not lie; for nothing is impossible with God, except to lie.[7] Let His faith therefore be stirred up again within us, and let us consider that all things are nigh unto Him. By the word of His might[8] He established all things, and by His word He can overthrow them. "Who shall say unto Him, What hast thou done? or, Who shall resist the power of His strength?"[9] When and as He pleases He will do all things, and none of the things determined by Him shall pass away.[10] All things are open before Him, and nothing can be hidden from His counsel. "The heavens[11] declare the glory of God, and the firmament showeth His handy-work. Day unto day uttereth speech, and night unto night showeth knowledge. And there are no words or speeches of which the voices are not heard."[12]

CHAP. XXVIII. — GOD SEES ALL THINGS: THEREFORE LET US AVOID TRANSGRESSION.

Since then all things are seen and heard [by God], let us fear Him, and forsake those wicked works which proceed from evil desires;[13] so that, through His mercy, we may be protected from the judgments to come. For whither can any of us flee from His mighty hand? Or what world will receive any of those who run away from Him? For the Scripture saith in a certain place, "Whither shall I go, and where shall I be hid from Thy presence? If I ascend into heaven, Thou art there; if I go away even to the uttermost parts of the earth, there is Thy right hand; if I make my bed in the abyss, there is Thy Spirit."[14] Whither, then, shall any one go, or where shall he escape from Him who comprehends all things?

CHAP. XXIX. — LET US ALSO DRAW NEAR TO GOD IN PURITY OF HEART.

Let us then draw near to Him with holiness of spirit, lifting up pure and undefiled hands unto Him, loving our gracious and merciful Father, who has made us partakers in the blessings of His elect.[15] For thus it is written, "When the Most High divided the nations, when He scattered[16] the sons of Adam, He fixed the bounds of the nations according to the number of the angels of God. His people Jacob became the portion of the Lord, and Israel the lot of His

---

[1] Comp. Luke viii. 5.
[2] This fable respecting the phœnix is mentioned by Herodotus (ii. 73) and by Pliny (*Nat. Hist.*, x. 2), and is used as above by Tertullian (*De Resurr.*, § 13) and by others of the Fathers.
[3] Literally, "the mightiness of His promise."
[4] Ps. xxviii. 7, or from some apocryphal book.
[5] Comp. Ps. iii. 6.
[6] Job xix. 25, 26.
[7] Comp. Tit. i. 2; Heb. vi. 18.
[8] Or, "majesty."
[9] Wisd. xii. 12, xi. 22.
[10] Comp. Matt. xxiv. 35.
[11] Literally, "If the heavens," etc.
[12] Ps. xix. 1-3.
[13] Literally, "abominable lusts of evil deeds."
[14] Ps. cxxxix. 7-10.
[15] Literally, "has made us to Himself a part of election."
[16] Literally, "sowed abroad."

inheritance."[1] And in another place [the Scripture] saith, "Behold, the Lord taketh unto Himself a nation out of the midst of the nations, as a man takes the first-fruits of his threshing-floor; and from that nation shall come forth the Most Holy.[2]

CHAP. XXX. — LET US DO THOSE THINGS THAT PLEASE GOD, AND FLEE FROM THOSE HE HATES, THAT WE MAY BE BLESSED.

Seeing, therefore, that we are the portion of the Holy One, let us do all those things which pertain to holiness, avoiding all evil-speaking, all abominable and impure embraces, together with all drunkenness, seeking after change,[3] all abominable lusts, detestable adultery, and execrable pride. "For God," saith [the Scripture], "resisteth the proud, but giveth grace to the humble."[4] Let us cleave, then, to those to whom grace has been given by God. Let us clothe ourselves with concord and humility, ever exercising self-control, standing far off from all whispering and evil-speaking, being justified by our works, and not our words. For [the Scripture] saith, "He that speaketh much, shall also hear much in answer. And does he that is ready in speech deem himself righteous? Blessed is he that is born of woman, who liveth but a short time: be not given to much speaking."[5] Let our praise be in God, and not of ourselves; for God hateth those that commend themselves. Let testimony to our good deeds be borne by others, as it was in the case of our righteous forefathers. Boldness, and arrogance, and audacity belong to those that are accursed of God; but moderation, humility, and meekness to such as are blessed by Him.

CHAP. XXXI. — LET US SEE BY WHAT MEANS WE MAY OBTAIN THE DIVINE BLESSING.

Let us cleave then to His blessing, and consider what are the means[6] of possessing it. Let us think[7] over the things which have taken place from the beginning. For what reason was our father Abraham blessed? was it not because he wrought righteousness and truth through faith?[8] Isaac, with perfect confidence, as if knowing what was to happen,[9] cheerfully yielded himself as a sacrifice.[10] Jacob, through reason[11] of his brother, went forth with humility from his own land, and came to Laban and served him; and there was given to him the sceptre of the twelve tribes of Israel.

CHAP. XXXII. — WE ARE JUSTIFIED NOT BY OUR OWN WORKS, BUT BY FAITH.

Whosoever will candidly consider each particular, will recognise the greatness of the gifts which were given by him.[12] For from him[13] have sprung the priests and all the Levites who minister at the altar of God. From him also [was descended] our Lord Jesus Christ according to the flesh.[14] From him [arose] kings, princes, and rulers of the race of Judah. Nor are his other tribes in small glory, inasmuch as God had promised, "Thy seed shall be as the stars of heaven."[15] All these, therefore, were highly honoured, and made great, not for their own sake, or for their own works, or for the righteousness which they wrought, but through the operation of His will. And we, too, being called by His will in Christ Jesus, are not justified by ourselves, nor by our own wisdom, or understanding, or godliness, or works which we have wrought in holiness of heart; but by that faith through which, from the beginning, Almighty God has justified all men; to whom be glory for ever and ever. Amen.

CHAP. XXXIII. — BUT LET US NOT GIVE UP THE PRACTICE OF GOOD WORKS AND LOVE. GOD HIMSELF IS AN EXAMPLE TO US OF GOOD WORKS.

What shall we do, then, brethren? Shall we become slothful in well-doing, and cease from the practice of love? God forbid that any such course should be followed by us! But rather let us hasten with all energy and readiness of mind to perform every good work. For the Creator and Lord of all Himself rejoices in His works. For by His infinitely great power He established the heavens, and by His incomprehensible wisdom He adorned them. He also divided the earth from the water which surrounds it, and fixed it upon the immoveable foundation of His own will. The animals also which are upon it He commanded by His own word[16] into existence. So likewise, when He had formed the sea, and the living creatures which are in it, He enclosed them [within their proper bounds] by His own power. Above all,[17] with His holy and undefiled hands He formed man, the most excellent [of His creatures], and truly great through the understanding given him — the express likeness of His own image. For

---

[1] Deut xxxii. 8, 9.
[2] Formed apparently from Num. xviii. 27 and 2 Chron. xxxi. 14. Literally, the closing words are, "the holy of holies."
[3] Some translate, "youthful lusts."
[4] Prov. iii. 34; James iv. 6; 1 Pet. v. 5.
[5] Job xi. 2, 3. The translation is doubtful. [But see Septuagint.]
[6] Literally, "what are the ways of His blessing."
[7] Literally, "unroll."
[8] Comp. James ii. 21.
[9] Some translate, "knowing what was to come."
[10] Gen. xxii.
[11] So Jacobson: Wotton reads, "fleeing from his brother."

[12] The meaning is here very doubtful. Some translate, "the gifts which were given to Jacob by Him," i.e., God.
[13] MS. αὐτῶν, referring to the gifts: we have followed the emendation αὐτοῦ, adopted by most editors. Some refer the word to God, and not Jacob.
[14] Comp. Rom. ix. 5.
[15] Gen. xxii. 17, xxviii. 4.
[16] Or, "commandment."
[17] Or, "in addition to all."

thus says God: "Let us make man in Our image, and after Our likeness. So God made man; male and female He created them."[1] Having thus finished all these things, He approved them, and blessed them, and said, "Increase and multiply."[2] We see,[3] then, how all righteous men have been adorned with good works, and how the Lord Himself, adorning Himself with His works, rejoiced. Having therefore such an example, let us without delay accede to His will, and let us work the work of righteousness with our whole strength.

CHAP. XXXIV. — GREAT IS THE REWARD OF GOOD WORKS WITH GOD. JOINED TOGETHER IN HARMONY, LET US IMPLORE THAT REWARD FROM HIM.

The good servant[4] receives the bread of his labour with confidence; the lazy and slothful cannot look his employer in the face. It is requisite, therefore, that we be prompt in the practice of well-doing; for of Him are all things. And thus He forewarns us: "Behold, the Lord [cometh], and His reward is before His face, to render to every man according to his work."[5] He exhorts us, therefore, with our whole heart to attend to this,[6] that we be not lazy or slothful in any good work. Let our boasting and our confidence be in Him. Let us submit ourselves to His will. Let us consider the whole multitude of His angels, how they stand ever ready to minister to His will. For the Scripture saith, "Ten thousand times ten thousand stood around Him, and thousands of thousands ministered unto Him,[7] and cried, Holy, holy, holy, [is] the Lord of Sabaoth; the whole creation is full of His glory."[8] And let us therefore, conscientiously gathering together in harmony, cry to Him earnestly, as with one mouth, that we may be made partakers of His great and glorious promises. For [the Scripture] saith, "Eye hath not seen, nor ear heard, neither have entered into the heart of man, the things which He hath prepared for them that wait for Him."[9]

CHAP. XXXV. — IMMENSE IS THIS REWARD. HOW SHALL WE OBTAIN IT?

How blessed and wonderful, beloved, are the gifts of God! Life in immortality, splendour in righteousness, truth in perfect confidence,[10] faith in assurance, self-control in holiness! And all these fall under the cognizance of our understandings [now]; what then shall those things be which are prepared for such as wait for Him? The Creator and Father of all worlds,[11] the Most Holy, alone knows their amount and their beauty. Let us therefore earnestly strive to be found in the number of those that wait for Him, in order that we may share in His promised gifts. But how, beloved, shall this be done? If our understanding be fixed by faith towards God; if we earnestly seek the things which are pleasing and acceptable to Him; if we do the things which are in harmony with His blameless will; and if we follow the way of truth, casting away from us all unrighteousness and iniquity, along with all covetousness, strife, evil practices, deceit, whispering, and evil-speaking, all hatred of God, pride and haughtiness, vainglory and ambition.[12] For they that do such things are hateful to God; and not only they that do them, but also those that take pleasure in them that do them.[13] For the Scripture saith, "But to the sinner God said, Wherefore dost thou declare my statutes, and take my covenant into thy mouth, seeing thou hatest instruction, and castest my words behind thee? When thou sawest a thief, thou consentedst with[14] him, and didst make thy portion with adulterers. Thy mouth has abounded with wickedness, and thy tongue contrived[15] deceit. Thou sittest, and speakest against thy brother; thou slanderest[16] thine own mother's son. These things thou hast done, and I kept silence; thou thoughtest, wicked one, that I should be like to thyself. But I will reprove thee, and set thyself before thee. Consider now these things, ye that forget God, lest He tear you in pieces, like a lion, and there be none to deliver. The sacrifice of praise will glorify Me, and a way is there by which I will show him the salvation of God."[17]

CHAP. XXXVI. — ALL BLESSINGS ARE GIVEN TO US THROUGH CHRIST.

This is the way, beloved, in which we find our Saviour,[18] even Jesus Christ, the High Priest of all our offerings, the defender and helper of our infirmity. By Him we look up to the heights of heaven. By Him we behold, as in a glass, His immaculate and most excellent visage. By Him are the eyes of our hearts opened. By Him our foolish and darkened understanding blossoms[19] up anew towards His marvellous light. By Him the Lord has willed that we should taste of im-

---

[1] Gen. i. 26, 27.
[2] Gen. i. 28.
[3] Or, "let us consider."
[4] Or, "labourer."
[5] Isa. xl. 10, lxii. 11; Rev. xxii. 12.
[6] The text here seems to be corrupt. Some translate, "He warns us with all His heart to this end, that," etc.
[7] Dan. vii. 10.
[8] Isa. vi. 3.
[9] 1 Cor. ii. 9.
[10] Some translate, "in liberty."
[11] Or, "of the ages."
[12] The reading is doubtful: some have ἀφιλοξενίαν, "want of a hospitable spirit." [So Jacobson.]
[13] Rom. i. 32.
[14] Literally, "didst run with."
[15] Literally, "didst weave."
[16] Or, "layest a snare for."
[17] Ps. l. 16-23. The reader will observe how the Septuagint followed by Clement differs from the Hebrew.
[18] Literally, "that which saves us."
[19] Or, "rejoices to behold."

mortal knowledge,[1] "who, being the brightness of His majesty, is by so much greater than the angels, as He hath by inheritance obtained a more excellent name than they."[2] For it is thus written, "Who maketh His angels spirits, and His ministers a flame of fire."[3] But concerning His Son[4] the Lord spoke thus: "Thou art my Son, to-day have I begotten Thee. Ask of Me, and I will give Thee the heathen for Thine inheritance, and the uttermost parts of the earth for Thy possession."[5] And again He saith to Him, "Sit Thou at My right hand, until I make Thine enemies Thy footstool."[6] But who are His enemies? All the wicked, and those who set themselves to oppose the will of God.[7]

CHAP. XXXVII. — CHRIST IS OUR LEADER, AND WE HIS SOLDIERS.

Let us then, men and brethren, with all energy act the part of soldiers, in accordance with His holy commandments. Let us consider those who serve under our generals, with what order, obedience, and submissiveness they perform the things which are commanded them. All are not prefects, nor commanders of a thousand, nor of a hundred, nor of fifty, nor the like, but each one in his own rank performs the things commanded by the king and the generals. The great cannot subsist without the small, nor the small without the great. There is a kind of mixture in all things, and thence arises mutual advantage.[8] Let us take our body for an example.[9] The head is nothing without the feet, and the feet are nothing without the head; yea, the very smallest members of our body are necessary and useful to the whole body. But all work[10] harmoniously together, and are under one common rule[11] for the preservation of the whole body.

CHAP. XXXVIII. — LET THE MEMBERS OF THE CHURCH SUBMIT THEMSELVES, AND NO ONE EXALT HIMSELF ABOVE ANOTHER.

Let our whole body, then, be preserved in Christ Jesus; and let every one be subject to his neighbour, according to the special gift[12] bestowed upon him. Let the strong not despise the weak, and let the weak show respect unto the strong. Let the rich man provide for the wants of the poor; and let the poor man bless God, because He hath given him one by whom his need may be supplied. Let the wise man display his wisdom, not by [mere] words, but through good deeds. Let the humble not bear testimony to himself, but leave witness to be borne to him by another.[13] Let him that is pure in the flesh not grow proud[14] of it, and boast, knowing that it was another who bestowed on him the gift of continence. Let us consider, then, brethren, of what matter we were made,—who and what manner of beings we came into the world, as it were out of a sepulchre, and from utter darkness.[15] He who made us and fashioned us, having prepared His bountiful gifts for us before we were born, introduced us into His world. Since, therefore, we receive all these things from Him, we ought for everything to give Him thanks; to whom be glory for ever and ever. Amen.

CHAP. XXXIX. — THERE IS NO REASON FOR SELF-CONCEIT.

Foolish and inconsiderate men, who have neither wisdom[16] nor instruction, mock and deride us, being eager to exalt themselves in their own conceits. For what can a mortal man do? or what strength is there in one made out of the dust? For it is written, "There was no shape before mine eyes, only I heard a sound,[17] and a voice [saying], What then? Shall a man be pure before the Lord? or shall such an one be [counted] blameless in his deeds, seeing He does not confide in His servants, and has charged[18] even His angels with perversity? The heaven is not clean in His sight: how much less they that dwell in houses of clay, of which also we ourselves were made! He smote them as a moth; and from morning even until evening they endure not. Because they could furnish no assistance to themselves, they perished. He breathed upon them, and they died, because they had no wisdom. But call now, if any one will answer thee, or if thou wilt look to any of the holy angels; for wrath destroys the foolish man, and envy killeth him that is in error. I have seen the foolish taking root, but their habitation was presently consumed. Let their sons be far from safety; let them be despised[19] before the gates of those less than themselves, and there shall be none to deliver. For what was prepared for them, the righteous shall eat; and they shall not be delivered from evil."[20]

---

[1] Or, "knowledge of immortality."
[2] Heb. i. 3, 4.
[3] Ps. civ. 4; Heb. i. 7.
[4] Some render, "to the Son."
[5] Ps. ii. 7, 8; Heb. i. 5.
[6] Ps. cx. 1; Heb i. 13.
[7] Some read, "who oppose their own will to that of God."
[8] Literally, " in these there is use."
[9] 1 Cor. xii. 12, etc.
[10] Literally, "all breathe together."
[11] Literally, "use one subjection."
[12] Literally, "according as he has been placed in his charism."

[13] Comp. Prov. xxvii. 2.
[14] The ms. is here slightly torn, and we are left to conjecture.
[15] Comp. Ps. cxxxix. 15.
[16] Literally, "and silly and uninstructed."
[17] Literally, "a breath."
[18] Or, "has perceived."
[19] Some render, "they perished at the gates."
[20] Job iv. 16-18, xv. 15, iv. 19-21, v. 1-5.

CHAP. XL. — LET US PRESERVE IN THE CHURCH THE ORDER APPOINTED BY GOD.

These things therefore being manifest to us, and since we look into the depths of the divine knowledge, it behoves us to do all things in [their proper] order, which the Lord has commanded us to perform at stated times.[1] He has enjoined offerings [to be presented] and service to be performed [to Him], and that not thoughtlessly or irregularly, but at the appointed times and hours. Where and by whom He desires these things to be done, He Himself has fixed by His own supreme will, in order that all things being piously done according to His good pleasure, may be acceptable unto Him.[2] Those, therefore, who present their offerings at the appointed times, are accepted and blessed; for inasmuch as they follow the laws of the Lord, they sin not. For his own peculiar services are assigned to the high priest, and their own proper place is prescribed to the priests, and their own special ministrations devolve on the Levites. The layman is bound by the laws that pertain to laymen.

CHAP. XLI. — CONTINUATION OF THE SAME SUBJECT.

Let every one of you, brethren, give thanks to God in his own order, living in all good conscience, with becoming gravity, and not going beyond the rule of the ministry prescribed to him. Not in every place, brethren, are the daily sacrifices offered, or the peace-offerings, or the sin-offerings and the trespass-offerings, but in Jerusalem only. And even there they are not offered in any place, but only at the altar before the temple, that which is offered being first carefully examined by the high priest and the ministers already mentioned. Those, therefore, who do anything beyond that which is agreeable to His will, are punished with death. Ye see,[3] brethren, that the greater the knowledge that has been vouchsafed to us, the greater also is the danger to which we are exposed.

CHAP. XLII. — THE ORDER OF MINISTERS IN THE CHURCH.

The apostles have preached the Gospel to us from[4] the Lord Jesus Christ; Jesus Christ [has done so] from[4] God. Christ therefore was sent forth by God, and the apostles by Christ. Both these appointments,[5] then, were made in an orderly way, according to the will of God. Having therefore received their orders, and being fully assured by the resurrection of our Lord Jesus Christ, and established[6] in the word of God, with full assurance of the Holy Ghost, they went forth proclaiming that the kingdom of God was at hand. And thus preaching through countries and cities, they appointed the first-fruits [of their labours], having first proved them by the Spirit,[7] to be bishops and deacons of those who should afterwards believe. Nor was this any new thing, since indeed many ages before it was written concerning bishops and deacons. For thus saith the Scripture in a certain place, "I will appoint their bishops[8] in righteousness, and their deacons[9] in faith."[10]

CHAP. XLIII. — MOSES OF OLD STILLED THE CONTENTION WHICH AROSE CONCERNING THE PRIESTLY DIGNITY.

And what wonder is it if those in Christ who were entrusted with such a duty by God, appointed those [ministers] before mentioned, when the blessed Moses also, "a faithful servant in all his house,"[11] noted down in the sacred books all the injunctions which were given him, and when the other prophets also followed him, bearing witness with one consent to the ordinances which he had appointed? For, when rivalry arose concerning the priesthood, and the tribes were contending among themselves as to which of them should be adorned with that glorious title, he commanded the twelve princes of the tribes to bring him their rods, each one being inscribed with the name[12] of the tribe. And he took them and bound them [together], and sealed them with the rings of the princes of the tribes, and laid them up in the tabernacle of witness on the table of God. And having shut the doors of the tabernacle, he sealed the keys, as he had done the rods, and said to them, Men and brethren, the tribe whose rod shall blossom has God chosen to fulfil the office of the priesthood, and to minister unto Him. And when the morning was come, he assembled all Israel, six hundred thousand men, and showed the seals to the princes of the tribes, and opened the tabernacle of witness, and brought forth the rods. And the rod of Aaron was found not only to have blossomed, but to bear fruit upon it.[13] What think ye, beloved? Did not Moses know beforehand that this would happen? Undoubtedly he knew; but he acted thus, that there might be no sedition in Israel, and that

---

[1] Some join κατὰ καιροὺς τεταγμένους, "at stated times," to the next sentence. [1 Cor. xvi. 1, 2.]
[2] Literally, "to His will." [Comp. Rom. xv. 15, 16, Greek.]
[3] Or, "consider." [This chapter has been cited to prove the earlier date for this Epistle. But the reference to Jerusalem may be an ideal present.]
[4] Or, "by the command of."
[5] Literally, "both things were done."
[6] Or, "confirmed by."
[7] Or, "having tested them in spirit."
[8] Or, "overseers."
[9] Or, "servants."
[10] Isa. lx. 17, Sept.; but the text is here altered by Clement. The LXX. have "I will give thy rulers in peace, and thy overseers in righteousness."
[11] Num. xii. 10; Heb. iii. 5.
[12] Literally, "every tribe being written according to its name."
[13] See Num. xvii.

the name of the true and only God might be glorified; to whom be glory for ever and ever. Amen.

CHAP. XLIV. — THE ORDINANCES OF THE APOSTLES, THAT THERE MIGHT BE NO CONTENTION RESPECTING THE PRIESTLY OFFICE.

Our apostles also knew, through our Lord Jesus Christ, and there would be strife on account of the office[1] of the episcopate. For this reason, therefore, inasmuch as they had obtained a perfect fore-knowledge of this, they appointed those [ministers] already mentioned, and afterwards gave instructions,[2] that when these should fall asleep, other approved men should succeed them in their ministry. We are of opinion, therefore, that those appointed by them,[3] or afterwards by other eminent men, with the consent of the whole Church, and who have blamelessly served the flock of Christ in a humble, peaceable, and disinterested spirit, and have for a long time possessed the good opinion of all, cannot be justly dismissed from the ministry. For our sin will not be small, if we eject from the episcopate[4] those who have blamelessly and holily fulfilled its duties.[5] Blessed are those presbyters who, having finished their course before now, have obtained a fruitful and perfect departure [from this world]; for they have no fear lest any one deprive them of the place now appointed them. But we see that ye have removed some men of excellent behaviour from the ministry, which they fulfilled blamelessly and with honour.

CHAP. XLV. — IT IS THE PART OF THE WICKED TO VEX THE RIGHTEOUS.

Ye are fond of contention, brethren, and full of zeal about things which do not pertain to salvation. Look carefully into the Scriptures, which are the true utterances of the Holy Spirit. Observe[6] that nothing of an unjust or counterfeit character is written in them. There[7] you will not find that the righteous were cast off by men who themselves were holy. The righteous were indeed persecuted, but only by the wicked. They were cast into prison, but only by the unholy; they were stoned, but only by transgressors; they were slain, but only by the accursed, and such as had conceived an unrighteous envy against them. Exposed to such sufferings, they endured them gloriously. For what shall we say, brethren? Was Daniel[8] cast into the den of lions by such as feared God? Were Ananias, and Azarias, and Mishael shut up in a furnace[9] of fire by those who observed[10] the great and glorious worship of the Most High? Far from us be such a thought! Who, then, were they that did such things? The hateful, and those full of all wickedness, were roused to such a pitch of fury, that they inflicted torture on those who served God with a holy and blameless purpose [of heart], not knowing that the Most High is the Defender and Protector of all such as with a pure conscience venerate[11] His all-excellent name; to whom be glory for ever and ever. Amen. But they who with confidence endured [these things] are now heirs of glory and honour, and have been exalted and made illustrious[12] by God in their memorial for ever and ever. Amen.

CHAP. XLVI. — LET US CLEAVE TO THE RIGHTEOUS: YOUR STRIFE IS PERNICIOUS.

Such examples, therefore, brethren, it is right that we should follow;[13] since it is written, "Cleave to the holy, for those that cleave to them shall [themselves] be made holy."[14] And again, in another place, [the Scripture] saith, "With a harmless man thou shalt prove[15] thyself harmless, and with an elect man thou shalt be elect, and with a perverse man thou shalt show[16] thyself perverse."[17] Let us cleave, therefore, to the innocent and righteous, since these are the elect of God. Why are there strifes, and tumults, and divisions, and schisms, and wars[18] among you? Have we not [all] one God and one Christ? Is there not one Spirit of grace poured out upon us? And have we not one calling in Christ?[19] Why do we divide and tear to pieces the members of Christ, and raise up strife against our own body, and have reached such a height of madness as to forget that "we are members one of another?"[20] Remember the words of our Lord Jesus Christ, how[21] He said, "Woe to that man [by whom[21] offences come]! It were better for him that he had never been born, than that he should cast a stumbling-block before one of my elect. Yea, it were better for him that a millstone should be

---

[1] Literally, "on account of the title of the oversight." Some understand this to mean, "in regard to the dignity of the episcopate;" and others simply, "on account of the oversight."
[2] The meaning of this passage is much controverted. Some render, "left a list of other approved persons;" while others translate the unusual word ἐπινομή, which causes the difficulty, by "testamentary direction," and many others deem the text corrupt. We have given what seems the simplest version of the text as it stands. [Comp. the versions of Wake, Chevallier, and others.]
[3] i.e., the apostles.
[4] Or, "oversight."
[5] Literally, "presented the offerings."
[6] Or, "Ye perceive."
[7] Or, "For."
[8] Dan. vi. 16.
[9] Dan. iii. 20.
[10] Literally, "worshipped."
[11] Literally, "serve."
[12] Or, "lifted up."
[13] Literally, "To such examples it is right that we should cleave."
[14] Not found in Scripture.
[15] Literally, "be."
[16] Or, "thou wilt overthrow."
[17] Ps. xviii. 25, 26.
[18] Or, "war." Comp. James iv. 1.
[19] Comp. Eph. iv. 4–6.
[20] Rom. xvii. 5.
[21] This clause is wanting in the text.

hung about [his neck], and he should be sunk in the depths of the sea, than that he should cast a stumbling-block before one of my little ones.[1] Your schism has subverted [the faith of] many, has discouraged many, has given rise to doubt in many, and has caused grief to us all. And still your sedition continueth.

CHAP. XLVII. — YOUR RECENT DISCORD IS WORSE THAN THE FORMER WHICH TOOK PLACE IN THE TIMES OF PAUL.

Take up the epistle of the blessed Apostle Paul. What did he write to you at the time when the Gospel first began to be preached?[2] Truly, under the inspiration[3] of the Spirit, he wrote to you concerning himself, and Cephas, and Apollos,[4] because even then parties[5] had been formed among you. But that inclination for one above another entailed less guilt upon you, inasmuch as your partialities were then shown towards apostles, already of high reputation, and towards a man whom they had approved. But now reflect who those are that have perverted you, and lessened the renown of your far-famed brotherly love. It is disgraceful, beloved, yea, highly disgraceful, and unworthy of your Christian profession,[6] that such a thing should be heard of as that the most stedfast and ancient Church of the Corinthians should, on account of one or two persons, engage in sedition against its presbyters. And this rumour has reached not only us, but those also who are unconnected[7] with us; so that, through your infatuation, the name of the Lord is blasphemed, while danger is also brought upon yourselves.

CHAP. XLVIII. — LET US RETURN TO THE PRACTICE OF BROTHERLY LOVE.

Let us therefore, with all haste, put an end[8] to this [state of things]; and let us fall down before the Lord, and beseech Him with tears, that He would mercifully[9] be reconciled to us, and restore us to our former seemly and holy practice of brotherly love. For [such conduct] is the gate of righteousness, which is set open for the attainment of life, as it is written, "Open to me the gates of righteousness; I will go in by them, and will praise the Lord: this is the gate of the Lord: the righteous shall enter in by it."[10] Although, therefore, many gates have been set open, yet this gate of righteousness is that gate in Christ by which blessed are all they that have entered in and have directed their way in holiness and righteousness, doing all things without disorder. Let a man be faithful: let him be powerful in the utterance of knowledge; let him be wise in judging of words; let him be pure in all his deeds; yet the more he seems to be superior to others [in these respects], the more humble-minded ought he to be, and to seek the common good of all, and not merely his own advantage.

CHAP. XLIX. — THE PRAISE OF LOVE.

Let him who has love in Christ keep the commandments of Christ. Who can describe the [blessed] bond of the love of God? What man is able to tell the excellence of its beauty, as it ought to be told? The height to which love exalts us is unspeakable. Love unites us to God. Love covers a multitude of sins.[11] Love beareth all things, is long-suffering in all things.[12] There is nothing base, nothing arrogant in love. Love admits of no schisms: love gives rise to no seditions: love does all things in harmony. By love have all the elect of God been made perfect; without love nothing is well-pleasing to God. In love has the Lord taken us to Himself. On account of the Love he bore us, Jesus Christ our Lord gave His blood for us by the will of God; His flesh for our flesh, and His soul for our souls.[13]

CHAP. L. — LET US PRAY TO BE THOUGHT WORTHY OF LOVE.

Ye see, beloved, how great and wonderful a thing is love, and that there is no declaring its perfection. Who is fit to be found in it, except such as God has vouchsafed to render so? Let us pray, therefore, and implore of His mercy, that we may live blameless in love, free from all human partialities for one above another. All the generations from Adam even unto this day have passed away; but those who, through the grace of God, have been made perfect in love, now possess a place among the godly, and shall be made manifest at the revelation[14] of the kingdom of Christ. For it is written, "Enter into thy secret chambers for a little time, until my wrath and fury pass away; and I will remember a propitious[15] day, and will raise you up out of your graves."[16] Blessed are we, beloved, if we keep the commandments of God in the harmony of love; that so through love our sins may be forgiven us. For it is written, "Blessed are they whose transgressions are forgiven, and whose sins are covered. Blessed is the man whose sin

---

[1] Comp. Matt. xviii. 6, xxvi. 24; Mark ix. 42; Luke xvii. 2.
[2] Literally, "in the beginning of the Gospel." [Comp. Philipp. iv. 15.]
[3] Or, "spiritually."
[4] 1 Cor. iii. 13, etc.
[5] Or, "inclinations for one above another."
[6] Literally, "of conduct in Christ."
[7] Or, "aliens from us," i.e., the Gentiles.
[8] Literally, "remove."
[9] Literally, "becoming merciful."
[10] Ps. cxviii. 19, 20.

[11] James v. 20; 1 Pet. iv. 8.
[12] Comp. 1 Cor. xiii. 4, etc.
[13] [Comp. Irenæus, v. 1; also Mathetes, Ep. to Diognetus, cap. ix.]
[14] Literally, "visitation."
[15] Or, "good."
[16] Isa. xxvi. 20.

the Lord will not impute to him, and in whose mouth there is no guile."[1] This blessedness cometh upon those who have been chosen by God through Jesus Christ our Lord; to whom be glory for ever and ever. Amen.

CHAP. LI. — LET THE PARTAKERS IN STRIFE ACKNOWLEDGE THEIR SINS.

Let us therefore implore forgiveness for all those transgressions which through any [suggestion] of the adversary we have committed. And those who have been the leaders of sedition and disagreement ought to have respect[2] to the common hope. For such as live in fear and love would rather that they themselves than their neighbours should be involved in suffering. And they prefer to bear blame themselves, rather than that the concord which has been well and piously[3] handed down to us should suffer. For it is better that a man should acknowledge his transgressions than that he should harden his heart, as the hearts of those were hardened who stirred up sedition against Moses the servant of God, and whose condemnation was made manifest [unto all]. For they went down alive into Hades, and death swallowed them up.[4] Pharaoh with his army and all the princes of Egypt, and the chariots with their riders, were sunk in the depths of the Red Sea, and perished,[5] for no other reason than that their foolish hearts were hardened, after so many signs and wonders had been wrought in the land of Egypt by Moses the servant of God.

CHAP. LII. — SUCH A CONFESSION IS PLEASING TO GOD.

The Lord, brethren, stands in need of nothing; and He desires nothing of any one, except that confession be made to Him. For, says the elect David, "I will confess unto the Lord; and that will please Him more than a young bullock that hath horns and hoofs. Let the poor see it, and be glad."[6] And again he saith, "Offer[7] unto God the sacrifice of praise, and pay thy vows unto the Most High. And call upon Me in the day of thy trouble: I will deliver thee, and thou shalt glorify Me."[8] For "the sacrifice of God is a broken spirit."[9]

CHAP. LIII. — THE LOVE OF MOSES TOWARDS HIS PEOPLE.

Ye understand, beloved, ye understand well the Sacred Scriptures, and ye have looked very earnestly into the oracles of God. Call then these things to your remembrance. When Moses went up into the mount, and abode there, with fasting and humiliation, forty days and forty nights, the Lord said unto him, "Moses, Moses, get thee down quickly from hence; for thy people whom thou didst bring out of the land of Egypt have committed iniquity. They have speedily departed from the way in which I commanded them to walk, and have made to themselves molten images."[10] And the Lord said unto him, "I have spoken to thee once and again, saying, I have seen this people, and, behold, it is a stiff-necked people: let Me destroy them, and blot out their name from under heaven; and I will make thee a great and wonderful nation, and one much more numerous than this."[11] But Moses said, "Far be it from Thee, Lord: pardon the sin of this people; else blot me also out of the book of the living."[12] O marvellous[13] love! O insuperable perfection! The servant speaks freely to his Lord, and asks forgiveness for the people, or begs that he himself might perish[14] along with them.

CHAP. LIV. — HE WHO IS FULL OF LOVE WILL INCUR EVERY LOSS, THAT PEACE MAY BE RESTORED TO THE CHURCH.

Who then among you is noble-minded? who compassionate? who full of love? Let him declare, "If on my account sedition and disagreement and schisms have arisen, I will depart, I will go away whithersoever ye desire, and I will do whatever the majority[15] commands; only let the flock of Christ live on terms of peace with the presbyters set over it." He that acts thus shall procure to himself great glory in the Lord; and every place will welcome[16] him. For "the earth is the Lord's, and the fulness thereof."[17] These things they who live a godly life, that is never to be repented of, both have done and always will do.

CHAP. LV. — EXAMPLES OF SUCH LOVE.

To bring forward some examples from among the heathen: Many kings and princes, in times of pestilence, when they had been instructed by an oracle, have given themselves up to death, in order that by their own blood they might deliver their fellow-citizens [from destruction]. Many have gone forth from their own cities, that so sedition might be brought to an end within

---

[1] Ps. xxxii. 1, 2.
[2] Or, "look to."
[3] Or, "righteously."
[4] Num. xvi.
[5] Ex. xiv.
[6] Ps. lxix. 31, 32.
[7] Or, "sacrifice."
[8] Ps. l. 14, 15.
[9] Ps. li. 17.

[10] Ex. xxxii. 7, etc.; Deut. ix. 12, etc.
[11] Ex. xxxii. 9, etc.
[12] Ex. xxxii. 32.
[13] Or, "mighty."
[14] Literally, "be wiped out."
[15] Literally, "the multitude." [Clement here puts words into the mouth of the Corinthian presbyters. It has been strangely quoted to strengthen a conjecture that he had humbly preferred Linus and Cletus when first called to preside.]
[16] Or, "receive."
[17] Ps. xxiv. 1; 1 Cor. x. 26, 28.

them. We know many among ourselves who have given themselves up to bonds, in order that they might ransom others. Many, too, have surrendered themselves to slavery, that with the price[1] which they received for themselves, they might provide food for others. Many women also, being strengthened by the grace of God, have performed numerous manly exploits. The blessed Judith, when her city was besieged, asked of the elders permission to go forth into the camp of the strangers; and, exposing herself to danger, she went out for the love which she bare to her country and people then besieged; and the Lord delivered Holofernes into the hands of a woman.[2] Esther also, being perfect in faith, exposed herself to no less danger, in order to deliver the twelve tribes of Israel from impending destruction. For with fasting and humiliation she entreated the everlasting God, who seeth all things; and He, perceiving the humility of her spirit, delivered the people for whose sake she had encountered peril.[3]

CHAP. LVI. — LET US ADMONISH AND CORRECT ONE ANOTHER.

Let us then also pray for those who have fallen into any sin, that meekness and humility may be given to them, so that they may submit, not unto us, but to the will of God. For in this way they shall secure a fruitful and perfect remembrance from us, with sympathy for them, both in our prayers to God, and our mention of them to the saints.[4] Let us receive correction, beloved, on account of which no one should feel displeased. Those exhortations by which we admonish one another are both good [in themselves] and highly profitable, for they tend to unite[5] us to the will of God. For thus saith the holy Word: "The Lord hath severely chastened me, yet hath not given me over to death."[6] "For whom the Lord loveth He chasteneth, and scourgeth every son whom He receiveth."[7] "The righteous," saith it, "shall chasten me in mercy, and reprove me; but let not the oil of sinners make fat my head."[8] And again he saith, "Blessed is the man whom the Lord reproveth, and reject not thou the warning of the Almighty. For He causes sorrow, and again restores [to gladness]; He woundeth, and His hands make whole. He shall deliver thee in six troubles, yea, in the seventh no evil shall touch thee. In famine He shall rescue thee from death, and in war He shall free thee from the power[9] of the sword. From the scourge of the tongue will He hide thee, and thou shalt not fear when evil cometh. Thou shalt laugh at the unrighteous and the wicked, and shalt not be afraid of the beasts of the field. For the wild beasts shall be at peace with thee: then shalt thou know that thy house shall be in peace, and the habitation of thy tabernacle shall not fail.[10] Thou shalt know also that thy seed shall be great, and thy children like the grass of the field. And thou shalt come to the grave like ripened corn which is reaped in its season, or like a heap of the threshing-floor which is gathered together at the proper time."[11] Ye see, beloved, that protection is afforded to those that are chastened of the Lord; for since God is good, He corrects us, that we may be admonished by His holy chastisement.

CHAP. LVII. — LET THE AUTHORS OF SEDITION SUBMIT THEMSELVES.

Ye therefore, who laid the foundation of this sedition, submit yourselves to the presbyters, and receive correction so as to repent, bending the knees of your hearts. Learn to be subject, laying aside the proud and arrogant self-confidence of your tongue. For it is better for you that ye should occupy[12] a humble but honourable place in the flock of Christ, than that, being highly exalted, ye should be cast out from the hope of His people.[13] For thus speaketh all-virtuous Wisdom:[14] "Behold, I will bring forth to you the words of My Spirit, and I will teach you My speech. Since I called, and ye did not hear; I held forth My words, and ye regarded not, but set at naught My counsels, and yielded not at My reproofs; therefore I too will laugh at your destruction; yea, I will rejoice when ruin cometh upon you, and when sudden confusion overtakes you, when overturning presents itself like a tempest, or when tribulation and oppression fall upon you. For it shall come to pass, that when ye call upon Me, I will not hear you; the wicked shall seek Me, and they shall not find Me. For they hated wisdom, and did not choose the fear of the Lord; nor would they listen to My counsels, but despised My reproofs. Wherefore they shall eat the fruits of their own way, and they shall be filled with their own ungodliness." . . .[15]

---

1 Literally, "and having received their prices, fed others." [Comp. Rom. xvi. 3, 4, and Phil. ii. 30.]
2 Judith viii. 30.
3 Esther vii., viii.
4 Literally, "there shall be to them a fruitful and perfect remembrance, with compassions both towards God and the saints."
5 Or, "they unite."
6 Ps. cxviii. 18.
7 Prov. iii. 12; Heb. xii. 6.
8 Ps. cxli. 5.
9 Literally, "hand."
10 Literally, "err" or "sin."
11 Job v. 17-26.
12 Literally, "to be found small and esteemed."
13 Literally, "His hope." [It has been conjectured that ἐλπίδος should be ἐπαυλιδος, and the reading, "out of the fold of his people." See Chevallier.]
14 Prov. i. 23-31. [Often cited by this name in primitive writers.]
15 Junius (Pat. Young), who examined the MS. before it was bound into its present form, stated that a whole leaf was here lost. The next letters that occur are ιπον, which have been supposed to indicate εἶπον or ἔλιπον. Doubtless some passages quoted by the ancients from the Epistle of Clement, and not now found in it, occurred in the portion which has thus been lost.

CHAP. LVIII. — BLESSINGS SOUGHT FOR ALL THAT CALL UPON GOD.

May God, who seeth all things, and who is the Ruler of all spirits and the Lord of all flesh — who chose our Lord Jesus Christ and us through Him to be a peculiar[1] people — grant to every soul that calleth upon His glorious and holy Name, faith, fear, peace, patience, long-suffering, self-control, purity, and sobriety, to the well-pleasing of His Name, through our High Priest and Protector, Jesus Christ, by whom be to Him glory, and majesty, and power, and honour, both now and for evermore. Amen.

CHAP. LIX. — THE CORINTHIANS ARE EXHORTED SPEEDILY TO SEND BACK WORD THAT PEACE HAS BEEN RESTORED. THE BENEDICTION.

Send back speedily to us in peace and with joy these our messengers to you: Claudius Ephebus and Valerius Bito, with Fortunatus: that they may the sooner announce to us the peace and harmony we so earnestly desire and long for [among you], and that we may the more quickly rejoice over the good order re-established among you. The grace of our Lord Jesus Christ be with you, and with all everywhere that are the called of God through Him, by whom be to Him glory, honour, power, majesty, and eternal dominion,[2] from everlasting to everlasting.[3] Amen.[4]

---

[1] Comp. Tit. ii. 14.
[2] Literally, "an eternal throne."
[3] Literally, "From the ages to the ages of ages."
[4] [Note St. Clement's frequent doxologies.]
    [N.B. — The language of Clement concerning the Western progress of St. Paul (cap. v.) is our earliest postscript to his Scripture biography. It is sufficient to refer the reader to the great works of Conybeare and Howson, and of Mr. Lewin, on the *Life and Epistles of St. Paul.* See more especially the valuable note of Lewin (vol. ii. p. 294) which takes notice of the opinion of some learned men, that the great Apostle of the Gentiles preached the Gospel in Britain.
    The whole subject of St. Paul's relations with British Christians is treated by Williams, in his *Antiquities of the Cymry*, with learning and in an attractive manner. But the reader will find more ready to his hand, perhaps, the interesting note of Mr. Lewin, on Claudia and Pudens (2 Tim x. 21), in his *Life and Epistles of St. Paul,* vol. ii. p. 392. See also Paley's *Horæ Paulinæ*, p. 40. London, 1820.]

INTRODUCTORY NOTE

TO THE

EPISTLE OF MATHETES TO DIOGNETUS

[A.D. 130.] THE anonymous author of this Epistle gives himself the title (Mathetes) "a *disciple*[1] of the Apostles," and I venture to adopt it as his name. It is about all we know of him, and it serves a useful end. I place his letter here, as a sequel to the Clementine Epistle, for several reasons, which I think scholars will approve: (1) It is full of the Pauline spirit, and exhales the same pure and primitive fragrance which is characteristic of Clement. (2) No theory as to its date very much conflicts with that which I adopt, and it is sustained by good authorities. (3) But, as a specimen of the persuasives against Gentilism which early Christians employed in their intercourse with friends who adhered to heathenism, it admirably illustrates the temper prescribed by St. Paul (2 Tim. ii. 24), and not less the peculiar social relations of converts to the Gospel with the more amiable and candid of their personal friends at this early period.

Mathetes was possibly a catechumen of St. Paul or of one of the apostle's associates. I assume that his correspondent was the tutor of M. Aurelius. Placed just here, it fills a *lacuna* in the series, and takes the place of the pseudo (second) Epistle of Clement, which is now relegated to its proper place with the works falsely ascribed to St. Clement.

Altogether, the Epistle is a gem of purest ray; and, while suggesting some difficulties as to interpretation and exposition, it is practically clear as to argument and intent. Mathetes is, perhaps, the first of the apologists.

THE following is the original introductory notice of the learned editors and translators: —

The following interesting and eloquent Epistle is anonymous, and we have no clue whatever as to its author. For a considerable period after its publication in 1592, it was generally ascribed to Justin Martyr. In recent times Otto has inserted it among the works of that writer, but Semisch and others contend that it cannot possibly be his. In dealing with this question, we depend entirely upon the internal evidence, no statement as to the authorship of the Epistle having descended to us from antiquity. And it can scarcely be denied that the whole tone of the Epistle, as well as special passages which it contains, points to some other writer than Justin. Accordingly, critics are now for the most part agreed that it is not his, and that it must be ascribed to one who lived at a still earlier date in the history of the Church. Several internal arguments have been brought forward in favour of this opinion. Supposing chap. xi. to be genuine, it has been supported by the fact that the writer there styles himself "a disciple of the apostles." But there is great suspicion that the two concluding chapters are spurious; and even though

---

[1] ἀποστόλων γενόμενος μαθητής. Cap. xi.

admitted to be genuine, the expression quoted evidently admits of a different explanation from that which implies the writer's personal acquaintance with the apostles: it might, indeed, be adopted by one even at the present day. More weight is to be attached to those passages in which the writer speaks of Christianity as still being a *new* thing in the world. Expressions to this effect occur in several places (chap. i., ii., ix.), and seem to imply that the author lived very little, if at all, after the apostolic age. There is certainly nothing in the epistle which is inconsistent with this opinion; and we may therefore believe, that in this beautiful composition we possess a genuine production of some apostolic man who lived not later than the beginning of the second century.

The names of Clement of Rome and of Apollos have both been suggested as those of the probable author. Such opinions, however, are pure fancies, which it is perhaps impossible to refute, but which rest on nothing more than conjecture. Nor can a single word be said as to the person named Diognetus, to whom the letter is addressed. We must be content to leave both points in hopeless obscurity, and simply accept the Epistle as written by an earnest and intelligent Christian to a sincere inquirer among the Gentiles, towards the close of the apostolic age.

It is much to be regretted that the text is often so very doubtful. Only three MSS. of the Epistle, all probably exhibiting the same original text, are known to exist; and in not a few passages the readings are, in consequence, very defective and obscure. But notwithstanding this drawback, and the difficulty of representing the full force and elegance of the original, this Epistle, as now presented to the English reader, can hardly fail to excite both his deepest interest and admiration.

[N.B. — Interesting speculations concerning this precious work may be seen in Bunsen's *Hippolytus and his Age*, vol. i. p. 188. The learned do not seem convinced by this author, but I have adopted his suggestion as to Diognetus the tutor of M. Aurelius.]

THE EPISTLE OF MATHETES TO DIOGNETUS

CHAP. I. — OCCASION OF THE EPISTLE.

SINCE I see thee, most excellent Diognetus, exceedingly desirous to learn the mode of worshipping God prevalent among the Christians, and inquiring very carefully and earnestly concerning them, what God they trust in, and what form of religion they observe,[1] so as all to look down upon the world itself, and despise death, while they neither esteem those to be gods that are reckoned such by the Greeks, nor hold to the superstition of the Jews; and what is the affection which they cherish among themselves; and why, in fine, this new kind or practice [of piety] has only now entered into the world,[2] and not long ago; I cordially welcome this thy desire, and I implore God, who enables us both to speak and to hear, to grant to me so to speak, that, above all, I may hear you have been edified,[3] and to you so to hear, that I who speak may have no cause of regret for having done so.

CHAP. II. — THE VANITY OF IDOLS.

Come, then, after you have freed[4] yourself from all prejudices possessing your mind, and laid aside what you have been accustomed to, as something apt to deceive[5] you, and being made, as if from the beginning, a new man, inasmuch as, according to your own confession, you are to be the hearer of a new [system of] doctrine; come and contemplate, not with your eyes only, but with your understanding, the substance and the form[6] of those whom ye declare and deem to be gods. Is not one of them a stone similar to that on which we tread? Is[7] not a second brass, in no way superior to those vessels which are constructed for our ordinary use? Is not a third wood, and that already rotten? Is not a fourth silver, which needs a man to watch it, lest it be stolen? Is not a fifth iron, consumed by rust? Is not a sixth earthenware, in no degree more valuable than that which is formed for the humblest purposes? Are not all these of corruptible matter? Are they not fabricated by means of iron and fire? Did not the sculptor fashion one of them, the brazier a second, the silversmith a third, and the potter a fourth? Was not every one of them, before they were formed by the arts of these [workmen] into the shape of these [gods], each in its[8] own way subject to change? Would not those things which are now vessels, formed of the same materials, become like to such, if they met with the same artificers? Might not these, which are now worshipped by you, again be made by men vessels similar to others? Are they not all deaf? Are they not blind? Are they not without life? Are they not destitute of feeling? Are they not incapable of motion? Are they not all liable to rot? Are they not all corruptible? These things ye call gods; these ye serve; these ye worship; and ye become altogether like to them. For this reason ye hate the Christians, because they do not deem *these* to be gods. But do not ye yourselves, who now think and suppose [such to be gods], much more cast contempt upon them than they [the Christians do]? Do ye not much more mock and insult them, when ye worship those that are made of stone and earthenware, without appointing any persons to guard them; but those made of silver and gold ye shut up by night, and appoint watchers to look after them by day, lest they be stolen? And by those gifts which ye mean to present to them, do ye not, if they are possessed of sense, rather punish [than honour] them? But if, on the other hand, they are destitute of sense, ye convict them of this fact, while ye worship them with blood and the smoke of sacrifices. Let any one of you suffer such indignities![9] Let any one of you endure to have such things done to himself! But not a single human being will, unless compelled to it,

---

[1] Literally, "trusting in what God, etc., they look down."
[2] Or, "life."
[3] Some read, "that you by hearing may be edified."
[4] Or, "purified."
[5] Literally, "which is deceiving."
[6] Literally, "of what substance, or of what form."
[7] Some make this and the following clauses affirmative instead of interrogative.

[8] The text is here corrupt. Several attempts at emendation have been made, but without any marked success.
[9] Some read, "Who of you would tolerate these things?" etc.

endure such treatment, since he is endowed with sense and reason. A stone, however, readily bears it, seeing it is insensible. Certainly you do not show [by your [1] conduct] that he [your God] is possessed of sense. And as to the fact that Christians are not accustomed to serve such gods, I might easily find many other things to say; but if even what has been said does not seem to any one sufficient, I deem it idle to say anything further.

CHAP. III. — SUPERSTITIONS OF THE JEWS.

And next, I imagine that you are most desirous of hearing something on this point, that the Christians do not observe the same forms of divine worship as do the Jews. The Jews, then, if they abstain from the kind of service above described, and deem it proper to worship one God as being Lord of all, [are right]; but if they offer Him worship in the way which we have described, they greatly err. For while the Gentiles, by offering such things to those that are destitute of sense and hearing, furnish an example of madness; they, on the other hand, by thinking to offer these things to God as if He needed them, might justly reckon it rather an act of folly than of divine worship. For He that made heaven and earth, and all that is therein, and gives to us all the things of which we stand in need, certainly requires none of those things which He Himself bestows on such as think of furnishing them to Him. But those who imagine that, by means of blood, and the smoke of sacrifices and burnt-offerings, they offer sacrifices [acceptable] to Him, and that by such honours they show Him respect, — these, by [2] supposing that they can give anything to Him who stands in need of nothing, appear to me in no respect to differ from those who studiously confer the same honour on things destitute of sense, and which therefore are unable to enjoy such honours.

CHAP. IV. — THE OTHER OBSERVANCES OF THE JEWS.

But as to their scrupulosity concerning meats, and their superstition as respects the Sabbaths, and their boasting about circumcision, and their fancies about fasting and the new moons, which are utterly ridiculous and unworthy of notice, — I do not [3] think that you require to learn anything from me. For, to accept some of those things which have been formed by God for the use of men as properly formed, and to reject others as useless and redundant, — how can this be lawful? And to speak falsely of God, as if He forbade us to do what is good on the Sabbath-days, — how is not this impious? And to glory in the circumcision [4] of the flesh as a proof of election, and as if, on account of it, they were specially beloved by God, — how is it not a subject of ridicule? And as to their observing months and days,[5] as if waiting upon [6] the stars and the moon, and their distributing,[7] according to their own tendencies, the appointments of God, and the vicissitudes of the seasons, some for festivities,[8] and others for mourning, — who would deem this a part of divine worship, and not much rather a manifestation of folly? I suppose, then, you are sufficiently convinced that the Christians properly abstain from the vanity and error common [to both Jews and Gentiles], and from the busy-body spirit and vain boasting of the Jews; but you must not hope to learn the mystery of their peculiar mode of worshipping God from any mortal.

CHAP. V. — THE MANNERS OF THE CHRISTIANS.

For the Christians are distinguished from other men neither by country, nor language, nor the customs which they observe. For they neither inhabit cities of their own, nor employ a peculiar form of speech, nor lead a life which is marked out by any singularity. The course of conduct which they follow has not been devised by any speculation or deliberation of inquisitive men; nor do they, like some, proclaim themselves the advocates of any merely human doctrines. But, inhabiting Greek as well as barbarian cities, according as the lot of each of them has determined, and following the customs of the natives in respect to clothing, food, and the rest of their ordinary conduct, they display to us their wonderful and confessedly striking [9] method of life. They dwell in their own countries, but simply as sojourners. As citizens, they share in all things with others, and yet endure all things as if foreigners. Every foreign land is to them as their native country, and every land of their birth as a land of strangers. They marry, as do all [others]; they beget children; but they do not destroy their offspring.[10] They

---

[1] The text is here uncertain, and the sense obscure. The meaning seems to be, that by sprinkling their gods with blood, etc., they tended to prove that these were not possessed of sense.
[2] The text is here very doubtful. We have followed that adopted by most critics.
[3] Otto, resting on MS. authority, omits the negative, but the sense seems to require its insertion.
[4] Literally, "lessening."
[5] Comp. Gal. iv. 10.
[6] This seems to refer to the practice of the Jews in fixing the beginning of the day, and consequently of the Sabbath, from the rising of the stars. They used to say, that when three stars of moderate magnitude appeared, it was night; when two, it was twilight; and when only one, that day had not yet departed. It thus came to pass (according to their *night-day* (νυχθήμερον) reckoning), that whosoever engaged in work on the evening of Friday, the beginning of the Sabbath, after three stars of moderate size were visible, was held to have sinned, and had to present a trespass-offering; and so on, according to the fanciful rule described.
[7] Otto supplies the *lacuna* which here occurs in the MSS. so as to read καταδιαιρεῖν.
[8] The great festivals of the Jews are here referred to on the one hand, and the day of atonement on the other.
[9] Literally, "paradoxical."
[10] Literally, "cast away fœtuses."

have a common table, but not a common bed.[1] They are in the flesh, but they do not live after the flesh.[2] They pass their days on earth, but they are citizens of heaven.[3] They obey the prescribed laws, and at the same time surpass the laws by their lives. They love all men, and are persecuted by all. They are unknown and are condemned; they are put to death, and restored to life.[4] They are poor, yet make many rich;[5] they are in lack of all things, and yet abound in all; they are dishonoured, and yet in their very dishonour are glorified. They are evil spoken of, and yet are justified; they are reviled, and bless;[6] they are insulted, and repay the insult with honour; they do good, yet are punished as evil-doers. When punished, they rejoice as if quickened into life; they are assailed by the Jews as foreigners, and are persecuted by the Greeks; yet those who hate them are unable to assign any reason for their hatred.

CHAP. VI. — THE RELATION OF CHRISTIANS TO THE WORLD.

To sum up all in one word — what the soul is in the body, that are Christians in the world. The soul is dispersed through all the members of the body, and Christians are scattered through all the cities of the world. The soul dwells in the body, yet is not of the body; and Christians dwell in the world, yet are not of the world.[7] The invisible soul is guarded by the visible body, and Christians are known indeed to be in the world, but their godliness remains invisible. The flesh hates the soul, and wars against it,[8] though itself suffering no injury, because it is prevented from enjoying pleasures; the world also hates the Christians, though in nowise injured, because they abjure pleasures. The soul loves the flesh that hates it, and [loves also] the members; Christians likewise love those that hate them. The soul is imprisoned in the body, yet preserves[9] that very body; and Christians are confined in the world as in a prison, and yet they are the preservers[9] of the world. The immortal soul dwells in a mortal tabernacle; and Christians dwell as sojourners in corruptible [bodies], looking for an incorruptible dwelling[10] in the heavens. The soul, when but ill-provided with food and drink, becomes better; in like manner, the Christians, though subjected day by day to punishment, increase the more in number.[11] God has assigned them this illustrious position, which it were unlawful for them to forsake.

CHAP. VII. — THE MANIFESTATION OF CHRIST.

For, as I said, this was no mere earthly invention which was delivered to them, nor is it a mere human system of opinion, which they judge it right to preserve so carefully, nor has a dispensation of mere human mysteries been committed to them, but truly God Himself, who is almighty, the Creator of all things, and invisible, has sent from heaven, and placed among men, [Him who is] the truth, and the holy and incomprehensible Word, and has firmly established Him in their hearts. He did not, as one might have imagined, send to men any servant, or angel, or ruler, or any one of those who bear sway over earthly things, or one of those to whom the government of things in the heavens has been entrusted, but the very Creator and Fashioner of all things — by whom He made the heavens — by whom he enclosed the sea within its proper bounds — whose ordinances[12] all the stars[13] faithfully observe — from whom the sun[14] has received the measure of his daily course to be observed[15] — whom the moon obeys, being commanded to shine in the night, and whom the stars also obey, following the moon in her course; by whom all things have been arranged, and placed within their proper limits, and to whom all are subject — the heavens and the things that are therein, the earth and the things that are therein, the sea and the things that are therein — fire, air, and the abyss — the things which are in the heights, the things which are in the depths, and the things which lie between. This [messenger] He sent to them. Was it then, as one[16] might conceive, for the purpose of exercising tyranny, or of inspiring fear and terror? By no means, but under the influence of clemency and meekness. As a king sends his son, who is also a king, so sent He Him; as God[17] He sent Him; as to men He sent Him; as a Saviour He sent Him, and as seeking to persuade, not to compel us; for violence has no place in the character of God. As calling us He sent Him, not as vengefully pursuing us; as loving us He sent Him, not as judging us. For He will yet send Him to judge us, and who shall endure His appearing?[18] . . . Do you not see them exposed to wild beasts,

---

[1] Otto omits " bed," which is an emendation, and gives the second " common " the sense of *unclean*.
[2] Comp. 2 Cor. x. 3.
[3] Comp. Phil. iii. 20.
[4] Comp. 2 Cor. vi. 9.
[5] Comp. 2 Cor. vi. 10.
[6] Comp. 2 Cor. iv. 12.
[7] John xvii. 11, 14, 16.
[8] Comp. 1 Pet. ii. 11.
[9] Literally, " keeps together."
[10] Literally, " incorruption."

[11] Or, " though punished, increase in number daily."
[12] Literally, " mysteries."
[13] Literally, " elements."
[14] The word " sun," though omitted in the MSS., should manifestly be inserted.
[15] Literally, " has received to observe."
[16] Literally, " one of men."
[17] " God " here refers to the person sent.
[18] [Comp. Mal. iii. 2. The Old Testament is frequently in mind, if not expressly quoted by Mathetes.] A considerable gap here occurs in the MSS.

that they may be persuaded to deny the Lord, and yet not overcome? Do you not see that the more of them are punished, the greater becomes the number of the rest? This does not seem to be the work of man: this is the power of God; these are the evidences of His manifestation.

CHAP. VIII. — THE MISERABLE STATE OF MEN BEFORE THE COMING OF THE WORD.

For, who of men at all understood before His coming what God is? Do you accept of the vain and silly doctrines of those who are deemed trustworthy philosophers? of whom some said that fire was God, calling that God to which they themselves were by and by to come; and some water; and others some other of the elements formed by God. But if any one of these theories be worthy of approbation, every one of the rest of created things might also be declared to be God. But such declarations are simply the startling and erroneous utterances of deceivers;[1] and no man has either seen Him, or made Him known,[2] but He has revealed Himself. And He has manifested Himself through faith, to which alone it is given to behold God. For God, the Lord and Fashioner of all things, who made all things, and assigned them their several positions, proved Himself not merely a friend of mankind, but also long-suffering [in His dealings with them.] Yea, He was always of such a character, and still is, and will ever be, kind and good, and free from wrath, and true, and the only one who is [absolutely] good;[3] and He formed in His mind a great and unspeakable conception, which He communicated to His Son alone. As long, then, as He held and preserved His own wise counsel in concealment,[4] He appeared to neglect us, and to have no care over us. But after He revealed and laid open, through His beloved Son, the things which had been prepared from the beginning, He conferred every blessing[5] all at once upon us, so that we should both share in His benefits, and see and be active[6] [in His service]. Who of us would ever have expected these things? He was aware, then, of all things in His own mind, along with His Son, according to the relation[7] subsisting between them.

CHAP. IX. — WHY THE SON WAS SENT SO LATE.

As long then as the former time[8] endured, He permitted us to be borne along by unruly impulses, being drawn away by the desire of pleasure and various lusts. This was not that He at all delighted in our sins, but that He simply endured them; nor that He approved the time of working iniquity which then was, but that He sought to form a mind conscious of righteousness,[9] so that being convinced in that time of our unworthiness of attaining life through our own works, it should now, through the kindness of God, be vouchsafed to us; and having made it manifest that in ourselves we were unable to enter into the kingdom of God, we might through the power of God be made able. But when our wickedness had reached its height, and it had been clearly shown that its reward,[10] punishment and death, was impending over us; and when the time had come which God had before appointed for manifesting His own kindness and power, how[11] the one love of God, through exceeding regard for men, did not regard us with hatred, nor thrust us away, nor remember our iniquity against us, but showed great long-suffering, and bore with us,[12] He Himself took on Him the burden of our iniquities, He gave His own Son as a ransom for us, the holy One for transgressors, the blameless One for the wicked, the righteous One for the unrighteous, the incorruptible One for the corruptible, the immortal One for them that are mortal. For what other thing was capable of covering our sins than His righteousness? By what other one was it possible that we, the wicked and ungodly, could be justified, than by the only Son of God? O sweet exchange! O unsearchable operation! O benefits surpassing all expectation! that the wickedness of many should be hid in a single righteous One, and that the righteousness of One should justify many transgressors![13] Having therefore convinced us in the former time[14] that our nature was unable to attain to life, and having now revealed the Saviour who is able to save even those things which it was [formerly] impossible to save, by both these facts He desired to lead us to trust in His kindness, to esteem Him our Nourisher, Father, Teacher, Counsellor, Healer, our Wisdom, Light, Honour, Glory, Power, and Life, so that we should not be anxious[15] concerning clothing and food.

---

[1] Literally, "these things are the marvels and error."
[2] Or, "known Him."
[3] Comp. Matt. xix. 17.
[4] Literally, "in a mystery."
[5] Literally, "all things."
[6] The sense is here very obscure. We have followed the text of Otto, who fills up the *lacuna* in the MS. as above. Others have, "to see, and to handle Him."
[7] Literally, "economically."
[8] Otto refers for a like contrast between these two times to Rom. iii. 21-26, v. 20, and Gal. iv. 4. [Comp. Acts xvii. 30.]

[9] The reading and sense are doubtful.
[10] Both the text and rendering are here somewhat doubtful, but the sense will in any case be much the same.
[11] Many variations here occur in the way in which the *lacuna* of the MSS. is to be supplied. They do not, however, greatly affect the meaning.
[12] In the MS. "saying" is here inserted, as if the words had been regarded as a quotation from Isa. liii. 11.
[13] [See Bossuet, who quotes it as from Justin Martyr (Tom. iii. p. 171). Sermon on the Circumcision.]
[14] That is, before Christ appeared.
[15] Comp. Matt. vi. 25, etc. [Mathetes, in a single sentence, expounds a most practical text with comprehensive views.]

CHAP. X.—THE BLESSINGS THAT WILL FLOW FROM FAITH.

If you also desire [to possess] this faith, you likewise shall receive first of all the knowledge of the Father.[1] For God has loved mankind, on whose account He made the world, to whom He rendered subject all the things that are in it,[2] to whom He gave reason and understanding, to whom alone He imparted the privilege of looking upwards to Himself, whom He formed after His own image, to whom He sent His only-begotten Son, to whom He has promised a kingdom in heaven, and will give it to those who have loved Him. And when you have attained this knowledge, with what joy do you think you will be filled? Or, how will you love Him who has first so loved you? And if you love Him, you will be an imitator of His kindness. And do not wonder that a man may become an imitator of God. He can, if he is willing. For it is not by ruling over his neighbours, or by seeking to hold the supremacy over those that are weaker, or by being rich, and showing violence towards those that are inferior, that happiness is found; nor can any one by these things become an imitator of God. But these things do not at all constitute His majesty. On the contrary he who takes upon himself the burden of his neighbour; he who, in whatsoever respect he may be superior, is ready to benefit another who is deficient; he who, whatsoever things he has received from God, by distributing these to the needy, becomes a god to those who receive [his benefits]: he is an imitator of God. Then thou shalt see, while still on earth, that God in the heavens rules over [the universe]; then thou shalt begin to speak the mysteries of God; then shalt thou both love and admire those that suffer punishment because they will not deny God; then shalt thou condemn the deceit and error of the world when thou shalt know what it is to live truly in heaven, when thou shalt despise that which is here esteemed to be death, when thou shalt fear what is truly death, which is reserved for those who shall be condemned to the eternal fire, which shall afflict those even to the end that are committed to it. Then shalt thou admire those who for righteousness' sake endure the fire that is but for a moment, and shalt count them happy when thou shalt know [the nature of] that fire.

CHAP. XI.—THESE THINGS ARE WORTHY TO BE KNOWN AND BELIEVED.

I do not speak of things strange to me, nor do I aim at anything inconsistent with right reason;[3] but having been a disciple of the Apostles, I am become a teacher of the Gentiles. I minister the things delivered to me to those that are disciples worthy of the truth. For who that is rightly taught and begotten by the loving[4] Word, would not seek to learn accurately the things which have been clearly shown by the Word to His disciples, to whom the Word being manifested has revealed them, speaking plainly [to them], not understood indeed by the unbelieving, but conversing with the disciples, who, being esteemed faithful by Him, acquired a knowledge of the mysteries of the Father? For which[5] reason He sent the Word, that He might be manifested to the world; and He, being despised by the people [of the Jews], was, when preached by the Apostles, believed on by the Gentiles.[6] This is He who was from the beginning, who appeared as if new, and was found old, and yet who is ever born afresh in the hearts of the saints. This is He who, being from everlasting, is to-day called[7] the Son; through whom the Church is enriched, and grace, widely spread, increases in the saints, furnishing understanding, revealing mysteries, announcing times, rejoicing over the faithful, giving[8] to those that seek, by whom the limits of faith are not broken through, nor the boundaries set by the fathers passed over. Then fear of the law is chanted, and the grace of the prophets is known, and the faith of the gospels is established, and the tradition of the Apostles is preserved, and the grace of the Church exults; which grace if you grieve not, you shall know those things which the Word teaches, by whom He wills, and when He pleases. For whatever things we are moved to utter by the will of the Word commanding us, we communicate to you with pains, and from a love of the things that have been revealed to us.

CHAP. XII.—THE IMPORTANCE OF KNOWLEDGE TO TRUE SPIRITUAL LIFE.

When you have read and carefully listened to these things, you shall know what God bestows on such as rightly love Him, being made [as ye are] a paradise of delight, presenting[9] in yourselves a tree bearing all kinds of produce and flourishing well, being adorned with various fruits. For in this place[10] the tree of knowledge and the tree of life have been planted; but it is not the tree of knowledge that destroys — it

---

[1] Thus Otto supplies the *lacuna;* others conjecture somewhat different supplements.
[2] So Böhl. Sylburgius and Otto read, "in the earth."
[3] Some render, "nor do I rashly seek to persuade others."
[4] Some propose to read, "and becoming a friend to the Word."
[5] It has been proposed to connect this with the preceding sentence, and read, "have known the mysteries of the Father, viz., for what purpose He sent the Word."
[6] [Comp. 1 Tim. iii. 16.]
[7] Or, "esteemed."
[8] Or, "given."
[9] Literally, "bringing forth."
[10] That is, in Paradise.

is disobedience that proves destructive. Nor truly are those words without significance which are written, how God from the beginning planted the tree of life in the midst of paradise, revealing through knowledge the way to life,[1] and when those who were first formed did not use this [knowledge] properly, they were, through the fraud of the Serpent, stripped naked.[2] For neither can life exist without knowledge, nor is knowledge secure without life. Wherefore both were planted close together. The Apostle, perceiving the force [of this conjunction], and blaming that knowledge which, without true doctrine, is admitted to influence life,[3] declares, "Knowledge puffeth up, but love edifieth." For he who thinks he knows anything without true knowledge, and such as is witnessed to by life, knows nothing, but is deceived by the Serpent, as not[4] loving life. But he who combines knowledge with fear, and seeks after life, plants in hope, looking for fruit. Let your heart be your wisdom; and let your life be true knowledge[5] inwardly received. Bearing this tree and displaying its fruit, thou shalt always gather[6] in those things which are desired by God, which the Serpent cannot reach, and to which deception does not approach; nor is Eve then corrupted,[7] but is trusted as a virgin; and salvation is manifested, and the Apostles are filled with understanding, and the Passover[8] of the Lord advances, and the choirs[9] are gathered together, and are arranged in proper order, and the Word rejoices in teaching the saints, — by whom the Father is glorified: to whom be glory for ever. Amen.[10]

---

[1] Literally, "revealing life."
[2] Or, "deprived of it."
[3] Literally, "knowledge without the truth of a command exercised to life." See 1 Cor. viii. 1.
[4] The MS. is here defective. Some read, "on account of the love of life."
[5] Or, "true word," or "reason."
[6] Or, "reap."
[7] The meaning seems to be, that if the tree of true knowledge and life be planted within you, you shall continue free from blemishes and sins.
[8] [This looks like a reference to the Apocalypse, Rev. v. 9., xix. 7., xx. 5.]
[9] [Here Bishop Wordsworth would read κλῆροι, cites 1 Pet. v. 3, and refers to Suicer (Lexicon) in voce κλῆρος.]
[10] [Note the Clement-like doxology.]

INTRODUCTORY NOTE

TO THE

EPISTLE OF POLYCARP TO THE PHILIPPIANS

[A.D. 65–100–155.] The Epistle of Polycarp is usually made a sort of preface to those of Ignatius, for reasons which will be obvious to the reader. Yet he was born later, and lived to a much later period. They seem to have been friends from the days of their common pupilage under St. John; and there is nothing improbable in the conjecture of Usher, that he was the "angel of the church in Smyrna," to whom the Master says, "Be thou faithful unto death, and I will give thee a crown of life." His pupil Irenæus gives us one of the very few portraits of an apostolic man which are to be found in antiquity, in a few sentences which are a picture: "I could describe the very place in which the blessed Polycarp sat and taught; his going out and coming in; the whole tenor of his life; his personal appearance; how he would speak of the conversations he had held with John and with others who had seen the Lord. How did he make mention of their words and of whatever he had heard from them respecting the Lord." Thus he unconsciously tantalizes our reverent curiosity. Alas! that such conversations were not written for our learning. But there is a wise Providence in what is withheld, as well as in the inestimable treasures we have received.

Irenæus will tell us more concerning him, his visit to Rome, his rebuke of Marcion, and incidental anecdotes, all which are instructive. The expression which he applied to Marcion is found in this Epistle. Other facts of interest are found in the Martyrdom, which follows in these pages. His death, in extreme old age under the first of the Antonines, has been variously dated; but we may accept the date we have given, as rendered probable by that of the Paschal question, which he so lovingly settled with Anicetus, Bishop of Rome.

The Epistle to the Philippians is the more interesting as denoting the state of that beloved church, the firstborn of European churches, and so greatly endeared to St. Paul. It abounds in practical wisdom, and is rich in Scripture and Scriptural allusions. It reflects the spirit of St. John, alike in its lamb-like and its aquiline features: he is as loving as the beloved disciple himself when he speaks of Christ and his church, but "the son of thunder" is echoed in his rebukes of threatened corruptions in faith and morals. Nothing can be more clear than his view of the doctrines of grace; but he writes like the disciple of St. John, though in perfect harmony with St. Paul's hymn-like eulogy of Christian love.

The following is the original INTRODUCTORY NOTICE: —

THE authenticity of the following Epistle can on no fair grounds be questioned. It is abundantly established by external testimony, and is also supported by the internal evidence. Irenæus says (*Adv. Hær.*, iii. 3): "There is extant an Epistle of Polycarp written to the Philippians, most satisfactory, from which those that have a mind to do so may learn the character of his faith," etc. This passage is embodied by Eusebius in his *Ecclesiastical History* (iv. 14) ; and in another place the same writer refers to the Epistle before us as an undoubted production of Polycarp (*Hist. Eccl.*, iii. 36). Other ancient testimonies might easily be added, but are superfluous, inasmuch as there is a general consent among scholars at the present day that we have in this letter an authentic production of the renowned Bishop of Smyrna.

Of Polycarp's life little is known, but that little is highly interesting. Irenæus was his disciple, and tells us that "Polycarp was instructed by the apostles, and was brought into contact with many who had seen Christ" (*Adv. Hær.*, iii. 3 ; Euseb. *Hist. Eccl.*, iv. 14). There is also a very graphic account given of Polycarp by Irenæus in his Epistle to Florinus, to which the reader is referred. It has been preserved by Eusebius (*Hist. Eccl.*, v. 20).

The Epistle before us is not perfect in any of the Greek MSS. which contain it. But the chapters wanting in Greek are contained in an ancient Latin version. While there is no ground for supposing, as some have done, that the whole Epistle is spurious, there seems considerable force in the arguments by which many others have sought to prove chap. xiii. to be an interpolation.

The date of the Epistle cannot be satisfactorily determined. It depends on the conclusion we reach as to some points, very difficult and obscure, connected with that account of the martyrdom of Polycarp which has come down to us. We shall not, however, probably be far wrong if we fix it about the middle of the second century.

THE EPISTLE OF POLYCARP TO THE PHILIPPIANS[1]

Polycarp, and the presbyters[2] with him, to the Church of God sojourning at Philippi: Mercy to you, and peace from God Almighty, and from the Lord Jesus Christ, our Saviour, be multiplied.

CHAP. I. — PRAISE OF THE PHILIPPIANS.

I have greatly rejoiced with you in our Lord Jesus Christ, because ye have followed the example[3] of true love [as displayed by God], and have accompanied, as became you, those who were bound in chains, the fitting ornaments of saints, and which are indeed the diadems of the true elect of God and our Lord; and because the strong root of your faith, spoken of in days[4] long gone by, endureth even until now, and bringeth forth fruit to our Lord Jesus Christ, who for our sins suffered even unto death, [but] "whom God raised from the dead, having loosed the bands of the grave."[5] "In whom, though now ye see Him not, ye believe, and believing, rejoice with joy unspeakable and full of glory;"[6] into which joy many desire to enter, knowing that "by grace ye are saved, not of works,"[7] but by the will of God through Jesus Christ.

CHAP. II. — AN EXHORTATION TO VIRTUE.

"Wherefore, girding up your loins,"[8] "serve the Lord in fear"[9] and truth, as those who have forsaken the vain, empty talk and error of the multitude, and "believed in Him who raised up our Lord Jesus Christ from the dead, and gave Him glory,"[10] and a throne at His right hand. To Him all things[11] in heaven and on earth are subject. Him every spirit serves. He comes as the Judge of the living and the dead.[12] His blood will God require of those who do not believe in Him.[13] But He who raised Him up from the dead will raise[14] up us also, if we do His will, and walk in His commandments, and love what He loved, keeping ourselves from all unrighteousness, covetousness, love of money, evil-speaking, falsewitness; "not rendering evil for evil, or railing for railing,"[15] or blow for blow, or cursing for cursing, but being mindful of what the Lord said in His teaching: "Judge not, that ye be not judged;[16] forgive, and it shall be forgiven unto you;[17] be merciful, that ye may obtain mercy;[18] with what measure ye mete, it shall be measured to you again;[19] and once more, "Blessed are the poor, and those that are persecuted for righteousness' sake, for theirs is the kingdom of God."[20]

CHAP. III. — EXPRESSIONS OF PERSONAL UNWORTHINESS.

These things, brethren, I write to you concerning righteousness, not because I take anything upon myself, but because ye have invited me to do so. For neither I, nor any other such one, can come up to the wisdom[21] of the blessed and glorified Paul. He, when among you, accurately and stedfastly taught the word of truth in the presence of those who were then alive. And when absent from you, he wrote you a letter,[22] which, if you carefully study, you will find to be the means of building you up in that faith which has been given you, and which, being followed by hope, and preceded by love towards God, and Christ, and our neighbour, "is the mother of us all."[23] For if any one be inwardly

---

[1] The title of this Epistle in most of the MSS. is, "The Epistle of St. Polycarp, Bishop of Smyrna, and holy martyr, to the Philippians."
[2] Or, "Polycarp, and those who with him are presbyters."
[3] Literally, "ye have received the patterns of true love."
[4] Phil. i. 5.
[5] Acts ii. 24. Literally, "having loosed the pains of Hades."
[6] 1 Pet. i. 8.
[7] Eph. ii. 8, 9.
[8] Comp. 1 Pet. i. 13; Eph. vi. 14.
[9] Ps. ii. 11.
[10] 1 Pet. i. 21.
[11] Comp. 1 Pet. iii. 22; Phil. ii. 10.
[12] Comp. Acts xvii. 31.
[13] Or, "who do not obey him."
[14] Comp. 1 Cor. vi. 14; 2 Cor. iv. 14; Rom. viii. 11.
[15] 1 Pet. iii. 9.
[16] Matt. vii. 1.
[17] Matt. vi. 12, 14; Luke vi. 37.
[18] Luke vi. 36.
[19] Matt. vii. 2; Luke vi. 38.
[20] Matt. v. 3, 10; Luke vi. 20.
[21] Comp. 2 Pet. iii. 15.
[22] The form is *plural*, but one Epistle is probably meant. [So, even in English, "letters" may be classically used for a single letter, as we say "by these presents." But even we might speak of St. Paul as having written his Epistles *to us;* so the Epistles to Thessalonica and Corinth might more naturally still be referred to here].
[23] Comp. Gal. iv. 26.

THE EPISTLE OF POLYCARP.

possessed of these graces, he hath fulfilled the command of righteousness, since he that hath love is far from all sin.

CHAP. IV. — VARIOUS EXHORTATIONS.

"But the love of money is the root of all evils."[1] Knowing, therefore, that "as we brought nothing into the world, so we can carry nothing out,"[2] let us arm ourselves with the armour of righteousness;[3] and let us teach, first of all, ourselves to walk in the commandments of the Lord. Next, [teach] your wives [to walk] in the faith given to them, and in love and purity tenderly loving their own husbands in all truth, and loving all [others] equally in all chastity; and to train up their children in the knowledge and fear of God. Teach the widows to be discreet as respects the faith of the Lord, praying continually[4] for all, being far from all slandering, evil-speaking, false-witnessing, love of money, and every kind of evil; knowing that they are the altar[5] of God, that He clearly perceives all things, and that nothing is hid from Him, neither reasonings, nor reflections, nor any one of the secret things of the heart.

CHAP. V. — THE DUTIES OF DEACONS, YOUTHS, AND VIRGINS.

Knowing, then, that "God is not mocked,"[6] we ought to walk worthy of His commandment and glory. In like manner should the deacons be blameless before the face of His righteousness, as being the servants of God and Christ,[7] and not of men. They must not be slanderers, double-tongued,[8] or lovers of money, but temperate in all things, compassionate, industrious, walking according to the truth of the Lord, who was the servant[9] of all. If we please Him in this present world, we shall receive also the future world, according as He has promised to us that He will raise us again from the dead, and that if we live[10] worthily of Him, "we shall also reign together with Him,"[11] provided only we believe. In like manner, let the young men also be blameless in all things, being especially careful to preserve purity, and keeping themselves in, as with a bridle, from every kind of evil. For it is well that they should be cut off from[12] the lusts that are in the world, since "every lust warreth against the spirit;"[13] and "neither fornicators, nor effeminate, nor abusers of themselves with mankind, shall inherit the kingdom of God,"[14] nor those who do things inconsistent and unbecoming. Wherefore, it is needful to abstain from all these things, being subject to the presbyters and deacons, as unto God and Christ. The virgins also must walk in a blameless and pure conscience.

CHAP. VI. — THE DUTIES OF PRESBYTERS AND OTHERS.

And let the presbyters be compassionate and merciful to all, bringing back those that wander, visiting all the sick, and not neglecting the widow, the orphan, or the poor, but always "providing for that which is becoming in the sight of God and man;"[15] abstaining from all wrath, respect of persons, and unjust judgment; keeping far off from all covetousness, not quickly crediting [an evil report] against any one, not severe in judgment, as knowing that we are all under a debt of sin. If then we entreat the Lord to forgive us, we ought also ourselves to forgive;[16] for we are before the eyes of our Lord and God, and "we must all appear at the judgment-seat of Christ, and must every one give an account of himself."[17] Let us then serve Him in fear, and with all reverence, even as He Himself has commanded us, and as the apostles who preached the Gospel unto us, and the prophets who proclaimed beforehand the coming of the Lord [have alike taught us]. Let us be zealous in the pursuit of that which is good, keeping ourselves from causes of offence, from false brethren, and from those who in hypocrisy bear the name of the Lord, and draw away vain men into error.

CHAP. VII. — AVOID THE DOCETÆ, AND PERSEVERE IN FASTING AND PRAYER.

"For whosoever does not confess that Jesus Christ has come in the flesh, is antichrist;"[18] and whosoever does not confess the testimony of the cross,[19] is of the devil; and whosoever perverts the oracles of the Lord to his own lusts, and says that there is neither a resurrection nor a judgment, he is the first-born of Satan.[20] Wherefore, forsaking the vanity of many, and their false doctrines, let us return to the word which has been handed down to us from[21] the beginning; "watching unto prayer,"[22] and persevering in fasting; beseeching in our supplications the all-seeing God "not to lead us into tempta-

---

[1] 1 Tim. vi. 10.
[2] 1 Tim. vi. 7.
[3] Comp. Eph. vi. 11.
[4] Comp. 1 Thess. v. 17.
[5] Some here read, "altars."
[6] Gal. vi. 7.
[7] Some read, "God in Christ."
[8] Comp. 1 Tim. iii. 8.
[9] Comp. Matt. xx. 28.
[10] Πολιτευσώμεθα, referring to the whole conduct; comp. Phil. i. 27.
[11] 2 Tim. ii. 12.
[12] Some read, ἀνακύπτεσθαι, "to emerge from." [So Chevallier, but not Wake nor Jacobson. See the note of latter, *ad loc.*]
[13] 1 Pet. ii. 11.
[14] 1 Cor vi. 9, 10.
[15] Rom. xii. 17; 2 Cor. viii. 31.
[16] Matt. vi. 12-14.
[17] Rom. xiv. 10-12; 2 Cor. v. 10.
[18] 1 John iv. 3.
[19] Literally, "the martyrdom of the cross," which some render, "His suffering on the cross."
[20] [The original, perhaps, of Eusebius (*Hist.* iv. cap. 14). It became a common-place expression in the Church.]
[21] Comp. Jude 3.
[22] 1 Pet. iv. 7.

tion,"[1] as the Lord has said: "The spirit truly is willing, but the flesh is weak."[2]

CHAP. VIII. — PERSEVERE IN HOPE AND PATIENCE.

Let us then continually persevere in our hope, and the earnest of our righteousness, which is Jesus Christ, "who bore our sins in His own body on the tree,"[3] "who did no sin, neither was guile found in His mouth,"[4] but endured all things for us, that we might live in Him.[5] Let us then be imitators of His patience; and if we suffer[6] for His name's sake, let us glorify Him.[7] For He has set us this example[8] in Himself, and we have believed that such is the case.

CHAP. IX. — PATIENCE INCULCATED.

I exhort you all, therefore, to yield obedience to the word of righteousness, and to exercise all patience, such as ye have seen [set] before your eyes, not only in the case of the blessed Ignatius, and Zosimus, and Rufus, but also in others among yourselves, and in Paul himself, and the rest of the apostles. [This do] in the assurance that all these have not run[9] in vain, but in faith and righteousness, and that they are [now] in their due place in the presence of the Lord, with whom also they suffered. For they loved not this present world, but Him who died for us, and for our sakes was raised again by God from the dead.

CHAP. X. — EXHORTATION TO THE PRACTICE OF VIRTUE.[10]

Stand fast, therefore, in these things, and follow the example of the Lord, being firm and unchangeable in the faith, loving the brotherhood,[11] and being attached to one another, joined together in the truth, exhibiting the meekness of the Lord in your intercourse with one another, and despising no one. When you can do good, defer it not, because "alms delivers from death."[12] Be all of you subject one to another,[13] having your conduct blameless among the Gentiles,"[14] that ye may both receive praise for your good works, and the Lord may not be blasphemed through you. But woe to him by whom the name of the Lord is blasphemed![15] Teach, therefore, sobriety to all, and manifest it also in your own conduct.

CHAP. XI. — EXPRESSION OF GRIEF ON ACCOUNT OF VALENS.

I am greatly grieved for Valens, who was once a presbyter among you, because he so little understands the place that was given him [in the Church]. I exhort you, therefore, that ye abstain from covetousness,[16] and that ye be chaste and truthful. "Abstain from every form of evil."[17] For if a man cannot govern himself in such matters, how shall he enjoin them on others? If a man does not keep himself from covetousness,[16] he shall be defiled by idolatry, and shall be judged as one of the heathen. But who of us are ignorant of the judgment of the Lord? "Do we not know that the saints shall judge the world?"[18] as Paul teaches. But I have neither seen nor heard of any such thing among you, in the midst of whom the blessed Paul laboured, and who are commended[19] in the beginning of his Epistle. For he boasts of you in all those Churches which alone then knew the Lord; but we [of Smyrna] had not yet known Him. I am deeply grieved, therefore, brethren, for him (Valens) and his wife; to whom may the Lord grant true repentance! And be ye then moderate in regard to this matter, and "do not count such as enemies,"[20] but call them back as suffering and straying members, that ye may save your whole body. For by so acting ye shall edify yourselves.[21]

CHAP. XII. — EXHORTATION TO VARIOUS GRACES.

For I trust that ye are well versed in the Sacred Scriptures, and that nothing is hid from you; but to me this privilege is not yet granted.[22] It is declared then in these Scriptures, "Be ye angry, and sin not,"[23] and, "Let not the sun go down upon your wrath."[24] Happy is he who remembers[25] this, which I believe to be the case with you. But may the God and Father of our Lord Jesus Christ, and Jesus Christ Himself, who is the Son of God, and our everlasting High Priest, build you up in faith and truth, and in all meekness, gentleness, patience, long-suffering, forbearance, and purity; and may He bestow on you a lot and portion among His saints, and on us with you, and on all that are under heaven, who shall believe in our Lord

---

[1] Matt. vi. 13, xxvi. 41.
[2] Matt. xxvi. 41; Mark xiv. 38.
[3] 1 Pet. ii. 24.
[4] 1 Pet. ii. 22.
[5] Comp. 1 John iv. 9.
[6] Comp. Acts v. 41; 1 Pet. iv. 16.
[7] Some read, "we glorify Him."
[8] Comp. 1 Pet. ii. 21.
[9] Comp. Phil. ii. 16; Gal. ii. 2.
[10] This and the two following chapters are preserved only in a Latin version. [See Jacobson, *ad loc.*]
[11] Comp. 1 Pet. ii. 17.
[12] Tobit iv. 10, xii. 9.
[13] Comp. 1 Pet. v. 5.
[14] 1 Pet. ii. 12.
[15] Isa. lii. 5.

[16] Some think that *incontinence* on the part of Valens and his wife is referred to. [For many reasons I am glad the translators have preferred the reading πλεονεξίας. The next word, *chaste*, sufficiently rebukes the example of Valens. For once I venture not to coincide with Jacobson's comment.]
[17] 1 Thess. v. 22.
[18] 1 Cor. vi. 2.
[19] Some read, "named;" comp. Phil. i. 5.
[20] 2 Thess. iii. 15.
[21] Comp. 1 Cor. xii. 26.
[22] This passage is very obscure. Some render it as follows: "But at present it is not granted unto me to practise that which is written, Be ye angry," etc.
[23] Ps. iv. 5.
[24] Eph. iv. 26.
[25] Some read, "believes."

Jesus Christ, and in His Father, who "raised Him from the dead."[1] Pray for all the saints. Pray also for kings,[2] and potentates, and princes, and for those that persecute and hate you,[3] and for the enemies of the cross, that your fruit may be manifest to all, and that ye may be perfect in Him.

CHAP. XIII. — CONCERNING THE TRANSMISSION OF EPISTLES.

Both you and Ignatius[4] wrote to me, that if any one went [from this] into Syria, he should carry your letter[5] with him; which request I will attend to if I find a fitting opportunity, either personally, or through some other acting for me, that your desire may be fulfilled. The Epistles of Ignatius written by him[6] to us, and all the rest [of his Epistles] which we have by us, we have sent to you, as you requested. They are subjoined to this Epistle, and by them ye may be greatly profited; for they treat of faith and patience, and all things that tend to edification in our Lord. Any[7] more certain information you may have obtained respecting both Ignatius himself, and those that were[8] with him, have the goodness to make known[9] to us.

CHAP. XIV. — CONCLUSION.

These things I have written to you by Crescens, whom up to the present[10] time I have recommended unto you, and do now recommend. For he has acted blamelessly among us, and I believe also among you. Moreover, ye will hold his sister in esteem when she comes to you. Be ye safe in the Lord Jesus Christ. Grace be with you all.[11] Amen.

---

[1] Gal. i. 1.
[2] Comp. 1 Tim. ii. 2.
[3] Matt. v. 44.
[4] Comp. Ep. of Ignatius to Polycarp, chap. viii.
[5] Or, "letters."
[6] Reference is here made to the two letters of Ignatius, one to Polycarp himself, and the other to the church at Smyrna.
[7] Henceforth, to the end, we have only the Latin version.
[8] The Latin version reads "are," which has been corrected as above.
[9] Polycarp was aware of the death of Ignatius (chap. ix.), but was as yet apparently ignorant of the circumstances attending it. [Who can fail to be touched by these affectionate yet entirely calm expressions as to his martyred friend and brother? Martyrdom was the habitual end of Christ's soldiers, and Polycarp expected his own; hence his restrained and temperate words of interest.]
[10] Some read, "in this present Epistle."
[11] Others read, "and in favour with all yours."

INTRODUCTORY NOTE

TO THE

EPISTLE CONCERNING THE MARTYRDOM OF POLYCARP

INTERNAL evidence goes far to establish the credit which Eusebius lends to this specimen of the martyrologies, certainly not the earliest if we accept that of Ignatius as genuine. As an encyclical of one of "the seven churches" to another of the same Seven, and as bearing witness to their aggregation with others into the unity of "the Holy and Catholic Church," it is a very interesting witness, not only to an article of the creed, but to the original meaning and acceptation of the same. More than this, it is evidence of the strength of Christ perfected in human weakness; and thus it affords us an assurance of grace equal to our day in every time of need. When I see in it, however, an example of what a noble army of martyrs, women and children included, suffered in those days "for the testimony of Jesus," and in order to hand down the knowledge of the Gospel to these boastful ages of our own, I confess myself edified by what I read, chiefly because I am humbled and abashed in comparing what a Christian used to be, with what a Christian is, in our times, even at his best estate.

That this Epistle has been interpolated can hardly be doubted, when we compare it with the unvarnished specimen, in Eusebius. As for the "fragrant smell" that came from the fire, many kinds of wood emit the like in burning; and, apart from Oriental warmth of colouring, there seems nothing incredible in the narrative if we except "the dove" (chap. xvi.), which, however, is probably a corrupt reading,[1] as suggested by our translators. The blade was thrust into the martyr's *left side;* and this, opening the heart, caused the outpouring of a flood, and not a mere trickling. But, though Greek thus amended is a plausible conjecture, there seems to have been nothing of the kind in the copy quoted by Eusebius. On the other hand, note the truly catholic and scriptural testimony: "We love the martyrs, but the Son of God we worship: it is impossible for us to worship any other."

Bishop Jacobson assigns more than fifty pages to this martyrology, with a Latin version and abundant notes. To these I must refer the student, who may wish to see this attractive history in all the light of critical scholarship and, often, of admirable comment.

The following is the original INTRODUCTORY NOTICE: —

THE following letter purports to have been written by the Church at Smyrna to the Church at Philomelium, and through that Church to the whole Christian world, in order to give a succinct account of the circumstances attending the martyrdom of Polycarp. It is the earliest of all the Martyria, and has generally been accounted both the most interesting and authentic. Not a few, however, deem it interpolated in several passages, and some refer it to a much later date than the

---

[1] See an ingenious conjecture in Bishop Wordsworth's *Hippolytus and the Church of Rome*, p. 318, C.

middle of the second century, to which it has been commonly ascribed. We cannot tell how much it may owe to the writers (chap. xxii.) who successively transcribed it. Great part of it has been engrossed by Eusebius in his *Ecclesiastical History* (iv. 15); and it is instructive to observe, that some of the most startling miraculous phenomena recorded in the text as it now stands, have no place in the narrative as given by that early historian of the Church. Much discussion has arisen respecting several particulars contained in this Martyrium; but into these disputes we do not enter, having it for our aim simply to present the reader with as faithful a translation as possible of this very interesting monument of Christian antiquity.

THE ENCYCLICAL EPISTLE OF THE CHURCH AT SMYRNA

CONCERNING THE MARTYRDOM OF THE HOLY POLYCARP

The Church of God which sojourns at Smyrna, to the Church of God sojourning in Philomelium,[1] and to all the congregations[2] of the Holy and Catholic Church in every place: Mercy, peace, and love from God the Father, and our Lord Jesus Christ, be multiplied.

CHAP. I. — SUBJECT OF WHICH WE WRITE.

We have written to you, brethren, as to what relates to the martyrs, and especially to the blessed Polycarp, who put an end to the persecution, having, as it were, set a seal upon it by his martyrdom. For almost all the events that happened previously [to this one], took place that the Lord might show us from above a martyrdom becoming the Gospel. For he waited to be delivered up, even as the Lord had done, that we also might become his followers, while we look not merely at what concerns ourselves, but have regard also to our neighbours. For it is the part of a true and well-founded love, not only to wish one's self to be saved, but also all the brethren.

CHAP. II. — THE WONDERFUL CONSTANCY OF THE MARTYRS.

All the martyrdoms, then, were blessed and noble which took place according to the will of God. For it becomes us who profess[3] greater piety than others, to ascribe the authority over all things to God. And truly,[4] who can fail to admire their nobleness of mind, and their patience, with that love towards their Lord which they displayed? — who, when they were so torn with scourges, that the frame of their bodies, even to the very inward veins and arteries, was laid open, still patiently endured, while even those that stood by pitied and bewailed them. But they reached such a pitch of magnanimity, that not one of them let a sigh or a groan escape them; thus proving to us all that those holy martyrs of Christ, at the very time when they suffered such torments, were absent from the body, or rather, that the Lord then stood by them, and communed with them. And, looking to the grace of Christ, they despised all the torments of this world, redeeming themselves from eternal punishment by [the suffering of] a single hour. For this reason the fire of their savage executioners appeared cool to them. For they kept before their view escape from that fire which is eternal and never shall be quenched, and looked forward with the eyes of their heart to those good things which are laid up for such as endure; things "which ear hath not heard, nor eye seen, neither have entered into the heart of man,"[5] but were revealed by the Lord to them, inasmuch as they were no longer men, but had already become angels. And, in like manner, those who were condemned to the wild beasts endured dreadful tortures, being stretched out upon beds full of spikes, and subjected to various other kinds of torments, in order that, if it were possible, the tyrant might, by their lingering tortures, lead them to a denial [of Christ].

CHAP. III. — THE CONSTANCY OF GERMANICUS. THE DEATH OF POLYCARP IS DEMANDED.

For the devil did indeed invent many things against them; but thanks be to God, he could not prevail over all. For the most noble Germanicus strengthened the timidity of others by his own patience, and fought heroically[6] with the wild beasts. For, when the proconsul sought to persuade him, and urged him[7] to

---

[1] Some read, "Philadelphia," but on inferior authority. Philomelium was a city of Phrygia.
[2] The word in the original is παροικίαις, from which the English "parishes" is derived.
[3] Literally, "who are more pious."
[4] The account now returns to the illustration of the statement made in the first sentence.
[5] 1 Cor. ii. 9.
[6] Or, "illustriously."
[7] Or, "said to him."

take pity upon his age, he attracted the wild beast towards himself, and provoked it, being desirous to escape all the more quickly from an unrighteous and impious world. But upon this the whole multitude, marvelling at the nobility of mind displayed by the devout and godly race of Christians,[1] cried out, "Away with the Atheists; let Polycarp be sought out!"

CHAP. IV. — QUINTUS THE APOSTATE.

Now one named Quintus, a Phrygian, who was but lately come from Phrygia, when he saw the wild beasts, became afraid. This was the man who forced himself and some others to come forward voluntarily [for trial]. Him the proconsul, after many entreaties, persuaded to swear and to offer sacrifice. Wherefore, brethren, we do not commend those who give themselves up [to suffering], seeing the Gospel does not teach so to do.[2]

CHAP. V. — THE DEPARTURE AND VISION OF POLYCARP.

But the most admirable Polycarp, when he first heard [that he was sought for], was in no measure disturbed, but resolved to continue in the city. However, in deference to the wish of many, he was persuaded to leave it. He departed, therefore, to a country house not far distant from the city. There he stayed with a few [friends], engaged in nothing else night and day than praying for all men, and for the Churches throughout the world, according to his usual custom. And while he was praying, a vision presented itself to him three days before he was taken; and, behold, the pillow under his head seemed to him on fire. Upon this, turning to those that were with him, he said to them prophetically, "I must be burnt alive."

CHAP. VI. — POLYCARP IS BETRAYED BY A SERVANT.

And when those who sought for him were at hand, he departed to another dwelling, whither his pursuers immediately came after him. And when they found him not, they seized upon two youths [that were there], one of whom, being subjected to torture, confessed. It was thus impossible that he should continue hid, since those that betrayed him were of his own household. The Irenarch[3] then (whose office is the same as that of the Cleronomus[4]), by name Herod, hastened to bring him into the stadium. [This all happened] that he might fulfil his special lot, being made a partaker of Christ, and that they who betrayed him might undergo the punishment of Judas himself.

CHAP. VII. — POLYCARP IS FOUND BY HIS PURSUERS.

His pursuers then, along with horsemen, and taking the youth with them, went forth at supper-time on the day of the preparation,[5] with their usual weapons, as if going out against a robber.[6] And being come about evening [to the place where he was], they found him lying down in the upper room of[7] a certain little house, from which he might have escaped into another place; but he refused, saying, "The will of God[8] be done."[9] So when he heard that they were come, he went down and spake with them. And as those that were present marvelled at his age and constancy, some of them said, "Was so much effort[10] made to capture such a venerable man?"[11] Immediately then, in that very hour, he ordered that something to eat and drink should be set before them, as much indeed as they cared for, while he besought them to allow him an hour to pray without disturbance. And on their giving him leave, he stood and prayed, being full of the grace of God, so that he could not cease[12] for two full hours, to the astonishment of them that heard him, insomuch that many began to repent that they had come forth against so godly and venerable an old man.

CHAP. VIII. — POLYCARP IS BROUGHT INTO THE CITY.

Now, as soon as he had ceased praying, having made mention of all that had at any time come in contact with him, both small and great, illustrious and obscure, as well as the whole Catholic Church throughout the world, the time of his departure having arrived, they set him upon an ass, and conducted him into the city, the day being that of the great Sabbath. And the Irenarch Herod, accompanied by his father Nicetes (both riding in a chariot[13]), met him, and taking him up into the chariot, they seated themselves beside him, and endeavoured to persuade him, saying, "What harm is there in saying, Lord Cæsar,[14] and in sacrificing, with the other ceremonies observed on such occasions, and so make sure of safety?" But he at first gave them no answer; and when they continued to urge him,

---

[1] Literally, "the nobleness of the God-loving and God-fearing race of Christians."
[2] Comp. Matt. x. 23.
[3] It was the duty of the Irenarch to apprehend all seditious troublers of the public peace.
[4] Some think that those magistrates bore this name that were elected by lot.
[5] That is, on Friday.
[6] Comp. Matt. xxvi. 55.
[7] Or, "in."
[8] Some read "the Lord."
[9] Comp. Matt vi. 10; Acts xxi 14.
[10] Or, "diligence."
[11] Jacobson reads, "and [marvelling] that they had used so great diligence to capture," etc.
[12] Or, "be silent."
[13] Jacobson deems these words an interpolation.
[14] Or, "Cæsar is Lord," all the MSS. having κύριος instead of κύριε, as usually printed.

he said, "I shall not do as you advise me." So they, having no hope of persuading him, began to speak bitter[1] words unto him, and cast him with violence out of the chariot,[2] insomuch that, in getting down from the carriage, he dislocated his leg[3] [by the fall]. But without being disturbed,[4] and as if suffering nothing, he went eagerly forward with all haste, and was conducted to the stadium, where the tumult was so great, that there was no possibility of being heard.

CHAP. IX. — POLYCARP REFUSES TO REVILE CHRIST.

Now, as Polycarp was entering into the stadium, there came to him a voice from heaven, saying, "Be strong, and show thyself a man, O Polycarp!" No one saw who it was that spoke to him; but those of our brethren who were present heard the voice. And as he was brought forward, the tumult became great when they heard that Polycarp was taken. And when he came near, the proconsul asked him whether he was Polycarp. On his confessing that he was, [the proconsul] sought to persuade him to deny [Christ], saying, "Have respect to thy old age," and other similar things, according to their custom, [such as], "Swear by the fortune of Cæsar; repent, and say, Away with the Atheists." But Polycarp, gazing with a stern countenance on all the multitude of the wicked heathen then in the stadium, and waving his hand towards them, while with groans he looked up to heaven, said, "Away with the Atheists."[5] Then, the proconsul urging him, and saying, "Swear, and I will set thee at liberty, reproach Christ;" Polycarp declared, "Eighty and six years have I served Him, and He never did me any injury: how then can I blaspheme my King and my Saviour?"

CHAP. X. — POLYCARP CONFESSES HIMSELF A CHRISTIAN.

And when the proconsul yet again pressed him, and said, "Swear by the fortune of Cæsar," he answered, "Since thou art vainly urgent that, as thou sayest, I should swear by the fortune of Cæsar, and pretendest not to know who and what I am, hear me declare with boldness, I am a Christian. And if you wish to learn what the doctrines[6] of Christianity are, appoint me a day, and thou shalt hear them." The proconsul replied, "Persuade the people." But Polycarp said, "To thee I have thought it right to offer an account [of my faith]; for we are taught to give all due honour (which entails no injury upon ourselves) to the powers and authorities which are ordained of God.[7] But as for *these*, I do not deem them worthy of receiving any account from me."[8]

CHAP. XI. — NO THREATS HAVE ANY EFFECT ON POLYCARP.

The proconsul then said to him, "I have wild beasts at hand; to these will I cast thee, except thou repent." But he answered, "Call them then, for we are not accustomed to repent of what is good in order to adopt that which is evil;[9] and it is well for me to be changed from what is evil to what is righteous."[10] But again the proconsul said to him, "I will cause thee to be consumed by fire, seeing thou despisest the wild beasts, if thou wilt not repent." But Polycarp said, "Thou threatenest me with fire which burneth for an hour, and after a little is extinguished, but art ignorant of the fire of the coming judgment and of eternal punishment, reserved for the ungodly. But why tarriest thou? Bring forth what thou wilt."

CHAP. XII. — POLYCARP IS SENTENCED TO BE BURNED.

While he spoke these and many other like things, he was filled with confidence and joy, and his countenance was full of grace, so that not merely did it not fall as if troubled by the things said to him, but, on the contrary, the proconsul was astonished, and sent his herald to proclaim in the midst of the stadium thrice, "Polycarp has confessed that he is a Christian." This proclamation having been made by the herald, the whole multitude both of the heathen and Jews, who dwelt at Smyrna, cried out with uncontrollable fury, and in a loud voice, "This is the teacher of Asia,[11] the father of the Christians, and the overthrower of our gods, he who has been teaching many not to sacrifice, or to worship the gods." Speaking thus, they cried out, and besought Philip the Asiarch[12] to let loose a lion upon Polycarp. But Philip answered that it was not lawful for him to do so, seeing the shows[13] of wild beasts were already finished. Then it seemed good to them to cry out with one consent, that Polycarp should be burnt alive. For thus it behooved the vision which was revealed to him in regard to his pillow to be fulfilled, when, seeing it on fire as he was praying, he turned about and said prophetically to the faithful that were with him, "I must be burnt alive."

---

[1] Or, "terrible."
[2] Or, "cast him down" simply, the following words being, as above, an interpolation.
[3] Or, "sprained his ankle."
[4] Or, "not turning back."
[5] Referring the words to the heathen, and not to the Christians, as was desired.
[6] Or, "an account of Christianity."
[7] Comp. Rom. xiii. 1–7; Tit. iii. 1.
[8] Or, "of my making any defence to them."
[9] Literally, "repentance from things better to things worse is a change impossible to us."
[10] That is, to leave this world for a better.
[11] Some read, "ungodliness," but the above seems preferable.
[12] The Asiarchs were those who superintended all arrangements connected with the games in the several provinces.
[13] Literally, "the baiting of dogs."

CHAP. XIII. — THE FUNERAL PILE IS ERECTED.

This, then, was carried into effect with greater speed than it was spoken, the multitudes immediately gathering together wood and fagots out of the shops and baths; the Jews especially, according to custom, eagerly assisting them in it. And when the funeral pile was ready, Polycarp, laying aside all his garments, and loosing his girdle, sought also to take off his sandals, — a thing he was not accustomed to do, inasmuch as every one of the faithful was always eager who should first touch his skin. For, on account of his holy life,[1] he was, even before his martyrdom, adorned[2] with every kind of good. Immediately then they surrounded him with those substances which had been prepared for the funeral pile. But when they were about also to fix him with nails, he said, "Leave me as I am; for He that giveth me strength to endure the fire, will also enable me, without your securing me by nails, to remain without moving in the pile."

CHAP. XIV. — THE PRAYER OF POLYCARP.

They did not nail him then, but simply bound him. And he, placing his hands behind him, and being bound like a distinguished ram [taken] out of a great flock for sacrifice, and prepared to be an acceptable burnt-offering unto God, looked up to heaven, and said, "O Lord God Almighty, the Father of thy beloved and blessed Son Jesus Christ, by whom we have received the knowledge of Thee, the God of angels and powers, and of every creature, and of the whole race of the righteous who live before thee, I give Thee thanks that Thou hast counted me worthy of this day and this hour, that I should have a part in the number of Thy martyrs, in the cup[3] of thy Christ, to the resurrection of eternal life, both of soul and body, through the incorruption [imparted] by the Holy Ghost. Among whom may I be accepted this day before Thee as a fat[4] and acceptable sacrifice, according as Thou, the ever-truthful[5] God, hast foreordained, hast revealed beforehand to me, and now hast fulfilled. Wherefore also I praise Thee for all things, I bless Thee, I glorify Thee, along with the everlasting and heavenly Jesus Christ, Thy beloved Son, with whom, to Thee, and the Holy Ghost, be glory both now and to all coming ages. Amen."[6]

CHAP. XV. — POLYCARP IS NOT INJURED BY THE FIRE.

When he had pronounced this *amen*, and so finished his prayer, those who were appointed for the purpose kindled the fire. And as the flame blazed forth in great fury,[7] we, to whom it was given to witness it, beheld a great miracle, and have been preserved that we might report to others what then took place. For the fire, shaping itself into the form of an arch, like the sail of a ship when filled with the wind, encompassed as by a circle the body of the martyr. And he appeared within not like flesh which is burnt, but as bread that is baked, or as gold and silver glowing in a furnace. Moreover, we perceived such a sweet odour [coming from the pile], as if frankincense or some such precious spices had been smoking[8] there.

CHAP. XVI. — POLYCARP IS PIERCED BY A DAGGER.

At length, when those wicked men perceived that his body could not be consumed by the fire, they commanded an executioner to go near and pierce him through with a dagger. And on his doing this, there came forth a dove,[9] and a great quantity of blood, so that the fire was extinguished; and all the people wondered that there should be such a difference between the unbelievers and the elect, of whom this most admirable Polycarp was one, having in our own times been an apostolic and prophetic teacher, and bishop of the Catholic Church which is in Smyrna. For every word that went out of his mouth either has been or shall yet be accomplished.

CHAP. XVII. — THE CHRISTIANS ARE REFUSED POLYCARP'S BODY.

But when the adversary of the race of the righteous, the envious, malicious, and wicked one, perceived the impressive[10] nature of his martyrdom, and [considered] the blameless life he had led from the beginning, and how he was now crowned with the wreath of immortality, having beyond dispute received his reward, he did his utmost that not the least memorial of him should be taken away by us, although many desired to do this, and to become possessors[11] of his holy flesh. For this end he suggested it to Nicetes, the father of Herod and brother of Alce, to go and entreat the governor not to give up his body to be buried, "lest," said he, "forsaking Him

---

[1] Literally, "good behaviour."
[2] Some think this implies that Polycarp's skin was believed to possess a miraculous efficacy.
[3] Comp. Matt. xx. 22, xxvi. 39; Mark x 38.
[4] Literally, "in a fat," etc., [or, "in a rich"].
[5] Literally, "the not false and true God."
[6] Eusebius (*Hist. Eccl.*, iv. 15) has preserved a great portion of this Martyrium, but in a text considerably differing from that we have followed. Here, instead of "and," he has "in the Holy Ghost."

[7] Literally, "a great flame shining forth."
[8] Literally, "breathing."
[9] Eusebius omits all mention of the *dove*, and many have thought the text to be here corrupt. It has been proposed to read ἐπ' ἀριστερᾷ, "on the left hand side," instead of περιστερά, "a dove."
[10] Literally, "greatness."
[11] The Greek, literally translated, is, "and to have fellowship with his holy flesh."

that was crucified, they begin to worship this one." This he said at the suggestion and urgent persuasion of the Jews, who also watched us, as we sought to take him out of the fire, being ignorant of this, that it is neither possible for us ever to forsake Christ, who suffered for the salvation of such as shall be saved throughout the whole world (the blameless one for sinners [1]), nor to worship any other. For Him indeed, as being the Son of God, we adore; but the martyrs, as disciples and followers of the Lord, we worthily love on account of their extraordinary [2] affection towards their own King and Master, of whom may we also be made companions [3] and fellow-disciples!

CHAP. XVIII. — THE BODY OF POLYCARP IS BURNED.

The centurion then, seeing the strife excited by the Jews, placed the body [4] in the midst of the fire, and consumed it. Accordingly, we afterwards took up his bones, as being more precious than the most exquisite jewels, and more purified [5] than gold, and deposited them in a fitting place, whither, being gathered together, as opportunity is allowed us, with joy and rejoicing, the Lord shall grant us to celebrate the anniversary [6] of his martyrdom, both in memory of those who have already finished their course,[7] and for the exercising and preparation of those yet to walk in their steps.

CHAP. XIX. — PRAISE OF THE MARTYR POLYCARP.

This, then, is the account of the blessed Polycarp, who, being the twelfth that was martyred in Smyrna (reckoning those also of Philadelphia), yet occupies a place of his own [8] in the memory of all men, insomuch that he is everywhere spoken of by the heathen themselves. He was not merely an illustrious teacher, but also a pre-eminent martyr, whose martyrdom all desire to imitate, as having been altogether consistent with the Gospel of Christ. For, having through patience overcome the unjust governor, and thus acquired the crown of immortality, he now, with the apostles and all the righteous [in heaven], rejoicingly glorifies God, even the Father, and blesses our Lord Jesus Christ, the Saviour of our souls, the Governor of our bodies, and the Shepherd of the Catholic Church throughout the world.[9]

CHAP. XX. — THIS EPISTLE IS TO BE TRANSMITTED TO THE BRETHREN.

Since, then, ye requested that we would at large make you acquainted with what really took place, we have for the present sent you this summary account through our brother Marcus. When, therefore, ye have yourselves read this Epistle,[10] be pleased to send it to the brethren at a greater distance, that they also may glorify the Lord, who makes such choice of His own servants. To Him who is able to bring us all by His grace and goodness [11] into his everlasting kingdom, through His only-begotten Son Jesus Christ, to Him be glory, and honour, and power, and majesty, for ever. Amen. Salute all the saints. They that are with us salute you, and Evarestus, who wrote this Epistle, with all his house.

CHAP. XXI. — THE DATE OF THE MARTYRDOM.

Now, the blessed Polycarp suffered martyrdom on the second day of the month Xanthicus just begun,[12] the seventh day before the Kalends of May, on the great Sabbath, at the eighth hour.[13] He was taken by Herod, Philip the Trallian being high priest,[14] Statius Quadratus being proconsul, but Jesus Christ being King for ever, to whom be glory, honour, majesty, and an everlasting throne, from generation to generation. Amen.

CHAP. XXII. — SALUTATION.

We wish you, brethren, all happiness, while you walk according to the doctrine of the Gospel of Jesus Christ; with whom be glory to God the Father and the Holy Spirit, for the salvation of His holy elect, after whose example [15] the blessed Polycarp suffered, following in whose steps may we too be found in the kingdom of Jesus Christ!

These things [16] Caius transcribed from the copy of Irenæus (who was a disciple of Polycarp), having himself been intimate with Irenæus. And I Socrates transcribed them at Corinth from the copy of Caius. Grace be with you all.

And I again, Pionius, wrote them from the previously written copy, having carefully searched into them, and the blessed Polycarp having

---

[1] This clause is omitted by Eusebius: it was probably interpolated by some transcriber, who had in his mind 1 Pet. iii. 18.
[2] Literally, "unsurpassable."
[3] Literally, "fellow-partakers."
[4] Or, "him."
[5] Or, "more tried."
[6] Literally, "the birth-day."
[7] Literally, "been athletes."
[8] Literally, "is alone remembered."
[9] Several additions are here made. One MS. has, "and the all-holy and life-giving Spirit;" while the old Latin version reads, "and the Holy Spirit, by whom we know all things."
[10] Literally, "having learned these things."
[11] Literally, "gift."
[12] The translation is here very doubtful. Wake renders the words μηνὸς ἱσταμένου, "of the *present* month."
[13] Great obscurity hangs over the chronology here indicated. According to Usher, the Smyrnæans began the month Xanthicus on the 25th of March. But the seventh day before the Kalends of May is the 25th of April. Some, therefore, read Ἀπριλλίων instead of Μαίων. The great Sabbath is that before the passover. The "eighth hour" may correspond either to our 8 A.M. or 2 P.M.
[14] Called before (chap. xii.) *Asiarch*.
[15] Literally, "according as."
[16] What follows is, of course, no part of the original Epistle.

manifested them to me through a revelation, even as I shall show in what follows. I have collected these things, when they had almost faded away through the lapse of time, that the Lord Jesus Christ may also gather me along with His elect into His heavenly kingdom, to whom, with the Father and the Holy Spirit, be glory for ever and ever. Amen.

INTRODUCTORY NOTE

TO THE

EPISTLE OF IGNATIUS TO THE EPHESIANS

[A.D. 30–107.] THE seductive myth which represents this Father as the little child whom the Lord placed in the midst of his apostles (St. Matt. xviii. 2) indicates at least the period when he may be supposed to have been born. That he and Polycarp were fellow-disciples under St. John, is a tradition by no means inconsistent with anything in the Epistles of either. His subsequent history is sufficiently indicated in the Epistles which follow.

Had not the plan of this series been so exclusively that of a mere revised reprint, the writings of Ignatius themselves would have made me diffident as to the undertaking. It seems impossible for any one to write upon the subject of these precious remains, without provoking controversy. This publication is designed as an *Eirenicon,* and hence "few words are best," from one who might be supposed incapable of an unbiassed opinion on most of the points which have been raised in connection with these Epistles. I must content myself therefore, by referring the studious reader to the originals as edited by Bishop Jacobson, with a Latin version and copious annotations. That revered and learned divine honoured me with his friendship; and his precious edition has been my frequent study, with theological students, almost ever since it appeared in 1840. It is by no means superannuated by the vigorous Ignatian literature which has since sprung up, and to which reference will he made elsewhere. But I am content to leave the whole matter, without comment, to the minds of Christians of whatever school and to their independent conclusions. It is a great thing to present them in a single volume with the shorter and longer Epistles duly compared, and with the Curetonian version besides. One luxury only I may claim, to relieve the drudging task-work of a mere reviser. Surely I may point out some of the proverbial wisdom of this great disciple, which has often stirred my soul, as with the trumpet heard by St. John in Patmos. In him, indeed, the lions encountered a lion, one truly begotten of "the Lion of the tribe of Judah." Take, then, as a specimen, these thrilling injunctions from his letter to Polycarp, to whom he bequeathed his own spirit, and in whom he well knew the Church would recognize a sort of survival of St. John himself. If the reader has any true perception of the rhythm and force of the Greek language, let him learn by heart the originals of the following aphorisms: —

    1. Find time to pray without ceasing.
    2. Every wound is not healed with the same remedy.
    3. The times demand thee, as pilots the haven.
    4. The crown is immortality.[1]
    5. Stand like a beaten anvil.[2]
    6. It is the part of a good athlete to be bruised and to prevail.

---

[1] Does not this seem a pointed allusion to Rev. ii. 10?
[2] Στῆθι ὡς ἄκμων τυπτόμενος.

7. Consider the times: look for Him who is above time.
8. Slight not the menservants and the handmaids.
9. Let your stewardship define your work.
10. A Christian is not his own master, but waits upon God.

Ignatius so delighted in his name Theophorus (sufficiently expounded in his own words to Trajan or his official representative), that it is worth noting how deeply the early Christians felt and believed in (2 Cor. vi. 16) the indwelling Spirit.

Ignatius has been censured for his language to the Romans, in which he seems to crave martyrdom. But he was already condemned, in law a dead man, and felt himself at liberty to glory in his tribulations. Is it more than modern Christians often too lightly sing? —

"Let cares like a wild deluge come,
And storms of sorrow fall," etc.

So the holy martyr adds, "Only let me attain unto Jesus Christ."

The Epistle to the Romans is utterly inconsistent with any conception on his part, that Rome was the see and residence of a bishop holding any other than fraternal relations with himself. It is very noteworthy that it is devoid of expressions, elsewhere made emphatic,[1] which would have been much insisted upon had they been found herein. Think what use would have been made of it, had the words which he addresses to the Smyrnæans (cap. viii.) to strengthen their fidelity to Polycarp, been found in this letter to the Romans, especially as in this letter we first find the use of the phrase "Catholic Church" in patristic writings. He defines it as to be found "where Jesus Christ is," words which certainly do not limit it to communion with a professed successor of St. Peter.

The following is the original INTRODUCTORY NOTICE: —

THE epistles ascribed to Ignatius have given rise to more controversy than any other documents connected with the primitive Church. As is evident to every reader on the very first glance at these writings, they contain numerous statements which bear on points of ecclesiastical order that have long divided the Christian world; and a strong temptation has thus been felt to allow some amount of prepossession to enter into the discussion of their authenticity or spuriousness. At the same time, this question has furnished a noble field for the display of learning and acuteness, and has, in the various forms under which it has been debated, given rise to not a few works of the very highest ability and scholarship. We shall present such an outline of the controversy as may enable the reader to understand its position at the present day.

There are, in all, fifteen Epistles which bear the name of Ignatius. These are the following: One to the Virgin Mary, two to the Apostle John, one to Mary of Cassobelæ, one to the Tarsians, one to the Antiochians, one to Hero, a deacon of Antioch, one to the Philippians; one to the Ephesians, one to the Magnesians, one to the Trallians, one to the Romans, one to the Philadelphians, one to the Smyrnæans, and one to Polycarp. The first three exist only in Latin: all the rest are extant also in Greek.

It is now the universal opinion of critics, that the first eight of these professedly Ignatian letters are spurious. They bear in themselves indubitable proofs of being the production of a later age than that in which Ignatius lived. Neither Eusebius nor Jerome makes the least reference to them; and they are now by common consent set aside as forgeries, which were at various dates, and to serve special purposes, put forth under the name of the celebrated Bishop of Antioch.

But after the question has been thus simplified, it still remains sufficiently complex. Of the seven Epistles which are acknowledged by Eusebius (*Hist. Eccl.*, iii. 36), we possess two Greek recensions, a shorter and a longer. It is plain that one or other of these exhibits a corrupt text, and

---

[1] See *To the Trallians*, cap. 13. Much might have been made, had it been found here, out of the reference to Christ the High Priest (Philadelphians, cap. 9).

scholars have for the most part agreed to accept the shorter form as representing the genuine letters of Ignatius. This was the opinion generally acquiesced in, from the time when critical editions of these Epistles began to be issued, down to our own day. Criticism, indeed, fluctuated a good deal as to which Epistles should be accepted and which rejected. Archp. Usher (1644), Isaac Vossius (1646), J. B. Cotelerius (1672), Dr. T. Smith (1709), and others, edited the writings ascribed to Ignatius in forms differing very considerably as to the order in which they were arranged, and the degree of authority assigned them, until at length, from about the beginning of the eighteenth century, the seven Greek Epistles, of which a translation is here given, came to be generally accepted in their *shorter* form as the genuine writings of Ignatius.

Before this date, however, there had not been wanting some who refused to acknowledge the authenticity of these Epistles in either of the recensions in which they were then known to exist. By far the most learned and elaborate work maintaining this position was that of Daillé (or Dallæus), published in 1666. This drew forth in reply the celebrated *Vindiciæ* of Bishop Pearson, which appeared in 1672. It was generally supposed that this latter work had established on an immoveable foundation the genuineness of the shorter form of the Ignatian Epistles; and, as we have stated above, this was the conclusion almost universally accepted down to our own day. The only considerable exception to this concurrence was presented by Whiston, who laboured to maintain in his *Primitive Christianity Revived* (1711) the superior claims of the longer recension of the Epistles, apparently influenced in doing so by the support which he thought they furnished to the kind of Arianism which he had adopted.

But although the shorter form of the Ignatian letters had been generally accepted in preference to the longer, there was still a pretty prevalent opinion among scholars, that even it could not be regarded as absolutely free from interpolations, or as of undoubted authenticity. Thus said Lardner, in his *Credibility of the Gospel History* (1743) : "I have carefully compared the two editions, and am very well satisfied, upon that comparison, that the larger are an interpolation of the smaller, and not the smaller an epitome or abridgment of the larger. . . . But whether the smaller themselves are the genuine writings of Ignatius, Bishop of Antioch, is a question that has been much disputed, and has employed the pens of the ablest critics. And whatever positiveness some may have shown on either side, I must own I have found it a very difficult question."

This expression of uncertainty was repeated in substance by Jortin (1751), Mosheim (1755), Griesbach (1768), Rosenmüller (1795), Neander (1826), and many others; some going so far as to deny that we have any authentic remains of Ignatius at all, while others, though admitting the seven shorter letters as being probably his, yet strongly suspected that they were not free from interpolation. Upon the whole, however, the shorter recension was, until recently, accepted without much opposition, and chiefly in dependence on the work of Bishop Pearson above mentioned, as exhibiting the genuine form of the Epistles of Ignatius.

But a totally different aspect was given to the question by the discovery of a Syriac version of three of these Epistles among the MSS. procured from the monastery of St. Mary Deipara, in the desert of Nitria, in Egypt. In the years 1838, 1839, and again in 1842, Archdeacon Tattam visited that monastery, and succeeded in obtaining for the English Government a vast number of ancient Syriac manuscripts. On these being deposited in the British Museum, the late Dr. Cureton, who then had charge of the Syriac department, discovered among them, first, the Epistle to Polycarp, and then again, the same Epistle, with those to the Ephesians and to the Romans, in two other volumes of manuscripts.

As the result of this discovery, Cureton published in 1845 a work, entitled, *The Ancient Syriac Version of the Epistles of St. Ignatius to St. Polycarp, the Ephesians, and the Romans*, etc., in which he argued that these Epistles represented more accurately than any formerly published what Ignatius had actually written. This, of course, opened up the controversy afresh. While some accepted the views of Cureton, others very strenuously opposed them. Among the former was the late Chev. Bunsen; among the latter, an anonymous writer in the *English Review*, and Dr. Hefele, in his third edition of the *Apostolic Fathers*. In reply to those who had controverted his arguments, Cureton published his *Vindiciæ Ignatianæ* in 1846, and his *Corpus Ignatianum* in 1849. He begins his introduction to the last-named work with the following sentences: "Exactly three centuries and a half intervened between the time when three Epistles in Latin, attributed to St. Ignatius, first issued from the press, and the publication in 1845 of three letters in Syriac bearing the name of the same apostolic writer. Very few years passed before the former were almost universally regarded as false and spurious; and it seems not improbable that scarcely a longer period will elapse before the latter be almost as generally acknowledged and received as the only true and genuine letters of the venerable Bishop of Antioch that have either come down to our times, or were ever known in the earliest ages of the Christian Church."

Had the somewhat sanguine hope thus expressed been realized, it would have been unnecessary for us to present to the English reader more than a translation of these three Syriac Epistles. But the Ignatian controversy is not yet settled. There are still those who hold that the balance of argument is in favour of the shorter Greek, as against these Syriac Epistles. They regard the latter as an epitome of the former, and think the harshness which, according to them, exists in the sequence of thoughts and sentences, clearly shows that this is the case. We have therefore given all the forms of the Ignatian letters which have the least claim on our attention.[1] The reader may judge, by comparison for himself, which of these is to be accepted as genuine, supposing him disposed to admit the claims of any one of them. We content ourselves with laying the materials for judgment before him, and with referring to the above-named works in which we find the whole subject discussed.

As to the personal history of Ignatius, almost nothing is known. The principal source of information regarding him is found in the account of his martyrdom, to which the reader is referred. Polycarp alludes to him in his Epistle to the Philippians (chap. ix.), and also to his letters (chap. xiii.). Irenæus quotes a passage from his Epistle to the Romans (*Adv. Hær.*, v. 28; *Epist. ad Rom.*, chap. iv.), without, however, naming him. Origen twice refers to him, first in the preface to his Comm. on the Song of Solomon, where he quotes a passage from the Epistle of Ignatius to the Romans, and again in his sixth homily on St. Luke, where he quotes from the Epistle to the Ephesians, both times naming the author. It is unnecessary to give later references.

Supposing the letters of Ignatius and the account of his martyrdom to be authentic, we learn from them that he voluntarily presented himself before Trajan at Antioch, the seat of his bishopric, when that prince was on his *first* expedition against the Parthians and Armenians (A.D. 107); and on professing himself a Christian, was condemned to the wild beasts. After a long and dangerous voyage he came to Smyrna, of which Polycarp was bishop, and thence wrote his four Epistles to the Ephesians, the Magnesians, the Trallians, and the Romans. From Smyrna he came to Troas, and tarrying there a few days, he wrote to the Philadelphians, the Smyrnæans, and Polycarp. He then came on to Neapolis, and passed through the whole of Macedonia. Finding a ship at Dyrrachium in Epirus about to sail into Italy, he embarked, and crossing the Adriatic, was brought to Rome, where he perished on the 20th of December 107, or, as some think, who deny a twofold expedition of Trajan against the Parthians, on the same day of the year A.D. 116.

---

[1] The other Epistles, bearing the name of Ignatius, will be found in the Appendix; so that the English reader possesses in this volume a complete collection of the Ignatian letters.

THE EPISTLE OF IGNATIUS TO THE EPHESIANS

SHORTER AND LONGER VERSIONS

Ignatius, who is also called Theophorus, to the Church which is at Ephesus, in Asia, deservedly most happy, being blessed in the greatness and fulness of God the Father, and predestinated before the beginning[1] of time, that it should be always for an enduring and unchangeable glory, being united[2] and elected through the true passion by the will of the Father, and Jesus Christ, our God: Abundant happiness through Jesus Christ, and His undefiled grace.

Ignatius, who is also called Theophorus, to the Church which is at Ephesus, in Asia, deservedly most happy, being blessed in the greatness and fulness of God the Father, and predestinated before the beginning[1] of time, that it should be always for an enduring and unchangeable glory, being united[2] and elected through the true passion by the will of God the Father, and of our Lord Jesus Christ our Saviour: Abundant happiness through Jesus Christ, and His undefiled joy.[3]

CHAP. I. — PRAISE OF THE EPHESIANS.

I HAVE become acquainted with your name, much-beloved in God, which ye have acquired by the habit of righteousness, according to the faith and love in Jesus Christ our Saviour. Being the followers[4] of God, and stirring up[5] yourselves by the blood of God, ye have perfectly accomplished the work which was beseeming to you. For, on hearing that I came bound from Syria for the common name and hope, trusting through your prayers to be permitted to fight with beasts at Rome, that so by martyrdom I may indeed become the disciple of Him "who gave Himself for us, an offering and a sacrifice to God,"[6] [ye hastened to see me[7]]. I received, therefore,[8] your whole multitude in the name of God, through Onesimus, a man of inexpressible love,[9] and your bishop in the flesh, whom I pray you by Jesus Christ to love, and that you would all seek to be like him. And blessed be He who has granted unto you, being worthy, to obtain such an excellent bishop.

I HAVE become acquainted with your greatly-desired name in God, which ye have acquired by the habit of righteousness, according to the faith and love in Christ Jesus our Saviour. Being the followers[4] of the love of God towards man, and stirring up[5] yourselves by the blood of Christ, you have perfectly accomplished the work which was beseeming to you. For, on hearing that I came bound from Syria for the sake of Christ, our common hope, trusting through your prayers to be permitted to fight with beasts at Rome, that so by martyrdom I may indeed become the disciple of Him "who gave Himself for us, an offering and a sacrifice to God,"[6] [ye hastened to see me[7]]. I have therefore received your whole multitude in the name of God, through Onesimus, a man of inexpressible love,[9] and who is your bishop, whom I pray you by Jesus Christ to love, and that you would all seek to be like him. Blessed be God, who has granted unto you, who are yourselves so excellent, to obtain such an excellent bishop.

---

[1] Literally, "before the ages." [2] These words may agree with "glory," but are better applied to the "Church."
[3] Some read, as in the shorter recension, "grace." [4] Literally, "imitators;" comp. Eph. v. 1. [5] Comp. in the Greek, 2 Tim. i. 6.
[6] Eph. v. 2. [7] This is wanting in the Greek. [8] Literally, "since therefore," without any apodosis. [9] Or, "unspeakably beloved."

CHAP. II. — CONGRATULATIONS AND ENTREATIES.

As to my fellow-servant Burrhus, your deacon in regard to God and blessed in all things,[1] I beg that he may continue longer, both for your honour and that of your bishop. And Crocus also, worthy both of God and you, whom I have received as the manifestation[2] of your love, hath in all things refreshed[3] me, as the Father of our Lord Jesus Christ shall also refresh[3] him; together with Onesimus, and Burrhus, and Euplus, and Fronto, by means of whom, I have, as to love, beheld all of you. May I always have joy of you, if indeed I be worthy of it. It is therefore befitting that you should in every way glorify Jesus Christ, who hath glorified you, that by a unanimous obedience "ye may be perfectly joined together in the same mind, and in the same judgment, and may all speak the same thing concerning the same thing,"[5] and that, being subject to the bishop and the presbytery, ye may in all respects be sanctified.

As to our fellow-servant Burrhus, your deacon in regard to God and blessed in all things, I pray that he may continue blameless for the honour of the Church, and of your most blessed bishop. Crocus also, worthy both of God and you, whom we have received as the manifestation[2] of your love to us, hath in all things refreshed[3] me, and "hath not been ashamed of my chain,"[4] as the Father of our Lord Jesus Christ will also refresh[3] him; together with Onesimus, and Burrhus, and Euplus, and Fronto, by means of whom I have, as to love, beheld all of you. May I always have joy of you, if indeed I be worthy of it. It is therefore befitting that you should in every way glorify Jesus Christ, who hath glorified you, that by a unanimous obedience "ye may be perfectly joined together in the same mind and in the same judgment, and may all speak the same thing concerning the same thing,"[5] and that, being subject to the bishop and the presbytery, ye may in all respects be sanctified.

CHAP. III. — EXHORTATIONS TO UNITY.

I do not issue orders to you, as if I were some great person. For though I am bound for the name [of Christ], I am not yet perfect in Jesus Christ. For now I begin to be a disciple, and I speak to you as fellow-disciples with me. For it was needful for me to have been stirred up by you in faith, exhortation, patience, and long-suffering. But inasmuch as love suffers me not to be silent in regard to you, I have therefore taken[6] upon me first to exhort you that ye would all run together in accordance with the will of God. For even Jesus Christ, our inseparable life, is the [manifested] will of the Father; as also bishops, settled everywhere to the utmost bounds [of the earth], are so by the will of Jesus Christ.

I do not issue orders to you, as if I were some great person. For though I am bound for His name, I am not yet perfect in Jesus Christ. For now I begin to be a disciple, and I speak to you as my fellow-servants. For it was needful for me to have been admonished by you in faith, exhortation, patience, and long-suffering. But inasmuch as love suffers me not to be silent in regard to you, I have therefore taken[6] upon me first to exhort you that ye would run together in accordance with the will of God. For even Jesus Christ does all things according to the will of the Father, as He Himself declares in a certain place, "I do always those things that please Him."[7] Wherefore it behoves us also to live according to the will of God in Christ, and to imitate Him as Paul did. For, says he, "Be ye followers of me, even as I also am of Christ."[8]

CHAP. IV. — THE SAME CONTINUED.

Wherefore it is fitting that ye should run together in accordance with the will of your bishop, which thing also ye do. For your justly renowned presbytery, worthy of God, is fitted as exactly to the bishop as the strings are to the harp. Therefore in your

Wherefore it is fitting that ye also should run together in accordance with the will of the bishop who by God's appointment[9] rules over you. Which thing ye indeed of yourselves do, being instructed by the Spirit. For your justly-renowned presbytery, being worthy of God, is fitted as exactly to the bishop as the strings are to the harp. Thus, being joined together in concord and harmonious

---

[1] Or, "your most blessed deacon in all things pertaining to God." [2] Literally, "pattern." [3] Comp. 1 Cor. xvi. 18, etc.
[4] Comp. 2 Tim. i. 16. [5] 1 Cor. i. 10. [6] Comp. Philem. 8, 9. [7] John viii. 29. [8] 1 Cor. xi. 1. [9] Literally, "according to God."

concord and harmonious love, Jesus Christ is sung. And do ye, man by man, become a choir, that being harmonious in love, and taking up the song of God in unison, ye may with one voice sing to the Father through Jesus Christ, so that He may both hear you, and perceive by your works that ye are indeed the members of His Son. It is profitable, therefore, that you should live in an unblameable unity, that thus ye may always enjoy communion with God.

love, of which Jesus Christ is the Captain and Guardian, do ye, man by man, become but one choir; so that, agreeing together in concord, and obtaining[1] a perfect unity with God, ye may indeed be one in harmonious feeling with God the Father, and His beloved Son Jesus Christ our Lord. For, says He, "Grant unto them, Holy Father, that as I and Thou are one, they also may be one in us."[2] It is therefore profitable that you, being joined together with God in an unblameable unity, should be the followers of the example of Christ, of whom also ye are members.

CHAP. V. — THE PRAISE OF UNITY.

For if I in this brief space of time, have enjoyed such fellowship with your bishop — I mean not of a mere human, but of a spiritual nature — how much more do I reckon you happy who are so joined to him as the Church is to Jesus Christ, and as Jesus Christ is to the Father, that so all things may agree in unity! Let no man deceive himself: if any one be not within the altar, he is deprived of the bread of God. For if the prayer of one or two possesses[4] such power, how much more that of the bishop and the whole Church! He, therefore, that does not assemble with the Church, has even[5] by this manifested his pride, and condemned himself. For it is written, "God resisteth the proud."[9] Let us be careful, then, not to set ourselves in opposition to the bishop, in order that we may be subject to God.

For if I, in this brief space of time, have enjoyed such fellowship with your bishop — I mean not of a mere human, but of a spiritual nature — how much more do I reckon you happy, who so depend[3] on him as the Church does on the Lord Jesus, and the Lord does on God and His Father, that so all things may agree in unity! Let no man deceive himself: if any one be not within the altar, he is deprived of the bread of God. For if the prayer of one or two possesses[4] such power that Christ stands in the midst of them, how much more will the prayer of the bishop and of the whole Church, ascending up in harmony to God, prevail for the granting of all their petitions in Christ! He, therefore, that separates himself from such, and does not meet in the society where sacrifices[6] are offered, and with "the Church of the first-born whose names are written in heaven," is a wolf in sheep's clothing,[7] while he presents a mild outward appearance. Do ye, beloved, be careful to be subject to the bishop, and the presbyters and the deacons. For he that is subject to these is obedient to Christ, who has appointed them; but he that is disobedient to these is disobedient to Christ Jesus. And "he that obeyeth not[8] the Son shall not see life, but the wrath of God abideth on him." For he that yields not obedience to his superiors is self-confident, quarrelsome, and proud. But "God," says [the Scripture] "resisteth the proud, but giveth grace to the humble;"[9] and, "The proud have greatly transgressed." The Lord also says to the priests, "He that heareth you, heareth Me; and he that heareth Me, heareth the Father that sent Me. He that despiseth you, despiseth Me; and he that despiseth Me, despiseth Him that sent Me."

CHAP. VI. — HAVE RESPECT TO THE BISHOP AS TO CHRIST HIMSELF.

Now the more any one sees the bishop keeping silence,[10] the more ought he to revere him. For we ought to receive every one whom the Master of the house sends to be over His household,[11] as we would do Him that sent him. It is manifest, therefore, that we should look upon the bishop even as we would upon the

The more, therefore, you see the bishop silent, the more do you reverence him. For we ought to receive every one whom the Master of the house sends to be over His household,[11] as we would do Him that sent him. It is manifest, therefore, that we should look upon the bishop even as we would look upon the Lord Himself, standing, as he does, before the Lord. For "it behoves the man who looks carefully about him, and is active in his business, to stand before kings, and not to stand before

---

[1] Literally, "receiving a union to God in oneness." [2] John xvii. 11, 12. [3] Some read, "mixed up with." [4] Matt. xviii. 19.
[5] Or, "already." [6] Literally, "in the assembly of sacrifices." [7] Matt. vii. 15. [8] Or, "believeth not" (John iii. 36).
[9] Prov. iii. 34; James iv. 6; 1 Pet. v. 5. [10] That is, "showing forbearance." [11] Comp. Matt. xxiv. 25.

Lord Himself. And indeed Onesimus himself greatly commends your good order in God, that ye all live according to the truth, and that no sect[2] has any dwelling-place among you. Nor, indeed, do ye hearken to any one rather than to Jesus Christ speaking in truth.	slothful men."[1] And indeed Onesimus himself greatly commends your good order in God, that ye all live according to the truth, and that no sect[2] has any dwelling-place among you. Nor indeed do ye hearken to any one rather than to Jesus Christ, the true Shepherd and Teacher. And ye are, as Paul wrote to you, "one body and one spirit, because ye have also been called in one hope of the faith.[3] Since also "there is one Lord, one faith, one baptism, one God and Father of all, who is over all, and through all, and in all."[4] Such, then, are ye, having been taught by such instructors, Paul the Christ-bearer, and Timothy the most faithful.

CHAP. VII. — BEWARE OF FALSE TEACHERS.

For some are in the habit of carrying about the name [of Jesus Christ] in wicked guile, while yet they practise things unworthy of God, whom ye must flee as ye would wild beasts. For they are ravening dogs, who bite secretly, against whom ye must be on your guard, inasmuch as they are men who can scarcely be cured. There is one Physician who is possessed both of flesh and spirit; both made and not made; God existing in flesh; true life in death; both of Mary and of God; first possible and then impossible, —[7] even Jesus Christ our Lord.	But some most worthless persons are in the habit of carrying about the name [of Jesus Christ] in wicked guile, while yet they practise things unworthy of God, and hold opinions contrary to the doctrine of Christ, to their own destruction, and that of those who give credit to them, whom you must avoid as ye would wild beasts. For "the righteous man who avoids them is saved for ever; but the destruction of the ungodly is sudden, and a subject of rejoicing."[5] For "they are dumb dogs, that cannot bark,"[6] raving mad, and biting secretly, against whom ye must be on your guard, since they labour under an incurable disease. But our Physician is the only true God, the unbegotten and unapproachable, the Lord of all, the Father and Begetter of the only-begotten Son. We have also as a Physician the Lord our God, Jesus the Christ, the only-begotten Son and Word, before time began,[8] but who afterwards became also man, of Mary the virgin. For "the Word was made flesh."[9] Being incorporeal, He was in the body; being impassible, He was in a passible body; being immortal, He was in a mortal body; being life, He became subject to corruption, that He might free our souls from death and corruption, and heal them, and might restore them to health, when they were diseased with ungodliness and wicked lusts.

CHAP. VIII. — RENEWED PRAISE OF THE EPHESIANS.

Let not then any one deceive you, as indeed ye are not deceived, inasmuch as ye are wholly devoted to God. For since there is no strife raging among you which might distress you, ye are certainly living in accordance with God's will. I am far inferior to you, and require to be sanctified by your Church of Ephesus, so renowned throughout the world. They that are carnal cannot do those things which are spiritual, nor they that are spiritual the things which are carnal; even as faith cannot do the works of un-	Let not then any one deceive you, as indeed ye are not deceived; for ye are wholly devoted to God. For when there is no evil desire within you, which might defile and torment you, then do ye live in accordance with the will of God, and are [the servants] of Christ. Cast ye out that which defiles[10] you, who are of the[11] most holy Church of the Ephesians, which is so famous and celebrated throughout the world. They that are carnal cannot do those things which are spiritual, nor they that are spiritual the things which are carnal; even as faith cannot do the works of unbelief, nor unbelief the works of faith. But ye, being full of the Holy Spirit, do nothing according to the flesh, but all things according to the Spirit. Ye are complete in Christ Jesus, "who is the Saviour of all men, specially of them that believe."[12]

---

[1] Prov. xxii. 29, after LXX. [2] Or, "heresy." [3] 1 Eph. iv. 4. [4] Eph. iv. 5, 6. [5] Prov. x. 25, xi. 3. [6] Isa. lvi. 10. [7] This clause is wanting in the Greek, and has been supplied from the ancient Latin version. [8] Or, "before the ages." [9] John i. 14. [10] It is difficult to translate περίψημα in this and similar passages; comp. 1 Cor. iv. 13. [11] Literally, "and the." [12] 1 Tim. iv. 10.

belief, nor unbelief the works of faith. But even those things which ye do according to the flesh are spiritual; for ye do all things in Jesus Christ.

CHAP. IX. — YE HAVE GIVEN NO HEED TO FALSE TEACHERS.

Nevertheless, I have heard of some who have passed on from this to you, having false doctrine, whom ye did not suffer to sow among you, but stopped your ears, that ye might not receive those things which were sown by them, as being stones[1] of the temple of the Father, prepared for the building of God the Father, and drawn up on high by the instrument of Jesus Christ, which is the cross,[2] making use of the Holy Spirit as a rope, while your faith was the means by which you ascended, and your love the way which led up to God. Ye, therefore, as well as all your fellow-travellers, are God-bearers, temple-bearers, Christ-bearers, bearers of holiness, adorned in all respects with the commandments of Jesus Christ, in whom also I exult that I have been thought worthy, by means of this Epistle, to converse and rejoice with you, because with respect to your Christian life[7] ye love nothing but God only.

Nevertheless, I have heard of some who have passed in among you, holding the wicked doctrine of the strange and evil spirit; to whom ye did not allow entrance to sow their tares, but stopped your ears that ye might not receive that error which was proclaimed by them, as being persuaded that that spirit which deceives the people does not speak the things of Christ, but his own, for he is a lying spirit. But the Holy Spirit does not speak His own things, but those of Christ, and that not from himself, but from the Lord; even as the Lord also announced to us the things that He received from the Father. For, says He, "the word which ye hear is not Mine, but the Father's, who sent Me."[3] And says He of the Holy Spirit, "He shall not speak of Himself, but whatsoever things He shall hear from Me."[4] And He says of Himself to the Father, "I have," says He, "glorified Thee upon the earth; I have finished the work which, Thou gavest Me; I have manifested Thy name to men."[5] And of the Holy Ghost, "He shall glorify Me, for He receives of Mine."[6] But the spirit of deceit preaches himself, and speaks his own things, for he seeks to please himself. He glorifies himself, for he is full of arrogance. He is lying, fraudulent, soothing, flattering, treacherous, rhapsodical, trifling, inharmonious, verbose, sordid, and timorous. From his power Jesus Christ will deliver you, who has founded you upon the rock, as being chosen stones, well fitted for the divine edifice of the Father, and who are raised up on high by Christ, who was crucified for you, making use of the Holy Spirit as a rope, and being borne up by faith, while exalted by love from earth to heaven, walking in company with those that are undefiled. For, says [the Scripture], "Blessed are the undefiled in the way, who walk in the law of the Lord."[8] Now the way is unerring, namely, Jesus Christ. For, says He, "I am the way and the life."[9] And this way leads to the Father. For "no man," says He, "cometh to the Father but by Me."[10] Blessed, then, are ye who are God-bearers, spirit-bearers, temple-bearers, bearers of holiness, adorned in all respects with the commandments of Jesus Christ, being "a royal priesthood, a holy nation, a peculiar people,"[11] on whose account I rejoice exceedingly, and have had the privilege, by this Epistle, of conversing with "the saints which are at Ephesus, the faithful in Christ Jesus."[12] I rejoice, therefore, over you, that ye do not give heed to vanity, and love nothing according to the flesh, but according to God.

CHAP. X. — EXHORTATIONS TO PRAYER, HUMILITY, ETC.

And pray ye without ceasing in behalf of other men. For there is in them hope of repentance that they

And pray ye without ceasing in behalf of other men; for there is hope of the repentance, that they may attain to God. For "cannot he that falls arise again, and he

---

[1] Comp. 1 Pet. ii. 5. [2] Comp. John xii. 32. [3] John xiv. 24. [4] John xvi. 13. [5] John xvii. 4, 6. [6] John xvi. 14.
[7] Literally, "according to the other life." [8] Ps. cxix. 1. [9] John xiv. 6. [10] John xiv. 6. [11] 1 Pet. ii. 9. [12] Eph. i. 1.

may attain to God. See,[2] then, that they be instructed by your works, if in no other way. Be ye meek in response to their wrath, humble in opposition to their boasting: to their blasphemies return[4] your prayers; in contrast to their error, be ye stedfast[5] in the faith; and for their cruelty, manifest your gentleness. While we take care not to imitate their conduct, let us be found their brethren in all true kindness; and let us seek to be followers of the Lord (who ever more unjustly treated, more destitute, more condemned?), that so no plant of the devil may be found in you, but ye may remain in all holiness and sobriety in Jesus Christ, both with respect to the flesh and spirit.

that goes astray return?"[1] Permit them, then, to be instructed by you. Be ye therefore the ministers of God, and the mouth of Christ. For thus saith the Lord, "If ye take forth the precious from the vile, ye shall be as my mouth."[3] Be ye humble in response to their wrath; oppose to their blasphemies your earnest prayers; while they go astray, stand ye stedfast in the faith. Conquer ye their harsh temper by gentleness, their passion by meekness. For "blessed are the meek;"[6] and Moses was meek above all men;[7] and David was exceeding meek.[8] Wherefore Paul exhorts as follows: "The servant of the Lord must not strive, but be gentle towards all men, apt to teach, patient, in meekness instructing those that oppose themselves."[9] Do not seek to avenge yourselves on those that injure you, for says [the Scripture], "If I have returned evil to those who returned evil to me."[10] Let us make them brethren by our kindness. For say ye to those that hate you, Ye are our brethren, that the name of the Lord may be glorified. And let us imitate the Lord, "who, when He was reviled, reviled not again;"[11] when He was crucified, He answered not; "when He suffered, He threatened not;"[12] but prayed for His enemies, "Father, forgive them; they know not what they do."[13] If any one, the more he is injured, displays the more patience, blessed is he. If any one is defrauded, if any one is despised, for the name of the Lord, he truly is the servant of Christ. Take heed that no plant of the devil be found among you, for such a plant is bitter and salt. "Watch ye, and be ye sober,"[14] in Christ Jesus.

CHAP. XI. — AN EXHORTATION TO FEAR GOD, ETC.

The last times are come upon us. Let us therefore be of a reverent spirit, and fear the long-suffering of God, that it tend not to our condemnation. For let us either stand in awe of the wrath to come, or show regard for the grace which is at present displayed — one of two things. Only [in one way or another] let us be found in Christ Jesus unto the true life. Apart from Him, let nothing attract[16] you, for whom I bear about these bonds, these spiritual jewels, by which may I arise through your prayers, of which I entreat I may always be a partaker, that I may be found in the lot of the Christians of Ephesus, who have always been of the same mind with the apostles through the power of Jesus Christ.

The last times are come upon us. Let us therefore be of a reverent spirit, and fear the long-suffering of God, lest we despise the riches of His goodness and forbearance.[15] For let us either fear the wrath to come, or let us love the present joy in the life that now is; and let our present and true joy be only this, to be found in Christ Jesus, that we may truly live. Do not at any time desire so much as even to breathe apart from Him. For He is my hope; He is my boast; He is my never-failing riches, on whose account I bear about with me these bonds from Syria to Rome, these spiritual jewels, in which may I be perfected through your prayers, and become a partaker of the sufferings of Christ, and have fellowship with Him in His death, His resurrection from the dead, and His everlasting life.[17] May I attain to this, so that I may be found in the lot of the Christians of Ephesus, who have always had intercourse with the apostles by the power of Jesus Christ, with Paul, and John, and Timothy the most faithful.

CHAP. XII. — PRAISE OF THE EPHESIANS.

I know both who I am, and to whom I write. I am a condemned man, ye have been the objects of

I know both who I am, and to whom I write. I am the very insignificant Ignatius, who have my lot with[18] those who are exposed to danger and condemnation.

---

[1] Jer. viii. 4. [2] Literally, "permit." [3] Jer. xv. 19. [4] The verb is here omitted in the original. [5] Comp. Col. i. 23. [6] Matt. v. 4. [7] Num. xii. 3. [8] Ps. cxxxi. 2. [9] 2 Tim. ii. 24, 25. [10] Ps. vii. 4. [11] 1 Pet. ii. 23. [12] 1 Pet. ii. 23. [13] Luke xxiii. 34. [14] 1 Pet. iv. 7. [15] Rom. ii. 4. [16] Literally, "let nothing become you." [17] Phil. iii. 10. [18] Literally, "am like to."

mercy; I am subject to danger, ye are established in safety. Ye are the persons through¹ whom those pass that are cut off for the sake of God. Ye are initiated into the mysteries of the Gospel with Paul, the holy, the martyred, the deservedly most happy, at whose feet⁴ may I be found, when I shall attain to God; who in all his Epistle⁵ makes mention of you in Christ Jesus.

But ye have been the objects of mercy, and are established in Christ. I am one delivered over [to death], but the least of all those that have been cut off for the sake of Christ, "from the blood of righteous Abel"² to the blood of Ignatius. Ye are initiated into the mysteries of the Gospel with Paul, the holy, the martyred, inasmuch as he was "a chosen vessel;"³ at whose feet may I be found, and at the feet of the rest of the saints, when I shall attain to Jesus Christ, who is always mindful of you in His prayers.

CHAP. XIII. — EXHORTATION TO MEET TOGETHER FREQUENTLY FOR THE WORSHIP OF GOD.

Take heed, then, often to come together to give thanks to God, and show forth His praise. For when ye assemble frequently in the same place, the powers of Satan are destroyed, and the destruction at which he aims⁷ is prevented by the unity of your faith. Nothing is more precious than peace, by which all war, both in heaven and earth,⁸ is brought to an end.

Take heed, then, often to come together to give thanks to God, and show forth His praise. For when ye come frequently together in the same place, the powers of Satan are destroyed, and his "fiery darts"⁶ urging to sin fall back ineffectual. For your concord and harmonious faith prove his destruction, and the torment of his assistants. Nothing is better than that peace which is according to Christ, by which all war, both of aërial and terrestrial spirits, is brought to an end. "For we wrestle not against blood and flesh, but against principalities and powers, and against the rulers of the darkness of this world, against spiritual wickedness in heavenly places."⁹

CHAP. XIV. — EXHORTATIONS TO FAITH AND LOVE.

None of these things is hid from you, if ye perfectly possess that faith and love towards Christ Jesus¹⁰ which are the beginning and the end of life. For the beginning is faith, and the end is love.¹¹ Now these two, being inseparably connected together,¹² are of God, while all other things which are requisite for a holy life follow after them. No man [truly] making a profession of faith sinneth;¹³ nor does he that possesses love hate any one. The tree is made manifest by its fruit;¹⁵ so those that profess themselves to be Christians shall be recognised by their conduct. For there is not now a demand for mere profession,¹⁶ but that a man be found continuing in the power of faith to the end.

Wherefore none of the devices of the devil shall be hidden from you, if, like Paul, ye perfectly possess that faith and love towards Christ¹⁰ which are the beginning and the end of life. The beginning of life is faith, and the end is love. And these two being inseparably connected together, do perfect the man of God; while all other things which are requisite to a holy life follow after them. No man making a profession of faith ought to sin, nor one possessed of love to hate his brother. For He that said, "Thou shalt love the Lord thy God,"¹⁴ said also, "and thy neighbour as thyself."¹⁴ Those that profess themselves to be Christ's are known not only by what they say, but by what they practise. "For the tree is known by its fruit."¹⁵

CHAP. XV. — EXHORTATION TO CONFESS CHRIST BY SILENCE AS WELL AS SPEECH.

It is better for a man to be silent and be [a Christian], than to talk and not to be one. It is good to teach, if he who speaks also acts. There is then one Teacher, who spake and it was done; while even those things which He did in silence are worthy of

It is better for a man to be silent and be [a Christian], than to talk and not to be one. "The kingdom of God is not in word, but in power."¹⁷ Men "believe with the heart, and confess with the mouth," the one "unto righteousness," the other "unto salvation."¹⁸ It is good to teach, if he who speaks also acts. For he who shall both "do and teach, the same shall be great in the kingdom."¹⁹

---

¹ Literally, "ye are the passage of." ² Matt. xxiii. 35. ³ Acts ix. 15. ⁴ Literally, "footsteps."
⁵ Some render, "in every Epistle." ⁶ Eph. vi. 16. ⁷ Literally, "his destruction." ⁸ Literally, "of heavenly and earthly things."
⁹ Eph. vi. 12. ¹⁰ 1 Tim. i. 14. ¹¹ 1 Tim. i. 5. ¹² Literally, "being in unity." ¹³ Comp. 1 John iii. 7. ¹⁴ Luke x. 27.
¹⁵ Matt. xii. 33. ¹⁶ Literally, "there is not now the work of profession." ¹⁷ 1 Cor. iv. 20. ¹⁸ Rom. x. 10. ¹⁹ Matt. v. 19.

the Father. He who possesses the word of Jesus, is truly able to hear even His very silence, that he may be perfect, and may both act as he speaks, and be recognised by his silence. There is nothing which is hid from God, but our very secrets are near to Him. Let us therefore do all things as those who have Him dwelling in us, that we may be His temples,[2] and He may be in us as our God, which indeed He is, and will manifest Himself before our faces. Wherefore we justly love Him.

Our Lord and God, Jesus Christ, the Son of the living God, first did and then taught, as Luke testifies, "whose praise is in the Gospel through all the Churches."[1] There is nothing which is hid from the Lord, but our very secrets are near to Him. Let us therefore do all things as those who have Him dwelling in us, that we may be His temples,[2] and He may be in us as God. Let Christ speak in us, even as He did in Paul. Let the Holy Spirit teach us to speak the things of Christ in like manner as He did.

CHAP. XVI. — THE FATE OF FALSE TEACHERS.

Do not err, my brethren.[3] Those that corrupt families shall not inherit the kingdom of God.[4] If, then, those who do this as respects the flesh have suffered death, how much more shall this be the case with any one who corrupts by wicked doctrine the faith of God, for which Jesus Christ was crucified! Such an one becoming defiled [in this way], shall go away into everlasting fire, and so shall every one that hearkens unto him.

Do not err, my brethren.[3] Those that corrupt families shall not inherit the kingdom of God.[4] And if those that corrupt mere human families are condemned to death, how much more shall those suffer everlasting punishment who endeavour to corrupt the Church of Christ, for which the Lord Jesus, the only-begotten Son of God, endured the cross, and submitted to death! Whosoever, "being waxen fat,"[5] and "become gross," sets at nought His doctrine, shall go into hell. In like manner, every one that has received from God the power of distinguishing, and yet follows an unskilful shepherd, and receives a false opinion for the truth, shall be punished. "What communion hath light with darkness? or Christ with Belial? Or what portion hath he that believeth with an infidel? or the temple of God with idols?"[6] And in like manner say I, what communion hath truth with falsehood? or righteousness with unrighteousness? or true doctrine with that which is false?

CHAP. XVII. — BEWARE OF FALSE DOCTRINES.

For this end did the Lord suffer the ointment to be poured upon His head,[7] that He might breathe immortality into His Church. Be not ye anointed with the bad odour of the doctrine of the prince of this world; let him not lead you away captive from the life which is set before you. And why are we not all prudent, since we have received the knowledge of God, which is Jesus Christ? Why do we foolishly perish, not recognising the gift which the Lord has of a truth sent to us?

For this end did the Lord suffer the ointment to be poured upon His head,[7] that His Church might breathe forth immortality. For saith [the Scripture], "Thy name is as ointment poured forth; therefore have the virgins loved Thee: they have drawn Thee; at the odour of Thine ointments we will run after Thee."[8] Let no one be anointed with the bad odour of the doctrine of [the prince of] this world; let not the holy Church of God be led captive by his subtlety, as was the first woman.[9] Why do we not, as gifted with reason, act wisely? When we had received from Christ, and had grafted in us the faculty of judging concerning God, why do we fall headlong into ignorance? and why, through a careless neglect of acknowledging the gift which we have received, do we foolishly perish?

CHAP. XVIII. — THE GLORY OF THE CROSS.

Let my spirit be counted as nothing[10] for the sake of the cross, which is a stumbling-block[11] to those that do not believe, but to us salvation and

The cross of Christ is indeed a stumbling-block to those that do not believe, but to the believing it is salvation and life eternal. "Where is the wise man? where the disputer?"[12] Where is the boasting of those who

---

[1] 2 Cor. viii. 18. [2] 1 Cor. vi. 19. [3] Comp. James i. 16. [4] 1 Cor. vi. 9, 10. [5] Deut. xxxii. 15. [6] 2 Cor. vi. 14-16. [7] Comp. John xii. 7. [8] Song of Sol. i. 3, 4. [9] Literally, "before the ages." [10] Again περίψημα, translated "offscouring," 1 Cor. iv. 13. [11] Comp. 1 Cor. i. 18. [12] 1 Cor. i. 20.

life eternal. "Where is the wise man? where the disputer?"[1] Where is the boasting of those who are styled prudent? For our God, Jesus Christ, was, according to the appointment[3] of God, conceived in the womb by Mary, of the seed of David, but by the Holy Ghost. He was born and baptized, that by His passion He might purify the water.

are called mighty? For the Son of God, who was begotten before time began,[2] and established all things according to the will of the Father, He was conceived in the womb of Mary, according to the appointment of God, of the seed of David, and by the Holy Ghost. For says [the Scripture], "Behold, a virgin shall be with child, and shall bring forth a son, and He shall be called Immanuel."[4] He was born and was baptized by John, that He might ratify the institution committed to that prophet.

CHAP. XIX. — THREE CELEBRATED MYSTERIES.

Now the virginity of Mary was hidden from the prince of this world, as was also her offspring, and the death of the Lord; three mysteries of renown,[5] which were wrought in silence by[6] God. How, then, was He manifested to the world?[7] A star shone forth in heaven above all the other stars, the light of which was inexpressible, while its novelty struck men with astonishment. And all the rest of the stars, with the sun and moon, formed a chorus to this star, and its light was exceedingly great above them all. And there was agitation felt as to whence this new spectacle came, so unlike to everything else [in the heavens]. Hence every kind of magic was destroyed, and every bond of wickedness disappeared; ignorance was removed, and the old kingdom abolished, God Himself being manifested in human form for the renewal of eternal life. And now that took a beginning which had been prepared by God. Henceforth all things were in a state of tumult, because He meditated the abolition of death.

Now the virginity of Mary was hidden from the prince of this world, as was also her offspring, and the death of the Lord; three mysteries of renown,[5] which were wrought in silence, but have been revealed to us. A star shone forth in heaven above all that were before it, and its light was inexpressible, while its novelty struck men with astonishment. And all the rest of the stars, with the sun and moon, formed a chorus to this star. It far exceeded them all in brightness, and agitation was felt as to whence this new spectacle [proceeded]. Hence worldly wisdom became folly; conjuration was seen to be mere trifling; and magic became utterly ridiculous. Every law[8] of wickedness vanished away; the darkness of ignorance was dispersed; and tyrannical authority was destroyed, God being manifested as a man, and man displaying power as God. But neither was the former a mere imagination,[9] nor did the second imply a bare humanity;[10] but the one was absolutely true,[11] and the other an economical arrangement.[12] Now that received a beginning which was perfected by God.[13] Henceforth all things were in a state of tumult, because He meditated the abolition of death.

CHAP. XX. — PROMISE OF ANOTHER LETTER.

If Jesus Christ shall graciously permit me through your prayers, and if it be His will, I shall, in a second little work which I will write to you, make further manifest to you [the nature of] the dispensation of which I have begun [to treat], with respect to the new man, Jesus Christ, in His faith and in His love, in His suffering and in His resurrection. Especially [will I do this[14]] if the Lord make known to me that ye come together

CHAP. XX. — EXHORTATIONS TO STEDFASTNESS AND UNITY.

Stand fast, brethren, in the faith of Jesus Christ, and in His love, in His passion, and in His resurrection. Do ye all come together in common, and individually,[15] through grace, in one faith of God the Father, and of Jesus Christ His only-begotten Son, and "the first-born of every creature,"[16] but of the seed of David according to the flesh, being under the guidance of the Comforter, in obedience to the bishop and the presbytery with an undivided mind, breaking one and the same bread, which is the medicine of immortality, and the antidote which prevents us from dying, but a cleansing remedy driving away evil, [which causes] that we should live in God through Jesus Christ.

---

[1] 1 Cor. i. 20. [2] Literally, "before the ages." [3] Or, "economy," or "dispensation." Comp. Col. i. 25; 1 Tim. i. 4. [4] Isa. vii. 14; Matt. i. 23. [5] Literally, "of noise." [6] Or, "in the silence of God" — divine silence. [7] Literally, "to the ages." [8] Some read, "bond." [9] Literally, "opinion." [10] Literally, "bareness." [11] Literally, "truth." [12] Literally, "an economy." [13] Or, "that which was perfect received a beginning from God." [14] The punctuation and meaning are here doubtful. [15] Literally, "by name." [16] Col. i. 15.

man by man in common through grace, individually,[1] in one faith, and in Jesus Christ, who was of the seed of David according to the flesh, being both the Son of man and the Son of God, so that ye obey the bishop and the presbytery with an undivided mind, breaking one and the same bread, which is the medicine of immortality, and the antidote to prevent us from dying, but [which causes] that we should live for ever in Jesus Christ.

CHAP. XXI. — CONCLUSION.

My soul be for yours and theirs[2] whom, for the honour of God, ye have sent to Smyrna; whence also I write to you, giving thanks unto the Lord, and loving Polycarp even as I do you. Remember me, as Jesus Christ also remembered you. Pray ye for the Church which is in Syria, whence I am led bound to Rome, being the last of the faithful who are there, even as I have been thought worthy to be chosen[4] to show forth the honour of God. Farewell in God the Father, and in Jesus Christ, our common hope.

My soul be for yours and theirs[2] whom, for the honour of God, ye have sent to Smyrna; whence also I write to you, giving thanks to the Lord, and loving Polycarp even as I do you. Remember me, as Jesus Christ also remembers you, who is blessed for evermore. Pray ye for the Church of Antioch which is in Syria, whence I am led bound to Rome, being the last of the faithful that are there, who[3] yet have been thought worthy to carry these chains to the honour of God. Fare ye well in God the Father, and the Lord Jesus Christ, our common hope, and in the Holy Ghost. Fare ye well. Amen. Grace [be with you].[5]

---

[1] Literally, "by name." [2] Some render, "May I, in my turn, be the means of refreshing you and those," etc. [3] Some read, "even as." [4] Literally, "to be found for." [5] Some omit, "Grace [be with you]."

THE EPISTLE OF IGNATIUS TO THE MAGNESIANS

SHORTER AND LONGER VERSIONS.

Ignatius, who is also called Theophorus, to the [Church] blessed in the grace of God the Father, in Jesus Christ our Saviour, in whom I salute the Church which is at Magnesia, near the Mæander, and wish it abundance of happiness in God the Father, and in Jesus Christ.

Ignatius, who is also called Theophorus, to the [Church] blessed in the grace of God the Father, in Jesus Christ our Saviour, in whom I salute the Church which is at Magnesia, near the Mæander, and wish it abundance of happiness in God the Father, and in Jesus Christ, our Lord, in whom may you have abundance of happiness.

CHAP. I. — REASON OF WRITING THE EPISTLE.

HAVING been informed of your godly[1] love, so well-ordered, I rejoiced greatly, and determined to commune with you in the faith of Jesus Christ. For as one who has been thought worthy of the most honourable of all names,[2] in those bonds which I bear about, I commend the Churches, in which I pray for a union both of the flesh and spirit of Jesus Christ, the constant source of our life, and of faith and love, to which nothing is to be preferred, but especially of Jesus and the Father, in whom, if we endure all the assaults of the prince of this world, and escape them, we shall enjoy God.

HAVING been informed of your godly[1] love, so well-ordered, I rejoiced greatly, and determined to commune with you in the faith of Jesus Christ. For as one who has been thought worthy of a divine and desirable name, in those bonds which I bear about, I commend the Churches, in which I pray for a union both of the flesh and spirit of Jesus Christ, "who is the Saviour of all men, but specially of them that believe;"[3] by whose blood ye were redeemed; by whom ye have known God, or rather have been known by Him;[4] in whom enduring, ye shall escape all the assaults of this world: for "He is faithful, who will not suffer you to be tempted above that which ye are able."[5]

CHAP. II. — I REJOICE IN YOUR MESSENGERS.

Since, then, I have had the privilege of seeing you, through Damas your most worthy bishop, and through your worthy presbyters Bassus and Apollonius, and through my fellow-servant the deacon Sotio, whose friendship may I ever enjoy, inasmuch as he is subject to the bishop as to the grace of God, and to the presbytery as to the law of Jesus Christ, [I now write[8] to you].

Since, then, I have had the privilege of seeing you, through Damas your most worthy[6] bishop, and through your worthy[6] presbyters Bassus and Apollonius, and through my fellow-servant the deacon Sotio, whose friendship may I ever enjoy,[7] inasmuch as he, by the grace of God, is subject to the bishop and presbytery, in the law of Jesus Christ, [I now write[8] to you].

---

[1] Literally, "according to God." [2] Literally, "of the most God-becoming name," referring either to the appellation "Theophorus," or to that of "martyr" or "confessor." [3] 1 Tim. iv. 10. [4] Comp. Gal. iv. 9. [5] 1 Cor. x. 13. [6] Literally, "worthy of God."
[7] Literally, "whom may I enjoy." [8] The apodosis is here wanting in the original, but must evidently be supplied in some such way as above.

CHAP. III. — HONOUR YOUR YOUTHFUL BISHOP.

Now it becomes you also not to treat your bishop too familiarly on account of his youth,[1] but to yield him all reverence, having respect to[2] the power of God the Father, as I have known even holy presbyters do, not judging rashly, from the manifest youthful appearance[3] [of their bishop], but as being themselves prudent in God, submitting to him, or rather not to him, but to the Father of Jesus Christ, the bishop of us all. It is therefore fitting that you should, after no hypocritical fashion, obey [your bishop], in honour of Him who has willed us [so to do], since he that does not so deceives not [by such conduct] the bishop that is visible, but seeks to mock Him that is invisible. And all such conduct has reference not to man,[10] but to God, who knows all secrets.	Now it becomes you also not to despise the age of your bishop, but to yield him all reverence, according to the will of God the Father, as I have known even holy presbyters do, not having regard to the manifest youth [of their bishop], but to his knowledge in God; inasmuch as "not the ancient are [necessarily] wise, nor do the aged understand prudence; but there is a spirit in men."[4] For Daniel the wise, at twelve years of age, became possessed of the divine Spirit, and convicted the elders, who in vain carried their grey hairs, of being false accusers, and of lusting after the beauty of another man's wife.[5] Samuel also, when he was but a little child, reproved Eli, who was ninety years old, for giving honour to his sons rather than to God.[6] In like manner, Jeremiah also received this message from God, "Say not, I am a child."[7] Solomon too, and Josiah, [exemplified the same thing.] The former, being made king at twelve years of age, gave that terrible and difficult judgment in the case of the two women concerning their children.[8] The latter, coming to the throne when eight years old,[9] cast down the altars and temples [of the idols], and burned down the groves, for they were dedicated to demons, and not to God. And he slew the false priests, as the corrupters and deceivers of men, and not the worshippers of the Deity. Wherefore youth is not to be despised when it is devoted to God. But he is to be despised who is of a wicked mind, although he be old, and full of wicked days.[11] Timothy the Christ-bearer was young, but hear what his teacher writes to him: "Let no man despise thy youth, but be thou an example of the believers in word and in conduct."[12] It is becoming, therefore, that ye also should be obedient to your bishop, and contradict him in nothing; for it is a fearful thing to contradict any such person. For no one does [by such conduct] deceive him that is visible, but does [in reality] seek to mock Him that is invisible, who, however, cannot be mocked by any one. And every such act has respect not to man, but to God. For God says to Samuel, "They have not mocked thee, but Me."[13] And Moses declares, "For their murmuring is not against us, but against the Lord God."[14] No one of those has, [in fact,] remained unpunished, who rose up against their superiors. For Dathan and Abiram did not speak against the law, but against Moses,[15] and were cast down alive into Hades. Korah also,[16] and the two hundred and fifty who conspired with him against Aaron, were destroyed by fire. Absalom, again,[17] who had slain his brother, became suspended on a tree, and had his evil-designing heart thrust through with darts. In like manner was Abeddadan[18] beheaded for the same reason. Uzziah,[19] when he presumed to oppose the priests and the priesthood, was smitten with leprosy. Saul also was dishonoured,[20] because he did not wait for Samuel the high priest. It behoves you, therefore, also to reverence your superiors.

---

[1] Literally, "to use the age of your bishop." [2] Literally, "according to." [3] Literally, "youthful condition."
[4] Job xxxii. 8, 9. [5] Dan. xiii. (Apoc.). [6] 1 Sam. iii 1. [7] Jer. i. 7. [8] 1 Kings iii. 16.
[9] 2 Kings xxii. xxiii. [10] Literally, "to flesh." [11] Dan. xiii. 52 (Apoc.). [12] 1 Tim. iv. 12.
[13] 1 Sam. viii. 7. [14] Ex. xvi. 8. [15] Num. xvi. 1. [16] Num. xvi. 31. [17] 2 Sam. xviii. 14.
[18] Sheba is referred to under this name: see 2 Sam xx. 22. [19] 2 Chron. xxvi. 20. [20] 1 Sam. xiii. 11.

CHAP. IV. — SOME WICKEDLY ACT INDEPENDENTLY OF THE BISHOP.

It is fitting, then, not only to be called Christians, but to be so in reality: as some indeed give one the title of bishop, but do all things without him. Now such persons seem to me to be not possessed of a good conscience, seeing they are not stedfastly gathered together according to the commandment.

It is fitting, then, not only to be called Christians, but to be so in reality. For it is not the being called so, but the being really so, that renders a man blessed. To those who indeed talk of the bishop, but do all things without him, will He who is the true and first Bishop, and the only High Priest by nature, declare, "Why call ye Me Lord, and do not the things which I say?"[1] For such persons seem to me not possessed of a good conscience, but to be simply dissemblers and hypocrites.

CHAP. V. — DEATH IS THE FATE OF ALL SUCH.

Seeing, then, all things have an end, these two things are simultaneously set before us — death and life; and every one shall go unto his own place. For as there are two kinds of coins, the one of God, the other of the world, and each of these has its special character stamped upon it, [so is it also here.][2] The unbelieving are of this world; but the believing have, in love, the character of God the Father by Jesus Christ, by whom, if we are not in readiness to die into His passion,[3] His life is not in us.

Seeing, then, all things have an end, and there is set before us life upon our observance [of God's precepts], but death as the result of disobedience, and every one, according to the choice he makes, shall go to his own place, let us flee from death, and make choice of life. For I remark, that two different characters are found among men — the one true coin, the other spurious. The truly devout man is the right kind of coin, stamped by God Himself. The ungodly man, again, is false coin, unlawful, spurious, counterfeit, wrought not by God, but by the devil. I do not mean to say that there are two different human natures, but that there is one humanity, sometimes belonging to God, and sometimes to the devil. If any one is truly religious, he is a man of God; but if he is irreligious, he is a man of the devil, made such, not by nature, but by his own choice. The unbelieving bear the image of the prince of wickedness. The believing possess the image of their Prince, God the Father, and Jesus Christ, through whom, if we are not in readiness to die for the truth into His passion,[3] His life is not in us.

CHAP. VI. — PRESERVE HARMONY.

Since therefore I have, in the persons before mentioned, beheld the whole multitude of you in faith and love, I exhort you to study to do all things with a divine harmony,[4] while your bishop presides in the place of God, and your presbyters in the place of the assembly of the apostles, along with your deacons, who are most dear to me, and are entrusted with the ministry of Jesus Christ, who was with the Father before the beginning of time,[5] and in the end was revealed. Do ye all then, imitating the same divine conduct,[7] pay respect to one another, and let no one look upon his neighbour after the flesh, but do ye continually love each other in Jesus Christ. Let nothing exist among you that may divide you; but be ye united with your bishop, and those that preside over you, as a type and evidence of your immortality.[8]

Since therefore I have, in the persons before mentioned, beheld the whole multitude of you in faith and love, I exhort you to study to do all things with a divine harmony,[4] while your bishop presides in the place of God, and your presbyters in the place of the assembly of the apostles, along with your deacons, who are most dear to me, and are entrusted with the ministry of Jesus Christ. He, being begotten by the Father before the beginning of time,[5] was God the Word, the only-begotten Son, and remains the same for ever; for "of His kingdom there shall be no end,"[6] says Daniel the prophet. Let us all therefore love one another in harmony, and let no one look upon his neighbour according to the flesh, but in Christ Jesus. Let nothing exist among you which may divide you; but be ye united with your bishop, being through him subject to God in Christ.

---

[1] Luke vi. 46.   [2] The apodosis is wanting in the original, and some prefer finding it in the following sentence.
[3] Or, "after the likeness of His passion."   [4] Literally, "in harmony of God."   [5] Literally, "before the ages."
[6] Dan. ii. 44, vii. 14, 27.   [7] Literally, "receiving the like manners of God."   [8] The meaning is here doubtful.

CHAP. VII. — DO NOTHING WITHOUT THE BISHOP AND PRESBYTERS.

As therefore the Lord did nothing without the Father, being united to Him, neither by Himself nor by the apostles, so neither do ye anything without the bishop and presbyters. Neither endeavour that anything appear reasonable and proper to yourselves apart; but being come together into the same place, let there be one prayer, one supplication, one mind, one hope, in love and in joy undefiled. There is one Jesus Christ, than whom nothing is more excellent. Do ye therefore all run together as into one temple of God, as to one altar, as to one Jesus Christ, who came forth from one Father, and is with and has gone to one.

As therefore the Lord does nothing without the Father, for says He, "I can of mine own self do nothing,"[1] so do ye, neither presbyter, nor deacon, nor layman, do anything without the bishop. Nor let anything appear commendable to you which is destitute of his approval.[2] For every such thing is sinful, and opposed [to the will of] God. Do ye all come together into the same place for prayer. Let there be one common supplication, one mind, one hope, with faith unblameable in Christ Jesus, than which nothing is more excellent. Do ye all, as one man, run together into the temple of God, as unto one altar, to one Jesus Christ, the High Priest of the unbegotten God.

CHAP. VIII. — CAUTION AGAINST FALSE DOCTRINES.

Be not deceived with strange doctrines, nor with old fables, which are unprofitable. For if we still live according to the Jewish law, we acknowledge that we have not received grace. For the divinest prophets lived according to Christ Jesus. On this account also they were persecuted, being inspired by His grace to fully convince the unbelieving that there is one God, who has manifested Himself by Jesus Christ His Son, who is His eternal Word, not proceeding forth from silence,[5] and who in all things pleased Him that sent Him.

Be not deceived with strange doctrines, "nor give heed to fables and endless genealogies,"[3] and things in which the Jews make their boast. "Old things are passed away: behold, all things have become new."[4] For if we still live according to the Jewish law, and the circumcision of the flesh, we deny that we have received grace. For the divinest prophets lived according to Jesus Christ. On this account also they were persecuted, being inspired by grace to fully convince the unbelieving that there is one God, the Almighty, who has manifested Himself by Jesus Christ His Son, who is His Word, not spoken, but essential. For He is not the voice of an articulate utterance, but a substance begotten by divine power, who has in all things pleased Him that sent Him.[6]

CHAP. IX. — LET US LIVE WITH CHRIST.

If, therefore, those who were brought up in the ancient order of things[7] have come to the possession of a new[8] hope, no longer observing the Sabbath, but living in the observance[10] of the Lord's Day, on which also our life has sprung up again by Him and by His death — whom some deny, by which mystery we have obtained faith,[12] and therefore endure, that we may be found the disciples of Jesus Christ, our only Master — how shall we be able to live apart from Him, whose disciples the prophets themselves in the Spirit did wait for Him as their Teacher? And therefore He whom they rightly waited for, being come, raised them from the dead.[16]

If, then, those who were conversant with the ancient Scriptures came to newness of hope, expecting the coming of Christ, as the Lord teaches us when He says, "If ye had believed Moses, ye would have believed Me, for he wrote of Me;"[9] and again, "Your father Abraham rejoiced to see My day, and he saw it, and was glad; for before Abraham was, I am;"[11] how shall we be able to live without Him? The prophets were His servants, and foresaw Him by the Spirit, and waited for Him as their Teacher, and expected Him as their Lord and Saviour, saying, "He will come and save us."[13] Let us therefore no longer keep the Sabbath after the Jewish manner, and rejoice in days of idleness; for "he that does not work, let him not eat."[14] For say the [holy] oracles, "In the sweat of thy face shalt thou eat thy bread."[15] But let every one of you keep the Sabbath after a spiritual manner, rejoicing in meditation on the law, not in relaxation of the body, admiring the work-

---

[1] John v. 30. [2] Or, "contrary to his judgment." [3] 1 Tim. i. 4. [4] 2 Cor. v. 17. [5] Some have argued that the Gnostic Σιγή, *silence*, is here referred to, and have consequently inferred that this epistle could not have been written by Ignatius.
[6] Some read ὑποστήσαντι, "that gave Him His *hypostasis*, or substance." [7] Literally, "in old things." [8] Or, "newness of."
[9] John v. 46. [10] Or, "according to." [11] John viii. 56, 58. [12] Literally, "we have received to believe." [13] Isa. xxxv. 4.
[14] 2 Thess. iii. 10. [15] Gen. iii. 19. [16] Comp. Matt. xxvii. 52.

manship of God, and not eating things prepared the day before, nor using lukewarm drinks, and walking within a prescribed space, nor finding delight in dancing and plaudits which have no sense in them.[1] And after the observance of the Sabbath, let every friend of Christ keep the Lord's Day as a festival, the resurrection-day, the queen and chief of all the days [of the week]. Looking forward to this, the prophet declared, "To the end, for the eighth day,"[2] on which our life both sprang up again, and the victory over death was obtained in Christ, whom the children of perdition, the enemies of the Saviour, deny, "whose god is their belly, who mind earthly things,"[3] who are "lovers of pleasure, and not lovers of God, having a form of godliness, but denying the power thereof."[4] These make merchandise of Christ, corrupting His word, and giving up Jesus to sale: they are corrupters of women, and covetous of other men's possessions, swallowing up wealth[5] insatiably; from whom may ye be delivered by the mercy of God through our Lord Jesus Christ!

CHAP. X. — BEWARE OF JUDAIZING.

Let us not, therefore, be insensible to His kindness. For were He to reward us according to our works, we should cease to be. Therefore, having become His disciples, let us learn to live according to the principles of Christianity.[7] For whosoever is called by any other name besides this, is not of God. Lay aside, therefore, the evil, the old, the sour leaven, and be ye changed into the new leaven, which is Jesus Christ. Be ye salted in Him, lest any one among you should be corrupted, since by your savour ye shall be convicted. It is absurd to profess [12] Christ Jesus, and to Judaize. For Christianity did not embrace [13] Judaism, but Judaism Christianity, that so every tongue which believeth might be gathered together to God.

Let us not, therefore, be insensible to His kindness. For were He to reward us according to our works, we should cease to be. For "if Thou, Lord, shalt mark iniquities, O Lord, who shall stand?"[6] Let us therefore prove ourselves worthy of that name which we have received. For whosoever is called by any other name besides this, he is not of God; for he has not received the prophecy which speaks thus concerning us: "The people shall be called by a new name, which the Lord shall name them, and shall be a holy people."[8] This was first fulfilled in Syria; for "the disciples were called Christians at Antioch,"[9] when Paul and Peter were laying the foundations of the Church. Lay aside, therefore, the evil, the old, the corrupt leaven,[10] and be ye changed into the new leaven of grace. Abide in Christ, that the stranger[11] may not have dominion over you. It is absurd to speak of Jesus Christ with the tongue, and to cherish in the mind a Judaism which has now come to an end. For where there is Christianity there cannot be Judaism. For Christ is one, in whom every nation that believes, and every tongue that confesses, is gathered unto God. And those that were of a stony heart have become the children of Abraham, the friend of God;[14] and in his seed all those have been blessed[15] who were ordained to eternal life[16] in Christ.

CHAP. XI. — I WRITE THESE THINGS TO WARN YOU.

These things [I address to you], my beloved, not that I know any of you to be in such a state;[17] but, as less than any of you, I desire to guard you beforehand, that ye fall not upon the hooks of vain doctrine, but that

These things [I address to you], my beloved, not that I know any of you to be in such a state;[17] but, as less than any of you, I desire to guard you beforehand, that ye fall not upon the hooks of vain doctrine, but that you may rather attain to a full assurance in Christ, who was begotten by the Father before all ages, but was afterwards

---

[1] Reference is here made to well-known Jewish opinions and practices with respect to the Sabbath. The Talmud fixes 2000 cubits as the space lawful to be traversed. Philo (*De Therap.*) refers to the dancing, etc. [2] Ps. vi. xii. (inscrip.). [3] Phil. iii. 18, 19.
[4] 2 Tim. iii. 4. [5] Literally, "whirlpools of wealth." [6] Ps. cxxx. 3. [7] Literally, "according to Christianity." [8] Isa. lxii. 2, 12.
[9] Acts xi. 26. [10] 1 Cor. v. 7. [11] Or, "enemy." [12] Some read, "to name." [13] Literally, "believe into," merge into.
[14] Matt. iii. 9; Isa xli. 8; James ii. 23. Some read, "children of God, friends of Abraham." [15] Gen. xxviii. 14. [16] Acts xiii. 48.
[17] i.e., addicted to the error of Judaizing.

ye attain to full assurance in regard to the birth, and passion, and resurrection which took place in the time of the government of Pontius Pilate, being truly and certainly accomplished by Jesus Christ, who is our hope,[1] from which may no one of you ever be turned aside.

born of the Virgin Mary without any intercourse with man. He also lived a holy life, and healed every kind of sickness and disease among the people, and wrought signs and wonders for the benefit of men; and to those who had fallen into the error of polytheism He made known the one and only true God, His Father, and underwent the passion, and endured the cross at the hands of the Christ-killing Jews, under Pontius Pilate the governor and Herod the king. He also died, and rose again, and ascended into the heavens to Him that sent Him, and is sat down at His right hand, and shall come at the end of the world, with His Father's glory, to judge the living and the dead, and to render to every one according to his works.[2] He who knows these things with a full assurance, and believes them, is happy; even as ye are now the lovers of God and of Christ, in the full assurance of our hope; from which may no one of us[3] ever be turned aside!

CHAP. XII. — YE ARE SUPERIOR TO ME.

May I enjoy you in all respects, if indeed I be worthy! For though I am bound, I am not worthy to be compared to any of you that are at liberty. I know that ye are not puffed up, for ye have Jesus Christ in yourselves. And all the more when I commend you, I know that ye cherish modesty[4] of spirit; as it is written, "The righteous man is his own accuser."[5]

May I enjoy you in all respects, if indeed I be worthy! For though I am bound, I am not worthy to be compared to one of you that are at liberty. I know that ye are not puffed up, for ye have Jesus in yourselves. And all the more when I commend you, I know that ye cherish modesty[4] of spirit; as it is written, "The righteous man is his own accuser;"[5] and again, "Declare thou first thine iniquities, that thou mayest be justified;"[6] and again, "When ye shall have done all things that are commanded you, say, We are unprofitable servants;"[7] "for that which is highly esteemed among men is abomination in the sight of God."[8] For says [the Scripture], "God be merciful to me a sinner."[9] Therefore those great ones, Abraham and Job,[10] styled themselves "dust and ashes"[11] before God. And David says, "Who am I before Thee, O Lord, that Thou hast glorified me hitherto?"[12] And Moses, who was "the meekest of all men,"[13] saith to God, "I am of a feeble voice, and of a slow tongue."[14] Be ye therefore also of a humble spirit, that ye may be exalted; for "he that abaseth himself shall be exalted, and he that exalteth himself shall be abased."[15]

CHAP. XIII. — BE ESTABLISHED IN FAITH AND UNITY.

Study, therefore, to be established in the doctrines of the Lord and the apostles, that so all things, whatsoever ye do, may prosper both in the flesh and spirit; in faith and love; in the Son, and in the Father, and in the Spirit; in the beginning and in the end; with your most admirable bishop, and the well-compacted spiritual crown of your presbytery, and the deacons who are according to God. Be ye subject to the bishop, and to one another, as Jesus Christ to the Father,

Study, therefore, to be established in the doctrines of the Lord and the apostles, that so all things, whatsoever ye do, may prosper, both in the flesh and spirit, in faith and love, with your most admirable bishop, and the well-compacted[16] spiritual crown of your presbytery, and the deacons who are according to God. Be ye subject to the bishop, and to one another, as Christ to the Father, that there may be a unity according to God among you.

---

[1] 1 Tim. i. 1. [2] 2 Tim. iv. 1; Rom. ii. 6. [3] Some read, "of you." [4] Literally, "are reverent." [5] Prov. xviii. 17 (LXX.).
[6] Isa. xliii. 26. [7] Luke xvii. 10. [8] Luke xvi. 15. [9] Luke xviii. 13. [10] Some read, "Jacob." [11] Gen. xviii. 27; Job xxx. 19.
[12] 1 Chron. xvii. 16. [13] Num. xii. 3. [14] Ex. iv. 10. [15] Luke xiv. 11. [16] Literally, "well-woven."

according to the flesh, and the apostles to Christ, and to the Father, and to the Spirit; that so there may be a union both fleshly and spiritual.

CHAP. XIV. — YOUR PRAYERS REQUESTED.

Knowing as I do that ye are full of God, I have but briefly exhorted you. Be mindful of me in your prayers, that I may attain to God; and of the Church which is in Syria, whence I am not worthy to derive my name: for I stand in need of your united prayer in God, and your love, that the Church which is in Syria may be deemed worthy of being refreshed [2] by your Church.

Knowing as I do that ye are full of all good, I have but briefly exhorted you in the love of Jesus Christ. Be mindful of me in your prayers, that I may attain to God; and of the Church which is in Syria, of whom I am not worthy to be called bishop. For I stand in need of your united prayer in God, and of your love, that the Church which is in Syria may be deemed worthy, by your good order, of being edified [1] in Christ.

CHAP. XV. — SALUTATIONS.

The Ephesians from Smyrna (whence I also write to you), who are here for the glory of God, as ye also are, who have in all things refreshed me, salute you, along with Polycarp, the bishop of the Smyrnæans. The rest of the Churches, in honour of Jesus Christ, also salute you. Fare ye well in the harmony of God, ye who have obtained the inseparable Spirit, who is Jesus Christ.

The Ephesians from Smyrna (whence I also write to you), who are here for the glory of God, as ye also are, who have in all things refreshed me, salute you, as does also Polycarp. The rest of the Churches, in honour of Jesus Christ, also salute you. Fare ye well in harmony, ye who have obtained the inseparable Spirit, in Christ Jesus, by the will of God.

---

[1] Literally, "of being fed as by a shepherd." [2] Literally, "of being sprinkled with dew."

[N.B. — In cap. ix., note 6, the reference is to the title of these two psalms, as rendered by the LXX. Εἰς τὸ τέλος ὑπὲρ τῆς ὀγδόης.]

THE EPISTLE OF IGNATIUS TO THE TRALLIANS

SHORTER AND LONGER VERSIONS

Ignatius, who is also called Theophorus, to the holy Church which is at Tralles, in Asia, beloved of God, the Father of Jesus Christ, elect, and worthy of God, possessing peace through the flesh, and blood, and passion of Jesus Christ, who is our hope, through our rising again to Him,[1] which also I salute in its fulness,[2] and in the apostolical character,[3] and wish abundance of happiness.

Ignatius, who is also called Theophorus, to the holy Church which is at Tralles, beloved by God the Father, and Jesus Christ, elect, and worthy of God, possessing peace through the flesh and Spirit of Jesus Christ, who is our hope, in His passion by the cross and death, and in His resurrection, which also I salute in its fulness,[2] and in the apostolical character,[3] and wish abundance of happiness.

CHAP. I.—ACKNOWLEDGMENT OF THEIR EXCELLENCE.

I know that ye possess an unblameable and sincere mind in patience, and that not only in present practice,[5] but according to inherent nature, as Polybius your bishop has shown me, who has come to Smyrna by the will of God and Jesus Christ, and so sympathized in the joy which I, who am bound in Christ Jesus, possess, that I beheld your whole multitude in him. Having therefore received through him the testimony of your good-will, according to God, I gloried to find you, as I knew you were, the followers of God.

I know that ye possess an unblameable and sincere mind in patience, and that not only for present use,[4] but as a permanent possession, as Polybius your bishop has shown me, who has come to Smyrna by the will of God the Father, and the Lord Jesus Christ, His Son, with the co-operation of the Spirit, and so sympathized in the joy which I, who am bound in Christ Jesus, possess, that I beheld your whole multitude in Him. Having therefore received through him the testimony of your good-will according to God, I gloried to find that you were the followers of Jesus Christ the Saviour.

CHAP. II.—BE SUBJECT TO THE BISHOP, ETC.

For, since ye are subject to the bishop as to Jesus Christ, ye appear to me to live not after the manner of men, but according to Jesus Christ, who died for us, in order, by believing in His death, ye may escape from death. It is therefore necessary that, as ye indeed do, so without the bishop ye should do nothing, but should also

Be ye subject to the bishop as to the Lord, for "he watches for your souls, as one that shall give account to God."[6] Wherefore also, ye appear to me to live not after the manner of men, but according to Jesus Christ, who died for us, in order that, by believing in His death, ye may by baptism be made partakers of His resurrection. It is therefore necessary, whatsoever things ye do, to do nothing without the bishop. And be ye subject also to the presbytery, as to the apostles of Jesus Christ, who is

---

[1] Some render, "in the resurrection which is by Him." [2] Either, "the whole members of the Church," or, "in the fulness of blessing."
[3] Either, "as an apostle," or, "in the apostolic form." [4] Literally, "not for use, but for a possession."
[5] Literally, "not according to use, but according to nature." [6] Heb. xiii. 17.

be subject to the presbytery, as to the apostle of Jesus Christ, who is our hope, in whom, if we live, we shall [at last] be found. It is fitting also that the deacons, as being [the ministers] of the mysteries of Jesus Christ, should in every respect be pleasing to all.[1] For they are not ministers of meat and drink, but servants of the Church of God. They are bound, therefore, to avoid all grounds of accusation [against them], as they would do fire.

our hope, in whom, if we live, we shall be found in Him. It behoves you also, in every way, to please the deacons, who are [ministers] of the mysteries of Christ Jesus; for they are not ministers of meat and drink, but servants of the Church of God. They are bound, therefore, to avoid all grounds of accusation [against them], as they would a burning fire. Let them, then, prove themselves to be such.

CHAP. III. — HONOUR THE DEACONS, etc.

In like manner, let all reverence the deacons as an appointment[2] of Jesus Christ, and the bishop as Jesus Christ, who is the Son of the Father, and the presbyters as the sanhedrim of God, and assembly of the apostles. Apart from these, there is no Church.[4] Concerning all this, I am persuaded that ye are of the same opinion. For I have received the manifestation[5] of your love, and still have it with me, in your bishop, whose very appearance is highly instructive,[6] and his meekness of itself a power; whom I imagine even the ungodly must reverence, seeing they are[7] also pleased that I do not spare myself. But shall I, when permitted to write on this point, reach such a height of self-esteem, that though being a condemned[8] man, I should issue commands to you as if I were an apostle?

And do ye reverence them as Christ Jesus, of whose place they are the keepers, even as the bishop is the representative of the Father of all things, and the presbyters are the sanhedrim of God, and assembly[3] of the apostles of Christ. Apart from these there is no elect Church, no congregation of holy ones, no assembly of saints. I am persuaded that ye also are of this opinion. For I have received the manifestation[5] of your love, and still have it with me, in your bishop, whose very appearance is highly instructive, and his meekness of itself a power; whom I imagine even the ungodly must reverence. Loving you as I do, I avoid writing in any severer strain to you, that I may not seem harsh to any, or wanting [in tenderness]. I am indeed bound for the sake of Christ, but I am not yet worthy of Christ. But when I am perfected, perhaps I shall then become so. I do not issue orders like an apostle.

CHAP. IV. — I HAVE NEED OF HUMILITY.

I have great knowledge in God,[9] but I restrain myself, lest I should perish through boasting. For now it is needful for me to be the more fearful, and not give heed to those that puff me up. For they that speak to me [in the way of commendation] scourge me. For I do indeed desire to suffer, but I know not if I be worthy to do so. For this longing, though it is not manifest to many, all the more vehemently assails me.[13] I therefore have need of meekness, by which the prince of this world is brought to nought.

But I measure myself, that I may not perish through boasting: but it is good to glory in the Lord.[10] And even though I were established[11] in things pertaining to God, yet then would it befit me to be the more fearful, and not give heed to those that vainly puff me up. For those that commend me scourge me. [I do indeed desire to suffer[12]], but I know not if I be worthy to do so. For the envy of the wicked one is not visible to many, but it wars against me. I therefore have need of meekness, by which the devil, the prince of this world, is brought to nought.

---

[1] It is doubtful whether this exhortation is addressed to the deacons or people; whether the former are urged in all respects to please the latter, or the latter in all points to be pleased with the former.   [2] Literally, "commandment."   The text, which is faulty in the MS., has been amended as above by Smith.   [3] Or, "conjunction."   [4] Literally, "no Church is called."   [5] Or, "pattern."
[6] Literally, "great instruction."   [7] Some here follow a text similar to that of the longer recension.
[8] Both the text and meaning are here very doubtful; some follow the reading of the longer recension.
[9] Literally, "I know many things in God."   [10] 1 Cor. i. 31.   [11] Or, "confirmed."   [12] Omitted in the MS.
[13] A different turn altogether is given to this passage in the longer recension.

CHAP. V. — I WILL NOT TEACH YOU PROFOUND DOCTRINES.

Am I not able to write to you of heavenly things? But I fear to do so, lest I should inflict injury on you who are but babes [in Christ]. Pardon me in this respect, lest, as not being able to receive [such doctrines], ye should be strangled by them. For even I, though I am bound [for Christ], yet am not on that account able to understand heavenly things, and the places [4] of the angels, and their gatherings under their respective princes, things visible and invisible. Without reference to such abstruse subjects, I am still but a learner [in other respects [5]]; for many things are wanting to us, that we come not short of God.

For might [1] not I write to you things more full of mystery? But I fear to do so, lest I should inflict injury on you who are but babes [in Christ]. Pardon me in this respect, lest, as not being able to receive their weighty import, [2] ye should be strangled by them. For even I, though I am bound [for Christ], and am able to understand heavenly things, the angelic orders, and the different sorts [3] of angels and hosts, the distinctions between powers and dominions, and the diversities between thrones and authorities, the mightiness of the Æons, and the pre-eminence of the cherubim and seraphim, the sublimity of the spirit, the kingdom of the Lord, and above all, the incomparable majesty of Almighty God — though I am acquainted with these things, yet am I not therefore by any means perfect; nor am I such a disciple as Paul or Peter. For many things are yet wanting to me, that I may not fall short of God.

CHAP. VI. — ABSTAIN FROM THE POISON OF HERETICS.

I therefore, yet not I, but the love of Jesus Christ, entreat you that ye use Christian nourishment only, and abstain from herbage of a different kind; I mean heresy. For those [7] [that are given to this] mix [11] up Jesus Christ with their own poison, speaking things which are unworthy of credit, like those who administer a deadly drug in sweet wine, which he who is ignorant of does greedily [13] take, with a fatal pleasure, [14] leading to his own death.

I therefore, yet not I, but the love of Jesus Christ, "entreat you that ye all speak the same thing, and that there be no divisions among you; but that ye be perfectly joined together in the same mind, and in the same judgment." [6] For there are some vain talkers [8] and deceivers, not Christians, but Christ-betrayers, [9] bearing about the name of Christ in deceit, and "corrupting the word" [10] of the Gospel; while they intermix the poison of their deceit with their persuasive talk, [12] as if they mingled aconite with sweet wine, that so he who drinks, being deceived in his taste by the very great sweetness of the draught, may incautiously meet with his death. One of the ancients gives us this advice, "Let no man be called good who mixes good with evil." [15] For they speak of Christ, not that they may preach Christ, but that they may reject Christ; and they speak [16] of the law, not that they may establish the law, but that they may proclaim things contrary to it. For they alienate Christ from the Father, and the law from Christ. They also calumniate His being born of the Virgin; they are ashamed of His cross; they deny His passion; and they do not believe His resurrection. They introduce God as a Being unknown; they suppose Christ to be unbegotten; and as to the Spirit, they do not admit that He exists. Some of them say that the Son is a mere man, and that the Father, Son, and Holy Spirit are but the same person, and that the creation is the work of God, not by Christ, but by some other strange power.

CHAP. VII. — THE SAME CONTINUED.

Be on your guard, therefore, against such persons. And this will be the case with you if you are not puffed up, and continue in intimate union with [17] Jesus Christ our God, and the

Be on your guard, therefore, against such persons, that ye admit not of a snare for your own souls. And act so that your life shall be without offence to all men, lest ye become as "a snare upon a watch-tower, and as a net which is spread out." [18] For "he that does not heal him-

---

[1] ἐβουλόμην apparently by mistake for ἐδυνάμην. [2] Literally, "their force." [3] Or, "varieties of." [4] Or, "stations." [5] Literally, "passing by this;" but both text and meaning are very doubtful. [6] 1 Cor. i. 10. [7] The ellipsis in the original is here very variously supplied. [8] Tit. i. 10. [9] Literally, "Christ-sellers." [10] 2 Cor. ii. 17. [11] Literally, "interweave." [12] Literally, "sweet address." [13] Or, "sweetly." [14] The construction is here difficult and doubtful. [15] *Apost. Constitutions*, vi. 13. [16] Supplied from the old Latin version. [17] Literally, "unseparated from." [18] Hos. v. 1.

bishop, and the enactments of the apostles. He that is within the altar is pure, but[2] he that is without is not pure; that is, he who does anything apart from the bishop, and presbytery, and deacons,[4] such a man is not pure in his conscience.

self in his own works, is the brother of him that destroys himself."[1] If, therefore, ye also put away conceit, arrogance, disdain, and haughtiness, it will be your privilege to be inseparably united to God, for "He is nigh unto those that fear Him."[3] And says He, "Upon whom will I look, but upon him that is humble and quiet, and that trembles at my words?"[5] And do ye also reverence your bishop as Christ Himself, according as the blessed apostles have enjoined you. He that is within the altar is pure, wherefore also he is obedient to the bishop and presbyters: but he that is without is one that does anything apart from the bishop, the presbyters, and the deacons. Such a person is defiled in his conscience, and is worse than an infidel. For what is the bishop but one who beyond all others possesses all power and authority, so far as it is possible for a man to possess it, who according to his ability has been made an imitator of the Christ of God?[6] And what is the presbytery but a sacred assembly, the counsellors and assessors of the bishop? And what are the deacons but imitators of the angelic powers,[7] fulfilling a pure and blameless ministry unto him, as the holy Stephen did to the blessed James, Timothy and Linus to Paul, Anencletus and Clement to Peter? He, therefore, that will not yield obedience to such, must needs be one utterly without God, an impious man who despises Christ, and depreciates His appointments.

CHAP. VIII. — BE ON YOUR GUARD AGAINST THE SNARES OF THE DEVIL.

Not that I know there is anything of this kind among you; but I put you on your guard, inasmuch as I love you greatly, and foresee the snares of the devil. Wherefore, clothing[11] yourselves with meekness, be ye renewed[12] in faith, that is the flesh of the Lord, and in love, that is the blood of Jesus Christ. Let no one of you cherish any grudge against his neighbour. Give no occasion to the Gentiles, lest by means of a few foolish men the whole multitude [of those that believe] in God be evil spoken of. For, "Woe to him by whose vanity my name is blasphemed among any."[17]

Now I write these things unto you, not that I know there are any such persons among you; nay, indeed I hope that God will never permit any such report to reach my ears, He "who spared not His Son for the sake of His holy Church."[8] But foreseeing the snares of the wicked one, I arm you beforehand by my admonitions, as my beloved and faithful children in Christ, furnishing you with the means of protection[9] against the deadly disease of unruly men, by which do ye flee from the disease[10] [referred to] by the good-will of Christ our Lord. Do ye therefore, clothing[11] yourselves with meekness, become the imitators of His sufferings, and of His love, wherewith[13] He loved us when He gave Himself a ransom[14] for us, that He might cleanse us by His blood from our old ungodliness, and bestow life on us when we were almost on the point of perishing through the depravity that was in us. Let no one of you, therefore, cherish any grudge against his neighbour. For says our Lord, "Forgive, and it shall be forgiven unto you."[15] Give no occasion to the Gentiles, lest "by means of a few foolish men the word and doctrine [of Christ] be blasphemed."[16] For says the prophet, as in the person of God, "Woe to him by whom my name is blasphemed among the Gentiles."[17]

CHAP. IX. — REFERENCE TO THE HISTORY OF CHRIST.

Stop your ears, therefore, when any one speaks to you at variance with[18]

Stop your ears, therefore, when any one speaks to you at variance with[18] Jesus Christ, the Son of God, who was

---

[1] Prov. xviii. 9 (LXX.). [2] This clause is inserted from the ancient Latin version. [3] Ps. lxxxv. 9. [4] The text has "deacon." [5] Isa. lxvi. 2. [6] Some render, "being a resemblance according to the power of Christ." [7] Some read, "imitators of Christ, ministering to the bishop, as Christ to the Father." [8] Rom. viii. 32. [9] Literally, "making you drink beforehand what will preserve you." [10] Or, "from which disease." [11] Literally, "taking up." [12] Or, "renew yourselves." [13] Comp. Eph. ii. 4. [14] Comp. 1 Tim. ii. 6. [15] Matt. vi. 14. [16] 1 Tim. vi. 1; Tit. ii. 5. [17] Isa. lii. 5. [18] Literally, "apart from."

Jesus Christ, who was descended from David, and was also of Mary; who was truly born, and did eat and drink. He was truly persecuted under Pontius Pilate; He was truly crucified, and [truly] died, in the sight of beings in heaven, and on earth, and under the earth. He was also truly raised from the dead, His Father quickening Him, even as after the same manner His Father will so raise up us who believe in Him by Christ Jesus, apart from whom we do not possess the true life.

descended from David, and was also of Mary; who was truly begotten of God and of the Virgin, but not after the same manner. For indeed God and man are not the same. He truly assumed a body; for "the Word was made flesh,"[1] and lived upon earth without sin. For says He, "Which of you convicteth me of sin?"[2] He did in reality both eat and drink. He was crucified and died under Pontius Pilate. He really, and not merely in appearance, was crucified, and died, in the sight of beings in heaven, and on earth, and under the earth. By those in heaven I mean such as are possessed of incorporeal natures; by those on earth, the Jews and Romans, and such persons as were present at that time when the Lord was crucified; and by those under the earth, the multitude that arose along with the Lord. For says the Scripture, "Many bodies of the saints that slept arose,"[3] their graves being opened. He descended, indeed, into Hades alone, but He arose accompanied by a multitude; and rent asunder that means[4] of separation which had existed from the beginning of the world, and cast down its partition-wall. He also rose again in three days, the Father raising Him up; and after spending forty days with the apostles, He was received up to the Father, and "sat down at His right hand, expecting till His enemies are placed under His feet."[5] On the day of the preparation, then, at the third hour, He received the sentence from Pilate, the Father permitting that to happen; at the sixth hour He was crucified; at the ninth hour He gave up the ghost; and before sunset He was buried.[6] During the Sabbath He continued under the earth in the tomb in which Joseph of Arimathæa had laid Him. At the dawning of the Lord's day He arose from the dead, according to what was spoken by Himself, "As Jonah was three days and three nights in the whale's belly, so shall the Son of man also be three days and three nights in the heart of the earth."[7] The day of the preparation, then, comprises the passion; the Sabbath embraces the burial; the Lord's Day contains the resurrection.

CHAP. X. — THE REALITY OF CHRIST'S PASSION.

But if, as some that are without God, that is, the unbelieving, say, that He only seemed to suffer (they themselves only seeming to exist), then why am I in bonds? Why do I long to be exposed to[8] the wild beasts? Do I therefore die in vain?[9] Am I not then guilty of falsehood[10] against [the cross of] the Lord?

But if, as some that are without God, that is, the unbelieving, say, He became man in appearance [only], that He did not in reality take unto Him a body, that He died in appearance [merely], and did not in very deed suffer, then for what reason am I now in bonds, and long to be exposed to[8] the wild beasts? In such a case, I die in vain, and am guilty of falsehood[10] against the cross of the Lord. Then also does the prophet in vain declare, "They shall look on Him whom they have pierced, and mourn over themselves as over one beloved."[11] These men, therefore, are not less unbelievers than were those that crucified Him. But as for me, I do not place my hopes in one who died for me in appearance, but in reality. For that which is false is quite abhorrent to the truth. Mary then did truly conceive a

---

[1] John i. 14. [2] John viii. 46. [3] Matt. xxvii. 52. [4] Literally, "hedge," or "fence." [5] Heb. x. 12, 13.
[6] Some read, "He was taken down from the cross, and laid in a new tomb." [7] Matt. xii. 40. [8] Literally, "to fight with."
[9] Some read this and the following clause affirmatively, instead of interrogatively. [10] The meaning is, that if they spoke the truth concerning the phantasmal character of Christ's death, then Ignatius was guilty of a practical falsehood in suffering for what was false.
[11] Zech. xii. 10.

body which had God inhabiting it. And God the Word was truly born of the Virgin, having clothed Himself with a body of like passions with our own. He who forms all men in the womb, was Himself really in the womb, and made for Himself a body of the seed of the Virgin, but without any intercourse of man. He was carried in the womb, even as we are, for the usual period of time; and was really born, as we also are; and was in reality nourished with milk, and partook of common meat and drink, even as we do. And when He had lived among men for thirty years, He was baptized by John, really and not in appearance; and when He had preached the Gospel three years, and done signs and wonders, He who was Himself the Judge was judged by the Jews, falsely so called, and by Pilate the governor; was scourged, was smitten on the cheek, was spit upon; He wore a crown of thorns and a purple robe; He was condemned: He was crucified in reality, and not in appearance, not in imagination, not in deceit. He really died, and was buried, and rose from the dead, even as He prayed in a certain place, saying, "But do Thou, O Lord, raise me up again, and I shall recompense them."[1] And the Father, who always hears Him,[2] answered and said, "Arise, O God, and judge the earth; for Thou shalt receive all the heathen for Thine inheritance."[3] The Father, therefore, who raised Him up, will also raise us up through Him, apart from whom no one will attain to true life. For says He, "I am the life; he that believeth in me, even though he die, shall live: and every one that liveth and believeth in me, even though he die, shall live for ever."[4] Do ye therefore flee from these ungodly heresies; for they are the inventions of the devil, that serpent who was the author of evil, and who by means of the woman deceived Adam, the father of our race.

CHAP. XI.—AVOID THE DEADLY ERRORS OF THE DOCETÆ.

Flee, therefore, those evil offshoots [of Satan], which produce death-bearing fruit, whereof if any one tastes, he instantly dies. For these men are not the planting of the Father. For if they were, they would appear as branches of the cross, and their fruit would be incorruptible. By it[9] He calls you through His passion, as being His members. The head, therefore, cannot be born by itself, without its members; God, who is [the Saviour] Himself, having promised their union.[10]

Do ye also avoid those wicked offshoots of his,[5] Simon his firstborn son, and Menander, and Basilides, and all his wicked mob of followers,[6] the worshippers of a man, whom also the prophet Jeremiah pronounces accursed.[7] Flee also the impure Nicolaitanes, falsely so called,[8] who are lovers of pleasure, and given to calumnious speeches. Avoid also the children of the evil one, Theodotus and Cleobulus, who produce death-bearing fruit, whereof if any one tastes, he instantly dies, and that not a mere temporary death, but one that shall endure for ever. These men are not the planting of the Father, but are an accursed brood. And says the Lord, "Let every plant which my heavenly Father has not planted be rooted up."[11] For if they had been branches of the Father, they would not have been "enemies of the cross of Christ,"[12] but rather of those who "killed the Lord of glory."[13] But now, by denying the cross, and being ashamed of the passion, they cover the transgression of the Jews, those fighters against God, those murderers of the Lord; for it were too little to style them merely

---

[1] Ps. xli. 10. [2] Comp. John xi. 42. [3] Ps. lxxxii. 8. [4] John xi. 25, 26. [5] i.e., Satan's. [6] Literally, "loud, confused noise." [7] The Ebionites, who denied the divine nature of our Lord, are here referred to. [8] It seems to be here denied that Nicolas was the founder of this school of heretics. [9] i.e., the cross. [10] Both text and meaning are here doubtful. [11] Matt. xv. 13. [12] Phil. iii. 18. [13] 1 Cor. ii. 8.

murderers of the prophets. But Christ invites you to [share in] His immortality, by His passion and resurrection, inasmuch as ye are His members.

CHAP. XII. — CONTINUE IN UNITY AND LOVE.

I salute you from Smyrna, together with the Churches of God which are with me, who have refreshed me in all things, both in the flesh and in the spirit. My bonds, which I carry about with me for the sake of Jesus Christ (praying that I may attain to God), exhort you. Continue in harmony among yourselves, and in prayer with one another; for it becomes every one of you, and especially the presbyters, to refresh the bishop, to the honour of the Father, of Jesus Christ, and of the apostles. I entreat you in love to hear me, that I may not, by having written, be a testimony against you. And do ye also pray for me, who have need of your love, along with the mercy of God, that I may be worthy of the lot for which I am destined, and that I may not be found reprobate.

I salute you from Smyrna, together with the Churches of God which are with me, whose rulers have refreshed me in every respect, both in the flesh and in the spirit. My bonds, which I carry about with me for the sake of Jesus Christ (praying that I may attain to God), exhort you. Continue in harmony among yourselves, and in supplication; for it becomes every one of you, and especially the presbyters, to refresh the bishop, to the honour of the Father, and to the honour of Jesus Christ and of the apostles. I entreat you in love to hear me, that I may not, by having thus written, be a testimony against you. And do ye also pray for me, who have need of your love, along with the mercy of God, that I may be thought worthy to attain the lot for which I am now designed, and that I may not be found reprobate.

CHAP. XIII. — CONCLUSION.

The love of the Smyrnæans and Ephesians salutes you. Remember in your prayers the Church which is in Syria, from which also I am not worthy to receive my appellation, being the last[1] of them. Fare ye well in Jesus Christ, while ye continue subject to the bishop, as to the command [of God], and in like manner to the presbytery. And do ye, every man, love one another with an undivided heart. Let my spirit be sanctified[2] by yours, not only now, but also when I shall attain to God. For I am as yet exposed to danger. But the Father is faithful in Jesus Christ to fulfil both mine and your petitions: in whom may ye be found unblameable.

The love of the Smyrnæans and Ephesians salutes you. Remember our Church which is in Syria, from which I am not worthy to receive my appellation, being the last[1] of those of that place. Fare ye well in the Lord Jesus Christ, while ye continue subject to the bishop, and in like manner to the presbyters and to the deacons. And do ye, every man, love one another with an undivided heart. My spirit salutes you,[2] not only now, but also when I shall have attained to God; for I am as yet exposed to danger. But the Father of Jesus Christ is faithful to fulfil both mine and your petitions: in whom may we be found without spot. May I have joy of you in the Lord.

---

[1] i.e., the least. [2] The shorter recension reads ἁγνίζετε, and the longer also hesitates between this and ἀσπάζεται. With the former reading the meaning is very obscure: it has been corrected as above to ἁγνίζηται.

THE EPISTLE OF IGNATIUS TO THE ROMANS

SHORTER AND LONGER VERSIONS

Ignatius, who is also called Theophorus, to the Church which has obtained mercy, through the majesty of the Most High Father, and Jesus Christ, His only-begotten Son; the Church which is beloved and enlightened by the will of Him that willeth all things which are according to the love of Jesus Christ our God, which also presides in the place of the region of the Romans, worthy of God, worthy of honour, worthy of the highest happiness, worthy of praise, worthy of obtaining her every desire, worthy of being deemed holy,[2] and which presides over love, is named from Christ, and from the Father, which I also salute in the name of Jesus Christ, the Son of the Father: to those who are united, both according to the flesh and spirit, to every one of His commandments; who are filled inseparably with the grace of God, and are purified from every strange taint, [I wish] abundance of happiness unblameably, in Jesus Christ our God.

Ignatius, who is also called Theophorus, to the Church which has obtained mercy, through the majesty of the Most High God the Father, and of Jesus Christ, His only-begotten Son; the Church which is sanctified and enlightened by the will of God, who formed all things that are according to the faith and love of Jesus Christ, our God and Saviour; the Church which presides in the place of the region of the Romans, and which is worthy of God, worthy of honour, worthy of the highest happiness, worthy of praise, worthy of credit,[1] worthy of being deemed holy,[2] and which presides over love, is named from Christ, and from the Father, and is possessed of the Spirit, which I also salute in the name of Almighty God, and of Jesus Christ His Son: to those who are united, both according to the flesh and spirit, to every one of His commandments, who are filled inseparably with all the grace of God, and are purified from every strange taint, [I wish] abundance of happiness unblameably, in God, even the Father, and our Lord Jesus Christ.

CHAP. I. — AS A PRISONER, I HOPE TO SEE YOU.

THROUGH prayer[3] to God I have obtained the privilege of seeing your most worthy faces,[4] and have even[5] been granted more than I requested; for I hope as a prisoner in Christ Jesus to salute you, if indeed it be the will of God that I be thought worthy of attaining unto the end. For the beginning has been well or-

THROUGH prayer to God I have obtained the privilege of seeing your most worthy faces,[4] even as I earnestly begged might be granted me; for as a prisoner in Christ Jesus I hope to salute you, if indeed it be the will [of God] that I be thought worthy of attaining unto the end. For the beginning has been well ordered, if I may obtain grace to cling to[6] my lot without hindrance unto the end. For I am afraid of your love,[7] lest it should do me an injury. For it is easy for you to accomplish what you please;

---

[1] Or as in the shorter recension. [2] Or, "most holy." [3] Some read, "since I have," leaving out the following "for," and finding the apodosis in "I hope to salute you." [4] Literally, "worthy of God." [5] Some read, "which I much desired to do." [6] Literally, "to receive."
[7] He probably refers here, and in what follows, to the influence which their earnest prayers in his behalf might have with God.

dered, if I may obtain grace to cling to[1] my lot without hindrance unto the end. For I am afraid of your love,[3] lest it should do me an injury. For it is easy for you to accomplish what you please; but it is difficult for me to attain to God, if ye spare me.

but it is difficult for me to attain to God, if ye do not spare me,[2] under the pretence of carnal affection.

CHAP. II. — DO NOT SAVE ME FROM MARTYRDOM.

For it is not my desire to act towards you as a man-pleaser,[4] but as pleasing God, even as also ye please Him. For neither shall I ever have such [another] opportunity of attaining to God; nor will ye, if ye shall now be silent, ever be entitled to[5] the honour of a better work. For if ye are silent concerning me, I shall become God's; but if you show your love to my flesh, I shall again have to run my race. Pray, then, do not seek to confer any greater favour upon me than that I be sacrificed to God while the altar is still prepared; that, being gathered together in love, ye may sing praise to the Father, through Christ Jesus, that God has deemed me, the bishop of Syria, worthy to be sent for[6] from the east unto the west. It is good to set from the world unto God, that I may rise again to Him.

For it is not my desire that ye should please men, but God, even as also ye do please Him. For neither shall I ever hereafter have such an opportunity of attaining to God; nor will ye, if ye shall now be silent, ever be entitled to[5] the honour of a better work. For if ye are silent concerning me, I shall become God's; but if ye show your love to my flesh, I shall again have to run my race. Pray, then, do not seek to confer any greater favour upon me than that I be sacrificed to God, while the altar is still prepared; that, being gathered together in love, ye may sing praise to the Father, through Christ Jesus, that God has deemed me, the bishop of Syria, worthy to be sent for[6] from the east unto the west, and to become a martyr[7] in behalf of His own precious[8] sufferings, so as to pass from the world to God, that I may rise again unto Him.

CHAP. III. — PRAY RATHER THAT I MAY ATTAIN TO MARTYRDOM.

Ye have never envied any one; ye have taught others. Now I desire that those things may be confirmed [by your conduct], which in your instructions ye enjoin [on others]. Only request in my behalf both inward and outward strength, that I may not only speak, but [truly] will; and that I may not merely be called a Christian, but really be found to be one. For if I be truly found [a Christian], I may also be called one, and be then deemed faithful, when I shall no longer appear to the world. Nothing visible is eternal.[9] "For the things which are seen are temporal, but the things which are not seen are eternal."[10] For our God, Jesus Christ, now that He is with[11] the Father, is all the more revealed [in

Ye have never envied any one; ye have taught others. Now I desire that those things may be confirmed [by your conduct], which in your instructions ye enjoin [on others]. Only request in my behalf both inward and outward strength, that I may not only speak, but [truly] will, so that I may not merely be called a Christian, but really found to be one. For if I be truly found [a Christian], I may also be called one, and be then deemed faithful, when I shall no longer appear to the world. Nothing visible is eternal. "For the things which are seen are temporal, but the things which are not seen are eternal."[10] The Christian is not the result[12] of persuasion, but of power.[13] When he is hated by the world, he is beloved of God. For says [the Scripture], "If ye were of this world, the world would love its own; but now ye are not of the world, but I have chosen you out of it: continue in fellowship with me."[14]

---

[1] Literally, "to receive." [2] Some read γε instead of μή, and translate as in shorter recension. [3] He probably refers here, and in what follows, to the influence which their earnest prayers in his behalf might have with God. [4] Some translate as in longer recension, but there is in the one case ὑμῖν, and in the other ὑμᾶς. [5] Literally, "have to be inscribed to." [6] Literally, "to be found and sent for." [7] The text is here in great confusion. [8] Literally, "beautiful." Some read, "it is good," etc. [9] Some read, "good." [10] 2 Cor. iv. 18. This quotation is not found in the old Latin version of the shorter recension. [11] Or, "in." [12] Literally, "work." [13] The meaning is here doubtful. [14] John xv. 19.

His glory]. Christianity is not a thing[1] of silence only, but also of [manifest] greatness.

CHAP. IV. — ALLOW ME TO FALL A PREY TO THE WILD BEASTS.

I write to the Churches, and impress on them all, that I shall willingly die for God, unless ye hinder me. I beseech of you not to show an unseasonable good-will towards me. Suffer me to become food for the wild beasts, through whose instrumentality it will be granted me to attain to God. I am the wheat of God, and let me be ground by the teeth of the wild beasts, that I may be found the pure bread of Christ. Rather entice the wild beasts, that they may become my tomb, and may leave nothing of my body; so that when I have fallen asleep [in death], I may be no trouble to any one. Then shall I truly be a disciple of Christ, when the world shall not see so much as my body. Entreat Christ for me, that by these instruments[2] I may be found a sacrifice [to God]. I do not, as Peter and Paul, issue commandments unto you. They were apostles; I am but a condemned man: they were free,[3] while I am, even until now, a servant. But when I suffer, I shall be the freedman of Jesus, and shall rise again emancipated in Him. And now, being a prisoner, I learn not to desire anything worldly or vain.

I write to all the Churches, and impress on them all, that I shall willingly die for God, unless ye hinder me. I beseech of you not to show an unseasonable good-will towards me. Suffer me to become food for the wild beasts, through whose instrumentality it will be granted me to attain to God. I am the wheat of God, and am ground by the teeth of the wild beasts, that I may be found the pure bread of God. Rather entice the wild beasts, that they may become my tomb, and may leave nothing of my body; so that when I have fallen asleep [in death], I may not be found troublesome to any one. Then shall I be a true disciple of Jesus Christ, when the world shall not see so much as my body. Entreat the Lord for me, that by these instruments[2] I may be found a sacrifice to God. I do not, as Peter and Paul, issue commandments unto you. They were apostles of Jesus Christ, but I am the very least [of believers]: they were free,[3] as the servants of God; while I am, even until now, a servant. But when I suffer, I shall be the freedman of Jesus Christ, and shall rise again emancipated in Him. And now, being in bonds for Him, I learn not to desire anything worldly or vain.

CHAP. V. — I DESIRE TO DIE.

From Syria even unto Rome I fight with beasts,[4] both by land and sea, both by night and day, being bound to ten leopards, I mean a band of soldiers, who, even when they receive benefits,[5] show themselves all the worse. But I am the more instructed by their injuries [to act as a disciple of Christ]; "yet am I not thereby justified."[6] May I enjoy the wild beasts that are prepared for me; and I pray they may be found eager to rush upon me, which also I will entice to devour me speedily, and not deal with me as with some, whom, out of fear, they have not touched. But if they be unwilling to assail me, I will compel them to do so. Pardon me

From Syria even unto Rome I fight with beasts,[4] both by land and sea, both by night and day, being bound to ten leopards, I mean a band of soldiers, who, even when they receive benefits,[5] show themselves all the worse. But I am the more instructed by their injuries [to act as a disciple of Christ]; "yet am I not thereby justified."[6] May I enjoy the wild beasts that are prepared for me; and I pray that they may be found eager to rush upon me, which also I will entice to devour me speedily, and not deal with me as with some, whom, out of fear, they have not touched. But if they be unwilling to assail me, I will compel them to do so. Pardon me [in this]: I know what is for my benefit. Now I begin to be a disciple, and have[7] no desire after anything visible or invisible, that I may attain to Jesus Christ. Let fire and the cross; let the crowds of wild beasts; let breakings, tearings, and separations of bones; let cutting off of members; let bruising to pieces of the whole body; and let

---

[1] Literally, "work." [2] i.e., by the teeth of the wild beasts. [3] "Free," probably from human infirmity. [4] Comp. 1 Cor. xv. 32, where the word is also used figuratively. [5] Probably the soldiers received gifts from the Christians, to treat Ignatius with kindness.
[6] 1 Cor. iv. 4. [7] In the shorter recension there is ζηλώσῃ, and in the longer ζηλῶσαι; hence the variety of rendering, but the translation is by no means certain.

[in this]: I know what is for my benefit. Now I begin to be a disciple. And let no one, of things visible or invisible, envy[1] me that I should attain to Jesus Christ. Let fire and the cross; let the crowds of wild beasts; let tearings,[2] breakings, and dislocations of bones; let cutting off of members; let shatterings of the whole body; and let all the dreadful[3] torments of the devil come upon me: only let me attain to Jesus Christ.

the very torment of the devil come upon me: only let me attain to Jesus Christ.

CHAP. VI. — BY DEATH I SHALL ATTAIN TRUE LIFE.

All the pleasures of the world, and all the kingdoms of this earth,[4] shall profit me nothing. It is better for me to die in behalf of[5] Jesus Christ, than to reign over all the ends of the earth. "For what shall a man be profited, if he gain the whole world, but lose his own soul?"[6] Him I seek, who died for us: Him I desire, who rose again for our sake. This is the gain which is laid up for me. Pardon me, brethren: do not hinder me from living, do not wish to keep me in a state of death;[7] and while I desire to belong to God, do not ye give me over to the world. Suffer me to obtain pure light: when I have gone thither, I shall indeed be a man of God. Permit me to be an imitator of the passion of my God. If any one has Him within himself, let him consider what I desire, and let him have sympathy with me, as knowing how I am straitened.

All the ends of the world, and all the kingdoms of this earth,[4] shall profit me nothing. It is better for me to die for the sake of Jesus Christ, than to reign over all the ends of the earth. "For what is a man profited, if he gain the whole world, but lose his own soul?" I long after the Lord, the Son of the true God and Father, even Jesus Christ. Him I seek, who died for us and rose again. Pardon me, brethren: do not hinder me in attaining to life; for Jesus is the life of believers. Do not wish to keep me in a state of death,[7] for life without Christ is death. While I desire to belong to God, do not ye give me over to the world. Suffer me to obtain pure light: when I have gone thither, I shall indeed be a man of God. Permit me to be an imitator of the passion of Christ, my God. If any one has Him within himself, let him consider what I desire, and let him have sympathy with me, as knowing how I am straitened.

CHAP. VII. — REASON OF DESIRING TO DIE.

The prince of this world would fain carry me away, and corrupt my disposition towards God. Let none of you, therefore, who are [in Rome] help him; rather be ye on my side, that is, on the side of God. Do not speak of Jesus Christ, and yet set your desires on the world. Let not envy find a dwelling-place among you; nor even should I, when present with you, exhort you to it, be ye persuaded to listen to me, but rather give credit to those things which I now write to you. For though I am alive while I write to you, yet I am eager to die. My love[8] has been crucified, and there is no

The prince of this world would fain carry me away, and corrupt my disposition towards God. Let none of you, therefore, who are [in Rome] help him; rather be ye on my side, that is, on the side of God. Do not speak of Jesus Christ, and yet prefer this world to Him. Let not envy find a dwelling-place among you; nor even should I, when present with you, exhort you to it, be ye persuaded, but rather give credit to those things which I now write to you. For though I am alive while I write to you, yet I am eager to die for the sake of Christ. My love[8] has been crucified, and there is no fire in me that loves anything; but there is living water springing up in me,[9] and which says to me inwardly, Come to the Father. I have no delight in corruptible food, nor in the pleasures of this life. I desire the bread of God, the heavenly bread, the bread of life, which is the flesh of Jesus Christ,

---

[1] In the shorter recension there is ζηλώσῃ, and in the longer ζηλῶσαι; hence the variety of rendering, but the translation is by no means certain. [2] Some deem this and the following word spurious. [3] Literally, "evil." [4] Literally, "this age." [5] Literally, "into." [6] Matt. xvi. 26. Some omit this quotation. [7] Literally, "to die." [8] Some understand by *love* in this passage, *Christ Himself;* others regard it as referring to *the natural desires of the heart*. [9] Comp. John iv. 14.

fire in me desiring to be fed;[1] but there is within me a water that liveth and speaketh,[2] saying to me inwardly, Come to the Father. I have no delight in corruptible food, nor in the pleasures of this life. I desire the bread of God, the heavenly bread, the bread of life, which is the flesh of Jesus Christ, the Son of God, who became afterwards of the seed of David and Abraham; and I desire the drink of God, namely His blood, which is incorruptible love and eternal life.

the Son of God, who became afterwards of the seed of David and Abraham; and I desire the drink, namely His blood, which is incorruptible love and eternal life.

CHAP. VIII. — BE YE FAVOURABLE TO ME.

I no longer wish to live after the manner of men, and my desire shall be fulfilled if ye consent. Be ye willing, then, that ye also may have your desires fulfilled. I entreat you in this brief letter; do ye give credit to me. Jesus Christ will reveal these things to you, [so that ye shall know] that I speak truly. He[5] is the mouth altogether free from falsehood, by which the Father has truly spoken. Pray ye for me, that I may attain [the object of my desire]. I have not written to you according to the flesh, but according to the will of God. If I shall suffer, ye have wished [well] to me; but if I am rejected, ye have hated me.

I no longer wish to live after the manner of men, and my desire shall be fulfilled if ye consent. "I am crucified with Christ: nevertheless I live; yet no longer I, since Christ liveth in me."[3] I entreat you in this brief letter: do not refuse me; believe me that I love Jesus, who was delivered [to death] for my sake. "What shall I render to the Lord for all His benefits towards me?"[4] Now God, even the Father, and the Lord Jesus Christ, shall reveal these things to you, [so that ye shall know] that I speak truly. And do ye pray along with me, that I may attain my aim in the Holy Spirit. I have not written to you according to the flesh, but according to the will of God. If I shall suffer, ye have loved me; but if I am rejected, ye have hated me.

CHAP. IX. — PRAY FOR THE CHURCH IN SYRIA.

Remember in your prayers the Church in Syria, which now has God for its shepherd, instead of me. Jesus Christ alone will oversee it, and your love [will also regard it]. But as for me, I am ashamed to be counted one of them; for indeed I am not worthy, as being the very last of them, and one born out of due time.[6] But I have obtained mercy to be somebody, if I shall attain to God. My spirit salutes you, and the love of the Churches that have received me in the name of Jesus Christ, and not as a mere passer-by. For even those Churches which were not[7] near to me in the way, I mean according to the flesh,[8] have gone before me,[9] city by city, [to meet me.]

Remember in your prayers the Church which is in Syria, which, instead of me, has now for its shepherd the Lord, who says, "I am the good Shepherd." And He alone will oversee it, as well as your love towards Him. But as for me, I am ashamed to be counted one of them; for I am not worthy, as being the very last of them, and one born out of due time. But I have obtained mercy to be somebody, if I shall attain to God. My spirit salutes you, and the love of the Churches which have received me in the name of Jesus Christ, and not as a mere passer-by. For even those Churches which were not near to me in the way, have brought me forward, city by city.

---

[1] Literally, "desiring material." [2] The text and meaning are here doubtful. We have followed Hefele, who understands by the water *the Holy Spirit*, and refers to John vii. 38. [3] Gal. ii. 20. [4] Ps. cxvi. 12. [5] Some refer this to Ignatius himself. [6] Comp. 1 Cor. xv. 8, 9. [7] Some refer this to the jurisdiction of Ignatius. [8] i.e., the outward road he had to travel. [9] Or, "have sent me forward;" comp. Tit. iii. 13.

CHAP. X. — CONCLUSION.

Now I write these things to you from Smyrna by the Ephesians, who are deservedly most happy. There is also with me, along with many others, Crocus, one dearly beloved by me.[1] As to those who have gone before me from Syria to Rome for the glory of God, I believe that you are acquainted with them; to whom, [then,] do ye make known that I am at hand. For they are all worthy, both of God and of you; and it is becoming that you should refresh them in all things. I have written these things unto you, on the day before the ninth of the Kalends of September (that[2] is, on the twenty-third day of August). Fare ye well to the end, in the patience of Jesus Christ. Amen.

Now I write these things to you from Smyrna by the Ephesians, who are deservedly most happy. There is also with me, along with many others, Crocus, one dearly beloved by me.[1] As to those who have gone before me from Syria to Rome for the glory of God, I believe that you are acquainted with them; to whom, [then,] do ye make known that I am at hand. For they are all worthy, both of God and of you; and it is becoming that you should refresh them in all things. I have written these things unto you on the day before the ninth of the Kalends of September. Fare ye well to the end, in the patience of Jesus Christ.

---

[1] Literally, "the name desired to me."   [2] This clause is evidently an explanatory gloss which has crept into the text.

THE EPISTLE OF IGNATIUS TO THE PHILADELPHIANS

SHORTER AND LONGER VERSIONS

Ignatius, who is also called Theophorus, to the Church of God the Father, and our Lord Jesus Christ, which is at Philadelphia, in Asia, which has obtained mercy, and is established in the harmony of God, and rejoiceth unceasingly[1] in the passion of our Lord, and is filled with all mercy through his resurrection; which I salute in the blood of Jesus Christ, who is our eternal and enduring joy, especially if [men] are in unity with the bishop, the presbyters, and the deacons, who have been appointed according to the mind of Jesus Christ, whom He has established in security, after His own will, and by His Holy Spirit.

Ignatius, who is also called Theophorus, to the Church of God the Father, and of the Lord Jesus Christ, which is at Philadelphia, which has obtained mercy through love, and is established in the harmony of God, and rejoiceth unceasingly,[1] in the passion of our Lord Jesus, and is filled with all mercy through His resurrection; which I salute in the blood of Jesus Christ, who is our eternal and enduring joy, especially to those who are in unity with the bishop, and the presbyters, and the deacons, who have been appointed by the will of God the Father, through the Lord Jesus Christ, who, according to His own will, has firmly established His Church upon a rock, by a spiritual building, not made with hands, against which the winds and the floods have beaten, yet have not been able to overthrow it:[2] yea, and may spiritual wickedness never be able to do so, but be thoroughly weakened by the power of Jesus Christ our Lord.

CHAP. I. — PRAISE OF THE BISHOP.

Which bishop,[3] I know, obtained the ministry which pertains to the common [weal], not of himself, neither by men,[4] nor through vainglory, but by the love of God the Father, and the Lord Jesus Christ; at whose meekness I am struck with admiration, and who by his silence is able to accomplish more than those who vainly talk. For he is in harmony with the commandments [of God], even as the harp is with its strings. Wherefore my soul declares his mind towards God a happy one, knowing it to be virtuous and perfect, and that his stability as well as freedom from all anger is after the example of the infinite[6] meekness of the living God.

Having beheld your bishop, I know that he was not selected to undertake the ministry which pertains to the common [weal], either by himself or by men,[4] or out of vainglory, but by the love of Jesus Christ, and of God the Father, who raised Him from the dead; at whose meekness I am struck with admiration, and who by His silence is able to accomplish more than they who talk a great deal. For he is in harmony with the commandments and ordinances of the Lord, even as the strings are with the harp, and is no less blameless than was Zacharias the priest.[5] Wherefore my soul declares his mind towards God a happy one, knowing it to be virtuous and perfect, and that his stability as well as freedom from all anger is after the example of the infinite meekness of the living God.

CHAP. II. — MAINTAIN UNION WITH THE BISHOP.

Wherefore, as children of light and truth, flee from division and wicked

Wherefore, as children of light and truth, avoid the dividing of your unity, and the wicked doctrine of the

---

[1] Or, "inseparably." [2] Comp. Matt. vii. 25. [3] The bishop previously referred to. [4] Comp. Gal. i. 1. [5] Luke i. 6. [6] Literally, "all."

doctrines; but where the shepherd is, there do ye as sheep follow. For there are many wolves that appear worthy of credit, who, by means of a pernicious pleasure, carry captive³ those that are running towards God; but in your unity they shall have no place.

heretics, from whom "a defiling influence has gone forth into all the earth."¹ But where the shepherd is, there do ye as sheep follow. For there are many wolves in sheep's clothing,² who, by means of a pernicious pleasure, carry captive³ those that are running towards God; but in your unity they shall have no place.

CHAP. III. — AVOID SCHISMATICS.

Keep yourselves from those evil plants which Jesus Christ does not tend, because they are not the planting of the Father. Not that I have found any division among you, but exceeding purity. For as many as are of God and of Jesus Christ are also with the bishop. And as many as shall, in the exercise of repentance, return into the unity of the Church, these, too, shall belong to God, that they may live according to Jesus Christ. Do not err, my brethren. If any man follows him that makes a schism in the Church, he shall not inherit the kingdom of God. If any one walks according to a strange⁵ opinion, he agrees not with the passion [of Christ].

Keep yourselves, then, from those evil plants which Jesus Christ does not tend, but that wild beast, the destroyer of men, because they are not the planting of the Father, but the seed of the wicked one. Not that I have found any division among you do I write these things; but I arm you beforehand, as the children of God. For as many as are of Christ are also with the bishop; but as many as fall away from him, and embrace communion with the accursed, these shall be cut off along with them. For they are not Christ's husbandry, but the seed of the enemy, from whom may you ever be delivered by the prayers of the shepherd, that most faithful and gentle shepherd who presides over you. I therefore exhort you in the Lord to receive with all tenderness those that repent and return to the unity of the Church, that through your kindness and forbearance they may recover⁴ themselves out of the snare of the devil, and becoming worthy of Jesus Christ, may obtain eternal salvation in the kingdom of Christ. Brethren, be not deceived. If any man follows him that separates from the truth, he shall not inherit the kingdom of God; and if any man does not stand aloof from the preacher of falsehood, he shall be condemned to hell. For it is obligatory neither to separate from the godly, nor to associate with the ungodly. If any one walks according to a strange⁵ opinion, he is not of Christ, nor a partaker of His passion; but is a fox,⁶ a destroyer of the vineyard of Christ. Have no fellowship⁷ with such a man, lest ye perish along with him, even should he be thy father, thy son, thy brother, or a member of thy family. For says [the Scripture], "Thine eye shall not spare him."⁸ You ought therefore to "hate those that hate God, and to waste away [with grief] on account of His enemies."⁹ I do not mean that you should beat them or persecute them, as do the Gentiles "that know not the Lord and God;"¹⁰ but that you should regard them as your enemies, and separate yourselves from them, while yet you admonish them, and exhort them to repentance, if it may be they will hear, if it may be they will submit themselves. For our God is a lover of mankind, and "will have all men to be saved, and to come to the knowledge of the truth."¹¹ Wherefore "He makes His sun to rise upon the evil and on the good, and sendeth rain on the just and on the unjust;"¹² of whose kindness the Lord, wishing us also to be imitators, says, "Be ye perfect, even as also your Father that is in heaven is perfect."¹³

---

¹ Jer. xxiii. 15. ² Comp. Matt. vii. 15. ³ Comp. 2 Tim. iii. 6. ⁴ 2 Tim. ii. 26. ⁵ i.e., heretical. ⁶ Comp. Song of Sol. ii. 15. ⁷ Comp. 1 Cor. v. 11. ⁸ Deut. xiii. 6, 8. ⁹ Ps. cxix. 21. ¹⁰ 1 Thess. iv. 5. ¹¹ 1 Tim. ii. 4. ¹² Matt. v. 45. ¹³ Matt. v. 48.

CHAP. IV. — HAVE BUT ONE EUCHARIST, ETC.

Take ye heed, then, to have but one Eucharist. For there is one flesh of our Lord Jesus Christ, and one cup to [show forth [1]] the unity of His blood; one altar; as there is one bishop, along with the presbytery and deacons, my fellow-servants: that so, whatsoever ye do, ye may do it according to [the will of] God.

I have confidence of you in the Lord, that ye will be of no other mind. Wherefore I write boldly to your love, which is worthy of God, and exhort you to have but one faith, and one [kind of] preaching, and one Eucharist. For there is one flesh of the Lord Jesus Christ; and His blood which was shed for us is one; one loaf also is broken to all [the communicants], and one cup is distributed among them all: there is but one altar for the whole Church, and one bishop, with the presbytery and deacons, my fellow-servants. Since, also, there is but one unbegotten Being, God, even the Father; and one only-begotten Son, God, the Word and man; and one Comforter, the Spirit of truth; and also one preaching, and one faith, and one baptism; [2] and one Church which the holy apostles established from one end of the earth to the other by the blood of Christ, and by their own sweat and toil; it behoves you also, therefore, as "a peculiar people, and a holy nation,"[3] to perform all things with harmony in Christ. Wives, be ye subject to your husbands in the fear of God;[4] and ye virgins, to Christ in purity, not counting marriage an abomination, but desiring that which is better, not for the reproach of wedlock, but for the sake of meditating on the law. Children, obey your parents, and have an affection for them, as workers together with God for your birth [into the world]. Servants, be subject to your masters in God, that ye may be the freedmen of Christ.[5] Husbands, love your wives, as fellow-servants of God, as your own body, as the partners of your life, and your co-adjutors in the procreation of children. Virgins, have Christ alone before your eyes, and His Father in your prayers, being enlightened by the Spirit. May I have pleasure in your purity, as that of Elijah, or as of Joshua the son of Nun, as of Melchizedek, or as of Elisha, as of Jeremiah, or as of John the Baptist, as of the beloved disciple, as of Timothy, as of Titus, as of Evodius, as of Clement, who departed this life in [perfect] chastity.[6] Not, however, that I blame the other blessed [saints] because they entered into the married state, of which I have just spoken.[7] For I pray that, being found worthy of God, I may be found at their feet in the kingdom, as at the feet of Abraham, and Isaac, and Jacob; as of Joseph, and Isaiah, and the rest of the prophets; as of Peter, and Paul, and the rest of the apostles, that were married men. For they entered into these marriages not for the sake of appetite, but out of regard for the propagation of mankind. Fathers, "bring up your children in the nurture and admonition of the Lord;"[8] and teach them the holy Scriptures, and also trades, that they may not indulge in idleness. Now [the Scripture] says, "A righteous father educates [his children] well; his heart shall rejoice in a wise son."[9] Masters, be gentle towards your servants, as holy Job has taught you;[10] for there is one nature, and one family of mankind. For "in Christ there is neither bond nor free."[11] Let governors be obedient to Cæsar; soldiers to those that command them; deacons to the presbyters, as

---

[1] Literally, "into." [2] Eph. iv. 5. [3] Tit. ii. 14; 1 Pet. ii. 9. [4] Eph. v. 22. [5] 1 Cor. vii. 22.
[6] There was a prevalent opinion among the ancient Christian writers, that all these holy men lived a life of [chaste] celibacy.
[7] Or, "it is not because, etc., that I have mentioned these." [8] Eph. vi. 4. [9] Prov. xxiii. 24. [10] Job xxxi. 13, 15. [11] Gal. iii. 28.

to high-priests; the presbyters, and deacons, and the rest of the clergy, together with all the people, and the soldiers, and the governors, and Cæsar [himself], to the bishop; the bishop to Christ, even as Christ to the Father. And thus unity is preserved throughout. Let not the widows be wanderers about, nor fond of dainties, nor gadders from house to house; but let them be like Judith, noted for her seriousness; and like Anna, eminent for her sobriety. I do not ordain these things as an apostle: for "who am I, or what is my father's house,"[1] that I should pretend to be equal in honour to them? But as your "fellow-soldier,"[2] I hold the position of one who [simply] admonishes you.

CHAP. V. — PRAY FOR ME.

My brethren, I am greatly enlarged in loving you; and rejoicing exceedingly [over you], I seek to secure your safety. Yet it is not I, but Jesus Christ, for whose sake being bound I fear the more, inasmuch as I am not yet perfect. But your prayer to God shall make me perfect, that I may attain to that portion which through mercy has been allotted me, while I flee to the Gospel as to the flesh of Jesus, and to the apostles as to the presbytery of the Church. And let us also love the prophets, because they too have proclaimed the Gospel,[4] and placed their hope in Him,[5] and waited for Him; in whom also believing, they were saved, through union to Jesus Christ, being holy men, worthy of love and admiration, having had witness borne to them by Jesus Christ, and being reckoned along with [us] in the Gospel of the common hope.

My brethren, I am greatly enlarged in loving you; and rejoicing exceedingly [over you], I seek to secure your safety. Yet it is not I, but the Lord Jesus through me; for whose sake being bound, I fear the more, for I am not yet perfect. But your prayer to God shall make me perfect, that I may attain that to which I have been called, while I flee to the Gospel as to the flesh of Jesus Christ, and to the apostles as the presbytery of the Church. I do also love the prophets as those who announced Christ, and as being partakers of the same Spirit with the apostles. For as the false prophets and the false apostles drew [to themselves] one and the same wicked, deceitful, and seducing[3] spirit; so also did the prophets and the apostles receive from God, through Jesus Christ, one and the same Holy Spirit, who is good, and sovereign,[6] and true, and the Author of [saving] knowledge.[7] For there is one God of the Old and New Testament, "one Mediator between God and men," for the creation of both intelligent and sensitive beings, and in order to exercise a beneficial and suitable providence [over them]. There is also one Comforter, who displayed[8] His power in Moses, and the prophets, and apostles. All the saints, therefore, were saved by Christ, hoping in Him, and waiting for Him; and they obtained through Him salvation, being holy ones, worthy of love and admiration, having testimony borne to them by Jesus Christ, in the Gospel of our common hope.

CHAP. VI. — DO NOT ACCEPT JUDAISM.

But if any one preach the Jewish law[9] unto you, listen not to him. For it is better to hearken to Christian doctrine from a man who has been circumcised, than to Judaism from one uncircumcised. But if either of such persons do not speak concerning Jesus Christ, they are in my judgment but as monuments and sepulchres of the dead, upon which are written only the names of men. Flee therefore the wicked devices and snares of the prince

If any one preaches the one God of the law and the prophets, but denies Christ to be the Son of God, he is a liar, even as also is his father the devil,[10] and is a Jew falsely so called, being possessed of[11] mere carnal circumcision. If any one confesses Christ Jesus the Lord, but denies the God of the law and of the prophets, saying that the Father of Christ is not the Maker of heaven and earth, he has not continued in the truth any more than his father the devil,[10] and is a disciple of Simon Magus, not of the Holy Spirit. If any one says there is one God, and also confesses Christ Jesus, but thinks the Lord to be a mere man, and not the only-begotten[12] God, and Wis-

---

[1] 1 Sam. xviii. 18; 2 Sam. vii. 18. [2] Phil. ii. 25. [3] Literally, "people-deceiving." [4] Literally, "have proclaimed in reference to the Gospel." [5] In Christ. [6] Comp. Ps. li. 12 (LXX.). [7] Literally, "teaching." [8] Or, "wrought." [9] Literally, "Judaism." [10] Comp. John viii. 44. [11] Literally, "beneath." [12] Comp. the reading sanctioned by the ancient authorities, John i. 18.

of this world, lest at any time being conquered[1] by his artifices,[2] ye grow weak in your love. But be ye all joined together[3] with an undivided heart. And I thank my God that I have a good conscience in respect to you, and that no one has it in his power to boast, either privately or publicly, that I have burdened[6] any one either in much or in little. And I wish for all among whom I have spoken, that they may not possess that for a testimony against them.

dom, and the Word of God, and deems Him to consist merely of a soul and body, such an one is a serpent, that preaches deceit and error for the destruction of men. And such a man is poor in understanding, even as by name he is an Ebionite.[4] If any one confesses the truths mentioned,[5] but calls lawful wedlock, and the procreation of children, destruction and pollution, or deems certain kinds of food abominable, such an one has the apostate dragon dwelling within him. If any one confesses the Father, and the Son, and the Holy Ghost, and praises the creation, but calls the incarnation merely an appearance, and is ashamed of the passion, such an one has denied the faith, not less than the Jews who killed Christ. If any one confesses these things, and that God the Word did dwell in a human body, being within it as the Word, even as the soul also is in the body, because it was God that inhabited it, and not a human soul, but affirms that unlawful unions are a good thing, and places the highest happiness[7] in pleasure, as does the man who is falsely called a Nicolaitan, this person can neither be a lover of God, nor a lover of Christ, but is a corrupter of his own flesh, and therefore void of the Holy Spirit, and a stranger to Christ. All such persons are but monuments and sepulchres of the dead, upon which are written only the names of dead men. Flee, therefore, the wicked devices and snares of the spirit which now worketh in the children of this world,[8] lest at any time being overcome,[1] ye grow weak in your love. But be ye all joined together[3] with an undivided heart and a willing mind, "being of one accord and of one judgment,"[9] being always of the same opinion about the same things, both when you are at ease and in danger, both in sorrow and in joy. I thank God, through Jesus Christ, that I have a good conscience in respect to you, and that no one has it in his power to boast, either privately or publicly, that I have burdened any one either in much or in little. And I wish for all among whom I have spoken, that they may not possess that for a testimony against them.

CHAP. VII.—I HAVE EXHORTED YOU TO UNITY.

For though some would have deceived me according to the flesh, yet the Spirit, as being from God, is not deceived. For it knows both whence it comes and whither it goes,[10] and detects the secrets [of the heart]. For, when I was among you, I cried, I spoke with a loud voice: Give heed to the bishop, and to the presbytery and deacons. Now, some suspected me of having spoken thus, as knowing beforehand the division caused by some among you.[11] But He is my witness, for whose sake I am in bonds, that I got no intelligence from any man.[13] But the Spirit proclaimed

For though some would have deceived me according to the flesh, yet my spirit is not deceived; for I have received it from God. For it knows both whence it comes and whither it goes, and detects the secrets [of the heart]. For when I was among you, I cried, I spoke with a loud voice—the word is not mine, but God's—Give heed to the bishop, and to the presbytery and deacons. But if ye suspect that I spake thus, as having learned beforehand the division caused by some among you, He is my witness, for whose sake I am in bonds, that I learned nothing of it from the mouth of any man. But the Spirit made an announcement to me, saying as follows: Do nothing without the bishop; keep your bodies[12] as the temples of God; love unity; avoid divisions; be ye followers of Paul, and of the rest of the apostles, even as they also were of Christ.

---

[1] Literally, "oppressed." [2] Or, "will." [3] Some render, "come together into the same place."
[4] From a Hebrew word meaning "poor." [5] Or, "these things." [6] Apparently by attempting to impose the yoke of Judaism.
[7] Literally, "the end of happiness." [8] Comp. Eph. ii. 2. [9] Phil. ii. 2. [10] John iii. 8. [11] Some translate, "as foreseeing the division to arise among you." [12] Literally, "your flesh." [13] Literally, "did not know from human flesh."

these words: Do nothing without the bishop; keep your bodies[1] as the temples of God;[2] love unity; avoid divisions; be the followers of Jesus Christ, even as He is of His Father.

CHAP. VIII. — THE SAME CONTINUED.

I therefore did what belonged to me, as a man devoted to[3] unity. For where there is division and wrath, God doth not dwell. To all them that repent, the Lord grants forgiveness, if they turn in penitence to the unity of God, and to communion with the bishop.[4] I trust [as to you] in the grace of Jesus Christ, who shall free you from every bond. And I exhort you to do nothing out of strife, but according to the doctrine of Christ. When I heard some saying, If I do not find it in the ancient[7] Scriptures, I will not believe the Gospel; on my saying to them, It is written, they answered me, That remains to be proved. But to me Jesus Christ is in the place of all that is ancient: His cross, and death, and resurrection, and the faith[8] which is by Him, are undefiled monuments of antiquity; by which I desire, through your prayers, to be justified.

I therefore did what belonged to me, as a man devoted to unity; adding this also, that where there is diversity of judgment, and wrath, and hatred, God does not dwell. To all them that repent, God grants forgiveness, if they with one consent return to the unity of Christ, and communion with the bishop.[4] I trust to the grace of Jesus Christ, that He will free you from every bond of wickedness.[5] I therefore exhort you that ye do nothing out of strife,[6] but according to the doctrine of Christ. For I have heard some saying, If I do not find the Gospel in the archives, I will not believe it. To such persons I say that my archives are Jesus Christ, to disobey whom is manifest destruction. My authentic archives are His cross, and death, and resurrection, and the faith which bears on these things, by which I desire, through your prayers, to be justified. He who disbelieves the Gospel disbelieves everything along with it. For the archives ought not to be preferred to the Spirit.[9] "It is hard to kick against the pricks;"[10] it is hard to disbelieve Christ; it is hard to reject the preaching of the apostles.

CHAP. IX. — THE OLD TESTAMENT IS GOOD: THE NEW TESTAMENT IS BETTER.

The priests[11] indeed are good, but the High Priest is better; to whom the holy of holies has been committed, and who alone has been trusted with the secrets of God. He is the door of the Father, by which enter in Abraham, and Isaac, and Jacob, and the prophets, and the apostles, and the Church. All these have for their object the attaining to the unity of God. But the Gospel possesses something transcendent [above the former dispensation], viz., the appearance of our Lord Jesus Christ, His passion and resurrection. For the beloved prophets announced Him,[17] but the Gospel is the perfection of immortality.[18] All these things are good together, if ye believe in love.

The priests[11] indeed, and the ministers of the word, are good; but the High Priest is better, to whom the holy of holies has been committed, and who alone has been entrusted with the secrets of God. The ministering powers of God are good. The Comforter is holy, and the Word is holy, the Son of the Father, by whom He made all things, and exercises a providence over them all. This is the Way[12] which leads to the Father, the Rock,[13] the Defence,[14] the Key, the Shepherd,[15] the Sacrifice, the Door[16] of knowledge, through which have entered Abraham, and Isaac, and Jacob, Moses and all the company of the prophets, and these pillars of the world, the apostles, and the spouse of Christ, on whose account He poured out His own blood, as her marriage portion, that He might redeem her. All these things tend towards the unity of the one and only true God. But the Gospel possesses something transcendent [above the former dispensation], viz., the appearing of our Saviour Jesus Christ, His passion, and the resurrection itself. For those things which the prophets announced, saying, "Until He come for whom it is reserved, and He shall be the expectation

---

[1] Literally, "your flesh." [2] Comp. 1 Cor. iii. 16, vi. 19. [3] Literally, "prepared for."
[4] Literally, "to the assembly of the bishop." [5] Comp. Isa. lviii. 6. [6] Phil. ii. 3.
[7] The meaning here is very doubtful. Some read ἐν τοῖς ἀρχαίοις, as translated above; others prefer ἐν τοῖς ἀρχείοις, as in the longer recension. [8] i.e., the system of Christian doctrine. [9] Or, "the archives of the Spirit are not exposed to all." [10] Acts xxvi. 14.
[11] i.e., the Jewish priests. [12] John xiv. 6. [13] 1 Cor. x. 4. [14] Literally, "the hedge." [15] John x. 11. [16] John x. 9.
[17] Literally, "proclaimed as to him." [18] The meaning is doubtful. Comp. 2 Tim. i. 10.

of the Gentiles,"[1] have been fulfilled in the Gospel, [our Lord saying,] "Go ye and teach all nations, baptizing them in the name of the Father, and of the Son, and of the Holy Ghost."[2] All then are good together, the law, the prophets, the apostles, the whole company [of others] that have believed through them: only if we love one another.

CHAP. X. — CONGRATULATE THE INHABITANTS OF ANTIOCH ON THE CLOSE OF THE PERSECUTION.

Since, according to your prayers, and the compassion which ye feel in Christ Jesus, it is reported to me that the Church which is at Antioch in Syria possesses peace, it will become you, as a Church of God, to elect a deacon to act as the ambassador of God [for you] to [the brethren there], that he may rejoice along with them when they are met together, and glorify the name [of God]. Blessed is he in Jesus Christ, who shall be deemed worthy of such a ministry; and ye too shall be glorified. And if ye are willing, it is not beyond your power to do this, for the sake[3] of God; as also the nearest Churches have sent, in some cases bishops, and in others presbyters and deacons.

Since, according to your prayers, and the compassion which ye feel in Christ Jesus, it is reported to me that the Church which is at Antioch in Syria possesses peace, it will become you, as a Church of God, to elect a bishop to act as the ambassador of God [for you] to [the brethren] there, that it may be granted them to meet together, and to glorify the name of God. Blessed is he in Christ Jesus, who shall be deemed worthy of such a ministry; and if ye be zealous [in this matter], ye shall receive glory in Christ. And if ye are willing, it is not altogether beyond your power to do this, for the sake of[3] God; as also the nearest Churches have sent, in some cases bishops, and in others presbyters and deacons.

CHAP. XI. — THANKS AND SALUTATION.

Now, as to Philo the deacon, of Cilicia, a man of reputation, who still ministers to me in the word of God, along with Rheus Agathopus, an elect man, who has followed me from Syria, not regarding[4] his life,—these bear witness in your behalf; and I myself give thanks to God for you, that ye have received them, even as the Lord you. But may those that dishonoured them be forgiven through the grace of Jesus Christ! The love of the brethren at Troas salutes you; whence also I write to you by Burrhus, who was sent along with me by the Ephesians and Smyrnæans, to show their respect.[7] May the Lord Jesus Christ honour them, in whom they hope, in flesh, and soul, and faith, and love, and concord! Fare ye well in Christ Jesus, our common hope.

Now, as to Philo the deacon, a man of Cilicia, of high reputation, who still ministers to me in the word of God, along with Gaius and Agathopus, an elect man, who has followed me from Syria, not regarding[4] his life, — these also bear testimony in your behalf. And I myself give thanks to God for you, because ye have received them: and the Lord will also receive you. But may those that dishonoured them be forgiven through the grace of Jesus Christ, " who wisheth not the death of the sinner, but his repentance."[5] The love of the brethren at Troas salutes you; whence also I write to you by Burrhus,[6] who was sent along with me by the Ephesians and Smyrnæans, to show their respect:[7] whom the Lord Jesus Christ will requite, in whom they hope, in flesh, and soul, and spirit, and faith, and love, and concord. Fare ye well in the Lord Jesus Christ, our common hope, in the Holy Ghost.

---

[1] Gen. xlix. 10. [2] Matt. xxviii. 19. [3] Literally, "for the name of." [4] Literally, "bidding farewell to."
[5] Comp. Ezek. xviii. 23, 32, xxxiii. 11; 2 Pet. iii. 9. [6] The MS. has "Burgus." [7] Or, "for the sake of honour."

THE EPISTLE OF IGNATIUS TO THE SMYRNÆANS

SHORTER AND LONGER VERSIONS

Ignatius, who is also called Theophorus, to the Church of God the Father, and of the beloved Jesus Christ, which has through mercy obtained every kind of gift, which is filled with faith and love, and is deficient in no gift, most worthy of God, and adorned with holiness:[1] *the Church which is at Smyrna, in Asia, wishes abundance of happiness, through the immaculate Spirit and word of God.*

Ignatius, who is also called Theophorus, to the Church of God the most high Father, and His beloved Son Jesus Christ, which has through mercy obtained every kind of gift, which is filled with faith and love, and is deficient in no gift, most worthy of God, and adorned with holiness:[1] *the Church which is at Smyrna, in Asia, wishes abundance of happiness, through the immaculate Spirit and word of God.*

CHAP. I. — THANKS TO GOD FOR YOUR FAITH.

I GLORIFY God, even Jesus Christ, who has given you such wisdom. For I have observed that ye are perfected in an immoveable faith, as if ye were nailed to the cross of our Lord Jesus Christ, both in the flesh and in the spirit, and are established in love through the blood of Christ, being fully persuaded with respect to our Lord, that He was truly of the seed of David according to the flesh,[3] and the Son of God according to the will and power[4] of God; that He was truly born of a virgin, was baptized by John, in order that all righteousness might be fulfilled[5] by Him; and was truly, under Pontius Pilate and Herod the tetrarch, nailed [to the cross] for us in His flesh. Of this fruit[7] we are by His divinely-blessed passion, that He might set up a standard[8] for all ages, through His resurrection, to all His holy and faithful [followers], whether among Jews or Gentiles, in the one body of His Church.

I GLORIFY the God and Father of our Lord Jesus Christ, who by Him has given you such wisdom. For I have observed that ye are perfected in an immoveable faith, as if ye were nailed to the cross of our Lord Jesus Christ, both in the flesh and in the spirit, and are established in love through the blood of Christ, being fully persuaded, in very truth, with respect to our Lord Jesus Christ, that He was the Son of God, "the first-born of every creature,"[2] God the Word, the only-begotten Son, and was of the seed of David according to the flesh,[3] by the Virgin Mary; was baptized by John, that all righteousness might be fulfilled[5] by Him; that He lived a life of holiness without sin, and was truly, under Pontius Pilate and Herod the tetrarch, nailed [to the cross] for us in His flesh. From whom we also derive our being,[6] from His divinely-blessed passion, that He might set up a standard for the ages, through His resurrection, to all His holy and faithful [followers], whether among Jews or Gentiles, in the one body of His Church.

---

[1] Literally, "holy-bearing." [2] Col. i. 15. [3] Rom. i. 3. [4] Theodoret, in quoting this passage, reads, "the Godhead and power." [5] Matt. iii. 15. [6] Literally, "we are." [7] i.e., the cross, "fruit" being put for *Christ on the tree.* [8] Isa. v. 26, xlix. 22.

CHAP. II. — CHRIST'S TRUE PASSION.

Now, He suffered all these things for our sakes, that we might be saved. And He suffered truly, even as also He truly raised up Himself, not, as certain unbelievers maintain, that He only seemed to suffer, as they themselves only seem to be [Christians]. And as they believe, so shall it happen unto them, when they shall be divested of their bodies, and be mere evil spirits.[3]

Now, He suffered all these things for us; and He suffered them really, and not in appearance only, even as also He truly rose again. But not, as some of the unbelievers, who are ashamed of the formation of man, and the cross, and death itself, affirm, that in appearance only, and not in truth, He took a body of the Virgin, and suffered only in appearance, forgetting, as they do, Him who said, "The Word was made flesh;"[1] and again, "Destroy this temple, and in three days I will raise it up;"[2] and once more, "If I be lifted up from the earth, I will draw all men unto Me."[4] The Word therefore did dwell in flesh, for "Wisdom built herself an house."[5] The Word raised up again His own temple on the third day, when it had been destroyed by the Jews fighting against Christ. The Word, when His flesh was lifted up, after the manner of the brazen serpent in the wilderness, drew all men to Himself for their eternal salvation.[6]

CHAP. III. — CHRIST WAS POSSESSED OF A BODY AFTER HIS RESURRECTION.

For I know that after His resurrection also He was still possessed of flesh,[7] and I believe that He is so now. When, for instance, He came to those who were with Peter, He said to them, "Lay hold, handle Me, and see that I am not an incorporeal spirit."[8] And immediately they touched Him, and believed, being convinced both by His flesh and spirit. For this cause also they despised death, and were found its conquerors.[12] And after his resurrection He did eat and drink with them, as being possessed of flesh, although spiritually He was united to the Father.

And I know that He was possessed of a body not only in His being born and crucified, but I also know that He was so after His resurrection, and believe that He is so now. When, for instance, He came to those who were with Peter, He said to them, "Lay hold, handle Me, and see that I am not an incorporeal spirit."[8] "For a spirit hath not flesh and bones, as ye see Me have."[9] And He says to Thomas, "Reach hither thy finger into the print of the nails, and reach hither thy hand, and thrust it into My side;"[10] and immediately they believed that He was Christ. Wherefore Thomas also says to Him, "My Lord, and my God."[11] And on this account also did they despise death, for it were too little to say, indignities and stripes. Nor was this all; but also after He had shown Himself to them, that He had risen indeed, and not in appearance only, He both ate and drank with them during forty entire days. And thus was He, with the flesh, received up in their sight unto Him that sent Him, being with that same flesh to come again, accompanied by glory and power. For, say the [holy] oracles, "This same Jesus, who is taken up from you into heaven, shall so come, in like manner as ye have seen Him go unto heaven."[13] But if they say that He will come at the end of the world without a body, how shall those "see Him that pierced Him,"[14] and when they recognise Him, "mourn for themselves?"[15] For incorporeal beings have neither form nor figure, nor the aspect[16] of an animal possessed of shape, because their nature is in itself simple.

CHAP. IV. — BEWARE OF THESE HERETICS.

I give you these instructions, beloved, assured that ye also hold the same opinions [as I do]. But I

I give you these instructions, beloved, assured that ye also hold the same opinions [as I do]. But I guard you beforehand from these beasts in the shape of men, from

---

[1] John i. 14. [2] John ii. 19. [3] Or, "seeing that they are phantasmal and diabolical," as some render; but the above is preferable. [4] John xii. 32. [5] Prov. ix. 1. [6] Num. xxi. 9; John iii. 14. [7] Literally, "in the flesh." [8] Literally, "demon." According to Jerome, this quotation is from the Gospel of the Nazarenes. Comp. Luke xxiv. 39. [9] Luke xxiv. 39. [10] John xx. 27.
[11] John xx. 28. [12] Literally, "above death." [13] Acts i. 11. [14] Rev. i. 7. [15] Zech. xii. 10. [16] Or, "mark."

guard you beforehand from those beasts in the shape of men, whom you must not only not receive, but, if it be possible, not even meet with; only you must pray to God for them, if by any means they may be brought to repentance, which, however, will be very difficult. Yet Jesus Christ, who is our true life, has the power of [effecting] this. But if these things were done by our Lord only in appearance, then am I also only in appearance bound. And why have I also surrendered myself to death, to fire, to the sword, to the wild beasts? But, [in fact,] he who is near to the sword is near to God; he that is among the wild beasts is in company with God; provided only he be so in the name of Jesus Christ. I undergo all these things that I may suffer together with Him, [1] He who became a perfect man inwardly strengthening me.[2]

whom you must not only turn away, but even flee from them. Only you must pray for them, if by any means they may be brought to repentance. For if the Lord were in the body in appearance only, and were crucified in appearance only, then am I also bound in appearance only. And why have I also surrendered myself to death, to fire, to the sword, to the wild beasts? But, [in fact,] I endure all things for Christ, not in appearance only, but in reality, that I may suffer together with Him, while He Himself inwardly strengthens me; for of myself I have no such ability.

CHAP. V. — THEIR DANGEROUS ERRORS.

Some ignorantly[3] deny Him, or rather have been denied by Him, being the advocates of death rather than of the truth. These persons neither have the prophets persuaded, nor the law of Moses, nor the Gospel even to this day, nor the sufferings we have individually endured. For they think also the same thing regarding us.[4] For what does any one profit me, if he commends me, but blasphemes my Lord, not confessing that He was [truly] possessed of a body?[5] But he who does not acknowledge this, has in fact altogether denied Him, being enveloped in death.[6] I have not, however, thought good to write the names of such persons, inasmuch as they are unbelievers. Yea, far be it from me to make any mention of them, until they repent and return to [a true belief in] Christ's passion, which is our resurrection.

Some have ignorantly denied Him, and advocate falsehood rather than the truth. These persons neither have the prophecies persuaded, nor the law of Moses, nor the Gospel even to this day, nor the sufferings we have individually endured. For they think also the same thing regarding us. For what does it profit, if any one commends me, but blasphemes my Lord, not owning Him to be God incarnate?[5] He that does not confess this, has in fact altogether denied Him, being enveloped in death. I have not, however, thought good to write the names of such persons, inasmuch as they are unbelievers; and far be it from me to make any mention of them, until they repent.

CHAP. VI. — UNBELIEVERS IN THE BLOOD OF CHRIST SHALL BE CONDEMNED.

Let no man deceive himself. Both the things which are in heaven, and the glorious angels,[7] and rulers, both visible and invisible, if they believe not in the blood of Christ, shall, in

Let no man deceive himself. Unless he believes that Christ Jesus has lived in the flesh, and shall confess His cross and passion, and the blood which He shed for the salvation of the world, he shall not obtain eternal life, whether he be a king, or a priest, or a ruler, or a private

---

[1] Comp. Rom. viii. 17.   [2] Comp. Phil. iv. 13.   [3] Or, "foolishly."   [4] i.e., As they imagine Christ to have suffered only in appearance, so they believe that we suffer in vain.   [5] Literally, "a flesh-bearer."   [6] Literally, "a death-bearer."
[7] Literally, "the glory of the angels."

consequence, incur condemnation.[1] "He that is able to receive it, let him receive it."[2] Let not [high] place puff any one up: for that which is worth all is[3] faith and love, to which nothing is to be preferred. But consider those who are of a different opinion with respect to the grace of Christ which has come unto us, how opposed they are to the will of God. They have no regard for love; no care for the widow, or the orphan, or the oppressed; of the bond, or of the free; of the hungry, or of the thirsty.

person, a master or a servant, a man or a woman. "He that is able to receive it, let him receive it."[2] Let no man's place, or dignity, or riches, puff him up; and let no man's low condition or poverty abase him. For the chief points are faith towards God, hope towards Christ, the enjoyment of those good things for which we look, and love towards God and our neighbour. For, "Thou shalt love the Lord thy God with all thy heart, and thy neighbour as thyself."[4] And the Lord says, "This is life eternal, to know the only true God, and Jesus Christ whom He has sent."[5] And again, "A new commandment give I unto you, that ye love one another. On these two commandments hang all the law and the prophets."[6] Do ye, therefore, notice those who preach other doctrines, how they affirm that the Father of Christ cannot be known, and how they exhibit enmity and deceit in their dealings with one another. They have no regard for love; they despise the good things we expect hereafter; they regard present things as if they were durable; they ridicule him that is in affliction; they laugh at him that is in bonds.

CHAP. VII.—LET US STAND ALOOF FROM SUCH HERETICS.

They abstain from the Eucharist and from prayer,[7] because they confess not the Eucharist to be the flesh of our Saviour Jesus Christ, which suffered for our sins, and which the Father, of His goodness, raised up again. Those, therefore, who speak against this gift of God, incur death[11] in the midst of their disputes. But it were better for them to treat it with respect,[13] that they also might rise again. It is fitting, therefore, that ye should keep aloof from such persons, and not to speak of[15] them either in private or in public, but to give heed to the prophets, and above all, to the Gospel, in which the passion [of Christ] has been revealed to us, and the resurrection has been fully proved.[16] But avoid all divisions, as the beginning of evils.

They are ashamed of the cross; they mock at the passion; they make a jest of the resurrection. They are the offspring of that spirit who is the author of all evil, who led Adam,[8] by means of his wife, to transgress the commandment, who slew Abel by the hands of Cain, who fought against Job, who was the accuser of Joshua[9] the son of Josedech, who sought to "sift the faith"[10] of the apostles, who stirred up the multitude of the Jews against the Lord, who also now "worketh in the children of disobedience;"[12] from whom the Lord Jesus Christ will deliver us, who prayed that the faith of the apostles might not fail,[14] not because He was not able of Himself to preserve it, but because He rejoiced in the pre-eminence of the Father. It is fitting, therefore, that ye should keep aloof from such persons, and neither in private nor in public to talk with[15] them; but to give heed to the law, and the prophets, and to those who have preached to you the word of salvation. But flee from all abominable heresies, and those that cause schisms, as the beginning of evils.

CHAP. VIII.—LET NOTHING BE DONE WITHOUT THE BISHOP.

See that ye all follow the bishop, even as Jesus Christ does the Father, and the presbytery as ye would the apostles; and reverence the deacons, as being the institution[17] of God. Let no man do anything connected with the Church without the bishop. Let that be deemed a proper[18] Eucharist, which is [administered] either

See that ye all follow the bishop, even as Christ Jesus does the Father, and the presbytery as ye would the apostles. Do ye also reverence the deacons, as those that carry out [through their office] the appointment of God. Let no man do anything connected with the Church without the bishop. Let that be deemed a proper[18] Eucharist, which is [administered] either by the bishop, or by one to whom he has entrusted it. Wherever the bishop shall appear, there let the multitude [of the people] also be;

---

[1] Literally, "judgment is to them." [2] Matt. xix. 12. [3] Literally, "the whole is." [4] Deut. vi. 5. [5] John xvii. 31.
[6] John xiii. 34; Matt. xxii. 40. [7] Theodoret, in quoting this passage, reads προσφοράς, "offering."
[8] Literally, "drove Adam out of." [9] Zech. iii. 1. [10] Luke xxii. 31. [11] Literally, "die disputing." [12] Eph. ii. 2.
[13] Literally, "to love." Some think there is a reference to the *agapæ*, or *love-feasts*. [14] Luke xxii. 32.
[15] The reading is περί in the one case, and μετά in the other, though the latter meaning seems preferable. Most of the MSS. of the longer recension read περί, as in the shorter. [16] Literally, "perfected." [17] Or, "command." [18] Or, "firm."

by the bishop, or by one to whom he has entrusted it. Wherever the bishop shall appear, there let the multitude [of the people] also be; even as, wherever Jesus Christ is, there is the Catholic Church. It is not lawful without the bishop either to baptize or to celebrate a love-feast; but whatsoever he shall approve of, that is also pleasing to God, so that everything that is done may be secure and valid.[2]

even as where Christ is, there does all the heavenly host stand by, waiting upon Him as the Chief Captain of the Lord's might, and the Governor of every intelligent nature. It is not lawful without the bishop either to baptize, or to offer, or to present sacrifice, or to celebrate a love-feast.[1] But that which seems good to him, is also well-pleasing to God, that everything ye do may be secure and valid.

CHAP. IX. — HONOUR THE BISHOP.

Moreover,[3] it is in accordance with reason that we should return to soberness [of conduct], and, while yet we have opportunity, exercise repentance towards God. It is well to reverence[5] both God and the bishop. He who honours the bishop has been honoured by God; he who does anything without the knowledge of the bishop, does [in reality] serve the devil. Let all things, then, abound to you through grace, for ye are worthy. Ye have refreshed me in all things, and Jesus Christ [shall refresh] you. Ye have loved me when absent as well as when present. May God recompense you, for whose sake, while ye endure all things, ye shall attain unto Him.

Moreover, it is in accordance with reason that we should return to soberness [of conduct], and, while yet we have opportunity, exercise repentance towards God. For "in Hades there is no one who can confess his sins."[4] For "behold the man, and his work is before him."[6] And [the Scripture saith], ".My son, honour thou God and the king."[7] And say I, Honour thou God indeed, as the Author and Lord of all things, but the bishop as the high-priest, who bears the image of God — of God, inasmuch as he is a ruler, and of Christ, in his capacity of a priest. After Him, we must also honour the king. For there is no one superior to God, or even like to Him, among all the beings that exist. Nor is there any one in the Church greater than the bishop, who ministers as a priest to God for the salvation of the whole world. Nor, again, is there any one among rulers to be compared with the king, who secures peace and good order to those over whom he rules. He who honours the bishop shall be honoured by God, even as he that dishonours him shall be punished by God. For if he that rises up against kings is justly held worthy of punishment, inasmuch as he dissolves public order, of how much sorer punishment, suppose ye, shall he be thought worthy,[8] who presumes to do anything without the bishop, thus both destroying the [Church's] unity, and throwing its order into confusion? For the priesthood is the very highest point of all good things among men, against which whosoever is mad enough to strive, dishonours not man, but God, and Christ Jesus, the First-born, and the only High Priest, by nature, of the Father. Let all things therefore be done by you with good order in Christ. Let the laity be subject to the deacons; the deacons to the presbyters; the presbyters to the bishop; the bishop to Christ, even as He is to the Father. As ye, brethren, have refreshed me, so will Jesus Christ refresh you. Ye have loved me when absent, as well as when present. God will recompense you, for whose sake ye have shown such kindness towards His prisoner. For even if I am not worthy of it, yet your zeal [to help me] is an admirable[9] thing. For "he who honours a prophet in the name of a prophet, shall receive a prophet's reward."[10] It is manifest also, that he who honours a prisoner of Jesus Christ shall receive the reward of the martyrs.

---

[1] Some refer the words to the Lord's Supper. [2] Or, "firm." [3] Or, "finally." [4] Ps. vi. 5. [5] Literally, "to know."
[6] Isa. lxii. 11. [7] Prov. xxiv. 21. [8] Comp. Heb. x. 29. [9] Or, "great." [10] Matt. x. 41.

CHAP. X. — ACKNOWLEDGMENT OF THEIR KINDNESS.

Ye have done well in receiving Philo and Rheus Agathopus as servants[1] of Christ our God, who have followed me for the sake of God, and who give thanks to the Lord in your behalf, because ye have in every way refreshed them. None of these things shall be lost to you. May my spirit be for you,[3] and my bonds, which ye have not despised or been ashamed of; nor shall Jesus Christ, our perfect hope, be ashamed of you.

Ye have done well in receiving Philo, and Gaius, and Agathopus, who, being the servants[1] of Christ, have followed me for the sake of God, and who greatly bless the Lord in your behalf, because ye have in every way refreshed them. None of those things which ye have done to them shall be passed by without being reckoned unto you. "The Lord grant" to you "that ye may find mercy of the Lord in that day!"[2] May my spirit be for you,[3] and my bonds, which ye have not despised or been ashamed of. Wherefore, neither shall Jesus Christ, our perfect hope, be ashamed of you.

CHAP. XI. — REQUEST TO THEM TO SEND A MESSENGER TO ANTIOCH.

Your prayer has reached to the Church which is at Antioch in Syria. Coming from that place bound with chains, most acceptable to God,[4] I salute all; I who am not worthy to be styled from thence, inasmuch as I am the least of them. Nevertheless, according to the will of God, I have been thought worthy [of this honour], not that I have any sense[5] [of having deserved it], but by the grace of God, which I wish may be perfectly given to me, that through your prayers I may attain to God. In order, therefore, that your work may be complete both on earth and in heaven, it is fitting that, for the honour of God, your Church should elect some worthy delegate;[6] so that he, journeying into Syria, may congratulate them that they are [now] at peace, and are restored to[7] their proper greatness, and that their proper constitution[8] has been re-established among them. It seems then to me a becoming thing, that you should send some one of your number with an epistle, so that, in company with them, he may rejoice[9] over the tranquillity which, according to the will of God, they have obtained, and because that, through your prayers, they have now reached the harbour. As persons who are perfect, ye should also aim at[10] those things which are perfect. For when ye are desirous to do well, God is also ready to assist you.

Your prayers have reached to the Church of Antioch, and it is at peace. Coming from that place bound, I salute all; I who am not worthy to be styled from thence, inasmuch as I am the least of them. Nevertheless, according to the will of God, I have been thought worthy [of this honour], not that I have any sense[5] [of having deserved it], but by the grace of God, which I wish may be perfectly given to me, that through your prayers I may attain to God. In order, therefore, that your work may be complete both on earth and in heaven, it is fitting that, for the honour of God, your Church should elect some worthy delegate;[6] so that he, journeying into Syria, may congratulate them that they are [now] at peace, and are restored to their proper greatness, and that their proper constitution[8] has been re-established among them. What appears to me proper to be done is this, that you should send some one of your number with an epistle, so that, in company with them, he may rejoice over the tranquillity which, according to the will of God, they have obtained, and because that, through your prayers, I have secured Christ as a safe harbour. As persons who are perfect, ye should also aim at[10] those things which are perfect. For when ye are desirous to do well, God is also ready to assist you.

CHAP. XII. — SALUTATIONS.

The love of the brethren at Troas salutes you; whence also I write to

The love of your brethren at Troas salutes you; whence also I write to you by Burgus, whom ye sent with

---

[1] Or, "deacons." [2] 2 Tim. i. 18. [3] Comp. Epistle of Ignatius to Ephesians, chap. xxi.; to Polycarp, chap ii. vi.
[4] Literally, "most becoming of God." [5] Or, "from any conscience." [6] Literally, "God-ambassador." [7] Or, "have received."
[8] Literally, "body." [9] Literally, "may glorify with them." [10] Or, "think of."

you by Burrhus, whom ye sent with me, together with the Ephesians, your brethren, and who has in all things refreshed me. And I would that all may imitate him, as being a pattern of a minister[1] of God. Grace will reward him in all things. I salute your most worthy[2] bishop, and your very venerable[3] presbytery, and your deacons, my fellow-servants, and all of you individually, as well as generally, in the name of Jesus Christ, and in His flesh and blood, in His passion and resurrection, both corporeal and spiritual, in union with God and you.[4] Grace, mercy, peace, and patience, be with you for evermore!

I salute the families of my brethren, with their wives and children, and the virgins who are called widows.[5] Be ye strong, I pray, in the power of the Holy Ghost. Philo, who is with me, greets you. I salute the house of Tavias, and pray that it may be confirmed in faith and love, both corporeal and spiritual. I salute Alce, my well-beloved,[6] and the incomparable Daphnus, and Eutecnus, and all by name. Fare ye well in the grace of God.

me, together with the Ephesians, your brethren, and who has in all things refreshed me. And I would that all may imitate him, as being a pattern of a minister of God. The grace of the Lord will reward him in all things. I salute your most worthy bishop Polycarp, and your venerable presbytery, and your Christ-bearing deacons, my fellow-servants, and all of you individually, as well as generally, in the name of Christ Jesus, and in His flesh and blood, in His passion and resurrection, both corporeal and spiritual, in union with God and you. Grace, mercy, peace, and patience, be with you in Christ for evermore!

CONCLUSION.

I salute the families of my brethren, with their wives and children, and those that are ever virgins, and the widows. Be ye strong, I pray, in the power of the Holy Ghost. Philo, my fellow-servant, who is with me, greets you. I salute the house of Tavias, and pray that it may be confirmed in faith and love, both corporeal and spiritual. I salute Alce, my well-beloved,[6] and the incomparable Daphnus, and Eutecnus, and all by name. Fare ye well in the grace of God, and of our Lord Jesus Christ, being filled with the Holy Spirit, and divine and sacred wisdom.

---

[1] Or, "the ministry." [2] Literally, "worthy of God." [3] Literally, "most becoming of God."
[4] Literally, "in the union of God and of you." [5] The *deaconesses* seem to have been called *widows*.
[6] Literally, "the name desired of me."

THE EPISTLE OF IGNATIUS TO POLYCARP

SHORTER AND LONGER VERSIONS

Ignatius, who is also called Theophorus, to Polycarp, Bishop of the Church of the Smyrnæans, or rather, who has, as his own bishop, God the Father, and the Lord Jesus Christ: [wishes] abundance of happiness.

Ignatius, bishop of Antioch, and a witness for Jesus Christ, to Polycarp, Bishop of the Church of the Smyrnæans, or rather, who has, as his own bishop, God the Father, and Jesus Christ: [wishes] abundance of happiness.

CHAP. I. — COMMENDATION AND EXHORTATION.

HAVING obtained good proof that thy mind is fixed in God as upon an immoveable rock, I loudly glorify [His name] that I have been thought worthy [to behold] thy blameless face,[1] which may I ever enjoy in God! I entreat thee, by the grace with which thou art clothed, to press forward in thy course, and to exhort all that they may be saved. Maintain thy position with all care, both in the flesh and spirit. Have a regard to preserve unity, than which nothing is better. Bear with all, even as the Lord does with thee. Support[2] all in love, as also thou doest. Give thyself to prayer without ceasing.[3] Implore additional understanding to what thou already hast. Be watchful, possessing a sleepless spirit. Speak to every man separately, as God enables thee.[4] Bear the infirmities of all, as being a perfect athlete [in the Christian life]: where the labour is great, the gain is all the more.

HAVING obtained good proof that thy mind is fixed in God as upon an immoveable rock, I loudly glorify [His name] that I have been thought worthy to behold thy blameless face,[1] which may I ever enjoy in God! I entreat thee, by the grace with which thou art clothed, to press forward in thy course, and to exhort all that they may be saved. Maintain thy position with all care, both in the flesh and spirit. Have a regard to preserve unity, than which nothing is better. Bear with all, even as the Lord does with thee. Support[2] all in love, as also thou doest. Give thyself to prayer without ceasing.[3] Implore additional understanding to what thou already hast. Be watchful, possessing a sleepless spirit. Speak to every man separately, as God enables thee.[4] Bear the infirmities of all, as being a perfect athlete [in the Christian life], even as does the Lord of all. For says [the Scripture], "He Himself took our infirmities, and bare our sicknesses."[5] Where the labour is great, the gain is all the more.

CHAP. II. — EXHORTATIONS.

If thou lovest the good disciples, no thanks are due to thee on that account; but rather seek by meekness to subdue the more troublesome. Every kind of wound is not healed with the same plaster. Mitigate vio-

If thou lovest the good disciples, no thanks are due to thee on that account; but rather seek by meekness to subdue the more troublesome. Every kind of wound is not healed with the same plaster. Mitigate violent attacks [of disease] by gentle applications.[6] Be in all things "wise as a serpent, and harmless always as a

---

[1] i.e., to make personal acquaintance with one esteemed so highly. [2] Or, "tolerate." [3] Comp. 1 Thess. v. 17. [4] Some read, "according to thy practice." [5] Matt. viii. 17. [6] Literally, "paroxysms by embrocations."

lent attacks [of disease] by gentle applications.¹ Be in all things "wise as a serpent, and harmless as a dove."² For this purpose thou art composed of both flesh and spirit, that thou mayest deal tenderly³ with those [evils] that present themselves visibly before thee. And as respects those that are not seen,⁴ pray that [God] would reveal them unto thee, in order that thou mayest be wanting in nothing, but mayest abound in every gift. The times call for thee, as pilots do for the winds, and as one tossed with tempest seeks for the haven, so that both thou [and those under thy care] may attain to God. Be sober as an athlete of God: the prize set before thee is immortality and eternal life, of which thou art also persuaded. In all things may my soul be for thine,⁵ and my bonds also, which thou hast loved.

dove."² For this purpose thou art composed of both soul and body, art both fleshly and spiritual, that thou mayest correct those [evils] that present themselves visibly before thee; and as respects those that are not seen, mayest pray that these should be revealed to thee, so that thou mayest be wanting in nothing, but mayest abound in every gift. The times call upon thee to pray. For as the wind aids the pilot of a ship, and as havens are advantageous for safety to a tempest-tossed vessel, so is also prayer to thee, in order that thou mayest attain to God. Be sober as an athlete of God, whose will is immortality and eternal life; of which thou art also persuaded. In all things may my soul be for thine,⁵ and my bonds also, which thou hast loved.

CHAP. III. — EXHORTATIONS.

Let not those who seem worthy of credit, but teach strange doctrines,⁶ fill thee with apprehension. Stand firm, as does an anvil which is beaten. It is the part of a noble⁷ athlete to be wounded, and yet to conquer. And especially, we ought to bear all things for the sake of God, that He also may bear with us. Be ever becoming more zealous than what thou art. Weigh carefully the times. Look for Him who is above all time, eternal and invisible, yet who became visible for our sakes; impalpable and impassible, yet who became passible on our account; and who in every kind of way suffered for our sakes.

Let not those who seem worthy of credit, but teach strange doctrines,⁶ fill thee with apprehension. Stand firm, as does an anvil which is beaten. It is the part of a noble⁷ athlete to be wounded, and yet to conquer. And especially we ought to bear all things for the sake of God, that He also may bear with us, and bring us into His kingdom. Add more and more to thy diligence; run thy race with increasing energy; weigh carefully the times. Whilst thou art here, be a conqueror; for here is the course, and there are the crowns. Look for Christ, the Son of God; who was before time, yet appeared in time; who was invisible by nature, yet visible in the flesh; who was impalpable, and could not be touched, as being without a body, but for our sakes became such, might be touched and handled in the body; who was impassible as God, but became passible for our sakes as man; and who in every kind of way suffered for our sakes.

CHAP. IV. — EXHORTATIONS.

Let not widows be neglected. Be thou, after the Lord, their protector⁸ and friend. Let nothing be done without thy consent; neither do thou anything without the approval of God, which indeed thou dost not, inasmuch as thou art stedfast. Let your assembling together be of frequent⁹ occurrence: seek after all by name.¹⁰ Do not despise either male or female slaves, yet neither let them be puffed up with conceit, but rather let them

Let not the widows be neglected. Be thou, after the Lord, their protector and friend. Let nothing be done without thy consent; neither do thou anything without the approval of God, which indeed thou doest not. Be thou stedfast. Let your assembling together be of frequent⁹ occurrence: seek after all by name.¹⁰ Do not despise either male or female slaves, yet neither let them be puffed up with conceit, but rather let them submit themselves¹¹ the more, for the glory of God, that they may obtain from God a better liberty. Let them not wish to be set free [from slavery] at the public expense, that they be not found slaves to their own desires.

---

¹ Literally, "paroxysms by embrocations." ² Matt. x. 16. ³ Literally, "flatter." ⁴ Some refer this to the mysteries of God and others to things yet future. ⁵ Comp. Epistle of Ignatius to the Ephesians, chap. xxi., etc. ⁶ Comp. 1 Tim. i. 3, vi. 3. ⁷ Literally, "great." ⁸ The word in the original (φροντιστής) denotes one who *thinks* or *cares* for another. ⁹ Some refer the words to more *frequent* meetings, and others to these meetings being more numerous; no comparison is necessarily implied. ¹⁰ i.e., so as to bring them out to the public assembly. ¹¹ Or, "act the part of slaves."

submit themselves[1] the more, for the glory of God, that they may obtain from God a better liberty. Let them not long to be set free [from slavery] at the public expense, that they be not found slaves to their own desires.

CHAP. V. — THE DUTIES OF HUSBANDS AND WIVES.

Flee evil arts; but all the more discourse in public regarding them.[2] Speak to my sisters, that they love the Lord, and be satisfied with their husbands both in the flesh and spirit. In like manner also, exhort my brethren, in the name of Jesus Christ, that they love their wives, even as the Lord the Church.[3] If any one can continue in a state of purity,[4] to the honour of Him who is Lord of the flesh,[5] let him so remain without boasting. If he begins to boast, he is undone; and if he reckon himself greater than the bishop, he is ruined. But it becomes both men and women who marry, to form their union with the approval of the bishop, that their marriage may be according to God, and not after their own lust. Let all things be done to the honour of God.[7]

Flee evil arts; but all the more discourse in public regarding them. Speak to my sisters, that they love the Lord, and be satisfied with their husbands both in the flesh and spirit. In like manner also, exhort my brethren, in the name of Jesus Christ, that they love their wives, even as the Lord the Church. If any one can continue in a state of purity,[4] to the honour of the flesh of the Lord, let him so remain without boasting. If he shall boast, he is undone; and if he seeks to be more prominent[6] than the bishop, he is ruined. But it becomes both men and women who marry, to form their union with the approval of the bishop, that their marriage may be according to the Lord, and not after their own lust. Let all things be done to the honour of God.[7]

CHAP. VI. — THE DUTIES OF THE CHRISTIAN FLOCK.

Give ye[8] heed to the bishop, that God also may give heed to you. My soul be for theirs[9] that are submissive to the bishop, to the presbyters, and to the deacons, and may my portion be along with them in God! Labour together with one another; strive in company together; run together; suffer together; sleep together; and awake together, as the stewards, and associates,[10] and servants of God. Please ye Him under whom ye fight, and from whom ye receive your wages. Let none of you be found a deserter. Let your baptism endure as your arms; your faith as your helmet; your love as your spear; your patience as a complete panoply. Let your works be the charge[12] assigned to you, that ye may receive a worthy recompense. Be long-suffering, therefore, with one another, in meekness, as God is towards you. May I have joy of you for ever![13]

Give ye[8] heed to the bishop, that God also may give heed to you. My soul be for theirs[9] that are submissive to the bishop, to the presbytery, and to the deacons: may I have my portion with them from God! Labour together with one another; strive in company together; run together; suffer together; sleep together; and awake together, as the stewards, and associates,[10] and servants of God. Please ye Him under whom ye fight, and from whom ye shall receive your wages. Let none of you be found a deserter. Let your baptism endure as your arms; your faith as your helmet; your love as your spear; your patience as a complete panoply. Let your works be the charge assigned to you, that you may obtain for them a most worthy[11] recompense. Be long-suffering, therefore, with one another, in meekness, and God shall be so with you. May I have joy of you for ever![13]

---

[1] Or, "act the part of slaves." [2] Some insert μή, and render, "rather do not even speak of them." [3] Eph. v. 25.
[4] i.e., in celibacy. [5] Some render, "to the honour of the flesh of the Lord," as in the longer recension.
[6] Literally, "if he be known beyond the bishop." [7] Comp. 1 Cor. x. 31. [8] As this Epistle, though sent to the bishop, was meant to be read to the people, Ignatius here directly addresses them. [9] Comp. chap. ii., etc. [10] Or, "assessors."
[11] Literally, "worthy of God." [12] A military reference, simply implying the idea of faithful effort leading to future reward.
[13] Comp. Ignatius' Epistle to the Ephesians, chap ii.

CHAP. VII. — REQUEST THAT POLYCARP WOULD SEND A MESSENGER TO ANTIOCH.

Seeing that the Church which is at Antioch in Syria is, as report has informed me, at peace, through your prayers, I also am the more encouraged, resting without anxiety in God,[1] if indeed by means of suffering I may attain to God, so that, through your prayers, I may be found a disciple [of Christ].[2] It is fitting, O Polycarp, most blessed in God, to assemble a very solemn[3] council, and to elect one whom you greatly love, and know to be a man of activity, who may be designated the messenger of God;[4] and to bestow on him this honour that he may go into Syria, and glorify your ever active love to the praise of Christ. A Christian has not power over himself, but must always be ready for[5] the service of God. Now, this work is both God's and yours, when ye shall have completed it to His glory.[6] For I trust that, through grace, ye are prepared for every good work pertaining to God. Knowing, therefore, your energetic love of the truth, I have exhorted you by this brief Epistle.

Seeing that the Church which is at Antioch in Syria is, as report has informed me, at peace, through your prayers, I also am the more encouraged, resting without anxiety in God,[1] if indeed by means of suffering I may attain to God, so that, through your prayers, I may be found a disciple [of Christ]. It is fitting, O Polycarp, most blessed in God, to assemble a very solemn[3] council, and to elect one whom you greatly love, and know to be a man of activity, who may be designated the messenger of God;[4] and to bestow on him the honour of going into Syria, so that, going into Syria, he may glorify your ever active love to the praise of God. A Christian has not power over himself, but must always be ready for[5] the service of God. Now, this work is both God's and yours, when ye shall have completed it. For I trust that, through grace, ye are prepared for every good work pertaining to God. Knowing your energetic love of the truth, I have exhorted you by this brief Epistle.

CHAP. VIII. — LET OTHER CHURCHES ALSO SEND TO ANTIOCH.

Inasmuch as I have not been able to write to all the Churches, because I must suddenly sail from Troas to Neapolis, as the will[7] [of the emperor] enjoins, [I beg that] thou, as being acquainted with the purpose[8] of God, wilt write to the adjacent Churches, that they also may act in like manner, such as are able to do so sending messengers,[9] and the others transmitting letters through those persons who are sent by thee, that thou[10] mayest be glorified by a work[11] which shall be remembered for ever, as indeed thou art worthy to be. I salute all by name, and in particular the wife of Epitropus, with all her house and children. I salute Attalus, my beloved. I salute him who shall be deemed worthy to go [from you] into Syria. Grace shall be with him for ever, and with Polycarp that sends him. I pray for your happiness for ever in our God, Jesus Christ, by whom continue ye in the unity and under the protection of God.[12] I salute Alce, my dearly beloved.[13] Fare ye well in the Lord.

Inasmuch, therefore, as I have not been able to write to all Churches, because I must suddenly sail from Troas to Neapolis, as the will[7] [of the emperor] enjoins, [I beg that] thou, as being acquainted with the purpose[8] of God, wilt write to the adjacent Churches, that they also may act in like manner, such as are able to do so sending messengers, and the others transmitting letters through those persons who are sent by thee, that thou mayest be glorified by a work[11] which shall be remembered for ever, as indeed thou art worthy to be. I salute all by name, and in particular the wife of Epitropus, with all her house and children. I salute Attalus, my beloved. I salute him who shall be deemed worthy to go [from you] into Syria. Grace shall be with him for ever, and with Polycarp that sends him. I pray for your happiness for ever in our God, Jesus Christ, by whom continue ye in the unity and under the protection of God. I salute Alce, my dearly beloved.[13] Amen. Grace [be with you]. Fare ye well in the Lord.

---

[1] Literally, "in freedom from care of God." [2] Some read, "in the resurrection." [3] Literally, "most befitting God." [4] Literally, "God-runner." [5] Literally, "at leisure for." [6] Literally, "to Him." [7] Some suppose the reference to be to the soldiers, or perhaps to God Himself. [8] Or, "as possessed of the judgment." [9] Literally, "men on foot." [10] Some have the plural "ye" here. [11] Literally, "an eternal work." [12] Some propose to read, "and of the bishop." [13] Literally, "name desired by me."

INTRODUCTORY NOTE

TO THE

SYRIAC VERSION OF THE IGNATIAN EPISTLES

When the Syriac version of the Ignatian Epistles was introduced to the English world in 1845, by Mr. Cureton, the greatest satisfaction was expressed by many, who thought the inveterate controversy about to be settled. Lord Russell made the learned divine a canon of Westminster Abbey, and the critical Chevalier Bunsen [1] committed himself as its patron. To the credit of the learned, in general, the work was gratefully received, and studied with scientific conscientiousness by Lightfoot and others. The literature of this period is valuable; and the result is decisive as to the Curetonian versions at least, which are fragmentary and abridged, and yet they are a valuable contribution to the study of the whole case.

The following is the original INTRODUCTORY NOTICE: —

Some account of the discovery of the Syriac version of the Ignatian Epistles has been already given. We have simply to add here a brief description of the MSS. from which the Syriac text has been printed. That which is named a by Cureton, contains only the Epistle to Polycarp, and exhibits the text of that Epistle which, after him, we have followed. He fixes its age somewhere in the first half of the sixth century, or before the year 550. The second MS., which Cureton refers to as β, is assigned by him to the seventh or eighth century. It contains the three Epistles of Ignatius, and furnishes the text here followed in the Epistles to the Ephesians and Romans. The third MS., which Cureton quotes as γ, has no date, but, as he tells us, "belonged to the collection acquired by Moses of Nisibis in A.D. 931, and was written apparently about three or four centuries earlier." It contains the three Epistles to Polycarp, the Ephesians, and the Romans. The text of all these MSS. is in several passages manifestly corrupt, and the translators appear at times to have mistaken the meaning of the Greek original.

[N.B. — Bunsen is forced to allow the fact that the discovery of the lost work of Hippolytus "throws new light on an obscure point of the Ignatian controversy," i.e., the *Sige* in the Epistle to the Magnesians (cap. viii.); but his treatment of the matter is unworthy of a candid scholar.]

---

[1] See the extraordinary passage and note in his *Hippolytus*, vol. i. p. 58, etc.

THE EPISTLE OF IGNATIUS TO POLYCARP[1]

Ignatius, who is [also called] Theophorus, to Polycarp, bishop of Smyrna, or rather, who has as his own bishop God the Father, and our Lord Jesus Christ: [wishes] abundance of happiness.

CHAP. I.

BECAUSE thy mind is acceptable to me, inasmuch as it is established in God, as on a rock which is immoveable, I glorify God the more exceedingly that I have been counted worthy of [seeing] thy face, which I longed after in God. Now I beseech thee, by the grace with which thou art clothed, to add [speed] to thy course, and that thou ever pray for all men that they may be saved, and that thou demand[2] things which are befitting, with all assiduity both of the flesh and spirit. Be studious of unity, than which nothing is more precious. Bear with all men, even as our Lord beareth with thee. Show patience[3] with all men in love, as [indeed] thou doest. Be stedfast in prayer. Ask for more understanding than that which thou [already] hast. Be watchful, as possessing a spirit which sleepeth not. Speak with every man according to the will of God. Bear the infirmities of all men as a perfect athlete; for where the labour is great, the gain is also great.

CHAP. II.

If thou lovest the good disciples only, thou hast no grace; [but] rather subdue those that are evil by gentleness. All [sorts of] wounds are not healed by the same medicine. Mitigate [the pain of] cutting[4] by tenderness. Be wise as the serpent in everything, and innocent, with respect to those things which are requisite, even as the dove. For this reason thou art [composed] of both flesh and spirit, that thou mayest entice[5] those things which are visible before thy face, and mayest ask, as to those which are concealed from thee, that they [too] may be revealed to thee, in order that thou be deficient in nothing, and mayest abound in all gifts. The time demands, even as a pilot does a ship, and as one who stands exposed to the tempest does a haven, that thou shouldst be worthy of God. Be thou watchful as an athlete of God. That which is promised to us is life eternal, which cannot be corrupted, of which things thou art also persuaded. In everything I will be instead[6] of thy soul, and my bonds which thou hast loved.

CHAP. III.

Let not those who seem to be somewhat, and teach strange doctrines, strike thee with apprehension; but stand thou in the truth, as an athlete[7] who is smitten, for it is [the part] of a great athlete to be smitten, and [yet] conquer. More especially is it fitting that we should bear everything for the sake of God, that He also may bear us. Be [still] more diligent than thou yet art. Be discerning of the times. Look for Him that is above the times, Him who has no times, Him who is invisible, Him who for our sakes became visible, Him who is impalpable, Him who is impassible, Him who for our sakes suffered, Him who endured everything in every form for our sakes.

CHAP. IV.

Let not the widows be overlooked; on account of[8] our Lord be thou their guardian, and let nothing be done without thy will; also do thou nothing without the will of God, as indeed thou doest not. Stand rightly. Let there be frequent[9] assemblies: ask every man [to them] by his name. Despise not slaves, either male or female; but neither let them be contemptuous, but let them labour the more as for the glory of

---

[1] The inscription varies in each of the three Syriac MSS., being in the first, "The Epistle of my lord Ignatius, the bishop;" in the second, "The Epistle of Ignatius;" and in the third, "The Epistle of Ignatius bishop of Antioch."
[2] For "vindicate thy place" in the Greek.
[3] Literally, "draw out thy spirit."
[4] Cureton observes, as one alternative here, that "the Syrian translator seems to have read παράξυσμα for παροξυσμούς."
[5] Or, "flatter," probably meaning to "deal gently with."
[6] Thus the Syriac renders ἀντίψυχον in the Greek.
[7] The Greek has ἄκμων, "an anvil."
[8] The Greek has μετά, "after."
[9] Or, "constant," "regular."

God, that they may be counted worthy of a more precious freedom, which is of God. Let them not desire to be set free out of the common [fund], lest they be found the slaves of lust.

CHAP. V.

Flee wicked arts; but all the more discourse regarding them. Speak to my sisters, that they love in our Lord, and that their husbands be sufficient for them in the flesh and spirit. Then, again, charge my brethren in the name of our Lord Jesus Christ, that they love their wives, as our Lord His Church. If any man is able in power to continue in purity,[1] to the honour of the flesh of our Lord, let him continue so without boasting; if he boasts, he is undone; if he become known apart from the bishop, he has destroyed himself.[2] It is becoming, therefore, to men and women who marry, that they marry with the counsel of the bishop, that the marriage may be in our Lord, and not in lust. Let everything, therefore, be [done] for the honour of God.

CHAP. VI.

Look ye to the bishop, that God also may look upon you. I will be instead of the souls of those who are subject to the bishop, and the presbyters, and the deacons; with them may I have a portion in the presence of God! Labour together with one another, act as athletes[3] together, run together, suffer together, sleep together, rise together. As stewards of God, and of His household,[4] and His servants, please Him and serve Him, that ye may receive from Him the wages [promised]. Let none of you be rebellious. Let your baptism be to you as armour, and faith as a spear, and love as a helmet, and patience as a panoply. Let your treasures be your good works, that ye may receive the gift of God, as is just. Let your spirit be long-suffering towards each other with meekness, even as God [is] toward you. As for me, I rejoice in you at all times.

CHAP. VII.

The Christian has not power over himself, but is [ever] ready to be subject to God.[5]

CHAP. VIII.

I salute him who is reckoned worthy to go to Antioch in my stead, as I commanded thee.[5]

---

[1] i.e., " in celibacy."
[2] Or, " corrupted himself."
[3] Literally, " make the contest."
[4] Literally, " sons of His house."
[5] These are the only parts of chaps. vii. and vi. in the Greek that are represented in the Syriac.

THE SECOND EPISTLE OF IGNATIUS TO THE EPHESIANS[1]

Ignatius, who is [also called] Theophorus, to the Church which is blessed in the greatness of God the Father, and perfected; to her who was selected[2] from eternity, that she might be at all times for glory, which abideth, and is unchangeable, and is perfected and chosen in the purpose of truth by the will of the Father of Jesus Christ our God; to her who is worthy of happiness; to her who is at Ephesus, in Jesus Christ, in joy which is unblameable: [wishes] abundance of happiness.

CHAP. I.

INASMUCH as your name, which is greatly beloved, is acceptable to me in God, [your name] which ye have acquired by nature, through a right and just will, and also by the faith and love of Jesus Christ our Saviour, and ye are imitators of God, and are fervent in the blood of God, and have speedily completed a work congenial to you; [for] when ye heard that I was bound,[3] so as to be able to do nothing for the sake of the common name and hope (and I hope, through your prayers, that I may be devoured by beasts at Rome, so that by means of this of which I have been accounted worthy, I may be endowed with strength to be a disciple of God), ye were diligent to come and see me. Seeing, then, that we have become acquainted with your multitude[4] in the name of God, by Onesimus, who is your bishop, in love which is unutterable, whom I pray that ye love in Jesus Christ our Lord, and that all of you imitate his example,[5] for blessed is He who has given you such a bishop, even as ye deserve [to have].[6]

CHAP. III.[7]

But inasmuch as love does not permit me to be silent in regard to you, on this account I have been forward to entreat of you that ye would be diligent in the will of God.

CHAP. VIII.[8]

For, so long as there is not implanted in you any one lust which is able to torment you, behold, ye live in God. I rejoice in you, and offer supplication[9] on account of you, Ephesians, a Church which is renowned in all ages. For those who are carnal are not able to do spiritual things, nor those that are spiritual carnal things; in like manner as neither can faith [do] those things which are foreign to faith, nor want of faith [do] what belongs to faith. For those things which ye have done in the flesh, even these are spiritual, because ye have done everything in Jesus Christ.

CHAP. IX.

And ye are prepared for the building of God the Father, and ye are raised up on high by the instrument of Jesus Christ, which is the cross; and ye are drawn by the rope, which is the Holy Spirit; and your pulley is your faith, and your love is the way which leadeth up on high to God.

CHAP. X.

Pray for all men; for there is hope of repentance for them, that they may be counted worthy of God. By your works especially let them be instructed. Against their harsh words be ye conciliatory, by meekness of mind and gentleness. Against their blasphemies do ye give yourselves to prayer; and against their error be ye armed with faith. Against their fierceness be ye peaceful and quiet, and be ye not astounded by them. Let us, then, be imitators of our Lord in meekness, and strive who shall more especially be injured, and oppressed, and defrauded.

---

[1] Another inscription is, "Epistle the Second, which is to the Ephesians."
[2] Literally, "separated."
[3] Literally, "bound from actions."
[4] Cureton renders, "have received your abundance," probably referring the words to gifts sent by the Ephesians to Ignatius.
[5] Literally, "be in his image."
[6] There is no Apodosis, unless it be found in what follows.
[7] The following clause is the whole of chap. iii. in the Greek, which is represented in the Syriac.

[8] Chaps. iv. v. vi. vii. of the Greek are totally omitted in the Syriac.
[9] Thus Cureton renders the words, referring in confirmation to the Peshito version of Phil. i. 4, but the meaning is doubtful.

CHAP. XIV.[1]

The work is not of promise,[2] unless a man be found in the power of faith, even to the end.

CHAP. XV.

It is better that a man should be silent while he is something, than that he should be talking when he is not; that by those things which he speaks he should act, and by those things of which he is silent he should be known.

CHAP. XVIII.[3]

My spirit bows in adoration to the cross, which is a stumbling-block to those who do not believe, but is to you for salvation and eternal life.

---

[1] Chaps. xi. xii. xiii. of the Greek are totally wanting in the Syriac, and only these few words of chaps. xiv. and xv. are represented.
[2] The meaning seems to be that mere profession, without continuous practice, is nothing.
[3] Chaps. xvi. and xvii. of the Greek are totally wanting in the Syriac.

CHAP. XIX.

There was concealed from the ruler of this world the virginity of Mary and the birth of our Lord, and the three renowned mysteries[4] which were done in the tranquillity of God from the star. And here, at the manifestation of the Son, magic began to be destroyed, and all bonds were loosed; and the ancient kingdom and the error of evil was destroyed. Henceforward all things were moved together, and the destruction of death was devised, and there was the commencement of that which was perfected in God.[5]

---

[4] Literally, "the mysteries of the shout." The meaning is here confused and obscure. See the Greek.
[5] Chaps. xx. and xxi. of the Greek are altogether wanting in the Syriac.

[N.B.—See spurious Epistle to Philippians, cap. 4, *infra*. This concealment from Satan of the mystery of the incarnation is the explanation, according to the Fathers, of his tempting the Messiah, and prompting His crucifixion. Also, Christ the more profoundly humbled himself, "*ne subtilis ille diaboli oculus magnum hoc pietatis deprehenderet sacramentum*" (St. Bernard, opp. ii. 1944). Bernard also uses this opinion very strikingly (opp. ii. 1953) in one of his sermons, supposing that Satan discovered the secret too late for his own purpose, and then prompted the outcry, *Come down from the cross*, to defeat the triumph of the second Adam. (Comp. St. Mark i. 24 and St. Luke iv. 34, where, after the first defeat of the tempter, this demon suspects the second Adam, and tries to extort the secret).]

THE THIRD EPISTLE OF THE SAME ST. IGNATIUS.[1]

Ignatius, who is [also called] Theophorus, to the Church which has received grace through the greatness of the Father Most High; to her who presideth in the place of the region of the Romans, who is worthy of God, and worthy of life, and happiness, and praise, and remembrance, and is worthy of prosperity, and presideth in love, and is perfected in the law of Christ unblameable: [wishes] abundance of peace.

CHAP. I.

FROM of old have I prayed to God, that I might be counted worthy to behold your faces which are worthy of God: now, therefore, being bound in Jesus Christ, I hope to meet you and salute you, if it be the will [of God] that I should be accounted worthy to the end. For the beginning is well arranged, if I be counted worthy to attain to the end, that I may receive my portion, without hindrance, through suffering. For I am in fear of your love, lest it should injure me. As to you, indeed, it is easy for you to do whatsoever ye wish; but as to me, it is difficult for me to be accounted worthy of God, if indeed ye spare me not.

CHAP. II.

For there is no other time such as this, that I should be accounted worthy of God; neither will ye, if ye be silent, [ever] be found in a better work than this. If ye let me alone, I shall be the word of God; but if ye love my flesh, again am I [only] to myself a voice. Ye cannot give me anything more precious than this, that I should be sacrificed to God, while the altar is ready; that ye may be in one concord in love, and may praise God the Father through Jesus Christ our Lord, because He has deemed a bishop worthy to be God's, having called him from the east to the west. It is good that I should set from the world in God, that I may rise in Him to life.[2]

CHAP. III.

Ye have never envied any man. Ye have taught others. Only pray ye for strength to be given to me from within and from without, that I may not only speak, but also may be willing, and that I may not merely be called a Christian, but also may be found to be [one]; for if I am found to be [so], I may then also be called [so]. Then [indeed] shall I be faithful, when I am no longer seen in the world. For there is nothing visible that is good. The work is not [a matter[3]] of persuasion; but Christianity is great when the world hateth it.

CHAP. IV.

I write to all the Churches, and declare to all men, that I willingly die for the sake of God, if so be that ye hinder me not. I entreat of you not to be [affected] towards me with a love which is unseasonable. Leave me to become [the prey of] the beasts, that by their means I may be accounted worthy of God. I am the wheat of God, and by the teeth of the beasts I shall be ground,[4] that I may be found the pure bread of God. Provoke ye greatly[5] the wild beasts, that they may be for me a grave, and may leave nothing of my body, in order that, when I have fallen asleep, I may not be a burden upon any one. Then shall I be in truth a disciple of Jesus Christ, when the world seeth not even my body. Entreat of our Lord in my behalf, that through these instruments I may be found a sacrifice to God. I do not, like Peter and Paul, issue orders unto you. They are[6] apostles, but I am one condemned; they indeed are free, but I am a slave, even until now. But if I suffer, I shall be the freed-man of Jesus Christ, and I shall rise in Him from the dead, free. And now being in bonds, I learn to desire nothing.

---

[1] Another inscription is, "The Third Epistle."
[2] Literally, "in life."
[3] The meaning is probably similar to that expressed in chap. xiv of the Epistle to the Ephesians.
[4] Literally, "I am ground."
[5] Literally, "with provoking, provoke."
[6] Literally, "they are who are."

CHAP. V.

From Syria, and even unto Rome, I am cast among wild beasts, by sea and by land, by night and by day, being bound between ten leopards, which are the band of soldiers, who, even when I do good to them, all the more do evil unto me. I, however, am the rather instructed by their injurious treatment;[1] but not on this account am I justified to myself. I rejoice in the beasts which are prepared for me, and I pray that they may in haste be found for me; and I will provoke them speedily to devour me, and not be as those which are afraid of some other men,[2] and will not approach them: even should they not be willing to approach me, I will go with violence against them. Know me from myself what is expedient for me.[3] Let no one[4] envy me of those things which are seen and which are not seen, that I should be accounted worthy of Jesus Christ. Fire, and the cross, and the beasts that are prepared, cutting off of the limbs, and scattering of the bones, and crushing of the whole body, harsh torments of the devil — let these come upon me, but[5] only let me be accounted worthy of Jesus Christ.

CHAP. VI.

The pains of the birth stand over against me.[6]

CHAP. VII.

And my love is crucified, and there is no fire in me for another love. I do not desire the food of corruption, neither the lusts of this world. I seek the bread of God, which is the flesh of Jesus Christ; and I seek His blood, a drink which is love incorruptible.

CHAP. IX.[7]

My spirit saluteth you, and the love of the Churches which received me as the name of Jesus Christ; for those also who were near to [my] way in the flesh, preceded me in every city.

[8] [Now therefore, being about to arrive shortly in Rome, I know many things in God; but I keep myself within measure, that I may not perish through boasting: for now it is needful for me to fear the more, and not pay regard to those who puff me up. For they who say such things to me scourge me; for I desire to suffer, but I do not know if I am worthy. For zeal is not visible to many, but with me it has war. I have need, therefore, of meekness, by which the prince of this world is destroyed. I am able to write to you of heavenly things, but I fear lest I should do you an injury. Know me from myself. For I am cautious lest ye should not be able to receive [such knowledge], and should be perplexed. For even I, not because I am in bonds, and am able to know heavenly things, and the places of angels, and the stations of the powers that are seen and that are not seen, am on this account a disciple; for I am far short of the perfection which is worthy of God.] Be ye perfectly strong[9] in the patience of Jesus Christ our God.

Here end the three Epistles of Ignatius, bishop and martyr.

---

[1] Literally, "by their injury."
[2] Literally, "and not as that which is afraid of some other men." So Cureton translates, but remarks that the passage is evidently corrupt. The reference plainly is to the fact that the beasts sometimes refused to attack their intended victims. See the case of Blandina, as reported by Eusebius (*Hist. Eccl.*, v. 1).
[3] Cureton renders interrogatively, "What is expedient for me?" and remarks that "the meaning of the Syriac appears to be, 'I crave your indulgence to leave the knowledge of what is expedient for me to my own conscience.'"
[4] Literally, "nothing."
[5] Literally, "and."
[6] The Latin version translates the Greek here, "He adds gain to me."

[7] Chap. viii. of the Greek is entirely omitted in the Syriac.
[8] The following passage is not found in this Epistle in the Greek recensions, but forms, in substance, chaps. iv. and v. of the Epistle to the Trallians. Diverse views are held by critics as to its proper place, according to the degree of authority they ascribe to the Syriac version. Cureton maintains that this passage has been transferred by the forger of the Epistle to the Trallians, "to give a fair colour to the fabrication by introducing a part of the genuine writing of Ignatius;" while Hefele asserts that it is bound by the "closest connection" to the preceding chapter in the Epistle to the Trallians.
[9] Or, as in the Greek, "Fare ye well, to the end."
[N.B. — The aphoristic genius of Ignatius seems to be felt by his Syrian abbreviator, who reduces whole chapters to mere maxims.]

INTRODUCTORY NOTE

TO THE

SPURIOUS EPISTLES OF IGNATIUS.

To the following introductory note of the translators nothing need be prefixed, except a grateful acknowledgment of the value of their labours and of their good judgment in giving us even these spurious writings for purposes of comparison. They have thus placed the materials for a complete understanding of the whole subject, before students who have a mind to subject it to a thorough and candid examination.

The following is the original INTRODUCTORY NOTICE: —

WE formerly stated that eight out of the fifteen Epistles bearing the name of Ignatius are now universally admitted to be spurious. None of them are quoted or referred to by any ancient writer previous to the sixth century. The style, moreover, in which they are written, so different from that of the other Ignatian letters, and allusions which they contain to heresies and ecclesiastical arrangements of a much later date than that of their professed author, render it perfectly certain that they are not the authentic production of the illustrious bishop of Antioch.

We cannot tell when or by whom these Epistles were fabricated. They have been thought to betray the same hand as the longer and interpolated form of the seven Epistles which are generally regarded as genuine. And some have conceived that the writer who gave forth to the world the "Apostolic Constitutions" under the name of Clement, was probably the author of these letters falsely ascribed to Ignatius, as well as of the longer recension of the seven Epistles which are mentioned by Eusebius.

It was a considerable time before editors in modern times began to discriminate between the true and the false in the writings attributed to Ignatius. The letters first published under his name were those three which exist only in Latin. These came forth in 1495 at Paris, being appended to a life of Becket, Archbishop of Canterbury. Some three years later, eleven Epistles, comprising those mentioned by Eusebius, and four others, were published in Latin, and passed through four or five editions. In 1536, the whole of the professedly Ignatian letters were published at Cologne in a Latin version; and this collection also passed through several editions. It was not till 1557 that the Ignatian Epistles appeared for the first time in Greek at Dillingen. After this date many editions came forth, in which the probably genuine were still mixed up with the certainly spurious, the three Latin letters only being rejected as destitute of authority. Vedelius of Geneva first made the distinction which is now universally accepted, in an edition of these Epistles which he published in 1623; and he was followed by Archbishop Usher and others, who entered more fully into that critical examination of these writings which has been continued down even to our own day.

The reader will have no difficulty in detecting the internal grounds on which these eight letters are set aside as spurious. The difference of style from the other Ignatian writings will strike him even in perusing the English version which we have given, while it is of course much more marked in the original. And other decisive proofs present themselves in every one of the Epistles. In that to the Tarsians there is found a plain allusion to the Sabellian heresy, which did not arise till after the middle of the third century. In the Epistle to the Antiochians there is an enumeration of various Church officers, who were certainly unknown at the period when Ignatius lived. The Epistle to Hero plainly alludes to Manichæan errors, and could not therefore have been written before the third century. There are equally decisive proofs of spuriousness to be found in the Epistle to the Philippians, such as the references it contains to the Patripassian heresy originated by Praxeas in the latter part of the second century, and the ecclesiastical feasts, etc., of which it makes mention. The letter to Maria Cassobolita is of a very peculiar style, utterly alien from that of the other Epistles ascribed to Ignatius. And it is sufficient simply to glance at the short Epistles to St. John and the Virgin Mary, in order to see that they carry the stamp of imposture on their front; and, indeed, no sooner were they published than by almost universal consent they were rejected.

But though the additional Ignatian letters here given are confessedly spurious, we have thought it not improper to present them to the English reader in an appendix to our first volume.[1] We have done so, because they have been so closely connected with the name of the bishop of Antioch, and also because they are in themselves not destitute of interest. We have, moreover, the satisfaction of thus placing for the first time within the reach of one acquainted only with our language, all the materials that have entered into the protracted agitation of the famous Ignatian controversy.

---

[1] [Spurious writings, if they can be traced to antiquity, are always useful. Sometimes they are evidence of facts, always of opinions, ideas and fancies of their date; and often they enable us to identify the origin of corruptions. Even interpolations prove what later partisans would be glad to find, if they could, in early writers. They bear unwilling testimony to the absence of *genuine* evidence in favour of their assumptions.]

THE EPISTLE OF IGNATIUS TO THE TARSIANS

Ignatius, who is also called Theophorus, to the Church which is at Tarsus, saved in Christ, worthy of praise, worthy of remembrance, and worthy of love: Mercy and peace from God the Father, and the Lord Jesus Christ, be ever multiplied.

CHAP. I. — HIS OWN SUFFERINGS: EXHORTATION TO STEDFASTNESS.

From Syria even unto Rome I fight with beasts: not that I am devoured by brute beasts, for these, as ye know, by the will of God, spared Daniel, but by beasts in the shape of men, in whom the merciless wild beast himself lies hid, and pricks and wounds me day by day. But none of these hardships "move me, neither count I my life dear unto myself,"[1] in such a way as to love it better than the Lord. Wherefore I am prepared for [encountering] fire, wild beasts, the sword, or the cross, so that only I may see Christ my Saviour and God, who died for me. I therefore, the prisoner of Christ, who am driven along by land and sea, exhort you: "stand fast in the faith,"[2] and be ye stedfast, "for the just shall live by faith;"[3] be ye unwavering, for "the Lord causes those to dwell in a house who are of one and the same character."[4]

CHAP. II. — CAUTIONS AGAINST FALSE DOCTRINE.

I have learned that certain of the ministers of Satan have wished to disturb you, some of them asserting that Jesus was born [only[5]] in appearance, was crucified in appearance, and died in appearance; others that He is not the Son of the Creator, and others that He is Himself God over all.[6] Others, again, hold that He is a mere man, and others that this flesh is not to rise again, so that our proper course is to live and partake of a life of pleasure, for that this is the chief good to beings who are in a little while to perish.

A swarm of such evils has burst in upon us.[7] But ye have not "given place by subjection to them, no, not for one hour."[8] For ye are the fellow-citizens as well as the disciples of Paul, who "fully preached the Gospel from Jerusalem, and round about unto Illyricum,"[9] and bare about "the marks of Christ" in his flesh.[10]

CHAP. III. — THE TRUE DOCTRINE RESPECTING CHRIST.

Mindful of him, do ye by all means know that Jesus the Lord was truly born of Mary, being made of a woman; and was as truly crucified. For, says he, "God forbid that I should glory, save in the cross of the Lord Jesus."[11] And He really suffered, and died, and rose again. For says [Paul], "If Christ should become passible, and should be the first to rise again from the dead."[12] And again, "In that He died, He died unto sin once: but in that He liveth, He liveth unto God."[13] Otherwise, what advantage would there be in [becoming subject to] bonds, if Christ has not died? what advantage in patience? what advantage in [enduring] stripes? And why such facts as the following: Peter was crucified; Paul and James were slain with the sword; John was banished to Patmos; Stephen was stoned to death by the Jews who killed the Lord? But, [in truth,] none of these sufferings were in vain; for the Lord was really crucified by the ungodly.

CHAP. IV. — CONTINUATION.

And [know ye, moreover], that He who was born of a woman was the Son of God, and He that was crucified was "the first-born of every creature,"[14] and God the Word, who also created all things. For says the apostle, "There is one God, the Father, of whom are all things; and

---

[1] Acts xx. 24.
[2] 1 Cor. xvi. 13.
[3] Hab. ii. 4; Gal. iii. 11.
[4] Ps. lxviii. 7 (after the LXX.).
[5] Some omit this.
[6] That is, as appears afterwards from chap. v., so as to have no personality distinct from the Father.
[7] The translation is here somewhat doubtful.
[8] Gal. ii. 5.
[9] Rom. xv. 19.
[10] Gal. vi. 17.
[11] Gal. vi. 14.
[12] Acts xxvi. 23 (somewhat inaccurately rendered in English version).
[13] Rom. vi. 10.
[14] Col. i. 15.

one Lord Jesus Christ, by whom are all things."[1] And again, "For there is one God, and one Mediator between God and man, the man Christ Jesus;"[2] and, "By Him were all things created that are in heaven, and on earth, visible and invisible; and He is before all things, and by Him all things consist."[3]

CHAP. V. — REFUTATION OF THE PREVIOUSLY MENTIONED ERRORS.

And that He Himself is not God over all, and the Father, but His Son, He [shows when He] says, "I ascend unto my Father and your Father, and to my God and your God."[4] And again, "When all things shall be subdued unto Him, then shall He also Himself be subject unto Him that put all things under Him, that God may be all in all."[5] Wherefore it is one [Person] who put all things under, and who is all in all, and another [Person] to whom they were subdued, who also Himself, along with all other things, becomes subject [to the former].

CHAP. VI. — CONTINUATION.

Nor is He a mere man, by whom and in whom all things were made; for "all things were made by Him."[6] "When He made the heaven, I was present with Him; and I was there with Him, forming [the world along with Him], and He rejoiced in me daily."[7] And how could a mere man be addressed in such words as these: "Sit Thou at My right hand?"[8] And how, again, could such an one declare: "Before Abraham was, I am?"[9] And, "Glorify Me with Thy glory which I had before the world was?"[10] What man could ever say, "I came down from heaven, not to do Mine own will, but the will of Him that sent Me?"[11] And of what man could it be said, "He was the true Light, which lighteth every man that cometh into the world: He was in the world, and the world was made by Him, and the world knew Him not. He came unto His own, and His own received Him not?"[12] How could such a one be a mere man, receiving the beginning of His existence from Mary, and not rather God the Word, and the only-begotten Son? For "in the beginning was the Word, and the Word was with God,[13] and the Word was God."[14] And in another place, "The Lord created Me, the beginning of His ways, for His ways, for His works. Before the world did He found Me, and before all the hills did He beget Me."[15]

CHAP. VII. — CONTINUATION.

And that our bodies are to rise again, He shows when He says, "Verily I say unto you, that the hour cometh, in the which all that are in the graves shall hear the voice of the Son of God; and they that hear shall live."[16] And [says] the apostle, "For this corruptible must put on incorruption, and this mortal must put on immortality."[17] And that we must live soberly and righteously, he [shows when he] says again, "Be not deceived: neither adulterers, nor effeminate persons, nor abusers of themselves with mankind, nor fornicators, nor revilers, nor drunkards, nor thieves, can inherit the kingdom of God."[18] And again, "If the dead rise not, then is not Christ raised; our preaching therefore is vain, and your faith is also vain: ye are yet in your sins. Then they also that are fallen asleep in Christ have perished. If in this life only we have hope in Christ, we are of all men most miserable. If the dead rise not, let us eat and drink, for to-morrow we die."[19] But if such be our condition and feelings, wherein shall we differ from asses and dogs, who have no care about the future, but think only of eating, and of indulging[20] such appetites as follow after eating? For they are unacquainted with any intelligence moving within them.

CHAP. VIII. — EXHORTATIONS TO HOLINESS AND GOOD ORDER.

May I have joy of you in the Lord! Be ye sober. Lay aside, every one of you, all malice and beast-like fury, evil-speaking, calumny, filthy speaking, ribaldry, whispering, arrogance, drunkenness, lust, avarice, vainglory, envy, and everything akin to these. "But put ye on the Lord Jesus Christ, and make no provision for the flesh, to fulfil the lusts thereof."[21] Ye presbyters, be subject to the bishop; ye deacons, to the presbyters; and ye, the people, to the presbyters and the deacons. Let my soul be for theirs who preserve this good order; and may the Lord be with them continually!

CHAP. IX. — EXHORTATIONS TO THE DISCHARGE OF RELATIVE DUTIES.

Ye husbands, love your wives; and ye wives, your husbands. Ye children, reverence your parents. Ye parents, "bring up your children in the nurture and admonition of the Lord."[22]

---

[1] 1 Cor. viii. 6.
[2] 1 Tim. ii. 5.
[3] Col. i. 16, 17.
[4] John xx. 17.
[5] 1 Cor. xv. 28.
[6] John i. 3.
[7] Prov. viii. 27, 30.
[8] Ps. cx. 1.
[9] John viii. 58.
[10] John xvii. 5.
[11] John vi. 38.
[12] John i. 9, 10, 11.
[13] John i. 1.
[14] Some insert here John i. 3.
[15] Prov. viii. 22, 23, 25.
[16] John v. 25, 28.
[17] 1 Cor. xv. 53.
[18] 1 Cor. vi. 9.
[19] 1 Cor. xv. 13, 14, 17, 18, 19, 32.
[20] Literally, "coming also to the appetite of those things after eating." The text is doubtful.
[21] Rom. xiii. 14.
[22] Eph. vi. 4.

Honour those [who continue] in virginity, as the priestesses of Christ; and the widows [that persevere] in gravity of behaviour, as the altar of God. Ye servants, wait upon your masters with [respectful] fear. Ye masters, issue orders to your servants with tenderness. Let no one among you be idle; for idleness is the mother of want. I do not enjoin these things as being a person of any consequence, although I am in bonds [for Christ]; but as a brother, I put you in mind of them. The Lord be with you!

CHAP. X. — SALUTATIONS.

May I enjoy your prayers! Pray ye that I may attain to Jesus. I commend unto you the Church which is at Antioch. The Churches of Philippi,[1] whence also I write to you, salute you. Philo, your deacon, to whom also I give thanks as one who has zealously ministered to me in all things, salutes you. Agathopus, the deacon from Syria, who follows me in Christ, salutes you. "Salute ye one another with a holy kiss."[2] I salute you all, both male and female, who are in Christ. Fare ye well in body, and soul, and in one Spirit; and do not ye forget me. The Lord be with you!

---

[1] Literally, "of the Philippians."
[2] 1 Pet. v. 14.

THE EPISTLE OF IGNATIUS TO THE ANTIOCHIANS

Ignatius, who is also called Theophorus, to the Church sojourning in Syria, which has obtained mercy from God, and been elected by Christ, and which first[1] received the name of Christ, [wishes] happiness in God the Father, and the Lord Jesus Christ.

CHAP. I. — CAUTIONS AGAINST ERROR.

THE Lord has rendered my bonds light and easy since I learnt that you are in peace, and that you live in all harmony both of the flesh and spirit. "I therefore, the prisoner of the Lord,[2] beseech you, that ye walk worthy of the vocation wherewith ye are called,"[3] guarding against those heresies of the wicked one which have broken in upon us, to the deceiving and destruction of those that accept of them; but that ye give heed to the doctrine of the apostles, and believe both the law and the prophets: that ye reject every Jewish and Gentile error, and neither introduce a multiplicity of gods, nor yet deny Christ under the pretence of [maintaining] the unity of God.

CHAP. II. — THE TRUE DOCTRINE RESPECTING GOD AND CHRIST.

For Moses, the faithful servant of God, when he said, "The Lord thy God is one Lord,"[4] and thus proclaimed that there was only one God, did yet forthwith confess also our Lord when he said, "The Lord rained upon Sodom and Gomorrah fire and brimstone from the Lord."[5] And again, "And God[6] said, Let Us make man after our image: and so God made man, after the image of God made He him."[7] And further, "In the image of God made He man."[8] And that [the Son of God] was to be made man, [Moses shows when] he says, "A prophet shall the Lord raise up unto you of your brethren, like unto me."[9]

CHAP. III. — THE SAME CONTINUED.

The prophets also, when they speak as in the person of God, [saying,] "I am God, the first [of beings], and I am also the last,[10] and besides Me there is no God,"[11] concerning the Father of the universe, do also speak of our Lord Jesus Christ. "A Son," they say, has been given to us, on whose shoulder the government is from above; and His name is called the Angel of great counsel, Wonderful, Counsellor, the strong and mighty God."[12] And concerning His incarnation, "Behold, a virgin shall be with Child, and shall bring forth a Son; and they shall call his name Immanuel."[13] And concerning the passion, "He was led as a sheep to the slaughter; and as a lamb before her shearers is dumb, I also was an innocent lamb led to be sacrificed."[14]

CHAP. IV. — CONTINUATION.

The Evangelists, too, when they declared that the one Father was "the only true God,"[15] did not omit what concerned our Lord, but wrote: "In the beginning was the Word, and the Word was with God, and the Word was God. The same was in the beginning with God. All things were made by Him, and without Him was not anything made that was made."[16] And concerning the incarnation: "The Word," says [the Scripture], "became flesh, and dwelt among us."[17] And again: "The book of the generation of Jesus Christ, the son of David, the son of Abraham."[18] And those very apostles, who said "that there is one God,"[19] said also that "there

---

[1] Comp. Acts xi. 26.
[2] Literally, "in the Lord."
[3] Eph. iv. 1.
[4] Deut. vi. 4; Mark xii. 29.
[5] Gen. xix. 24.
[6] The MS. has "Lord."
[7] Gen. i. 26, 27.
[8] Gen v. 1, ix. 6.
[9] Deut. xviii. 15; Acts iii. 22, vii. 37.
[10] Literally, "after these things."
[11] Isa. xliv. 6.
[12] Isa. ix. 6.
[13] Isa. vii. 14; Matt. i. 23.
[14] Isa. liii. 7; Jer. xi. 19.
[15] John xvii. 3.
[16] John i. 1.
[17] John i. 14.
[18] Matt. i. 1.
[19] 1 Cor. viii. 4, 6; Gal. iii. 20.

is one Mediator between God and men."[1] Nor were they ashamed of the incarnation and the passion. For what says [one]? "The man Christ Jesus, who gave Himself"[2] for the life and salvation of the world.

CHAP. V. — DENUNCIATION OF FALSE TEACHERS.

Whosoever, therefore, declares that there is but one God, only so as to take away the divinity of Christ, is a devil,[3] and an enemy of all righteousness. He also that confesseth Christ, yet not as the Son of the Maker of the world, but of some other unknown[4] being, different from Him whom the law and the prophets have proclaimed, this man is an instrument of the devil. And he that rejects the incarnation, and is ashamed of the cross for which I am in bonds, this man is antichrist.[5] Moreover, he who affirms Christ to be a mere man is accursed, according to the [declaration of the] prophet,[6] since he puts not his trust in God, but in man. Wherefore also he is unfruitful, like the wild myrtle-tree.

CHAP. VI. — RENEWED CAUTIONS.

These things I write to you, thou new olive-tree of Christ, not that I am aware you hold any such opinions, but that I may put you on your guard, as a father does his children. Beware, therefore, of those that hasten to work mischief, those "enemies of the cross of Christ, whose end is destruction, whose glory is in their shame."[7] Beware of those "dumb dogs," those trailing serpents, those scaly[8] dragons, those asps, and basilisks, and scorpions. For these are subtle wolves,[9] and apes that mimic the appearance of men.

CHAP. VII. — EXHORTATION TO CONSISTENCY OF CONDUCT.

Ye have been the disciples of Paul and Peter; do not lose what was committed to your trust. Keep in remembrance Euodias,[10] your deservedly-blessed pastor, into whose hands the government over you was first entrusted by the apostles. Let us not bring disgrace upon our Father. Let us prove ourselves His true-born children, and not bastards. Ye know after what manner I have acted among you. The things which, when present, I spoke to you, these same, when absent, I now write to you. "If any man love not the Lord Jesus Christ, let him be Anathema."[11] Be ye followers of me.[12] My soul be for yours, when I attain to Jesus. Remember my bonds.[13]

CHAP. VIII. — EXHORTATIONS TO THE PRESBYTERS AND OTHERS.

Ye presbyters, "feed the flock which is among you,"[14] till God shall show who is to hold the rule over you. For "I am now ready to be offered,"[15] that I "may win Christ."[16] Let the deacons know of what dignity they are, and let them study to be blameless, that they may be the followers of Christ. Let the people be subject to the presbyters and the deacons. Let the virgins know to whom they have consecrated themselves.

CHAP. IX. — DUTIES OF HUSBANDS, WIVES, PARENTS, AND CHILDREN.

Let the husbands love their wives, remembering that, at the creation, one woman, and not many, was given to one man. Let the wives honour their husbands, as their own flesh; and let them not presume to address them by their names.[17] Let them also be chaste, reckoning their husbands as their only partners, to whom indeed they have been united according to the will of God. Ye parents, impart a holy training to your children. Ye children, "honour your parents, that it may be well with you."[18]

CHAP. X. — DUTIES OF MASTERS AND SERVANTS.

Ye masters, do not treat your servants with haughtiness, but imitate patient Job, who declares, "I did not despise[19] the cause[20] of my man-servant, or of my maid-servant, when they contended with me. For what in that case shall I do when the Lord makes an inquisition regarding me?"[21] And you know what follows. Ye servants, do not provoke your masters to anger in anything, lest ye become the authors of incurable mischiefs to yourselves.

CHAP. XI. — INCULCATION OF VARIOUS MORAL DUTIES.

Let no one addicted to idleness eat,[22] lest he become a wanderer about, and a whoremonger. Let drunkenness, anger, envy, reviling, clamour, and blasphemy "be not so much as named among you."[23] Let not the widows live a life of pleasure, lest they wax wanton against the word.[24] Be subject to Cæsar in everything in which subjection implies no [spiritual] danger.

---

[1] Eph. iv. 5, 6; 1 Tim. ii. 5.
[2] 1 Tim. ii. 5.
[3] Comp. John vi. 70. Some read, "the son of the devil."
[4] Or, "that cannot be known."
[5] Comp. 1 John ii. 22, iv. 3; 2 John 7.
[6] Jer. xvii. 5.
[7] Phil. iii. 18, 19.
[8] The text is here doubtful.
[9] Literally, "fox-like thoes," lynxes being perhaps intended.
[10] Some think that this is the same person as the Euodias referred to by St. Paul, Phil. iv. 2; but, as appears from the Greek (ver. 3, αἵτινες), the two persons there mentioned were *women*.
[11] 1 Cor. xvi. 22.
[12] Comp. 1 Cor. iv. 16.
[13] Comp. Col. iv. 18.
[14] 1 Pet. v. 2.
[15] 2 Tim. iv. 6.
[16] Phil. iii. 8.
[17] Comp. 1 Pet. iii. 6.
[18] Eph. vi. 1, 3.
[19] Literally, "If I did despise."
[20] Or, "judgment."
[21] Job xxxi. 13, 14.
[22] Comp. 2 Thess. iii. 10.
[23] Eph. v. 3.
[24] 1 Tim. v. 6, 11.

Provoke not those that rule over you to wrath, that you may give no occasion against yourselves to those that seek for it. But as to the practice of magic, or the impure love of boys, or murder, it is superfluous to write to you, since such vices are forbidden to be committed even by the Gentiles. I do not issue commands on these points as if I were an apostle; but, as your fellow-servant, I put you in mind of them.

CHAP. XII. — SALUTATIONS.

I salute the holy presbytery. I salute the sacred deacons, and that person most dear to me,[1] whom may I behold, through the Holy Spirit, occupying my place when I shall attain to Christ. My soul be in place of his. I salute the sub-deacons, the readers, the singers, the doorkeepers, the labourers,[2] the exorcists, the confessors.[3] I salute the keepers of the holy gates, the deaconesses in Christ. I salute the virgins betrothed to Christ, of whom may I have joy in the Lord Jesus.[4] I salute the people of the Lord, from the smallest to the greatest, and all my sisters in the Lord.

---
[1] Literally, "the name desirable to me," referring to Hero the deacon.
[2] A class of persons connected with the Church, whose duty it was to bury the bodies of the martyrs and others.
[3] Such as voluntarily confessed Christ before Gentile rulers.
[4] Some insert here a clause referring to *widows*.

CHAP. XIII. — SALUTATIONS CONTINUED.

I salute Cassian and his partner in life, and their very dear children. Polycarp, that most worthy bishop, who is also deeply interested in you, salutes you; and to him I have commended you in the Lord. The whole Church of the Smyrnæans, indeed, is mindful of you in their prayers in the Lord. Onesimus, the pastor of the Ephesians, salutes you. Damas,[5] the bishop of Magnesia, salutes you. Polybius, bishop of the Trallians, salutes you. Philo and Agathopus, the deacons, my companions, salute you, "Salute one another with a holy kiss."[6]

CHAP. XIV. — CONCLUSION.

I write this letter to you from Philippi. May He who is alone unbegotten, keep you stedfast both in the spirit and in the flesh, through Him who was begotten before time[7] began! And may I behold you in the kingdom of Christ! I salute him who is to bear rule over you in my stead: may I have joy of him in the Lord! Fare ye well in God, and in Christ, being enlightened by the Holy Spirit.

---
[5] Or, as some read, "Demas."
[6] 2 Cor. xiii. 12.
[7] Literally, "before ages."

THE EPISTLE OF IGNATIUS TO HERO

A DEACON OF ANTIOCH

Ignatius, who is also called Theophorus, to Hero, the deacon of Christ, and the servant of God, a man honoured by God, and most dearly loved as well as esteemed, who carries Christ and the Spirit within him, and who is mine own son in faith and love: Grace, mercy, and peace from Almighty God, and from Christ Jesus our Lord, His only-begotten Son, "who gave Himself for our sins, that He might deliver us from the present evil world,"[1] *and preserve us unto His heavenly kingdom.*

CHAP. I. — EXHORTATIONS TO EARNESTNESS AND MODERATION.

I EXHORT thee in God, that thou add [speed] to thy course, and that thou vindicate thy dignity. Have a care to preserve concord with the saints. Bear [the burdens of] the weak, that "thou mayest fulfil the law of Christ."[2] Devote[3] thyself to fasting and prayer, but not beyond measure, lest thou destroy thyself[4] thereby. Do not altogether abstain from wine and flesh, for these things are not to be viewed with abhorrence, since [the Scripture] saith, "Ye shall eat the good things of the earth."[5] And again, "Ye shall eat flesh even as herbs."[6] And again, "Wine maketh glad the heart of man, and oil exhilarates, and bread strengthens him."[7] But all are to be used with moderation, as being the gifts of God. "For who shall eat or who shall drink without Him? For if anything be beautiful, it is His; and if anything be good, it is His."[8] Give attention to reading,[9] that thou mayest not only thyself know the laws, but mayest also explain them to others, as the earnest servant[10] of God. "No man that warreth entangleth himself with the affairs of this life, that he may please him who hath chosen him to be a soldier; and if a man also strive for masteries, yet is he not crowned except he strive lawfully."[11] I that am in bonds pray that my soul may be in place of yours.

CHAP. II. — CAUTIONS AGAINST FALSE TEACHERS.

Every one that teaches anything beyond what is commanded, though he be [deemed] worthy of credit, though he be in the habit of fasting, though he live in continence, though he work miracles, though he have the gift of prophecy, let him be in thy sight as a wolf in sheep's clothing,[12] labouring for the destruction of the sheep. If any one denies the cross, and is ashamed of the passion, let him be to thee as the adversary himself. "Though he gives all his goods to feed the poor, though he remove mountains, though he give his body to be burned,"[13] let him be regarded by thee as abominable. If any one makes light of the law or the prophets, which Christ fulfilled at His coming, let him be to thee as antichrist. If any one says that the Lord is a mere man, he is a Jew, a murderer of Christ.

CHAP. III. — EXHORTATIONS AS TO ECCLESIASTICAL DUTIES.

"Honour widows that are widows indeed."[14] Be the friend of orphans; for God is "the Father of the fatherless, and the Judge of the widows."[15] Do nothing without the bishops; for they are priests, and thou a servant of the priests. They baptize, offer sacrifice,[16] ordain, and lay on hands; but thou ministerest to them, as the holy Stephen

---

[1] Gal. i. 4.
[2] Gal. vi. 2.
[3] Literally, "have leisure for."
[4] Literally, "cast thyself down."
[5] Isa. i. 19.
[6] Gen. ix. 3.
[7] Ps. civ. 15.
[8] Eccles. ii. 25 (after LXX.); Zech. ix. 17.
[9] Comp. 1. Tim. iv. 13.
[10] Literally, "athlete."
[11] 2 Tim. ii. 4.
[12] Comp. Matt. vii. 15.
[13] 1 Cor. xiii. 2.
[14] 1 Tim. v. 3.
[15] Ps. lxviii. 5.
[16] The term ἱερουργέω, which we have translated as above, is one whose signification is disputed. It occurs once in the New Testament (Rom. xv. 16) where it is translated in our English version simply "ministering." Etymologically, it means "to act as a priest," and we have in our translation followed Hesychius (Cent. iv.), who explains it as meaning "to offer sacrifice." [The whole passage in the Epistle to the Romans, where this word occurs may be compared (original Greek) with Mal. i. 11, Heb. v. 1, etc.]

did at Jerusalem to James and the presbyters. Do not neglect the sacred meetings[1] [of the saints]; inquire after every one by name. "Let no man despise thy youth, but be thou an example to the believers, both in word and conduct."[2]

CHAP. IV. — SERVANTS AND WOMEN ARE NOT TO BE DESPISED.

Be not ashamed of servants, for we possess the same nature in common with them. Do not hold women in abomination, for they have given thee birth, and brought thee up. It is fitting, therefore, to love those that were the authors of our birth (but only in the Lord), inasmuch as a man can produce no children without a woman. It is right, therefore, that we should honour those who have had a part in giving us birth. "Neither is the man without the woman, nor the woman without the man,"[3] except in the case of those who were first formed. For the body of Adam was made out of the four elements, and that of Eve out of the side of Adam. And, indeed, the altogether peculiar birth of the Lord was of a virgin alone. [This took place] not as if the lawful union [of man and wife] were abominable, but such a kind of birth was fitting to God. For it became the Creator not to make use of the ordinary method of generation, but of one that was singular and strange, as being the Creator.

CHAP. V. — VARIOUS RELATIVE DUTIES.

Flee from haughtiness, "for the Lord resisteth the proud."[4] Abhor falsehood, for says [the Scripture], "Thou shalt destroy all them that speak lies."[5] Guard against envy, for its author is the devil, and his successor Cain, who envied his brother, and out of envy committed murder. Exhort my sisters to love God, and be content with their own husbands only. In like manner, exhort my brethren also to be content with their own wives. Watch over the virgins, as the precious treasures of Christ. Be long-suffering,[6] that thou mayest be great in wisdom. Do not neglect the poor, in so far as thou art prosperous. For "by alms and fidelity sins are purged away."[7]

CHAP. VI — EXHORTATIONS TO PURITY AND CAUTION.

Keep thyself pure as the habitation of God. Thou art the temple of Christ. Thou art the instrument of the Spirit. Thou knowest in what way I have brought thee up. Though I am the least of men, do thou seek to follow me, be thou an imitator of my conduct. I do not glory in the world, but in the Lord. I exhort Hero, my son; "but let him that glorieth, glory in the Lord."[8] May I have joy of thee, my dear son, whose guardian may He be who is the only unbegotten God, and the Lord Jesus Christ! Do not believe all persons, do not place confidence in all; nor let any man get the better of thee by flattery. For many are the ministers of Satan; and "he that is hasty to believe is light of heart."[9]

CHAP. VII. — SOLEMN CHARGE TO HERO, AS FUTURE BISHOP OF ANTIOCH.

Keep God in remembrance, and thou shalt never sin. Be not double-minded[10] in thy prayers; for blessed is he who doubteth not. For I believe in the Father of the Lord Jesus Christ, and in His only-begotten Son, that God will show me, Hero, upon my throne. Add speed, therefore,[11] to thy course. I charge thee before the God of the universe, and before Christ, and in the presence of the Holy Spirit, and of the ministering ranks [of angels], keep in safety that deposit which I and Christ have committed to thee, and do not judge thyself unworthy of those things which have been shown by God [to me] concerning thee. I hand over to thee the Church of Antioch. I have commended you to Polycarp in the Lord Jesus Christ.

CHAP. VIII. — SALUTATIONS.

The bishops, Onesimus, Bitus, Damas, Polybius, and all they of Philippi (whence also I have written to thee), salute thee in Christ. Salute the presbytery worthy of God: salute my holy fellow-deacons, of whom may I have joy in Christ, both in the flesh and in the spirit. Salute the people of the Lord, from the smallest to the greatest, every one by name; whom I commit to thee as Moses did [the Israelites] to Joshua, who was their leader after him. And do not reckon this which I have said presumptuous on my part; for although we are not such as they were, yet we at least pray that we may be so, since indeed we are the children of Abraham. Be strong, therefore, O Hero, like a hero, and like a man. For from henceforth thou shalt lead[12] in and out the people of the Lord that are in Antioch, and so "the congregation of the Lord shall not be as sheep which have no shepherd."[13]

CHAP. IX. — CONCLUDING SALUTATIONS AND INSTRUCTIONS.

Salute Cassian, my host, and his most serious-minded partner in life, and their very dear chil-

---

[1] Specially, assemblies for the celebration of the Lord's Supper.
[2] 1 Tim. iv. 12.
[3] 1 Cor. xi. 11.
[4] Jas. iv. 6; 1 Pet. v. 5.
[5] Ps. v. 6.
[6] Prov. xiv. 29.
[7] Prov. xv. 27 (after LXX.: xvi. 6 in English version)
[8] 1 Cor. i. 31; 2 Cor. x. 17.
[9] Ecclus. xix. 4.
[10] Comp. Jas. i. 6, 8.
[11] Comp. Epistle to the Antiochians, chap. xii.
[12] Comp. Deut. xxxi. 7, 23.
[13] Num. xxvii. 17.

dren, to whom may "God grant that they find mercy of the Lord in that day,"[1] on account of their ministrations to us, whom also I commend to thee in Christ. Salute by name all the faithful in Christ that are at Laodicea. Do not neglect those at Tarsus, but look after them steadily, confirming them in the Gospel. I salute in the Lord, Maris the bishop of Neapolis, near Anazarbus. Salute thou also Mary my daughter, distinguished both for gravity and erudition, as also "the Church which is in her house."[2] May my soul be in place of hers: she is the very pattern of pious women. May the Father of Christ, by His only-begotten Son, preserve thee in good health, and of high repute in all things, to a very old age, for the benefit of the Church of God! Farewell in the Lord, and pray thou that I may be perfected.

---

[1] 2 Tim. i. 18.

[2] Col. iv. 15.

THE EPISTLE OF IGNATIUS TO THE PHILIPPIANS

Ignatius, who is also called Theophorus, to the Church of God which is at Philippi, which has obtained mercy in faith, and patience, and love unfeigned: Mercy and peace from God the Father, and the Lord Jesus Christ, "who is the Saviour of all men, specially of them that believe." [1]

CHAP. I. — REASON FOR WRITING THE EPISTLE.

BEING mindful of your love and of your zeal in Christ, which ye have manifested towards us, we thought it fitting to write to you, who display such a godly and spiritual love to the brethren,[2] to put you in remembrance of your Christian course,[3] "that ye all speak the same thing, being of one mind, thinking the same thing, and walking by the same rule of faith,"[4] as Paul admonished you. For if there is one God of the universe, the Father of Christ, "of whom are all things;"[5] and one Lord Jesus Christ, our [Lord], "by whom are all things;"[5] and also one Holy Spirit, who wrought[6] in Moses, and in the prophets and apostles; and also one baptism, which is administered that we should have fellowship with the death of the Lord;[7] and also one elect Church; there ought likewise to be but one faith in respect to Christ. For "there is one Lord, one faith, one baptism; one God and Father of all, who is through all, and in all."[8]

CHAP. II. — UNITY OF THE THREE DIVINE PERSONS.

There is then one God and Father, and not two or three; One who is; and there is no other besides Him, the only true [God]. For "the Lord thy God," saith [the Scripture], "is one Lord."[9] And again, "Hath not one God created us? Have we not all one Father?"[10] And there is also one Son, God the Word. For "the only-begotten Son," saith [the Scripture], "who is in the bosom of the Father."[11] And again, "One Lord Jesus Christ."[12] And in another place, "What is His name, or what His Son's name, that we may know?"[13] And there is also one Paraclete.[14] For "there is also," saith [the Scripture], "one Spirit,"[15] since "we have been called in one hope of our calling."[16] And again, "We have drunk of one Spirit,"[15] with what follows. And it is manifest that all these gifts [possessed by believers] "worketh one and the self-same Spirit."[17] There are not then either three Fathers,[18] or three Sons, or three Paracletes, but one Father, and one Son, and one Paraclete. Wherefore also the Lord, when He sent forth the apostles to make disciples of all nations, commanded them to "baptize in the name of the Father, and of the Son, and of the Holy Ghost,"[19] not unto one [person] having three names, nor into three [persons] who became incarnate, but into three possessed of equal honour.

CHAP. III. — CHRIST WAS TRULY BORN, AND DIED, ETC.

For there is but One that became incarnate, and that neither the Father nor the Paraclete, but the Son only, [who became so] not in appearance or imagination, but in reality. For "the Word became flesh."[20] For "Wisdom builded for herself a house."[21] And God the Word was born as man, with a body, of the Virgin, without any intercourse of man. For [it is written], "A virgin shall conceive in her womb, and bring forth a son."[22] He was then truly born, truly grew up, truly ate and drank, was truly crucified, and died, and rose again. He who believes these things, as they really were,

---

[1] 1 Tim. iv. 10.
[2] Literally, "to your brother-loving spiritual love according to God."
[3] Literally, "course in Christ."
[4] 1 Cor. i. 10; Phil. ii. 2, iii. 16.
[5] 1 Cor. viii. 6.
[6] 1 Cor. xii. 11.
[7] Literally, "which is given unto the death of the Lord."
[8] Eph. iv. 5.
[9] Deut. vi. 4; Mark xii. 29.
[10] Mal. ii. 10.
[11] John i. 18.
[12] 1 Cor. viii. 6.
[13] Prov. xxx. 4.
[14] i.e., "Advocate" or "Comforter;" comp. John xiv. 16.
[15] Eph. iv. 4.
[16] 1 Cor. xii. 13.
[17] 1 Cor. xii. 11.
[18] Comp. Athanasian Creed.
[19] Matt. xxviii. 19.
[20] John i. 14.
[21] Prov. ix. 1.
[22] Isa. vii. 14.

and as they really took place, is blessed. He who believeth them not is no less accursed than those who crucified the Lord. For the prince of this world rejoiceth when any one denies the cross, since he knows that the confession of the cross is his own destruction. For that is the trophy which has been raised up against his power, which when he sees, he shudders, and when he hears of, is afraid.

CHAP. IV. — THE MALIGNITY AND FOLLY OF SATAN.

And indeed, before the cross was erected, he (Satan) was eager that it should be so; and he "wrought" [for this end] "in the children of disobedience."[1] He wrought in Judas, in the Pharisees, in the Sadducees, in the old, in the young, and in the priests. But when it was just about to be erected, he was troubled, and infused repentance into the traitor, and pointed him to a rope to hang himself with, and taught him [to die by] strangulation. He terrified also the silly woman, disturbing her by dreams; and he, who had tried every means to have the cross prepared, now endeavoured to put a stop to its erection;[2] not that he was influenced by repentance on account of the greatness of his crime (for in that case he would not be utterly depraved), but because he perceived his own destruction [to be at hand]. For the cross of Christ was the beginning of his condemnation, the beginning of his death, the beginning of his destruction. Wherefore, also, he works in some that they should deny the cross, be ashamed of the passion, call the death an appearance, mutilate and explain away the birth of the Virgin, and calumniate the [human] nature[3] itself as being abominable. He fights along with the Jews to a denial of the cross, and with the Gentiles to the calumniating of Mary,[4] who are heretical in holding that Christ possessed a mere phantasmal body.[5] For the leader of all wickedness assumes manifold[6] forms, beguiler of men as he is, inconsistent, and even contradicting himself, projecting one course and then following another. For he is wise to do evil, but as to what good may be he is totally ignorant. And indeed he is full of ignorance, on account of his voluntary want of reason: for how can he be deemed anything else who does not perceive reason when it lies at his very feet?

CHAP. V. — APOSTROPHE TO SATAN.

For if the Lord were a mere man, possessed of a soul and body only, why dost thou mutilate and explain away His being born with the common nature of humanity? Why dost thou call the passion a mere appearance, as if it were any strange thing happening to a [mere] man? And why dost thou reckon the death of a mortal to be simply an imaginary death? But if, [on the other hand,] He is both God and man, then why dost thou call it unlawful to style Him "the Lord of glory,"[7] who is by nature unchangeable? Why dost thou say that it is unlawful to declare of the Lawgiver who possesses a human soul, "The Word was made flesh,"[8] and was a perfect man, and not merely one dwelling in a man? But how came this magician into existence, who of old formed all nature that can be apprehended either by the senses or intellect, according to the will of the Father; and, when He became incarnate, healed every kind of disease and infirmity?[9]

CHAP. VI. — CONTINUATION.

And how can He be but God, who raises up the dead, sends away the lame sound of limb, cleanses the lepers, restores sight to the blind, and either increases or transmutes existing substances, as the five loaves and the two fishes, and the water which became wine, and who puts to flight thy whole host by a mere word? And why dost thou abuse the nature of the Virgin, and style her members disgraceful, since thou didst of old display such in public processions,[10] and didst order them to be exhibited naked, males in the sight of females, and females to stir up the unbridled lust of males? But now these are reckoned by thee disgraceful, and thou pretendest to be full of modesty, thou spirit of fornication, not knowing that then only anything becomes disgraceful when it is polluted by wickedness. But when sin is not present, none of the things that have been created are shameful, none of them evil, but all very good. But inasmuch as thou art blind, thou revilest these things.

CHAP. VII. — CONTINUATION: INCONSISTENCY OF SATAN.

And how, again, does Christ not at all appear to thee to be of the Virgin, but to be God over all,[11] and the Almighty? Say, then, who sent Him? Who was Lord over Him? And whose will did He obey? And what laws did He fulfil, since He was subject neither to the will nor power of any one? And while you deny that Christ was born,[12] you affirm that the unbegotten was begotten, and that He who had no begin-

---

[1] Eph. ii. 2.
[2] [This is the idea worked out by St. Bernard. See my note (*supra*) suffixed to the Syriac Epistle to Ephesians.]
[3] The various Gnostic sects are here referred to, who held that matter was essentially evil, and therefore denied the reality of our Lord's incarnation.
[4] The MS. has μαγείας, "of magic;" we have followed the emendation proposed by Faber.
[5] Literally, "heretical in respect to phantasy."
[6] Literally, is "various," or "manifold."
[7] 1 Cor. ii. 8.
[8] John i. 14.
[9] Matt. iv. 23, ix. 35.
[10] Reference seems here to be made to obscene heathen practices.
[11] i.e., so as to have no separate personality from the Father. Comp. Epistle to the Tarsians, chap. ii.
[12] Literally, "and taking away Christ from being born."

ning was nailed to the cross, by whose permission I am unable to say. But thy changeable tactics do not escape me, nor am I ignorant that thou art wont to walk with slanting and uncertain[1] steps. And thou art ignorant who really was born, thou who pretendest to know everything.

CHAP. VIII. — CONTINUATION: IGNORANCE OF SATAN.

For many things are unknown[2] to thee; [such as the following]: the virginity of Mary; the wonderful birth; Who it was that became incarnate; the star which guided those who were in the east; the Magi who presented gifts; the salutation of the archangel to the Virgin; the marvellous conception of her that was betrothed; the announcement of the boy-forerunner respecting the son of the Virgin, and his leaping in the womb on account of what was foreseen; the songs of the angels over Him that was born; the glad tidings announced to the shepherds; the fear of Herod lest his kingdom should be taken from him; the command to slay the infants; the removal into Egypt, and the return from that country to the same region; the infant swaddling-bands; the human registration; the nourishing by means of milk; the name of father given to Him who did not beget; the manger because there was not room [elsewhere]; no human preparation [for the Child]; the gradual growth, human speech, hunger, thirst, journeyings, weariness; the offering of sacrifices, and then also circumcision, baptism; the voice of God over Him that was baptized, as to who He was and whence [He had come]; the testimony of the Spirit and the Father from above; the voice of John the prophet when it signified the passion by the appellation of "the Lamb;" the performance of divers miracles, manifold healings; the rebuke of the Lord ruling both the sea and the winds; evil spirits expelled; thou thyself subjected to torture, and, when afflicted by the power of Him who had been manifested, not having it in thy power to do anything.

CHAP. IX. — CONTINUATION: IGNORANCE OF SATAN.

Seeing these things, thou wast in utter perplexity.[3] And thou wast ignorant that it was a virgin that should bring forth; but the angels' song of praise struck thee with astonishment, as well as the adoration of the Magi, and the appearance of the star. Thou didst revert to thy state of [wilful] ignorance, because all the circumstances seemed to thee trifling;[4] for thou didst deem the swaddling-bands, the circumcision, and the nourishment by means of milk contemptible:[5] these things appeared to thee unworthy of God. Again, thou didst behold a man who remained forty days and nights without tasting human food, along with ministering angels at whose presence thou didst shudder, when first of all thou hadst seen Him baptized as a common man, and knewest not the reason thereof. But after His [lengthened] fast thou didst again assume thy wonted audacity, and didst tempt Him when hungry, as if He had been an ordinary man, not knowing who He was. For thou saidst, "If thou be the Son of God, command that these stones be made bread."[6] Now, this expression, "If thou be the Son," is an indication of ignorance. For if thou hadst possessed real knowledge, thou wouldst have understood that the Creator can with equal ease both create what does not exist, and change that which already has a being. And thou temptedst by means of hunger[7] Him who nourisheth all that require food. And thou temptedst the very "Lord of glory,"[8] forgetting in thy malevolence that "man shall not live by bread alone, but by every word that proceedeth out of the mouth of God." For if thou hadst known that He was the Son of God, thou wouldst also have understood that He who had kept his[9] body from feeling any want for forty days and as many nights, could have also done the same for ever. Why, then, does He suffer hunger? In order to prove that He had assumed a body subject to the same feelings as those of ordinary men. By the first fact He showed that He was God, and by the second that He was also man.

CHAP. X. — CONTINUATION: AUDACITY OF SATAN.

Darest thou, then, who didst fall "as lightning"[10] from the very highest glory, to say to the Lord, "Cast thyself down from hence[11] [to Him] to whom the things that are not are reckoned as if they were,[12] and to provoke to a display of vainglory Him that was free from all ostentation? And didst thou pretend to read in Scripture concerning Him: "For He hath given His angels charge concerning Thee, and in their hands they shall bear Thee up, lest thou shouldest dash Thy foot against a stone?"[13] At the same time thou didst pretend to be ignorant of the rest, furtively concealing what [the Scripture] predicted concerning thee and thy servants: "Thou shalt tread upon the adder and the basilisk; the lion and the dragon shalt thou trample under foot."[14]

---

[1] Literally, "double."
[2] According to many of the Fathers, Satan was in great ignorance as to a multitude of points connected with Christ. [See my note at end of the Syriac Epistle to Ephesians, *supra*.]
[3] Literally, "thou wast dizzy in the head."
[4] Literally, "on account of the paltry things."
[5] Literally, "small."
[6] Matt. iv. 3.
[7] Or, "the belly."
[8] 1 Cor. ii. 8.
[9] Some insert, "corruptible."
[10] Luke x. 18.
[11] Matt. iv. 6.
[12] Comp. Rom. iv. 17.
[13] Matt. iv. 6.
[14] Ps. xci. 13.

CHAP. XI.—CONTINUATION: AUDACITY OF SATAN.

If, therefore, thou art trodden down under the feet of the Lord, how dost thou tempt Him that cannot be tempted, forgetting that precept of the lawgiver, "Thou shall not tempt the Lord thy God?"[1] Yea, thou even darest, most accursed one, to appropriate the works of God to thyself, and to declare that the dominion over these was delivered to thee.[2] And thou dost set forth thine own fall as an example to the Lord, and dost promise to give Him what is really His own, if He would fall down and worship thee.[3] And how didst thou not shudder, O thou spirit more wicked through thy malevolence than all other wicked spirits, to utter such words against the Lord? Through thine appetite[4] was thou overcome, and through thy vainglory wast thou brought to dishonour: through avarice and ambition dost thou [now] draw on [others] to ungodliness. Thou, O Belial, dragon, apostate, crooked serpent, rebel against God, outcast from Christ, alien from the Holy Spirit, exile from the ranks of the angels, reviler of the laws of God, enemy of all that is lawful, who didst rise up against the first-formed of men, and didst drive forth [from obedience to] the commandment [of God] those who had in no respect injured thee; thou who didst raise up against Abel the murderous Cain; thou who didst take arms against Job: dost thou say to the Lord, "If Thou wilt fall down and worship me?" Oh what audacity! Oh what madness! Thou runaway slave, thou incorrigible[5] slave, dost thou rebel against the good Lord? Dost thou say to so great a Lord, the God of all that either the mind or the senses can perceive, "If Thou wilt fall down and worship me?"

CHAP. XII.—THE MEEK REPLY OF CHRIST.

But the Lord is long-suffering, and does not reduce to nothing him who in his ignorance dares [to utter] such words, but meekly replies, "Get thee hence, Satan."[6] He does not say, "Get thee behind *Me*," for it is not possible that he should be converted; but, "Begone, Satan," to the course which thou hast chosen. "Begone" to those things to which, through thy malevolence, thou hast been called. For I know Who I am, and by Whom I have been sent, and Whom it behoves Me to worship. For "thou shalt worship the Lord thy God, and Him only shalt thou serve."[7] I know the one [God]; I am acquainted with the only [Lord] from whom thou hast become an apostate. I am not an enemy of God; I acknowledge His pre-eminence; I know the Father, who is the author of my generation.

CHAP. XIII.—VARIOUS EXHORTATIONS AND DIRECTIONS.

These things, brethren, out of the affection which I entertain for you, I have felt compelled to write, exhorting you with a view to the glory of God, not as if I were a person of any consequence, but simply as a brother. Be ye subject to the bishop, to the presbyters, and to the deacons. Love one another in the Lord, as being the images of God. Take heed, ye husbands, that ye love your wives as your own members. Ye wives also, love your husbands, as being one with them in virtue of your union. If any one lives in chastity or continence, let him not be lifted up, lest he lose his reward. Do not lightly esteem the festivals. Despise not the period of forty days, for it comprises an imitation of the conduct of the Lord. After the week of the passion, do not neglect to fast on the fourth and sixth days, distributing at the same time of thine abundance to the poor. If any one fasts on the Lord's Day or on the Sabbath, except on the paschal Sabbath only, he is a murderer of Christ.

CHAP. XIV.—FAREWELLS AND CAUTIONS.

Let your prayers be extended to the Church of Antioch, whence also I as a prisoner am being led to Rome. I salute the holy bishop Polycarp; I salute the holy bishop Vitalius, and the sacred presbytery, and my fellow-servants the deacons; in whose stead may my soul be found. Once more I bid farewell to the bishop, and to the presbyters in the Lord. If any one celebrates the passover along with the Jews, or receives the emblems of their feast, he is a partaker with those that killed the Lord and His apostles.

CHAP. XV.—SALUTATIONS. CONCLUSION.

Philo and Agathopus the deacons salute you. I salute the company of virgins, and the order of widows; of whom may I have joy! I salute the people of the Lord, from the least unto the greatest. I have sent you this letter through Euphanius the reader, a man honoured of God, and very faithful, happening to meet with him at Rhegium, just as he was going on board ship. Remember my bonds,[8] that I may be made perfect in Christ. Fare ye well in the flesh, the soul, and the spirit, while ye think of things perfect, and turn yourselves away from the workers of iniquity, who corrupt the word of truth, and are strengthened inwardly by the grace of our Lord Jesus Christ.

---

[1] Deut. vi. 16.
[2] Luke iv. 6.
[3] Matt. iv. 9.
[4] Or, "belly."
[5] Or, "that always needs whipping."
[6] Matt. iv. 10.
[7] Matt. iv. 10; Deut. vi. 13.
[8] Comp. Col. iv. 18.

THE EPISTLE OF MARIA THE PROSELYTE TO IGNATIUS

MARY OF CASSOBELÆ[1] TO IGNATIUS.

Maria, a proselyte of Jesus Christ, to Ignatius Theophorus, most blessed bishop of the apostolic Church which is at Antioch, beloved in God the Father, and Jesus: Happiness and safety. We all[2] beg for thee joy and health in Him.

CHAP. I. — OCCASION OF THE EPISTLE.

Since Christ has, to our wonder,[3] been made known among us to be the Son of the living God, and to have become man in these last times by means of the Virgin Mary,[4] of the seed of David and Abraham, according to the announcements previously made regarding Him and through Him by the company of the prophets, we therefore beseech and entreat that, by thy wisdom, Maris our friend, bishop of our native Neapolis,[5] which is near Zarbus,[6] and Eulogius, and Sobelus the presbyter, be sent to us, that we be not destitute of such as preside over the divine word; as Moses also says, "Let the Lord God look out a man who shall guide this people, and the congregation of the Lord shall not be as sheep which have no shepherd."[7]

CHAP. II. — YOUTH MAY BE ALLIED WITH PIETY AND DISCRETION.

But as to those whom we have named being young men, do not, thou blessed one, have any apprehension. For I would have you know that they are wise about the flesh, and are insensible to its passions, they themselves glowing with all the glory of a hoary head through their own[8] intrinsic merits, and though but recently called as young men to the priesthood.[9] Now, call thou into exercise[10] thy thoughts through the Spirit that God has given to thee by Christ, and thou wilt remember[11] that Samuel, while yet a little child, was called a seer, and was reckoned in the company of the prophets, that he reproved the aged Eli for transgression, since he had honoured his infatuated sons above God the author of all things, and had allowed them to go unpunished, when they turned the office of the priesthood into ridicule, and acted violently towards thy people.

CHAP. III. — EXAMPLES OF YOUTHFUL DEVOTEDNESS.

Moreover, the wise Daniel, while he was a young man, passed judgment on certain vigorous old men,[12] showing them that they were abandoned wretches, and not [worthy to be reckoned] elders, and that, though Jews by extraction, they were Canaanites in practice. And Jeremiah, when on account of his youth he declined the office of a prophet entrusted to him by God, was addressed in these words: "Say not, I am a youth; for thou shalt go to all those to whom I send thee, and thou shalt speak according to all that I command thee; because I am with thee."[13] And the wise Solomon, when only in the twelfth year of his age,[14] had wisdom to decide the important question concerning the children of the two women,[15] when it was unknown to whom these respectively belonged; so that the whole people were astonished at such wisdom in a child, and venerated him as being not a mere youth, but a full-grown man. And he solved the hard questions of the queen of the Ethiopians, which had profit in them as the streams of the Nile [have fertility], in such a manner that that woman,

---

[1] Nothing can be said with certainty as to the place here referred to. Some have conceived that the ordinary reading, *Maria Cassobolita*, is incorrect, and that it should be changed to *Maria Castabalitis*, supposing the reference to be to Castabala, a well-known city of Cilicia. But this and other proposed emendations rest upon mere conjecture.
[2] Some propose to read, "always."
[3] Or, "wonderfully."
[4] The MS. has, "and."
[5] The MS. has Ἠμελάπης, which Vossius and others deem a mistake for ἡμεδαπῆς, as translated above.
[6] The same as Azarbus (comp. Epist. to Hero, chap. ix.).
[7] Num. xxvii. 16, 17.
[8] Literally, "in themselves."
[9] Literally, "in recent newness of priesthood."
[10] Literally, "call up."
[11] Literally, "know."
[12] The ancient Latin version translates ὠμογέροντας "cruel old men," which perhaps suits the reference better.
[13] Jer. i. 7.
[14] Comp. for similar statements to those here made, Epistle to the Magnesians (longer), chap. iii.
[15] Literally, "understood the great question of the ignorance of the women respecting their children."

though herself so wise, was beyond measure astonished.[1]

CHAP. IV.— THE SAME SUBJECT CONTINUED.

Josiah also, beloved of God, when as yet he could scarcely speak articulately, convicts those who were possessed of a wicked spirit as being false in their speech, and deceivers of the people. He also reveals the deceit of the demons, and openly exposes those that are no gods; yea, while yet an infant he slays their priests, and overturns their altars, and defiles the place where sacrifices were offered with dead bodies, and throws down the temples, and cuts down the groves, and breaks in pieces the pillars, and breaks open the tombs of the ungodly, that not a relic of the wicked might any longer exist.[2] To such an extent did he display zeal in the cause of godliness, and prove himself a punisher of the ungodly, while he as yet faltered in speech like a child. David, too, who was at once a prophet and a king, and the root of our Saviour according to the flesh, while yet a youth is anointed by Samuel to be king.[3] For he himself says in a certain place, "I was small among my brethren, and the youngest in the house of my father." [4]

CHAP. V.— EXPRESSIONS OF RESPECT FOR IGNATIUS.

But time would fail me if I should endeavour to enumerate [5] all those that pleased God in their youth, having been entrusted by God with either the prophetical, the priestly, or the kingly office. And those which have been mentioned may suffice, by way of bringing the subject to thy remembrance. But I entreat thee not to reckon me presumptuous or ostentatious [in writing as I have done]. For I have set forth these statements, not as instructing thee, but simply as suggesting the matter to the remembrance of my father in God. For I know my own place,[6] and do not compare myself with such as you. I salute thy holy clergy, and thy Christ-loving people who are ruled under thy care as their pastor. All the faithful with us salute thee. Pray, blessed shepherd, that I may be in health as respects God.

---

[1] Literally, "out of herself."
[2] 2 Kings xxii. xxiii.
[3] 1 Sam. xvi.

[4] Ps. cl. 1 (in the Septuagint; not found at all in Hebrew).
[5] Literally, "to trace up."
[6] Literally, "measure" or "limits."

THE EPISTLE OF IGNATIUS TO MARY AT NEAPOLIS, NEAR ZARBUS.

Ignatius, who is also called Theophorus, to her who has obtained mercy through the grace of the most high God the Father, and Jesus Christ the Lord, who died for us, to Mary, my daughter, most faithful, worthy of God, and bearing Christ [in her heart], wishes abundance of happiness in God.

CHAP. I. — ACKNOWLEDGMENT OF HER EXCELLENCE AND WISDOM.

SIGHT indeed is better than writing, inasmuch as, being one[1] of the company of the senses, it not only, by communicating proofs of friendship, honours him who receives them, but also, by those which it in turn receives, enriches the desire for better things. But the second harbour of refuge, as the phrase runs, is the practice of writing, which we have received, as a convenient haven, by thy faith, from so great a distance, seeing that by means of a letter we have learned the excellence that is in thee. For the souls of the good, O thou wisest[2] of women! resemble fountains of the purest water; for they allure by their beauty passers-by to drink of them, even though these should not be thirsty. And thy intelligence invites us, as by a word of command, to participate in those divine draughts which gush forth so abundantly in thy soul.

CHAP. II. — HIS OWN CONDITION.

But I, O thou blessed woman, not being now so much my own master as in the power of others, am driven along by the varying wills of many adversaries,[3] being in one sense in exile, in another in prison, and in a third in bonds. But I pay no regard to these things. Yea, by the injuries inflicted on me through them, I acquire all the more the character of a disciple, that I may attain to Jesus Christ. May I enjoy the torments which are prepared for me, seeing that "the sufferings of this present time are not worthy [to be compared] with the glory which shall be revealed in us."[4]

CHAP. III. — HE HAD COMPLIED WITH HER REQUEST.

I have gladly acted as requested in thy letter,[5] having no doubt respecting those persons whom thou didst prove to be men of worth. For I am sure that thou barest testimony to them in the exercise of a godly judgment,[6] and not through the influence of carnal favour. And thy numerous quotations of Scripture passages exceedingly delighted me, which, when I had read, I had no longer a single doubtful thought respecting the matter. For I did not hold that those things were simply to be glanced over by my eyes, of which I had received from thee such an incontrovertible demonstration. May I be in place of thy soul, because thou lovest Jesus, the Son of the living God. Wherefore also He Himself says to thee, "I love them that love Me; and those that seek Me shall find peace."[7]

CHAP. IV. — COMMENDATION AND EXHORTATION.

Now it occurs to me to mention, that the report is true which I heard of thee whilst thou wast at Rome with the blessed father[8] Linus, whom the deservedly-blessed Clement, a hearer of Peter and Paul, has now succeeded. And by this time thou hast added a hundred-fold to thy reputation; and may thou, O woman! still further increase it. I greatly desired to come unto you, that I might have rest with you; but "the way of man is not in himself."[9] For the military guard [under which I am kept] hinders my purpose, and does not permit me to go further. Nor indeed, in the state I am now in, can I either do or suffer anything. Wherefore deeming the practice of writing the second resource

---

[1] Literally, "a part."
[2] Literally, "all-wise."
[3] Literally, "by the many wills of the adversaries."
[4] Rom. viii. 18.
[5] Literally, "I have gladly fulfilled the things commanded by thee in the letter."
[6] Literally, "by a judgment of God."
[7] Prov. viii. 17 (loosely quoted from LXX.).
[8] The original is πάπα,]common to primitive bishops.]
[9] Jer. x. 23.

of friends for their mutual encouragement, I salute thy sacred soul, beseeching of thee to add still further to thy vigour. For our present labour is but little, while the reward which is expected is great.

CHAP. V.—SALUTATIONS AND GOOD WISHES.

Avoid those that deny the passion of Christ, and His birth according to the flesh: and there are many at present who suffer under this disease. But it would be absurd to admonish thee on other points, seeing that thou art perfect in every good work and word, and able also to exhort others in Christ. Salute all that are like-minded with thyself, and who hold fast to their salvation in Christ. The presbyters and deacons, and above all the holy Hero, salute thee. Cassian my host salutes thee, as well as my sister, his wife, and their very dear children. May the Lord sanctify thee for evermore in the enjoyment both of bodily and spiritual health, and may I see thee in Christ obtaining the crown!

THE EPISTLE OF IGNATIUS TO ST. JOHN THE APOSTLE

Ignatius, and the brethren who are with him, to John the holy presbyter.

WE are deeply grieved at thy delay in strengthening us by thy addresses and consolations. If thy absence be prolonged, it will disappoint many of us. Hasten then to come, for we believe that it is expedient. There are also many of our women here, who are desirous to see Mary [the mother] of Jesus, and wish day by day to run off from us to you, that they may meet with her, and touch those breasts of hers which nourished the Lord Jesus, and may inquire of her respecting some rather secret matters. But Salome also, [the daughter of Anna,] whom thou lovest, who stayed with her five months at Jerusalem, and some other well-known persons, relate that she is full of all graces and all virtues, after the manner of a virgin, fruitful in virtue and grace. And, as they report, she is cheerful in persecutions and afflictions, free from murmuring in the midst of penury and want, grateful to those that injure her, and rejoices when exposed to troubles: she sympathizes with the wretched and the afflicted as sharing in their afflictions, and is not slow to come to their assistance. Moreover, she shines forth gloriously as contending in the fight of faith against the pernicious conflicts of vicious[1] principles or conduct. She is the lady of our new religion and repentance,[2] and the handmaid among the faithful of all works of piety. She is indeed devoted to the humble, and she humbles herself more devotedly than the devoted, and is wonderfully magnified by all, while at the same time she suffers detraction from the Scribes and Pharisees. Besides these points, many relate to us numerous other things regarding her. We do not, however, go so far as to believe all in every particular; nor do we mention such to thee. But, as we are informed by those who are worthy of credit, there is in Mary the mother of Jesus an angelic purity of nature allied with the nature of humanity.[3] And such reports as these have greatly excited our emotions, and urge us eagerly to desire a sight of this (if it be lawful so to speak) heavenly prodigy and most sacred marvel. But do thou in haste comply with this our desire; and fare thou well. Amen.

---

[1] Literally, "of vices."
[2] Some MSS. and editions seem with propriety to omit this word.
[3] Literally, "a nature of angelic purity is allied to human nature."

A SECOND EPISTLE OF IGNATIUS TO ST. JOHN

His friend[1] Ignatius to John the holy presbyter.

IF thou wilt give me leave, I desire to go up to Jerusalem, and see the faithful[2] saints who are there, especially Mary the mother, whom they report to be an object of admiration and of affection to all. For who would not rejoice to behold and to address her who bore the true God from her[3] own womb, provided he is a friend of our faith and religion? And in like manner [I desire to see] the venerable James, who is surnamed Just, whom they relate to be very like Christ Jesus in appearance,[4] in life, and in method of conduct, as if he were a twin-brother of the same womb. They say that, if I see him, I see also Jesus Himself, as to all the features and aspect of His body. Moreover, [I desire to see] the other saints, both male and female. Alas! why do I delay? Why am I kept back? Kind[5] teacher, bid me hasten [to fulfil my wish], and fare thou well. Amen.

---

[1] Literally, "his own."
[2] Some omit this word.
[3] Literally, "of herself." Some read, instead of "*de se*," "*deorum*," when the translation will be, "the true God of gods."
[4] Or, "face." Some omit the word.
[5] Or, "good."

THE EPISTLE OF IGNATIUS TO THE VIRGIN MARY

Her friend[1] Ignatius to the Christ-bearing Mary.

THOU oughtest to have comforted and consoled me who am a neophyte, and a disciple of thy [beloved] John. For I have heard things wonderful to tell respecting thy [son] Jesus, and I am astonished by such a report. But I desire with my whole heart to obtain information concerning the things which I have heard from thee, who wast always intimate and allied with Him, and who wast acquainted with [all] His secrets. I have also written to thee at another time, and have asked thee concerning the same things. Fare thou well; and let the neophytes who are with me be comforted of thee, and by thee, and in thee. Amen.

---

[1] Literally, "her own." [Mary is here called χριστοτόκος, and not θεοτόκος, which suggests a Nestorian forgery.]

REPLY OF THE BLESSED VIRGIN TO THIS LETTER.

The lowly handmaid of Christ Jesus to Ignatius, her beloved fellow-disciple.

THE things which thou hast heard and learned from John concerning Jesus are true. Believe them, cling to them, and hold fast the profession of that Christianity which thou hast embraced, and conform thy habits and life to thy profession. Now I will come in company with John to visit thee, and those that are with thee. Stand fast in the faith,[2] and show thyself a man; nor let the fierceness of persecution move thee, but let thy spirit be strong and rejoice in God thy Saviour.[3] Amen.

---

[2] 1 Cor. xvi. 13.
[3] Luke i. 47.

INTRODUCTORY NOTE
TO THE
MARTYRDOM OF IGNATIUS

THE learned dissertation of Pearson, on the difficulties of reconciling the supposed year of the martyrdom with the history of Trajan, etc., is given entire in Jacobson (vol. ii. p. 524), against the decision of Usher for A.D. 107. Pearson accepts A.D. 116. Consult also the preface of Dr. Thomas Smith,[1] in the same work (p. 518), on the text of the original and of the Latin versions, and on the credibility of the narrative. Our learned translators seem to think the text they have used, to be without interpolation. If the simple-minded faithful of those days, so near the age of miracles, appear to us, in some degree, enthusiasts, let us remember the vision of Col. Gardiner, accredited by Doddridge, Lord Lyttleton's vision (see Boswell, *anno* 1784, chap. xi.), accepted by Johnson and his contemporaries, and the interesting narrative of the pious Mr. Tennent of New Jersey, attested by so many excellent and intelligent persons, almost of our own times.

The following is the INTRODUCTORY NOTICE of the translators: —

THE following account of the martyrdom of Ignatius professes, in several passages, to have been written by those who accompanied him on his voyage to Rome, and were present on the occasion of his death (chaps. v. vi. vii.). And if the genuineness of this narrative, as well as of the Ignatian Epistles, be admitted, there can be little doubt that the persons in question were Philo and Agathopus, with Crocus perhaps, all of whom are mentioned by Ignatius (*Epist. to Smyr.*, chap. x.; *to Philad.*, chap. xi.; *to Rom.*, chap. x.) as having attended him on that journey to Rome which resulted in his martyrdom. But doubts have been started, by Daille and others, as to the date and authorship of this account. Some of these rest upon internal considerations, but the weightiest objection is found in the fact that no reference to this narrative is to be traced during the first six centuries of our era.[2] This is certainly a very suspicious circumstance, and may well give rise to some hesitation in ascribing the authorship to the immediate companions and friends of Ignatius. On the other hand, however, this account of the death of Ignatius is in perfect harmony with the particulars recounted by Eusebius and Chrysostom regarding him. Its comparative simplicity, too, is greatly in its favour. It makes no reference to the legends which by and by connected themselves with the name of Ignatius. As is well known, he came in course of time to be identified with the child whom Christ (Matt. xviii. 2) set before His disciples as a pattern of humility. It was said that the Saviour took him up in His arms, and that hence Ignatius

---

[1] He published an edition of Ignatius, Oxford, 1709.
[2] [A most remarkable statement. "References" may surely be *traced*, at least in Eusebius (iii. 36) and Irenæus (*Adv. Hares.* v. 28), if not in Jerome, etc. But the sermon of St. Chrysostom (Opp. ii., 593) seems almost, in parts, a paraphrase.]

derived his name of *Theophorus;*[1] that is, according to the explanation which this legend gives of the word, *one carried by God.* But in chap. ii. of the following narrative we find the term explained to mean, "one who has Christ in his breast;" and this simple explanation, with the entire silence preserved as to the marvels afterwards connected with the name of Ignatius, is certainly a strong argument in favour of the early date and probable genuineness of the account. Some critics, such as Usher and Grabe, have reckoned the latter part of the narrative spurious, while accepting the former; but there appears to be a unity about it which requires us either to accept it *in toto*, or to reject it altogether.[2]

---

[1] [See on this matter Jacobson's note (vol. ii. p. 262), and reference to Pearson (*Vind. Ignat.*, part ii. cap. 12). The false accentuation (Θεόφορος) occurs in some copies to support the myth of the child Ignatius as the *God-borne* instead of the *God-bearing;* i.e., carried by Christ, instead of carrying the Spirit of Christ within.]

[2] [But see the note in Jacobson, vol. ii. p. 557.]

THE MARTYRDOM OF IGNATIUS

CHAP. I. — DESIRE OF IGNATIUS FOR MARTYRDOM.

When Trajan, not long since,[1] succeeded to the empire of the Romans, Ignatius, the disciple of John the apostle, a man in all respects of an apostolic character, governed the Church of the Antiochians with great care, having with difficulty escaped the former storms of the many persecutions under Domitian, inasmuch as, like a good pilot, by the helm of prayer and fasting, by the earnestness of his teaching, and by his [constant[2]] spiritual labour, he resisted the flood that rolled against him, fearing [only] lest he should lose any of those who were deficient in courage, or apt to suffer from their simplicity.[3] Wherefore he rejoiced over the tranquil state of the Church, when the persecution ceased for a little time, but was grieved as to himself, that he had not yet attained to a true love to Christ, nor reached the perfect rank of a disciple. For he inwardly reflected, that the confession which is made by martyrdom, would bring him into a yet more intimate relation to the Lord. Wherefore, continuing a few years longer with the Church, and, like a divine lamp, enlightening every one's understanding by his expositions of the [Holy[4]] Scriptures, he [at length] attained the object of his desire.

CHAP. II. — IGNATIUS IS CONDEMNED BY TRAJAN.

For Trajan, in the ninth[5] year of his reign, being lifted up [with pride], after the victory he had gained over the Scythians and Dacians, and many other nations, and thinking that the religious body of the Christians were yet wanting to complete the subjugation of all things to himself, and [thereupon] threatening them with persecution unless they should agree to[6] worship dæmons, as did all other nations, thus compelled[7] all who were living godly lives either to sacrifice [to idols] or die. Wherefore the noble soldier of Christ [Ignatius], being in fear for the Church of the Antiochians, was, in accordance with his own desire, brought before Trajan, who was at that time staying at Antioch, but was in haste [to set forth] against Armenia and the Parthians. And when he was set before the emperor Trajan, [that prince] said unto him, "Who art thou, wicked wretch,[8] who settest[9] thyself to transgress our commands, and persuadest others to do the same, so that they should miserably perish?" Ignatius replied, "No one ought to call Theophorus[10] wicked; for all evil spirits[11] have departed from the servants of God. But if, because I am an enemy to these [spirits], you call me wicked in respect to them, I quite agree with you; for inasmuch as I have Christ the King of heaven [within me], I destroy all the devices of these [evil spirits]." Trajan answered, "And who is Theophorus?" Ignatius replied, "He who has Christ within his breast." Trajan said, "Do *we* not then seem to you to have the gods in our mind, whose assistance we enjoy in fighting against our enemies?" Ignatius answered, "Thou art in error when thou callest the dæmons of the nations gods. For there is but one God, who made heaven, and earth, and the sea, and all that are in them; and one Jesus Christ, the only-begotten Son of God, whose kingdom may I enjoy." Trajan said, "Do you mean Him who was crucified under Pontius Pilate?" Ignatius replied, "I mean Him who crucified my sin, with him who was the inventor of it,[12] and who has condemned [and cast down] all the deceit and malice of the devil under the feet of those who carry Him in their heart." Trajan said, "Dost thou then carry within thee Him that was crucified?" Ignatius replied, "Truly so; for it is written, 'I will dwell in them, and walk in

---

[1] The date of Trajan's accession was A.D. 98.
[2] The text here is somewhat doubtful.
[3] Literally, "any of the faint-hearted and more guileless."
[4] This word is of doubtful authority.
[5] The numeral is uncertain. In the old Latin version we find "the fourth," which Grabe has corrected into the nineteenth. The choice lies between "ninth" and "nineteenth," i.e., A.D 107 or 116.
[6] Literally, "would choose to submit to."
[7] Some read, "fear compelled."

[8] Literally, "evil-dæmon."
[9] Literally, "art zealous."
[10] Or, "one who carries God."
[11] Literally, "the dæmons."
[12] The Latin version reads, "Him who bore my sin, with its inventor, upon the cross."

them.'"¹ Then Trajan pronounced sentence as follows: "We command that Ignatius, who affirms that he carries about within him Him that was crucified, be bound by soldiers, and carried to the great [city] Rome, there to be devoured by the beasts, for the gratification of the people." When the holy martyr heard this sentence, he cried out with joy, "I thank thee, O Lord, that Thou hast vouchsafed to honour me with a perfect love towards Thee, and hast made me to be bound with iron chains, like² Thy Apostle Paul." Having spoken thus, he then, with delight, clasped the chains about him; and when he had first prayed for the Church, and commended it with tears to the Lord, he was hurried away by the savage³ cruelty of the soldiers, like a distinguished ram,⁴ the leader of a goodly flock, that he might be carried to Rome, there to furnish food to the bloodthirsty beasts.

CHAP. III. — IGNATIUS SAILS TO SMYRNA.

Wherefore, with great alacrity and joy, through his desire to suffer, he came down from Antioch to Seleucia, from which place he set sail. And after a great deal of suffering he came to Smyrna, where he disembarked with great joy, and hastened to see the holy Polycarp, [formerly] his fellow-disciple, and [now] bishop of Smyrna. For they had both, in old times, been disciples of St. John the Apostle. Being then brought to him, and having communicated to him some spiritual gifts, and glorying in his bonds, he entreated of him to labour⁵ along with him for the fulfilment of his desire; earnestly indeed asking this of the whole Church (for the cities and Churches of Asia had welcomed⁶ the holy man through their bishops, and presbyters, and deacons, all hastening to meet him, if by any means they might receive from him some⁷ spiritual gift), but above all, the holy Polycarp, that, by means of the wild beasts, he soon disappearing from this world, might be manifested before the face of Christ.

CHAP. IV. — IGNATIUS WRITES TO THE CHURCHES.

And these things he thus spake, and thus testified, extending his love to Christ so far as one who was about to⁸ secure heaven through his good confession, and the earnestness of those who joined their prayers to his in regard to his [approaching] conflict; and to give a recompense to the Churches, who came to meet him through their rulers, sending⁹ letters of thanksgiving to them, which dropped spiritual grace, along with prayer and exhortation. Wherefore, seeing all men so kindly affected towards him, and fearing lest the love of the brotherhood should hinder his zeal towards the Lord,¹⁰ while a fair door of suffering martyrdom was opened to him, he wrote to the Church of the Romans the Epistle which is here subjoined.

(See the Epistle as formerly given.)

CHAP. V. — IGNATIUS IS BROUGHT TO ROME.

Having therefore, by means of this Epistle, settled,¹¹ as he wished, those of the brethren at Rome who were unwilling [for his martyrdom]; and setting sail from Smyrna (for Christophorus was pressed by the soldiers to hasten to the public spectacles in the mighty [city] Rome, that, being given up to the wild beasts in the sight of the Roman people, he might attain to the crown for which he strove), he [next] landed at Troas. Then, going on from that place to Neapolis, he went [on foot] by Philippi through Macedonia, and on to that part of Epirus which is near Epidamnus; and finding a ship in one of the seaports, he sailed over the Adriatic Sea, and entering from it on the Tyrrhene, he passed by the various islands and cities, until, when Puteoli came in sight, he was eager there to disembark, having a desire to tread in the footsteps of the Apostle Paul.¹² But a violent wind arising did not suffer him to do so, the ship being driven rapidly forwards;¹³ and, simply expressing his delight¹⁴ over the love of the brethren in that place, he sailed by. Wherefore, continuing to enjoy fair winds, we were reluctantly hurried on in one day and a night, mourning [as we did] over the coming departure from us of this righteous man. But to him this happened just as he wished, since he was in haste as soon as possible to leave this world, that he might attain to the Lord whom he loved. Sailing then into the Roman harbour, and the unhallowed sports being just about to close, the soldiers began to be annoyed at our slowness, but the bishop rejoicingly yielded to their urgency.

CHAP. VI. — IGNATIUS IS DEVOURED BY THE BEASTS AT ROME.

They pushed forth therefore from the place which is called Portus;¹⁵ and (the¹⁶ fame of all relating to the holy martyr being already spread

---
¹ 2 Cor. vi. 16.
² Literally, "with."
³ Or, "beast-like."
⁴ [Better, "like the noble leader," etc.; remitting κριὸς to the margin, as an ignoble word to English ears.]
⁵ It is doubtful if this clause should be referred to Polycarp.
⁶ Or, "received."
⁷ Literally, "a portion of."
⁸ The Latin version has, "that he was to." [But compare the martyr's Epistle to the Romans (cap. 5), "yet am I not thereby justified," — a double reference to St. Paul's doctrine, 1 Cor. iv. 4 and xiii. 3. See also his quotation (*Sept.*, Prov. xviii. 17). Epistle to Magnesians, cap. 12.]

⁹ The punctuation and construction are here doubtful.
¹⁰ Or, "should prevent him from hastening to the Lord."
¹¹ Or, "corrected."
¹² Comp. Acts xxviii. 13, 14.
¹³ Literally, "the ship being driven onwards from the stern."
¹⁴ Literally, "declaring happy."
¹⁵ [Of which we shall learn more when we come to Hippolytus. Trajan had just improved the work of Claudius at this haven, near Ostia.]
¹⁶ Literally, "for the."

abroad) we met the brethren full of fear and joy; rejoicing indeed because they were thought worthy to meet with Theophorus, but struck with fear because so eminent a man was being led to death. Now he enjoined some to keep silence who, in their fervent zeal, were saying[1] that they would appease the people, so that they should not demand the destruction of this just one. He being immediately aware of this through the Spirit,[2] and having saluted them all, and begged of them to show a true affection towards him, and having dwelt [on this point] at greater length than in his Epistle,[3] and having persuaded them not to envy him hastening to the Lord, he then, after he had, with all the brethren kneeling [beside him], entreated the Son of God in behalf of the Churches, that a stop might be put to the persecution, and that mutual love might continue among the brethren, was led with all haste into the amphitheatre. Then, being immediately thrown in, according to the command of Cæsar given some time ago, the public spectacles being just about to close (for it was then a solemn day, as they deemed it, being that which is called the thirteenth[4] in the Roman tongue, on which the people were wont to assemble in more than ordinary numbers[5]), he was thus cast to the wild beasts close beside the temple,[6] that so by them the desire of the holy martyr Ignatius should be fulfilled, according to that which is written, "The desire of the righteous is acceptable[7] [to God]," to the effect that he might not be troublesome to any of the brethren by the gathering of his remains, even as he had in his Epistle expressed a wish beforehand that so his end might be. For only the harder portions of his holy remains were left, which were conveyed to Antioch and wrapped[8] in linen, as an inestimable treasure left to the holy Church by the grace which was in the martyr.

CHAP. VII. — IGNATIUS APPEARS IN A VISION AFTER HIS DEATH.

Now these things took place on the thirteenth day before the Kalends of January, that is, on the twentieth of December,[9] Sura and Senecio being then the consuls of the Romans for the second time. Having ourselves been eye-witnesses of these things, and having spent the whole night in tears within the house, and having entreated the Lord, with bended knees and much prayer, that He would give us weak men full assurance respecting the things which were done,[10] it came to pass, on our falling into a brief slumber, that some of us saw the blessed Ignatius suddenly standing by us and embracing us, while others beheld him again praying for us, and others still saw him dropping with sweat, as if he had just come from his great labour, and standing by the Lord. When, therefore, we had with great joy witnessed these things, and had compared our several visions[11] together, we sang praise to God, the giver of all good things, and expressed our sense of the happiness of the holy [martyr]; and now we have made known to you both the day and the time [when these things happened], that, assembling ourselves together according to the time of his martyrdom, we may have fellowship with the champion and noble martyr of Christ, who trode under foot the devil, and perfected the course which, out of love to Christ, he had desired, in Christ Jesus our Lord; by whom, and with whom, be glory and power to the Father, with the Holy Spirit, for evermore! Amen.

---

[1] Literally, "boiling, and saying."
[2] Or, "in spirit."
[3] i.e., in his Epistle to the Romans.
[4] The Saturnalia were then celebrated.
[5] Literally, "they came together zealously."
[6] The amphitheatre itself was sacred to several of the gods. [But (παρὰ τῷ ναῷ) the original indicates the *cella*, or shrine, in the centre of the amphitheatre where the image of Pluto was exhibited. A plain cross, until the late excavations, marked the very spot.]
[7] Prov. x. 24.

[8] Or, "deposited."
[9] [The Greeks celebrate this martyrdom, to this day, on the twentieth of December.]
[10] To the effect, viz., that the martyrdom of Ignatius had been acceptable to God.
[11] Literally, "the visions of the dreams."

INTRODUCTORY NOTE

TO THE

EPISTLE OF BARNABAS

[A.D. 100.] The writer of this Epistle is supposed to have been an Alexandrian Jew of the times of Trajan and Hadrian. He was a layman; but possibly he bore the name of "Barnabas," and so has been confounded with his holy and apostolic name-sire. It is more probable that the Epistle, being anonymous, was attributed to St. Barnabas, by those who supposed that apostle to be the author of the Epistle to the Hebrews, and who discovered similarities in the plan and purpose of the two works. It is with great reluctance that I yield to modern scholars, in dismissing the ingenious and temperate argument of Archbishop Wake[1] for the apostolic origin of this treatise. The learned Lardner[2] shares his convictions; and the very interesting and ingenious views of Jones[3] never appeared to me satisfactory, weighed with preponderating arguments, on the other side.[4]

The Maccabæan spirit of the Jews never burned more furiously than after the destruction of Jerusalem, and while it was kindling the conflagration that broke out under Barchochebas, and blazed so terribly in the insurrection against Hadrian.[5] It is not credible that the Jewish Christians at Alexandria and elsewhere were able to emancipate themselves from their national spirit; and accordingly the old Judaizing, which St. Paul had anathematized and confuted, would assert itself again. If such was the occasion of this Epistle, as I venture to suppose, a higher character must be ascribed to it than could otherwise be claimed. This accounts, also, for the degree of favour with which it was accepted by the primitive faithful.

It is interesting as a specimen of their conflicts with a persistent Judaism which St. Paul had defeated and anathematized, but which was ever cropping out among believers originally of the Hebrews.[6] Their own habits of allegorizing, and their Oriental tastes, must be borne in mind, if we are readily disgusted with our author's fancies and refinements. St. Paul himself pays a practical tribute to their modes of thought, in his Epistle to the Galatians (iv. 24). This is the *ad hominem* form of rhetoric, familiar to all speakers, which laid even the apostle open to the slander of enemies (2 Cor. xii. 16), — that he was "crafty," and caught men with guile. It is interesting to note the more Occidental spirit of Cyprian, as compared with our author, when he also contends with Judaism. Doubtless we have in the pseudo-Barnabas something of that *œconomy* which

---

[1] Discourse (p. 148) to his *Genuine Epistles of the Apostolical Fathers.* Philadelphia, 1846.
[2] Works, ii. 250, note; and iv. 128.
[3] On the Canon, vol. ii. p. 431.
[4] To those who may adhere to the older opinion, let me commend the eloquent and instructive chapter (xxiii.) in Farrar's *Life of St. Paul.*
[5] Hadrian's purpose to rebuild their city seems to be pointed at in chap. xvi.
[6] M. Renan may be read with pain, and yet with profit, in much that his Gallio-spirit suggests on this subject. Chap. v., *St. Paul,* Paris, 1884.

is always capable of abuse, and which was destined too soon to overleap the bounds of its moral limitations.

It is to be observed that this writer sometimes speaks as a Gentile, a fact which some have found it difficult to account for, on the supposition that he was a Hebrew, if not a Levite as well. But so, also, St. Paul sometimes speaks as a Roman, and sometimes as a Jew; and, owing to the mixed character of the early Church, he writes to the Romans (iv. 1) as if they were all Israelites, and again to the same Church (Rom. xi. 13) as if they were all Gentiles. So this writer sometimes identifies himself with Jewish thought as a son of Abraham, and again speaks from the Christian position as if he were a Gentile, thus identifying himself with the catholicity of the Church.

But the subject thus opened is vast; and "the Epistle of Barnabas," so called, still awaits a critical editor, who at the same time shall be a competent expositor. Nobody can answer these requisitions, who is unable, for this purpose, to be a Christian of the days of Trajan.

But it will be observed that this version has great advantages over any of its predecessors, and is a valuable acquisition to the student. The learned translators have had before them the entire Greek text of the fourth century, disfigured it is true by corruptions, but still very precious, the rather as they have been able to compare it with the text of Hilgenfeld. Their editorial notes are sufficient for our own plan; and little has been left for me to do, according to the scheme of this publication, save to revise the "copy" for printing. I am glad to presume no further into such a labyrinth, concerning which the learned and careful Wake modestly professes, "I have endeavoured to attain to the sense of my author, and to make him as plain and easy as I was able. If in anything I have chanced to mistake him, I have only this to say for myself: that he must be better acquainted with the road than I pretend to be, who will undertake to travel so long a journey in the dark and never to miss his way."

The following is the original INTRODUCTORY NOTICE: —

NOTHING certain is known as to the author of the following Epistle. The writer's name is Barnabas, but scarcely any scholars now ascribe it to the illustrious friend and companion of St. Paul. External and internal evidence here come into direct collision. The ancient writers who refer to this Epistle unanimously attribute it to Barnabas the Levite, of Cyprus, who held such an honourable place in the infant Church. Clement of Alexandria does so again and again (*Strom.*, ii. 6, ii. 7, etc.). Origen describes it as "a Catholic Epistle" (*Cont. Cels.*, i. 63), and seems to rank it among the Sacred Scriptures (*Comm. in Rom.*, i. 24). Other statements have been quoted from the fathers, to show that they held this to be an authentic production of the apostolic Barnabas; and certainly no other name is ever hinted at in Christian antiquity as that of the writer. But notwithstanding this, the internal evidence is now generally regarded as conclusive against this opinion. On perusing the Epistle, the reader will be in circumstances to judge of this matter for himself. He will be led to consider whether the spirit and tone of the writing, as so decidedly opposed to all respect for Judaism — the numerous inaccuracies which it contains with respect to Mosaic enactments and observances — the absurd and trifling interpretations of Scripture which it suggests — and the many silly vaunts of superior knowledge in which its writer indulges — can possibly comport with its ascription to the fellow-labourer of St. Paul. When it is remembered that no one ascribes the Epistle to the apostolic Barnabas till the times of Clement of Alexandria, and that it is ranked by Eusebius among the "spurious" writings, which, however much known and read in the Church, were never regarded as authoritative, little doubt can remain that the external evidence is of itself weak, and should not make us hesitate for a moment in refusing to ascribe this writing to Barnabas the Apostle.

The date, object, and intended readers of the Epistle can only be doubtfully inferred from some statements which it contains. It was clearly written after the destruction of Jerusalem, since reference is made to that event (chap. xvi.), but how long after is matter of much dispute. The general opinion is, that its date is not later than the middle of the second century, and that it cannot be placed earlier than some twenty or thirty years before. In point of style, both as respects thought and expression, a very low place must be assigned it. We know nothing certain of the region in which the author lived, or where the first readers were to be found. The intention of the writer, as he himself states (chap. i.), was "to perfect the knowledge" of those to whom he wrote. Hilgenfeld, who has devoted much attention to this Epistle, holds that "it was written at the close of the first century by a Gentile Christian of the school of Alexandria, with the view of winning back, or guarding from a Judaic form of Christianity, those Christians belonging to the same class as himself."

Until the recent discovery of the Codex Sinaiticus by Tischendorf, the first four and a half chapters were known only in an ancient Latin version. The whole Greek text is now happily recovered, though it is in many places very corrupt. We have compared its readings throughout, and noted the principal variations from the text represented in our version. We have also made frequent reference to the text adopted by **Hilgenfeld in his recent edition of the** Epistle (Lipsiæ, T. O. Weigel, 1866).

THE EPISTLE OF BARNABAS[1]

CHAP. I. — AFTER THE SALUTATION, THE WRITER DECLARES THAT HE WOULD COMMUNICATE TO HIS BRETHREN SOMETHING OF THAT WHICH HE HAD HIMSELF RECEIVED.

ALL hail, ye sons and daughters, in the name of our Lord[2] Jesus Christ, who loved us in peace.

Seeing that the divine fruits[3] of righteousness abound among you, I rejoice exceedingly and above measure in your happy and honoured spirits, because ye have with such effect received the engrafted[4] spiritual gift. Wherefore also I inwardly rejoice the more, hoping to be saved, because I truly perceive in you the Spirit poured forth from the rich Lord[5] of love. Your greatly desired appearance has thus filled me with astonishment over you.[6] I am therefore pursuaded of this, and fully convinced in my own mind, that since I began to speak among you I understand many things, because the Lord hath accompanied me in the way of righteousness. I am also on this account bound[7] by the strictest obligation to love you above my own soul, because great are the faith and love dwelling in you, while you hope for the life which He has promised.[8] Considering this, therefore, that if I should take the trouble to communicate to you some portion of what I have myself received, it will prove to me a sufficient reward that I minister to such spirits, I have hastened briefly to write unto you, in order that, along with your faith, ye might have perfect knowledge. The doctrines of the Lord, then, are three:[9] the hope of life, the beginning and the completion of it. For the Lord hath made known to us by the prophets both the things which are past and present, giving us also the first-fruits of the knowledge[10] of things to come, which things as we see accomplished, one by one, we ought with the greater richness of faith[11] and elevation of spirit to draw near to Him with reverence.[12] I then, not as your teacher, but as one of yourselves, will set forth a few things by which in present circumstances ye may be rendered the more joyful.

CHAP. II. — THE JEWISH SACRIFICES ARE NOW ABOLISHED.

Since, therefore, the days are evil, and Satan[13] possesses the power of this world, we ought to give heed to ourselves, and diligently inquire into the ordinances of the Lord. Fear and patience, then, are helpers of our faith; and long-suffering and continence are things which fight on our side. While these remain pure in what respects the Lord, Wisdom, Understanding, Science, and Knowledge rejoice along with them.[14] For He hath revealed to us by all the prophets that He needs neither sacrifices, nor burnt-offerings, nor oblations, saying thus, "What is the multitude of your sacrifices unto Me, saith the Lord? I am full of burnt-offerings, and desire not the fat of lambs, and the blood of bulls and goats, not when ye come to appear before

---

[1] The Codex Sinaiticus has simply "Epistle of Barnabas" for title; Dressel gives, "Epistle of Barnabas the Apostle," from the Vatican MS. of the Latin text.
[2] The Cod. Sin. has simply, "the Lord."
[3] Literally, "the judgments of God being great and rich towards you;" but, as Hefele remarks, δικαίωμα seems here to have the meaning of *righteousness*, as in Rom. v. 18.
[4] This appears to be the meaning of the Greek, and is confirmed by the ancient Latin version. Hilgenfeld, however, following Cod. Sin., reads "thus," instead of "because," and separates the clauses.
[5] The Latin reads, "a spirit infused into you from the honourable fountain of God."
[6] This sentence is entirely omitted in the Latin.
[7] The Latin text is here quite different, and seems evidently corrupt. We have followed the Cod. Sin., as does Hilgenfeld.
[8] Literally, "in the hope of His life."
[9] The Greek is here totally unintelligible: it seems impossible either to punctuate or construe it. We may attempt to represent it as follows: "The doctrines of the Lord, then, are three: Life, Faith, and Hope, our beginning and end; and Righteousness, the beginning and the end of judgment; Love and Joy and the Testimony of gladness for works of righteousness." We have followed the ancient Latin text, which Hilgenfeld also adopts, though Weitzäcker and others prefer the Greek.
[10] Instead of "knowledge" (γνώσεως), Cod. Sin. has "taste" (γεύσεως).
[11] Literally, "we ought more richly and loftily to approach His fear."
[12] Instead of "to Him with fear," the reading of Cod. Sin., the Latin has, "to His altar," which Hilgenfeld adopts.
[13] The Latin text is literally, "the adversary;" the Greek has, "and he that worketh possesseth power;" Hilgenfeld reads, "he that worketh against," the idea expressed above being intended.
[14] Or, "while these things continue, those which respect the Lord rejoice in purity along with them — Wisdom," etc.

Me: for who hath required these things at your hands? Tread no more My courts, not though ye bring with you fine flour. Incense is a vain abomination unto Me, and your new moons and sabbaths I cannot endure."[1] He has therefore abolished these things, that the new law of our Lord Jesus Christ, which is without the yoke of necessity, might have a human oblation.[2] And again He says to them, "Did I command your fathers, when they went out from the land of Egypt, to offer unto Me burnt-offerings and sacrifices? But this rather I commanded them, Let no one of you cherish any evil in his heart against his neighbour, and love not an oath of falsehood."[3] We ought therefore, being possessed of understanding, to perceive the gracious intention of our Father; for He speaks to us, desirous that we, not[4] going astray like them, should ask how we may approach Him. To us, then, He declares, "A sacrifice [pleasing] to God is a broken spirit; a smell of sweet savour to the Lord is a heart that glorifieth Him that made it."[5] We ought therefore, brethren, carefully to inquire concerning our salvation, lest the wicked one, having made his entrance by deceit, should hurl[6] us forth from our [true] life.

CHAP. III. — THE FASTS OF THE JEWS ARE NOT TRUE FASTS, NOR ACCEPTABLE TO GOD.

He says then to them again concerning these things, "Why do ye fast to Me as on this day, saith the Lord, that your voice should be heard with a cry? I have not chosen this fast, saith the Lord, that a man should humble his soul. Nor, though ye bend your neck like a ring, and put upon you sackcloth and ashes, will ye call it an acceptable fast."[7] To us He saith, "Behold, this is the fast that I have chosen, saith the Lord, not that a man should humble his soul, but that he should loose every band of iniquity, untie the fastenings of harsh agreements, restore to liberty them that are bruised, tear in pieces every unjust engagement, feed the hungry with thy bread, clothe the naked when thou seest him, bring the homeless into thy house, not despise the humble if thou behold him, and not [turn away] from the members of thine own family. Then shall thy dawn break forth, and thy healing shall quickly spring up, and righteousness shall go forth before thee, and the glory of God shall encompass thee; and then thou shalt call, and God shall hear thee; whilst thou art yet speaking, He shall say, Behold, I am with thee; if thou take away from thee the chain [binding others], and the stretching forth of the hands[8] [to swear falsely], and words of murmuring, and give cheerfully thy bread to the hungry, and show compassion to the soul that has been humbled."[9] To this end, therefore, brethren, He is long-suffering, foreseeing how the people whom He has prepared shall with guilelessness believe in His Beloved. For He revealed all these things to us beforehand, that we should not rush forward as rash acceptors of their laws.[10]

CHAP. IV. — ANTICHRIST IS AT HAND: LET US THEREFORE AVOID JEWISH ERRORS.

It therefore behoves us, who inquire much concerning events at hand,[11] to search diligently into those things which are able to save us. Let us then utterly flee from all the works of iniquity, lest these should take hold of us; and let us hate the error of the present time, that we may set our love on the world to come: let us not give loose reins to our soul, that it should have power to run with sinners and the wicked, lest we become like them. The final stumbling-block (or source of danger) approaches, concerning which it is written, as Enoch[12] says, "For for this end the Lord has cut short the times and the days, that His Beloved may hasten; and He will come to the inheritance." And the prophet also speaks thus: "Ten kingdoms shall reign upon the earth, and a little king shall rise up after them, who shall subdue under one three of the kings.[13] In like manner Daniel says concerning the same, "And I beheld the fourth beast, wicked and powerful, and more savage than all the beasts of the earth, and how from it sprang up ten horns, and out of them a little budding horn, and how it subdued under one three of the great horns."[14] Ye ought therefore to understand. And this also I further beg of you, as being one of you, and loving you both individually and collectively more than my own soul, to take heed now to yourselves, and not to be like some, adding largely to your sins, and saying, "The covenant is both theirs and ours."[15] But they thus finally lost it, after Moses had already received it. For the Scripture saith, "And Moses was fasting in

---

[1] Isa. i. 11–14, from the Sept., as is the case throughout. We have given the quotation as it stands in Cod. Sin.
[2] Thus in the Latin. The Greek reads, "might not have a man-made oblation." The Latin text seems preferable, implying that, instead of the outward sacrifices of the law, there is now required a dedication of *man himself*. Hilgenfeld follows the Greek.
[3] Jer. vii. 22; Zech. viii. 17.
[4] So the Greek. Hilgenfeld, with the Latin, omits "not."
[5] Ps. li. 19. There is nothing in Scripture corresponding to the last clause.
[6] Literally, "sling us out."
[7] Isa. lviii. 4, 5.
[8] The original here is χειροτονίαν, from the LXX. Hefele remarks, that it may refer to the stretching forth of the hands, either to swear falsely, or to mock and insult one's neighbour.
[9] Isa. lviii. 6–10.
[10] The Greek is here unintelligible: the Latin has, "that we should not rush on, as if proselytes to their law."
[11] Or it might be rendered, "things present." Cotelerius reads, "de his instantibus."
[12] The Latin reads "Daniel" instead of "Enoch;" comp. Dan. ix. 24–27.
[13] Dan. vii. 24, very loosely quoted.
[14] Dan. vii. 7, 8, also very inaccurately cited.
[15] We here follow the Latin text in preference to the Greek, which reads merely, "the covenant is ours." What follows seems to show the correctness of the Latin, as the author proceeds to deny that the Jews had any further interest in the promises.

the mount forty days and forty nights, and received the covenant from the Lord, tables of stone written with the finger of the hand of the Lord;"[1] but turning away to idols, they lost it. For the Lord speaks thus to Moses: "Moses, go down quickly; for the people whom thou hast brought out of the land of Egypt have transgressed."[2] And Moses understood [the meaning of God], and cast the two tables out of his hands; and their covenant was broken, in order that the covenant of the beloved Jesus might be sealed upon our heart, in the hope which flows from believing in Him.[3] Now, being desirous to write many things to you, not as your teacher, but as becometh one who loves you, I have taken care not to fail to write to you from what I myself possess, with a view to your purification.[4] We take earnest[5] heed in these last days; for the whole [past] time of your faith will profit you nothing, unless now in this wicked time we also withstand coming sources of danger, as becometh the sons of God. That the Black One[6] may find no means of entrance, let us flee from every vanity, let us utterly hate the works of the way of wickedness. Do not, by retiring apart, live a solitary life, as if you were already [fully] justified; but coming together in one place, make common inquiry concerning what tends to your general welfare. For the Scripture saith, "Woe to them who are wise to themselves, and prudent in their own sight!"[7] Let us be spiritually-minded: let us be a perfect temple to God. As much as in us lies, let us meditate upon the fear of God, and let us keep His commandments, that we may rejoice in His ordinances. The Lord will judge the world without respect of persons. Each will receive as he has done: if he is righteous, his righteousness will precede him; if he is wicked, the reward of wickedness is before him. Take heed, lest resting at our ease, as those who are the called [of God], we should fall asleep in our sins, and the wicked prince, acquiring power over us, should thrust us away from the kingdom of the Lord. And all the more attend to this, my brethren, when ye reflect and behold, that after so great signs and wonders were wrought in Israel, they were thus [at length] abandoned. Let us beware lest we be found [fulfilling that saying], as it is written, "Many are called, but few are chosen."[8]

CHAP. V.—THE NEW COVENANT, FOUNDED ON THE SUFFERINGS OF CHRIST, TENDS TO OUR SALVATION, BUT TO THE JEWS' DESTRUCTION.

For to this end the Lord endured to deliver up His flesh to corruption, that we might be sanctified through the remission of sins, which is effected by His blood of sprinkling. For it is written concerning Him, partly with reference to Israel, and partly to us; and [the Scripture] saith thus: "He was wounded for our transgressions, and bruised for our iniquities: with His stripes we are healed. He was brought as a sheep to the slaughter, and as a lamb which is dumb before its shearer."[9] Therefore we ought to be deeply grateful to the Lord, because He has both made known to us things that are past, and hath given us wisdom concerning things present, and hath not left us without understanding in regard to things which are to come. Now, the Scripture saith, "Not unjustly are nets spread out for birds."[10] This means that the man perishes justly, who, having a knowledge of the way of righteousness, rushes off into the way of darkness. And further, my brethren: if the Lord endured to suffer for our soul, He being Lord of all the world, to whom God said at the foundation of the world, "Let us make man after our image, and after our likeness,"[11] understand how it was that He endured to suffer at the hand of men. The prophets, having obtained grace from Him, prophesied concerning Him. And He (since it behoved Him to appear in flesh), that He might abolish death, and reveal the resurrection from the dead, endured [what and as He did], in order that He might fulfill the promise made unto the fathers, and by preparing a new people for Himself, might show, while He dwelt on earth, that He, when He has raised mankind, will also judge them. Moreover, teaching Israel, and doing so great miracles and signs, He preached [the truth] to him, and greatly loved him. But when He chose His own apostles who where to preach His Gospel, [He did so from among those] who were sinners above all sin, that He might show He came "not to call the righteous, but sinners to repentance."[12] Then He manifested Himself to be the Son of God. For if He had not come in the flesh, how could men have been saved by beholding Him?[13] Since looking upon

---

[1] Ex. xxxi. 18, xxxiv. 28.
[2] Ex. xxxii. 7; Deut. ix. 12.
[3] Literally, "in hope of His faith."
[4] The Greek is here incorrect and unintelligible; and as the Latin omits the clause, our translation is merely conjectural. Hilgenfeld's text, if we give a somewhat peculiar meaning to ἐλλιπεῖν, may be translated: "but as it is becoming in one who loves you not to fail in giving you what we ha e, I, though the very offscouring of you, have been eager to write to you"
[5] So the Cod. Sin. Hilgenfeld reads, with the Latin, "let us take."
[6] The Latin here departs entirely from the Greek text, and quotes as a saying of "the Son of God" the following precept, nowhere to be found in the New Testament: "Let us resist all iniquity, and hold it in hatred." Hilgenfeld joins this clause to the former sentence.
[7] Isa. v. 21.

[8] An exact quotation from Matt. xx. 16 or xxii. 14. It is worthy of notice that this is the first example in the writings of the Fathers of a citation from any book of the New Testament, preceded by the authoritative formula, "it is written."
[9] Isa. liii. 5, 7.
[10] Prov. i. 17, from the LXX., which has mistaken the meaning.
[11] Gen. i. 26.
[12] Matt. ix. 13; Mark ii. 17; Luke v. 32.
[13] The Cod Sin. reads, "neither would men have been saved by seeing Him."

the sun which is to cease to exist, and is the work of His hands, their eyes are not able to bear his rays. The Son of God therefore came in the flesh with this view, that He might bring to a head the sum of their sins who had persecuted His prophets[1] to the death. For this purpose, then, He endured. For God saith, "The stroke of his flesh is from them;"[2] and[3] "when I shall smite the Shepherd, then the sheep of the flock shall be scattered."[4] He himself willed thus to suffer, for it was necessary that He should suffer on the tree. For says he who prophesies regarding Him, "Spare my soul from the sword,[5] fasten my flesh with nails; for the assemblies of the wicked have risen up against me."[6] And again he says, "Behold, I have given my back to scourges, and my cheeks to strokes, and I have set my countenance as a firm rock."[7]

CHAP. VI. — THE SUFFERINGS OF CHRIST, AND THE NEW COVENANT, WERE ANNOUNCED BY THE PROPHETS.

When, therefore, He has fulfilled the commandment, what saith He? "Who is he that will contend with Me? let him oppose Me: or who is he that will enter into judgment with Me? let him draw near to the servant of the Lord."[8] "Woe unto you, for ye shall all wax old, like a garment, and the moth shall eat you up."[9] And again the prophet says, "Since[10] as a mighty stone He is laid for crushing, behold I cast down for the foundations of Zion a stone, precious, elect, a corner-stone, honourable." Next, what says He? "And he who shall trust[11] in it shall live for ever." Is our hope, then, upon a stone? Far from it. But [the language is used] inasmuch as He laid his flesh [as a foundation] with power; for He says, "And He placed me as a firm rock."[12] And the prophet says again, "The stone which the builders rejected, the same has become the head of the corner."[13] And again he says, "This is the great and wonderful day which the Lord hath made."[14] I write the more simply unto you, that ye may understand. I am the offscouring of your love.[15] What, then, again says the prophet? "The assembly of the wicked surrounded me; they encompassed me as bees do a honeycomb,"[16] and "upon my garment they cast lots."[17] Since, therefore, He was about to be manifested and to suffer in the flesh, His suffering was foreshown. For the prophet speaks against Israel, "Woe to their soul, because they have counselled an evil counsel against themselves,[18] saying, Let us bind the just one, because he is displeasing to us."[19] And Moses also says to them,[20] "Behold these things, saith the Lord God: Enter into the good land which the Lord sware [to give] to Abraham, and Isaac, and Jacob, and inherit ye it, a land flowing with milk and honey."[21] What, then, says Knowledge?[22] Learn: "Trust," she says, "in Him who is to be manifested to you in the flesh — that is, Jesus." For man is earth in a suffering state, for the formation of Adam was from the face of the earth. What, then, meaneth this: "into the good land, a land flowing with milk and honey?" Blessed be our Lord, who has placed in us wisdom and understanding of secret things. For the prophet says, "Who shall understand the parable of the Lord, except him who is wise and prudent, and who loves his Lord?"[23] Since, therefore, having renewed us by the remission of our sins, He hath made us after another pattern, [it is His purpose] that we should possess the soul of children, inasmuch as He has created us anew by His Spirit.[24] For the Scripture says concerning us, while He speaks to the Son, "Let Us make man after Our image, and after Our likeness; and let them have dominion over the beasts of the earth, and the fowls of heaven, and the fishes of the sea."[25] And the Lord said, on beholding the fair creature[26] man, "Increase, and multiply, and replenish the earth."[27] These things [were spoken] to the Son. Again, I will show thee how, in respect to us,[28] He has accomplished a second fashioning in these last days. The Lord says, "Behold, I will make[29] the last like the first."[30] In reference to this, then, the prophet proclaimed, "Enter ye into the land

---

[1] Cod. Sin. has, "their prophets," but the corrector has changed it as above.
[2] A very loose reference to Isa. liii. 8.
[3] Cod. Sin. omits "and," and reads, "when they smite their own shepherd, then the sheep of the pasture shall be scattered and fail."
[4] Zech. xiii. 7.
[5] Cod. Sin. inserts "and."
[6] These are inaccurate and confused quotations from Ps. xxii. 21, 17, and cxix. 120.
[7] Isa. l. 6, 7.
[8] Isa. l. 8.
[9] Isa. l. 9.
[10] The Latin omits "since," but it is found in all the Greek MSS.
[11] Cod. Sin. has "believe." Isa. viii. 14, xxviii. 16.
[12] Isa. l. 7.
[13] Ps. cxviii. 22.
[14] Ps. cxviii. 24.
[15] Comp. 1 Cor. iv. 13. The meaning is, "My love to you is so great, that I am ready to be or to do all things for you."
[16] Ps. xxii. 17, cxviii. 12.
[17] Ps. xxii. 19.
[18] Isa. iii. 9.
[19] Wisd. ii. 12. This apocryphal book is thus quoted as Scripture, and intertwined with it.
[20] Cod. Sin. reads, "What says the other prophet Moses unto them?"
[21] Ex. xxxiii. 1; Lev. xx. 24.
[22] The original word is "Gnosis," the knowledge peculiar to advanced Christians, by which they understand the mysteries of Scripture.
[23] Not found in Scripture. Comp. Isa. xl. 13; Prov. i. 6. Hilgenfeld, however, changes the usual punctuation, which places a colon after prophet, and reads, "For the prophet speaketh the parable of the Lord. Who shall understand," etc.
[24] The Greek is here very elliptical and obscure: "His Spirit" is inserted above, from the Latin.
[25] Gen. i. 26.
[26] Cod. Sin. has "our fair formation."
[27] Gen. i. 28.
[28] Cod. Sin. inserts, "the Lord says."
[29] Cod. Sin. has "I make."
[30] Not in Scripture, but comp. Matt. xx. 16, and 2 Cor. v. 17.

flowing with milk and honey, and have dominion over it."[1] Behold, therefore, we have been refashioned, as again He says in another prophet, "Behold, saith the Lord, I will take away from these, that is, from those whom the Spirit of the Lord foresaw, their stony hearts, and I will put hearts of flesh within them,"[2] because He[3] was to be manifested in flesh, and to sojourn among us. For, my brethren, the habitation of our heart is a holy temple to the Lord.[4] For again saith the Lord, "And wherewith shall I appear before the Lord my God, and be glorified?"[5] He says,[6] "I will confess to thee in the Church in the midst[7] of my brethren; and I will praise thee in the midst of the assembly of the saints."[8] We, then, are they whom He has led into the good land. What, then, mean the milk and honey? This, that as the infant is kept alive first by honey, and then by milk, so also we, being quickened and kept alive by the faith of the promise and by the word, shall live ruling over the earth. But He said above,[9] "Let them increase, and rule over the fishes."[10] Who then is able to govern the beasts, or the fishes, or the fowls of heaven? For we ought to perceive that to govern implies authority, so that one should command and rule. If, therefore, this does not exist at present, yet still He has promised it to us. When? When we ourselves also have been made perfect [so as] to become heirs of the covenant of the Lord.[11]

CHAP. VII. — FASTING, AND THE GOAT SENT AWAY, WERE TYPES OF CHRIST.

Understand, then, ye children of gladness, that the good Lord has foreshown all things to us, that we might know to whom we ought for everything to render thanksgiving and praise. If therefore the Son of God, who is Lord [of all things], and who will judge the living and the dead, suffered, that His stroke might give us life, let us believe that the Son of God could not have suffered except for our sakes. Moreover, when fixed to the cross, He had given Him to drink vinegar and gall. Hearken how the priests of the people[12] gave previous indications of this. His commandment having been written, the Lord enjoined, that whosoever did not keep the fast should be put to death, because He also Himself was to offer in sacrifice for our sins the vessel of the Spirit, in order that the type established in Isaac when he was offered upon the altar might be fully accomplished. What, then, says He in the prophet? "And let them eat of the goat which is offered, with fasting, for all their sins."[13] Attend carefully: "And let all the priests alone eat the inwards, unwashed with vinegar." Wherefore? Because to me, who am to offer my flesh for the sins of my new people, ye are to give gall with vinegar to drink: eat ye alone, while the people fast and mourn in sackcloth and ashes. [These things were done] that He might show that it was necessary for Him to suffer for them.[14] How,[15] then, ran the commandment? Give your attention. Take two goats of goodly aspect, and similar to each other, and offer them. And let the priest take one as a burnt-offering for sins.[16] And what should they do with the other? "Accursed," says He, "is the one." Mark how the type of Jesus[17] now comes out. "And all of you spit upon it, and pierce it, and encircle its head with scarlet wool, and thus let it be driven into the wilderness." And when all this has been done, he who bears the goat brings it into the desert, and takes the wool off from it, and places that upon a shrub which is called *Rachia*,[18] of which also we are accustomed to eat the fruits[19] when we find them in the field. Of this[20] kind of shrub alone the fruits are sweet. Why then, again, is this? Give good heed. [You see] "one upon the altar, and the other accursed;" and why [do you behold] the one that is accursed crowned? Because they shall see Him then in that day having a scarlet robe about his body down to his feet; and they shall say, Is not this He whom we once despised, and pierced, and mocked, and crucified? Truly this is[21] He who then declared Himself to be the Son of God. For how like is He to Him![22] With a view to this, [He required] the goats to be of goodly aspect, and similar, that, when they see Him then coming, they may be amazed by the likeness of the goat. Behold, then,[23] the type of Jesus who was to suffer. But why is it that they

---

[1] Ex. xxxiii. 3.
[2] Ezek. xi. 19, xxxvi. 26.
[3] Cod. Sin. inserts "Himself;" comp. John i. 14.
[4] Comp. Eph. ii. 21.
[5] Comp. Ps. xlii. 2.
[6] Cod. Sin. omits "He says."
[7] Cod. Sin. omits "in the midst."
[8] Ps. xxii. 23; Heb. ii. 12.
[9] Cod. Sin. has "But we said above."
[10] Gen. i. 28.
[11] These are specimens of the "Gnosis," or faculty of bringing out the hidden spiritual meaning of Scripture referred to before. Many more such interpretations follow.
[12] Cod. Sin. reads "temple," which is adopted by Hilgenfeld.
[13] Not to be found in Scripture, as is the case also with what follows. Hefele remarks, that "certain false traditions respecting the Jewish rites seem to have prevailed among the Christians of the second century, of which Barnabas here adopts some, as do Justin (*Dial. c. Try.* 40) and Tertullian (*adv. Jud.* 14; *adv. Marc.* iii. 7)."
[14] Cod. Sin. has "by them."
[15] Cod. Sin. reads, "what commanded He?"
[16] Cod. Sin. reads, "one as a burnt-offering, and one for sins."
[17] Cod. Sin. reads, "type of God," but it has been corrected to Jesus.
[18] In Cod. Sin. we find "*Rachel*." The orthography is doubtful, but there is little question that a kind of bramble-bush is intended.
[19] Thus the Latin interprets; others render "shoots."
[20] Cod. Sin. has "thus" instead of "this."
[21] Literally, "was."
[22] The text is here in great confusion, though the meaning is plain. Dressel reads, "For how are they alike, and why [does He enjoin] that the goats should be good and alike?" The Cod. Sin. reads, "How is He like Him? For this that," etc.
[23] Cod. Sin. here inserts "the goat."

place the wool in the midst of thorns? It is a type of Jesus set before the view of the Church. [They[1] place the wool among thorns], that any one who wishes to bear it away may find it necessary to suffer much, because the thorn is formidable, and thus obtain it only as the result of suffering. Thus also, says He, "Those who wish to behold Me, and lay hold of My kingdom, must through tribulation and suffering obtain Me."[2]

CHAP. VIII. — THE RED HEIFER A TYPE OF CHRIST.

Now what do you suppose this to be a type of, that a command was given to Israel, that men of the greatest wickedness[3] should offer a heifer, and slay and burn it, and, that then boys should take the ashes, and put these into vessels, and bind round a stick[4] purple wool along with hyssop, and that thus the boys should sprinkle the people, one by one, in order that they might be purified from their sins? Consider how He speaks to you with simplicity. The calf[5] is Jesus: the sinful men offering it are those who led Him to the slaughter. But now the men are no longer guilty, are no longer regarded as sinners.[6] And the boys that sprinkle are those that have proclaimed to us the remission of sins and purification of heart. To these He gave authority to preach the Gospel, being twelve in number, corresponding to the twelve tribes[7] of Israel. But why are there three boys that sprinkle? To correspond[8] to Abraham, and Isaac, and Jacob, because these were great with God. And why was the wool [placed] upon the wood? Because by wood Jesus holds His kingdom, so that [through the cross] those believing on Him shall live for ever. But why was hyssop joined with the wool? Because in His kingdom the days will be evil and polluted in which we shall be saved, [and] because he who suffers in body is cured through the cleansing[9] efficacy of hyssop. And on this account the things which stand thus are clear to us, but obscure to them, because they did not hear the voice of the Lord.

CHAP. IX. — THE SPIRITUAL MEANING OF CIRCUMCISION.

He speaks moreover concerning our ears, how He hath circumcised both them and our heart. The Lord saith in the prophet, "In the hearing of the ear they obeyed me."[10] And again He saith, "By hearing, those shall hear who are afar off; they shall know what I have done."[11] And, "Be ye circumcised in your hearts, saith the Lord."[12] And again He says, "Hear, O Israel, for these things saith the Lord thy God."[13] And once more the Spirit of the Lord proclaims, "Who is he that wishes to live for ever? By hearing let him hear the voice of my servant."[14] And again He saith, "Hear, O heaven, and give ear, O earth, for God[15] hath spoken."[16] These are in proof.[17] And again He saith, "Hear the word of the Lord, ye rulers of this people."[18] And again He saith, "Hear, ye children, the voice of one crying in the wilderness."[19] Therefore He hath circumcised our ears, that we might hear His word and believe, for the circumcision in which they trusted is abolished.[20] For He declared that circumcision was not of the flesh, but they transgressed because an evil angel deluded them.[21] He saith to them, "These things saith the Lord your God"— (here[22] I find a new[23] commandment) — "Sow not among thorns, but circumcise yourselves to the Lord."[24] And why speaks He thus: "Circumcise the stubbornness of your heart, and harden not your neck?"[25] And again: "Behold, saith the Lord, all the nations are uncircumcised[26] in the flesh, but this people are uncircumcised in heart."[27] But thou wilt say, "Yea, verily the people are circumcised for a seal." But so also is every Syrian and Arab, and all the priests of idols: are these then also within the bond of His covenant?[28] Yea, the Egyptians also practise circumcision. Learn then, my children, concerning all things richly,[29] that Abraham, the first who enjoined circumcision, looking forward in spirit to Jesus, practised that rite, having received the mysteries[30] of the three letters. For [the Scripture] saith, "And Abraham circum-

---

[1] Cod. Sin. reads, "for as he who . . . so, says he," etc.
[2] Comp. Acts xiv. 22.
[3] Literally, "men in whom sins are perfect." Of this, and much more that follows, no mention is made in Scripture.
[4] Cod. Sin. has "upon sticks," and adds, "Behold again the type of the cross, both the scarlet wool and the hyssop," — adopted by Hilgenfeld.
[5] Cod. Sin. has, "the law is Christ Jesus," corrected to the above.
[6] The Greek text is, "then no longer [sinful] men, no longer the glory of sinners," which Dressel defends and Hilgenfeld adopts, but which is surely corrupt.
[7] Literally, "in witness of the tribes."
[8] "In witness of."
[9] Thus the sense seems to require, and thus Dressel translates, though it is difficult to extract such a meaning from the Greek text.

[10] Ps. xviii. 44.
[11] Isa. xxxiii. 13.
[12] Jer. iv. 4.
[13] Jer. vii. 2.
[14] Ps. xxxiv. 11-13. The first clause of this sentence is wanting in Cod. Sin.
[15] Cod. Sin. has "Lord."
[16] Isa. i. 2.
[17] In proof of the spiritual meaning of circumcision; but Hilgenfeld joins the words to the preceding sentence.
[18] Isa. i. 10.
[19] Cod. Sin. reads, "it is the voice," corrected, however, as above.
[20] Cod. Sin. has, "that we might hear the word, and not only believe," plainly a corrupt text.
[21] Cod. Sin., at first hand, has "slew them," but is corrected as above.
[22] The meaning is here very obscure, but the above rendering and punctuation seem preferable to any other.
[23] Cod. Sin., with several other MSS., leaves out "new."
[24] Jer. iv. 3. Cod. Sin. has "God" instead of "Lord."
[25] Deut. x. 16.
[26] This contrast seems to be marked in the original. Cod. Sin. has, "Behold, receive again."
[27] Jer. ix. 25, 26.
[28] Dressel and Hilgenfeld read, "their covenant," as does Cod. Sin.; we have followed Hefele.
[29] Cod. Sin. has "children of love," omitting "richly," and inserting it before "looking forward."
[30] Literally, "doctrines."

cised ten, and eight, and three hundred men of his household."[1] What, then, was the knowledge given to him in this? Learn the eighteen first, and then the three hundred.[2] The ten and the eight are thus denoted — Ten by I, and Eight by H.[3] You have [the initials of the name of] Jesus. And because[4] the cross was to express the grace [of our redemption] by the letter T, he says also, "Three Hundred." He signifies, therefore, Jesus by two letters, and the cross by one. He knows this, who has put within us the engrafted[5] gift of His doctrine. No one has been admitted by me to a more excellent piece of knowledge[6] than this, but I know that ye are worthy.

CHAP. X. — SPIRITUAL SIGNIFICANCE OF THE PRECEPTS OF MOSES RESPECTING DIFFERENT KINDS OF FOOD.

Now, wherefore did Moses say, "Thou shalt not eat the swine, nor the eagle, nor the hawk, nor the raven, nor any fish which is not possessed of scales?"[7] He embraced three doctrines in his mind [in doing so]. Moreover, the Lord saith to them in Deuteronomy, "And I will establish my ordinances among this people."[8] Is there then not a command of God that they should not eat [these things]? There is, but Moses spoke with a spiritual reference.[9] For this reason he named the swine, as much as to say, "Thou shalt not join thyself to men who resemble swine." For when they live in pleasure, they forget their Lord; but when they come to want, they acknowledge the Lord. And [in like manner] the swine, when it has eaten, does not recognize its master; but when hungry it cries out, and on receiving food is quiet again. "Neither shalt thou eat," says he "the eagle, nor the hawk, nor the kite, nor the raven." "Thou shalt not join thyself," he means, "to such men as know not how to procure food for themselves by labour and sweat, but seize on that of others in their iniquity, and although wearing an aspect of simplicity, are on the watch to plunder others."[10] So these birds, while they sit idle, inquire how they may devour the flesh of others, proving themselves pests [to all] by their wickedness. "And thou shalt not eat," he says, "the lamprey, or the polypus, or the cuttlefish." He means, "Thou shalt not join thyself or be like to such men as are ungodly to the end, and are condemned[11] to death." In like manner as those fishes, above accursed, float in the deep, not swimming [on the surface] like the rest, but make their abode in the mud which lies at the bottom. Moreover, "Thou shalt not," he says, "eat the hare." Wherefore? "Thou shalt not be a corrupter of boys, nor like unto such."[12] Because the hare multiplies, year by year, the places of its conception; for as many years as it lives so many[13] it has. Moreover, "Thou shalt not eat the hyena." He means, "Thou shalt not be an adulterer, nor a corrupter, nor be like to them that are such." Wherefore? Because that animal annually changes its sex, and is at one time male, and at another female. Moreover, he has rightly detested the weasel. For he means, "Thou shalt not be like to those whom we hear of as committing wickedness with the mouth,[14] on account of their uncleanness; nor shalt thou be joined to those impure women who commit iniquity with the mouth. For this animal conceives by the mouth." Moses then issued[15] three doctrines concerning meats with a spiritual significance; but they received them according to fleshly desire, as if he had merely spoken of [literal] meats. David, however, comprehends the knowledge of the three doctrines, and speaks in like manner: "Blessed is the man who hath not walked in the counsel of the ungodly,"[16] even as the fishes [referred to] go in darkness to the depths [of the sea]; "and hath not stood in the way of sinners," even as those who profess to fear the Lord, but go astray like swine; "and hath not sat in the seat of scorners,"[17] even as those birds that lie in wait for prey. Take a full and firm grasp of this spiritual[18] knowledge. But Moses says still further, "Ye shall eat every animal that is cloven-footed and ruminant." What does he mean? [The ruminant animal denotes him] who, on receiving food, recognizes Him that nourishes him, and being satisfied by Him,[19] is visibly made glad. Well spake [Moses], having respect to the commandment.

---

[1] Not found in Scripture; but comp. Gen. xvii. 26, 27, xiv. 14.
[2] Cod. Sin. inserts, "and then making a pause."
[3] This sentence is altogether omitted by inadvertence in Cod. Sin.
[4] Some MSS. here read, "and further:" the above is the reading in Cod. Sin., and is also that of Hefele.
[5] This is rendered in the Latin, "the more profound gift," referring, as it does, to the *Gnosis* of the initiated. The same word is used in chap. i.
[6] Literally, "has learned a more germane (or genuine) word from me," being an idle vaunt on account of the ingenuity in interpreting Scripture he has just displayed.
[7] Cod. Sin. has "portion," corrected, however, as above. See Lev. xi. and Deut. xiv.
[8] Deut. iv. 1.
[9] Literally, "in spirit."
[10] Cod. Sin. inserts, "and gaze about for some way of escape on account of their greediness, even as these birds alone do not procure food for themselves (by labour), but sitting idle, seek to devour the flesh of others." The text as above seems preferable: Hilgenfeld, however, follows the Greek.

[11] Cod. Sin. has, "condemned already."
[12] Dressel has a note upon this passage, in which he refers the words we have rendered "corrupters of boys," to those who by their dissolute lives waste their fortunes, and so entail destruction on their children; but this does not appear satisfactory. Comp. Clem. Alex. *Pædag.* ii. 10.
[13] We have left τρύπας untranslated. [Cavities, i.e. of conception].
[14] Cod. Sin. has, "with the body through uncleanness," and so again in the last clause.
[15] Cod. Sin. inserts, "having received."
[16] Ps. i. 1.
[17] Literally, "of the pestilent."
[18] Cod. Sin. reads "perfectly" instead of "perfect," as do most MSS.; but, according to Dressel, we should read, "have a perfect knowledge concerning the food." Hilgenfeld follows the Greek.
[19] Or, "resting upon Him."

What, then, does he mean? That we ought to join ourselves to those that fear the Lord, those who meditate in their heart on the commandment which they have received, those who both utter the judgments of the Lord and observe them, those who know that meditation is a work of gladness, and who ruminate[1] upon the word of the Lord. But what means the cloven-footed? That the righteous man also walks in this world, yet looks forward to the holy state[2] [to come]. Behold how well Moses legislated. But how was it possible for them to understand or comprehend these things? We then, rightly understanding his commandments,[3] explain them as the Lord intended. For this purpose He circumcised our ears and our hearts, that we might understand these things.

CHAP. XI. — BAPTISM AND THE CROSS PREFIGURED IN THE OLD TESTAMENT.

Let us further inquire whether the Lord took any care to foreshadow the water [of baptism] and the cross. Concerning the water, indeed, it is written, in reference to the Israelites, that they should not receive that baptism which leads to the remission of sins, but should procure[4] another for themselves. The prophet therefore declares, "Be astonished, O heaven, and let the earth tremble[5] at this, because this people hath committed two great evils: they have forsaken Me, a living fountain, and have hewn out for themselves broken cisterns.[6] Is my holy hill Zion a desolate rock? For ye shall be as the fledglings of a bird, which fly away when the nest is removed."[7] And again saith the prophet, "I will go before thee and make level the mountains, and will break the brazen gates, and bruise in pieces the iron bars; and I will give thee the secret,[8] hidden, invisible treasures, that they may know that I am the Lord God."[9] And "He shall dwell in a lofty cave of the strong rock."[10] Furthermore, what saith He in reference to the Son? "His water is sure;[11] ye shall see the King in His glory, and your soul shall meditate on the fear of the Lord."[12] And again He saith in another prophet, "The man who doeth these things shall be like a tree planted by the courses of waters, which shall yield its fruit in due season; and his leaf shall not fade, and all that he doeth shall prosper. Not so are the ungodly, not so, but even as chaff, which the wind sweeps away from the face of the earth. Therefore the ungodly shall not stand in judgment, nor sinners in the counsel of the just; for the Lord knoweth the way of the righteous, but the way of the ungodly shall perish."[13] Mark how He has described at once both the water and the cross. For these words imply, Blessed are they who, placing their trust in the cross, have gone down into the water; for, says He, they shall receive their reward in due time: then He declares, I will recompense them. But now He saith,[14] "Their leaves shall not fade." This meaneth, that every word which proceedeth out of your mouth in faith and love shall tend to bring conversion and hope to many. Again, another prophet saith, "And the land of Jacob shall be extolled above every land."[15] This meaneth the vessel of His Spirit, which He shall glorify. Further, what says He? "And there was a river flowing on the right, and from it arose beautiful trees; and whosoever shall eat of them shall live for ever."[16] This meaneth,[17] that we indeed descend into the water full of sins and defilement, but come up, bearing fruit in our heart, having the fear [of God] and trust in Jesus in our spirit. "And whosoever shall eat of these shall live for ever." This meaneth: Whosoever, He declares, shall hear thee speaking, and believe, shall live for ever.

CHAP. XII. — THE CROSS OF CHRIST FREQUENTLY ANNOUNCED IN THE OLD TESTAMENT.

In like manner He points to the cross of Christ in another prophet, who saith,[18] "And when shall these things be accomplished? And the Lord saith, When a tree shall be bent down, and again arise, and when blood shall flow out of wood."[19] Here again you have an intimation concerning the cross, and Him who should be crucified. Yet again He speaks of this[20] in Moses, when Israel was attacked by strangers. And that He might remind them, when assailed, that it was on account of their sins they were delivered to death, the Spirit speaks to the heart of Moses, that he should make a figure of the cross,[21] and of Him about to suffer thereon; for unless they put their trust in Him, they shall be overcome for ever. Moses therefore placed one weapon above another in the midst of the hill,[22] and

---

[1] Cod. Sin. here has the singular, "one who ruminates."
[2] Literally, "holy age."
[3] Cod. Sin. inserts again, "rightly."
[4] Literally, "should build."
[5] Cod. Sin. has, "confine still more," corrected to "tremble still more."
[6] Cod. Sin. has, "have dug a pit of death." See Jer. ii. 12, 13.
[7] Comp. Isa. xvi. 1, 2.
[8] Literally, "dark." Cod. Sin. has, "of darkness."
[9] Isa. xlv. 2, 3.
[10] Isa. xxxiii. 16. Cod. Sin. has, "thou shalt dwell."
[11] Cod. Sin. entirely omits the question given above, and joins "the water is sure" to the former sentence.
[12] Isa. xxxiii. 16-18.
[13] Ps. i. 3-6.
[14] Cod. Sin has, "what meaneth?"
[15] Zeph. iii. 19.
[16] Ezek. xlvii. 12.
[17] Omitted in Cod. Sin.
[18] Cod. Sin. refers this to *God*, and not to the prophet.
[19] From some unknown apocryphal book. Hilgenfeld compares Hab. ii. 11.
[20] Cod. Sin. reads, "He speaks to Moses."
[21] Cod. Sin. omits "and."
[22] Cod. Sin. reads πυγμῆς, which must here be translated "heap" or "mass." According to Hilgenfeld, however, πυγμή is here equivalent to πυγμαχία, "a fight." The meaning would then be, that "Moses piled weapon upon weapon in the midst of the *battle*," instead of "hill" (πήγης), as above.

standing upon it, so as to be higher than all the people, he stretched forth his hands,[1] and thus again Israel acquired the mastery. But when again he let down his hands, they were again destroyed. For what reason? That they might know that they could not be saved unless they put their trust in Him.[2] And in another prophet He declares, "All day long I have stretched forth My hands to an unbelieving people, and one that gainsays My righteous way."[3] And again Moses makes a type of Jesus, [signifying] that it was necessary for Him to suffer, [and also] that He would be the author of life[4] [to others], whom they believed to have destroyed on the cross[5] when Israel was falling. For since transgression was committed by Eve through means of the serpent, [the Lord] brought it to pass that every [kind of] serpents bit them, and they died,[6] that He might convince them, that on account of their transgression they were given over to the straits of death. Moreover Moses, when he commanded, "Ye shall not have any graven or molten [image] for your God,"[7] did so that he might reveal a type of Jesus. Moses then makes a brazen serpent, and places it upon a beam,[8] and by proclamation assembles the people. When, therefore, they were come together, they besought Moses that he would offer sacrifice[9] in their behalf, and pray for their recovery. And Moses spake unto them, saying, "When any one of you is bitten, let him come to the serpent placed on the pole; and let him hope and believe, that even though dead, it is able to give him life, and immediately he shall be restored."[10] And they did so. Thou hast in this also [an indication of] the glory of Jesus; for in Him and to Him are all things.[11] What, again, says Moses to Jesus (Joshua) the son of Nave, when he gave him[12] this name, as being a prophet, with this view only, that all the people might hear that the Father would reveal all things concerning His Son Jesus to the son[13] of Nave? This name then being given him when he sent him to spy out the land, he said, "Take a book into thy hands, and write what the Lord declares, that the Son of God will in the last days cut off from the roots all the house of Amalek."[14] Behold again: Jesus who was manifested, both by type and in the flesh,[15] is not the Son of man, but the Son of God. Since, therefore, they were to say that Christ was the son[16] of David, fearing and understanding the error of the wicked, he saith, "The Lord said unto my Lord, Sit at My right hand, until I make Thine enemies Thy footstool."[17] And again, thus saith Isaiah, "The Lord said to Christ,[18] my Lord, whose right hand I have holden,[19] that the nations should yield obedience before Him; and I will break in pieces the strength of kings."[20] Behold how David calleth Him Lord and the Son of God.

CHAP. XIII. — CHRISTIANS, AND NOT JEWS, THE HEIRS OF THE COVENANT.

But let us see if this people[21] is the heir, or the former, and if the covenant belongs to us or to them. Hear ye now what the Scripture saith concerning the people. Isaac prayed for Rebecca his wife, because she was barren; and she conceived.[22] Furthermore also, Rebecca went forth to inquire of the Lord; and the Lord said to her, "Two nations are in thy womb, and two peoples in thy belly; and the one people shall surpass the other, and the elder shall serve the younger."[23] You ought to understand who was Isaac, who Rebecca, and concerning what persons He declared that this people should be greater than that. And in another prophecy Jacob speaks more clearly to his son Joseph, saying, "Behold, the Lord hath not deprived me of thy presence; bring thy sons to me, that I may bless them."[24] And he brought Manasseh and Ephraim, desiring that Manasseh[25] should be blessed, because he was the elder. With this view Joseph led him to the right hand of his father Jacob. But Jacob saw in spirit the type of the people to arise afterwards. And what says [the Scripture]? And Jacob changed the direction of his hands, and laid his right hand upon the head of Ephraim, the second and younger, and blessed him. And Joseph said to Jacob, "Transfer thy right hand to the head of Manasseh,[25] for he is my first-born son."[26] And Jacob said, "I know it, my son, I know it; but the elder shall serve the younger: yet he also shall be blessed."[27] Ye see on whom he laid[28] [his hands], that this people should be first, and

---

[1] Thus standing in the form of a cross.
[2] Or, as some read, "in the cross."
[3] Isa. lxv. 2.
[4] Cod. Sin. has, "and He shall make him alive."
[5] Literally, "the sign."
[6] Comp. Num. xxi. 6–9; John iii. 14–18.
[7] Deut. xxvii. 15. Cod. Sin. reads, "molten or graven."
[8] Instead of ἐν δοκῷ, "on a beam," Cod. Sin. with other MSS. has ἐνδόξως, "manifestly," which is adopted by Hilgenfeld.
[9] Cod. Sin. simply reads, "offer supplication."
[10] Num. xxi. 9.
[11] Comp. Col. i. 16.
[12] Cod. Sin. has the imperative, "Put on him;" but it is connected as above.
[13] Cod. Sin. closes the sentence with *Jesus*, and inserts, "Moses said therefore to Jesus."
[14] Ex. xvii. 14.
[15] Comp. 1 Tim. iii. 16.
[16] That is, merely human: a reference is supposed to the Ebionites.
[17] Ps. cx. 1; Matt. xxii. 43–45.
[18] Cod. Sin. corrects "to Cyrus," as LXX.
[19] Cod. Sin. has, "he has taken hold."
[20] Isa. xlv. 1.
[21] That is, "Christians."
[22] Gen. xxv. 21.
[23] Gen. xxv. 23.
[24] Gen. xlviii. 11, 9.
[25] Cod. Sin. reads each time "Ephraim," by a manifest mistake, instead of Manasseh.
[26] Gen. xlviii. 18.
[27] Gen. xlviii. 19.
[28] Or, "of whom he willed."

heir of the covenant. If then, still further, the same thing was intimated through Abraham, we reach the perfection of our knowledge. What, then, says He to Abraham? "Because thou hast believed,[1] it is imputed to thee for righteousness: behold, I have made thee the father of those nations who believe in the Lord while in [a state of] uncircumcision."[2]

CHAP. XIV.—THE LORD HATH GIVEN US THE TESTAMENT WHICH MOSES RECEIVED AND BROKE.

Yes [it is even so]; but let us inquire if the Lord has really given that testament which He swore to the fathers that He would give[3] to the people. He did give it; but they were not worthy to receive it, on account of their sins. For the prophet declares, "And Moses was fasting forty days and forty nights on Mount Sinai, that he might receive the testament of the Lord for the people."[4] And he received from the Lord[5] two tables, written in the spirit by the finger of the hand of the Lord. And Moses having received them, carried them down to give to the people. And the Lord said to Moses, "Moses, Moses, go down quickly; for thy people hath sinned, whom thou didst bring out of the land of Egypt."[6] And Moses understood that they had again[7] made molten images; and he threw the tables out of his hands, and the tables of the testament of the Lord were broken. Moses then received it, but they proved themselves unworthy. Learn now how *we* have received it. Moses, as a servant,[8] received it; but the Lord himself, having suffered in our behalf, hath given it to us, that we should be the people of inheritance. But He was manifested, in order that they might be perfected in their iniquities, and that we, being constituted heirs through Him,[9] might receive the testament of the Lord Jesus, who was prepared for this end, that by His personal manifestation, redeeming our hearts (which were already wasted by death, and given over to the iniquity of error) from darkness, He might by His word enter into a covenant with us. For it is written how the Father, about to redeem[10] us from darkness, commanded Him to prepare[11] a holy people for Himself. The prophet therefore declares, "I, the Lord Thy God, have called Thee in righteousness, and will hold Thy hand, and will strengthen Thee; and I have given Thee for a covenant to the people, for a light to the nations, to open the eyes of the blind, and to bring forth from fetters them that are bound, and those that sit in darkness out of the prison-house."[12] Ye perceive,[13] then, whence we have been redeemed. And again, the prophet says, "Behold, I have appointed Thee as a light to the nations, that Thou mightest be for salvation even to the ends of the earth, saith the Lord God that redeemeth thee."[14] And again, the prophet saith, "The Spirit of the Lord is upon me; because He hath anointed me to preach the Gospel to the humble: He hath sent me to heal the broken-hearted, to proclaim deliverance to the captives, and recovery of sight to the blind; to announce the acceptable year of the Lord, and the day of recompense; to comfort all that mourn."[15]

CHAP. XV.—THE FALSE AND THE TRUE SABBATH.

Further,[16] also, it is written concerning the Sabbath in the Decalogue which [the Lord] spoke, face to face, to Moses on Mount Sinai, "And sanctify ye the Sabbath of the Lord with clean hands and a pure heart."[17] And He says in another place, "If my sons keep the Sabbath, then will I cause my mercy to rest upon them."[18] The Sabbath is mentioned at the beginning of the creation [thus]: "And God made in six days the works of His hands, and made an end on the seventh day, and rested on it, and sanctified it."[19] Attend, my children, to the meaning of this expression, "He finished in six days." This implieth that the Lord will finish all things in six thousand years, for a day is[20] with Him a thousand years. And He Himself testifieth,[21] saying, "Behold, to-day[22] will be as a thousand years."[23] Therefore, my children, in six days, that is, in six thousand years, all things will be finished. "And He rested on the seventh day." This meaneth: when His Son, coming [again], shall destroy the time of the wicked man,[24] and judge the ungodly, and change the sun, and the moon,[25] and the stars, then shall He truly rest on the seventh day. Moreover, He says, "Thou shalt sanctify it with pure hands and a pure heart." If, therefore, any one can now sanctify

---

[1] Cod. Sin. has, "when alone believing," and is followed by Hilgenfeld to this effect: "What, then, says He to Abraham, when, alone believing, he was placed in righteousness? Behold," etc.
[2] Gen. xv. 6, xvii. 5; comp. Rom. iv. 3.
[3] Cod. Sin. absurdly repeats "to give."
[4] Ex. xxiv. 18.
[5] Ex. xxxi. 18.
[6] Ex. xxxii. 7; Deut. ix. 12.
[7] Cod. Sin. reads, "for themselves."
[8] Comp. Heb. iii. 5.
[9] Cod. Sin. and other MSS. read, "through Him who inherited."
[10] Cod. Sin. refers this to Christ.
[11] Cod. Sin. reads, "be prepared." Hilgenfeld follows Cod. Sin. so far, and reads, "For it is written how the Father commanded Him who was to redeem us from darkness (αὐτῷ — λυτρωσάμενος) to prepare a holy people for Himself."
[12] Isa. xlii. 6, 7.
[13] Cod. Sin. has, "we know."
[14] Isa. xlix. 6. The text of Cod. Sin., and of the other MSS., is here in great confusion: we have followed that given by Hefele.
[15] Isa. lxi. 1, 2.
[16] Cod. Sin. reads "because," but this is corrected to "moreover."
[17] Ex. xx. 8; Deut. v. 12.
[18] Jer. xvii. 24, 25.
[19] Gen. ii. 2. The Hebrew text is here followed, the Septuagint reading "sixth" instead of "seventh."
[20] Cod. Sin. reads "signifies."
[21] Cod. Sin. adds, "to me."
[22] Cod. Sin. reads, "The day of the Lord shall be as a thousand years."
[23] Ps. xc. 4; 2 Pet. iii. 8.
[24] Cod. Sin. seems properly to omit "of the wicked man."
[25] Cod. Sin. places *stars* before *moon*.

the day which God hath sanctified, except he is pure in heart in all things,[1] we are deceived.[2] Behold, therefore:[3] certainly then one properly resting sanctifies it, when we ourselves, having received the promise, wickedness no longer existing, and all things having been made new by the Lord, shall be able to work righteousness.[4] Then we shall be able to sanctify it, having been first sanctified ourselves.[5] Further, He says to them, "Your new moons and your Sabbaths I cannot endure."[6] Ye perceive how He speaks: Your present Sabbaths are not acceptable to Me, but that is which I have made, [namely this,] when, giving rest to all things, I shall make a beginning of the eighth day, that is, a beginning of another world. Wherefore, also, we keep the eighth day with joyfulness, the day also on which Jesus rose again from the dead.[7] And[8] when He had manifested Himself, He ascended into the heavens.

CHAP. XVI. — THE SPIRITUAL TEMPLE OF GOD.

Moreover, I will also tell you concerning the temple, how the wretched [Jews], wandering in error, trusted not in God Himself, but in the temple, as being the house of God. For almost after the manner of the Gentiles they worshipped Him in the temple.[9] But learn how the Lord speaks, when abolishing it: "Who hath meted out heaven with a span, and the earth with his palm? Have not I?"[10] "Thus saith the Lord, Heaven is My throne, and the earth My footstool: what kind of house will ye build to Me, or what is the place of My rest?"[11] Ye perceive that their hope is vain. Moreover, He again says, "Behold, they who have cast down this temple, even they shall build it up again."[12] It has so happened.[13] For through their going to war, it was destroyed by their enemies; and now they, as the servants of their enemies, shall rebuild it. Again, it was revealed that the city and the temple and the people of Israel were to be given up. For the Scripture saith, "And it shall come to pass in the last days, that the Lord will deliver up the sheep of His pasture, and their sheep-fold and tower, to destruction."[14] And it so happened as the Lord had spoken. Let us inquire, then, if there still is a temple of God. There is — where He himself declared He would make and finish it. For it is written, "And it shall come to pass, when the week is completed, the temple of God shall be built in glory in the name of the Lord."[15] I find, therefore, that a temple does exist. Learn, then, how it shall be built in the name of the Lord. Before we believed in God, the habitation of our heart was corrupt and weak, as being indeed like a temple made with hands. For it was full of idolatry, and was a habitation of demons, through our doing such things as were opposed to [the will of] God. But it shall be built, observe ye, in the name of the Lord, in order that the temple of the Lord may be built in glory. How? Learn [as follows]. Having received the forgiveness of sins, and placed our trust in the name of the Lord, we have become new creatures, formed again from the beginning. Wherefore in our habitation God truly dwells in us. How? His word of faith; His calling[16] of promise; the wisdom of the statutes; the commands of the doctrine; He himself prophesying in us; He himself dwelling in us; opening to us who were enslaved by death the doors of the temple, that is, the mouth; and by giving us repentance introduced us into the incorruptible temple.[17] He then, who wishes to be saved, looks not to man,[18] but to Him who dwelleth in him, and speaketh in him, amazed at never having either heard him utter such words with his mouth, nor himself having ever desired to hear them.[19] This is the spiritual temple built for the Lord.

CHAP. XVII. — CONCLUSION OF THE FIRST PART OF THE EPISTLE.

As far as was possible, and could be done with perspicuity, I cherish the hope that, according to my desire, I have omitted none[20] of those things at present [demanding consideration], which bear upon your salvation. For if I should write to you about things future,[21] ye would not understand, because such knowledge is hid in parables. These things then are so.

---

[1] Cod. Sin. reads "again," but is corrected as above.
[2] The meaning is, "If the Sabbaths of the Jews were the true Sabbath, we should have been deceived by God, who demands pure hands and a pure heart." — HEFELE.
[3] Cod. Sin. has, "But if not." Hilgenfeld's text of this confused passage reads as follows: "Who then can sanctify the day which God has sanctified, except the man who is of a pure heart? We are deceived (or mistaken) in all things. Behold, therefore," etc.
[4] Cod. Sin. reads, "resting aright, we shall sanctify it, having been justified, and received the promise, iniquity no longer existing, but all things having been made new by the Lord."
[5] Cod. Sin. reads, "Shall we not then?"
[6] Isa. i. 13.
[7] "Barnabas here bears testimony to the observance of the Lord's Day in early times." — HEFELE.
[8] We here follow the punctuation of Dressel: Hefele places only a comma between the clauses, and inclines to think that the writer implies that the ascension of Christ took place on the first day of the week.
[9] That is, "they worshipped the temple instead of Him."
[10] Isa. xl. 12.
[11] Isa. lxvi. 1.
[12] Comp. Isa. xlix. 17 (Sept.).
[13] Cod. Sin. omits this.

[14] Comp. Isa. v., Jer. xxv.; but the words do not occur in Scripture.
[15] Dan. ix. 24-27; Hagg. ii. 10.
[16] Cod. Sin. reads, "the calling."
[17] Cod. Sin. gives the clauses of this sentence separately, each occupying a line.
[18] That is, the man who is engaged in preaching the Gospel.
[19] Such is the punctuation adopted by Hefele, Dressel, and Hilgenfeld.
[20] Cod. Sin. reads, "my soul hopes that it has not omitted anything."
[21] Cod. Sin., "about things present or future." Hilgenfeld's text of this passage is as follows: "My mind and soul hopes that, according to my desire, I have omitted none of the things that pertain to salvation. For if I should write to you about things present or future," etc. Hefele gives the text as above, and understands the meaning to be, "points bearing on the *present* argument."

CHAP. XVIII. — SECOND PART OF THE EPISTLE. THE TWO WAYS.

But let us now pass to another sort of knowledge and doctrine. There are two ways of doctrine and authority, the one of light, and the other of darkness. But there is a great difference between these two ways. For over one are stationed the light-bringing angels of God, but over the other the angels[1] of Satan. And He indeed (i.e., God) is Lord for ever and ever, but he (i.e., Satan) is prince of the time[2] of iniquity.

CHAP. XIX. — THE WAY OF LIGHT.

The way of light, then, is as follows. If any one desires to travel to the appointed place, he must be zealous in his works. The knowledge, therefore, which is given to us for the purpose of walking in this way, is the following. Thou shalt love Him that created thee:[3] thou shalt glorify Him that redeemed thee from death. Thou shalt be simple in heart, and rich in spirit. Thou shalt not join thyself to those who walk in the way of death. Thou shalt hate doing what is unpleasing to God: thou shalt hate all hypocrisy. Thou shalt not forsake the commandments of the Lord. Thou shalt not exalt thyself, but shalt be of a lowly mind.[4] Thou shalt not take glory to thyself. Thou shalt not take evil counsel against thy neighbour. Thou shalt not allow over-boldness to enter into thy soul.[5] Thou shalt not commit fornication: thou shalt not commit adultery: thou shalt not be a corrupter of youth. Thou shalt not let the word of God issue from thy lips with any kind of impurity.[6] Thou shalt not accept persons when thou reprovest any one for transgression. Thou shalt be meek: thou shalt be peaceable. Thou shalt tremble at the words which thou hearest.[7] Thou shalt not be mindful of evil against thy brother. Thou shalt not be of doubtful mind[8] as to whether a thing shall be or not. Thou shalt not take the name[9] of the Lord in vain. Thou shalt love thy neighbour more than thine own soul.[10] Thou shalt not slay the child by procuring abortion; nor, again, shalt thou destroy it after it is born. Thou shalt not withdraw thy hand from thy son, or from thy daughter, but from their infancy thou shalt teach them the fear of the Lord.[11] Thou shalt not covet what is thy neighbour's, nor shalt thou be avaricious. Thou shalt not be joined in soul with the haughty, but thou shalt be reckoned with the righteous and lowly. Receive thou as good things the trials[12] which come upon thee.[13] Thou shalt not be of double mind or of double tongue,[14] for a double tongue is a snare of death. Thou shalt be subject[15] to the Lord, and to [other] masters as the image of God, with modesty and fear. Thou shalt not issue orders with bitterness to thy maid-servant or thy man-servant, who trust in the same [God[16]], lest thou shouldst not[17] reverence that God who is above both; for He came to call men not according to their outward appearance,[18] but according as the Spirit had prepared them.[19] Thou shalt communicate in all things with thy neighbour; thou shalt not call[20] things thine own; for if ye are partakers in common of things which are incorruptible,[21] how much more [should you be] of those things which are corruptible![22] Thou shalt not be hasty with thy tongue, for the mouth is a snare of death. As far as possible, thou shalt be pure in thy soul. Do not be ready to stretch forth thy hands to take, whilst thou contractest them to give. Thou shalt love, as the apple of thine eye, every one that speaketh to thee the word of the Lord. Thou shalt remember the day of judgment, night and day. Thou shalt seek out every day the faces of the saints,[23] either by word examining them, and going to exhort them, and meditating how to save a soul by the word,[24] or by thy hands thou shalt labour for the redemption of thy sins. Thou shalt not hesitate to give, nor murmur when thou givest. "Give to every one that asketh thee,"[25] and thou shalt know who is the good Recompenser of the reward. Thou shalt preserve what thou hast received [in charge], neither adding to it nor taking from it. To the last thou shalt hate the wicked[26] [one].[27] Thou shalt judge righteously. Thou shalt not make a schism, but thou shalt pacify those that contend by bringing them together. Thou shalt

---

[1] Comp. 2 Cor. xii. 7.
[2] Cod. Sin. reads, "of the present time of iniquity."
[3] Cod. Sin. inserts, "Thou shalt fear Him that formed thee."
[4] Cod. Sin. adds, "in all things."
[5] Literally, "shalt not give insolence to thy soul."
[6] "That is, while proclaiming the Gospel, thou shalt not in any way be of corrupt morals." — HEFELE.
[7] Isa. lxvi. 2. All the preceding clauses are given in Cod. Sin. in distinct lines.
[8] Comp. James i. 8.
[9] Cod. Sin. has "thy name," but this is corrected as above.
[10] Cod. Sin. corrects to, "as thine own soul."
[11] Cod. Sin. has, "of God."
[12] "Difficulties," or "troubles."
[13] Cod. Sin. adds, "knowing that without God nothing happens."
[14] Cod. Sin. has "talkative," and omits the following clause.
[15] Cod. Sin. has, "Thou shalt be subject (ὑποταγήσῃ — untouched by the corrector) to masters as a type of God."
[16] Inserted in Cod. Sin.
[17] Cod. Sin. has, "they should not."
[18] Comp. Eph. vi. 9.
[19] Comp. Rom. viii. 29, 30.
[20] Cod. Sin. has, "and not call."
[21] Cod. Sin. has, "in that which is incorruptible."
[22] Cod. Sin. has, "in things that are subject to death," but is corrected as above.
[23] Or, "the persons of the saints." Cod. Sin. omits this clause, but it is added by a corrector.
[24] The text is here confused in all the editions; we have followed that of Dressel. Cod. Sin. is defective. Hilgenfeld's text reads, "Thou shalt seek out every day the faces of the saints, either labouring by word and going to exhort them, and meditating to save a soul by the word, or by thy hands thou shalt labour for the redemption of thy sins" — almost identical with that given above.
[25] Cod. Sin. omits this quotation from Matt. v. 42 or Luke vi. 30 but it is added by a corrector.
[26] Cod. Sin. has, "hate evil."
[27] Cod. Sin. inserts "and."

confess thy sins. Thou shalt not go to prayer with an evil conscience. This is the way of light.[1]

CHAP. XX. — THE WAY OF DARKNESS.

But the way of darkness[2] is crooked, and full of cursing; for it is the way of eternal[3] death with punishment, in which way are the things that destroy the soul, viz., idolatry, over-confidence, the arrogance of power, hypocrisy, double-heartedness, adultery, murder, rapine, haughtiness, transgression,[4] deceit, malice, self-sufficiency, poisoning, magic, avarice,[5] want of the fear of God. [In this way, too,] are those who persecute the good, those who hate truth, those who love falsehood, those who know not the reward of righteousness, those who cleave not to that which is good, those who attend not with just judgment to the widow and orphan, those who watch not to the fear of God, [but incline] to wickedness, from whom meekness and patience are far off; persons who love vanity, follow after a reward, pity not the needy, labour not in aid of him who is overcome with toil; who are prone to evil-speaking, who know not Him that made them, who are murderers of children, destroyers of the workmanship of God; who turn away him that is in want, who oppress the afflicted, who are advocates of the rich, who are unjust judges of the poor, and who are in every respect transgressors.

CHAP. XXI. — CONCLUSION.

It is well, therefore,[6] that he who has learned the judgments of the Lord, as many as have been written, should walk in them. For he who keepeth these shall be glorified in the kingdom of God; but he who chooseth other things[7] shall be destroyed with his works. On this account there will be a resurrection,[8] on this account a retribution. I beseech you who are superiors, if you will receive any counsel of my good-will, have among yourselves those to whom you may show kindness: do not forsake them. For the day is at hand on which all things shall perish with the evil [one]. The Lord is near, and His reward. Again, and yet again, I beseech you: be good lawgivers[9] to one another; continue faithful counsellors of one another; take away from among you all hypocrisy. And may God, who ruleth over all the world, give to you wisdom, intelligence, understanding, knowledge of His judgments,[10] with patience. And be ye[11] taught of God, inquiring diligently what the Lord asks from you; and do it that ye may be safe in the day of judgment.[12] And if you have any remembrance of what is good, be mindful of me, meditating on these things, in order that both my desire and watchfulness may result in some good. I beseech you, entreating this as a favour. While yet you are in this fair vessel,[13] do not fail in any one of those things,[14] but unceasingly seek after them, and fulfil every commandment; for these things are worthy.[15] Wherefore I have been the more earnest to write to you, as my ability served,[16] that I might cheer you. Farewell, ye children of love and peace. The Lord of glory and of all grace be with your spirit. Amen.[17]

---

[1] Cod. Sin. omits this clause: it is inserted by a corrector.
[2] Literally, " of the Black One."
[3] Cod. Sin. joins " eternal " with *way*, instead of *death*.
[4] Cod. Sin. reads " transgressions."
[5] Cod. Sin. omits " magic, avarice."
[6] Cod. Sin. omits " therefore."
[7] The things condemned in the previous chapter.
[8] Cod. Sin. has " resurrections," but is corrected as above.
[9] Cod. Sin. has, " lawgivers of good things."
[10] Cod. Sin. omits the preposition.
[11] Cod. Sin. omits this.
[12] Cod. Sin. reads, " that ye may be found in the day of judgment," which Hilgenfeld adopts.
[13] Literally, " While yet the good vessel is with you," i.e., as long as you are in the body.
[14] Cod. Sin. reads, " fail not in any one of yourselves," which is adopted by Hilgenfeld.
[15] Corrected in Cod. Sin. to, " it is worthy."
[16] Cod. Sin. omits this clause, but it is inserted by the corrector.
[17] Cod. Sin. omits " Amen," and adds at the close, " Epistle of Barnabas."

INTRODUCTORY NOTE

TO THE

FRAGMENTS OF PAPIAS

[A.D. 70–155.] It seems unjust to the holy man of whose comparatively large contributions to early Christian literature such mere relics have been preserved, to set them forth in these versions, unaccompanied by the copious annotations of Dr. Routh. If even such crumbs from his table are not by any means without a practical value, with reference to the Canon and other matters, we may well credit the testimony (though disputed) of Eusebius, that he was a learned man, and well versed in the Holy Scripture.[1] All who name poor Papias are sure to do so with the apologetic qualification of that historian, that he was of slender capacity. Nobody who attributes to him the millenarian fancies, of which he was but a narrator, as if these were the characteristics rather than the blemishes of his works, can fail to accept this estimate of our author. But more may be said when we come to the great name of Irenæus, who seems to make himself responsible for them.[2]

Papias has the credit of association with Polycarp, in the friendship of St. John himself, and of "others who had seen the Lord." He is said to have been bishop of Hierapolis, in Phrygia, and to have died about the same time that Polycarp suffered; but even this is questioned. So little do we know of one whose lost books, could they be recovered, might reverse the received judgment, and establish his claim to the disputed tribute which makes him, like Apollos, "an eloquent man, and mighty in the Scriptures."

The following is the original INTRODUCTORY NOTICE: —

THE principal information in regard to Papias is given in the extracts made among the fragments from the works of Irenæus and Eusebius. He was bishop of the Church in Hierapolis, a city of Phrygia, in the first half of the second century. Later writers affirm that he suffered martyrdom about A.D. 163; some saying that Rome, others that Pergamus, was the scene of his death.

He was a hearer of the Apostle John, and was on terms of intimate intercourse with many who had known the Lord and His apostles. From these he gathered the floating traditions in regard to the sayings of our Lord, and wove them into a production divided into five books. This work does not seem to have been confined to an exposition of the sayings of Christ, but to have contained much historical information.

---

[1] See Lardner, ii. p. 119.
[2] *Against Heresies*, book v. chap. xxxiii. See the prudent note of Canon Robertson (*History of the Christ. Church*, vol. i. p. 116).

Eusebius [1] speaks of Papias as a man most learned in all things, and well acquainted with the Scriptures. In another passage [2] he describes him as of small capacity. The fragments of Papias are translated from the text given in Routh's *Reliquiæ Sacræ*, vol. i. [3]

---

[1] *Hist. Eccl.*, iii. 39.
[2] *Ibid.*
[3] [Where the fragments with learned annotations and elucidations fill forty-four pages.]

FRAGMENTS OF PAPIAS

I.

FROM THE EXPOSITION OF THE ORACLES OF THE LORD.[1]

[THE writings of Papias in common circulation are five in number, and these are called an Exposition of the Oracles of the Lord. Irenæus makes mention of these as the only works written by him, in the following words: "Now testimony is borne to these things in writing by Papias, an ancient man, who was a hearer of John, and a friend of Polycarp, in the fourth of his books; for five books were composed by him." Thus wrote Irenæus. Moreover, Papias himself, in the introduction to his books, makes it manifest that he was not himself a hearer and eye-witness of the holy apostles; but he tells us that he received the truths of our religion[2] from those who were aquainted with them [the apostles] in the following words:]

But I shall not be unwilling to put down, along with my interpretations,[3] whatsoever instructions I received with care at any time from the elders, and stored up with care in my memory, assuring you at the same time of their truth. For I did not, like the multitude, take pleasure in those who spoke much, but in those who taught the truth; nor in those who related strange commandments,[4] but in those who rehearsed the commandments given by the Lord to faith,[5] and proceeding from truth itself. If, then, any one who had attended on the elders came, I asked minutely after their sayings,—what Andrew or Peter said, or what was said by Philip, or by Thomas, or by James, or by John, or by Matthew, or by any other of the Lord's disciples: which things[6] Aristion and the presbyter John, the disciples of the Lord, say. For I imagined that what was to be got from books was not so profitable to me as what came from the living and abiding voice.

II.[7]

[The early Christians] *called those who practised a godly guilelessness,*[8] *children,* [as is stated by Papias in the first book of the Lord's Expositions, and by Clemens Alexandrinus in his *Pædagogue.*]

III.[9]

Judas walked about in this world a sad[10] example of impiety; for his body having swollen to such an extent that he could not pass where a chariot could pass easily, he was crushed by the chariot, so that his bowels gushed out.[11]

IV.[12]

[As the elders who saw John the disciple of the Lord remembered that they had heard from him how the Lord taught in regard to those times, and said]: "The days will come in which vines shall grow, having each ten thousand branches, and in each branch ten thousand twigs, and in each true twig ten thousand shoots, and in every one of the shoots ten thousand clusters, and on every one of the clusters ten thousand grapes, and every grape when pressed will give five-and-twenty metretes of wine. And when any one of the saints shall lay hold of a cluster, another shall cry out, 'I am a better cluster, take me; bless the Lord through me.' In like manner, [He said] that a grain of wheat would

---

[1] This fragment is found in Eusebius, *Hist. Eccl.*, iii. 39.
[2] Literally, " the things of faith."
[3] Papias states that he will give an exact account of what the elders said; and that, in addition to this, he will accompany this account with an explanation of the meaning and import of the statements.
[4] Literally, " commandments belonging to others," and therefore strange and novel to the followers of Christ.
[5] *Given to faith* has been variously understood. Either not stated in direct language, but like parables given in figures, so that only the faithful could understand; or entrusted to faith, that is, to those who were possessed of faith, the faithful.
[6] *Which things*: this is usually translated, "what Aristion and John say;" and the translation is admissible. But the words more naturally mean, that John and Aristion, even at the time of his writing, were telling him some of the sayings of the Lord.
[7] This fragment is found in the *Scholia* of Maximus on the works of Dionysius the Areopagite.
[8] Literally, "a guilelessness according to God."
[9] This fragment is found in Œcumenius.
[10] Literally, " great."
[11] Literally, " were emptied out." Theophylact, after quoting this passage, adds other particulars, as if they were derived from Papias. [But see Routh, i. pp. 26, 27.] He says that Judas's eyes were so swollen that they could not see the light; that they were so sunk that they could not be seen, even by the optical instruments of physicians; and that the rest of his body was covered with runnings and worms. He further states, that he died in a solitary spot, which was left desolate until his time; and no one could pass the place without stopping up his nose with his hands.
[12] From Irenæus, *Hær.*, v. 32. [Hearsay at second-hand, and handed about among many, amounts to nothing as evidence. Note the reports of sermons, also, as they appear in our daily Journals. Whose reputation can survive if such be credited?]

produce ten thousand ears, and that every ear would have ten thousand grains, and every grain would yield ten pounds of clear, pure, fine flour; and that apples, and seeds, and grass would produce in similar proportions; and that all animals, feeding then only on the productions of the earth, would become peaceable and harmonious, and be in perfect subjection to man."[1] [Testimony is borne to these things in writing by Papias, an ancient man, who was a hearer of John and a friend of Polycarp, in the fourth of his books; for five books were composed by him. And he added, saying, "Now these things are credible to believers. And Judas the traitor," says he, "not believing, and asking, 'How shall such growths be accomplished by the Lord?' the Lord said, 'They shall see who shall come to them.' These, then, are the times mentioned by the prophet Isaiah: 'And the wolf shall lie down with the lamb,' etc. (Isa. xi. 6 ff.)."]

V.[2]

As the presbyters say, then[3] those who are deemed worthy of an abode in heaven shall go there, others shall enjoy the delights of Paradise, and others shall possess the splendour of the city;[4] for everywhere the Saviour will be seen, according as they shall be worthy who see Him. But that there is this distinction between the habitation of those who produce an hundred-fold, and that of those who produce sixty-fold, and that of those who produce thirty-fold; for the first will be taken up into the heavens, the second class will dwell in Paradise, and the last will inhabit the city; and that on this account the Lord said, "In my Father's house are many mansions:"[5] for all things belong to God, who supplies all with a suitable dwelling-place, even as His word says, that a share is given to all by the Father,[6] according as each one is or shall be worthy. And this is the couch[7] in which they shall recline who feast, being invited to the wedding. The presbyters, the disciples of the apostles, say that this is the gradation and arrangement of those who are saved, and that they advance through steps of this nature; and that, moreover, they ascend through the Spirit to the Son, and through the Son to the Father; and that in due time the Son will yield up His work to the Father, even as it is said by the apostle, "For He must reign till He hath put all enemies under His feet. The last enemy that shall be destroyed is death."[8] For in the times of the kingdom the just man who is on the earth shall forget to die. "But when He saith all things are put under Him, it is manifest that He is excepted which did put all things under Him. And when all things shall be subdued unto Him, then shall the Son also Himself be subject unto Him that put all things under Him, that God may be all in all."[9]

VI.[10]

[Papias, who is now mentioned by us, affirms that he received the sayings of the apostles from those who accompanied them, and he moreover asserts that he heard in person Aristion and the presbyter John.[11] Accordingly he mentions them frequently by name, and in his writings gives their traditions. Our notice of these circumstances may not be without its use. It may also be worth while to add to the statements of Papias already given, other passages of his in which he relates some miraculous deeds, stating that he acquired the knowledge of them from tradition. The residence of the Apostle Philip with his daughters in Hierapolis has been mentioned above. We must now point out how Papias, who lived at the same time, relates that he had received a wonderful narrative from the daughters of Philip. For he relates that a dead man was raised to life in his day.[12] He also mentions another miracle relating to Justus, surnamed Barsabas, how he swallowed a deadly poison, and received no harm, on account of the grace of the Lord. The same person, moreover, has set down other things as coming to him from unwritten tradition, amongst these some strange parables and instructions of the Saviour, and some other things of a more fabulous nature.[13] Amongst these he says that there will be a millennium after the resurrection from the dead, when the personal reign of Christ will be established on this earth. He moreover hands down, in his own writing, other narratives given by the previously mentioned Aristion of the Lord's sayings, and the traditions of the presbyter John. For information on these points, we can merely refer our readers to the books themselves; but now, to the extracts already made, we shall add, as being a matter of primary importance, a tradition regarding Mark who wrote the Gospel, which he [Papias] has given in the following words]: And the presbyter said this. Mark having become the

---

[1] [See Grabe, *apud* Routh, 1. 29.]
[2] This fragment is found in Irenæus, *Hær.*, v. 36; but it is a mere guess that the saying of the presbyters is taken from the work of Papias.
[3] In the future state.
[4] The new Jerusalem on earth.
[5] John xiv. 2.
[6] Commentators suppose that the reference here is to Matt. xx. 23.
[7] Matt. xxii. 10.
[8] 1 Cor. xv. 25, 26.
[9] 1 Cor. xv. 27, 28.
[10] From Eusebius, *Hist. Eccl.*, iii. 39.
[11] [A certain presbyter, of whom see *Apost. Constitutions*, vii. 46, where he is said to have been ordained by St. John, the Evangelist.]
[12] "In his day" may mean "in the days of Papias," or "in the days of Philip." As the narrative came from the daughters of Philip, it is more likely that Philip's days are meant.
[13] [Again, note the reduplicated hearsay. Not even Irenæus, much less Eusebius, should be accepted, otherwise than as retailing vague reports.]

interpreter of Peter, wrote down accurately whatsoever he remembered. It was not, however, in exact order that he related the sayings or deeds of Christ. For he neither heard the Lord nor accompanied Him. But afterwards, as I said, he accompanied Peter, who accommodated his instructions to the necessities [of his hearers], but with no intention of giving a regular narrative of the Lord's sayings. Wherefore Mark made no mistake in thus writing some things as he remembered them. For of one thing he took especial care, not to omit anything he had heard, and not to put anything fictitious into the statements. [This is what is related by Papias regarding Mark; but with regard to Matthew he has made the following statements]: Matthew put together the oracles [of the Lord] in the Hebrew language, and each one interpreted them as best he could. [The same person uses proofs from the First Epistle of John, and from the Epistle of Peter in like manner. And he also gives another story of a woman[1] who was accused of many sins before the Lord, which is to be found in the Gospel according to the Hebrews.]

VII.[2]

Papias thus speaks, word for word: To some of them [angels] He gave dominion over the arrangement of the world, and He commissioned them to exercise their dominion well. *And he says, immediately after this:* but it happened that their arrangement came to nothing.[3]

VIII.[4]

With regard to the inspiration of the book (Revelation), we deem it superfluous to add another word; for the blessed Gregory Theologus and Cyril, and even men of still older date, Papias, Irenæus, Methodius, and Hippolytus, bore entirely satisfactory testimony to it.

IX.[5]

Taking occasion from Papias of Hierapolis, the illustrious, a disciple of the apostle who leaned on the bosom of Christ, and Clemens, and Pantænus the priest of [the Church] of the Alexandrians, and the wise Ammonius, the ancient and first expositors, who agreed with each other, who understood the work of the six days as referring to Christ and the whole Church.

X.[6]

(1.) Mary the mother of the Lord; (2.) Mary the wife of Cleophas or Alphæus, who was the mother of James the bishop and apostle, and of Simon and Thaddeus, and of one Joseph; (3.) Mary Salome, wife of Zebedee, mother of John the evangelist and James; (4.) Mary Magdalene. These four are found in the Gospel. James and Judas and Joseph were sons of an aunt (2) of the Lord's. James also and John were sons of another aunt (3) of the Lord's. Mary (2), mother of James the Less and Joseph, wife of Alphæus was the sister of Mary the mother of the Lord, whom John names of Cleophas, either from her father or from the family of the clan, or for some other reason. Mary Salome (3) is called Salome either from her husband or her village. Some affirm that she is the same as Mary of Cleophas, because she had two husbands.

---

[1] Rufinus supposes this story to be the same as that now found in the *textus receptus* of John's Gospel, viii. 1-11,—the woman taken in adultery.
[2] This extract is made from Andreas Cæsariensis, [Bishop of Cæsarea in Cappadocia, *circiter*, A.D 500].
[3] That is, that government of the world's affairs was a failure. An ancient writer takes τάξις to mean the arraying of the evil angels in battle against God.
[4] This also is taken from Andreas Cæsariensis. [See Lardner, vol. v. 77.]
[5] This fragment, or rather reference, is taken from Anastasius Sinaita. Routh gives, as another fragment, the repetition of the same statement by Anastasius.
[6] This fragment was found by Grabe in a MS. of the Bodleian Library, with the inscription on the margin, "Papia." Westcott states that it forms part of a dictionary written by "a mediæval Papias. [He seems to have added the words, "Maria is called *Illuminatrix*, or *Star of the Sea*," etc, a middle-age device.] The dictionary exists in MS. both at Oxford and Cambridge."

JUSTIN MARTYR

INTRODUCTORY NOTE

TO THE

FIRST APOLOGY OF JUSTIN MARTYR

[A.D. 110-165.] JUSTIN was a Gentile, but born in Samaria, near Jacob's well. He must have been well educated: he had travelled extensively, and he seems to have been a person enjoying at least a competence. After trying all other systems, his elevated tastes and refined perceptions made him a disciple of Socrates and Plato. So he climbed towards Christ. As he himself narrates the story of his conversion, it need not be anticipated here. What Plato was feeling after, he found in Jesus of Nazareth. The conversion of such a man marks a new era in the gospel history. The sub-apostolic age begins with the first Christian author, — the founder of theological literature. It introduced to mankind, as the mother of true philosophy, the despised teaching of those Galileans to whom their Master had said, "Ye are the light of the world."

And this is the epoch which forced this great truth upon the attention of contemplative minds. It was more than a hundred years since the angels had sung " Good-will to men ; " and that song had now been heard for successive generations, breaking forth from the lips of sufferers on the cross, among lions, and amid blazing faggots. Here was a nobler Stoicism that needed interpretation. Not only choice spirits, despising the herd and boasting of a loftier intellectual sphere, were its professors; but thousands of men, women, and children, withdrawing themselves not at all from the ordinary and humble lot of the people, were inspired by it to live and die heroically and sublimely, — exhibiting a superiority to revenge and hate entirely unaccountable, praying for their enemies, and seeking to glorify their God by love to their fellow-men.

And in spite of Gallios and Neros alike, the gospel was dispelling the gross darkness. Of this, Pliny's letter to Trajan is decisive evidence. Even in Seneca we detect reflections of the daybreak. Plutarch writes as never a Gentile could have written until now. Plato is practically surpassed by him in his thoughts upon the " delays [1] of the Divine Justice." Hadrian's address to his soul, in his dying moments, is a tribute to the new ideas which had been sown in the popular mind. And now the Antonines, impelled by something in the age, came forward to reign as "philosophers." At this moment, Justin Martyr confronts them like a Daniel. The "little stone" smites the imperial image in the face, not yet "in the toes." He tells the professional philosophers on a throne how false and hollow is all wisdom that is not meant for all humanity, and that is not capable of leavening the masses. He exposes the impotency of even Socratic philosophy: he shows, in contrast, the force that works in the words of Jesus; he points out their regenerating power. It is the mission of Justin to be a star in the West, leading its Wise Men to the cradle of Bethlehem.

---

[1] See Amyot's translation, and a more modern one by De Maistre (*Œuvres*, vol. ii. Paris, 1833). An edition of *The Delays* (the original, with notes by Professor Hackett) has appeared in America (Andover, *circ.*, 1842), and is praised by Tayler Lewis.

The writings of Justin are deficient in charms of style; and, for us, there is something the reverse of attractive in the forms of thought which he had learned from the philosophers.[1] If Plato had left us nothing but the Timæus, a Renan would doubtless have reproached him as of feeble intellectual power. So a dancing-master might criticise the movements of an athlete, or the writhings of St. Sebastian shot with arrows. The practical wisdom of Justin using the rhetoric of his times, and discomfiting false philosophy with its own weapons, is not appreciated by the fastidious Parisian. But the manly and heroic pleadings of the man, for a despised people with whom he had boldly identified himself; the intrepidity with which he defends them before despots, whose mere caprice might punish him with death; above all, the undaunted spirit with which he exposes the shame and absurdity of their inveterate superstition and reproaches the memory of Hadrian whom Antoninus had deified, as he had deified Antinous of loathsome history, — these are characteristics which every instinct of the unvitiated soul delights to honour. Justin cannot be refuted by a sneer.

He wore his philosopher's gown after his conversion, as a token that he had attained the only true philosophy. And seeing, that, after the conflicts and tests of ages, it is the only philosophy that lasts and lives and triumphs, its discoverer deserves the homage of mankind. Of the philosophic gown we shall hear again when we come to Tertullian.[2]

The residue of Justin's history may be found in "The Martyrdom" and other pages soon to follow, as well as in the following INTRODUCTORY NOTE of the able translators, Messrs. Dods and Reith: —

JUSTIN MARTYR was born in Flavia Neapolis, a city of Samaria, the modern Nablous. The date of his birth is uncertain, but may be fixed about A.D. 114. His father and grandfather were probably of Roman origin. Before his conversion to Christianity he studied in the schools of the philosophers, searching after some knowledge which should satisfy the cravings of his soul. At last he became acquainted with Christianity, being at once impressed with the extraordinary fearlessness which the Christians displayed in the presence of death, and with the grandeur, stability, and truth of the teachings of the Old Testament. From this time he acted as an evangelist, taking every opportunity to proclaim the gospel as the only safe and certain philosophy, the only way to salvation. It is probable that he travelled much. We know that he was some time in Ephesus, and he must have lived for a considerable period in Rome. Probably he settled in Rome as a Christian teacher. While he was there, the philosophers, especially the Cynics, plotted against him, and he sealed his testimony to the truth by martyrdom.

The principal facts of Justin's life are gathered from his own writings. There is little clue to dates. It is agreed on all hands that he lived in the reign of Antoninus Pius, and the testimony of Eusebius and most credible historians renders it nearly certain that he suffered martyrdom in the reign of Marcus Aurelius. The *Chronicon Paschale* gives as the date 165 A.D.

The writings of Justin Martyr are among the most important that have come down to us from the second century. He was not the first that wrote an Apology in behalf of the Christians, but his Apologies are the earliest extant. They are characterized by intense Christian fervour, and they give us an insight into the relations existing between heathens and Christians in those days. His other principal writing, the Dialogue with Trypho, is the first elaborate exposition of the reasons for regarding Christ as the Messiah of the Old Testament, and the first systematic attempt to exhibit the false position of the Jews in regard to Christianity.

Many of Justin's writings have perished. Those works which have come to us bearing his name have been divided into three classes.

---

[1] He quotes Plato's reference, e.g., to the X.; but the Orientals delighted in such conceits. Compare the Hebrew critics on the ה (in Gen. i. 4), on which see Nordheimer, *Gram.*, vol. i. p. 7, New York, 1838.

[2] It survives in the pulpits of Christendom — Greek, Latin, Anglican, Lutheran, etc. — to this day, in slightly different forms.

The first class embraces those which are unquestionably genuine, viz. the two Apologies, and the Dialogue with Trypho. Some critics have urged objections against Justin's authorship of the Dialogue; but the objections are regarded now as possessing no weight.

The second class consists of those works which are regarded by some critics as Justin's, and by others as not his. They are: 1. An Address to the Greeks; 2. A Hortatory Address to the Greeks; 3. On the Sole Government of God; 4. An Epistle to Diognetus; 5. Fragments from a work on the Resurrection; 6. And other Fragments. Whatever difficulty there may be in settling the authorship of these treatises, there is but one opinion as to their earliness. The latest of them, in all probability, was not written later than the third century.

The third class consists of those that are unquestionably not the works of Justin. These are: 1. An Exposition of the True Faith; 2. Replies to the Orthodox; 3. Christian Questions to Gentiles; 4. Gentile Questions to Christians; 5. Epistle to Zenas and Serenus; and 6. A Refutation of certain Doctrines of Aristotle. There is no clue to the date of the two last. There can be no doubt that the others were written after the Council of Nicæa, though, immediately after the Reformation, Calvin and others appealed to the first as a genuine writing of Justin's.

There is a curious question connected with the Apologies of Justin which have come down to us. Eusebius mentions two Apologies,— one written in the reign of Antoninus Pius, the other in the reign of Marcus Aurelius. Critics have disputed much whether we have these two Apologies in those now extant. Some have maintained, that what is now called the Second Apology was the preface of the first, and that the second is lost. Others have tried to show, that the so-called Second Apology is the continuation of the first, and that the second is lost. Others have supposed that the two Apologies which we have are Justin's two Apologies, but that Eusebius was wrong in affirming that the second was addressed to Marcus Aurelius; and others maintain, that we have in our two Apologies the two Apologies mentioned by Eusebius, and that our first is his first, and our second his second.

THE FIRST APOLOGY OF JUSTIN

CHAP. I. — ADDRESS.

To the Emperor Titus Ælius Adrianus Antoninus Pius Augustus Cæsar, and to his son Verissimus the Philosopher, and to Lucius the Philosopher, the natural son of Cæsar, and the adopted son of Pius, a lover of learning, and to the sacred Senate, with the whole People of the Romans, I, Justin, the son of Priscus and grandson of Bacchius, natives of Flavia Neapolis in Palestine, present this address and petition in behalf of those of all nations who are unjustly hated and wantonly abused, myself being one of them.

CHAP. II. — JUSTICE DEMANDED.

Reason directs those who are truly pious and philosophical to honour and love only what is true, declining to follow traditional opinions,[1] if these be worthless. For not only does sound reason direct us to refuse the guidance of those who did or taught anything wrong, but it is incumbent on the lover of truth, by all means, and if death be threatened, even before his own life, to choose to do and say what is right. Do you, then, since ye are called pious and philosophers, guardians of justice and lovers of learning, give good heed, and hearken to my address; and if ye are indeed such, it will be manifested. For we have come, not to flatter you by this writing, nor please you by our address, but to beg that you pass judgment, after an accurate and searching investigation, not flattered by prejudice or by a desire of pleasing superstitious men, nor induced by irrational impulse or evil rumours which have long been prevalent, to give a decision which will prove to be against yourselves. For as for us, we reckon that no evil can be done us, unless we be convicted as evil-doers, or be proved to be wicked men; and you, you can kill, but not hurt us.

CHAP. III. — CLAIM OF JUDICIAL INVESTIGATION.

But lest any one think that this is an unreasonable and reckless utterance, we demand that the charges against the Christians be investigated, and that, if these be substantiated, they be punished as they deserve; [or rather, indeed, we ourselves will punish them.][2] But if no one can convict us of anything, true reason forbids you, for the sake of a wicked rumour, to wrong blameless men, and indeed rather yourselves, who think fit to direct affairs, not by judgment, but by passion. And every sober-minded person will declare this to be the only fair and equitable adjustment, namely, that the subjects render an unexceptional account of their own life and doctrine; and that, on the other hand, the rulers should give their decision in obedience, not to violence and tyranny, but to piety and philosophy. For thus would both rulers and ruled reap benefit. For even one of the ancients somewhere said, "Unless both rulers and ruled philosophize, it is impossible to make states blessed."[3] It is our task, therefore, to afford to all an opportunity of inspecting our life and teachings, lest, on account of those who are accustomed to be ignorant of our affairs, we should incur the penalty due to them for mental blindness;[4] and it is your business, when you hear us, to be found, as reason demands, good judges. For if, when ye have learned the truth, you do not what is just, you will be before God without excuse.

CHAP. IV. — CHRISTIANS UNJUSTLY CONDEMNED FOR THEIR MERE NAME.

By the mere application of a name, nothing is decided, either good or evil, apart from the actions implied in the name; and indeed, so far at least as one may judge from the name we are accused of, we are most excellent people.[5] But

---

[1] Literally, "the opinions of the ancients."
[2] Thirlby regarded the clause in brackets as an interpolation. There is considerable variety of opinion as to the exact meaning of the words amongst those who regard them as genuine.
[3] Plat. *Rep.*, v. 18.
[4] That is to say, if the Christians refused or neglected to make their real opinions and practices known, they would share the guilt of those whom they thus kept in darkness.
[5] Justin avails himself here of the similarity in sound of the words Χριστός (Christ) and χρηστός (good, worthy, excellent). The play upon these words is kept up throughout this paragraph, and cannot be always represented to the English reader. [But Justin was merely quoting and using, *ad hominem*, the popular blunder of which Suetonius (*Life of Claudius*, cap. 25) gives us an example, "impulsore Chresto." It will be observed again in others of these Fathers.]

as we do not think it just to beg to be acquitted on account of the name, if we be convicted as evil-doers, so, on the other hand, if we be found to have committed no offence, either in the matter of thus naming ourselves, or of our conduct as citizens, it is your part very earnestly to guard against incurring just punishment, by unjustly punishing those who are not convicted. For from a name neither praise nor punishment could reasonably spring, unless something excellent or base in action be proved. And those among yourselves who are accused you do not punish before they are convicted; but in our case you receive the name as proof against us, and this although, so far as the name goes, you ought rather to punish our accusers. For we are accused of being Christians, and to hate what is *excellent* (Chrestian) is unjust. Again, if any of the accused deny the name, and say that he is not a Christian, you acquit him, as having no evidence against him as a wrong-doer; but if any one acknowledge that he is a Christian, you punish him on account of this acknowledgment. Justice requires that you inquire into the life both of him who confesses and of him who denies, that by his deeds it may be apparent what kind of man each is. For as some who have been taught by the Master, Christ, not to deny Him, give encouragement to others when they are put to the question, so in all probability do those who lead wicked lives give occasion to those who, without consideration, take upon them to accuse all the Christians of impiety and wickedness. And this also is not right. For of philosophy, too, some assume the name and the garb who do nothing worthy of their profession; and you are well aware, that those of the ancients whose opinions and teachings were quite diverse, are yet all called by the one name of philosophers. And of these some taught atheism; and the poets who have flourished among you raise a laugh out of the uncleanness of Jupiter with his own children. And those who now adopt such instruction are not restrained by you; but, on the contrary, you bestow prizes and honours upon those who euphoniously insult the gods.

CHAP. V. — CHRISTIANS CHARGED WITH ATHEISM.

Why, then, should this be? In our case, who pledge ourselves to do no wickedness, nor to hold these atheistic opinions, you do not examine the charges made against us; but, yielding to unreasoning passion, and to the instigation of evil demons, you punish us without consideration or judgment. For the truth shall be spoken; since of old these evil demons, effecting apparitions of themselves, both defiled women and corrupted boys, and showed such fearful sights to men, that those who did not use their reason in judging of the actions that were done, were struck with terror; and being carried away by fear, and not knowing that these were demons, they called them gods, and gave to each the name which each of the demons chose for himself.[1] And when Socrates endeavoured, by true reason and examination, to bring these things to light, and deliver men from the demons, then the demons themselves, by means of men who rejoiced in iniquity, compassed his death, as an atheist and a profane person, on the charge that "he was introducing new divinities;" and in our case they display a similar activity. For not only among the Greeks did reason (Logos) prevail to condemn these things through Socrates, but also among the Barbarians were they condemned by Reason (or the Word, the Logos) Himself, who took shape, and became man, and was called Jesus Christ; and in obedience to Him, we not only deny that they who did such things as these are gods,[2] but assert that they are wicked and impious demons,[2] whose actions will not bear comparison with those even of men desirous of virtue.

CHAP. VI. — CHARGE OF ATHEISM REFUTED.

Hence are we called atheists. And we confess that we are atheists, so far as gods of this sort are concerned, but not with respect to the most true God, the Father of righteousness and temperance and the other virtues, who is free from all impurity. But both Him, and the Son (who came forth from Him and taught us these things, and the host of the other good angels who follow and are made like to Him),[3] and the prophetic Spirit, we worship and adore, knowing them in reason and truth, and declaring without grudging to every one who wishes to learn, as we have been taught.

CHAP. VII. — EACH CHRISTIAN MUST BE TRIED BY HIS OWN LIFE.

But some one will say, Some have ere now been arrested and convicted as evil-doers. For

---

[1] [1. Cor. x. 20. Milton's admirable economy in working this truth into his great poem (i. 378) affords a sublime exposition of the mind of the Fathers on the origin of mythologies.]

[2] The word δαίμων means in Greek a god, but the Christians used the word to signify an evil spirit. Justin uses the same word here for god and demon. The connection which Justin and other Christian writers supposed to exist between evil spirits and the gods of the heathens will be apparent from Justin's own statements. The word διάβολος, devil, is not applied to these demons. There is but one devil, but many demons.

[3] This is the literal and obvious translation of Justin's words. But from c. 13, 16, and 61, it is evident that he did not desire to inculcate the worship of angels. We are therefore driven to adopt another translation of this passage, even though it be somewhat harsh. Two such translations have been proposed: the first connecting " us " and " the host of the other good angels " as the common object of the verb " taught; " the second connecting " these things " with " the host of," etc., and making these two together the subject taught. In the first case the translation would stand, " taught these things to us and to the host," etc.; in the second case the translation would be, " taught us about these things, and about the host of the others who follow Him, viz. the good angels." [I have ventured to insert parenthetic marks in the text, an obvious and simple resource to suggest the manifest intent of the author. Grabe's note *in loc*. gives another and very ingenious exegesis, but the simplest is best.]

you condemn many, many a time, after inquiring into the life of each of the accused severally, but not on account of those of whom we have been speaking.[1] And this we acknowledge, that as among the Greeks those who teach such theories as please themselves are all called by the one name "Philosopher," though their doctrines be diverse, so also among the Barbarians this name on which accusations are accumulated is the common property of those who are and those who seem wise. For all are called Christians. Wherefore we demand that the deeds of all those who are accused to you be judged, in order that each one who is convicted may be punished as an evil-doer, and not as a Christian; and if it is clear that any one is blameless, that he may be acquitted, since by the mere fact of his being a Christian he does no wrong.[2] For we will not require that you punish our accusers;[3] they being sufficiently punished by their present wickedness and ignorance of what is right.

CHAP. VIII. — CHRISTIANS CONFESS THEIR FAITH IN GOD.

And reckon ye that it is for your sakes we have been saying these things; for it is in our power, when we are examined, to deny that we are Christians; but we would not live by telling a lie. For, impelled by the desire of the eternal and pure life, we seek the abode that is with God, the Father and Creator of all, and hasten to confess our faith, persuaded and convinced as we are that they who have proved to God[4] by their works that they followed Him, and loved to abide with Him where there is no sin to cause disturbance, can obtain these things. This, then, to speak shortly, is what we expect and have learned from Christ, and teach. And Plato, in like manner, used to say that Rhadamanthus and Minos would punish the wicked who came before them; and we say that the same thing will be done, but at the hand of Christ, and upon the wicked in the same bodies united again to their spirits which are now to undergo everlasting punishment; and not only, as Plato said, for a period of a thousand years. And if any one say that this is incredible or impossible, this error of ours is one which concerns ourselves only, and no other person, so long as you cannot convict us of doing any harm.

CHAP. IX. — FOLLY OF IDOL WORSHIP.

And neither do we honour with many sacrifices and garlands of flowers such deities as men have formed and set in shrines and called gods; since we see that these are soulless and dead, and have not the form of God (for we do not consider that God has such a form as some say that they imitate to His honour), but have the names and forms of those wicked demons which have appeared. For why need we tell you who already know, into what forms the craftsmen,[5] carving and cutting, casting and hammering, fashion the materials? And often out of vessels of dishonour, by merely changing the form, and making an image of the requisite shape, they make what they call a god; which we consider not only senseless, but to be even insulting to God, who, having ineffable glory and form, thus gets His name attached to things that are corruptible, and require constant service. And that the artificers of these are both intemperate, and, not to enter into particulars, are practised in every vice, you very well know; even their own girls who work along with them they corrupt. What infatuation! that dissolute men should be said to fashion and make gods for your worship, and that you should appoint such men the guardians of the temples where they are enshrined; not recognising that it is unlawful even to think or say that men are the guardians of gods.

CHAP. X. — HOW GOD IS TO BE SERVED.

But we have received by tradition that God does not need the material offerings which men can give, seeing, indeed, that He Himself is the provider of all things. And we have been taught, and are convinced, and do believe, that He accepts those only who imitate the excellences which reside in Him, temperance, and justice, and philanthropy, and as many virtues as are peculiar to a God who is called by no proper name. And we have been taught that He in the beginning did of His goodness, for man's sake, create all things out of unformed matter; and if men by their works show themselves worthy of this His design, they are deemed worthy, and so we have received — of reigning in company with Him, being delivered from corruption and suffering. For as in the beginning He created us when we were not, so do we consider that, in like manner, those who choose what is pleasing to Him are, on account of their choice, deemed worthy of incorruption and of fellowship with Him. For the coming into being at first was not in our own power; and in order that we may follow those things which please Him, choosing them by means of the rational faculties He has Himself endowed us with, He both persuades us and leads us to faith. And we think it for the advantage of all men that they are not restrained from learning these

---

[1] i.e., according to Otto, "not on account of the sincere Christians of whom we have been speaking." According to Trollope, "not on account of (or at the instigation of) the demons before mentioned."
[2] Or, "as a Christian who has done no wrong."
[3] Compare the Rescript of Adrian appended to this Apology.
[4] Literally, "persuaded God."

[5] [Isa. xliv. 9-20; Jer. x. 3.]

things, but are even urged thereto. For the restraint which human laws could not effect, the Word, inasmuch as He is divine, would have effected, had not the wicked demons, taking as their ally the lust of wickedness which is in every man, and which draws variously to all manner of vice, scattered many false and profane accusations, none of which attach to us.

CHAP. XI. — WHAT KINGDOM CHRISTIANS LOOK FOR.

And when you hear that we look for a kingdom, you suppose, without making any inquiry, that we speak of a human kingdom; whereas we speak of that which is with God, as appears also from the confession of their faith made by those who are charged with being Christians, though they know that death is the punishment awarded to him who so confesses. For if we looked for a human kingdom, we should also deny our Christ, that we might not be slain; and we should strive to escape detection, that we might obtain what we expect. But since our thoughts are not fixed on the present, we are not concerned when men cut us off; since also death is a debt which must at all events be paid.

CHAP. XII. — CHRISTIANS LIVE AS UNDER GOD'S EYE.

And more than all other men are we your helpers and allies in promoting peace, seeing that we hold this view, that it is alike impossible for the wicked, the covetous, the conspirator, and for the virtuous, to escape the notice of God, and that each man goes to everlasting punishment or salvation according to the value of his actions. For if all men knew this, no one would choose wickedness even for a little, knowing that he goes to the everlasting punishment of fire; but would by all means restrain himself, and adorn himself with virtue, that he might obtain the good gifts of God, and escape the punishments. For those who, on account of the laws and punishments you impose, endeavour to escape detection when they offend (and they offend, too, under the impression that it is quite possible to escape your detection, since you are but men), those persons, if they learned and were convinced that nothing, whether actually done or only intended, can escape the knowledge of God, would by all means live decently on account of the penalties threatened, as even you yourselves will admit. But you seem to fear lest all men become righteous, and you no longer have any to punish. Such would be the concern of public executioners, but not of good princes. But, as we before said, we are persuaded that these things are prompted by evil spirits, who demand sacrifices and service even from those who live unreasonably; but as for you, we presume that you who aim at [a reputation for] piety and philosophy will do nothing unreasonable. But if you also, like the foolish, prefer custom to truth, do what you have power to do. But just so much power have rulers who esteem opinion more than truth, as robbers have in a desert. And that you will not succeed is declared by the Word, than whom, after God who begat Him, we know there is no ruler more kingly and just. For as all shrink from succeeding to the poverty or sufferings or obscurity of their fathers, so whatever the Word forbids us to choose, the sensible man will not choose. That all these things should come to pass, I say, our Teacher foretold, He who is both Son and Apostle of God the Father of all and the Ruler, Jesus Christ; from whom also we have the name of Christians. Whence we become more assured of all the things He taught us, since whatever He beforehand foretold should come to pass, is seen in fact coming to pass; and this is the work of God, to tell of a thing before it happens, and as it was foretold so to show it happening. It were possible to pause here and add no more, reckoning that we demand what is just and true; but because we are well aware that it is not easy suddenly to change a mind possessed by ignorance, we intend to add a few things, for the sake of persuading those who love the truth, knowing that it is not impossible to put ignorance to flight by presenting the truth.

CHAP. XIII. — CHRISTIANS SERVE GOD RATIONALLY.

What sober-minded man, then, will not acknowledge that we are not atheists, worshipping as we do the Maker of this universe, and declaring, as we have been taught, that He has no need of streams of blood and libations and incense; whom we praise to the utmost of our power by the exercise of prayer and thanksgiving for all things wherewith we are supplied, as we have been taught that the only honour that is worthy of Him is not to consume by fire what He has brought into being for our sustenance, but to use it for ourselves and those who need, and with gratitude to Him to offer thanks by invocations and hymns [1] for our creation, and for all the means of health, and for the various qualities of the different kinds of things, and for the changes of the seasons; and to present before Him petitions for our existing again in incorruption through faith in Him. Our teacher of these things is Jesus Christ, who also was born for this purpose, and was crucified under Pontius Pilate, procurator of Judæa, in the times of Tiberius Cæsar; and that we reasonably worship Him, having learned that He is the Son of the true

---

[1] πομπὰς καὶ ὕμνους. "Grabe, and it should seem correctly, understands πομπὰς to be *solemn prayers*. . . . He also remarks, that the ὕμνοι were either psalms of David, or some of those psalms and songs made by the primitive Christians, which are mentioned in Eusebius, *H. E.*, v. 28."—TROLLOPE.

God Himself, and holding Him in the second place, and the prophetic Spirit in the third, we will prove. For they proclaim our madness to consist in this, that we give to a crucified man a place second to the unchangeable and eternal God, the Creator of all; for they do not discern the mystery that is herein, to which, as we make it plain to you, we pray you to give heed.

CHAP. XIV. — THE DEMONS MISREPRESENT CHRISTIAN DOCTRINE.

For we forewarn you to be on your guard, lest those demons whom we have been accusing should deceive you, and quite divert you from reading and understanding what we say. For they strive to hold you their slaves and servants; and sometimes by appearances in dreams, and sometimes by magical impositions, they subdue all who make no strong opposing effort for their own salvation. And thus do we also, since our persuasion by the Word, stand aloof from them (i.e., the demons), and follow the only unbegotten God through His Son — we who formerly delighted in fornication, but now embrace chastity alone; we who formerly used magical arts, dedicate ourselves to the good and unbegotten God; we who valued above all things the acquisition of wealth and possessions, now bring what we have into a common stock, and communicate to every one in need; we who hated and destroyed one another, and on account of their different manners would not live[1] with men of a different tribe, now, since the coming of Christ, live familiarly with them, and pray for our enemies, and endeavour to persuade those who hate us unjustly to live comformably to the good precepts of Christ, to the end that they may become partakers with us of the same joyful hope of a reward from God the ruler of all. But lest we should seem to be reasoning sophistically, we consider it right, before giving you the promised[2] explanation, to cite a few precepts given by Christ Himself. And be it yours, as powerful rulers, to inquire whether we have been taught and do teach these things truly. Brief and concise utterances fell from Him, for He was no sophist, but His word was the power of God.

CHAP. XV. — WHAT CHRIST HIMSELF TAUGHT.

Concerning chastity, He uttered such sentiments as these:[3] "Whosoever looketh upon a woman to lust after her, hath committed adultery with her already in his heart before God." And, "If thy right eye offend thee, cut it out; for it is better for thee to enter into the kingdom of heaven with one eye, than, having two eyes, to be cast into everlasting fire." And, "Whosoever shall marry her that is divorced from another husband, committeth adultery."[4] And, "There are some who have been made eunuchs of men, and some who were born eunuchs, and some who have made themselves eunuchs for the kingdom of heaven's sake; but all cannot receive this saying."[5] So that all who, by human law, are twice married,[6] are in the eye of our Master sinners, and those who look upon a woman to lust after her. For not only he who in act commits adultery is rejected by Him, but also he who desires to commit adultery: since not only our works, but also our thoughts, are open before God. And many, both men and women, who have been Christ's disciples from childhood, remain pure at the age of sixty or seventy years; and I boast that I could produce such from every race of men. For what shall I say, too, of the countless multitude of those who have reformed intemperate habits, and learned these things? For Christ called not the just nor the chaste to repentance, but the ungodly, and the licentious, and the unjust; His words being, "I came not to call the righteous, but sinners to repentance."[7] For the heavenly Father desires rather the repentance than the punishment of the sinner. And of our love to all, He taught thus: "If ye love them that love you, what new thing do ye? for even fornicators do this. But I say unto you, Pray for your enemies, and love them that hate you, and bless them that curse you, and pray for them that despitefully use you."[8] And that we should communicate to the needy, and do nothing for glory, He said, "Give to him that asketh, and from him that would borrow turn not away; for if ye lend to them of whom ye hope to receive, what new thing do ye? even the publicans do this. Lay not up for yourselves treasure upon earth, where moth and rust doth corrupt, and where robbers break through; but lay up for yourselves treasure in heaven, where neither moth nor rust doth corrupt. For what is a man profited, if he shall gain the whole world, and lose his own soul? or what shall a man give in exchange for it? Lay up treasure, therefore, in heaven, where neither moth nor rust doth corrupt."[9] And, "Be ye kind and merciful, as your Father also is kind and merciful, and maketh His sun to rise on sinners, and the righteous, and the wicked.

---

[1] Literally, "would not use the same hearth or fire."
[2] See the end of chap. xii.
[3] The reader will notice that Justin quotes from memory, so that there are some slight discrepancies between the words of Jesus as here cited, and the same sayings as recorded in our Gospels.
[4] Matt. v. 28, 29, 32.
[5] Matt. xix. 12.
[6] διγαμίας ποιούμενοι, lit. contracting a double marriage. Of double marriages there are three kinds: the first, marriage with a second wife while the first is still alive and recognised as a lawful wife, or bigamy; the second, marriage with a second wife after divorce from the first. and third, marriage with a second wife after the death of the first. It is thought that Justin here refers to the second case.
[7] Matt. ix. 13.
[8] Matt. v. 46, 44; Luke vi. 28.
[9] Luke vi. 30, 34; Matt. vi. 19, xvi. 26, vi. 20.

Take no thought what ye shall eat, or what ye shall put on: are ye not better than the birds and the beasts? And God feedeth them. Take no thought, therefore, what ye shall eat, or what ye shall put on; for your heavenly Father knoweth that ye have need of these things. But seek ye the kingdom of heaven, and all these things shall be added unto you. For where his treasure is, there also is the mind of a man."[1] And, "Do not these things to be seen of men; otherwise ye have no reward from your Father which is in heaven."[2]

CHAP. XVI. — CONCERNING PATIENCE AND SWEARING.

And concerning our being patient of injuries, and ready to serve all, and free from anger, this is what He said: "To him that smiteth thee on the one cheek, offer also the other; and him that taketh away thy cloak or coat, forbid not. And whosoever shall be angry, is in danger of the fire. And every one that compelleth thee to go with him a mile, follow him two. And let your good works shine before men, that they, seeing them, may glorify your Father which is in heaven."[3] For we ought not to strive; neither has He desired us to be imitators of wicked men, but He has exhorted us to lead all men, by patience and gentleness, from shame and the love of evil. And this indeed is proved in the case of many who once were of your way of thinking, but have changed their violent and tyrannical disposition, being overcome either by the constancy which they have witnessed in their neighbours' lives,[4] or by the extraordinary forbearance they have observed in their fellow-travellers when defrauded, or by the honesty of those with whom they have transacted business.

And with regard to our not swearing at all, and always speaking the truth, He enjoined as follows: "Swear not at all; but let your yea be yea, and your nay, nay; for whatsoever is more than these cometh of evil."[5] And that we ought to worship God alone, He thus persuaded us: "The greatest commandment is, Thou shalt worship the Lord thy God, and Him only shalt thou serve, with all thy heart, and with all thy strength, the Lord God that made thee."[6] And when a certain man came to Him and said, "Good Master," He answered and said, "There is none good but God only, who made all things."[7] And let those who are not found living as He taught, be understood to be no Christians, even though they profess with the lip the precepts of Christ; for not those who make profession, but those who do the works, shall be saved, according to His word: "Not every one who saith to Me, Lord, Lord, shall enter into the kingdom of heaven, but he that doeth the will of My Father which is in heaven. For whosoever heareth Me, and doeth My sayings, heareth Him that sent Me. And many will say unto Me, Lord, Lord, have we not eaten and drunk in Thy name, and done wonders? And then will I say unto them, Depart from Me, ye workers of iniquity. Then shall there be wailing and gnashing of teeth, when the righteous shall shine as the sun, and the wicked are sent into everlasting fire. For many shall come in My name, clothed outwardly in sheep's clothing, but inwardly being ravening wolves. By their works ye shall know them. And every tree that bringeth not forth good fruit, is hewn down and cast into the fire."[8] And as to those who are not living pursuant to these His teachings, and are Christians only in name, we demand that all such be punished by you.

CHAP. XVII. — CHRIST TAUGHT CIVIL OBEDIENCE.

And everywhere we, more readily than all men, endeavour to pay to those appointed by you the taxes both ordinary and extraordinary,[9] as we have been taught by Him; for at that time some came to Him and asked Him, if one ought to pay tribute to Cæsar; and He answered, "Tell Me, whose image does the coin bear?" And they said, "Cæsar's." And again He answered them, "Render therefore to Cæsar the things that are Cæsar's, and to God the things that are God's."[10] Whence to God alone we render worship, but in other things we gladly serve you, acknowledging you as kings and rulers of men, and praying that with your kingly power you be found to possess also sound judgment. But if you pay no regard to our prayers and frank explanations, we shall suffer no loss, since we believe (or rather, indeed, are persuaded) that every man will suffer punishment in eternal fire according to the merit of his deed, and will render account according to the power he has received from God, as Christ intimated when He said, "To whom God has given more, of him shall more be required."[11]

CHAP. XVIII. — PROOF OF IMMORTALITY AND THE RESURRECTION.

For reflect upon the end of each of the preceding kings, how they died the death common to all, which, if it issued in insensibility, would

---

[1] Luke vi. 36; Matt. v. 45, vi. 25, 26, 33, 21.
[2] Matt. vi. 1.
[3] Luke vi. 29; Matt. vi. 22, 41, 16.
[4] i.e., Christian neighbours.
[5] Matt. v. 34, 27.
[6] Mark xii. 30.
[7] Matt. xix. 6, 17.

[8] Matt. vii. 21, etc.; Luke xiii. 26; Matt. xiii. 42, vii. 15, 16, 19.
[9] φόρους καὶ εἰσφοράς. The former is the annual tribute; the latter, any occasional assessment. See Otto's Note, and Thucyd. iii. 19.
[10] Matt. xxii. 17, 19, 20, 21.
[11] Luke xii. 48.

be a godsend[1] to all the wicked. But since sensation remains to all who have ever lived, and eternal punishment is laid up (i.e., for the wicked), see that ye neglect not to be convinced, and to hold as your belief, that these things are true. For let even necromancy, and the divinations you practise by immaculate children,[2] and the evoking of departed human souls,[3] and those who are called among the magi, Dream-senders and Assistant-spirits (Familiars),[4] and all that is done by those who are skilled in such matters — let these persuade you that even after death souls are in a state of sensation; and those who are seized and cast about by the spirits of the dead, whom all call dæmoniacs or madmen;[5] and what you repute as oracles, both of Amphilochus, Dodana, Pytho, and as many other such as exist; and the opinions of your authors, Empedocles and Pythagoras, Plato and Socrates, and the pit of Homer,[6] and the descent of Ulysses to inspect these things, and all that has been uttered of a like kind. Such favour as you grant to these, grant also to us, who not less but more firmly than they believe in God; since we expect to receive again our own bodies, though they be dead and cast into the earth, for we maintain that with God nothing is impossible.

CHAP. XIX. — THE RESURRECTION POSSIBLE.

And to any thoughtful person would anything appear more incredible, than, if we were not in the body, and some one were to say that it was possible that from a small drop of human seed bones and sinews and flesh be formed into a shape such as we see? For let this now be said hypothetically: if you yourselves were not such as you now are, and born of such parents [and causes], and one were to show you human seed and a picture of a man, and were to say with confidence that from such a substance such a being could be produced, would you believe before you saw the actual production? No one will dare to deny [that such a statement would surpass belief]. In the same way, then, you are now incredulous because you have never seen a dead man rise again. But as at first you would not have believed it possible that such persons could be produced from the small drop, and yet now you see them thus produced, so also judge ye that it is not impossible that the bodies of men, after they have been dissolved, and like seeds resolved into earth, should in God's appointed time rise again and put on incorruption. For what power worthy of God those imagine who say, that each thing returns to that from which it was produced, and that beyond this not even God Himself can do anything, we are unable to conceive; but this we see clearly, that they would not have believed it possible that they could have become such and produced from such materials, as they now see both themselves and the whole world to be. And that it is better to believe even what is impossible to our own nature and to men, than to be unbelieving like the rest of the world, we have learned; for we know that our Master Jesus Christ said, that "what is impossible with men is possible with God,"[7] and, "Fear not them that kill you, and after that can do no more; but fear Him who after death is able to cast both soul and body into hell."[8] And hell is a place where those are to be punished who have lived wickedly, and who do not believe that those things which God has taught us by Christ will come to pass.

CHAP. XX. — HEATHEN ANALOGIES TO CHRISTIAN DOCTRINE.

And the Sibyl[9] and Hystaspes said that there should be a dissolution by God of things corruptible. And the philosophers called Stoics teach that even God Himself shall be resolved into fire, and they say that the world is to be formed anew by this revolution; but we understand that God, the Creator of all things, is superior to the things that are to be changed. If, therefore, on some points we teach the same things as the poets and philosophers whom you honour, and on other points are fuller and more divine in our teaching, and if we alone afford proof of what we assert, why are we unjustly hated more than all others? For while we say that all things have been produced and arranged into a world by God, we shall seem to utter the doctrine of

---

[1] ἕρμαιον, a piece of unlooked-for luck, Hermes being the reputed giver of such gifts: vid. Liddell and Scott's Lex.; see also the Scholiast, quoted by Stallbaum in Plato's Phaed., p. 107, on a passage singularly analogous to this.

[2] Boys and girls, or even children prematurely taken from the womb, were slaughtered, and their entrails inspected, in the belief that the souls of the victims (being still conscious, as Justin is arguing) would reveal things hidden and future. Instances are abundantly cited by Otto and Trollope.

[3] This form of spirit-rapping was familiar to the ancients, and Justin again (Dial. c. Tryph., c. 105) uses the invocation of Samuel by the witch of Endor as a proof of the immortality of the soul.

[4] Valesius (on Euseb. H. E., iv. 7) states that the magi had two kinds of familiars: the first, who were sent to inspire men with dreams which might give them intimations of things future; and the second, who were sent to watch over men, and protect them from diseases and misfortunes. The first, he says, they called (as here) ὀνειροπομπούς, and the second παρέδρους.

[5] Justin is not the only author in ancient or recent times who has classed dæmoniacs and maniacs together; neither does he stand alone among the ancients in the opinion that dæmoniacs were possessed by the spirits of departed men. References will be found in Trollope's note. [See this matter more fully illustrated in Kaye's Justin Martyr, pp. 105-111.]

[6] See the Odyssey, book xi. line 25, where Ulysses is described as digging a pit or trench with his sword, and pouring libations, in order to collect around him the souls of the dead.

[7] Matt. xix. 26.
[8] Matt. x. 28.
[9] The Sibylline Oracles are now generally regarded as heathen fragments largely interpolated by unscrupulous men during the early ages of the Church. For an interesting account of these somewhat perplexing documents, see Burton's Lectures on the Ecclesiastical History of the First Three Centuries, Lect. xvii. The prophecies of Hystaspes were also commonly appealed to as genuine by the early Christians. [See (on the Sibyls and Justin M.) Casaubon, Exercitationes, pp. 65 and 80. This work is a most learned and diversified thesaurus, in the form of strictures on Card. Baronius. Geneva, 1663.]

Plato; and while we say that there will be a burning up of all, we shall seem to utter the doctrine of the Stoics: and while we affirm that the souls of the wicked, being endowed with sensation even after death, are punished, and that those of the good being delivered from punishment spend a blessed existence, we shall seem to say the same things as the poets and philosophers; and while we maintain that men ought not to worship the works of their hands, we say the very things which have been said by the comic poet Menander, and other similar writers, for they have declared that the workman is greater than the work.

CHAP. XXI. — ANALOGIES TO THE HISTORY OF CHRIST.

And when we say also that the Word, who is the first-birth[1] of God, was produced without sexual union, and that He, Jesus Christ, our Teacher, was crucified and died, and rose again, and ascended into heaven, we propound nothing different from what you believe regarding those whom you esteem sons of Jupiter. For you know how many sons your esteemed writers ascribed to Jupiter: Mercury, the interpreting word and teacher of all; Æsculapius, who, though he was a great physician, was struck by a thunderbolt, and so ascended to heaven; and Bacchus too, after he had been torn limb from limb; and Hercules, when he had committed himself to the flames to escape his toils; and the sons of Leda, and Dioscuri; and Perseus, son of Danae; and Bellerophon, who, though sprung from mortals, rose to heaven on the horse Pegasus. For what shall I say of Ariadne, and those who, like her, have been declared to be set among the stars? And what of the emperors who die among yourselves, whom you deem worthy of deification, and in whose behalf you produce some one who swears he has seen the burning Cæsar rise to heaven from the funeral pyre? And what kind of deeds are recorded of each of these reputed sons of Jupiter, it is needless to tell to those who already know. This only shall be said, that they are written for the advantage and encouragement[2] of youthful scholars; for all reckon it an honourable thing to imitate the gods. But far be such a thought concerning the gods from every well-conditioned soul, as to believe that Jupiter himself, the governor and creator of all things, was both a parricide and the son of a parricide, and that being overcome by the love of base and shameful pleasures, he came in to Ganymede and those many women whom he had violated and that his sons did like actions. But, as we said above, wicked devils perpetrated these things. And we have learned that those only are deified who have lived near to God in holiness and virtue; and we believe that those who live wickedly and do not repent are punished in everlasting fire.

CHAP. XXII. — ANALOGIES TO THE SONSHIP OF CHRIST.

Moreover, the Son of God called Jesus, even if only a man by ordinary generation, yet, on account of His wisdom, is worthy to be called the Son of God; for all writers call God the Father of men and gods. And if we assert that the Word of God was born of God in a peculiar manner, different from ordinary generation, let this, as said above, be no extraordinary thing to you, who say that Mercury is the angelic word of God. But if any one objects that He was crucified, in this also He is on a par with those reputed sons of Jupiter of yours, who suffered as we have now enumerated. For their sufferings at death are recorded to have been not all alike, but diverse; so that not even by the peculiarity of His sufferings does He seem to be inferior to them; but, on the contrary, as we promised in the preceding part of this discourse, we will now prove Him superior — or rather have already proved Him to be so — for the superior is revealed by His actions. And if we even affirm that He was born of a virgin, accept this in common with what you accept of Perseus. And in that we say that He made whole the lame, the paralytic, and those born blind, we seem to say what is very similar to the deeds said to have been done by Æsculapius.

CHAP. XXIII. — THE ARGUMENT.

And that this may now become evident to you — (firstly[3]) that whatever we assert in conformity with what has been taught us by Christ, and by the prophets who preceded Him, are alone true, and are older than all the writers who have existed; that we claim to be acknowledged, not because we say the same things as these writers said, but because we say true things: and (secondly) that Jesus Christ is the only proper Son who has been begotten by God, being His Word and first-begotten, and power; and, becoming man according to His will, He

---

[1] i.e., first-born.
[2] διαφοράν καὶ προτροπήν. The irony here is so obvious as to make the proposed reading (διαφθοράν καὶ παρατροπήν, corruption and depravation) unnecessary. Otto prefers the reading adopted above. Trollope, on the other hand, inclines to the latter reading, mainly on the score of the former expressions being unusual. See his very sensible note *in loc.*

[3] The Benedictine editor, Maranus, Otto, and Trollope, here note that Justin in this chapter promises to make good three distinct positions: 1st, That Christian doctrines alone are true, and are to be received, not on account of their resemblance to the sentiments of poets or philosophers, but on their own account; 2d, that Jesus Christ is the incarnate Son of God, and our teacher; 3d, that before His incarnation, the demons, having some knowledge of what He would accomplish, enabled the heathen poets and priests in some points to anticipate, though in a distorted form, the facts of the incarnation. The first he establishes in chap. xxiv.-xxix.; the second in chap xxx.-liii.; and the third in chap. liv. et sq.

taught us these things for the conversion and restoration of the human race: and (thirdly) that before He became a man among men, some, influenced by the demons before mentioned, related beforehand, through the instrumentality of the poets, those circumstances as having really happened, which, having fictitiously devised, they narrated, in the same manner as they have caused to be fabricated the scandalous reports against us of infamous and impious actions,[1] of which there is neither witness nor proof — we shall bring forward the following proof.

CHAP. XXIV. — VARIETIES OF HEATHEN WORSHIP.

In the first place [we furnish proof], because, though we say things similar to what the Greeks say, we only are hated on account of the name of Christ, and though we do no wrong, are put to death as sinners; other men in other places worshipping trees and rivers, and mice and cats and crocodiles, and many irrational animals. Nor are the same animals esteemed by all; but in one place one is worshipped, and another in another, so that all are profane in the judgment of one another, on account of their not worshipping the same objects. And this is the sole accusation you bring against us, that we do not reverence the same gods as you do, nor offer to the dead libations and the savour of fat, and crowns for their statues,[2] and sacrifices. For you very well know that the same animals are with some esteemed gods, with others wild beasts, and with others sacrificial victims.

CHAP. XXV. — FALSE GODS ABANDONED BY CHRISTIANS.

And, secondly, because we — who, out of every race of men, used to worship Bacchus the son of Semele, and Apollo the son of Latona (who in their loves with men did such things as it is shameful even to mention), and Proserpine and Venus (who were maddened with love of Adonis, and whose mysteries also you celebrate), or Æsculapius, or some one or other of those who are called gods — have now, through Jesus Christ, learned to despise these, though we be threatened with death for it, and have dedicated ourselves to the unbegotten and impassible God; of whom we are persuaded that never was he goaded by lust of Antiope, or such other women, or of Ganymede, nor was rescued by that hundred-handed giant whose aid was obtained through Thetis, nor was anxious on this account[3] that her son Achilles should destroy many of the Greeks because of his concubine Briseis. Those who believe these things we pity, and those who invented them we know to be devils.

CHAP. XXVI. — MAGICIANS NOT TRUSTED BY CHRISTIANS.

And, thirdly, because after Christ's ascension into heaven the devils put forward certain men who said that they themselves were gods; and they were not only not persecuted by you, but even deemed worthy of honours. There was a Samaritan, Simon, a native of the village called Gitto, who in the reign of Claudius Cæsar, and in your royal city of Rome, did mighty acts of magic, by virtue of the art of the devils operating in him. He was considered a god, and as a god was honoured by you with a statue, which statue was erected on the river Tiber, between the two bridges, and bore this inscription, in the language of Rome: —

"Simoni Deo Sancto,"[4]
"To Simon the holy God."

And almost all the Samaritans, and a few even of other nations, worship him, and acknowledge him as the first god; and a woman, Helena, who went about with him at that time, and had formerly been a prostitute, they say is the first idea generated by him. And a man, Meander, also a Samaritan, of the town Capparetæa, a disciple of Simon, and inspired by devils, we know to have deceived many while he was in Antioch by his magical art. He persuaded those who adhered to him that they should never die, and even now there are some living who hold this opinion of his. And there is Marcion, a man of Pontus, who is even at this day alive, and teaching his disciples to believe in some other god greater than the Creator. And he, by the aid of the devils, has caused many of every nation to speak blasphemies, and to deny that God is the maker of this universe, and to assert that some other being, greater than He, has done greater works. All who take their opinions from these men, are, as we before said,[5] called Christians; just as also those who do not agree with

---

[1] We have here followed the reading and rendering of Trollope. [But see reading of Langus, and Grabe's note, in the edition already cited, 1. 46.]
[2] ἐν γραφαῖς στεφάνους. The only conjecture which seems at all probable is that of the Benedictine editor followed here. [Grabe after Salmasius reads ἐν ῥαφαῖς and quotes Martial, *Sutilis aptetur rosa crinibus.* Translate, "patch-work garlands."]
[3] i.e., on account of the assistance gained for him by Thetis, and in return for it.
[4] It is very generally supposed that Justin was mistaken in understanding this to have been a statue erected to Simon Magus. This supposition rests on the fact that in the year 1574 there was dug up in the island of the Tiber a fragment of marble, with the inscription "Semoni Sanco Deo," etc., being probably the base of a statue erected to the Sabine deity Semo Sancus. This inscription Justin is supposed to have mistaken for the one he gives above. This has always seemed to us very slight evidence on which to reject so precise a statement as Justin here makes; a statement which he would scarcely have hazarded in an apology addressed to Rome, where every person had the means of ascertaining its accuracy. If, as is supposed, he made a mistake, it must have been at once exposed, and other writers would not have so frequently repeated the story as they have done. See *Burton's Bampton Lectures*, p. 374. [See Note in Grabe (1. 51), and also mine, at end.]
[5] See chap. vii.

the philosophers in their doctrines, have yet in common with them the name of philosophers given to them. And whether they perpetrate those fabulous and shameful deeds[1] — the upsetting of the lamp, and promiscuous intercourse, and eating human flesh — we know not; but we do know that they are neither persecuted nor put to death by you, at least on account of their opinions. But I have a treatise against all the heresies that have existed already composed, which, if you wish to read it, I will give you.

CHAP. XXVII. — GUILT OF EXPOSING CHILDREN.

But as for us, we have been taught that to expose newly-born children is the part of wicked men; and this we have been taught lest we should do any one an injury, and lest we should sin against God, first, because we see that almost all so exposed (not only the girls, but also the males) are brought up to prostitution. And as the ancients are said to have reared herds of oxen, or goats, or sheep, or grazing horses, so now we see you rear children only for this shameful use; and for this pollution a multitude of females and hermaphrodites, and those who commit unmentionable iniquities, are found in every nation. And you receive the hire of these, and duty and taxes from them, whom you ought to exterminate from your realm. And any one who uses such persons, besides the godless and infamous and impure intercourse, may possibly be having intercourse with his own child, or relative, or brother. And there are some who prostitute even their own children and wives, and some are openly mutilated for the purpose of sodomy; and they refer these mysteries to the mother of the gods, and along with each of those whom you esteem gods there is painted a serpent,[2] a great symbol and mystery. Indeed, the things[3] which you do openly and with applause, as if the divine light were overturned and extinguished, these you lay to our charge; which, in truth, does no harm to us who shrink from doing any such things, but only to those who do them and bear false witness against us.

CHAP. XXVIII. — GOD'S CARE FOR MEN.

For among us the prince of the wicked spirits is called the serpent, and Satan, and the devil, as you can learn by looking into our writings. And that he would be sent into the fire with his host, and the men who follow him, and would be punished for an endless duration, Christ foretold. For the reason why God has delayed to do this, is His regard for the human race. For He foreknows that some are to be saved by repentance, some even that are perhaps not yet born.[4] In the beginning He made the human race with the power of thought and of choosing the truth and doing right, so that all men are without excuse before God; for they have been born rational and contemplative. And if any one disbelieves that God cares for these things,[5] he will thereby either insinuate that God does not exist, or he will assert that though He exists He delights in vice, or exists like a stone, and that neither virtue nor vice are anything, but only in the opinion of men these things are reckoned good or evil. And this is the greatest profanity and wickedness.

CHAP. XXIX. — CONTINENCE OF CHRISTIANS.

And again [we fear to expose children], lest some of them be not picked up, but die, and we become murderers. But whether we marry, it is only that we may bring up children; or whether we decline marriage, we live continently. And that you may understand that promiscuous intercourse is not one of our mysteries, one of our number a short time ago presented to Felix the governor in Alexandria a petition, craving that permission might be given to a surgeon to make him an eunuch. For the surgeons there said that they were forbidden to do this without the permission of the governor. And when Felix absolutely refused to sign such a permission, the youth remained single, and was satisfied with his own approving conscience, and the approval of those who thought as he did. And it is not out of place, we think, to mention here Antinous, who was alive but lately, and whom all were prompt, through fear, to worship as a god, though they knew both who he was and what was his origin.[6]

CHAP. XXX. — WAS CHRIST NOT A MAGICIAN?

But lest any one should meet us with the question, What should prevent that He whom we call Christ, being a man born of men, performed what we call His mighty works by magical art, and by this appeared to be the Son of God? we will now offer proof, not trusting mere assertions, but being of necessity persuaded by those who prophesied [of Him] before these things came to pass, for with our own eyes we behold things that have happened and are happening just as

---

[1] Which were commonly charged against the Christians.
[2] Thirlby remarks that the serpent was the symbol specially of eternity, of power, and of wisdom, and that there was scarcely any divine attribute to which the heathen did not find some likeness in this animal. See also Hardwick's *Christ and other Masters*, vol. ii. 146 (2d ed.).
[3] [Note how he retaliates upon the calumny (cap. xxvi.) of the "upsetting of the lamp."]
[4] Literally, "For He foreknows some about to be saved by repentance, and some not yet perhaps born."
[5] Those things which concern the salvation of man; so Trollope and the other interpreters, except Otto, who reads τούτων masculine, and understands it of the men first spoken of. [See Plato (*De Legibus*, opp. ix. p. 98, Bipont., 1786), and the valuable edition of Book X. by Professor Tayler Lewis (p. 52. etc.), New York, 1845.]
[6] For a sufficient account of the infamous history here alluded to and the extravagant grief of Hadrian, and the servility of the people, see Smith's *Dictionary of Biography*: "Antinous." [Note, " all were prompt, *through fear*," etc. Thus we may measure the defiant intrepidity of this stinging sarcasm addressed to the "philosophers," with whose sounding titles this Apology begins.]

they were predicted; and this will, we think, appear even to you the strongest and truest evidence.

CHAP. XXXI. — OF THE HEBREW PROPHETS.

There were, then, among the Jews certain men who were prophets of God, through whom the prophetic Spirit published beforehand things that were to come to pass, ere ever they happened. And their prophecies, as they were spoken and when they were uttered, the kings who happened to be reigning among the Jews at the several times carefully preserved in their possession, when they had been arranged in books by the prophets themselves in their own Hebrew language. And when Ptolemy king of Egypt formed a library, and endeavoured to collect the writings of all men, he heard also of these prophets, and sent to Herod, who was at that time king of the Jews,[1] requesting that the books of the prophets be sent to him. And Herod the king did indeed send them, written, as they were, in the foresaid Hebrew language. And when their contents were found to be unintelligible to the Egyptians, he again sent and requested that men be commissioned to translate them into the Greek language. And when this was done, the books remained with the Egyptians, where they are until now. They are also in the possession of all Jews throughout the world; but they, though they read, do not understand what is said, but count us foes and enemies; and, like yourselves, they kill and punish us whenever they have the power, as you can well believe. For in the Jewish war which lately raged, Barchochebas, the leader of the revolt of the Jews, gave orders that Christians alone should be led to cruel punishments, unless they would deny Jesus Christ and utter blasphemy. In these books, then, of the prophets we found Jesus our Christ foretold as coming, born of a virgin, growing up to man's estate, and healing every disease and every sickness, and raising the dead, and being hated, and unrecognised, and crucified, and dying, and rising again, and ascending into heaven, and being, and being called, the Son of God. We find it also predicted that certain persons should be sent by Him into every nation to publish these things, and that rather among the Gentiles [than among the Jews] men should believe on Him. And He was predicted before He appeared, first 5000 years before, and again 3000, then 2000, then 1000, and yet again 800; for in the succession of generations prophets after prophets arose.

CHAP. XXXII. — CHRIST PREDICTED BY MOSES.

Moses then, who was the first of the prophets, spoke in these very words: "The sceptre shall not depart from Judah, nor a lawgiver from between his feet, until He come for whom it is reserved; and He shall be the desire of the nations, binding His foal to the vine, washing His robe in the blood of the grape."[2] It is yours to make accurate inquiry, and ascertain up to whose time the Jews had a lawgiver and king of their own. Up to the time of Jesus Christ, who taught us, and interpreted the prophecies which were not yet understood, [they had a lawgiver] as was foretold by the holy and divine Spirit of prophecy through Moses, "that a ruler would not fail the Jews until He should come for whom the kingdom was reserved" (for Judah was the forefather of the Jews, from whom also they have their name of Jews); and after He (i.e., Christ) appeared, you began to rule the Jews, and gained possession of all their territory. And the prophecy, "He shall be the expectation of the nations," signified that there would be some of all nations who should look for Him to come again. And this indeed you can see for yourselves, and be convinced of by fact. For of all races of men there are some who look for Him who was crucified in Judæa, and after whose crucifixion the land was straightway surrendered to you as spoil of war. And the prophecy, "binding His foal to the vine, and washing His robe in the blood of the grape," was a significant symbol of the things that were to happen to Christ, and of what He was to do. For the foal of an ass stood bound to a vine at the entrance of a village, and He ordered His acquaintances to bring it to Him then; and when it was brought, He mounted and sat upon it, and entered Jerusalem, where was the vast temple of the Jews which was afterwards destroyed by you. And after this He was crucified, that the rest of the prophecy might be fulfilled. For this "washing His robe in the blood of the grape" was predictive of the passion He was to endure, cleansing by His blood those who believe on Him. For what is called by the Divine Spirit through the prophet "His robe," are those men who believe in Him in whom abideth the seed[3] of God, the Word. And what is spoken of as "the blood of the grape," signifies that He who should appear would have blood, though not of the seed of man, but of the power of God. And the first power after God the Father and Lord of all is the Word, who is also the Son; and of Him we will, in what follows, relate how He took flesh and became man. For as man did not make the blood of the vine, but God, so it was hereby intimated that the blood should not be of human seed, but of divine

---

[1] Some attribute this blunder in chronology to Justin, others to his transcribers: it was Eleazar the high priest to whom Ptolemy applied.

[2] Gen. xlix. 10.

[3] Grabe would here read, not σπέρμα, but πνεῦμα, the spirit; but the Benedictine, Otto, and Trollope all think that no change should be made.

power, as we have said above. And Isaiah, another prophet, foretelling the same things in other words, spoke thus: "A star shall rise out of Jacob, and a flower shall spring from the root of Jesse; and His arm shall the nations trust."[1] And a star of light has arisen, and a flower has sprung from the root of Jesse — this Christ. For by the power of God He was conceived by a virgin of the seed of Jacob, who was the father of Judah, who, as we have shown, was the father of the Jews; and Jesse was His forefather according to the oracle, and He was the son of Jacob and Judah according to lineal descent.

CHAP. XXXIII. — MANNER OF CHRIST'S BIRTH PREDICTED.

And hear again how Isaiah in express words foretold that He should be born of a virgin; for he spoke thus: "Behold, a virgin shall conceive, and bring forth a son, and they shall say for His name, 'God with us.'"[2] For things which were incredible and seemed impossible with men, these God predicted by the Spirit of prophecy as about to come to pass, in order that, when they came to pass, there might be no unbelief, but faith, because of their prediction. But lest some, not understanding the prophecy now cited, should charge us with the very things we have been laying to the charge of the poets who say that Jupiter went in to women through lust, let us try to explain the words. This, then, "Behold, a virgin shall conceive," signifies that a virgin should conceive without intercourse. For if she had had intercourse with any one whatever, she was no longer a virgin; but the power of God having come upon the virgin, overshadowed her, and caused her while yet a virgin to conceive. And the angel of God who was sent to the same virgin at that time brought her good news, saying, "Behold, thou shalt conceive of the Holy Ghost, and shalt bear a Son, and He shall be called the Son of the Highest, and thou shalt call His name Jesus; for He shall save His people from their sins,"[3] — as they who have recorded all that concerns our Saviour Jesus Christ have taught, whom we believed, since by Isaiah also, whom we have now adduced, the Spirit of prophecy declared that He should be born as we intimated before. It is wrong, therefore, to understand the Spirit and the power of God as anything else than the Word, who is also the first-born of God, as the foresaid prophet Moses declared; and it was this which, when it came upon the virgin and overshadowed her, caused her to conceive, not by intercourse, but by power. And the name Jesus in the Hebrew language means $\Sigma\omega\tau\acute{\eta}\rho$ (Saviour) in the Greek tongue. Wherefore, too, the angel said to the virgin, "Thou shalt call His name Jesus, for He shall save His people from their sins." And that the prophets are inspired[4] by no other than the Divine Word, even you, as I fancy, will grant.

CHAP. XXXIV. — PLACE OF CHRIST'S BIRTH FORETOLD.

And hear what part of earth He was to be born in, as another prophet, Micah, foretold. He spoke thus: "And thou, Bethlehem, the land of Judah, art not the least among the princes of Judah; for out of thee shall come forth a Governor, who shall feed My people."[5] Now there is a village in the land of the Jews, thirty-five stadia from Jerusalem, in which Jesus Christ was born, as you can ascertain also from the registers of the taxing made under Cyrenius, your first procurator in Judæa.

CHAP. XXXV. — OTHER FULFILLED PROPHECIES.

And how Christ after He was born was to escape the notice of other men until He grew to man's estate, which also came to pass, hear what was foretold regarding this. There are the following predictions:[6] — "Unto us a child is born, and unto us a young man is given, and the government shall be upon His shoulders;"[7] which is significant of the power of the cross, for to it, when He was crucified, He applied His shoulders, as shall be more clearly made out in the ensuing discourse. And again the same prophet Isaiah, being inspired by the prophetic Spirit, said, "I have spread out my hands to a disobedient and gainsaying people, to those who walk in a way that is not good. They now ask of me judgment, and dare to draw near to God."[8] And again in other words, through another prophet, He says, "They pierced My hands and My feet, and for My vesture they cast lots."[9] And indeed David, the king and prophet, who uttered these things, suffered none of them; but Jesus Christ stretched forth His hands, being crucified by the Jews speaking against Him, and denying that He was the Christ. And as the prophet spoke, they tormented Him, and set Him on the judgment-seat, and said, Judge us. And the expression, "They pierced my hands and my feet," was used in reference to the nails of the cross which were fixed in His hands and feet. And after He was crucified they cast lots upon His vesture, and they

---

[1] Isa. xi. 1.
[2] Isa. vii. 14.
[3] Luke i. 32; Matt. i. 21.
[4] θεοφοροῦνται, lit. are borne by a god — a word used of those who were supposed to be wholly under the influence of a deity.
[5] Micah v. 2.
[6] These predictions have so little reference to the point Justin intends to make out, that some editors have supposed that a passage has here been lost. Others think the irrelevancy an insufficient ground for such a supposition. [See below, cap. xl.]
[7] Isa. ix. 6.
[8] Isa. lxv. 2, lviii. 2.
[9] Ps. xxii. 16.

that crucified Him parted it among them. And that these things did happen, you can ascertain from the Acts of Pontius Pilate.[1] And we will cite the prophetic utterances of another prophet, Zephaniah,[2] to the effect that He was foretold expressly as to sit upon the foal of an ass and to enter Jerusalem. The words are these: "Rejoice greatly, O daughter of Zion; shout, O daughter of Jerusalem: behold, thy King cometh unto thee; lowly, and riding upon an ass, and upon a colt the foal of an ass."[3]

CHAP. XXXVI. — DIFFERENT MODES OF PROPHECY.

But when you hear the utterances of the prophets spoken as it were personally, you must not suppose that they are spoken by the inspired themselves, but by the Divine Word who moves them. For sometimes He declares things that are to come to pass, in the manner of one who foretells the future; sometimes He speaks as from the person of God the Lord and Father of all; sometimes as from the person of Christ; sometimes as from the person of the people answering the Lord or His Father, just as you can see even in your own writers, one man being the writer of the whole, but introducing the persons who converse. And this the Jews who possessed the books of the prophets did not understand, and therefore did not recognise Christ even when He came, but even hate us who say that He has come, and who prove that, as was predicted, He was crucified by them.

CHAP. XXXVII. — UTTERANCES OF THE FATHER.

And that this too may be clear to you, there were spoken from the person of the Father, through Isaiah the prophet, the following words: "The ox knoweth his owner, and the ass his master's crib; but Israel doth not know, and My people hath not understood. Woe, sinful nation, a people full of sins, a wicked seed, children that are transgressors, ye have forsaken the Lord."[4] And again elsewhere, when the same prophet speaks in like manner from the person of the Father, "What is the house that ye will build for Me? saith the Lord. The heaven is My throne, and the earth is My footstool."[5] And again, in another place, "Your new moons and your sabbaths My soul hateth; and the great day of the fast and of ceasing from labour I cannot away with; nor, if ye come to be seen of Me, will I hear you: your hands are full of blood; and if ye bring fine flour, incense, it is abomination unto Me: the fat of lambs and the blood of bulls I do not desire. For who hath required this at your hands? But loose every bond of wickedness, tear asunder the tight knots of violent contracts, cover the houseless and naked deal thy bread to the hungry."[6] What kind of things are taught through the prophets from [the person of] God, you can now perceive.

CHAP. XXXVIII. — UTTERANCES OF THE SON.

And when the Spirit of prophecy speaks from the person of Christ, the utterances are of this sort: "I have spread out My hands to a disobedient and gainsaying people, to those who walk in a way that is not good."[7] And again: "I gave My back to the scourges, and My cheeks to the buffetings; I turned not away My face from the shame of spittings; and the Lord was My helper: therefore was I not confounded: but I set My face as a firm rock; and I knew that I should not be ashamed, for He is near that justifieth Me."[8] And again, when He says, "They cast lots upon My vesture, and pierced My hands and My feet. And I lay down and slept, and rose again, because the Lord sustained Me."[9] And again, when He says, "They spake with their lips, they wagged the head, saying, Let Him deliver Himself."[10] And that all these things happened to Christ at the hands of the Jews, you can ascertain. For when He was crucified, they did shoot out the lip, and wagged their heads, saying, "Let Him who raised the dead save Himself."[11]

CHAP. XXXIX. — DIRECT PREDICTIONS BY THE SPIRIT.

And when the Spirit of prophecy speaks as predicting things that are to come to pass, He speaks in this way: "For out of Zion shall go forth the law, and the word of the Lord from Jerusalem. And He shall judge among the nations, and shall rebuke many people; and they shall beat their swords into ploughshares, and their spears into pruning-hooks: nation shall not lift up sword against nation, neither shall they learn war any more."[12] And that it did so come to pass, we can convince you. For from Jerusalem there went out into the world, men, twelve in number, and these illiterate, of no ability in speaking: but by the power of God they proclaimed to every race of men that they were sent

---

[1] ἄκτων. These Acts of Pontius Pilate, or regular accounts of his procedure sent by Pilate to the Emperor Tiberius, are supposed to have been destroyed at an early period, possibly in consequence of the unanswerable appeals which the Christians constantly made to them. There exists a forgery in imitation of these Acts. See Trollope.
[2] The reader will notice that these are not the words of Zephaniah, but of Zechariah (ix. 9), to whom also Justin himself refers them in the *Dial. Tryph.*, c. 53. [Might be corrected in the text, therefore, as a clerical slip of the pen.]
[3] Zech. ix.9.
[4] Isa. i. 3. This quotation varies only in one word from that of the LXX.
[5] Isa. lxvi. 1.
[6] Isa. i. 14, xviii. 6.
[7] Isa. lxv. 2.
[8] Isa. l. 6.
[9] Ps. xxii. 18, iii. 5.
[10] Ps. xxii. 7.
[11] Comp. Matt. xxvii. 39.
[12] Isa. ii. 3.

by Christ to teach to all the word of God; and we who formerly used to murder one another do not only now refrain from making war upon our enemies, but also, that we may not lie nor deceive our examiners, willingly die confessing Christ. For that saying, " The tongue has sworn, but the mind is unsworn," [1] might be imitated by us in this matter. But if the soldiers enrolled by you, and who have taken the military oath, prefer their allegiance to their own life, and parents, and country, and all kindred, though you can offer them nothing incorruptible, it were verily ridiculous if we, who earnestly long for incorruption, should not endure all things, in order to obtain what we desire from Him who is able to grant it.

CHAP. XL. — CHRIST'S ADVENT FORETOLD.

And hear how it was foretold concerning those who published His doctrine and proclaimed His appearance, the above-mentioned prophet and king speaking thus by the Spirit of prophecy: " Day unto day uttereth speech, and night unto night showeth knowledge. There is no speech nor language where their voice is not heard. Their voice has gone out into all the earth, and their words to the ends of the world. In the sun hath He set His tabernacle, and he as a bridegroom going out of his chamber shall rejoice as a giant to run his course." [2] And we have thought it right and relevant to mention some other prophetic utterances of David besides these; from which you may learn how the Spirit of prophecy exhorts men to live, and how He foretold the conspiracy which was formed against Christ by Herod the king of the Jews, and the Jews themselves, and Pilate, who was your governor among them, with his soldiers; and how He should be believed on by men of every race; and how God calls Him His Son, and has declared that He will subdue all His enemies under Him; and how the devils, as much as they can, strive to escape the power of God the Father and Lord of all, and the power of Christ Himself; and how God calls all to repentance before the day of judgment comes. These things were uttered thus: " Blessed is the man who hath not walked in the counsel of the ungodly, nor stood in the way of sinners, nor sat in the seat of the scornful: but his delight is in the law of the Lord; and in His law will he meditate day and night. And he shall be like a tree planted by the rivers of waters, which shall give his fruit in his season; and his leaf shall not wither, and whatsoever he doeth shall prosper. The ungodly are not so, but are like the chaff which the wind driveth away from the face of the earth. Therefore the ungodly shall not stand in the judgment, nor sinners in the council of the righteous. For the Lord knoweth the way of the righteous; but the way of the ungodly shall perish. Why do the heathen rage, and the people imagine new things? The kings of the earth set themselves, and the rulers take counsel together, against the Lord, and against His Anointed, saying, Let us break their bands asunder, and cast their yoke from us. He that dwelleth in the heavens shall laugh at them, and the Lord shall have them in derision. Then shall He speak to them in His wrath, and vex them in His sore displeasure. Yet have I been set by Him a King on Zion His holy hill, declaring the decree of the Lord. The Lord said to Me, Thou art My Son; this day have I begotten Thee. Ask of Me, and I shall give Thee the heathen for Thine inheritance, and the uttermost parts of the earth as Thy possession. Thou shalt herd them with a rod of iron; as the vessels of a potter shalt Thou dash them in pieces. Be wise now, therefore, O ye kings; be instructed, all ye judges of the earth. Serve the Lord with fear, and rejoice with trembling. Embrace instruction, lest at any time the Lord be angry, and ye perish from the right way, when His wrath has been suddenly kindled. Blessed are all they that put their trust in Him." [3]

CHAP. XLI. — THE CRUCIFIXION PREDICTED.

And again, in another prophecy, the Spirit of prophecy, through the same David, intimated that Christ, after He had been crucified, should reign, and spoke as follows: " Sing to the Lord, all the earth, and day by day declare His salvation. For great is the Lord, and greatly to be praised, to be feared above all the gods. For all the gods of the nations are idols of devils; but God made the heavens. Glory and praise are before His face, strength and glorying are in the habitation of His holiness. Give Glory to the Lord, the Father everlasting. Receive grace, and enter His presence, and worship in His holy courts. Let all the earth fear before His face; let it be established, and not shaken. Let them rejoice among the nations. The Lord hath reigned from the tree." [4]

CHAP. XLII. — PROPHECY USING THE PAST TENSE.

But when the Spirit of prophecy speaks of things that are about to come to pass as if they had already taken place, — as may be observed even in the passages already cited by me, — that

---

[1] Eurip., *Hipp.*, 608.
[2] Ps. xix. 2, etc. [Note how J. excuses himself for the apparent irrelevancy of some of his citations (cap. xxxv., note), though quite in the manner of Plato himself. These Scriptures were of novel interest, and he was stimulating his readers to study the Septuagint.]
[3] Ps. i. ii.
[4] Ps. xcvi. 1, etc. This last clause, which is not extant in our copies, either of the LXX. or of the Hebrew, Justin charged the Jews with erasing. See *Dial. Tryph.*, c. 73. [Concerning the eighteen Jewish alterations, see *Pearson on the Creed*, art. iv. p. 335. Ed. London, 1824.]

this circumstance may afford no excuse to readers [for misinterpreting them], we will make even this also quite plain. The things which He absolutely knows will take place, He predicts as if already they had taken place. And that the utterances must be thus received, you will perceive, if you give your attention to them. The words cited above, David uttered 1500[1] years before Christ became a man and was crucified; and no one of those who lived before Him, nor yet of His contemporaries, afforded joy to the Gentiles by being crucified. But our Jesus Christ, being crucified and dead, rose again, and having ascended to heaven, reigned; and by those things which were published in His name among all nations by the apostles, there is joy afforded to those who expect the immortality promised by Him.

CHAP. XLIII. — RESPONSIBILITY ASSERTED.

But lest some suppose, from what has been said by us, that we say that whatever happens, happens by a fatal necessity, because it is foretold as known beforehand, this too we explain. We have learned from the prophets, and we hold it to be true, that punishments, and chastisements, and good rewards, are rendered according to the merit of each man's actions. Since if it be not so, but all things happen by fate, neither is anything at all in our own power. For if it be fated that this man, e.g., be good, and this other evil, neither is the former meritorious nor the latter to be blamed. And again, unless the human race have the power of avoiding evil and choosing good by free choice, they are not accountable for their actions, of whatever kind they be. But that it is by free choice they both walk uprightly and stumble, we thus demonstrate. We see the same man making a transition to opposite things. Now, if it had been fated that he were to be either good or bad, he could never have been capable of both the opposites, nor of so many transitions. But not even would some be good and others bad, since we thus make fate the cause of evil, and exhibit her as acting in opposition to herself; or that which has been already stated would seem to be true, that neither virtue nor vice is anything, but that things are only reckoned good or evil by opinion; which, as the true word shows, is the greatest impiety and wickedness. But this we assert is inevitable fate, that they who choose the good have worthy rewards, and they who choose the opposite have their merited awards. For not like other things, as trees and quadrupeds, which cannot act by choice, did God make man : for neither would he be worthy of reward or praise did he not of himself choose the good, but were created for this end;[2] nor, if he were evil, would he be worthy of punishment, not being evil of himself, but being able to be nothing else than what he was made.

CHAP. XLIV. — NOT NULLIFIED BY PROPHECY.

And the holy Spirit of prophecy taught us this, telling us by Moses that God spoke thus to the man first created : " Behold, before thy face are good and evil : choose the good."[3] And again, by the other prophet Isaiah, that the following utterance was made as if from God the Father and Lord of all : " Wash you, make you clean ; put away evils from your souls ; learn to do well ; judge the orphan, and plead for the widow : and come and let us reason together, saith the Lord : And if your sins be as scarlet, I will make them white as wool ; and if they be red like as crimson, I will make them white as snow. And if ye be willing and obey Me, ye shall eat the good of the land ; but if ye do not obey Me, the sword shall devour you : for the mouth of the Lord hath spoken it."[4] And that expression, "The sword shall devour you," does not mean that the disobedient shall be slain by the sword, but the sword of God is fire, of which they who choose to do wickedly become the fuel. Wherefore He says, "The sword shall devour you : for the mouth of the Lord hath spoken it." And if He had spoken concerning a sword that cuts and at once despatches, He would not have said, shall *devour*. And so, too, Plato, when he says, " The blame is his who chooses, and God is blameless,"[5] took this from the prophet Moses and uttered it. For Moses is more ancient than all the Greek writers. And whatever both philosophers and poets have said concerning the immortality of the soul, or punishments after death, or contemplation of things heavenly, or doctrines of the like kind, they have received such suggestions from the prophets as have enabled them to understand and interpret these things. And hence there seem to be seeds of truth among all men ; but they are charged with not accurately understanding [the truth] when they assert contradictories. So that what we say about future events being foretold, we do not say it as if they came about by a fatal necessity; but God foreknowing all that shall be done by all men, and it being His decree that the future actions of men shall all be recompensed according to their several value, He foretells by the Spirit of prophecy that He will bestow meet rewards according to the merit of the actions done, always urging the human

---

[1] A chronological error, whether of the copyist or of Justin himself cannot be known.

[2] Or, " but were made so." The words are, ἀλλὰ τοῦτο γενόμενος and the meaning of Justin is sufficiently clear.
[3] Deut. xxx. 15, 19.
[4] Isa. i. 16, etc.
[5] Plato, Rep. x. [On this remarkable passage refer to Biog. Note above. See, also, brilliant note of the sophist De Maistre, Œuvres, ii. p. 105. Ed. Paris, 1853.]

race to effort and recollection, showing that He cares and provides for men. But by the agency of the devils death has been decreed against those who read the books of Hystaspes, or of the Sibyl,[1] or of the prophets, that through fear they may prevent men who read them from receiving the knowledge of the good, and may retain them in slavery to themselves; which, however, they could not always effect. For not only do we fearlessly read them, but, as you see, bring them for your inspection, knowing that their contents will be pleasing to all. And if we persuade even a few, our gain will be very great; for, as good husbandmen, we shall receive the reward from the Master.

CHAP. XLV. — CHRIST'S SESSION IN HEAVEN FORETOLD.

And that God the Father of all would bring Christ to heaven after He had raised Him from the dead, and would keep Him there[2] until He has subdued His enemies the devils, and until the number of those who are foreknown by Him as good and virtuous is complete, on whose account He has still delayed the consummation — hear what was said by the prophet David. These are his words: "The Lord said unto My Lord, Sit Thou at My right hand, until I make Thine enemies Thy footstool. The Lord shall send to Thee the rod of power out of Jerusalem; and rule Thou in the midst of Thine enemies. With Thee is the government in the day of Thy power, in the beauties of Thy saints: from the womb of morning[3] have I begotten Thee."[4] That which he says, "He shall send to Thee the rod of power out of Jerusalem," is predictive of the mighty word, which His apostles, going forth from Jerusalem, preached everywhere; and though death is decreed against those who teach or at all confess the name of Christ, we everywhere both embrace and teach it. And if you also read these words in a hostile spirit, ye can do no more, as I said before, than kill us; which indeed does no harm to us, but to you and all who unjustly hate us, and do not repent, brings eternal punishment by fire.

CHAP. XLVI. — THE WORD IN THE WORLD BEFORE CHRIST.

But lest some should, without reason, and for the perversion of what we teach, maintain that we say that Christ was born one hundred and fifty years ago under Cyrenius, and subsequently, in the time of Pontius Pilate, taught what we say He taught; and should cry out against us as though all men who were born before Him were irresponsible — let us anticipate and solve the difficulty. We have been taught that Christ is the first-born of God, and we have declared above that He is the Word of whom every race of men were partakers; and those who lived reasonably[5] are Christians, even though they have been thought atheists; as, among the Greeks, Socrates and Heraclitus, and men like them; and among the barbarians, Abraham, and Ananias, and Azarias, and Misael, and Elias, and many others whose actions and names we now decline to recount, because we know it would be tedious. So that even they who lived before Christ, and lived without reason, were wicked and hostile to Christ, and slew those who lived reasonably. But who, through the power of the Word, according to the will of God the Father and Lord of all, He was born of a virgin as a man, and was named Jesus, and was crucified, and died, and rose again, and ascended into heaven, an intelligent man will be able to comprehend from what has been already so largely said. And we, since the proof of this subject is less needful now, will pass for the present to the proof of those things which are urgent.

CHAP. XLVII. — DESOLATION OF JUDÆA FORETOLD.

That the land of the Jews, then, was to be laid waste, hear what was said by the Spirit of prophecy. And the words were spoken as if from the person of the people wondering at what had happened. They are these: "Sion is a wilderness, Jerusalem a desolation. The house of our sanctuary has become a curse, and the glory which our fathers blessed is burned up with fire, and all its glorious things are laid waste: and Thou refrainest Thyself at these things, and hast held Thy peace, and hast humbled us very sore."[6] And ye are convinced that Jerusalem has been laid waste, as was predicted. And concerning its desolation, and that no one should be permitted to inhabit it, there was the following prophecy by Isaiah: "Their land is desolate, their enemies consume it before them, and none of them shall dwell therein."[7] And that it is guarded by you lest any one dwell in it, and that death is decreed against a Jew apprehended entering it, you know very well.[8]

CHAP. XLVIII. — CHRIST'S WORK AND DEATH FORETOLD.

And that it was predicted that our Christ

---

[1] [On the Orphica and Sibyllina, see Bull, Works, vol. vi. pp. 291-298.]
[2] So Thirlby, Otto, and Trollope seem all to understand the word κατέχειν; yet it seems worth considering whether Justin has not borrowed both the sense and the word from 2 Thess. ii. 6, 7.
[3] Or, "before the morning star."
[4] Ps. cx. 1, etc.

[5] μετὰ λόγου, "with reason," or "the Word." [This remarkable passage on the salvability and accountability of the heathen is noteworthy. See, on St. Matt. xxv. 32, *Morsels of Criticism* by the eccentric but thoughtful Ed. King, p. 341. London, 1788].
[6] Isa. lxiv. 10-12.
[7] Isa. i. 7.
[8] [*Ad hominem*, referring to the cruel decree of Hadrian, which the philosophic Antonines did not annul.]

should heal all diseases and raise the dead, hear what was said. There are these words: "At His coming the lame shall leap as an hart, and the tongue of the stammerer shall be clear speaking: the blind shall see, and the lepers shall be cleansed; and the dead shall rise, and walk about."[1] And that He did those things, you can learn from the Acts of Pontius Pilate. And how it was predicted by the Spirit of prophecy that He and those who hoped in Him should be slain, hear what was said by Isaiah. These are the words: "Behold now the righteous perisheth, and no man layeth it to heart; and just men are taken away, and no man considereth. From the presence of wickedness is the righteous man taken, and his burial shall be in peace: he is taken from our midst."[2]

CHAP. XLIX.—HIS REJECTION BY THE JEWS FORETOLD.

And again, how it was said by the same Isaiah, that the Gentile nations who were not looking for Him should worship Him, but the Jews who always expected Him should not recognize Him when He came. And the words are spoken as from the person of Christ; and they are these: "I was manifest to them that asked not for Me; I was found of them that sought Me not: I said, Behold Me, to a nation that called not on My name. I spread out My hands to a disobedient and gainsaying people, to those who walked in a way that is not good, but follow after their own sins; a people that provoketh Me to anger to My face."[3] For the Jews having the prophecies, and being always in expectation of the Christ to come, did not recognise Him, and not only so, but even treated Him shamefully. But the Gentiles, who had never heard anything about Christ, until the apostles set out from Jerusalem and preached concerning Him, and gave them the prophecies, were filled with joy and faith, and cast away their idols, and dedicated themselves to the Unbegotten God through Christ. And that it was foreknown that these infamous things should be uttered against those who confessed Christ, and that those who slandered Him, and said that it was well to preserve the ancient customs, should be miserable, hear what was briefly said by Isaiah; it is this: "Woe unto them that call sweet bitter, and bitter sweet."[4]

CHAP. L.—HIS HUMILIATION PREDICTED.

But that, having become man for our sakes, He endured to suffer and to be dishonoured, and that He shall come again with glory, hear the prophecies which relate to this; they are these:

"Because they delivered His soul unto death, and He was numbered with the transgressors, He has borne the sin of many, and shall make intercession for the transgressors. For, behold, My Servant shall deal prudently, and shall be exalted, and shall be greatly extolled. As many were astonished at Thee, so marred shall Thy form be before men, and so hidden from them Thy glory; so shall many nations wonder, and the kings shall shut their mouths at Him. For they to whom it was not told concerning Him, and they who have not heard, shall understand. O Lord, who hath believed our report? and to whom is the arm of the Lord revealed? We have declared before Him as a child, as a root in a dry ground. He had no form, nor glory; and we saw Him, and there was no form nor comeliness: but His form was dishonoured and marred more than the sons of men. A man under the stroke, and knowing how to bear infirmity, because His face was turned away: He was despised, and of no reputation. It is He who bears our sins, and is afflicted for us; yet we did esteem Him smitten, stricken, and afflicted. But He was wounded for our transgressions, He was bruised for our iniquities, the chastisement of peace was upon Him, by His stripes we are healed. All we, like sheep, have gone astray; every man has wandered in his own way. And He delivered Him for our sins; and He opened not His mouth for all His affliction. He was brought as a sheep to the slaughter, and as a lamb before his shearer is dumb, so He openeth not His mouth. In His humiliation, His judgment was taken away."[5] Accordingly, after He was crucified, even all His acquaintances forsook Him, having denied Him; and afterwards, when He had risen from the dead and appeared to them, and had taught them to read the prophecies in which all these things were foretold as coming to pass, and when they had seen Him ascending into heaven, and had believed, and had received power sent thence by Him upon them, and went to every race of men, they taught these things, and were called apostles.

CHAP. LI.—THE MAJESTY OF CHRIST.

And that the Spirit of prophecy might signify to us that He who suffers these things has an ineffable origin, and rules His enemies, He spake thus: "His generation who shall declare? because His life is cut off from the earth: for their transgressions He comes to death. And I will give the wicked for His burial, and the rich for His death; because He did no violence, neither was any deceit in His mouth. And the Lord is pleased to cleanse Him from the stripe. If He be given for sin, your soul shall see His seed

---

[1] Isa. xxxv. 6.
[2] Isa. lvii. 1.
[3] Isa. lxv. 1-3.
[4] Isa. v. 20.

[5] Isa. lii. 13-15, liii. 1-8.

prolonged in days. And the Lord is pleased to deliver His soul from grief, to show Him light, and to form Him with knowledge, to justify the righteous who richly serveth many. And He shall bear our iniquities. Therefore He shall inherit many, and He shall divide the spoil of the strong; because His soul was delivered to death: and He was numbered with the transgressors; and He bare the sins of many, and He was delivered up for their transgressions."[1] Hear, too, how He was to ascend into heaven according to prophecy. It was thus spoken: "Lift up the gates of heaven; be ye opened, that the King of glory may come in. Who is this King of glory? The Lord, strong and mighty."[2] And how also He should come again out of heaven with glory, hear what was spoken in reference to this by the prophet Jeremiah.[3] His words are: "Behold, as the Son of man He cometh in the clouds of heaven, and His angels with Him."[4]

CHAP. LII. — CERTAIN FULFILMENT OF PROPHECY.

Since, then, we prove that all things which have already happened had been predicted by the prophets before they came to pass, we must necessarily believe also that those things which are in like manner predicted, but are yet to come to pass, shall certainly happen. For as the things which have already taken place came to pass when foretold, and even though unknown, so shall the things that remain, even though they be unknown and disbelieved, yet come to pass. For the prophets have proclaimed two advents of His: the one, that which is already past, when He came as a dishonoured and suffering Man; but the second, when, according to prophecy, He shall come from heaven with glory, accompanied by His angelic host, when also He shall raise the bodies of all men who have lived, and shall clothe those of the worthy with immortality, and shall send those of the wicked, endued with eternal sensibility, into everlasting fire with the wicked devils. And that these things also have been foretold as yet to be, we will prove. By Ezekiel the prophet it was said: "Joint shall be joined to joint, and bone to bone, and flesh shall grow again; and every knee shall bow to the Lord, and every tongue shall confess Him."[5] And in what kind of sensation and punishment the wicked are to be, hear from what was said in like manner with reference to this; it is as follows: "Their worm shall not rest, and their fire shall not be quenched;"[6] and then shall they repent, when it profits them not. And what the people of the Jews shall say and do, when they see Him coming in glory, has been thus predicted by Zechariah the prophet: "I will command the four winds to gather the scattered children; I will command the north wind to bring them, and the south wind, that it keep not back. And then in Jerusalem there shall be great lamentation, not the lamentation of mouths or of lips, but the lamentation of the heart; and they shall rend not their garments, but their hearts. Tribe by tribe they shall mourn, and then they shall look on Him whom they have pierced; and they shall say, Why, O Lord, hast Thou made us to err from Thy way? The glory which our fathers blessed, has for us been turned into shame."[7]

CHAP. LIII. — SUMMARY OF THE PROPHECIES.

Though we could bring forward many other prophecies, we forbear, judging these sufficient for the persuasion of those who have ears to hear and understand; and considering also that those persons are able to see that we do not make mere assertions without being able to produce proof, like those fables that are told of the so-called sons of Jupiter. For with what reason should we believe of a crucified man that He is the first-born of the unbegotten God, and Himself will pass judgment on the whole human race, unless we had found testimonies concerning Him published before He came and was born as man, and unless we saw that things had happened accordingly — the devastation of the land of the Jews, and men of every race persuaded by His teaching through the apostles, and rejecting their old habits, in which, being deceived, they had had their conversation; yea, seeing ourselves too, and knowing that the Christians from among the Gentiles are both more numerous and more true than those from among the Jews and Samaritans? For all the other human races are called Gentiles by the Spirit of prophecy; but the Jewish and Samaritan races are called the tribe of Israel, and the house of Jacob. And the prophecy in which it was predicted that there should be more believers from the Gentiles than from the Jews and Samaritans, we will produce: it ran thus: "Rejoice, O barren, thou that dost not bear; break forth and shout, thou that dost not travail, because many more are the children of the desolate than of her that hath an husband."[8] For all the Gentiles were "desolate" of the true God, serving the works of their hands; but the Jews and Samaritans, having the word of God delivered to them by the prophets, and always expecting the Christ, did not recognise Him when He came, except some few, of whom the Spirit of prophecy by Isaiah had predicted that

---

[1] Isa. liii 8-12.
[2] Ps. xxiv. 7.
[3] This prophecy occurs not in Jeremiah, but in Dan. vii. 13.
[4] Dan. vii. 13.
[5] Ezek. xxxvii. 7, 8; Isa. xlv. 24.
[6] Isa. lxvi. 24.
[7] Zech. xii. 3-14; Isa. lxiii. 17, lxiv. 11.
[8] Isa. liv. 1.

they should be saved. He spoke as from their person: "Except the Lord had left us a seed, we should have been as Sodom and Gomorrah."[1] For Sodom and Gomorrah are related by Moses to have been cities of ungodly men, which God burned with fire and brimstone, and overthrew, no one of their inhabitants being saved except a certain stranger, a Chaldæan by birth, whose name was Lot; with whom also his daughters were rescued. And those who care may yet see their whole country desolate and burned, and remaining barren. And to show how those from among the Gentiles were foretold as more true and more believing, we will cite what was said by Isaiah[2] the prophet; for he spoke as follows: "Israel is uncircumcised in heart, but the Gentiles are uncircumcised in the flesh." So many things therefore, as these, when they are seen with the eye, are enough to produce conviction and belief in those who embrace the truth, and are not bigoted in their opinions, nor are governed by their passions.

CHAP. LIV. — ORIGIN OF HEATHEN MYTHOLOGY.

But those who hand down the myths which the poets have made, adduce no proof to the youths who learn them; and we proceed to demonstrate that they have been uttered by the influence of the wicked demons, to deceive and lead astray the human race. For having heard it proclaimed through the prophets that the Christ was to come, and that the ungodly among men were to be punished by fire, they put forward many to be called sons of Jupiter, under the impression that they would be able to produce in men the idea that the things which were said with regard to Christ were mere marvellous tales, like the things which were said by the poets. And these things were said both among the Greeks and among all nations where they [the demons] heard the prophets foretelling that Christ would specially be believed in; but that in hearing what was said by the prophets they did not accurately understand it, but imitated what was said of our Christ, like men who are in error, we will make plain. The prophet Moses, then, was, as we have already said, older than all writers; and by him, as we have also said before, it was thus predicted: "There shall not fail a prince from Judah, nor a lawgiver from between his feet, until He come for whom it is reserved; and He shall be the desire of the Gentiles, binding His foal to the vine, washing His robe in the blood of the grape."[3] The devils, accordingly, when they heard these prophetic words, said that Bacchus was the son of Jupiter, and gave out that he was the discoverer of the vine, and they number wine[4] [or, the ass] among his mysteries; and they taught that, having been torn in pieces, he ascended into heaven. And because in the prophecy of Moses it had not been expressly intimated whether He who was to come was the Son of God, and whether He would, riding on the foal, remain on earth or ascend into heaven, and because the name of "foal" could mean either the foal of an ass or the foal of a horse, they, not knowing whether He who was foretold would bring the foal of an ass or of a horse as the sign of His coming, nor whether He was the Son of God, as we said above, or of man, gave out that Bellerophon, a man born of man, himself ascended to heaven on his horse Pegasus. And when they heard it said by the other prophet Isaiah, that He should be born of a virgin, and by His own means ascend into heaven, they pretended that Perseus was spoken of. And when they knew what was said, as has been cited above, in the prophecies written aforetime, "Strong as a giant to run his course,"[5] they said that Hercules was strong, and had journeyed over the whole earth. And when, again, they learned that it had been foretold that He should heal every sickness, and raise the dead, they produced Æsculapius.

CHAP. LV. — SYMBOLS OF THE CROSS.

But in no instance, not even in any of those called sons of Jupiter, did they imitate the being crucified; for it was not understood by them, all the things said of it having been put symbolically. And this, as the prophet foretold, is the greatest symbol of His power and rule; as is also proved by the things which fall under our observation. For consider all the things in the world, whether without this form they could be administered or have any community. For the sea is not traversed except that trophy which is called a sail abide safe in the ship; and the earth is not ploughed without it: diggers and mechanics do not their work, except with tools which have this shape. And the human form differs from that of the irrational animals in nothing else than in its being erect and having the hands extended, and having on the face extending from the forehead what is called the nose, through which there is respiration for the living creature; and this shows no other form than that of the cross. And so it was said by the prophet, "The breath before our face is the Lord Christ."[6] And the power of this form is shown by your own symbols on what are called "vexilla" [banners] and

---

[1] Isa. i. 9.
[2] The following words are found, not in Isaiah, but in Jer. ix. 26.
[3] Gen. xlix. 10.
[4] In the MS. the reading is οἶνον (wine); but as Justin's argument seems to require ὄνον (an ass), Sylburg inserted this latter word in his edition; and this reading is approved by Grabe and Thirlby, and adopted by Otto and Trollope. It may be added, that ἀναγράφουσι is much more suitable to ὄνον than to οἶνον.
[5] Ps. xix. 5.
[6] From Lam. iv. 20 (Sept.).

trophies, with which all your state possessions are made, using these as the insignia of your power and government, even though you do so unwittingly.[1] And with this form you consecrate the images of your emperors when they die, and you name them gods by inscriptions. Since, therefore, we have urged you both by reason and by an evident form, and to the utmost of our ability, we know that now we are blameless even though you disbelieve; for our part is done and finished.

CHAP. LVI. — THE DEMONS STILL MISLEAD MEN.

But the evil spirits were not satisfied with saying, before Christ's appearance, that those who were said to be sons of Jupiter were born of him; but after He had appeared and been born among men, and when they learned how He had been foretold by the prophets, and knew that He should be believed on and looked for by every nation, they again, as was said above, put forward other men, the Samaritans Simon and Menander, who did many mighty works by magic, and deceived many, and still keep them deceived. For even among yourselves, as we said before,[2] Simon was in the royal city Rome in the reign of Claudius Cæsar, and so greatly astonished the sacred senate and people of the Romans, that he was considered a god, and honoured, like the others whom you honour as gods, with a statue. Wherefore we pray that the sacred senate and your people may, along with yourselves, be arbiters of this our memorial, in order that if any one be entangled by that man's doctrines, he may learn the truth, and so be able to escape error; and as for the statue, if you please, destroy it.

CHAP. LVII. — AND CAUSE PERSECUTION.

Nor can the devils persuade men that there will be no conflagration for the punishment of the wicked; as they were unable to effect that Christ should be hidden after He came. But this only can they effect, that they who live irrationally, and were brought up licentiously in wicked customs, and are prejudiced in their own opinions, should kill and hate us; whom we not only do not hate, but, as is proved, pity and endeavour to lead to repentance. For we do not fear death, since it is acknowledged we must surely die; and there is nothing new, but all things continue the same in this administration of things; and if satiety overtakes those who enjoy even one year of these things, they ought to give heed to our doctrines, that they may live eternally free both from suffering and from want. But if they believe that there is nothing after death, but declare that those who die pass into insensibility, then they become our benefactors when they set us free from sufferings and necessities of this life, and prove themselves to be wicked, and inhuman, and bigoted. For they kill us with no intention of delivering us, but cut us off that we may be deprived of life and pleasure.

CHAP. LVIII. — AND RAISE UP HERETICS.

And, as we said before, the devils put forward Marcion of Pontus, who is even now teaching men to deny that God is the maker of all things in heaven and on earth, and that the Christ predicted by the prophets is His Son, and preaches another god besides the Creator of all, and likewise another son. And this man many have believed, as if he alone knew the truth, and laugh at us, though they have no proof of what they say, but are carried away irrationally as lambs by a wolf, and become the prey of atheistical doctrines, and of devils. For they who are called devils attempt nothing else than to seduce men from God who made them, and from Christ His first-begotten; and those who are unable to raise themselves above the earth they have riveted, and do now rivet, to things earthly, and to the works of their own hands; but those who devote themselves to the contemplation of things divine, they secretly beat back; and if they have not a wise sober-mindedness, and a pure and passionless life, they drive them into godlessness.

CHAP. LIX. — PLATO'S OBLIGATION TO MOSES.

And that you may learn that it was from our teachers — we mean the account given through the prophets — that Plato borrowed his statement that God, having altered matter which was shapeless, made the world, hear the very words spoken through Moses, who, as above shown, was the first prophet, and of greater antiquity than the Greek writers; and through whom the Spirit of prophecy, signifying how and from what materials God at first formed the world, spake thus: "In the beginning God created the heaven and the earth. And the earth was invisible and unfurnished, and darkness was upon the face of the deep; and the Spirit of God moved over the waters. And God said, Let there be light; and it was so." So that both Plato and they who agree with him, and we ourselves, have learned, and you also can be convinced, that by the word of God the whole world was made out of the substance spoken of before by Moses. And that which the poets call Erebus, we know was spoken of formerly by Moses.[3]

---

[1] [The Orientals delight in such refinements, but the "scandal of the cross" led the early Christians thus to retort upon the heathen; and the *Labarum* may have been the fruit of this very suggestion.]
[2] [See cap. xxvi. above, and note p. 187, below.]
[3] Comp. Deut. xxxii. 22.

CHAP. LX. — PLATO'S DOCTRINE OF THE CROSS.

And the physiological discussion[1] concerning the Son of God in the *Timæus* of Plato, where he says, "He placed him crosswise[2] in the universe," he borrowed in like manner from Moses; for in the writings of Moses it is related how at that time, when the Israelites went out of Egypt and were in the wilderness, they fell in with poisonous beasts, both vipers and asps, and every kind of serpent, which slew the people; and that Moses, by the inspiration and influence of God, took brass, and made it into the figure of a cross, and set it in the holy tabernacle, and said to the people, "If ye look to this figure, and believe, ye shall be saved thereby."[3] And when this was done, it is recorded that the serpents died, and it is handed down that the people thus escaped death. Which things Plato reading, and not accurately understanding, and not apprehending that it was the figure of the cross, but taking it to be a placing crosswise, he said that the power next to the first God was placed crosswise in the universe. And as to his speaking of a third, he did this because he read, as we said above, that which was spoken by Moses, "that the Spirit of God moved over the waters." For he gives the second place to the Logos which is with God, who he said was placed crosswise in the universe; and the third place to the Spirit who was said to be borne upon the water, saying, "And the third around the third."[4] And hear how the Spirit of prophecy signified through Moses that there should be a conflagration. He spoke thus: "Everlasting fire shall descend, and shall devour to the pit beneath."[5] It is not, then, that we hold the same opinions as others, but that all speak in imitation of ours. Among us these things can be heard and learned from persons who do not even know the forms of the letters, who are uneducated and barbarous in speech, though wise and believing in mind; some, indeed, even maimed and deprived of eyesight; so that you may understand that these things are not the effect of human wisdom, but are uttered by the power of God.

CHAP. LXI. — CHRISTIAN BAPTISM.

I will also relate the manner in which we dedicated ourselves to God when we had been made new through Christ; lest, if we omit this, we seem to be unfair in the explanation we are making. As many as are persuaded and believe that what we teach and say is true, and undertake to be able to live accordingly, are instructed to pray and to entreat God with fasting, for the remission of their sins that are past, we praying and fasting with them. Then they are brought by us where there is water, and are regenerated in the same manner in which we were ourselves regenerated. For, in the name of God, the Father and Lord of the universe, and of our Saviour Jesus Christ, and of the Holy Spirit, they then receive the washing with water. For Christ also said, "Except ye be born again, ye shall not enter into the kingdom of heaven."[6] Now, that it is impossible for those who have once been born to enter into their mothers' wombs, is manifest to all. And how those who have sinned and repent shall escape their sins, is declared by Esaias the prophet, as I wrote above;[7] he thus speaks: "Wash you, make you clean; put away the evil of your doings from your souls; learn to do well; judge the fatherless, and plead for the widow: and come and let us reason together, saith the Lord. And though your sins be as scarlet, I will make them white like wool; and though they be as crimson, I will make them white as snow. But if ye refuse and rebel, the sword shall devour you: for the mouth of the Lord hath spoken it."[8]

And for this [rite] we have learned from the apostles this reason. Since at our birth we were born without our own knowledge or choice, by our parents coming together, and were brought up in bad habits and wicked training; in order that we may not remain the children of necessity and of ignorance, but may become the children of choice and knowledge, and may obtain in the water the remission of sins formerly committed, there is pronounced over him who chooses to be born again, and has repented of his sins, the name of God the Father and Lord of the universe; he who leads to the laver the person that is to be washed calling him by this name alone. For no one can utter the name of the ineffable God; and if any one dare to say that there is a name, he raves with a hopeless madness. And this washing is called illumination, because they who learn these things are illuminated in their understandings. And in the name of Jesus Christ, who was crucified under Pontius Pilate, and in the name of the Holy Ghost, who through the prophets foretold all things about Jesus, he who is illuminated is washed.

CHAP. LXII. — ITS IMITATION BY DEMONS.

And the devils, indeed, having heard this washing published by the prophet, instigated

---

[1] Literally, "that which is treated physiologically."
[2] He impressed him as a χίασμα, i.e., in the form of the letter χ upon the universe." Plato is speaking of the soul of the universe. [Timæus, Opp., vol. ix. p. 314. And see note of Langus (p. 37) on p. 113 of Grabe. Here crops out the Platonic philosopher speaking after the fashion of his contemporaries, perhaps to conciliate his sovereign. See Professor Jowett's Introduction to the *Timæus*, which will aid the students.]
[3] Num. xxi. 8.
[4] Τὰ δὲ τρίτα περὶ τὸν τρίτον.
[5] Deut. xxxii. 22.
[6] John iii. 5.
[7] Chap. xliv.
[8] Isa. i. 16–20.

those who enter their temples, and are about to approach them with libations and burnt-offerings, also to sprinkle themselves; and they cause them also to wash themselves entirely, as they depart [from the sacrifice], before they enter into the shrines in which their images are set. And the command, too, given by the priests to those who enter and worship in the temples, that they take off their shoes, the devils, learning what happened to the above-mentioned prophet Moses, have given in imitation of these things. For at that juncture, when Moses was ordered to go down into Egypt and lead out the people of the Israelites who were there, and while he was tending the flocks of his maternal uncle[1] in the land of Arabia, our Christ conversed with him under the appearance of fire from a bush, and said, "Put off thy shoes, and draw near and hear." And he, when he had put off his shoes and drawn near, heard that he was to go down into Egypt and lead out the people of the Israelites there; and he received mighty power from Christ, who spoke to him in the appearance of fire, and went down and led out the people, having done great and marvellous things; which, if you desire to know, you will learn them accurately from his writings.

CHAP. LXIII. — HOW GOD APPEARED TO MOSES.

And all the Jews even now teach that the nameless God spake to Moses; whence the Spirit of prophecy, accusing them by Isaiah the prophet mentioned above, said "The ox knoweth his owner, and the ass his master's crib; but Israel doth not know Me, and My people do not understand."[2] And Jesus the Christ, because the Jews knew not what the Father was, and what the Son, in like manner accused them; and Himself said, "No one knoweth the Father, but the Son; nor the Son, but the Father, and they to whom the Son revealeth Him."[3] Now the Word of God is His Son, as we have before said. And He is called Angel and Apostle; for He declares whatever we ought to know, and is sent forth to declare whatever is revealed; as our Lord Himself says, "He that heareth Me, heareth Him that sent Me."[4] From the writings of Moses also this will be manifest; for thus it is written in them, "And the Angel of God spake to Moses, in a flame of fire out of the bush, and said, I am that I am, the God of Abraham, the God of Isaac, the God of Jacob, the God of thy fathers; go down into Egypt, and bring forth My people."[5] And if you wish to learn what follows, you can do so from the same writings; for it is impossible to relate the whole here. But so much is written for the sake of proving that Jesus the Christ is the Son of God and His Apostle, being of old the Word, and appearing sometimes in the form of fire, and sometimes in the likeness of angels; but now, by the will of God, having become man for the human race, He endured all the sufferings which the devils instigated the senseless Jews to inflict upon Him; who, though they have it expressly affirmed in the writings of Moses, "And the angel of God spake to Moses in a flame of fire in a bush, and said, I am that I am, the God of Abraham, and the God of Isaac, and the God of Jacob," yet maintain that He who said this was the Father and Creator of the universe. Whence also the Spirit of prophecy rebukes them, and says, "Israel doth not know Me, my people have not understood Me."[6] And again, Jesus, as we have already shown, while He was with them, said, "No one knoweth the Father, but the Son; nor the Son but the Father, and those to whom the Son will reveal Him."[7] The Jews, accordingly, being throughout of opinion that it was the Father of the universe who spake to Moses, though He who spake to him was indeed the Son of God, who is called both Angel and Apostle, are justly charged, both by the Spirit of prophecy and by Christ Himself, with knowing neither the Father nor the Son. For they who affirm that the Son is the Father, are proved neither to have become acquainted with the Father, nor to know that the Father of the universe has a Son; who also, being the first-begotten Word of God, is even God. And of old He appeared in the shape of fire and in the likeness of an angel to Moses and to the other prophets; but now in the times of your reign,[8] having, as we before said, become Man by a virgin, according to the counsel of the Father, for the salvation of those who believe on Him, He endured both to be set at nought and to suffer, that by dying and rising again He might conquer death. And that which was said out of the bush to Moses, "I am that I am, the God of Abraham, and the God of Isaac, and the God of Jacob, and the God of your fathers,"[9] this signified that they, even though dead, are yet in existence, and are men belonging to Christ Himself. For they were the first of all men to busy themselves in the search after God; Abraham being the father of Isaac, and Isaac of Jacob, as Moses wrote.

CHAP. LXIV. — FURTHER MISREPRESENTATIONS OF THE TRUTH.

From what has been already said, you can

---

[1] Thirlby conjectures that Justin here confused in his mind the histories of Moses and Jacob.
[2] Isa. i. 3.
[3] Matt. xi. 27.
[4] Luke x. 16.
[5] Ex. iii. 6.
[6] Isa. i. 3.
[7] Matt. xi. 27.
[8] [Rather, "of your empire."]
[9] Ex. iii. 6.

understand how the devils, in imitation of what was said by Moses, asserted that Proserpine was the daughter of Jupiter, and instigated the people to set up an image of her under the name of Kore [Cora, i.e., the maiden or daughter] at the spring-heads. For, as we wrote above,[1] Moses said, " In the beginning God made the heaven and the earth. And the earth was without form and unfurnished : and the Spirit of God moved upon the face of the waters." In imitation, therefore, of what is here said of the Spirit of God moving on the waters, they said that Proserpine [or Cora] was the daughter of Jupiter.[2] And in like manner also they craftily feigned that Minerva was the daughter of Jupiter, not by sexual union, but, knowing that God conceived and made the world by the Word, they say that Minerva is the first conception [ἔννοια] ; which we consider to be very absurd, bringing forward the form of the conception in a female shape. And in like manner the actions of those others who are called sons of Jupiter sufficiently condemn them.

CHAP. LXV. — ADMINISTRATION OF THE SACRAMENTS.

But we, after we have thus washed him who has been convinced and has assented to our teaching, bring him to the place where those who are called brethren are assembled, in order that we may offer hearty prayers in common for ourselves and for the baptized [illuminated] person, and for all others in every place, that we may be counted worthy, now that we have learned the truth, by our works also to be found good citizens and keepers of the commandments, so that we may be saved with an everlasting salvation. Having ended the prayers, we salute one another with a kiss.[3] There is then brought to the president of the brethren[4] bread and a cup of wine mixed with water ; and he taking them, gives praise and glory to the Father of the universe, through the name of the Son and of the Holy Ghost, and offers thanks at considerable length for our being counted worthy to receive these things at His hands. And when he has concluded the prayers and thanksgivings, all the people present express their assent by saying Amen. This word Amen answers in the Hebrew language to γένοιτο [so be it]. And when the president has given thanks, and all the people have expressed their assent, those who are called by us deacons give to each of those present to partake of the bread and wine mixed with water over which the thanksgiving was pronounced, and to those who are absent they carry away a portion.

CHAP. LXVI. — OF THE EUCHARIST.

And this food is called among us Εὐχαριστία[5] [the Eucharist], of which no one is allowed to partake but the man who believes that the things which we teach are true, and who has been washed with the washing that is for the remission of sins, and unto regeneration, and who is so living as Christ has enjoined. For not as common bread and common drink do we receive these ; but in like manner as Jesus Christ our Saviour, having been made flesh by the Word of God, had both flesh and blood for our salvation, so likewise have we been taught that the food which is blessed by the prayer of His word, and from which our blood and flesh by transmutation are nourished, is the flesh and blood of that Jesus who was made flesh.[6] For the apostles, in the memoirs composed by them, which are called Gospels, have thus delivered unto us what was enjoined upon them ; that Jesus took bread, and when He had given thanks, said, " This do ye in remembrance of Me,[7] this is My body ; " and that, after the same manner, having taken the cup and given thanks, He said, " This is My blood ; " and gave it to them alone. Which the wicked devils have imitated in the mysteries of Mithras, commanding the same thing to be done. For, that bread and a cup of water are placed with certain incantations in the mystic rites of one who is being initiated, you either know or can learn.

CHAP. LXVII. — WEEKLY WORSHIP OF THE CHRISTIANS.

And we afterwards continually remind each other of these things. And the wealthy among us help the needy ; and we always keep together ; and for all things wherewith we are supplied, we bless the Maker of all through His Son

---

[1] Chap. lix.
[2] And therefore caused her to preside over the waters, as above.
[3] The kiss of charity, the kiss of peace, or "the peace" (ἡ εἰρήνη), was enjoined by the Apostle Paul in his Epistles to the Corinthians, Thessalonians, and Romans, and thence passed into a common Christian usage. It was continued in the Western Church, under regulations to prevent its abuse, until the thirteenth century. Stanley remarks (*Corinthians*, i. 414), "It is still continued in the worship of the Coptic Church."
[4] τῷ προεστῶτι τῶν ἀδελφῶν. This expression may quite legitimately be translated, "to that one of the brethren who was presiding."
[5] Literally, thanksgiving. See Matt. xxvi. 27.
[6] This passage is claimed alike by Calvinists, Lutherans, and Romanists; and, indeed, the language is so inexact, that each party may plausibly maintain that their own opinion is advocated by it. [But the same might be said of the words of our Lord himself; and, if such widely separated Christians can all adopt this passage, who can be sorry?] The expression, "the prayer of His word," or of the word we have from Him, seems to signify the prayer pronounced over the elements, in imitation of our Lord's thanksgiving before breaking the bread. [I must dissent from the opinion that the language is "inexact:" he expresses himself naturally as one who believes it is bread, but yet not "common bread." So Gelasius, Bishop of Rome (A.D. 490.), " By the sacraments we are made partakers of the divine nature, and yet the substance and nature of bread and wine do not cease to be in them," etc. (See the original in *Bingham's Antiquities*, book xv. cap. 5. See Chrysost., *Epist. ad. Cæsarium*, tom. iii. p. 753. Ed. Migne.) Those desirous to pursue this inquiry will find the Patristic authorities in *Historia Transubstantionis Papalis*, etc., *Edidit* F. Meyrick, Oxford, 1858. The famous tractate of Ratranin (A.D. 840) was published at Oxford, 1838, with the homily of Ælfric (A.D. 960) in a cheap edition.]
[7] Luke xxii. 19.

Jesus Christ, and through the Holy Ghost. And on the day called Sunday,[1] all who live in cities or in the country gather together to one place, and the memoirs of the apostles or the writings of the prophets are read, as long as time permits; then, when the reader has ceased, the president verbally instructs, and exhorts to the imitation of these good things. Then we all rise together and pray, and, as we before said, when our prayer is ended, bread and wine and water are brought, and the president in like manner offers prayers and thanksgivings, according to his ability,[2] and the people assent, saying Amen; and there is a distribution to each, and a participation of that over which thanks have been given,[3] and to those who are absent a portion is sent by the deacons. And they who are well to do, and willing, give what each thinks fit; and what is collected is deposited with the president, who succours the orphans and widows, and those who, through sickness or any other cause, are in want, and those who are in bonds, and the strangers sojourning among us, and in a word takes care of all who are in need. But Sunday is the day on which we all hold our common assembly, because it is the first day on which God, having wrought a change in the darkness and matter, made the world; and Jesus Christ our Saviour on the same day rose from the dead. For He was crucified on the day before that of Saturn (Saturday); and on the day after that of Saturn, which is the day of the Sun, having appeared to His apostles and disciples, He taught them these things, which we have submitted to you also for your consideration.

CHAP. LXVIII. — CONCLUSION.

And if these things seem to you to be reasonable and true, honour them; but if they seem nonsensical, despise them as nonsense, and do not decree death against those who have done no wrong, as you would against enemies. For we forewarn you, that you shall not escape the coming judgment of God, if you continue in your injustice; and we ourselves will invite you to do that which is pleasing to God. And though from the letter of the greatest and most illustrious Emperor Adrian, your father, we could demand that you order judgment to be given as we have desired, yet we have made this appeal and explanation, not on the ground of Adrian's decision, but because we know that what we ask is just. And we have subjoined the copy of Adrian's epistle, that you may know that we are speaking truly about this. And the following is the copy: —

EPISTLE OF ADRIAN[4] IN BEHALF OF THE CHRISTIANS.

I have received the letter addressed to me by your predecessor Serenius Granianus, a most illustrious man; and this communication I am unwilling to pass over in silence, lest innocent persons be disturbed, and occasion be given to the informers for practising villany. Accordingly, if the inhabitants of your province will so far sustain this petition of theirs as to accuse the Christians in some court of law, I do not prohibit them from doing so. But I will not suffer them to make use of mere entreaties and outcries. For it is far more just, if any one desires to make an accusation, that you give judgment upon it. If, therefore, any one makes the accusation, and furnishes proof that the said men do anything contrary to the laws, you shall adjudge punishments in proportion to the offences. And this, by Hercules, you shall give special heed to, that if any man shall, through mere calumny, bring an accusation against any of these persons, you shall award to him more severe punishments in proportion to his wickedness.

EPISTLE OF ANTONINUS TO THE COMMON ASSEMBLY OF ASIA.[5]

The Emperor Cæsar Titus Ælius Adrianus Antoninus Augustus Pius, Supreme Pontiff, in the fifteenth year of his tribuneship, Consul for the third time, Father of the fatherland, to the Common Assembly of Asia, greeting: I should have thought that the gods themselves would see to it that such offenders should not escape. For if they had the power, they themselves would much rather punish those who refuse to worship them; but it is you who bring trouble on these persons, and accuse as the opinion of atheists that which they hold, and lay to their charge certain other things which we are unable to prove. But it would be advantageous to them that they should be thought to die for that of which they are accused, and they conquer you by being lavish of their lives rather than yield that obedience which you require of them. And regarding the earthquakes which have already happened and are now occurring, it is not seemly that you remind us of them, losing heart whenever they occur, and thus set your conduct in contrast with that of these men; for they have much greater confidence towards God than you yourselves have. And you, indeed, seem at such times to ignore the gods, and you neglect the temples, and make

---

[1] τῇ τοῦ Ἡλίου λεγομένῃ ἡμέρᾳ.

[2] ὅση δύναμις αὐτῷ, — a phrase over which there has been much contention, but which seems to admit of no other meaning than that given above. [No need of any "contention." Langus renders, *Pro virili suâ*, and Grabe illustrates by reference to *Apost. Const.*, lib. viii. cap. 12. Our own learned translators render the same phrase (cap. xiii., above) "to the utmost of our power." Some say this favours extemporary prayers, and others object. Oh! what matter either way? We all sing hymns, "according to our ability."]

[3] Or, of the eucharistic elements.

[4] Addressed to Minucius Fundanus. [Generally credited as genuine.]

[5] [Regarded as spurious.]

no recognition of the worship of God. And hence you are jealous of those who do serve Him, and persecute them to the death. Concerning such persons, some others also of the governors of provinces wrote to my most divine father; to whom he replied that they should not at all disturb such persons, unless they were found to be attempting anything against the Roman government. And to myself many have sent intimations regarding such persons, to whom I also replied in pursuance of my father's judgment. But if any one has a matter to bring against any person of this class, merely as such a person,[1] let the accused be acquitted of the charge, even though he should be found to be such an one; but let the accuser be amenable to justice.

EPISTLE OF MARCUS AURELIUS TO THE SENATE, IN WHICH HE TESTIFIES THAT THE CHRISTIANS WERE THE CAUSE OF HIS VICTORY.[2]

The Emperor Cæsar Marcus Aurelius Antoninus, Germanicus, Parthicus, Sarmaticus, to the People of Rome, and to the sacred Senate, greeting: I explained to you my grand design, and what advantages I gained on the confines of Germany, with much labour and suffering, in consequence of the circumstance that I was surrounded by the enemy; I myself being shut up in Carnuntum by seventy-four cohorts, nine miles off. And the enemy being at hand, the scouts pointed out to us, and our general Pompeianus showed us that there was close on us a mass of a mixed multitude of 977,000 men, which indeed we saw; and I was shut up by this vast host, having with me only a battalion composed of the first, tenth, double and marine legions. Having then examined my own position, and my host, with respect to the vast mass of barbarians and of the enemy, I quickly betook myself to prayer to the gods of my country. But being disregarded by them, I summoned those who among us go by the name of Christians. And having made inquiry, I discovered a great number and vast host of them, and raged against them, which was by no means becoming; for afterwards I learned their power. Wherefore they began the battle, not by preparing weapons, nor arms, nor bugles; for such preparation is hateful to them, on account of the God they bear about in their conscience. Therefore it is probable that those whom we suppose to be atheists, have God as their ruling power entrenched in their conscience. For having cast themselves on the ground, they prayed not only for me, but also for the whole army as it stood, that they might be delivered from the present thirst and famine. For during five days we had got no water, because there was none; for we were in the heart of Germany, and in the enemy's territory. And simultaneously with their casting themselves on the ground, and praying to God (a God of whom I am ignorant), water poured from heaven, upon us most refreshingly cool, but upon the enemies of Rome a withering[3] hail. And immediately we recognised the presence of God following on the prayer — a God unconquerable and indestructible. Founding upon this, then, let us pardon such as are Christians, lest they pray for and obtain such a weapon against ourselves. And I counsel that no such person be accused on the ground of his being a Christian. But if any one be found laying to the charge of a Christian that he is a Christian, I desire that it be made manifest that he who is accused as a Christian, and acknowledges that he is one, is accused of nothing else than only this, that he is a Christian; but that he who arraigns him be burned alive. And I further desire, that he who is entrusted with the government of the province shall not compel the Christian, who confesses and certifies such a matter, to retract; neither shall he commit him. And I desire that these things be confirmed by a decree of the Senate. And I command this my edict to be published in the Forum of Trajan, in order that it may be read. The prefect Vitrasius Pollio will see that it be transmitted to all the provinces round about, and that no one who wishes to make use of or to possess it be hindered from obtaining a copy from the document I now publish.

---

[1] That is, if any one accuses a Christian merely on the ground of his being a Christian.

[2] [Spurious, no doubt; but the literature of the subject is very rich. See text and notes, Milman's *Gibbon*, vol. ii. 46.]

[3] Literally, "fiery."

[Note 1. (See capp. xxvi. and lvi.)
In 1851 I recognised this stone in the Vatican, and read it with emotion. I copied it, as follows:
"Semoni
Sanco
Deo Fidio
Sacrvm
Sex. Pompeius. S. P. F. Col. Mussianvs.
Quinquennalis Decur Bidentalis Donum dedit."
The explanation is possibly this: Simon Magus was actually recognised as the God *Semo*, just as Barnabas and Paul were supposed to be Zeus and Hermes (Acts xiv. 12.), and were offered divine honours accordingly. Or the Samaritans may so have informed Justin on their understanding of this inscription, and with pride in the success of their countryman (Acts viii. 10), whom they had recognised " as the great power of God." See *Orelli* (No. 1860), *Insc.*, vol. i. 337.

Note II. (The Thundering Legion.)
The bas-relief on the column of Antonine, in Rome, is a very striking complement of the story, but an answer to prayer is not a miracle. I simply transcribe from the American Translation of Alzog's *Universal Church History* the references there given to the *Legio Fulminatrix*: "Tertull., Apol., cap. 5; Ad Scap., cap. 4; Euseb., v. 5; Greg. Nyss. Or., 11 in Martyr.; Oros., vii. 15; Dio. Cass. Epit.: Xiphilin., lib. lxxi. cap. 8; Jul. Capitol. in Marc. Antonin., cap. 24."]

THE SECOND APOLOGY OF JUSTIN

FOR THE CHRISTIANS

ADDRESSED TO THE ROMAN SENATE

CHAP. I. — INTRODUCTION.

ROMANS, the things which have recently[1] happened in your city under Urbicus,[2] and the things which are likewise being everywhere unreasonably done by the governors, have compelled me to frame this composition for your sakes, who are men of like passions, and brethren, though ye know it not, and though ye be unwilling to acknowledge it on account of your glorying in what you esteem dignities.[3] For everywhere, whoever is corrected by father, or neighbour, or child, or friend, or brother, or husband, or wife, for a fault, for being hard to move, for loving pleasure and being hard to urge to what is right (except those who have been persuaded that the unjust and intemperate shall be punished in eternal fire, but that the virtuous and those who lived like Christ shall dwell with God in a state that is free from suffering, — we mean, those who have become Christians), and the evil demons, who hate us, and who keep such men as these subject to themselves, and serving them in the capacity of judges, incite them, as rulers actuated by evil spirits, to put us to death. But that the cause of all that has taken place under Urbicus may become quite plain to you, I will relate what has been done.

CHAP. II. — URBICUS CONDEMNS THE CHRISTIANS TO DEATH.

A certain woman lived with an intemperate[4] husband; she herself, too, having formerly been intemperate. But when she came to the knowledge of the teachings of Christ she became sober-minded, and endeavoured to persuade her husband likewise to be temperate, citing the teaching of Christ, and assuring him that there shall be punishment in eternal fire inflicted upon those who do not live temperately and conformably to right reason. But he, continuing in the same excesses, alienated his wife from him by his actions. For she, considering it wicked to live any longer as a wife with a husband who sought in every way means of indulging in pleasure contrary to the law of nature, and in violation of what is right, wished to be divorced from him. And when she was overpersuaded by her friends, who advised her still to continue with him, in the idea that some time or other her husband might give hope of amendment, she did violence to her own feeling and remained with him. But when her husband had gone into Alexandria, and was reported to be conducting himself worse than ever, she — that she might not, by continuing in matrimonial connection with him, and by sharing his table and his bed, become a partaker also in his wickednesses and impieties — gave him what you call a bill of divorce,[5] and was separated from him. But this noble husband of hers, — while he ought to have been rejoicing that those actions which formerly she unhesitatingly committed with the servants and hirelings, when she delighted in drunkenness and every vice, she had now given up, and desired that he too should give up the same, — when she had gone from him without his desire, brought an accusation against her, affirming that she was a Christian. And she presented a paper to thee, the Emperor,[6] requesting that first she be permitted to arrange her affairs, and afterwards to make her defence against the accusation, when her affairs were set in order. And this you granted. And

---

[1] Literally, "both yesterday and the day before."
[2] [See Grabe's note on the conjecture of Valesius that this prefect was Lollius Urbicus, the historian (vol. i. p. 1, and notes, p. 1).]
[3] [He has addressed them as "Romans," because in this they gloried together, — emperor, senate, soldiers, and citizens.]
[4] ἀκολασταίνοντι, which word includes unchastity, as well as the other forms of intemperance. [As we say, dissolute.]
[5] ῥεπούδιον, i.e., "repudium," a bill of repudiation.
[6] [Rather, "to thee, autocrat:" a very bold apostrophe, like that of Huss to the Emperor Sigismund, which crimsoned his forehead with a blush of shame.]

her *quondam* husband, since he was now no longer able to prosecute her, directed his assaults against a man, Ptolemæus, whom Urbicus punished, and who had been her teacher in the Christian doctrines. And this he did in the following way. He persuaded a centurion — who had cast Ptolemæus into prison, and who was friendly to himself — to take Ptolemæus and interrogate him on this sole point: whether he were a Christian? And Ptolemæus, being a lover of truth, and not of a deceitful or false disposition, when he confessed himself to be a Christian, was bound by the centurion, and for a long time punished in the prison. And, at last, when the man¹ came to Urbicus, he was asked this one question only: whether he was a Christian? And again, being conscious of his duty, and the nobility of it through the teaching of Christ, he confessed his discipleship in the divine virtue. For he who denies anything, either denies it because he condemns the thing itself, or he shrinks from confession because he is conscious of his own unworthiness or alienation from it; neither of which cases is that of the true Christian. And when Urbicus ordered him to be led away to punishment, one Lucius, who was also himself a Christian, seeing the unreasonable judgment that had thus been given, said to Urbicus: "What is the ground of this judgment? Why have you punished this man, not as an adulterer, nor fornicator, nor murderer, nor thief, nor robber, nor convicted of any crime at all, but who has only confessed that he is called by the name of Christian? This judgment of yours, O Urbicus, does not become the Emperor Pius, nor the philosopher, the son of Cæsar, nor the sacred senate." ² And he said nothing else in answer to Lucius than this: "You also seem to me to be such an one." And when Lucius answered, "Most certainly I am," he again ordered him also to be led away. And he professed his thanks, knowing that he was delivered from such wicked rulers, and was going to the Father and King of the heavens. And still a third having come forward, was condemned to be punished.

CHAP. III. — JUSTIN ACCUSES CRESCENS OF IGNORANT PREJUDICE AGAINST THE CHRISTIANS.

I too, therefore, expect to be plotted against and fixed to the stake, by some of those I have named, or perhaps by Crescens, that lover of bravado and boasting;³ for the man is not worthy of the name of philosopher who publicly bears witness against us in matters which he does not understand, saying that the Christians are atheists and impious, and doing so to win favour with the deluded mob, and to please them. For if he assails us without having read the teachings of Christ, he is thoroughly depraved, and far worse than the illiterate, who often refrain from discussing or bearing false witness about matters they do not understand. Or, if he has read them and does not understand the majesty that is in them, or, understanding it, acts thus that he may not be suspected of being such [a Christian], he is far more base and thoroughly depraved, being conquered by illiberal and unreasonable opinion and fear. For I would have you to know that I proposed to him certain questions on this subject, and interrogated him, and found most convincingly that he, in truth, knows nothing. And to prove that I speak the truth, I am ready, if these disputations have not been reported to you, to conduct them again in your presence. And this would be an act worthy of a prince. But if my questions and his answers have been made known to you, you are already aware that he is acquainted with none of our matters; or, if he is acquainted with them, but, through fear of those who might hear him, does not dare to speak out, like Socrates, he proves himself, as I said before, no philosopher, but an opionative man;⁴ at least he does not regard that Socratic and most admirable saying: "But a man must in no wise be honoured before the truth." ⁵ But it is impossible for a Cynic, who makes indifference his end, to know any good but indifference.

CHAP. IV. — WHY THE CHRISTIANS DO NOT KILL THEMSELVES.

But lest some one say to us, "Go then all of you and kill yourselves, and pass even now to God, and do not trouble us," I will tell you why we do not so, but why, when examined, we fearlessly confess. We have been taught that God did not make the world aimlessly, but for the sake of the human race; and we have before stated that He takes pleasure in those who imitate His properties, and is displeased with those that embrace what is worthless either in word or deed. If, then, we all kill ourselves, we shall become the cause, as far as in us lies, why no one should be born, or instructed in the divine doctrines, or even why the human race should not exist; and we shall, if we so act, be ourselves acting in opposition to the will of God. But when we are examined, we make no denial, because we are not conscious of any evil, but count it impious not to speak the truth in all things, which also we know is pleasing to God, and be-

---
¹ i e., Ptolemæus.
² On this passage, see Donaldson's *Critical History*, etc., vol. ii. p. 79.
³ Words resembling "philosopher" in sound, viz. φιλοψόφου καὶ φιλοκομπου. [This passage is found elsewhere. See note, cap. viii., in the text preferred by Grabe.]

⁴ φιλόδοξος, which may mean a lover of vainglory.
⁵ See Plato, *Rep.*, p. 595.

cause we are also now very desirous to deliver you from an unjust prejudice.

CHAP. V. — HOW THE ANGELS TRANSGRESSED.

But if this idea take possession of some one, that if we acknowledge God as our helper, we should not, as we say, be oppressed and persecuted by the wicked; this, too, I will solve. God, when He had made the whole world, and subjected things earthly to man, and arranged the heavenly elements for the increase of fruits and rotation of the seasons, and appointed this divine law — for these things also He evidently made for man — committed the care of men and of all things under heaven to angels whom He appointed over them. But the angels transgressed this appointment, and were captivated by love of women, and begat children who are those that are called demons; and besides, they afterwards subdued the human race to themselves, partly by magical writings, and partly by fears and the punishments they occasioned, and partly by teaching them to offer sacrifices, and incense, and libations, of which things they stood in need after they were enslaved by lustful passions; and among men they sowed murders, wars, adulteries, intemperate deeds, and all wickedness. Whence also the poets and mythologists, not knowing that it was the angels and those demons who had been begotten by them that did these things to men, and women, and cities, and nations, which they related, ascribed them to god himself, and to those who were accounted to be his very offspring, and to the offspring of those who were called his brothers, Neptune and Pluto, and to the children again of these their offspring. For whatever name each of the angels had given to himself and his children, by that name they called them.

CHAP. VI. — NAMES OF GOD AND OF CHRIST, THEIR MEANING AND POWER.

But to the Father of all, who is unbegotten, there is no name given. For by whatever name He be called, He has as His elder the person who gives Him the name. But these words, Father, and God, and Creator, and Lord, and Master, are not names, but appellations derived from His good deeds and functions. And His Son, who alone is properly called Son, the Word, who also was with Him and was begotten before the works, when at first He created and arranged all things by Him, is called Christ, in reference to His being anointed and God's ordering all things through Him; this name itself also containing an unknown significance; as also the appellation "God" is not a name, but an opinion implanted in the nature of men of a thing that can hardly be explained. But "Jesus," His name as man and Saviour, has also significance. For He was made man also, as we before said, having been conceived according to the will of God the Father, for the sake of believing men, and for the destruction of the demons. And now you can learn this from what is under your own observation. For numberless demoniacs throughout the whole world, and in your city, many of our Christian men exorcising them in the name of Jesus Christ, who was crucified under Pontius Pilate, have healed and do heal, rendering helpless and driving the possessing devils out of the men, though they could not be cured by all the other exorcists, and those who used incantations and drugs.

CHAP. VII. — THE WORLD PRESERVED FOR THE SAKE OF CHRISTIANS. MAN'S RESPONSIBILITY.

Wherefore God delays causing the confusion and destruction of the whole world, by which the wicked angels and demons and men shall cease to exist, because of the seed of the Christians, who know that they are the cause of preservation in nature.[1] Since, if it were not so, it would not have been possible for you to do these things, and to be impelled by evil spirits; but the fire of judgment would descend and utterly dissolve all things, even as formerly the flood left no one but him only with his family who is by us called Noah, and by you Deucalion, from whom again such vast numbers have sprung, some of them evil and others good. For so we say that there will be the conflagration, but not as the Stoics, according to their doctrine of all things being changed into one another, which seems most degrading. But neither do we affirm that it is by fate that men do what they do, or suffer what they suffer, but that each man by free choice acts rightly or sins; and that it is by the influence of the wicked demons that earnest men, such as Socrates and the like, suffer persecution and are in bonds, while Sardanapalus, Epicurus, and the like, seem to be blessed in abundance and glory. The Stoics, not observing this, maintained that all things take place according to the necessity of fate. But since God in the beginning made the race of angels and men with free-will, they will justly suffer in eternal fire the punishment of whatever sins they have committed. And this is the nature of all that is made, to be capable of vice and virtue. For neither would any of them be praiseworthy unless there were power to turn to both [virtue and vice]. And this also is shown by those men everywhere who have made laws and philosophised according to right reason, by their prescribing to do some things and refrain from others. Even the Stoic philosophers, in their

---

[1] This is Dr. Donaldson's rendering of a clause on which the editors differ both as to reading and rendering.

doctrine of morals, steadily honour the same things, so that it is evident that they are not very felicitous in what they say about principles and incorporeal things. For if they say that human actions come to pass by fate, they will maintain either that God is nothing else than the things which are ever turning, and altering, and dissolving into the same things, and will appear to have had a comprehension only of things that are destructible, and to have looked on God Himself as emerging both in part and in whole in every wickedness;[1] or that neither vice nor virtue is anything; which is contrary to every sound idea, reason, and sense.

CHAP. VIII. — ALL HAVE BEEN HATED IN WHOM THE WORD HAS DWELT.

And those of the Stoic school — since, so far as their moral teaching went, they were admirable, as were also the poets in some particulars, on account of the seed of reason [the Logos] implanted in every race of men — were, we know, hated and put to death, — Heraclitus for instance, and, among those of our own time, Musonius and others. For, as we intimated, the devils have always effected, that all those who anyhow live a reasonable and earnest life, and shun vice, be hated. And it is nothing wonderful; if the devils are proved to cause those to be much worse hated who live not according to a part only of the word diffused [among men], but by the knowledge and contemplation of the whole Word, which is Christ. And they, having been shut up in eternal fire, shall suffer their just punishment and penalty. For if they are even now overthrown by men through the name of Jesus Christ, this is an intimation of the punishment in eternal fire which is to be inflicted on themselves and those who serve them. For thus did both all the prophets foretell, and our own teacher Jesus teach.[2]

CHAP. IX. — ETERNAL PUNISHMENT NOT A MERE THREAT.

And that no one may say what is said by those who are deemed philosophers, that our assertions that the wicked are punished in eternal fire are big words and bugbears, and that we wish men to live virtuously through fear, and not because such a life is good and pleasant; I will briefly reply to this, that if this be not so, God does not exist; or, if He exists, He cares not for men, and neither virtue nor vice is anything, and, as we said before, lawgivers unjustly punish those who transgress good commandments. But since these are not unjust, and their Father teaches them by the word to do the same things as Himself, they who agree with them are not unjust. And if one object that the laws of men are diverse, and say that with some, one thing is considered good, another evil, while with others what seemed bad to the former is esteemed good, and what seemed good is esteemed bad, let him listen to what we say to this. We know that the wicked angels appointed laws conformable to their own wickedness, in which the men who are like them delight; and the right Reason,[3] when He came, proved that not all opinions nor all doctrines are good, but that some are evil, while others are good. Wherefore, I will declare the same and similar things to such men as these, and, if need be, they shall be spoken of more at large. But at present I return to the subject.

CHAP. X. — CHRIST COMPARED WITH SOCRATES.

Our doctrines, then, appear to be greater than all human teaching; because Christ, who appeared for our sakes, became the whole rational being, both body, and reason, and soul. For whatever either lawgivers or philosophers uttered well, they elaborated by finding and contemplating some part of the Word. But since they did not know the whole of the Word, which is Christ, they often contradicted themselves. And those who by human birth were more ancient than Christ, when they attempted to consider and prove things by reason, were brought before the tribunals as impious persons and busybodies. And Socrates, who was more zealous in this direction than all of them, was accused of the very same crimes as ourselves. For they said that he was introducing new divinities, and did not consider those to be gods whom the state recognised. But he cast out from the state both Homer[4] and the rest of the poets, and taught men to reject the wicked demons and those who did the things which the poets related; and he exhorted them to become acquainted with the God who was to them unknown, by means of the investigation of reason, saying, "That it is neither easy to find the Father and Maker of all, nor, having found Him, is. it safe to declare Him to all."[5] But these things our Christ did through His own power. For no one trusted in Socrates so as to die for this doctrine, but in Christ, who was partially known even by Socrates (for He was and is the Word who is in every man, and who foretold the things that were to come to pass both through the prophets and in His own person when He was made of like passions, and taught these things), not only philosophers and scholars believed, but also artisans and people entirely uneducated, despising both glory, and fear, and

---

[1] Literally, "becoming (γινόμενον) both through the parts and through the whole in every wickedness.
[2] [Here, in Grabe's text, comes in the passage about Crescens.]
[3] These words can be taken of the Logos as well as of the right reason diffused among men by Him.
[4] Plato, *Rep.*, x c. i. p. 595.
[5] Plat., *Timæus*, p. 28, C. (but "possible," and not "safe," is the word used by Plato).

death; since He is a power of the ineffable Father, and not the mere instrument of human reason.[1]

CHAP. XI. — HOW CHRISTIANS VIEW DEATH.

But neither should we be put to death, nor would wicked men and devils be more powerful than we, were not death a debt due by every man that is born. Wherefore we give thanks when we pay this debt. And we judge it right and opportune to tell here, for the sake of Crescens and those who rave as he does, what is related by Xenophon. Hercules, says Xenophon, coming to a place where three ways met, found Virtue and Vice, who appeared to him in the form of women: Vice, in a luxurious dress, and with a seductive expression rendered blooming by such ornaments, and her eyes of a quickly melting tenderness,[2] said to Hercules that if he would follow her, she would always enable him to pass his life in pleasure and adorned with the most graceful ornaments, such as were then upon her own person; and Virtue, who was of squalid look and dress, said, But if you obey me, you shall adorn yourself not with ornament nor beauty that passes away and perishes, but with everlasting and precious graces. And we are persuaded that every one who flees those things that seem to be good, and follows hard after what are reckoned difficult and strange, enters into blessedness. For Vice, when by imitation of what is incorruptible (for what is really incorruptible she neither has nor can produce) she has thrown around her own actions, as a disguise, the properties of Virtue, and qualities which are really excellent, leads captive earthly-minded men, attaching to Virtue her own evil properties. But those who understood the excellences which belong to that which is real, are also uncorrupt in virtue. And this every sensible person ought to think both of Christians and of the athletes, and of those who did what the poets relate of the so-called gods, concluding as much from our contempt of death, even when it could be escaped.[3]

CHAP. XII. — CHRISTIANS PROVED INNOCENT BY THEIR CONTEMPT OF DEATH.

For I myself, too, when I was delighting in the doctrines of Plato, and heard the Christians slandered, and saw them fearless of death, and of all other things which are counted fearful, perceived that it was impossible that they could be living in wickedness and pleasure. For what sensual or intemperate man, or who that counts it good to feast on human flesh,[4] could welcome death that he might be deprived of his enjoyments, and would not rather continue always the present life, and attempt to escape the observation of the rulers; and much less would he denounce himself when the consequence would be death? This also the wicked demons have now caused to be done by evil men. For having put some to death on account of the accusations falsely brought against us, they also dragged to the torture our domestics, either children or weak women, and by dreadful torments forced them to admit those fabulous actions which they themselves openly perpetrate; about which we are the less concerned, because none of these actions are really ours, and we have the unbegotten and ineffable God as witness both of our thoughts and deeds. For why did we not even publicly profess that these were the things which we esteemed good, and prove that these are the divine philosophy, saying that the mysteries of Saturn are performed when we slay a man, and that when we drink our fill of blood, as it is said we do, we are doing what you do before that idol you honour, and on which you sprinkle the blood not only of irrational animals, but also of men, making a libation of the blood of the slain by the hand of the most illustrious and noble man among you? And imitating Jupiter and the other gods in sodomy and shameless intercourse with woman, might we not bring as our apology the writings of Epicurus and the poets? But because we persuade men to avoid such instruction, and all who practise them and imitate such examples, as now in this discourse we have striven to persuade you, we are assailed in every kind of way. But we are not concerned, since we know that God is a just observer of all. But would that even now some one would mount a lofty rostrum, and shout with a loud voice,[5] "Be ashamed, be ashamed, ye who charge the guiltless with those deeds which yourselves openly commit, and ascribe things which apply to yourselves and to your gods to those who have not even the slightest sympathy with them. Be ye converted; become wise."

CHAP. XIII. — HOW THE WORD HAS BEEN IN ALL MEN.

For I myself, when I discovered the wicked disguise which the evil spirits had thrown around the divine doctrines of the Christians, to turn aside others from joining them, laughed both at those who framed these falsehoods, and at the disguise itself, and at popular opinion; and I confess that I both boast and with all my strength

---

[1] [Certainly the author of this chapter, and others like it, cannot be accused of a feeble rhetoric.]
[2] Another reading is πρὸς τὰς ὄψεις, referring to the eyes of the beholder; and which may be rendered, "speedily fascinating to the sight."
[3] Καὶ φευκτοῦ θανάτου may also be rendered, "even of death which men flee from."
[4] Alluding to the common accusation against the Christians.
[5] Literally, "with a tragic voice," — the loud voice in which the Greek tragedies were recited through the *mask* [*persona*].

strive to be found a Christian; not because the teachings of Plato are different from those of Christ, but because they are not in all respects similar, as neither are those of the others, Stoics, and poets, and historians. For each man spoke well in proportion to the share he had of the spermatic word,[1] seeing what was related to it. But they who contradict themselves on the more important points appear not to have possessed the heavenly[2] wisdom, and the knowledge which cannot be spoken against. Whatever things were rightly said among all men, are the property of us Christians. For next to God, we worship and love the Word who is from the unbegotten and ineffable God, since also He became man for our sakes, that, becoming a partaker of our sufferings, He might also bring us healing. For all the writers were able to see realities darkly through the sowing of the implanted word that was in them. For the seed and imitation imparted according to capacity is one thing, and quite another is the thing itself, of which there is the participation and imitation according to the grace which is from Him.

CHAP. XIV. — JUSTIN PRAYS THAT THIS APPEAL BE PUBLISHED.

And we therefore pray you to publish this little book, appending what you think right, that our opinions may be known to others, and that these persons may have a fair chance of being freed from erroneous notions and ignorance of good, who by their own fault are become subject to punishment; that so these things may be published to men, because it is in the nature of man to know good and evil; and by their condemning us, whom they do not understand, for actions which they say are wicked, and by delighting in the gods who did such things, and even now require similar actions from men, and by inflicting on us death or bonds or some other such punishment, as if we were guilty of these things, they condemn themselves, so that there is no need of other judges.

CHAP. XV. — CONCLUSION.

And I despised the wicked and deceitful doctrine of Simon[3] of my own nation. And if you give this book your authority, we will expose him before all, that, if possible, they may be converted. For this end alone did we compose this treatise. And our doctrines are not shameful, according to a sober judgment, but are indeed more lofty than all human philosophy; and if not so, they are at least unlike the doctrines of the Sotadists, and Philænidians, and Dancers, and Epicureans, and such other teachings of the poets, which all are allowed to acquaint themselves with, both as acted and as written. And henceforth we shall be silent, having done as much as we could, and having added the prayer that all men everywhere may be counted worthy of the truth. And would that you also, in a manner becoming piety and philosophy,[4] would for your own sakes judge justly!

---

[1] The word disseminated among men. [St. James i. 21.]
[2] Literally, dimly seen at a distance.
[3] [Simon Magus appears to be one with whom Justin is perfectly familiar, and hence we are not to conclude rashly that he blundered as to the divine honours rendered to him as the Sabine God.]
[4] [Another apostrophe, and a home thrust for "Pius the philosopher" and emperor.]

DIALOGUE OF JUSTIN, PHILOSOPHER AND MARTYR,

WITH

TRYPHO, A JEW

CHAP. I. — INTRODUCTION.

WHILE I was going about one morning in the walks of the Xystus,[1] a certain man, with others in his company, having met me, and said, "Hail, O philosopher!" And immediately after saying this, he turned round and walked along with me; his friends likewise followed him. And I in turn having addressed him, said, "What is there important?"

And he replied, "I was instructed," says he, "by Corinthus the Socratic in Argos, that I ought not to despise or treat with indifference those who array themselves in this dress,[2] but to show them all kindness, and to associate with them, as perhaps some advantage would spring from the intercourse either to some such man or to myself. It is good, moreover, for both, if either the one or the other be benefited. On this account, therefore, whenever I see any one in such costume, I gladly approach him, and now, for the same reason, have I willingly accosted you; and these accompany me, in the expectation of hearing for themselves something profitable from you."

"But who are you, most excellent man?" So I replied to him in jest.[3]

Then he told me frankly both his name and his family. "Trypho," says he, "I am called; and I am a Hebrew of the circumcision,[4] and having escaped from the war[5] lately carried on there, I am spending my days in Greece, and chiefly at Corinth."

"And in what," said I, "would you be profited by philosophy so much as by your own lawgiver and the prophets?"

"Why not?" he replied. "Do not the philosophers turn every discourse on God? and do not questions continually arise to them about His unity and providence? Is not this truly the duty of philosophy, to investigate the Deity?"

"Assuredly," said I, "so we too have believed. But the most[6] have not taken thought of this, whether there be one or more gods, and whether they have a regard for each one of us or no, as if this knowledge contributed nothing to our happiness; nay, they moreover attempt to persuade us that God takes care of the universe with its genera and species, but not of me and you, and each individually, since otherwise we would surely not need to pray to Him night and day. But it is not difficult to understand the upshot of this; for fearlessness and license in speaking result to such as maintain these opinions, doing and saying whatever they choose, neither dreading punishment nor hoping for any benefit from God. For how could they? They affirm that the same things shall always happen; and, further, that I and you shall again live in like manner, having become neither better men nor worse. But there are some others,[7] who, having supposed the soul to be immortal and immaterial, believe that though they have committed evil they will not suffer punishment (for that which is immaterial is insensible), and that the soul, in consequence of its immortality, needs nothing from God."

And he, smiling gently, said, "Tell us your opinion of these matters, and what idea you entertain respecting God, and what your philosophy is."

---

[1] This Xystus, on the authority of Euseb. (iv. 18), was at Ephesus. There, Philostratus mentions, Appolonius was wont to have disputations. — OTTO.
[2] Euseb. (iv. 11): "Justin, in philosopher's garb, preached the word of God."
[3] In jest, no doubt, because quoting a line from Homer, *Il.*, vi. 123. τίς δὲ σύ ἐσσι, φέριστε, καταθνητῶν ἀνθρώπων.
[4] [i.e., "A Hebrew of the Hebrews" (Phil. iii. 5).]
[5] The war instigated by Bar Cochba.

[6] The opinions of Stoics. — OTTO.
[7] The Platonists.

CHAP. II. — JUSTIN DESCRIBES HIS STUDIES IN PHILOSOPHY.

"I will tell you," said I, "what seems to me; for philosophy is, in fact, the greatest possession, and most honourable before God,[1] to whom it leads us and alone commends us; and these are truly holy men who have bestowed attention on philosophy. What philosophy is, however, and the reason why it has been sent down to men, have escaped the observation of most; for there would be neither Platonists, nor Stoics, nor Peripatetics, nor Theoretics,[2] nor Pythagoreans, this knowledge being *one*.[3] I wish to tell you why it has become many-headed. It has happened that those who first handled it [i.e., philosophy], and who were therefore esteemed illustrious men, were succeeded by those who made no investigations concerning truth, but only admired the perseverance and self-discipline of the former, as well as the novelty of the doctrines; and each thought that to be true which he learned from his teacher: then, moreover, those latter persons handed down to *their* successors such things, and others similar to them; and this system was called by the name of him who was styled the father of the doctrine. Being at first desirous of personally conversing with one of these men, I surrendered myself to a certain Stoic; and having spent a considerable time with him, when I had not acquired any further knowledge of God (for he did not know himself, and said such instruction was unnecessary), I left him and betook myself to another, who was called a Peripatetic, and as *he* fancied, shrewd. And this man, after having entertained me for the first few days, requested me to settle the fee, in order that our intercourse might not be unprofitable. Him, too, for this reason I abandoned, believing him to be no philosopher at all. But when my soul was eagerly desirous to hear the peculiar and choice philosophy, I came to a Pythagorean, very celebrated — a man who thought much of his own wisdom. And then, when I had an interview with him, willing to become his hearer and disciple, he said, 'What then? Are you acquainted with music, astronomy, and geometry? Do you expect to perceive any of those things which conduce to a happy life, if you have not been first informed on those points which wean the soul from sensible objects, and render it fitted for objects which appertain to the mind, so that it can contemplate that which is honourable in its essence and that which is good in its essence?'

Having commended many of these branches of learning, and telling me that they were necessary, he dismissed me when I confessed to him my ignorance. Accordingly I took it rather impatiently, as was to be expected when I failed in my hope, the more so because I deemed the man had some knowledge; but reflecting again on the space of time during which I would have to linger over those branches of learning, I was not able to endure longer procrastination. In my helpless condition it occurred to me to have a meeting with the Platonists, for their fame was great. I thereupon spent as much of my time as possible with one who had lately settled in our city,[4] — a sagacious man, holding a high position among the Platonists, — and I progressed, and made the greatest improvements daily. And the perception of immaterial things quite overpowered me, and the contemplation of ideas furnished my mind with wings,[5] so that in a little while I supposed that I had become wise; and such was my stupidity, I expected forthwith to look upon God, for this is the end of Plato's philosophy.

CHAP. III. — JUSTIN NARRATES THE MANNER OF HIS CONVERSION.

"And while I was thus disposed, when I wished at one period to be filled with great quietness, and to shun the path of men, I used to go into a certain field not far from the sea. And when I was near that spot one day, which having reached I purposed to be by myself, a certain old man, by no means contemptible in appearance, exhibiting meek and venerable manners, followed me at a little distance. And when I turned round to him, having halted, I fixed my eyes rather keenly on him.

"And he said, 'Do you know me?'

"I replied in the negative.

"'Why, then,' said he to me, 'do you so look at me?'

"'I am astonished,' I said, 'because you have chanced to be in my company in the same place; for I had not expected to see any man here.'

"And he says to me, 'I am concerned about some of my household. These are gone away from me; and therefore have I come to make personal search for them, if, perhaps, they shall make their appearance somewhere. But why are you here?' said he to me.

"'I delight,' said I, 'in such walks, where my attention is not distracted, for converse with myself is uninterrupted; and such places are most fit for philology.'[6]

"'Are you, then, a philologian,'[7] said he, 'but

---

[1] ᾧ some omit, and put θεῷ of prev. cl. in this cl., reading so: "Philosophy is the greatest possession, and most honourable, and introduces us to God," etc.
[2] Maranus thinks that those who are different from the masters of practical philosophy are called *Theoretics*. I do not know whether they may be better designated *Sceptics* or *Pyrrhonists*. — OTTO.
[3] Julian, *Orat.* vi., says: "Let no one divide our philosophy into many parts, or cut it into many parts, and especially let him not make many out of *one*: for as truth is one, so also is philosophy."
[4] Either Flavia Neapolis is indicated, or Ephesus. — OTTO.
[5] Narrating his progress in the study of Platonic philosophy, he elegantly employs this trite phrase of Plato's. — OTTO.
[6] Philology, used here to denote the exercise of the *reason*.
[7] Philology, used here to denote the exercise of *speech*. The twofold use of λόγος — *oratio* and *ratio* — ought to be kept in view. The old man uses it in the former, Justin in the latter, sense.

no lover of deeds or of truth? and do you not aim at being a practical man so much as being a sophist?'

"'What greater work,' said I, 'could one accomplish than this, to show the reason which governs all, and having laid hold of it, and being mounted upon it, to look down on the errors of others, and their pursuits? But without philosophy and right reason, prudence would not be present to any man. Wherefore it is necessary for every man to philosophize, and to esteem this the greatest and most honourable work; but other things only of second-rate or third-rate importance, though, indeed, if they be made to depend on philosophy, they are of moderate value, and worthy of acceptance; but deprived of it, and not accompanying it, they are vulgar and coarse to those who pursue them.'

"'Does philosophy, then, make happiness?' said he, interrupting.

"'Assuredly,' I said, 'and it alone.'

"'What, then, is philosophy?' he says; 'and what is happiness? Pray tell me, unless something hinders you from saying.'

"'Philosophy, then,' said I, 'is the knowledge of that which really exists, and a clear perception of the truth; and happiness is the reward of such knowledge and wisdom.'

"'But what do you call God?' said he.

"'That which always maintains the same nature, and in the same manner, and is the cause of all other things — that, indeed, is God.' So I answered him; and he listened to me with pleasure, and thus again interrogated me: —

"'Is not knowledge a term common to different matters? For in arts of all kinds, he who knows any one of them is called a skilful man, in the art of generalship, or of ruling, or of healing equally. But in divine and human affairs it is not so. Is there a knowledge which affords understanding of human and divine things, and then a thorough acquaintance with the divinity and the righteousness of them?'

"'Assuredly,' I replied.

"'What, then? Is it in the same way we know man and God, as we know music, and arithmetic, and astronomy, or any other similar branch?'

"'By no means,' I replied.

"'You have not answered me correctly, then,' he said; 'for some [branches of knowledge] come to us by learning, or by some employment, while of others we have knowledge by sight. Now, if one were to tell you that there exists in India an animal with a nature unlike all others, but of such and such a kind, multiform and various, you would not know it before you saw it; but neither would you be competent to give any account of it, unless you should hear from one who had seen it.'

"'Certainly not,' I said.

"'How then,' he said, 'should the philosophers judge correctly about God, or speak any truth, when they have no knowledge of Him, having neither seen Him at any time, nor heard Him?'

"'But, father,' said I, 'the Deity cannot be seen merely by the eyes, as other living beings can, but is discernible to the mind alone, as Plato says; and I believe him.'

CHAP. IV. — THE SOUL OF ITSELF CANNOT SEE GOD.

"'Is there then,' says he, 'such and so great power in our mind? Or can a man not perceive by sense sooner? Will the mind of man see God at any time, if it is uninstructed by the Holy Spirit?'

"'Plato indeed says,' replied I, 'that the mind's eye is of such a nature, and has been given for this end, that we may see that very Being when the mind is pure itself, who is the cause of all discerned by the mind, having no colour, no form, no greatness — nothing, indeed, which the bodily eye looks upon; but It is something of this sort, he goes on to say, that is beyond all essence, unutterable and inexplicable, but alone honourable and good, coming suddenly into souls well-dispositioned, on account of their affinity to and desire of seeing Him.'

"'What affinity, then,' replied he, 'is there between us and God? Is the soul also divine and immortal, and a part of that very regal mind? And even as that sees God, so also is it attainable by us to conceive of the Deity in our mind, and thence to become happy?'

"'Assuredly,' I said.

"'And do all the souls of all living beings comprehend Him?' he asked; 'or are the souls of men of one kind and the souls of horses and of asses of another kind?'

"'No; but the souls which are in all are similar,' I answered.

"'Then,' says he, 'shall both horses and asses see, or have they seen at some time or other, God?'

"'No,' I said; 'for the majority of men will not, saving such as shall live justly, purified by righteousness, and by every other virtue.'

"'It is not, therefore,' said he, 'on account of his affinity, that a man sees God, nor because he has a mind, but because he is temperate and righteous?'

"'Yes,' said I; 'and because he has that whereby he perceives God.'

"'What then? Do goats or sheep injure any one?'

"'No one in any respect,' I said.

"'Therefore these animals will see [God] according to your account,' says he.

"'No; for their body being of such a nature, is an obstacle to them.'

"He rejoined, 'If these animals could assume speech, be well assured that they would with greater reason ridicule our body; but let us now dismiss this subject, and let it be conceded to you as you say. Tell me, however, this: Does the soul see [God] so long as it is in the body, or after it has been removed from it?'

"'So long as it is in the form of a man, it is possible for it,' I continue, 'to attain to this by means of the mind; but especially when it has been set free from the body, and being apart by itself, it gets possession of that which it was wont continually and wholly to love.'

"'Does it remember this, then [the sight of God], when it is again in the man?'

"'It does not appear to me so,' I said.

"'What, then, is the advantage to those who have seen [God]? or what has he who has seen more than he who has not seen, unless he remember this fact, that he *has* seen?'

"'I cannot tell,' I answered.

"'And what do those suffer who are judged to be unworthy of this spectacle?' said he.

"'They are imprisoned in the bodies of certain wild beasts, and this is their punishment.'

"'Do they know, then, that it is for this reason they are in such forms, and that they have committed some sin?'

"'I do not think so.'

"'Then these reap no advantage from their punishment, as it seems: moreover, I would say that they are not punished unless they are conscious of the punishment.'

"'No indeed.'

"'Therefore souls neither see God nor transmigrate into other bodies; for they would know that so they are punished, and they would be afraid to commit even the most trivial sin afterwards. But that they can perceive that God exists, and that righteousness and piety are honourable, I also quite agree with you,' said he.

"'You are right,' I replied.

CHAP. V.—THE SOUL IS NOT IN ITS OWN NATURE IMMORTAL.

"'These philosophers know nothing, then, about these things; for they cannot tell what a soul is.'

"'It does not appear so.'

"'Nor ought it to be called immortal; for if it is immortal, it is plainly unbegotten.'

"'It is both unbegotten and immortal, according to some who are styled Platonists.'

"'Do you say that the world is also unbegotten?'

"'Some say so. I do not, however, agree with them.'

"'You are right; for what reason has one for supposing that a body so solid, possessing resistance, composite, changeable, decaying, and renewed every day, has not arisen from some cause? But if the world is begotten, souls also are necessarily begotten; and perhaps at one time they were not in existence, for they were made on account of men and other living creatures, if you will say that they have been begotten wholly apart, and not along with their respective bodies.'

"'This seems to be correct.'

"'They are not, then, immortal?'

"'No; since the world has appeared to us to be begotten.'

"'But I do not say, indeed, that all souls die; for that were truly a piece of good fortune to the evil. What then? The souls of the pious remain in a better place, while those of the unjust and wicked are in a worse, waiting for the time of judgment. Thus some which have appeared worthy of God never die; but others are punished so long as God wills them to exist and to be punished.'

"'Is what you say, then, of a like nature with that which Plato in *Timæus* hints about the world, when he says that it is indeed subject to decay, inasmuch as it has been created, but that it will neither be dissolved nor meet with the fate of death on account of the will of God? Does it seem to you the very same can be said of the soul, and generally of all things? For those things which exist after[1] God, or shall at any time exist,[2] these have the nature of decay, and are such as may be blotted out and cease to exist; for God alone is unbegotten and incorruptible, and therefore He is God, but all other things after Him are created and corruptible. For this reason souls both die and are punished: since, if they were unbegotten, they would neither sin, nor be filled with folly, nor be cowardly, and again ferocious; nor would they willingly transform into swine, and serpents, and dogs; and it would not indeed be just to compel them, if they be unbegotten. For that which is unbegotten is similar to, equal to, and the same with that which is unbegotten; and neither in power nor in honour should the one be preferred to the other, and hence there are not many things which are unbegotten: for if there were some difference between them, you would not discover the cause of the difference, though you searched for it; but after letting the mind ever wander to infinity, you would at length, wearied out, take your stand on one Unbegotten, and say that this is the Cause of all. Did such escape the observation of Plato and Pythagoras, those wise men,'

---

[1] "Beside."
[2] Otto says: If the old man begins to speak here, then ἔχει must be read tor ἔχειν. The received text makes it appear that Justin continues a quotation, or the substance of it, from Plato.

I said, 'who have been as a wall and fortress of philosophy to us?'

CHAP. VI. — THESE THINGS WERE UNKNOWN TO PLATO AND OTHER PHILOSOPHERS.

"'It makes no matter to me,' said he, 'whether Plato or Pythagoras, or, in short, any other man, held such opinions. For the truth is so; and you would perceive it from this. The soul assuredly is or has life. If, then, it is life, it would cause something else, and not itself, to live, even as motion would move something else than itself. Now, that the soul lives, no one would deny. But if it lives, it lives not as being life, but as the partaker of life; but that which partakes of anything, is different from that of which it does partake. Now the soul partakes of life, since God wills it to live. Thus, then, it will not even partake [of life] when God does not will it to live. For to live is not its attribute, as it is God's; but as a man does not live always, and the soul is not for ever conjoined with the body, since, whenever this harmony must be broken up, the soul leaves the body, and the man exists no longer; even so, whenever the soul must cease to exist, the spirit of life is removed from it, and there is no more soul, but it goes back to the place from whence it was taken.'

CHAP. VII. — THE KNOWLEDGE OF TRUTH TO BE SOUGHT FROM THE PROPHETS ALONE.

"'Should any one, then, employ a teacher?' I say, 'or whence may any one be helped, if not even in them there is truth?'

"'There existed, long before this time, certain men more ancient than all those who are esteemed philosophers, both righteous and beloved by God, who spoke by the Divine Spirit, and foretold events which would take place, and which are now taking place. They are called prophets. These alone both saw and announced the truth to men, neither reverencing nor fearing any man, not influenced by a desire for glory, but speaking those things alone which they saw and which they heard, being filled with the Holy Spirit. Their writings are still extant, and he who has read them is very much helped in his knowledge of the beginning and end of things, and of those matters which the philosopher ought to know, provided he has believed them. For they did not use demonstration in their treatises, seeing that they were witnesses to the truth above all demonstration, and worthy of belief; and those events which have happened, and those which are happening, compel you to assent to the utterances made by them, although, indeed, they were entitled to credit on account of the miracles which they performed, since they both glorified the Creator, the God and Father of all things, and proclaimed His Son, the Christ [sent] by Him: which, indeed, the false prophets, who are filled with the lying unclean spirit, neither have done nor do, but venture to work certain wonderful deeds for the purpose of astonishing men, and glorify the spirits and demons of error. But pray that, above all things, the gates of light may be opened to you; for these things cannot be perceived or understood by all, but only by the man to whom God and His Christ have imparted wisdom.'

CHAP. VIII. — JUSTIN BY HIS COLLOQUY IS KINDLED WITH LOVE TO CHRIST.

"When he had spoken these and many other things, which there is no time for mentioning at present, he went away, bidding me attend to them; and I have not seen him since. But straightway a flame was kindled in my soul; and a love of the prophets, and of those men who are friends of Christ, possessed me; and whilst revolving his words in my mind, I found this philosophy alone to be safe and profitable. Thus, and for this reason, I am a philosopher. Moreover, I would wish that all, making a resolution similar to my own, do not keep themselves away from the words of the Saviour. For they possess a terrible power in themselves, and are sufficient to inspire those who turn aside from the path of rectitude with awe; while the sweetest rest is afforded those who make a diligent practice of them. If, then, you have any concern for yourself, and if you are eagerly looking for salvation, and if you believe in God, you may — since you are not indifferent to the matter,[1] — become acquainted with the Christ of God, and, after being initiated,[2] live a happy life."

When I had said this, my beloved friends[3] those who were with Trypho laughed; but he, smiling, says, "I approve of your other remarks, and admire the eagerness with which you study divine things; but it were better for you still to abide in the philosophy of Plato, or of some other man, cultivating endurance, self-control, and moderation, rather than be deceived by false words, and follow the opinions of men of no reputation. For if you remain in that mode of philosophy, and live blamelessly, a hope of a better destiny were left to you; but when you have forsaken God, and reposed confidence in man, what safety still awaits you? If, then, you are willing to listen to me (for I have already considered you a friend), first be circumcised, then observe what ordinances have been enacted with respect to the Sabbath, and the feasts, and

---

[1] According to one interpretation, this clause is applied to God: "If you believe in God, seeing He is not indifferent to the matter," etc. Maranus says that it means: A Jew who reads so much of Christ in the Old Testament, cannot be indifferent to the things which pertain to Him.
[2] Literally: having become perfect. Some refer the words to perfection of character; some to initiation by baptism.
[3] Latin version, "beloved Pompeius."

the new moons of God; and, in a word, do all things which have been written in the law: and then perhaps you shall obtain mercy from God. But Christ — if He has indeed been born, and exists anywhere — is unknown, and does not even know Himself, and has no power until Elias come to anoint Him, and make Him manifest to all. And you, having accepted a groundless report, invent a Christ for yourselves, and for his sake are inconsiderately perishing."

CHAP. IX. — THE CHRISTIANS HAVE NOT BELIEVED GROUNDLESS STORIES.

"I excuse and forgive you, my friend," I said. "For you know not what you say, but have been persuaded by teachers who do not understand the Scriptures; and you speak, like a diviner, whatever comes into your mind. But if you are willing to listen to an account of Him, how we have not been deceived, and shall not cease to confess Him, — although men's reproaches be heaped upon us, although the most terrible tyrant compel us to deny Him, — I shall prove to you as you stand here that we have not believed empty fables, or words without any foundation, but words filled with the Spirit of God, and big with power, and flourishing with grace."

Then again those who were in his company laughed, and shouted in an unseemly manner. Then I rose up and was about to leave; but he, taking hold of my garment, said I should not accomplish that[1] until I had performed what I promised. "Let not, then, your companions be so tumultuous, or behave so disgracefully," I said. "But if they wish, let them listen in silence; or, if some better occupation prevent them, let them go away; while we, having retired to some spot, and resting there, may finish the discourse." It seemed good to Trypho that we should do so; and accordingly, having agreed upon it, we retired to the middle space of the Xystus. Two of his friends, when they had ridiculed and made game of our zeal, went off. And when we were come to that place, where there are stone seats on both sides, those with Trypho, having seated themselves on the one side, conversed with each other, some one of them having thrown in a remark about the war waged in Judæa.

CHAP. X. — TRYPHO BLAMES THE CHRISTIANS FOR THIS ALONE — THE NON-OBSERVANCE OF THE LAW.

And when they ceased, I again addressed them thus: —

"Is there any other matter, my friends, in which we are blamed, than this, that we live not after the law, and are not circumcised in the flesh as your forefathers were, and do not observe sabbaths as you do? Are our lives and customs also slandered among you? And I ask this: have you also believed concerning us, that we eat men; and that after the feast, having extinguished the lights, we engage in promiscuous concubinage? Or do you condemn us in this alone, that we adhere to such tenets, and believe in an opinion, untrue, as you think?"

"This is what we are amazed at," said Trypho, "but those things about which the multitude speak are not worthy of belief; for they are most repugnant to human nature. Moreover, I am aware that your precepts in the so-called Gospel are so wonderful and so great, that I suspect no one can keep them; for I have carefully read them. But this is what we are most at a loss about: that you, professing to be pious, and supposing yourselves better than others, are not in any particular separated from them, and do not alter your mode of living from the nations, in that you observe no festivals or sabbaths, and do not have the rite of circumcision; and further, resting your hopes on a man that was crucified, you yet expect to obtain some good thing from God, while you do not obey His commandments. Have you not read, that that soul shall be cut off from his people who shall not have been circumcised on the eighth day? And this has been ordained for strangers and for slaves equally. But you, despising this covenant rashly, reject the consequent duties, and attempt to persuade yourselves that you know God, when, however, you perform none of those things which they do who fear God. If, therefore, you can defend yourself on these points, and make it manifest in what way you hope for anything whatsoever, even though you do not observe the law, this we would very gladly hear from you, and we shall make other similar investigations."

CHAP. XI. — THE LAW ABROGATED; THE NEW TESTAMENT PROMISED AND GIVEN BY GOD.

"There will be no other God, O Trypho, nor was there from eternity any other existing" (I thus addressed him), "but He who made and disposed all this universe. Nor do we think that there is one God for us, another for you, but that He alone is God who led your fathers out from Egypt with a strong hand and a high arm. Nor have we trusted in any other (for there is no other), but in Him in whom you also have trusted, the God of Abraham, and of Isaac, and of Jacob. But we do not trust through Moses or through the law; for then we would do the same as yourselves. But now[2] — (for I have read that there shall be a final law, and a covenant, the chiefest

---

[1] According to another reading, "I did not *leave*."

[2] Editors suppose that Justin inserts a long parenthesis here, from "for" to "Egypt." It is more natural to take this as an anacoluthon. Justin was going to say "But now we trust through Christ," but feels that such a statement requires a preliminary explanation.

of all, which it is now incumbent on all men to observe, as many as are seeking after the inheritance of God. For the law promulgated on Horeb is now old, and belongs to yourselves alone; but *this* is for all universally. Now, law placed against law has abrogated that which is before it, and a covenant which comes after in like manner has put an end to the previous one; and an eternal and final law — namely, Christ — has been given to us, and the covenant is trustworthy, after which there shall be no law, no commandment, no ordinance. Have you not read this which Isaiah says: 'Hearken unto Me, hearken unto Me, my people; and, ye kings, give ear unto Me: for a law shall go forth from Me, and My judgment shall be for a light to the nations. My righteousness approaches swiftly, and My salvation shall go forth, and nations shall trust in Mine arm?'[1] And by Jeremiah, concerning this same new covenant, He thus speaks: 'Behold, the days come, saith the Lord, that I will make a new covenant with the house of Israel and with the house of Judah; not according to the covenant which I made with their fathers, in the day that I took them by the hand, to bring them out of the land of Egypt'[2]). If, therefore, God proclaimed a new covenant which was to be instituted, and this for a light of the nations, we see and are persuaded that men approach God, leaving their idols and other unrighteousness, through the name of Him who was crucified, Jesus Christ, and abide by their confession even unto death, and maintain piety. Moreover, by the works and by the attendant miracles, it is possible for all to understand that He is the new law, and the new covenant, and the expectation of those who out of every people wait for the good things of God. For the true spiritual Israel, and descendants of Judah, Jacob, Isaac, and Abraham (who in uncircumcision was approved of and blessed by God on account of his faith, and called the father of many nations), are we who have been led to God through this crucified Christ, as shall be demonstrated while we proceed.

CHAP. XII. — THE JEWS VIOLATE THE ETERNAL LAW, AND INTERPRET ILL THAT OF MOSES.

I also adduced another passage in which Isaiah exclaims: "'Hear My words, and your soul shall live; and I will make an everlasting covenant with you, even the sure mercies of David. Behold, I have given Him for a witness to the people: nations which know not Thee shall call on Thee; peoples who know not Thee shall escape to Thee, because of thy God, the Holy One of Israel; for He has glorified Thee.'[3]

This same law you have despised, and His new holy covenant you have slighted; and now you neither receive it, nor repent of your evil deeds. 'For your ears are closed, your eyes are blinded, and the heart is hardened,' Jeremiah[4] has cried; yet not even then do you listen. The Lawgiver is present, yet you do not see Him; to the poor the Gospel is preached, the blind see, yet you do not understand. You have now need of a second circumcision, though you glory greatly in the flesh. The new law requires you to keep perpetual sabbath, and you, because you are idle for one day, suppose you are pious, not discerning why this has been commanded you: and if you eat unleavened bread, you say the will of God has been fulfilled. The Lord our God does not take pleasure in such observances: if there is any perjured person or a thief among you, let him cease to be so; if any adulterer, let him repent; then he has kept the sweet and true sabbaths of God. If any one has impure hands, let him wash and be pure.

CHAP. XIII. — ISAIAH TEACHES THAT SINS ARE FORGIVEN THROUGH CHRIST'S BLOOD.

"For Isaiah did not send you to a bath, there to wash away murder and other sins, which not even all the water of the sea were sufficient to purge; but, as might have been expected, this was that saving bath of the olden time which followed[5] those who repented, and who no longer were purified by the blood of goats and of sheep, or by the ashes of an heifer, or by the offerings of fine flour, but by faith through the blood of Christ, and through His death, who died for this very reason, as Isaiah himself said, when he spake thus: 'The Lord shall make bare His holy arm in the eyes of all the nations, and all the nations and the ends of the earth shall see the salvation of God. Depart ye, depart ye, depart ye,[6] go ye out from thence, and touch no unclean thing; go ye out of the midst of her, be ye clean that bear the vessels of the Lord, for[7] ye go not with haste. For the Lord shall go before you; and the Lord, the God of Israel, shall gather you together. Behold, my servant shall deal prudently; and He shall be exalted, and be greatly glorified. As many were astonished at Thee, so Thy form and Thy glory shall be marred more than men. So shall many nations be astonished at Him, and the kings shall shut their mouths; for that which had not been told them concerning Him shall they see, and that which they had not heard shall they consider. Lord,

---

[1] According to the LXX., Isa. li. 4, 5.
[2] Jer. xxxi. 31, 32.
[3] Isa. lv. 3 ff. according to LXX.
[4] Not in Jeremiah; some would insert, in place of Jeremiah, Isaiah or John. [St. John xii. 40; Isa. vi. 10: where see full references in the English margin. But comp. Jeremiah vii. 24, 26, xi. 8, and xvii. 23.]
[5] 1. Cor. x. 4. Otto reads: which he mentioned and which was for those who repented.
[6] Three times in Justin, not in LXX.
[7] Deviating slightly from LXX., omitting a clause.

who hath believed our report? and to whom is the arm of the Lord revealed? We have announced Him as a child before Him, as a root in a dry ground. He hath no form or comeliness, and when we saw Him He had no form or beauty; but His form is dishonoured, and fails more than the sons of men. He is a man in affliction, and acquainted with bearing sickness, because His face has been turned away; He was despised, and we esteemed Him not. He bears our sins, and is distressed for us; and we esteemed Him to be in toil and in affliction, and in evil treatment. But He was wounded for our transgressions, He was bruised for our iniquities; the chastisement of our peace was upon Him. With His stripes we are healed. All we, like sheep, have gone astray. Every man has turned to his own way; and the Lord laid on Him our iniquities, and by reason of His oppression He opens not His mouth. He was brought as a sheep to the slaughter; and as a lamb before her shearer is dumb, so He openeth not His mouth. In His humiliation His judgment was taken away. And who shall declare His generation? For His life is taken from the earth. Because of the transgressions of my people He came unto death. And I will give the wicked for His grave, and the rich for His death, because He committed no iniquity, and deceit was not found in His mouth. And the Lord wills to purify Him from affliction. If he has been given for sin, your soul shall see a long-lived seed. And the Lord wills to take His soul away from trouble, to show Him light, and to form Him in understanding, to justify the righteous One who serves many well. And He shall bear our sins; therefore He shall inherit many, and shall divide the spoil of the strong, because His soul was delivered to death; and He was numbered with the transgressors, and He bare the sins of many, and was delivered for their transgression. Sing, O barren, who bearest not; break forth and cry aloud, thou who dost not travail in pain: for more are the children of the desolate than the children of the married wife. For the Lord said, Enlarge the place of thy tent and of thy curtains; fix them, spare not, lengthen thy cords, and strengthen thy stakes; stretch forth to thy right and thy left; and thy seed shall inherit the Gentiles, and thou shalt make the desolate cities to be inherited. Fear not because thou art ashamed, neither be thou confounded because thou hast been reproached; for thou shalt forget everlasting shame, and shalt not remember the reproach of thy widowhood, because the Lord has made a name for Himself, and He who has redeemed thee shall be called through the whole earth the God of Israel. The Lord has called thee as [1] a woman forsaken and grieved in spirit, as [1] a woman hated from her youth.' [2]

CHAP. XIV. — RIGHTEOUSNESS IS NOT PLACED IN JEWISH RITES, BUT IN THE CONVERSION OF THE HEART GIVEN IN BAPTISM BY CHRIST.

" By reason, therefore, of this laver of repentance and knowledge of God, which has been ordained on account of the transgression of God's people, as Isaiah cries, we have believed, and testify that that very baptism which he announced is alone able to purify those who have repented; and this is the water of life. But the cisterns which you have dug for yourselves are broken and profitless to you. For what is the use of that baptism which cleanses the flesh and body alone? Baptize the soul from wrath and from covetousness, from envy, and from hatred; and, lo! the body is pure. For this is the symbolic significance of unleavened bread, that you do not commit the old deeds of wicked leaven. But you have understood all things in a carnal sense, and you suppose it to be piety if you do such things, while your souls are filled with deceit, and, in short, with every wickedness. Accordingly, also, after the seven days of eating unleavened bread, God commanded them to mingle new leaven, that is, the performance of other works, and not the imitation of the old and evil works. And because this is what this new Lawgiver demands of you, I shall again refer to the words which have been quoted by me, and to others also which have been passed over. They are related by Isaiah to the following effect: 'Hearken to me, and your soul shall live; and I will make with you an everlasting covenant, even the sure mercies of David. Behold, I have given Him for a witness to the people, a leader and commander to the nations. Nations which know not Thee shall call on Thee; and peoples who know not Thee shall escape unto Thee, because of Thy God, the Holy One of Israel, for He has glorified Thee. Seek ye God; and when you find Him, call on Him, so long as He may be nigh you. Let the wicked forsake his ways, and the unrighteous man his thoughts; and let him return unto the Lord, and he will obtain mercy, because He will abundantly pardon your sins. For my thoughts are not as your thoughts, neither are my ways as your ways; but as far removed as the heavens are from the earth, so far is my way removed from your way, and your thoughts from my thoughts. For as the snow or the rain descends from heaven, and shall not return till it waters the earth, and makes it bring forth and bud, and gives seed to the sower and bread for food, so shall My word be that goeth forth out of My mouth: it shall not return until it shall have

---

[1] LXX. "*not* as," etc.   [2] Isa. lii. 10 ff. following the LXX. on to liv. 6.

accomplished all that I desired, and I shall make My commandments prosperous. For ye shall go out with joy, and be taught with gladness. For the mountains and the hills shall leap while they expect you, and all the trees of the fields shall applaud with their branches: and instead of the thorn shall come up the cypress, and instead of the brier shall come up the myrtle. And the Lord shall be for a name, and for an everlasting sign, and He shall not fail!'[1] Of these and such like words written by the prophets, O Trypho," said I, "some have reference to the first advent of Christ, in which He is preached as inglorious, obscure, and of mortal appearance: but others had reference to His second advent, when He shall appear in glory and above the clouds; and your nation shall see and know Him whom they have pierced, as Hosea, one of the twelve prophets, and Daniel, foretold.

CHAP. XV. — IN WHAT THE TRUE FASTING CONSISTS.

"Learn, therefore, to keep the true fast of God, as Isaiah says, that you may please God. Isaiah has cried thus: 'Shout vehemently, and do not spare: lift up thy voice as with a trumpet, and show My people their transgressions, and the house of Jacob their sins. They seek Me from day to day, and desire to know My ways, as a nation that did righteousness, and forsook not the judgment of God. They ask of Me now righteous judgment, and desire to draw near to God, saying, Wherefore have we fasted, and Thou seest not? and afflicted our souls, and Thou hast not known? Because in the days of your fasting you find your own pleasure, and oppress all those who are subject to you. Behold, ye fast for strifes and debates, and smite the humble with your fists. Why do ye fast for Me, as to-day, so that your voice is heard aloud? This is not the fast which I have chosen, the day in which a man shall afflict his soul. And not even if you bend your neck like a ring, or clothe yourself in sackcloth and ashes, shall you call this a fast, and a day acceptable to the Lord. This is not the fast which I have chosen, saith the Lord; but loose every unrighteous bond, dissolve the terms of wrongous covenants, let the oppressed go free, and avoid every iniquitous contract. Deal thy bread to the hungry, and lead the homeless poor under thy dwelling; if thou seest the naked, clothe him; and do not hide thyself from thine own flesh. Then shall thy light break forth as the morning, and thy garments[2] shall rise up quickly: and thy righteousness shall go before thee, and the glory of God shall envelope thee. Then shalt thou cry, and the Lord shall hear thee: while thou art speaking, He will say, Behold, I am here. And if thou take away from thee the yoke, and the stretching out of the hand, and the word of murmuring; and shalt give heartily thy bread to the hungry, and shalt satisfy the afflicted soul; then shall thy light arise in the darkness, and thy darkness shall be as the noon-day: and thy God shall be with thee continually, and thou shalt be satisfied according as thy soul desireth, and thy bones shall become fat, and shall be as a watered garden, and as a fountain of water, or as a land where water fails not.'[3] 'Circumcise, therefore, the foreskin of your heart,' as the words of God in all these passages demand."

CHAP. XVI. — CIRCUMCISION GIVEN AS A SIGN, THAT THE JEWS MIGHT BE DRIVEN AWAY FOR THEIR EVIL DEEDS DONE TO CHRIST AND THE CHRISTIANS.

"And God himself proclaimed by Moses, speaking thus: 'And circumcise the hardness of your hearts, and no longer stiffen the neck. For the Lord your God is both Lord of lords, and a great, mighty, and terrible God, who regardeth not persons, and taketh not rewards.'[4] And in Leviticus: 'Because they have transgressed against Me, and despised Me, and because they have walked contrary to Me, I also walked contrary to them, and I shall cut them off in the land of their enemies. Then shall their uncircumcised heart be turned.'[5] For the circumcision according to the flesh, which is from Abraham, was given for a sign; that you may be separated from other nations, and from us; and that you alone may suffer that which you now justly suffer; and that your land may be desolate, and your cities burned with fire; and that strangers may eat your fruit in your presence, and not one of you may go up to Jerusalem.'[6] For you are not recognised among the rest of men by any other mark than your fleshly circumcision. For none of you, I suppose, will venture to say that God neither did nor does foresee the events, which are future, nor foreordained his deserts for each one. Accordingly, these things have happened to you in fairness and justice, for you have slain the Just One, and His prophets before Him; and now you reject those who hope in Him, and in Him who sent Him — God the Almighty and Maker of all things — cursing in your synagogues those that believe on Christ. For you have not the power to lay hands upon us, on account of those who now have the mastery. But as often as you could, you did so. Wherefore God, by Isaiah, calls to you, saying, 'Behold how the righteous

---

[1] Isa. lv. 3 to end.
[2] ἱμάτια: some read ἰάματα, as in LXX., "thy health," the better reading probably.
[3] Isa. lviii. 1–12.
[4] Deut. x. 16 f.
[5] Lev. xxvi. 40, 41.
[6] See *Apol.*, i. 47. The Jews [By Hadrian's recent edict] were prohibited by law from entering Jerusalem on pain of death. And so Justin sees in circumcision their own punishment.

man perished, and no one regards it. For the righteous man is taken away from before iniquity. His grave shall be in peace, he is taken away from the midst. Draw near hither, ye lawless children, seed of the adulterers, and children of the whore. Against whom have you sported yourselves, and against whom have you opened the mouth, and against whom have you loosened the tongue?'[1]

CHAP. XVII. — THE JEWS SENT PERSONS THROUGH THE WHOLE EARTH TO SPREAD CALUMNIES ON CHRISTIANS.

"For other nations have not inflicted on us and on Christ this wrong to such an extent as you have, who in very deed are the authors of the wicked prejudice against the Just One, and us who hold by Him. For after that you had crucified Him, the only blameless and righteous Man, — through whose stripes those who approach the Father by Him are healed, — when you knew that He had risen from the dead and ascended to heaven, as the prophets foretold He would, you not only did not repent of the wickedness which you had committed, but at that time you selected and sent out from Jerusalem chosen men through all the land to tell that the godless heresy of the Christians had sprung up, and to publish those things which all they who knew us not speak against us. So that you are the cause not only of your own unrighteousness, but in fact of that of all other men. And Isaiah cries justly: 'By reason of you, My name is blasphemed among the Gentiles.'[2] And: 'Woe unto their soul! because they have devised an evil device against themselves, saying, Let us bind the righteous, for he is distasteful to us. Therefore they shall eat the fruit of their doings. Woe unto the wicked! evil shall be rendered to him according to the works of his hands.' And again, in other words:[3] 'Woe unto them that draw their iniquity as with a long cord, and their transgressions as with the harness of a heifer's yoke: who say, Let his speed come near; and let the counsel of the Holy One of Israel come, that we may know it. Woe unto them that call evil good, and good evil; that put light for darkness, and darkness for light; that put bitter for sweet, and sweet for bitter!'[4] Accordingly, you displayed great zeal in publishing throughout all the land bitter and dark and unjust things against the only blameless and righteous Light sent by God.

For He appeared distasteful to you when He cried among you, 'It is written, My house is the house of prayer; but ye have made it a den of thieves!'[5] He overthrew also the tables of the money-changers in the temple, and exclaimed, 'Woe unto you, Scribes and Pharisees, hypocrites! because ye pay tithe of mint and rue, but do not observe the love of God and justice. Ye whited sepulchres! appearing beautiful outward, but are within full of dead men's bones.'[6] And to the Scribes, 'Woe unto you, Scribes! for ye have the keys, and ye do not enter in yourselves, and them that are entering in ye hinder; ye blind guides!'

CHAP. XVIII. — CHRISTIANS WOULD OBSERVE THE LAW, IF THEY DID NOT KNOW WHY IT WAS INSTITUTED.

"For since you have read, O Trypho, as you yourself admitted, the doctrines taught by our Saviour, I do not think that I have done foolishly in adding some short utterances of His to the prophetic statements. Wash therefore, and be now clean, and put away iniquity from your souls, as God bids you be washed in this laver, and be circumcised with the true circumcision. For we too would observe the fleshly circumcision, and the Sabbaths, and in short all the feasts, if we did not know for what reason they were enjoined you, — namely, on account of your transgressions and the hardness of your hearts. For if we patiently endure all things contrived against us by wicked men and demons, so that even amid cruelties unutterable, death and torments, we pray for mercy to those who inflict such things upon us, and do not wish to give the least retort to any one, even as the new Lawgiver commanded us: how is it, Trypho, that we would not observe those rites which do not harm us, — I speak of fleshly circumcision, and Sabbaths, and feasts?

CHAP. XIX. — CIRCUMCISION UNKNOWN BEFORE ABRAHAM. THE LAW WAS GIVEN BY MOSES ON ACCOUNT OF THE HARDNESS OF THEIR HEARTS.

"It is this about which we are at a loss, and with reason, because, while you endure such things, you do not observe all the other customs which we are now discussing."

"This circumcision is not, however, necessary for all men, but for you alone, in order that, as I have already said, you may suffer these things which you now justly suffer. Nor do we receive that useless baptism of cisterns, for it has nothing to do with this baptism of life. Wherefore also God has announced that you have forsaken Him, the living fountain, and digged for yourselves broken cisterns which can hold no water. Even you, who are the circumcised according to the flesh, have need of our circumcision; but we, having the latter, do not require the former. For if it were necessary, as you suppose, God

---

[1] Isa. lvii. 1-4.
[2] Isa. lii. 5.
[3] Isa. iii. 9 ff.
[4] Isa. v. 18, 20.
[5] Matt. xxi. 13.

[6] This and following quotation taken promiscuously from Matt. xxiii. and Luke xi.

would not have made Adam uncircumcised; would not have had respect to the gifts of Abel when, being uncircumcised, he offered sacrifice; and would not have been pleased with the uncircumcision of Enoch, who was not found, because God had translated him. Lot, being uncircumcised, was saved from Sodom, the angels themselves and the Lord sending him out. Noah was the beginning of our race; yet, uncircumcised, along with his children he went into the ark. Melchizedek, the priest of the Most High, was uncircumcised; to whom also Abraham, the first who received circumcision after the flesh, gave tithes, and he blessed him: after whose order God declared, by the mouth of David, that He would establish the everlasting priest. Therefore to you alone this circumcision was necessary, in order that the people may be no people, and the nation no nation; as also Hosea,[1] one of the twelve prophets, declares. Moreover, all those righteous men already mentioned, though they kept no Sabbaths,[2] were pleasing to God; and after them Abraham with all his descendants until Moses, under whom your nation appeared unrighteous and ungrateful to God, making a calf in the wilderness: wherefore God, accommodating Himself to that nation, enjoined them also to offer sacrifices, as if to His name, in order that you might not serve idols. Which precept, however, you have not observed; nay, you sacrificed your children to demons. And you were commanded to keep Sabbaths, that you might retain the memorial of God. For His word makes this announcement, saying, 'That ye may know that I am God who redeemed you.'[3]

CHAP. XX. — WHY CHOICE OF MEATS WAS PRESCRIBED.

"Moreover, you were commanded to abstain from certain kinds of food, in order that you might keep God before your eyes while you ate and drank, seeing that you were prone and very ready to depart from His knowledge, as Moses also affirms: 'The people ate and drank, and rose up to play.'[4] And again: 'Jacob ate, and was satisfied, and waxed fat; and he who was beloved kicked: he waxed fat, he grew thick, he was enlarged, and he forsook God who had made him.'[5] For it was told you by Moses in the book of Genesis, that God granted to Noah, being a just man, to eat of every animal, but not of flesh with the blood, which is *dead*."[6] And as he was ready to say, "as the green herbs," I anticipated him: "Why do you not receive this statement, 'as the green herbs,' in the sense in which it was given by God, to wit, that just as God has granted the herbs for sustenance to man, even so has He given the animals for the diet of flesh? But, you say, a distinction was laid down thereafter to Noah, because we do not eat certain herbs. As you interpret it, the thing is incredible. And first I shall not occupy myself with this, though able to say and to hold that every vegetable is food, and fit to be eaten. But although we discriminate between green herbs, not eating all, we refrain from eating some, not because they are common or unclean, but because they are bitter, or deadly, or thorny. But we lay hands on and take of all herbs which are sweet, very nourishing and good, whether they are marine or land plants. Thus also God by the mouth of Moses commanded you to abstain from unclean and improper[7] and violent animals: when, moreover, though you were eating manna in the desert, and were seeing all those wondrous acts wrought for you by God, you made and worshipped the golden calf.[8] Hence he cries continually, and justly, 'They are foolish children, in whom is no faith.'[9]

CHAP. XXI. — SABBATHS WERE INSTITUTED ON ACCOUNT OF THE PEOPLE'S SINS, AND NOT FOR A WORK OF RIGHTEOUSNESS.

"Moreover, that God enjoined you to keep the Sabbath, and impose on you other precepts for a sign, as I have already said, on account of your unrighteousness, and that of your fathers, — as He declares that for the sake of the nations, lest His name be profaned among them, therefore He permitted some of you to remain alive,— these words of His can prove to you: they are narrated by Ezekiel thus: I am the Lord your God; walk in My statutes, and keep My judgments, and take no part in the customs of Egypt; and hallow My Sabbaths; and they shall be a sign between Me and you, that ye may know that I am the Lord your God. Notwithstanding ye rebelled against Me, and your children walked not in My statutes, neither kept My judgments to do them: which if a man do, he shall live in them. But they polluted My Sabbaths. And I said that I would pour out My fury upon them in the wilderness, to accomplish My anger upon them; yet I did it not; that My name might not be altogether profaned in the sight of the heathen. I led them out before their eyes, and

---

[1] Hos. i. and ii.
[2] [They did not *Sabbatize;* but Justin does not deny what is implied in many Scriptures, that they marked the week, and noted the seventh day. Gen. ii. 3, viii. 10, 12.]
[3] Ezek. xx. 12.
[4] Ex. xxxii. 6.
[5] Deut. xxxii. 15.
[6] νεκριμαῖον, or "dieth of itself;" com. reading was ἐκριμαῖον, which was supposed to be derived from ἐκρίπτω, and to mean "which ought to be cast out:" the above was suggested by H. Stephanus.

[7] ἄδικος καὶ παράνομος.
[8] "The reasoning of St. Justin is not quite clear to interpreters. As we abstain from some herbs, not because they are forbidden by law, but because they are deadly; so the law of abstinence from improper and violent animals was imposed not on Noah, but on you as a yoke on account of your sins." — MARANUS.
[9] Deut. xxxii. 6, 20.

I lifted up Mine hand unto them in the wilderness, that I would scatter them among the heathen, and disperse them through the countries; because they had not executed My judgments, but had despised My statutes, and polluted My Sabbaths, and their eyes were after the devices of their fathers. Wherefore I gave them also statutes which were not good, and judgments whereby they shall not live. And I shall pollute them in their own gifts, that I may destroy all that openeth the womb, when I pass through them.'[1]

CHAP. XXII. — SO ALSO WERE SACRIFICES AND OBLATIONS.

"And that you may learn that it was for the sins of your own nation, and for their idolatries, and not because there was any necessity for such sacrifices, that they were likewise enjoined, listen to the manner in which He speaks of these by Amos, one of the twelve, saying: 'Woe unto you that desire the day of the Lord! to what end is this day of the Lord for you? It is darkness and not light, as when a man flees from the face of a lion, and a bear meets him; and he goes into his house, and leans his hands against the wall, and the serpent bites him. Shall not the day of the Lord be darkness and not light, even very dark, and no brightness in it? I have hated, I have despised your feast-days, and I will not smell in your solemn assemblies: wherefore, though ye offer Me your burnt-offerings and sacrifices, I will not accept them; neither will I regard the peace-offerings of your presence. Take thou away from Me the multitude of thy songs and psalms; I will not hear thine instruments. But let judgment be rolled down as water, and righteousness as an impassable torrent. Have ye offered unto Me victims and sacrifices in the wilderness, O house of Israel? saith the Lord. And have ye taken up the tabernacle of Moloch, and the star of your god Raphan, the figures which ye made for yourselves? And I will carry you away beyond Damascus, saith the Lord, whose name is the Almighty God. Woe to them that are at ease in Zion, and trust in the mountain of Samaria: those who are named among the chiefs have plucked away the first-fruits of the nations: the house of Israel have entered for themselves. Pass all of you unto Calneh, and see; and from thence go ye unto Hamath the great, and go down thence to Gath of the strangers, the noblest of all these kingdoms, if their boundaries are greater than your boundaries. Ye who come to the evil day, who are approaching, and who hold to false Sabbaths; who lie on beds of ivory, and are at ease upon their couches; who eat the lambs out of the flock, and the sucking calves out of the midst of the herd; who applaud at the sound of the musical instruments; they reckon them as stable, and not as fleeting, who drink wine in bowls, and anoint themselves with the chief ointments, but they are not grieved for the affliction of Joseph. Wherefore now they shall be captives, among the first of the nobles who are carried away; and the house of evil-doers shall be removed, and the neighing of horses shall be taken away from Ephraim.[2] And again by Jeremiah: 'Collect your flesh, and sacrifices, and eat: for concerning neither sacrifices nor libations did I command your fathers in the day in which I took them by the hand to lead them out of Egypt.[3] And again by David, in the forty-ninth Psalm, He thus said: 'The God of gods, the Lord hath spoken, and called the earth, from the rising of the sun unto the going down thereof. Out of Zion is the perfection of His beauty. God, even our God, shall come openly, and shall not keep silence. Fire shall burn before Him, and it shall be very temptestuous round about Him. He shall call to the heavens above, and to the earth, that He may judge His people. Assemble to Him His saints; those that have made a covenant with Him by sacrifices. And the heavens shall declare His righteousness, for God is judge. Hear, O My people, and I will speak to thee; O Israel, and I will testify to thee, I am God, even thy God. I will not reprove thee for thy sacrifices; thy burnt-offerings are continually before me. I will take no bullocks out of thy house, nor he-goats out of thy folds: for all the beasts of the field are Mine, the herds and the oxen on the mountains. I know all the fowls of the heavens, and the beauty of the field is Mine. If I were hungry, I would not tell thee; for the world is Mine, and the fulness thereof. Will I eat the flesh of bulls, or drink the blood of goats? Offer unto God the sacrifice of praise, and pay thy vows unto the Most High, and call upon Me in the day of trouble, and I will deliver thee, and thou shalt glorify Me. But unto the wicked God saith, What hast thou to do to declare My statutes, and to take My covenant into thy mouth? But thou hast hated instruction, and cast My words behind thee. When thou sawest a thief, thou consentedst with him; and hast been partaker with the adulterer. Thy mouth has framed evil, and thy tongue has enfolded deceit. Thou sittest and speakest against thy brother; thou slanderest thine own mother's son. These things hast thou done, and I kept silence; thou thoughtest that I would be like thyself in wickedness. I will reprove thee, and set thy sins in order before thine eyes. Now consider this, ye that forget God, lest He tear you in pieces, and there be none to deliver. The

---

[1] Ezek. xx. 19-26.
[2] Amos v. 18 to end, vi, 1-7.
[3] Jer. vii. 21 f.

sacrifice of praise shall glorify Me; and there is the way in which I shall show him My salvation.[1] Accordingly He neither takes sacrifices from you nor commanded them at first to be offered because they are needful to Him, but because of your sins. For indeed the temple, which is called the temple in Jerusalem, He admitted to be His house or court, not as though He needed it, but in order that you, in this view of it, giving yourselves to Him, might not worship idols. And that this is so, Isaiah says: 'What house have ye built Me? saith the Lord. Heaven is My throne, and earth is My footstool.'[2]

CHAP. XXXIII.—THE OPINION OF THE JEWS REGARDING THE LAW DOES AN INJURY TO GOD.

"But if we do not admit this, we shall be liable to fall into foolish opinions, as if it were not the same God who existed in the times of Enoch and all the rest, who neither were circumcised after the flesh, nor observed Sabbaths, nor any other rites, seeing that Moses enjoined such observances; or that God has not wished each race of mankind continually to perform the same righteous actions: to admit which, seems to be ridiculous and absurd. Therefore we must confess that He, who is ever the same, has commanded these and such like institutions on account of sinful men, and we must declare Him to be benevolent, foreknowing, needing nothing, righteous and good. But if this be not so, tell me, sir, what you think of those matters which we are investigating." And when no one responded: "Wherefore, Trypho, I will proclaim to you, and to those who wish to become proselytes, the divine message which I heard from that man.[3] Do you see that the elements are not idle, and keep no Sabbaths? Remain as you were born. For if there was no need of circumcision before Abraham, or of the observance of Sabbaths, of feasts and sacrifices, before Moses; no more need is there of them now, after that, according to the will of God, Jesus Christ the Son of God has been born without sin, of a virgin sprung from the stock of Abraham. For when Abraham himself was in uncircumcision, he was justified and blessed by reason of the faith which he reposed in God, as the Scripture tells. Moreover, the Scriptures and the facts themselves compel us to admit that He received circumcision for a sign, and not for righteousness. So that it was justly recorded concerning the people, that the soul which shall not be circumcised on the eighth day shall be cut off from his family. And, furthermore, the inability of the female sex to receive fleshly circumcision, proves that this circumcision has been given for a sign, and not for a work of righteousness. For God has given likewise to women the ability to observe all things which are righteous and virtuous; but we see that the bodily form of the male has been made different from the bodily form of the female; yet we know that neither of them is righteous or unrighteous merely for this cause, but [is considered righteous] by reason of piety and righteousness.

CHAP. XXIV.—THE CHRISTIANS' CIRCUMCISION FAR MORE EXCELLENT.

"Now, sirs," I said, "it is possible for us to show how the eighth day possessed a certain mysterious import, which the seventh day did not possess, and which was promulgated by God through these rites. But lest I appear now to diverge to other subjects, understand what I say: the blood of that circumcision is obsolete, and we trust in the blood of salvation; there is now another covenant, and another law has gone forth from Zion. Jesus Christ circumcises all who will—as was declared above—with knives of stone;[4] that they may be a righteous nation, a people keeping faith, holding to the truth, and maintaining peace. Come then with me, all who fear God, who wish to see the good of Jerusalem. Come, let us go to the light of the Lord; for He has liberated His people, the house of Jacob. Come, all nations; let us gather ourselves together at Jerusalem, no longer plagued by war for the sins of her people. 'For I was manifest to them that sought Me not; I was found of them that asked not for Me;'[5] He exclaims by Isaiah: 'I said, Behold Me, unto nations which were not called by My name. I have spread out My hands all the day unto a disobedient and gainsaying people, which walked in a way that was not good, but after their own sins. It is a people that provoketh Me to my face.'[5]

CHAP. XXV.—THE JEWS BOAST IN VAIN THAT THEY ARE SONS OF ABRAHAM.

"Those who justify themselves, and say they are sons of Abraham, shall be desirous even in a small degree to receive the inheritance along with you;[6] as the Holy Spirit, by the mouth of Isaiah, cries, speaking thus while he personates them: 'Return from heaven, and behold from the habitation of Thy holiness and glory. Where is Thy zeal and strength? Where is the multitude of Thy mercy? for Thou hast sustained us, O Lord. For Thou art our Father, because Abraham is ignorant of us, and Israel has not recognised us. But Thou, O Lord, our Father,

---

[1] Ps. i. (in E. V.).
[2] Isa. lxvi. 1.
[3] The man he met by the sea-shore.
[4] Josh. v. 2; Isa. xxvi. 2, 3.
[5] Isa. lxv. 1–3.
[6] Other edd. have, "with us."

deliver us: from the beginning Thy name is upon us. O Lord, why hast Thou made us to err from Thy way? and hardened our hearts, so that we do not fear Thee? Return for Thy servants' sake, the tribes of Thine inheritance, that we may inherit for a little Thy holy mountain. We were as from the beginning, when Thou didst not bear rule over us, and when Thy name was not called upon us. If Thou wilt open the heavens, trembling shall seize the mountains before Thee: and they shall be melted, as wax melts before the fire; and fire shall consume the adversaries, and Thy name shall be manifest among the adversaries; the nations shall be put into disorder before Thy face. When Thou shalt do glorious things, trembling shall seize the mountains before Thee. From the beginning we have not heard, nor have our eyes seen a God besides Thee: and Thy works,[1] the mercy which Thou shalt show to those who repent. He shall meet those who do righteousness, and they shall remember Thy ways. Behold, Thou art wroth, and we were sinning. Therefore we have erred and become all unclean, and all our righteousness is as the rags of a woman set apart: and we have faded away like leaves by reason of our iniquities; thus the wind will take us away. And there is none that calleth upon Thy name, or remembers to take hold of Thee; for Thou hast turned away Thy face from us, and hast given us up on account of our sins. And now return, O Lord, for we are all Thy people. The city of Thy holiness has become desolate. Zion has become as a wilderness, Jerusalem a curse; the house, our holiness, and the glory which our fathers blessed, has been burned with fire; and all the glorious nations[2] have fallen along with it. And in addition to these [misfortunes], O Lord, Thou hast refrained Thyself, and art silent, and hast humbled us very much.'"[3]

And Trypho remarked, "What is this you say? that none of us shall inherit anything on the holy mountain of God?"

CHAP. XXVI. — NO SALVATION TO THE JEWS EXCEPT THROUGH CHRIST.

And I replied, "I do not say so; but those who have persecuted and do persecute Christ, if they do not repent, shall not inherit anything on the holy mountain. But the Gentiles, who have believed on Him, and have repented of the sins which they have committed, they shall receive the inheritance along with the patriarchs and the prophets, and the just men who are descended from Jacob, even although they neither keep the Sabbath, nor are circumcised, nor observe the feasts. Assuredly they shall receive the holy inheritance of God. For God speaks by Isaiah thus: 'I, the Lord God, have called Thee in righteousness, and will hold Thine hand, and will strengthen Thee; and I have given Thee for a covenant of the people, for a light of the Gentiles, to open the eyes of the blind, to bring out them that are bound from the chains, and those who sit in darkness from the prison-house.'[4] And again: 'Lift up a standard[5] for the people; for, lo, the Lord has made it heard unto the end of the earth. Say ye to the daughters of Zion, Behold, thy Saviour has come; having His reward, and His work before His face: and He shall call it a holy nation, redeemed by the Lord. And thou shalt be called a city sought out, and not forsaken. Who is this that cometh from Edom? in red garments from Bosor? This that is beautiful in apparel, going up with great strength? I speak righteousness, and the judgment of salvation. Why are Thy garments red, and Thine apparel as from the trodden wine-press? Thou art full of the trodden grape. I have trodden the wine-press all alone, and of the people there is no man with Me; and I have trampled them in fury, and crushed them to the ground, and spilled their blood on the earth. For the day of retribution has come upon them, and the year of redemption is present. And I looked, and there was none to help; and I considered, and none assisted: and My arm delivered; and My fury came on them, and I trampled them in My fury, and spilled their blood on the earth.'"[6]

CHAP. XXVII. — WHY GOD TAUGHT THE SAME THINGS BY THE PROPHETS AS BY MOSES.

And Trypho said, "Why do you select and quote whatever you wish from the prophetic writings, but do not refer to those which expressly command the Sabbath to be observed? For Isaiah thus speaks: 'If thou shalt turn away thy foot from the Sabbaths, so as not to do thy pleasure on the holy day, and shalt call the Sabbaths the holy delights of thy God; if thou shalt not lift thy foot to work, and shalt not speak a word from thine own mouth; then thou shalt trust in the Lord, and He shall cause thee to go up to the good things of the land; and He shall feed thee with the inheritance of Jacob thy father: for the mouth of the Lord hath spoken it.'"[7]

And I replied, "I have passed them by, my friends, not because such prophecies were contrary to me, but because you have understood, and

---

[1] Otto reads: "Thy works which Thou shalt do to those who wait for mercy."
[2] Some suppose the correct reading to be, "our glorious *institutions* [manners, customs, or ordinances] have," etc., ἔθη for ἔθνη.
[3] Isa. lxiii. 15 to end, and lxiv.
[4] Isa. xlii. 6, 7.
[5] συσσεισμόν, "a shaking," is the original reading; but LXX. has σύσσημον, a standard or signal, and this most edd. adopt.
[6] Isa. lxii. 10 to end, lxiii. 1-6.
[7] Isa. lviii. 13, 14.

do understand, that although God commands you by all the prophets to do the same things which He also commanded by Moses, it was on account of the hardness of your hearts, and your ingratitude towards Him, that He continually proclaims them, in order that, even in this way, if you repented, you might please Him, and neither sacrifice your children to demons, nor be partakers with thieves, nor lovers of gifts, nor hunters after revenge, nor fail in doing judgment for orphans, nor be inattentive to the justice due to the widow, nor have your hands full of blood. 'For the daughters of Zion have walked with a high neck, both sporting by winking with their eyes, and sweeping along their dresses.'[1] For they are all gone aside,' He exclaims, 'they are all become useless. There is none that understands, there is not so much as one. With their tongues they have practised deceit, their throat is an open sepulchre, the poison of asps is under their lips, destruction and misery are in their paths, and the way of peace they have not known.'[2] So that, as in the beginning, these things were enjoined you because of your wickedness, in like manner because of your stedfastness in it, or rather your increased proneness to it, by means of the same precepts He calls you to a remembrance or knowledge of it. But you are a people hard-hearted and without understanding, both blind and lame, children in whom is no faith, as He Himself says, honouring Him only with your lips, far from Him in your hearts, teaching doctrines that are your own and not His. For, tell me, did God wish the priests to sin when they offer the sacrifices on the Sabbaths? or those to sin, who are circumcised and do circumcise on the Sabbaths; since He commands that on the eighth day — even though it happen to be a Sabbath — those who are born shall be always circumcised? or could not the infants be operated upon one day previous or one day subsequent to the Sabbath, if He knew that it is a sinful act upon the Sabbaths? Or why did He not teach those — who are called righteous and pleasing to Him, who lived before Moses and Abraham, who were not circumcised in their foreskin, and observed no Sabbaths — to keep these institutions?"

CHAP. XXVIII. — TRUE RIGHTEOUSNESS IS OBTAINED BY CHRIST.

And Trypho replied, "We heard you adducing this consideration a little ago, and we have given it attention: for, to tell the truth, it is worthy of attention; and that answer which pleases most — namely, that so it seemed good to Him — does not satisfy me. For this is ever the shift to which those have recourse who are unable to answer the question."

Then I said, "Since I bring from the Scriptures and the facts themselves both the proofs and the inculcation of them, do not delay or hesitate to put faith in me, although I am an uncircumcised man; so short a time is left you in which to become proselytes. If Christ's coming shall have anticipated you, in vain you will repent, in vain you will weep; for He will not hear you. 'Break up your fallow ground,' Jeremiah has cried to the people, 'and sow not among thorns. Circumcise yourselves to the Lord, and circumcise the foreskin of your heart.'[3] Do not sow, therefore, among thorns, and in untilled ground, whence you can have no fruit. Know Christ; and behold the fallow ground, good, good and fat, is in your hearts. 'For, behold, the days come, saith the Lord, that I will visit all them that are circumcised in their foreskins; Egypt, and Judah,[4] and Edom, and the sons of Moab. For all the nations are uncircumcised, and all the house of Israel are uncircumcised in their hearts.'[5] Do you see how that God does not mean this circumcision which is given for a sign? For it is of no use to the Egyptians, or the sons of Moab, or the sons of Edom. But though a man be a Scythian or a Persian, if he has the knowledge of God and of His Christ, and keeps the everlasting righteous decrees, he is circumcised with the good and useful circumcision, and is a friend of God, and God rejoices in his gifts and offerings. But I will lay before you, my friends, the very words of God, when He said to the people by Malachi, one of the twelve prophets, 'I have no pleasure in you, saith the Lord; and I shall not accept your sacrifices at your hands: for from the rising of the sun unto its setting My name shall be glorified among the Gentiles; and in every place a sacrifice is offered unto My name, even a pure sacrifice: for My name is honoured among the Gentiles, saith the Lord; but ye profane it.'[6] And by David He said, 'A people whom I have not known, served Me; at the hearing of the ear they obeyed Me.'[7]

CHAP. XXIX. — CHRIST IS USELESS TO THOSE WHO OBSERVE THE LAW.

"Let us glorify God, all nations gathered together; for He has also visited us. Let us glorify Him by the King of glory, by the Lord of hosts. For He has been gracious towards the Gentiles also; and our sacrifices He esteems more grateful than yours. What need, then, have I of circumcision, who have been witnessed to by God? What need have I of that other baptism, who

---

[1] Isa. iii. 16.
[2] Various passages strung together; comp. Rom. iii. 10, and foll. verses.
[3] Jer. iv. 3.
[4] So in A. V., but supposed to be Idumæa.
[5] Jer. ix. 25 f.
[6] Mal. i. 10, etc.
[7] Ps. xviii. 43.

have been baptized with the Holy Ghost? I think that while I mention this, I would persuade even those who are possessed of scanty intelligence. For these words have neither been prepared by me, nor embellished by the art of man; but David sung them, Isaiah preached them, Zechariah proclaimed them, and Moses wrote them. Are you acquainted with them, Trypho? They are contained in your Scriptures, or rather not yours, but ours.[1] For we believe them; but you, though you read them, do not catch the spirit that is in them. Be not offended at, or reproach us with, the bodily uncircumcision with which God has created us; and think it not strange that we drink hot water on the Sabbaths, since God directs the government of the universe on this day equally as on all others; and the priests, as on other days, so on this, are ordered to offer sacrifices; and there are so many righteous men who have performed none of these legal ceremonies, and yet are witnessed to by God Himself.

CHAP. XXX. — CHRISTIANS POSSESS THE TRUE RIGHTEOUSNESS.

"But impute it to your own wickedness, that God even can be accused by those who have no understanding, of not having always instructed all in the same righteous statutes. For such institutions seemed to be unreasonable and unworthy of God to many men, who had not received grace to know that your nation were called to conversion and repentance of spirit,[2] while they were in a sinful condition and labouring under spiritual disease; and that the prophecy which was announced subsequent to the death of Moses is everlasting. And this is mentioned in the Psalm, my friends.[3] And that we, who have been made wise by them, confess that the statutes of the Lord are sweeter than honey and the honey-comb, is manifest from the fact that, though threatened with death, we do not deny His name. Moreover, it is also manifest to all, that we who believe in Him pray to be kept by Him from strange, i.e., from wicked and deceitful, spirits; as the word of prophecy, personating one of those who believe in Him, figuratively declares. For we do continually beseech God by Jesus Christ to preserve us from the demons which are hostile to the worship of God, and whom we of old time served, in order that, after our conversion by Him to God, we may be blameless. For we call Him Helper and Redeemer, the power of whose name even the demons do fear; and at this day, when they are exorcised in the name of Jesus Christ, crucified under Pontius Pilate, governor of Judæa, they are overcome. And thus it is manifest to all, that His Father has given Him so great power, by virtue of which demons are subdued to His name, and to the dispensation of His suffering.

CHAP. XXXI. — IF CHRIST'S POWER BE NOW SO GREAT, HOW MUCH GREATER AT THE SECOND ADVENT!

"But if so great a power is shown to have followed and to be still following the dispensation of His suffering, how great shall that be which shall follow His glorious advent! For He shall come on the clouds as the Son of man, so Daniel foretold, and His angels shall come with Him. These are the words: 'I beheld till the thrones were set; and the Ancient of days did sit, whose garment was white as snow, and the hair of His head like the pure wool. His throne was like a fiery flame, His wheels as burning fire. A fiery stream issued and came forth from before Him. Thousand thousands ministered unto Him, and ten thousand times ten thousand stood before Him. The books were opened, and the judgment was set. I beheld then the voice of the great words which the horn speaks: and the beast was beat down, and his body destroyed, and given to the burning flame. And the rest of the beasts were taken away from their dominion, and a period of life was given to the beasts until a season and time. I saw in the vision of the night, and, behold, one like the Son of man coming with the clouds of heaven; and He came to the Ancient of days, and stood before Him. And they who stood by brought Him near; and there were given Him power and kingly honour, and all nations of the earth by their families, and all glory, serve Him. And His dominion is an everlasting dominion, which shall not be taken away; and His kingdom shall not be destroyed. And my spirit was chilled within my frame, and the visions of my head troubled me. I came near unto one of them that stood by, and inquired the precise meaning of all these things. In answer he speaks to me, and showed me the judgment of the matters: These great beasts are four kingdoms, which shall perish from the earth, and shall not receive dominion for ever, even for ever and ever. Then I wished to know exactly about the fourth beast, which destroyed all [the others] and was very terrible, its teeth of iron, and its nails of brass; which devoured, made waste, and stamped the residue with its feet: also about the ten horns upon its head, and of the one which came up, by means of which three of the former fell. And that horn had eyes, and a mouth speaking great things; and its countenance excelled the

---

[1] [This striking claim of the Old Testament Scriptures is noteworthy.]
[2] Or, "repentance of the Father;" πατρός for πνεύματος. Maranus explains the confusion on the ground of the similarity between the contractions for the words, πρς and πνς.
[3] Ps. xix.

rest. And I beheld that horn waging war against the saints, and prevailing against them, until the Ancient of days came; and He gave judgment for the saints of the Most High. And the time came, and the saints of the Most High possessed the kingdom. And it was told me concerning the fourth beast: There shall be a fourth kingdom upon earth, which shall prevail over all these kingdoms, and shall devour the whole earth, and shall destroy and make it thoroughly waste. And the ten horns are ten kings that shall arise; and one shall arise after them;[1] and he shall surpass the first in evil deeds, and he shall subdue three kings, and he shall speak words against the Most High, and shall overthrow the rest of the saints of the Most High, and shall expect to change the seasons and the times. And it shall be delivered into his hands for a time, and times, and half a time. And the judgment sat, and they shall take away his dominion, to consume and to destroy it unto the end. And the kingdom, and the power, and the great places of the kingdoms under the heavens, were given to the holy people of the Most High, to reign in an everlasting kingdom: and all powers shall be subject to Him, and shall obey Him. Hitherto is the end of the matter. I, Daniel, was possessed with a very great astonishment, and my speech was changed in me; yet I kept the matter in my heart.'"[2]

CHAP. XXXII. — TRYPHO OBJECTING THAT CHRIST IS DESCRIBED AS GLORIOUS BY DANIEL, JUSTIN DISTINGUISHES TWO ADVENTS.

And when I had ceased, Trypho said, "These and such like Scriptures, sir, compel us to wait for Him who, as Son of man, receives from the Ancient of days the everlasting kingdom. But this so-called Christ of yours was dishonourable and inglorious, so much so that the last curse contained in the law of God fell on him, for he was crucified."

Then I replied to him, "If, sirs, it were not said by the Scriptures which I have already quoted, that His form was inglorious, and His generation not declared, and that for His death the rich would suffer death, and with His stripes we should be healed, and that He would be led away like a sheep; and if I had not explained that there would be two advents of His,— one in which He was pierced by you; a second, when you shall know Him whom you have pierced, and your tribes shall mourn, each tribe by itself, the women apart, and the men apart, — then I must have been speaking dubious and obscure things. But now, by means of the contents of those Scriptures esteemed holy and prophetic amongst you, I attempt to prove all [that I have adduced], in the hope that some one of you may be found to be of that remnant which has been left by the grace of the Lord of Sabaoth for the eternal salvation. In order, therefore, that the matter inquired into may be plainer to you, I will mention to you other words also spoken by the blessed David, from which you will perceive that the Lord is called the Christ by the Holy Spirit of prophecy; and that the Lord, the Father of all, has brought Him again from the earth, setting Him at His own right hand, until He makes His enemies His footstool; which indeed happens from the time that our Lord Jesus Christ ascended to heaven, after He rose again from the dead, the times now running on to their consummation; and he whom Daniel foretells would have dominion for a time, and times, and an half, is even already at the door, about to speak blasphemous and daring things against the Most High. But you, being ignorant of how long he will have dominion, hold another opinion. For you interpret the 'time' as being a hundred years. But if this is so, the man of sin must, at the shortest, reign three hundred and fifty years, in order that we may compute that which is said by the holy Daniel—'and times'—to be *two* times only. All this I have said to you in digression, in order that you at length may be persuaded of what has been declared against you by God, that you are foolish sons; and of this, 'Therefore, behold, I will proceed to take away this people, and shall take them away; and I will strip the wise of their wisdom, and will hide the understanding of their prudent men;'[3] and may cease to deceive yourselves and those who hear you, and may learn of us, who have been taught wisdom by the grace of Christ. The words, then, which were spoken by David, are these:[4] 'The Lord said unto My Lord, Sit Thou at My right hand, until I make Thine enemies Thy footstool. The Lord shall send the rod of Thy strength out of Sion: rule Thou also in the midst of Thine enemies. With Thee shall be, in the day, the chief of Thy power, in the beauties of Thy saints. From the womb, before the morning star, have I begotten Thee. The Lord hath sworn, and will not repent: Thou art a priest for ever after the order of Melchizedek. The Lord is at Thy right hand: He has crushed kings in the day of His wrath: He shall judge among the heathen, He shall fill [with] the dead bodies.[5] He shall drink of the brook in the way; therefore shall He lift up the head.'

---

[1] Literally, "And the ten horns, ten kings shall arise after them."
[2] Dan. vii. 9-28.
[3] Isa. xxix. 14.
[4] Ps. cx.
[5] πληρώσει πτώματα; Lat. version, *implebit ruinas*. Thirlby suggested that an omission has taken place in the MSS. by the transcriber's fault.

CHAP. XXXIII.—PS. CX. IS NOT SPOKEN OF HEZEKIAH. HE PROVES THAT CHRIST WAS FIRST HUMBLE, THEN SHALL BE GLORIOUS.

"And," I continued, "I am not ignorant that you venture to expound this psalm as if it referred to king Hezekiah; but that you are mistaken, I shall prove to you from these very words forthwith. 'The Lord hath sworn, and will not repent,' it is said; and, 'Thou art a priest for ever, after the order of Melchizedek,' with what follows and precedes. Not even you will venture to object that Hezekiah was either a priest, or is the everlasting priest of God; but that this is spoken of our Jesus, these expressions show. But your ears are shut up, and your hearts are made dull.[1] For by this statement, 'The Lord hath sworn, and will not repent: Thou art a priest for ever, after the order of Melchizedek,' with an oath God has shown Him (on account of your unbelief) to be the High Priest after the order of Melchizedek; i.e., as Melchizedek was described by Moses as the priest of the Most High, and he was a priest of those who were in uncircumcision, and blessed the circumcised Abraham who brought him tithes, so God has shown that His everlasting Priest, called also by the Holy Spirit Lord, would be Priest of those in uncircumcision. Those too in circumcision who approach Him, that is, believing Him and seeking blessings from Him, He will both receive and bless. And that He shall be first humble as a man, and then exalted, these words at the end of the Psalm show: 'He shall drink of the brook in the way,' and then, 'Therefore shall He lift up the head.'

CHAP. XXXIV.—NOR DOES PS. LXXII. APPLY TO SOLOMON, WHOSE FAULTS CHRISTIANS SHUDDER AT.

"Further, to persuade you that you have not understood anything of the Scriptures, I will remind you of another psalm, dictated to David by the Holy Spirit, which you say refers to Solomon, who was also your king. But it refers also to our Christ. But you deceive yourselves by the ambiguous forms of speech. For where it is said, 'The law of the Lord is perfect,' you do not understand it of the law which was to be after Moses, but of the law which was given by Moses, although God declared that He would establish a new law and a new covenant. And where it has been said, 'O God, give Thy judgment to the king,' since Solomon was king, you say that the Psalm refers to him, although the words of the Psalm expressly proclaim that reference is made to the everlasting King, i.e., to Christ. For Christ is King, and Priest, and God, and Lord, and angel, and man, and captain, and stone, and a Son born, and first made subject to suffering, then returning to heaven, and again coming with glory, and He is preached as having the everlasting kingdom: so I prove from all the Scriptures. But that you may perceive what I have said, I quote the words of the Psalm; they are these: 'O God, give Thy judgment to the king, and Thy righteousness unto the king's son, to judge Thy people with righteousness, and Thy poor with judgment. The mountains shall take up peace to the people, and the little hills righteousness. He shall judge the poor of the people, and shall save the children of the needy, and shall abase the slanderer. He shall co-endure with the sun, and before the moon unto all generations. He shall come down like rain upon the fleece, as drops falling on the earth. In His days shall righteousness flourish, and abundance of peace until the moon be taken away. And He shall have dominion from sea to sea, and from the rivers unto the ends of the earth. Ethiopians shall fall down before Him, and His enemies shall lick the dust. The kings of Tarshish and the isles shall offer gifts; the kings of Arabia and Seba shall offer gifts; and all the kings of the earth shall worship Him, and all the nations shall serve Him: for He has delivered the poor from the man of power, and the needy that hath no helper. He shall spare the poor and needy, and shall save the souls of the needy: He shall redeem their souls from usury and injustice, and His name shall be honourable before them. And He shall live, and to Him shall be given of the gold of Arabia, and they shall pray continually for Him: they shall bless Him all the day. And there shall be a foundation on the earth, it shall be exalted on the tops of the mountains: His fruit shall be on Lebanon, and they of the city shall flourish like grass of the earth. His name shall be blessed for ever. His name shall endure before the sun; and all tribes of the earth shall be blessed in Him, all nations shall call Him blessed. Blessed be the Lord, the God of Israel, who only doeth wondrous things; and blessed be His glorious name for ever, and for ever and ever; and the whole earth shall be filled with His glory. Amen, amen.'[2] And at the close of this Psalm which I have quoted, it is written, 'The hymns of David the son of Jesse are ended.'[3] Moreover, that Solomon was a renowned and great king, by whom the temple called that at Jerusalem was built, I know; but that none of those things mentioned in the Psalm happened to him, is evident. For neither did all kings worship him; nor did he reign to the ends of the earth; nor did his enemies, falling before him, lick the dust. Nay, also, I venture to repeat what is

---

[1] πεπήρωνται. Maranus thinks πεπώρωνται more probable, "hardened."
[2] Ps. lxxii.
[3] [A striking passage in De Maistre (Œuvres, vol. vi. p. 275) is worthy of comparison.]

written in the book of Kings as committed by him, how through a woman's influence he worshipped the idols of Sidon, which those of the Gentiles who know God, the Maker of all things through Jesus the crucified, do not venture to do, but abide every torture and vengeance even to the extremity of death, rather than worship idols, or eat meat offered to idols."

CHAP. XXXV. — HERETICS CONFIRM THE CATHOLICS IN THE FAITH.

And Trypho said, "I believe, however, that many of those who say that they confess Jesus, and are called Christians, eat meats offered to idols, and declare that they are by no means injured in consequence." And I replied, "The fact that there are such men confessing themselves to be Christians, and admitting the crucified Jesus to be both Lord and Christ, yet not teaching His doctrines, but those of the spirits of error, causes us who are disciples of the true and pure doctrine of Jesus Christ, to be more faithful and stedfast in the hope announced by Him. For what things He predicted would take place in His name, these we do see being actually accomplished in our sight. For he said, 'Many shall come in My name, clothed outwardly in sheep's clothing, but inwardly they are ravening wolves.'[1] And, 'There shall be schisms and heresies.'[2] And, 'Beware of false prophets, who shall come to you clothed outwardly in sheep's clothing, but inwardly they are ravening wolves.'[1] And, 'Many false Christs and false apostles shall arise, and shall deceive many of the faithful.'[3] There are, therefore, and there were many, my friends, who, coming forward in the name of Jesus, taught both to speak and act impious and blasphemous things; and these are called by us after the name of the men from whom each doctrine and opinion had its origin. (For some in one way, others in another, teach to blaspheme the Maker of all things, and Christ, who was foretold by Him as coming, and the God of Abraham, and of Isaac, and of Jacob, with whom we have nothing in common, since we know them to be atheists, impious, unrighteous, and sinful, and confessors of Jesus in name only, instead of worshippers of Him. Yet they style themselves Christians, just as certain among the Gentiles inscribe the name of God upon the works of their own hands, and partake in nefarious and impious rites.) Some are called Marcians, and some Valentinians, and some Basilidians, and some Saturnilians, and others by other names; each called after the originator of the individual opinion, just as each one of those who consider themselves philosophers, as I said before, thinks he must bear the name of the philosophy which he follows, from the name of the father of the particular doctrine. So that, in consequence of these events, we know that Jesus foreknew what would happen after Him, as well as in consequence of many other events which He foretold would befall those who believed on and confessed Him, the Christ. For all that we suffer, even when killed by friends, He foretold would take place; so that it is manifest no word or act of His can be found fault with. Wherefore we pray for you and for all other men who hate us; in order that you, having repented along with us, may not blaspheme Him who, by His works, by the mighty deeds even now wrought through His name, by the words He taught, by the prophecies announced concerning Him, is the blameless, and in all things irreproachable, Christ Jesus; but, believing on Him, may be saved in His second glorious advent, and may not be condemned to fire by Him."

CHAP. XXXVI. — HE PROVES THAT CHRIST IS CALLED LORD OF HOSTS.

Then he replied, "Let these things be so as you say — namely, that it was foretold Christ would suffer, and be called a stone; and after His first appearance, in which it had been announced He would suffer, would come in glory, and be Judge finally of all, and eternal King and Priest. Now show if this man be He of whom these prophecies were made."

And I said, "As you wish, Trypho, I shall come to these proofs which you seek in the fitting place; but now you will permit me first to recount the prophecies, which I wish to do in order to prove that Christ is called both God and Lord of hosts, and Jacob, in parable by the Holy Spirit; and your interpreters, as God says, are foolish, since they say that reference is made to Solomon and not to Christ, when he bore the ark of testimony into the temple which he built. The Psalm of David is this: 'The earth is the Lord's, and the fulness thereof; the world, and all that dwell therein. He hath founded it upon the seas, and prepared it upon the floods. Who shall ascend into the hill of the Lord? or who shall stand in His holy place? He that is clean of hands and pure of heart: who has not received his soul in vain, and has not sworn guilefully to his neighbour: he shall receive blessing from the Lord, and mercy from God his Saviour. This is the generation of them that seek the Lord, that seek the face of the God of Jacob.[4] Lift up your gates, ye rulers;

---

[1] Matt. vii. 15.
[2] 1 Cor. xi. 19.
[3] Matt. xxiv. 11.
[4] Maranus remarks from Thirlby: "As Justin wrote a little before, 'and is called Jacob in parable,' it seems to convince us that Justin wrote, 'thy face, O Jacob.'" [The meaning in this latter case becomes plain, if we observe that "O Israel" is equivalent to, and means, "O house of Jacob:" an apostrophe to the Church of the ancient people.]

and be ye lift up, ye everlasting doors; and the King of glory shall come in. Who is this King of glory? The Lord strong and mighty in battle. Lift up your gates, ye rulers; and be ye lift up, ye everlasting doors; and the King of glory shall come in. Who is this King of glory? The Lord of hosts, He is the King of glory.'[1] Accordingly, it is shown that Solomon is not the Lord of hosts; but when our Christ rose from the dead and ascended to heaven, the rulers in heaven, under appointment of God, are commanded to open the gates of heaven, that He who is King of glory may enter in, and having ascended, may sit on the right hand of the Father until He make the enemies His footstool, as has been made manifest by another Psalm. For when the rulers of heaven saw Him of uncomely and dishonoured appearance, and inglorious, not recognising Him, they inquired, 'Who is this King of glory?' And the Holy Spirit, either from the person of His Father, or from His own person, answers them, 'The Lord of hosts, He is this King of glory.' For every one will confess that not one of those who presided over the gates of the temple at Jerusalem would venture to say concerning Solomon, though he was so glorious a king, or concerning the ark of testimony, 'Who is this King of glory?'

CHAP. XXXVII. — THE SAME IS PROVED FROM OTHER PSALMS.

"Moreover, in the diapsalm of the forty-sixth Psalm, reference is thus made to Christ: 'God went up with a shout, the Lord with the sound of a trumpet. Sing ye to our God, sing ye: sing to our King, sing ye; for God is King of all the earth: sing with understanding. God has ruled over the nations. God sits upon His holy throne. The rulers of the nations were assembled along with the God of Abraham, for the strong ones of God are greatly exalted on the earth.'[2] And in the ninety-eighth Psalm, the Holy Spirit reproaches you, and predicts Him whom you do not wish to be king to be King and Lord, both of Samuel, and of Aaron, and of Moses, and, in short, of all the others. And the words of the Psalm are these: 'The Lord has reigned, let the nations be angry: [it is] He who sits upon the cherubim, let the earth be shaken. The Lord is great in Zion, and He is high above all the nations. Let them confess Thy great name, for it is fearful and holy, and the honour of the King loves judgment. Thou hast prepared equity; judgment and righteousness hast Thou performed in Jacob. Exalt the Lord our God, and worship the footstool of His feet; for He is holy. Moses and Aaron among His priests, and Samuel among those who call upon His name. They called (says the Scripture) on the Lord, and He heard them. In the pillar of the cloud He spake to them; for[3] they kept His testimonies, and the commandment which he gave them. O Lord our God, Thou heardest them: O God, Thou wert propitious to them, and [yet] taking vengeance on all their inventions. Exalt the Lord our God, and worship at His holy hill; for the Lord our God is holy.'"[4]

CHAP. XXXVIII. — IT IS AN ANNOYANCE TO THE JEW THAT CHRIST IS SAID TO BE ADORED. JUSTIN CONFIRMS IT, HOWEVER, FROM PS. XLV.

And Trypho said, "Sir, it were good for us if we obeyed our teachers, who laid down a law that we should have no intercourse with any of you, and that we should not have even any communication with you on these questions. For you utter many blasphemies, in that you seek to persuade us that this crucified man was with Moses and Aaron, and spoke to them in the pillar of the cloud; then that he became man, was crucified, and ascended up to heaven, and comes again to earth, and ought to be worshipped."

Then I answered, " I know that, as the word of God says, this great wisdom of God, the Maker of all things, and the Almighty, is hid from you. Wherefore, in sympathy with you, I am striving to the utmost that you may understand these matters which to you are paradoxical; but if not, that I myself may be innocent in the day of judgment. For you shall hear other words which appear still more paradoxical; but be not confounded, nay, rather remain still more zealous hearers and investigators, despising the tradition of your teachers, since they are convicted by the Holy Spirit of inability to perceive the truths taught by God, and of preferring to teach their own doctrines. Accordingly, in the forty-fourth [forty-fifth] Psalm, these words are in like manner referred to Christ: 'My heart has brought forth a good matter;[5] I tell my works to the King. My tongue is the pen of a ready writer. Fairer in beauty than the sons of men: grace is poured forth into Thy lips: therefore hath God blessed Thee for ever. Gird Thy sword upon Thy thigh, O mighty One. Press on in Thy fairness and in Thy beauty, and prosper and reign, because of truth, and of meekness, and of righteousness: and Thy right hand shall instruct Thee marvellously. Thine arrows are sharpened, O mighty One; the people shall fall under Thee; in the heart of the enemies of the King [the arrows are fixed]. Thy throne, O God, is for ever and ever: a sceptre of equity

---

[1] Ps. xxiv.
[2] Ps. xlvi. 5–9. [The *diapsalm* is here used for what follows the "Selah."]
[3] "For" wanting in both Codd.
[4] Ps. xcix.
[5] [Hebrew and Greek, " a good word," i.e. the Logos.]

is the sceptre of Thy kingdom. Thou hast loved righteousness, and hast hated iniquity; therefore thy God[1] hath anointed Thee with the oil of gladness above Thy fellows. [He hath anointed Thee] with myrrh,[2] and oil, and cassia, from Thy garments; from the ivory palaces, whereby they made Thee glad. Kings' daughters are in Thy honour. The queen stood at Thy right hand, clad in garments[3] embroidered with gold. Hearken, O daughter, and behold, and incline thine ear, and forget thy people and the house of thy father: and the King shall desire thy beauty; because He is thy Lord, they shall worship Him also. And the daughter of Tyre [shall be there] with gifts. The rich of the people shall entreat Thy face. All the glory of the King's daughter [is] within, clad in embroidered garments of needlework. The virgins that follow her shall be brought to the King; her neighbours shall be brought unto Thee: they shall be brought with joy and gladness: they shall be led into the King's shrine. Instead of thy fathers, thy sons have been born: Thou shalt appoint them rulers over all the earth. I shall remember Thy name in every generation: therefore the people shall confess Thee for ever, and for ever and ever.'

CHAP. XXXIX. — THE JEWS HATE THE CHRISTIANS WHO BELIEVE THIS. HOW GREAT THE DISTINCTION IS BETWEEN BOTH!

"Now it is not surprising," I continued, "that you hate us who hold these opinions, and convict you of a continual hardness of heart.[4] For indeed Elijah, conversing with God concerning you, speaks thus: 'Lord, they have slain Thy prophets, and digged down Thine altars: and I am left alone, and they seek my life.' And He answers him: 'I have still seven thousand men who have not bowed the knee to Baal.'[5] Therefore, just as God did not inflict His anger on account of those seven thousand men, even so He has now neither yet inflicted judgment, nor does inflict it, knowing that daily some [of you] are becoming disciples in the name of Christ, and quitting the path of error; who are also receiving gifts, each as he is worthy, illumined through the name of this Christ. For one receives the spirit of understanding, another of counsel, another of strength, another of healing, another of foreknowledge, another of teaching, and another of the fear of God."

To this Trypho said to me, "I wish you knew that you are beside yourself, talking these sentiments."

And I said to him, "Listen, O friend,[6] for I am not mad or beside myself; but it was prophesied that, after the ascent of Christ to heaven, He would deliver[7] us from error and give us gifts. The words are these: 'He ascended up on high; He led captivity captive; He gave gifts to men.'[8] Accordingly, we who have received gifts from Christ, who has ascended up on high, prove from the words of prophecy that you, 'the wise in yourselves, and the men of understanding in your own eyes,'[9] are foolish, and honour God and His Christ by lip only. But we, who are instructed in the whole truth,[10] honour Them both in acts, and in knowledge, and in heart, even unto death. But you hesitate to confess that He is Christ, as the Scriptures and the events witnessed and done in His name prove, perhaps for this reason, lest you be persecuted by the rulers, who, under the influence of the wicked and deceitful spirit, the serpent, will not cease putting to death and persecuting those who confess the name of Christ until He come again, and destroy them all, and render to each his deserts."

And Trypho replied, "Now, then, render us the proof that this man who you say was crucified and ascended into heaven is the Christ of God. For you have sufficiently proved by means of the Scriptures previously quoted by you, that it is declared in the Scriptures that Christ must suffer, and come again with glory, and receive the eternal kingdom over all the nations, every kingdom being made subject to Him: now show us that this man is He."

And I replied, "It has been already proved, sirs, to those who have ears, even from the facts which have been conceded by you; but that you may not think me at a loss, and unable to give proof of what you ask, as I promised, I shall do so at a fitting place. At present, I resume the consideration of the subject which I was discussing.

CHAP. XL. — HE RETURNS TO THE MOSAIC LAWS, AND PROVES THAT THEY WERE FIGURES OF THE THINGS WHICH PERTAIN TO CHRIST.

"The mystery, then, of the lamb which God enjoined to be sacrificed as the passover, was a type of Christ; with whose blood, in proportion to their faith in Him, they anoint their houses, i.e., themselves, who believe on Him. For that the creation which God created — to wit, Adam — was a house for the spirit which proceeded from God, you all can understand. And that

---

[1] Or, "God, thy God."
[2] στακτή.
[3] Literally, "garments of gold, variegated."
[4] Literally, "of a hard-hearted opinion."
[5] 1 Kings xix. 14, 18.
[6] ὦ οὗτος. [Or, Look you, listen!]
[7] Literally, "carry us captive."
[8] Ps. lxviii. 19.
[9] Isa. v. 21.
[10] Constrasting either Catholics with heretics, or Christians with Jews. [Note this word *Catholic*, as here used in its legitimate primitive sense.]

this injunction was temporary, I prove thus. God does not permit the lamb of the passover to be sacrificed in any other place than where His name was named; knowing that the days will come, after the suffering of Christ, when even the place in Jerusalem shall be given over to your enemies, and all the offerings, in short, shall cease; and that lamb which was commanded to be wholly roasted was a symbol of the suffering of the cross which Christ would undergo. For the lamb,[1] which is roasted, is roasted and dressed up in the form of the cross. For one spit is transfixed right through from the lower parts up to the head, and one across the back, to which are attached the legs of the lamb. And the two goats which were ordered to be offered during the fast, of which one was sent away as the scape [goat], and the other sacrificed, were similarly declarative of the two appearances of Christ: the first, in which the elders of your people, and the priests, having laid hands on Him and put Him to death, sent Him away as the scape [goat]; and His second appearance, because in the same place in Jerusalem you shall recognise Him whom you have dishonoured, and who was an offering for all sinners willing to repent, and keeping the fast which Isaiah speaks of, loosening the terms[2] of the violent contracts, and keeping the other precepts, likewise enumerated by him, and which I have quoted,[3] which those believing in Jesus do. And further, you are aware that the offering of the two goats, which were enjoined to be sacrificed at the fast, was not permitted to take place similarly anywhere else, but only in Jerusalem.

CHAP. XLI. — THE OBLATION OF FINE FLOUR WAS A FIGURE OF THE EUCHARIST.

"And the offering of fine flour, sirs," I said, "which was prescribed to be presented on behalf of those purified from leprosy, was a type of the bread of the Eucharist, the celebration of which our Lord Jesus Christ prescribed, in remembrance of the suffering which He endured on behalf of those who are purified in soul from all iniquity, in order that we may at the same time thank God for having created the world, with all things therein, for the sake of man, and for delivering us from the evil in which we were, and for utterly overthrowing[4] principalities and powers by Him who suffered according to His will. Hence God speaks by the mouth of Malachi, one of the twelve [prophets], as I said before,[5] about the sacrifices at that time presented by you: 'I have no pleasure in you, saith the Lord; and I will not accept your sacrifices at your hands: for, from the rising of the sun unto the going down of the same, My name has been glorified among the Gentiles, and in every place incense is offered to My name, and a pure offering: for My name is great among the Gentiles, saith the Lord: but ye profane it.'[6] [So] He then speaks of those Gentiles, namely us, who in every place offer sacrifices to Him, i.e., the bread of the Eucharist, and also the cup of the Eucharist, affirming both that we glorify His name, and that you profane [it]. The command of circumcision, again, bidding [them] always circumcise the children on the eighth day, was a type of the true circumcision, by which we are circumcised from deceit and iniquity through Him who rose from the dead on the first day after the Sabbath, [namely through] our Lord Jesus Christ. For the first day after the Sabbath, remaining the first[7] of all the days, is called, however, the eighth, according to the number of all the days of the cycle, and [yet] remains the first.

CHAP. XLII. — THE BELLS ON THE PRIEST'S ROBE WERE A FIGURE OF THE APOSTLES.

"Moreover, the prescription that twelve bells[8] be attached to the [robe] of the high priest, which hung down to the feet, was a symbol of the twelve apostles, who depend on the power of Christ, the eternal Priest; and through their voice it is that all the earth has been filled with the glory and grace of God and of His Christ. Wherefore David also says: 'Their sound has gone forth into all the earth, and their words to the ends of the world.'[9] And Isaiah speaks as if he were personating the apostles, when they say to Christ that they believe not in their own report, but in the power of Him who sent them. And so he says: 'Lord, who hath believed our report? and to whom is the arm of the Lord revealed? We have preached before Him as if [He were] a child, as if a root in a dry ground.'[10] (And what follows in order of the prophecy already quoted.[11]) But when the passage speaks as from the lips of many, 'We have preached before Him,' and adds, 'as if a child,' it signifies that the wicked shall become subject to Him, and shall obey His command, and that all shall become as one child. Such a thing as you may witness in the body: although the members are enumerated as many, all are called *one*, and are a *body*. For, indeed, a commonwealth and a church,[12] though many individuals in number,

---

[1] Some think this particularly refers to the paschal lamb, others to any lamb which is roasted.
[2] Literally, "cords."
[3] Chap. xv.
[4] Literally, "overthrowing with a perfect overthrow."
[5] Chap. xxviii.
[6] Mal. i. 10–12.
[7] Or, "being the first."
[8] Ex. xxviii. 33 gives no definite number of bells. Otto presumes Justin to have confounded the bells and the gems, which were twelve in number.
[9] Ps. xix. 4.
[10] Isa. liii. 1, 2.
[11] Chap. xiii.
[12] ἐκκλησία. Lat. vers. has *conventus*.

are in fact as one, called and addressed by one appellation. And in short, sirs," said I, "by enumerating all the other appointments of Moses, I can demonstrate that they were types, and symbols, and declarations of those things which would happen to Christ, of those who it was foreknown were to believe in Him, and of those things which would also be done by Christ Himself. But since what I have now enumerated appears to me to be sufficient, I revert again to the order of the discourse.[1]

CHAP. XLIII. — HE CONCLUDES THAT THE LAW HAD AN END IN CHRIST, WHO WAS BORN OF THE VIRGIN.

"As, then, circumcision began with Abraham, and the Sabbath and sacrifices and offerings and feasts with Moses, and it has been proved they were enjoined on account of the hardness of your people's heart, so it was necessary, in accordance with the Father's will, that they should have an end in Him who was born of a virgin, of the family of Abraham and tribe of Judah, and of David; in Christ the Son of God, who was proclaimed as about to come to all the world, to be the everlasting law and the everlasting covenant, even as the forementioned prophecies show. And we, who have approached God through Him, have received not carnal, but spiritual circumcision, which Enoch and those like him observed. And we have received it through baptism, since we were sinners, by God's mercy; and all men may equally obtain it. But since the mystery of His birth now demands our attention, I shall speak of it. Isaiah then asserted in regard to the generation of Christ, that it could not be declared by man, in words already quoted:[2] 'Who shall declare His generation? for His life is taken from the earth: for the transgressions of my people was He led[3] to death.'[4] The Spirit of prophecy thus affirmed that the generation of Him who was to die, that we sinful men might be healed by His stripes, was such as could not be declared. Furthermore, that the men who believe in Him may possess the knowledge of the manner in which He came into the world,[5] the Spirit of prophecy by the same Isaiah foretold how it would happen thus: 'And the Lord spoke again to Ahaz, saying, Ask for thyself a sign from the Lord thy God, in the depth, or in the height. And Ahaz said, I will not ask, neither will I tempt the Lord. And Isaiah said, Hear then, O house of David; Is it a small thing for you to contend with men, and how do you contend with the Lord? Therefore the Lord Himself will give you a sign. Behold, the virgin shall conceive, and shall bear a son, and his name shall be called Immanuel. Butter and honey shall he eat, before he knows or prefers the evil, and chooses out the good;[6] for before the child knows good or ill, he rejects evil[7] by choosing out the good. For before the child knows how to call father or mother, he shall receive the power of Damascus and the spoil of Samaria in presence of the king of Assyria. And the land shall be forsaken,[8] which thou shalt with difficulty endure in consequence of the presence of its two kings.[9] But God shall bring on thee, and on thy people, and on the house of thy father, days which have not yet come upon thee since the day in which Ephraim took away from Judah the king of Assyria.'[10] Now it is evident to all, that in the race of Abraham according to the flesh no one has been born of a virgin, or is said to have been born [of a virgin], save this our Christ. But since you and your teachers venture to affirm that in the prophecy of Isaiah it is not said, 'Behold, the virgin shall conceive,' but, 'Behold, the young woman shall conceive, and bear a son;' and [since] you explain the prophecy as if [it referred] to Hezekiah, who was your king, I shall endeavor to discuss shortly this point in opposition to you, and to show that reference is made to Him who is acknowledged by us as Christ.

CHAP. XLIV. — THE JEWS IN VAIN PROMISE THEMSELVES SALVATION, WHICH CANNOT BE OBTAINED EXCEPT THROUGH CHRIST.

" For thus, so far as you are concerned, I shall be found in all respects innocent, if I strive earnestly to persuade you by bringing forward demonstrations. But if you remain hard-hearted, or weak in [forming] a resolution, on account of death, which is the lot of the Christians, and are unwilling to assent to the truth, you shall appear as the authors of your own [evils]. And you deceive yourselves while you fancy that, because you are the seed of Abraham after the flesh, therefore you shall fully inherit the good things announced to be bestowed by God through Christ. For no one, not even of them,[11] has anything to look for, but only those who in mind are assimilated to the faith of Abraham, and who have

---

[1] Literally, " to the discourse in order."
[2] Chap. xiii.
[3] Or, " was I led."
[4] Isa. liii. 8.
[5] Literally, " He was in the world, being born."
[6] See Chap. lxvi.
[7] Literally, "disobeys evil" (ἀπειθεῖ πονηρά). Conjectured: ἀπωθεῖ, and ἀπειθεῖ πονηρία.
[8] The MSS. of Justin read, " shall be taken:" καταληφθήσεται. This is plainly a mistake for καταλειφθήσεται; but whether the mistake is Justin's or the transcribers', it would be difficult to say, as Thirlby remarks.
[9] The rendering of this is doubtful: literally, " from the face of the two kings," and the words might go with " shall be forsaken."
[10] Isa. vii. 10-17 with Isa. viii. 4 inserted. The last clause may also be translated, " in which He took away from Judah Ephraim, even the king of Assyria."
[11] i.e., of Abraham's seed.

recognised all the mysteries: for I say,[1] that some injunctions were laid on you in reference to the worship of God and practice of righteousness; but some injunctions and acts were likewise mentioned in reference to the mystery of Christ, on account of[2] the hardness of your people's hearts. And that this is so, God makes known in Ezekiel, [when] He said concerning it: 'If Noah and Jacob[3] and Daniel should beg either sons or daughters, the request would not be granted them.'[4] And in Isaiah, of the very same matter He spake thus: 'The Lord God said, they shall both go forth and look on the members [of the bodies] of the men that have transgressed. For their worm shall not die, and their fire shall not be quenched, and they shall be a gazing-stock to all flesh.'[5] So that it becomes you to eradicate this hope from your souls, and hasten to know in what way forgiveness of sins, and a hope of inheriting the promised good things, shall be yours. But there is no other [way] than this, — to become acquainted with this Christ, to be washed in the fountain[6] spoken of by Isaiah for the remission of sins; and for the rest, to live sinless lives."

CHAP. XLV. — THOSE WHO WERE RIGHTEOUS BEFORE AND UNDER THE LAW SHALL BE SAVED BY CHRIST.

And Trypho said, "If I seem to interrupt these matters, which you say must be investigated, yet the question which I mean to put is urgent. Suffer me first."

And I replied, "Ask whatever you please, as it occurs to you; and I shall endeavour, after questions and answers, to resume and complete the discourse."

Then he said, "Tell me, then, shall those who lived according to the law given by Moses, live in the same manner with Jacob, Enoch, and Noah, in the resurrection of the dead, or not?"

I replied to him, "When I quoted, sir, the words spoken by Ezekiel, that 'even if Noah and Daniel and Jacob were to beg sons and daughters, the request would not be granted them,' but that each one, that is to say, shall be saved by his own righteousness, I said also, that those who regulated their lives by the law of Moses would in like manner be saved. For what in the law of Moses is naturally good, and pious, and righteous, and has been prescribed to be done by those who obey it;[7] and what was appointed to be performed by reason of the hardness of the people's hearts; was similarly recorded, and done also by those who were under the law. Since those who did that which is universally, naturally, and eternally good are pleasing to God, they shall be saved through this Christ in the resurrection equally with those righteous men who were before them, namely Noah, and Enoch, and Jacob, and whoever else there be, along with those who have known[8] this Christ, Son of God, who was before the morning star and the moon, and submitted to become incarnate, and be born of this virgin of the family of David, in order that, by this dispensation, the serpent that sinned from the beginning, and the angels like him, may be destroyed, and that death may be contemned, and for ever quit, at the second coming of the Christ Himself, those who believe in Him and live acceptably, — and be no more: when some are sent to be punished unceasingly into judgment and condemnation of fire; but others shall exist in freedom from suffering, from corruption, and from grief, and in immortality."

CHAP. XLVI. — TRYPHO ASKS WHETHER A MAN WHO KEEPS THE LAW EVEN NOW WILL BE SAVED. JUSTIN PROVES THAT IT CONTRIBUTES NOTHING TO RIGHTEOUSNESS.

"But if some, even now, wish to live in the observance of the institutions given by Moses, and yet believe in this Jesus who was crucified, recognising Him to be the Christ of God, and that it is given to Him to be absolute Judge of all, and that His is the everlasting kingdom, can they also be saved?" he inquired of me.

And I replied, "Let us consider that also together, whether one may now observe all the Mosaic institutions."

And he answered, "No. For we know that, as you said, it is not possible either anywhere to sacrifice the lamb of the passover, or to offer the goats ordered for the fast; or, in short, [to present] all the other offerings."

And I said, "Tell [me] then yourself, I pray, some things which can be observed; for you will be persuaded that, though a man does not keep or has not performed the eternal[6] decrees, he may assuredly be saved."

Then he replied, "To keep the Sabbath, to be circumcised, to observe months, and to be washed if you touch anything prohibited by Moses, or after sexual intercourse."

And I said, "Do you think that Abraham, Isaac, Jacob, Noah, and Job, and all the rest be-

---

[1] Justin distinguishes between such essential acts as related to God's worship and the establishment of righteousness, and such ceremonial observances as had a mere temporary significance. The recognition of this distinction he alleges to be necessary to salvation: necessary in this sense, that justification must be placed not on the latter, but on the former; and without such recognition, a Jew would, as Justin says, rest his hopes on his noble descent from Abraham.
[2] More probably, "or on account of," etc.
[3] In Bible, "Job;" Maranus prefers "Jacob," and thinks the mention of his name very suitable to disprove the arrogant claims of Jacob's posterity.
[4] Ezek. xiv. 20.
[5] Isa. lxvi. 24.
[6] Some refer this to Christ's baptism. See Cyprian, *Adv. Jud.* i. 24. — OTTO.
[7] It, i.e., the law, or "what in the law," etc.
[8] Those who live after Christ.
[9] "Eternal," i.e., as the Jew thinks.

fore or after them equally righteous, also Sarah the wife of Abraham, Rebekah the wife of Isaac, Rachel the wife of Jacob, and Leah, and all the rest of them, until the mother of Moses the faithful servant, who observed none of these [statutes], will be saved?"

And Trypho answered, "Were not Abraham and his descendants circumcised?"

And I said, "I know that Abraham and his descendants were circumcised. The reason why circumcision was given to them I stated at length in what has gone before; and if what has been said does not convince you,[1] let us again search into the matter. But you are aware that, up to Moses, no one in fact who was righteous observed any of these rites at all of which we are talking, or received one commandment to observe, except that of circumcision, which began from Abraham."

And he replied, "We know it, and admit that they are saved."

Then I returned answer, "You perceive that God by Moses laid all such ordinances upon you on account of the hardness of your people's hearts, in order that, by the large number of them, you might keep God continually, and in every action, before your eyes, and never begin to act unjustly or impiously. For He enjoined you to place around you [a fringe] of purple dye,[2] in order that you might not forget God; and He commanded you to wear a phylactery,[3] certain characters, which indeed we consider holy, being engraved on very thin parchment; and by these means stirring you up[4] to retain a constant remembrance of God: at the same time, however, convincing you, that in your hearts you have not even a faint remembrance of God's worship. Yet not even so were you dissuaded from idolatry: for in the times of Elijah, when [God] recounted the number of those who had not bowed the knee to Baal, He said the number was seven thousand; and in Isaiah He rebukes you for having sacrificed your children to idols. But we, because we refuse to sacrifice to those to whom we were of old accustomed to sacrifice, undergo extreme penalties, and rejoice in death, — believing that God will raise us up by His Christ, and will make us incorruptible, and undisturbed, and immortal; and we know that the ordinances imposed by reason of the hardness of your people's hearts, contribute nothing to the performance of righteousness and of piety."

CHAP. XLVII. — JUSTIN COMMUNICATES WITH CHRISTIANS WHO OBSERVE THE LAW. NOT A FEW CATHOLICS DO OTHERWISE.

And Trypho again inquired, "But if some one, knowing that this is so, after he recognises that this man is Christ, and has believed in and obeys Him, wishes, however, to observe these [institutions], will he be saved?"

I said, "In my opinion, Trypho, such an one will be saved, if he does not strive in every way to persuade other men, — I mean those Gentiles who have been circumcised from error by Christ, to observe the same things as himself, telling them that they will not be saved unless they do so. This you did yourself at the commencement of the discourse, when you declared that I would not be saved unless I observe these institutions."

Then he replied, "Why then have you said, 'In my opinion, such an one will be saved,' unless there are some [5] who affirm that such will not be saved?"

"There are such people, Trypho," I answered; "and these do not venture to have any intercourse with or to extend hospitality to such persons; but I do not agree with them. But if some, through weak-mindedness, wish to observe such institutions as were given by Moses, from which they expect some virtue, but which we believe were appointed by reason of the hardness of the people's hearts, along with their hope in this Christ, and [wish to perform] the eternal and natural acts of righteousness and piety, yet choose to live with the Christians and the faithful, as I said before, not inducing them either to be circumcised like themselves, or to keep the Sabbath, or to observe any other such ceremonies, then I hold that we ought to join ourselves to such, and associate with them in all things as kinsmen and brethren. But if, Trypho," I continued, "some of your race, who say they believe in this Christ, compel those Gentiles who believe in this Christ to live in all respects according to the law given by Moses, or choose not to associate so intimately with them, I in like manner do not approve of them. But I believe that even those, who have been persuaded by them to observe the legal dispensation along with their confession of God in Christ, shall probably be saved. And I hold, further, that such as have confessed and known this man to be Christ, yet who have gone back from some cause to the legal dispensation, and have denied that this man is Christ, and have repented not before death, shall by no means be saved. Further, I hold that those of the seed of Abraham who live according to the law, and do not believe in this Christ before death, shall likewise not be saved, and especially those who have anathematized and do anathematize this very Christ in the synagogues, and everything by which they might obtain salvation and escape the vengeance of fire.[6] For the goodness and the loving-kindness

---

[1] Literally, "put you out of countenance."
[2] Num. xv. 38.
[3] Deut. vi. 6.
[4] Literally, "importuning."
[5] "Or, Are there not some," etc.
[6] The text seems to be corrupt. Otto reads: "Do anathematize those who put their trust in this very Christ so as to obtain salvation," etc.

of God, and His boundless riches, hold righteous and sinless the man who, as Ezekiel[1] tells, repents of sins; and reckons sinful, unrighteous, and impious the man who falls away from piety and righteousness to unrighteousness and ungodliness. Wherefore also our Lord Jesus Christ said, 'In whatsoever things I shall take you, in these I shall judge you.'"[2]

CHAP. XLVIII. — BEFORE THE DIVINITY OF CHRIST IS PROVED, HE [TRYPHO] DEMANDS THAT IT BE SETTLED THAT HE IS CHRIST.

And Trypho said, "We have heard what you think of these matters. Resume the discourse where you left off, and bring it to an end. For some of it appears to me to be paradoxical, and wholly incapable of proof. For when you say that this Christ existed as God before the ages, then that He submitted to be born and become man, yet that He is not man of man, this [assertion] appears to me to be not merely paradoxical, but also foolish."

And I replied to this, "I know that the statement does appear to be paradoxical, especially to those of your race, who are ever unwilling to understand or to perform the [requirements] of God, but [ready to perform] those of your teachers, as God Himself declares.[3] Now assuredly, Trypho," I continued, "[the proof] that this man[4] is the Christ of God does not fail, though I be unable to prove that He existed formerly as Son of the Maker of all things, being God, and was born a man by the Virgin. But since I have certainly proved that this man is the Christ of God, whoever He be, even if I do not prove that He pre-existed, and submitted to be born a man of like passions with us, having a body, according to the Father's will; in this last matter alone is it just to say that I have erred, and not to deny that He is the Christ, though it should appear that He was born man of men, and [nothing more] is proved [than this], that He has become Christ by election. For there are some, my friends," I said, " of our race,[5] who admit that He is Christ, while holding Him to be man of men; with whom I do not agree, nor would I,[6] even though most of those who have [now] the same opinions as myself should say so; since we were enjoined by Christ Himself to put no faith in human doctrines,[7] but in those proclaimed by the blessed prophets and taught by Himself."

CHAP. XLIX. — TO THOSE WHO OBJECT THAT ELIJAH HAS NOT YET COME, HE REPLIES THAT HE IS THE PRECURSOR OF THE FIRST ADVENT.

And Trypho said, "Those who affirm him to have been a man, and to have been anointed by election, and then to have become Christ, appear to me to speak more plausibly than you who hold those opinions which you express. For we all expect that Christ will be a man [born] of men, and that Elijah when he comes will anoint him. But if this man appear to be Christ, he must certainly be known as man [born] of men; but from the circumstance that Elijah has not yet come, I infer that this man is not He [the Christ]."

Then I inquired of him, "Does not Scripture, in the book of Zechariah,[8] say that Elijah shall come before the great and terrible day of the Lord?"

And he answered, "Certainly."

"If therefore Scripture compels you to admit that two advents of Christ were predicted to take place, — one in which He would appear suffering, and dishonoured, and without comeliness; but the other in which He would come glorious, and Judge of all, as has been made manifest in many of the fore-cited passages, — shall we not suppose that the word of God has proclaimed that Elijah shall be the precursor of the great and terrible day, that is, of His second advent?"

"Certainly," he answered.

"And, accordingly, our Lord in His teaching," I continued, "proclaimed that this very thing would take place, saying that Elijah would also come. And we know that this shall take place when our Lord Jesus Christ shall come in glory from heaven; whose first manifestation the Spirit of God who was in Elijah preceded as herald in [the person of] John, a prophet among your nation; after whom no other prophet appeared among you. He cried, as he sat by the river Jordan: 'I baptize you with water to repentance; but He that is stronger than I shall come, whose shoes I am not worthy to bear: He shall baptize you with the Holy Ghost and with fire: whose fan is in His hand, and He will thoroughly purge His floor, and will gather the wheat into the barn; but the chaff He will burn up with unquenchable fire.'[9] And this very prophet your king Herod had shut up in prison; and when his birth-day was celebrated, and the niece[10] of the same Herod by her dancing had pleased him, he told her to ask whatever she pleased.

---

[1] Ezek. xxxiii. 11-20.
[2] [Comp. St. John xii. 47, 48.] Grabius thinks this taken from the [apocryphal] Gospel according to the Hebrews. It is not in the New or Old Testament. [Query. Is it not, rather, one of the traditional sayings preserved among early Christians?]
[3] Comp. Isa. xxix. 13.
[4] Or, "such a man."
[5] Some read, "of *your* race," referring to the *Ebionites*. Maranus believes the reference is to the Ebionites, and supports in a long note the reading "our," inasmuch as Justin would be more likely to associate these Ebionites with Christians than with Jews, even though they were heretics.
[6] Langus translates: "Nor would, indeed, many who are of the same opinion as myself say so."
[7] [Note this emphatic testimony of primitive faith.]
[8] Mal. iv. 5.
[9] Matt. iii. 11, 12.
[10] Literally, "cousin."

Then the mother of the maiden instigated her to ask the head of John, who was in prison; and having asked it, [Herod] sent and ordered the head of John to be brought in on a charger. Wherefore also our Christ said, [when He was] on earth, to those who were affirming that Elijah must come before Christ: 'Elijah shall come, and restore all things; but I say unto you, that Elijah has already come, and they knew him not, but have done to him whatsoever they chose.'[1] And it is written, 'Then the disciples understood that He spake to them about John the Baptist.'"

And Trypho said, "This statement also seems to me paradoxical; namely, that the prophetic Spirit of God, who was in Elijah, was also in John."

To this I replied, "Do you not think that the same thing happened in the case of Joshua the son of Nave (Nun), who succeeded to the command of the people after Moses, when Moses was commanded to lay his hands on Joshua, and God said to him, 'I will take of the spirit which is in thee, and put it on him?'"[2]

And he said, "Certainly."

"As therefore," I say, "while Moses was still among men, God took of the spirit which was in Moses and put it on Joshua, even so God was able to cause [the spirit] of Elijah to come upon John; in order that, as Christ at His first coming appeared inglorious, even so the first coming of the spirit, which remained always pure in Elijah[3] like that of Christ, might be perceived to be inglorious. For the Lord said He would wage war against Amalek with concealed hand; and you will not deny that Amalek fell. But if it is said that only in the glorious advent of Christ war will be waged with Amalek, how great will the fulfilment[4] of Scripture be which says, 'God will wage war against Amalek with concealed hand!' You can perceive that the concealed power of God was in Christ the crucified, before whom demons, and all the principalities and powers of the earth, tremble."

CHAP. L.—IT IS PROVED FROM ISAIAH THAT JOHN IS THE PRECURSOR OF CHRIST.

And Trypho said, "You seem to me to have come out of a great conflict with many persons about all the points we have been searching into, and therefore quite ready to return answers to all questions put to you. Answer me then, first, how you can show that there is another God besides the Maker of all things; and then you will show, [further], that He submitted to be born of the Virgin."

I replied, "Give me permission first of all to quote certain passages from the prophecy of Isaiah, which refer to the office of forerunner discharged by John the Baptist and prophet before this our Lord Jesus Christ."

"I grant it," said he.

Then I said, "Isaiah thus foretold John's forerunning: 'And Hezekiah said to Isaiah, Good is the word of the Lord which He spake: Let there be peace and righteousness in my days.'[5] And, 'Encourage the people; ye priests, speak to the heart of Jerusalem, and encourage her, because her humiliation is accomplished. Her sin is annulled; for she has received of the Lord's hand double for her sins. A voice of one crying in the wilderness, Prepare the ways of the Lord; make straight the paths of our God. Every valley shall be filled up, and every mountain and hill shall be brought low: and the crooked shall be made straight, and the rough way shall be plain ways; and the glory of the Lord thall be seen, and all flesh shall see the salvation of God: for the Lord hath spoken it. A voice of one saying, Cry; and I said, What shall I cry? All flesh is grass, and all the glory of man as the flower of grass. The grass has withered, and the flower of it has fallen away; but the word of the Lord endureth for ever. Thou that bringest good tidings to Zion, go up to the high mountain; thou that bringest good tidings to Jerusalem, lift up thy voice with strength. Lift ye up, be not afraid; tell the cities of Judah, Behold your God! Behold, the Lord comes with strength, and [His] arm comes with authority. Behold, His reward is with Him, and His work before Him. As a shepherd He will tend His flock, and will gather the lambs with [His] arm, and cheer on her that is with young. Who has measured the water with [his] hand, and the heaven with a span, and all the earth with [his] fist? Who has weighed the mountains, and [put] the valleys into a balance? Who has known the mind of the Lord? And who has been His counsellor, and who shall advise Him? Or with whom did He take counsel, and he instructed Him? Or who showed Him judgment? Or who made Him to know the way of understanding? All the nations are reckoned as a drop of a bucket, and as a turning of a balance, and shall be reckoned as spittle. But Lebanon is not sufficient to burn, nor the beasts sufficient for a burnt-offering; and all the nations are considered nothing, and for nothing.'"[6]

CHAP. LI.—IT IS PROVED THAT THIS PROPHECY HAS BEEN FULFILLED.

And when I ceased, Trypho said, "All the words of the prophecy you repeat, sir, are am-

---

[1] Matt. xvii. 12.
[2] Num. xi. 17, spoken of the seventy elders. Justin confuses what is said here with Num. xxvii 18 and Deut. xxxiv. 9.
[3] The meaning is, that no division of person took place. Elijah remained the same after as before his spirit was shed on John.
[4] Literally, "fruit."
[5] Isa. xxxix. 8.
[6] Isa. xl. 1-17.

biguous, and have no force in proving what you wish to prove." Then I answered, "If the prophets had not ceased, so that there were no more in your nation, Trypho, after this John, it is evident that what I say in reference to Jesus Christ might be regarded perhaps as ambiguous. But if John came first calling on men to repent, and Christ, while [John] still sat by the river Jordan, having come, put an end to his prophesying and baptizing, and preached also Himself, saying that the kingdom of heaven is at hand, and that He must suffer many things from the Scribes and Pharisees, and be crucified, and on the third day rise again, and would appear again in Jerusalem, and would again eat and drink with His disciples; and foretold that in the interval between His [first and second] advent, as I previously said,[1] priests and false prophets would arise in His name, which things do actually appear; then how can they be ambiguous, when you may be persuaded by the facts? Moreover, He referred to the fact that there would be no longer in your nation any prophet, and to the fact that men recognised how that the New Testament, which God formerly announced [His intention of] promulgating, was then present, i.e., Christ Himself; and in the following terms: 'The law and the prophets were until John the Baptist; from that time the kingdom of heaven suffereth violence, and the violent take it by force. And if you can[2] receive it, he is Elijah, who was to come. He that hath ears to hear, let him hear.'[3]

CHAP. LII. — JACOB PREDICTED TWO ADVENTS OF CHRIST.

"And it was prophesied by Jacob the patriarch[4] that there would be two advents of Christ, and that in the first He would suffer, and that after He came there would be neither prophet nor king in your nation (I proceeded), and that the nations who believed in the suffering Christ would look for His future appearance. And for this reason the Holy Spirit had uttered these truths in a parable, and obscurely: for," I added, "it is said, 'Judah, thy brethren have praised thee: thy hands [shall be] on the neck of thine enemies; the sons of thy father shall worship thee. Judah is a lion's whelp; from the germ, my son, thou art sprung up. Reclining, he lay down like a lion, and like [a lion's] whelp: who shall raise him up? A ruler shall not depart from Judah, or a leader from his thighs, until that which is laid up in store for him shall come; and he shall be the desire of nations, binding his foal to the vine, and the foal of his ass to the tendril of the vine. He shall wash his garments in wine, and his vesture in the blood of the grape. His eyes shall be bright with [5] wine, and his teeth white like milk.'[6] Moreover, that in your nation there never failed either prophet or ruler, from the time when they began until the time when this Jesus Christ appeared and suffered, you will not venture shamelessly to assert, nor can you prove it. For though you affirm that Herod, after[7] whose [reign] He suffered, was an Ashkelonite, nevertheless you admit that there was a high priest in your nation; so that you then had one who presented offerings according to the law of Moses, and observed the other legal ceremonies; also [you had] prophets in succession until John, (even then, too, when your nation was carried captive to Babylon, when your land was ravaged by war, and the sacred vessels carried off); there never failed to be a prophet among you, who was lord, and leader, and ruler of your nation. For the Spirit which was in the prophets anointed your kings, and established them. But after the manifestation and death of our Jesus Christ in your nation, there was and is nowhere any prophet: nay, further, you ceased to exist under your own king, your land was laid waste, and forsaken like a lodge in a vineyard; and the statement of Scripture, in the mouth of Jacob, 'And He shall be the desire of nations,' meant symbolically His two advents, and that the nations would believe in Him; which facts you may now at length discern. For those out of all the nations who are pious and righteous through the faith of Christ, look for His future appearance.

CHAP. LIII. — JACOB PREDICTED THAT CHRIST WOULD RIDE ON AN ASS, AND ZECHARIAH CONFIRMS IT.

"And that expression, 'binding his foal to the vine, and the ass's foal to the vine tendril,' was a declaring beforehand both of the works wrought by Him at His first advent, and also of that belief in Him which the nations would repose. For they were like an unharnessed foal, which was not bearing a yoke on its neck, until this Christ came, and sent His disciples to instruct them; and they bore the yoke of His word, and yielded the neck to endure all [hardships], for the sake of the good things promised by Himself, and expected by them. And truly our Lord Jesus Christ, when He intended to go into Jerusalem, requested His disciples to bring Him a certain ass, along with its foal, which was bound in an entrance of a village called Bethphage; and having seated Himself on it, He

---

[1] Chap. xxv.
[2] "Are willing."
[3] Matt. xi. 12–15.
[4] [Gen. xlix. 5, 8, 9, 10, 11, 18, 24. These texts are frequently referred to by Justin.]
[5] Or, "in comparison of."
[6] Gen. xlix. 8–12.
[7] ἀφ' οὗ; many translated "under whom," as if ἐφ' οὗ. This would be erroneous. Conjectured also ἔφυγε for ἔπαθεν.

entered into Jerusalem. And as this was done by Him in the manner in which it was prophesied in precise terms that it would be done by the Christ, and as the fulfilment was recognised, it became a clear proof that He was the Christ. And though all this happened and is proved from Scripture, you are still hard-hearted. Nay, it was prophesied by Zechariah, one of the twelve [prophets], that such would take place, in the following words : ' Rejoice greatly, daughter of Zion ; shout, and declare, daughter of Jerusalem ; behold, thy King shall come to thee, righteous, bringing salvation, meek, and lowly, riding on an ass, and the foal of an ass.'[1] Now, that the Spirit of prophecy, as well as the patriarch Jacob, mentioned both an ass and its foal, which would be used by Him ; and, further, that He, as I previously said, requested His disciples to bring both beasts ; [this fact] was a prediction that you of the synagogue, along with the Gentiles, would believe in Him. For as the unharnessed colt was a symbol of the Gentiles, even so the harnessed ass was a symbol of your nation. For you possess the law which was imposed [upon you] by the prophets. Moreover, the prophet Zechariah foretold that this same Christ would be smitten, and His disciples scattered : which also took place. For after His crucifixion, the disciples that accompanied Him were dispersed, until He rose from the dead, and persuaded them that so it had been prophesied concerning Him, that He would suffer ; and being thus persuaded, they went into all the world, and taught these truths. Hence also we are strong in His faith and doctrine, since we have [this our] persuasion both from the prophets, and from those who throughout the world are seen to be worshippers of God in the name of that crucified One. The following is said, too, by Zechariah : ' O sword, rise up against My Shepherd, and against the man of My people, saith the Lord of hosts. Smite the Shepherd, and His flock shall be scattered.'[2]

CHAP. LIV. — WHAT THE BLOOD OF THE GRAPE SIGNIFIES.

"And that expression which was committed to writing[3] by Moses, and prophesied by the patriarch Jacob, namely, ' He shall wash His garments with wine, and His vesture with the blood of the grape,' signified that He would wash those that believe in Him with His own blood. For the Holy Spirit called those who receive remission of sins through Him, His garments ; amongst whom He is always present in power, but will be manifestly present at His second coming. That the Scripture mentions the blood of the grape has been evidently designed, because Christ derives blood not from the seed of man, but from the power of God. For as God, and not man, has produced the blood of the vine, so also [the Scripture] has predicted that the blood of Christ would be not of the seed of man, but of the power of God. But this prophecy, sirs, which I repeated, proves that Christ is not man of men, begotten in the ordinary course of humanity."

CHAP. LV. — TRYPHO ASKS THAT CHRIST BE PROVED GOD, BUT WITHOUT METAPHOR. JUSTIN PROMISES TO DO SO.

And Trypho answered, "We shall remember this your exposition, if you strengthen [your solution of] this difficulty by other arguments : but now resume the discourse, and show us that the Spirit of prophecy admits another God besides the Maker of all things, taking care not to speak of the sun and moon, which, it is written,[4] God has given to the nations to worship as gods ; and oftentimes the prophets, employing[5] this manner of speech, say that ' thy God is a God of gods, and a Lord of lords,' adding frequently, ' the great and strong and terrible [God].' For such expressions are used, not as if they really were gods, but because the Scripture is teaching us that the true God, who made all things, is Lord alone of those who are reputed gods and lords. And in order that the Holy Spirit may convince [us] of this, He said by the holy David, ' The gods of the nations, reputed gods, are idols of demons, and not gods ; '[6] and He denounces a curse on those who worship them."

And I replied, "I would not bring forward these proofs, Trypho, by which I am aware those who worship these [idols] and such like are condemned, but such [proofs] as no one could find any objection to. They will appear strange to you, although you read them every day ; so that even from this fact we[7] understand that, because of your wickedness, God has withheld from you the ability to discern the wisdom of His Scriptures ; yet [there are] some exceptions, to whom, according to the grace of His long-suffering, as Isaiah said, He has left a seed of[8] salvation, lest your race be utterly destroyed, like Sodom and Gomorrah. Pay attention, therefore, to what I shall record out of the holy Scriptures, which[9] do not need to be expounded, but only listened to.

---

[1] Zech. ix. 9.
[2] Zech. xiii. 7.
[3] Literally, "inquired into."
[4] Deut. iv. 19, an apparent [i.e., evident] misinterpretation of the passage. [But see St. John x. 33-36.]
[5] Or, "misusing."
[6] Ps. xcvi. 5.
[7] Com. reading, "you;" evidently wrong.
[8] Literally, "for."
[9] Two constructions, "which" referring either to Scriptures as whole, or to what he records from them. Last more probable.

CHAP. LVI. — GOD WHO APPEARED TO MOSES IS DISTINGUISHED FROM GOD THE FATHER.

"Moses, then, the blessed and faithful servant of God, declares that He who appeared to Abraham under the oak in Mamre is God, sent with the two angels in His company to judge Sodom by Another who remains ever in the supercelestial places, invisible to all men, holding personal intercourse with none, whom we believe to be Maker and Father of all things; for he speaks thus: 'God appeared to him under the oak in Mamre, as he sat at his tent-door at noontide. And lifting up his eyes, he saw, and behold, three men stood before him; and when he saw them, he ran to meet them from the door of his tent; and he bowed himself toward the ground, and said;'"[1] (and so on;)[2] "'Abraham gat up early in the morning to the place where he stood before the Lord: and he looked toward Sodom and Gomorrah, and toward the adjacent country, and beheld, and, lo, a flame went up from the earth, like the smoke of a furnace.'" And when I had made an end of quoting these words, I asked them if they had understood them.

And they said they had understood them, but that the passages adduced brought forward no proof that there is any other God or Lord, or that the Holy Spirit says so, besides the Maker of all things.

Then I replied, "I shall attempt to persuade you, since you have understood the Scriptures, [of the truth] of what I say, that there is, and that there is said to be, another God and Lord subject to[3] the Maker of all things; who is also called an Angel, because He announces to men whatsoever the Maker of all things — above whom there is no other God — wishes to announce to them." And quoting once more the previous passage, I asked Trypho, "Do you think that God appeared to Abraham under the oak in Mamre, as the Scripture asserts?"

He said, "Assuredly."

"Was He one of those three," I said, "whom Abraham saw, and whom the Holy Spirit of prophecy describes as men?"

He said, "No; but God appeared to him, before the vision of the three. Then those three whom the Scripture calls men, were angels; two of them sent to destroy Sodom, and one to announce the joyful tidings to Sarah, that she would bear a son; for which cause he was sent, and having accomplished his errand, went away."[4]

"How then," said I, "does the one of the three, who was in the tent, and who said, 'I shall return to thee hereafter, and Sarah shall have a son,'[5] appear to have returned when Sarah had begotten a son, and to be there declared, by the prophetic word, God? But that you may clearly discern what I say, listen to the words expressly employed by Moses; they are these: 'And Sarah saw the son of Hagar the Egyptian bond-woman, whom she bore to Abraham, sporting with Isaac her son, and said to Abraham, Cast out this bond-woman and her son; for the son of this bond-woman shall not share the inheritance of my son Isaac. And the matter seemed very grievous in Abraham's sight, because of his son. But God said to Abraham, Let it not be grievous in thy sight because of the son, and because of the bond-woman. In all that Sarah hath said unto thee, hearken to her voice; for in Isaac shall thy seed be called.'[6] Have you perceived, then, that He who said under the oak that He would return, since He knew it would be necessary to advise Abraham to do what Sarah wished him, came back as it is written; and is God, as the words declare, when they so speak: 'God said to Abraham, Let it not be grievous in thy sight because of the son, and because of the bond-woman?'" I inquired. And Trypho said, "Certainly; but you have not proved from this that there is another God besides Him who appeared to Abraham, and who also appeared to the other patriarchs and prophets. You have proved, however, that we were wrong in believing that the three who were in the tent with Abraham were all angels."

I replied again, "If I could not have proved to you from the Scriptures that one of those three is God, and is called Angel,[7] because, as I already said, He brings messages to those to whom God the Maker of all things wishes [messages to be brought], then in regard to Him who appeared to Abraham on earth in human form in like manner as the two angels who came with Him, and who was God even before the creation of the world, it were reasonable for you to entertain the same belief as is entertained by the whole of your nation."

"Assuredly," he said, "for up to this moment this has been our belief."

Then I replied, "Reverting to the Scriptures, I shall endeavour to persuade you, that He who is said to have appeared to Abraham, and to Jacob, and to Moses, and who is called God, is distinct from Him who made all things, — numerically, I mean, not [distinct] in will. For I affirm that He has never at any time done[8] any-

---

[1] Gen. xviii. 1, 2.
[2] Gen. xix. 27, 28; "and so on" inserted probably not by Justin, but by some copyist, as is evident from succeeding words.
[3] Some, "besides;" but probably as above.
[4] Or, "going away, departed."
[5] Gen. xviii. 10.
[6] Gen. xxi. 9-12.
[7] Or, "Messenger." [The "Jehovah-angel" of the Pentateuch, *passim*.] In the various passages in which Justin assigns the reason for Christ being called angel or messenger, Justin uses also the verb ἀγγέλλω, to convey messages, to announce. The similarity between ἄγγελος and ἀγγέλλω cannot be retained in English, and therefore the point of Justin's remarks is lost to the English reader.
[8] Some supply, "or said."

thing which He who made the world — above whom there is no other God — has not wished Him both to do and to engage Himself with."

And Trypho said, "Prove now that this is the case, that we also may agree with you. For we do not understand you to affirm that He has done or said anything contrary to the will of the Maker of all things."

Then I said, "The Scripture just quoted by me will make this plain to you. It is thus: 'The sun was risen on the earth, and Lot entered into Segor (Zoar); and the Lord rained on Sodom sulphur and fire from the Lord out of heaven, and overthrew these cities and all the neighbourhood.'"[1]

Then the fourth of those who had remained with Trypho said, "It[2] must therefore necessarily be said that one of the two angels who went to Sodom, and is named by Moses in the Scripture Lord, is different from Him who also is God, and appeared to Abraham."[3]

"It is not on this ground solely," I said, "that it must be admitted absolutely that some other one is called Lord by the Holy Spirit besides Him who is considered Maker of all things; not solely [for what is said] by Moses, but also [for what is said] by David. For there is written by him: 'The Lord says to my Lord, Sit on My right hand, until I make Thine enemies Thy footstool,'[4] as I have already quoted. And again, in other words: 'Thy throne, O God, is for ever and ever. A sceptre of equity is the sceptre of Thy kingdom: Thou hast loved righteousness and hated iniquity: therefore God, even Thy God, hath anointed Thee with the oil of gladness above Thy fellows.'[5] If, therefore, you assert that the Holy Spirit calls some other one God and Lord, besides the Father of all things and His Christ, answer me; for I undertake to prove to you from Scriptures themselves, that He whom the Scripture calls Lord is not one of the two angels that went to Sodom, but He who was with them, and is called God, that appeared to Abraham."

And Trypho said, "Prove this; for, as you see, the day advances, and we are not prepared for such perilous replies; since never yet have we heard any man investigating, or searching into, or proving these matters; nor would we have tolerated your conversation, had you not referred everything to the Scriptures:[6] for you are very zealous in adducing proofs from them; and you are of opinion that there is no God above the Maker of all things."

Then I replied, "You are aware, then, that the Scripture says, 'And the Lord said to Abraham, Why did Sarah laugh, saying, Shall I truly conceive? for I am old. Is anything impossible with God? At the time appointed shall I return to thee according to the time of life, and Sarah shall have a son.'[7] And after a little interval: 'And the men rose up from thence, and looked towards Sodom and Gomorrah; and Abraham went with them, to bring them on the way. And the Lord said, I will not conceal from Abraham, my servant, what I do.'[8] And again, after a little, it thus says: 'The Lord said, The cry of Sodom and Gomorrah is great,[9] and their sins are very grievous. I will go down now, and see whether they have done altogether according to their cry which has come unto me; and if not, that I may know. And the men turned away thence, and went to Sodom. But Abraham was standing before the Lord; and Abraham drew near, and said, Wilt Thou destroy the righteous with the wicked?'"[10] (and so on,[11] for I do not think fit to write over again the same words, having written them all before, but shall of necessity give those by which I established the proof to Trypho and his companions. Then I proceeded to what follows, in which these words are recorded:) "'And the Lord went His way as soon as He had left communing with Abraham; and [Abraham] went to his place. And there came two angels to Sodom at even. And Lot sat in the gate of Sodom;'[12] and what follows until, 'But the men put forth their hands, and pulled Lot into the house to them, and shut to the door of the house;'[13] and what follows till, 'And the angels laid hold on his hand, and on the hand of his wife, and on the hands of his daughters, the Lord being merciful to him. And it came to pass, when they had brought them forth abroad, that they said, Save, save thy life. Look not behind thee, nor stay in all the neighbourhood; escape to the mountain, lest thou be taken along with [them]. And Lot said to them, I beseech [Thee], O Lord, since Thy servant hath found grace in Thy sight, and Thou hast magnified Thy righteousness, which Thou showest towards me in saving my life; but I cannot escape to the mountain, lest evil overtake me, and I die. Behold, this city is near to flee unto, and it is small: there I shall be safe, since it is small; and my soul shall live. And He said to him, Behold, I have accepted thee [14] also in this mat-

---

[1] Gen. xix. 23.
[2] Or, "We must of necessity think, that besides the one of the two angels who came down to Sodom, and whom the Scripture by Moses calls Lord, God Himself appeared to Abraham."
[3] This passage is rather confused: the translation is necessarily free, but, it is believed, correct. Justin's friend wishes to make out that *two* distinct individuals are called *Lord* or *God* in the narrative.
[4] Ps. cx. 1.
[5] Ps. xlv. 6, 7.
[6] [Note again the fidelity of Justin to this principle, and the fact that in no other way could a Jew be persuaded to listen to a Christian. Acts xvii. 11.]

[7] Gen. xviii. 13, 14.
[8] Gen. xviii. 16, 17.
[9] Literally, "is multiplied."
[10] Gen. xviii. 20–23.
[11] Comp. Note 2, p. 223.
[12] Gen. xviii. 33, xix. 1.
[13] Gen. xix. 10.
[14] Literally, "I have admired thy face."

ter, so as not to destroy the city for which thou hast spoken. Make haste to save thyself there; for I shall not do anything till thou be come thither. Therefore he called the name of the city Segor (Zoar). The sun was risen upon the earth; and Lot entered into Segor (Zoar). And the Lord rained on Sodom and Gomorrah sulphur and fire from the Lord out of heaven; and He overthrew these cities, and all the neighbourhood.'"[1] And after another pause I added: "And now have you not perceived, my friends, that one of the three, who is both God and Lord, and ministers to Him who is in the heavens, is Lord of the two angels? For when [the angels] proceeded to Sodom, He remained behind, and communed with Abraham in the words recorded by Moses; and when He departed after the conversation, Abraham went back to his place. And when he came [to Sodom], the two angels no longer conversed with Lot, but Himself, as the Scripture makes evident; and He is the Lord who received commission from the Lord who [remains] in the heavens, i.e., the Maker of all things, to inflict upon Sodom and Gomorrah the [judgments] which the Scripture describes in these terms: 'The Lord rained down upon Sodom and Gomorrah sulphur and fire from the Lord out of heaven.'"

CHAP. LVII. — THE JEW OBJECTS, WHY IS HE SAID TO HAVE EATEN, IF HE BE GOD? ANSWER OF JUSTIN.

Then Trypho said when I was silent, "That Scripture compels us to admit this, is manifest; but there is a matter about which we are deservedly at a loss — namely, about what was said to the effect that [the Lord] ate what was prepared and placed before him by Abraham; and you would admit this."

I answered, "It is written that they ate; and if we believe[2] that it is said the three ate, and not the two alone — who were really angels, and are nourished in the heavens, as is evident to us, even though they are not nourished by food similar to that which mortals use — (for, concerning the sustenance of manna which supported your fathers in the desert, Scripture speaks thus, that they ate angels' food): [if we believe that three ate], then I would say that the Scripture which affirms they ate bears the same meaning as when we would say about fire that it has devoured all things; yet it is not certainly understood that they ate, masticating with teeth and jaws. So that not even here should we be at a loss about anything, if we are acquainted even slightly with figurative modes of expression, and able to rise above them."

And Trypho said, "It is possible that [the question] about the mode of eating may be thus explained: [the mode, that is to say,] in which it is written, they took and ate what had been prepared by Abraham: so that you may now proceed to explain to us how this God who appeared to Abraham, and is minister to God the Maker of all things, being born of the Virgin, became man, of like passions with all, as you said previously."

Then I replied, "Permit me first, Trypho, to collect some other proofs on this head, so that you, by the large number of them, may be persuaded of [the truth of] it, and thereafter I shall explain what you ask."

And he said, "Do as seems good to you; for I shall be thoroughly pleased."

CHAP. LVIII. — THE SAME IS PROVED FROM THE VISIONS WHICH APPEARED TO JACOB.

Then I continued, "I purpose to quote to you Scriptures, not that I am anxious to make merely an artful display of words; for I possess no such faculty, but God's grace alone has been granted to me to the understanding of His Scriptures, of which grace I exhort all to become partakers freely and bounteously, in order that they may not, through want of it,[3] incur condemnation in the judgment which God the Maker of all things shall hold through my Lord Jesus Christ."

And Trypho said, "What you do is worthy of the worship of God; but you appear to me to feign ignorance when you say that you do not possess a store of artful words."

I again replied, "Be it so, since you think so; yet I am persuaded that I speak the truth.[4] But give me your attention, that I may now rather adduce the remaining proofs."

"Proceed," said he.

And I continued: "It is again written by Moses, my brethren, that He who is called God and appeared to the patriarchs is called both Angel and Lord, in order that from this you may understand Him to be minister to the Father of all things, as you have already admitted, and may remain firm, persuaded by additional arguments. The word of God, therefore, [recorded] by Moses, when referring to Jacob the grandson of Abraham, speaks thus: 'And it came to pass, when the sheep conceived, that I saw them with my eyes in the dream: And, behold, the he-goats and the rams which leaped upon the sheep and she-goats were spotted with white, and speckled and sprinkled with a dun colour. And the Angel of God said to me in the dream, Jacob, Jacob. And I said, What is it, Lord? And He said, Lift up thine eyes, and see that the he-goats and rams leaping on the sheep and she-goats are spotted

---

[1] Gen. xix. 16-25.
[2] Literally, "hear."
[3] Literally, "for this sake." [Note here and elsewhere the primitive rule as to the duty of all men to search the Scriptures.]
[4] Or, "speak otherwise."

with white, speckled, and sprinkled with a dun colour. For I have seen what Laban doeth unto thee. I am the God who appeared to thee in Bethel,[1] where thou anointedst a pillar and vowedst a vow unto Me. Now therefore arise, and get thee out of this land, and depart to the land of thy birth, and I shall be with thee.[2] And again, in other words, speaking of the same Jacob, it thus says: 'And having risen up that night, he took the two wives, and the two women-servants, and his eleven children, and passed over the ford Jabbok; and he took them and went over the brook, and sent over all his belongings. But Jacob was left behind alone, and an Angel[3] wrestled with him until morning. And He saw that He is not prevailing against him, and He touched the broad part of his thigh; and the broad part of Jacob's thigh grew stiff while he wrestled with Him. And He said, Let Me go, for the day breaketh. But he said, I will not let Thee go, except Thou bless me. And He said to him, What is thy name? And he said, Jacob. And He said, Thy name shall be called no more Jacob, but Israel shall be thy name; for thou hast prevailed with God, and with men shalt be powerful. And Jacob asked Him, and said, Tell me Thy name. But he said, Why dost thou ask after My name? And He blessed him there. And Jacob called the name of that place Peniel,[4] for I saw God face to face, and my soul rejoiced.'[5] And again, in other terms, referring to the same Jacob, it says the following: 'And Jacob came to Luz, in the land of Canaan, which is Bethel, he and all the people that were with him. And there he built an altar, and called the name of that place Bethel; for there God appeared to him when he fled from the face of his brother Esau. And Deborah, Rebekah's nurse, died, and was buried beneath Bethel under an oak: and Jacob called the name of it The Oak of Sorrow. And God appeared again to Jacob in Luz, when he came out from Mesopotamia in Syria, and He blessed him. And God said to him, Thy name shall be no more called Jacob, but Israel shall be thy name.'[6] He is called God, and He is and shall be God." And when all had agreed on these grounds, I continued: "Moreover, I consider it necessary to repeat to you the words which narrate how He who is both Angel and God and Lord, and who appeared as a man to Abraham, and who wrestled in human form with Jacob, was seen by him when he fled from his brother Esau. They are as follows: 'And Jacob went out from the well of the oath,[7] and went toward Charran.[8] And he lighted on a spot, and slept there, for the sun was set; and he gathered of the stones of the place, and put them under his head. And he slept in that place; and he dreamed, and, behold, a ladder was set up on the earth, whose top reached to heaven; and the angels of God ascended and descended upon it. And the Lord stood[9] above it, and He said, I am the Lord, the God of Abraham thy father, and of Isaac; be not afraid: the land whereon thou liest, to thee will I give it, and to thy seed; and thy seed shall be as the dust of the earth, and shall be extended to the west, and south, and north, and east: and in thee, and in thy seed, shall all families of the earth be blessed. And, behold, I am with thee, keeping thee in every way wherein thou goest, and will bring thee again into this land; for I will not leave thee, until I have done all that I have spoken to thee of. And Jacob awaked out of his sleep, and said, Surely the Lord is in this place, and I knew it not. And he was afraid, and said, How dreadful is this place! this is none other than the house of God, and this is the gate of heaven. And Jacob rose up in the morning, and took the stone which he had placed under his head, and he set it up for a pillar, and poured oil upon the top of it; and Jacob called the name of the place The House of God, and the name of the city formerly was Ulammaus.'"[10]

CHAP. LIX. — GOD DISTINCT FROM THE FATHER CONVERSED WITH MOSES.

When I had spoken these words, I continued: "Permit me, further, to show you from the book of Exodus how this same One, who is both Angel, and God, and Lord, and man, and who appeared in human form to Abraham and Isaac,[11] appeared in a flame of fire from the bush, and conversed with Moses." And after they said they would listen cheerfully, patiently, and eagerly, I went on: "These words are in the book which bears the title of Exodus: 'And after many days the king of Egypt died, and the children of Israel groaned by reason of the works;'[12] and so on until, 'Go and gather the elders of Israel, and thou shalt say unto them, The Lord God of your fathers, the God of Abraham, the God of Isaac, and the God of Jacob, hath appeared to me, saying, I am surely beholding you, and the things which have befallen you in Egypt.'"[13] In addition to these words, I went on: "Have you perceived, sirs, that this very God whom Moses speaks of as an Angel that talked to him in the flame of fire, declares to

---

[1] Literally, "in the place of God."
[2] Gen. xxxi. 10–13.
[3] Some read, "a man."
[4] Literally, "the face of God."
[5] Gen. xxxii. 22–30.
[6] Gen. xxxv. 6–10.
[7] Or, "Beersheba."
[8] So LXX. and N. T.; Heb. "Haran."
[9] Literally, "was set up."
[10] Gen. xxviii. 10–19. [Οὐλαμλούς. Sept. Luz Eng.]
[11] Some conjecture "Jacob," others insert "Jacob" after "Isaac." [Gen. xxii. The Jehovah-angel was seen no doubt by Isaac, as well as by his father.]
[12] Ex. ii. 23.
[13] Ex. iii. 16.

Moses that He is the God of Abraham, of Isaac, and of Jacob?"

CHAP. LX.— OPINIONS OF THE JEWS WITH REGARD TO HIM WHO APPEARED IN THE BUSH.

Then Trypho said, "We do not perceive this from the passage quoted by you, but [only this], that it was an angel who appeared in the flame of fire, but God who conversed with Moses; so that there were really two persons in company with each other, an angel and God, that appeared in that vision."

I again replied, "Even if this were so, my friends, that an angel and God were together in the vision seen by Moses, yet, as has already been proved to you by the passages previously quoted, it will not be the Creator of all things that is the God that said to Moses that He was the God of Abraham, and the God of Isaac, and the God of Jacob, but it will be He who has been proved to you to have appeared to Abraham, ministering to the will of the Maker of all things, and likewise carrying into execution His counsel in the judgment of Sodom; so that, even though it be as you say, that there were two—an angel and God—he who has but the smallest intelligence will not venture to assert that the Maker and Father of all things, having left all supercelestial matters, was visible on a little portion of the earth."

And Trypho said, "Since it has been previously proved that He who is called God and Lord, and appeared to Abraham, received from the Lord, who is in the heavens, that which He inflicted on the land of Sodom, even although an angel had accompanied the God who appeared to Moses, we shall perceive that the God who communed with Moses from the bush was not the Maker of all things, but He who has been shown to have manifested Himself to Abraham and to Isaac and to Jacob; who also is called and is perceived to be the Angel of God the Maker of all things, because He publishes to men the commands of the Father and Maker of all things."

And I replied, "Now assuredly, Trypho, I shall show that, in the vision of Moses, this same One alone who is called an Angel, and who is God, appeared to and communed with Moses. For the Scripture says thus: 'The Angel of the Lord appeared to him in a flame of fire from the bush; and he sees that the bush burns with fire, but the bush was not consumed. And Moses said, I will turn aside and see this great sight, for the bush is not burnt. And when the Lord saw that he is turning aside to behold, the Lord called to him out of the bush.'[1] In the same manner, therefore, in which the Scripture calls Him who appeared to Jacob in the dream an Angel, then [says] that the same Angel who appeared in the dream spoke to him,[2] saying, 'I am the God that appeared to thee when thou didst flee from the face of Esau thy brother;' and [again] says that, in the judgment which befell Sodom in the days of Abraham, the Lord had inflicted the punishment[3] of the Lord who [dwells] in the heavens;—even so here, the Scripture, in announcing that the Angel of the Lord appeared to Moses, and in afterwards declaring him to be Lord and God, speaks of the same One, whom it declares by the many testimonies already quoted to be minister to God, who is above the world, above whom there is no other [God].

CHAP. LXI— WISDOM IS BEGOTTEN OF THE FATHER, AS FIRE FROM FIRE.

"I shall give you another testimony, my friends," said I, "from the Scriptures, that God begat before all creatures a Beginning,[4] [who was] a certain rational power [proceeding] from Himself, who is called by the Holy Spirit, now the Glory of the Lord, now the Son, again Wisdom, again an Angel, then God, and then Lord and Logos; and on another occasion He calls Himself Captain, when He appeared in human form to Joshua the son of Nave (Nun). For He can be called by all those names, since He ministers to the Father's will, and since He was begotten of the Father by an act of will;[5] just as we see[6] happening among ourselves: for when we give out some word, we beget the word; yet not by abscission, so as to lessen the word[7] [which remains] in us, when we give it out: and just as we see also happening in the case of a fire, which is not lessened when it has kindled [another], but remains the same; and that which has been kindled by it likewise appears to exist by itself, not diminishing that from which it was kindled. The Word of Wisdom, who is Himself this God begotten of the Father of all things, and Word, and Wisdom, and Power, and the Glory of the Begetter, will bear evidence to me, when He speaks by Solomon the following: 'If I shall declare to you what happens daily, I shall call to mind events from everlasting, and review them. The Lord made me the

---

[1] Ex. iii. 2-4.
[2] Gen. xxxv. 7.
[3] Literally, "judgment."
[4] Or, "in the beginning, before all creatures." [Justin's reference to Joshua (i. 13-15) deserves special consideration; for he supposes that the true Joshua (JESUS) was the substance, and the true "captain of salvation," of whom this one was but a shadow (Heb. iv. 8, *margin*), type, and pledge. See cap. lxii.]
[5] The act of will or volition is on the part of the Father.
[6] Or, "Do we not see," etc.
[7] The word λόγος, translated "word," means both the thinking power or reason which produces ideas and the expression of these ideas. And Justin passes here from the one meaning to the other. When we utter a thought, the utterance of it does not diminish the power of thought in us, though in one sense the thought has gone away from us.

beginning of His ways for His works. From everlasting He established me in the beginning, before He had made the earth, and before He had made the deeps, before the springs of the waters had issued forth, before the mountains had been established. Before all the hills He begets me. God made the country, and the desert, and the highest inhabited places under the sky. When He made ready the heavens, I was along with Him, and when He set up His throne on the winds: when He made the high clouds strong, and the springs of the deep safe, when He made the foundations of the earth, I was with Him arranging. I was that in which He rejoiced; daily and at all times I delighted in His countenance, because He delighted in the finishing of the habitable world, and delighted in the sons of men. Now, therefore, O son, hear me. Blessed is the man who shall listen to me, and the mortal who shall keep my ways, watching[1] daily at my doors, observing the posts of my ingoings. For my outgoings are the outgoings of life, and [my] will has been prepared by the Lord. But they who sin against me, trespass against their own souls; and they who hate me love death.'[2]

CHAP. LXII. — THE WORDS "LET US MAKE MAN" AGREE WITH THE TESTIMONY OF PROVERBS.

"And the same sentiment was expressed, my friends, by the word of God [written] by Moses, when it indicated to us, with regard to Him whom it has pointed out,[3] that God speaks in the creation of man with the very same design, in the following words: 'Let Us make man after our image and likeness. And let them have dominion over the fish of the sea, and over the fowl of the heaven, and over the cattle, and over all the earth, and over all the creeping things that creep on the earth. And God created man: after the image of God did He create him; male and female created He them. And God blessed them, and said, Increase and multiply, and fill the earth, and have power over it.[4] And that you may not change the [force of the] words just quoted, and repeat what your teachers assert, — either that God said to Himself, 'Let Us make,' just as we, when about to do something, oftentimes say to ourselves, 'Let us make;' or that God spoke to the elements, to wit, the earth and other similar substances of which we believe man was formed, 'Let Us make,' — I shall quote again the words narrated by Moses himself, from which we can indisputably learn that [God] conversed with some one who was numerically distinct from Himself, and also a rational Being. These are the words: 'And God said, Behold, Adam has become as one of us, to know good and evil.'[5] In saying, therefore, ' as one of us,' [Moses] has declared that [there is a certain] number of persons associated with one another, and that they are at least two. For I would not say that the dogma of that heresy[6] which is said to be among you[7] is true, or that the teachers of it can prove that [God] spoke to angels, or that the human frame was the workmanship of angels. But this Offspring, which was truly brought forth from the Father, was with the Father before all the creatures, and the Father communed with Him; even as the Scripture by Solomon has made clear, that He whom Solomon calls Wisdom, was begotten as a Beginning before all His creatures and as Offspring by God, who has also declared this same thing in the revelation made by Joshua the son of Nave (Nun). Listen, therefore, to the following from the book of Joshua, that what I say may become manifest to you; it is this: 'And it came to pass, when Joshua was near Jericho, he lifted up his eyes, and sees a man standing over against him. And Joshua approached to Him, and said, Art thou for us, or for our adversaries? And He said to him, I am Captain of the Lord's host: now have I come. And Joshua fell on his face on the ground, and said to Him, Lord, what commandest Thou Thy servant? And the Lord's Captain says to Joshua, Loose the shoes off thy feet; for the place whereon thou standest is holy ground. And Jericho was shut up and fortified, and no one went out of it. And the Lord said to Joshua, Behold, I give into thine hand Jericho, and its king, [and] its mighty men.'"[8]

CHAP. LXIII. — IT IS PROVED THAT THIS GOD WAS INCARNATE.

And Trypho said, "This point has been proved to me forcibly, and by many arguments, my friend. It remains, then, to prove that He submitted to become man by the Virgin, according to the will of His Father; and to be crucified, and to die. Prove also clearly, that after this He rose again and ascended to heaven."

I answered, "This, too, has been already de-

---

[1] The MSS. of Justin read "sleeping," but this is regarded as the mistake of some careless transcriber.
[2] Prov. viii. 21 ff.
[3] Justin, since he is of opinion that the Word is the beginning of the universe, thinks that by these words, "in the beginning," Moses indicated the Word, like many other writers. Hence also he says in Ap. i. 23, that Moses declares the Word "to be begotten first by God." If this explanation does not satisfy, read, "with regard to Him whom I have pointed out" (Maranus).
[4] Gen. i. 26, 28.
[5] Gen. iii. 22.
[6] Heresy or sect.
[7] Or, "among us." Maranus pronounces against this latter reading for the following reasons: (1.) The Jews had their own heresies which supplied many things to the Christian heresies, especially to Menander and Saturninus. (2.) The sect which Justin here refutes was of opinion that God spoke to angels. But those angels, as Menander and Saturninus invented, "exhorted themselves, saying, Let us make," etc. (3.) The expression διδάσκαλοι suits the rabbins well. So Justin frequently calls them. (4.) Those teachers seem for no other cause to have put the words in the angels' mouths than to eradicate the testimony by which they proved divine persons.
[8] Josh. v. 13 ad fin., and vi. 1, 2.

monstrated by me in the previously quoted words of the prophecies, my friends; which, by recalling and expounding for your sakes, I shall endeavour to lead you to agree with me also about this matter. The passage, then, which Isaiah records, 'Who shall declare His generation? for His life is taken away from the earth,[1]—does it not appear to you to refer to One who, not having descent from men, was said to be delivered over to death by God for the transgressions of the people?—of whose blood, Moses (as I mentioned before), when speaking in parable, said, that He would wash His garments in the blood of the grape; since His blood did not spring from the seed of man, but from the will of God. And then, what is said by David, 'In the splendours of Thy holiness have I begotten Thee from the womb, before the morning star.[2] The Lord hath sworn, and will not repent, Thou art a priest for ever, after the order of Melchizedek,'[3]—does this not declare to you[4] that [He was] from of old,[5] and that the God and Father of all things intended Him to be begotten by a human womb? And speaking in other words, which also have been already quoted, [he says]: 'Thy throne, O God, is for ever and ever: a sceptre of rectitude is the sceptre of Thy kingdom. Thou hast loved righteousness, and hast hated iniquity: therefore God, even thy God, hath anointed Thee with the oil of gladness above Thy fellows. [He hath anointed Thee] with myrrh, and oil, and cassia from Thy garments, from the ivory palaces, whereby they made Thee glad. Kings' daughters are in Thy honour. The queen stood at Thy right hand, clad in garments embroidered with gold.[6] Hearken, O daughter, and behold, and incline thine ear, and forget thy people and the house of thy father; and the King shall desire thy beauty: because he is thy Lord, and thou shalt worship Him.'[7] Therefore these words testify explicitly that He is witnessed to by Him who established these things,[8] as deserving to be worshipped, as God and as Christ. Moreover, that the word of God speaks to those who believe in Him as being one soul, and one synagogue, and one church, as to a daughter; that it thus addresses the church which has sprung from His name and partakes of His name (for we are all called Christians), is distinctly proclaimed in like manner in the following words, which teach us also to forget [our] old ancestral customs, when they speak thus:[9] 'Hearken, O daughter, and behold, and incline thine ear; forget thy people and the house of thy father, and the King shall desire thy beauty: because He is thy Lord, and thou shalt worship Him.'"

CHAP. LXIV.—JUSTIN ADDUCES OTHER PROOFS TO THE JEW, WHO DENIES THAT HE NEEDS THIS CHRIST.

Here Trypho said, "Let Him be recognised as Lord and Christ and God, as the Scriptures declare, by you of the Gentiles, who have from His name been all called Christians; but we who are servants of God that made this same [Christ], do not require to confess or worship Him."

To this I replied, "If I were to be quarrelsome and light-minded like you, Trypho, I would no longer continue to converse with you, since you are prepared not to understand what has been said, but only to return some captious answer;[10] but now, since I fear the judgment of God, I do not state an untimely opinion concerning any one of your nation, as to whether or not some of them may be saved by the grace of the Lord of Sabaoth. Therefore, although you act wrongfully, I shall continue to reply to any proposition you shall bring forward, and to any contradiction which you make; and, in fact, I do the very same to all men of every nation, who wish to examine along with me, or make inquiry at me, regarding this subject. Accordingly, if you had bestowed attention on the Scriptures previously quoted by me, you would already have understood, that those who are saved of your own nation are saved through this [11] [man], and partake of His lot; and you would not certainly have asked me about this matter. I shall again repeat the words of David previously quoted by me, and beg of you to comprehend them, and not to act wrongfully, and stir each other up to give merely some contradiction. The words which David speaks, then, are these: 'The Lord has reigned; let the nations be angry: [it is] He who sits upon the cherubim; let the earth be shaken. The Lord is great in Zion; and He is high above all the nations. Let them confess Thy great name, for it is fearful and holy; and the honour of the king loves judgment. Thou hast prepared equity; judgment and righteousness hast Thou performed in Jacob. Exalt the Lord our God, and worship the footstool of His feet; for He is holy. Moses and Aaron among His priests, and Samuel among them that call upon His name; they called on the Lord, and He heard them. In the pillar of the cloud He spake to them; for they kept His testimonies and His commandments which He gave them.'[12] And

---

[1] Isa. liii. 8.
[2] Note this beautiful rendering, Ps. cx. 3.
[3] Ps. cx. 4.
[4] Or, "to us."
[5] ἄνωθεν; in Lat. vers. *antiquitus*, which Maranus prefers.
[6] Literally, "garments of gold, variegated."
[7] Ps. xlv. 6-11.
[8] The incarnation, etc.
[9] "Being so," literally.

[10] Literally, "but only sharpen yourselves to say something."
[11] [Or, "this one."]
[12] Ps. xcix. 1-7.

from the other words of David, also previously quoted, which you foolishly affirm refer to Solomon, [because] inscribed for Solomon, it can be proved that they do not refer to Solomon, and that this [Christ] existed before the sun, and that those of your nation who are saved shall be saved through Him. [The words] are these: 'O God, give Thy judgment to the king, and Thy righteousness unto the king's son. He shall judge[1] Thy people with righteousness, and Thy poor with judgment. The mountains shall take up peace to the people, and the little hills righteousness. He shall judge the poor of the people, and shall save the children of the needy, and shall abase the slanderer: and He shall co-endure with the sun, and before the moon unto all generations;' and so on until, 'His name endureth before the sun, and all tribes of the earth shall be blessed in Him. All nations shall call Him blessed. Blessed be the Lord, the God of Israel, who only doeth wondrous things: and blessed be His glorious name for ever and ever: and the whole earth shall be filled with His glory. Amen, Amen.'[2] And you remember from other words also spoken by David, and which I have mentioned before, how it is declared that He would come forth from the highest heavens, and again return to the same places, in order that you may recognise Him as God coming forth from above, and man living among men; and [how it is declared] that He will again appear, and they who pierced Him shall see Him, and shall bewail Him. [The words] are these: 'The heavens declare the glory of God, and the firmament showeth His handiwork. Day unto day uttereth speech, and night unto night showeth knowledge. They are not speeches or words whose voices are heard. Their sound has gone out through all the earth, and their words to the ends of the world. In the sun has he set his habitation; and he, like a bridegroom going forth from his chamber, will rejoice as a giant to run his race: from the highest heaven is his going forth, and he returns to the highest heaven, and there is not one who shall be hidden from his heat.'"[3]

CHAP. LXV.—THE JEW OBJECTS THAT GOD DOES NOT GIVE HIS GLORY TO ANOTHER. JUSTIN EXPLAINS THE PASSAGE.

And Trypho said, "Being shaken[4] by so many Scriptures, I know not what to say about the Scripture which Isaiah writes, in which God says that He gives not His glory to another, speaking thus: 'I am the Lord God; this is my name; my glory will I not give to another, nor my virtues.'"[5]

And I answered, "If you spoke these words, Trypho, and then kept silence in simplicity and with no ill intent, neither repeating what goes before nor adding what comes after, you must be forgiven; but if [you have done so] because you imagined that you could throw doubt on the passage, in order that I might say the Scriptures contradicted each other, you have erred. But I shall not venture to suppose or to say such a thing; and if a Scripture which appears to be of such a kind be brought forward, and if there be a pretext [for saying] that it is contrary [to some other], since I am entirely convinced that no Scripture contradicts another, I shall admit rather that I do not understand what is recorded, and shall strive to persuade those who imagine that the Scriptures are contradictory, to be rather of the same opinion as myself. With what intent, then, you have brought forward the difficulty, God knows. But I shall remind you of what the passage says, in order that you may recognise even from this very [place] that God gives glory to His Christ alone. And I shall take up some short passages, sirs, those which are in connection with what has been said by Trypho, and those which are also joined on in consecutive order. For I will not repeat those of another section, but those which are joined together in one. Do you also give me your attention. [The words] are these: 'Thus saith the Lord, the God that created the heavens, and made[6] them fast, that established the earth, and that which is in it; and gave breath to the people upon it, and spirit to them who walk therein: I the Lord God have called Thee in righteousness, and will hold Thine hand, and will strengthen Thee; and I have given Thee for a covenant of the people, for a light of the Gentiles, to open the eyes of the blind, to bring out them that are bound from the chains, and those who sit in darkness from the prison-house. I am the Lord God; this is my name: my glory will I not give to another, nor my virtues to graven images. Behold, the former things are come to pass; new things which I announce, and before they are announced they are made manifest to you. Sing unto the Lord a new song: His sovereignty [is] from the end of the earth. [Sing], ye who descend into the sea, and continually sail[7] [on it]; ye islands, and inhabitants thereof. Rejoice, O wilderness, and the villages thereof, and the houses; and the inhabitants of Cedar shall rejoice, and the inhabitants of the rock shall cry aloud from the top of the mountains: they shall give glory to God; they shall publish His virtues among the islands. The Lord God of hosts shall go forth, He shall destroy war utterly, He shall stir up

---

[1] Or, "to judge," as in chap. xxxiv.
[2] Ps. lxxii. 1, etc.
[3] Ps. xix. 1–6.
[4] Literally, "importuned."
[5] Isa. xlii. 8.

[6] Literally, "fixed."
[7] Or, "ye islands which sail on it;" or without "continually."

zeal, and He shall cry aloud to the enemies with strength.'"[1] And when I repeated this, I said to them, "Have you perceived, my friends, that God says He will give Him whom He has established as a light of the Gentiles, glory, and to no other; and not, as Trypho said, that God was retaining the glory to Himself?"

Then Trypho answered, "We have perceived this also; pass on therefore to the remainder of the discourse."

CHAP. LXVI. — HE PROVES FROM ISAIAH THAT GOD WAS BORN FROM A VIRGIN.

And I, resuming the discourse where I had left off[2] at a previous stage, when proving that He was born of a virgin, and that His birth of a virgin had been predicted by Isaiah, quoted again the same prophecy. It is as follows: 'And the Lord spoke again to Ahaz, saying, Ask for thyself a sign from the Lord thy God, in the depth or in the height. And Ahaz said, I will not ask, neither will I tempt the Lord. And Isaiah said, Hear then, O house of David; Is it no small thing for you to contend with men? And how do you contend with the Lord? Therefore the Lord Himself will give you a sign; Behold, the virgin shall conceive, and shall bear a son, and they shall call his name Immanuel. Butter and honey shall he eat; before he knows or prefers the evil he will choose out the good. For before the child knows ill or good, he rejects evil by choosing out the good. For before the child knows how to call father or mother, he shall receive the power of Damascus, and the spoil of Samaria, in presence of the king of Assyria. And the land shall be forsaken, which[3] thou shalt with difficulty endure in consequence of the presence of its two kings. But God shall bring on thee, and on thy people, and on the house of thy father, days which have not yet come upon thee since the day in which Ephraim took away from Judah the king of Assyria.'"[4] And I continued: "Now it is evident to all, that in the race of Abraham according to the flesh no one has been born of a virgin, or is said to have been born [of a virgin], save this our Christ."

CHAP. LXVII. — TRYPHO COMPARES JESUS WITH PERSEUS; AND WOULD PREFER [TO SAY] THAT HE WAS ELECTED [TO BE CHRIST] ON ACCOUNT OF OBSERVANCE OF THE LAW. JUSTIN SPEAKS OF THE LAW AS FORMERLY.

And Trypho answered, "The Scripture has not, 'Behold, the virgin shall conceive, and bear a son,' but, 'Behold, the young woman shall conceive, and bear a son,' and so on, as you quoted. But the whole prophecy refers to Hezekiah, and it is proved that it was fulfilled in him, according to the terms of this prophecy. Moreover, in the fables of those who are called Greeks, it is written that Perseus was begotten of Danae, who was a virgin; he who was called among them Zeus having descended on her in the form of a golden shower. And you ought to feel ashamed when you make assertions similar to theirs, and rather [should] say that this Jesus was born man of men. And if you prove from the Scriptures that He is the Christ, and that on account of having led a life conformed to the law, and perfect, He deserved the honour of being elected to be Christ, [it is well]; but do not venture to tell monstrous phenomena, lest you be convicted of talking foolishly like the Greeks."

Then I said to this, "Trypho, I wish to persuade you, and all men in short, of this, that even though you talk worse things in ridicule and in jest, you will not move me from my fixed design; but I shall always adduce from the words which you think can be brought forward [by you] as proof [of your own views], the demonstration of what I have stated along with the testimony of the Scriptures. You are not, however, acting fairly or truthfully in attempting to undo those things in which there has been constantly agreement between us; namely, that certain commands were instituted by Moses on account of the hardness of your people's hearts. For you said that, by reason of His living conformably to law, He was elected and became Christ, if indeed He were proved to be so."

And Trypho said, "You admitted[5] to us that He was both circumcised, and observed the other legal ceremonies ordained by Moses."

And I replied, "I have admitted it, and do admit it: yet I have admitted that He endured all these not as if He were justified by them, but completing the dispensation which His Father, the Maker of all things, and Lord and God, wished Him [to complete]. For I admit that He endured crucifixion and death, and the incarnation, and the suffering of as many afflictions as your nation put upon Him. But since again you dissent from that to which you but lately assented, Trypho, answer me: Are those righteous patriarchs who lived before Moses, who observed none of those [ordinances] which, the Scripture shows, received the commencement of [their] institution from Moses, saved, [and have they attained to] the inheritance of the blessed?"

---

[1] Isa. xlii. 5-13.
[2] Chap. xliii.
[3] ἦν, which is in chap. xliii., is here omitted, but ought to be inserted without doubt.
[4] Isa. vii. 10-17, with Isa. viii. 4 inserted between vers. 16 and 17.

[5] We have not seen that Justin admitted this; but it is not to be supposed that the passage where he did admit it has been lost, as Perionius suspected; for sometimes Justin refers to passages at other places, which he did not relate in their own place. — MARANUS.

And Trypho said, "The Scriptures compel me to admit it."

"Likewise I again ask you," said I, "did God enjoin your fathers to present the offerings and sacrifices because He had need of them, or because of the hardness of their hearts and tendency to idolatry?"

"The latter," said he, "the Scriptures in like manner compel us to admit."

"Likewise," said I, "did not the Scriptures predict that God promised to dispense a new covenant besides that which [was dispensed] in the mountain Horeb?"

This, too, he replied, had been predicted.

Then I said again, "Was not the old covenant laid on your fathers with fear and trembling, so that they could not give ear to God?"

He admitted it.

"What then?" said I: "God promised that there would be another covenant, not like that old one, and said that it would be laid on them without fear, and trembling, and lightnings, and that it would be such as to show what kind of commands and deeds God knows to be eternal and suited to every nation, and what commandments He has given, suiting them to the hardness of your people's hearts, as He exclaims also by the prophets."

"To this also," said he, "those who are lovers of truth and not lovers of strife must assuredly assent."

Then I replied, "I know not how you speak of persons very fond of strife, [since] you yourself oftentimes were plainly acting in this very manner, frequently contradicting what you had agreed to."

CHAP. LXVIII. — HE COMPLAINS OF THE OBSTINACY OF TRYPHO; HE ANSWERS HIS OBJECTION; HE CONVICTS THE JEWS OF BAD FAITH.

And Trypho said, "You endeavour to prove an incredible and well-nigh impossible thing; [namely], that God endured to be born and become man."

"If I undertook," said I, "to prove this by doctrines or arguments of man, you should not bear with me. But if I quote frequently Scriptures, and so many of them, referring to this point, and ask you to comprehend them, you are hard-hearted in the recognition of the mind and will of God. But if you wish to remain for ever so, I would not be injured at all; and for ever retaining the same [opinions] which I had before I met with you, I shall leave you."

And Trypho said, "Look, my friend, you made yourself master of these [truths] with much labour and toil.[1] And we accordingly must diligently scrutinize all that we meet with, in order to give our assent to those things which the Scriptures compel us [to believe]."

Then I said to this, "I do not ask you not to strive earnestly by all means, in making an investigation of the matters inquired into; but [I ask you], when you have nothing to say, not to contradict those things which you said you had admitted."

And Trypho said, "So we shall endeavour to do."

I continued again: "In addition to the questions I have just now put to you, I wish to put more: for by means of these questions I shall strive to bring the discourse to a speedy termination."

And Trypho said, "Ask the questions."

Then I said, "Do you think that any other one is said to be worthy of worship and called Lord and God in the Scriptures, except the Maker of all, and Christ, who by so many Scriptures was proved to you to have become man?"

And Trypho replied, "How can we admit this, when we have instituted so great an inquiry as to whether there is any other than the Father alone?"

Then I again said, "I must ask you this also, that I may know whether or not you are of a different opinion from that which you admitted some time ago."[2]

He replied, "It is not, sir."

Then again I, "Since you certainly admit these things, and since Scripture says, 'Who shall declare His generation?' ought you not now to suppose that He is not the seed of a human race?"

And Trypho said, "How then does the Word say to David, that out of his loins God shall take to Himself a Son, and shall establish His kingdom, and shall set Him on the throne of His glory?"

And I said, "Trypho, if the prophecy which Isaiah uttered, 'Behold, the virgin shall conceive,' is said not to the house of David, but to another house of the twelve tribes, perhaps the matter would have some difficulty; but since this prophecy refers to the house of David, Isaiah has explained how that which was spoken by God to David in mystery would take place. But perhaps you are not aware of this, my friends, that there were many sayings written obscurely, or parabolically, or mysteriously, and symbolical actions, which the prophets who lived after the persons who said or did them expounded."

"Assuredly," said Trypho.

"If, therefore, I shall show that this prophecy of Isaiah refers to our Christ, and not to Hezekiah, as you say, shall I not in this matter, too, compel you not to believe your teachers, who venture to assert that the explanation which your

---

[1] [Note the courteous admission of Trypho, and the consent of both parties to the duty of searching the Scriptures.]

[2] τέως: Vulg. παρὰ Θεῷ, *vitiose*. — OTTO.

seventy elders that were with Ptolemy the king of the Egyptians gave, is untrue in certain respects? For some statements in the Scriptures, which appear explicitly to convict them of a foolish and vain opinion, these they venture to assert have not been so written. But other statements, which they fancy they can distort and harmonize with human actions,[1] these, they say, refer not to this Jesus Christ of ours, but to him of whom they are pleased to explain them. Thus, for instance, they have taught you that this Scripture which we are now discussing refers to Hezekiah, in which, as I promised, I shall show they are wrong. And since they are compelled, they agree that some Scriptures which we mention to them, and which expressly prove that Christ was to suffer, to be worshipped, and [to be called] God, and which I have already recited to you, do refer indeed to Christ, but they venture to assert that this man is not Christ. But they admit that He will come to suffer, and to reign, and to be worshipped, and to be God;[2] and this opinion I shall in like manner show to be ridiculous and silly. But since I am pressed to answer first to what was said by you in jest, I shall make answer to it, and shall afterwards give replies to what follows.

CHAP. LXIX. — THE DEVIL, SINCE HE EMULATES THE TRUTH, HAS INVENTED FABLES ABOUT BACCHUS, HERCULES, AND ÆSCULAPIUS.

"Be well assured, then, Trypho," I continued, "that I am established in the knowledge of and faith in the Scriptures by those counterfeits which he who is called the devil is said to have performed among the Greeks; just as some were wrought by the Magi in Egypt, and others by the false prophets in Elijah's days. For when they tell that Bacchus, son of Jupiter, was begotten by [Jupiter's] intercourse with Semele, and that he was the discoverer of the vine; and when they relate, that being torn in pieces, and having died, he rose again, and ascended to heaven; and when they introduce wine[3] into his mysteries, do I not perceive that [the devil] has imitated the prophecy announced by the patriarch Jacob, and recorded by Moses? And when they tell that Hercules was strong, and travelled over all the world, and was begotten by Jove of Alcmene, and ascended to heaven when he died, do I not perceive that the Scripture which speaks of Christ, 'strong as a giant to run his race,'[4] has been in like manner imitated? And when he [the devil] brings forward Æsculapius as the raiser of the dead and healer of all diseases, may I not say that in this matter likewise he has imitated the prophecies about Christ? But since I have not quoted to you such Scripture as tells that Christ will do these things, I must necessarily remind you of one such: from which you can understand, how that to those destitute of a knowledge of God, I mean the Gentiles, who, 'having eyes, saw not, and having a heart, understood not,' worshipping the images of wood, [how even to them] Scripture prophesied that they would renounce these [vanities], and hope in this Christ. It is thus written: 'Rejoice, thirsty wilderness: let the wilderness be glad, and blossom as the lily: the deserts of the Jordan shall both blossom and be glad: and the glory of Lebanon was given to it, and the honour of Carmel. And my people shall see the exaltation of the Lord, and the glory of God. Be strong, ye careless hands and enfeebled knees. Be comforted, ye faint in soul: be strong, fear not. Behold, our God gives, and will give, retributive judgment. He shall come and save us. Then the eyes of the blind shall be opened, and the ears of the deaf shall hear. Then the lame shall leap as an hart, and the tongue of the stammerers shall be distinct: for water has broken forth in the wilderness, and a valley in the thirsty land; and the parched ground shall become pools, and a spring of water shall [rise up] in the thirsty land.'[5] The spring of living water which gushed forth from God in the land destitute of the knowledge of God, namely the land of the Gentiles, was this Christ, who also appeared in your nation, and healed those who were maimed, and deaf, and lame in body from their birth, causing them to leap, to hear, and to see, by His word. And having raised the dead, and causing them to live, by His deeds He compelled the men who lived at that time to recognise Him. But though they saw such works, they asserted it was magical art. For they dared to call Him a magician, and a deceiver of the people. Yet He wrought such works, and persuaded those who were [destined to] believe on Him; for even if any one be labouring under a defect of body, yet be an observer of the doctrines delivered by Him, He shall raise him up at His second advent perfectly sound, after He has made him immortal, and incorruptible, and free from grief.

CHAP. LXX. — SO ALSO THE MYSTERIES OF MITHRAS ARE DISTORTED FROM THE PROPHECIES OF DANIEL AND ISAIAH.

"And when those who record the mysteries of Mithras say that he was begotten of a rock, and call the place where those who believe in him are initiated a cave, do I not perceive here that the utterance of Daniel, that a stone with-

---

[1] The text is corrupt, and various emendations have been proposed.
[2] Or, "and to be worshipped as God."
[3] Or, "an ass." The ass was sacred to Bacchus; and many fluctuate between οἶνον and ὄνον.
[4] Ps. xix. 5.
[5] Isa. xxxv. 1-7.

out hands was cut out of a great mountain, has been imitated by them, and that they have attempted likewise to imitate the whole of Isaiah's[1] words?[2] For they[3] contrived that the words of righteousness be quoted also by them.[4] But I must repeat to you the words of Isaiah referred to, in order that from them you may know that these things are so. They are these: 'Hear, ye that are far off, what I have done; those that are near shall know my might. The sinners in Zion are removed; trembling shall seize the impious. Who shall announce to you the everlasting place? The man who walks in righteousness, speaks in the right way, hates sin and unrighteousness, and keeps his hands pure from bribes, stops the ears from hearing the unjust judgment of blood, closes the eyes from seeing unrighteousness: he shall dwell in the lofty cave of the strong rock. Bread shall be given to him, and his water [shall be] sure. Ye shall see the King with glory, and your eyes shall look far off. Your soul shall pursue diligently the fear of the Lord. Where is the scribe? where are the counsellors? where is he that numbers those who are nourished,— the small and great people? with whom they did not take counsel, nor knew the depth of the voices, so that they heard not. The people who are become depreciated, and there is no understanding in him who hears.'[5] Now it is evident, that in this prophecy [allusion is made] to the bread which our Christ gave us to eat,[6] in remembrance of His being made flesh for the sake of His believers, for whom also He suffered; and to the cup which He gave us to drink,[6] in remembrance of His own blood, with giving of thanks. And this prophecy proves that we shall behold this very King with glory; and the very terms of the prophecy declare loudly, that the people foreknown to believe in Him were foreknown to pursue diligently the fear of the Lord. Moreover, these Scriptures are equally explicit in saying, that those who are reputed to know the writings of the Scriptures, and who hear the prophecies, have no understanding. And when I hear, Trypho," said I, "that Perseus was begotten of a virgin, I understand that the deceiving serpent counterfeited also this.

CHAP. LXXI.—THE JEWS REJECT THE INTERPRETATION OF THE LXX., FROM WHICH, MOREOVER, THEY HAVE TAKEN AWAY SOME PASSAGES.

"But I am far from putting reliance in your teachers, who refuse to admit that the interpretation made by the seventy elders who were with Ptolemy [king] of the Egyptians is a correct one; and they attempt to frame another. And I wish you to observe, that they have altogether taken away many Scriptures from the translations effected by those seventy elders who were with Ptolemy, and by which this very man who was crucified is proved to have been set forth expressly as God, and man, and as being crucified, and as dying; but since I am aware that this is denied by all of your nation, I do not address myself to these points, but I proceed[7] to carry on my discussions by means of those passages which are still admitted by you. For you assent to those which I have brought before your attention, except that you contradict the statement, 'Behold, the virgin shall conceive,' and say it ought to be read, 'Behold, the young woman shall conceive.' And I promised to prove that the prophecy referred, not, as you were taught, to Hezekiah, but to this Christ of mine: and now I shall go to the proof."

Here Trypho remarked, "We ask you first of all to tell us some of the Scriptures which you allege have been completely cancelled."

CHAP. LXXII.—PASSAGES HAVE BEEN REMOVED BY THE JEWS FROM ESDRAS AND JEREMIAH.

And I said, "I shall do as you please. From the statements, then, which Esdras made in reference to the law of the passover, they have taken away the following: 'And Esdras said to the people, This passover is our Saviour and our refuge. And if you have understood, and your heart has taken it in, that we shall humble Him on a standard, and[8] thereafter hope in Him, then this place shall not be forsaken for ever, says the God of hosts. But if you will not believe Him, and will not listen to His declaration, you shall be a laughing-stock to the nations.'[9] And from the sayings of Jeremiah they have cut out the following: 'I [was] like a lamb that is brought to the slaughter: they devised a device against me, saying, Come, let us lay on wood on His bread, and let us blot Him out from the land of the living; and His name shall no more be remembered.'[10] And since this passage from the sayings of Jeremiah is still written in some copies

---

[1] The text here has ταῦτα ποιῆσαι ὁμοίως. Maranus suggests Ἡσαίου for ποιῆσαι; and so we have translated.
[2] Justin says that the priests of Mithras imitated all the words of Isaiah about to be quoted; and to prove it, is content with a single example, namely, the precepts of righteousness, which they were wont to relate to him, as in these words of Isaiah: "He who walks in righteousness," etc. Justin omitted many other passages, as easy and obvious. For since Mithras is the same as fire, it manifestly answers to the fire of which Isaiah speaks. And since Justin reminded them who are initiated, that they are said to be initiated by Mithras himself, it was not necessary to remind them that the words of Isaiah are imitated in this: "You shall see the King with glory." Bread and water are referred to by Isaiah: so also in these mysteries of Mithras, Justin testifies that bread and a cup of water are placed before them (Apol. i.).—MARANUS.
[3] i.e., the devils.
[4] i.e., the priests of Mithras.
[5] Isa. xxxiii. 13–19.
[6] Literally, "to do," ποιεῖν. [The horrible charge of banqueting on blood, etc., constantly repeated against Christians, was probably based on the Eucharist. See Kaye's *Illustrations from Tatian, Athenagorus, and Theoph. Antioch.*, cap. ix. p. 153.]
[7] Or, "profess."
[8] Or, "even if we."
[9] It is not known where this passage comes from.
[10] Jer. xi. 19.

[of the Scriptures] in the synagogues of the Jews (for it is only a short time since they were cut out), and since from these words it is demonstrated that the Jews deliberated about the Christ Himself, to crucify and put Him to death, He Himself is both declared to be led as a sheep to the slaughter, as was predicted by Isaiah, and is here represented as a harmless lamb; but being in a difficulty about them, they give themselves over to blasphemy. And again, from the sayings of the same Jeremiah these have been cut out: 'The Lord God remembered His dead people of Israel who lay in the graves; and He descended to preach to them His own salvation.'[1]

CHAP. LXXIII. — [THE WORDS] "FROM THE WOOD" HAVE BEEN CUT OUT OF PS. XCVI.

"And from the ninety-fifth (ninety-sixth) Psalm they have taken away this short saying of the words of David: 'From the wood.'[2] For when the passage said, 'Tell ye among the nations, the Lord hath reigned from the wood,' they have left, 'Tell ye among the nations, the Lord hath reigned.' Now no one of your people has ever been said to have reigned as God and Lord among the nations, with the exception of Him only who was crucified, of whom also the Holy Spirit affirms in the same Psalm that He was raised again, and freed from [the grave], declaring that there is none like Him among the gods of the nations: for they are idols of demons. But I shall repeat the whole Psalm to you, that you may perceive what has been said. It is thus: 'Sing unto the Lord a new song; sing unto the Lord, all the earth. Sing unto the Lord, and bless His name; show forth His salvation from day to day. Declare His glory among the nations, His wonders among all people. For the Lord is great, and greatly to be praised: He is to be feared above all the gods. For all the gods of the nations are demons but the Lord made the heavens. Confession and beauty are in His presence; holiness and magnificence are in His sanctuary. Bring to the Lord, O ye countries of the nations, bring to the Lord glory and honour, bring to the Lord glory in His name. Take sacrifices, and go into His courts; worship the Lord in His holy temple. Let the whole earth be moved before Him: tell ye among the nations, the Lord hath reigned.[3] For He hath established the world, which shall not be moved; He shall judge the nations with equity. Let the heavens rejoice, and the earth be glad; let the sea and its fulness shake. Let the fields and all therein be joyful. Let all the trees of the wood be glad before the Lord: for He comes, for He comes to judge the earth. He shall judge the world with righteousness, and the people with His truth.'"

Here Trypho remarked, "Whether [or not] the rulers of the people have erased any portion of the Scriptures, as you affirm, God knows; but it seems incredible."

"Assuredly," said I, "it does seem incredible. For it is more horrible than the calf which they made, when satisfied with manna on the earth; or than the sacrifice of children to demons; or than the slaying of the prophets. But," said I, "you appear to me not to have heard the Scriptures which I said they had stolen away. For such as have been quoted are more than enough to prove the points in dispute, besides those which are retained by us,[4] and shall yet be brought forward."

CHAP. LXXIV. — THE BEGINNING OF PS. XCVI. IS ATTRIBUTED TO THE FATHER [BY TRYPHO]. BUT [IT REFERS] TO CHRIST BY THESE WORDS: "TELL YE AMONG THE NATIONS THAT THE LORD," ETC.

Then Trypho said, "We know that you quoted these because we asked you. But it does not appear to me that this Psalm which you quoted last from the words of David refers to any other than the Father and Maker of the heavens and earth. You, however, asserted that it referred to Him who suffered, whom you also are eagerly endeavouring to prove to be Christ."

And I answered, "Attend to me, I beseech you, while I speak of the statement which the Holy Spirit gave utterance to in this Psalm; and you shall know that I speak not sinfully, and that we[5] are not really bewitched; for so you shall be enabled of yourselves to understand many other statements made by the Holy Spirit. 'Sing unto the Lord a new song; sing unto the Lord, all the earth: sing unto the Lord, and bless His name; show forth His salvation from day to day, His wonderful works among all people.' He bids the inhabitants of all the earth, who have known the mystery of this salvation, i.e., the suffering of Christ, by which He saved them, sing and give praises to God the Father of all things, and recognise that He is to be praised and feared, and that He is the Maker of heaven and earth, who effected this salvation in behalf of the human race, who also was crucified and was dead, and who was deemed worthy by Him (God) to reign over all the earth. As [is clearly seen[6]] also by the land into which [He said] He would

---

[1] This is wanting in our Scriptures: it is cited by Iren., iii. 20, under the name of Isaiah, and in iv. 22 under that of Jeremiah. — MARANUS.
[2] These words were not taken away by the Jews, but added by some Christian. — OTTO. [A statement not proved.]
[3] It is strange that "from the wood" is not added; but the audacity of the copyists in such matters is well known. — MARANUS.
[4] Many think, "you."
[5] In text, "you." Maranus suggests, as far better, "we."
[6] Something is here wanting; the suggested reading of Maranus has been adopted. [As to omissions between this chapter and the next, critics are not agreed. The Benedictine editors see no proofs of them.]

bring [your fathers]; [for He thus speaks]:¹ 'This people [shall go a whoring after other gods], and shall forsake Me, and shall break my covenant which I made with them in that day; and I will forsake them, and will turn away My face from them; and they shall be devoured,² and many evils and afflictions shall find them out; and they shall say in that day, Because the Lord my God is not amongst us, these misfortunes have found us out. And I shall certainly turn away My face from them in that day, on account of all the evils which they have committed, in that they have turned to other gods.'³

CHAP. LXXV. — IT IS PROVED THAT JESUS WAS THE NAME OF GOD IN THE BOOK OF EXODUS.

"Moreover, in the book of Exodus we have also perceived that the name of God Himself, which, He says, was not revealed to Abraham or to Jacob, was Jesus, and was declared mysteriously through Moses. Thus it is written: 'And the Lord spake to Moses, Say to this people, Behold, I send My angel before thy face, to keep thee in the way, to bring thee into the land which I have prepared for thee. Give heed to Him, and obey Him; do not disobey Him. For He will not draw back from you; for My name is in Him.'⁴ Now understand that He who led your fathers into the land is called by this name Jesus, and first called Auses⁵ (Oshea). For if you shall understand this, you shall likewise perceive that the name of Him who said to Moses, 'for My name is in Him,' was Jesus. For, indeed, He was also called Israel, and Jacob's name was changed to this also. Now Isaiah shows that those prophets who are sent to publish tidings from God are called His angels and apostles. For Isaiah says in a certain place, 'Send me.'⁶ And that the prophet whose name was changed, Jesus [Joshua], was strong and great, is manifest to all. If, then, we know that God revealed Himself in so many forms to Abraham, and to Jacob, and to Moses, how are we at a loss, and do not believe that, according to the will of the Father of all things, it was possible for Him to be born man of the Virgin, especially after we have such⁷ Scriptures, from which it can be plainly perceived that He became so according to the will of the Father?

CHAP. LXXVI. — FROM OTHER PASSAGES THE SAME MAJESTY AND GOVERNMENT OF CHRIST ARE PROVED.

"For when Daniel speaks of 'one like unto the Son of man' who received the everlasting kingdom, does he not hint at this very thing? For he declares that, in saying 'like unto the Son of man,' He appeared, and was man, but not of human seed. And the same thing he proclaimed in mystery when he speaks of this stone which was cut out without hands. For the expression 'it was cut out without hands' signified that it is not a work of man, but [a work] of the will of the Father and God of all things, who brought Him forth. And when Isaiah says, 'Who shall declare His generation?' he meant that His descent could not be declared. Now no one who is a man of men has a descent that cannot be declared. And when Moses says that He will wash His garments in the blood of the grape, does not this signify what I have now often told you is an obscure prediction, namely, that He had blood, but not from men; just as not man, but God, has begotten the blood of the vine? And when Isaiah calls Him the Angel of mighty counsel,⁸ did he not foretell Him to be the Teacher of those truths which He did teach when He came [to earth]? For He alone taught openly those mighty counsels which the Father designed both for all those who have been and shall be well-pleasing to Him, and also for those who have rebelled against His will, whether men or angels, when He said: 'They shall come from the east [and from the west⁹], and shall sit down with Abraham, and Isaac, and Jacob, in the kingdom of heaven: but the children of the kingdom shall be cast out into outer darkness.'¹⁰ And, 'Many shall say to Me in that day, Lord, Lord, have we not eaten, and drunk, and prophesied, and cast out demons in Thy name? And I will say to them, Depart from Me.'¹¹ Again, in other words, by which He shall condemn those who are unworthy of salvation, He said, 'Depart into outer darkness, which the Father has prepared for Satan and his angels.'¹² And again, in other words, He said, 'I give unto you power to tread on serpents, and on scorpions, and on *scolopendras*, and on all the might of the enemy.'¹³ And now we, who believe on our Lord Jesus, who was crucified under Pontius Pilate, when we exorcise all demons and evil spirits, have them subjected to us. For if the prophets declared obscurely that Christ would suffer, and thereafter be Lord of all, yet that [declaration] could not be understood by any man until He Himself persuaded the apostles that such statements were expressly related in the Scriptures. For He exclaimed before His crucifixion: 'The Son of man must suffer many

---

¹ Deut. xxxi. 16-18.
² Literally, "for food."
³ The first conference seems to have ended hereabout. [It occupied two days. But the student must consult the learned note of Kaye (*Justin Martyr*, p. 20. Rivingtons, London. 1853).]
⁴ Ex. xxiii. 20, 21.
⁵ [Num. xiii. 16.]
⁶ Isa. vi. 8.
⁷ Or, "so many."
⁸ [Is. ix. 6, according to LXX.]
⁹ Not in all edd.
¹⁰ Matt. viii. 11.
¹¹ Matt. vii. 22.
¹² Matt. xxv. 41.
¹³ Luke x. 19. ["And on *scolopendras*" (i.e. *centipedes*) not in the original.]

things, and be rejected by the Scribes and Pharisees, and be crucified, and on the third day rise again.'[1] And David predicted that He would be born from the womb before sun and moon,[2] according to the Father's will, and made Him known, being Christ, as God strong and to be worshipped."

CHAP. LXXVII. — HE RETURNS TO EXPLAIN THE PROPHECY OF ISAIAH.

Then Trypho said, "I admit that such and so great arguments are sufficient to persuade one; but I wish [you] to know that I ask you for the proof which you have frequently proposed to give me. Proceed then to make this plain to us, that we may see how you prove that that [passage] refers to this Christ of yours. For we assert that the prophecy relates to Hezekiah." And I replied, "I shall do as you wish. But show me yourselves first of all how it is said of Hezekiah, that before he knew how to call father or mother, he received the power of Damascus and the spoils of Samaria in the presence of the king of Assyria. For it will not be conceded to you, as you wish to explain it, that Hezekiah waged war with the inhabitants of Damascus and Samaria in presence of the king of Assyria. 'For before the child knows how to call father or mother,' the prophetic word said, 'He shall take the power of Damascus and spoils of Samaria in presence of the king of Assyria.' For if the Spirit of prophecy had not made the statement with an addition, 'Before the child knows how to call father or mother, he shall take the power of Damascus and spoils of Samaria,' but had only said, 'And shall bear a son, and he shall take the power of Damascus and spoils of Samaria,' then you might say that God foretold that he would take these things, since He foreknew it. But now the prophecy has stated it with this addition: 'Before the child knows how to call father or mother, he shall take the power of Damascus and spoils of Samaria.' And you cannot prove that such a thing ever happened to any one among the Jews. But we are able to prove that it happened in the case of our Christ. For at the time of His birth, Magi who came from Arabia worshipped Him, coming first to Herod, who then was sovereign in your land, and whom the Scripture calls king of Assyria on account of his ungodly and sinful character. For you know," continued I, "that the Holy Spirit oftentimes announces such events by parables and similitudes; just as He did towards all the people in Jerusalem, frequently saying to them, 'Thy father is an Amorite, and thy mother a Hittite.'[3]

CHAP. LXXVIII. — HE PROVES THAT THIS PROPHECY HARMONIZES WITH CHRIST ALONE, FROM WHAT IS AFTERWARDS WRITTEN.

"Now this king Herod, at the time when the Magi came to him from Arabia, and said they knew from a star which appeared in the heavens that a King had been born in your country, and that they had come to worship Him, learned from the elders of your people that it was thus written regarding Bethlehem in the prophet: 'And thou, Bethlehem, in the land of Judah, art by no means least among the princes of Judah; for out of thee shall go forth the leader who shall feed my people.'[4] Accordingly the Magi from Arabia came to Bethlehem and worshipped the Child, and presented Him with gifts, gold and frankincense, and myrrh; but returned not to Herod, being warned in a revelation after worshipping the Child in Bethlehem. And Joseph, the spouse of Mary, who wished at first to put away his betrothed Mary, supposing her to be pregnant by intercourse with a man, i.e., from fornication, was commanded in a vision not to put away his wife; and the angel who appeared to him told him that what is in her womb is of the Holy Ghost. Then he was afraid, and did not put her away; but on the occasion of the first census which was taken in Judæa, under Cyrenius, he went up from Nazareth, where he lived, to Bethlehem, to which he belonged, to be enrolled; for his family was of the tribe of Judah, which then inhabited that region. Then along with Mary he is ordered to proceed into Egypt, and remain there with the Child until another revelation warn them to return into Judæa. But when the Child was born in Bethlehem, since Joseph could not find a lodging in that village, he took up his quarters in a certain cave near the village; and while they were there Mary brought forth the Christ and placed Him in a manger, and here the Magi who came from Arabia found Him. I have repeated to you," I continued, "what Isaiah foretold about the sign which foreshadowed the cave; but for the sake of those who have come with us to-day, I shall again remind you of the passage." Then I repeated the passage from Isaiah which I have already written, adding that, by means of those words, those who presided over the mysteries of Mithras were stirred up by the devil to say that in a place, called among them a cave, they were initiated by him.[5] "So Herod, when the Magi

---

[1] Luke ix. 22.
[2] Justin puts "sun and moon" instead of "Lucifer." [Ps. cx. 3, Sept, compounded with Prov. viii. 27.] Maranus says, David did predict, not that Christ would be born of Mary before sun and moon, but that it would happen before sun and moon that He would be born of a virgin.
[3] Ezek. xvi. 3.
[4] Mic. v. 2.
[5] Text has, by "them;" but Maranus says the artifice lay in the priest's compelling the initiated to say that Mithras himself was the initiator in the cave.

from Arabia did not return to him, as he had asked them to do, but had departed by another way to their own country, according to the commands laid on them; and when Joseph, with Mary and the Child, had now gone into Egypt, as it was revealed to them to do; as he did not know the Child whom the Magi had gone to worship, ordered simply the whole of the children then in Bethlehem to be massacred. And Jeremiah prophesied that this would happen, speaking by the Holy Ghost thus: 'A voice was heard in Ramah, lamentation and much wailing, Rachel weeping for her children; and she would not be comforted, because they are not.'[1] Therefore, on account of the voice which would be heard from Ramah, i.e., from Arabia (for there is in Arabia at this very time a place called Rama), wailing would come on the place where Rachel the wife of Jacob called Israel, the holy patriarch, has been buried, i.e., on Bethlehem; while the women weep for their own slaughtered children, and have no consolation by reason of what has happened to them. For that expression of Isaiah, 'He shall take the power of Damascus and spoils of Samaria,' foretold that the power of the evil demon that dwelt in Damascus should be overcome by Christ as soon as He was born; and this is proved to have happened. For the Magi, who were held in bondage[2] for the commission of all evil deeds through the power of that demon, by coming to worship Christ, shows that they have revolted from that dominion which held them captive; and this [dominion] the Scripture has showed us to reside in Damascus. Moreover, that sinful and unjust power is termed well in parable, Samaria.[3] And none of you can deny that Damascus was, and is, in the region of Arabia, although now it belongs to what is called Syrophœnicia. Hence it would be becoming for you, sirs, to learn what you have not perceived, from those who have received grace from God, namely, from us Christians; and not to strive in every way to maintain your own doctrines, dishonouring those of God. Therefore also this grace has been transferred to us, as Isaiah says, speaking to the following effect: 'This people draws near to Me, they honour Me with their lips, but their heart is far from Me; but in vain they worship Me, teaching the commands and doctrines of men. Therefore, behold, I will proceed[4] to remove this people, and I shall remove them; and I shall take away the wisdom of their wise men, and bring to nothing the understanding of the prudent men.'"[5]

CHAP. LXXIX. — HE PROVES AGAINST TRYPHO THAT THE WICKED ANGELS HAVE REVOLTED FROM GOD.

On this, Trypho, who was somewhat angry, but respected the Scriptures, as was manifest from his countenance, said to me, "The utterances of God are holy, but your expositions are mere contrivances, as is plain from what has been explained by you; nay, even blasphemies, for you assert that angels sinned and revolted from God."

And I, wishing to get him to listen to me, answered in milder tones, thus: "I admire, sir, this piety of yours; and I pray that you may entertain the same disposition towards Him to whom angels are recorded to minister, as Daniel says; for [one] like the Son of man is led to the Ancient of days, and every kingdom is given to Him for ever and ever. But that you may know, sir," continued I, "that it is not our audacity which has induced us to adopt this exposition, which you reprehend, I shall give you evidence from Isaiah himself; for he affirms that evil angels have dwelt and do dwell in Tanis, in Egypt. These are [his] words: 'Woe to the rebellious children! Thus saith the Lord, You have taken counsel, but not through Me; and [made] agreements, but not through My Spirit, to add sins to sins; who have sinned[6] in going down to Egypt (but they have not inquired at Me), that they may be assisted by Pharaoh, and be covered with the shadow of the Egyptians. For the shadow of Pharaoh shall be a disgrace to you, and a reproach to those who trust in the Egyptians; for the princes in Tanis[7] are evil angels. In vain will they labour for a people which will not profit them by assistance, but [will be] for a disgrace and a reproach [to them].'[8] And, further, Zechariah tells, as you yourself have related, that the devil stood on the right hand of Joshua the priest, to resist him; and [the Lord] said, 'The Lord, who has taken[9] Jerusalem, rebuke thee.'[10] And again, it is written in Job,[11] as you said yourself, how that the angels came to stand before the Lord, and the devil came with them. And we have it recorded by Moses in the beginning of Genesis, that the serpent beguiled Eve, and was cursed. And we know that in Egypt there were magicians who emulated[12] the mighty power displayed by God through the faithful servant Moses. And you are aware that David said, 'The gods of the nations are demons.'"[13]

---

[1] Jer. xxxi. 15.
[2] Literally, "spoiled."
[3] Justin thinks the "spoils of Samaria" denote spoils of Satan; Tertull. thinks that they are spoils of Christ.
[4] Literally, "add."
[5] Isa. xxix. 13, 14.

[6] LXX. "who walk," πορευόμενοι for πονηρευόμενοι.
[7] In E. V. "Zoan."
[8] Isa. xxx. 1-5.
[9] ἐκδεξάμενος; in chap. cxv. inf. it is ἐκλεξάμενος.
[10] Zech. iii. 1.
[11] Job i. 6.
[12] Maranus suggests the insertion of ἐποίησαν or ἐπείρασαν before ἐξισοῦσθαι.
[13] Ps. xcvi. 5.

CHAP. LXXX. — THE OPINION OF JUSTIN WITH REGARD TO THE REIGN OF A THOUSAND YEARS. SEVERAL CATHOLICS REJECT IT.

And Trypho to this replied, " I remarked to you sir, that you are very anxious to be safe in all respects, since you cling to the Scriptures. But tell me, do you really admit that this place, Jerusalem, shall be rebuilt; and do you expect your people to be gathered together, and made joyful with Christ and the patriarchs, and the prophets, both the men of our nation, and other proselytes who joined them before your Christ came? or have you given way, and admitted this in order to have the appearance of worsting us in the controversies?"

Then I answered, " I am not so miserable a fellow, Trypho, as to say one thing and think another. I admitted to you formerly,[1] that I and many others are of this opinion, and [believe] that such will take place, as you assuredly are aware;[2] but, on the other hand, I signified to you that many who belong to the pure and pious faith, and are true Christians, think otherwise. Moreover, I pointed out to you that some who are called Christians, but are godless, impious heretics, teach doctrines that are in every way blasphemous, atheistical, and foolish. But that you may know that I do not say this before you alone, I shall draw up a statement, so far as I can, of all the arguments which have passed between us; in which I shall record myself as admitting the very same things which I admit to you.[3] For I choose to follow not men or men's doctrines, but God and the doctrines [delivered] by Him. For if you have fallen in with some who are called Christians, but who do not admit this [truth],[4] and venture to blaspheme the God of Abraham, and the God of Isaac, and the God of Jacob; who say there is no resurrection of the dead, and that their souls, when they die, are taken to heaven; do not imagine that they are Christians, even as one, if he would rightly consider it, would not admit that the Sadducees, or similar sects of Genistæ, Meristæ,[5] Galilæans, Hellenists,[6] Pharisees, Baptists, are Jews (do not hear me impatiently when I tell you what I think), but are [only] called Jews and children of Abraham, worshipping God with the lips, as God Himself declared, but the heart was far from Him. But I and others, who are right-minded Christians on all points, are assured that there will be a resurrection of the dead, and a thousand years[7] in Jerusalem, which will then be built, adorned, and enlarged, [as] the prophets Ezekiel and Isaiah and others declare.

CHAP. LXXXI. — HE ENDEAVOURS TO PROVE THIS OPINION FROM ISAIAH AND THE APOCALYPSE.

" For Isaiah spake thus concerning this space of a thousand years : ' For there shall be the new heaven and the new earth, and the former shall not be remembered, or come into their heart; but they shall find joy and gladness in it, which things I create. For, Behold, I make Jerusalem a rejoicing, and My people a joy; and I shall rejoice over Jerusalem, and be glad over My people. And the voice of weeping shall be no more heard in her, or the voice of crying. And there shall be no more there a person of immature years, or an old man who shall not fulfil his days.[8] For the young man shall be an hundred years old ;[9] but the sinner who dies an hundred years old,[9] he shall be accursed. And they shall build houses, and shall themselves inhabit them ; and they shall plant vines, and shall themselves eat the produce of them, and drink the wine. They shall not build, and others inhabit ; they shall not plant, and others eat. For according to the days of the tree of life shall be the days of my people ; the works of their toil shall abound.[10] Mine elect shall not toil fruitlessly, or beget children to be cursed ; for they shall be a seed righteous and blessed by the Lord, and their offspring with them. And it shall come to pass, that before they call I will hear; while they are still speaking, I shall say, What is it? Then shall the wolves and the lambs feed together, and the lion shall eat straw like the ox ; but the serpent [shall eat] earth as bread. They shall not hurt or maltreat each other on the holy mountain, saith the Lord.'[11] Now we have understood that the expression used among these words, ' According to the days of the tree [of life[12]] shall be the days of my people ; the works of their toil shall abound,' obscurely predicts a thousand years. For as Adam was told that in the day he ate of the tree he would die, we know that he did not

---

[1] Justin made no previous allusion to this point, so far as we know from the writing preserved.
[2] Or, " so as to believe thoroughly that such will take place "(after "opinion").
[3] [A hint of the origin of this work. See Kaye's Note, p. 18].
[4] i.e., resurrection.
[5] Maranus says, Hieron. thinks the *Genistæ* were so called because they were sprung from Abraham (γένος) the *Meristæ* so called because they separated the Scriptures. Josephus bears testimony to the fact that the sects of the Jews differed in regard to fate and providence; the Pharisees submitting all things indeed to God, with the exception of human will; the Essenes making no exceptions, and submitting all to God. I believe therefore that the *Genistæ* were so called because they believed the world to be in general governed by God; the *Meristæ*, because they believed that a fate or providence belonged to each man.
[6] Otto says, the author and chief of this sect of *Galilæans* was Judas Galilæus, who, after the exile of king Archelaus, when the Romans wished to raise a tax in Judæa, excited his countrymen to the retaining of their former liberty. — The *Hellenists*, or rather *Hellenæans*. No one mentions this sect but Justin; perhaps *Herodians* or *Hillelæans* (from R. Hillel).

[7] We have translated the text of Justin as it stands. Commentators make the sense, " and that there will be a thousand years in Jerusalem," or " that the saints will live a thousand years in Jerusalem."
[8] Literally, " time."
[9] Literally, " the son of an hundred years. "
[10] Or, as in margin of A. V., " they shall make the works of their toil continue long," so reading παλαιώσουσιν for πλεονάσουσιν: thus also LXX.
[11] Isa. lxv. 17 to end.
[12] These words are not found in the MSS.

complete a thousand years. We have perceived, moreover, that the expression, 'The day of the Lord is as a thousand years,'[1] is connected with this subject. And further, there was a certain man with us, whose name was John, one of the apostles of Christ, who prophesied, by a revelation that was made to him, that those who believed in our Christ would dwell[2] a thousand years in Jerusalem; and that thereafter the general, and, in short, the eternal resurrection and judgment of all men would likewise take place. Just as our Lord also said, 'They shall neither marry nor be given in marriage, but shall be equal to the angels, the children of the God of the resurrection.'[3]

CHAP. LXXXII. — THE PROPHETICAL GIFTS OF THE JEWS WERE TRANSFERRED TO THE CHRISTIANS.

"For the prophetical gifts remain with us, even to the present time. And hence you ought to understand that [the gifts] formerly among your nation have been transferred to us. And just as there were false prophets contemporaneous with your holy prophets, so are there now many false teachers amongst us, of whom our Lord forewarned us to beware; so that in no respect are we deficient, since we know that He foreknew all that would happen to us after His resurrection from the dead and ascension to heaven. For He said we would be put to death, and hated for His name's sake; and that many false prophets and false Christs would appear in His name, and deceive many: and so has it come about. For many have taught godless, blasphemous, and unholy doctrines, forging them in His name; have taught, too, and even yet are teaching, those things which proceed from the unclean spirit of the devil, and which were put into their hearts. Therefore we are most anxious that you be persuaded not to be misled by such persons, since we know that every one who can speak the truth, and yet speaks it not, shall be judged by God, as God testified by Ezekiel, when He said, 'I have made thee a watchman to the house of Judah. If the sinner sin, and thou warn him not, he himself shall die in his sin; but his blood will I require at thine hand. But if thou warn him, thou shalt be innocent.'[4] And on this account we are, through fear, very earnest in desiring to converse [with men] according to the Scriptures, but not from love of money, or of glory, or of pleasure. For no man can convict us of any of these [vices]. No more do we wish to live like the rulers of your people, whom God reproaches when He says, 'Your rulers are companions of thieves, lovers of bribes, followers of the rewards.'[5] Now, if you know certain amongst us to be of this sort, do not for their sakes blaspheme the Scriptures and Christ, and do not assiduously strive to give falsified interpretations.

CHAP. LXXXIII. — IT IS PROVED THAT THE PSALM, "THE LORD SAID TO MY LORD," ETC., DOES NOT SUIT HEZEKIAH.

"For your teachers have ventured to refer the passage, 'The Lord says to my Lord, Sit at my right hand, till I make Thine enemies Thy footstool,' to Hezekiah; as if he were requested to sit on the right side of the temple, when the king of Assyria sent to him and threatened him; and he was told by Isaiah not to be afraid. Now we know and admit that what Isaiah said took place; that the king of Assyria desisted from waging war against Jerusalem in Hezekiah's days, and the angel of the Lord slew about 185,000 of the host of the Assyrians. But it is manifest that the Psalm does not refer to him. For thus it is written, 'The Lord says to my Lord, Sit at My right hand, till I make Thine enemies Thy footstool. He shall send forth a rod of power over[6] Jerusalem, and it shall rule in the midst of Thine[7] enemies. In the splendour of the saints before the morning star have I begotten Thee. The Lord hath sworn, and will not repent, Thou art a priest for ever after the order of Melchizedek.' Who does not admit, then, that Hezekiah is no priest for ever after the order of Melchizedek? And who does not know that he is not the redeemer of Jerusalem? And who does not know that he neither sent a rod of power into Jerusalem, nor ruled in the midst of his enemies; but that it was God who averted from him the enemies, after he mourned and was afflicted? But our Jesus, who has not yet come in glory, has sent into Jerusalem a rod of power, namely, the word of calling and repentance [meant] for all nations over which demons held sway, as David says, 'The gods of the nations are demons.' And His strong word has prevailed on many to forsake the demons whom they used to serve, and by means of it to believe in the Almighty God because the gods of the nations are demons.[8] And we mentioned formerly that the statement, 'In the splendour of the saints before the morning star have I begotten Thee from the womb,' is made to Christ.

---

[1] Ps. xc. 4; 2 Pet. iii. 8.
[2] Literally, "make." [A very noteworthy passage, as a primitive exposition of Rev. xx. 4-5. See Kaye, chap. v.]
[3] Luke xx. 35 f.
[4] Ezek. iii. 17, 18, 19.
[5] Isa. i. 23.
[6] ἐπί, but afterwards εἰς. Maranus thinks that ἐπί is the insertion of some copyist.
[7] Or better, "His." This quotation from Ps. cx. is put very differently from the previous quotation of the same Psalm in chap. xxxii. [Justin often quotes from memory. Kaye, cap. viii.]
[8] This last clause is thought to be an interpolation.

CHAP. LXXXIV. — THAT PROPHECY, "BEHOLD, A VIRGIN," ETC., SUITS CHRIST ALONE.

"Moreover, the prophecy, 'Behold, the virgin shall conceive, and bear a son,' was uttered respecting Him. For if He to whom Isaiah referred was not to be begotten of a virgin, of whom[1] did the Holy Spirit declare, 'Behold, the Lord Himself shall give us a sign: behold, the virgin shall conceive, and bear a son?' For if He also were to be begotten of sexual intercourse, like all other first-born sons, why did God say that He would give a sign which is not common to all the first-born sons? But that which is truly a sign, and which was to be made trustworthy to mankind, — namely, that the first-begotten of all creation should become incarnate by the Virgin's womb, and be a child, — this he anticipated by the Spirit of prophecy, and predicted it, as I have repeated to you, in various ways; in order that, when the event should take place, it might be known as the operation of the power and will of the Maker of all things; just as Eve was made from one of Adam's ribs, and as all living beings were created in the beginning by the word of God. But you in these matters venture to pervert the expositions which your elders that were with Ptolemy king of Egypt gave forth, since you assert that the Scripture is not so as they have expounded it, but says, 'Behold, the young woman shall conceive,' as if great events were to be inferred if a woman should beget from sexual intercourse: which indeed all young women, with the exception of the barren, do; but even these, God, if He wills, is able to cause [to bear]. For Samuel's mother, who was barren, brought forth by the will of God; and so also the wife of the holy patriarch Abraham; and Elisabeth, who bore John the Baptist, and other such. So that you must not suppose that it is impossible for God to do anything He wills. And especially when it was predicted that this would take place, do not venture to pervert or misinterpret the prophecies, since you will injure yourselves alone, and will not harm God.

CHAP. LXXXV. — HE PROVES THAT CHRIST IS THE LORD OF HOSTS FROM PS. XXIV., AND FROM HIS AUTHORITY OVER DEMONS.

"Moreover, some of you venture to expound the prophecy which runs, 'Lift up your gates, ye rulers; and be ye lift up, ye everlasting doors, that the King of glory may enter,'[2] as if it referred likewise to Hezekiah, and others of you [expound it] of Solomon; but neither to the latter nor to the former, nor, in short, to any of your kings, can it be proved to have reference, but to this our Christ alone, who appeared without comeliness, and inglorious, as Isaiah and David and all the Scriptures said; who is the Lord of hosts, by the will of the Father who conferred on Him [the dignity]; who also rose from the dead, and ascended to heaven, as the Psalm and the other Scriptures manifested when they announced Him to be Lord of hosts; and of this you may, if you will, easily be persuaded by the occurrences which take place before your eyes. For every demon, when exorcised in the name of this very Son of God — who is the First-born of every creature, who became man by the Virgin, who suffered, and was crucified under Pontius Pilate by your nation, who died, who rose from the dead, and ascended into heaven — is overcome and subdued. But though you exorcise any demon in the name of any of those who were amongst you — either kings, or righteous men, or prophets, or patriarchs — it will not be subject to you. But if any of you exorcise it in [the name of] the God of Abraham, and the God of Isaac, and the God of Jacob, it will perhaps be subject to you. Now assuredly your exorcists, I have said,[3] make use of craft when they exorcise, even as the Gentiles do, and employ fumigations and incantations.[4] But that they are angels and powers whom the word of prophecy by David [commands] to lift up the gates, that He who rose from the dead, Jesus Christ, the Lord of hosts, according to the will of the Father, might enter, the word of David has likewise showed; which I shall again recall to your attention for the sake of those who were not with us yesterday, for whose benefit, moreover, I sum up many things I said yesterday. And now, if I say this to you, although I have repeated it many times, I know that it is not absurd so to do. For it is a ridiculous thing to see the sun, and the moon, and the other stars, continually keeping the same course, and bringing round the different seasons; and to see the computer who may be asked how many are twice two, because he has frequently said that they are four, not ceasing to say again that they are four; and equally so other things, which are confidently admitted, to be continually mentioned and admitted in like manner; yet that he who founds his discourse on the prophetic Scriptures should leave them and abstain from constantly referring to the same Scriptures, because it is thought he can bring forth something better than Scripture. The passage, then, by which I proved that God reveals that there are both angels and hosts in heaven is this: 'Praise

---

[1] Or, "why was it."
[2] Ps. xxiv. 7.
[3] Chap. lxxvi.
[4] καταδεσμοι, by some thought to be verses by which evil spirits, once expelled, were kept from returning. Plato (*Rep.*) speaks of incantations by which demons were summoned to the help of those who practised such rites; but Justin refers to them only as being expelled. Others regard them as drugs.

the Lord from the heavens: praise Him in the highest. Praise Him, all His angels: praise Him, all His hosts.'"[1]

Then one of those who had come with them on the second day, whose name was Mnaseas, said, "We are greatly pleased that you undertake to repeat the same things on our account." And I said, "Listen, my friends, to the Scripture which induces me to act thus. Jesus commanded [us] to love even [our] enemies, as was predicted by Isaiah in many passages, in which also is contained the mystery of our own regeneration, as well, in fact, as the regeneration of all who expect that Christ will appear in Jerusalem, and by their works endeavour earnestly to please Him. These are the words spoken by Isaiah: 'Hear the word of the Lord, ye that tremble at His word. Say, our brethren, to them that hate you and detest you, that the name of the Lord has been glorified. He has appeared to your joy, and they shall be ashamed. A voice of noise from the city, a voice from the temple,[2] a voice of the Lord who rendereth recompense to the proud. Before she that travailed brought forth, and before the pains of labour came, she brought forth a male child. Who hath heard such a thing? and who hath seen such a thing? has the earth brought forth in one day? and has she produced a nation at once? for Zion has travailed and borne her children. But I have given such an expectation even to her that does not bring forth, said the Lord. Behold, I have made her that begetteth, and her that is barren, saith the Lord. Rejoice, O Jerusalem, and hold a joyous assembly, all ye that love her. Be glad, all ye that mourn for her, that ye may suck and be filled with the breast of her consolation, that having suck ye may be delighted with the entrance of His glory.'"[3]

CHAP. LXXXVI. — THERE ARE VARIOUS FIGURES IN THE OLD TESTAMENT OF THE WOOD OF THE CROSS BY WHICH CHRIST REIGNED.

And when I had quoted this, I added, "Hear, then, how this Man, of whom the Scriptures declare that He will come again in glory after His crucifixion, was symbolized both by the tree of life, which was said to have been planted in paradise, and by those events which should happen to all the just. Moses was sent with a rod to effect the redemption of the people; and with this in his hands at the head of the people, he divided the sea. By this he saw the water gushing out of the rock; and when he cast a tree into the waters of Marah, which were bitter, he made them sweet. Jacob, by putting rods into the water-troughs, caused the sheep of his uncle to conceive, so that he should obtain their young. With his rod the same Jacob boasts that he had crossed the river. He said he had seen a ladder, and the Scripture has declared that God stood above it. But that this was not the Father, we have proved from the Scriptures. And Jacob, having poured oil on a stone in the same place, is testified to by the very God who appeared to him, that he had anointed a pillar to the God who appeared to him. And that the stone symbolically proclaimed Christ, we have also proved by many Scriptures; and that the unguent, whether it was of oil, or of *stacte*,[4] or of any other compounded sweet balsams, had reference to Him, we have also proved,[5] inasmuch as the word says: 'Therefore God, even Thy God, hath anointed Thee with the oil of gladness above Thy fellows.'[6] For indeed all kings and anointed persons obtained from Him their share in the names of kings and anointed: just as He Himself received from the Father the titles of King, and Christ, and Priest, and Angel, and such like other titles which He bears or did bear. Aaron's rod, which blossomed, declared him to be the high priest. Isaiah prophesied that a rod would come forth from the root of Jesse, [and this was] Christ. And David says that the righteous man is 'like the tree that is planted by the channels of waters, which should yield its fruit in its season, and whose leaf should not fade.'[7] Again, the righteous is said to flourish like the palm-tree. God appeared from a tree to Abraham, as it is written, near the oak in Mamre. The people found seventy willows and twelve springs after crossing the Jordan.[8] David affirms that God comforted him with a rod and staff. Elisha, by casting a stick[9] into the river Jordan, recovered the iron part of the axe with which the sons of the prophets had gone to cut down trees to build the house in which they wished to read and study the law and commandments of God; even as our Christ, by being crucified on the tree, and by purifying [us] with water, has redeemed us, though plunged in the direst offences which we have committed, and has made [us] a house of prayer and adoration. Moreover, it was a rod that pointed out Judah to be the father of Tamar's sons by a great mystery."

CHAP. LXXXVII. — TRYPHO MAINTAINS IN OBJECTION THESE WORDS: "AND SHALL REST ON HIM," ETC. THEY ARE EXPLAINED BY JUSTIN.

Hereupon Trypho, after I had spoken these

---

[1] Ps. cxlviii. 1, 2. [Kaye's citations (chap. ix. p. 181) from Tatian, concerning angels and demons, are valuable aids to the understanding of Justin in his frequent references to this subject.]
[2] In both MSS. "people."
[3] Isa. lxvi. 5-11.
[4] [Myrrh. Christ the (Anointed) Rock is also referred to by Jacob (Gen. xlix. 24).]
[5] In chap. lxiii. probably, where the same Psalm is quoted.
[6] Ps. xlv. 7.
[7] Ps. i. 3.
[8] The Red Sea, not the Jordan. [Ex. xv. 27.]
[9] Literally, "a tree."

words, said, "Do not now suppose that I am endeavouring, by asking what I do ask, to overturn the statements you have made; but I wish to receive information respecting those very points about which I now inquire. Tell me, then, how, when the Scripture asserts by Isaiah, 'There shall come forth a rod from the root of Jesse; and a flower shall grow up from the root of Jesse; and the Spirit of God shall rest upon Him, the spirit of wisdom and understanding, the spirit of counsel and might, the spirit of knowledge and piety: and the spirit of the fear of the Lord shall fill Him:'[1] (now you admitted to me," continued he, "that this referred to Christ, and you maintain Him to be pre-existent God, and having become incarnate by God's will, to be born man by the Virgin:) how He can be demonstrated to have been pre-existent, who is filled with the powers of the Holy Ghost, which the Scripture by Isaiah enumerates, as if He were in lack of them?"

Then I replied, "You have inquired most discreetly and most prudently, for truly there does seem to be a difficulty; but listen to what I say, that you may perceive the reason of this also. The Scripture says that these enumerated powers of the Spirit have come on Him, not because He stood in need of them, but because they would rest in Him, i.e., would find their accomplishment in Him, so that there would be no more prophets in your nation after the ancient custom: and this fact you plainly perceive. For after Him no prophet has arisen among you. Now, that [you may know that] your prophets, each receiving some one or two powers from God, did and spoke the things which we have learned from the Scriptures, attend to the following remarks of mine. Solomon possessed the spirit of wisdom, Daniel that of understanding and counsel, Moses that of might and piety, Elijah that of fear, and Isaiah that of knowledge; and so with the others: each possessed one power, or one joined alternately with another; also Jeremiah, and the twelve [prophets], and David, and, in short, the rest who existed amongst you. Accordingly He[2] rested, i.e., ceased, when *He* came, after whom, in the times of this dispensation wrought out by Him amongst men,[3] it was requisite that such gifts should cease from you; and having received their rest in Him, should again, as had been predicted, become gifts which, from the grace of His Spirit's power, He imparts to those who believe in Him, according as He deems each man worthy thereof. I have already said, and do again say, that it had been prophesied that this would be done by Him after His ascension to heaven. It is accordingly said,[4] 'He ascended on high, He led captivity captive, He gave gifts unto the sons of men.' And again, in another prophecy it is said: 'And it shall come to pass after this, I will pour out My Spirit on all flesh, and on My servants, and on My handmaids, and they shall prophesy.'[5]

CHAP. LXXXVIII. — CHRIST HAS NOT RECEIVED THE HOLY SPIRIT ON ACCOUNT OF POVERTY.

"Now, it is possible to see amongst us women and men who possess gifts of the Spirit of God; so that it was prophesied that the powers enumerated by Isaiah would come upon Him, not because He needed power, but because these would not continue after Him. And let this be a proof to you, namely, what I told you was done by the Magi from Arabia, who as soon as the Child was born came to worship Him, for even at His birth He was in possession of His power; and as He grew up like all other men, by using the fitting means, He assigned its own [requirements] to each development, and was sustained by all kinds of nourishment, and waited for thirty years, more or less, until John appeared before Him as the herald of His approach, and preceded Him in the way of baptism, as I have already shown. And then, when Jesus had gone to the river Jordan, where John was baptizing, and when He had stepped into the water, a fire[6] was kindled in the Jordan; and when He came out of the water, the Holy Ghost lighted on Him like a dove, [as] the apostles of this very Christ of ours wrote. Now, we know that he did not go to the river because He stood in need of baptism, or of the descent of the Spirit like a dove; even as He submitted to be born and to be crucified, not because He needed such things, but because of the human race, which from Adam had fallen under the power of death and the guile of the serpent, and each one of which had committed personal transgression. For God, wishing both angels and men, who were endowed with freewill, and at their own disposal, to do whatever He had strengthened each to do, made them so, that if they chose the things acceptable to Himself, He would keep them free from death and from punishment; but that if they did evil, He would punish each as He sees fit. For it was not His entrance into Jerusalem sitting on an ass, which we have showed was prophesied, that empowered Him to be Christ, but it furnished men with a proof that He is the Christ; just as it was necessary in the time of John that men have

---

[1] Isa. xi. 1 ff.
[2] He, that is, the Spirit. The following "He" is Christ.
[3] Or, "wrought out amongst His people." So Otto.
[4] Literally, "He said accordingly." Ps. lxviii. 18.

[5] Joel ii 28 f.
[6] [The *Shechinah* probably attended the descent of the Holy Spirit, and what follows in the note seems a gratuitous explanation. The Ebionite corruption of a truth need not be resorted to. See chap. cxxviii: The fire in the bush.] Justin learned this either from tradition or from apocryphal books. Mention is made of a fire both in the Ebionite Gospel and in another publication called *Pauli prædicatio*, the readers and users of which denied that the rite of baptism had been duly performed, unless *quam mox in aquam descenderunt, statim super aquam ignis appareat*.

proof, that they might know who is Christ. For when John remained[1] by the Jordan, and preached the baptism of repentance, wearing only a leathern girdle and a vesture made of camels' hair, eating nothing but locusts and wild honey, men supposed him to be Christ; but he cried to them, 'I am not the Christ, but the voice of one crying; for He that is stronger than I shall come, whose shoes I am not worthy to bear.'[2] And when Jesus came to the Jordan, He was considered to be the son of Joseph the carpenter; and He appeared without comeliness, as the Scriptures declared; and He was deemed a carpenter (for He was in the habit of working as a carpenter when among men, making ploughs and yokes; by which He taught the symbols of righteousness and an active life); but then the Holy Ghost, and for man's sake, as I formerly stated, lighted on Him in the form of a dove, and there came at the same instant from the heavens a voice, which was uttered also by David when he spoke, personating Christ, what the Father would say to Him: 'Thou art My Son: this day have I begotten Thee;'[3] [the Father] saying that His generation would take place for men, at the time when they would become acquainted with Him: 'Thou art My Son; this day have I begotten thee.'"[4]

CHAP. LXXXIX. — THE CROSS ALONE IS OFFENSIVE TO TRYPHO ON ACCOUNT OF THE CURSE, YET IT PROVES THAT JESUS IS CHRIST.

Then Trypho remarked, "Be assured that all our nation waits for Christ; and we admit that all the Scriptures which you have quoted refer to Him. Moreover, I do also admit that the name of Jesus, by which the the son of Nave (Nun) was called, has inclined me very strongly to adopt this view. But whether Christ should be so shamefully crucified, this we are in doubt about. For whosoever is crucified is said in the law to be accursed, so that I am exceedingly incredulous on this point. It is quite clear, indeed, that the Scriptures announce that Christ had to suffer; but we wish to learn if you can prove it to us whether it was by the suffering cursed in the law."

I replied to him, "If Christ was not to suffer, and the prophets had not foretold that He would be led to death on account of the sins of the people, and be dishonoured and scourged, and reckoned among the transgressors, and as a sheep be led to the slaughter, whose generation, the prophet says, no man can declare, then you would have good cause to wonder. But if these are to be characteristic of Him and mark Him out to all, how is it possible for us to do anything else than believe in Him most confidently? And will not as many as have understood the writings of the prophets, whenever they hear merely that He was crucified, say that this is He and no other?"

CHAP. XC. — THE STRETCHED-OUT HANDS OF MOSES SIGNIFIED BEFOREHAND THE CROSS.

"Bring us on, then," said [Trypho], "by the Scriptures, that we may also be persuaded by you; for we know that He should suffer and be led as a sheep. But prove to us whether He must be crucified and die so disgracefully and so dishonourably by the death cursed in the law.[5] For we cannot bring ourselves even to think of this."

"You know," said I, "that what the prophets said and did they veiled by parables and types, as you admitted to us; so that it was not easy for all to understand the most [of what they said], since they concealed the truth by these means, that those who are eager to find out and learn it might do so with much labour."

They answered, "We admitted this."

"Listen, therefore," say I, "to what follows; for Moses first exhibited this seeming curse of Christ's by the signs which he made."

"Of what [signs] do you speak?" said he.

"When the people," replied I, "waged war with Amalek, and the son of Nave (Nun) by name Jesus (Joshua), led the fight, Moses himself prayed to God, stretching out both hands, and Hur with Aaron supported them during the whole day, so that they might not hang down when he got wearied. For if he gave up any part of this sign, which was an imitation of the cross, the people were beaten, as is recorded in the writings of Moses; but if he remained in this form, Amalek was proportionally defeated, and he who prevailed prevailed by the cross. For it was not because Moses so prayed that the people were stronger, but because, while one who bore the name of Jesus (Joshua) was in the forefront of the battle, he himself made the sign of the cross. For who of you knows not that the prayer of one who accompanies it with lamentation and tears, with the body prostrate, or with bended knees, propitiates God most of all? But in such a manner neither he nor any other one, while sitting on a stone, prayed. Nor even the stone symbolized Christ, as I have shown.

CHAP. XCI. — THE CROSS WAS FORETOLD IN THE BLESSINGS OF JOSEPH, AND IN THE SERPENT THAT WAS LIFTED UP.

"And God by Moses shows in another way the force of the mystery of the cross, when He said in the blessing wherewith Joseph was blessed,

---

[1] Literally, "sat."
[2] Isa. i. 27.
[3] Ps. ii. 7.
[4] The repetition seems quite superfluous.

[5] [This intense abhorrence of the cross made it worth while to show that these similitudes existed under the law. They were *ad hominem* appeals, and suited to Jewish modes of thought.]

'From the blessing of the Lord is his land; for the seasons of heaven, and for the dews, and for the deep springs from beneath, and for the seasonable fruits of the sun,[1] and for the coming together of the months, and for the heights of the everlasting mountains, and for the heights of the hills, and for the ever-flowing rivers, and for the fruits of the fatness of the earth; and let the things accepted by Him who appeared in the bush come on the head and crown of Joseph. Let him be glorified among his brethren;[2] his beauty is [like] the firstling of a bullock; his horns the horns of an unicorn: with these shall he push the nations from one end of the earth to another.'[3] Now, no one could say or prove that the horns of an unicorn represent any other fact or figure than the type which portrays the cross. For the one beam is placed upright, from which the highest extremity is raised up into a horn, when the other beam is fitted on to it, and the ends appear on both sides as horns joined on to the one horn. And the part which is fixed in the centre, on which are suspended those who are crucified, also stands out like a horn; and it also looks like a horn conjoined and fixed with the other horns. And the expression, 'With these shall he push as with horns the nations from one end of the earth to another,' is indicative of what is now the fact among all the nations. For some out of all the nations, through the power of this mystery, having been so pushed, that is, pricked in their hearts, have turned from vain idols and demons to serve God. But the same figure is revealed for the destruction and condemnation of the unbelievers; even as Amalek was defeated and Israel victorious when the people came out of Egypt, by means of the type of the stretching out of Moses' hands, and the name of Jesus (Joshua), by which the son of Nave (Nun) was called. And it seems that the type and sign, which was erected to counteract the serpents which bit Israel, was intended for the salvation of those who believe that death was declared to come thereafter on the serpent through Him that would be crucified, but salvation to those who had been bitten by him and had betaken themselves to Him that sent His Son into the world to be crucified.[4] For the Spirit of prophecy by Moses did not teach us to believe in the serpent, since it shows us that he was cursed by God from the beginning; and in Isaiah tells us that he shall be put to death as an enemy by the mighty sword, which is Christ.

CHAP. XCII. — UNLESS THE SCRIPTURES BE UNDERSTOOD THROUGH GOD'S GREAT GRACE, GOD WILL NOT APPEAR TO HAVE TAUGHT ALWAYS THE SAME RIGHTEOUSNESS.

"Unless, therefore, a man by God's great grace receives the power to understand what has been said and done by the prophets, the appearance of being able to repeat the words or the deeds will not profit him, if he cannot explain the argument of them. And will they not assuredly appear contemptible to many, since they are related by those who understood them not? For if one should wish to ask you why, since Enoch, Noah with his sons, and all others in similar circumstances, who neither were circumcised nor kept the Sabbath, pleased God, God demanded by other leaders, and by the giving of the law after the lapse of so many generations, that those who lived between the times of Abraham and of Moses be justified by circumcision, and that those who lived after Moses be justified by circumcision and the other ordinances — to wit, the Sabbath, and sacrifices, and libations,[5] and offerings; [God will be slandered] unless you show, as I have already said, that God who foreknew was aware that your nation would deserve expulsion from Jerusalem, and that none would be permitted to enter into it. (For[6] you are not distinguished in any other way than by the fleshly circumcision, as I remarked previously. For Abraham was declared by God to be righteous, not on account of circumcision, but on account of faith. For before he was circumcised the following statement was made regarding him: 'Abraham believed God, and it was accounted unto him for righteousness.'[7] And we, therefore, in the uncircumcision of our flesh, believing God through Christ, and having that circumcision which is of advantage to us who have acquired it — namely, that of the heart — we hope to appear righteous before and well-pleasing to God: since already we have received His testimony through the words of the prophets.) [And, further, God will be slandered unless you show] that you were commanded to observe the Sabbath, and to present offerings, and that the Lord submitted to have a place called by the name of God, in order that, as has been said, you might not become impious and godless by worshipping idols and forgetting God, as indeed you do always appear to have been. (Now, that God enjoined the ordinances of Sabbaths and offerings for these reasons, I have proved in what I previously remarked; but for the sake of those who came to-day, I

---

[1] There is a variety of reading here: either ἀβύσσου πηγῶν κάτωθεν καθαρῶν: or, ἀβύσσου πηγῶν κάτωθεν, καὶ καθ' ὥραν γεννημάτων, κ.τ.λ., which we prefer.
[2] The translation in the text is a rendering of the Septuagint. The MSS. of Justin read: "Being glorified as the first-born among his brethren."
[3] Deut. xxxiii. 13-17.
[4] [A clumsy exposition of St. John, iii. 14.]
[5] Or, "ashes," σποδῶν for σπονδῶν.
[6] We have adopted the parenthesis inserted by Maranus. Langus would insert before it, τί ἕξετε ἀποκρίνασθαι; "What will you have to answer?"
[7] Gen. xv. 6.

wish to repeat nearly the whole.) For if this is not the case, God will be slandered,[1] as having no foreknowledge, and as not teaching all men to know and to do the same acts of righteousness (for many generations of men appear to have existed before Moses); and the Scripture is not true which affirms that 'God is true and righteous, and all His ways are judgments, and there is no unrighteousness in him.' But since the Scripture is true, God is always willing that such even as you be neither foolish nor lovers of yourselves, in order that you may obtain the salvation of Christ,[2] who pleased God, and received testimony from Him, as I have already said, by alleging proof from the holy words of prophecy.

CHAP. XCIII. — THE SAME KIND OF RIGHTEOUSNESS IS BESTOWED ON ALL. CHRIST COMPREHENDS IT IN TWO PRECEPTS.

"For [God] sets before every race of mankind that which is always and universally just, as well as all righteousness; and every race knows that adultery, and fornication, and homicide,[3] and such like, are sinful; and though they all commit such practices, yet they do not escape from the knowledge that they act unrighteously whenever they so do, with the exception of those who are possessed with an unclean spirit, and who have been debased by education, by wicked customs, and by sinful institutions, and who have lost, or rather quenched and put under, their natural ideas. For we may see that such persons are unwilling to submit to the same things which they inflict upon others, and reproach each other with hostile consciences for the acts which they perpetrate. And hence I think that our Lord and Saviour Jesus Christ spoke well when He summed up all righteousness and piety in two commandments. They are these: 'Thou shalt love the Lord thy God with all thy heart, and with all thy strength, and thy neighbour as thyself.'[4] For the man who loves God with all the heart, and with all the strength, being filled with a God-fearing mind, will reverence no other god; and since God wishes it, he would reverence that angel who is beloved by the same Lord and God. And the man who loves his neighbour as himself will wish for him the same good things that he wishes for himself, and no man will wish evil things for himself. Accordingly, he who loves his neighbour would pray and labour that his neighbour may be possessed of the same benefits as himself. Now nothing else is neighbour to man than that similarly-affectioned and reasonable being — man. Therefore, since all righteousness is divided into two branches, namely, in so far as it regards God and men, whoever, says the Scripture, loves the Lord God with all the heart, and all the strength, and his neighbour as himself, would be truly a righteous man. But you were never shown to be possessed of friendship or love either towards God, or towards the prophets, or towards yourselves, but, as is evident, you are ever found to be idolaters and murderers of righteous men, so that you laid hands even on Christ Himself; and to this very day you abide in your wickedness, execrating those who prove that this man who was crucified by you is the Christ. Nay, more than this, you suppose that He was crucified as hostile to and cursed by God, which supposition is the product of your most irrational mind. For though you have the means of understanding that this man is Christ from the signs given by Moses, yet you will not; but, in addition, fancying that we can have no arguments, you put whatever question comes into your minds, while you yourselves are at a loss for arguments whenever you meet with some firmly established Christian.

CHAP. XCIV. — IN WHAT SENSE HE WHO HANGS ON A TREE IS CURSED.

"For tell me, was it not God who commanded by Moses that no image or likeness of anything which was in heaven above or which was on the earth should be made, and yet who caused the brazen serpent to be made by Moses in the wilderness, and set it up for a sign by which those bitten by serpents were saved? Yet is He free from unrighteousness. For by this, as I previously remarked, He proclaimed the mystery, by which He declared that He would break the power of the serpent which occasioned the transgression of Adam, and [would bring] to them that believe on Him [who was foreshadowed] by this sign, i.e., Him who was to be crucified, salvation from the fangs of the serpent, which are wicked deeds, idolatries, and other unrighteous acts. Unless the matter be so understood, give me a reason why Moses set up the brazen serpent for a sign, and bade those that were bitten gaze at it, and the wounded were healed; and this, too, when he had himself commanded that no likeness of anything whatsoever should be made."

On this, another of those who came on the second day said, "You have spoken truly: we cannot give a reason. For I have frequently interrogated the teachers about this matter, and none of them gave me a reason: therefore continue what you are speaking; for we are paying attention while you unfold the mystery, on account of which the doctrines of the prophets are falsely slandered."

---

[1] We have supplied this phrase twice above.
[2] Literally, salvation along with Christ, that is, salvation by the aid of Christ.
[3] ἀνδρομανία is read in MSS. for ἀνδροφονία.
[4] Matt. xxii. 37.

Then I replied, "Just as God commanded the sign to be made by the brazen serpent, and yet He is blameless; even so, though a curse lies in the law against persons who are crucified, yet no curse lies on the Christ of God, by whom all that have committed things worthy of a curse are saved.[1]

CHAP. XCV. — CHRIST TOOK UPON HIMSELF THE CURSE DUE TO US.

"For the whole human race will be found to be under a curse. For it is written in the law of Moses, 'Cursed is every one that continueth not in all things that are written in the book of the law to do them.'[2] And no one has accurately done all, nor will you venture to deny this; but some more and some less than others have observed the ordinances enjoined. But if those who are under this law appear to be under a curse for not having observed all the requirements, how much more shall all the nations appear to be under a curse who practise idolatry, who seduce youths, and commit other crimes? If, then, the Father of all wished His Christ for the whole human family to take upon Him the curses of all, knowing that, after He had been crucified and was dead, He would raise Him up, why do you argue about Him, who submitted to suffer these things according to the Father's will, as if He were accursed, and do not rather bewail yourselves? For although His Father caused Him to suffer these things in behalf of the human family, yet you did not commit the deed as in obedience to the will of God. For you did not practise piety when you slew the prophets. And let none of you say: If His Father wished Him to suffer this, in order that by His stripes the human race might be healed, we have done no wrong. If, indeed, you repent of your sins, and recognise Him to be Christ, and observe His commandments, then you may assert this; for, as I have said before, remission of sins shall be yours. But if you curse Him and them that believe on Him, and, when you have the power, put them to death, how is it possible that requisition shall not be made of you, as of unrighteous and sinful men, altogether hard-hearted and without understanding, because you laid your hands on Him?

CHAP. XCVI. — THAT CURSE WAS A PREDICTION OF THE THINGS WHICH THE JEWS WOULD DO.

"For the statement in the law, 'Cursed is every one that hangeth on a tree,'[3] confirms our hope which depends on the crucified Christ, not because He who has been crucified is cursed by God, but because God foretold that which would be done by you all, and by those like to you, who do not know[4] that this is He who existed before all, who is the eternal Priest of God, and King, and Christ. And you clearly see that this has come to pass. For you curse in your synagogues all those who are called[5] from Him Christians; and other nations effectively carry out the curse, putting to death those who simply confess themselves to be Christians; to all of whom we say, You are our brethren; rather recognise the truth of God. And while neither they nor you are persuaded by us, but strive earnestly to cause us to deny the name of Christ, we choose rather and submit to death, in the full assurance that all the good which God has promised through Christ He will reward us with. And in addition to all this we pray for you, that Christ may have mercy upon you. For He taught us to pray for our enemies also, saying, 'Love your enemies; be kind and merciful, as your heavenly Father is.'[6] For we see that the Almighty God is kind and merciful, causing His sun to rise on the unthankful and on the righteous, and sending rain on the holy and on the wicked; all of whom He has taught us He will judge.

CHAP. XCVII. — OTHER PREDICTIONS OF THE CROSS OF CHRIST.

"For it was not without design that the prophet Moses, when Hur and Aaron upheld his hands, remained in this form until evening. For indeed the Lord remained upon the tree almost until evening, and they buried Him at eventide; then on the third day He rose again. This was declared by David thus: 'With my voice I cried to the Lord, and He heard me out of His holy hill. I laid me down, and slept; I awaked, for the Lord sustained me.'[7] And Isaiah likewise mentions concerning Him the manner in which He would die, thus: 'I have spread out My hands unto a people disobedient, and gainsaying, that walk in a way which is not good.'[8] And that He would rise again, Isaiah himself said: 'His burial has been taken away from the midst, and I will give the rich for His death.'[9] And again, in other words, David in the twenty-first[10] Psalm thus refers to the suffering and to the cross in a parable of mystery: 'They pierced my hands and my feet; they counted all my bones. They considered and gazed on me; they parted my garments among themselves, and cast lots upon my vesture.' For when they crucified Him, driving in the nails, they pierced His hands and feet; and those who crucified Him parted

---

[1] [Gal. iii. 13.]
[2] Deut. xxvii. 26.
[3] Deut. xxi. 23.
[4] We read ἐπισταμένων for ἐπιστάμενον. Otherwise to be translated: "God foretold that which you did not know," etc.
[5] λεγομένων for γενομένων.
[6] Luke vi. 35.
[7] Ps. iii. 4, 5.
[8] Isa. lxv. 2; comp. also Rom. x. 21.
[9] Isa. liii. 9.
[10] That is, Ps. xxii. 16-18.

His garments among themselves, each casting lots for what he chose to have, and receiving according to the decision of the lot. And this very Psalm you maintain does not refer to Christ; for you are in all respects blind, and do not understand that no one in your nation who has been called King or Christ has ever had his hands or feet pierced while alive, or has died in this mysterious fashion — to wit, by the cross — save this Jesus alone.

CHAP. XCVIII. — PREDICTIONS OF CHRIST IN PS. XXII.

" I shall repeat the whole Psalm, in order that you may hear His reverence to the Father, and how He refers all things to Him, and prays to be delivered by Him from this death; at the same time declaring in the Psalm who they are that rise up against Him, and showing that He has truly become man capable of suffering. It is as follows: 'O God, my God, attend to me: why hast Thou forsaken me? The words of my transgressions are far from my salvation. O my God, I will cry to Thee in the day-time, and Thou wilt not hear; and in the night-season, and it is not for want of understanding in me. But Thou, the Praise of Israel, inhabitest the holy place. Our fathers trusted in Thee; they trusted, and Thou didst deliver them. They cried unto Thee, and were delivered: they trusted in Thee, and were not confounded. But I am a worm, and no man; a reproach of men, and despised of the people. All they that see me laughed me to scorn; they spake with the lips, they shook the head: He trusted on the Lord: let Him deliver him, let Him save him, since he desires Him. For Thou art He that took me out of the womb; my hope from the breasts of my mother: I was cast upon Thee from the womb. Thou art my God from my mother's belly: be not far from me, for trouble is near; for there is none to help. Many calves have compassed me; fat bulls have beset me round. They opened their mouth upon me, as a ravening and roaring lion. All my bones are poured out and dispersed like water. My heart has become like wax melting in the midst of my belly. My strength is dried up like a potsherd; and my tongue has cleaved to my throat; and Thou hast brought me into the dust of death. For many dogs have surrounded me; the assembly of the wicked have beset me round. They pierced my hands and my feet, they did tell all my bones. They did look and stare upon me; they parted my garments among them, and cast lots upon my vesture. But do not Thou remove Thine assistance from me, O Lord: give heed to help me; deliver my soul from the sword, and my [1] only-begotten from the hand of the dog. Save me from the lion's mouth, and my humility from the horns of the unicorns. I will declare Thy name to my brethren; in the midst of the Church will I praise Thee. Ye that fear the Lord, praise Him: all ye the seed of Jacob, glorify Him. Let all the seed of Israel fear Him.'"

CHAP. XCIX. — IN THE COMMENCEMENT OF THE PSALM ARE CHRIST'S DYING WORDS.

And when I had said these words, I continued: "Now I will demonstrate to you that the whole Psalm refers thus to Christ, by the words which I shall again explain. What is said at first — 'O God, my God, attend to me: why hast Thou forsaken me?' — announced from the beginning that which was to be said in the time of Christ. For when crucified, He spake: 'O God, my God, why hast Thou forsaken me?' And what follows: 'The words of my transgressions are far from my salvation. O my God, I will cry to Thee in the day-time, and Thou wilt not hear; and in the night-season, and it is not for want of understanding in me.' These, as well as the things which He was to do, were spoken. For on the day on which He was to be crucified,[2] having taken three of His disciples to the hill called Olivet, situated opposite to the temple in Jerusalem, He prayed in these words: 'Father, if it be possible, let this cup pass from me.'[3] And again He prayed: "Not as I will, but as Thou wilt;'[4] showing by this that He had become truly a suffering man. But lest any one should say, He did not know then that He had to suffer, He adds immediately in the Psalm: 'And it is not for want of understanding in me.' Even as there was no ignorance on God's part when He asked Adam where he was, or asked Cain where Abel was; but [it was done] to convince each what kind of man he was, and in order that through the record [of Scripture] we might have a knowledge of all: so likewise Christ declared that ignorance was not on His side, but on theirs, who thought that He was not the Christ, but fancied they would put Him to death, and that He, like some common mortal, would remain in Hades.

CHAP. C. — IN WHAT SENSE CHRIST IS [CALLED] JACOB, AND ISRAEL, AND SON OF MAN.

"Then what follows — 'But Thou, the praise of Israel, inhabitest the holy place' — declared that He is to do something worthy of praise and wonderment, being about to rise again from the dead on the third day after the crucifixion; and this He has obtained from the Father. For I

---

[1] Probably should be "Thy."

[2] [Jewish computation of the evening as part of the succeeding day.]
[3] Matt. xxvi. 39.
[4] Ibid.

have showed already that Christ is called both Jacob and Israel; and I have proved that it is not in the blessing of Joseph and Judah alone that what relates to Him was proclaimed mysteriously, but also in the Gospel it is written that He said: 'All things are delivered unto me by My Father;' and, 'No man knoweth the Father but the Son; nor the Son but the Father, and they to whom the Son will reveal Him.'[1] Accordingly He revealed to us all that we have perceived by His grace out of the Scriptures, so that we know Him to be the first-begotten of God, and to be before all creatures; likewise to be the Son of the patriarchs, since He assumed flesh by the Virgin of their family, and submitted to become a man without comeliness, dishonoured, and subject to suffering. Hence, also, among His words He said, when He was discoursing about His future sufferings: 'The Son of man must suffer many things, and be rejected by the Pharisees and Scribes, and be crucified, and on the third day rise again.'[2] He said then that He was the Son of man, either because of His birth by the Virgin, who was, as I said, of the family of David,[3] and Jacob, and Isaac, and Abraham; or because Adam[4] was the father both of Himself and of those who have been first enumerated from whom Mary derives her descent. For we know that the fathers of women are the fathers likewise of those children whom their daughters bear. For [Christ] called one of His disciples — previously known by the name of Simon — Peter; since he recognised Him to be Christ the Son of God, by the revelation of His Father: and since we find it recorded in the memoirs of His apostles that He is the Son of God, and since we call Him the Son, we have understood that He proceeded before all creatures from the Father by His power and will (for He is addressed in the writings of the prophets in one way or another as Wisdom, and the Day,[5] and the East, and a Sword, and a Stone, and a Rod, and Jacob, and Israel); and that He became man by the Virgin, in order that the disobedience which proceeded from the serpent might receive its destruction in the same manner in which it derived its origin. For Eve, who was a virgin and undefiled, having conceived the word of the serpent, brought forth disobedience and death. But the Virgin Mary received faith and joy, when the angel Gabriel announced the good tidings to her that the Spirit of the Lord would come upon her, and the power of the Highest would overshadow her: wherefore also the Holy Thing begotten of her is the Son of God;[6] and she replied, 'Be it unto me according to thy word.'"[7] And by her has He been born, to whom we have proved so many Scriptures refer, and by whom God destroys both the serpent and those angels and men who are like him; but works deliverance from death to those who repent of their wickedness and believe upon Him.

CHAP. CI. — CHRIST REFERS ALL THINGS TO THE FATHER.

"Then what follows of the Psalm is this, in which He says: 'Our fathers trusted in Thee; they trusted, and Thou didst deliver them. They cried unto Thee, and were not confounded. But I am a worm, and no man; a reproach of men, and despised of the people;' which show that He admits them to be His fathers, who trusted in God and were saved by Him, who also were the fathers of the Virgin, by whom He was born and became man; and He foretells that He shall be saved by the same God, but boasts not in accomplishing anything through His own will or might. For when on earth He acted in the very same manner, and answered to one who addressed Him as 'Good Master:' 'Why callest thou me good? One is good, my Father who is in heaven.'[8] But when He says, 'I am a worm, and no man; a reproach of men, and despised of the people,' He prophesied the things which do exist, and which happen to Him. For we who believe on Him are everywhere a reproach, 'despised of the people;' for, rejected and dishonoured by your nation, He suffered those indignities which you planned against Him. And the following: 'All they that see me laughed me to scorn; they spake with the lips, they shook the head: He trusted in the Lord; let Him deliver him, since he desires Him;' this likewise He foretold should happen to Him. For they that saw Him crucified shook their heads each one of them, and distorted their lips, and twisting their noses to each other,[9] they spake in mockery the words which are recorded in the memoirs of His apostles: 'He said he was the Son of God: let him come down; let God save him.'

CHAP. CII. — THE PREDICTION OF THE EVENTS WHICH HAPPENED TO CHRIST WHEN HE WAS BORN. WHY GOD PERMITTED IT.

"And what follows — 'My hope from the

---

[1] Matt. xi. 27.
[2] Matt. xvi. 21.
[3] [Note this testimony to Mary's descent from David.]
[4] The text is, αὐτὸν τὸν Ἀβραὰμ πατέρα. Thirlby proposed αὐτὸν τὸν Ἀδάμ: Maranus changed this into αὐτοῦ τὸν Ἀδὰμ πατέρα.
[5] It is not easy, says Maranus, to say in what Scripture Christ is so called. [Clearly he refers to the Dayspring (St. Luke, ii. 78) as the LXX. render many texts of the O. T. See Zech. iii. 8.] Perhaps Justin had in his mind the passage, "This is the *day* which the Lord hath made" (Ps. cxviii. 24). Clem. Alex. teaches that Christ is here referred to.
[6] Luke i. 35. See Meyer *in loc.*
[7] Luke i. 38.
[8] Luke xviii. 18 f.
[9] The text is corrupt, and the meaning doubtful. Otto translates: *naribus inter se certantes.*

breasts of my mother. On Thee have I been cast from the womb; from my mother's belly Thou art my God: for there is no helper. Many calves have compassed me; fat bulls have beset me round. They opened their mouth upon me, as a ravening and a roaring lion. All my bones are poured out and dispersed like water. My heart has become like wax melting in the midst of my belly. My strength is become dry like a potsherd; and my tongue has cleaved to my throat'—foretold what would come to pass; for the statement, 'My hope from the breasts of my mother,' [is thus explained]. As soon as He was born in Bethlehem, as I previously remarked, king Herod, having learned from the Arabian Magi about Him, made a plot to put Him to death; and by God's command Joseph took Him with Mary and departed into Egypt. For the Father had decreed that He whom He had begotten should be put to death, but not before He had grown to manhood, and proclaimed the word which proceeded from Him. But if any of you say to us, Could not God rather have put Herod to death? I return answer by anticipation: Could not God have cut off in the beginning the serpent, so that he exist not, rather than have said, 'And I will put enmity between him and the woman, and between his seed and her seed?'[1] Could He not have at once created a multitude of men? But yet, since He knew that it would be good, He created both angels and men free to do that which is righteous, and He appointed periods of time during which He knew it would be good for them to have the exercise of free-will; and because He likewise knew it would be good, He made general and particular judgments; each one's freedom of will, however, being guarded. Hence Scripture says the following, at the destruction of the tower, and division and alteration of tongues: 'And the Lord said, Behold, the people is one, and they have all one language; and this they have begun to do: and now nothing will be restrained from them of all which they have attempted to do.'[2] And the statement, 'My strength is become dry like a potsherd, and my tongue has cleaved to my throat,' was also a prophecy of what would be done by Him according to the Father's will. For the power of His strong word, by which He always confuted the Pharisees and Scribes, and, in short, all your nation's teachers that questioned Him, had a cessation like a plentiful and strong spring, the waters of which have been turned off, when He kept silence, and chose to return no answer to any one in the presence of Pilate; as has been declared in the memoirs of His apostles, in order that what is recorded by Isaiah might have efficacious fruit, where it is written, 'The Lord gives me a tongue, that I may know when I ought to speak.'[3] Again, when He said, 'Thou art my God; be not far from me,' He taught that all men ought to hope in God who created all things, and seek salvation and help from Him alone; and not suppose, as the rest of men do, that salvation can be obtained by birth, or wealth, or strength, or wisdom. And such have ever been your practices: at one time you made a calf, and always you have shown yourselves ungrateful, murderers of the righteous, and proud of your descent. For if the Son of God evidently states that He can be saved, [neither][4] because He is a son, nor because He is strong or wise, but that without God He cannot be saved, even though He be sinless, as Isaiah declares in words to the effect that even in regard to His very language He committed no sin (for He committed no iniquity or guile with His mouth), how do you or others who expect to be saved without this hope, suppose that you are not deceiving yourselves?

CHAP. CIII.—THE PHARISEES ARE THE BULLS: THE ROARING LION IS HEROD OR THE DEVIL.

"Then what is next said in the Psalm—'For trouble is near, for there is none to help me. Many calves have compassed me; fat bulls have beset me round. They opened their mouth upon me as a ravening and roaring lion. All my bones are poured out and dispersed like water,'—was likewise a prediction of the events which happened to Him. For on that night when some of your nation, who had been sent by the Pharisees and Scribes, and teachers,[5] came upon Him from the Mount[6] of Olives, those whom Scripture called butting and prematurely destructive calves surrounded Him. And the expression, 'Fat bulls have beset me round,' He spoke beforehand of those who acted similarly to the calves, when He was led before your teachers. And the Scripture described them as bulls, since we know that bulls are authors of calves' existence. As therefore the bulls are the begetters of the calves, so your teachers were the cause why their children went out to the Mount of Olives to take Him and bring Him to them. And the expression, 'For there is none to help,' is also indicative of what took place. For there was not even a single man to assist Him as an innocent person. And the expression, 'They opened their mouth upon me like a roaring lion,'

---

[1] Gen. iii. 15.
[2] Gen. xi. 6.
[3] Isa. l. 4.
[4] Not found in MSS.
[5] καὶ τῶν διδασκάλων, adopted instead of κατὰ τὴν διδασκαλίαν, "according to their instructions."
[6] ἀπὸ τοῦ ὄρους. Justin seems to have supposed that the Jews came on Christ from some point of the hill while He was in the valley below. Ἐπὶ τοῦ ὄρους and ἐπὶ τὸ ὄρος have been suggested.

designates him who was then king of the Jews, and was called Herod, a successor of the Herod who, when Christ was born, slew all the infants in Bethlehem born about the same time, because he imagined that amongst them He would assuredly be of whom the Magi from Arabia had spoken; for he was ignorant of the will of Him that is stronger than all, how He had commanded Joseph and Mary to take the Child and depart into Egypt, and there to remain until a revelation should again be made to them to return into their own country. And there they did remain until Herod, who slew the infants in Bethlehem, was dead, and Archelaus had succeeded him. And he died before Christ came to the dispensation on the cross which was given Him by His Father. And when Herod succeeded Archelaus, having received the authority which had been allotted to him, Pilate sent to him by way of compliment Jesus bound; and God foreknowing that this would happen, had thus spoken: 'And they brought Him to the Assyrian, a present to the king.'[1] Or He meant the devil by the lion roaring against Him: whom Moses calls the serpent, but in Job and Zechariah he is called the devil, and by Jesus is addressed as Satan, showing that a compounded name was acquired by him from the deeds which he performed. For 'Sata' in the Jewish and Syrian tongue means apostate; and 'Nas' is the word from which he is called by interpretation the *serpent*, i.e., according to the interpretation of the Hebrew term, from both of which there arises the single word *Satanas*. For this devil, when [Jesus] went up from the river Jordan, at the time when the voice spake to Him, 'Thou art my Son: this day have I begotten Thee,'[2] is recorded in the memoirs of the apostles to have come to Him and tempted Him, even so far as to say to Him, 'Worship me;' and Christ answered him, 'Get thee behind me, Satan: thou shalt worship the Lord thy God, and Him only shalt thou serve.'[3] For as he had deceived Adam, so he hoped[4] that he might contrive some mischief against Christ also. Moreover, the statement, 'All my bones are poured out[5] and dispersed like water; my heart has become like wax, melting in the midst of my belly,' was a prediction of that which happened to Him on that night when men came out against Him to the Mount of Olives to seize Him. For in the memoirs which I say were drawn up by His apostles and those who followed them, [it is recorded] that His sweat fell down like drops of blood while He was praying, and saying, 'If it be possible, let this cup pass:'[6]

His heart and also His bones trembling; His heart being like wax melting in His belly:[7] in order that we may perceive that the Father wished His Son really[8] to undergo such sufferings for our sakes, and may not say that He, being the Son of God, did not feel what was happening to Him and inflicted on Him. Further, the expression, 'My strength is dried up like a potsherd, and my tongue has cleaved to my throat,' was a prediction, as I previously remarked, of that silence, when He who convicted all your teachers of being unwise returned no answer at all.

CHAP. CIV. — CIRCUMSTANCES OF CHRIST'S DEATH ARE PREDICTED IN THIS PSALM.

"And the statement, 'Thou hast brought me into the dust of death; for many dogs have surrounded me: the assembly of the wicked have beset me round. They pierced my hands and my feet. They did tell all my bones. They did look and stare upon me. They parted my garments among them, and cast lots upon my vesture,'— was a prediction, as I said before, of the death to which the synagogue of the wicked would condemn Him, whom He calls both dogs and hunters, declaring that those who hunted Him were both gathered together and assiduously striving to condemn Him. And this is recorded to have happened in the memoirs of His apostles. And I have shown that, after His crucifixion, they who crucified Him parted His garments among them.

CHAP. CV. — THE PSALM ALSO PREDICTS THE CRUCIFIXION AND THE SUBJECT OF THE LAST PRAYERS OF CHRIST ON EARTH.

" And what follows of the Psalm, — ' But Thou, Lord, do not remove Thine assistance from me; give heed to help me. Deliver my soul from the sword, and my[9] only-begotten from the hand of the dog; save me from the lion's mouth, and my humility from the horns of the unicorns,' — was also information and prediction of the events which should befall Him. For I have already proved that He was the only-begotten of the Father of all things, being begotten in a peculiar manner Word and Power by Him, and having afterwards become man through the Virgin, as we have learned from the memoirs. Moreover, it is similarly foretold that He would die by crucifixion. For the passage, 'Deliver my soul from the sword, and my[10] only-begotten from the hand of the dog; save me from the lion's mouth, and my humility from the horns of the unicorns,' is indicative of the suffering by which He should

---
[1] Hos. x. 6.
[2] Ps. ii. 7; comp. Matt. iii. 17.
[3] Matt. iv. 9, 10.
[4] Literally, "said."
[5] Maranus says it is hardly to be doubted that Justin read, "I am poured out like water," etc.
[6] Luke xxii. 44, 42.
[7] [Breast, rather. The (κοίλη) cavity of the nobler *viscera*.]
[8] Justin refers to the opinion of the Docetes, that Christ suffered in appearance merely, and not in reality.
[9] See note on chap. xcviii.
[10] *Ibid.*

die, i.e., by crucifixion. For the 'horns of the unicorns,' I have already explained to you, are the figure of the cross only. And the prayer that His soul should be saved from the sword, and lion's mouth, and hand of the dog, was a prayer that no one should take possession of His soul: so that, when we arrive at the end of life, we may ask the same petition from God, who is able to turn away every shameless evil angel from taking our souls. And that the souls survive, I have shown[1] to you from the fact that the soul of Samuel was called up by the witch, as Saul demanded. And it appears also, that all the souls of similiar righteous men and prophets fell under the dominion of such powers, as is indeed to be inferred from the very facts in the case of that witch. Hence also God by His Son teaches[2] us for whose sake these things seem to have been done, always to strive earnestly, and at death to pray that our souls may not fall into the hands of any such power. For when Christ was giving up His spirit on the cross, He said, 'Father, into Thy hands I commend my spirit,'[3] as I have learned also from the memoirs. For He exhorted His disciples to surpass the pharisaic way of living, with the warning, that if they did not, they might be sure they could not be saved; and these words are recorded in the memoirs: 'Unless your righteousness exceed that of the Scribes and Pharisees, ye shall not enter into the kingdom of heaven.'[4]

CHAP. CVI.—CHRIST'S RESURRECTION IS FORETOLD IN THE CONCLUSION OF THE PSALM.

"The remainder of the Psalm makes it manifest that He knew His Father would grant to Him all things which He asked, and would raise Him from the dead; and that He urged all who fear God to praise Him because He had compassion on all races of believing men, through the mystery of Him who was crucified; and that He stood in the midst of His brethren the apostles (who repented of their flight from Him when He was crucified, after He rose from the dead, and after they were persuaded by Himself that, before His passion He had mentioned to them that He must suffer these things, and that they were announced beforehand by the prophets), and when living with them sang praises to God, as is made evident in the memoirs of the apostles. The words are the following: 'I will declare Thy name to my brethren; in the midst of the Church will I praise Thee. Ye that fear the Lord, praise Him; all ye, the seed of Jacob, glorify Him. Let all the seed of Israel fear Him.' And when it is said that He changed the name of one of the apostles to Peter; and when it is written in the memoirs of Him that this so happened, as well as that He changed the names of other two brothers, the sons of Zebedee, to Boanerges, which means sons of thunder; this was an announcement of the fact that it was He by whom Jacob was called Israel, and Oshea called Jesus (Joshua), under whose name the people who survived of those that came from Egypt were conducted into the land promised to the patriarchs. And that He should arise like a star from the seed of Abraham, Moses showed beforehand when he thus said, 'A star shall arise from Jacob, and a leader from Israel;'[5] and another Scripture says, 'Behold a man; the East is His name.'[6] Accordingly, when a star rose in heaven at the time of His birth, as is recorded in the memoirs of His apostles, the Magi from Arabia, recognising the sign by this, came and worshipped Him.

CHAP. CVII.—THE SAME IS TAUGHT FROM THE HISTORY OF JONAH.

"And that He would rise again on the third day after the crucifixion, it is written[7] in the memoirs that some of your nation, questioning Him, said, 'Show us a sign;' and He replied to them, 'An evil and adulterous generation seeketh after a sign; and no sign shall be given them, save the sign of Jonah.' And since He spoke this obscurely, it was to be understood by the audience that after His crucifixion He should rise again on the third day. And He showed that your generation was more wicked and more adulterous than the city of Nineveh; for the latter, when Jonah preached to them, after he had been cast up on the third day from the belly of the great fish, that after three (in other versions, forty)[8] days they should all perish, proclaimed a fast of all creatures, men and beasts, with sackcloth, and with earnest lamentation, with true repentance from the heart, and turning away from unrighteousness, in the belief that God is merciful and kind to all who turn from wickedness; so that the king of that city himself, with his nobles also, put on sackcloth and remained fasting and praying, and obtained their request that the city should not be overthrown. But when Jonah was grieved that on the (fortieth) third day, as he proclaimed, the city was not overthrown, by the dispensation of a gourd[9] springing up from the earth for him, under which he sat

---

[1] This demonstration is not given. [It *could not be.* The woman was herself frightened by the direct interposition of God. 1. Sam. xxviii. 12, 13.]
[2] Sylburg proposed δικαίους γίνεσθαι for δι᾽ οὓς γίν, "to strive earnestly to become righteous, and at death to pray."
[3] Luke xxiii. 46.
[4] Matt. v. 20.
[5] Num. xxiv. 17.
[6] [Or, "Dayspring."] Zech. vi. 12 (according to LXX.).
[7] Matt. xii. 38 f.
[8] In the LXX. only *three* days are recorded, though in the Hebrew and other versions *forty*. The parenthetic clause is probably the work of a transcriber.
[9] Read κικυῶνα for σικυῶνα.

and was shaded from the heat (now the gourd had sprung up suddenly, and Jonah had neither planted nor watered it, but it had come up all at once to afford him shade), and by the other dispensation of its withering away, for which Jonah grieved, [God] convicted him of being unjustly displeased because the city of Nineveh had not been overthrown, and said, 'Thou hast had pity on the gourd, for the which thou hast not laboured, neither madest it grow; which came up in a night, and perished in a night. And shall I not spare Nineveh, the great city, wherein dwell more than six score thousand persons that cannot discern between their right hand and their left hand; and also much cattle?'[1]

CHAP. CVIII. — THE RESURRECTION OF CHRIST DID NOT CONVERT THE JEWS. BUT THROUGH THE WHOLE WORLD THEY HAVE SENT MEN TO ACCUSE CHRIST.

"And though all the men of your nation knew the incidents in the life of Jonah, and though Christ said amongst you that He would give the sign of Jonah, exhorting you to repent of your wicked deeds at least after He rose again from the dead, and to mourn before God as did the Ninevites, in order that your nation and city might not be taken and destroyed, as they have been destroyed; yet you not only have not repented, after you learned that He rose from the dead, but, as I said before,[2] you have sent chosen and ordained men throughout all the world to proclaim that a godless and lawless heresy had sprung from one Jesus, a Galilæan deceiver, whom we crucified, but his disciples stole him by night from the tomb, where he was laid when unfastened from the cross, and now deceive men by asserting that he has risen from the dead and ascended to heaven. Moreover, you accuse Him of having taught those godless, lawless, and unholy doctrines which you mention to the condemnation of those who confess Him to be Christ, and a Teacher from and Son of God. Besides this, even when your city is captured, and your land ravaged, you do not repent, but dare to utter imprecations on Him and all who believe in Him. Yet we do not hate you or those who, by your means, have conceived such prejudices against us; but we pray that even now all of you may repent and obtain mercy from God, the compassionate and long-suffering Father of all.

CHAP. CIX. — THE CONVERSION OF THE GENTILES HAS BEEN PREDICTED BY MICAH.

"But that the Gentiles would repent of the evil in which they led erring lives, when they heard the doctrine preached by His apostles from Jerusalem, and which they learned[3] through them, suffer me to show you by quoting a short statement from the prophecy of Micah, one of the twelve [minor prophets]. This is as follows: 'And in the last days the mountain of the Lord shall be manifest, established on the top of the mountains; it shall be exalted above the hills, and people shall flow unto it.[4] And many nations shall go, and say, Come, let us go up to the mountain of the Lord, and to the house of the God of Jacob; and they shall enlighten us in His way, and we shall walk in His paths: for out of Zion shall go forth the law, and the word of the Lord from Jerusalem. And He shall judge among many peoples, and shall rebuke strong nations afar off; and they shall beat their swords into ploughshares, and their spears into sickles: nation shall not lift up a sword against nation, neither shall they learn war any more. And each man shall sit under his vine and under his fig tree; and there shall be none to terrify: for the mouth of the Lord of hosts hath spoken it. For all people will walk in the name of their gods; but we will walk in the name of the Lord our God for ever. And it shall come to pass in that day, that I will assemble her that is afflicted, and gather her that is driven out, and whom I had plagued; and I shall make her that is afflicted a remnant, and her that is oppressed a strong nation. And the Lord shall reign over them in Mount Zion from henceforth, and even for ever.'"[5]

CHAP. CX. — A PORTION OF THE PROPHECY ALREADY FULFILLED IN THE CHRISTIANS: THE REST SHALL BE FULFILLED AT THE SECOND ADVENT.

And when I had finished these words, I continued: "Now I am aware that your teachers, sirs, admit the whole of the words of this passage to refer to Christ; and I am likewise aware that they maintain He has not yet come; or if they say that He has come, they assert that it is not known who He is; but when He shall become manifest and glorious, then it shall be known who He is. And then, they say, the events mentioned in this passage shall happen, just as if there was no fruit as yet from the words of the prophecy. O unreasoning men! understanding not what has been proved by all these passages, that two advents of Christ have been announced: the one, in which He is set forth as suffering, inglorious, dishonoured, and crucified; but the other, in which He shall come from heaven with glory, when the man of apostasy,[6] who speaks strange things against the Most

---
[1] Jonah iv. 10 f.
[2] Chap. xvii.
[3] Read μαθόντα for παθόντα.
[4] Literally, "people shall place a river in it."
[5] Mic. iv. 1 ff.
[6] 2 Thess. ii. 3; and see chap. xxxii.

High, shall venture to do unlawful deeds on the earth against us the Christians, who, having learned the true worship of God from the law, and the word which went forth from Jerusalem by means of the apostles of Jesus, have fled for safety to the God of Jacob and God of Israel; and we who were filled with war, and mutual slaughter, and every wickedness, have each through the whole earth changed our warlike weapons,—our swords into ploughshares, and our spears into implements of tillage,—and we cultivate piety, righteousness, philanthropy, faith, and hope, which we have from the Father Himself through Him who was crucified; and sitting each under his vine, i.e., each man possessing his own married wife. For you are aware that the prophetic word says, 'And his wife shall be like a fruitful vine.'[1] Now it is evident that no one can terrify or subdue us who have believed in Jesus over all the world. For it is plain that, though beheaded, and crucified, and thrown to wild beasts, and chains, and fire, and all other kinds of torture, we do not give up our confession; but the more such things happen, the more do others and in larger numbers become faithful, and worshippers of God through the name of Jesus. For just as if one should cut away the fruit-bearing parts of a vine, it grows up again, and yields other branches flourishing and fruitful; even so the same thing happens with us. For the vine planted by God and Christ the Saviour is His people. But the rest of the prophecy shall be fulfilled at His second coming. For the expression, 'He that is afflicted [and driven out],' i.e., from the world, [implies] that, so far as you and all other men have it in your power, each Christian has been driven out not only from his own property, but even from the whole world; for you permit no Christian to live. But you say that the same fate has befallen your own nation. Now, if you have been cast out after defeat in battle, you have suffered such treatment justly indeed, as all the Scriptures bear witness; but we, though we have done no such [evil acts] after we knew the truth of God, are testified to by God, that, together with the most righteous, and only spotless and sinless Christ, we are taken away out of the earth. For Isaiah cries, 'Behold how the righteous perishes, and no man lays it to heart; and righteous men are taken away, and no man considers it.'[2]

CHAP. CXI.—THE TWO ADVENTS WERE SIGNIFIED BY THE TWO GOATS. OTHER FIGURES OF THE FIRST ADVENT, IN WHICH THE GENTILES ARE FREED BY THE BLOOD OF CHRIST.

"And that it was declared by symbol, even in the time of Moses, that there would be two advents of this Christ, as I have mentioned previously, [is manifest] from the symbol of the goats presented for sacrifice during the fast. And again, by what Moses and Joshua did, the same thing was symbolically announced and told beforehand. For the one of them, stretching out his hands, remained till evening on the hill, his hands being supported; and this reveals a type of no other thing than of the cross: and the other, whose name was altered to Jesus (Joshua), led the fight, and Israel conquered. Now this took place in the case of both those holy men and prophets of God, that you may perceive how one of them could not bear up both the mysteries: I mean, the type of the cross and the type of the name. For this is, was, and shall be the strength of Him alone, whose name every power dreads, being very much tormented because they shall be destroyed by Him. Therefore our suffering and crucified Christ was not cursed by the law, but made it manifest that He alone would save those who do not depart from His faith. And the blood of the passover, sprinkled on each man's doorposts and lintel, delivered those who were saved in Egypt, when the first-born of the Egyptians were destroyed. For the passover was Christ, who was afterwards sacrificed, as also Isaiah said, 'He was led as a sheep to the slaughter.'[3] And it is written, that on the day of the passover you seized Him, and that also during the passover you crucified Him. And as the blood of the passover saved those who were in Egypt, so also the blood of Christ will deliver from death those who have believed. Would God, then, have been deceived if this sign had not been above the doors? I do not say that; but I affirm that He announced beforehand the future salvation for the human race through the blood of Christ. For the sign of the scarlet thread, which the spies, sent to Jericho by Joshua, son of Nave (Nun), gave to Rahab the harlot, telling her to bind it to the window through which she let them down to escape from their enemies, also manifested the symbol of the blood of Christ, by which those who were at one time harlots and unrighteous persons out of all nations are saved, receiving remission of sins, and continuing no longer in sin.

CHAP. CXII.—THE JEWS EXPOUND THESE SIGNS JEJUNELY AND FEEBLY, AND TAKE UP THEIR ATTENTION ONLY WITH INSIGNIFICANT MATTERS.

"But you, expounding these things in a low [and earthly] manner, impute much weakness to God, if you thus listen to them merely, and do not investigate the force of the words spoken. Since even Moses would in this way be con-

---

[1] Ps. cxxviii. 3.
[2] Isa. lvii. 1.
[3] Isa. liii. 7.

sidered a transgressor: for he enjoined that no likeness of anything in heaven, or on earth, or in the sea, be made; and then he himself made a brazen serpent and set it on a standard, and bade those who were bitten look at it: and they were saved when they looked at it. Will the serpent, then, which (I have already said) God had in the beginning cursed and cut off by the great sword, as Isaiah says,[1] be understood as having preserved at that time the people? and shall we receive these things in the foolish acceptation of your teachers, and [regard] them not as signs? And shall we not rather refer the standard to the resemblance of the crucified Jesus, since also Moses by his outstretched hands, together with him who was named Jesus (Joshua), achieved a victory for your people? For in this way we shall cease to be at a loss about the things which the lawgiver did, when he, without forsaking God, persuaded the people to hope in a beast through which transgression and disobedience had their origin. And this was done and said by the blessed prophet with much intelligence and mystery; and there is nothing said or done by any one of the prophets, without exception, which one can justly reprehend, if he possess the knowledge which is in them. But if your teachers only expound to you why female camels are spoken of in this passage, and are not in that; or why so many measures of fine flour and so many measures of oil [are used] in the offerings; and do so in a low and sordid manner, while they never venture either to speak of or to expound the points which are great and worthy of investigation, or command you to give no audience to us while we expound them, and to come not into conversation with us; will they not deserve to hear what our Lord Jesus Christ said to them: 'Whited sepulchres, which appear beautiful outward, and within are full of dead men's bones; which pay tithe of mint, and swallow a camel: ye blind guides!'[2] If, then, you will not despise the doctrines of those who exalt themselves and wish to be called Rabbi, Rabbi, and come with such earnestness and intelligence to the words of prophecy as to suffer the same inflictions from your own people which the prophets themselves did, you cannot receive any advantage whatsoever from the prophetic writings.

CHAP. CXIII.—JOSHUA WAS A FIGURE OF CHRIST.

"What I mean is this. Jesus (Joshua), as I have now frequently remarked, who was called Oshea, when he was sent to spy out the land of Canaan, was named by Moses Jesus (Joshua). Why he did this you neither ask, nor are at a loss about it, nor make strict inquiries. Therefore Christ has escaped your notice; and though you read, you understand not; and even now, though you hear that Jesus is our Christ, you consider not that the name was bestowed on Him not purposelessly nor by chance. But you make a theological discussion as to why one 'α' was added to Abraham's first name; and as to why one 'ρ' was added to Sarah's name, you use similar high-sounding disputations.[3] But why do you not similarly investigate the reason why the name of Oshea the son of Nave (Nun), which his father gave him, was changed to Jesus (Joshua)? But since not only was his name altered, but he was also appointed successor to Moses, being the only one of his contemporaries who came out from Egypt, he led the surviving people into the Holy Land; and as he, not Moses, led the people into the Holy Land, and as he distributed it by lot to those who entered along with him, so also Jesus the Christ will turn again the dispersion of the people, and will distribute the good land to each one, though not in the same manner. For the former gave them a temporary inheritance, seeing he was neither Christ who is God, nor the Son of God; but the latter, after the holy resurrection,[4] shall give us the eternal possession. The former, after he had been named Jesus (Joshua), and after he had received strength from His Spirit, caused the sun to stand still. For I have proved that it was Jesus who appeared to and conversed with Moses, and Abraham, and all the other patriarchs without exception, ministering to the will of the Father; who also, I say, came to be born man by the Virgin Mary, and lives for ever. For the latter is He after [5] whom and by whom the Father will renew both the heaven and the earth; this is He who shall shine an eternal light in Jerusalem; this is he who is the king of Salem after the order of Melchizedek, and the eternal Priest of the Most High. The former is said to have circumcised the people a second time with knives of stone (which was a sign of this circumcision with which Jesus Christ Himself has circumcised us from the idols made of stone and of other materials), and to have collected together those who were circumcised from the uncircumcision, i.e., from the error of the world, in every place by the knives of stone, to wit, the words of our Lord Jesus. For I have shown that Christ was proclaimed by the prophets in parables a Stone and a Rock. Accordingly, the knives of stone we shall take to mean His words, by means of

---

[1] Isa. xxvii. 1.
[2] Matt. xxiii. 27, 23, 24. [Note the examples he gives of the rabbinical expositions. He consents to their principle, but gives nobler analogies.]
[3] According to the LXX., Σάρα was altered to Σάρρα, and Ἀβραμ to Ἀβρααμ.
[4] Or, "resurrection of the saints."
[5] Justin seems to mean that the renewal of heaven and earth dates from the incarnation of Christ. [St. Matt. xix. 28.]

which so many who were in error have been circumcised from uncircumcision with the circumcision of the heart, with which God by Jesus commanded those from that time to be circumcised who derived their circumcision from Abraham, saying that Jesus (Joshua) would circumcise a second time with knives of stone those who entered into that holy land.

CHAP. CXIV. — SOME RULES FOR DISCERNING WHAT IS SAID ABOUT CHRIST. THE CIRCUMCISION OF THE JEWS IS VERY DIFFERENT FROM THAT WHICH CHRISTIANS RECEIVE.

"For the Holy Spirit sometimes brought about that something, which was the type of the future, should be done clearly; sometimes He uttered words about what was to take place, as if it was then taking place, or had taken place. And unless those who read perceive this art, they will not be able to follow the words of the prophets as they ought. For example's sake, I shall repeat some prophetic passages, that you may understand what I say. When He speaks by Isaiah, 'He was led as a sheep to the slaughter, and like a lamb before the shearer,'[1] He speaks as if the suffering had already taken place. And when He says again, 'I have stretched out my hands to a disobedient and gainsaying people;'[2] and when He says, 'Lord, who hath believed our report?'[3] — the words are spoken as if announcing events which had already come to pass. For I have shown that Christ is oftentimes called a Stone in parable, and in figurative speech Jacob and Israel. And again, when He says, 'I shall behold the heavens, the works of Thy fingers,'[4] unless I understand His method of using words,[5] I shall not understand intelligently, but just as your teachers suppose, fancying that the Father of all, the unbegotten God, has hands and feet, and fingers, and a soul, like a composite being; and they for this reason teach that it was the Father Himself who appeared to Abraham and to Jacob. Blessed therefore are we who have been circumcised the second time with knives of stone. For your first circumcision was and is performed by iron instruments, for you remain hard-hearted; but our circumcision, which is the second, having been instituted after yours, circumcises us from idolatry and from absolutely every kind of wickedness by sharp stones, i.e., by the words [preached] by the apostles of the corner-stone cut out without hands. And our hearts are thus circumcised from evil, so that we are happy to die for the name of the good Rock, which causes living water to burst forth for the hearts of those who by Him have loved the Father of all, and which gives those who are willing to drink of the water of life. But you do not comprehend me when I speak these things; for you have not understood what it has been prophesied that Christ would do, and you do not believe us who draw your attention to what has been written. For Jeremiah thus cries: 'Woe unto you! because you have forsaken the living fountain, and have digged for yourselves broken cisterns that can hold no water. Shall there be a wilderness where Mount Zion is, because I gave Jerusalem a bill of divorce in your sight?'[6]

CHAP. CXV. — PREDICTION ABOUT THE CHRISTIANS IN ZECHARIAH. THE MALIGNANT WAY WHICH THE JEWS HAVE IN DISPUTATIONS.

"But you ought to believe Zechariah when he shows in parable the mystery of Christ, and announces it obscurely. The following are his words: 'Rejoice, and be glad, O daughter of Zion: for, lo, I come, and I shall dwell in the midst of thee, saith the Lord. And many nations shall be added to the Lord in that day. And they shall be my people, and I will dwell in the midst of thee; and they shall know that the Lord of hosts hath sent me unto thee. And the Lord shall inherit Judah his portion in the holy land, and He shall choose Jerusalem again. Let all flesh fear before the Lord, for He is raised up out of His holy clouds. And He showed me Jesus (Joshua) the high priest standing before the angel [of the Lord[7]]; and the devil stood at his right hand to resist him. And the Lord said to the devil, The Lord who hath chosen Jerusalem rebuke thee. Behold, is not this a brand plucked out of the fire?'"[8]

As Trypho was about to reply and contradict me, I said, "Wait and hear what I say first: for I am not to give the explanation which you suppose, as if there had been no priest of the name of Joshua (Jesus) in the land of Babylon, where your nation were prisoners. But even if I did, I have shown that if there[9] was a priest named Joshua (Jesus) in your nation, yet the prophet had not seen him in his revelation, just as he had not seen either the devil or the angel of the Lord by eyesight, and in his waking condition, but in a trance, at the time when the revelation was made to him.[10] But I now say, that as [Scripture] said that the Son of Nave (Nun) by the name Jesus (Joshua) wrought powerful works and exploits which proclaimed beforehand what would be performed by our Lord; so I proceed now to show

---

[1] Isa. liii. 7.
[2] Isa. lxv. 2.
[3] Isa. liii. 1.
[4] Ps. viii. 3.
[5] Literally, "the operation of His words." Editors have changed τῶν λόγων into τὸν λόγον or τοῦ λόγου: but there is no need of change.

[6] Jer. ii. 13.
[7] Omitted by Justin in this place.
[8] Zech. ii. 10-13, iii. 1, 2.
[9] The reading suggested by Maranus, εἰ μὲν ἦν.
[10] [Noteworthy as to prophetic vision.]

that the revelation made among your people in Babylon in the days of Jesus (Joshua) the priest, was an announcement of the things to be accomplished by our Priest, who is God, and Christ the Son of God the Father of all.

"Indeed, I wondered," continued I, "why a little ago you kept silence while I was speaking, and why you did not interrupt me when I said that the son of Nave (Nun) was the only one of contemporaries who came out of Egypt that entered the Holy Land along with the men described as younger than that generation. For you swarm and light on sores like flies. For though one should speak ten thousand words well, if there happen to be one little word displeasing to you, because not sufficiently intelligible or accurate, you make no account of the many good words, but lay hold of the little word, and are very zealous in setting it up as something impious and guilty; in order that, when you are judged with the very same judgment by God, you may have a much heavier account to render for your great audacities, whether evil actions, or bad interpretations which you obtain by falsifying the truth. For with what judgment you judge, it is righteous that you be judged withal.

CHAP. CXVI. — IT IS SHOWN HOW THIS PROPHECY SUITS THE CHRISTIANS.

"But to give you the account of the revelation of the holy Jesus Christ, I take up again my discourse, and I assert that even that revelation was made for us who believe on Christ the High Priest, namely this crucified One; and though we lived in fornication and all kinds of filthy conversation, we have by the grace of our Jesus, according to His Father's will, stripped ourselves of all those filthy wickednesses with which we were imbued. And though the devil is ever at hand to resist us, and anxious to seduce all to himself, yet the Angel of God, i.e., the Power of God sent to us through Jesus Christ, rebukes him, and he departs from us. And we are just as if drawn out from the fire, when purified from our former sins, and [rescued] from the affliction and the fiery trial by which the devil and all his coadjutors try us; out of which Jesus the Son of God has promised again to deliver us,[1] and invest us with prepared garments, if we do His commandments; and has undertaken to provide an eternal kingdom [for us]. For just as that Jesus (Joshua), called by the prophet a priest, evidently had on filthy garments because he is said to have taken a harlot for a wife,[2] and is called a brand plucked out of the fire, because he had received remission of sins when the devil that resisted him was rebuked; even so we, who through the name of Jesus have believed as one man in God the Maker of all, have been stripped, through the name of His first-begotten Son, of the filthy garments, i.e., of our sins; and being vehemently inflamed by the word of His calling, we are the true high priestly race of God, as even God Himself bears witness, saying that in every place among the Gentiles sacrifices are presented to Him well-pleasing and pure. Now God receives sacrifices from no one, except through His priests.[3]

CHAP. CXVII. — MALACHI'S PROPHECY CONCERNING THE SACRIFICES OF THE CHRISTIANS. IT CANNOT BE TAKEN AS REFERRING TO THE PRAYERS OF JEWS OF THE DISPERSION.

"Accordingly, God, anticipating all the sacrifices which we offer through this name, and which Jesus the Christ enjoined us to offer, i.e., in the Eucharist of the bread and the cup, and which are presented by Christians in all places throughout the world, bears witness that they are well-pleasing to Him. But He utterly rejects those presented by you and by those priests of yours, saying, 'And I will not accept your sacrifices at your hands; for from the rising of the sun to its setting my name is glorified among the Gentiles (He says); but ye profane it.'[4] Yet even now, in your love of contention, you assert that God does not accept the sacrifices of those who dwelt then in Jerusalem, and were called Israelites; but says that He is pleased with the prayers of the individuals of that nation then dispersed, and calls their prayers sacrifices. Now, that prayers and giving of thanks, when offered by worthy men, are the only perfect and well-pleasing sacrifices to God, I also admit. For such alone Christians have undertaken to offer, and in the remembrance effected by their solid and liquid food, whereby the suffering of the Son of God[5] which He endured is brought to mind, whose name the high priests of your nation and your teachers have caused to be profaned and blasphemed over all the earth. But these filthy garments, which have been put by you on all who have become Christians by the name of Jesus, God shows shall be taken away from us, when He shall raise all men from the dead, and appoint some to be incorruptible, immortal, and free from sorrow in the everlasting and imperishable kingdom; but shall send others away to the everlasting punishment of fire. But as to you and your teachers deceiving yourselves when you interpret what the Scripture says as referring to

---

[1] Maranus changed ἀποσπᾷ into ἀποσπᾶν, an emendation adopted in our translation. Otto retains the reading of the MS., "out of which Jesus the Son of God again snatches us. He promised that He would clothe us with," etc.
[2] Justin either confuses Joshua son of Josedech with Hosea the prophet, or he refers to the Jewish tradition that "filthy garments" signified either an illicit marriage, or sins of the people, or the squalor of captivity.
[3] [Isaiah lxvi. 21; Rom. xv. 15, 16, 17 (*Greek*); 1 Pet. ii. 9.]
[4] Mal. i. 10-12.
[5] Or, "God of God."

those of your nation then in dispersion, and maintain that their prayers and sacrifices offered in every place are pure and well-pleasing, learn that you are speaking falsely, and trying by all means to cheat yourselves: for, first of all, not even now does your nation extend from the rising to the setting of the sun, but there are nations among which none of your race ever dwelt. For there is not one single race of men, whether barbarians, or Greeks, or whatever they may be called, nomads, or vagrants, or herdsmen living in tents, among whom prayers and giving of thanks are not offered through the name of the crucified Jesus.[1] And then,[2] as the Scriptures show, at the time when Malachi wrote this, your dispersion over all the earth, which now exists, had not taken place.

CHAP. CXVIII. — HE EXHORTS TO REPENTANCE BEFORE CHRIST COMES; IN WHOM CHRISTIANS, SINCE THEY BELIEVE, ARE FAR MORE RELIGIOUS THAN JEWS.

"So that you ought rather to desist from the love of strife, and repent before the great day of judgment come, wherein all those of your tribes who have pierced this Christ shall mourn, as I have shown has been declared by the Scriptures. And I have explained that the Lord swore, 'after the order of Melchizedek,'[3] and what this prediction means; and the prophecy of Isaiah which says, 'His burial is taken away from the midst,'[4] I have already said, referred to the future burying and rising again of Christ; and I have frequently remarked that this very Christ is the Judge of all the living and the dead. And Nathan likewise, speaking to David about Him, thus continued: 'I will be His Father, and He shall be my Son; and my mercy shall I not take away from Him, as I did from them that went before Him; and I will establish Him in my house, and in His kingdom for ever.'[5] And Ezekiel says, 'There shall be no other prince in the house but He.'[6] For He is the chosen Priest and eternal King, the Christ, inasmuch as He is the Son of God; and do not suppose that Isaiah or the other prophets speak of sacrifices of blood or libations being presented at the altar on His second advent, but of true and spiritual praises and giving of thanks. And we have not in vain believed in Him, and have not been led astray by those who taught us such doctrines; but this has come to pass through the wonderful foreknowledge of God, in order that we, through the calling of the new and eternal covenant, that is, of Christ, might be found more intelligent and God-fearing than yourselves, who are considered to be lovers of God and men of understanding, but are not. Isaiah, filled with admiration of this, said: 'And kings shall shut their mouths: for those to whom no announcement has been made in regard to Him[7] shall see; and those who heard not shall understand. Lord, who hath believed our report? and to whom is the arm of the Lord revealed?'[8]

"And in repeating this,[9] Trypho," I continued, "as far as is allowable, I endeavour to do so for the sake of those who came with you to-day, yet briefly and concisely."

Then he replied, "You do well; and though you repeat the same things at considerable length, be assured that I and my companions listen with pleasure."

CHAP. CXIX. — CHRISTIANS ARE THE HOLY PEOPLE PROMISED TO ABRAHAM. THEY HAVE BEEN CALLED LIKE ABRAHAM.

Then I said again, "Would you suppose, sirs, that we could ever have understood these matters in the Scriptures, if we had not received grace to discern by the will of Him whose pleasure it was? in order that the saying of Moses[10] might come to pass, 'They provoked me with strange [gods], they provoked me to anger with their abominations. They sacrificed to demons whom they knew not; new gods that came newly up, whom their fathers knew not. Thou hast forsaken God that begat thee, and forgotten God that brought thee up. And the Lord saw, and was jealous, and was provoked to anger by reason of the rage of His sons and daughters: and He said, I will turn My face away from them, and I will show what shall come on them at the last; for it is a very froward generation, children in whom is no faith. They have moved Me to jealousy with that which is not God, they have provoked Me to anger with their idols; and I will move them to jealousy with that which is not a nation, I will provoke them to anger with a foolish people. For a fire is kindled from Mine anger, and it shall burn to Hades. It shall consume the earth and her increase, and set on fire the foundations of the mountains; I will heap mischief on them.'[11] And after that Righteous One was put to death, we flourished as another people, and shot forth as new and prosperous corn; as the prophets said, 'And many nations shall betake themselves to the Lord in that day for a people: and they shall dwell in the midst of all the earth.'[12] But we are not

---

[1] [Note this testimony to the catholicity of the Church in the second century. And see Kaye (compare with Gibbon), cap. vi. 112.]
[2] εἶτα δὲ for εἰδότες.
[3] Ps. cx. 4.
[4] Isa. liii. 8.
[5] 2 Sam. vii. 14 f.
[6] Ezek. xliv. 3.

[7] The MSS. read "them." Otto has changed it to "Him."
[8] Isa. lii. 15, liii. 1.
[9] [Let this apology be noted.]
[10] Literally, "in the time of Moses."
[11] Deut. xxxii. 16-23.
[12] Zech. ii. 11.

only a people, but also a holy people, as we have shown already.[1] 'And they shall call them the holy people, redeemed by the Lord.'[2] Therefore we are not a people to be despised, nor a barbarous race, nor such as the Carian and Phrygian nations; but God has even chosen us, and He has become manifest to those who asked not after Him. 'Behold, I am God,' He says, 'to the nation which called not on My name.'[3] For this is that nation which God of old promised to Abraham, when He declared that He would make him a father of many nations; not meaning, however, the Arabians, or Egyptians, or Idumæans, since Ishmael became the father of a mighty nation, and so did Esau; and there is now a great multitude of Ammonites. Noah, moreover, was the father of Abraham, and in fact of all men; and others were the progenitors of others. What larger measure of grace, then, did Christ bestow on Abraham? This, namely, that He called him with His voice by the like calling, telling him to quit the land wherein he dwelt. And He has called all of us by that voice, and we have left already the way of living in which we used to spend our days, passing our time in evil after the fashions of the other inhabitants of the earth; and along with Abraham we shall inherit the holy land, when we shall receive the inheritance for an endless eternity, being children of Abraham through the like faith. For as he believed the voice of God, and it was imputed to him for righteousness, in like manner we, having believed God's voice spoken by the apostles of Christ, and promulgated to us by the prophets, have renounced even to death all the things of the world. Accordingly, He promises to him a nation of similar faith, God-fearing, righteous, and delighting the Father; but it is not you, 'in whom is no faith.'

CHAP. CXX. — CHRISTIANS WERE PROMISED TO ISAAC, JACOB, AND JUDAH.

"Observe, too, how the same promises are made to Isaac and to Jacob. For thus He speaks to Isaac: 'And in thy seed shall all the nations of the earth be blessed.'[4] And to Jacob: 'And in thee and in thy seed shall all families of the earth be blessed.'[5] He says that neither to Esau nor to Reuben, nor to any other; only to those of whom the Christ should arise, according to the dispensation, through the Virgin Mary. But if you would consider the blessing of Judah, you would perceive what I say. For the seed is divided from Jacob, and comes down through Judah, and Phares, and Jesse, and David. And this was a symbol of the fact that some of your nation would be found children of Abraham, and found, too, in the lot of Christ; but that others, who are indeed children of Abraham, would be like the sand on the sea-shore, barren and fruitless, much in quantity, and without number indeed, but bearing no fruit whatever, and only drinking the water of the sea. And a vast multitude in your nation are convicted of being of this kind, imbibing doctrines of bitterness and godlessness, but spurning the word of God. He speaks therefore in the passage relating to Judah: 'A prince shall not fail from Judah, nor a ruler from his thighs, till that which is laid up for him come; and He shall be the expectation of the nations.'[6] And it is plain that this was spoken not of Judah, but of Christ. For all we out of all nations do expect not Judah, but Jesus, who led your fathers out of Egypt. For the prophecy referred even to the advent of Christ: 'Till He come for whom this is laid up, and He shall be the expectation of nations.' Jesus came, therefore, as we have shown at length, and is expected again to appear above the clouds; whose name you profane, and labour hard to get it profaned over all the earth. It were possible for me, sirs," I continued, "to contend against you about the reading which you so interpret, saying it is written, 'Till the things laid up for Him come;' though the Seventy have not so explained it, but thus, 'Till He comes for whom this is laid up.' But since what follows indicates that the reference is to Christ (for it is, 'and He shall be the expectation of nations'), I do not proceed to have a mere verbal controversy with you, as I have not attempted to establish proof about Christ from the passages of Scripture which are not admitted by you,[7] which I quoted from the words of Jeremiah the prophet, and Esdras, and David; but from those which are even now admitted by you, which had your teachers comprehended, be well assured they would have deleted them, as they did those about the death of Isaiah, whom you sawed asunder with a wooden saw. And this was a mysterious type of Christ being about to cut your nation in two, and to raise those worthy of the honour to the everlasting kingdom along with the holy patriarchs and prophets; but He has said that He will send others to the condemnation of the unquenchable fire along with similar disobedient and impenitent men from all the nations. 'For they shall come,' He said, 'from the west and from the east, and shall sit down with Abraham, and Isaac, and Jacob in the kingdom of heaven; but the children of the kingdom shall be cast out into outer darkness.'[8] And I have mentioned

---

[1] See chap. cx.
[2] Isa. lxii. 12.
[3] Isa. lxv. 1.
[4] Gen. xxvi. 4.
[5] Gen. xxviii. 14.
[6] Gen. xlix. 10.
[7] [Note this important point. He forbears to cite the New Testament.]
[8] Matt. viii. 11 f.

these things, taking nothing whatever into consideration, except the speaking of the truth, and refusing to be coerced by any one, even though I should be forthwith torn in pieces by you. For I gave no thought to any of my people, that is, the Samaritans, when I had a communication in writing with Cæsar,[1] but stated that they were wrong in trusting to the magician Simon of their own nation, who, they say, is God above all power, and authority, and might."

CHAP. CXXI. — FROM THE FACT THAT THE GENTILES BELIEVE IN JESUS, IT IS EVIDENT THAT HE IS CHRIST.

And as they kept silence, I went on: " [The Scripture], speaking by David about this Christ, my friends, said no longer that 'in His seed' the nations should be blessed, but 'in Him.' So it is here: 'His name shall rise up for ever above the sun; and in Him shall all nations be blessed.'[2] But if all nations are blessed in Christ, and we of all nations believe in Him, then He is indeed the Christ, and we are those blessed by Him. God formerly gave the sun as an object of worship,[3] as it is written, but no one ever was seen to endure death on account of his faith in the sun; but for the name of Jesus you may see men of every nation who have endured and do endure all sufferings, rather than deny Him. For the word of His truth and wisdom is more ardent and more light-giving than the rays of the sun, and sinks down into the depths of heart and mind. Hence also the Scripture said, 'His name shall rise up above the sun.' And again, Zechariah says, 'His name is the East.'[4] And speaking of the same, he says that 'each tribe shall mourn.'[5] But if He so shone forth and was so mighty in His first advent (which was without honour and comeliness, and very contemptible), that in no nation He is unknown, and everywhere men have repented of the old wickedness in each nation's way of living, so that even demons were subject to His name, and all powers and kingdoms feared His name more than they feared all the dead, shall He not on His glorious advent destroy by all means all those who hated Him, and who unrighteously departed from Him, but give rest to His own, rewarding them with all they have looked for? To us, therefore, it has been granted to hear, and to understand, and to be saved by this Christ, and to recognise all the [truths revealed] by the Father. Wherefore He said to Him: 'It is a great thing for Thee to be called my servant, to raise up the tribes of Jacob, and turn again the dispersed of Israel. I have appointed Thee for a light to the Gentiles, that Thou mayest be their salvation unto the end of the earth.'[6]

CHAP. CXXII. — THE JEWS UNDERSTAND THIS OF THE PROSELYTES WITHOUT REASON.

" You think that these words refer to the stranger[7] and the proselytes, but in fact they refer to us who have been illumined by Jesus. For Christ would have borne witness even to them; but now you are become twofold more the children of hell, as He said Himself.[8] Therefore what was written by the prophets was spoken not of those persons, but of us, concerning whom the Scripture speaks: 'I will lead the blind by a way which they knew not; and they shall walk in paths which they have not known. And I am witness, saith the Lord God, and my servant whom I have chosen.'[9] To whom, then, does Christ bear witness? Manifestly to those who have believed. But the proselytes not only do not believe, but twofold more than yourselves blaspheme His name, and wish to torture and put to death us who believe in Him; for in all points they strive to be like you. And again in other words He cries: 'I the Lord have called Thee in righteousness, and will hold Thine hand, and will strengthen Thee, and will give Thee for a covenant of the people, for a light of the Gentiles, to open the eyes of the blind, to bring out the prisoners from their bonds.'[10] These words, indeed, sirs, refer also to Christ, and concern the enlightened nations; or will you say again, He speaks to them of the law and the proselytes?"

Then some of those who had come on the second day cried out as if they had been in a theatre, "But what? does He not refer to the law, and to those illumined by it? Now these are proselytes."

"No," I said, looking towards Trypho, "since, if the law were able to enlighten the nations and those who possess it, what need is there of a new covenant? But since God announced beforehand that He would send a new covenant, and an everlasting law and commandment, we will not understand this of the old law and its proselytes, but of Christ and His proselytes, namely us Gentiles, whom He has illumined, as He says somewhere: 'Thus saith the Lord, In an acceptable time have I heard Thee, and in a day of salvation have I helped Thee, and I have given Thee for a covenant of the people, to establish the earth, and to inherit the deserted.'[11] What, then, is Christ's inheritance? Is it not the nations? What is the covenant of God? Is it not

---

[1] The *Apology*, i. chap. xxvi.; ii. chap. xv.
[2] Ps. lxxii. 17.
[3] So Justin concludes from Deut. iv. 19; comp. chap. lv. [The explanation is not very difficult (see Rom. i. 28), but the language of Justin is unguarded.]
[4] Zech. vi. 12.
[5] Zech. xii. 12.
[6] Isa. xlix. 6.
[7] Γηόρα or Γειόρα. Found in LXX., Ex. xii. 19 and Isa. xiv. 1.
[8] Matt. xxiii. 15.
[9] Isa. xlii. 16, xliii. 10.
[10] Isa. xlii. 6.
[11] Isa. xlix. 8.

Christ? As He says in another place: 'Thou art my Son; this day have I begotten Thee. Ask of Me, and I shall give Thee the nations for Thine inheritance, and the uttermost parts of the earth for Thy possession.'[1]

CHAP. CXXIII. — RIDICULOUS INTERPRETATIONS OF THE JEWS. CHRISTIANS ARE THE TRUE ISRAEL.

"As, therefore, all these latter prophecies refer to Christ and the nations, you should believe that the former refer to Him and them in like manner. For the proselytes have no need of a covenant, if, since there is one and the same law imposed on all that are circumcised, the Scripture speaks about them thus: 'And the stranger shall also be joined with them, and shall be joined to the house of Jacob;'[2] and because the proselyte, who is circumcised that he may have access to the people, becomes like one of themselves,[3] while we who have been deemed worthy to be called a people are yet Gentiles, because we have not been circumcised. Besides, it is ridiculous for you to imagine that the eyes of the proselytes are to be opened while your own are not, and that you be understood as blind and deaf while they are enlightened. And it will be still more ridiculous for you, if you say that the law has been given to the nations, but you have not known it. For you would have stood in awe of God's wrath, and would not have been lawless, wandering sons; being much afraid of hearing God always say, 'Children in whom is no faith. And who are blind, but my servants? and deaf, but they that rule over them? And the servants of God have been made blind. You see often, but have not observed; your ears have been opened, and you have not heard.'[4] Is God's commendation of you honourable? and is God's testimony seemly for His servants? You are not ashamed though you often hear these words. You do not tremble at God's threats, for you are a people foolish and hard-hearted. 'Therefore, behold, I will proceed to remove this people,' saith the Lord; 'and I will remove them, and destroy the wisdom of the wise, and hide the understanding of the prudent.'[5] Deservedly too: for you are neither wise nor prudent, but crafty and unscrupulous; wise only to do evil, but utterly incompetent to know the hidden counsel of God, or the faithful covenant of the Lord, or to find out the everlasting paths. 'Therefore, saith the Lord, I will raise up to Israel and to Judah the seed of men and the seed of beasts.'[6] And by Isaiah He speaks thus concerning another Israel: 'In that day shall there be a third Israel among the Assyrians and the Egyptians, blessed in the land which the Lord of Sabaoth hath blessed, saying, blessed shall my people in Egypt and in Assyria be, and Israel mine inheritance.'[7] Since then God blesses this people, and calls them Israel, and declares them to be His inheritance, how is it that you repent not of the deception you practise on yourselves, as if you alone were the Israel, and of execrating the people whom God has blessed? For when He speaks to Jerusalem and its environs, He thus added: 'And I will beget men upon you, even my people Israel; and they shall inherit you, and you shall be a possession for them; and you shall be no longer bereaved of them.'"[8]

"What, then?" says Trypho; "are you Israel? and speaks He such things of you?"

"If, indeed," I replied to him, "we had not entered into a lengthy[9] discussion on these topics, I might have doubted whether you ask this question in ignorance; but since we have brought the matter to a conclusion by demonstration and with your assent, I do not believe that you are ignorant of what I have just said, or desire again mere contention, but that you are urging me to exhibit the same proof to these men." And in compliance with the assent expressed in his eyes, I continued: "Again in Isaiah, if you have ears to hear it, God, speaking of Christ in parable, calls Him Jacob and Israel. He speaks thus: 'Jacob is my servant, I will uphold Him; Israel is mine elect, I will put my Spirit upon Him, and He shall bring forth judgment to the Gentiles. He shall not strive, nor cry, neither shall any one hear His voice in the street: a bruised reed He shall not break, and smoking flax He shall not quench; but He shall bring forth judgment to truth: He shall shine,[10] and shall not be broken till He have set judgment on the earth. And in His name shall the Gentiles trust.'[11] As therefore from the one man Jacob, who was surnamed Israel, all your nation has been called Jacob and Israel; so we from Christ, who begat us unto God, like Jacob, and Israel, and Judah, and Joseph, and David, are called and are the true sons of God, and keep the commandments of Christ."

CHAP. CXXIV. — CHRISTIANS ARE THE SONS OF GOD.

And when I saw that they were perturbed because I said that we are the sons of God, I anticipated their questioning, and said, "Listen, sirs, how the Holy Ghost speaks of this people, saying that they are all sons of the Highest; and how this very Christ will be present in their assembly, rendering judgment to all men. The

---
[1] Ps. ii. 7 f.
[2] Isa. xiv. 1.
[3] Literally, "a native of the land."
[4] Deut. xxxii. 20; Isa. xlii. 19 f.
[5] Isa. xxix. 14.
[6] Jer. xxxi. 27.
[7] Isa. xix. 24 f.
[8] Ezek. xxxvi. 12.
[9] [I cannot forbear to note this "Americanism" in the text.]
[10] LXX. ἀναλάμψει, as above. The reading of the text is ἀναλνψει.
[11] Isa. xlii. 1–4.

words are spoken by David, and are, according to your version of them, thus: 'God standeth in the congregation of gods; He judgeth among the gods. How long do ye judge unjustly, and accept the persons of the wicked? Judge for the orphan and the poor, and do justice to the humble and needy. Deliver the needy, and save the poor out of the hand of the wicked. They know not, neither have they understood; they walk on in darkness: all the foundations of the earth shall be shaken. I said, Ye are gods, and are all children of the Most High. But ye die like men, and fall like one of the princes. Arise, O God! judge the earth, for Thou shalt inherit all nations.'[1] But in the version of the Seventy it is written, 'Behold, ye die like men, and fall like one of the princes,'[2] in order to manifest the disobedience of men,—I mean of Adam and Eve,—and the fall of one of the princes, i.e., of him who was called the serpent, who fell with a great overthrow, because he deceived Eve. But as my discourse is not intended to touch on this point, but to prove to you that the Holy Ghost reproaches men because they were made like God, free from suffering and death, provided that they kept His commandments, and were deemed deserving of the name of His sons, and yet they, becoming like Adam and Eve, work out death for themselves; let the interpretation of the Psalm be held just as you wish, yet thereby it is demonstrated that all men are deemed worthy of becoming "gods," and of having power to become sons of the Highest; and shall be each by himself judged and condemned like Adam and Eve. Now I have proved at length that Christ is called God.

CHAP. CXXV.—HE EXPLAINS WHAT FORCE THE WORD ISRAEL HAS, AND HOW IT SUITS CHRIST.

"I wish, sirs," I said, "to learn from you what is the force of the name Israel." And as they were silent, I continued: "I shall tell you what I know: for I do not think it right, when I know, not to speak; or, suspecting that you do know, and yet from envy or from voluntary ignorance deceive yourselves,[3] to be continually solicitous; but I speak all things simply and candidly, as my Lord said: 'A sower went forth to sow the seed; and some fell by the wayside, and some among thorns, and some on stony ground, and some on good ground.'[4] I must speak, then, in the hope of finding good ground somewhere; since that Lord of mine, as One strong and powerful, comes to demand back His own from all, and will not condemn His steward if He recognises that he, by the knowledge that the Lord is powerful and has come to demand His own, has given it to every bank, and has not digged for any cause whatsoever. Accordingly the name Israel signifies this, A man who overcomes power; for *Isra* is a man overcoming, and *El* is power.[5] And that Christ would act so when He became man was foretold by the mystery of Jacob's wrestling with Him who appeared to him, in that He ministered to the will of the Father, yet nevertheless is God, in that He is the first-begotten of all creatures. For when He became man, as I previously remarked, the devil came to Him—i.e., that power which is called the serpent and Satan—tempting Him, and striving to effect His downfall by asking Him to worship him. But He destroyed and overthrew the devil, having proved him to be wicked, in that he asked to be worshipped as God, contrary to the Scripture; who is an apostate from the will of God. For He answers him, 'It is written, Thou shalt worship the Lord thy God, and Him only shalt thou serve.'[6] Then, overcome and convicted, the devil departed at that time. But since our Christ was to be numbed, i.e., by pain and experience of suffering, He made a previous intimation of this by touching Jacob's thigh, and causing it to shrink. But Israel was His name from the beginning, to which He altered the name of the blessed Jacob when He blessed him with His own name, proclaiming thereby that all who through Him have fled for refuge to the Father, constitute the blessed Israel. But you, having understood none of this, and not being prepared to understand, since you are the children of Jacob after the fleshly seed, expect that you shall be assuredly saved. But that you deceive yourselves in such matters, I have proved by many words.

CHAP. CXXVI.—THE VARIOUS NAMES OF CHRIST ACCORDING TO BOTH NATURES. IT IS SHOWN THAT HE IS GOD, AND APPEARED TO THE PATRIARCHS.

"But if you knew, Trypho," continued I, "who He is that is called at one time the Angel of great counsel,[7] and a Man by Ezekiel, and like the Son of man by Daniel, and a Child by Isaiah, and Christ and God to be worshipped by David, and Christ and a Stone by many, and Wisdom by Solomon, and Joseph and Judah and a Star by Moses, and the East by Zechariah, and the Suffering One and Jacob and Israel by Isaiah again, and a Rod, and Flower, and Corner-Stone, and Son of God, you would not have blasphemed Him who has now come, and been

---

[1] Ps. lxxxii.
[2] In the text there is certainly no distinction given. But if we read ὡς ἄνθρωπος (כְּאָדָם), "as a man," in the first quotation we shall be able to follow Justin's argument.
[3] The reading here is ἐπίσταμαι αὐτός, which is generally abandoned for ἀπατᾶν ἑαυτούς.
[4] Matt. xiii. 3.
[5] [On Justin's Hebrew, see Kaye, p. 19.]
[6] Matt. iv. 10.
[7] [By Isaiah. "Counsellor" in English version.]

born, and suffered, and ascended to heaven; who shall also come again, and then your twelve tribes shall mourn. For if you had understood what has been written by the prophets, you would not have denied that He was God, Son of the only, unbegotten, unutterable God. For Moses says somewhere in Exodus the following: 'The Lord spake to Moses, and said to him, I am the Lord, and I appeared to Abraham, to Isaac, and to Jacob, being their God; and my name I revealed not to them, and I established my covenant with them.'[1] And thus again he says, 'A man wrestled with Jacob,'[2] and asserts it was God; narrating that Jacob said, 'I have seen God face to face, and my life is preserved.' And it is recorded that he called the place where He wrestled with him, appeared to and blessed him, the Face of God (Peniel). And Moses says that God appeared also to Abraham near the oak in Mamre, when he was sitting at the door of his tent at mid-day. Then he goes on to say: 'And he lifted up his eyes and looked, and, behold, three men stood before him; and when he saw them, he ran to meet them.'[3] After a little, one of them promises a son to Abraham: 'Wherefore did Sarah laugh, saying, Shall I of a surety bear a child, and I am old? Is anything impossible with God? At the time appointed I will return, according to the time of life, and Sarah shall have a son. And they went away from Abraham.'[4] Again he speaks of them thus: 'And the men rose up from thence, and looked toward Sodom.'[5] Then to Abraham He who was and is again speaks: 'I will not hide from Abraham, my servant, what I intend to do.'"[6] And what follows in the writings of Moses I quoted and explained; "from which I have demonstrated," I said, "that He who is described as God appeared to Abraham, to Isaac, and to Jacob, and the other patriarchs, was appointed under the authority of the Father and Lord, and ministers to His will." Then I went on to say what I had not said before: "And so, when the people desired to eat flesh, and Moses had lost faith in Him, who also there is called the Angel, and who promised that God would give them to satiety, He who is both God and the Angel, sent by the Father, is described as saying and doing these things. For thus the Scripture says: 'And the Lord said to Moses, Will the Lord's hand not be sufficient? thou shalt know now whether my word shall conceal thee or not.'[7] And again, in other words, it thus says: 'But the Lord spake unto me, Thou shalt not go over this Jordan: the Lord thy God, who goeth before thy face, He shall cut off the nations.'[8]

CHAP. CXXVII. — THESE PASSAGES OF SCRIPTURE DO NOT APPLY TO THE FATHER, BUT TO THE WORD.

"These and other such sayings are recorded by the lawgiver and by the prophets; and I suppose that I have stated sufficiently, that wherever[9] God says, 'God went up from Abraham,'[10] or, 'The Lord spake to Moses,'[11] and 'The Lord came down to behold the tower which the sons of men had built,'[12] or when 'God shut Noah into the ark,'[13] you must not imagine that the unbegotten God Himself came down or went up from any place. For the ineffable Father and Lord of all neither has come to any place, nor walks, nor sleeps, nor rises up, but remains in His own place, wherever that is, quick to behold and quick to hear, having neither eyes nor ears, but being of indescribable might; and He sees all things, and knows all things, and none of us escapes His observation; and He is not moved or confined to a spot in the whole world, for He existed before the world was made. How, then, could He talk with any one, or be seen by any one, or appear on the smallest portion of the earth, when the people at Sinai were not able to look even on the glory of Him who was sent from Him; and Moses himself could not enter into the tabernacle which he had erected, when it was filled with the glory of God; and the priest could not endure to stand before the temple when Solomon conveyed the ark into the house in Jerusalem which he had built for it? Therefore neither Abraham, nor Isaac, nor Jacob, nor any other man, saw the Father and ineffable Lord of all, and also of Christ, but [saw] Him who was according to His will His Son, being God, and the Angel because He ministered to His will; whom also it pleased Him to be born man by the Virgin; who also was fire when He conversed with Moses from the bush. Since, unless we thus comprehend the Scriptures, it must follow that the Father and Lord of all had not been in heaven when what Moses wrote took place: 'And the Lord rained upon Sodom fire and brimstone from the Lord out of heaven;'[14] and again, when it is thus said by David: 'Lift up your gates, ye rulers; and be ye lift up, ye everlasting gates; and the King of glory shall enter;'[15] and again, when He says: 'The Lord says to my Lord, Sit at My right hand, till I make Thine enemies Thy footstool.'[16]

---

[1] Ex. vi. 2 ff.
[2] Gen. xxxii. 24, 30.
[3] Gen. xviii. 2.
[4] Gen. xviii. 13 f.
[5] Gen. xviii. 16.
[6] Gen. xviii. 17.
[7] Num. xi. 23.
[8] Deut. xxxi. 2 f.
[9] ὅταν που instead of ὅταν μου.
[10] Gen. xviii. 22.
[11] Ex. vi. 29.
[12] Gen. xi. 5.
[13] Gen. vii. 16.
[14] Gen. xix. 24.
[15] Ps. xxiv. 7.
[16] Ps. cx. 1.

CHAP. CXXVIII. — THE WORD IS SENT NOT AS AN INANIMATE POWER, BUT AS A PERSON BEGOTTEN OF THE FATHER'S SUBSTANCE.

"And that Christ being Lord, and God the Son of God, and appearing formerly in power as Man, and Angel, and in the glory of fire as at the bush, so also was manifested at the judgment executed on Sodom, has been demonstrated fully by what has been said." Then I repeated once more all that I had previously quoted from Exodus, about the vision in the bush, and the naming of Joshua (Jesus), and continued: "And do not suppose, sirs, that I am speaking superfluously when I repeat these words frequently: but it is because I know that some wish to anticipate these remarks, and to say that the power sent from the Father of all which appeared to Moses, or to Abraham, or to Jacob, is called an Angel because He came to men (for by Him the commands of the Father have been proclaimed to men); is called Glory, because He appears in a vision sometimes that cannot be borne; is called a Man, and a human being, because He appears arrayed in such forms as the Father pleases; and they call Him the Word, because He carries tidings from the Father to men: but maintain that this power is indivisible and inseparable from the Father, just as they say that the light of the sun on earth is indivisible and inseparable from the sun in the heavens; as when it sinks, the light sinks along with it; so the Father, when He chooses, say they, causes His power to spring forth, and when He chooses, He makes it return to Himself. In this way, they teach, He made the angels. But it is proved that there are angels who always exist, and are never reduced to that form out of which they sprang. And that this power which the prophetic word calls God, as has been also amply demonstrated, and Angel, is not numbered [as different] in name only like the light of the sun, but is indeed something numerically distinct, I have discussed briefly in what has gone before; when I asserted that this power was begotten from the Father, by His power and will, but not by abscission, as if the essence of the Father were divided; as all other things partitioned and divided are not the same after as before they were divided: and, for the sake of example, I took the case of fires kindled from a fire, which we see to be distinct from it, and yet that from which many can be kindled is by no means made less, but remains the same.

CHAP. CXXIX. — THAT IS CONFIRMED FROM OTHER PASSAGES OF SCRIPTURE.

"And now I shall again recite the words which I have spoken in proof of this point. When Scripture says, 'The Lord rained fire from the Lord out of heaven,' the prophetic word indicates that there were two in number: One upon the earth, who, it says, descended to behold the cry of Sodom; Another in heaven, who also is Lord of the Lord on earth, as He is Father and God; the cause of His power and of His being Lord and God. Again, when the Scripture records that God said in the beginning, 'Behold, Adam has become like one of Us,'[1] this phrase, 'like one of Us,' is also indicative of number; and the words do not admit of a figurative meaning, as the sophists endeavour to affix on them, who are able neither to tell nor to understand the truth. And it is written in the book of Wisdom: 'If I should tell you daily events, I would be mindful to enumerate them from the beginning. The Lord created me the beginning of His ways for His works. From everlasting He established me in the beginning, before He formed the earth, and before He made the depths, and before the springs of waters came forth, before the mountains were settled; He begets me before all the hills.'"[2] When I repeated these words, I added: "You perceive, my hearers, if you bestow attention, that the Scripture has declared that this Offspring was begotten by the Father before all things created; and that that which is begotten is numerically distinct from that which begets, any one will admit."

CHAP. CXXX. — HE RETURNS TO THE CONVERSION OF THE GENTILES, AND SHOWS THAT IT WAS FORETOLD.

And when all had given assent, I said: "I would now adduce some passages which I had not recounted before. They are recorded by the faithful servant Moses in parable, and are as follows: 'Rejoice, O ye heavens, with Him, and let all the angels of God worship Him;'"[3] and I added what follows of the passage: "'Rejoice, O ye nations, with His people, and let all the angels of God be strengthened in Him: for the blood of His sons He avenges, and will avenge, and will recompense His enemies with vengeance, and will recompense those that hate Him; and the Lord will purify the land of His people.' And by these words He declares that we, the nations, rejoice with His people, — to wit, Abraham, and Isaac, and Jacob, and the prophets, and, in short, all of that people who are well-pleasing to God, according to what has been already agreed on between us. But we will not receive it of all your nation; since we know from Isaiah[4] that the members of those who have transgressed shall be consumed

---

[1] Gen. iii. 22.
[2] Prov. viii. 22 ff.
[3] Deut. xxxii. 43.
[4] Isa. lxvi. 24.

by the worm and unquenchable fire, remaining immortal; so that they become a spectacle to all flesh. But in addition to these, I wish, sirs," said I, "to add some other passages from the very words of Moses, from which you may understand that God has from of old dispersed all men according to their kindreds and tongues; and out of all kindreds has taken to Himself your kindred, a useless, disobedient, and faithless generation; and has shown that those who were selected out of every nation have obeyed His will through Christ, — whom He calls also Jacob, and names Israel, — and these, then, as I mentioned fully previously, must be Jacob and Israel. For when He says, 'Rejoice, O ye nations, with His people,' He allots the same inheritance to them, and does not call them by the same name;[1] but when He says that they as Gentiles rejoice with His people, He calls them Gentiles to reproach you. For even as you provoked Him to anger by your idolatry, so also He has deemed those who were idolaters worthy of knowing His will, and of inheriting His inheritance.

CHAP. CXXXI. — HOW MUCH MORE FAITHFUL TO GOD THE GENTILES ARE WHO ARE CONVERTED TO CHRIST THAN THE JEWS.

"But I shall quote the passage by which it is made known that God divided all the nations. It is as follows: 'Ask thy father, and he will show thee; thine elders, and they will tell thee; when the Most High divided the nations, as He dispersed the sons of Adam. He set the bounds of the nations according to the numbers of the children of Israel; and the Lord's portion became His people Jacob, and Israel was the lot of His inheritance.'"[2] And having said this, I added: "The Seventy have translated it, 'He set the bounds of the nations according to the number of the angels of God.' But because my argument is again in nowise weakened by this, I have adopted your exposition. And you yourselves, if you will confess the truth, must acknowledge that we, who have been called by God through the despised and shameful mystery of the cross (for the confession of which, and obedience to which, and for our piety, punishments even to death have been inflicted on us by demons, and by the host of the devil, through the aid ministered to them by you), and endure all torments rather than deny Christ even by word, through whom we are called to the salvation prepared beforehand by the Father, are more faithful to God than you, who were redeemed from Egypt with a high hand and a visitation of great glory, when the sea was parted for you, and a passage left dry, in which [God] slew those who pursued you with a very great equipment, and splendid chariots, bringing back upon them the sea which had been made a way for your sakes; on whom also a pillar of light shone, in order that you, more than any other nation in the world, might possess a peculiar light, never-failing and never-setting; for whom He rained manna as nourishment, fit for the heavenly angels, in order that you might have no need to prepare your food; and the water at Marah was made sweet; and a sign of Him that was to be crucified was made, both in the matter of the serpents which bit you, as I already mentioned (God anticipating before the proper times these mysteries, in order to confer grace upon you, to whom you are always convicted of being thankless), as well as in the type of the extending of the hands of Moses, and of Oshea being named Jesus (Joshua); when you fought against Amalek: concerning which God enjoined that the incident be recorded, and the name of Jesus laid up in your understandings; saying that this is He who would blot out the memorial of Amalek from under heaven. Now it is clear that the memorial of Amalek remained after the son of Nave (Nun): but He makes it manifest through Jesus, who was crucified, of whom also those symbols were fore-announcements of all that would happen to Him, the demons would be destroyed, and would dread His name, and that all principalities and kingdoms would fear Him; and that they who believe in Him out of all nations would be shown as God-fearing and peaceful men; and the facts already quoted by me, Trypho, indicate this. Again, when you desired flesh, so vast a quantity of quails was given you, that they could not be told; for whom also water gushed from the rock; and a cloud followed you for a shade from heat, and covering from cold, declaring the manner and signification of another and new heaven; the latchets of your shoes did not break, and your shoes waxed not old, and your garments wore not away, but even those of the children grew along with them.

CHAP. CXXXII. — HOW GREAT THE POWER WAS OF THE NAME OF JESUS IN THE OLD TESTAMENT.

"Yet after this you made a calf, and were very zealous in committing fornication with the daughters of strangers, and in serving idols. And again, when the land was given up to you with so great a display of power, that you witnessed[3] the sun stand still in the heavens by the order of that man whose name was Jesus (Joshua), and not go down for thirty-six hours,

---

[1] The reading is, "and calls them by the same name." But the whole argument shows that the Jews and Gentiles are distinguished by name. [But that Gentiles are also called (Israel) by the same name is the point here.]
[2] Deut. xxxii. 7 ff.

[3] {Another Americanism. Greek, θεάσασθαι.}

as well as all the other miracles which were wrought for you as time served;[1] and of these it seems good to me now to speak of another, for it conduces to your hereby knowing Jesus, whom we also know to have been Christ the Son of God, who was crucified, and rose again, and ascended to heaven, and will come again to judge all men, even up to Adam himself. You are aware, then," I continued, "that when the ark of the testimony was seized by the enemies of Ashdod,[2] and a terrible and incurable malady had broken out among them, they resolved to place it on a cart to which they yoked cows that had recently calved, for the purpose of ascertaining by trial whether or not they had been plagued by God's power on account of the ark, and if God wished it to be taken back to the place from which it had been carried away. And when they had done this, the cows, led by no man, went not to the place whence the ark had been taken, but to the fields of a certain man whose name was Oshea, the same as his whose name was altered to Jesus (Joshua), as has been previously mentioned, who also led the people into the land and meted it out to them: and when the cows had come into these fields they remained there, showing to you thereby that they were guided by the name of power;[3] just as formerly the people who survived of those that came out of Egypt, were guided into the land by him who had received the name Jesus (Joshua), who before was called Oshea.

CHAP. CXXXIII. — THE HARD-HEARTEDNESS OF THE JEWS, FOR WHOM THE CHRISTIANS PRAY.

" Now, although these and all other such unexpected and marvellous works were wrought amongst and seen by you at different times, yet you are convicted by the prophets of having gone to such a length as offering your own children to demons; and besides all this, of having dared to do such things against Christ; and you still dare to do them: for all which may it be granted to you to obtain mercy and salvation from God and His Christ. For God, knowing before that you would do such things, pronounced this curse upon you by the prophet Isaiah: 'Woe unto their soul! they have devised evil counsel against themselves, saying, Let us bind the righteous man, for he is distasteful to us. Therefore they shall eat the fruit of their own doings. Woe to the wicked! evil, according to the works of his hands, shall befall him. O my people, your exactors glean you, and those who extort from you shall rule over you. O my people, they who call you blessed cause you to err, and disorder the way of your paths. But now the Lord shall sist His people to judgment, and He shall enter into judgment with the elders of the people and the princes thereof. But why have you burnt up my vineyard? and why is the spoil of the poor found in your houses? Why do you wrong my people, and put to shame the countenance of the humble?'[4] Again, in other words, the same prophet spake to the same effect: 'Woe unto them that draw their iniquity as with a long cord, and their transgressions as with the harness of an heifer's yoke: who say, Let His speed come near, and let the counsel of the Holy One of Israel come, that we may know it. Woe unto them that call evil good, and good evil! that put light for darkness, and darkness for light! that put bitter for sweet, and sweet for bitter! Woe unto them that are wise in their own eyes, and prudent in their own sight! Woe unto those that are mighty among you, who drink wine, who are men of strength, who mingle strong drink! who justify the wicked for a reward, and take away justice from the righteous! Therefore, as the stubble shall be burnt by the coal of fire, and utterly consumed by the burning flame, their root shall be as wool, and their flower shall go up like dust. For they would not have the law of the Lord of Sabaoth, but despised[5] the word of the Lord, the Holy One of Israel. And the Lord of Sabaoth was very angry, and laid His hands upon them, and smote them; and He was provoked against the mountains, and their carcases were in the midst like dung on the road. And for all this they have not repented,[6] but their hand is still high.'[7] For verily your hand is high to commit evil, because ye slew the Christ, and do not repent of it; but so far from that, ye hate and murder us who have believed through Him in the God and Father of all, as often as ye can; and ye curse Him without ceasing, as well as those who side with Him; while all of us pray for you, and for all men, as our Christ and Lord taught us to do, when He enjoined us to pray even for our enemies, and to love them that hate us, and to bless them that curse us.

CHAP. CXXXIV. — THE MARRIAGES OF JACOB ARE A FIGURE OF THE CHURCH.

" If, then, the teaching of the prophets and of Himself moves you, it is better for you to follow God than your imprudent and blind masters, who even till this time permit each man to have four or five wives; and if any one see a beautiful woman and desire to have her, they quote the doings of Jacob [called] Israel, and of the other

---

[1] The anacolouthon is in the original.
[2] See 1 Sam. v.
[3] Or, "by the power of the name." [2 Sam. vi. 14. Joshua in English version.]
[4] Isa. iii. 9-15.
[5] Literally, "provoked."
[6] Literally, "turned away."
[7] Isa. v. 18-25.

patriarchs, and maintain that it is not wrong to do such things; for they are miserably ignorant in this matter. For, as I before said, certain dispensations of weighty mysteries were accomplished in each act of this sort. For in the marriages of Jacob I shall mention what dispensation and prophecy were accomplished, in order that you may thereby know that your teachers never looked at the divine motive which prompted each act, but only at the grovelling and corrupting passions. Attend therefore to what I say. The marriages of Jacob were types of that which Christ was about to accomplish. For it was not lawful for Jacob to marry two sisters at once. And he serves Laban for [one of] the daughters; and being deceived in [the obtaining of] the younger, he again served seven years. Now Leah is your people and synagogue; but Rachel is our Church. And for these, and for the servants in both, Christ even now serves. For while Noah gave to the two sons the seed of the third as servants, now on the other hand Christ has come to restore both the free sons and the servants amongst them, conferring the same honour on all of them who keep His commandments; even as the children of the free women and the children of the bond women born to Jacob were all sons, and equal in dignity. And it was foretold what each should be according to rank and and according to fore-knowledge. Jacob served Laban for speckled and many-spotted sheep; and Christ served, even to the slavery of the cross, for the various and many-formed races of mankind, acquiring them by the blood and mystery of the cross. Leah was weak eyed; for the eyes of your souls are excessively weak. Rachel stole the gods of Laban, and has hid them to this day; and we have lost our paternal and material gods. Jacob was hated for all time by his brother; and we now, and our Lord Himself, are hated by you and by all men, though we are brothers by nature. Jacob was called Israel; and Israel has been demonstrated to be the Christ, who is, and is called, Jesus.

CHAP. CXXXV. — CHRIST IS KING OF ISRAEL, AND CHRISTIANS ARE THE ISRAELITIC RACE.

"And when Scripture says, 'I am the Lord God, the Holy One of Israel, who have made known Israel your King,'[1] will you not understand that truly Christ is the everlasting King? For you are aware that Jacob the son of Isaac was never a king. And therefore Scripture again, explaining to us, says what king is meant by Jacob and Israel: 'Jacob is my Servant, I will uphold Him; and Israel is mine Elect, my soul shall receive Him. I have given Him my Spirit; and He shall bring forth judgment to the Gentiles.

He shall not cry, and His voice shall not be heard without. The bruised reed He shall not break, and the smoking flax He shall not quench, until He shall bring forth judgment to victory. He shall shine, and shall not be broken, until He set judgment on the earth. And in His name shall the Gentiles trust.'[2] Then is it Jacob the patriarch in whom the Gentiles and yourselves shall trust? or is it not Christ? As, therefore, Christ is the Israel and the Jacob, even so we, who have been quarried out from the bowels of Christ, are the true Israelitic race. But let us attend rather to the very word: 'And I will bring forth,' He says, 'the seed out of Jacob, and out of Judah: and it shall inherit My holy mountain; and Mine Elect and My servants shall possess the inheritance, and shall dwell there; and there shall be folds of flocks in the thicket, and the valley of Achor shall be a resting-place of cattle for the people who have sought Me. But as for you, who forsake Me, and forget My holy mountain, and prepare a table for demons, and fill out drink for the demon, I shall give you to the sword. You shall all fall with a slaughter; for I called you, and you hearkened not, and did evil before me, and did choose that wherein I delighted not.'[3] Such are the words of Scripture; understand, therefore, that the seed of Jacob now referred to is something else, and not, as may be supposed, spoken of your people. For it is not possible for the seed of Jacob to leave an entrance for the descendants of Jacob, or for [God] to have accepted the very same persons whom He had reproached with unfitness for the inheritance, and promise it to them again; but as there the prophet says, 'And now, O house of Jacob, come and let us walk in the light of the Lord; for He has sent away His people, the house of Jacob, because their land was full, as at the first, of soothsayers and divinations;'[4] even so it is necessary for us here to observe that there are two seeds of Judah, and two races, as there are two houses of Jacob: the one begotten by blood and flesh, the other by faith and the Spirit.

CHAP. CXXXVI. — THE JEWS, IN REJECTING CHRIST, REJECTED GOD WHO SENT HIM.

"For you see how He now addresses the people, saying a little before: 'As the grape shall be found in the cluster, and they will say, Destroy it not, for a blessing is in it; so will I do for My servant's sake: for His sake I will not destroy them all.'[5] And thereafter He adds: 'And I shall bring forth the seed out of Jacob, and out of Judah.' It is plain then that if He thus be angry with them, and threaten to leave very few

---

[1] Isa. xliii. 15.
[2] Isa. xlii. 1–4.
[3] Isa. lxv. 9–12.
[4] Isa. ii. 5 f.
[5] Isa. lxv. 8 f.

of them, He promises to bring forth certain others, who shall dwell in His mountain. But these are the persons whom He said He would sow and beget. For you neither suffer Him when He calls you, nor hear Him when He speaks to you, but have done evil in the presence of the Lord. But the highest pitch of your wickedness lies in this, that you hate the Righteous One, and slew Him; and so treat those who have received from Him all that they are and have, and who are pious, righteous, and humane. Therefore 'woe unto their soul,' says the Lord,[1] 'for they have devised an evil counsel against themselves, saying, Let us take away the righteous, for he is distasteful to us.' For indeed you are not in the habit of sacrificing to Baal, as were your fathers, or of placing cakes in groves and on high places for the host of heaven: but you have not accepted God's Christ. For he who knows not Him, knows not the will of God; and he who insults and hates Him, insults and hates Him that sent Him. And whoever believes not in Him, believes not the declarations of the prophets, who preached and proclaimed Him to all.

CHAP. CXXXVII. — HE EXHORTS THE JEWS TO BE CONVERTED.

"Say no evil thing, my brothers, against Him that was crucified, and treat not scornfully the stripes wherewith all may be healed, even as we are healed. For it will be well if, persuaded by the Scriptures, you are circumcised from hardheartedness: not that circumcision which you have from the tenets that are put into you; for that was given for a sign, and not for a work of righteousness, as the Scriptures compel you [to admit]. Assent, therefore, and pour no ridicule on the Son of God; obey not the Pharisaic teachers, and scoff not at the King of Israel, as the rulers of your synagogues teach you to do after your prayers: for if he that touches those who are not pleasing[2] to God, is as one that touches the apple of God's eye, how much more so is he that touches His beloved! And that this is He, has been sufficiently demonstrated."

And as they kept silence, I continued: "My friends, I now refer to the Scriptures as the Seventy have interpreted them; for when I quoted them formerly as you possess them, I made proof of you [to ascertain] how you were disposed.[3] For, mentioning the Scripture which says, 'Woe unto them! for they have devised evil counsel against themselves, saying[4] (as the Seventy have translated, I continued): 'Let us take away the righteous, for he is distasteful to us;' whereas at the commencement of the discussion I added what your version has: 'Let us bind the righteous, for he is distasteful to us.' But you had been busy about some other matter, and seem to have listened to the words without attending to them. But now, since the day is drawing to a close, for the sun is about to set, I shall add one remark to what I have said, and conclude. I have indeed made the very same remark already, but I think it would be right to bestow some consideration on it again.

CHAP. CXXXVIII. — NOAH IS A FIGURE OF CHRIST, WHO HAS REGENERATED US BY WATER, AND FAITH, AND WOOD: [i.e., *the Cross.*]

"You know, then, sirs," I said, "that God has said in Isaiah to Jerusalem: 'I saved thee in the deluge of Noah.'[5] By this which God said was meant that the mystery of saved men appeared in the deluge. For righteous Noah, along with the other mortals at the deluge, i.e., with his own wife, his three sons and their wives, being eight in number, were a symbol of the eighth day, wherein Christ appeared when He rose from the dead, for ever the first in power. For Christ, being the first-born of every creature, became again the chief of another race regenerated by Himself through water, and faith, and wood, containing the mystery of the cross; even as Noah was saved by wood when he rode over the waters with his household. Accordingly, when the prophet says, 'I saved thee in the times of Noah,' as I have already remarked, he addresses the people who are equally faithful to God, and possess the same signs. For when Moses had the rod in his hands, he led your nation through the sea. And you believe that this was spoken to your nation only, or to the land. But the whole earth, as the Scripture says, was inundated, and the water rose in height fifteen cubits above all the mountains: so that it is evident this was not spoken to the land, but to the people who obeyed Him: for whom also He had before prepared a resting-place in Jerusalem, as was previously demonstrated by all the symbols of the deluge; I mean, that by water, faith, and wood, those who are afore-prepared, and who repent of the sins which they have committed, shall escape from the impending judgment of God.

CHAP. CXXXIX. — THE BLESSINGS, AND ALSO THE CURSE, PRONOUNCED BY NOAH WERE PROPHECIES OF THE FUTURE.

"For another mystery was accomplished and predicted in the days of Noah, of which you are

---

[1] Isa. iii. 9.
[2] Zech. ii. 8.
[3] [Justin's varied quotations of the same text seem to have been of purpose. But consult Kaye's most useful note as to the text of the LXX., in answer to objections of Wetstein, p. 20. ff.]
[4] Isa. iii. 9.
[5] Isa. liv. 9 comes nearer to these words than any other passage; but still the exact quotation is not in Isaiah, or in any other part of Scripture. [It is quite probable that Isa. liv. 9 was thus misunderstood by the Jews, as Trypho seems to acquiesce.]

not aware. It is this: in the blessings wherewith Noah blessed his two sons, and in the curse pronounced on his son's son. For the Spirit of prophecy would not curse the son that had been by God blessed along with [his brothers]. But since the punishment of the sin would cleave to the whole descent of the son that mocked at his father's nakedness, he made the curse originate with *his* son.[1] Now, in what he said, he foretold that the descendants of Shem would keep in retention the property and dwellings of Canaan: and again, that the descendants of Japheth would take possession of the property of which Shem's descendants had dispossessed Canaan's descendants; and spoil the descendants of Shem, even as they plundered the sons of Canaan. And listen to the way in which it has so come to pass. For you, who have derived your lineage from Shem, invaded the territory of the sons of Canaan by the will of God; and you possessed it. And it is manifest that the sons of Japheth, having invaded you in turn by the judgment of God, have taken your land from you, and have possessed it. Thus it is written: 'And Noah awoke from the wine, and knew what his younger son had done unto him; and he said, Cursed be Canaan, the servant; a servant shall he be unto his brethren. And he said, Blessed be the Lord God of Shem; and Canaan shall be his servant. May the Lord enlarge Japheth, and let him dwell in the houses of Shem; and let Canaan be his servant.'[2] Accordingly, as two peoples were blessed, — those from Shem, and those from Japheth, — and as the offspring of Shem were decreed first to possess the dwellings of Canaan, and the offspring of Japheth were predicted as in turn receiving the same possessions, and to the two peoples there was the one people of Canaan handed over for servants; so Christ has come according to the power given Him from the Almighty Father, and summoning men to friendship, and blessing, and repentance, and dwelling together, has promised, as has already been proved, that there shall be a future possession for all the saints in this same land. And hence all men everywhere, whether bond or free, who believe in Christ, and recognise the truth in His own words and those of His prophets, know that they shall be with Him in that land, and inherit everlasting and incorruptible good.

CHAP. CXL. — IN CHRIST ALL ARE FREE. THE JEWS HOPE FOR SALVATION IN VAIN BECAUSE THEY ARE SONS OF ABRAHAM.

"Hence also Jacob, as I remarked before, being himself a type of Christ, had married the two handmaids of his two free wives, and of them begat sons, for the purpose of indicating beforehand that Christ would receive even all those who amongst Japheth's race are descendants of Canaan, equally with the free, and would have the children fellow-heirs. And we are such; but you cannot comprehend this, because you cannot drink of the living fountain of God, but of broken cisterns which can hold no water, as the Scripture says.[3] But they are cisterns broken, and holding no water, which your own teachers have digged, as the Scripture also expressly asserts, 'teaching for doctrines the commandments of men.'[4] And besides, they beguile themselves and you, supposing that the everlasting kingdom will be assuredly given to those of the dispersion who are of Abraham after the flesh, although they be sinners, and faithless, and disobedient towards God, which the Scriptures have proved is not the case. For if so, Isaiah would never have said this: 'And unless the Lord of Sabaoth had left us a seed, we would have been like Sodom and Gomorrah.'[5] And Ezekiel: 'Even if Noah, and Jacob, and Daniel were to pray for sons or daughters, their request should not be granted.'[6] But neither shall the father perish for the son, nor the son for the father; but every one for his own sin, and each shall be saved for his own righteousness.[7] And again Isaiah says: 'They shall look on the carcases[8] of them that have transgressed: their worm shall not cease, and their fire shall not be quenched; and they shall be a spectacle to all flesh.'[9] And our Lord, according to the will of Him that sent Him, who is the Father and Lord of all, would not have said, 'They shall come from the east, and from the west, and shall sit down with Abraham, and Isaac, and Jacob in the kingdom of heaven. But the children of the kingdom shall be cast out into outer darkness.'[10] Furthermore, I have proved in what has preceded,[11] that those who were foreknown to be unrighteous, whether men or angels, are not made wicked by God's fault, but each man by his own fault is what he will appear to be.

CHAP. CXLI. — FREE-WILL IN MEN AND ANGELS.

"But that you may not have a pretext for saying that Christ must have been crucified, and that those who transgressed must have been among your nation, and that the matter could not have been otherwise, I said briefly by antici-

---

[1] [But Justin goes on to show that it was prophetic foresight only: the curse cleaves only to wicked descendants, the authors of idolatry. It was removed by Christ. St. Matt. xv. 22-28.]
[2] Gen. ix. 24-27.
[3] Jer. ii. 13.
[4] Isa. xxix. 13.
[5] Isa. i. 9.
[6] Ezek. xiv. 18, 20.
[7] Ezek. xviii. 20.
[8] Literally, "limbs."
[9] Isa. lxvi. 24.
[10] Matt. viii. 11 f.
[11] Chap. lxxxviii. cii.

pation, that God, wishing men and angels to follow His will, resolved to create them free to do righteousness; possessing reason, that they may know by whom they are created, and through whom they, not existing formerly, do now exist; and with a law that they should be judged by Him, if they do anything contrary to right reason: and of ourselves we, men and angels, shall be convicted of having acted sinfully, unless we repent beforehand. But if the word of God foretells that some angels and men shall be certainly punished, it did so because it foreknew that they would be unchangeably [wicked], but not because God had created them so. So that if they repent, all who wish for it can obtain mercy from God: and the Scripture foretells that they shall be blessed, saying, 'Blessed is the man to whom the Lord imputeth not sin;'[1] that is, having repented of his sins, that he may receive remission of them from God; and not as you deceive yourselves, and some others who resemble you in this, who say, that even though they be sinners, but know God, the Lord will not impute sin to them. We have as proof of this the one fall of David, which happened through his boasting, which was forgiven then when he so mourned and wept, as it is written. But if even to such a man no remission was granted before repentance, and only when this great king, and anointed one, and prophet, mourned and conducted himself so, how can the impure and utterly abandoned, if they weep not, and mourn not, and repent not, entertain the hope that the Lord will not impute to them sin? And this one fall of David, in the matter of Uriah's wife, proves, sirs," I said, "that the patriarchs had many wives, not to commit fornication, but that a certain dispensation and all mysteries might be accomplished by them; since, if it were allowable to take any wife, or as many wives as one chooses, and how he chooses, which the men of your nation do over all the earth, wherever they sojourn, or wherever they have been sent, taking women under the name of marriage, much more would David have been permitted to do this."

When I had said this, dearest Marcus Pompeius, I came to an end.

CHAP. CXLII. — THE JEWS RETURN THANKS, AND LEAVE JUSTIN.

Then Trypho, after a little delay, said, "You see that it was not intentionally that we came to discuss these points. And I confess that I have been particularly pleased with the conference; and I think that these are of quite the same opinion as myself. For we have found more than we expected, and more than it was possible to have expected. And if we could do this more frequently, we should be much helped in the searching of the Scriptures themselves. But since," he said, "you are on the eve of departure, and expect daily to set sail, do not hesitate to remember us as friends when you are gone."

"For my part," I replied, "if I had remained, I would have wished to do the same thing daily. But now, since I expect, with God's will and aid, to set sail, I exhort you to give all diligence in this very great struggle for your own salvation, and to be earnest in setting a higher value on the Christ of the Almighty God than on your own teachers."

After this they left me, wishing me safety in my voyage, and from every misfortune. And I, praying for them, said, "I can wish no better thing for you, sirs, than this, that, recognising in this way that intelligence is given to every man, you may be of the same opinion as ourselves, and believe that Jesus is the Christ of God."[2]

---

[1] Ps. xxxii. 2.

[2] The last sentence is very dubious. For παντὶ ἀνθρώπινον νοῦν read παντὶ ἀνθρώπῳ τὸν νοῦν. For ποιήσητε read πιστεύσητε. And lastly, for τὸ ἡμῶν read τὸν Ἰησοῦν.
[But there is no doubt about the touching beauty of this close: and truly Trypho seems "not far from the kingdom of God." Note the marvellous knowledge of the Old Testament Scriptures, which Justin had acquired, and which he could use in conversation. His quotations from the Psalms, *memoriter*, are more accurate than others. See Kaye, p. 141.]

THE DISCOURSE TO THE GREEKS

[TRANSLATED BY THE REV M. DODS, M.A.]

CHAP. I. — JUSTIN JUSTIFIES HIS DEPARTURE FROM GREEK CUSTOMS.

Do not suppose, ye Greeks, that my separation from your customs is unreasonable and unthinking; for I found in them nothing that is holy or acceptable to God. For the very compositions of your poets are monuments of madness and intemperance. For any one who becomes the scholar of your most eminent instructor, is more beset by difficulties than all men besides. For first they say that Agamemnon, abetting the extravagant lust of his brother, and his madness and unrestrained desire, readily gave even his daughter to be sacrificed, and troubled all Greece that he might rescue Helen, who had been ravished by the leprous[1] shepherd. But when in the course of the war they took captives, Agamemnon was himself taken captive by Chryseis, and for Briseis' sake kindled a feud with the son of Thetis. And Pelides himself, who crossed the river,[2] overthrew Troy, and subdued Hector, this your hero became the slave of Polyxena, and was conquered by a dead Amazon; and putting off the god-fabricated armour, and donning the hymeneal robe, he became a sacrifice of love in the temple of Apollo. And the Ithacan Ulysses made a virtue of a vice.[3] And indeed his sailing past the Sirens[4] gave evidence that he was destitute of worthy prudence, because he could not depend on his prudence for stopping his ears. Ajax, son of Telamon, who bore the shield of sevenfold ox-hide, went mad when he was defeated in the contest with Ulysses for the armour. Such things I have no desire to be instructed in. Of such virtue I am not covetous, that I should believe the myths of Homer. For the whole rhapsody, the beginning and end both of the Iliad and the Odyssey is — a woman.

---

[1] Potter would here read λιπαροῦ, "elegant" [ironically for effeminate]; but the above reading is defended by Sylburg, on the ground that shepherds were so greatly despised, that this is not too hard an epithet to apply to Paris.
[2] Of the many attempts to amend this clause, there seems to be none satisfactory.
[3] Or, won the reputation of the virtue of wisdom by the vice of deceit.
[4] That is, the manner in which he did it, stopping his companions' ears with wax, and having himself bound to the mast of his ship.

CHAP. II. — THE GREEK THEOGONY EXPOSED.

But since, next to Homer, Hesiod wrote his *Works and Days*, who will believe his drivelling theogony? For they say that Chronos, the son of Ouranos,[5] in the beginning slew his father, and possessed himself of his rule; and that, being seized with a panic lest he should himself suffer in the same way, he preferred devouring his children; but that, by the craft of the Curetes, Jupiter was conveyed away and kept in secret, and afterwards bound his father with chains, and divided the empire; Jupiter receiving, as the story goes, the air, and Neptune the deep, and Pluto the portion of Hades. But Pluto ravished Proserpine; and Ceres sought her child wandering through the deserts. And this myth was celebrated in the Eleusinian fire.[6] Again, Neptune ravished Melanippe when she was drawing water, besides abusing a host of Nereids not a few, whose names, were we to recount them, would cost us a multitude of words. And as for Jupiter, he was a various adulterer, with Antiope as a satyr, with Danaë as gold, and with Europa as a bull; with Leda, moreover, he assumed wings. For the love of Semele proved both his unchastity and the jealousy of Semele. And they say that he carried off the Phrygian Ganymede to be his cup-bearer. These, then, are the exploits of the sons of Saturn. And your illustrious son of Latona [Apollo], who professed soothsaying, convicted himself of lying. He pursued Daphne, but did not gain possession of her; and to Hyacinthus,[7] who loved him, he did not foretell his death. And I say nothing of the masculine character of Minerva, nor of the feminine nature of Bacchus, nor of the fornicating disposition of Venus. Read to Jupiter, ye Greeks, the law against parricides, and the penalty of adultery, and the ignominy of pæderasty. Teach Minerva and Diana the works of women, and Bacchus the works of men. What seemliness is

---

[5] Or, Saturn son of Heaven.
[6] In the mysteries of Eleusis, the return of Proserpine from the lower world was celebrated.
[7] Apollo accidentally killed Hyacinthus by striking him on the head with a quoit.

there in a woman's girding herself with armour, or in a man's decorating himself with cymbals, and garlands, and female attire, and accompanied by a herd of bacchanalian women?

CHAP. III. — FOLLIES OF THE GREEK MYTHOLOGY.

For Hercules, celebrated by his three nights,[1] sung by the poets for his successful labours, the son of Jupiter, who slew the lion and destroyed the many-headed hydra; who put to death the fierce and mighty boar, and was able to kill the fleet man-eating birds, and brought up from Hades the three-headed dog; who effectually cleansed the huge Augean building from its dung, and killed the bulls and the stag whose nostrils breathed fire, and plucked the golden fruit from the tree, and slew the poisonous serpent (and for some reason, which it is not lawful to utter, killed Achelous, and the guest-slaying Busiris), and crossed the mountains that he might get water which gave forth an articulate speech, as the story goes: he who was able to do so many and such like and so great deeds as these, how childishly he was delighted to be stunned by the cymbals of the satyrs, and to be conquered by the love of woman, and to be struck on the hips by the laughing Lyda! And at last, not being able to put off the tunic of Nessus, himself kindling his own funeral pile, so he died. Let Vulcan lay aside his envy, and not be jealous if he is hated because he is old and club-footed, and Mars loved, because young and beautiful. Since, therefore, ye Greeks, your gods are convicted of intemperance, and your heroes are effeminate, as the histories on which your dramas are founded have declared, such as the curse of Atreus, the bed of Thyestes,[2] and the taint in the house of Pelops, and Danaus murdering through hatred and making Ægyptus childless in the intoxication of his rage, and the Thyestean banquet spread by the Furies.[3] And Procne is to this day flitting about, lamenting; and her sister of Athens shrills with her tongue cut out. For what need is there of speaking of the goad[4] of Œdipus, and the murder of Laius, and the marrying his mother, and the mutual slaughter of those who were at once his brothers and his sons?

CHAP. IV. — SHAMELESS PRACTICES OF THE GREEKS.

And your public assemblies I have come to hate. For there are excessive banquetings, and subtle flutes which provoke to lustful movements, and useless and luxurious anointings, and crowning with garlands. With such a mass of evils do you banish shame; and ye fill your minds with them, and are carried away by intemperance, and indulge as a common practice in wicked and insane fornication. And this further I would say to you, why are you, being a Greek, indignant at your son when he imitates Jupiter, and rises against you and defrauds you of your own wife? Why do you count him your enemy, and yet worship one that is like him? And why do you blame your wife for living in unchastity, and yet honour Venus with shrines? If indeed these things had been related by others, they would have seemed to be mere slanderous accusations, and not truth. But now your own poets sing these things, and your histories noisily publish them.

CHAP. V. — CLOSING APPEAL.

Henceforth, ye Greeks, come and partake of incomparable wisdom, and be instructed by the Divine Word, and acquaint yourselves with the King immortal; and do not recognise those men as heroes who slaughter whole nations. For our own Ruler,[5] the Divine Word, who even now constantly aids us, does not desire strength of body and beauty of feature, nor yet the high spirit of earth's nobility, but a pure soul, fortified by holiness, and the watchwords of our King, holy actions, for through the Word power passes into the soul. O trumpet of peace to the soul that is at war! O weapon that puttest to flight terrible passions! O instruction that quenches the innate fire of the soul! The Word exercises an influence which does not make poets: it does not equip philosophers nor skilled orators, but by its instruction it makes mortals immortal, mortals gods; and from the earth transports them to the realms above Olympus. Come, be taught; become as I am, for I, too, was as ye are.[6] These have conquered me — the divinity of the instruction, and the power of the Word: for as a skilled serpent-charmer lures the terrible reptile from his den and causes it to flee, so the Word drives the fearful passions of our sensual nature from the very recesses of the soul; first driving forth lust, through which every ill is begotten — hatreds, strife, envy, emulations, anger, and such like. Lust being once banished, the soul becomes calm and serene. And being set free from the ills in which it was sunk up to the neck, it returns to Him who made it. For it is fit that it be restored to that state whence it departed, whence every soul was or is.

---

[1] Τριέσπερον, so called, as some think, [from his origin: "*ex concubitu trium noctium.*"]
[2] Thyestes seduced the wife of his brother Atreus, whence the tragic career of the family.
[3] There is no apodosis in the Greek.
[4] Not, as the editors dispute, either the tongue of the buckle with which he put out his eyes, nor the awl with which his heels were bored through, but the goad with which he killed his father.

[5] Αὐτὸς γὰρ ἡμῶν.
[6] [He seems to quote Gal. iv. 12.]
[N. B. — It should be stated that modern critics consider this work as not improbably by another author.]

JUSTIN'S HORTATORY ADDRESS TO THE GREEKS

[TRANSLATED BY THE REV. M. DODS, M.A.]

CHAP. I. — REASONS FOR ADDRESSING THE GREEKS.

As I begin this hortatory address to you, ye men of Greece, I pray God that I may know what I ought to say to you, and that you, shaking off your habitual[1] love of disputing, and being delivered from the error of your fathers, may now choose what is profitable; not fancying that you commit any offence against your forefathers, though the things which you formerly considered by no means salutary should now seem useful to you. For accurate investigation of matters, putting truth to the question with a more searching scrutiny, often reveals that things which have passed for excellent are of quite another sort. Since, then, we propose to discourse of the true religion (than which, I think, there is nothing which is counted more valuable by those who desire to pass through life without danger, on account of the judgment which is to be after the termination of this life, and which is announced not only by our forefathers according to God, to wit the prophets and lawgivers, but also by those among yourselves who have been esteemed wise, not poets alone, but also philosophers, who professed among you that they had attained the true and divine knowledge), I think it well first of all to examine the teachers of religion, both our own and yours, who they were, and how great, and in what times they lived; in order that those who have formerly received from their fathers the false religion, may now, when they perceive this, be extricated from that inveterate error; and that we may clearly and manifestly show that we ourselves follow the religion of our forefathers according to God.

CHAP. II. — THE POETS ARE UNFIT TO BE RELIGIOUS TEACHERS.

Whom, then, ye men of Greece, do ye call your teachers of religion? The poets? It will do your cause no good to say so to men who know the poets; for they know how very ridiculous a theogony they have composed, — as we can learn from Homer, your most distinguished and prince of poets. For he says, first, that the gods were in the beginning generated from water; for he has written thus:[2] —

"Both ocean, the origin of the gods, and their mother Tethys."

And then we must also remind you of what he further says of him whom ye consider the first of the gods, and whom he often calls "the father of gods and men;" for he said:[3] —

"Zeus, who is the dispenser of war to men."

Indeed, he says that he was not only the dispenser of war to the army, but also the cause of perjury to the Trojans, by means of his daughter;[4] and Homer introduces him in love, and bitterly complaining, and bewailing himself, and plotted against by the other gods, and at one time exclaiming concerning his own son:[5] —

"Alas! he falls, my most beloved of men!
Sarpedon, vanquished by Patroclus, falls.
So will the fates."

And at another time concerning Hector:[6] —

"Ah! I behold a warrior dear to me
Around the walls of Ilium driven, and grieve
For Hector."

And what he says of the conspiracy of the other gods against Zeus, they know who read these words:[7] "When the other Olympians — Juno, and Neptune, and Minerva — wished to bind him." And unless the blessed gods had feared him whom gods call Briareus, Zeus would have been bound by them. And what Homer says of his intemperate loves, we must remind you in the very words he used. For he said that Zeus spake thus to Juno:[8] —

---

[1] Literally, "former."
[2] *Iliad*, xiv. 302.
[3] *Iliad*, xix. 224.
[4] That is, Venus, who, after Paris had sworn that the war should be decided by single combat between himself and Menelaus, carried him off, and induced him, though defeated, to refuse performance of the articles agreed upon.
[5] *Iliad*, xvi. 433. Sarpedon was a son of Zeus.
[6] *Iliad*, xxii. 168.
[7] *Iliad*, i. 399, etc.
[8] *Iliad*, xiv. 315. (The passage is here given in full from Cowper's translation. In Justin's quotation one or two lines are omitted.)

> "For never goddess pour'd, nor woman yet,
> So full a tide of love into my breast;
> I never loved Ixion's consort thus,
> Nor sweet Acrisian Danaë, from whom
> Sprang Perseus, noblest of the race of man;
> Nor Phœnix' daughter fair, of whom were born
> Minos, unmatch'd but by the powers above,
> And Rhadamanthus; nor yet Semele,
> Nor yet Alcmene, who in Thebes produced
> The valiant Hercules; and though my son
> By Semele were Bacchus, joy of man;
> Nor Ceres golden-hair'd, nor high-enthron'd
> Latona in the skies; no — nor thyself
> As now I love thee, and my soul perceive
> O'erwhelm'd with sweetness of intense desire."

It is fit that we now mention what one can learn from the work of Homer of the other gods, and what they suffered at the hands of men. For he says that Mars and Venus were wounded by Diomed, and of many others of the gods he relates the sufferings. For thus we can gather from the case of Dione consoling her daughter; for she said to her:[1] —

> "Have patience, dearest child; though much enforc'd
> Restrain thine anger: we, in heav'n who dwell,
> Have much to bear from mortals; and ourselves
> Too oft upon each other suff'rings lay:
> Mars had his suff'rings; by Alöeus' sons,
> Otus and Ephialtes, strongly bound,
> He thirteen months in brazen fetters lay:
> Juno, too, suffer'd, when Amphitryon's son
> Thro' her right breast a three-barb'd arrow sent:
> Dire, and unheard of, were the pangs she bore,
> Great Pluto's self the stinging arrow felt,
> When that same son of Ægis-bearing Jove
> Assail'd him in the very gates of hell,
> And wrought him keenest anguish; pierced with pain,
> To high Olympus, to the courts of Jove,
> He came; the bitter shaft remain'd
> Deep in his shoulder fix'd, and griev'd his soul."

But if it is right to remind you of the battle of the gods, opposed to one another, your own poet himself will recount it, saying:[2] —

> "Such was the shock when gods in battle met;
> For there to royal Neptune stood oppos'd
> Phœbus Apollo with his arrows keen;
> The blue-eyed Pallas to the god of war;
> To Juno, Dian, heav'nly archeress,
> Sister of Phœbus, golden-shafted queen.
> Stout Hermes, helpful god, Latona fac'd."

These and such like things did Homer teach you; and not Homer only, but also Hesiod. So that if you believe your most distinguished poets, who have given the genealogies of your gods, you must of necessity either suppose that the gods are such beings as these, or believe that there are no gods at all.

CHAP. III. — OPINIONS OF THE SCHOOL OF THALES.

And if you decline citing the poets, because you say it is allowable for them to frame myths, and to relate in a mythical way many things about the gods which are far from true, do you suppose you have some others for your religious teachers, or how do you say that they themselves[3] have learned this religion of yours? For it is impossible that any should know matters so great and divine, who have not themselves learned them first from the initiated.[4] You will no doubt say, "The sages and philosophers." For to them, as to a fortified wall, you are wont to flee, when any one quotes the opinions of your poets about the gods. Therefore, since it is fit that we commence with the ancients and the earliest, beginning thence I will produce the opinion of each, much more ridiculous as it is than the theology of the poets. For Thales of Miletus, who took the lead in the study of natural philosophy, declared that water was the first principle of all things; for from water he says that all things are, and that into water all are resolved. And after him Anaximander, who came from the same Miletus, said that the infinite was the first principle of all things; for that from this indeed all things are produced, and into this do all decay. Thirdly, Anaximenes — and he too was from Miletus — says that air is the first principle of all things; for he says that from this all things are produced, and into this all are resolved. Heraclitus and Hippasus, from Metapontus, say that fire is the first principle of all things; for from fire all things proceed, and in fire do all things terminate. Anaxagoras of Clazomenæ said that the homogeneous parts are the first principles of all things. Archelaus, the son of Apollodorus, an Athenian, says that the infinite air and its density and rarity are the first principle of all things. All these, forming a succession from Thales, followed the philosophy called by themselves physical.

CHAP. IV. — OPINIONS OF PYTHAGORAS AND EPICURUS.

Then, in regular succession from another starting-point, Pythagoras the Samian, son of Mnesarchus, calls numbers, with their proportions and harmonies, and the elements composed of both, the first principles; and he includes also unity and the indefinite binary.[5] Epicurus, an Athenian, the son of Neocles, says that the first principles of the things that exist are bodies perceptible by reason, admitting no vacuity,[6] unbegotten, indestructible, which can neither be broken, nor admit of any formation of their parts, nor alteration, and are therefore perceptible by reason. Empedocles of Agrigentum,

---

[1] *Iliad*, v. 382 (from Lord Derby's translation).
[2] *Iliad*, xx. 66 (from Lord Derby's translation).
[3] i.e., these teachers.
[4] Literally, "those who knew."
[5] μονάδα καὶ τὴν ἀόριστον δυάδα. One, or unity, was considered by Pythagoras as the essence of number, and also as God. Two, or the indefinite binary, was the equivalent of evil. So Plutarch, *De placit. philosoph.*, c. 7; from which treatise the above opinions of the various sects are quoted, generally *verbatim*.
[6] ἀμέτοχα κενοῦ: the void being that in which these bodies move, while they themselves are of a different nature from it.

son of Meton, maintained that there were four elements — fire, air, water, earth; and two elementary powers — love and hate,[1] of which the former is a power of union, the latter of separation. You see, then, the confusion of those who are considered by you to have been wise men, whom you assert to be your teachers of religion: some of them declaring that water is the first principle of all things; others, air; others, fire; and others, some other of these fore-mentioned elements; and all of them employing persuasive arguments for the establishment of their own errors, and attempting to prove their own peculiar dogma to be the most valuable. These things were said by them. How then, ye men of Greece, can it be safe for those who desire to be saved, to fancy that they can learn the true religion from these philosophers, who were neither able so to convince themselves as to prevent sectarian wrangling with one another, and not to appear definitely opposed to one another's opinions?

CHAP. V. — OPINIONS OF PLATO AND ARISTOTLE.

But possibly those who are unwilling to give up the ancient and inveterate error, maintain that they have received the doctrine of their religion not from those who have now been mentioned, but from those who are esteemed among them as the most renowned and finished philosophers, Plato and Aristotle. For these, they say, have learned the perfect and true religion. But I would be glad to ask, first of all, from those who say so, from whom they say that these men have learned this knowledge; for it is impossible that men who have not learned these so great and divine matters from some who knew them, should either themselves know them, or be able correctly to teach others; and, in the second place, I think we ought to examine the opinions even of these sages. For we shall see whether each of these does not manifestly contradict the other. But if we find that even they do not agree with each other, I think it is easy to see clearly that they too are ignorant. For Plato, with the air of one that has descended from above, and has accurately ascertained and seen all that is in heaven, says that the most high God exists in a fiery substance.[2] But Aristotle, in a book addressed to Alexander of Macedon, giving a compendious explanation of his own philosophy, clearly and manifestly overthrows the opinion of Plato, saying that God does not exist in a fiery substance: but inventing, as a fifth substance, some kind of ætherial and unchangeable body, says that God exists in it. Thus, at least, he wrote: "Not, as some of those who have erred regarding the Deity say, that God exists in a fiery substance." Then, as if he were not satisfied with this blasphemy against Plato, he further, for the sake of proving what he says about the ætherial body, cites as a witness him whom Plato had banished from his republic as a liar, and as being an imitator of the images of truth at three removes,[3] for so Plato calls Homer; for he wrote: "Thus at least did Homer speak,[4] 'And Zeus obtained the wide heaven in the air and the clouds,'" wishing to make his own opinion appear more worthy of credit by the testimony of Homer; not being aware that if he used Homer as a witness to prove that he spoke truth, many of his tenets would be proved untrue. For Thales of Miletus, who was the founder of philosophy among them, taking occasion from him,[5] will contradict his first opinions about first principles. For Aristotle himself, having said that God and matter are the first principles of all things, Thales, the eldest of all their sages, says that water is the first principle of the things that exist; for he says that all things are from water, and that all things are resolved into water. And he conjectures this, first, from the fact that the seed of all living creatures, which is their first principle, is moist; and secondly, because all plants grow and bear fruit in moisture, but when deprived of moisture, wither. Then, as if not satisfied with his conjectures, he cites Homer as a most trustworthy testimony, who speaks thus: —

"Ocean, who is the origin of all."[6]

May not Thales, then, very fairly say to him, "What is the reason, Aristotle, why you give heed to Homer, as if he spoke truth, when you wish to demolish the opinions of Plato; but when you promulgate an opinion contrary to ours, you think Homer untruthful?"

CHAP. VI. — FURTHER DISAGREEMENTS BETWEEN PLATO AND ARISTOTLE.

And that these very wonderful sages of yours do not even agree in other respects, can be easily learned from this. For while Plato says that there are three first principles of all things, God, and matter, and form, — God, the maker of all; and matter, which is the subject of the first production of all that is produced, and affords to God opportunity for His workmanship; and form, which is the type of each of the things

---

[1] Or, accord and discord, attraction and repulsion.
[2] Or, "is of a fiery nature."
[3] See the *Republic*, x. 2. By the Platonic doctrine, the ideas of things in the mind of God were the realities; the things themselves, as seen by us, were the images of these realities; and poetry, therefore, describing the images of realities, was only at the third remove from nature. As Plato puts it briefly in this same passage, "the painter, the bed-maker, God — these three are the masters of three species of beds."
[4] *Iliad*, xv. 192.
[5] i.e., from Homer; using Homer's words as suggestive and confirmatory of his doctrine.
[6] *Iliad*, xiv. 246.

produced, — Aristotle makes no mention at all of form as a first principle, but says that there are two, God and matter. And again, while Plato says that the highest God and the ideas exist in the first place of the highest heavens, and in fixed sphere, Aristotle says that, next to the most high God, there are, not ideas, but certain gods, who can be perceived by the mind. Thus, then, do they differ concerning things heavenly. So that one can see that they not only are unable to understand our earthly matters, but also, being at variance among themselves regarding these things, they will appear unworthy of credit when they treat of things heavenly. And that even their doctrine regarding the human soul as it now is does not harmonize, is manifest from what has been said by each of them concerning it. For Plato says that it is of three parts, having the faculty of reason, of affection, and of appetite.[1] But Aristotle says that the soul is not so comprehensive as to include also corruptible parts, but only reason. And Plato loudly maintains that "the whole soul is immortal." But Aristotle, naming it "the actuality,"[2] would have it to be mortal, not immortal. And the former says it is always in motion; but Aristotle says that it is immoveable, since it must itself precede all motion.

CHAP. VII. — INCONSISTENCIES OF PLATO'S DOCTRINE.

But in these things they are convicted of thinking in contradiction to each other. And if any one will accurately criticise their writings, they have chosen to abide in harmony not even with their own opinions. Plato, at any rate, at one time says that there are three first principles of the universe — God, and matter, and form; but at another time four, for he adds the universal soul. And again, when he has already said that matter is eternal,[3] he afterwards says that it is produced; and when he has first given to form its peculiar rank as a first principle, and has asserted for its self-subsistence, he afterwards says that this same thing is among the things perceived by the understanding. Moreover, having first declared that everything that is made is mortal,[4] he afterwards states that some of the things that are made are indestructible and immortal. What, then, is the cause why those who have been esteemed wise among you disagree not only with one another, but also with themselves? Manifestly, their unwillingness to learn from those who know, and their desire to attain accurate knowledge of things heavenly by their own human excess of wisdom; though they were able to understand not even earthly matters. Certainly some of your philosophers say that the human soul is in us; others, that it is around us. For not even in this did they choose to agree with one another, but, distributing, as it were, ignorance in various ways among themselves, they thought fit to wrangle and dispute with one another even about the soul. For some of them say that the soul is fire, and some that it is the air; and others, the mind; and others, motion; and others, an exhalation; and certain others say that it is a power flowing from the stars; and others, number capable of motion; and others, a generating water. And a wholly confused and inharmonious opinion has prevailed among them, which only in this one respect appears praiseworthy to those who can form a right judgment, that they have been anxious to convict one another of error and falsehood.

CHAP. VIII. — ANTIQUITY, INSPIRATION, AND HARMONY OF CHRISTIAN TEACHERS.

Since therefore it is impossible to learn anything true concerning religion from your teachers, who by their mutual disagreement have furnished you with sufficient proof of their own ignorance, I consider it reasonable to recur to our progenitors, who both in point of time have by a great way the precedence of your teachers, and who have taught us nothing from their own private fancy, nor differed with one another, nor attempted to overturn one another's positions, but without wrangling and contention received from God the knowledge which also they taught to us. For neither by nature nor by human conception is it possible for men to know things so great and divine, but by the gift which then descended from above upon the holy men, who had no need of rhetorical art,[5] nor of uttering anything in a contentious or quarrelsome manner, but to present themselves pure [6] to the energy of the Divine Spirit, in order that the divine plectrum itself, descending from heaven, and using righteous men as an instrument like a harp or lyre, might reveal to us the knowledge of things divine and heavenly. Wherefore, as if with one mouth and one tongue, they have in succession, and in harmony with one another, taught us both concerning God, and the creation of the world, and the formation of man, and concerning the immortality of the human soul, and the judgment which is to be after this life, and concerning all things which it is needful for us to know, and thus in divers times and places have afforded us the divine instruction.[7]

---

[1] τὸ λογικόν, τὸ θυμικόν, τὸ ἐπιθυμητικόν, — corresponding to what we roughly speak of as reason, the heart, and the appetites.
[2] ἐντελέχεια, — the completion or actuality to which each thing, by virtue of its peculiar nature (or potentiality, δύναμις), can arrive.
[3] Literally, "unbegotten."
[4] Or, "liable to destruction."
[5] Literally, "the art of words."
[6] Literally, "clean," free from other influences.
[7] [The diversities of Christian theology are to be regretted; but Justin here shows the harmony and order of truths, such as are everywhere received by Christians, to be an inestimable advantage.]

CHAP. IX. — THE ANTIQUITY OF MOSES PROVED BY GREEK WRITERS.

I will begin, then, with our first prophet and lawgiver, Moses; first explaining the times in which he lived, on authorities which among you are worthy of all credit. For I do not propose to prove these things only from our own divine histories, which as yet you are unwilling to credit on account of the inveterate error of your forefathers, but also from your own histories, and such, too, as have no reference to our worship, that you may know that, of all your teachers, whether sages, poets, historians, philosophers, or lawgivers, by far the oldest, as the Greek histories show us, was Moses, who was our first religious teacher.[1] For in the times of Ogyges and Inachus, whom some of your poets suppose to have been earth-born,[2] Moses is mentioned as the leader and ruler of the Jewish nation. For in this way he is mentioned both by Polemon in the first book of his *Hellenics*, and by Apion son of Posidonius in his book against the Jews, and in the fourth book of his history, where he says that during the reign of Inachus over Argos the Jews revolted from Amasis king of the Egyptians, and that Moses led them. And Ptolemæus the Mendesian, in relating the history of Egypt, concurs in all this. And those who write the Athenian history, Hellanicus and Philochorus (the author of *The Attic History*), Castor and Thallus, and Alexander Polyhistor, and also the very well informed writers on Jewish affairs, Philo and Josephus, have mentioned Moses as a very ancient and time-honoured prince of the Jews. Josephus, certainly, desiring to signify even by the title of his work the antiquity and age of the history, wrote thus at the commencement of the history: "The Jewish antiquities[3] of Flavius Josephus," — signifying the oldness of the history by the word "antiquities." And your most renowned historian Diodorus, who employed thirty whole years in epitomizing the libraries, and who, as he himself wrote, travelled over both Asia and Europe for the sake of great accuracy, and thus became an eye-witness of very many things, wrote forty entire books of his own history. And he in the first book, having said that he had learned from the Egyptian priests that Moses was an ancient lawgiver, and even the first, wrote of him in these very words: "For subsequent to the ancient manner of living in Egypt which gods and heroes are fabled to have regulated, they say that Moses[4] first persuaded the people to use written laws, and to live by them; and he is recorded to have been a man both great of soul and of great faculty in social matters." Then, having proceeded a little further, and wishing to mention the ancient lawgivers, he mentions Moses first. For he spoke in these words: "Among the Jews they say that Moses ascribed his laws[5] to that God who is called Jehovah, whether because they judged it a marvellous and quite divine conception which promised to benefit a multitude of men, or because they were of opinion that the people would be the more obedient when they contemplated the majesty and power of those who were said to have invented the laws. And they say that Sasunchis was the second Egyptian legislator, a man of excellent understanding. And the third, they say, was Sesonchosis the king, who not only performed the most brilliant military exploits of any in Egypt, but also consolidated that warlike race by legislation. And the fourth lawgiver, they say, was Bocchoris the king, a wise and surpassingly skilful man. And after him it is said that Amasis the king acceded to the government, whom they relate to have regulated all that pertains to the rulers of provinces, and to the general administration of the government of Egypt. And they say that Darius, the father of Xerxes, was the sixth who legislated for the Egyptians."

CHAP. X. — TRAINING AND INSPIRATION OF MOSES.[6]

These things, ye men of Greece, have been recorded in writing concerning the antiquity of Moses by those who were not of our religion; and they said that they learned all these things from the Egyptian priests, among whom Moses was not only born, but also was thought worthy of partaking of all the education of the Egyptians, on account of his being adopted by the king's daughter as her son; and for the same reason was thought worthy of great attention, as the wisest of the historians relate, who have chosen to record his life and actions, and the rank of his descent, — I speak of Philo and Josephus. For these, in their narration of the history of the Jews, say that Moses was sprung from the race of the Chaldæans, and that he was born in Egypt when his forefathers had migrated on account of famine from Phœnicia to that country; and him God chose to honour on account of his exceeding virtue, and judged him worthy to become the leader and lawgiver of his own race, when He thought it right that the people of the Hebrews should return out of Egypt into their own land. To him first did God communicate that divine and prophetic gift which in those days descended upon the holy men, and him also did He first

---

[1] The incongruity in this sentence is Justin's.
[2] [Autochthones]. That is, sprung from the soil; and hence the oldest inhabitants, the aborigines.
[3] Literally, archæology.
[4] Unfortunately, Justin here mistook Menes for Moses. [But he may have so read the name in his copy. See Grabe's note on Diodorus, and the quotation following in another note.]

[5] This sentence must be so completed from the context in Diodorus. See the note of Maranus.
[6] [Consult the ponderous learning of Warburton's *Divine Legation, passim.*]

furnish that he might be our teacher in religion, and then after him the rest of the prophets, who both obtained the same gift as he, and taught us the same doctrines concerning the same subjects. These we assert to have been our teachers, who taught us nothing from their own human conception, but from the gift vouchsafed to them by God from above.

CHAP. XI. — HEATHEN ORACLES TESTIFY OF MOSES.

But as you do not see the necessity of giving up the ancient error of your forefathers in obedience to these teachers [of ours], what teachers of your own do you maintain to have lived worthy of credit in the matter of religion? For, as I have frequently said, it is impossible that those who have not themselves learned these so great and divine things from such persons as are acquainted with them, should either themselves know them, or be able rightly to teach others. Since, therefore, it has been sufficiently proved that the opinions of your philosophers are obviously full of all ignorance and deceit, having now perhaps wholly abandoned the philosophers as formerly you abandoned the poets, you will turn to the deceit of the oracles; for in this style I have heard some speaking. Therefore I think it fit to tell you at this step in our discourse what I formerly heard among you concerning their utterances. For when one inquired at your oracle — it is your own story — what religious men had at any time happened to live, you say that the oracle answered thus: "Only the Chaldæans have obtained wisdom, and the Hebrews, who worship God Himself, the self-begotten King."

Since, therefore, you think that the truth can be learned from your oracles, when you read the histories and what has been written regarding the life of Moses by those who do not belong to our religion, and when you know that Moses and the rest of the prophets were descended from the race of the Chaldæans and Hebrews, do not think that anything incredible has taken place if a man sprung from a godly line, and who lived worthily of the godliness of his fathers, was chosen by God to be honoured with this great gift and to be set forth as the first of all the prophets.

CHAP. XII. — ANTIQUITY OF MOSES PROVED.

And I think it necessary also to consider the times in which your philosophers lived, that you may see that the time which produced them for you is very recent, and also short. For thus you will be able easily to recognise also the antiquity of Moses. But lest, by a complete survey of the periods, and by the use of a greater number of proofs, I should seem to be prolix, I thing it may be sufficiently demonstrated from the following. For Socrates was the teacher of Plato, and Plato of Aristotle. Now these men flourished in the time of Philip and Alexander of Macedon, in which time also the Athenian orators flourished, as the Philippics of Demosthenes plainly show us. And those who have narrated the deeds of Alexander sufficiently prove that during his reign Aristotle associated with him. From all manner of proofs, then, it is easy to see that the history of Moses is by far more ancient than all profane[1] histories. And, besides, it is fit that you recognise this fact also, that nothing has been accurately recorded by Greeks before the era of the Olympiads, and that there is no ancient work which makes known any action of the Greeks or Barbarians. But before that period existed only the history of the prophet Moses, which he wrote in the Hebrew character by the divine inspiration. For the Greek character was not yet in use, as the teachers of language themselves prove, telling us that Cadmus first brought the letters from Phœnicia, and communicated them to the Greeks. And your first of philosophers, Plato, testifies that they were a recent discovery. For in the *Timæus*[2] he wrote that Solon, the wisest of the wise men, on his return from Egypt, said to Critias that he had heard this from a very aged Egyptian priest, who said to him, "O Solon, Solon, you Greeks are ever children, and aged Greek there is none." Then again he said, "You are all youths in soul, for you hold no ancient opinion derived through remote tradition, nor any system of instruction hoary with time; but all these things escape your knowledge, because for many generations the posterity of these ancient ages died mute, not having the use of letters." It is fit, therefore, that you understand that it is the fact that every history has been written in these recently-discovered Greek letters; and if any one would make mention of old poets, or legislators, or historians, or philosophers, or orators, he will find that they wrote their own works in the Greek character.

CHAP. XIII. — HISTORY OF THE SEPTUAGINT.

But if any one says that the writings of Moses and of the rest of the prophets were also written in the Greek character, let him read profane histories, and know that Ptolemy, king of Egypt, when he had built the library in Alexandria, and by gathering books from every quarter had filled it, then learnt that very ancient histories written in Hebrew happened to be carefully preserved; and wishing to know their contents, he sent for seventy wise men from Jerusalem, who were acquainted with both the Greek and Hebrew language, and appointed them to translate the books; and that in freedom from all disturb-

---
[1] Literally, "without," not belonging to the true faith.
[2] C. 3.

ance they might the more speedily complete the translation, he ordered that there should be constructed, not in the city itself, but seven stadia off (where the Pharos was built), as many little cots as there were translators, so that each by himself might complete his own translation; and enjoined upon those officers who were appointed to this duty, to afford them all attendance, but to prevent communication with one another, in order that the accuracy of the translation might be discernible even by their agreement. And when he ascertained that the seventy men had not only given the same meaning, but had employed the same words, and had failed in agreement with one another not even to the extent of one word, but had written the same things, and concerning the same things, he was struck with amazement, and believed that the translation had been written by divine power, and perceived that the men were worthy of all honour, as beloved of God; and with many gifts ordered them to return to their own country. And having, as was natural, marvelled at the books, and concluded them to be divine, he consecrated them in that library. These things, ye men of Greece, are no fable, nor do we narrate fictions; but we ourselves having been in Alexandria, saw the remains of the little cots at the Pharos still preserved, and having heard these things from the inhabitants, who had received them as part of their country's tradition,[1] we now tell to you what you can also learn from others, and specially from those wise and esteemed men who have written of these things, Philo and Josephus, and many others. But if any of those who are wont to be forward in contradiction should say that these books do not belong to us, but to the Jews, and should assert that we in vain profess to have learnt our religion from them, let him know, as he may from those very things which are written in these books, that not to them, but to us, does the doctrine of them refer. That the books relating to our religion are to this day preserved among the Jews, has been a work of Divine Providence on our behalf; for lest, by producing them out of the Church, we should give occasion to those who wish to slander us to charge us with fraud, we demand that they be produced from the synagogue of the Jews, that from the very books still preserved among them it might clearly and evidently appear, that the laws which were written by holy men, for instruction pertain to us.

CHAP. XIV. — A WARNING APPEAL TO THE GREEKS.

It is therefore necessary, ye Greeks, that you contemplate the things that are to be, and consider the judgment which is predicted by all, not only by the godly, but also by those who are irreligious, that ye do not without investigation commit yourselves to the error of your fathers, nor suppose that if they themselves have been in error, and have transmitted it to you, that this which they have taught you is true; but looking to the danger of so terrible a mistake, inquire and investigate carefully into those things which are, as you say, spoken of even by your own teachers. For even unwillingly they were on your account forced to say many things by the Divine regard for mankind, especially those of them who were in Egypt, and profited by the godliness of Moses and his ancestry. For I think that some of you, when you read even carelessly the history of Diodorus, and of those others who wrote of these things, cannot fail to see that both Orpheus, and Homer, and Solon, who wrote the laws of the Athenians, and Pythagoras, and Plato, and some others, when they had been in Egypt, and had taken advantage of the history of Moses, afterwards published doctrines concerning the gods quite contrary to those which formerly they had erroneously promulgated.

CHAP. XV. — TESTIMONY OF ORPHEUS TO MONOTHEISM.

At all events, we must remind you what Orpheus, who was, as one might say, your first teacher of polytheism, latterly addressed to his son Musæus, and to the other legitimate auditors, concerning the one and only God. And he spoke thus: —

"I speak to those who lawfully may hear:
All others, ye profane, now close the doors,
And, O Musæus! hearken thou to me,
Who offspring art of the light-bringing moon:
The words I utter now are true indeed;
And if thou former thoughts of mine hast seen,
Let them not rob thee of the blessed life,
But rather turn the depths of thine own heart
Unto the place where light and knowledge dwell.
Take thou the word divine to guide thy steps,
And walking well in the straight certain path,
Look to the one and universal King —
One, self-begotten, and the only One —
Of whom all things and we ourselves are sprung.
All things are open to His piercing gaze,
While He Himself is still invisible.
Present in all His works, though still unseen,
He gives to mortals evil out of good,
Sending both chilling wars and tearful griefs;
And other than the great King there is none.
The clouds for ever settle round His throne,
And mortal eyeballs in mere mortal eyes
Are weak, to see Jove reigning over all.
He sits established in the brazen heavens
Upon His golden throne; under His feet
He treads the earth, and stretches His right hand
To all the ends of ocean, and around
Tremble the mountain ranges and the streams,
The depths, too, of the blue and hoary sea."

---

[1] [Doubtless Justin relates the tradition as he received it. Consult Dr. Selwyn's full account of the fables concerning the LXX., in *Smith's Dict. of the Bible*, iii. p. 1203 ff.]

And again, in some other place he says:—

"There is one Zeus alone, one sun, one hell,
One Bacchus; and in all things but one God;
Nor of all these as diverse let me speak."

And when he swears he says:—

"Now I adjure thee by the highest heaven,
The work of the great God, the only wise;
And I adjure thee by the Father's voice,
Which first He uttered when He stablished
The whole world by His counsel."

What does he mean by "I adjure thee by the Father's voice, which first He uttered?" It is the Word of God which he here names "the voice," by whom heaven and earth and the whole creation were made, as the divine prophecies of the holy men teach us; and these he himself also paid some attention to in Egypt, and understood that all creation was made by the Word of God; and therefore, after he says, "I adjure thee by the Father's voice, which first He uttered," he adds this besides, "when by His counsel He established the whole world." Here he calls the Word "voice," for the sake of the poetical metre. And that this is so, is manifest from the fact, that a little further on, where the metre permits him, he names it "Word." For he said:—

"Take thou the *Word* divine to guide thy steps."

CHAP. XVI.—TESTIMONY OF THE SIBYL.

We must also mention what the ancient and exceedingly remote Sibyl, whom Plato and Aristophanes, and others besides, mention as a prophetess, taught you in her oracular verses concerning one only God. And she speaks thus:—

"There is one only unbegotten God,
Omnipotent, invisible, most high,
All-seeing, but Himself seen by no flesh."

Then elsewhere thus:—

"But we have strayed from the Immortal's ways,
And worship with a dull and senseless mind
Idols, the workmanship of our own hands,
And images and figures of dead men."

And again somewhere else:—

"Blessed shall be those men upon the earth
Who shall love the great God before all else,
Blessing Him when they eat and when they drink;
Trusting in this their piety alone.
Who shall abjure all shrines which they may see,
All altars and vain figures of dumb stones,
Worthless and stained with blood of animals,
And sacrifice of the four-footed tribes,
Beholding the great glory of One God."

These are the Sibyl's words.

CHAP. XVII.—TESTIMONY OF HOMER.

And the poet Homer, using the license of poetry, and rivalling the original opinion of Orpheus regarding the plurality of the gods, mentions, indeed, several gods in a mythical style, lest he should seem to sing in a different strain from the poem of Orpheus, which he so distinctly proposed to rival, that even in the first line of his poem he indicated the relation he held to him. For as Orpheus in the beginning of his poem had said, "O goddess, sing the wrath of Demeter, who brings the goodly fruit," Homer began thus, "O goddess, sing the wrath of Achilles, son of Peleus," preferring, as it seems to me, even to violate the poetical metre in his first line, than that he should seem not to have remembered before all else the names of the gods. But shortly after he also clearly and explicitly presents his own opinion regarding one God only, somewhere [1] saying to Achilles by the mouth of Phœnix, "Not though God Himself were to promise that He would peel off my old age, and give me the vigour of my youth," where he indicates by the pronoun the real and true God. And somewhere [2] he makes Ulysses address the host of the Greeks thus: "The rule of many is not a good thing; let there be one ruler." And that the rule of many is not a good thing, but on the contrary an evil, he proposed to evince by fact, recounting the wars which took place on account of the multitude of rulers, and the fights and factions, and their mutual counterplots. For monarchy *is* free from contention. So far the poet Homer.

CHAP. XVIII.—TESTIMONY OF SOPHOCLES.

And if it is needful that we add testimonies concerning one God, even from the dramatists, hear even Sophocles speaking thus:—

"There is one God, in truth there is but one,
Who made the heavens and the broad earth beneath,
The glancing waves of ocean and the winds
But many of us mortals err in heart,
And set up for a solace in our woes
Images of the gods in stone and wood,
Or figures carved in brass or ivory,
And, furnishing for these our handiworks,
Both sacrifice and rite magnificent,
We think that thus we do a pious work."

Thus, then, Sophocles.

CHAP. XIX.—TESTIMONY OF PYTHAGORAS.

And Pythagoras, son of Mnesarchus, who expounded the doctrines of his own philosophy, mystically by means of symbols, as those who have written his life show, himself seems to have entertained thoughts about the unity of God not unworthy of his foreign residence in Egypt. For when he says that unity is the first principle of all things, and that it is the cause of all good, he teaches by an allegory that God is one, and alone.[3] And that this is so, is evident from his saying that

---

[1] *Iliad*, ix. 445.
[2] *Iliad*, ii. 204.
[3] Has no fellow.

unity and one differ widely from one another. For he says that unity belongs to the class of things perceived by the mind, but that one belongs to numbers. And if you desire to see a clearer proof of the opinion of Pythagoras concerning one God, hear his own opinion, for he spoke as follows: "God is one; and He Himself does not, as some suppose, exist outside the world, but in it, He being wholly present in the whole circle, and beholding all generations; being the regulating ingredient of all the ages, and the administrator of His own powers and works, the first principle of all things, the light of heaven, and Father of all, the intelligence and animating soul of the universe, the movement of all orbits." Thus, then, Pythagoras.

CHAP. XX. — TESTIMONY OF PLATO.

But Plato, though he accepted, as is likely, the doctrine of Moses and the other prophets regarding one only God, which he learned while in Egypt, yet fearing, on account of what had befallen Socrates, lest he also should raise up some Anytus or Meletus against himself, who should accuse him before the Athenians, and say, "Plato is doing harm, and making himself mischievously busy, not acknowledging the gods recognised by the state;" in fear of the hemlock-juice, contrives an elaborate and ambiguous discourse concerning the gods, furnishing by his treatise gods to those who wish them, and none for those who are differently disposed, as may readily be seen from his own statements. For when he has laid down that everything that is made is mortal, he afterwards says that the gods were made. If, then, he would have God and matter to be the origin of all things, manifestly it is inevitably necessary to say that the gods were made of matter; but if of matter, out of which he said that evil also had its origin, he leaves right-thinking persons to consider what kind of beings the gods should be thought who are produced out of matter. For, for this very reason did he say that matter was eternal,[1] that he might not seem to say that God is the creator of evil. And regarding the gods who were made by God, there is no doubt he said this: "Gods of gods, of whom I am the creator." And he manifestly held the correct opinion concerning the really existing God. For having heard in Egypt that God had said to Moses, when He was about to send him to the Hebrews, "I am that I am,"[2] he understood that God had not mentioned to him His own proper name.

CHAP. XXI. — THE NAMELESSNESS OF GOD.

For God cannot be called by any proper name, for names are given to mark out and distinguish their subject-matters, because these are many and diverse; but neither did any one exist before God who could give Him a name, nor did He Himself think it right to name Himself, seeing that He is one and unique, as He Himself also by His own prophets testifies, when He says, "I God am the first," and after this, "And beside me there is no other God."[3] On this account, then, as I before said, God did not, when He sent Moses to the Hebrews, mention any name, but by a participle He mystically teaches them that He is the one and only God. "For," says He, "I am the *Being;*" manifestly contrasting Himself, "the Being," with those who are not,[4] that those who had hitherto been deceived might see that they were attaching themselves, not to beings, but to those who had no being. Since, therefore, God knew that the first men remembered the old delusion of their forefathers, whereby the misanthropic demon contrived to deceive them when he said to them, "If ye obey me in transgressing the commandment of God, ye shall be as gods," calling those gods which had no being, in order that men, supposing that there were other gods in existence, might believe that they themselves could become gods. On this account He said to Moses, "I am the Being," that by the participle "being" He might teach the difference between God who is and those who are not.[5] Men, therefore, having been duped by the deceiving demon, and having dared to disobey God, were cast out of Paradise, remembering the name of gods, but no longer being taught by God that there are no other gods. For it was not just that they who did not keep the first commandment, which it was easy to keep, should any longer be taught, but should rather be driven to just punishment. Being therefore banished from Paradise, and thinking that they were expelled on account of their disobedience only, not knowing that it was also because they had believed in the existence of gods which did not exist, they gave the name of gods even to the men who were afterwards born of themselves. This first false fancy, therefore, concerning gods, had its origin with the father of lies. God, therefore, knowing that the false opinion about the plurality of gods was burdening the soul of man like some disease, and wishing to remove and eradicate it, appeared first to Moses, and said to him, "I am He who is." For it was necessary, I think, that he who was to be the ruler and leader of the Hebrew people should first of all know the living God. Wherefore, having appeared to him first, as it was possible for God to appear to a man, He said to him, "I am He who is;" then, being about to

---

[1] Or, "uncreated."
[2] ὁ ὤν, "He who is; the Being."
[3] Isa. xliv. 6.
[4] Literally, "with the not-beings."
[5] Literally, "between the God being and not-beings."

send him to the Hebrews, He further orders him to say, "He who is hath sent me to you."

CHAP. XXII. — STUDIED AMBIGUITY OF PLATO.

Plato accordingly having learned this in Egypt, and being greatly taken with what was said about one God, did indeed consider it unsafe to mention the name of Moses, on account of his teaching the doctrine of one only God, for he dreaded the Areopagus; but what is very well expressed by him in his elaborate treatise, the *Timæus*, he has written in exact correspondence with what Moses said regarding God, though he has done so, not as if he had learned it from him, but as if he were expressing his own opinion. For he said, "In my opinion, then, we must first define what that is which exists eternally, and has no generation,[1] and what that is which is always being generated, but never really is." Does not this, ye men of Greece, seem to those who are able to understand the matter to be one and the same thing, saving only the difference of the article? For Moses said, "*He* who is," and Plato, "That which is." But either of the expressions seems to apply to the ever-existent God. For He is the only one who eternally exists, and has no generation. What, then, that other thing is which is contrasted with the ever-existent, and of which he said, "And what that is which is always being generated, but never really is," we must attentively consider. For we shall find him clearly and evidently saying that He who is unbegotten is eternal, but that those that are begotten and made are generated and perish[2] — as he said of the same class, "gods of gods, of whom I am maker" — for he speaks in the following words: "In my opinion, then, we must first define what that is which is always existent and has no birth, and what that is which is always being generated but never really is. The former, indeed, which is apprehended by reflection combined with reason, always exists in the same way;[3] while the latter, on the other hand, is conjectured by opinion formed by the perception of the senses unaided by reason, since it never really is, but is coming into being and perishing." These expressions declare to those who can rightly understand them the death and destruction of the gods that have been brought into being. And I think it necessary to attend to this also, that Plato never names him the creator, but the fashioner[4] of the gods, although, in the opinion of Plato, there is considerable difference between these two. For the creator creates the creature by his own capability and power, being in need of nothing else; but the fashioner frames his production when he has received from matter the capability for his work.

CHAP. XXIII. — PLATO'S SELF-CONTRADICTION.

But, perhaps, some who are unwilling to abandon the doctrines of polytheism, will say that to these fashioned gods the maker said, "Since ye have been produced, ye are not immortal, nor at all imperishable; yet shall ye not perish nor succumb to the fatality of death, because you have obtained my will,[5] which is a still greater and mightier bond." Here Plato, through fear of the adherents of polytheism, introduces his "maker" uttering words which contradict himself. For having formerly stated that he said that everything which is produced is perishable, he now introduces him saying the very opposite; and he does not see that it is thus absolutely impossible for him to escape the charge of falsehood. For he either at first uttered what is false when he said that everything which is produced is perishable, or now, when he propounds the very opposite to what he had formerly said. For if, according to his former definition, it is absolutely necessary that every created thing be perishable, how can he consistently make that possible which is absolutely impossible? So that Plato seems to grant an empty and impossible prerogative to his "maker," when he propounds that those who were once perishable because made from matter should again, by his intervention, become imperishable and enduring. For it is quite natural that the power of matter, which, according to Plato's opinion, is uncreated, and contemporary and coæval with the maker, should resist his will. For he who has not created has no power, in respect of that which is uncreated, so that it is not possible that it (matter), being free, can be controlled by any external necessity. Wherefore Plato himself, in consideration of this, has written thus: "It is necessary to affirm that God cannot suffer violence."

CHAP. XXIV. — AGREEMENT OF PLATO AND HOMER.

How, then, does Plato banish Homer from his republic, since, in the embassy to Achilles, he represents Phœnix as saying to Achilles, "Even the gods themselves are not inflexible,"[6] though Homer said this not of the king and Platonic maker of the gods, but of some of the multitude whom the Greeks esteem as gods, as one can gather from Plato's saying, "gods of gods?" For Homer, by that golden chain,[7] refers all power and might to the one highest

---

[1] That is, "is not produced or created; has no birth."
[2] Or, "are born and die."
[3] κατὰ ταὐτά, "according to the same things," i.e., in eternal immutability.
[4] Or, "demiurge or maker."
[5] That is, "my will to the contrary." See Plato, *Tim.*, p. 41, [cap 13].
[6] *Iliad*, ix. 497.
[7] That is, by the challenge of the chain introduced — *Iliad,* viii. 18.

God. And the rest of the gods, he said, were so far distant from his divinity, that he thought fit to name them even along with men. At least he introduces Ulysses saying of Hector to Achilles, "He is raging terribly, trusting in Zeus, and values neither men nor gods."[1] In this passage Homer seems to me without doubt to have learnt in Egypt, like Plato, concerning the one God, and plainly and openly to declare this, that he who trusts in the really existent God makes no account of those that do not exist. For thus the poet, in another passage, and employing another but equivalent word, to wit, a pronoun, made use of the same participle employed by Plato to designate the really existent God, concerning whom Plato said, "What that is which always exists, and has no birth." For not without a double sense does this expression of Phœnix seem to have been used: "Not even if God Himself were to promise me, that, having burnished off my old age, He should set me forth in the flower of youth." For the pronoun "Himself" signifies the really existing God. For thus, too, the oracle which was given to you concerning the Chaldæans and Hebrews signifies. For when some one inquired what men had ever lived godly, you say the answer was:—

"Only the Chaldæans and the Hebrews found wisdom,
Worshipping God *Himself*, the unbegotten King."

CHAP. XXV. — PLATO'S KNOWLEDGE OF GOD'S ETERNITY.

How, then, does Plato blame Homer for saying that the gods are not inflexible, although, as is obvious from the expressions used, Homer said this for a useful purpose? For it is the property of those who expect to obtain mercy by prayer and sacrifices, to cease from and repent of their sins. For those who think that the Deity is inflexible, are by no means moved to abandon their sins, since they suppose that they will derive no benefit from repentance. How, then, does Plato the philosopher condemn the poet Homer for saying, "Even the gods themselves are not inflexible," and yet himself represent the maker of the gods as so easily turned, that he sometimes declares the gods to be mortal, and at other times declares the same to be immortal? And not only concerning them, but also concerning matter, from which, as he says, it is necessary that the created gods have been produced, he sometimes says that it is uncreated, and at other times that it is created; and yet he does not see that he himself, when he says that the maker of the gods is so easily turned, is convicted of having fallen into the very errors for which he blames Homer, though Homer said the very opposite concerning the maker of the gods. For he said that he spoke thus of himself:—

"For ne'er my promise shall deceive, or fail,
Or be recall'd, if with a nod confirm'd."[2]

But Plato, as it seems, unwillingly entered into these strange dissertations concerning the gods, for he feared those who were attached to polytheism. And whatever he thinks fit to tell of all that he had learned from Moses and the prophets concerning one God, he preferred delivering in a mystical style, so that those who desired to be worshippers of God might have an inkling of his own opinion. For being charmed with that saying of God to Moses, "I am the really existing," and accepting with a great deal of thought the brief participial expression, he understood that God desired to signify to Moses His eternity, and therefore said, "I am the really existing;" for this word "existing" expresses not one time only, but the three — the past, the present, and the future. For when Plato says, "and which never really is," he uses the verb "is" of time indefinite. For the word "never" is not spoken, as some suppose, of the past, but of the future time. And this has been accurately understood even by profane writers. And therefore, when Plato wished, as it were, to interpret to the uninitiated what had been mystically expressed by the participle concerning the eternity of God, he employed the following language: "God indeed, as the old tradition runs, includes the beginning, and end, and middle of all things." In this sentence he plainly and obviously names the law of Moses "the old tradition," fearing, through dread of the hemlock-cup, to mention the name of Moses; for he understood that the teaching of the man was hateful to the Greeks; and he clearly enough indicates Moses by the antiquity of the tradition. And we have sufficiently proved from Diodorus and the rest of the historians, in the foregoing chapters, that the law of Moses is not only old, but even the first. For Diodorus says that he was the first of all lawgivers; the letters which belong to the Greeks, and which they employed in the writing of their histories, having not yet been discovered.

CHAP. XXVI. — PLATO INDEBTED TO THE PROPHETS.

And let no one wonder that Plato should believe Moses regarding the eternity of God. For you will find him mystically referring the true knowledge of realities to the prophets, next in order after the really existent God. For, discoursing in the *Timæus* about certain first principles, he wrote thus: "This we lay down as the first principle of fire and the other bodies,

---

[1] *Iliad*, ix. 238.   [2] *Iliad*, i. 526.

proceeding according to probability and necessity. But the first principles of these again God above knows, and whosoever among men is beloved of Him." [1] And what men does he think beloved of God, but Moses and the rest of the prophets? For their prophecies he read, and, having learned from them the doctrine of the judgment, he thus proclaims it in the first book of the *Republic*: "When a man begins to think he is soon to die, fear invades him, and concern about things which had never before entered his head. And those stories about what goes on in Hades, which tell us that the man who has here been unjust must there be punished, though formerly ridiculed, now torment his soul with apprehensions that they may be true. And he, either through the feebleness of age, or even because he is now nearer to the things of the other world, views them more attentively. He becomes, therefore, full of apprehension and dread, and begins to call himself to account, and to consider whether he has done any one an injury. And that man who finds in his life many iniquities, and who continually starts from his sleep as children do, lives in terror, and with a forlorn prospect. But to him who is conscious of no wrong-doing, sweet hope is the constant companion and good nurse of old age, as Pindar says.[2] For this, Socrates, he has elegantly expressed, that 'whoever leads a life of holiness and justice, him sweet hope, the nurse of age, accompanies, cheering his heart, for she powerfully sways the changeful mind of mortals.'"[3] This Plato wrote in the first book of the *Republic*.

CHAP. XXVII. — PLATO'S KNOWLEDGE OF THE JUDGMENT.

And in the tenth book he plainly and manifestly wrote what he had learned from the prophets about the judgment, not as if he had learned it from them, but, on account of his fear of the Greeks, as if he had heard it from a man who had been slain in battle — for this story he thought fit to invent — and who, when he was about to be buried on the twelfth day, and was lying on the funeral pile, came to life again, and described the other world. The following are his very words: [4] "For he said that he was present when one was asked by another person where the great Ardiæus was. This Ardiæus had been prince in a certain city of Pamphylia, and had killed his aged father and his elder brother, and done many other unhallowed deeds, as was reported. He said, then, that the person who was asked said: He neither comes nor ever will come hither. For we saw, among other terrible sights, this also. When we were close to the mouth [of the pit], and were about to return to the upper air, and had suffered everything else, we suddenly beheld both him and others likewise, most of whom were tyrants. But there were also some private sinners who had committed great crimes. And these, when they thought they were to ascend, the mouth would not permit, but bellowed when any of those who were so incurably wicked attempted to ascend, unless they had paid the full penalty. Then fierce men, fiery to look at, stood close by, and hearing the din,[5] took some and led them away; but Ardiæus and the rest, having bound hand and foot, and striking their heads down, and flaying, they dragged to the road outside, tearing them with thorns, and signifying to those who were present the cause of their suffering these things, and that they were leading them away to cast them into Tartarus. Hence, he said, that amidst all their various fears, this one was the greatest, lest the mouth should bellow when they ascended, since if it were silent each one would most gladly ascend; and that the punishments and torments were such as these, and that, on the other hand, the rewards were the reverse of these." Here Plato seems to me to have learnt from the prophets not only the doctrine of the judgment, but also of the resurrection, which the Greeks refuse to believe. For his saying that the soul is judged along with the body, proves nothing more clearly than that he believed the doctrine of the resurrection. Since how could Ardiæus and the rest have undergone such punishment in Hades, had they left on earth the body, with its head, hands, feet, and skin? For certainly they will never say that the soul has a head and hands, and feet and skin. But Plato, having fallen in with the testimonies of the prophets in Egypt, and having accepted what they teach concerning the resurrection of the body, teaches that the soul is judged in company with the body.

CHAP. XXVIII. — HOMER'S OBLIGATIONS TO THE SACRED WRITERS.

And not only Plato, but Homer also, having received similar enlightenment in Egypt, said that Tityus was in like manner punished. For Ulysses speaks thus to Alcinous when he is recounting his divination by the shades of the dead: [6] —

"There Tityus, large and long, in fetters bound,
O'erspread nine acres of infernal ground;
Two ravenous vultures, furious for their food,
Scream o'er the fiend, and riot in his blood,
Incessant gore the liver in his breast,
Th' immortal liver grows, and gives th' immortal feast."

---

[1] Plato, *Tim.*, p. 53 D, [cap. 20].
[2] Pind., *Fr.*, 233, a fragment preserved in this place.
[3] Plato. *Rep.*, p. 330 D.
[4] Plato, *Rep.*, p. 615, [lib. x. p. 325. Ed. Bipont, 1785.]
[5] The bellowing of the mouth of the pit.
[6] *Odyssey*, xi. 576 (Pope's translation, line 709).

For it is plain that it is not the soul, but the body, which has a liver. And in the same manner he has described both Sisyphus and Tantalus as enduring punishment with the body. And that Homer had been in Egypt, and introduced into his own poem much of what he there learnt, Diodorus, the most esteemed of historians, plainly enough teaches us. For he said that when he was in Egypt he had learnt that Helen, having received from Theon's wife, Polydamna, a drug, "lulling all sorrow and melancholy, and causing forgetfulness of all ills,"[1] brought it to Sparta. And Homer said that by making use of that drug Helen put an end to the lamentation of Menelaus, caused by the presence of Telemachus. And he also called Venus "golden," from what he had seen in Egypt. For he had seen the temple which in Egypt is called "the temple of golden Venus," and the plain which is named "the plain of golden Venus." And why do I now make mention of this? To show that the poet transferred to his own poem much of what is contained in the divine writings of the prophets. And first he transferred what Moses had related as the beginning of the creation of the world. For Moses wrote thus: "In the beginning God created the heaven and the earth,"[2] then the sun, and the moon, and the stars. For having learned this in Egypt, and having been much taken with what Moses had written in the Genesis of the world, he fabled that Vulcan had made in the shield of Achilles a kind of representation of the creation of the world. For he wrote thus:[3] —

"There he described the earth, the heaven, the sea,
The sun that rests not, and the moon full-orb'd;
There also, all the stars which round about,
As with a radiant frontlet, bind the skies."

And he contrived also that the garden of Alcinous should preserve the likeness of Paradise, and through this likeness he represented it as ever-blooming and full of all fruits. For thus he wrote:[4] —

"Tall thriving trees confess'd the fruitful mould;
The reddening apple ripens here to gold.
Here the blue fig with luscious juice o'erflows,
With deeper red the full pomegranate glows;
The branch here bends beneath the weighty pear,
And verdant olives flourish round the year.
The balmy spirit of the western gale
Eternal breathes on fruits, untaught to fail;
Each dropping pear a following pear supplies,
On apples apples, figs on figs arise.
The same mild season gives the blooms to blow,
The buds to harden, and the fruits to grow.
Here order'd vines in equal ranks appear,
With all th' united labours of the year.
Some to unload the fertile branches run,
Some dry the blackening clusters in the sun,
Others to tread the liquid harvest join.
The groaning presses foam with floods of wine.
Here are the vines in early flower descry'd
Here grapes discoloured on the sunny side,
And there in autumn's richest purple dy'd."

Do not these words present a manifest and clear imitation of what the first prophet Moses said about Paradise? And if any one wish to know something of the building of the tower by which the men of that day fancied they would obtain access to heaven, he will find a sufficiently exact allegorical imitation of this in what the poet has ascribed to Otus and Ephialtes. For of them he wrote thus:[5] —

"Proud of their strength, and more than mortal size,
The gods they challenge, and affect the skies.
Heav'd on Olympus tottering Ossa stood;
On Ossa, Pelion nods with all his wood."

And the same holds good regarding the enemy of mankind who was cast out of heaven, whom the Sacred Scriptures call the Devil,[6] a name which he obtained from his first devilry against man; and if any one would attentively consider the matter, he would find that the poet, though he certainly never mentions the name of "the devil," yet gives him a name from his wickedest action. For the poet, calling him Ate,[7] says that he was hurled from heaven by their god, just as if he had a distinct remembrance of the expressions which Isaiah the prophet had uttered regarding him. He wrote thus in his own poem:[8] —

"And, seizing by her glossy locks
The goddess Ate, in his wrath he swore
That never to the starry skies again,
And the Olympian heights, he would permit
The universal mischief to return.
Then, whirling her around, he cast her down
To earth. She, mingling with all works of men,
Caused many a pang to Jove."

CHAP. XXIX. — ORIGIN OF PLATO'S DOCTRINE OF FORM.

And Plato, too, when he says that form is the third original principle next to God and matter, has manifestly received this suggestion from no other source than from Moses, having learned, indeed, from the words of Moses the name of form, but not having at the same time been instructed by the initiated, that without mystic insight it is impossible to have any distinct knowledge of the writings of Moses. For Moses wrote that God had spoken to him regarding the tabernacle in the following words: "And thou shalt make for me according to all that I show thee in the mount, the pattern of the tabernacle."[9] And again: "And thou shalt erect the taber-

---

[1] *Odyssey*, iv. 221; [Milton's Comus, line 675].
[2] Gen. i. 1.
[3] *Iliad*, xviii. 483.
[4] *Odyssey*, vii. 114 (Pope's translation, line 146).
[5] *Odyssey*, xi. 312 (Pope's translation, line 385).
[6] The false accuser; one who does injury by slanderous accusations.
[7] Ἄτη, the goddess of mischief, from whom spring all rash, blind deeds and their results.
[8] *Iliad*, xix. 126.
[9] Ex. xxv. 9.

nacle according to the pattern of all the instruments thereof, even so shalt thou make it."[1] And again, a little afterwards: "Thus then thou shalt make it according to the pattern which was showed to thee in the mount."[2] Plato, then, reading these passages, and not receiving what was written with the suitable insight, thought that form had some kind of separate existence before that which the senses perceive, and he often calls it the pattern of the things which are made, since the writing of Moses spoke thus of the tabernacle: "According to the form showed to thee in the mount, so shalt thou make it."

CHAP. XXX. — HOMER'S KNOWLEDGE OF MAN'S ORIGIN.

And he was obviously deceived in the same way regarding the earth and heaven and man; for he supposes that there are "ideas" of these. For as Moses wrote thus, "In the beginning God created the heaven and the earth," and then subjoins this sentence, "And the earth was invisible and unfashioned," he thought that it was the pre-existent earth which was spoken of in the words, "The earth was," because Moses said, "And the earth was invisible and unfashioned;" and he thought that the earth, concerning which he says, "God created the heaven and the earth," was that earth which we perceive by the senses, and which God made according to the pre-existent form. And so also, of the heaven which was created, he thought that the heaven which was created — and which he also called the firmament — was that creation which the senses perceive; and that the heaven which the intellect perceives is that other of which the prophet said, "The heaven of heavens is the Lord's, but the earth hath He given to the children of men."[3] And so also concerning man: Moses first mentions the name of man, and then after many other creations he makes mention of the formation of man, saying, "And God made man, taking dust from the earth."[4] He thought, accordingly, that the man first so named existed before the man who was made, and that he who was formed of the earth was afterwards made according to the pre-existent form. And that man was formed of earth, Homer, too, having discovered from the ancient and divine history which says, "Dust thou art, and unto dust shalt thou return,"[5] calls the lifeless body of Hector dumb clay. For in condemnation of Achilles dragging the corpse of Hector after death, he says somewhere:[6] —

"On the dumb clay he cast indignity,
Blinded with rage."

And again, somewhere else,[7] he introduces Menelaus, thus addressing those who were not accepting Hector's challenge to single combat with becoming alacrity, —

"To earth and water may you all return," —

resolving them in his violent rage into their original and pristine formation from earth. These things Homer and Plato, having learned in Egypt from the ancient histories, wrote in their own words.

CHAP. XXXI. — FURTHER PROOF OF PLATO'S ACQUAINTANCE WITH SCRIPTURE.

For from what other source, if not from his reading the writings of the prophets, could Plato have derived the information he gives us, that Jupiter drives a winged chariot in heaven? For he knew this from the following expressions of the prophet about the cherubim: "And the glory of the Lord went out from the house and rested on the cherubim; and the cherubim lift up their wings, and the wheels beside them; and the glory of the Lord God of Israel was over them above."[8] And borrowing this idea, the magniloquent Plato shouts aloud with vast assurance, "The great Jove, indeed, driving his winged chariot in heaven." For from what other source, if not from Moses and the prophets, did he learn this and so write? And whence did he receive the suggestion of his saying that God exists in a fiery substance? Was it not from the third book of the history of the Kings, where it is written, "The Lord was not in the wind; and after the wind an earthquake, but the Lord was not in the earthquake; and after the earthquake a fire, but the Lord was not in the fire; and after the fire a still small voice?"[9] But these things pious men must understand in a higher sense with profound and meditative insight. But Plato, not attending to the words with the suitable insight, said that God exists in a fiery substance.

CHAP. XXXII. — PLATO'S DOCTRINE OF THE HEAVENLY GIFT.

And if any one will attentively consider the gift that descends from God on the holy men, — which gift the sacred prophets call the Holy Ghost, — he shall find that this was announced under another name by Plato in the dialogue with Meno. For, fearing to name the gift of God "the Holy Ghost," lest he should seem, by following the teaching of the prophets, to be an enemy to the Greeks, he acknowledges, indeed, that it comes down from God, yet does not think fit to name it the Holy Ghost, but virtue.

---

[1] Ex. xxv. 9.
[2] Ex. xxv. 40.
[3] Ps. cxv. 16.
[4] Gen. ii. 7.
[5] Gen. iii. 19.
[6] *Iliad*, xxii.

[7] *Iliad*, vii. 99.
[8] Ezek. xi. 22.
[9] 1 Kings xix. 11, 12.

For so in the dialogue with Meno, concerning reminiscence, after he had put many questions regarding virtue, whether it could be taught or whether it could not be taught, but must be gained by practice, or whether it could be attained neither by practice nor by learning, but was a natural gift in men, or whether it comes in some other way, he makes this declaration in these very words: "But if now through this whole dialogue we have conducted our inquiry and discussion aright, virtue must be neither a natural gift, nor what one can receive by teaching, but comes to those to whom it does come by divine destiny." These things, I think, Plato having learned from the prophets regarding the Holy Ghost, he has manifestly transferred to what he calls virtue. For as the sacred prophets say that one and the same spirit is divided into seven spirits, so he also, naming it one and the same virtue, says this is divided into four virtues; wishing by all means to avoid mention of the Holy Spirit, but clearly declaring in a kind of allegory what the prophets said of the Holy Spirit. For to this effect he spoke in the dialogue with Meno towards the close: "From this reasoning, Meno, it appears that virtue comes to those to whom it does come by a divine destiny. But we shall know clearly about this, in what kind of way virtue comes to men, when, as a first step, we shall have set ourselves to investigate, as an independent inquiry, what virtue itself is." You see how he calls only by the name of virtue, the gift that descends from above; and yet he counts it worthy of inquiry, whether it is right that this [gift] be called virtue or some other thing, fearing to name it openly the Holy Spirit, lest he should seem to be following the teaching of the prophets.

CHAP. XXXIII. — PLATO'S IDEA OF THE BEGINNING OF TIME DRAWN FROM MOSES.

And from what source did Plato draw the information that time was created along with the heavens? For he wrote thus: "Time, accordingly, was created along with the heavens; in order that, coming into being together, they might also be together dissolved, if ever their dissolution should take place." Had he not learned this from the divine history of Moses? For he knew that the creation of time had received its original constitution from days and months and years. Since, then, the first day which was created along with the heavens constituted the beginning of all time (for thus Moses wrote, "In the beginning God created the heavens and the earth," and then immediately subjoins, "And one day was made," as if he would designate the whole of time by one part of it), Plato names the day "time," lest, if he mentioned the "day," he should seem to lay himself open to the accusation of the Athenians, that he was completely adopting the expressions of Moses. And from what source did he derive what he has written regarding the dissolution of the heavens? Had he not learned this, too, from the sacred prophets, and did he not think that this was their doctrine?

CHAP. XXXIV. — WHENCE MEN ATTRIBUTED TO GOD HUMAN FORM.

And if any person investigates the subject of images, and inquires on what ground those who first fashioned your gods conceived that they had the forms of men, he will find that this also was derived from the divine history. For seeing that Moses' history, speaking in the person of God, says, "Let Us make man in our image and likeness," these persons, under the impression that this meant that men were like God in form, began thus to fashion their gods, supposing they would make a likeness from a likeness. But why, ye men of Greece, am I now induced to recount these things? That ye may know that it is not possible to learn the true religion from those who were unable, even on those subjects by which they won the admiration of the heathen,[1] to write anything original, but merely propounded by some allegorical device in their own writings what they had learned from Moses and the other prophets.

CHAP. XXXV. — APPEAL TO THE GREEKS.

The time, then, ye men of Greece, is now come, that ye, having been persuaded by the secular histories that Moses and the rest of the prophets were far more ancient than any of those who have been esteemed sages among you, abandon the ancient delusion of your forefathers, and read the divine histories of the prophets, and ascertain from them the true religion; for they do not present to you artful discourses, nor speak speciously and plausibly — for this is the property of those who wish to rob you of the truth — but use with simplicity the words and expressions which offer themselves, and declare to you whatever the Holy Ghost, who descended upon them, chose to teach through them to those who are desirous to learn the true religion. Having then laid aside all false shame, and the inveterate error of mankind, with all its bombastic parade and empty noise, though by means of it you fancy you are possessed of all advantages, do you give yourselves to the things that profit you. For neither will you commit any offence against your fathers, if you now show a desire to betake yourselves to that which is quite opposed to their error, since it is likely enough that they

---

[1] Literally, "those without."

themselves are now lamenting in Hades, and repenting with a too late repentance; and if it were possible for them to show you thence what had befallen them after the termination of this life, ye would know from what fearful ills they desired to deliver you. But now, since it is not possible in this present life that ye either learn from them, or from those who here profess to teach that philosophy which is falsely so called, it follows as the one thing that remains for you to do, that, renouncing the error of your fathers, ye read the prophecies of the sacred writers,[1] not requiring from them unexceptionable diction (for the matters of our religion lie in works,[2] not in words), and learn from them what will give you life everlasting. For those who bootlessly disgrace the name of philosophy are convicted of knowing nothing at all, as they are themselves forced, though unwillingly, to confess, since not only do they disagree with each other, but also expressed their own opinions sometimes in one way, sometimes in another.

CHAP. XXXVI. — TRUE KNOWLEDGE NOT HELD BY THE PHILOSOPHERS.

And if "the discovery of the truth" be given among them as one definition of philosophy, how are they who are not in possession of the true knowledge worthy of the name of philosophy? For if Socrates, the wisest of your wise men, to whom even your oracle, as you yourselves say, bears witness, saying, "Of all men, Socrates is the wisest"—if he confesses that he knows nothing, how did those who came after him profess to know even things heavenly? For Socrates said that he was on this account called wise, because, while other men pretended to know what they were ignorant of, he himself did not shrink from confessing that he knew nothing. For he said, "I seem to myself to be wisest by this little particular, that what I do not know, I do not suppose I know." Let no one fancy that Socrates ironically feigned ignorance, because he often used to do so in his dialogues. For the last expression of his apology which he uttered as he was being led away to the prison, proves that in seriousness and truth he was confessing his ignorance: "But now it is time to go away, I indeed to die, but you to live. And which of us goes to the better state, is hidden to all but God." Socrates, indeed, having uttered this last sentence in the Areopagus, departed to the prison, ascribing to God alone the knowledge of those things which are hidden from us; but those who came after him, though they are unable to comprehend even earthly things, profess to understand things heavenly as if they had seen them. Aristotle at least — as if he had seen things heavenly with greater accuracy than Plato — declared that God did not exist, as Plato said, in the fiery substance (for this was Plato's doctrine) but in the fifth element, air. And while he demanded that concerning these matters he should be believed on account of the excellence of his language, he yet departed this life because he was overwhelmed with the infamy and disgrace of being unable to discover even the nature of the Euripus in Chalcis.[3] Let not any one, therefore, of sound judgment prefer the elegant diction of these men to his own salvation, but let him, according to that old story, stop his ears with wax, and flee the sweet hurt which these sirens would inflict upon him. For the above-mentioned men, presenting their elegant language as a kind of bait, have sought to seduce many from the right religion, in imitation of him who dared to teach the first men polytheism. Be not persuaded by these persons, I entreat you, but read the prophecies of the sacred writers.[4] And if any slothfulness or old hereditary superstition prevents you from reading the prophecies of the holy men through which you can be instructed regarding the one only God, which is the first article of the true religion, yet believe him who, though at first he taught you polytheism, yet afterwards preferred to sing a useful and necessary recantation — I mean Orpheus, who said what I quoted a little before; and believe the others who wrote the same things concerning one God. For it was the work of Divine Providence on your behalf, that they, though unwillingly, bore testimony that what the prophets said regarding one God was true, in order that, the doctrine of a plurality of gods being rejected by all, occasion might be afforded you of knowing the truth.

CHAP. XXXVII. — OF THE SIBYL.[5]

And you may in part easily learn the right religion from the ancient Sibyl, who by some kind of potent inspiration teaches you, through her oracular predictions, truths which seem to be much akin to the teaching of the prophets. She, they say, was of Babylonian extraction, being the daughter of Berosus, who wrote the Chaldæan History; and when she had crossed over (how, I know not) into the region of Campania, she there uttered her oracular sayings in a city called Cumæ, six miles from Baiæ, where the hot springs of Campania are found. And being in that city, we saw also a certain place, in which we were shown a very large basilica[6] cut out of one stone; a vast affair, and worthy of all admiration. And they who had heard it from their fathers as part of their country's tradition, told us that it was

---

[1] Literally, "sacred men."
[2] [A noteworthy apology for early Christian writers.]
[3] This is now supposed to be fable.
[4] Literally, "sacred men."
[5] [In Grabe's edition consult notes of Lang and Kortholt, ii. p. 45.]
[6] [Travellers must recognise the agreement of Justin's story with the traditional cave still shown in this region.]

here she used to publish her oracles. And in the middle of the basilica they showed us three receptacles cut out of one stone, in which, when filled with water, they said that she washed, and having put on her robe again, retires into the inmost chamber of the basilica, which is still a part of the one stone; and sitting in the middle of the chamber on a high rostrum and throne, thus proclaims her oracles. And both by many other writers has the Sibyl been mentioned as a prophetess, and also by Plato in his *Phædrus*. And Plato seems to me to have counted prophets divinely inspired when he read her prophecies. For he saw that what she had long ago predicted was accomplished; and on this account he expresses in the Dialogue with Meno his wonder at and admiration of prophets in the following terms: "Those whom we now call prophetic persons we should rightly name divine. And not least would we say that they are divine, and are raised to the prophetic ecstasy by the inspiration and possession of God, when they correctly speak of many and important matters, and yet know nothing of what they are saying,"—plainly and manifestly referring to the prophecies of the Sibyl. For, unlike the poets who, after their poems are penned, have power to correct and polish, specially in the way of increasing the accuracy of their verse, she was filled indeed with prophecy at the time of the inspiration, but as soon as the inspiration ceased, there ceased also the remembrance of all she had said. And this indeed was the cause why some only, and not all, the metres of the verses of the Sibyl were preserved. For we ourselves, when in that city, ascertained from our *cicerone*, who showed us the places in which she used to prophesy, that there was a certain coffer made of brass in which they said that her remains were preserved. And besides all else which they told us as they had heard it from their fathers, they said also that they who then took down her prophecies, being illiterate persons, often went quite astray from the accuracy of the metres; and this, they said, was the cause of the want of metre in some of the verses, the prophetess having no remembrance of what she had said, after the possession and inspiration ceased, and the reporters having, through their lack of education, failed to record the metres with accuracy. And on this account, it is manifest that Plato had an eye to the prophecies of the Sibyl when he said this about prophets, for he said, "When they correctly speak of many and important matters, and yet know nothing of what they are saying."

CHAP. XXXVIII. — CONCLUDING APPEAL.

But since, ye men of Greece, the matters of the true religion lie not in the metrical numbers of poetry, nor yet in that culture which is highly esteemed among you, do ye henceforward pay less devotion to accuracy of metres and of language; and giving heed without contentiousness to the words of the Sibyl, recognise how great are the benefits which she will confer upon you by predicting, as she does in a clear and patent manner, the advent of our Saviour Jesus Christ;[1] who, being the Word of God, inseparable from Him in power, having assumed man, who had been made in the image and likeness of God, restored to us the knowledge of the religion of our ancient forefathers, which the men who lived after them abandoned through the bewitching counsel of the envious devil, and turned to the worship of those who were no gods. And if you still hesitate and are hindered from belief regarding the formation of man, believe those whom you have hitherto thought it right to give heed to, and know that your own oracle, when asked by some one to utter a hymn of praise to the Almighty God, in the middle of the hymn spoke thus, "Who formed the first of men, and called him Adam." And this hymn is preserved by many whom we know, for the conviction of those who are unwilling to believe the truth which all bear witness to. If therefore, ye men of Greece, ye do not esteem the false fancy concerning those that are no gods at a higher rate than your own salvation, believe, as I said, the most ancient and time-honoured Sibyl, whose books are preserved in all the world, and who by some kind of potent inspiration both teaches us in her oracular utterances concerning those that are called gods, that have no existence; and also clearly and manifestly prophesies concerning the predicted advent of our Saviour Jesus Christ, and concerning all those things which were to be done by Him. For the knowledge of these things will constitute your necessary preparatory training for the study of the prophecies of the sacred writers. And if any one supposes that he has learned the doctrine concerning God from the most ancient of those whom you name philosophers, let him listen to Ammon and Hermes:[2] to Ammon, who in his discourse concerning God calls Him wholly hidden; and to Hermes, who says plainly and distinctly, "that it is difficult to comprehend God, and that it is impossible even for the man who can comprehend Him to declare Him to others." From every point of view, therefore, it must be seen that in no other way than only from the prophets who teach us by divine inspiration, is it at all possible to learn anything concerning God and the true religion.

---

[1] [The fascinating use made of this by Virgil must not be overlooked: —
"Ultima Cumæi venit jam carminis ætas," etc.
Ecl., iv. (Pollio) 4.]

[2] [Hermes Trismegistus. Milton (Penseroso, line 88,) translates this name.]

[N.B. — This work is not supposed to be Justin's by modern critics.]

JUSTIN ON THE SOLE GOVERNMENT OF GOD.[1]

[TRANSLATED BY THE REV. G. REITH, M.A.]

CHAP. I.—OBJECT OF THE AUTHOR.

ALTHOUGH human nature at first received a union of intelligence and safety to discern the truth, and the worship due to the one Lord of all, yet envy, insinuating the excellence of human greatness, turned men away to the making of idols; and this superstitious custom, after continuing for a long period, is handed down to the majority as if it were natural and true. It is the part of a lover of man, or rather of a lover of God, to remind men who have neglected it of that which they ought to know. For the truth is of itself sufficient to show forth, by means of those things which are contained under the pole of heaven, the order [instituted by] Him who has created them. But forgetfulness having taken possession of the minds of men, through the long-suffering of God, has acted recklessly in transferring to mortals the name which is applicable to the only true God; and from the few the infection of sin spread to the many, who were blinded by popular usage to the knowledge of that which was lasting and unchangeable. For the men of former generations, who instituted private and public rites in honour of such as were more powerful, caused forgetfulness of the Catholic[2] faith to take possession of their posterity; but I, as I have just stated, along with a God-loving mind, shall employ the speech of one who loves man, and set it before those who have intelligence, which all ought to have who are privileged to observe the administration of the universe, so that they should worship unchangeably Him who knows all things. This I shall do, not by mere display of words, but by altogether using demonstration drawn from the old poetry in Greek literature,[3] and from writings very common amongst all. For from these the famous men who have handed down idol-worship as law to the multitudes, shall be taught and convicted by their own poets and literature of great ignorance.

CHAP. II.—TESTIMONIES TO THE UNITY OF GOD.

First, then, Æschylus,[4] in expounding the arrangement of his work,[5] expressed himself also as follows respecting the only God:—

"Afar from mortals place the holy God,
Nor ever think that He, like to thyself,
In fleshly robes is clad; for all unknown
Is the great God to such a worm as thou.
Divers similitudes He bears; at times
He seems as a consuming fire that burns
Unsated; now like water, then again
In sable folds of darkness shrouds Himself.
Nay, even the very beasts of earth reflect
His sacred image; whilst the wind, clouds, rain,
The roll of thunder and the lightning flash,
Reveal to men their great and sovereign Lord.
Before Him sea and rocks, with every fount,
And all the water floods, in reverence bend;
And as they gaze upon His awful face,
Mountains and earth, with the profoundest depths
Of ocean, and the highest peaks of hills,
Tremble: for He is Lord Omnipotent;
And this the glory is of God Most High."

But he was not the only man initiated in the knowledge of God; for Sophocles also thus describes the nature of the only Creator of all things, the One God:—

"There is one God, in truth there is but one,
Who made the heavens and the broad earth beneath,
The glancing waves of ocean, and the winds;
But many of us mortals err in heart,
And set up, for a solace in our woes,
Images of the gods in stone and brass,
Or figures carved in gold or ivory;
And, furnishing for these, our handiworks,
Both sacrifice and rite magnificent,
We think that thus we do a pious work."

And Philemon also, who published many explanations of ancient customs, shares in the knowledge of the truth; and thus he writes:—

"Tell me what thoughts of God we should conceive?
One, all things seeing, yet Himself unseen."

Even Orpheus, too, who introduces three hundred and sixty gods, will bear testimony in my

---

[1] Θεοῦ is omitted in MSS., but μοναρχία of itself implies it.
[2] i.e., the doctrine that God only is to be worshipped.
[3] Literally, "history."
[4] Grotius supposes this to be Æschylus the younger in some prologue.
[5] This may also be translated: "expounding the set of opinions prevalent in his day."

favour from the tract called *Diathecæ*, in which he appears to repent of his error by writing the following: —

"I'll speak to those who lawfully may hear;
All others, ye profane, now close the doors!
And, O Musæus, hearken thou to me,
Who offspring art of the light-bringing moon.
The words I tell thee now are true indeed,
And if thou former thoughts of mine hast seen,
Let them not rob thee of the blessed life;
But rather turn the depths of thine own heart
Unto that place where light and knowledge dwell.
Take thou the word divine to guide thy steps;
And walking well in the straight certain path,
Look to the one and universal King,
One, self-begotten, and the only One
Of whom all things, and we ourselves, are sprung.
All things are open to His piercing gaze,
While He Himself is still invisible;
Present in all His works, though still unseen,
He gives to mortals evil out of good,
Sending both chilling wars and tearful griefs;
And other than the Great King there is none.
The clouds for ever settle round His throne;
And mortal eyeballs in mere mortal eyes
Are weak to see Jove, reigning over all.
He sits established in the brazen heavens
Upon His throne; and underneath His feet
He treads the earth, and stretches His right hand
To all the ends of ocean, and around
Tremble the mountain ranges, and the streams,
The depths, too, of the blue and hoary sea."

He speaks indeed as if he had been an eye-witness of God's greatness. And Pythagoras[1] agrees with him when he writes: —

"Should one in boldness say, Lo, I am God!
Besides the One — Eternal — Infinite,
Then let him from the throne he has usurped
Put forth his power and form another globe,
Such as we dwell in, saying, This is mine.
Nor only so, but in this new domain
For ever let him dwell. If this he can,
Then verily he is a god proclaimed."

CHAP. III. — TESTIMONIES TO A FUTURE JUDGMENT.

Then further concerning Him, that He alone is powerful, both to institute judgment on the deeds performed in life, and on the ignorance of the Deity [displayed by men], I can adduce witnesses from your own ranks; and first Sophocles,[2] who speaks as follows: —

"That time of times shall come, shall surely come,
When from the golden ether down shall fall
Fire's teeming treasure, and in burning flames
All things of earth and heaven shall be consumed;
And then, when all creation is dissolved,
The sea's last wave shall die upon the shore,
The bald earth stript of trees, the burning air
No winged thing upon its breast shall bear.
There are two roads to Hades, well we know;[3]
By this the righteous, and by that the bad,
On to their separate fates shall tend; and He,
Who all things had destroyed, shall all things save."

And Philemon[4] again: —

"Think'st thou, Nicostratus, the dead, who here
Enjoyed whate'er of good life offers man,
Escape the notice of Divinity,
As if they might forgotten be of Him?
Nay, there's an eye of Justice watching all;
For if the good and bad find the same end,
Then go thou, rob, steal, plunder, at thy will,
Do all the evil that to thee seems good.
Yet be not thou deceived; for underneath
There is a throne and place of judgment set,
Which God the Lord of all shall occupy;
Whose name is terrible, nor shall I dare
To breathe it forth in feeble human speech."

And Euripides:[5] —

"Not grudgingly he gives a lease of life,
That we the holders may be fairly judged;
And if a mortal man doth think to hide
His daily guilt from the keen eye of God,
It is an evil thought; so if perchance
He meets with leisure-taking Justice, she
Demands him as her lawful prisoner:
But many of you hastily commit
A twofold sin, and say there is no God.
But, ah! there is; there is. Then see that he
Who, being wicked, prospers, may redeem
The time so precious, else hereafter waits
For him the due reward of punishment."

CHAP. IV. — GOD DESIRES NOT SACRIFICES, BUT RIGHTEOUSNESS.

And that God is not appeased by the libations and incense of evil-doers, but awards vengeance in righteousness to each one, Philemon[6] again shall bear testimony to me: —

"If any one should dream, O Pamphilus,
By sacrifice of bulls or goats — nay, then,
By Jupiter — of any such like things;
Or by presenting gold or purple robes,
Or images of ivory and gems;
If thus he thinks he may propitiate God,
He errs, and shows himself a silly one.
But let him rather useful be, and good,
Committing neither theft nor lustful deeds,
Nor murder foul, for earthly riches' sake.
Let him of no man covet wife or child,
His splendid house, his wide-spread property,
His maiden, or his slave born in his house,
His horses, or his cattle, or his beeves.
Nay, covet not a pin, O Pamphilus,
For God, close by you, sees whate'er you do.
He ever with the wicked man is wroth,
But in the righteous takes a pleasure still,
Permitting him to reap fruit of his toil,
And to enjoy the bread his sweat has won.
But being righteous, see thou pay thy vows,
And unto God the giver offer gifts.
Place thy adorning not in outward shows,
But in an inward purity of heart;
Hearing the thunder then, thou shalt not fear,
Nor shalt thou flee, O master, at its voice,
For thou art conscious of no evil deed,
And God, close by you, sees whate'er you do."

Again, Plato, in *Timæus*,[7] says: "But if any one on consideration should actually institute

---
[1] "Pythagorei cujusdam fetus." — OTTO, after Goezius.
[2] [Langus compares 2. Pet. iii. 7.]
[3] Some propose to insert these three lines in the centre of the next quotation from Philemon, after the line, "Nay, there's an eye," etc.
[4] Some say *Diphilus*.
[5] Grotius joins these lines to the preceding. Clement of Alexandria assigns them, and the others, which are under the name of Euripides, to Diphilus.
[6] Some attribute these lines to Menander, others regard them as spurious.
[7] P. 68, D, [cap. 30.]

a rigid inquiry, he would be ignorant of the distinction between the human and the divine nature; because God mingles many[1] things up into one, [and again is able to dissolve one into many things,] seeing that He is endued with knowledge and power; but no man either is, or ever shall be, able to perform any of these."

CHAP. V. — THE VAIN PRETENSIONS OF FALSE GODS.

But concerning those who think that they shall share the holy and perfect name, which some have received by a vain tradition as if they were gods, Menander in the *Auriga* says: —

"If there exists a god who walketh out
  With an old woman, or who enters in
  By stealth to houses through the folding-doors,
He ne'er can please me; nay, but only he
Who stays at home, a just and righteous God,
To give salvation to His worshippers."

The same Menander, in the *Sacerdos*, says: —

"There is no God, O woman, that can save
  One man by another; if indeed a man,
  With sound of tinkling cymbals, charm a god
  Where'er he listeth, then assuredly
  He who doth so is much the greater god.
  But these, O Rhode, are but the cunning schemes
  Which daring men of intrigue, unabashed,
  Invent to earn themselves a livelihood,
  And yield a laughing-stock unto the age."

Again, the same Menander, stating his opinion about those who are received as gods, proving rather that they are not so, says: —

"Yea, if I this beheld, I then should wish
  That back to me again my soul returned.
  For tell me where, O Getas, in the world
  'Tis possible to find out righteous gods?"

And in the *Depositum*: —

"There's an unrighteous judgment, as it seems,
  Even with the gods."

And Euripides the tragedian, in *Orestes*, says: —

"Apollo having caused by his command
  The murder of the mother, knoweth not
  What honesty and justice signify.
  We serve the gods, whoever they may be;
  But from the central regions of the earth
  You see Apollo plainly gives response
  To mortals, and whate'er he says we do.
  I him obeyed, when she that bore me fell
  Slain by my hand: *he* is the wicked man.
  Then slay him, for 'twas he that sinned, not I.
  What could I do? Think you not that the god
  Should free me from the blame which I do bear?"

The same also in *Hippolytus*: —

"But on these points the gods do not judge right."

And in *Ion*: —

"But in the daughter of Erechtheus
  What interest have I? for that pertains
  Not unto such as me. But when I come
  With golden vessels for libations, I
  The dew shall sprinkle, and yet needs must warn
  Apollo of his deeds; for when he weds
  Maidens by force, the children secretly
  Begotten he betrays, and then neglects
  When dying. Thus not you; but while you may
  Always pursue the virtues, for the gods
  Will surely punish men of wickedness.
  How is it right that you, who have prescribed
  Laws for men's guidance, live unrighteously?
  But ye being absent, I shall freely speak,
  And ye to men shall satisfaction give
  For marriage forced, thou Neptune, Jupiter,
  Who over heaven presides. The temples ye
  Have emptied, while injustice ye repay.
  And though ye laud the prudent to the skies,
  Yet have ye filled your hands with wickedness.
  No longer is it right to call men ill
  If they do imitate the sins[2] of gods;[3]
  Nay, evil let their teachers rather be."

And in *Archelaus*: —

"Full oft, my son, do gods mankind perplex."

And in *Bellerophon*: —

"They are no gods, who do not what is right."

And again in the same: —

"Gods reign in heaven most certainly, says one;
  But it is false, — yea, false: and let not him
  Who speaks thus, be so foolish as to use
  Ancient tradition, or to pay regard
  Unto my words: but with unclouded eye
  Behold the matter in its clearest light.
  Power absolute, I say, robs men of life
  And property; transgresses plighted faith;
  Nor spares even cities, but with cruel hand
  Despoils and devastates them ruthlessly.
  But they that do these things have more success
  Than those who live a gentle pious life;
  And cities small, I know, which reverence gods,
  Submissive bend before the many spears
  Of larger impious ones; yea, and methinks
  If any man lounge idly, and abstain
  From working with his hands for sustenance,
  Yet pray the gods; he very soon will know
  If they from him misfortunes will avert."

And Menander in *Diphilus*:[4] —

"Therefore ascribe we praise and honour great
  To Him who Father is, and Lord of all;
  Sole maker and preserver of mankind,
  And who with all good things our earth has stored."

The same also in the *Piscatores*: —

"For I deem that which nourishes my life
  Is God; but he whose custom 'tis to meet
  The wants of men, — He needs not at our hands
  Renewed supplies, Himself being all in all."[5]

The same in the *Fratres*: —

"God ever is intelligence to those
  Who righteous are: so wisest men have thought."

And in the *Tibicinæ*: —

"Good reason finds a temple in all things
  Wherein to worship; for what is the mind,
  But just the voice of God within us placed?"

---

[1] The MSS. are corrupt here. They seem to read, and one actually does read, "all" for "many." "Many" is in Plato, and the clause in brackets is taken from Plato to fill up the sense.

[2] κακά in Euripedes, καλά in text.
[3] [See Warburton's *Divine Legation* (book ii. § 4), vol. ii. p. 20. Ed. London, 1811.]
[4] These lines are assigned to Diphilus.
[5] The words from "but" to "all" are assigned by Otto to Justin, not to Menander.

And the tragedian in *Phrixus*: —

"But if the pious and the impious
Share the same lot, how could we think it just,
If Jove, the best, judges not uprightly?"

In *Philoctetes*: —

"You see how honourable gain is deemed
Even to the gods; and how he is admired
Whose shrine is laden most with yellow gold.
What, then, doth hinder thee, since it is good
To be like gods, from thus accepting gain?"

In *Hecuba*: —

"O Jupiter! whoever thou mayest be,
Of whom except in word all knowledge fails;"

and, —

"Jupiter, whether thou art indeed
A great necessity, or the mind of man,
I worship thee!"

CHAP. VI. — WE SHOULD ACKNOWLEDGE ONE ONLY GOD.

Here, then, is a proof of virtue, and of a mind loving prudence, to recur to the communion of the unity,[1] and to attach one's self to prudence for salvation, and make choice of the better things according to the free-will placed in man; and not to think that those who are possessed of human passions are lords of all, when they shall not appear to have even equal power with men.

For in Homer,[2] Demodocus says he is self-taught —

"God inspired me with strains" —

though he is a mortal. Æsculapius and Apollo are taught to heal by Chiron the Centaur, — a very novel thing indeed, for gods to be taught by a man. What need I speak of Bacchus, who the poet says is mad? or of Hercules, who he says is unhappy? What need to speak of Mars and Venus, the leaders of adultery; and by means of all these to establish the proof which has been undertaken? For if some one, in ignorance, should imitate the deeds which are said to be divine, he would be reckoned among impure men, and a stranger to life and humanity; and if any one does so knowingly, he will have a plausible excuse for escaping vengeance, by showing that imitation of godlike deeds of audacity is no sin. But if any one should blame these deeds, he will take away their well-known names, and not cover them up with specious and plausible words. It is necessary, then, to accept the true and invariable Name, not proclaimed by my words only, but by the words of those who have introduced us to the elements of learning, in order that we may not, by living idly in this present state of existence, not only as those who are ignorant of the heavenly glory, but also as having proved ourselves ungrateful, render our account to the Judge.

---

[1] See chap. i., the opening sentence.

[2] *Odyssey*, xxii. 347.
[N. B. — This tractate is probably the genuine work of Justin.]

FRAGMENTS OF THE LOST WORK OF JUSTIN ON THE RESURRECTION

[TRANSLATED BY THE REV. M. DODS, M.A.]

CHAP. I. — THE SELF-EVIDENCING POWER OF TRUTH.

THE word of truth is free, and carries its own authority, disdaining to fall under any skilful argument, or to endure the logical scrutiny of its hearers. But it would be believed for its own nobility, and for the confidence due to Him who sends it. Now the word of truth is sent from God; wherefore the freedom claimed by the truth is not arrogant. For being sent with authority, it were not fit that it should be required to produce proof of what is said; since neither is there any proof beyond itself, which is God. For every proof is more powerful and trustworthy than that which it proves; since what is disbelieved, until proof is produced, gets credit when such proof is produced, and is recognised as being what it was stated to be. But nothing is either more powerful or more trustworthy than the truth; so that he who requires proof of this, is like one who wishes it demonstrated why the things that appear to the senses do appear. For the test of those things which are received through the reason, is sense; but of sense itself there is no test beyond itself. As then we bring those things which reason hunts after, to sense, and by it judge what kind of things they are, whether the things spoken be true or false, and then sit in judgment no longer, giving full credit to its decision; so also we refer all that is said regarding men and the world to the truth, and by it judge whether it be worthless or no. But the utterances of truth we judge by no separate test, giving full credit to itself. And God, the Father of the universe, who is the perfect intelligence, is the truth. And the Word, being His Son, came to us, having put on flesh, revealing both Himself and the Father, giving to us in Himself resurrection from the dead, and eternal life afterwards. And this is Jesus Christ, our Saviour and Lord. He, therefore, is Himself both the faith and the proof of Himself and of all things. Wherefore those who follow Him, and know Him, having faith in Him as their proof, shall rest in Him. But since the adversary does not cease to resist many, and uses many and divers arts to ensnare them, that he may seduce the faithful from their faith, and that he may prevent the faithless from believing, it seems to me necessary that we also, being armed with the invulnerable doctrines of the faith, do battle against him in behalf of the weak.

CHAP. II. — OBJECTIONS TO THE RESURRECTION OF THE FLESH.

They who maintain the wrong opinion say that there is no resurrection of the flesh; giving as their reason that it is impossible that what is corrupted and dissolved should be restored to the same as it had been. And besides the impossibility, they say that the salvation of the flesh is disadvantageous; and they abuse the flesh, adducing its infirmities, and declare that it only is the cause of our sins, so that if the flesh, say they, rise again, our infirmities also rise with it. And such sophistical reasons as the following they elaborate: If the flesh rise again, it must rise either entire and possessed of all its parts, or imperfect. But its rising imperfect argues a want of power on God's part, if some parts could be saved, and others not; but if all the parts are saved, then the body will manifestly have all its members. But is it not absurd to say that these members will exist after the resurrection from the dead, since the Saviour said, "They neither marry, nor are given in marriage, but shall be as the angels in heaven?"[1] And the angels, say they, have neither flesh, nor do they eat, nor have sexual intercourse; therefore there shall be no resurrection of the flesh. By

---

[1] Mark xii. 25.

these and such like arguments, they attempt to distract men from the faith. And there are some who maintain that even Jesus Himself appeared only as spiritual, and not in flesh, but presented merely the appearance of flesh: these persons seek to rob the flesh of the promise. First, then, let us solve those things which seem to them to be insoluble; then we will introduce in an orderly manner the demonstration concerning the flesh, proving that it partakes of salvation.

CHAP. III. — IF THE MEMBERS RISE, MUST THEY DISCHARGE THE SAME FUNCTIONS AS NOW?

They say, then, if the body shall rise entire, and in possession of all its members, it necessarily follows that the functions of the members shall also be in existence; that the womb shall become pregnant, and the male also discharge his function of generation, and the rest of the members in like manner. Now let this argument stand or fall by this one assertion. For this being proved false, their whole objection will be removed. Now it is indeed evident that the members which discharge functions discharge those functions which in the present life we see; but it does not follow that they necessarily discharge the same functions from the beginning. And that this may be more clearly seen, let us consider it thus. The function of the womb is to become pregnant; and of the member of the male to impregnate. But as, though these members are destined to discharge such functions, it is not therefore necessary that they from the beginning discharge them (since we see many women who do not become pregnant, as those that are barren, even though they have wombs), so pregnancy is not the immediate and necessary consequence of having a womb; but those even who are not barren abstain from sexual intercourse, some being virgins from the first, and others from a certain time. And we see men also keeping themselves virgins, some from the first, and some from a certain time; so that by their means, marriage, made lawless through lust, is destroyed.[1] And we find that some even of the lower animals, though possessed of wombs, do not bear, such as the mule; and the male mules do not beget their kind. So that both in the case of men and the irrational animals we can see sexual intercourse abolished; and this, too, before the future world. And our Lord Jesus Christ was born of a virgin, for no other reason than that He might destroy the begetting by lawless desire, and might show to the ruler[2] that the formation of man was possible to God without human intervention. And when He had been born, and had submitted to the other conditions of the flesh, — I mean food, drink, and clothing, — this one condition only of discharging the sexual function He did not submit to; for, regarding the desires of the flesh, He accepted some as necessary, while others, which were unnecessary, He did not submit to. For if the flesh were deprived of food, drink, and clothing, it would be destroyed; but being deprived of lawless desire, it suffers no harm. And at the same time He foretold that, in the future world, sexual intercourse should be done away with; as He says, "The children of this world marry, and are given in marriage; but the children of the world to come neither marry nor are given in marriage, but shall be like the angels in heaven."[3] Let not, then, those that are unbelieving marvel, if in the world to come He do away with those acts of our fleshly members which even in this present life are abolished.

CHAP. IV. — MUST THE DEFORMED RISE DEFORMED?

Well, they say, if then the flesh rise, it must rise the same as it falls; so that if it die with one eye, it must rise one-eyed; if lame, lame; if defective in any part of the body, in this part the man must rise deficient. How truly blinded are they in the eyes of their hearts! For they have not seen on the earth blind men seeing again, and the lame walking by His word. All things which the Saviour did, He did in the first place in order that what was spoken concerning Him in the prophets might be fulfilled, "that the blind should receive sight, and the deaf hear,"[4] and so on; but also to induce the belief that in the resurrection the flesh shall rise entire. For if on earth He healed the sicknesses of the flesh, and made the body whole, much more will He do this in the resurrection, so that the flesh shall rise perfect and entire. In this manner, then, shall those dreaded difficulties of theirs be healed.

CHAP. V. — THE RESURRECTION OF THE FLESH IS NOT IMPOSSIBLE.

But again, of those who maintain that the flesh has no resurrection, some assert that it is impossible; others that, considering how vile and despicable the flesh is, it is not fit that God should raise it; and others, that it did not at the first receive the promise. First, then, in respect of those who say that it is impossible for God to raise it, it seems to me that I should show that they are ignorant, professing as they do in word that they are believers, yet by their works proving themselves to be unbelieving, even more

---

[1] That is to say, their lives are a protest against entering into marriage for any other purpose than that of begetting children.
[2] i.e., to the devil. [St. John xii. 31, xiv. 30, xvi. 11.]
[3] Luke xx. 34, 35.
[4] Isa. xxxv. 5.

unbelieving than the unbelievers. For, seeing that all the heathen believe in their idols, and are persuaded that to them all things are possible (as even their poet Homer says,[1] "The gods can do all things, and that easily;" and he added the word "easily" that he might bring out the greatness of the power of the gods), many do seem to be more unbelieving than they. For if the heathen believe in their gods, which are idols ("which have ears, and they hear not; they have eyes, and they see not"[2]), that they can do all things, though they be but devils, as saith the Scripture, "The gods of the nations are devils,"[3] much more ought we, who hold the right, excellent, and true faith, to believe in our God, since also we have proofs [of His power], first in the creation of the first man, for he was made from the earth by God; and this is sufficient evidence of God's power; and then they who observe things can see how men are generated one by another, and can marvel in a still greater degree that from a little drop of moisture so grand a living creature is formed. And certainly if this were only recorded in a promise, and not seen accomplished, this too would be much more incredible than the other; but it is rendered more credible by accomplishment.[4] But even in the case of the resurrection the Saviour has shown us accomplishments, of which we will in a little speak. But now we are demonstrating that the resurrection of the flesh is possible, asking pardon of the children of the Church if we adduce arguments which seem to be secular[5] and physical:[6] first, because to God nothing is secular, not even the world itself, for it is His workmanship; and secondly, because we are conducting our argument so as to meet unbelievers. For if we argued with believers, it were enough to say that we believe; but now we must proceed by demonstrations. The foregoing proofs are indeed quite sufficient to evince the possibility of the resurrection of the flesh; but since these men are exceedingly unbelieving, we will further adduce a more convincing argument still, — an argument drawn not from faith, for they are not within its scope, but from their own mother unbelief, — I mean, of course, from physical reasons. For if by such arguments we prove to them that the resurrection of the flesh is possible, they are certainly worthy of great contempt if they can be persuaded neither by the deliverances of faith nor by the arguments of the world.

[1] *Odyssey*, ii. 304.
[2] Ps. cxv. 5.
[3] Ps. xcvi. 5.
[4] i.e., by actually happening under our observation.
[5] ἔξωθεν, "without" or "outside," to which reference is made in the next clause, which may be translated, "because nothing is outside God," or, "because to God nothing is ' without.'"
[6] κοσμικῶν, arguments drawn from the laws by which the world is governed.

CHAP. VI. — THE RESURRECTION CONSISTENT WITH THE OPINIONS OF THE PHILOSOPHERS.

Those, then, who are called natural philosophers, say, some of them, as Plato, that the universe is matter and God; others, as Epicurus, that it is atoms and the void;[7] others, like the Stoics, that it is these four — fire, water, air, earth. For it is sufficient to mention the most prevalent opinions. And Plato says that all things are made from matter by God, and according to His design; but Epicurus and his followers say that all things are made from the atom and the void by some kind of self-regulating action of the natural movement of the bodies; and the Stoics, that all are made of the four elements, God pervading them. But while there is such discrepancy among them, there are some doctrines acknowledged by them all in common, one of which is that neither can anything be produced from what is not in being, nor anything be destroyed or dissolved into what has not any being, and that the elements exist indestructible out of which all things are generated. And this being so, the regeneration of the flesh will, according to all these philosophers, appear to be possible. For if, according to Plato, it is matter and God, both these are indestructible and God; and God indeed occupies the position of an artificer, to wit, a potter; and matter occupies the place of clay or wax, or some such thing. That, then, which is formed of matter, be it an image or a statue, is destructible; but the matter itself is indestructible, such as clay or wax, or any other such kind of matter. Thus the artist designs in the clay or wax, and makes the form of a living animal; and again, if his handiwork be destroyed, it is not impossible for him to make the same form, by working up the same material, and fashioning it anew. So that, according to Plato, neither will it be impossible for God, who is Himself indestructible, and has also indestructible material, even after that which has been first formed of it has been destroyed, to make it anew again, and to make the same form just as it was before. But according to the Stoics even, the body being produced by the mixture of the four elementary substances, when this body has been dissolved into the four elements, these remaining indestructible, it is possible that they receive a second time the same fusion and composition, from God pervading them, and so re-make the body which they formerly made. Like as if a man shall make a composition of gold and silver, and brass and tin, and then shall wish to dissolve it again, so that each element exist separately, having again mixed them, he may, if he pleases, make the very same composition as he had for-

[7] τὸ κενόν, the void of space in which the infinity of atoms moved.

merly made. Again, according to Epicurus, the atoms and the void being indestructible, it is by a definite arrangement and adjustment of the atoms as they come together, that both all other formations are produced, and the body itself; and it being in course of time dissolved, is dissolved again into those atoms from which it was also produced. And as these remain indestructible, it is not at all impossible, that by coming together again, and receiving the same arrangement and position, they should make a body of like nature to what was formerly produced by them; as if a jeweller should make in mosaic the form of an animal, and the stones should be scattered by time or by the man himself who made them, he having still in his possession the scattered stones, may gather them together again, and having gathered, may dispose them in the same way, and make the same form of an animal. And shall not God be able to collect again the decomposed members of the flesh, and make the same body as was formerly produced by Him?

CHAP. VII. — THE BODY VALUABLE IN GOD'S SIGHT.

But the proof of the possibility of the resurrection of the flesh I have sufficiently demonstrated, in answer to men of the world. And if the resurrection of the flesh is not found impossible on the principles even of unbelievers, how much more will it be found in accordance with the mind of believers! But following our order, we must now speak with respect to those who think meanly of the flesh, and say that it is not worthy of the resurrection nor of the heavenly economy,[1] because, first, its substance is earth; and besides, because it is full of all wickedness, so that it forces the soul to sin along with it. But these persons seem to be ignorant of the whole work of God, both of the genesis and formation of man at the first, and why the things in the world were made.[2] For does not the word say, "Let Us make man in our image, and after our likeness?"[3] What kind of man? Manifestly He means fleshly man. For the word says, "And God took dust of the earth, and made man."[4] It is evident, therefore, that man made in the image of God was of flesh. Is it not, then, absurd to say, that the flesh made by God in His own image is contemptible, and worth nothing? But that the flesh is with God a precious possession is manifest, first from its being formed by Him, if at least the image is valuable to the former and artist; and besides, its value can be gathered from the creation of the rest of the world. For that on account of which the rest is made, is the most precious of all to the maker.

CHAP. VIII. — DOES THE BODY CAUSE THE SOUL TO SIN?

Quite true, say they; yet the flesh is a sinner, so much so, that it forces the soul to sin along with it. And thus they vainly accuse it, and lay to its charge alone the sins of both. But in what instance can the flesh possibly sin by itself, if it have not the soul going before it and inciting it? For as in the case of a yoke of oxen, if one or other is loosed from the yoke, neither of them can plough alone; so neither can soul or body alone effect anything, if they be unyoked from their communion. And if it is the flesh that is the sinner, then on its account alone did the Saviour come, as He says, "I am not come to call the righteous, but sinners to repentance."[5] Since, then, the flesh has been proved to be valuable in the sight of God, and glorious above all His works, it would very justly be saved by Him.

We must meet, therefore, those who say, that even though it be the special handiwork of God, and beyond all else valued by Him, it would not immediately follow that it has the promise of the resurrection. Yet is it not absurd, that that which has been produced with such circumstance, and which is beyond all else valuable, should be so neglected by its Maker, as to pass to nonentity? Then the sculptor and painter, if they wish the works they have made to endure, that they may win glory by them, renew them when they begin to decay; but God would so neglect His own possession and work, that it becomes annihilated, and no longer exists. Should we not call this labour in vain? As if a man who has built a house should forthwith destroy it, or should neglect it, though he sees it falling into decay, and is able to repair it: we would blame him for labouring in vain; and should we not so blame God? But not such an one is the Incorruptible, — not senseless is the Intelligence of the universe. Let the unbelieving be silent, even though they themselves do not believe.

But, in truth, He has even called the flesh to the resurrection, and promises to it everlasting life. For where He promises to save man, there He gives the promise to the flesh. For what is man but the reasonable animal composed of body and soul? Is the soul by itself man? No; but the soul of man. Would the body be called man? No, but it is called the body of man. If, then, neither of these is by itself man, but that which is made up of the two together is called man, and God has called *man* to life and

---

[1] Or, "citizenship."
[2] This might also be rendered, "and the things in the world, on account of which he was made;" but the subsequent argument shows the propriety of the above rendering.
[3] Gen. i. 26.
[4] Gen. ii. 7.

[5] Mark ii. 17.

resurrection, He has called not a part, but the whole, which is the soul and the body. Since would it not be unquestionably absurd, if, while these two are in the same being and according to the same law, the one were saved and the other not? And if it be not impossible, as has already been proved, that the flesh be regenerated, what is the distinction on the ground of which the soul is saved and the body not? Do they make God a grudging God? But He is good, and will have all to be saved. And by God and His proclamation, not only has your soul heard and believed on Jesus Christ, and with it the flesh,[1] but both were washed, and both wrought righteousness. They make God, then, ungrateful and unjust, if, while both believe on Him, He desires to save one and not the other. Well, they say, but the soul is incorruptible, being a part of God and inspired by Him, and therefore He desires to save what is peculiarly His own and akin to Himself; but the flesh is corruptible, and not from Him, as the soul is. Then what thanks are due to Him, and what manifestation of His power and goodness is it, if He purposed to save what is by nature saved and exists as a part of Himself? For it had its salvation from itself; so that in saving the soul, God does no great thing. For to be saved is its natural destiny, because it is a part of Himself, being His inspiration. But no thanks are due to one who saves what is his own; for this is to save himself. For he who saves a part of himself, saves himself by his own means, lest he become defective in that part; and this is not the act of a good man. For not even when a man does good to his children and offspring, does one call him a good man; for even the most savage of the wild beasts do so, and indeed willingly endure death, if need be, for the sake of their cubs. But if a man were to perform the same acts in behalf of his slaves, that man would justly be called good. Wherefore the Saviour also taught us to love our enemies, since, says He, what thank have ye? So that He has shown us that it is a good work not only to love those that are begotten of Him, but also those that are without. And what He enjoins upon us, He Himself first of all does.[2]

. . . .

CHAP. IX. — THE RESURRECTION OF CHRIST PROVES THAT THE BODY RISES.

If He had no need of the flesh, why did He heal it? And what is most forcible of all, He raised the dead. Why? Was it not to show what the resurrection should be? How then did He raise the dead? Their souls or their bodies? Manifestly both. If the resurrection were only spiritual, it was requisite that He, in raising the dead, should show the body lying apart by itself, and the soul living apart by itself. But now He did not do so, but raised the body, confirming in it the promise of life. Why did He rise in the flesh in which He suffered, unless to show the resurrection of the flesh? And wishing to confirm this, when His disciples did not know whether to believe He had truly risen in the body, and were looking upon Him and doubting, He said to them, "Ye have not yet faith, see that it is I;"[3] and He let them handle Him, and showed them the prints of the nails in His hands. And when they were by every kind of proof persuaded that it was Himself, and in the body, they asked Him to eat with them, that they might thus still more accurately ascertain that He had in verity risen bodily; and He did eat honey-comb and fish. And when He had thus shown them that there is truly a resurrection of the flesh, wishing to show them this also, that it is not impossible for flesh to ascend into heaven (as He had said that our dwelling-place is in heaven), "He was taken up into heaven while they beheld,"[4] as He was in the flesh. If, therefore, after all that has been said, any one demand demonstration of the resurrection, he is in no respect different from the Sadducees, since resurrection of the flesh is the power of God, and, being above all reasoning, is established by faith, and seen in works.

. . . .

CHAP. X. — THE BODY SAVED, AND WILL THEREFORE RISE.

The resurrection is a resurrection of the flesh which died. For the spirit dies not; the soul is in the body, and without a soul it cannot live. The body, when the soul forsakes it, is not. For the body is the house of the soul; and the soul the house of the spirit. These three, in all those who cherish a sincere hope and unquestioning faith in God, will be saved. Considering, therefore, even such arguments as are suited to this world, and finding that, even according to them, it is not impossible that the flesh be regenerated; and seeing that, besides all these proofs, the Saviour in the whole Gospel shows that there is salvation for the flesh, why do we any longer endure those unbelieving and dangerous arguments, and fail to see that we are retrograding when we listen to such an argument as this: that the soul is immortal, but the body mortal, and incapable of being revived? For this we used to hear from Pythagoras and Plato,

---

[1] Migne proposes to read here καὶ οὐ σὺν αὐτῇ, "without the flesh," which gives a more obvious meaning. The above reading is, however, defensible. Justin means that the flesh was not merely partaking of the soul's faith and promise, but had rights of its own.

[2] It is supposed that a part of the treatise has been here dropped out.

[3] Comp. Luke xxiv. 32, etc.
[4] Acts i. 9.

even before we learned the truth. If then the Saviour said this, and proclaimed salvation to the soul alone, what new thing, beyond what we heard from Pythagoras and Plato and all their band, did He bring us? But now He has come proclaiming the glad tidings of a new and strange hope to men. For indeed it was a strange and new thing for God to promise that He would not keep incorruption in incorruption, but would make corruption incorruption. But because the prince of wickedness could in no other way corrupt the truth, he sent forth his apostles (evil men who introduced pestilent doctrines), choosing them from among those who crucified our Saviour; and these men bore the name of the Saviour, but did the works of him that sent them, through whom the name itself has been spoken against. But if the flesh do not rise, why is it also guarded, and why do we not rather suffer it to indulge its desires? Why do we not imitate physicians, who, it is said, when they get a patient that is despaired of and incurable, allow him to indulge his desires? For they know that he is dying; and this indeed those who hate the flesh surely do, casting it out of its inheritance, so far as they can; for on this account they also despise it, because it is shortly to become a corpse. But if our physician Christ, God, having rescued us from our desires, regulates our flesh with His own wise and temperate rule, it is evident that He guards it from sins because it possesses a hope of salvation, as physicians do not suffer men whom they hope to save to indulge in what pleasures they please.

[N.B. — These fragments are probably genuine.]

OTHER FRAGMENTS FROM THE LOST WRITINGS OF JUSTIN

[TRANSLATED BY THE REV. A. ROBERTS, D.D.]

I.

THE most admirable Justin rightly declared that the aforesaid demons[1] resembled robbers. — TATIAN'S *Address to the Greeks,* chap. xviii.

II.

And Justin well said in his book against Marcion, that he would not have believed the Lord Himself, if He had announced any other God than the Fashioner and Maker [of the world], and our Nourisher. But since, from the one God, who both made this world and formed us, and contains as well as administers all things, there came to us the only-begotten Son, summing up His own workmanship in Himself, my faith in Him is stedfast, and my love towards the Father is immoveable, God bestowing both upon us. — IRENÆUS: *Heresies,* iv. 6.

III.

Justin well said: Before the advent of the Lord, Satan never ventured to blaspheme God, inasmuch as he was not yet sure of his own damnation, since that was announced concerning him by the prophets only in parables and allegories. But after the advent of the Lord, learning plainly from the discourses of Christ and His apostles that eternal fire was prepared for him who voluntarily departed from God, and for all who, without repentance, persevere in apostasy, then, by means of a man of this sort, he, as if already condemned, blasphemes that God who inflicts judgment upon him, and imputes the sin of his apostasy to his Maker, instead of to his own will and predilection. — IRENÆUS: *Heresies,* v. 26.

IV.

Expounding the reason of the incessant plotting of the devil against us, he declares: Before the advent of the Lord, the devil did not so plainly know the measure of his own punishment, inasmuch as the divine prophets had but enigmatically announced it; as, for instance, Isaiah, who in the person of the Assyrian tragically revealed the course to be followed against the devil. But when the Lord appeared, and the devil clearly understood that eternal fire was laid up and prepared for him and his angels, he then began to plot without ceasing against the faithful, being desirous to have many companions in his apostasy, that he might not by himself endure the shame of condemnation, comforting himself by this cold and malicious consolation. — *From the writings of* JOHN OF ANTIOCH.

V.

And Justin of Neapolis, a man who was not far separated from the apostles either in age or excellence, says that that which is mortal is inherited, but that which is immortal inherits; and that the flesh indeed dies, but the kingdom of heaven lives. — *From* METHODIUS *On the Resurrection, in Photius.*

VI.

Neither is there straitness with God, nor anything that is not absolutely perfect. — *From manuscript of the writings of* JUSTIN.

VII.

We shall not injure God by remaining ignorant of Him, but shall deprive ourselves of His friendship.

VIII.

The unskilfulness of the teacher proves destructive to his disciples, and the carelessness of the disciples entails danger on the teacher, and especially should they owe their negligence to his want of knowledge.

IX.

The soul can with difficulty be recalled to those good things from which it has fallen, and

---

[1] [See, on the Resurrection, cap. vi.; and compare, —
"And of those demons that are found
In fire, air, flood, or under ground," etc.
Milton, *Pens.*, line 93.]

is with difficulty dragged away from those evils to which it has become accustomed. If at any time thou showest a disposition to blame thyself, then perhaps, through the medicine of repentance, I should cherish good hopes regarding thee. But when thou altogether despisest fear, and rejectest with scorn the very faith of Christ, it were better for thee that thou hadst never been born from the womb. — *From the writings of* JOHN OF DAMASCUS.

X.

By the two birds[1] Christ is denoted, both dead as man, and living as God. He is likened to a bird, because He is understood and declared to be from above, and from heaven. And the living bird, having been dipped in the blood of the dead one, was afterwards let go. For the living and divine Word was in the crucified and dead temple [of the body], as being a partaker of the passion, and yet impassible to God.

By that which took place in the running[2] water, in which the wood and the hyssop and the scarlet were dipped, is set forth the bloody passion of Christ on the cross for the salvation of those who are sprinkled with the Spirit, and the water, and the blood. Wherefore the material for purification was not provided chiefly with reference to leprosy, but with regard to the forgiveness of sins, that both leprosy might be understood to be an emblem of sin, and the things which were sacrificed an emblem of Him who was to be sacrificed for sins.

For this reason, consequently, he ordered that the scarlet should be dipped at the same time in the water, thus predicting that the flesh should no longer possess its natural [evil] properties. For this reason, also, were there the two birds, the one being sacrificed in the water, and the other dipped both in the blood and in the water, and then sent away, just as is narrated also respecting the goats.

The goat that was sent away presented a type of Him who taketh away the sins of men. But the two contained a representation of the one economy of God incarnate. For He was wounded for our transgressions, and He bare the sins of many, and He was delivered for our iniquities. — *From manuscript of writings of* JUSTIN.

XI.

When God formed man at the beginning, He suspended the things of nature on his will, and made an experiment by means of one commandment. For He ordained that, if he kept this, he should partake of immortal existence; but if he transgressed it, the contrary should be his lot. Man having been thus made, and immediately looking towards transgression, naturally became subject to corruption. Corruption then becoming inherent in nature, it was necessary that He who wished to save should be one who destroyed the efficient cause of corruption. And this could not otherwise be done than by the life which is according to nature being united to that which had received the corruption, and so destroying the corruption, while preserving as immortal for the future that which had received it. It was therefore necessary that the Word should become possessed of a body, that He might deliver us from the death of natural corruption. For if, as ye[3] say, He had simply by a nod warded off death from us, death indeed would not have approached us on account of the expression of His will; but none the less would we again have become corruptible, inasmuch as we carried about in ourselves that natural corruption. — LEONTIUS *against Eutychians*, etc., book ii.

XII.

As it is inherent in all bodies formed by God to have a shadow, so it is fitting that God, who is just, should render to those who choose what is good, and to those who prefer what is evil, to every one according to his deserts. — *From the writings of* JOHN OF DAMASCUS.

XIII.

He speaks not of the Gentiles in foreign lands, but concerning [the people] who agree with the Gentiles, according to that which is spoken by Jeremiah: "It is a bitter thing for thee, that thou hast forsaken me, saith the Lord thy God, that of old thou hast broken thy yoke, and torn asunder thy bands, and said, I will not serve Thee, but will go to every high hill, and underneath every tree, and there shall I become dissolute in my fornication."[4] — *From manuscript of the writings of* JUSTIN.

XIV.

Neither shall light ever be darkness as long as light exists, nor shall the truth of the things pertaining to us be controverted. For truth is that than which nothing is more powerful. Every one who might speak the truth, and speaks it not, shall be judged by God. — *Manuscript and works of* JOHN OF DAMASCUS.

XV.

And the fact that it was not said of the seventh day equally with the other days, "And there was evening, and there was morning," is a distinct indication of the consummation which is to take place in it before it is finished, as the

---

[1] See Lev. xiv. 49–53.
[2] Literally, "living."
[3] The Gentiles are here referred to, who saw no necessity for the incarnation.
[4] Jer. ii. 19, etc. (LXX.)

fathers declare, especially St. Clement, and Irenæus, and Justin the martyr and philosopher, who, commenting with exceeding wisdom on the number six of the sixth day, affirms that the intelligent soul of man and his five susceptible senses were the six works of the sixth day. Whence also, having discoursed at length on the number six, he declares that all things which have been framed by God are divided into six classes, — viz., into things intelligent and immortal, such as are the angels; into things reasonable and mortal, such as mankind; into things sensitive and irrational, such as cattle, and birds, and fishes; into things that can advance, and move, and are insensible, such as the winds, and the clouds, and the waters, and the stars; into things which increase and are immoveable, such as the trees; and into things which are insensible and immoveable, such as the mountains, the earth, and such like. For all the creatures of God, in heaven and on earth, fall under one or other of these divisions, and are circumscribed by them. — *From the writings of* ANASTASIUS.

XVI.

Sound doctrine does not enter into the hard and disobedient heart; but, as if beaten back, enters anew into itself.

XVII.

As the good of the body is health, so the good of the soul is knowledge, which is indeed a kind of health of soul, by which a likeness to God is attained. — *From the writings of* JOHN OF DAMASCUS.

XVIII.

To yield and give way to our passions is the lowest slavery, even as to rule over them is the only liberty.

The greatest of all good is to be free from sin, the next is to be justified; but he must be reckoned the most unfortunate of men, who, while living unrighteously, remains for a long time unpunished.

Animals in harness cannot but be carried over a precipice by the inexperience and badness of their driver, even as by his skilfulness and excellence they will be saved.

The end contemplated by a philosopher is likeness to God, so far as that is possible. — *From the writings of* ANTONIUS MELISSA.

XIX.

[The words] of St. Justin, philosopher and martyr, from the fifth part of his *Apology:*[1] — I reckon prosperity, O men, to consist in nothing else than in living according to truth. But we do not live properly, or according to truth, unless we understand the nature of things.

It escapes them apparently, that he who has by a true faith come forth from error to the truth, has truly known himself, not, as they say, as being in a state of frenzy, but as free from the unstable and (as to every variety of error) changeable corruption, by the simple and ever identical truth. — *From the writings of* JOHN OF DAMASCUS.

---

[1] It is doubtful if these words are really Justin's, or, if so, from which, or what part, of his *Apologies* they are derived.

INTRODUCTORY NOTE

TO THE

MARTYRDOM OF JUSTIN MARTYR

CRESCENS, a cynic, has the ill-renown of stirring up the persecution in which Justin and his friends suffered for Christ. The story that he died by the hemlock seems to have originated among the Greeks, who naturally gave this turn to the sufferings of a philosopher.

The following INTRODUCTORY NOTICE of the translator supplies all that need be added.

THOUGH nothing is known as to the date or authorship of the following narrative, it is generally reckoned among the most trustworthy of the Martyria. An absurd addition was in some copies made to it, to the effect that Justin died by means of hemlock. Some have thought it necessary, on account of this story, to conceive of two Justins, one of whom, the celebrated defender of the Christian faith whose writings are given in this volume, died through poison, while the other suffered in the way here described, along with several of his friends. But the description of Justin given in the following account, is evidently such as compels us to refer it to the famous apologist and martyr of the second century.[1]

---

[1] [See Cave, *Lives of the Fathers*, i. 243. Epiphanius, by fixing the martyrdom under the prefecture of Rusticus, seems to identify this history; but, then, he also connects it with the reign of Hadrian. Ed. Oëhler, tom. ii. 709. Berlin, 1859.]

THE MARTYRDOM OF THE HOLY MARTYRS

JUSTIN, CHARITON, CHARITES, PÆON, AND LIBERIANUS, WHO SUFFERED AT ROME.

[TRANSLATED BY THE REV. M. DODS, M.A.]

CHAP. I. — EXAMINATION OF JUSTIN BY THE PREFECT.

In the time of the lawless partisans of idolatry, wicked decrees were passed against the godly Christians in town and country, to force them to offer libations to vain idols; and accordingly the holy men, having been apprehended, were brought before the prefect of Rome, Rusticus by name. And when they had been brought before his judgment-seat, Rusticus the prefect said to Justin, "Obey the gods at once, and submit to the kings."[1] Justin said, "To obey the commandments of our Saviour Jesus Christ is worthy neither of blame nor of condemnation." Rusticus the prefect said, "What kind of doctrines do you profess?" Justin said, "I have endeavoured to learn all doctrines; but I have acquiesced at last in the true doctrines, those namely of the Christians, even though they do not please those who hold false opinions." Rusticus the prefect said, "Are those the doctrines that please you, you utterly wretched man?" Justin said, "Yes, since I adhere to them with right dogma."[2] Rusticus the prefect said, "What is the dogma?" Justin said, "That according to which we worship the God of the Christians, whom we reckon to be one from the beginning, the maker and fashioner of the whole creation, visible and invisible; and the Lord Jesus Christ, the Son of God, who had also been preached beforehand by the prophets as about to be present with the race of men, the herald of salvation and teacher of good disciples. And I, being a man, think that what I can say is insignificant in comparison with His boundless divinity, acknowledging a certain prophetic power,[3] since it was prophesied concerning Him of whom now I say that He is the Son of God. For I know that of old the prophets foretold His appearance among men."

CHAP. II. — EXAMINATION OF JUSTIN CONTINUED.

Rusticus the prefect said, "Where do you assemble?" Justin said, "Where each one chooses and can: for do you fancy that we all meet in the very same place? Not so; because the God of the Christians is not circumscribed by place; but being invisible, fills heaven and earth, and everywhere is worshipped and glorified by the faithful." Rusticus the prefect said, "Tell me where you assemble, or into what place do you collect your followers?" Justin said, "I live above one Martinus, at the Timiotinian Bath; and during the whole time (and I am now living in Rome for the second time) I am unaware of any other meeting than his. And if any one wished to come to me, I communicated to him the doctrines of truth." Rusticus said, "Are you not, then, a Christian?" Justin said, "Yes, I am a Christian."

CHAP. III. — EXAMINATION OF CHARITON AND OTHERS.

Then said the prefect Rusticus to Chariton, "Tell me further, Chariton, are you also a Christian?" Chariton said, "I am a Christian by the command of God." Rusticus the prefect asked the woman Charito, "What say you, Charito?" Charito said, "I am a Christian by the grace of God." Rusticus said to Euelpistus, "And what are you?" Euelpistus, a servant of Cæsar, answered, "I too am a Christian, having been freed by Christ; and by the grace of Christ I partake of the same hope." Rusticus the prefect said to Hierax, "And you, are you a Christian?" Hierax said, "Yes, I am a Christian, for I revere and worship the same God." Rusticus the pre-

---

[1] i.e., the emperors.
[2] Μετὰ δόγματος ὀρθοῦ, orthodoxy.
[3] That is, that a prophetic inspiration is required to speak worthily of Christ.

fect said, "Did Justin make you Christians?" Hierax said, "I was a Christian, and will be a Christian." And Pæon stood up and said, "I too am a Christian." Rusticus the prefect said, "Who taught you?" Pæon said, "From our parents we received this good confession." Euelpistus said, "I willingly heard the words of Justin. But from my parents also I learned to be a Christian." Rusticus the prefect said, "Where are your parents?" Euelpistus said, "In Cappadocia." Rusticus says to Hierax, "Where are your parents?" And he answered, and said, "Christ is our true father, and faith in Him is our mother; and my earthly parents died; and I, when I was driven from Iconium in Phrygia, came here." Rusticus the prefect said to Liberianus, "And what say you? Are you a Christian, and unwilling to worship [the gods]?" Liberianus said, "I too am a Christian, for I worship and reverence the only true God."

CHAP. IV. — RUSTICUS THREATENS THE CHRISTIANS WITH DEATH.

The prefect says to Justin, "Hearken, you who are called learned, and think that you know true doctrines; if you are scourged and beheaded, do you believe you will ascend into heaven?" Justin said, "I hope that, if I endure these things, I shall have His gifts.[1] For I know that, to all who have thus lived, there abides the divine favour until the completion of the whole world." Rusticus the prefect said, "Do you suppose, then, that you will ascend into heaven to receive some recompense?" Justin said, "I do not suppose it, but I know and am fully persuaded of it." Rusticus the prefect said, "Let us, then, now come to the matter in hand, and which presses. Having come together, offer sacrifice with one accord to the gods." Justin said, "No right-thinking person falls away from piety to impiety." Rusticus the prefect said, "Unless ye obey, ye shall be mercilessly punished." Justin said, "Through prayer we can be saved on account of our Lord Jesus Christ, even when we have been punished,[2] because this shall become to us salvation and confidence at the more fearful and universal judgment-seat of our Lord and Saviour." Thus also said the other martyrs: "Do what you will, for we are Christians, and do not sacrifice to idols."

CHAP. V. — SENTENCE PRONOUNCED AND EXECUTED.

Rusticus the prefect pronounced sentence, saying, "Let those who have refused to sacrifice to the gods and to yield to the command of the emperor be scourged,[3] and led away to suffer the punishment of decapitation, according to the laws." The holy martyrs having glorified God, and having gone forth to the accustomed place, were beheaded, and perfected their testimony in the confession of the Saviour. And some of the faithful having secretly removed their bodies, laid them in a suitable place, the grace of our Lord Jesus Christ having wrought along with them, to whom be glory for ever and ever. Amen.

---

[1] Another reading is δόγματα, which may be translated, "I shall have what He teaches [us to expect]."

[2] This passage admits of another rendering. Lord Hailes, following the common Latin version, thus translates: "It was our chief wish to endure tortures for the sake of our Lord Jesus Christ, and so to be saved."

[3] [This wholesale sentence implies a great indifference to the probable Roman citizenship of some of them, if not of our heroic martyr himself; but Acts xxii. 25-29 seems to allow that the *condemned* were not protected by the law.]

IRENÆUS

INTRODUCTORY NOTE

TO

IRENÆUS AGAINST HERESIES

[A.D. 120–202.] THIS history introduces us to the Church in her Western outposts. We reach the banks of the Rhone, where for nearly a century Christian missions have flourished. Between Marseilles and Smyrna there seems to have been a brisk trade, and Polycarp had sent Pothinus into Celtic Gaul at an early date as its evangelist. He had fixed his see at Lyons, when Irenæus joined him as a presbyter, having been his fellow-pupil under Polycarp. There, under the "good Aurelius," as he is miscalled (A.D. 177), arose the terrible persecution which made "the martyrs of Lyons and Vienne" so memorable. It was during this persecution that Irenæus was sent to Rome with letters of remonstrance against the rising pestilence of heresy; and he was probably the author of the account of the sufferings of the martyrs which is appended to their testimony.[1] But he had the mortification of finding the Montanist heresy patronized by Eleutherus the Bishop of Rome; and there he met an old friend from the school of Polycarp, who had embraced the Valentinian heresy. We cannot doubt that to this visit we owe the life-long struggle of Irenæus against the heresies that now came in, like locusts, to devour the harvests of the Gospel. But let it be noted here, that, so far from being "the mother and mistress" of even the Western Churches, Rome herself is a mission of the Greeks;[2] Southern Gaul is evangelized from Asia Minor, and Lyons checks the heretical tendencies of the Bishop at Rome. Ante-Nicene Christianity, and indeed the Church herself, appears in Greek costume which lasts through the synodical period; and Latin Christianity, when it begins to appear, is African, and not Roman. It is strange that those who have recorded this great historical fact have so little perceived its bearings upon Roman pretensions in the Middle Ages and modern times.

Returning to Lyons, our author found that the venerable Pothinus had closed his holy career by a martyr's death; and naturally Irenæus became his successor. When the emissaries of heresy followed him, and began to disseminate their licentious practices and foolish doctrines by the aid of "silly women," the great work of his life began. He condescended to study these diseases of the human mind like a wise physician; and, sickening as was the process of classifying and describing them, he made this also his laborious task, that he might enable others to withstand and to overcome them. The works he has left us are monuments of his fidelity to Christ, and to the charges of St. Paul, St. Peter, and St. Jude, whose solemn warnings now proved to be prophecies. No marvel that the great apostle, "night and day with tears," had forewarned the churches of "the grievous wolves" which were to make havoc of the fold.

If it shocks the young student of the virgin years of Christianity to find such a state of things, let him reflect that it was all foretold by Christ himself, and demonstrates the malice and power of the adversary. "An enemy hath done this," said the Master. The spirit that was then work-

---

[1] Eusebius, book v. to the twenty-seventh chapter, should be read as an introduction to this author.
[2] Milman, *Hist. Latin Christianity*, b. i. pp. 27, 28, and the notes.

ing "in the children of disobedience," now manifested itself. The awful visions of the Apocalypse began to be realized. It was now evident in what sense "the Prince of peace" had pronounced His mission, "not peace, but a sword." In short, it became a conspicuous fact, that the Church here on earth is "militant;" while, at the same time, there was seen to be a profound philosophy in the apostolic comment,[1] "There must be also heresies among you, that they which are approved may be made manifest." In the divine economy of Providence it was permitted that every form of heresy which was ever to infest the Church should now exhibit its essential principle, and attract the censures of the faithful. Thus testimony to primitive truth was secured and recorded: the language of catholic orthodoxy was developed and defined, and landmarks of faith were set up for perpetual memorial to all generations. It is a striking example of this divine economy, that the see of Rome was allowed to exhibit its fallibility very conspicuously at this time, and not only to receive the rebukes of Irenæus, but to accept them as wholesome and necessary; so that the heresy of Eleutherus, and the spirit of Diotrephes in Victor, have enabled reformers ever since, and even in the darkest days of pontifical despotism, to testify against the manifold errors patronized by Rome. Hilary and other Gallicans have been strengthened by the example of Irenæus, and by his faithful words of reproof and exhortation, to resist Rome, even down to our own times.

That the intolerable absurdities of Gnosticism should have gained so many disiciples, and proved itself an adversary to be grappled with and not despised, throws light on the condition of the human mind under heathenism, even when it professed "knowledge" and "philosophy." The task of Irenæus was twofold: (1) to render it impossible for any one to confound Gnosticism with Christianity, and (2) to make it impossible for such a monstrous system to survive, or ever to rise again. His task was a nauseous one; but never was the spirit enjoined by Scripture more patiently exhibited, nor with more entire success.[2] If Julian had found Gnosticism just made to his hand, and powerful enough to suit his purposes, the whole history of his attempt to revive Paganism would have been widely different. Irenæus demonstrated its essential unity with the old mythology, and with heathen systems of philosophy. If the fog and malaria that rose with the Day-star, and obscured it, were speedily dispersed, our author is largely to be identified with the radiance which flowed from the Sun of righteousness, and with the breath of the Spirit that banished them for ever.

The Episcopate of Irenæus was distinguished by labours, "in season and out of season," for the evangelization of Southern Gaul; and he seems to have sent missionaries into other regions of what we now call France. In spite of Paganism and heresy, he rendered Lyons a Christian city; and Marcus seems to have retreated before his terrible castigation, taking himself off to regions beyond the Pyrenees.[3] But the pacific name he bears, was rendered yet more illustrious by his interposition to compose the Easter Controversy, then threatening to impair, if not to destroy, the unity of the Church. The beautiful *concordat* between East and West, in which Polycarp and Anicetus had left the question, was now disturbed by Victor, Bishop of Rome, whose turbulent spirit would not accept the compromise of his predecessor. Irenæus remonstrates with him in a catholic spirit, and overrules his impetuous temper. At the Council of Nice, the rule for the observance of Easter was finally settled by the whole Church; and the forbearing example of Irenæus, no doubt contributed greatly to this happy result. The blessed peacemaker survived this great triumph, for a short time only, closing his life, like a true shepherd, with thousands of his flock, in the massacre (A.D. 202) stimulated by the wolfish Emperor Severus.

The INTRODUCTORY NOTICE of the learned translators[4] is as follows:—

---

[1] 1 Cor. xi. 19.   [2] 2 Tim. ii. 24, 25, 26.

[3] On the authority of St. Jerome. See Guettee, *De l'église de France*, vol. 1. p. 27.

[4] The first two books of Irenæus *Against Heresies* have been translated by Dr. Roberts. The groundwork of the translation of the third book, and that portion of the fourth book which is continued in this volume, has been furnished by the Rev. W. H. Rambaut. An attempt has been made, in rendering this important author into English, to adhere as closely as possible to the original. It would have been far easier to give a loose and flowing translation of the obscure and involved sentences of Irenæus; but the object has been studiously kept in view, to place the English reader, as much as possible, in the position of one who has immediate access to the Greek or Latin text.

INTRODUCTORY NOTE.

The work of Irenæus *Against Heresies* is one of the most precious remains of early Christian antiquity. It is devoted, on the one hand, to an account and refutation of those multiform Gnostic heresies which prevailed in the latter half of the second century; and, on the other hand, to an exposition and defence of the Catholic faith.

In the prosecution of this plan, the author divides his work into five books. The first of these contains a minute description of the tenets of the various heretical sects, with occasional brief remarks in illustration of their absurdity, and in confirmation of the truth to which they were opposed. In his second book, Irenæus proceeds to a more complete demolition of those heresies which he has already explained, and argues at great length against them, on grounds principally of reason. The three remaining books set forth more directly the true doctrines of revelation, as being in utter antagonism to the views held by the Gnostic teachers. In the course of this argument, many passages of Scripture are quoted and commented on; many interesting statements are made, bearing on the rule of faith; and much important light is shed on the doctrines held, as well as the practices observed, by the Church of the second century.

It may be made matter of regret, that so large a portion of the work of Irenæus is given to an exposition of the manifold Gnostic speculations. Nothing more absurd than these has probably ever been imagined by rational beings. Some ingenious and learned men have indeed endeavoured to reconcile the wild theories of these heretics with the principles of reason; but, as Bishop Kaye remarks (*Eccl. Hist. of the Second and Third Centuries*, p. 524), "a more arduous or unpromising undertaking cannot well be conceived." The fundamental object of the Gnostic speculations was doubtless to solve the two grand problems of all religious philosophy, viz., How to account for the existence of evil; and, How to reconcile the finite with the infinite. But these ancient theorists were not more successful in grappling with such questions than have been their successors in modern times. And by giving loose reins to their imagination, they built up the most incongruous and ridiculous systems; while, by deserting the guidance of Scripture they were betrayed into the most pernicious and extravagant errors.

Accordingly, the patience of the reader is sorely tried, in following our author through those mazes of absurdity which he treads, in explaining and refuting these Gnostic speculations. This is especially felt in the perusal of the first two books, which, as has been said, are principally devoted to an exposition and subversion of the various heretical systems. But the vagaries of the human mind, however melancholy in themselves, are never altogether destitute of instruction. And in dealing with those set before us in this work, we have not only the satisfaction of becoming acquainted with the currents of thought prevalent in these early times, but we obtain much valuable information regarding the primitive Church, which, had it not been for these heretical schemes, might never have reached our day.

Not a little of what is contained in the following pages will seem almost unintelligible to the English reader. And it is scarcely more comprehensible to those who have pondered long on the original. We have inserted brief notes of explanation where these seemed specially necessary. But we have not thought it worth while to devote a great deal of space to the elucidation of those obscure Gnostic views which, in so many varying forms, are set forth in this work. For the same reason, we give here no account of the origin, history, and successive phases of Gnosticism. Those who wish to know the views of the learned on these points, may consult the writings of Neander, Baur, and others, among the Germans, or the lectures of Dr. Burton in English; while a succinct description of the whole matter will be found in the "Preliminary Observations on the Gnostic System," prefixed to Harvey's edition of Irenæus.

The great work of Irenæus, now for the first time translated into English, is unfortunately no longer extant in the original. It has come down to us only in an ancient Latin version, with the exception of the greater part of the first book, which has been preserved in the original Greek, through means of copious quotations made by Hippolytus and Epiphanius. The text, both Latin and Greek, is often most uncertain. Only three MSS. of the work *Against Heresies* are at present known to exist. Others, however, were used in the earliest printed editions put forth by Erasmus. And as these codices were more ancient than any now available, it is greatly to be regretted that they have disappeared or perished. One of our difficulties throughout, has been to fix the readings we should adopt, especially in the first book. Varieties of reading, actual or conjectural, have been noted only when some point of special importance seemed to be involved.

After the text has been settled, according to the best judgment which can be formed, the work of translation remains; and that is, in this case, a matter of no small difficulty. Irenæus, even in the original Greek, is often a very obscure writer. At times he expresses himself with remarkable clearness and terseness; but, upon the whole, his style is very involved and prolix. And the Latin version adds to these difficulties of the original, by being itself of the most barbarous character. In fact, it is often necessary to make a conjectural re-translation of it into Greek, in order to obtain some inkling of what the author wrote. Dodwell supposes this Latin version to have been made about the end of the fourth century; but as Tertullian seems to have used it, we must rather place it in the beginning of the third. Its author is unknown, but he was certainly little qualified for his task. We have endeavoured to give as close and accurate a translation of the work as possible, but there are not a few passages in which a guess can only be made as to the probable meaning.

Irenæus had manifestly taken great pains to make himself acquainted with the various heretical systems which he describes. His mode of exposing and refuting these is generally very effective. It is plain that he possessed a good share of learning, and that he had a firm grasp of the doctrines of Scripture. Not unfrequently he indulges in a kind of sarcastic humour, while inveighing against the folly and impiety of the heretics. But at times he gives expression to very strange opinions. He is, for example, quite peculiar in imagining that our Lord lived to be an *old* man, and that His public ministry embraced at least *ten* years. But though, on these and some other points, the judgment of Irenæus is clearly at fault, his work contains a vast deal of sound and valuable exposition of Scripture, in opposition to the fanciful systems of interpretation which prevailed in his day.

We possess only very scanty accounts of the personal history of Irenæus. It has been generally supposed that he was a native of Smyrna, or some neighbouring city, in Asia Minor. Harvey, however, thinks that he was probably born in Syria, and removed in boyhood to Smyrna. He himself tells us (iii. 3, 4) that he was in early youth acquainted with Polycarp, the illustrious bishop of that city. A sort of clue is thus furnished as to the date of his birth. Dodwell supposes that he was born so early as A.D. 97, but this is clearly a mistake; and the general date assigned to his birth is somewhere between A.D. 120 and A.D. 140.

It is certain that Irenæus was bishop of Lyons, in France, during the latter quarter of the second century. The exact period or circumstances of his ordination cannot be determined. Eusebius states (*Hist. Eccl.*, v. 4) that he was, while yet a presbyter, sent with a letter, from certain members of the Church of Lyons awaiting martyrdom, to Eleutherus, bishop of Rome; and that (v. 5) he succeeded Pothinus as bishop of Lyons, probably about A.D. 177. His great work *Against Heresies* was, we learn, written during the episcopate of Eleutherus, that is, between A.D. 182 and A.D. 188, for Victor succeeded to the bishopric of Rome in A.D. 189. This new bishop of Rome took very harsh measures for enforcing uniformity throughout the Church as to the observance of the paschal solemnities. On account of the severity thus evinced, Irenæus addressed to him a letter (only a fragment of which remains), warning him that if he persisted in the course on which he had entered, the effect would be to rend the Catholic Church in pieces. This letter had the desired result; and the question was more temperately debated, until finally settled by the Council of Nice.

The full title of the principal work of Irenæus, as given by Eusebius (*Hist. Eccl.*, v. 7), and

INTRODUCTORY NOTE.

indicated frequently by the author himself, was *A Refutation and Subversion of Knowledge falsely so called*, but it is generally referred to under the shorter title, *Against Heresies*. Several other smaller treatises are ascribed to Irenæus; viz., *An Epistle to Florinus*, of which a small fragment has been preserved by Eusebius; a treatise *On the Valentinian Ogdoad;* a work called forth by the paschal controversy, entitled *On Schism*, and another *On Science;* all of which that remain will be found in our next volume of his writings. Irenæus is supposed to have died about A.D. 202; but there is probably no real ground for the statement of Jerome, repeated by subsequent writers, that he suffered martyrdom, since neither Tertullian nor Eusebius, nor other early authorities, make any mention of such a fact.

As has been already stated, the first printed copy of our author was given to the world by Erasmus. This was in the year 1526. Between that date and 1571, a number of reprints were produced in both folio and octavo. All these contained merely the ancient barbarous Latin version, and were deficient towards the end by five entire chapters. These latter were supplied by the edition of Feuardent, Professor of Divinity at Paris, which was published in 1575, and went through six subsequent editions. Previously to this, however, another had been set forth by Gallasius, a minister of Geneva, which contained the first portions of the Greek text from Epiphanius. Then, in 1702, came the edition of Grabe, a learned Prussian, who had settled in England. It was published at Oxford, and contained considerable additions to the Greek text, with fragments. Ten years after this there appeared the important Paris edition by the Benedictine monk Massuet. This was reprinted at Venice in the year 1724, in two thin folio volumes, and again at Paris in a large octavo, by the Abbé Migne, in 1857. A German edition was published by Stieren in 1853.

In the year 1857 there was also brought out a Cambridge edition, by the Rev. Wigan Harvey, in two octavo volumes. The two principal features of this edition are: the additions which have been made to the Greek text from the recently discovered *Philosophoumena* of Hippolytus; and the further addition of thirty-two fragments of a Syriac version of the Greek text of Irenæus, culled from the Nitrian collection of Syriac MSS. in the British Museum. These fragments are of considerable interest, and in some instances rectify the readings of the barbarous Latin version, where, without such aid, it would have been unintelligible. The edition of Harvey will be found constantly referred to in the notes appended to our translation.

IRENÆUS AGAINST HERESIES

BOOK I

PREFACE.

1. INASMUCH[1] as certain men have set the truth aside, and bring in lying words and vain genealogies, which, as the apostle says,[2] "minister questions rather than godly edifying which is in faith," and by means of their craftily-constructed plausibilities draw away the minds of the inexperienced and take them captive, [I have felt constrained, my dear friend, to compose the following treatise in order to expose and counteract their machinations.] These men falsify the oracles of God, and prove themselves evil interpreters of the good word of revelation. They also overthrow the faith of many, by drawing them away, under a pretence of [superior] knowledge, from Him who founded and adorned the universe; as if, forsooth, they had something more excellent and sublime to reveal, than that God who created the heaven and the earth, and all things that are therein. By means of specious and plausible words, they cunningly allure the simple-minded to inquire into their system; but they nevertheless clumsily destroy them, while they initiate them into their blasphemous and impious opinions respecting the Demiurge;[3] and these simple ones are unable, even in such a matter, to distinguish falsehood from truth.

2. Error, indeed, is never set forth in its naked deformity, lest, being thus exposed, it should at once be detected. But it is craftily decked out in an attractive dress, so as, by its outward form, to make it appear to the inexperienced (ridiculous as the expression may seem) more true than the truth itself. One[4] far superior to me has well said, in reference to this point, "A clever imitation in glass casts contempt, as it were, on that precious jewel the emerald (which is most highly esteemed by some), unless it come under the eye of one able to test and expose the counterfeit. Or, again, what inexperienced person can with ease detect the presence of brass when it has been mixed up with silver?" Lest, therefore, through my neglect, some should be carried off, even as sheep are by wolves, while they perceive not the true character of these men,—because they outwardly are covered with sheep's clothing (against whom the Lord has enjoined[5] us to be on our guard), and because their language resembles ours, while their sentiments are very different,—I have deemed it my duty (after reading some of the *Commentaries*, as they call them, of the disciples of Valentinus, and after making myself acquainted with their tenets through personal intercourse with some of them) to unfold to thee, my friend, these portentous and profound mysteries, which do not fall within the range of every intellect, because all have not sufficiently purged[6] their brains. I do this, in order that thou, obtaining an acquaintance with these things, mayest in turn explain them to all those with whom thou art connected, and exhort them to avoid such an abyss of madness and of blasphemy against Christ. I intend, then, to the best of my ability, with brevity and clearness to set forth the opinions of those who are now

---

[1] The Greek original of the work of Irenæus is from time to time recovered through the numerous quotations made from it by subsequent writers, especially by the author's pupil Hippolytus, and by Epiphanius. The latter preserves (*Hær.*, xxxi. secs. 9-32) the preface of Irenæus, and most of the first book. An important difference of reading occurs between the Latin and Greek in the very first word. The translator manifestly read ἐπεί, *quatenus*, while in Epiphanius we find ἐπί, *against*. The former is probably correct, and has been followed in our version. We have also supplied a clause, in order to avoid the extreme length of the sentence in the original, which runs on without any apodosis to the words ἀναγκαῖον ἡγησάμην, "I have judged it necessary."
[2] 1 Tim. i. 4. The Latin has here *genealogias infinitas*, "endless genealogies," as in *textus receptus* of New Testament.
[3] As will be seen by and by, this fancied being was, in the Valentinian system, the creator of the material universe, but far inferior to the supreme ruler Bythus.
[4] There are frequent references in Irenæus to some venerable men who had preceded him in the Church. It is supposed that Pothinus, whom he succeeded at Lyons, is generally meant; but the reference may sometimes be to Polycarp, with whom in early life he had been acquainted.
[5] Comp. Matt. vii. 15.
[6] The original is ἐγκέφαλον ἐξεπτύκασιν, which the Latin translator renders simply, "have not sufficient brains." He probably followed a somewhat different reading. Various emendations have been proposed, but the author may be understood by the ordinary text to be referring ironically to the boasted subtlety and sublimity of the Gnostics.

promulgating heresy. I refer especially to the disciples of Ptolemæus, whose school may be described as a bud from that of Valentinus. I shall also endeavour, according to my moderate ability, to furnish the means of overthrowing them, by showing how absurd and inconsistent with the truth are their statements. Not that I am practised either in composition or eloquence; but my feeling of affection prompts me to make known to thee and all thy companions those doctrines which have been kept in concealment until now, but which are at last, through the goodness of God, brought to light. "For there is nothing hidden which shall not be revealed, nor secret that shall not be made known."[1]

3. Thou wilt not expect from me, who am resident among the Keltæ,[2] and am accustomed for the most part to use a barbarous dialect, any display of rhetoric, which I have never learned, or any excellence of composition, which I have never practised, or any beauty and persuasiveness of style, to which I make no pretensions. But thou wilt accept in a kindly spirit what I in a like spirit write to thee simply, truthfully, and in my own homely way; whilst thou thyself (as being more capable than I am) wilt expand those ideas of which I send thee, as it were, only the seminal principles; and in the comprehensiveness of thy understanding, wilt develop to their full extent the points on which I briefly touch, so as to set with power before thy companions those things which I have uttered in weakness. In fine, as I (to gratify thy long-cherished desire for information regarding the tenets of these persons) have spared no pains, not only to make these doctrines known to thee, but also to furnish the means of showing their falsity; so shalt thou, according to the grace given to thee by the Lord, prove an earnest and efficient minister to others, that men may no longer be drawn away by the plausible system of these heretics, which I now proceed to describe.[3]

CHAP. I. — ABSURD IDEAS OF THE DISCIPLES OF VALENTINUS AS TO THE ORIGIN, NAME, ORDER, AND CONJUGAL PRODUCTIONS OF THEIR FANCIED ÆONS, WITH THE PASSAGES OF SCRIPTURE WHICH THEY ADAPT TO THEIR OPINIONS.

1. THEY maintain, then, that in the invisible and ineffable heights above there exists a certain perfect, pre-existent Æon,[4] whom they call Proarche, Propator, and Bythus, and describe as being invisible and incomprehensible. Eternal and unbegotten, he remained throughout innumerable cycles of ages in profound serenity and quiescence. There existed along with him Ennœa, whom they also call Charis and Sige.[5] At last this Bythus determined to send forth from himself the beginning of all things, and deposited this production (which he had resolved to bring forth) in his contemporary Sige, even as seed is deposited in the womb. She then, having received this seed, and becoming pregnant, gave birth to Nous, who was both similar and equal to him who had produced him, and was alone capable of comprehending his father's greatness. This Nous they call also Monogenes, and Father, and the Beginning of all Things. Along with him was also produced Aletheia; and these four constituted the first and first-begotten Pythagorean Tetrad, which they also denominate the root of all things. For there are first Bythus and Sige, and then Nous and Aletheia. And Monogenes, perceiving for what purpose he had been produced, also himself sent forth Logos and Zoe, being the father of all those who were to come after him, and the beginning and fashioning of the entire Pleroma. By the conjunction of Logos and Zoe were brought forth Anthropos and Ecclesia; and thus was formed the first-begotten Ogdoad, the root and substance of all things, called among them by four names, viz., Bythus, and Nous, and Logos, and Anthropos. For each of these is masculo-feminine, as follows: Propator was united by a conjunction with his Ennœa; then Monogenes, that is Nous, with Aletheia; Logos with Zoe, and Anthropos with Ecclesia.

2. These Æons having been produced for the glory of the Father, and wishing, by their own efforts, to effect this object, sent forth emanations by means of conjunction. Logos and Zoe, after producing Anthropos and Ecclesia, sent forth other ten Æons, whose names are the following: Bythius and Mixis, Ageratos and Henosis, Autophyes and Hedone, Acinetos and Syncrasis, Monogenes and Macaria.[6] These are

---

[1] Matt. x. 26.
[2] As Cæsar informs us (*Comm.*, i. 1), Gaul was divided into three parts, one of which was called Celtic Gaul, lying between the Seine and the Garonne. Of this division Lyons is the principal city.
[3] [The reader will find a logical and easy introduction to the crabbed details which follow, by turning to chap. xxiii., and reading through succeeding chapters down to chap. xxix.]
[4] This term Æon (Αἰών) seems to have been formed from the words ἀεὶ ὤν, *ever-existing*. "We may take αἰών, therefore," says Harvey (*Irenæus*, cxix.), "in the Valentinian acceptation of the word, to mean an emanation from the divine substance, subsisting co-ordinately and co-eternally with the Deity, the Pleroma still remaining one."
[5] Sige, however, was no true consort of Bythus, who included in himself the idea of male and female, and was the one cause of all things: comp. Hippolytus, *Philosop.*, vi. 29. There seems to have been considerable disagreement among these heretics as to the completion of the mystical number thirty. Valentinus himself appears to have considered Bythus as a monad, and Sige as a mere nonentity. The two latest Æons, Christ and the Holy Spirit, would then complete the number thirty. But other Gnostic teachers included both Bythus and Sige in that mystical number.
[6] It may be well to give here the English equivalents of the names of these Æons and their authors. They are as follows: Bythus, *Profundity;* Proarche, *First-Beginning;* Propator, *First-Father;* Ennœa, *Idea;* Charis, *Grace;* Sige, *Silence;* Nous, *Intelligence;* Aletheia, *Truth;* Logos, *Word;* Zoe, *Life;* Anthropos, *Man;* Ecclesia, *Church;* Bythius, *Deep;* Mixis, *Mingling;* Ageratos, *Undecaying;* Henosis, *Union;* Autophyes, *Self-existent;* Hedone, *Pleasure;* Acinetos, *Immoveable;* Syncrasis, *Blending;* Monogenes, *Only-Begotten;* Macaria, *Happiness;* Paracletus, *Advocate;* Pistis, *Faith;* Patricos, *Ancestral;* Elpis, *Hope;* Metricos, *Metrical;* Agape, *Love;* Ainos, *Praise;* Synesis, *Understanding;* Ecclesiasticus, *Ecclesiastical;* Macariotes, *Felicity;* Theletos, *Desiderated;* Sophia, *Wisdom.*

the ten Æons whom they declare to have been produced by Logos and Zoe. They then add that Anthropos himself, along with Ecclesia, produced twelve Æons, to whom they give the following names: Paracletus and Pistis, Patricos and Elpis, Metricos and Agape, Ainos and Synesis, Ecclesiasticus and Macariotes, Theletos and Sophia.

3. Such are the thirty Æons in the erroneous system of these men; and they are described as being wrapped up, so to speak, in silence, and known to none [except these professing teachers]. Moreover, they declare that this invisible and spiritual Pleroma of theirs is tripartite, being divided into an Ogdoad, a Decad, and a Duodecad. And for this reason they affirm it was that the "Saviour"—for they do not please to call Him "Lord"—did no work in public during the space of thirty years,[1] thus setting forth the mystery of these Æons. They maintain also, that these thirty Æons are most plainly indicated in the parable[2] of the labourers sent into the vineyard. For some are sent about the first hour, others about the third hour, others about the sixth hour, others about the ninth hour, and others about the eleventh hour. Now, if we add up the numbers of the hours here mentioned, the sum total will be thirty: for one, three, six, nine, and eleven, when added together, form thirty. And by the hours, they hold that the Æons were pointed out; while they maintain that these are great, and wonderful, and hitherto unspeakable mysteries which it is their special function to develop; and so they proceed when they find anything in the multitude[3] of things contained in the Scriptures which they can adopt and accommodate to their baseless speculations.

CHAP. II. — THE PROPATOR WAS KNOWN TO MONOGENES ALONE. AMBITION, DISTURBANCE, AND DANGER INTO WHICH SOPHIA FELL; HER SHAPELESS OFFSPRING: SHE IS RESTORED BY HOROS. THE PRODUCTION OF CHRIST AND OF THE HOLY SPIRIT, IN ORDER TO THE COMPLETION OF THE ÆONS. MANNER OF THE PRODUCTION OF JESUS.

1. They proceed to tell us that the Propator of their scheme was known only to Monogenes, who sprang from him; in other words, only to Nous, while to all the others he was invisible and incomprehensible. And, according to them, Nous alone took pleasure in contemplating the Father, and exulting in considering his immeasurable greatness; while he also meditated how he might communicate to the rest of the Æons the greatness of the Father, revealing to them how vast and mighty he was, and how he was without beginning, — beyond comprehension, and altogether incapable of being seen. But, in accordance with the will of the Father, Sige restrained him, because it was his design to lead them all to an acquaintance with the aforesaid Propator, and to create within them a desire of investigating his nature. In like manner, the rest of the Æons also, in a kind of quiet way, had a wish to behold the Author of their being, and to contemplate that First Cause which had no beginning.

2. But there rushed forth in advance of the rest that Æon who was much the latest of them, and was the youngest of the Duodecad which sprang from Anthropos and Ecclesia, namely Sophia, and suffered passion apart from the embrace of her consort Theletos. This passion, indeed, first arose among those who were connected with Nous and Aletheia, but passed as by contagion to this degenerate Æon, who acted under a pretence of love, but was in reality influenced by temerity, because she had not, like Nous, enjoyed communion with the perfect Father. This passion, they say, consisted in a desire to search into the nature of the Father; for she wished, according to them, to comprehend his greatness. When she could not attain her end, inasmuch as she aimed at an impossibility, and thus became involved in an extreme agony of mind, while both on account of the vast profundity as well as the unsearchable nature of the Father, and on account of the love she bore him, she was ever stretching herself forward, there was danger lest she should at last have been absorbed by his sweetness, and resolved into his absolute essence, unless she had met with that Power which supports all things, and preserves them outside of the unspeakable greatness. This power they term Horos; by whom, they say, she was restrained and supported; and that then, having with difficulty been brought back to herself, she was convinced that the Father is incomprehensible, and so laid aside her original design, along with that passion which had arisen within her from the overwhelming influence of her admiration.

3. But others of them fabulously describe the passion and restoration of Sophia as follows: They say that she, having engaged in an impossible and impracticable attempt, brought forth an amorphous substance, such as her female nature enabled her to produce.[4] When she looked upon it, her first feeling was one of grief, on account of the imperfection of its generation, and then of fear lest this should end[5] her own existence. Next she lost, as it were, all com-

---

[1] Luke iii. 23.
[2] Matt. xx. 1-16.
[3] Some omit ἐν πλήθει, while others render the words "a definite number," thus: "And if there is anything else in Scripture which is referred to by a definite number."
[4] Alluding to the Gnostic notion that, in generation, the male gives form, the female substance. Sophia, therefore, being a female Æon, gave to her enthymesis substance alone, without form. Comp. Hippol., *Philosop.*, vi. 30.
[5] Some render this obscure clause, "lest it should never attain perfection," but the above seems preferable. See Hippol., vi. 31, where the fear referred to is extended to the whole Pleroma.

mand of herself, and was in the greatest perplexity while endeavouring to discover the cause of all this, and in what way she might conceal what had happened. Being greatly harassed by these passions, she at last changed her mind, and endeavoured to return anew to the Father. When, however, she in some measure made the attempt, strength failed her, and she became a suppliant of the Father. The other Æons, Nous in particular, presented their supplications along with her. And hence they declare material substance[1] had its beginning from ignorance and grief, and fear and bewilderment.

4. The Father afterwards produces, in his own image, by means of Monogenes, the above-mentioned Horos, without conjunction,[2] masculo-feminine. For they maintain that sometimes the Father acts in conjunction with Sige, but that at other times he shows himself independent both of male and female. They term this Horos both Stauros and Lytrotes, and Carpistes, and Horothetes, and Metagoges.[3] And by this Horos they declare that Sophia was purified and established, while she was also restored to her proper conjunction. For her enthymesis (or inborn idea) having been taken away from her, along with its supervening passion, she herself certainly remained within the Pleroma; but her enthymesis, with its passion, was separated from her by Horos, fenced[4] off, and expelled from that circle. This enthymesis was, no doubt, a spiritual substance, possessing some of the natural tendencies of an Æon, but at the same time shapeless and without form, because it had received nothing.[5] And on this account they say that it was an imbecile and feminine production.[6]

5. After this substance had been placed outside of the Pleroma of the Æons, and its mother restored to her proper conjunction, they tell us that Monogenes, acting in accordance with the prudent forethought of the Father, gave origin to another conjugal pair, namely Christ and the Holy Spirit (lest any of the Æons should fall into a calamity similar to that of Sophia), for the purpose of fortifying and strengthening the Pleroma, and who at the same time completed the number of the Æons. Christ then instructed them as to the nature of their conjunction, and taught them that those who possessed a comprehension of the Unbegotten were sufficient for themselves.[7] He also announced among them what related to the knowledge of the Father,— namely, that he cannot be understood or comprehended, nor so much as seen or heard, except in so far as he is known by Monogenes only. And the reason why the rest of the Æons possess perpetual existence is found in that part of the Father's nature which is incomprehensible; but the reason of their origin and formation was situated in that which may be comprehended regarding him, that is, in the Son.[8] Christ, then, who had just been produced, effected these things among them.

6. But the Holy Spirit[9] taught them to give thanks on being all rendered equal among themselves, and led them to a state of true repose. Thus, then, they tell us that the Æons were constituted equal to each other in form and sentiment, so that all became as Nous, and Logos, and Anthropos, and Christus. The female Æons, too, became all as Aletheia, and Zoe, and Spiritus, and Ecclesia. Everything, then, being thus established, and brought into a state of perfect rest, they next tell us that these beings sang praises with great joy to the Propator, who himself shared in the abounding exaltation. Then, out of gratitude for the great benefit which had been conferred on them, the whole Pleroma of the Æons, with one design and desire, and with the concurrence of Christ and the Holy Spirit, their Father also setting the seal of His approval on their conduct, brought together whatever each one had in himself of the greatest beauty and preciousness; and uniting all these contributions so as skilfully to blend the whole, they produced, to the honour and glory of Bythus, a being of most perfect beauty, the very star of the Pleroma, and the perfect fruit [of it], namely Jesus. Him they also speak of under the name of Saviour, and Christ, and patronymically, Logos, and Everything, because He was formed from the contributions of all. And then we are told that, by way of honour, angels of the same nature as Himself were simultaneously produced, to act as His body-guard.

---

[1] "The reader will observe the parallel; as the enthymesis of Bythus produced intelligent substance, so the enthymesis of Sophia resulted in the formation of material substance."— HARVEY.

[2] Some propose reading these words in the dative rather than the accusative, and thus to make them refer to the *image of the Father*.

[3] The meaning of these terms is as follows: Stauros means primarily *a stake*, and then *a cross;* Lytrotes is *a Redeemer;* Carpistes, according to Grabe, means *an Emancipator*, according to Neander *a Reaper;* Horothetes is *one that fixes boundaries;* and Metagoges is explained by Neander as being *one that brings back*, from the supposed function of Horos, to bring back all that sought to wander from the special grade of being assigned them.

[4] The common text has ἀποστερηθῆναι, *was deprived;* but Billius proposes to read ἀποσταυρωθῆναι, in conformity with the ancient Latin version, "crucifixam."

[5] That is, had not shared in any male influence, but was a purely female production.

[6] Literally, "fruit." Harvey remarks on this expression, "that what we understand by *emanations*, the Gnostic described as spiritual *fructification;* and as the seed of a tree is in itself, even in the embryo state, so these various Æons, as existing always in the divine nature, were co-eternal with it."

[7] This is an exceedingly obscure and difficult passage. Harvey's rendering is: "For, say they, Christ taught them the nature of their copulæ, (namely,) that being cognisant of their (limited) perception of the Unbegotten they needed no higher knowledge, and that He enounced," etc. The words seem scarcely capable of yielding this sense: we have followed the interpretation of Billius.

[8] Both the text and meaning are here very doubtful. Some think that the import of the sentence is, that the knowledge that the Father is incomprehensible secured the continued safety of the Æons, while the same knowledge conferred upon Monogenes his origin and form.

[9] The Greek text inserts ἕν, *one*, before "Holy Spirit."

CHAP. III.—TEXTS OF HOLY SCRIPTURE USED BY THESE HERETICS TO SUPPORT THEIR OPINIONS.

1. Such, then, is the account they give of what took place within the Pleroma; such the calamities that flowed from the passion which seized upon the Æon who has been named, and who was within a little of perishing by being absorbed in the universal substance, through her inquisitive searching after the Father; such the consolidation[1] [of that Æon] from her condition of agony by Horos, and Stauros, and Lytrotes, and Carpistes, and Horothetes, and Metagoges.[2] Such also is the account of the generation of the later Æons, namely of the first Christ and of the Holy Spirit, both of whom were produced by the Father after the repentance[3] [of Sophia], and of the second[4] Christ (whom they also style Saviour), who owed his being to the joint contributions [of the Æons]. They tell us, however, that this knowledge has not been openly divulged, because all are not capable of receiving it, but has been mystically revealed by the Saviour through means of parables to those qualified for understanding it. This has been done as follows. The thirty Æons are indicated (as we have already remarked) by the thirty years during which they say the Saviour performed no public act, and by the parable of the labourers in the vineyard. Paul also, they affirm, very clearly and frequently names these Æons, and even goes so far as to preserve their order, when he says, "To all the generations of the Æons of the Æon."[5] Nay, we ourselves, when at the giving[6] of thanks we pronounce the words, "To Æons of Æons" (for ever and ever), do set forth these Æons. And, in fine, wherever the words *Æon* or *Æons* occur, they at once refer them to these beings.

2. The production, again, of the Duodecad of the Æons, is indicated by the fact that the Lord was *twelve*[7] years of age when He disputed with the teachers of the law, and by the election of the apostles, for of these there were twelve.[8] The other eighteen Æons are made manifest in this way: that the Lord, [according to them,] conversed with His disciples for eighteen months[9] after His resurrection from the dead. They also affirm that these eighteen Æons are strikingly indicated by the first two letters of His name ['Ιησοῦς], namely *Iota*[10] and *Eta*. And, in like manner, they assert that the ten Æons are pointed out by the letter *Iota*, which begins His name; while, for the same reason, they tell us the Saviour said, "One *Iota*, or one tittle, shall by no means pass away until all be fulfilled."[11]

3. They further maintain that the passion which took place in the case of the twelfth Æon is pointed at by the apostasy of Judas, who was the twelfth apostle, and also by the fact that Christ suffered in the twelfth month. For their opinion is, that He continued to preach for one year only after His baptism. The same thing is also most clearly indicated by the case of the woman who suffered from an issue of blood. For after she had been thus afflicted during twelve years, she was healed by the advent of the Saviour, when she had touched the border of His garment; and on this account the Saviour said, "Who touched me?"[12]—teaching his disciples the mystery which had occurred among the Æons, and the healing of that Æon who had been involved in suffering. For she who had been afflicted twelve years represented that power whose essence, as they narrate, was stretching itself forth, and flowing into immensity; and unless she had touched the garment of the Son,[13] that is, Aletheia of the first Tetrad, who is denoted by the hem spoken of, she would have been dissolved into the general essence[14] [of which she participated]. She stopped short, however, and ceased any longer to suffer. For the power that went forth from the Son (and this power they term Horos) healed her, and separated the passion from her.

4. They moreover affirm that the Saviour[15] is shown to be derived from all the Æons, and to be in Himself *everything* by the following passage: "Every male that openeth the womb."[16] For He, being everything, opened the womb[17] of the enthymesis of the suffering Æon, when

---

[1] The reading is here very doubtful. We have followed the text of Grabe (approved by Harvey), ἐξ ἀγῶνος σύμπηξις.
[2] These are all names of the same person: see above, ii. 4. Hence some have proposed the reading ἐξαιώνιος instead of ἐξ ἀγῶνος, alluding to the *sixfold* appellation of the Æon Horos.
[3] Billius renders, "from the repentance of the Father," but the above seems preferable.
[4] Harvey remarks, "Even in their Christology the Valentinians must have their part and counterpart."
[5] Or, "to all the generations of the ages of the age." See Eph. iii. 21. The apostle, of course, simply uses these words as a strong expression to denote "for ever."
[6] Literally, "at the thanksgiving," or "eucharist." Massuet, the Benedictine editor, refers this to the Lord's Supper, and hence concludes that some of the ancient liturgies still extant must even then have been in use. Harvey and others, however, deny that there is any necessity for supposing the Holy Eucharist to be referred to; the ancient Latin version translates in the plural, "in gratiarum actionibus."
[7] Luke ii. 42.
[8] Luke vi. 13.
[9] This opinion is in positive contradiction to the *forty days* mentioned by St. Luke (Acts i. 3). But the Valentinians seem to have followed a spurious writing of their own called "The Gospel of Truth." See iii. 11, 8.
[10] The numeral value of *Iota* in Greek is ten, and of *Eta*, eight.
[11] Matt. v. 18.
[12] Mark v. 31.
[13] The Latin reads "filii," which we have followed. Reference is made in this word to Nous, who was, as we have already seen, also called *Son*, and who interested himself in the recovery of Sophia. Aletheia was his consort, and was typified by the hem of the Saviour's garment.
[14] Her individuality (μορφή) would have been lost, while her substance (οὐσία) would have survived in the common essence of the Æons.
[15] That is, the "second Christ" referred to above, sec. 1. [It is much to be wished that this *second* were always distinguished by the untranslated name *Soter*.]
[16] Ex. xiii. 2; Luke ii. 23.
[17] Not as being born of it, but as fecundating it, and so producing a manifold offspring. See below.

it had been expelled from the Pleroma. This they also style the second Ogdoad, of which we shall speak presently. And they state that it was clearly on this account that Paul said, "And He Himself is all things;"[1] and again, "All things are to Him, and of Him are all things;"[2] and further, "In Him dwelleth all the fulness of the Godhead;"[3] and yet again, "All things are gathered together by God in Christ."[4] Thus do they interpret these and any like passages to be found in Scripture.

5. They show, further, that that Horos of theirs, whom they call by a variety of names, has two faculties, — the one of supporting, and the other of separating; and in so far as he supports and sustains, he is Stauros, while in so far as he divides and separates, he is Horos. They then represent the Saviour as having indicated this twofold faculty: first, the sustaining power, when He said, "Whosoever doth not bear his cross (Stauros), and follow after me, cannot be my disciple;"[5] and again, "Taking up the cross, follow me;"[6] but the separating power when He said, "I came not to send peace, but a sword."[7] They also maintain that John indicated the same thing when he said, "The fan is in His hand, and He will thoroughly purge the floor, and will gather the wheat into His garner; but the chaff He will burn with fire unquenchable."[8] By this declaration He set forth the faculty of Horos. For that fan they explain to be the cross (Stauros), which consumes, no doubt, all material[9] objects, as fire does chaff, but it purifies all them that are saved, as a fan does wheat. Moreover, they affirm that the Apostle Paul himself made mention of this cross in the following words: "The doctrine of the cross is to them that perish foolishness, but to us who are saved it is the power of God."[10] And again: "God forbid that I should glory in anything[11] save in the cross of Christ, by whom the world is crucified to me, and I unto the world."

6. Such, then, is the account which they all give of their Pleroma, and of the formation[12] of the universe, striving, as they do, to adapt the good words of revelation to their own wicked inventions. And it is not only from the writings of the evangelists and the apostles that they endeavour to derive proofs for their opinions by means of perverse interpretations and deceitful expositions: they deal in the same way with the law and the prophets, which contain many parables and allegories that can frequently be drawn into various senses, according to the kind of exegesis to which they are subjected. And others[13] of them, with great craftiness, adapted such parts of Scripture to their own figments, lead away captive from the truth those who do not retain a stedfast faith in one God, the Father Almighty, and in one Lord Jesus Christ, the Son of God.

CHAP. IV. — ACCOUNT GIVEN BY THE HERETICS OF THE FORMATION OF ACHAMOTH; ORIGIN OF THE VISIBLE WORLD FROM HER DISTURBANCES.

1. The following are the transactions which they narrate as having occurred outside of the Pleroma: The enthymesis of that Sophia who dwells above, which they also term Achamoth,[14] being removed from the Pleroma, together with her passion, they relate to have, as a matter of course, become violently excited in those places of darkness and vacuity [to which she had been banished]. For she was excluded from light[15] and the Pleroma, and was without form or figure, like an untimely birth, because she had received nothing[16] [from a male parent]. But the Christ dwelling on high took pity upon her; and having extended himself through and beyond Stauros,[17] he imparted a figure to her, but merely as respected substance, and not so as to convey intelligence.[18] Having effected this, he withdrew his influence, and returned, leaving Achamoth to herself, in order that she, becoming sensible of her suffering as being severed from the Pleroma, might be influenced by the desire of better things, while she possessed in the meantime a kind of odour of immortality left in her by Christ and the Holy Spirit. Wherefore also she is called by two names — Sophia after her father (for Sophia is spoken of as being her father), and Holy Spirit from that Spirit who is along with Christ. Having then obtained a form, along with intelligence, and being immediately deserted by that Logos who had been invisibly present with her — that is, by Christ — she strained herself to discover that light which had forsaken her, but could not

---

[1] Col. iii. 11.
[2] Rom. xi. 36.
[3] Col. ii. 9.
[4] Eph. i. 10.
[5] Luke xiv. 27. It will be observed that the quotations of Scripture made by Irenæus often vary somewhat from the received text. This may be due to various reasons — his quoting from memory; his giving the texts in the form in which they were quoted by the heretics; or, as Harvey conjectures, from his having been more familiar with a Syriac version of the New Testament than with the Greek original.
[6] Matt. x. 21.
[7] Matt. x. 34.
[8] Luke iii. 17.
[9] Hence Stauros was called by the agricultural name Carpistes, as separating what was gross and material from the spiritual and heavenly.
[10] 1 Cor. i. 18.
[11] Gal. vi. 14. The words ἐν μηδενί do not occur in the Greek text.
[12] Billius renders, "of their opinion."

[13] The punctuation and rendering are here slightly doubtful.
[14] This term, though Tertullian declares himself to have been ignorant of its derivation, was evidently formed from the Hebrew word חָכְמָה — chockmah, *wisdom*.
[15] The reader will observe that *light* and *fulness* are the exact correlatives of the *darkness* and *vacuity* which have just been mentioned.
[16] As above stated (ii. 3), the Gnostics held that form and figure were due to the male, substance to the female parent.
[17] The Valentinian Stauros was the boundary fence of the Pleroma beyond which Christ extended himself to assist the enthymesis of Sophia.
[18] The peculiar *gnosis* which Nous received from his father, and communicated to the other Æons.

effect her purpose, inasmuch as she was prevented by Horos. And as Horos thus obstructed her further progress, he exclaimed, IAO,[1] whence, they say, this name *Iao* derived its origin. And when she could not pass by Horos on account of that passion in which she had been involved, and because she alone had been left without, she then resigned herself to every sort of that manifold and varied state of passion to which she was subject; and thus she suffered grief on the one hand because she had not obtained the object of her desire, and fear on the other hand, lest life itself should fail her, as light had already done, while, in addition, she was in the greatest perplexity. All these feelings were associated with ignorance. And this ignorance of hers was not, like that of her mother, the first Sophia, an Æon, due to degeneracy by means of passion, but to an [innate] opposition [of nature to knowledge].[2] Moreover, another kind of passion fell upon her (Achamoth), namely, that of desiring to return to him who gave her life.

2. This collection [of passions] they declare was the substance of the matter from which this world was formed. For from [her desire of] returning [to him who gave her life], every soul belonging to this world, and that of the Demiurge[3] himself, derived its origin. All other things owed their beginning to her terror and sorrow. For from her tears all that is of a liquid nature was formed; from her smile all that is lucent; and from her grief and perplexity all the corporeal elements of the world. For at one time, as they affirm, she would weep and lament on account of being left alone in the midst of darkness and vacuity; while, at another time, reflecting on the light which had forsaken her, she would be filled with joy, and laugh; then, again, she would be struck with terror; or, at other times, would sink into consternation and bewilderment.

3. Now what follows from all this? No light tragedy comes out of it, as the fancy of every man among them pompously explains, one in one way, and another in another, from what kind of passion and from what element being derived its origin. They have good reason, as seems to me, why they should not feel inclined to teach these things to all in public, but only to such as are able to pay a high price for an acquaintance with such profound mysteries. For these doctrines are not at all similar to those of which our Lord said, " Freely ye have received, freely give."[4] They are, on the contrary, abstruse, and portentous, and profound mysteries, to be got at only with great labour by such as are in love with falsehood. For who would not expend all that he possessed, if only he might learn in return, that from the tears of the enthymesis of the Æon involved in passion, seas, and fountains, and rivers, and every liquid substance derived its origin; that light burst forth from her smile; and that from her perplexity and consternation the corporeal elements of the world had their formation?

4. I feel somewhat inclined myself to contribute a few hints towards the development of their system. For when I perceive that waters are in part fresh, such as fountains, rivers, showers, and so on, and in part salt, such as those in the sea, I reflect with myself that all such waters cannot be derived from her tears, inasmuch as these are of a saline quality only. It is clear, therefore, that the waters which are salt are alone those which are derived from her tears. But it is probable that she, in her intense agony and perplexity, was covered with perspiration. And hence, following out their notion, we may conceive that fountains and rivers, and all the fresh water in the world, are due to this source. For it is difficult, since we know that all tears are of the same quality, to believe that waters both salt and fresh proceeded from them. The more plausible supposition is, that some are from her tears, and some from her perspiration. And since there are also in the world certain waters which are hot and acrid in their nature, thou must be left to guess their origin, how and whence. Such are some of the results of their hypothesis.

5. They go on to state that, when the mother Achamoth had passed through all sorts of passion, and had with difficulty escaped from them, she turned herself to supplicate the light which had forsaken her, that is, Christ. He, however, having returned to the Pleroma, and being probably unwilling again to descend from it, sent forth to her the Paraclete, that is, the Saviour.[5] This being was endowed with all power by the Father, who placed everything under his authority, the Æons[6] doing so likewise, so that " by him were all things, visible and invisible, created, thrones, divinities, dominions."[7] He then was sent to her along with his contemporary angels. And they related that Achamoth, filled with reverence, at first veiled herself through modesty, but that by and by, when she had looked upon him with all his endowments, and had acquired strength from his appearance, she ran forward to meet him. He then imparted to her form as respected intelligence, and brought healing to her passions, separating them from her, but not

---

[1] Probably corresponding to the Hebrew יהוה, *Jehovah.*
[2] This sentence is very elliptical in the original, but the sense is as given above. Sophia fell from *Gnosis* by degradation; Achamoth never possessed this knowledge, her nature being from the first opposed to it.
[3] " The Demiurge derived from Enthymesis an animal, and not a spiritual nature." — HARVEY.
[4] Matt. x. 8.
[5] " Jesus, or Soter, was also called the Paraclete in the sense of Advocate, or one acting as the representative of others." — HARVEY.
[6] Both the Father and the other Æons constituting Soter an impersonation of the entire Pleroma.
[7] Col. i. 16.

so as to drive them out of thought altogether. For it was not possible that they should be annihilated as in the former case,[1] because they had already taken root and acquired strength [so as to possess an indestructible existence]. All that he could do was to separate them and set them apart, and then commingle and condense them, so as to transmute them from incorporeal passion into unorganized matter.[2] He then by this process conferred upon them a fitness and a nature to become concretions and corporeal structures, in order that two substances should be formed, — the one evil, resulting from the passions, and the other subject indeed to suffering, but originating from her conversion. And on this account (i.e., on account of this hypostatizing of ideal matter) they say that the Saviour virtually[3] created the world. But when Achamoth was freed from her passion, she gazed with rapture on the dazzling vision of the angels that were with him; and in her ecstasy, conceiving by them, they tell us that she brought forth new beings, partly after her own image, and partly a spiritual progeny after the image of the Saviour's attendants.

CHAP. V. — FORMATION OF THE DEMIURGE; DESCRIPTION OF HIM. HE IS THE CREATOR OF EVERYTHING OUTSIDE OF THE PLEROMA.

1. These three kinds of existence, then, having, according to them, been now formed, — one from the passion, which was matter; a second from the conversion, which was animal; and the third, that which she (Achamoth) herself brought forth, which was spiritual, — she next addressed herself to the task of giving these form. But she could not succeed in doing this as respected the spiritual existence, because it was of the same nature with herself. She therefore applied herself to give form to the animal substance which had proceeded from her own conversion, and to bring forth to light the instructions of the Saviour.[4] And they say she first formed out of animal substance him who is Father and King of all things, both of these which are of the same nature with himself, that is, animal substances, which they also call right-handed, and those which sprang from the passion, and from matter, which they call left-handed. For they affirm that he formed all the things which came into existence after him, being secretly impelled thereto by his mother. From this circumstance they style him Metropator,[5] Apator, Demiurge, and Father, saying that he is Father of the substances on the right hand, that is, of the animal, but Demiurge of those on the left, that is, of the material, while he is at the same time the king of all. For they say that this Enthymesis, desirous of making all things to the honour of the Æons, formed images of them, or rather that the Saviour[6] did so through her instrumentality. And she, in the image[7] of the invisible Father, kept herself concealed from the Demiurge. But he was in the image of the only-begotten Son, and the angels and archangels created by him were in the image of the rest of the Æons.

2. They affirm, therefore, that he was constituted the Father and God of everything outside of the Pleroma, being the creator of all animal and material substances. For he it was that discriminated these two kinds of existence hitherto confused, and made corporeal from incorporeal substances, fashioned things heavenly and earthly, and became the Framer (Demiurge) of things material and animal, of those on the right and those on the left, of the light and of the heavy, and of those tending upwards as well as of those tending downwards. He created also seven heavens, above which they say that he, the Demiurge, exists. And on this account they term him Hebdomas, and his mother Achamoth Ogdoads, preserving the number of the first-begotten and primary Ogdoad as the Pleroma. They affirm, moreover, that these seven heavens are intelligent, and speak of them as being angels, while they refer to the Demiurge himself as being an angel bearing a likeness to God; and in the same strain, they declare that Paradise, situated above the third heaven, is a fourth angel possessed of power, from whom Adam derived certain qualities while he conversed with him.

3. They go on to say that the Demiurge imagined that he created all these things of himself, while he in reality made them in conjunction with the productive power of Achamoth. He formed the heavens, yet was ignorant of the heavens; he fashioned man, yet knew not man; he brought to light the earth, yet had no acquaintance with the earth; and, in like manner, they declare that he was ignorant of the forms of all that he made, and knew not even of the existence of his own mother, but imagined that he himself was all things. They further affirm

---

[1] That is, as in the case of her mother Sophia, who is sometimes called "the Sophia above," Achamoth being "the Sophia below," or "the second Sophia."
[2] Thus Harvey renders ἀσώματον ὕλην: so Baur, *Chr. Gnos.*, as quoted by Stieren. Billius proposes to read ἐνσώματον, *corporeal*.
[3] Though not actually, for that was the work of the Demiurge. See next chapter.
[4] "In order that," says Grabe, "this formation might not be merely *according to essence*, but also *according to knowledge*, as the formation of the mother Achamoth was characterized above."

[5] Metropator, as proceeding only from his mother Achamoth: Apator, as having no male progenitor.
[6] Harvey remarks, "The Valentinian Saviour being an aggregation of all the æonic perfections, the images of them were reproduced by the spiritual conception of Achamoth beholding the glory of Σωτήρ. The reader will not fail to observe that every successive development is the reflex of a more divine antecedent."
[7] The relation indicated seems to be as follows: Achamoth, after being formed "according to knowledge," was outside of the Pleroma as the image of Propator, the Demiurge was as Nous, and the mundane angels which he formed corresponded to the other Æons of the Pleroma.

that his mother originated this opinion in his mind, because she desired to bring him forth possessed of such a character that he should be the head and source of his own essence, and the absolute ruler over every kind of operation [that was afterwards attempted]. This mother they also call Ogdoad, Sophia, Terra, Jerusalem, Holy Spirit, and, with a masculine reference, Lord.[1] Her place of habitation is an intermediate one, above the Demiurge indeed, but below and outside of the Pleroma, even to the end.[2]

4. As, then, they represent all material substance to be formed from three passions, viz., fear, grief, and perplexity, the account they give is as follows: Animal substances originated from fear and from conversion; the Demiurge they also describe as owing his origin to conversion; but the existence of all the other animal substances they ascribe to fear, such as the souls of irrational animals, and of wild beasts, and men. And on this account, he (the Demiurge), being incapable of recognising any spiritual essences, imagined himself to be God alone, and declared through the prophets, "I am God, and besides me there is none else."[3] They further teach that the spirits of wickedness derived their origin from grief. Hence the devil, whom they also call Cosmocrator (the ruler of the world), and the demons, and the angels, and every wicked spiritual being that exists, found the source of their existence. They represent the Demiurge as being the son of that mother of theirs (Achamoth), and Cosmocrator as the creature of the Demiurge. Cosmocrator has knowledge of what is above himself, because he is a *spirit* of wickedness; but the Demiurge is ignorant of such things, inasmuch as he is merely *animal.* Their mother dwells in that place which is above the heavens, that is, in the intermediate abode; the Demiurge in the heavenly place, that is, in the hebdomad; but the Cosmocrator in this our world. The corporeal elements of the world, again, sprang, as we before remarked, from bewilderment and perplexity, as from a more ignoble source. Thus the earth arose from her state of stupor; water from the agitation caused by her fear; air from the consolidation of her grief; while fire, producing death and corruption, was inherent in all these elements, even as they teach that ignorance also lay concealed in these three passions.

5. Having thus formed the world, he (the Demiurge) also created the earthy [part of] man, not taking him from this dry earth, but from an invisible substance consisting of fusible and fluid matter, and then afterwards, as they define the process, breathed into him the animal part of his nature. It was this latter which was created after his image and likeness. The material part, indeed, was very near to God, so far as the image went, but not of the same substance with him. The animal, on the other hand, was so in respect to likeness; and hence his substance was called the spirit of life, because it took its rise from a spiritual outflowing. After all this, he was, they say, enveloped all round with a covering of skin; and by this they mean the outward sensitive flesh.

6. But they further affirm that the Demiurge himself was ignorant of that offspring of his mother Achamoth, which she brought forth as a consequence of her contemplation of those angels who waited on the Saviour, and which was, like herself, of a spiritual nature. She took advantage of this ignorance to deposit it (her production) in him without his knowledge, in order that, being by his instrumentality infused into that animal soul proceeding from himself, and being thus carried as in a womb in this material body, while it gradually increased in strength, might in course of time become fitted for the reception of perfect rationality.[4] Thus it came to pass, then, according to them, that, without any knowledge on the part of the Demiurge, the man formed by his inspiration was at the same time, through an unspeakable providence, rendered a spiritual man by the simultaneous inspiration received from Sophia. For, as he was ignorant of his mother, so neither did he recognise her offspring. This [offspring] they also declare to be the Ecclesia, an emblem of the Ecclesia which is above. This, then, is the kind of man whom they conceive of: he has his animal soul from the Demiurge, his body from the earth, his fleshy part from matter, and his spiritual man from the mother Achamoth.

CHAP. VI. — THE THREEFOLD KIND OF MAN FEIGNED BY THESE HERETICS: GOOD WORKS NEEDLESS FOR THEM, THOUGH NECESSARY TO OTHERS: THEIR ABANDONED MORALS.

1. There being thus three kinds of substances, they declare of all that is material (which they also describe as being "on the left hand") that it must of necessity perish, inasmuch as it is incapable of receiving any *afflatus* of incorruption. As to every animal existence (which they also denominate "on the right hand"), they hold that, inasmuch as it is a mean between the spiritual and the material, it passes to the side to

---

[1] "Achamoth by these names must be understood to have an intermediate position between the divine prototypal idea and creation: she was the reflex of the one, and therefore *masculo-feminine;* she was the pattern to be realized in the latter, and therefore was named *Earth and Jerusalem.*" — HARVEY.
[2] But after the consummation here referred to, Achamoth regained the Pleroma: see below, chap. vii. 1.
[3] Isa. xlv. 5, 6, xlvi. 9.

[4] An account is here given of the infusion of a spiritual principle into mankind. The Demiurge himself could give no more than the animal soul; but, unwittingly to himself, he was made the instrument of conveying that spiritual essence from Achamoth, which had grown up within her from the contemplation of those angels who accompanied the Saviour.

which inclination draws it. Spiritual substance, again, they describe as having been sent forth for this end, that, being here united with that which is animal, it might assume shape, the two elements being simultaneously subjected to the same discipline. And this they declare to be "the salt"¹ and "the light of the world." For the animal substance had need of training by means of the outward senses; and on this account they affirm that the world was created, as well as that the Saviour came to the animal substance (which was possessed of free-will), that He might secure for it salvation. For they affirm that He received the first-fruits of those whom He was to save [as follows], from Achamoth that which was spiritual, while He was invested by the Demiurge with the animal Christ, but was begirt² by a [special] dispensation with a body endowed with an animal nature, yet constructed with unspeakable skill, so that it might be visible and tangible, and capable of enduring suffering. At the same time, they deny that He assumed anything material [into His nature], since indeed matter is incapable of salvation. They further hold that the consummation of all things will take place when all that is spiritual has been formed and perfected by Gnosis (knowledge); and by this they mean spiritual men who have attained to the perfect knowledge of God, and been initiated into these mysteries by Achamoth. And they represent themselves to be these persons.

2. Animal men, again, are instructed in animal things; such men, namely, as are established by their works, and by a mere faith, while they have not perfect knowledge. We of the Church, they say, are these persons.³ Wherefore also they maintain that good works are necessary to us, for that otherwise it is impossible we should be saved. But as to themselves, they hold that they shall be entirely and undoubtedly saved, not by means of conduct, but because they are spiritual by nature.⁴ For, just as it is impossible that material substance should partake of salvation (since, indeed, they maintain that it is incapable of receiving it), so again it is impossible that spiritual substance (by which they mean themselves) should ever come under the power of corruption, whatever the sort of actions in which they indulged. For even as gold, when submersed in filth, loses not on that account its beauty, but retains its own native qualities, the filth having no power to injure the gold, so they affirm that they cannot in any measure suffer hurt, or lose their spiritual substance, whatever the material actions in which they may be involved.

3. Wherefore also it comes to pass, that the "most perfect" among them addict themselves without fear to all those kinds of forbidden deeds of which the Scriptures assure us that "they who do such things shall not inherit the kingdom of God."⁵ For instance, they make no scruple about eating meats offered in sacrifice to idols, imagining that they can in this way contract no defilement. Then, again, at every heathen festival celebrated in honour of the idols, these men are the first to assemble; and to such a pitch do they go, that some of them do not even keep away from that bloody spectacle hateful both to God and men, in which gladiators either fight with wild beasts, or singly encounter one another. Others of them yield themselves up to the lusts of the flesh with the utmost greediness, maintaining that carnal things should be allowed to the carnal nature, while spiritual things are provided for the spiritual. Some of them, moreover, are in the habit of defiling those women to whom they have taught the above doctrine, as has frequently been confessed by those women who have been led astray by certain of them, on their returning to the Church of God, and acknowledging this along with the rest of their errors. Others of them, too, openly and without a blush, having become passionately attached to certain women, seduce them away from their husbands, and contract marriages of their own with them. Others of them, again, who pretend at first to live in all modesty with them as with sisters, have in course of time been revealed in their true colours, when the sister has been found with child by her [pretended] brother.

4. And committing many other abominations and impieties, they run us down (who from the fear of God guard against sinning even in thought or word) as utterly contemptible and ignorant persons, while they highly exalt themselves, and claim to be perfect, and the elect seed. For they declare that we simply receive grace for use, wherefore also it will again be taken away from us; but that they themselves have grace as their own special possession, which has descended from above by means of an unspeakable and indescribable conjunction; and on this account more will be given them.⁶ They maintain, therefore, that in every way it is always necessary for them to practise the mystery of conjunction. And that they may persuade the thoughtless to believe this, they are in the habit of using these very words, "Whosoever being *in* this world does not so love a woman as to

---

¹ Matt. v. 13, 14.
² "The doctrine of Valentinus, therefore," says Harvey, "as regards the human nature of Christ, was essentially Docetic. His body was *animal*, but not *material*, and only visible and tangible as having been formed κατ' οἰκονομίαν and κατεσκευασμένον ἀρρήτῳ τέχνῃ."
³ [That is, *carnal;* men of the carnal mind, *psychic* instead of *pneumatic*. Rom. viii. 6.]
⁴ On account of what they had received from Achamoth.
⁵ Gal. v. 21.
⁶ Comp. Luke xix. 26.

obtain possession of her, is not of the truth, nor shall attain to the truth. But whosoever being *of*[1] this world has intercourse with woman, shall not attain to the truth, because he has so acted under the power of concupiscence." On this account, they tell us that it is necessary for us whom they call *animal* men, and describe as being *of* the world, to practise continence and good works, that by this means we may attain at length to the intermediate habitation, but that to them who are called "the spiritual and perfect" such a course of conduct is not at all necessary. For it is not conduct of any kind which leads into the Pleroma, but the seed sent forth thence in a feeble, immature state, and here brought to perfection.

CHAP. VII. — THE MOTHER ACHAMOTH, WHEN ALL HER SEED ARE PERFECTED, SHALL PASS INTO THE PLEROMA, ACCOMPANIED BY THOSE MEN WHO ARE SPIRITUAL; THE DEMIURGE, WITH ANIMAL MEN, SHALL PASS INTO THE INTERMEDIATE HABITATION; BUT ALL MATERIAL MEN SHALL GO INTO CORRUPTION. THEIR BLASPHEMOUS OPINIONS AGAINST THE TRUE INCARNATION OF CHRIST BY THE VIRGIN MARY. THEIR VIEWS AS TO THE PROPHECIES. STUPID IGNORANCE OF THE DEMIURGE.

1. When all the seed shall have come to perfection, they state that then their mother Achamoth shall pass from the intermediate place, and enter in within the Pleroma, and shall receive as her spouse the Saviour, who sprang from all the Æons, that thus a conjunction may be formed between the Saviour and Sophia, that is, Achamoth. These, then, are the bridegroom and bride, while the nuptial chamber is the full extent of the Pleroma. The spiritual seed, again, being divested of their animal souls,[2] and becoming intelligent spirits, shall in an irresistible and invisible manner enter in within the Pleroma, and be bestowed as brides on those angels who wait upon the Saviour. The Demiurge himself will pass into the place of his mother Sophia;[3] that is, the intermediate habitation. In this intermediate place, also, shall the souls of the righteous repose; but nothing of an animal nature shall find admittance to the Pleroma. When these things have taken place as described, then shall that fire which lies hidden in the world blaze forth and burn; and while destroying all matter, shall also be extinguished along with it, and have no further existence. They affirm that the Demiurge was acquainted with none of these things before the advent of the Saviour.

2. There are also some who maintain that he also produced Christ as his own proper son, but of an animal nature, and that mention was[4] made of him by the prophets. This Christ passed through Mary[5] just as water flows through a tube; and there descended upon him in the form of a dove at the time of his baptism, that Saviour who belonged to the Pleroma, and was formed by the combined efforts of all its inhabitants. In him there existed also that spiritual seed which proceeded from Achamoth. They hold, accordingly, that our Lord, while preserving the type of the first-begotten and primary tetrad, was compounded of these four substances, — of that which is spiritual, in so far as He was from Achamoth; of that which is animal, as being from the Demiurge by a special dispensation, inasmuch as He was formed [corporeally] with unspeakable skill; and of the Saviour, as respects that dove which descended upon Him. He also continued free from all suffering, since indeed it was not possible that He should suffer who was at once incomprehensible and invisible. And for this reason the Spirit of Christ, who had been placed within Him, was taken away when He was brought before Pilate. They maintain, further, that not even the seed which He had received from the mother [Achamoth] was subject to suffering; for it, too, was impassible, as being spiritual, and invisible even to the Demiurge himself. It follows, then, according to them, that the animal Christ, and that which had been formed mysteriously by a special dispensation, underwent suffering, that the mother might exhibit through him a type of the Christ above, namely, of him who extended himself through Stauros,[6] and imparted to Achamoth shape, so far as substance was concerned. For they declare that all these transactions were counterparts of what took place above.

3. They maintain, moreover, that those souls which possess the seed of Achamoth are superior to the rest, and are more dearly loved by the Demiurge than others, while he knows not the true cause thereof, but imagines that they are what they are through his favour towards them. Wherefore, also, they say he distributed them to prophets, priests, and kings; and they declare that many things were spoken[7] by this seed through the prophets, inasmuch as it was endowed with a transcendently lofty nature. The

---

[1] Comp. John xvii. 16. The Valentinians, while *in the world*, claimed to be not *of the world*, as animal men were.
[2] Their spiritual substance was received from Achamoth; their animal souls were created by the Demiurge. These are now separated; the spirit enters the Pleroma, while the soul remains in heaven.
[3] Viz., Achamoth.
[4] A Syriac fragment here reads, "He spake by the prophets through him."
[5] "Thus," says Harvey, "we may trace back to the Gnostic period the Apollinarian error, closely allied to the Docetic, that the body of Christ was not derived from the blessed Virgin, but that it was of heavenly substance, and was only brought forth into the world through her instrumentality."
[6] By thus extending himself through Stauros, who bounded the Pleroma, the Christ above became the type of the Christ below, who was extended upon the cross.
[7] Billius, following the old Latin version, reads, "They interpret many things, spoken by the prophets, of this seed."

mother also, they say, spake much about things above, and that both through him and through the souls which were formed by him. Then, again, they divide the prophecies [into different classes], maintaining that one portion was uttered by the mother, a second by her seed, and a third by the Demiurge. In like manner, they hold that Jesus uttered some things under the influence of the Saviour, others under that of the mother, and others still under that of the Demiurge, as we shall show further on in our work.

4. The Demiurge, while ignorant of those things which were higher than himself, was indeed excited by the announcements made [through the prophets], but treated them with contempt, attributing them sometimes to one cause and sometimes to another; either to the prophetic spirit (which itself possesses the power of self-excitement), or to [mere unassisted] man, or that it was simply a crafty device of the lower [and baser order of men].[1] He remained thus ignorant until the appearing of the Lord. But they relate that when the Saviour came, the Demiurge learned all things from Him, and gladly with all his power joined himself to Him. They maintain that he is the centurion mentioned in the Gospel, who addressed the Saviour in these words: "For I also am one having soldiers and servants under my authority; and whatsoever I command they do."[2] They further hold that he will continue administering the affairs of the world as long as that is fitting and needful, and specially that he may exercise a care over the Church; while at the same time he is influenced by the knowledge of the reward prepared for him, namely, that he may attain to the habitation of his mother.

5. They conceive, then, of three kinds of men, spiritual, material, and animal, represented by Cain, Abel, and Seth. These three natures are no longer found in one person,[3] but constitute various kinds [of men]. The material goes, as a matter of course, into corruption. The animal, if it make choice of the better part, finds repose in the intermediate place; but if the worse, it too shall pass into destruction. But they assert that the spiritual principles which have been sown by Achamoth, being disciplined and nourished here from that time until now in righteous souls (because when given forth by her they were yet but weak), at last attaining to perfection, shall be given as brides to the angels of the Saviour, while their animal souls of necessity rest for ever with the Demiurge in the intermediate place. And again subdividing the animal souls themselves, they say that some are by nature good, and others by nature evil. The good are those who become capable of receiving the [spiritual] seed; the evil by nature are those who are never able to receive that seed.

CHAP. VIII. — HOW THE VALENTINIANS PERVERT THE SCRIPTURES TO SUPPORT THEIR OWN IMPIOUS OPINIONS.

1. Such, then, is their system, which neither the prophets announced, nor the Lord taught, nor the apostles delivered, but of which they boast that beyond all others they have a perfect knowledge. They gather their views from other sources than the Scriptures;[4] and, to use a common proverb, they strive to weave ropes of sand, while they endeavour to adapt with an air of probability to their own peculiar assertions the parables of the Lord, the sayings of the prophets, and the words of the apostles, in order that their scheme may not seem altogether without support. In doing so, however, they disregard the order and the connection of the Scriptures, and so far as in them lies, dismember and destroy the truth. By transferring passages, and dressing them up anew, and making one thing out of another, they succeed in deluding many through their wicked art in adapting the oracles of the Lord to their opinions. Their manner of acting is just as if one, when a beautiful image of a king has been constructed by some skilful artist out of precious jewels, should then take this likeness of the man all to pieces, should re-arrange the gems, and so fit them together as to make them into the form of a dog or of a fox, and even that but poorly executed; and should then maintain and declare that *this* was the beautiful image of the king which the skilful artist constructed, pointing to the jewels which had been admirably fitted together by the first artist to form the image of the king, but have been with bad effect transferred by the latter one to the shape of a dog, and by thus exhibiting the jewels, should deceive the ignorant who had no conception what a king's form was like, and persuade them that that miserable likeness of the fox was, in fact, the beautiful image of the king. In like manner do these persons patch together old wives' fables, and then endeavour, by violently drawing away from their proper connection, words, expressions, and parables whenever found, to adapt the oracles of God to their baseless fictions. We have already stated how far they proceed in this way with respect to the interior of the Pleroma.

2. Then, again, as to those things outside of their Pleroma, the following are some specimens of what they attempt to accommodate out of the Scriptures to their opinions. They affirm that

---

[1] Such appears to be the meaning of this sentence, but the original is very obscure. The writer seems to refer to the spiritual, the animal, and the material classes of men, and to imply that the Demiurge supposed some propehcies to be due to one of these classes, and some to the others.
[2] Matt. viii. 9; Luke vii. 8.
[3] As was the case at first, in Adam.
[4] Literally, "reading from things unwritten."

the Lord came in the last times of the world to endure suffering, for this end, that He might indicate the passion which occurred to the last of the Æons, and might by His own end announce the cessation of that disturbance which had risen among the Æons. They maintain, further, that that girl of twelve years old, the daughter of the ruler of the synagogue,[1] to whom the Lord approached and raised her from the dead, was a type of Achamoth, to whom their Christ, by extending himself, imparted shape, and whom he led anew to the perception of that light which had forsaken her. And that the Saviour appeared to her when she lay outside of the Pleroma as a kind of abortion, they affirm Paul to have declared in his Epistle to the Corinthians [in these words], "And last of all, He appeared to me also, as to one born out of due time."[2] Again, the coming of the Saviour with His attendants to Achamoth is declared in like manner by him in the same Epistle, when he says, "A woman ought to have a veil upon her head, because of the angels."[3] Now, that Achamoth, when the Saviour came to her, drew a veil over herself through modesty, Moses rendered manifest when he put a veil upon his face. Then, also, they say that the passions which she endured were indicated by the Lord upon the cross. Thus, when He said, "My God, my God, why hast Thou forsaken Me?"[4] He simply showed that Sophia was deserted by the light, and was restrained by Horos from making any advance forward. Her anguish, again, was indicated when He said, "My soul is exceeding sorrowful, even unto death;"[5] her fear by the words, "Father, if it be possible, let this cup pass from Me;"[6] and her perplexity, too, when He said, "And what I shall say, I know not."[7]

3. And they teach that He pointed out the three kinds of men as follows: the *material*, when He said to him that asked Him, "Shall I follow Thee?"[8] "The Son of man hath not where to lay His head;"—the *animal*, when He said to him that declared, "I will follow Thee, but suffer me first to bid them farewell that are in my house," "No man, putting his hand to the plough, and looking back, is fit for the kingdom of heaven"[9] (for this man they declare to be of the intermediate class, even as they do that other who, though he professed to have wrought a large amount of righteousness, yet refused to follow Him, and was so overcome by [the love of] riches, as never to reach perfection)—this one it pleases them to place in the animal class;—the *spiritual*, again, when He said, "Let the dead bury their dead, but go thou and preach the kingdom of God,"[10] and when He said to Zaccheus the publican, "Make haste, and come down, for to-day I must abide in thine house"[11]—for these they declared to have belonged to the spiritual class. Also the parable of the leaven which the woman is described as having hid in three measures of meal, they declare to make manifest the three classes. For, according to their teaching, the woman represented Sophia; the three measures of meal, the three kinds of men—spiritual, animal, and material; while the leaven denoted the Saviour Himself. Paul, too, very plainly set forth the material, animal, and spiritual, saying in one place, "As is the earthy, such are they also that are earthy;"[12] and in another place, "But the animal man receiveth not the things of the Spirit;"[13] and again: "He that is spiritual judgeth all things."[14] And this, "The animal man receiveth not the things of the Spirit," they affirm to have been spoken concerning the Demiurge, who, as being animal, knew neither his mother who was spiritual, nor her seed, nor the Æons in the Pleroma. And that the Saviour received first-fruits of those whom He was to save, Paul declared when he said, "And if the first-fruits be holy, the lump is also holy,"[15] teaching that the expression "first-fruits" denoted that which is spiritual, but that "the lump" meant us, that is, the animal Church, the lump of which they say He assumed, and blended it with Himself, inasmuch as He is "the leaven."

4. Moreover, that Achamoth wandered beyond the Pleroma, and received form from Christ, and was sought after by the Saviour, they declare that He indicated when He said, that He had come after that sheep which was gone astray.[16] For they explain the wandering sheep to mean their mother, by whom they represent the Church as having been sown. The wandering itself denotes her stay outside of the Pleroma in a state of varied passion, from which they maintain that matter derived its origin. The woman, again, who sweeps the house and finds the piece of money, they declare to denote the Sophia above, who, having lost her enthymesis, afterwards recovered it, on all things

---

[1] Luke viii. 41.
[2] 1 Cor. xv. 8.
[3] 1 Cor. xi. 10. Irenæus here reads κάλυμμα, *veil*, instead of ἐξουσίαν, *power*, as in the received text. [An interesting fact, as it betokens an old gloss, which may have slipped into the text of some ancient MSS.]
[4] Matt. xxvii. 46.
[5] Matt. xxvi. 38.
[6] Matt. xxvi. 39.
[7] John xii. 27. The Valentinians seem, for their own purposes, to have added οὐκ οἶδα to this text.
[8] Luke ix. 57, 58.
[9] Luke ix. 61, 62.
[10] Luke ix. 60.
[11] Luke xix. 5.
[12] 1 Cor. xv. 48.
[13] 1 Cor. ii. 14.
[14] 1 Cor. ii. 15.
[15] Rom. xi. 16.
[16] Luke xv. 4, 8.

being purified by the advent of the Saviour. Wherefore this substance also, according to them, was reinstated in Pleroma. They say, too, that Simeon, "who took Christ into his arms, and gave thanks to God, and said, Lord, now lettest Thou Thy servant depart in peace, according to Thy word,"[1] was a type of the Demiurge, who, on the arrival of the Saviour, learned his own change of place, and gave thanks to Bythus. They also assert that by Anna, who is spoken of in the gospel[2] as a prophetess, and who, after living seven years with her husband, passed all the rest of her life in widowhood until she saw the Saviour, and recognised Him, and spoke of Him to all, was most plainly indicated Achamoth, who, having for a little while looked upon the Saviour with His associates, and dwelling all the rest of the time in the intermediate place, waited for Him till He should come again, and restore her to her proper consort. Her name, too, was indicated by the Saviour, when He said, "Yet wisdom is justified by her children."[3] This, too, was done by Paul in these words, "But we speak wisdom among them that are perfect."[4] They declare also that Paul has referred to the conjunctions within the Pleroma, showing them forth by means of one; for, when writing of the conjugal union in this life, he expressed himself thus: "This is a great mystery, but I speak concerning Christ and the Church."[5]

5. Further, they teach that John, the disciple of the Lord, indicated the first Ogdoad, expressing themselves in these words: John, the disciple of the Lord, wishing to set forth the origin of all things, so as to explain how the Father produced the whole, lays down a certain principle,—that, namely, which was first-begotten by God, which Being he has termed both the only-begotten Son and God, in whom the Father, after a seminal manner, brought forth all things. By him the Word was produced, and in him the whole substance of the Æons, to which the Word himself afterwards imparted form. Since, therefore, he treats of the first origin of things, he rightly proceeds in his teaching from the beginning, that is, from God and the Word. And he expresses himself thus: "In the beginning was the Word, and the Word was with God, and the Word was God; the same was in the beginning with God."[6] Having first of all distinguished these three—God, the Beginning, and the Word—he again unites them, that he may exhibit the production of each of them, that is, of the Son and of the Word, and may at the same time show their union with one another, and with the Father. For "the beginning" is in the Father, and of the Father, while "the Word" is in the beginning, and of the beginning. Very properly, then, did he say, "In the beginning was the Word," for He was in the Son; "and the Word was with God," for He was the beginning; "and the Word was God," of course, for that which is begotten of God is God. "The same was in the beginning with God"—this clause discloses the order of production. "All things were made by Him, and without Him was nothing made;"[7] for the Word was the author of form and beginning to all the Æons that came into existence after Him. But "what was made in Him," says John, "is life."[8] Here again he indicated conjunction; for all things, he said, were made *by* Him, but *in* Him was life. This, then, which is in Him, is more closely connected with Him than those things which were simply made by Him, for it exists along with Him, and is developed by Him. When, again, he adds, "And the life was the light of men," while thus mentioning Anthropos, he indicated also Ecclesia by that one expression, in order that, by using only one name, he might disclose their fellowship with one another, in virtue of their conjunction. For Anthropos and Ecclesia spring from Logos and Zoe. Moreover, he styled life (Zoe) the light of men, because they are enlightened by her, that is, formed and made manifest. This also Paul declares in these words: "For whatsoever doth make manifest is light."[9] Since, therefore, Zoe manifested and begat both Anthropos and Ecclesia, she is termed their light. Thus, then, did John by these words reveal both other things and the second Tetrad, Logos and Zoe, Anthropos and Ecclesia. And still further, he also indicated the first Tetrad. For, in discoursing of the Saviour, and declaring that all things beyond the Pleroma received form from Him, he says that He is the fruit of the entire Pleroma. For he styles Him a "light which shineth in darkness, and which was not comprehended"[10] by it, inasmuch as, when He imparted form to all those things which had their origin from passion, He was not known by it.[11] He also styles Him Son, and Aletheia, and Zoe, and the "Word made flesh, whose glory," he says, "we beheld; and His glory was as that of the Only-begotten (given to Him by the Father), full of grace and truth."[12] (But what John really does

---

[1] Luke ii. 28.
[2] Luke ii. 36.
[3] Luke vii. 35.
[4] 1 Cor. ii. 6.
[5] Eph. v. 32.
[6] John i. 1, 2.
[7] John i. 3.
[8] John i. 3, 4. The punctuation here followed is different from that commonly adopted, but is found in many of the Fathers, and in some of the most ancient MSS.
[9] Eph. v. 13.
[10] John i. 5.
[11] ὑπ' αὐτῆς, occurring twice, is rendered both times in the old Latin version, "ab eis." The reference is to σκοτία, *darkness*, i.e., all those not belonging to the spiritual seed.
[12] Comp. John i. 14.

say is this: "And the Word was made flesh, and dwelt among us; and we beheld His glory, the glory as of the only-begotten of the Father, full of grace and truth."[1]) Thus, then, does he [according to them] distinctly set forth the first Tetrad, when he speaks of the Father, and Charis, and Monogenes, and Aletheia. In this way, too, does John tell of the first Ogdoad, and that which is the mother of all the Æons. For he mentions the Father, and Charis, and Monogenes, and Aletheia, and Logos, and Zoe, and Anthropos, and Ecclesia. Such are the views of Ptolemæus.[2]

CHAP. IX. — REFUTATION OF THE IMPIOUS INTERPRETATIONS OF THESE HERETICS.

1. You see, my friend, the method which these men employ to deceive themselves, while they abuse the Scriptures by endeavouring to support their own system out of them. For this reason, I have brought forward their modes of expressing themselves, that thus thou mightest understand the deceitfulness of their procedure, and the wickedness of their error. For, in the first place, if it had been John's intention to set forth that Ogdoad above, he would surely have preserved the order of its production, and would doubtless have placed the primary Tetrad first, as being, according to them, most venerable, and would then have annexed the second, that, by the sequence of the names, the order of the Ogdoad might be exhibited, and not after so long an interval, as if forgetful for the moment; and then again calling the matter to mind, he, last of all, made mention of the primary Tetrad. In the next place, if he had meant to indicate their conjunctions, he certainly would not have omitted the name of Ecclesia; while, with respect to the other conjunctions, he either would have been satisfied with the mention of the male [Æons] (since the others [like Ecclesia] might be understood), so as to preserve a uniformity throughout; or if he enumerated the conjunctions of the rest, he would also have announced the spouse of Anthropos, and would not have left us to find out her name by divination.

2. The fallacy, then, of this exposition is manifest. For when John, proclaiming one God, the Almighty, and one Jesus Christ, the Only-begotten, by whom all things were made, declares that this was the Son of God, this the Only-begotten, this the Former of all things, this the true Light who enlighteneth every man, this the Creator of the world, this He that came to His own, this He that became flesh and dwelt among us, — these men, by a plausible kind of exposition, perverting these statements, maintain that there was another Monogenes, according to production, whom they also style Arche. They also maintain that there was another Saviour, and another Logos, the son of Monogenes, and another Christ produced for the re-establishment of the Pleroma. Thus it is that, wresting from the truth every one of the expressions which have been cited, and taking a bad advantage of the names, they have transferred them to their own system; so that, according to them, in all these terms John makes no mention of the Lord Jesus Christ. For if he has named the Father, and Charis, and Monogenes, and Aletheia, and Logos, and Zoe, and Anthropos, and Ecclesia, according to their hypothesis, he has, by thus speaking, referred to the primary Ogdoad, in which there was as yet no Jesus, and no Christ, the teacher of John. But that the apostle did not speak concerning their conjunctions, but concerning our Lord Jesus Christ, whom he also acknowledges as the Word of God, he himself has made evident. For, summing up his statements respecting the Word previously mentioned by him, he further declares, "And the Word was made flesh, and dwelt among us." But, according to their hypothesis, the Word did not become flesh at all, inasmuch as He never went outside of the Pleroma, but that Saviour [became flesh] who was formed by a special dispensation [out of all the Æons], and was of later date than the Word.

3. Learn then, ye foolish men, that Jesus who suffered for us, and who dwelt among us, is Himself the Word of God. For if any other of the Æons had become flesh for our salvation, it would have been probable that the apostle spoke of another. But if the Word of the Father who descended is the same also that ascended, He, namely, the Only-begotten Son of the only God, who, according to the good pleasure of the Father, became flesh for the sake of men, the apostle certainly does not speak regarding any other, or concerning any Ogdoad, but respecting our Lord Jesus Christ. For, according to them, the Word did not originally become flesh. For they maintain that the Saviour assumed an animal body, formed in accordance with a special dispensation by an unspeakable providence, so as to become visible and palpable. But *flesh* is that which was of old formed for Adam by God out of the dust, and it is this that John has declared the Word of God became. Thus is their primary and first-begotten Ogdoad brought to nought. For, since Logos, and Monogenes, and Zoe, and Phōs, and Soter, and Christus, and the Son of God, and He who became incarnate for us, have been proved to be one and the same, the Ogdoad which they have built up at once falls to pieces. And when this is destroyed,

---

[1] This is parenthetically inserted by the author, to show the misquotation of Scripture by these heretics.
[2] These words are wanting in the Greek, but are inserted in the old Latin version.

their whole system sinks into ruin, — a system which they falsely dream into existence, and thus inflict injury on the Scriptures, while they build up their own hypothesis.

4. Then, again, collecting a set of expressions and names scattered here and there [in Scripture], they twist them, as we have already said, from a natural to a non-natural sense. In so doing, they act like those who bring forward any kind of hypothesis they fancy, and then endeavour to support[1] them out of the poems of Homer, so that the ignorant imagine that Homer actually composed the verses bearing upon that hypothesis, which has, in fact, been but newly constructed; and many others are led so far by the regularly-formed sequence of the verses, as to doubt whether Homer may not have composed them. Of this kind[2] is the following passage, where one, describing Hercules as having been sent by Eurystheus to the dog in the infernal regions, does so by means of these Homeric verses, — for there can be no objection to our citing these by way of illustration, since the same sort of attempt appears in both: —

"Thus saying, there sent forth from his house deeply groaning." — *Od*., x. 76.
"The hero Hercules conversant with mighty deeds." — *Od*., xxi. 26.
Eurystheus, the son of Sthenelus, descended from Perseus." — *Il*., xix. 123.
"That he might bring from Erebus the dog of gloomy Pluto." — *Il*., viii. 368.
"And he advanced like a mountain-bred lion confident of strength." — *Od*., vi. 130.
"Rapidly through the city, while all his friends followed." — *Il*., xxiv. 327.
"Both maidens, and youths, and much-enduring old men." — *Od*., xi. 38.
"Mourning for him bitterly as one going forward to death." — *Il*., xxiv. 328.
"But Mercury and the blue-eyed Minerva conducted him." — *Od*., xi. 626.
"For she knew the mind of her brother, how it laboured with grief." — *Il*., ii. 409.

Now, what simple-minded man, I ask, would not be led away by such verses as these to think that Homer actually framed them so with reference to the subject indicated? But he who is acquainted with the Homeric writings will recognise the verses indeed, but not the subject to which they are applied, as knowing that some of them were spoken of Ulysses, others of Hercules himself, others still of Priam, and others again of Menelaus and Agamemnon. But if he takes them and restores each of them to its proper position, he at once destroys the narrative in question. In like manner he also who retains unchangeable[3] in his heart the rule of the truth which he received by means of baptism, will doubtless recognise the names, the expressions, and the parables taken from the Scriptures, but will by no means acknowledge the blasphemous use which these men make of them. For, though he will acknowledge the gems, he will certainly not receive the fox instead of the likeness of the king. But when he has restored every one of the expressions quoted to its proper position, and has fitted it to the body of the truth, he will lay bare, and prove to be without any foundation, the figment of these heretics.

5. But since what may prove a finishing-stroke[4] to this exhibition is wanting, so that any one, on following out their farce to the end, may then at once append an argument which shall overthrow it, we have judged it well to point out, first of all, in what respects the very fathers of this fable differ among themselves, as if they were inspired by different spirits of error. For this very fact forms an *a priori* proof that the truth proclaimed by the Church is immoveable,[5] and that the theories of these men are but a tissue of falsehoods.

CHAP. X. — UNITY OF THE FAITH OF THE CHURCH THROUGHOUT THE WHOLE WORLD.

1. The Church, though dispersed throughout the whole world, even to the ends of the earth, has received from the apostles and their disciples this faith: [She believes] in one God, the Father Almighty, Maker of heaven, and earth, and the sea, and all things that are in them; and in one Christ Jesus, the Son of God, who became incarnate for our salvation; and in the Holy Spirit, who proclaimed through the prophets the dispensations[6] of God, and the advents, and the birth from a virgin, and the passion, and the resurrection from the dead, and the ascension into heaven in the flesh of the beloved Christ Jesus, our Lord, and His [future] manifestation from heaven in the glory of the Father "to gather all things in one,"[7] and to raise up anew all flesh of the whole human race, in order that to Christ Jesus, our Lord, and God, and Saviour, and King, according to the will of the invisible Father, "every knee should bow, of things in heaven, and things in earth, and things under the earth, and that every tongue should confess"[8] to Him, and that He should execute just judgment towards all; that He may send "spiritual wickednesses,"[9] and

---

[1] It is difficult to give an exact rendering of μελετᾶν in this passage; the old Lat. version translates it by *meditari*, which Massuet proposes to render " skilfully to fit."
[2] Tertullian refers (*Præscrip. Hær.*) to those Homeric centos of which a specimen follows. We have given each line as it stands in the original: the text followed by Irenæus differs slightly from the received text.
[3] Literally, " immoveable in himself," the word ἀκλινῆ being used with an apparent reference to the original meaning of κανόνα, *a builder's rule*.
[4] The meaning of the word ἀπολύτρωσις here is not easily determined; but it is probably a scenic term equivalent to ἀπόλυσις, and may be rendered as above.
[5] [The Creed, in the sublime simplicity of its fundamental articles, is established; that is, by the impossibility of framing anything to take their place.]
[6] " Of God" is added from the old Latin.
[7] Eph. i. 10.
[8] Phil. ii. 10, 11.
[9] Eph. vi. 12.

the angels who transgressed and became apostates, together with the ungodly, and unrighteous, and wicked, and profane among men, into everlasting fire; but may, in the exercise of His grace, confer immortality on the righteous, and holy, and those who have kept His commandments, and have persevered in His love, some from the beginning [of their Christian course], and others from [the date of] their repentance, and may surround them with everlasting glory.

2. As I have already observed, the Church, having received this preaching and this faith, although scattered throughout the whole world, yet, as if occupying but one house, carefully preserves it. She also believes these points [of doctrine] just as if she had but one soul, and one and the same heart, and she proclaims them, and teaches them, and hands them down, with perfect harmony, as if she possessed only one mouth. For, although the languages of the world are dissimilar, yet the import of the tradition is one and the same. For the Churches which have been planted in Germany do not believe or hand down anything different, nor do those in Spain, nor those in Gaul, nor those in the East, nor those in Egypt, nor those in Libya, nor those which have been established in the central regions[1] of the world. But as the sun, that creature of God, is one and the same throughout the whole world, so also the preaching of the truth shineth everywhere, and enlightens all men that are willing to come to a knowledge of the truth. Nor will any one of the rulers in the Churches, however highly gifted he may be in point of eloquence, teach doctrines different from these (for no one is greater than the Master); nor, on the other hand, will he who is deficient in power of expression inflict injury on the tradition. For the faith being ever one and the same, neither does one who is able at great length to discourse regarding it, make any addition to it, nor does one, who can say but little, diminish it.

3. It does not follow because men are endowed with greater and less degrees of intelligence, that they should therefore change the subject-matter [of the faith] itself, and should conceive of some other God besides Him who is the Framer, Maker, and Preserver of this universe, (as if He were not sufficient[2] for them), or of another Christ, or another Only-begotten. But the fact referred to simply implies this, that one may [more accurately than another] bring out the meaning of those things which have been spoken in parables, and accommodate them to the general scheme of the faith; and explain [with special clearness] the operation and dispensation of God connected with human salvation; and show that God manifested longsuffering in regard to the apostasy of the angels who transgressed, as also with respect to the disobedience of men; and set forth why it is that one and the same God has made some things temporal and some eternal, some heavenly and others earthly; and understand for what reason God, though invisible, manifested Himself to the prophets not under one form, but differently to different individuals; and show why it was that more covenants than one were given to mankind; and teach what was the special character of each of these covenants; and search out for what reason "God[3] hath concluded every man[4] in unbelief, that He may have mercy upon all;" and gratefully[5] describe on what account the Word of God became flesh and suffered; and relate why the advent of the Son of God took place in these last times, that is, in the end, rather than in the beginning [of the world]; and unfold what is contained in the Scriptures concerning the end [itself], and things to come; and not be silent as to how it is that God has made the Gentiles, whose salvation was despaired of, fellow-heirs, and of the same body, and partakers with the saints; and discourse how it is that "this mortal body shall put on immortality, and this corruptible shall put on incorruption;"[6] and proclaim in what sense [God] says, "That is a people who was not a people; and she is beloved who was not beloved;"[7] and in what sense He says that "more are the children of her that was desolate, than of her who possessed a husband."[8] For in reference to these points, and others of a like nature, the apostle exclaims: "Oh! the depth of the riches both of the wisdom and knowledge of God; how unsearchable are His judgments, and His ways past finding out!"[9] But [the superior skill spoken of] is not found in this, that any one should, beyond the Creator and Framer [of the world], conceive of the Enthymesis of an erring Æon, their mother and his, and should thus proceed to such a pitch of blasphemy; nor does it consist in this, that he should again falsely imagine, as being above this [fancied being], a Pleroma at one time supposed to contain thirty, and at another time an innumerable tribe of Æons, as these teachers who are destitute of truly divine wisdom maintain; while the Catholic Church pos-

---

[1] Probably referring to the Churches in Palestine.
[2] The text here is ἀρκουμένους τούτους, which is manifestly corrupt. Various emendations have been proposed: we prefer reading ἀρκούμενος τούτοις, and have translated accordingly.
[3] Rom. xi. 32.
[4] Irenæus here reads πάντα instead of πάντας, as in Text. Rec. of New Testament.
[5] εὐχαριστεῖν — this word has been deemed corrupt, as it certainly appears out of keeping with the other verbs; but it may be rendered as above.
[6] 1 Cor. xv. 54.
[7] Hos. ii. 23; Rom. ix. 25.
[8] Isa. liv. 1; Gal. iv. 27.
[9] Rom. xi. 33.

sesses one and the same faith throughout the whole world, as we have already said.

CHAP. XI. — THE OPINIONS OF VALENTINUS, WITH THOSE OF HIS DISCIPLES AND OTHERS.

1. Let us now look at the inconsistent opinions of those heretics (for there are some two or three of them), how they do not agree in treating the same points, but alike, in things and names, set forth opinions mutually discordant. The first[1] of them, Valentinus, who adapted the principles of the heresy called "Gnostic" to the peculiar character of his own school, taught as follows: He maintained that there is a certain Dyad (twofold being), who is inexpressible by any name, of whom one part should be called Arrhetus (unspeakable), and the other Sige (silence). But of this Dyad a second was produced, one part of whom he names Pater, and the other Aletheia. From this Tetrad, again, arose Logos and Zoe, Anthropos and Ecclesia. These constitute the primary Ogdoad. He next states that from Logos and Zoe ten powers were produced, as we have before mentioned. But from Anthropos and Ecclesia proceeded twelve, one of which separating from the rest, and falling from its original condition, produced the rest[2] of the universe. He also supposed two beings of the name of Horos, the one of whom has his place between Bythus and the rest of the Pleroma, and divides the created Æons from the uncreated Father, while the other separates their mother from the Pleroma. Christ also was not produced from the Æons within the Pleroma, but was brought forth by the mother who had been excluded from it, in virtue of her remembrance of better things, but not without a kind of shadow. He, indeed, as being masculine, having severed the shadow from himself, returned to the Pleroma; but his mother being left with the shadow, and deprived of her spiritual substance, brought forth another son, namely, the Demiurge, whom he also styles the supreme ruler of all those things which are subject to him. He also asserts that, along with the Demiurge, there was produced a left-hand power, in which particular he agrees with those falsely called Gnostics, of whom to we have yet to speak. Sometimes, again, he maintains that Jesus was produced from him who was separated from their mother, and united to the rest, that is, from Theletus, sometimes as springing from him who returned into the Pleroma, that is, from Christ; and at other times still as derived from Anthropos and Ecclesia. And he declares that the Holy Spirit was produced by Aletheia[3] for the inspection and fructification of the Æons, by entering invisibly into them, and that, in this way, the Æons brought forth the plants of truth.

2. Secundus again affirms that the primary Ogdoad consists of a right hand and a left hand Tetrad, and teaches that the one of these is called light, and the other darkness. But he maintains that the power which separated from the rest, and fell away, did not proceed directly from the thirty Æons, but from their fruits.

3. There is another,[4] who is a renowned teacher among them, and who, struggling to reach something more sublime, and to attain to a kind of higher knowledge, has explained the primary Tetrad as follows: There is [he says] a certain Proarche who existed before all things, surpassing all thought, speech, and nomenclature, whom I call Monotes (unity). Together with this Monotes there exists a power, which again I term Henotes (oneness). This Henotes and Monotes, being one, produced, yet not so as to bring forth [apart from themselves, as an emanation] the beginning of all things, an intelligent, unbegotten, and invisible being, which beginning language terms "Monad." With this Monad there co-exists a power of the same essence, which again I term Hen (One). These powers then — Monotes, and Henotes, and Monas, and Hen — produced the remaining company of the Æons.

4. Iu, Iu! Pheu, Pheu! — for well may we utter these tragic exclamations at such a pitch of audacity in the coining of names as he has displayed without a blush, in devising a nomenclature for his system of falsehood. For when he declares: There is a certain Proarche before all things, surpassing all thought, whom I call Monotes; and again, with this Monotes there co-exists a power which I also call Henotes, — it is most manifest that he confesses the things which have been said to be his own invention, and that he himself has given names to his scheme of things, which had never been previously suggested by any other. It is manifest also, that he himself is the one who has had sufficient audacity to coin these names; so that, unless *he* had appeared in the world, the truth would still have been destitute of a name. But, in that case, nothing hinders any other, in dealing with the same subject, to affix names after such a fashion as the following: There[5] is a certain Proarche, royal, surpassing all thought, a power existing before every other substance, and extended into space in every direction. But along with it there exists a power which I term a *Gourd;* and along

---

[1] That is, the first of the two or three here referred to, not the first of the Gnostic teachers, as some have imagined. [The Gnosticism of one age may be essentially the same in spirit as the Agnosticism of another.]
[2] Viz., all outside of the Pleroma.
[3] Corrected from *Ecclesia* in the text.
[4] Some have supposed that the name of this teacher was *Epiphanes*, and that the old Latin mistakenly translates this by *clarus;* others think that Colorbasus is the teacher in question.
[5] The Greek text is wanting till the end of this section.

with this Gourd there exists a power which again I term *Utter-Emptiness*. This Gourd and Emptiness, since they are one, produced (and yet did not simply produce, so as to be apart from themselves) a fruit, everywhere visible, eatable, and delicious, which fruit-language calls a *Cucumber*. Along with this Cucumber exists a power of the same essence, which again I call a *Melon*. These powers, the Gourd, Utter-Emptiness, the Cucumber, and the Melon, brought forth the remaining multitude of the delirious melons of Valentinus.[1] For if it is fitting that that language which is used respecting the universe be transformed to the primary Tetrad, and if any one may assign names at his pleasure, who shall prevent us from adopting these names, as being much more credible [than the others], as well as in general use, and understood by all?

5. Others still, however, have called their primary and first-begotten Ogdoad by the following names: first, Proarche; then Anennoetos; thirdly, Arrhetos; and fourthly, Aoratos. Then, from the first, Proarche, there was produced, in the first and fifth place, Arche; from Anennoetos, in the second and sixth place, Acataleptos; from Arrhetos, in the third and seventh place, Anonomastos; and from Aoratos, in the fourth and eighth place, Agennetos. This is the Pleroma of the first Ogdoad. They maintain that these powers were anterior to Bythus and Sige, that they may appear more perfect than the perfect, and more knowing than the very Gnostics! To these persons one may justly exclaim: "O ye trifling sophists!" since, even respecting Bythus himself, there are among them many and discordant opinions. For some declare him to be without a consort, and neither male nor female, and, in fact, nothing at all; while others affirm him to be masculo-feminine, assigning to him the nature of a hermaphrodite; others, again, allot Sige to him as a spouse, that thus may be formed the first conjunction.

CHAP. XII. — THE DOCTRINES OF THE FOLLOWERS OF PTOLEMY AND COLORBASUS.

1. But the followers of Ptolemy say[2] that he [Bythos] has two consorts, which they also name *Diatheses* (affections), viz., Ennœa and Thelesis. For, as they affirm, he first conceived the thought of producing something, and then willed to that effect. Wherefore, again, these two affections, or powers, Ennœa and Thelesis, having intercourse, as it were, between themselves, the production of Monogenes and Aletheia took place according to conjunction. These two came forth as types and images of the two affections of the Father, — visible representations of those that were invisible, — Nous (i.e., Monogenes) of Thelesis, and Aletheia of Ennœa, and accordingly the image resulting from Thelesis was masculine,[3] while that from Ennœa was feminine. Thus Thelesis (will) became, as it were, a faculty of Ennœa (thought). For Ennœa continually yearned after offspring; but she could not of herself bring forth that which she desired. But when the power of Thelesis (the faculty of will) came upon her, then she brought forth that on which she had brooded.

2. These fancied beings[4] (like the Jove of Homer, who is represented[5] as passing an anxious sleepless night in devising plans for honouring Achilles and destroying numbers of the Greeks) will not appear to you, my dear friend, to be possessed of greater knowledge than He who is the God of the universe. He, as soon as He thinks, also performs what He has willed; and as soon as He wills, also thinks that which He has willed; then thinking when He wills, and then willing when He thinks, since He is all thought, [all will, all mind, all light,][6] all eye, all ear, the one entire fountain of all good things.

3. Those of them, however, who are deemed more skilful than the persons who have just been mentioned, say that the first Ogdoad was not produced gradually, so that one Æon was sent forth by another, but that all[7] the Æons were brought into existence at once by Propator and his Ennœa. He (Colorbasus) affirms this as confidently as if he had assisted at their birth. Accordingly, he and his followers maintain that Anthropos and Ecclesia were not produced,[8] as others hold, from Logos and Zoe; but, on the contrary, Logos and Zoe from Anthropos and Ecclesia. But they express this in another form, as follows: When the Propator conceived the thought of producing something, he received the name of *Father*. But because what he did produce was *true*, it was named Aletheia. Again, when he wished to reveal himself, this was termed Anthropos. Finally, when he produced those whom he had previously thought of, these were named Ecclesia. Anthropos, by speaking, formed Logos: this is the first-born son. But Zoe followed upon Logos; and thus the first Ogdoad was completed.

4. They have much contention also among themselves respecting the Saviour. For some

---

[1] [1 Kings xviii. 27. "It came to pass that Elijah mocked them," etc. This *reductio ad absurdum* of our author is singularly applicable to certain forms of what is called "Modern Thought."]
[2] We here follow the Greek as preserved by Hippolytus (*Philosoph.*, vi. 38). The text followed by Epiphanius (*Hær.*, xxxiii. 1) does not so well agree with the Latin.
[3] The text is here hopelessly corrupt; but the general meaning seems to be that given above.
[4] This sentence exists only in the Latin version, and we can give only a free translation.
[5] *Iliad*, ii. 1, etc.
[6] These words are found in *Epiphanius*, but omitted in the old Latin version. The Latin gives "sense" instead of "light."
[7] The text is here very uncertain. Some propose to read *six* Æons instead of *all*.
[8] Here again the text is corrupt and obscure. We have followed what seems the most probable emendation.

maintain that he was formed out of all; wherefore also he was called Eudocetos, because the whole Pleroma was *well pleased* through him to glorify the Father. But others assert that he was produced from those ten Æons alone who sprung from Logos and Zoe, and that on this account he was called Logos and Zoe, thus preserving the ancestral names.[1] Others, again, affirm that he had his being from those twelve Æons who were the offspring of Anthropos and Ecclesia; and on this account he acknowledges himself the Son of man, as being a descendant of Anthropos. Others still, assert that he was produced by Christ and the Holy Spirit, who were brought forth for the security of the Pleroma; and that on this account he was called Christ, thus preserving the appellation of the Father, by whom he was produced. And there are yet others among them who declare that the Propator of the whole, Proarche, and Proanennoetos is called Anthropos; and that this is the great and abstruse mystery, namely, that the Power which is above all others, and contains all in his embrace, is termed Anthropos; hence does the Saviour style himself the "Son of man."

CHAP. XIII. — THE DECEITFUL ARTS AND NEFARIOUS PRACTICES OF MARCUS.

1. But[2] there is another among these heretics, Marcus by name, who boasts himself as having improved upon his master. He is a perfect adept in magical impostures, and by this means drawing away a great number of men, and not a few women, he has induced them to join themselves to him, as to one who is possessed of the greatest knowledge and perfection, and who has received the highest power from the invisible and ineffable regions above. Thus it appears as if he really were the precursor of Antichrist. For, joining the buffooneries of Anaxilaus[3] to the craftiness of the *magi*, as they are called, he is regarded by his senseless and cracked-brain followers as working miracles by these means.

2. Pretending[4] to consecrate cups mixed with wine, and protracting to great length the word of invocation, he contrives to give them a purple and reddish colour, so that Charis,[5] who is one of those that are superior to all things, should be thought to drop her own blood into that cup through means of his invocation, and that thus those who are present should be led to rejoice to taste of that cup, in order that, by so doing, the Charis, who is set forth by this magician, may also flow into them. Again, handing mixed cups to the women, he bids them consecrate these in his presence. When this has been done, he himself produces another cup of much larger size than that which the deluded woman has consecrated, and pouring from the smaller one consecrated by the woman into that which has been brought forward by himself, he at the same time pronounces these words: "May that Charis who is before all things, and who transcends all knowledge and speech, fill thine inner man, and multiply in thee her own knowledge, by sowing the grain of mustard seed in thee as in good soil." Repeating certain other like words, and thus goading on the wretched woman [to madness], he then appears a worker of wonders when the large cup is seen to have been filled out of the small one, so as even to overflow by what has been obtained from it. By accomplishing several other similar things, he has completely deceived many, and drawn them away after him.

3. It appears probable enough that this man possesses a demon as his familiar spirit, by means of whom he seems able to prophesy,[6] and also enables as many as he counts worthy to be partakers of his Charis themselves to prophesy. He devotes himself especially to women, and those such as are well-bred, and elegantly attired, and of great wealth, whom he frequently seeks to draw after him, by addressing them in such seductive words as these: "I am eager to make thee a partaker of my Charis, since the Father of all doth continually behold thy angel before His face. Now the place of thy angel is among us:[7] it behoves us to become one. Receive first from me and by me [the gift of] Charis. Adorn thyself as a bride who is expecting her bridegroom, that thou mayest be what I am, and I what thou art. Establish the germ of light in thy nuptial chamber. Receive from me a spouse, and become receptive of him, while thou art received by him. Behold Charis has descended upon thee; open thy mouth and prophesy." On the woman replying, "I have never at any time prophesied, nor do I know how to prophesy;" then engaging, for the second time, in certain invocations, so as to astound his deluded victim, he says to her, "Open thy mouth, speak whatsoever occurs to thee, and thou shalt prophesy." She then, vainly puffed up and elated by these words, and greatly excited in soul by the expectation that it is herself who is to prophesy, her heart beating violently [from emotion], reaches the requisite pitch of audacity, and idly as well as impudently utters some nonsense as it happens to occur to her, such as might be ex-

---

[1] Harvey justly remarks, that "one cause of perplexity in unravelling the Valentinian scheme is the recurrence of similar names at different points of the system, e.g., the Enthymesis of Sophia was called Sophia and Spiritus; and Pater, Arche, Monogenes, Christus, Anthropos, Ecclesia, were all of them terms of a double denomination."
[2] The Greek text of this section is preserved both by Epiphanius (*Hær.*, xxxiv. 1) and by Hippolytus (*Philosoph.*, vi. 39, 40). Their citations are somewhat discordant, and we therefore follow the old Latin version.
[3] Pliny, *Hist. Nat.*, xxxv. 15, etc.
[4] Epiphanius now gives the Greek text *verbatim*, to which, therefore, we return.
[5] Probably referring to Sige, the consort of Bythus.
[6] [Comp. Acts xvi. 16.]
[7] Literally, "the place of thy mightiness is in us."

pected from one heated by an empty spirit. (Referring to this, one superior to me has observed, that the soul is both audacious and impudent when heated with empty air.) Henceforth she reckons herself a prophetess, and expresses her thanks to Marcus for having imparted to her of his own Charis. She then makes the effort to reward him, not only by the gift of her possessions (in which way he has collected a very large fortune), but also by yielding up to him her person, desiring in every way to be united to him, that she may become altogether one with him.

4. But already some of the most faithful women, possessed of the fear of God, and not being deceived (whom, nevertheless, he did his best to seduce like the rest by bidding them prophesy), abhorring and execrating him, have withdrawn from such a vile company of revellers. This they have done, as being well aware that the gift of prophecy is not conferred on men by Marcus, the magician, but that only those to whom God sends His grace from above possess the divinely-bestowed power of prophesying; and then they speak where and when God pleases, and not when Marcus orders them to do so. For that which commands is greater and of higher authority than that which is commanded, inasmuch as the former rules, while the latter is in a state of subjection. If, then, Marcus, or any one else, does command,—as these are accustomed continually at their feasts to play at drawing lots, and [in accordance with the lot] to command one another to prophesy, giving forth as oracles what is in harmony with their own desires,—it will follow that he who commands is greater and of higher authority than the prophetic spirit, though he is but a man, which is impossible. But such spirits as are commanded by these men, and speak when they desire it, are earthly and weak, audacious and impudent, sent forth by Satan for the seduction and perdition of those who do not hold fast that well-compacted faith which they received at first through the Church.

5. Moreover, that this Marcus compounds philters and love-potions, in order to insult the persons of some of these women, if not of all, those of them who have returned to the Church of God — a thing which frequently occurs — have acknowledged, confessing, too, that they have been defiled by him, and that they were filled with a burning passion towards him. A sad example of this occurred in the case of a certain Asiatic, one of our deacons, who had received him (Marcus) into his house. His wife, a woman of remarkable beauty, fell a victim both in mind and body to this magician, and, for a long time, travelled about with him. At last, when, with no small difficulty, the brethren had converted her, she spent her whole time in the exercise of public confession,[1] weeping over and lamenting the defilement which she had received from this magician.

6. Some of his disciples, too, addicting themselves[2] to the same practices, have deceived many silly women, and defiled them. They proclaim themselves as being "perfect," so that no one can be compared to them with respect to the immensity of their knowledge, nor even were you to mention Paul or Peter, or any other of the apostles. They assert that they themselves know more than all others, and that they alone have imbibed the greatness of the knowledge of that power which is unspeakable. They also maintain that they have attained to a height above all power, and that therefore they are free in every respect to act as they please, having no one to fear in anything. For they affirm, that because of the "Redemption"[3] it has come to pass that they can neither be apprehended, nor even seen by the judge. But even if he should happen to lay hold upon them, then they might simply repeat these words, while standing in his presence along with the "Redemption:" "O thou, who sittest beside God,[4] and the mystical, eternal Sige, thou through whom the angels (mightiness), who continually behold the face of the Father, having thee as their guide and introducer, do derive their forms[5] from above, which she in the greatness of her daring inspiring with mind on account of the goodness of the Propator, produced us as their images, having her mind then intent upon the things above, as in a dream,— behold, the judge is at hand, and the crier orders me to make my defence. But do thou, as being acquainted with the affairs of both, present the cause of both of us to the judge, inasmuch as it is in reality but one cause."[6] Now, as soon as the Mother hears these words, she puts the Homeric[7] helmet of Pluto upon them, so that they may invisibly escape the judge. And then she immediately catches them up, conducts them into the bridal chamber, and hands them over to their consorts.

---

[1] [Note this manner of primitive "confession;" and see Bingham, *Antiquities*, book xv. cap. 8.]
[2] We here follow the rendering of Billius, " in iisdem studiis versantes." Others adhere to the received text, and translate περιπολίζοντες " going about idly."
[3] Grabe is of opinion that reference is made in this term to an imprecatory formula in use among the Marcosians, analogous to the form of thanksgiving employed night and morning by the Jews for their redemption from Egypt. Harvey refers the word to the *second* baptism practised among these and other heretics, by which it was supposed they were removed from the cognizance of the Demiurge, who is styled the "judge" in the close of the above sentence.
[4] That is, Sophia, of whom Achamoth, afterwards referred to, was the emanation.
[5] The angels accompanying Soter were the consorts of spiritual Gnostics, to whom they were restored after death.
[6] The syntax in this long sentence is very confused, but the meaning is tolerably plain. The gist of it is, that these Gnostics, as being the spiritual seed, claimed a consubstantiality with Achamoth, and consequently escaped from the material Demiurge, and attained at last to the Pleroma.
[7] Rendering the wearer invisible. See *Il.*, v. 844.

7. Such are the words and deeds by which, in our own district of the Rhone, they have deluded many women, who have their consciences seared as with a hot iron.[1] Some of them, indeed, make a public confession of their sins; but others of them are ashamed to do this, and in a tacit kind of way, despairing of [attaining to] the life of God, have, some of them, apostatized altogether; while others hesitate between the two courses, and incur that which is implied in the proverb, "neither without nor within;" possessing this as the fruit from the seed of the children of knowledge.

CHAP. XIV. — THE VARIOUS HYPOTHESES OF MARCUS AND OTHERS. THEORIES RESPECTING LETTERS AND SYLLABLES.

1. This Marcus[2] then, declaring that he alone was the matrix and receptacle of the Sige of Colorbasus, inasmuch as he was only-begotten, has brought to the birth in some such way as follows that which was committed to him of the defective Enthymesis. He declares that the infinitely exalted Tetrad descended upon him from the invisible and indescribable places in the form of a woman (for the world could not have borne it coming in its male form), and expounded to him alone its own nature, and the origin of all things, which it had never before revealed to any one either of gods or men. This was done in the following terms: When first the unoriginated, inconceivable Father, who is without material substance,[3] and is neither male nor female, willed to bring forth that which is ineffable to Him, and to endow with form that which is invisible, He opened His mouth, and sent forth the Word similar to Himself, who, standing near, showed Him what He Himself was, inasmuch as He had been manifested in the form of that which was invisible. Moreover, the pronunciation of His name took place as follows: — He spake the first word of it, which was the beginning[4] [of all the rest], and that utterance consisted of four letters. He added the second, and this also consisted of four letters. Next He uttered the third, and this again embraced ten letters. Finally, He pronounced the fourth, which was composed of twelve letters. Thus took place the enunciation of the whole name, consisting of thirty letters, and four distinct utterances. Each of these elements has its own peculiar letters, and character, and pronunciation, and forms, and images, and there is not one of them that perceives the shape of that [utterance] of which it is an element. Neither does any one know[5] itself, nor is it acquainted with the pronunciation of its neighbour, but each one imagines that by its own utterance it does in fact name the whole. For while every one of them is a part of the whole, it imagines its own sound to be the whole name, and does not leave off sounding until, by its own utterance, it has reached the last letter of each of the elements. This teacher declares that the restitution of all things will take place, when all these, mixing into one letter, shall utter one and the same sound. He imagines that the emblem of this utterance is found in *Amen*, which we pronounce in concert.[6] The diverse sounds (he adds) are those which give form to that Æon who is without material substance and unbegotten, and these, again, are the forms which the Lord has called angels, who continually behold the face of the Father.[7]

2. Those names of the elements which may be told, and are common, he has called Æons, and words, and roots, and seeds, and fulnesses, and fruits. He asserts that each of these, and all that is peculiar to every one of them, is to be understood as contained in the name Ecclesia. Of these elements, the last letter of the last one uttered its voice, and this sound[8] going forth generated its own elements after the image of the [other] elements, by which he affirms, that both the things here below were arranged into the order they occupy, and those that preceded them were called into existence. He also maintains that the letter itself, the sound of which followed that sound below, was received up again by the syllable to which it belonged, in order to the completion of the whole, but that the sound remained below as if cast outside. But the element itself from which the letter with its special pronunciation descended to that below, he affirms to consist of thirty letters, while each of these letters, again, contains other letters in itself, by means of which the name of the letter is expressed. And thus, again, others are named by other letters, and others still by others, so that the multitude of letters swells out into infinitude. You may more clearly understand what I mean by the following example: — The word *Delta* con-

---

[1] 2 Tim. iii. 6.
[2] This sentence has completely baffled all the critics. [Its banter, or mock gravity, has not been self-evident.] We cannot enter upon the wide field of discussion which it has opened up, but would simply state that Irenæus here seems to us, as often, to be playing upon the terms which were in common use among these heretics. Marcus probably received his system from Colorbasus, and is here declared, by the use of that jargon which Irenæus means to ridicule while so employing it, to have proceeded to develop it in the way described.
[3] Such appears to be the meaning of ἀνούσιος in this passage. The meaning of οὐσία fluctuated for a time in the early Church, and was sometimes used to denote *material substance*, instead of its usual significance of *being*.
[4] The old Latin preserves ἀοχή untranslated, implying that this was the first word which the Father spoke. Some modern editors adopt this view, while others hold the meaning simply to be, as given above, that that first sound which the Father uttered was the origin of all the rest.
[5] The letters are here confounded with the Æons, which they represented.
[6] [1 Cor. xiv. 16.]
[7] Matt. xviii. 10.
[8] By this Achamoth is denoted, who was said to give rise to the material elements, after the image of the Divine.

tains five letters, viz., D, E, L, T, A : these letters, again, are written by other letters,[1] and others still by others. If, then, the entire composition of the word Delta [when thus analyzed] runs out into infinitude, letters continually generating other letters, and following one another in constant succession, how much vaster than that [one] word is the [entire] ocean of letters ! And if even one letter be thus infinite, just consider the immensity of the letters in the entire name; out of which the Sige of Marcus has taught us the Propator is composed. For which reason the Father, knowing the incomprehensibleness of His own nature, assigned to the elements, which He also terms Æons, [the power] of each one uttering its own enunciation, because no one of them was capable by itself of uttering the whole.

3. Moreover, the Tetrad, explaining these things to him more fully, said : — I wish to show thee Aletheia (Truth) herself; for I have brought her down from the dwellings above, that thou mayest see her without a veil, and understand her beauty — that thou mayest also hear her speaking, and admire her wisdom. Behold, then, her head on high, *Alpha* and *Omega;* her neck, *Beta* and *Psi;* her shoulders with her hands, *Gamma* and *Chi;* her breast, *Delta* and *Phi;* her diaphragm, *Epsilon* and *Upsilon;* her back, *Zeta* and *Tau;* her belly, *Eta* and *Sigma;* her thighs, *Theta* and *Rho;* her knees, *Iota* and *Pi;* her legs, *Kappa* and *Omicron;* her ancles, *Lambda* and *Xi;* her feet, *Mu* and *Nu*. Such is the body of Truth, according to this magician, such the figure of the element, such the character of the letter. And he calls this element Anthropos (Man), and says that is the fountain of all speech, and the beginning of all sound, and the expression of all that is unspeakable, and the mouth of the silent Sige. This indeed is the body of Truth. But do thou, elevating the thoughts of thy mind on high, listen from the mouth of Truth to the self-begotten Word, who is also the dispenser of the bounty of the Father.

4. When she (the Tetrad) had spoken these things, Aletheia looked at him, opened her mouth, and uttered a word. That word was a name, and the name was this one which we do know and speak of, viz., Christ Jesus. When she had uttered this name, she at once relapsed into silence. And as Marcus waited in the expectation that she would say something more, the Tetrad again came forward and said, " Thou hast reckoned as contemptible that word which thou hast heard from the mouth of Aletheia. This which thou knowest and seemest to possess, is not an ancient name. For thou possessest the sound of it merely, whilst thou art ignorant of its power. For Jesus ('Ιησοῦς) is a name arithmetically [2] symbolical, consisting of six letters, and is known by all those that belong to the called. But that which is among the Æons of the Pleroma consists of many parts, and is of another form and shape, and is known by those [angels] who are joined in affinity with Him, and whose figures (mightinesses) are always present with Him.

5. Know, then, that the four-and-twenty letters which you possess are symbolical emanations of the three powers that contain the entire number of the elements above. For you are to reckon thus — that the nine mute [3] letters are [the images] of Pater and Aletheia, because they are without voice, that is, of such a nature as cannot be uttered or pronounced. But the semi-vowels [4] represent Logos and Zoe, because they are, as it were, midway between the consonants and the vowels, partaking [5] of the nature of both. The vowels, again, are representative of Anthropos and Ecclesia, inasmuch as a voice proceeding from Anthropos gave being to them all; for the sound of the voice imparted to them form. Thus, then, Logos and Zoe possess eight [of these letters] ; Anthropos and Ecclesia seven ; and Pater and Aletheia nine. But since the number allotted to each was unequal, He who existed in the Father came down, having been specially sent by Him from whom He was separated, for the rectification of what had taken place, that the unity of the Pleromas, being endowed with equality, might develop in all that one power which flows from all. Thus that division which had only seven letters, received the power of eight,[6] and the three sets were rendered alike in point of number, all becoming Ogdoads ; which three, when brought together, constitute the number four-and-twenty. The three elements, too (which he declares to exist in conjunction with three powers,[7] and thus form the six from which have flowed the twenty-four letters), being quadrupled by the word of the ineffable Tetrad, give rise to the same number with them ; and these elements he maintains to belong to Him who cannot be named. These, again, were endowed by the three powers with a resemblance to Him who is invisible. And he says that those letters which we call double [8] are the images of

---

[1] That is, their names are spelt by other letters.

[2] The old Latin version renders ἐπίσημον, *insigne, illustrious,* but there seems to be a reference to the Valentinian notion of the mystic number of 888 formed (10+8+200+70+400+200) by the numerical value of the letters in the word 'Ιησοῦς.

[3] The mutes are π, κ, τ, β, γ, δ, φ, χ, θ.

[4] The semi-vowels are λ, μ, ν, ρ, σ, ζ, ξ, ψ.

[5] It seems scarcely possible to give a more definite rendering of this clause: it may be literally translated thus: " And because they receive the outflow of those above, but the turning back again of those below."

[6] The ninth letter being taken from the mutes and added to the semi-vowels, an equal division of the twenty-four was thus secured.

[7] Viz., Pater, Athropos, and Logos.

[8] Viz., ζ, ξ, ψ = δς, κς, πς.

the images of these elements; and if these be added to the four-and-twenty letters, by the force of analogy they form the number thirty.

6. He asserts that the fruit of this arrangement and analogy has been manifested in the likeness of an image, namely, Him who, after six days, ascended[1] into the mountain along with three others, and then became one of six (the sixth),[2] in which character He descended, and was contained in the Hebdomad, since He was the illustrious Ogdoad,[3] and contained in Himself the entire number of the elements, which the descent of the dove (who is Alpha and Omega) made clearly manifest, when He came to be baptized; for the number of the dove is eight hundred and one.[4] And for this reason did Moses declare that man was formed on the sixth day; and then, again, according to arrangement, it was on the sixth day, which is the preparation, that the last man appeared, for the regeneration of the first. Of this arrangement, both the beginning and the end were formed at that sixth hour, at which He was nailed to the tree. For that perfect being Nous, knowing that the number six had the power both of formation and regeneration, declared to the children of light, that regeneration which has been wrought out by Him who appeared as the *Episemon* in regard to that number. Whence also he declares it is that the double letters[5] contain the Episemon number; for this Episemon, when joined to the twenty-four elements, completed the name of thirty letters.

7. He employed as his instrument, as the Sige of Marcus declares, the power of seven letters,[6] in order that the fruit of the independent will [of Achamoth] might be revealed. "Consider this present *Episemon*," she says — "Him who was formed after the [original] *Episemon*, as being, as it were, divided or cut into two parts, and remaining outside; who, by His own power and wisdom, through means of that which had been produced by Himself, gave life to this world, consisting of seven powers,[7] after the likeness of the power of the Hebdomad, and so formed it, that it is the soul of everything visible. And He indeed uses this work Himself as if it had been formed by His own free will; but the rest, as being images of what cannot be [fully] imitated, are subservient to the Enthymesis of the mother. And the first heaven indeed pronounces *Alpha*, the next to this *Epsilon*, the third *Eta*, the fourth, which is also in the midst of the seven, utters the sound of *Iota*, the fifth *Omicron*, the sixth *Upsilon*, the seventh, which is also the fourth from the middle, utters the elegant *Omega*," — as the Sige of Marcus, talking a deal of nonsense, but uttering no word of truth, confidently asserts. "And these powers," she adds, "being all simultaneously clasped in each other's embrace, do sound out the glory of Him by whom they were produced; and the glory of that sound is transmitted upwards to the Propator." She asserts, moreover, that "the sound of this uttering of praise, having been wafted to the earth, has become the Framer and the Parent of those things which are on the earth."

8. He instances, in proof of this, the case of infants who have just been born, the cry of whom, as soon as they have issued from the womb, is in accordance with the sound of every one of these elements. As, then, he says, the seven powers glorify the Word, so also does the complaining soul of infants.[8] For this reason, too, David said: "Out of the mouth of babes and sucklings Thou hast perfected praise;"[9] and again: "The heavens declare the glory of God."[10] Hence also it comes to pass, that when the soul is involved in difficulties and distresses, for its own relief it calls out, "Oh" (Ω), in honour of the letter in question,[11] so that its cognate soul above may recognise [its distress], and send down to it relief.

9. Thus it is, that in regard to the whole name,[12] which consists of thirty letters, and Bythus, who receives his increase from the letters of this [name], and, moreover, the body of Aletheia, which is composed of twelve members, each of which consists of two letters, and the voice which she uttered without having spoken at all, and in regard to the analysis of that name which cannot be expressed in words, and the soul of the world and of man, according as they possess that arrangement, which is after the image [of things above], he has uttered his nonsensical opinions. It remains that I relate how the Tetrad showed him from the names a power equal in number; so that nothing, my friend, which I have received as spoken by him, may remain unknown to thee; and thus thy request, often proposed to me, may be fulfilled.

---

[1] Matt. xvii. 7; Mark ix. 2.
[2] Moses and Elias being added to the company.
[3] Referring to the word Χρειστός, according to Harvey, who remarks, that "generally the Ogdoad was the receptacle of the spiritual seed."
[4] The Saviour, as Alpha and Omega, was symbolized by the dove, the sum of the Greek numerals, π, ε, ρ, ι, σ, τ, ε, ρ, α (περιστερά, *dove*), being, like that of Α and Ω, 801.
[5] That is, the letters ζ, ξ, ψ all contain ς, whose value is *six*, and which was called ἐπίσημον by the Greeks.
[6] Referring to *Aletheia*, which, in Greek, contains seven letters.
[7] By these seven powers are meant the seven heavens (also called angels), formed by the Demiurge.

[8] We here follow the text of Hippolytus: the ordinary text and the old Latin read, "So does the soul of infants, weeping and mourning over Marcus, deify him."
[9] Ps. viii. 2.
[10] Ps. xix. 1.
[11] The text is here altogether uncertain: we have given the probable meaning.
[12] That is, the name of Soter, the perfect result of the whole Pleroma.

CHAP. XV.—SIGE RELATES TO MARCUS THE GENERATION OF THE TWENTY-FOUR ELEMENTS AND OF JESUS. EXPOSURE OF THESE ABSURDITIES.

1. The all-wise Sige then announced the production of the four-and-twenty elements to him as follows:—Along with Monotes there co-existed Henotes, from which sprang two productions, as we have remarked above, Monas and Hen, which, added to the other two, make four, for twice two are four. And again, two and four, when added together, exhibit the number six. And further, these six being quadrupled, give rise to the twenty-four forms. And the names of the first Tetrad, which are understood to be most holy, and not capable of being expressed in words, are known by the Son alone, while the father also knows what they are. The other names which are to be uttered with respect, and faith, and reverence, are, according to him, Arrhetos and Sige, Pater and Aletheia. Now the entire number of this Tetrad amounts to four-and-twenty letters; for the name Arrhetos contains in itself seven letters, Seige[1] five, Pater five, and Aletheia seven. If all these be added together —twice five, and twice seven—they complete the number twenty-four. In like manner, also, the second Tetrad, Logos and Zoe, Anthropos and Ecclesia, reveal the same number of elements. Moreover, that name of the Saviour which may be pronounced, viz., Jesus ['Ιησοῦς], consists of six letters, but His unutterable name comprises four-and-twenty letters. The name Christ the Son[2] (υἱὸς Χρειστός) comprises twelve letters, but that which is unpronounceable in Christ contains thirty letters. And for this reason he declares that He is *Alpha* and *Omega*, that he may indicate the dove, inasmuch as that bird has this number [in its name].

2. But Jesus, he affirms, has the following unspeakable origin. From the mother of all things, that is, the first Tetrad, there came forth the second Tetrad, after the manner of a daughter; and thus an Ogdoad was formed, from which, again, a Decad proceeded: thus was produced a Decad and an Ogdoad. The Decad, then, being joined with the Ogdoad, and multiplying it ten times, gave rise to the number *eighty;* and, again, multiplying eighty ten times, produced the number *eight hundred*. Thus, then, the whole number of the letters proceeding from the Ogdoad [multiplied] into the Decad, is eight hundred and eighty-eight.[3] This is the name of Jesus; for this name, if you reckon up the numerical value of the letters, amounts to eight hundred and eighty-eight. Thus, then, you have a clear statement of their opinion as to the origin of the supercelestial Jesus. Wherefore, also, the alphabet of the Greeks contains eight Monads, eight Decads, and eight Hecatads[4], which present the number eight hundred and eighty-eight, that is, *Jesus*, who is formed of all numbers; and on this account He is called *Alpha* and *Omega*, indicating His origin from all. And, again, they put the matter thus: If the first Tetrad be added up according to the progression of number, the number ten appears. For one, and two, and three, and four, when added together, form ten; and this, as they will have it, is Jesus. Moreover, Chreistus, he says, being a word of eight letters, indicates the first Ogdoad, and this, when multiplied by ten, gives birth to Jesus (888). And Christ the Son, he says, is also spoken of, that is, the Duodecad. For the name Son, (υἱός) contains four letters, and Christ (Chreistus) eight, which, being combined, point out the greatness of the Duodecad. But, he alleges, before the *Episemon* of this name appeared, that is Jesus the Son, mankind were involved in great ignorance and error. But when this name of six letters was manifested (the person bearing it clothing Himself in flesh, that He might come under the apprehension of man's senses, and having in Himself these six and twenty-four letters), then, becoming acquainted with Him, they ceased from their ignorance, and passed from death unto life, this name serving as their guide to the Father of truth.[5] For the Father of all had resolved to put an end to ignorance, and to destroy death. But this abolishing of ignorance was just the knowledge of Him. And therefore that man (Anthropos) was chosen according to His will, having been formed after the image of the [corresponding] power above.

3. As to the Æons, they proceeded from the Tetrad, and in that Tetrad were Anthropos and Ecclesia, Logos and Zoe. The powers, then, he declares, who emanated from these, generated that Jesus who appeared upon the earth. The angel Gabriel took the place of Logos, the Holy Spirit that of Zoe, the Power of the Highest that of Anthropos, while the Virgin pointed out the place of Ecclesia. And thus, by a special dispensation, there was generated by Him, through Mary, that man, whom, as He passed through the womb, the Father of all chose to [obtain] the knowledge of Himself by means of the Word. And on His coming to the water [of baptism], there descended on Him, in the form of a dove,

---

[1] Manifestly to be so spelt here, as in the sequel *Chreistus*, for Christus.
[2] The text is here altogether uncertain, and the meaning obscure.
[3] The reading is exceedingly doubtful: some prefer the number *eighty-eight*.
[4] There were, as Harvey here observes, three extraneous characters introduced into the Greek alphabet for the sake of numeration — the three *episema* for 6, 90, and 900 respectively. The true alphabet, then, as employed to denote number, included eight units, eight tens, and eight hundreds.
[5] Or, according to the Greek text, "being as the way to the Father;" comp. John xiv. 6.

that Being who had formerly ascended on high, and completed the twelfth number, in whom there existed the seed of those who were produced contemporaneously with Himself, and who descended and ascended along with Him. Moreover, he maintains that that power which descended was the seed of the Father, which had in itself both the Father and the Son, as well as that power of Sige which is known by means of them, but cannot be expressed in language, and also all the Æons. And this was that Spirit who spoke by the mouth of Jesus, and who confessed that He was the son of Man as well as revealed the Father, and who, having descended into Jesus, was made one with Him. And he says that the Saviour formed by special dispensation did indeed destroy death, but that Christ made known the Father.[1] He maintains, therefore, that Jesus is the name of that man formed by a special dispensation, and that He was formed after the likeness and form of that [heavenly] Anthropos, who was about to descend upon Him. After He had received that Æon, He possessed Anthropos himself, and Logos himself, and Pater, and Arrhetus, and Sige, and Aletheia, and Ecclesia, and Zoe.

4. Such ravings, we may now well say, go beyond *Iu, Iu, Pheu, Pheu,* and every kind of tragic exclamation or utterance of misery.[2] For who would not detest one who is the wretched contriver of such audacious falsehoods, when he perceives the truth turned by Marcus into a mere image, and that punctured all over with the letters of the alphabet? The Greeks confess that they first received sixteen letters from Cadmus, and that but recently, as compared with the beginning, [the vast antiquity of which is implied] in the common proverb: "Yesterday and before;"[3] and afterwards, in the course of time, they themselves invented at one period the aspirates, and at another the double letters, while, last of all, they say Palamedes added the long letters to the former. Was it so, then, that until these things took place among the Greeks, truth had no existence? For, according to thee, Marcus, the body of truth is posterior to Cadmus and those who preceded him — posterior also to those who added the rest of the letters — posterior even to thyself! For thou alone hast formed that which is called by thee the truth into an [outward, visible] image.

5. But who will tolerate thy nonsensical Sige, who names Him that cannot be named, and expounds the nature of Him that is unspeakable, and searches out Him that is unsearchable, and declares that He whom thou maintainest to be destitute of body and form, opened His mouth and sent forth the Word, as if He were included among organized beings; and that His Word, while like to His Author, and bearing the image of the invisible, nevertheless consisted of thirty elements and four syllables? It will follow, then, according to thy theory, that the Father of all, in accordance with the likeness of the Word, consists of thirty elements and four syllables! Or, again, who will tolerate thee in thy juggling with forms and numbers, — at one time thirty, at another twenty-four, and at another, again, only six, — whilst thou shuttest up [in these] the Word of God, the Founder, and Framer, and Maker of all things; and then, again, cutting Him up piecemeal into four syllables and thirty elements; and bringing down the Lord of all who founded the heavens to the number eight hundred and eighty-eight, so that He should be similar to the alphabet; and subdividing the Father, who cannot be contained, but contains all things, into a Tetrad, and an Ogdoad, and a Decad, and a Duodecad; and by such multiplications, setting forth the unspeakable and inconceivable nature of the Father, as thou thyself declarest it to be? And showing thyself a very Dædalus for evil invention, and the wicked architect of the supreme power, thou dost construct a nature and substance for Him whom thou callest incorporeal and immaterial, out of a multitude of letters, generated the one by the other. And that power whom thou affirmest to be indivisible, thou dost nevertheless divide into consonants, and vowels, and semivowels; and, falsely ascribing those letters which are mute to the Father of all things, and to His Ennœa (thought), thou hast driven on all that place confidence in thee to the highest point of blasphemy, and to the grossest impiety.[4]

6. With good reason, therefore, and very fittingly, in reference to thy rash attempt, has that divine elder[5] and preacher of the truth burst forth in verse against thee as follows: —

"Marcus, thou former of idols, inspector of portents,
Skill'd in consulting the stars, and deep in the black arts of magic,
Ever by tricks such as these confirming the doctrines of error,
Furnishing signs unto those involved by thee in deception,
Wonders of power that is utterly severed from God and apostate,
Which Satan, thy true father, enables thee still to accomplish,
By means of Azazel, that fallen and yet mighty angel, —
Thus making thee the precursor of his own impious actions."

Such are the words of the saintly elder. And I shall endeavour to state the remainder of their mystical system, which runs out to great length, in brief compass, and to bring to the light what

---

[1] The text is here uncertain: we follow that suggested by Grabe.
[2] [Comp. cap. xi. 4, *supra*.]
[3] Comp. Gen. xxxi. 2. — We here follow the punctuation of Scaliger, now generally accepted by the editors, though entirely different from the old Latin.
[4] [Mosheim thinks this Marcus was a lunatic.]
[5] [Some think Pothinus.]

has for a long time been concealed. For in this way such things will become easily susceptible of exposure by all.

CHAP. XVI. — ABSURD INTERPRETATIONS OF THE MARCOSIANS.

1. Blending in one the production of their own Æons, and the straying and recovery of the sheep [spoken of in the Gospel [1]], these persons endeavour to set forth things in a more mystical style, while they refer everything to numbers, maintaining that the universe has been formed out of a Monad and a Dyad. And then, reckoning from unity on to four, they thus generate the Decad. For when one, two, three, and four are added together, they give rise to the number of the ten Æons. And, again, the Dyad advancing from itself [by twos] up to six — two, and four, and six — brings out the Duodecad. Once more, if we reckon in the same way up to ten, the number thirty appears, in which are found eight, and ten, and twelve. They therefore term the Duodecad — because it contains the Episemon,[2] and because the Episemon [so to speak] waits upon it — the passion. And for this reason, because an error occurred in connection with the twelfth number,[3] the sheep frisked off, and went astray; for they assert that a defection took place from the Duodecad. In the same way they oracularly declare, that one power having departed also from the Duodecad, has perished; and this was represented by the woman who lost the drachma,[4] and, lighting a lamp, again found it. Thus, therefore, the numbers that were left, viz., nine, as respects the pieces of money, and eleven in regard to the sheep,[5] when multiplied together, give birth to the number ninety-nine, for nine times eleven are ninety-nine. Wherefore also they maintain the word "Amen" contains this number.

2. I will not, however, weary thee by recounting their other interpretations, that you may perceive the results everywhere. They maintain, for instance, that the letter *Eta* (η) along with the *Episemon* (ς) constitutes an Ogdoad, inasmuch as it occupies the eighth place from the first letter. Then, again, without the *Episemon*, reckoning the number of the letters, and adding them up till we come to *Eta*, they bring out the Triacontad. For if one begins at *Alpha* and ends with *Eta*, omitting the *Episemon*, and adds together the value of the letters in succession, he will find their number altogether to amount to thirty. For up to *Epsilon* (ϵ) fifteen are formed; then adding seven to that number, the sum of twenty-two is reached. Next, *Eta* being added to these, since its value is eight, the most wonderful Triacontad is completed. And hence they give forth that the Ogdoad is the mother of the thirty Æons. Since, therefore, the number thirty is composed of three powers [the Ogdoad, Decad, and Duodecad], when multiplied by three, it produces ninety, for three times thirty are ninety. Likewise this Triad, when multiplied by itself, gives rise to nine. Thus the Ogdoad generates, by these means, ninety-nine. And since the twelfth Æon, by her defection, left eleven in the heights above, they maintain that therefore the position of the letters is a true co-ordinate of the method of their calculation [6] (for Lambda is the eleventh in order among the letters, and represents the number thirty), and also forms a representation of the arrangement of affairs above, since, on from Alpha, omitting *Episemon*, the number of the letters up to Lambda, when added together according to the successive value of the letters, and including *Lambda* itself, forms the sum of ninety-nine; but that this *Lambda*, being the eleventh in order, descended to seek after one equal to itself, so as to complete the number of twelve letters, and when it found such a one, the number was completed, is manifest from the very configuration of the letter; for *Lambda* being engaged, as it were, in the quest of one similar to itself, and finding such an one, and clasping it to itself, thus filled up the place of the twelfth, the letter *Mu* (M) being composed of two *Lambdas* (ΛΛ). Wherefore also they, by means of their "knowledge," avoid the place of ninety-nine, that is, the defection — a type of the left hand,[7] — but endeavour to secure *one* more, which, when added to the ninety and nine, has the effect of changing their reckoning to the right hand.

3. I well know, my dear friend, that when thou hast read through all this, thou wilt indulge in a hearty laugh over this their inflated wise folly! But those men are really worthy of being mourned over, who promulgate such a kind of religion, and who so frigidly and perversely pull to pieces the greatness of the truly unspeakable power, and the dispensations of God in themselves so striking, by means of Alpha and Beta, and through the aid of numbers. But as many as separate from the Church, and give heed to such old wives' fables as these, are truly self-condemned; and these men Paul commands us, "after a first and second admonition, to avoid." [8]

---

[1] Luke xv. 4.
[2] All the editors, Grabe, Massuet, Stieren, and Harvey, differ as to the text and interpretation of this sentence. We have given what seems the simplest rendering of the text as it stands.
[3] Referring to the last of the twelve Æons.
[4] Luke xv. 8.
[5] Meaning the Æon who left the Duodecad, when eleven remained, and not referring to the lost sheep of the parable.
[6] Harvey gives the above paraphrase of the very obscure original; others propose to read λ' instead of λόγου.
[7] Massuet explains this and the following reference, by remarking that the ancients used the fingers of the hand in counting; by the left hand they indicated all the numbers below a hundred, but by the right hand all above that sum. — Comp. Juvenal, *Sat.*, x. 249.
[8] Tit. iii. 10.

And John, the disciple of the Lord, has intensified their condemnation, when he desires us not even to address to them the salutation of "good-speed;" for, says he, "He that bids them be of good-speed is a partaker with their evil deeds;"[1] and that with reason, "for there is no good-speed to the ungodly,"[2] saith the LORD. Impious indeed, beyond all impiety, are these men, who assert that the Maker of heaven and earth, the only God Almighty, besides whom there is no God, was produced by means of a defect, which itself sprang from another defect, so that, according to them, He was the product of the third defect.[3] Such an opinion we should detest and execrate, while we ought everywhere to flee far apart from those that hold it; and in proportion as they vehemently maintain and rejoice in their fictitious doctrines, so much the more should we be convinced that they are under the influence of the wicked spirits of the Ogdoad, — just as those persons who fall into a fit of frenzy, the more they laugh, and imagine themselves to be well, and do all things as if they were in good health [both of body and mind], yea, some things better than those who really are so, are only thus shown to be the more seriously diseased. In like manner do these men, the more they seem to excel others in wisdom, and waste their strength by drawing the bow too tightly,[4] the greater fools do they show themselves. For when the unclean spirit of folly has gone forth, and when afterwards he finds them not waiting upon God, but occupied with mere worldly questions, then, "taking seven other spirits more wicked than himself,"[5] and inflating the minds of these men with the notion of their being able to conceive of something beyond God, and having fitly prepared them for the reception of deceit, he implants within them the Ogdoad of the foolish spirits of wickedness.

CHAP. XVII. — THE THEORY OF THE MARCOSIANS, THAT CREATED THINGS WERE MADE AFTER THE IMAGE OF THINGS INVISIBLE.

1. I wish also to explain to thee their theory as to the way in which the creation itself was formed through the mother by the Demiurge (as it were without his knowledge), after the image of things invisible. They maintain, then, that first of all the four elements, fire, water, earth, and air, were produced after the image of the primary Tetrad above, and that then, if we add their operations, viz., heat, cold, dryness, and humidity, an exact likeness of the Ogdoad is presented. They next reckon up ten powers in the following manner: — There are seven globular bodies, which they also call heavens; then that globular body which contains these, which also they name the eighth heaven; and, in addition to these, the sun and moon. These, being ten in number, they declare to be types of the invisible Decad, which proceeded from Logos and Zoe. As to the Duodecad, it is indicated by the zodiacal circle, as it is called; for they affirm that the twelve signs do most manifestly shadow forth the Duodecad, the daughter of Anthropos and Ecclesia. And since the highest heaven, bearing upon the very sphere [of the seventh heaven], has been linked with the most rapid precession of the whole system, as a check, and balancing that system with its own gravity, so that it completes the cycle from sign to sign in thirty years, — they say that this is an image of Horus, encircling their thirty-named mother.[6] And then, again, as the moon travels through her allotted space of heaven in thirty days, they hold, that by these days she expresses the number of the thirty Æons. The sun also, who runs through his orbit in twelve months, and then returns to the same point in the circle, makes the Duodecad manifest by these twelve months; and the days, as being measured by twelve hours, are a type of the invisible Duodecad. Moreover, they declare that the hour, which is the twelfth part of the day, is composed[7] of thirty parts, in order to set forth the image of the Triacontad. Also the circumference of the zodiacal circle itself contains three hundred and sixty degrees (for each of its signs comprises thirty); and thus also they affirm, that by means of this circle an image is preserved of that connection which exists between the twelve and the thirty. Still further, asserting that the earth is divided into twelve zones, and that in each zone it receives power from the heavens, according to the perpendicular [position of the sun above it], bringing forth productions corresponding to that power which sends down its influence upon it, they maintain that this is a most evident type of the Duodecad and its offspring.

2. In addition to these things, they declare that the Demiurge, desiring to imitate the infinitude, and eternity, and immensity, and freedom from all measurement by time of the Ogdoad above, but, as he was the fruit of defect, being unable to express its permanence and eternity, had recourse to the expedient of spreading out its eternity into times, and seasons, and vast numbers of years, imagining, that by the multitude of such times he might imitate its immen-

---

[1] 2 John 10, 11.
[2] Isa. xlviii. 22.
[3] The Demiurge being the fruit of the abortive conversion of the abortive passion of Achamoth, who, again, was the abortive issue of Sophia.
[4] i.e., by aiming at what transcends their ability, they fall into absurdity, as a bow is broken by bending it too far.
[5] Matt. xii. 43.

[6] Such is the translation which Harvey, following the text preserved by Hippolytus, gives of the above intricate and obscure sentence.
[7] Literally, "is adorned with."

sity. They declare further, that the truth having escaped him, he followed that which was false, and that, for this reason, when the times are fulfilled, his work shall perish.

CHAP. XVIII. — PASSAGES FROM MOSES, WHICH THE HERETICS PERVERT TO THE SUPPORT OF THEIR HYPOTHESIS.

1. And while they affirm such things as these concerning the creation, every one of them generates something new, day by day, according to his ability; for no one is deemed "perfect," who does not develop among them some mighty fictions. It is thus necessary, first, to indicate what things they metamorphose [to their own use] out of the prophetical writings, and next, to refute them. Moses, then, they declare, by his mode of beginning the account of the creation, has at the commencement pointed out the mother of all things when he says, " In the beginning God created the heaven and the earth;"[1] for, as they maintain, by naming these four, — God, beginning, heaven, and earth, — he set forth their Tetrad. Indicating also its invisible and hidden nature, he said, " Now the earth was invisible and unformed."[2] They will have it, moreover, that he spoke of the second Tetrad, the offspring of the first, in this way — by naming an abyss and darkness, in which were also water, and the Spirit moving upon the water. Then, proceeding to mention the Decad, he names light, day, night, the firmament, the evening, the morning, dry land, sea, plants, and, in the tenth place, trees. Thus, by means of these ten names, he indicated the ten Æons. The power of the Duodecad, again, was shadowed forth by him thus: — He names the sun, moon, stars, seasons, years, whales, fishes, reptiles, birds, quadrupeds, wild beasts, and after all these, in the twelfth place, man. Thus they teach that the Triacontad was spoken of through Moses by the Spirit. Moreover, man also, being formed after the image of the power above, had in himself that ability which flows from the one source. This ability was seated in the region of the brain, from which four faculties proceed, after the image of the Tetrad above, and these are called: the first, *sight*, the second, *hearing*, the third, *smell*, and the fourth,[3] *taste*. And they say that the Ogdoad is indicated by man in this way: that he possesses two ears, the like number of eyes, also two nostrils, and a twofold taste, namely, of bitter and sweet. Moreover, they teach that the whole man contains the entire image of the Triacontad as follows: In his hands, by means of his fingers, he bears the Decad; and in his whole body the Duodecad, inasmuch as his body is divided into twelve members; for they portion that out, as the body of Truth is divided by them — a point of which we have already spoken.[4] But the Ogdoad, as being unspeakable and invisible, is understood as hidden in the viscera.

2. Again, they assert that the sun, the great light-giver, was formed on the fourth day, with a reference to the number of the Tetrad. So also, according to them, the courts[5] of the tabernacle constructed by Moses, being composed of fine linen, and blue, and purple, and scarlet, pointed to the same image. Moreover, they maintain that the long robe of the priest falling over his feet, as being adorned with four rows of precious stones,[6] indicates the Tetrad; and if there are any other things in the Scriptures which can possibly be dragged into the number *four*, they declare that these had their being with a view to the Tetrad. The Ogdoad, again, was shown as follows: — They affirm that man was formed on the eighth day, for sometimes they will have him to have been made on the sixth day, and sometimes on the eighth, unless, perchance, they mean that his earthly part was formed on the sixth day, but his fleshly part on the eighth, for these two things are distinguished by them. Some of them also hold that one man was formed after the image and likeness of God, masculo-feminine, and that this was the spiritual man; and that another man was formed out of the earth.

3. Further, they declare that the arrangement made with respect to the ark in the Deluge, by means of which eight persons were saved,[7] most clearly indicates the Ogdoad which brings salvation. David also shows forth the same, as holding the eighth place in point of age among his brethren.[8] Moreover, that circumcision which took place on the eighth day,[9] represented the circumcision of the Ogdoad above. In a word, whatever they find in the Scriptures capable of being referred to the number *eight*, they declare to fulfil the mystery of the Ogdoad. With respect, again, to the Decad, they maintain that it is indicated by those ten nations which God promised to Abraham for a possession.[10] The arrangement also made by Sarah when, after ten years, she gave[11] her handmaid Hagar to him, that by her he might have a son, showed the same thing. Moreover, the servant of Abraham who was sent to Rebekah, and presented her at the well with ten bracelets of gold, and her

---

[1] Gen. i. 1.
[2] Gen. i. 2.
[3] One of the senses was thus capriciously cancelled by these heretics.
[4] See above, chap. xiv. 2.
[5] Or, rather, perhaps "curtains." Ex. xxvi. 1.
[6] Ex. xxviii. 17.
[7] Gen. vi. 18; 1 Pet. iii. 20.
[8] 1 Sam. xvi. 10.
[9] Gen. xvii. 12.
[10] Gen. xv. 19.
[11] Gen. xvi. 2.

brethren who detained her for ten days;[1] Jeroboam also, who received the ten sceptres[2] (tribes), and the ten courts[3] of the tabernacle, and the columns of ten cubits[4] [high], and the ten sons of Jacob who were at first sent into Egypt to buy corn,[5] and the ten apostles to whom the Lord appeared after His resurrection, — Thomas[6] being absent, — represented, according to them, the invisible Decad.

4. As to the Duodecad, in connection with which the mystery of the passion of the defect occurred, from which passion they maintain that all things visible were framed, they assert that is to be found strikingly and manifestly everywhere [in Scripture]. For they declare that the twelve sons of Jacob,[7] from whom also sprung twelve tribes, — the breastplate of the high priest, which bore twelve precious stones and twelve little bells,[8] — the twelve stones which were placed by Moses at the foot of the mountain,[9] — the same number which was placed by Joshua in the river,[10] and again, on the other side, the bearers of the ark of the covenant,[11] — those stones which were set up by Elijah when the heifer was offered as a burnt-offering;[12] the number, too, of the apostles; and, in fine, every event which embraces in it the number *twelve*, — set forth their Duodecad. And then the union of all these, which is called the Triacontad, they strenuously endeavour to demonstrate by the ark of Noah, the height of which was thirty cubits;[13] by the case of Samuel, who assigned Saul the chief place among thirty guests;[14] by David, when for thirty days he concealed himself in the field;[15] by those who entered along with him into the cave; also by the fact that the length (height) of the holy tabernacle was thirty cubits;[16] and if they meet with any other like numbers, they still apply these to their Triacontad.

CHAP. XIX. — PASSAGES OF SCRIPTURE BY WHICH THEY ATTEMPT TO PROVE THAT THE SUPREME FATHER WAS UNKNOWN BEFORE THE COMING OF CHRIST.

1. I judge it necessary to add to these details also what, by garbling passages of Scripture, they try to persuade us concerning their Propator, who was unknown to all before the coming of Christ. Their object in this is to show that our Lord announced another Father than the Maker of this universe, whom, as we said before, they impiously declare to have been the fruit of a defect. For instance, when the prophet Isaiah says, " But Israel hath not known Me, and My people have not understood Me,"[17] they pervert his words to mean ignorance of the invisible Bythus. And that which is spoken by Hosea, "There is no truth in them, nor the knowledge of God,"[18] they strive to give the same reference. And, "There is none that understandeth, or that seeketh after God: they have all gone out of the way, they are together become unprofitable,"[19] they maintain to be said concerning ignorance of Bythus. Also that which is spoken by Moses, "No man shall see God and live,"[20] has, as they would persuade us, the same reference.

2. For they falsely hold, that the Creator was seen by the prophets. But this passage, "No man shall see God and live," they would interpret as spoken of His greatness unseen and unknown by all; and indeed that these words, "No man shall see God," are spoken concerning the invisible Father, the Maker of the universe, is evident to us all; but that they are not used concerning that Bythus whom they conjure into existence, but concerning the Creator (and He is the invisible God), shall be shown as we proceed. They maintain that Daniel also set forth the same thing when he begged of the angels explanations of the parables, as being himself ignorant of them. But the angel, hiding from him the great mystery of Bythus, said unto him, "Go thy way quickly, Daniel, for these sayings are closed up until those who have understanding do understand them, and those who are white be made white."[21] Moreover, they vaunt themselves as being the *white* and the men of *good understanding*.

CHAP. XX. — THE APOCRYPHAL AND SPURIOUS SCRIPTURES OF THE MARCOSIANS, WITH PASSAGES OF THE GOSPELS WHICH THEY PERVERT.

1. Besides the above [misrepresentations], they adduce an unspeakable number of apocryphal and spurious writings, which they themselves have forged, to bewilder the minds of foolish men, and of such as are ignorant of the Scriptures of truth. Among other things, they bring forward that false and wicked story[22] which

---

[1] Gen. xxiv. 22, 25.
[2] 1 Kings xi. 31.
[3] Ex. xxvi. 1, xxxvi. 8.
[4] Ex. xxxvi. 21.
[5] Gen. xlii. 3.
[6] John xx. 24.
[7] Gen. xxxv. 22, xlix. 28.
[8] Ex. xxviii. 2. — There is no mention of the *number* of the bells in Scripture.
[9] Ex. xxiv. 4.
[10] Josh. iv. 3.
[11] Josh. iii. 12.
[12] 1 Kings xviii. 31.
[13] Gen. vi. 15.
[14] 1 Sam. ix. 22.
[15] 1 Sam. xx. 5.
[16] Ex. xxvi. 8. *Numbers* appear to have been often capriciously introduced by these heretics to give a colour of support to their own theories.
[17] Isa. i. 3.
[18] Hos. iv. 1.
[19] Rom. iii. 11; Ps. xiv. 3.
[20] Ex. xxxiii. 20.
[21] Dan. xii. 9, 10. The words in the above quotation not occurring in the Hebrew text of the passage, seem to have been interpolated by these heretics.
[22] [From the *Protevangel of Thomas*. Compare the curious work of Dominic Deodati, *De Christo Græce loquente*, p. 95. London, 1843.]

relates that our Lord, when He was a boy learning His letters, on the teacher saying to Him, as is usual, "Pronounce Alpha," replied [as He was bid], "Alpha." But when, again, the teacher bade Him say, "Beta," the Lord replied, "Do thou first tell me what Alpha is, and then I will tell thee what Beta is." This they expound as meaning that He alone knew the Unknown, which He revealed under its type Alpha.

2. Some passages, also, which occur in the Gospels, receive from them a colouring of the same kind, such as the answer which He gave His mother when He was twelve years of age: "Wist ye not that I must be about My Father's business?"[1] Thus, they say, He announced to them the Father of whom they were ignorant. On this account, also, He sent forth the disciples to the twelve tribes, that they might proclaim to them the unknown God. And to the person who said to Him, "Good Master,"[2] He confessed that God who is truly good, saying, "Why callest thou Me good: there is One who is good, the Father in the heavens;"[3] and they assert that in this passage the Æons receive the name of heavens. Moreover, by His not replying to those who said to Him, "By what power doest Thou this?"[4] but by a question on His own side, put them to utter confusion; by His thus not replying, according to their interpretation, He showed the unutterable nature of the Father. Moreover, when He said, "I have often desired to hear one of these words, and I had no one who could utter it,"[5] they maintain, that by this expression "one" He set forth the one true God whom they knew not. Further, when, as He drew nigh to Jerusalem, He wept over it and said, "If thou hadst known, even thou, in this thy day, the things that belong unto thy peace, but they are hidden from thee,"[6] by this word "hidden" He showed the abstruse nature of Bythus. And again, when He said, "Come unto Me all ye that labour and are heavy laden, and I will give you rest, and learn of Me,"[7] He announced the Father of truth. For what they knew not, these men say that He promised to teach them.

3. But they adduce the following passage as the highest testimony,[8] and, as it were, the very crown of their system: — "I thank Thee, O Father, Lord of heaven and earth, because Thou hast hid these things from the wise and prudent, and hast revealed them to babes. Even so, my Father; for so it seemed good in Thy sight. All things have been delivered to Me by My Father; and no one knoweth the Father but the Son, or the Son but the Father, and he to whom the Son will reveal Him."[9] In these words they affirm that He clearly showed that the Father of truth, conjured into existence by them, was known to no one before His advent. And they desire to construe the passage as if teaching that the Maker and Framer [of the world] was always known by all, while the Lord spoke these words concerning the Father unknown to all, whom they now proclaim.

CHAP. XXI. — THE VIEWS OF REDEMPTION ENTERTAINED BY THESE HERETICS.

1. It happens that their tradition respecting *redemption*[10] is invisible and incomprehensible, as being the mother of things which are incomprehensible and invisible; and on this account, since it is fluctuating, it is impossible simply and all at once to make known its nature, for every one of them hands it down just as his own inclination prompts. Thus there are as many schemes of "redemption" as there are teachers of these mystical opinions. And when we come to refute them, we shall show in its fitting-place, that this class of men have been instigated by Satan to a denial of that baptism which is regeneration to God, and thus to a renunciation of the whole [Christian] faith.

2. They maintain that those who have attained to perfect knowledge must of necessity be regenerated into that power which is above all. For it is otherwise impossible to find admittance within the Pleroma, since this [regeneration] it is which leads them down into the depths of Bythus. For the baptism instituted by the visible Jesus was for the remission of sins, but the redemption brought in by that Christ who descended upon Him, was for perfection; and they allege that the former is animal, but the latter spiritual. And the baptism of John was proclaimed with a view to repentance, but the redemption by Jesus[11] was brought in for the sake of perfection. And to this He refers when He says, "And I have another baptism to be baptized with, and I hasten eagerly towards it."[12] Moreover, they affirm that the Lord added this redemption to the sons of Zebedee, when their mother asked that they might sit, the one on His right hand, and the other on His left, in His kingdom, saying, "Can ye be baptized with the baptism which I shall be baptized with?"[13] Paul, too, they declare, has often set forth, in express terms, the redemption which is in Christ

---

[1] Luke ii. 49.
[2] Mark x. 17.
[3] Luke xviii. 18.
[4] Matt. xxi. 23.
[5] Taken from some apocryphal writing.
[6] Luke xix. 42, loosely quoted.
[7] Matt. xi. 28.
[8] The translator evidently read τῶν for τήν, in which case the rendering will be "proof of those most high," but the Greek text seems preferable.
[9] Matt. xi. 25–27.
[10] Comp. chap. xiii. 6.
[11] The Latin reads "Christ."
[12] Luke xii. 50. The text was probably thus corrupted by the heretics.
[13] Mark x. 38.

Jesus; and this was the same which is handed down by them in so varied and discordant forms.

3. For some of them prepare a nuptial couch, and perform a sort of mystic rite (pronouncing certain expressions) with those who are being initiated, and affirm that it is a spiritual marriage which is celebrated by them, after the likeness of the conjunctions above. Others, again, lead them to a place where water is, and baptize them, with the utterance of these words, "Into the name of the unknown Father of the universe — into truth, the mother of all things — into Him who descended on Jesus — into union, and redemption, and communion with the powers." Others still repeat certain Hebrew words, in order the more thoroughly to bewilder those who are being initiated, as follows: "Basema, Chamosse, Baœnaora, Mistadia, Ruada, Kousta, Babaphor, Kalachthei."[1] The interpretation of these terms runs thus: "I invoke that which is above every power of the Father, which is called light, and good Spirit, and life, because Thou hast reigned in the body." Others, again, set forth the redemption thus: The name which is hidden from every deity, and dominion, and truth, which Jesus of Nazareth was clothed with in the lives[2] of the light of Christ — of Christ, who lives by the Holy Ghost, for the angelic redemption. The name of restitution stands thus: Messia, Uphareg, Namempsœman, Chaldœaur, Mosomedœa, Acphranœ, Psaua, Jesus Nazaria.[3] The interpretation of these words is as follows: "I do not divide the Spirit of Christ, neither the heart nor the supercelestial power which is merciful; may I enjoy Thy name, O Saviour of truth!" Such are words of the initiators; but he who is initiated, replies, "I am established, and I am redeemed; I redeem my soul from this age (world), and from all things connected with it in the name of Iao, who redeemed his own soul into redemption in Christ who liveth." Then the bystanders add these words, "Peace be to all on whom this name rests." After this they anoint the initiated person with balsam; for they assert that this unguent is a type of that sweet odour which is above all things.

4. But there are some of them who assert that it is superfluous to bring persons to the water, but mixing oil and water together, they place this mixture on the heads of those who are to be initiated, with the use of some such expressions as we have already mentioned. And this they maintain to be the redemption. They, too, are accustomed to anoint with balsam. Others, however, reject all these practices, and maintain that the mystery of the unspeakable and invisible power ought not to be performed by visible and corruptible creatures, nor should that of those [beings] who are inconceivable, and incorporeal, and beyond the reach of sense, [be performed] by such as are the objects of sense, and possessed of a body. These hold that the knowledge of the unspeakable Greatness is itself perfect redemption. For since both defect and passion flowed from ignorance, the whole substance of what was thus formed is destroyed by knowledge; and therefore knowledge is the redemption of the inner man. This, however, is not of a corporeal nature, for the body is corruptible; nor is it animal, since the animal soul is the fruit of a defect, and is, as it were, the abode of the spirit. The redemption must therefore be of a spiritual nature; for they affirm that the inner and spiritual man is redeemed by means of knowledge, and that they, having acquired the knowledge of all things, stand thenceforth in need of nothing else. This, then, is the true redemption.

5. Others still there are who continue to redeem persons even up to the moment of death, by placing on their heads oil and water, or the pre-mentioned ointment with water, using at the same time the above-named invocations, that the persons referred to may become incapable of being seized or seen by the principalities and powers, and that their inner man may ascend on high in an invisible manner, as if their body were left among created things in this world, while their soul is sent forward to the Demiurge. And they instruct them, on their reaching the principalities and powers, to make use of these words: "I am a son from the Father — the Father who had a pre-existence, and a son in Him who is pre-existent. I have come to behold all things, both those which belong to myself and others, although, strictly speaking, they do not belong to others, but to Achamoth, who is female in nature, and made these things for herself. For I derive being from Him who is pre-existent, and I come again to my own place whence I went forth." And they affirm that, by saying these things, he escapes from the powers. He then advances to the companions of the Demiurge, and thus addresses them: — "I am a vessel more precious than the female who formed you. If your mother is ignorant of her own descent, I know myself, and am aware where I am, and I call upon the incorruptible Sophia, who is in the Father, and is the mother of your mother, who has no father, nor any male consort; but a female springing from a female formed you, while ignorant of her own mother, and imagining that she alone existed; but I call upon her mother." And they declare, that when the companions of the Demiurge hear these words, they are greatly agitated, and upbraid their origin and the race of their mother. But he goes into his own place, having

---

[1] We have given these words as they stand in the Greek text: a very different list, but equally unmeaning, is found in the Latin.
[2] The Latin reads *zonis*, "zones," instead of "lives," as in the Greek.
[3] Here, again, are many variations.

thrown [off] his chain, that is, his animal nature. These, then, are the particulars which have reached us respecting "redemption."[1] But since they differ so widely among themselves both as respects doctrine and tradition, and since those of them who are recognised as being most modern make it their effort daily to invent some new opinion, and to bring out what no one ever before thought of, it is a difficult matter to describe all their opinions.

CHAP. XXII. — DEVIATIONS OF HERETICS FROM THE TRUTH.

1. The rule[2] of truth which we hold, is, that there is one God Almighty, who made all things by His Word, and fashioned and formed, out of that which had no existence, all things which exist. Thus saith the Scripture, to that effect: "By the Word of the Lord were the heavens established, and all the might of them, by the spirit of His mouth."[3] And again, "All things were made by Him, and without Him was nothing made."[4] There is no exception or deduction stated; but the Father made all things by Him, whether visible or invisible, objects of sense or of intelligence, temporal, on account of a certain character given them, or eternal; and these eternal[5] things He did not make by angels, or by any powers separated from His Ennœa. For God needs none of all these things, but is He who, by His Word and Spirit, makes, and disposes, and governs all things, and commands all things into existence, — He who formed the world (for the world is of all), — He who fashioned man, — He [who][6] is the God of Abraham, and the God of Isaac, and the God of Jacob, above whom there is no other God, nor initial principle, nor power, nor pleroma, — He is the Father of our Lord Jesus Christ, as we shall prove. Holding, therefore, this rule, we shall easily show, notwithstanding the great variety and multitude of their opinions, that these men have deviated from the truth; for almost all the different sects of heretics admit that there is one God; but then, by their pernicious doctrines, they change [this truth into error], even as the Gentiles do through idolatry, — thus proving themselves ungrateful to Him that created them. Moreover, they despise the workmanship of God, speaking against their own salvation, becoming their own bitterest accusers, and being false witnesses [against themselves]. Yet, reluctant as they may be, these men shall one day rise again in the flesh, to confess the power of Him who raises them from the dead; but they shall not be numbered among the righteous on account of their unbelief.

2. Since, therefore, it is a complex and multiform task to detect and convict all the heretics, and since our design is to reply to them all according to their special characters, we have judged it necessary, first of all, to give an account of their source and root, in order that, by getting a knowledge of their most exalted Bythus, thou mayest understand the nature of the tree which has produced such fruits.

CHAP. XXIII. — DOCTRINES AND PRACTICES OF SIMON MAGUS AND MENANDER.

1. Simon the Samaritan was that magician of whom Luke, the disciple and follower of the apostles, says, "But there was a certain man, Simon by name, who beforetime used magical arts in that city, and led astray the people of Samaria, declaring that he himself was some great one, to whom they all gave heed, from the least to the greatest, saying, This is the power of God, which is called great. And to him they had regard, because that of long time he had driven them mad by his sorceries."[7] This Simon, then — who feigned faith, supposing that the apostles themselves performed their cures by the art of magic, and not by the power of God; and with respect to their filling with the Holy Ghost, through the imposition of hands, those that believed in God through Him who was preached by them, namely, Christ Jesus — suspecting that even this was done through a kind of greater knowledge of magic, and offering money to the apostles, thought he, too, might receive this power of bestowing the Holy Spirit on whomsoever he would, — was addressed in these words by Peter: "Thy money perish with thee, because thou hast thought that the gift of God can be purchased with money: thou hast neither part nor lot in this matter, for thy heart is not right in the sight of God; for I perceive that thou art in the gall of bitterness, and in the bond of iniquity."[8] He, then, not putting faith in God a whit the more, set himself eagerly to contend against the apostles, in order that he himself might seem to be a wonderful being, and applied himself with still greater zeal to the study of the whole magic art, that he might the better bewilder and overpower multitudes of men. Such was his procedure in the reign of Claudius Cæsar, by whom also he is said to have been honoured with a statue, on account of his

---

[1] The Greek text, which has hitherto been preserved almost entire, ends at this point. With only brief extracts from the original, now and then, we are henceforth exclusively dependent on the old Latin version, with some Syriac and Armenian fragments recently discovered.
[2] The Latin here begins with the words "cum teneamus," and the apodosis is found afterwards at "facile arguimus." But we have broken up the one long sentence into several.
[3] Ps. xxxiii. 6.
[4] John i. 3.
[5] The text is here uncertain and obscure: eternal things seem to be referred to, not as regarded *substance*, but the *forms* assigned them.
[6] This word would perhaps be better cancelled.
[7] Acts viii. 9-11.
[8] Acts viii. 20, 21, 23.

magical power.[1] This man, then, was glorified by many as if he were a god; and he taught that it was himself who appeared among the Jews as the Son, but descended in Samaria as the Father, while he came to other nations in the character of the Holy Spirit. He represented himself, in a word, as being the loftiest of all powers, that is, the Being who is the Father over all, and he allowed himself to be called by whatsoever title men were pleased to address him.

2. Now this Simon of Samaria, from whom all sorts of heresies derive their origin, formed his sect out of the following materials: — Having redeemed from slavery at Tyre, a city of Phœnicia, a certain woman named Helena, he was in the habit of carrying her about with him, declaring that this woman was the first conception of his mind, the mother of all, by whom, in the beginning, he conceived in his mind [the thought] of forming angels and archangels. For this Ennœa leaping forth from him, and comprehending the will of her father, descended to the lower regions [of space], and generated angels and powers, by whom also he declared this world was formed. But after she had produced them, she was detained by them through motives of jealousy, because they were unwilling to be looked upon as the progeny of any other being. As to himself, they had no knowledge of him whatever; but his Ennœa was detained by those powers and angels who had been produced by her. She suffered all kinds of contumely from them, so that she could not return upwards to her father, but was even shut up in a human body, and for ages passed in succession from one female body to another, as from vessel to vessel. She was, for example, in that Helen on whose account the Trojan war was undertaken; for whose sake also Stesichorus[2] was struck blind, because he had cursed her in his verses, but afterwards, repenting and writing what are called *palinodes*, in which he sang her praise, he was restored to sight. Thus she, passing from body to body, and suffering insults in every one of them, at last became a common prostitute; and she it was that was meant by the lost sheep.[3]

3. For this purpose, then, he had come that he might win her first, and free her from slavery, while he conferred salvation upon men, by making himself known to them. For since the angels ruled the world ill because each one of them coveted the principal power for himself, he had come to amend matters, and had descended, transfigured and assimilated to powers and principalities and angels, so that he might appear among men to be a man, while yet he was not a man; and that thus he was thought to have suffered in Judæa, when he had not suffered. Moreover, the prophets uttered their predictions under the inspiration of those angels who formed the world; for which reason those who place their trust in him and Helena no longer regarded them, but, as being free, live as they please; for men are saved through his grace, and not on account of their own righteous actions. For such deeds are not righteous in the nature of things, but by mere accident, just as those angels who made the world, have thought fit to constitute them, seeking, by means of such precepts, to bring men into bondage. On this account, he pledged himself that the world should be dissolved, and that those who are his should be freed from the rule of them who made the world.

4. Thus, then, the mystic priests belonging to this sect both lead profligate lives and practise magical arts, each one to the extent of his ability. They use exorcisms and incantations. Love-potions, too, and charms, as well as those beings who are called "Paredri" (familiars) and "Oniropompi" (dream-senders), and whatever other curious arts can be had recourse to, are eagerly pressed into their service. They also have an image of Simon fashioned after the likeness of Jupiter, and another of Helena in the shape of Minerva; and these they worship. In fine, they have a name derived from Simon, the author of these most impious doctrines, being called Simonians; and from them "knowledge, falsely so called,"[4] received its beginning, as one may learn even from their own assertions.

5. The successor of this man was Menander, also a Samaritan by birth, and he, too, was a perfect adept in the practice of magic. He affirms that the primary Power continues unknown to all, but that he himself is the person who has been sent forth from the presence of the invisible beings as a saviour, for the deliverance of men. The world was made by angels, whom, like Simon, he maintains to have been produced by Ennœa. He gives, too, as he affirms, by means of that magic which he teaches, knowledge to this effect, that one may overcome those very angels that made the world; for his disciples obtain the *resurrection* by being baptized into him, and can die no more, but remain in the possession of immortal youth.

CHAP. XXIV. — DOCTRINES OF SATURNINUS AND BASILIDES.

1. Arising among these men, Saturninus (who was of that Antioch which is near Daphne) and Basilides laid hold of some favourable opportunities, and promulgated different systems of

---

[1] Comp. Just. Mart., *Apol.*, i. 26. It is generally supposed that Simon Magus was thus confounded with the Sabine god, Semo Sancus; but see our note, *loc. cit.* [And mine at end of the First Apology. Consult *Orelli's Inscriptions* there noted.]
[2] A lyric poet of Sicily, said to have been dealt with, as stated above, by Castor and Pollux.
[3] Matt. xviii. 12.
[4] 1 Tim. vi. 20.

doctrine — the one in Syria, the other at Alexandria. Saturninus, like Menander, set forth one father unknown to all, who made angels, archangels, powers, and potentates. The world, again, and all things therein, were made by a certain company of seven angels. Man, too, was the workmanship of angels, a shining image bursting forth below from the presence of the supreme power; and when they could not, he says, keep hold of this, because it immediately darted upwards again, they exhorted each other, saying, " Let us make man after our image and likeness." [1] He was accordingly formed, yet was unable to stand erect, through the inability of the angels to convey to him that power, but wriggled [on the ground] like a worm. Then the power above taking pity upon him, since he was made after his likeness, sent forth a spark of life, which gave man an erect posture, compacted his joints, and made him live. He declares, therefore, that this spark of life, after the death of a man, returns to those things which are of the same nature with itself, and the rest of the body is decomposed into its original elements.

2. He has also laid it down as a truth, that the Saviour was without birth, without body, and without figure, but was, by supposition, a visible man; and he maintained that the God of the Jews was one of the angels; and, on this account, because all the powers wished to annihilate his father, Christ came to destroy the God of the Jews, but to save such as believe in him; that is, those who possess the spark of his life. This heretic was the first to affirm that two kinds of men were formed by the angels, — the one wicked, and the other good. And since the demons assist the most wicked, the Saviour came for the destruction of evil men and of the demons, but for the salvation of the good. They declare also, that marriage and generation are from Satan.[2] Many of those, too, who belong to his school, abstain from animal food, and draw away multitudes by a feigned temperance of this kind. They hold, moreover, that some of the prophecies were uttered by those angels who made the world, and some by Satan; whom Saturninus represents as being himself an angel, the enemy of the creators of the world, but especially of the God of the Jews.

3. Basilides again, that he may appear to have discovered something more sublime and plausible, gives an immense development to his doctrines. He sets forth that Nous was first born of the unborn father, that from him, again, was born Logos, from Logos Phronesis, from Phronesis Sophia and Dynamis, and from Dynamis and Sophia the powers, and principalities, and angels, whom he also calls the *first;* and that by them the first heaven was made. Then other powers, being formed by emanation from these, created another heaven similar to the first; and in like manner, when others, again, had been formed by emanation from them, corresponding exactly to those above them, these, too, framed another third heaven; and then from this third, in downward order, there was a fourth succession of descendants; and so on, after the same fashion, they declare that more and more principalities and angels were formed, and three hundred and sixty-five heavens.[3] Wherefore the year contains the same number of days in conformity with the number of the heavens.

4. Those angels who occupy the lowest heaven, that, namely, which is visible to us, formed all the things which are in the world, and made allotments among themselves of the earth and of those nations which are upon it. The chief of them is he who is thought to be the God of the Jews; and inasmuch as he desired to render the other nations subject to his own people, that is, the Jews, all the other princes resisted and opposed him. Wherefore all other nations were at enmity with his nation. But the father without birth and without name, perceiving that they would be destroyed, sent his own first-begotten Nous (he it is who is called Christ) to bestow deliverance on them that believe in him, from the power of those who made the world. He appeared, then, on earth as a man, to the nations of these powers, and wrought miracles. Wherefore he did not himself suffer death, but Simon, a certain man of Cyrene, being compelled, bore the cross in his stead; so that this latter being transfigured by him, that he might be thought to be Jesus, was crucified, through ignorance and error, while Jesus himself received the form of Simon, and, standing by, laughed at them. For since he was an incorporeal power, and the Nous (mind) of the unborn father, he transfigured himself as he pleased, and thus ascended to him who had sent him, deriding them, inasmuch as he could not be laid hold of, and was invisible to all. Those, then, who know these things have been freed from the principalities who formed the world; so that it is not incumbent on us to confess him who was crucified, but him who came in the form of a man, and was thought to be crucified, and was called Jesus, and was sent by the father, that by this dispensation he might destroy the works of the makers of the world. If any one, therefore, he declares, confesses the crucified, that man is still a slave, and under the power of those who formed our bodies; but he who denies him has been freed from these beings, and is acquainted with the dispensation of the unborn father.

---

[1] Gen. i. 26.
[2] [1. Tim. iv. 3.]
[3] The ordinary text reads, " three hundred and seventy-five," but it should manifestly be corrected as above.

5. Salvation belongs to the soul alone, for the body is by nature subject to corruption. He declares, too, that the prophecies were derived from those powers who were the makers of the world, but the law was specially given by their chief, who led the people out of the land of Egypt. He attaches no importance to [the question regarding] meats offered in sacrifice to idols, thinks them of no consequence, and makes use of them without any hesitation; he holds also the use of other things, and the practice of every kind of lust, a matter of perfect indifference. These men, moreover, practise magic, and use images, incantations, invocations, and every other kind of curious art. Coining also certain names as if they were those of the angels, they proclaim some of these as belonging to the first, and others to the second heaven; and then they strive to set forth the names, principles, angels, and powers of the three hundred and sixty-five imagined heavens. They also affirm that the barbarous name in which the Saviour ascended and descended, is Caulacau.[1]

6. He, then, who has learned [these things], and known all the angels and their causes, is rendered invisible and incomprehensible to the angels and all the powers, even as Caulacau also was. And as the son was unknown to all, so must they also be known by no one; but while they know all, and pass through all, they themselves remain invisible and unknown to all; for, " Do thou," they say, " know all, but let nobody know thee." For this reason, persons of such a persuasion are also ready to recant [their opinions], yea, rather, it is impossible that they should suffer on account of a mere name, since they are like to all. The multitude, however, cannot understand these matters, but only one out of a thousand, or two out of ten thousand. They declare that they are no longer Jews, and that they are not yet Christians; and that it is not at all fitting to speak openly of their mysteries, but right to keep them secret by preserving silence.

7. They make out the local position of the three hundred and sixty-five heavens in the same way as do mathematicians. For, accepting the theorems of these latter, they have transferred them to their own type of doctrine. They hold that their chief is *Abraxas;*[2] and, on this account, that word contains in itself the numbers amounting to three hundred and sixty-five.

---

[1] This sentence is wholly unintelligible as it stands in the Latin version. Critics differ greatly as to its meaning; Harvey tries to bring out of it something like the translation given above. [This name is manufactured from a curious abuse of (קַו לָקָו) Isaiah xxviii. 10-13, which is variously understood. See (Epiphanius ed. Oehler, vol. i.) *Philastr.*, p. 38.]

[2] So written in Latin, but in Greek Ἀβρασάξ, the numerical value of the letters in which is three hundred and sixty-five. [See *Aug.* (ed. *Migne*), vol. viii. p. 26.] It is doubtful to whom or what this word refers; probably to the heavens.

CHAP. XXV. — DOCTRINES OF CARPOCRATES.

1. Carpocrates, again, and his followers maintain that the world and the things which are therein were created by angels greatly inferior to the unbegotten Father. They also hold that Jesus was the son of Joseph, and was just like other men, with the exception that he differed from them in this respect, that inasmuch as his soul was stedfast and pure, he perfectly remembered those things which he had witnessed[3] within the sphere of the unbegotten God. On this account, a power descended upon him from the Father, that by means of it he might escape from the creators of the world; and they say that it, after passing through them all, and remaining in all points free, ascended again to him, and to the powers,[4] which in the same way embraced like things to itself. They further declare, that the soul of Jesus, although educated in the practices of the Jews, regarded these with contempt, and that for this reason he was endowed with faculties, by means of which he destroyed those passions which dwelt in men as a punishment [for their sins].

2. The soul, therefore, which is like that of Christ can despise those rulers who were the creators of the world, and, in like manner, receives power for accomplishing the same results. This idea has raised them to such a pitch of pride, that some of them declare themselves similar to Jesus; while others, still more mighty, maintain that they are superior to his disciples, such as Peter and Paul, and the rest of the apostles, whom they consider to be in no respect inferior to Jesus. For their souls, descending from the same sphere as his, and therefore despising in like manner the creators of the world, are deemed worthy of the same power, and again depart to the same place. But if any one shall have despised the things in this world more than he did, he thus proves himself superior to him.

3. They practise also magical arts and incantations; philters, also, and love-potions; and have recourse to familiar spirits, dream-sending demons, and other abominations, declaring that they possess power to rule over, even now, the princes and formers of this world; and not only them, but also all things that are in it. These men, even as the Gentiles, have been sent forth by Satan[5] to bring dishonour upon the Church, so that, in one way or another, men hearing the things which they speak, and imagining that we all are such as they, may turn away their ears from the preaching of the truth; or, again, seeing the things they practise, may speak evil of

---

[3] [I note again this " Americanism."]
[4] Such seems to be the meaning of the Latin, but the original text is conjectural.
[5] [See cap. xxvii. 3.]

us all, who have in fact no fellowship with them, either in doctrine or in morals, or in our daily conduct. But they lead a licentious life,[1] and, to conceal their impious doctrines, they abuse the name [of Christ], as a means of hiding their wickedness; so that "their condemnation is just,"[2] when they receive from God a recompense suited to their works.

4. So unbridled is their madness, that they declare they have in their power all things which are irreligious and impious, and are at liberty to practise them; for they maintain that things are evil or good, simply in virtue of human opinion.[3] They deem it necessary, therefore, that by means of transmigration from body to body, souls should have experience of every kind of life as well as every kind of action (unless, indeed, by a single incarnation, one may be able to prevent any need for others, by once for all, and with equal completeness, doing all those things which we dare not either speak or hear of, nay, which we must not even conceive in our thoughts, nor think credible, if any such thing is mooted among those persons who are our fellow-citizens), in order that, as their writings express it, their souls, having made trial of every kind of life, may, at their departure, not be wanting in any particular. It is necessary[4] to insist upon this, lest, on account of some one thing being still wanting to their deliverance, they should be compelled once more to become incarnate. They affirm that for this reason Jesus spoke the following parable:—"Whilst thou art with thine adversary in the way, give all diligence, that thou mayest be delivered from him, lest he give thee up to the judge, and the judge surrender thee to the officer, and he cast thee into prison. Verily, I say unto thee, thou shalt not go out thence until thou pay the very last farthing."[5] They also declare the "adversary" is one of those angels who are in the world, whom they call the Devil, maintaining that he was formed for this purpose, that he might lead those souls which have perished from the world to the Supreme Ruler. They describe him also as being chief among the makers of the world, and maintain that he delivers such souls [as have been mentioned] to another angel, who ministers to him, that he may shut them up in other bodies; for they declare that the body is "the prison." Again, they interpret these expressions, "Thou shalt not go out thence until thou pay the very last farthing," as meaning that no one can escape from the power of those angels who made the world, but that he must pass from body to body, until he has experience of every kind of action which can be practised in this world, and when nothing is longer wanting to him, then his liberated soul should soar upwards to that God who is above the angels, the makers of the world. In this way also all souls are saved, whether their own which, guarding against all delay, participate in all sorts of actions during one incarnation, or those, again, who, by passing from body to body, are set free, on fulfilling and accomplishing what is requisite in every form of life into which they are sent, so that at length they shall no longer be [shut up] in the body.

5. And thus, if ungodly, unlawful, and forbidden actions are committed among them, I can no longer find ground for believing them to be such.[6] And in their writings we read as follows, the interpretation which they give [of their views], declaring that Jesus spoke in a mystery to His disciples and apostles privately, and that they requested and obtained permission to hand down the things thus taught them, to others who should be worthy and believing. We are saved, indeed, by means of faith and love; but all other things, while in their nature indifferent, are reckoned by the opinion of men — some good and some evil, there being nothing really evil by nature.

6. Others of them employ outward marks, branding their disciples inside the lobe of the right ear. From among these also arose Marcellina, who came to Rome under [the episcopate of] Anicetus, and, holding these doctrines, she led multitudes astray. They style themselves Gnostics. They also possess images, some of them painted, and others formed from different kinds of material; while they maintain that a likeness of Christ was made by Pilate at that time when Jesus lived among them.[7] They crown these images, and set them up along with the images of the philosophers of the world; that is to say, with the images of Pythagoras, and Plato, and Aristotle, and the rest. They have also other modes of honouring these images, after the same manner of the Gentiles.

CHAP. XXVI. — DOCTRINES OF CERINTHUS, THE EBIONITES, AND NICOLAITANES.

1. Cerinthus, again, a man who was educated[8] in the wisdom of the Egyptians, taught that the world was not made by the primary God, but by a certain Power far separated from him, and at a distance from that Principality who is su-

---

[1] The text is here defective, but the above meaning seems to be indicated by Epiphanius.
[2] Rom. iii. 8.
[3] [Isaiah v. 20. Horne Tooke derives our word *Truth* from what any one *troweth*.]
[4] The text here has greatly puzzled the editors. We follow the simple emendation proposed by Harvey.
[5] Matt. v. 25, 26; Luke xii. 58.
[6] The meaning is here very doubtful, but Tertullian understood the words as above. If sinning were a *necessity*, then it could no longer be regarded as evil.
[7] [This censure of images as a Gnostic peculiarity, and as a heathenish corruption, should be noted.]
[8] We here follow the text as preserved by Hippolytus. The Latin has, "a certain man in Asia."

preme over the universe, and ignorant of him who is above all. He represented Jesus as having not been born of a virgin, but as being the son of Joseph and Mary according to the ordinary course of human generation, while he nevertheless was more righteous, prudent, and wise than other men. Moreover, after his baptism, Christ descended upon him in the form of a dove from the Supreme Ruler, and that then he proclaimed the unknown Father, and performed miracles. Bnt at last Christ departed from Jesus, and that then Jesus suffered and rose again, while Christ remained impassible, inasmuch as he was a spiritual being.

2. Those who are called Ebionites agree that the world was made by God; but their opinions with respect to the Lord are similar to those of Cerinthus and Carpocrates. They use the Gospel according to Matthew only, and repudiate the Apostle Paul, maintaining that he was an apostate from the law. As to the prophetical writings, they endeavour to expound them in a somewhat singular manner: they practise circumcision, persevere in the observance of those customs which are enjoined by the law, and are so Judaic in their style of life, that they even adore Jerusalem as if it were the house of God.

3. The Nicolaitanes are the followers of that Nicolas who was one of the seven first ordained to the diaconate by the apostles.[1] They lead lives of unrestrained indulgence. The character of these men is very plainly pointed out in the Apocalypse of John, [when they are represented] as teaching that it is a matter of indifference to practise adultery, and to eat things sacrificed to idols. Wherefore the Word has also spoken of them thus: "But this thou hast, that thou hatest the deeds of the Nicolaitanes, which I also hate."[2]

CHAP. XXVII. — DOCTRINES OF CERDO AND MARCION.

1. Cerdo was one who took his system from the followers of Simon, and came to live at Rome in the time of Hyginus, who held the ninth place in the episcopal succession from the apostles downwards. He taught that the God proclaimed by the law and the prophets was not the Father of our Lord Jesus Christ. For the former was known, but the latter unknown; while the one also was righteous, but the other benevolent.

2. Marcion of Pontus succeeded him, and developed his doctrine. In so doing, he advanced the most daring blasphemy against Him who is proclaimed as God by the law and the prophets, declaring Him to be the author of evils, to take delight in war, to be infirm of purpose, and even to be contrary to Himself. But Jesus being derived from that father who is above the God that made the world, and coming into Judæa in the times of Pontius Pilate the governor, who was the procurator of Tiberius Cæsar, was manifested in the form of a man to those who were in Judæa, abolishing the prophets and the law, and all the works of that God who made the world, whom also he calls Cosmocrator. Besides this, he mutilates the Gospel which is according to Luke, removing all that is written respecting the generation of the Lord, and setting aside a great deal of the teaching of the Lord, in which the Lord is recorded as most clearly confessing that the Maker of this universe is His Father. He likewise persuaded his disciples that he himself was more worthy of credit than are those apostles who have handed down the Gospel to us, furnishing them not with the Gospel, but merely a fragment of it. In like manner, too, he dismembered the Epistles of Paul, removing all that is said by the apostle respecting that God who made the world, to the effect that He is the Father of our Lord Jesus Christ, and also those passages from the prophetical writings which the apostle quotes, in order to teach us that they announced beforehand the coming of the Lord.

3. Salvation will be the attainment only of those souls which had learned his doctrine; while the body, as having been taken from the earth, is incapable of sharing in salvation. In addition to his blasphemy against God Himself, he advanced this also, truly speaking as with the mouth of the devil, and saying all things in direct opposition to the truth, — that Cain, and those like him, and the Sodomites, and the Egyptians, and others like them, and, in fine, all the nations who walked in all sorts of abomination, were saved by the Lord, on His descending into Hades, and on their running unto Him, and that He welcomed Him into their kingdom. But the serpent[3] which was in Marcion declared that Abel, and Enoch, and Noah, and those other righteous men who sprang[4] from the patriarch Abraham, with all the prophets, and those who were pleasing to God, did not partake in salvation. For since these men, he says, knew that their God was constantly tempting them, so now they suspected that He was tempting them, and did not run to Jesus, or believe His announcement: and for this reason he declared that their souls remained in Hades.

4. But since this man is the only one who has dared openly to mutilate the Scriptures, and unblushingly above all others to inveigh against God, I purpose specially to refute him, convict-

---

[1] [This is disputed by other primitive authorities.]
[2] Rev. ii. 6.
[3] [Comp. cap. xxv. 3.]
[4] We here follow the amended version proposed by the Benedictine editor.

ing him out of his own writings; and, with the help of God, I shall overthrow him out of those [1] discourses of the Lord and the apostles, which are of authority with him, and of which he makes use. At present, however, I have simply been led to mention him, that thou mightest know that all those who in any way corrupt the truth, and injuriously affect the preaching of the Church, are the disciples and successors of Simon Magus of Samaria. Although they do not confess the name of their master, in order all the more to seduce others, yet they do teach his doctrines. They set forth, indeed, the name of Christ Jesus as a sort of lure, but in various ways they introduce the impieties of Simon; and thus they destroy multitudes, wickedly disseminating their own doctrines by the use of a good name, and, through means of its sweetness and beauty, extending to their hearers the bitter and malignant poison of the serpent, the great author of apostasy.[2]

CHAP. XXVIII. — DOCTRINES OF TATIAN, THE ENCRATITES, AND OTHERS.

1. Many offshoots of numerous heresies have already been formed from those heretics we have described. This arises from the fact that numbers of them — indeed, we may say all — desire themselves to be teachers, and to break off from the particular heresy in which they have been involved. Forming one set of doctrines out of a totally different system of opinions, and then again others from others, they insist upon teaching something new, declaring themselves the inventors of any sort of opinion which they may have been able to call into existence. To give an example: Springing from Saturninus and Marcion, those who are called Encratites (self-controlled) preached against marriage, thus setting aside the original creation of God, and indirectly blaming Him who made the male and female for the propagation of the human race. Some of those reckoned among them have also introduced abstinence from animal food, thus proving themselves ungrateful to God, who formed all things. They deny, too, the salvation of him who was first created. It is but lately, however, that this opinion has been invented among them. A certain man named Tatian first introduced the blasphemy. He was a hearer of Justin's, and as long as he continued with him he expressed no such views; but after his martyrdom he separated from the Church, and, excited and puffed up by the thought of being a teacher, as if he were superior to others, he composed his own peculiar type of doctrine. He invented a system of certain invisible Æons, like the followers of Valen-

tinus; while, like Marcion and Saturninus, he declared that marriage was nothing else than corruption and fornication.[3] But his denial of Adam's salvation was an opinion due entirely to himself.

2. Others, again, following upon Basilides and Carpocrates, have introduced promiscuous intercourse and a plurality of wives, and are indifferent about eating meats sacrificed to idols, maintaining that God does not greatly regard such matters. But why continue? For it is an impracticable attempt to mention all those who, in one way or another, have fallen away from the truth.

CHAP. XXIX. — DOCTRINES OF VARIOUS OTHER GNOSTIC SECTS, AND ESPECIALLY OF THE BARBELIOTES OR BORBORIANS.

1. Besides those, however, among these heretics who are Simonians, and of whom we have already spoken, a multitude of Gnostics have sprung up, and have been manifested like mushrooms growing out of the ground. I now proceed to describe the principal opinions held by them. Some of them, then, set forth a certain Æon who never grows old, and exists in a virgin spirit: him they style Barbelos.[4] They declare that somewhere or other there exists a certain father who cannot be named, and that he was desirous to reveal himself to this Barbelos. Then this Ennœa went forward, stood before his face, and demanded from him Prognosis (prescience). But when Prognosis had, [as was requested,] come forth, these two asked for Aphtharsia (incorruption), which also came forth, and after that Zoe Aionios (eternal life). Barbelos, glorying in these, and contemplating their greatness, and in conception [5] [thus formed], rejoicing in this greatness, generated light similar to it. They declare that this was the beginning both of light and of the generation of all things; and that the Father, beholding this light, anointed it with his own benignity, that it might be rendered perfect. Moreover, they maintain that this was Christ, who again, according to them, requested that Nous should be given him as an assistant; and Nous came forth accordingly. Besides these, the Father sent forth Logos. The conjunctions of Ennœa and Logos, and of Aphtharsia and Christ, will thus be formed; while Zoe Aionios was united to Thelema, and Nous to Prognosis. These, then, magnified the great light and Barbelos.

2. They also affirm that Autogenes was afterwards sent forth from Ennœa and Logos, to be

---

[1] A promise never fulfilled: comp. book iii. 12, and Euseb., *Hist. Eccl.*, v. 8.
[2] [Rev. xii. 9.]
[3] [The whole casuistical system of the Trent divines, *De Matrimonio*, proceeds on this principle: marriage is licensed evil.]
[4] Harvey supposes this name to be derived from two Syriac words, meaning "God in a Tetrad." Matter again derives it from two Hebrew words, denoting "Daughter of the Lord."
[5] Both the text and meaning are here altogether doubtful.

a representation of the great light, and that he was greatly honoured, all things being rendered subject unto him. Along with him was sent forth Aletheia, and a conjunction was formed between Autogenes and Aletheia. But they declare that from the Light, which is Christ, and from Aphtharsia, four luminaries were sent forth to surround Autogenes; and again from Thelema and Zoe Aionios four other emissions took place, to wait upon these four luminaries; and these they name Charis (grace), Thelesis (will), Synesis (understanding), and Phronesis (prudence). Of these, Charis is connected with the great and first luminary: him they represent as Soter (Saviour), and style Armogenes.[1] Thelesis, again, is united to the second luminary, whom they also name Raguel; Synesis to the third, whom they call David; and Phronesis to the fourth, whom they name Eleleth.

3. All these, then, being thus settled, Autogenes moreover produces a perfect and true man, whom they also call Adamas, inasmuch as neither has he himself ever been conquered, nor have those from whom he sprang; he also was, along with the first light, severed from Armogenes. Moreover, perfect knowledge was sent forth by Autogenes along with man, and was united to him; hence he attained to the knowledge of him that is above all. Invincible power was also conferred on him by the virgin spirit; and all things then rested in him, to sing praises to the great Æon. Hence also they declare were manifested the mother, the father, the son; while from Anthropos and Gnosis that Tree was produced which they also style Gnosis itself.

4. Next they maintain, that from the first angel, who stands by the side of Monogenes, the Holy Spirit has been sent forth, whom they also term Sophia and Prunicus.[2] He then, perceiving that all the others had consorts, while he himself was destitute of one, searched after a being to whom he might be united; and not finding one, he exerted and extended himself to the uttermost, and looked down into the lower regions, in the expectation of there finding a consort; and still not meeting with one, he leaped forth [from his place] in a state of great impatience, [which had come upon him] because he had made his attempt without the good-will of his father. Afterwards, under the influence of simplicity and kindness, he produced a work in which were to be found ignorance and audacity. This work of his they declare to be Protarchontes, the former of this [lower] creation. But they relate that a mighty power carried him away from his mother, and that he settled far away from her in the lower regions, and formed the firmament of heaven, in which also they affirm that he dwells. And in his ignorance he formed those powers which are inferior to himself — angels, and firmaments, and all things earthly. They affirm that he, being united to Authadia (audacity), produced Kakia (wickedness), Zelos (emulation), Phthonos (envy), Erinnys (fury), and Epithymia (lust). When these were generated, the mother Sophia deeply grieved, fled away, departed into the upper regions, and became the last of the Ogdoad, reckoning it downwards. On her thus departing, he imagined he was the only being in existence; and on this account declared, "I am a jealous God, and besides me there is no one."[3] Such are the falsehoods which these people invent.

CHAP. XXX. — DOCTRINES OF THE OPHITES AND SETHIANS.

1. Others, again, portentously declare that there exists, in the power of Bythus, a certain primary light, blessed, incorruptible, and infinite: this is the Father of all, and is styled the first man. They also maintain that his Ennœa, going forth from him, produced a son, and that this is the son of man — the second man. Below these, again, is the Holy Spirit, and under this superior spirit the elements were separated from each other, viz., water, darkness, the abyss, chaos, above which they declare the Spirit was borne, calling him the first woman. Afterwards, they maintain, the first man, with his son, delighting over the beauty of the Spirit — that is, of the woman — and shedding light upon her, begat by her an incorruptible light, the third male, whom they call Christ, — the son of the first and second man, and of the Holy Spirit, the first woman.

2. The father and son thus both had intercourse with the woman (whom they also call the mother of the living). When, however,[4] she could not bear nor receive into herself the greatness of the lights, they declare that she was filled to repletion, and became ebullient on the left side; and that thus their only son Christ, as belonging to the right side, and ever tending to what was higher, was immediately caught up with his mother to form an incorruptible Æon. This constitutes the true and holy Church, which has become the appellation, the meeting together, and the union of the father of all, of the first man, of the son, of the second man, of Christ their son, and of the woman who has been mentioned.

3. They teach, however, that the power which proceeded from the woman by ebullition, being besprinkled with light, fell downward from the place occupied by its progenitors, yet possessing

---

[1] Harvey refers to the cabbalistic books in explanation of this and the following names, but their meanings are very uncertain.
[2] Various explanations of this word have been proposed, but its signification remains altogether doubtful.
[3] Ex. xx. 5; Isa. xlv. 5, 6.
[4] The punctuation is here difficult and doubtful.

by its own will that besprinkling of light; and it they call Sinistra, Prunicus, and Sophia, as well as masculo-feminine. This being, in its simplicity, descended into the waters while they were yet in a state of immobility, and imparted motion to them also, wantonly acting upon them even to their lowest depths, and assumed from them a body. For they affirm that all things rushed towards and clung to that sprinkling of light, and begirt it all round. Unless it had possessed that, it would perhaps have been totally absorbed in, and overwhelmed by, material substance. Being therefore bound down by a body which was composed of matter, and greatly burdened by it, this power regretted the course it had followed, and made an attempt to escape from the waters and ascend to its mother: it could not effect this, however, on account of the weight of the body lying over and around it. But feeling very ill at ease, it endeavoured at least to conceal that light which came from above, fearing lest it too might be injured by the inferior elements, as had happened to itself. And when it had received power from that besprinkling of light which it possessed, it sprang back again, and was borne aloft; and being on high, it extended itself, covered [a portion of space], and formed this visible heaven out of its body; yet remained under the heaven which it made, as still possessing the form of a watery body. But when it had conceived a desire for the light above, and had received power by all things, it laid down this body, and was freed from it. This body which they speak of that power as having thrown off, they call a female from a female.

4. They declare, moreover, that her son had also himself a certain breath of incorruption left him by his mother, and that through means of it he works; and becoming powerful, he himself, as they affirm, also sent forth from the waters a son without a mother; for they do not allow him either to have known a mother. His son, again, after the example of his father, sent forth another son. This third one, too, generated a fourth; the fourth also generated a son: they maintain that again a son was generated by the fifth; and the sixth, too, generated a seventh. Thus was the Hebdomad, according to them, completed, the mother possessing the eighth place; and as in the case of their generations, so also in regard to dignities and powers, they precede each other in turn.

5. They have also given names to [the several persons] in their system of falsehood, such as the following: he who was the first descendant of the mother is called Ialdabaoth;[1] he, again, descended from him, is named Iao; he, from this one, is called Sabaoth; the fourth is named Adoneus; the fifth, Eloeus; the sixth, Oreus; and the seventh and last of all, Astanphæus. Moreover, they represent these heavens, potentates, powers, angels, and creators, as sitting in their proper order in heaven, according to their generation, and as invisibly ruling over things celestial and terrestrial. The first of them, namely Ialdabaoth, holds his mother in contempt, inasmuch as he produced sons and grandsons without the permission of any one, yea, even angels, archangels, powers, potentates, and dominions. After these things had been done, his sons turned to strive and quarrel with him about the supreme power, — conduct which deeply grieved Ialdabaoth, and drove him to despair. In these circumstances, he cast his eyes upon the subjacent dregs of matter, and fixed his desire upon it, to which they declare his son owes his origin. This son is Nous himself, twisted into the form of a serpent;[2] and hence were derived the spirit, the soul, and all mundane things: from this too were generated all oblivion, wickedness, emulation, envy, and death. They declare that the father imparted[3] still greater crookedness to this serpent-like and contorted Nous of theirs, when he was with their father in heaven and Paradise.

6. On this account, Ialdabaoth, becoming uplifted in spirit, boasted himself over all those things that were below him, and exclaimed, "I am father, and God, and above me there is no one." But his mother, hearing him speak thus, cried out against him, "Do not lie, Ialdabaoth: for the father of all, the first Anthropos (man), is above thee; and so is Anthropos the son of Anthropos." Then, as all were disturbed by this new voice, and by the unexpected proclamation, and as they were inquiring whence the noise proceeded, in order to lead them away and attract them to himself, they affirm that Ialdabaoth exclaimed, "Come, let us make man after our image."[4] The six powers, on hearing this, and their mother furnishing them with the idea of a man (in order that by means of him she might empty them of their original power), jointly formed a man of immense size, both in regard to breadth and length. But as he could merely writhe along the ground, they carried him to their father; Sophia so labouring in this matter, that she might empty him (Ialdabaoth) of the light with which he had been sprinkled, so that he might no longer, though still powerful, be able to lift up himself against the powers above. They declare, then, that by breathing

---

[1] The probable meaning of this and the following names is thus given by Harvey: Ialdabaoth, *Lord God of the Fathers;* Iao, *Jehovah;* Oreus, *Light;* Astanphæus, *Crown*: Sabaoth, of course, means *Hosts;* Adoneus, *Lord;* and Eloeus, *God*. All the names are derived from the cabbalistic theology of the Jews.

[2] Hence their name of Ophites, from ὄφις, *a serpent*.
[3] The Latin has *evertisse*, implying that thus Nous was more degraded.
[4] Gen. i. 26.

into man the spirit of life, he was secretly emptied of his power; that hence man became a possessor of nous (intelligence) and enthymesis (thought); and they affirm that these are the faculties which partake in salvation. He [they further assert] at once gave thanks to the first Anthropos (man), forsaking those who had created him.

7. But Ialdabaoth, feeling envious at this, was pleased to form the design of again emptying man by means of woman, and produced a woman from his own enthymesis, whom that Prunicus [above mentioned] laying hold of, imperceptibly emptied her of power. But the others coming and admiring her beauty, named her Eve, and falling in love with her, begat sons by her, whom they also declare to be the angels. But their mother (Sophia) cunningly devised a scheme to seduce Eve and Adam, by means of the serpent, to transgress the command of Ialdabaoth. Eve listened to this as if it had proceeded from a son of God, and yielded an easy belief. She also persuaded Adam to eat of the tree regarding which God had said that they should not eat of it. They then declare that, on their thus eating, they attained to the knowledge of that power which is above all, and departed from those who had created them.[1] When Prunicus perceived that the powers were thus baffled by their own creature, she greatly rejoiced, and again cried out, that since the father was incorruptible, he (Ialdabaoth) who formerly called himself the father was a liar; and that, while Anthropos and the first woman (the Spirit) existed previously, this one (Eve) sinned by committing adultery.

8. Ialdabaoth, however, through that oblivion in which he was involved, and not paying any regard to these things, cast Adam and Eve out of Paradise, because they had transgressed his commandment. For he had a desire to beget sons by Eve, but did not accomplish his wish, because his mother opposed him in every point, and secretly emptied Adam and Eve of the light with which they had been sprinkled, in order that that spirit which proceeded from the supreme power might participate neither in the curse nor opprobrium [caused by transgression]. They also teach that, thus being emptied of the divine substance, they were cursed by him, and cast down from heaven to this world.[2] But the serpent also, who was acting against the father, was cast down by him into this lower world; he reduced, however, under his power the angels here, and begat six sons, he himself forming the seventh person, after the example of that Hebdomad which surrounds the father. They further declare that these are the seven mundane demons, who always oppose and resist the human race, because it was on their account that their father was cast down to this lower world.

9. Adam and Eve previously had light, and clear, and as it were spiritual bodies, such as they were at their creation; but when they came to this world, these changed into bodies more opaque, and gross, and sluggish. Their soul also was feeble and languid, inasmuch as they had received from their creator a merely mundane inspiration. This continued until Prunicus, moved with compassion towards them, restored to them the sweet savour of the besprinkling of light, by means of which they came to a remembrance of themselves, and knew that they were naked, as well as that the body was a material substance, and thus recognised that they bore death about with them. They thereupon became patient, knowing that only for a time they would be enveloped in the body. They also found out food, through the guidance of Sophia; and when they were satisfied, they had carnal knowledge of each other, and begat Cain, whom the serpent, that had been cast down along with his sons, immediately laid hold of and destroyed by filling him with mundane oblivion, and urging into folly and audacity, so that, by slaying his brother Abel, he was the first to bring to light envy and death. After these, they affirm that, by the forethought of Prunicus, Seth was begotten, and then Norea,[3] from whom they represent all the rest of mankind as being descended. They were urged on to all kinds of wickedness by the inferior Hebdomad, and to apostasy, idolatry, and a general contempt for everything by the superior holy Hebdomad,[4] since the mother was always secretly opposed to them, and carefully preserved what was peculiarly her own, that is, the besprinkling of light. They maintain, moreover, that the holy Hebdomad is the seven stars which they call planets; and they affirm that the serpent cast down has two names, Michael and Samael.

10. Ialdabaoth, again, being incensed with men, because they did not worship or honour him as father and God, sent forth a deluge upon them, that he might at once destroy them all. But Sophia opposed him in this point also, and Noah and his family were saved in the ark by means of the besprinkling of that light which proceeded from her, and through it the world was again filled with mankind. Ialdabaoth himself chose a certain man named Abraham from among these, and made a covenant with him, to the effect that, if his seed continued to serve him, he would give to them the earth for an inheritance. Afterwards, by means of Moses, he

---

[1] That is, from Ialdabaoth, etc. [*Philastr.* (*ut supra*), Oehler, i. p. 38.]
[2] There is constant reference in this section to rabbinical conceits and follies.
[3] A name probably derived from the Hebrew נַעֲרָה, *girl*, but of the person referred to we know nothing.
[4] We here follow the emendation of Grabe: the defection of Prunicus is intended.

brought forth Abraham's descendants from Egypt, and gave them the law, and made them the Jews. Among that people he chose seven days,[1] which they also call the holy Hebdomad. Each of these receives his own herald for the purpose of glorifying and proclaiming God; so that, when the rest hear these praises, they too may serve those who are announced as gods by the prophets.

11. Moreover, they distribute the prophets in the following manner: Moses, and Joshua the son of Nun, and Amos, and Habakkuk, belonged to Ialdabaoth; Samuel, and Nathan, and Jonah, and Micah, to Iao; Elijah, Joel, and Zechariah, to Sabaoth; Isaiah, Ezekiel, Jeremiah, and Daniel, to Adonai; Tobias and Haggai to Eloi; Michaiah and Nahum to Oreus; Esdras and Zephaniah to Astanphæus. Each one of these, then, glorifies his own father and God, and they maintain that Sophia· herself has also spoken many things through them regarding the first Anthropos (man),[2] and concerning that Christ who is above, thus admonishing and reminding men of the incorruptible light, the first Anthropos, and of the descent of Christ. The [other] powers being terrified by these things, and marvelling at the novelty of those things which were announced by the prophets, Prunicus brought it about by means of Ialdabaoth (who knew not what he did), that emissions of two men took place, the one from the barren Elizabeth, and the other from the Virgin Mary.

12. And since she herself had no rest either in heaven or on earth, she invoked her mother to assist her in her distress. Upon this, her mother, the first woman, was moved with compassion towards her daughter, on her repentance, and begged from the first man that Christ should be sent to her assistance, who, being sent forth, descended to his sister, and to the besprinkling of light. When he recognised her (that is, the Sophia below), her brother descended to her, and announced his advent through means of John, and prepared the baptism of repentance, and adopted Jesus beforehand, in order that on Christ descending he might find a pure vessel, and that by the son of that Ialdabaoth the woman might be announced by Christ. They further declare that he descended through the seven heavens, having assumed the likeness of their sons, and gradually emptied them of their power. For they maintain that the whole besprinkling of light rushed to him, and that Christ, descending to this world, first clothed his sister Sophia [with it], and that then both exulted in the mutual refreshment they felt in each other's society: this scene they describe as relating to bridegroom and bride. But Jesus, inasmuch as he was begotten of the Virgin through the agency of God, was wiser, purer, and more righteous than all other men: Christ united to Sophia descended into him, and thus Jesus Christ was produced.

13. They affirm that many of his disciples were not aware of the descent of Christ into him; but that, when Christ did descend on Jesus, he then began to work miracles, and heal, and announce the unknown Father, and openly to confess himself the son of the first man. The powers and the father of Jesus were angry at these proceedings, and laboured to destroy him; and when he was being led away for this purpose, they say that Christ himself, along with Sophia, departed from him into the state of an incorruptible Æon, while Jesus was crucified. Christ, however, was not forgetful of his Jesus, but sent down a certain energy into him from above, which raised him up again in the body, which they call both animal and spiritual; for he sent the mundane parts back again into the world. When his disciples saw that he had risen, they did not recognise him — no, not even Jesus himself, by whom he rose again from the dead. And they assert that this very great error prevailed among his disciples, that they imagined he had risen in a mundane body, not knowing that "flesh[3] and blood do not attain to the kingdom of God."

14. They strove to establish the descent and ascent of Christ, by the fact that neither before his baptism, nor after his resurrection from the dead, do his disciples state that he did any mighty works, not being aware that Jesus was united to Christ, and the incorruptible Æon to the Hebdomad; and they declare his mundane body to be of the same nature as that of animals. But after his resurrection he tarried [on earth] eighteen months; and knowledge descending into him from above, he taught what was clear. He instructed a few of his disciples, whom he knew to be capable of understanding so great mysteries, in these things, and was then received up into heaven, Christ sitting down at the right hand of his father Ialdabaoth, that he may receive to himself the souls of those who have known them,[4] after they have laid aside their mundane flesh, thus enriching himself without the knowledge or perception of his father; so that, in proportion as Jesus enriches himself with holy souls, to such an extent does his father suffer loss and is diminished, being emptied of his own power by these souls. For he will not now possess holy souls to send them down again into

---

[1] The Latin here is "ex quibus," and the meaning is exceedingly obscure. Harvey thinks it is the representative ἐξ ὧν (χρόνων) in the Greek, but we prefer to refer it to "Judæos," as above. The next sentence seems unintelligible: but, according to Harvey, "each deified day of the week had his ministering prophets."

[2] The common text inserts "et incorruptibili Æone," but this seems better rejected as a glossarial interpolation.

[3] 1 Cor. xv. 50. The Latin text reads "apprehendunt," which can scarcely be the translation of κληρονομῆσαι in the Greek text of the New Testament.

[4] That is, Christ and Jesus.

the world, except those only which are of his substance, that is, those into which he has breathed. But the consummation [of all things] will take place, when the whole besprinkling of the spirit of light is gathered together, and is carried off to form an incorruptible Æon.

15. Such are the opinions which prevail among these persons, by whom, like the Lernæan hydra, a many-headed beast has been generated from the school of Valentinus. For some of them assert that Sophia herself became the serpent; on which account she was hostile to the creator of Adam, and implanted knowledge in men, for which reason the serpent was called wiser than all others. Moreover, by the position of our intestines, through which the food is conveyed, and by the fact that they possess such a figure, our internal configuration [1] in the form of a serpent reveals our hidden generatrix.

CHAP. XXXI. — DOCTRINES OF THE CAINITES.

1. Others again declare that Cain derived his being from the Power above, and acknowledge that Esau, Korah, the Sodomites, and all such persons, are related to themselves. On this account, they add, they have been assailed by the Creator, yet no one of them has suffered injury. For Sophia was in the habit of carrying off that which belonged to her from them to herself. They declare that Judas the traitor was thoroughly acquainted with these things, and that he alone, knowing the truth as no others did, accomplished the mystery of the betrayal; by him all things, both earthly and heavenly, were thus thrown into confusion. They produce a fictitious history of this kind, which they style the Gospel of Judas.

2. I have also made a collection of their writings in which they advocate the abolition of the doings of Hystera.[2] Moreover, they call this Hystera the creator of heaven and earth. They also hold, like Carpocrates, that men cannot be saved until they have gone through all kinds of experience. An angel, they maintain, attends them in every one of their sinful and abominable actions, and urges them to venture on audacity and incur pollution. Whatever may be the nature[3] of the action, they declare that they do it in the name of the angel, saying, "O thou angel, I use thy work; O thou power, I accomplish thy operation!" And they maintain that this is "perfect knowledge," without shrinking to rush into such actions as it is not lawful even to name.

3. It was necessary clearly to prove, that, as their very opinions and regulations exhibit them, those who are of the school of Valentinus derive their origin from such mothers, fathers, and ancestors, and also to bring forward their doctrines, with the hope that perchance some of them, exercising repentance and returning to the only Creator, and God the Former of the universe, may obtain salvation, and that others may not henceforth be drawn away by their wicked, although plausible, persuasions, imagining that they will obtain from them the knowledge of some greater and more sublime mysteries. But let them rather, learning to good effect from us the wicked tenets of these men, look with contempt upon their doctrines, while at the same time they pity those who, still cleaving to these miserable and baseless fables, have reached such a pitch of arrogance as to reckon themselves superior to all others on account of such knowledge, or, as it should rather be called, ignorance. They have now been fully exposed; and simply to exhibit their sentiments, is to obtain a victory over them.

4. Wherefore I have laboured to bring forward, and make clearly manifest, the utterly ill-conditioned carcase of this miserable little fox.[4] For there will not now be need of many words to overturn their system of doctrine, when it has been made manifest to all. It is as when, on a beast hiding itself in a wood, and by rushing forth from it is in the habit of destroying multitudes, one who beats round the wood and thoroughly explores it, so as to compel the animal to break cover, does not strive to capture it, seeing that it is truly a ferocious beast; but those present can then watch and avoid its assaults, and can cast darts at it from all sides, and wound it, and finally slay that destructive brute. So, in our case, since we have brought their hidden mysteries, which they keep in silence among themselves, to the light, it will not now be necessary to use many words in destroying their system of opinions. For it is now in thy power, and in the power of all thy associates, to familiarize yourselves with what has been said, to overthrow their wicked and undigested doctrines, and to set forth doctrines agreeable to the truth. Since then the case is so, I shall, according to promise, and as my ability serves, labour to overthrow them, by refuting them all in the following book. Even to give an account of them is a tedious affair, as thou seest.[5] But I shall furnish means for overthrowing them, by meeting all their opinions in the order in which they have been described, that I may not only expose the wild beast to view, but may inflict wounds upon it from every side.

---

[1] The text of this sentence is hopelessly corrupt, but the meaning is as given above.
[2] According to Harvey, Hystera corresponds to the "passions" of Achamoth. [Note the "Americanism," *advocate* used as a verb.]
[3] The text is here imperfect, and the translation only conjectural.

[4] [Cant. ii. 15; St. Luke xiii. 32.]
[5] [Let the reader bear in mind that the Greek of this original and very precious author exists only in fragments. We are reading the translation of a translation; the Latin very rude, and the subject itself full of difficulties. It may yet be discovered that some of the faults of the work are not chargeable to Irenæus.]

IRENÆUS AGAINST HERESIES

BOOK II

PREFACE.

1. IN the first book, which immediately precedes this, exposing "knowledge falsely so called,"[1] I showed thee, my very dear friend, that the whole system devised, in many and opposite ways, by those who are of the school of Valentinus, was false and baseless. I also set forth the tenets of their predecessors, proving that they not only differed among themselves, but had long previously swerved from the truth itself. I further explained, with all diligence, the doctrine as well as practice of Marcus the magician, since he, too, belongs to these persons; and I carefully noticed[2] the passages which they garble from the Scriptures, with the view of adapting them to their own fictions. Moreover, I minutely narrated the manner in which, by means of numbers, and by the twenty-four letters of the alphabet, they boldly endeavour to establish [what they regard as] truth. I have also related how they think and teach that creation at large was formed after the image of their invisible Pleroma, and what they hold respecting the Demiurge, declaring at the same time the doctrine of Simon Magus of Samaria, their progenitor, and of all those who succeeded him. I mentioned, too, the multitude of those Gnostics who are sprung from him, and noticed[2] the points of difference between them, their several doctrines, and the order of their succession, while I set forth all those heresies which have been originated by them. I showed, moreover, that all these heretics, taking their rise from Simon, have introduced impious and irreligious doctrines into this life; and I explained the nature of their "redemption," and their method of initiating those who are rendered "perfect," along with their invocations and their mysteries. I proved also that there is one God, the Creator, and that He is not the fruit of any defect, nor is there anything either above Him, or after Him.

2. In the present book, I shall establish those points which fit in with my design, so far as time permits, and overthrow, by means of lengthened treatment under distinct heads, their whole system; for which reason, since it is an exposure and subversion of their opinions, I have so entitled the composition of this work. For it is fitting, by a plain revelation and overthrow of their conjunctions, to put an end to these hidden alliances,[3] and to Bythus himself, and thus to obtain a demonstration that he never existed at any previous time, nor now has any existence.

CHAP. I.— THERE IS BUT ONE GOD: THE IMPOSSIBILITY OF ITS BEING OTHERWISE.

1. IT is proper, then, that I should begin with the first and most important head, that is, God the Creator, who made the heaven and the earth, and all things that are therein (whom these men blasphemously style the fruit of a defect), and to demonstrate that there is nothing either above Him or after Him; nor that, influenced by any one, but of His own free will, He created all things, since He is the only God, the only Lord, the only Creator, the only Father, alone containing all things, and Himself commanding all things into existence.

2. For how can there be any other Fulness, or Principle, or Power, or God, above Him, since it is matter of necessity that God, the Pleroma (Fulness) of all these, should contain all things in His immensity, and should be contained by no one? But if there *is* anything beyond Him, He is not then the Pleroma of all, nor does He contain all. For that which they declare to be beyond Him will be wanting to the Pleroma, or, [in other words,] to that God who is above all things. But that which is wanting, and falls in any way short, is not the

---

[1] 1 Tim. vi. 20.
[2] [Note this "Americanism."]
[3] This passage is very obscure: we have supplied "et," which, as Harvey conjectures, may have dropped out of the text.

Pleroma of all things. In such a case, He would have both beginning, middle, and end, with respect to those who are beyond Him. And if He has an end in regard to those things which are below, He has also a beginning with respect to those things which are above. In like manner, there is an absolute necessity that He should experience the very same thing at all other points, and should be held in, bounded, and enclosed by those existences that are outside of Him. For that being who is the end downwards, necessarily circumscribes and surrounds him who finds his end in it. And thus, according to them, the Father of all (that is, He whom they call Proön and Proarche), with their Pleroma, and the good God of Marcion, is established and enclosed in some other, and is surrounded from without by another mighty Being, who must of necessity be greater, inasmuch as that which contains is greater than that which is contained. But then that which is greater is also stronger, and in a greater degree Lord; and that which is greater, and stronger, and in a greater degree Lord — must be God.

3. Now, since there exists, according to them, also something else which they declare to be outside of the Pleroma, into which they further hold there descended that higher power who went astray, it is in every way necessary that the Pleroma either contains that which is beyond, yet is contained (for otherwise, it will not be beyond the Pleroma; for if there is anything beyond the Pleroma, there will be a Pleroma within this very Pleroma which they declare to be outside of the Pleroma, and the Pleroma will be contained by that which is beyond: and with the Pleroma is understood also the first God); or, again, they must be an infinite distance separated from each other — the Pleroma [I mean], and that which is beyond it. But if they maintain this, there will then be a third kind of existence, which separates by immensity the Pleroma and that which is beyond it. This third kind of existence will therefore bound and contain both the others, and will be greater both than the Pleroma, and than that which is beyond it, inasmuch as it contains both in its bosom. In this way, talk might go on for ever concerning those things which are contained, and those which contain. For if this third existence has its beginning above, and its end beneath, there is an absolute necessity that it be also bounded on the sides, either beginning or ceasing at certain other points, [where new existences begin.] These, again, and others which are above and below, will have their beginnings at certain other points, and so on *ad infinitum;* so that their thoughts would never rest in one God, but, in consequence of seeking after more than exists, would wander away to that which has no existence, and depart from the true God.

4. These remarks are, in like manner, applicable against the followers of Marcion. For his two gods will also be contained and circumscribed by an immense interval which separates them from one another. But then there is a necessity to suppose a multitude of gods separated by an immense distance from each other on every side, beginning with one another, and ending in one another. Thus, by that very process of reasoning on which they depend for teaching that there is a certain Pleroma or God above the Creator of heaven and earth, any one who chooses to employ it may maintain that there is another Pleroma above the Pleroma, above that again another, and above Bythus another ocean of Deity, while in like manner the same successions hold with respect to the sides; and thus, their doctrine flowing out into immensity, there will always be a necessity to conceive of other Pleromata, and other Bythi, so as never at any time to stop, but always to continue seeking for others besides those already mentioned. Moreover, it will be uncertain whether these which we conceive of are below, or are, in fact, themselves the things which are above; and, in like manner, [it will be doubtful] respecting those things which are said by them to be above, whether they are really above or below; and thus our opinions will have no fixed conclusion or certainty, but will of necessity wander forth after worlds without limits, and gods that cannot be numbered.

5. These things, then, being so, each deity will be contented with his own possessions, and will not be moved with any curiosity respecting the affairs of others; otherwise he would be unjust, and rapacious, and would cease to be what God is. Each creation, too, will glorify its own maker, and will be contented with him, not knowing any other; otherwise it would most justly be deemed an apostate by all the others, and would receive a richly-deserved punishment. For it must be either that there is one Being who contains all things, and formed in His own territory all those things which have been created, according to His own will; or, again, that there are numerous unlimited creators and gods, who begin from each other, and end in each other on every side; and it will then be necessary to allow that all the rest are contained from without by some one who is greater, and that they are each of them shut up within their own territory, and remain in it. No one of them all, therefore, is God. For there will be [much] wanting to every one of them, possessing [as he will do] only a very small part when compared with all the rest. The name of the Omnipotent will thus be brought to an end, and such an opinion will of necessity fall into impiety.

CHAP. II. — THE WORLD WAS NOT FORMED BY ANGELS, OR BY ANY OTHER BEING, CONTRARY TO THE WILL OF THE MOST HIGH GOD, BUT WAS MADE BY THE FATHER THROUGH THE WORD.[1]

1. Those, moreover, who say that the world was formed by angels, or by any other maker of it, contrary to the will of Him who is the Supreme Father, err first of all in this very point, that they maintain that angels formed such and so mighty a creation, contrary to the will of the Most High God. This would imply that angels were more powerful than God; or if not so, that He was either careless, or inferior, or paid no regard to those things which took place among His own possessions, whether they turned out ill or well, so that He might drive away and prevent the one, while He praised and rejoiced over the other. But if one would not ascribe such conduct even to a man of any ability, how much less to God!

2. Next let them tell us whether these things have been formed within the limits which are contained by Him, and in His proper territory, or in regions belonging to others, and lying beyond Him? But if they say [that these things were done] beyond Him, then all the absurdities already mentioned will face them, and the Supreme God will be enclosed by that which is beyond Him, in which also it will be necessary that He should find His end. If, on the other hand, [these things were done] within His own proper territory, it will be very idle to say that the world was thus formed within His proper territory against His will by angels who are themselves under His power, or by any other being, as if either He Himself did not behold all things which take place among His own possessions, or[2] was not aware of the things to be done by angels.

3. If, however, [the things referred to were done] not against His will, but with His concurrence and knowledge, as some [of these men] think, the angels, or the Former of the world [whoever that may have been], will no longer be the causes of that formation, but the will of God. For if He is the Former of the world, He too made the angels, or at least was the cause of their creation; and *He* will be regarded as having made the world who prepared the causes of its formation. Although they maintain that the angels were made by a long succession downwards, or that the Former of the world [sprang] from the Supreme Father, as Basilides asserts; nevertheless that which is the cause of those things which have been made will still be traced to Him who was the Author of such a succession. [The case stands] just as regards success in war, which is ascribed to the king who prepared those things which are the cause of victory; and, in like manner, the creation of any state, or of any work, is referred to him who prepared materials for the accomplishment of those results which were afterwards brought about. Wherefore, we do not say that it was the axe which cut the wood, or the saw which divided it; but one would very properly say that the *man* cut and divided it who formed the axe and the saw for this purpose, and [who also formed] at a much earlier date all the tools by which the axe and the saw themselves were formed. With justice, therefore, according to an analogous process of reasoning, the Father of all will be declared the Former of this world, and not the angels, nor any other [so-called] former of the world, other than He who was its Author, and had formerly [3] been the cause of the preparation for a creation of this kind.

4. This manner of speech may perhaps be plausible or persuasive to those who know not God, and who liken Him to needy human beings, and to those who cannot immediately and without assistance form anything, but require many instrumentalities to produce what they intend. But it will not be regarded as at all probable by those who know that God stands in need of nothing, and that He created and made all things by His Word, while He neither required angels to assist Him in the production of those things which are made, nor of any power greatly inferior to Himself, and ignorant of the Father, nor of any defect or ignorance, in order that he who should know Him might become man.[4] But He Himself in Himself, after a fashion which we can neither describe nor conceive, predestinating all things, formed them as He pleased, bestowing harmony on all things, and assigning them their own place, and the beginning of their creation. In this way He conferred on spiritual things a spiritual and invisible nature, on supercelestial things a celestial, on angels an angelical, on animals an animal, on beings that swim a nature suited to the water, and on those that live on the land one fitted for the land — on all, in short, a nature suitable to the character of the life assigned them — while He formed all things that were made by His Word that never wearies.

5. For this is a peculiarity of the pre-eminence of God, not to stand in need of other instruments for the creation of those things which are summoned into existence. His own Word is both suitable and sufficient for the formation of all things, even as John, the disciple of the Lord,

---

[1] [This noble chapter is a sort of homily on Hebrews i.]
[2] The common text has "ut:" we prefer to read "aut" with Erasmus and others.
[3] Vossius and others read "primus" instead of "prius," but on defective MS. authority.
[4] Harvey here observes: "Grabe misses the meaning by applying to the redeemed that which the author says of the Redeemer;" but it may be doubted if this is really the case. Perhaps Massuet's rendering of the clause, "that that man might be formed who should know Him," is, after all, preferable to that given above.

declares regarding Him: "All things were made by Him, and without Him was nothing made."[1] Now, among the "all things" our world must be embraced. It too, therefore, was made by His Word, as Scripture tells us in the book of Genesis that He made all things connected with our world by His Word. David also expresses the same truth [when he says], "For He spake, and they were made; He commanded, and they were created."[2] Whom, therefore, shall we believe as to the creation of the world — these heretics who have been mentioned that prate so foolishly and inconsistently on the subject, or the disciples of the Lord, and Moses, who was both a faithful servant of God and a prophet? He at first narrated the formation of the world in these words: "In the beginning God created the heaven and the earth,"[3] and all other things in succession; but neither gods nor angels [had any share in the work].

Now, that this God is the Father of our Lord Jesus Christ, Paul the apostle also has declared, [saying,] "There is one God, the Father, who is above all, and through all things, and in us all."[4] I have indeed proved already that there is only one God; but I shall further demonstrate this from the apostles themselves, and from the discourses of the Lord. For what sort of conduct would it be, were we to forsake the utterances of the prophets, of the Lord, and of the apostles, that we might give heed to these persons, who speak not a word of sense?

CHAP. III. — THE BYTHUS AND PLEROMA OF THE VALENTINIANS, AS WELL AS THE GOD OF MARCION, SHOWN TO BE ABSURD; THE WORLD WAS ACTUALLY CREATED BY THE SAME BEING WHO HAD CONCEIVED THE IDEA OF IT, AND WAS NOT THE FRUIT OF DEFECT OR IGNORANCE.

1. The Bythus, therefore, whom they conceive of with his Pleroma, and the God of Marcion, are inconsistent. If indeed, as they affirm, he has something subjacent and beyond himself, which they style vacuity and shadow, this vacuum is then proved to be greater than their Pleroma. But it is inconsistent even to make this statement, that while he contains all things within himself, the creation was formed by some other. For it is absolutely necessary that they acknowledge a certain void and chaotic kind of existence (below the spiritual Pleroma) in which this universe was formed, and that the Propator purposely left this chaos as it was, either[5] knowing beforehand what things were to happen in it, or being ignorant of them. If he was really ignorant, then God will not be prescient of all things. But they will not even [in that case] be able to assign a reason on what account He thus left this place void during so long a period of time. If, again, He is prescient, and contemplated mentally that creation which was about to have a being in that place, then He Himself created it who also formed it beforehand [ideally] in Himself.

2. Let them cease, therefore, to affirm that the world was made by any other; for as soon as God formed a conception in His mind, that was also done which He had thus mentally conceived. For it was not possible that one Being should mentally form the conception, and another actually produce the things which had been conceived by Him in His mind. But God, according to these heretics, mentally conceived either an eternal world or a temporal one, *both* of which suppositions cannot be true. Yet if He had mentally conceived of it as eternal, spiritual,[6] and visible, it would also have been formed such. But if it was formed such as it really is, then *He* made it such who had mentally conceived of it as such; or He willed it to exist in the ideality[7] of the Father, according to the conception of His mind, such as it now is, compound, mutable, and transient. Since, then, it is just such as the Father had [ideally] formed in counsel with Himself, it must be worthy of the Father. But to affirm that what was mentally conceived and pre-created by the Father of all, just as it has been actually formed, is the fruit of defect, and the production of ignorance, is to be guilty of great blasphemy. For, according to them, the Father of all will thus be [regarded as] generating in His breast, according to His own mental conception, the emanations of defect and the fruits of ignorance, since the things which He had conceived in His mind have actually been produced.

CHAP. IV. — THE ABSURDITY OF THE SUPPOSED VACUUM AND DEFECT OF THE HERETICS IS DEMONSTRATED.

1. The cause, then, of such a dispensation on the part of God, is to be inquired after; but the formation of the world is not to be ascribed to any other. And all things are to be spoken of as having been so prepared by God beforehand, that they should be made as they have been

---

[1] John i. 3.
[2] Ps. xxxiii. 9, cxlviii. 5.
[3] Gen. i. 1.
[4] Eph. iv. 6, differing somewhat from Text. Rec. of New Testament.
[5] In the barbarous Latin version we here find *utrum . . . an* as the translation of ἤ . . . ἤ, instead of *aut . . . aut*.

[6] We have translated the text as it here stands in the MSS. Grabe omits *spiritalem et;* Massuet proposes to read *et invisibilem*, and Stieren *invisibilem*.
[7] *In præsentia:* Grabe proposes *in præscientia*, but without MS. authority. "The reader," says Harvey, "will observe that there are three suppositions advanced by the author: that the world, as some heretics asserted, was eternal; that it was created in time, with no previous idea of it in the divine mind; or that it existed as a portion of the divine counsels from all eternity, though with no temporal subsistence until the time of its creation, — and of this the author now speaks." The whole passage is most obscurely expressed.

made; but shadow and vacuity are not to be conjured into existence. But whence, let me ask, came this vacuity [of which they speak]? If it was indeed produced by Him who, according to them, is the Father and Author of all things, then it is both equal in honour and related to the rest of the Æons, perchance even more ancient than they are. Moreover, if it proceeded from the same source [as they did], it must be similar in nature to Him who produced it, as well as to those along with whom it was produced. There will therefore be an absolute necessity, both that the Bythus of whom they speak, along with Sige, be similar in nature to a vacuum, that is, that He really is a vacuum; and that the rest of the Æons, since they are the brothers of vacuity, should also be devoid[1] of substance. If, on the other hand, it has not been thus produced, it must have sprung from and been generated by itself, and in that case it will be equal in point of age to that Bythus who is, according to them, the Father of all; and thus vacuity will be of the same nature and of the same honour with Him who is, according to them, the universal Father. For it must of necessity have been either produced by some one, or generated by itself, and sprung from itself. But if, in truth, vacuity was produced, then its producer Valentinus is also a vacuum, as are likewise his followers. If, again, it was not produced, but was generated by itself, then that which is really a vacuum is similar to, and the brother of, and of the same honour with, that Father who has been proclaimed by Valentinus; while it is more ancient, and dating its existence from a period greatly anterior, and more exalted in honour than the remaining Æons of Ptolemy himself, and Heracleon, and all the rest[2] who hold the same opinions.

2. But if, driven to despair in regard to these points, they confess that the Father of all contains all things, and that there is nothing whatever outside of the Pleroma (for it is an absolute necessity that, [if there be anything outside of it,] it should be bounded and circumscribed by something greater than itself), and that they speak of what is *without* and what *within* in reference to knowledge and ignorance, and not with respect to local distance; but that, in the Pleroma, or in those things which are contained by the Father, the whole creation which we know to have been formed, having been made by the Demiurge, or by the angels, is contained by the unspeakable greatness, as the centre is in a circle, or as a spot is in a garment, — then, in the first place, what sort of a being must that Bythus be, who allows a stain to have place in His own bosom, and permits another one to create or produce within His territory, contrary to His own will? Such a mode of acting would truly entail [the charge of] degeneracy upon the entire Pleroma, since it might from the first have cut off that defect, and those emanations which derived their origin from it,[3] and not have agreed to permit the formation of creation either in ignorance, or passion, or in defect. For he who can afterwards rectify a defect, and does, as it were, wash away a stain,[4] could at a much earlier date have taken care that no such stain should, even at first, be found among his possessions. Or if at the first he allowed that the things which were made [should be as they are], since they could not, in fact, be formed otherwise, then it follows that they must always continue in the same condition. For how is it possible, that those things which cannot at the first obtain rectification, should subsequently receive it? Or how can men say that they are called to perfection, when those very beings who are the causes from which men derive their origin — either the Demiurge himself, or the angels — are declared to exist in defect? And if, as is maintained, [the Supreme Being,] inasmuch as He is benignant, did at last take pity upon men, and bestow on them perfection, He ought at first to have pitied those who were the creators of man, and to have conferred on them perfection. In this way, men too would verily have shared in His compassion, being formed perfect by those that were perfect. For if He pitied the *work* of these beings, He ought long before to have pitied *themselves*, and not to have allowed them to fall into such awful blindness.

3. Their talk also about shadow and vacuity, in which they maintain that the creation with which we are concerned was formed, will be brought to nothing, if the things referred to were created within the territory which is contained by the Father. For if they hold that the light of their Father is such that it fills all things which are inside of Him, and illuminates them all, how can any vacuum or shadow possibly exist within that territory which is contained by the Pleroma, and by the light of the Father? For, in that case, it behoves them to point out some place within the Propator, or within the Pleroma, which is not illuminated, nor kept possession of by any one, and in which either the angels or the Demiurge formed whatever they pleased. Nor will it be a small amount of space in which such and so great a creation can be

---

[1] Literally, "should also possess a vacant substance."
[2] The text has "reliquis omnibus," which would refer to the Æons; but we follow the emendation proposed by Massuet, "reliquorum omnium," as the reference manifestly is to other heretics.
[3] "*Ab eo*:" some refer "eo" to the Demiurge, but it is not unusual for the Latin translator to follow the Greek gender, although different from that of the Latin word which he has himself employed. We may therefore here refer "eo" to "labem," which is the translation of the neuter noun ὑστέρημα.
[4] *Labem* is here repeated, probably by mistake.

conceived of as having been formed. There will therefore be an absolute necessity that, within the Pleroma, or within the Father of whom they speak, they should conceive[1] of some place, void, formless, and full of darkness, in which those things were formed which have been formed. By such a supposition, however, the light of their Father would incur a reproach, as if He could not illuminate and fill those things which are within Himself. Thus, then, when they maintain that these things were the fruit of defect and the work of error, they do moreover introduce defect and error within the Pleroma, and into the bosom of the Father.

CHAP. V. — THIS WORLD WAS NOT FORMED BY ANY OTHER BEINGS WITHIN THE TERRITORY WHICH IS CONTAINED BY THE FATHER.

1. The remarks, therefore, which I made a little while ago[2] are suitable in answer to those who assert that this world was formed outside of the Pleroma, or under a "good God;" and such persons, with the Father they speak of, will be quite cut off from that which is outside the Pleroma, in which, at the same time, it is necessary that they should finally rest.[3] In answer to those, again, who maintain that this world was formed by certain other beings within that territory which is contained by the Father, all those points which have now[4] been noticed will present themselves [as exhibiting their] absurdities and incoherencies; and they will be compelled either to acknowledge all those things which are within the Father, lucid, full, and energetic, or to accuse the light of the Father as if He could not illuminate all things; or, as a portion of their Pleroma [is so described], the whole of it must be confessed to be void, chaotic, and full of darkness. And they accuse all other created things as if these were merely temporal, or [at the best], if eternal,[5] yet material. But[6] these (the Æons) ought to be regarded as beyond the reach of such accusations, since they are within the Pleroma, or the charges in question will equally fall against the entire Pleroma; and thus the Christ of whom they speak is discovered to be the author of ignorance. For, according to their statements, when He had given a form so far as substance was concerned to the Mother they conceive of, He cast her outside of the Pleroma; that is, He cut her off from knowledge. He, therefore, who separated her from knowledge, did in reality produce ignorance in her. How then could the very same person bestow the gift of knowledge on the rest of the Æons, those who were anterior to Him [in production], and yet be the author of ignorance to His Mother? For He placed her beyond the pale of knowledge, when He cast her outside of the Pleroma.

2. Moreover, if they explain being within and without the Pleroma as implying knowledge and ignorance respectively, as certain of them do (since he who has knowledge is within that which knows), then they must of necessity grant that the Saviour Himself (whom they designate *All Things*) was in a state of ignorance. For they maintain that, on His coming forth outside of the Pleroma, He imparted form to their Mother [Achamoth]. If, then, they assert that whatever is outside [the Pleroma] is ignorant of all things, and if the Saviour went forth to impart form to their Mother, then He was situated beyond the pale of the knowledge of all things; that is, He was in ignorance. How then could He communicate knowledge to her, when He Himself was beyond the pale of knowledge? For we, too, they declare to be outside the Pleroma, inasmuch as we are outside of the knowledge which they possess. And once more.: If the Saviour really went forth beyond the Pleroma to seek after the sheep which was lost, but the Pleroma is [co-extensive with] knowledge, then He placed Himself beyond the pale of knowledge, that is, in ignorance. For it is necessary either that they grant that what is outside the Pleroma is so in a local sense, in which case all the remarks formerly made will rise up against them; or if they speak of that which is within in regard to knowledge, and of that which is without in respect to ignorance, then their Saviour, and Christ long before Him, must have been formed in ignorance, inasmuch as they went forth beyond the Pleroma, that is, beyond the pale of knowledge, in order to impart form to their Mother.

3. These arguments may, in like manner, be adapted to meet the case of all those who, in any way, maintain that the world was formed either by angels or by any other one than the true God. For the charges which they bring against the Demiurge, and those things which were made material and temporal, will in truth fall back on the Father; if indeed the[7] very things which

---

[1] The Latin is *fieri eos:* Massuet conjectures that the Greek had been ποιεῖσθαι αὐτούς, and that the translator rendered ποιεῖσθαι as a passive instead of a middle verb, *fieri* for *facere*.
[2] See above, chap. i.
[3] The Latin text here is, "et concludentur tales cum patre suo ab eo qui est extra Pleroma, in quo etiam et desinere eos necesse est." None of the editors notice the difficulty or obscurity of the clause, but it appears to us absolutely untranslateable. We have rendered it as if the reading were "ab eo *quod*," though, if the strict grammatical construction be followed, the translation must be, "from *Him* who." But then to what does "in quo," which follows, refer? It may be ascribed either to the immediate antecedent *Pleroma*, or to *Him* who is described as being beyond it.
[4] Chap. ii., iii., iv.
[5] This is an extremely difficult passage. We follow the reading *æternochoica* adopted by Massuet, but Harvey reads *æterna choica*, and renders, "They charge all other substance (i.e., spiritual) with the imperfections of the material creation, as though Æon substance were equally ephemeral and choic."
[6] The common reading is "aut;" we adopt Harvey's conjectural emendation of "at."
[7] The above clause is very obscure; Massuet reads it interrogatively.

were formed in the bosom of the Pleroma began by and by in fact to be dissolved, in accordance with the permission and good-will of the Father. The [immediate] Creator, then, is not the [real] Author of this work, thinking, as He did, that He formed it very good, but *He* who allows and approves of the productions of defect, and the works of error having a place among his own possessions, and that temporal things should be mixed up with eternal, corruptible with incorruptible, and those which partake of error with those which belong to truth. If, however, these things were formed without the permission or approbation of the Father of all, then that Being must be more powerful, stronger, and more kingly, who made these things within a territory which properly belongs to Him (the Father), and did so without His permission. If again, as some say, their Father permitted these things without approving of them, then He gave the permission on account of some necessity, being either able to prevent [such procedure], or not able. But if indeed He could not [hinder it], then He is weak and powerless; while, if He could, He is a seducer, a hypocrite, and a slave of necessity, inasmuch as He does not consent [to such a course], and yet allows it as if He did consent. And allowing error to arise at the first, and to go on increasing, He endeavours in later times to destroy it, when already many have miserably perished on account of the [original] defect.

4. It is not seemly, however, to say of Him who is God over all, since He is free and independent, that He was a slave to necessity, or that anything takes place with His permission, yet against His desire; otherwise they will make necessity greater and more kingly than God, since that which has the most power is superior [1] to all [others]. And He ought at the very beginning to have cut off the causes of [the fancied] necessity, and not to have allowed Himself to be shut up to yielding to that necessity, by permitting anything besides that which became Him. For it would have been much better, more consistent, and more God-like, to cut off at the beginning the principle of this kind of necessity, than afterwards, as if moved by repentance, to endeavour to extirpate the results of necessity when they had reached such a development. And if the Father of all be a slave to necessity, and must yield to fate, while He unwillingly tolerates the things which are done, but is at the same time powerless to do anything in opposition to necessity and fate (like the Homeric Jupiter, who says of necessity, "I have willingly given thee, yet with unwilling mind"), then, according to this reasoning, the Bythus of whom they speak will be found to be the slave of necessity and fate.

CHAP. VI.—THE ANGELS AND THE CREATOR OF THE WORLD COULD NOT HAVE BEEN IGNORANT OF THE SUPREME GOD.

1. How, again, could either the angels, or the Creator of the world, have been ignorant of the Supreme God, seeing they were His property, and His creatures, and were contained by Him? He might indeed have been invisible to them on account of His superiority, but He could by no means have been unknown to them on account of His providence. For though it is true, as they declare, that they were very far separated from Him through their inferiority [of nature], yet, as His dominion extended over all of them, it behoved them to know their Ruler, and to be aware of this in particular, that He who created them is Lord of all. For since His invisible essence is mighty, it confers on all a profound mental intuition and perception of His most powerful, yea, omnipotent greatness. Wherefore, although "no one knows the Father, except the Son, nor the Son except the Father, and those to whom the Son will reveal Him," [2] yet all [beings] do know this one fact at least, because reason, implanted in their minds, moves them, and reveals to them [the truth] that there is one God, the Lord of all.

2. And on this account all things have been [by general consent] placed under the sway of Him who is styled the Most High, and the Almighty. By calling upon Him, even before the coming of our Lord, men were saved both from most wicked spirits, and from all kinds of demons, and from every sort of apostate power. This was the case, not as if earthly spirits or demons had seen Him, but because they knew of the existence of Him who is God over all, at whose invocation they trembled, as there does tremble every creature, and principality, and power, and every being endowed with energy under His government. By way of parallel, shall not those who live under the empire of the Romans, although they have never seen the emperor, but are far separated from him both by land and sea, know very well, as they experience his rule, who it is that possesses the principal power in the state? How then could it be, that those angels who were superior to us [in nature], or even He whom they call the Creator of the world, did not know the Almighty, when even dumb animals tremble and yield at the invocation of His name? And as, although they have not seen Him, yet all things are subject to the name of our Lord,[3] so must they also be to His who made and established all things by His word, since it was no other than He who formed the world. And for this reason do the Jews even now put demons to flight by means

---

[1] The text has "antiquius," literally "more ancient," but it may here be rendered as above.
[2] Matt. xi. 27.
[3] Massuet refers this to the Roman emperor.

of this very adjuration, inasmuch as all beings fear the invocation of Him who created them.

3. If, then, they shrink from affirming that the angels are more irrational than the dumb animals, they will find that it behoved these, although they had not seen Him who is God over all, to know His power and sovereignty. For it will appear truly ridiculous, if they maintain that they themselves indeed, who dwell upon the earth, know Him who is God over all whom they have never seen, but will not allow Him who, according to their opinion, formed them and the whole world, although He dwells in the heights and above the heavens, to know those things with which they themselves, though they dwell below, are acquainted. [This is the case], unless perchance they maintain that Bythus lives in Tartarus below the earth, and that on this account they have attained to a knowledge of Him before those angels who have their abode on high. Thus do they rush into such an abyss of madness as to pronounce the Creator of the world void of understanding. They are truly deserving of pity, since with such utter folly they affirm that He (the Creator of the world) neither knew His Mother, nor her seed, nor the Pleroma of the Æons, nor the Propator, nor what the things were which He made; but that these are images of those things which are within the Pleroma, the Saviour having secretly laboured that they should be so formed [by the unconscious Demiurge], in honour of those things which are above.

CHAP. VII. — CREATED THINGS ARE NOT THE IMAGES OF THOSE ÆONS WHO ARE WITHIN THE PLEROMA.

1. While the Demiurge was thus ignorant of all things, they tell us that the Saviour conferred honour upon the Pleroma by the creation [which he summoned into existence] through means of his Mother, inasmuch as he produced similitudes and images of those things which are above. But I have already shown that it was impossible that anything should exist *beyond* the Pleroma (in which external region they tell us that images were made of those things which are within the Pleroma), or that this world was formed by any other one than the Supreme God. But if it is a pleasant thing to overthrow them on every side, and to prove them vendors of falsehood; let us say, in opposition to them, that if these things were made by the Saviour to the honour of those which are above, after their likeness, then it behoved them always to endure, that those things which have been honoured should perpetually continue in honour. But if they do in fact pass away, what is the use of this very brief period of honour, — an honour which at one time had no existence, and which shall again come to nothing? In that case I shall prove that the Saviour is rather an aspirant after vainglory, than [1] one who honours those things which are above. For what honour can those things which are temporal confer on such as are eternal and endure for ever? or those which pass away on such as remain? or those which are corruptible on such as are incorruptible? — since, even among men who are themselves mortal, there is no value attached to that honour which speedily passes away, but to that which endures as long as it possibly can. But those things which, as soon as they are made, come to an end, may justly be said rather to have been formed for the contempt of such as are thought to be honoured by them; and that that which is eternal is contumeliously treated when its image is corrupted and dissolved. But what if their Mother had not wept, and laughed, and been involved in despair? The Saviour would not then have possessed any means of honouring the Fulness, inasmuch as her last state of confusion [2] did not have substance of its own by which it might honour the Propator.

2. Alas for the honour of vainglory which at once passes away, and no longer appears! There will be some [3] Æon, in whose case such honour will not be thought at all to have had an existence, and then the things which are above will be unhonoured; or it will be necessary to produce once more another Mother weeping, and in despair, in order to the honour of the Pleroma. What a dissimilar, and at the same time blasphemous image! Do you tell me that an image of the Only-begotten was produced by the former [4] of the world, whom [5] again ye wish to be considered the Nous (mind) of the Father of all, and [yet maintain] that this image was ignorant of itself, ignorant of creation, — ignorant, too, of the Mother, — ignorant of everything that exists, and of those things which were made by it; and are you not ashamed while, in opposition to yourselves, you ascribe ignorance even to the Only-begotten Himself? For if these things [below] were made by the Saviour after the similitude of those which are above, while He (the Demiurge) who was made after such similitude was in so great ignorance, it necessarily follows that around Him, and in accordance with Him, after whose likeness he that is thus ignorant was formed, ignorance of the kind in question spiritually exists.

---

[1] Harvey supposes that the translator here read ἢ *quam* instead of ἢ *quâ* (gloria); but Grabe, Massuet, and Stieren prefer to delete *erit*.

[2] Reference is here made to the supposed wretched state of Achamoth as lying in the region of shadow, vacuity, and, in fact, non-existence, until compassionated by the Christ above, who gave her form as respected *substance*.

[3] We have literally translated the above very obscure sentence. According to Massuet, the sense is: "There will some time be, or perhaps even now there is, some Æon utterly destitute of such honour, inasmuch as those things which the Saviour, for the sake of honouring it, had formed after its image, have been destroyed; and then those things which are above will remain without honour," etc.

[4] The Saviour is here referred to, as having formed all things through means of Achamoth and the Demiurge.

[5] Massuet deletes *quem*, and reads *nūn* as a genitive.

For it is not possible, since both were produced spiritually, and neither fashioned nor composed, that in some the likeness was preserved, while in others the likeness of the image was spoiled, that image which was here produced that it might be according to the image of that production which is above. But if it is not similar, the charge will then attach to the Saviour, who produced a dissimilar image, — of being, so to speak, an incompetent workman. For it is out of their power to affirm that the Saviour had not the faculty of production, since they style Him *All Things*. If, then, the image is dissimilar, he is a poor workman, and the blame lies, according to their hypothesis, with the Saviour. If, on the other hand, it is similar, then the same ignorance will be found to exist in the Nous (mind) of their Propator, that is, in the Only-begotten. The Nous of the Father, in that case, was ignorant of Himself; ignorant, too, of the Father; ignorant, moreover, of those very things which were formed by Him. But if *He* has knowledge, it necessarily follows also that he who was formed after his likeness by the Saviour should know the things which are like; and thus, according to their own principles, their monstrous blasphemy is overthrown.

3. Apart from this, however, how can those things which belong to creation, various, manifold, and innumerable as they are, be the images of those thirty Æons which are within the Pleroma, whose names, as these men fix them, I have set forth in the book which precedes this? And not only will they be unable to adapt the [vast] variety of creation at large to the [comparative] smallness of their Pleroma, but they cannot do this even with respect to any one part of it, whether [that possessed by] celestial or terrestrial beings, or those that live in the waters. For they themselves testify that their Pleroma consists of thirty Æons; but any one will undertake to show that, in a single department of those [created beings] which have been mentioned, they reckon that there are not thirty, but many thousands of species. How then can those things, which constitute such a multiform creation, which are opposed in nature to each other, and disagree among themselves, and destroy the one the other, be the images and likenesses of the thirty Æons of the Pleroma, if indeed, as they declare, these being possessed of one nature, are of equal and similar properties, and exhibit no differences [among themselves]? For it was incumbent, if these things are images of those Æons, — inasmuch as they declare that some men are wicked by nature, and some, on the other hand, naturally good, — to point out such differences also among their Æons, and to maintain that some of them were produced naturally good, while some were naturally evil, so that the supposition of the likeness of those things might harmonize with the Æons. Moreover, since there are in the world some creatures that are gentle, and others that are fierce, some that are innocuous, while others are hurtful and destroy the rest; some have their abode on the earth, others in the water, others in the air, and others in the heaven; in like manner, they are bound to show that the Æons possess such properties, if indeed the one are the images of the others. And besides; "the eternal fire which the Father has prepared for the devil and his angels,"[2] — they ought to show of which of those Æons that are above it is the image; for it, too, is reckoned part of the creation.

4. If, however, they say that these things are the images of the Enthymesis of that Æon who fell into passion, then, first of all, they will act impiously against their Mother, by declaring her to be the first cause of evil and corruptible images. And then, again, how can those things which are manifold, and dissimilar, and contrary in their nature, be the images of one and the same Being? And if they say that the angels of the Pleroma are numerous, and that those things which are many are the images of these — not in this way either will the account they give be satisfactory. For, in the first place, they are then bound to point out differences among the angels of the Pleroma, which are mutually opposed to each other, even as the images existing below are of a contrary nature among themselves. And then, again, since there are many, yea, innumerable angels who surround the Creator, as all the prophets acknowledge, — [saying, for instance,] "Ten thousand times ten thousand stood beside Him, and many thousands of thousands ministered unto Him,"[2] — then, according[3] to them, the angels of the Pleroma will have as images the angels of the Creator, and the entire creation remains in the image of the Pleroma, but so that the thirty Æons no longer correspond to the manifold variety of the creation.

5. Still further, if these things [below] were made after the similitude of those [above], after the likeness of which again will those then be made? For if the Creator of the world did not form these things directly from His own[4] conception, but, like an architect of no ability, or a boy receiving his first lesson, copied them from archetypes furnished by others, then whence did their Bythus obtain the forms of that creation which He at first produced? It clearly follows

---
[1] Matt. xxv. 41.
[2] Dan. vii. 10, agreeing neither with the Greek nor Hebrew text.
[3] This clause is exceedingly obscure. Harvey remarks upon it as follows: "The reasoning of Irenæus seems to be this: According to the Gnostic theory, the Æons and angels of the Pleroma were homogeneous. They were also the archetypes of things created. But things created are heterogeneous: therefore either these Æons are heterogeneous, which is contrary to theory; or things created are homogeneous, which is contrary to fact."
[4] Literally, "from Himself."

that He must have received the model from some other one who is above Him, and that one, in turn, from another. And none the less [for these suppositions], the talk about images, as about gods, will extend to infinity, if we do not at once fix our mind on one Artificer, and on one God, who of Himself formed those things which have been created. Or is it really the case that, in regard to mere men, one will allow that they have of themselves invented what is useful for the purposes of life, but will not grant to that God who formed the world, that of Himself He created the forms of those things which have been made, and imparted to it its orderly arrangement?

6. But, again, how can these things [below] be images of those [above], since they are really contrary to them, and can in no respect have sympathy with them? For those things which are contrary to each other may indeed be destructive of those to which they are contrary, but can by no means be their images — as, for instance, water and fire; or, again, light and darkness, and other such things, can never be the images of one another. In like manner, neither can those things which are corruptible and earthly, and of a compound nature, and transitory, be the images of those which, according to these men, are spiritual; unless these very things themselves be allowed to be compound, limited in space, and of a definite shape, and thus no longer spiritual, and diffused, and spreading into vast extent, and incomprehensible. For they must of necessity be possessed of a definite figure, and confined within certain limits, that they may be true images; and then it is decided that they are not spiritual. If, however, these men maintain that they are spiritual, and diffused, and incomprehensible, how can those things which are possessed of figure, and confined within certain limits, be the images of such as are destitute of figure and incomprehensible?

7. If, again, they affirm that neither according to configuration nor formation, but according to number and the order of production, those things [above] are the images [of these below], then, in the first place, these things [below] ought not to be spoken of as images and likenesses of those Æons that are above. For how can the things which have neither the fashion nor shape of those [above] be their images? And, in the next place, they would adapt both the numbers and productions of the Æons above, so as to render them identical with and similar to those that belong to the creation [below]. But now, since they refer to only thirty Æons, and declare that the vast multitude of things which are embraced within the creation [below] are images of those that are but thirty, we may justly condemn them as utterly destitute of sense.

CHAP. VIII. — CREATED THINGS ARE NOT A SHADOW OF THE PLEROMA.

1. If, again, they declare that these things [below] are a shadow of those [above], as some of them are bold enough to maintain, so that in this respect they are images, then it will be necessary for them to allow that those things which are above are possessed of bodies. For those bodies which are above do cast a shadow, but spiritual substances do not, since they can in no degree darken others. If, however, we also grant them this point (though it is, in fact, an impossibility), that there is a shadow belonging to those essences which are spiritual and lucent, into which they declare their Mother descended; yet, since those things [which are above] are eternal, and that shadow which is cast by them endures for ever, [it follows that] these things [below] are also not transitory, but endure along with those which cast their shadow over them. If, on the other hand, these things [below] are transitory, it is a necessary consequence that those [above] also, of which these are the shadow, pass away; while, if they endure, their shadow likewise endures.

2. If, however, they maintain that the shadow spoken of does not exist as being produced by the shade of [those above], but simply in this respect, that [the things below] are far separated from those [above], they will then charge the light of their Father with weakness and insufficiency, as if it cannot extend so far as these things, but fails to fill that which is empty, and to dispel the shadow, and that when no one is offering any hindrance. For, according to them, the light of their Father will be changed into darkness and buried in obscurity, and will come to an end in those places which are characterized by emptiness, since it cannot penetrate and fill all things. Let them then no longer declare that their Bythus is the fulness of all things, if indeed he has neither filled nor illuminated that which is vacuum and shadow; or, on the other hand, let them cease talking of vacuum and shadow, if the light of their Father does in truth fill all things.

3. Beyond the primary Father, then — that is, the God who is over all — there can neither be any Pleroma into which they declare the Enthymesis of that Æon who suffered passion, descended (so that the Pleroma itself, or the primary God, should not be limited and circumscribed by that which is beyond, and should, in fact, be contained by it); nor can vacuum or shadow have any existence, since the Father exists beforehand, so that His light cannot fail, and find end in a vacuum. It is, moreover, irrational and impious to conceive of a place in which He who is, according to them, Propator, and Proarche, and Father of all, and of this

Pleroma, ceases and has an end. Nor, again, is it allowable, for the reasons[1] already stated, to allege that some other being formed so vast a creation in the bosom of the Father, either with or without His consent. For it is equally impious and infatuated to affirm that so great a creation was[2] formed by angels, or by some particular production ignorant of the true God in that territory which is His own. Nor is it possible that those things which are earthly and material could have been formed within their Pleroma, since that is wholly spiritual. And further, it is not even possible that those things which belong to a multiform creation, and have been formed with mutually opposite qualities, [could have been created] after the image of the things above, since these (i.e., the Æons) are said to be few, and of a like formation, and homogeneous. Their talk, too, about the shadow of *kenoma* — that is, of a vacuum — has in all points turned out false. Their figment, then, [in what way soever viewed,] has been proved groundless,[3] and their doctrines untenable. Empty, too, are those who listen to them, and are verily descending into the abyss of perdition.

CHAP. IX. — THERE IS BUT ONE CREATOR OF THE WORLD, GOD THE FATHER: THIS THE CONSTANT BELIEF OF THE CHURCH.

1. That God is the Creator of the world is accepted even by those very persons who in many ways speak against Him, and yet acknowledge Him, styling Him the Creator, and an angel, not to mention that all the Scriptures call out [to the same effect], and the Lord teaches us of this Father[4] who is in heaven, and no other, as I shall show in the sequel of this work. For the present, however, that proof which is derived from those who allege doctrines opposite to ours, is of itself sufficient, — all men, in fact, consenting to this truth: the ancients on their part preserving with special care, from the tradition of the first-formed man, this persuasion, while they celebrate the praises of one God, the Maker of heaven and earth; others, again, after them, being reminded of this fact by the prophets of God, while the very heathen learned it from creation itself. For even creation reveals Him who formed it, and the very work made suggests Him who made it, and the world manifests Him who ordered it. The Universal Church, moreover, through the whole world, has received this tradition from the apostles.

2. This God, then, being acknowledged, as I have said, and receiving testimony from all to the fact of His existence, that Father whom they conjure into existence is beyond doubt untenable, and has no witnesses [to his existence]. Simon Magus was the first who said that he himself was God over all, and that the world was formed by his angels. Then those who succeeded him, as I have shown in the first book,[5] by their several opinions, still further depraved [his teaching] through their impious and irreligious doctrines against the Creator. These [heretics now referred to],[6] being the disciples of those mentioned, render such as assent to them worse than the heathen. For the former "serve the creature rather than the Creator,"[7] and "those which are not gods,"[8] notwithstanding that they ascribe the first place in Deity to that God who was the Maker of this universe. But the latter maintain that He, [i.e., the Creator of this world,] is the fruit of a defect, and describe Him as being of an animal nature, and as not knowing that Power which is above Him, while He also exclaims, "I am God, and besides Me there is no other God."[9] Affirming that He lies, they are themselves liars, attributing all sorts of wickedness to Him; and conceiving of one who is not above this Being as really having an existence, they are thus convicted by their own views of blasphemy against that God who really exists, while they conjure into existence a god who has no existence, to their own condemnation. And thus those who declare themselves "perfect," and as being possessed of the knowledge of all things, are found to be worse than the heathen, and to entertain more blasphemous opinions even against their own Creator.

CHAP. X. — PERVERSE INTERPRETATIONS OF SCRIPTURE BY THE HERETICS: GOD CREATED ALL THINGS OUT OF NOTHING, AND NOT FROM PRE-EXISTENT MATTER.

1. It is therefore in the highest degree irrational, that we should take no account of Him who is truly God, and who receives testimony from all, while we inquire whether there is above Him that [other being] who really has no existence, and has never been proclaimed by any one. For that nothing has been clearly spoken regarding Him, they themselves furnish testimony; for since they, with wretched success, transfer to that being who has been conceived of by them, those parables [of Scripture] which, whatever the form in which they have been spoken, are sought after [for this purpose], it is manifest that they now generate another [god], who was

---

[1] See above, chap. ii. and v.
[2] The text has *fabricásse*, for which, says Massuet, should be read *fabricatam esse;* or *fabricásse* itself must be taken in a passive signification. It is possible, however, to translate, as Harvey indicates, "that He (Bythus) formed so great a creation by angels," etc., though this seems harsh and unsuitable.
[3] Literally, *empty:* there is a play on the words *vacuum* and *vacui* (which immediately follows), as there had been in the original Greek.
[4] Comp. e.g., Matt. v. 16, v. 45, vi. 9, etc.
[5] See chap. xxiii. etc.
[6] Viz., the Valentinians.
[7] Rom. i. 25.
[8] Gal. iv. 8.
[9] Isa. xlvi. 9.

never previously sought after. For by the fact that they thus endeavour to explain ambiguous passages of Scripture (ambiguous, however, not as if referring to another god, but as regards the dispensations of [the true] God), they have constructed another god, weaving, as I said before, ropes of sand, and affixing a more important to a less important question. For no question can be solved by means of another which itself awaits solution; nor, in the opinion of those possessed of sense, can an ambiguity be explained by means of another ambiguity, or enigmas by means of another greater enigma, but things of such character receive their solution from those which are manifest, and consistent, and clear.

2. But these [heretics], while striving to explain passages of Scripture and parables, bring forward another more important, and indeed impious question, to this effect, "Whether there be really another god above that God who was the Creator of the world?" They are not in the way of solving the questions [which they propose]; for how could they find means of doing so? But they append an important question to one of less consequence, and thus insert [in their speculations] a difficulty incapable of solution. For in order that they may [1] know "knowledge" itself (yet not learning this fact, that the Lord, when thirty years old, came to the baptism of truth), they do impiously despise that God who was the Creator, and who sent Him for the salvation of men. And that they may be deemed capable of informing us whence is the substance of matter, while they believe not that God, according to His pleasure, in the exercise of His own will and power, formed all things (so that those things which now are should have an existence) out of what did not previously exist, they have collected [a multitude of] vain discourses. They thus truly reveal their infidelity; they do not believe in that which really exists, and they have fallen away into [the belief of] that which has, in fact, no existence.

3. For, when they tell us that all moist substance proceeded from the tears of Achamoth, all lucid substance from her smile, all solid substance from her sadness, all mobile substance from her terror, and that thus they have sublime knowledge on account of which they are superior to others, — how can these things fail to be regarded as worthy of contempt, and truly ridiculous? They do not believe that God (being powerful, and rich in all resources) created matter itself, inasmuch as they know not how much a spiritual and divine essence can accomplish. But they do believe that their Mother, whom they style a female from a female, produced from her passions aforesaid the so vast material substance of creation. They inquire, too, whence the substance of creation was supplied to the Creator; but they do not inquire whence [were supplied] to their Mother (whom they call the Enthymesis and impulse of the Æon that went astray) so great an amount of tears, or perspiration, or sadness, or that which produced the remainder of matter.

4. For, to attribute the substance of created things to the power and will of Him who is God of all, is worthy both of credit and acceptance. It is also agreeable [to reason], and there may be well said regarding such a belief, that "the things which are impossible with men are possible with God."[2] While men, indeed, cannot make anything out of nothing, but only out of matter already existing, yet God is in this point preeminently superior to men, that He Himself called into being the substance of His creation, when previously it had no existence. But the assertion that matter was produced from the Enthymesis of an Æon going astray, and that the Æon [referred to] was far separated from her Enthymesis, and that, again, her passion and feeling, apart from herself, became matter — is incredible, infatuated, impossible, and untenable.

CHAP. XI. — THE HERETICS, FROM THEIR DISBELIEF OF THE TRUTH, HAVE FALLEN INTO AN ABYSS OF ERROR: REASONS FOR INVESTIGATING THEIR SYSTEMS.

1. They do not believe that He, who is God above all, formed by His Word, in His own territory, as He Himself pleased, the various and diversified [works of creation which exist], inasmuch as He is the former of all things, like a wise architect, and a most powerful monarch. But they believe that angels, or some power separate from God, and who was ignorant of Him, formed this universe. By this course, therefore, not yielding credit to the truth, but wallowing in falsehood, they have lost the bread of true life, and have fallen into vacuity[3] and an abyss of shadow. They are like the dog of Æsop, which dropped the bread, and made an attempt at seizing its shadow, thus losing the [real] food. It is easy to prove from the very words of the Lord, that He acknowledges one Father and Creator of the world, and Fashioner of man, who was proclaimed by the law and the prophets, while He knows no other, and that this One is really God over all; and that He teaches that adoption of sons pertaining to the Father, which is eternal life, takes place through Himself, conferring it [as He does] on all the righteous.

---

[1] This clause is unintelligible in the Latin text: by a conjectural restoration of the Greek we have given the above translation.

[2] Luke xviii. 27.

[3] Playing upon the doctrines of the heretics with respect to *vacuity* and *shade*.

2. But since these men delight in attacking us, and in their true character of cavillers assail us with points which really tell not at all against us, bringing forward in opposition to us a multitude of parables and [captious] questions, I have thought it well, on the other side, first of all to put to them the following inquiries concerning their own doctrines, to exhibit their improbability, and to put an end to their audacity. After this has been done, [I intend] to bring forward the discourses of the Lord, so that they may not only be rendered destitute of the means of attacking us, but that, since they will be unable reasonably to reply to those questions which are put, they may see that their plan of argument is destroyed; so that, either returning to the truth, and humbling themselves, and ceasing from their multifarious phantasies, they may propitiate God for those blasphemies they have uttered against Him, and obtain salvation; or that, if they still persevere in that system of vainglory which has taken possession of their minds, they may at least find it necessary to change their kind of argument against us.

CHAP. XII. — THE TRIACONTAD OF THE HERETICS ERRS BOTH BY DEFECT AND EXCESS: SOPHIA COULD NEVER HAVE PRODUCED ANYTHING APART FROM HER CONSORT; LOGOS AND SIGE COULD NOT HAVE BEEN CONTEMPORARIES.

1. We may [1] remark, in the first place, regarding their Triacontad, that the whole of it marvellously falls to ruin on both sides, that is, both as respects defect and excess. They say that to indicate it the Lord came to be baptized at the age of thirty years. But this assertion really amounts to a manifest subversion of their entire argument. As to defect, this happens as follows: first of all, because they reckon the Propator among the other Æons. For the Father of all ought not to be counted with other productions; He who was not produced with that which was produced; He who was unbegotten with that which was born; He whom no one comprehends with that which is comprehended by Him, and who is on this account [Himself] incomprehensible; and He who is without figure with that which has a definite shape. For inasmuch as He is superior to the rest, He ought not to be numbered with them, and that so that He who is impassible and not in error should be reckoned with an Æon subject to passion, and actually in error. For I have shown in the book which immediately precedes this, that, beginning with Bythus, they reckon up the Tricontad to Sophia, whom they describe as the erring Æon; and I have also there set forth the names of their [Æons]; but if He be not reckoned, there are no longer, on their own showing, thirty productions of Æons, but these then become only twenty-nine.

2. Next, with respect to the first production Ennœa, whom they also term Sige, from whom again they describe Nous and Aletheia as having been sent forth, they err in both particulars. For it is impossible that the thought (Ennœa) of any one, or his silence (Sige), should be understood apart from himself; and that, being sent forth beyond him, it should possess a special figure of its own. But if they assert that the (Ennœa) was not sent forth beyond Him, but continued one with the Propator, why then do they reckon her with the other Æons — with those who were not one [with the Father], and are on this account ignorant of His greatness? If, however, she was so united (let us take this also into consideration), there is then an absolute necessity, that from this united and inseparable conjunction, which constitutes but one being, there [2] should proceed an unseparated and united production, so that it should not be dissimilar to Him who sent it forth. But if this be so, then just as Bythus and Sige, so also Nous and Aletheia will form one and the same being, ever cleaving mutually together. And inasmuch as the one cannot be conceived of without the other, just as water cannot [be conceived of] without [the thought of] moisture, or fire without [the thought of] heat, or a stone without [the thought] of hardness (for these things are mutually bound together, and the one cannot be separated from the other, but always co-exists with it), so it behoves Bythus to be united in the same way with Ennœa, and Nous with Aletheia. Logos and Zoe again, as being sent forth by those that are thus united, ought themselves to be united, and to constitute only one being. But, according to such a process of reasoning, Homo and Ecclesia too, and indeed all the remaining conjunctions of the Æons produced, ought to be united, and always to co-exist, the one with the other. For there is a necessity in their opinion, that a female Æon should exist side by side with a male one, inasmuch as she is, so to speak, [the forthputting of] his affection.

3. These things being so, and such opinions being proclaimed by them, they again venture, without a blush, to teach that the younger Æon of the Duodecad, whom they also style Sophia, did, apart from union with her consort, whom they call Theletus, endure passion, and separately, without any assistance from him, gave birth to a production which they name "a female from a female." They thus rush into such utter frenzy, as to form two most clearly opposite opinions respecting the same point. For if

---

[1] The text vacillates between "dicemus" and "dicamus."

[2] This sentence is confused in the Latin text, but the meaning is evidently that given above.

Bythus is ever one with Sige, Nous with Aletheia, Logos with Zoe, and so on, as respects the rest, how could Sophia, without union with her consort, either suffer or generate anything? And if, again, she did really suffer passion apart from him, it necessarily follows that the other conjunctions also admit of disjunction and separation among themselves, — a thing which I have already shown to be impossible. It is also impossible, therefore, that Sophia suffered passion apart from Theletus; and thus, again, their whole system of argument is overthrown. For they have yet[1] again derived the whole of remaining [material substance], like the composition of a tragedy, from that passion which they affirm she experienced apart from union with her consort.

4. If, however, they impudently maintain, in order to preserve from ruin their vain imaginations, that the rest of the conjunctions also were disjoined and separated from one another on account of this latest conjunction, then [I reply that], in the first place, they rest upon a thing which is impossible. For how can they separate the Propator from his Ennœa, or Nous from Aletheia, or Logos from Zoe, and so on with the rest? And how can they themselves maintain that they tend again to unity, and are, in fact, all at one, if indeed these very conjunctions, which are within the Pleroma, do not preserve unity, but are separate from one another; and that to such a degree, that they both endure passion and perform the work of generation without union one with another, just as hens do apart from intercourse with cocks.

5. Then, again, their first and first-begotten Ogdoad will be overthrown as follows: They must admit that Bythus and Sige, Nous and Aletheia, Logos and Zoe, Anthropos and Ecclesia, do individually dwell in the same Pleroma. But it is impossible that Sige (silence) can exist in the presence of Logos (speech), or again, that Logos can manifest himself in the presence of Sige. For these are mutually destructive of each other, even as light and darkness can by no possibility exist in the same place: for if light prevails, there cannot be darkness; and if darkness, there cannot be light, since, where light appears, darkness is put to flight. In like manner, where Sige is, there cannot be Logos; and where Logos is, there certainly cannot be Sige. But if they say that Logos simply exists within[2] (unexpressed), Sige also will exist within, and will not the less be destroyed by the Logos within. But that he really is not merely conceived of in the mind, the very order of the production of their (Æons) shows.

6. Let them not then declare that the first and principal Ogdoad consists of Logos and Sige, but let them [as a matter of necessity] exclude either Sige or Logos; and then their first and principal Ogdoad is at an end. For if they describe the conjunctions [of the Æons] as united, then their whole argument falls to pieces. Since, if they were united, how could Sophia have generated a defect without union with her consort? If, on the other hand, they maintain that, as in production, each of the Æons possesses his own peculiar substance, then how can Sige and Logos manifest themselves in the same place? So far, then, with respect to defect.

7. But again, their Triacontad is overthrown as to excess by the following considerations. They represent Horos (whom they call by a variety of names which I have mentioned in the preceding book) as having been produced by Monogenes just like the other Æons. Some of them maintain that this Horos was produced by Monogenes, while others affirm that he was sent forth by the Propator himself in His own image. They affirm further, that a production was formed by Monogenes — Christ and the Holy Spirit; and they do not reckon these in the number of the Pleroma, nor the Saviour either, whom they also declare to be *Totum*[3] (all things). Now, it is evident even to a blind man, that not merely thirty productions, as they maintain, were sent forth, but four more along with these thirty. For they reckon the Propator himself in the Pleroma, and those too, who in succession were produced by one another. Why is it, then, that those [other beings] are not reckoned as existing with these in the same Pleroma, since they were produced in the same manner? For what just reason can they assign for not reckoning along with the other Æons, either Christ, whom they describe as having, according to the Father's will, been produced by Monogenes, or the Holy Spirit, or Horos, whom they also call Soter[4] (Saviour), and not even the Saviour Himself, who came to impart assistance and form to their Mother? Whether is this as if these latter were weaker than the former, and therefore unworthy of the name of Æons, or of being numbered among them, or as if they were superior and more excellent? But how could they be weaker, since they were produced for the establishment and rectification of the others? And then, again, they cannot possibly be superior to the first and principal Tetrad, by which they were also produced; for it, too, is reckoned in the number above men-

---

[1] It is difficult to see the meaning of "iterum" here. Harvey begins a new paragraph with this sentence.
[2] ἐνδιάθετος — simply *conceived* in the mind — used in opposition to προφορικός, *expressed*.
[3] Harvey remarks that "the author perhaps wrote Ὅρον (*Horos*), which was read by the translator" Ὅλον (*totum*).
[4] Since *Soter* does not occur among the various appellations of Horos mentioned by Irenæus (i. 11, 4), Grabe proposes to read *Stauros*, and Massuet *Lytrotes;* but Harvey conceives that the difficulty is explained by the fact that Horos was a *power* of Soter (i. 3, 3).

tioned. These latter beings, then, ought also to have been numbered in the Pleroma of the Æons, or that should be deprived of the honour of those Æons which bear this appellation (the Tetrad).

8. Since, therefore, their Triacontad is thus brought to nought, as I have shown, both with respect to defect and excess (for in dealing with such a number, either excess or defect [to any extent] will render the number untenable, and how much more so great variations?), it follows that what they maintain respecting their Ogdoad and Duodecad is a mere fable which cannot stand. Their whole system, moreover, falls to the ground, when their very foundation is destroyed and dissolved into Bythus,[1] that is, into what has no existence. Let them, then, henceforth seek to set forth some other reasons why the Lord came to be baptized at the age of thirty years, and [explain in some other way] the Duodecad of the apostles; and [the fact stated regarding] her who suffered from an issue of blood; and all the other points respecting which they so madly labour in vain.

CHAP. XIII. — THE FIRST ORDER OF PRODUCTION MAINTAINED BY THE HERETICS IS ALTOGETHER INDEFENSIBLE.

1. I now proceed to show, as follows, that the first order of production, as conceived of by them, must be rejected. For they maintain that Nous and Aletheia were produced from Bythus and his Ennœa, which is proved to be a contradiction. For Nous is that which is itself chief, and highest, and, as it were, the principle and source of all understanding. Ennœa, again, which arises from him, is any sort of emotion concerning any subject. It cannot be, therefore, that Nous was produced by Bythus and Ennœa; it would be more like the truth for them to maintain that Ennœa was produced as the daughter of the Propator and this Nous. For Ennœa is not the daughter of Nous, as they assert, but Nous becomes the father of Ennœa. For how can Nous have been produced by the Propator, when he holds the chief and primary place of that hidden and invisible affection which is within Him? By this affection sense is produced, and Ennœa, and Enthymesis, and other things which are simply synonyms for Nous himself. As I have said already, they are merely certain definite exercises in thought of that very power concerning some particular subject. We understand the [several] terms according to their[2] length and breadth of meaning, not according to any [fundamental] change [of signification]; and the [various exercises of thought] are limited by [the same sphere of] knowledge, and are expressed together by [the same] term, the [very same] sense remaining within, and creating, and administering, and freely governing even by its own power, and as it pleases, the things which have been previously mentioned.

2. For the first exercise of that [power] respecting anything, is styled Ennœa; but when it continues, and gathers strength, and takes possession of the whole soul, it is called Enthymesis. This Enthymesis, again, when it exercises itself a long time on the same point, and has, as it were, been proved, is named Sensation. And this Sensation, when it is much developed, becomes Counsel. The increase, again, and greatly developed exercise of this Counsel becomes the Examination of thought (Judgment); and this remaining in the mind is most properly termed Logos (reason), from which the spoken Logos (word) proceeds.[3] But all the [exercises of thought] which have been mentioned are [fundamentally] one and the same, receiving their origin from Nous, and obtaining [different] appellation according to their increase. Just as the human body, which is at one time young, then in the prime of life, and then old, has received [different] appellations according to its increase and continuance, but not according to any change of substance, or on account of any [real] loss of body, so is it with those [mental exercises]. For, when one [mentally] contemplates anything, he also thinks of it; and when he thinks of it, he has also knowledge regarding it; and when he knows it, he also considers it; and when he considers it, he also mentally handles it; and when he mentally handles it, he also speaks of it. But, as I have already said, it is Nous who governs all these [mental processes], while He is himself invisible, and utters speech of himself by means of those processes which have been mentioned, as it were by rays [proceeding from Him], but He himself is not sent forth by any other.

3. These things may properly be said to hold good in men, since they are compound by nature, and consist of a body and a soul. But those who affirm that Ennœa was sent forth from God, and Nous from Ennœa, and then, in succession, Logos from these, are, in the first place, to be blamed as having improperly used these productions; and, in the next place, as describing the affections, and passions, and mental tendencies of men, while they [thus prove them-

---

[1] Irenæus here, after his custom, plays upon the word *Bythus* (profundity), which, in the phraseology of the Valentinians, was a name of the Propator, but is in this passage used to denote *an unfathomable abyss*.
[2] This sentence appears to us, after long study, totally untranslateable. The general meaning seems to be, that whatever name is given to mental acts, whether they are called *Ennœa, Enthymesis,* or by whatever other appellation, they are all but exercises of the same fundamental power, styled *Nous*. Compare the following section.
[3] "The following," says Harvey, "may be considered to be consecutive steps in the evolution of λόγος as a psychological entity. Ennœa, *conception;* Enthymesis, *intention;* Sensation, *thought;* Consilium, *reasoning;* Cogitationis Examinatio, *judgment;* in Mente Perseverans, Λόγος ἐνδιάθετος; Emissibile Verbum, Λόγος προφορικός."

selves] ignorant of God. By their manner of speaking, they ascribe those things which apply to men to the Father of all, whom they also declare to be unknown to all; and they deny that He himself made the world, to guard against attributing want of power[1] to Him; while, at the same time, they endow Him with human affections and passions. But if they had known the Scriptures, and been taught by the truth, they would have known, beyond doubt, that God is not as men are; and that His thoughts are not like the thoughts of men.[2] For the Father of all is at a vast distance from those affections and passions which operate among men. He is a simple, uncompounded Being, without diverse members,[3] and altogether like, and equal to Himself, since He is wholly understanding, and wholly spirit, and wholly thought, and wholly intelligence, and wholly reason, and wholly hearing, and wholly seeing, and wholly light, and the whole source of all that is good — even as the religious and pious are wont to speak concerning God.

4. He is, however, above [all] these properties, and therefore indescribable. For He may well and properly be called an Understanding which comprehends all things, but He is not [on that account] like the understanding of men; and He may most properly be termed Light, but He is nothing like that light with which we are acquainted. And so, in all other particulars, the Father of all is in no degree similar to human weakness. He is spoken of in these terms according to the love [we bear Him]; but in point of greatness, our thoughts regarding Him transcend these expressions. If then, even in the case of human beings, understanding itself does not arise from emission, nor is that intelligence which produces other things separated from the living man, while its motions and affections come into manifestation, much more will the mind of God, who is all understanding, never by any means be separated from Himself; nor can anything[4] [in His case] be produced as if by a different Being.

5. For if He produced intelligence, then He who did thus produce intelligence must be understood, in accordance with their views, as a compound and corporeal Being; so that God, who sent forth [the intelligence referred to], is separate from it, and the intelligence which was sent forth separate [from Him]. But if they affirm that intelligence was sent forth from intelligence, they then cut asunder the intelligence of God, and divide it into parts. And whither has it gone? Whence was it sent forth? For whatever is sent forth from any place, passes of necessity into some other. But what existence was there more ancient than the intelligence of God, into which they maintain it was sent forth? And what a vast region that must have been which was capable of receiving and containing the intelligence of God! If, however, they affirm [that this emission took place] just as a ray proceeds from the sun, then, as the subjacent air which receives the ray must have had an existence prior to it, so [by such reasoning] they will indicate that there was something in existence, into which the intelligence of God was sent forth, capable of containing it, and more ancient than itself. Following upon this, we must hold that, as we see the sun, which is less than all things, sending forth rays from himself to a great distance, so likewise we say that the Propator sent forth a ray beyond, and to a great distance from, Himself. But what can be conceived of beyond, or at a distance from, God, into which He sent forth this ray?

6. If, again, they affirm that that [intelligence] was not sent forth beyond the Father, but within the Father Himself, then, in the first place, it becomes superfluous to say that it was sent forth at all. For how could it have been sent forth if it continued within the Father? For an emission is the manifestation of that which is emitted, beyond him who emits it. In the next place, this [intelligence] being sent forth, both that Logos who springs from Him will still be within the Father, as will also be the future emissions proceeding from Logos. These, then, cannot in such a case be ignorant of the Father, since they are within Him; nor, being all equally surrounded by the Father, can any one know Him less [than another] according to the descending order of their emission. And all of them must also in an equal measure continue impassible, since they exist in the bosom of their Father, and none of them can ever sink into a state of degeneracy or degradation. For with the Father there is no degeneracy, unless perchance as in a great circle a smaller is contained, and within this one again a smaller; or unless they affirm of the Father, that, after the manner of a sphere or a square, He contains within Himself on all sides the likeness of a sphere, or the production of the rest of the Æons in the form of a square, each one of these being surrounded by that one who is above him in greatness, and surrounding in turn that one who is after him in smallness; and that on this account, the smallest and the last of all, having its place in the centre, and thus being far separated from the Father, was really ignorant of the Propator. But if they maintain any such hypothesis, they must shut up their Bythus with

---

[1] That is, lest He should be thought destitute of power, as having been unable to prevent evil from having a place in creation.
[2] Isa. lv. 8.
[3] The Latin expression is "similimembrius," which some regard as the translation of ὁμοιόκωλος, and others of ὁμοιομερής; but in either case the meaning will be as given above.
[4] That is, His Nous, Ennœa, etc., can have no independent existence. The text fluctuates between "emittitur" and "emittetur."

in a definite form and space, while He both surrounds others, and is surrounded by them; for they must of necessity acknowledge that there is something outside of Him which surrounds Him. And none the less will the talk concerning those that contain, and those that are contained, flow on into infinitude; and all [the Æons] will most clearly appear to be bodies enclosed [by one another].

7. Further, they must also confess either that He is mere vacuity, or that the entire universe is within Him; and in that case all will in like degree partake of the Father. Just as, if one forms circles in water, or round or square figures, all these will equally partake of water; just as those, again, which are framed in the air, must necessarily partake of air, and those which [are formed] in light, of light; so must those also who are within Him all equally partake of the Father, ignorance having no place among them. Where, then, is this partaking of the Father who fills [all things]? If, indeed, He has filled [all things], there will be no ignorance among them. On this ground, then, their work of [supposed] degeneracy is brought to nothing, and the production of matter with the formation of the rest of the world; which things they maintain to have derived their substance from passion and ignorance. If, on the other hand, they acknowledge that He is vacuity, then they fall into the greatest blasphemy; they deny His spiritual nature. For how can He be a spiritual being, who cannot fill even those things which are within Him?

8. Now, these remarks which have been made concerning the emission of intelligence are in like manner applicable in opposition to those who belong to the school of Basilides, as well as in opposition to the rest of the Gnostics, from whom these also (the Valentinians) have adopted the ideas about emissions, and were refuted in the first book. But I have now plainly shown that the first production of Nous, that is, of the intelligence they speak of, is an untenable and impossible opinion. And let us see how the matter stands with respect to the rest [of the Æons]. For they maintain that Logos and Zoe were sent forth by him (i.e., Nous) as fashioners of this Pleroma; while they conceive of an emission of Logos, that is, the Word after the analogy of human feelings, and rashly form conjectures respecting God, as if they had discovered something wonderful in their assertion that Logos was produced by Nous. All indeed have a clear perception that this may be logically affirmed with respect to men.[1] But in Him who is God over all, since He is all Nous, and all Logos, as I have said before, and has in Himself nothing more ancient or late than another, and nothing at variance with another, but continues altogether equal, and similar, and homogeneous, there is no longer ground for conceiving of such production in the order which has been mentioned. Just as he does not err who declares that God is all vision, and all hearing (for in what manner He sees, in that also He hears; and in what manner He hears, in that also He sees), so also he who affirms that He is all intelligence, and all word, and that, in whatever respect He is intelligence, in that also He is word, and that this Nous is His Logos, will still indeed have only an inadequate conception of the Father of all, but will entertain far more becoming [thoughts regarding Him] than do those who transfer the generation of the word to which men gave utterance to the eternal Word of God, assigning a beginning and course of production [to Him], even as they do to their own word. And in what respect will the Word of God — yea, rather God Himself, since He is the Word — differ from the word of men, if He follows the same order and process of generation?

9. They have fallen into error, too, respecting Zoe, by maintaining that she was produced in the sixth place, when it behoved her to take precedence of all [the rest], since God is life, and incorruption, and truth. And these and such like attributes have not been produced according to a gradual scale of descent, but they are names of those perfections which always exist in God, so far as it is possible and proper for men to hear and to speak of God. For with the name of God the following words will harmonize: intelligence, word, life, incorruption, truth, wisdom, goodness, and such like. And neither can any one maintain that intelligence is more ancient than life, for intelligence itself is life; nor that life is later than intelligence, so that He who is the intellect of all, that is God, should at one time have been destitute of life. But if they affirm that life was indeed [previously] in the Father, but was produced in the sixth place in order that the Word might live, surely it ought long before, [according to such reasoning,] to have been sent forth, in the fourth place, that Nous might have life; and still further, even before Him, [it should have been] with Bythus, that their Bythus might live. For to reckon Sige, indeed, along with their Propator, and to assign her to Him as His consort, while they do not join Zoe to the number, — is not this to surpass all other madness?

10. Again, as to the second production which proceeds from these [Æons who have been mentioned], — that, namely, of Homo and Ecclesia, — their very fathers, falsely styled Gnostics, strive among themselves, each one seeking to make good his own opinions, and thus convicting themselves of being wicked thieves.

---

[1] That is, in human beings no doubt, *thought* (Nous) precedes *speech* (Logos).

They maintain that it is more suitable to [the theory of] production — as being, in fact, truthlike — that the Word was produced by man, and not man by the Word; and that man existed prior to the Word, and that this is really He who is God over all. And thus it is, as I have previously remarked, that heaping together with a kind of plausibility all human feelings, and mental exercises, and formation of intentions, and utterances of words, they have lied with no plausibility at all against God. For while they ascribe the things which happen to men, and whatsoever they recognise themselves as experiencing, to the divine reason, they seem to those who are ignorant of God to make statements suitable enough. And by these human passions, drawing away their intelligence, while they describe the origin and production of the Word of God in the fifth place, they assert that thus they teach wonderful mysteries, unspeakable and sublime, known to no one but themselves. It was, [they affirm,] concerning these that the Lord said, "Seek, and ye shall find,"[1] that is, that they should inquire how Nous and Aletheia proceeded from Bythus and Sige; whether Logos and Zoe again derive their origin from these; and then, whether Anthropos and Ecclesia proceed from Logos and Zoe.

CHAP. XIV. — VALENTINUS AND HIS FOLLOWERS DERIVED THE PRINCIPLES OF THEIR SYSTEM FROM THE HEATHEN; THE NAMES ONLY ARE CHANGED.

1. Much more like the truth, and more pleasing, is the account which Antiphanes,[2] one of the ancient comic poets, gives in his *Theogony* as to the origin of all things. For he speaks of Chaos as being produced from Night and Silence; relates that then Love[3] sprang from Chaos and Night; from this again, Light; and that from this, in his opinion, were derived all the rest of the first generation of the gods. After these he next introduces a second generation of gods, and the creation of the world; then he narrates the formation of mankind by the second order of the gods. These men (the heretics), adopting this fable as their own, have ranged their opinions round it, as if by a sort of natural process, changing only the names of the things referred to, and setting forth the very same beginning of the generation of all things, and their production. In place of Night and Silence they substitute Bythus and Sige; instead of Chaos, they put Nous; and for Love (by whom, says the comic poet, all other things were set in order) they have brought forward the Word; while for the primary and greatest gods they have formed the Æons; and in place of the secondary gods, they tell us of that creation by their mother which is outside of the Pleroma, calling it the second Ogdoad. They proclaim to us, like the writer referred to, that from this (Ogdoad) came the creation of the world and the formation of man, maintaining that they alone are acquainted with these ineffable and unknown mysteries. Those things which are everywhere acted in the theatres by comedians with the clearest voices they transfer to their own system, teaching them undoubtedly through means of the same arguments, and merely changing the names.

2. And not only are they convicted of bringing forward, as if their own [original ideas], those things which are to be found among the comic poets, but they also bring together the things which have been said by all those who were ignorant of God, and who are termed philosophers; and sewing together, as it were, a motley garment out of a heap of miserable rags, they have, by their subtle manner of expression, furnished themselves with a cloak which is really not their own. They do, it is true, introduce a new kind of doctrine, inasmuch as by a new sort of art it has been substituted [for the old]. Yet it is in reality both old and useless, since these very opinions have been sewed together out of ancient dogmas redolent of ignorance and irreligion. For instance, Thales[4] of Miletus affirmed that water was the generative and initial principle of all things. Now it is just the same thing whether we say *water* or *Bythus*. The poet Homer,[5] again, held the opinion that Oceanus, along with mother Tethys, was the origin of the gods: this idea these men have transferred to Bythus and Sige. Anaximander laid it down that infinitude is the first principle of all things, having seminally in itself the generation of them all, and from this he declares the immense worlds [which exist] were formed: this, too, they have dressed up anew, and referred to Bythus and their Æons. Anaxagoras, again, who has also been surnamed "Atheist," gave it as his opinion that animals were formed from seeds falling down from heaven upon earth. This thought, too, these men have transferred to "the seed" of their Mother, which they maintain to be themselves; thus acknowledging at once, in the judgment of such as are possessed of sense, that they themselves are the offspring of the irreligious Anaxagoras.

3. Again, adopting the [ideas of] shade and vacuity from Democritus and Epicurus, they

---

[1] Matt. vii. 7.
[2] Nothing is known of this writer. Several of the same name are mentioned by the ancients, but to none of them is a work named *Theogonia* ascribed. He is supposed to be the same poet as is cited by Athenæus, but that writer quotes from a work styled Ἀφροδίτης γοναί.
[3] The Latin is "Cupidinem;" and Harvey here refers to Aristotle, who "quotes the authority of Hesiod and Parmenides as saying that Love is the eternal intellect, reducing Chaos into order."
[4] Compare, on the opinions of the philosophers referred to in this chapter, Hippolytus, *Philosoph.*, book i.
[5] *Iliad*, xiv. 201; vii. 99.

have fitted these to their own views, following upon those [teachers] who had already talked a great deal about a vacuum and atoms, the one of which they called *that which is*, and the other *that which is not*. In like manner, these men call those things which are within the Pleroma real existences, just as those philosophers did the atoms; while they maintain that those which are without the Pleroma have no true existence, even as those did respecting the vacuum. They have thus banished themselves in this world (since they are here outside of the Pleroma) into a place which has no existence. Again, when they maintain that these things [below] are images of those which have a true existence [above], they again most manifestly rehearse the doctrine of Democritus and Plato. For Democritus was the first who maintained that numerous and diverse figures were stamped, as it were, with the forms [of things above], and descended from universal space into this world. But Plato, for his part, speaks of matter, and exemplar,[1] and God. These men, following those distinctions, have styled what he calls ideas, and exemplar, the *images* of those things which are above; while, through a mere change of name, they boast themselves as being discoverers and contrivers of this kind of imaginary fiction.

4. This opinion, too, that they hold the Creator formed the world out of previously existing matter, both Anaxagoras, Empedocles, and Plato expressed before them; as, forsooth, we learn they also do under the inspiration of their Mother. Then again, as to the opinion that everything of necessity passes away to those things out of which they maintain it was also formed, and that God is the slave of this necessity, so that He cannot impart immortality to what is mortal, or bestow incorruption on what is corruptible, but every one passes into a substance similar in nature to itself, both those who are named Stoics from the portico (στοὰ), and indeed all that are ignorant of God, poets and historians alike, make the same affirmation.[2] Those [heretics] who hold the same [system of] infidelity have ascribed, no doubt, their own proper region to spiritual beings, — that, namely, which is within the Pleroma, but to animal beings the intermediate space, while to corporeal they assign that which is material. And they assert that God Himself can do no otherwise, but that every one of the [different kinds of substance] mentioned passes away to those things which are of the same nature [with itself].

5. Moreover, as to their saying that the Saviour was formed out of all the Æons, by every one of them depositing, so to speak, in Him his own special flower, they bring forward nothing new that may not be found in the Pandora of Hesiod. For what he says respecting her, these men insinuate concerning the Saviour, bringing Him before us as Pandoros (All-gifted), as if each of the Æons had bestowed on Him what He possessed in the greatest perfection. Again, their opinion as to the indifference of [eating of] meats and other actions, and as to their thinking that, from the nobility of their nature, they can in no degree at all contract pollution, whatever they eat or perform, they have derived it from the Cynics, since they do in fact belong to the same society as do these [philosophers]. They also strive to transfer to [the treatment of matters of] faith that hairsplitting and subtle mode of handling questions which is, in fact, a copying of Aristotle.

6. Again, as to the desire they exhibit to refer this whole universe to numbers, they have learned it from the Pythagoreans. For these were the first who set forth numbers as the initial principle of all things, and [described] that initial principle of theirs as being both equal and unequal, out of which [two properties] they conceived that both things sensible [3] and immaterial derived their origin. And [they held] that one set of first principles [4] gave rise to the matter [of things], and another to their form. They affirm that from these first principles all things have been made, just as a statue is of its metal and its special form. Now, the heretics have adapted this to the things which are outside of the Pleroma. The [Pythagoreans] maintained that the [5] principle of intellect is proportionate to the energy wherewith mind, as a recipient of the comprehensible, pursues its inquiries, until, worn out, it is resolved at length in the Indivisible and One. They further affirm that Hen — that is, One — is the first principle of all things, and the substance of all that has been formed. From this again proceeded the Dyad, the Tetrad, the Pentad, and the manifold generation of the others. These things the heretics repeat, word for word, with a reference to their Pleroma and Bythus.

---

[1] The Latin has here *exemplum*, corresponding doubtless to παράδειγμα, and referring to those ἰδέαι of all things which Plato supposed to have existed for ever in the divine mind.

[2] [Our author's demonstration of the essential harmony of Gnosticism with the old mythologies, and the philosophies of the heathen, explains the hold it seems to have gained among nominal converts to Christianity, and also the necessity for a painstaking refutation of what seem to us mere absurdities. The great merit of Irenæus is thus illustrated: he gave the death-blow to heathenism in extirpating heresy.]

[3] The Latin text reads "sensibilia et insensata;" but these words, as Harvey observes, must be the translation of αἰσθητὰ καὶ ἀναίσθητα, — "the former referring to material objects of sense, the latter to the immaterial world of intellect."

[4] This clause is very obscure, and we are not sure if the above rendering brings out the real meaning of the author. Harvey takes a different view of it, and supposes the original Greek to have been, καὶ ἄλλας μὲν τῆς ὑποστάσεως ἀρχὰς εἶναι ἄλλας δὲ τῆς αἰσθήσεως καὶ τῆς οὐσίας. He then remarks: "The reader will observe that the word ὑπόστασις here means *intellectual substance*, οὐσία *material;* as in V. c. ult. The meaning therefore of the sentence will be, *And they affirmed that the first principles of intellectual substance and of sensible and material existence were diverse,* viz., unity was the exponent of the first, duality of the second."

[5] All the editors confess the above sentence hopelessly obscure. We have given Harvey's conjectural translation.

From the same source, too, they strive to bring into vogue those conjunctions which proceed from unity. Marcus boasts of such views as if they were his own, and as if he were seen to have discovered something more novel than others, while he simply sets forth the Tetrad of Pythagoras as the originating principle and mother of all things.

7. But I will merely say, in opposition to these men — Did all those who have been mentioned, with whom you have been proved to coincide in expression, know, or not know, the truth? If they knew it, then the descent of the Saviour into this world was superfluous. For why [in that case] did He descend? Was it that He might bring that truth which was [already] known to the knowledge of those who knew it? If, on the other hand, these men did *not* know it, then how is it that, while you express yourselves in the same terms as do those who knew not the truth, ye boast that yourselves alone possess that knowledge which is above all things, although they who are ignorant of God [likewise] possess it? Thus, then, by a complete perversion[1] of language, they style ignorance of the truth knowledge: and Paul well says [of them, that [they make use of] "novelties of words of false knowledge."[2] For that knowledge of theirs is truly found to be false. If, however, taking an impudent course with respect to these points, they declare that men indeed did not know the truth, but that their Mother,[3] the seed of the Father, proclaimed the mysteries of truth through such men, even as also through the prophets, while the Demiurge was ignorant [of the proceeding], then I answer, in the first place, that the things which were predicted were not of such a nature as to be intelligible to no one; for the men themselves knew what they were saying, as did also their disciples, and those again succeeded these. And, in the next place, if either the Mother or her seed knew and proclaimed those things which were of the truth (and the Father[4] is truth), then on their theory the Saviour spake falsely when He said, "No one knoweth the Father but the Son,"[5] unless indeed they maintain that their seed or Mother is *No-one*.

8. Thus far, then, by means of [ascribing to their Æons] human feelings, and by the fact that they largely coincide in their language with many of those who are ignorant of God, they have been seen plausibly drawing a certain number away [from the truth]. They lead them on by the use of those [expressions] with which they have been familiar, to that sort of discourse which treats of all things, setting forth the production of the Word of God, and of Zoe, and of Nous, and bringing into the world, as it were, the [successive] emanations of the Deity. The views, again, which they propound, without either plausibility or parade, are simply lies from beginning to end. Just as those who, in order to lure and capture any kind of animals, place their accustomed food before them, gradually drawing them on by means of the familiar aliment, until at length they seize it, but, when they have taken them captive, they subject them to the bitterest of bondage, and drag them along with violence whithersoever they please; so also do these men gradually and gently persuading [others], by means of their plausible speeches, to accept of the emission which has been mentioned, then bring forward things which are not consistent, and forms of the remaining emissions which are not such as might have been expected. They declare, for instance, that [ten][6] Æons were sent forth by Logos and Zoe, while from Anthropos and Ecclesia there proceeded twelve, although they have neither proof, nor testimony, nor probability, nor anything whatever of such a nature [to support these assertions]; and with equal folly and audacity do they wish it to be believed that from Logos and Zoe, being Æons, were sent forth Bythus and Mixis, Ageratos and Henosis, Autophyes and Hedone, Acinetos and Syncrasis, Monogenes and Macaria. Moreover, [as they affirm,] there were sent forth, in a similar way, from Anthropos and Ecclesia, being Æons, Paracletus and Pistis, Patricos and Elpis, Metricos and Agape, Ainos and Synesis, Ecclesiasticus and Macariotes, Theletos and Sophia.

9. The passions and error of this Sophia, and how she ran the risk of perishing through her investigation [of the nature] of the Father, as they relate, and what took place outside of the Pleroma, and from what sort of a defect they teach that the Maker of the world was produced, I have set forth in the preceding book, describing in it, with all diligence, the opinions of these heretics. [I have also detailed their views] respecting Christ, whom they describe as having been produced subsequently to all these, and also regarding Soter, who, [according to them,] derived his being from those Æons who were formed within the Pleroma.[7] But I have of necessity mentioned their names at present, that from these the absurdity of their falsehood may be made manifest, and also the confused nature of the nomenclature they have devised. For

---

[1] Literally, "antiphrasis."
[2] 1 Tim. vi. 20. The text is, "Vocum novitates falsæ agnitionis," καινοφωνίας having apparently been read in the Greek instead of κενοφωνίας as in Text. Rec.
[3] Grabe and others insert " vel " between these words.
[4] It seems necessary to regard these words as parenthetical, though the point is overlooked by all the editors.
[5] Matt. xi. 27.
[6] "Decem" is of doubtful authority.
[7] The text has "qui in labe facti sunt;" but, according to Harvey, "the sense requires πληρώματι instead of ἐκτρώματι in the original."

they themselves detract from [the dignity of] their Æons by a multitude of names of this sort. They give out names plausible and credible to the heathen, [as being similar] to those who are called their twelve gods,[1] and even these they will have to be images of their twelve Æons. But the images [so called] can produce names [of their own] much more seemly, and more powerful through their etymology to indicate divinity [than are those of their fancied prototypes].

CHAP. XV. — NO ACCOUNT CAN BE GIVEN OF THESE PRODUCTIONS.

1. But let us return to the fore-mentioned question as to the production [of the Æons]. And, in the first place, let them tell us the reason of the production of the Æons being of such a kind that they do not come in contact with any of those things which belong to creation. For they maintain that those things [above] were not made on account of creation, but creation on account of them; and that the former are not images of the latter, but the latter of the former. As, therefore, they render a reason for the images, by saying that the month has thirty days on account of the thirty Æons, and the day twelve hours, and the year twelve months, on account of the twelve Æons which are within the Pleroma, with other such nonsense of the same kind, let them now tell us also the reason for that production of the Æons, why it was of such a nature, for what reason the first and first-begotten *Ogdoad* was sent forth, and not a Pentad, or a Triad, or a Septenad, or any one of those which are defined by a different number? Moreover, how did it come to pass, that from Logos and Zoe were sent forth ten Æons, and neither more nor less; while again from Anthropos and Ecclesia proceeded twelve, although these might have been either more or less numerous?

2. And then, again, with reference to the entire Pleroma, what reason is there that it should be divided into these three — an Ogdoad, a Decad, and a Duodecad — and not into some other number different from these? Moreover, with respect to the division itself, why has it been made into *three* parts, and not into four, or five, or six, or into some other number among those which have no connection with such numbers[2] as belong to creation? For they describe those [Æons above] as being more ancient than these [created things below], and it behoves them to possess their principle [of being] in themselves, one which existed before creation, and not after the pattern of creation, all exactly agreeing as to the point.[3]

3. The account which *we* give of creation is one harmonious with that regular order [of things prevailing in the world], for this scheme of ours is adapted to the [4] things which have [actually] been made; but it is a matter of necessity that they, being unable to assign any reason belonging to the things themselves, with regard to those beings that existed before [creation], and were perfected by themselves, should fall into the greatest perplexity. For, as to the points on which they interrogate us as knowing nothing of creation, they themselves, when questioned in turn respecting the Pleroma, either make mention of mere human feelings, or have recourse to that sort of speech which bears only upon that harmony observable in creation, improperly giving us replies concerning things which are secondary, and not concerning those which, as they maintain, are primary. For we do not question them concerning that harmony which belongs to creation, nor concerning human feelings; but because they must acknowledge, as to their octiform, deciform, and duodeciform Pleroma (the image of which they declare creation to be), that their Father formed it of that figure vainly and thoughtlessly, and must ascribe to Him deformity, if He made anything without a reason. Or, again, if they declare that the Pleroma was so produced in accordance with the foresight of the Father, for the sake of creation, as if He had thus symmetrically arranged its very essence, then it follows that the Pleroma can no longer be regarded as having been formed on its own account, but for the sake of that [creation] which was to be its image as possessing its likeness (just as the clay model is not moulded for its own sake, but for the sake of the statue in brass, or gold, or silver about to be formed), then creation will have greater honour than the Pleroma, if, for its sake, those things [above] were produced.

CHAP. XVI. — THE CREATOR OF THE WORLD EITHER PRODUCED OF HIMSELF THE IMAGES OF THINGS TO BE MADE, OR THE PLEROMA WAS FORMED AFTER THE IMAGE OF SOME PREVIOUS SYSTEM; AND SO ON AD INFINITUM.

1. But if they will not yield assent to any one of these conclusions, since in that case they would be proved by us as incapable of rendering any reason for such a production of their Pleroma, they will of necessity be shut up to this — that they confess that, above the Pleroma, there was some other system more spiritual and more powerful, after the image of which their Pleroma was

---

[1] Viz., the "Dii majorum gentium" of the Gentiles.
[2] Referring to numbers like 4, 5, 6, which do not correspond to any important fact in creation, as 7 e.g., does to the number of the planets.
[3] The Latin text is here scarcely intelligible, and is variously pointed by the editors.
[4] Harvey explains " his " as here denoting " in his," but we are at a loss to know how he would translate the passage. It is in the highest degree obscure.

formed. For if the Demiurge did not of himself construct that figure of creation which exists, but made it after the form of those things which are above, then from whom did their Bythus — who, to be sure, brought it about that the Pleroma should be possessed of a configuration of this kind — receive the figure of those things which existed before Himself? For it must needs be, either that the intention [of creating] dwelt in that god who made the world, so that of his own power, and from himself, he obtained the model of its formation; or, if any departure is made from this being, then there will arise a necessity for constantly asking whence there came to that one who is above him the configuration of those things which have been made; what, too, was the number of the productions; and what the substance of the model itself? If, however, it was in the power of Bythus to impart of himself such a configuration to the Pleroma, then why may it not have been in the power of the Demiurge to form of himself such a world as exists? And then, again, if creation be an image of those things [above], why should we not affirm that those are, in turn, images of others above them, and those above these again, of others, and thus go on supposing innumerable images of images?

2. This difficulty presented itself to Basilides after he had utterly missed the truth, and was conceiving that, by an infinite succession of those beings that were formed from one another, he might escape such perplexity. When he had proclaimed that three hundred and sixty-five heavens were formed through succession and similitude by one another, and that a manifest proof [of the existence] of these was found in the number of the days of the year, as I stated before; and that above these there was a power which they also style Unnameable, and its dispensation — he did not even in this way escape such perplexity. For, when asked whence came the image of its configuration to that heaven which is above all, and from which he wishes the rest to be regarded as having been formed by means of succession, he will say, from that dispensation which belongs to the Unnameable. He must then say, either that the Unspeakable formed it of himself, or he will find it necessary to acknowledge that there is some other power above this being, from whom his unnameable One derived such vast numbers of configurations as do, according to him, exist.

3. How much safer and more accurate a course is it, then, to confess at once that which is true: that this God, the Creator, who formed the world, is the only God, and that there is no other God besides Him — He Himself receiving from Himself the model and figure of those things which have been made — than that, after wearying ourselves with such an impious and circuitous description, we should be compelled, at some point or another, to fix the mind on some One, and to confess that from Him proceeded the configuration of things created.

4. As to the accusation brought against us by the followers of Valentinus, when they declare that we continue in that Hebdomad which is below, as if we could not lift our minds on high, nor understand those things which are above, because we do not accept their monstrous assertions: this very charge do the followers of Basilides bring in turn against them, inasmuch as they (the Valentinians) keep circling about those things which are below, [going] as far as the first and second Ogdoad, and because they unskilfully imagine that, immediately after the thirty Æons, they have discovered Him who is above all things Father, not following out in thought their investigations to that Pleroma which is above the three hundred and sixty-five heavens, which[1] is above forty-five Ogdoads. And any one, again, might bring against them the same charge, by imagining four thousand three hundred and eighty heavens, or Æons, since the days of the year contain that number of hours. If, again, some one adds also the nights, thus doubling the hours which have been mentioned, imagining that [in this way] he has discovered a great multitude of Ogdoads, and a kind of innumerable company[2] of Æons, and thus, in opposition to Him who is above all things Father, conceiving himself more perfect than all [others], he will bring the same charge against all, inasmuch as they are not capable of rising to the conception of such a multitude of heavens or Æons as he has announced, but are either so deficient as to remain among those things which are below, or continue in the intermediate space.

CHAP. XVII. — INQUIRY INTO THE PRODUCTION OF THE ÆONS: WHATEVER ITS SUPPOSED NATURE, IT IS IN EVERY RESPECT INCONSISTENT; AND ON THE HYPOTHESIS OF THE HERETICS, EVEN NOUS AND THE FATHER HIMSELF WOULD BE STAINED WITH IGNORANCE.

1. That system, then, which has respect to their Pleroma, and especially that part of it which refers to the primary Ogdoad being thus burdened with so great contradictions and perplexities, let me now go on to examine the remainder of their scheme. [In doing so] on account of their madness, I shall be making inquiry respecting things which have no real existence; yet it is necessary to do this, since the treatment of this subject has been entrusted to me, and since I desire all men

---

[1] The text is here doubtful: Harvey proposes to read "qui" instead of "quæ," but we prefer "quod" with Grabe. The meaning is, that three hundred and sixty-five is more than forty-five Ogdoads ($45 \times 8 = 360$).

[2] "Operositatem," corresponding to πραγματείαν, lit. *manufacture*.

to come to the knowledge of the truth, as well as because thou thyself hast asked to receive from me full and complete means for overturning [the views of] these men.

2. I ask, then, in what manner were the rest of the Æons produced? Was it so as to be united with Him who produced them, even as the solar rays are with the sun; or was it actually[1] and separately, so that each of them possessed an independent existence and his own special form, just as has a man from another man, and one herd of cattle from another? Or was it after the manner of germination, as branches from a tree? And were they of the same substance with those who produced them, or did they derive their substance from some other [kind of] substance? Also, were they produced at the same time, so as to be contemporaries; or after a certain order, so that some of them were older, and others younger? And, again, are they uncompounded and uniform, and altogether equal and similar among themselves, as spirit and light are produced; or are they compounded and different, unlike [to each other] in their members?

3. If each of them was produced, after the manner of men, actually and according to its own generation, then either those thus generated by the Father will be of the same substance with Him, and similar to their Author; or if[2] they appear dissimilar, then it must of necessity be acknowledged that they are [formed of] some different substance. Now, if the beings generated by the Father be similar to their Author, then those who have been produced must remain for ever impassible, even as is He who produced them; but if, on the other hand, they are of a different substance, which is capable of passion, then whence came this dissimilar substance to find a place within the incorruptible Pleroma? Further, too, according to this principle, each one of them must be understood as being completely separated from every other, even as men are not mixed with nor united the one to the other, but each having a distinct shape of his own, and a definite sphere of action, while each one of them, too, is formed of a particular size, — qualities characteristic of a body, and not of a spirit. Let them therefore no longer speak of the Pleroma as being *spiritual*, or of themselves as "spiritual," if indeed their Æons sit feasting with the Father, just as if they were men, and He Himself is of such a configuration as those reveal Him to be who were produced by Him.

4. If, again, the Æons were derived from Logos, Logos from Nous, and Nous from Bythus, just as lights are kindled from a light — as, for example, torches are from a torch — then they may no doubt differ in generation and size from one another; but since they are of the same substance with the Author of their production, they must either all remain for ever impassible, or their Father Himself must participate in passion. For the torch which has been kindled subsequently cannot be possessed of a different kind of light from that which preceded it. Wherefore also their lights, when blended in one, return to the original identity, since that one light is then formed which has existed even from the beginning. But we cannot speak, with respect to light itself, of some part being more recent in its origin, and another being more ancient (for the whole is but one light); nor can we so speak even in regard to those torches which have received the light (for these are all contemporary as respects their material substance, for the substance of torches is one and the same), but simply as to [the time of] its being kindled, since one was lighted a little while ago, and another has just now been kindled.

5. The defect, therefore, of that passion which has regard to ignorance, will either attach alike to their whole Pleroma, since [all its members] are of the same substance; and the Propator will share in this defect of ignorance — that is, will be ignorant of Himself; or, on the other hand, all those lights which are within the Pleroma will alike remain for ever impassible. Whence, then, comes the passion of the youngest Æon, if the light of the Father is that from which all other lights have been formed, and which is by nature impassible? And how can one Æon be spoken of as either younger or older among themselves, since there is but one light in the entire Pleroma? And if any one calls them stars, they will all nevertheless appear to participate in the same nature. For if "one star differs from another star in glory,"[3] but not in qualities, nor substance, nor in the fact of being passible or impassible; so all these, since they are alike derived from the light of the Father, must either be naturally impassible and immutable, or they must all, in common with the light of the Father, be passible, and are capable of the varying phases of corruption.

6. The same conclusion will follow, although they affirm that the production of Æons sprang from Logos, as branches from a tree, since Logos has his generation from their Father. For all [the Æons] are formed of the same substance with the Father, differing from one another only in size, and not in nature, and filling up the greatness of the Father, even as the fingers com-

---

[1] *Efficabiliter* in the Latin text is thought to correspond to ἐνεργῶς in the original Greek.
[2] *Si* is inserted by most of the editors; and although Harvey argues for its omission, we agree with Massuet in deeming it indispensable.

[3] 1 Cor. xv. 41.

plete the hand. If therefore He exists in passion and ignorance, so must also those Æons who have been generated by Him. But if it is impious to ascribe ignorance and passion to the Father of all, how can they describe an Æon produced by Him as being passible; and while they ascribe the same impiety to the very wisdom (Sophia) of God, how can they still call themselves religious men?

7. If, again, they declare that their Æons were sent forth just as rays are from the sun, then, since all are of the same substance and sprung from the same source, all must either be capable of passion along with Him who produced them, or all will remain impassible for ever. For they can no longer maintain that, of beings so produced, some are impassible and others passible. If, then, they declare all impassible, they do themselves destroy their own argument. For how could the youngest Æon have suffered passion if all were impassible? If, on the other hand, they declare that all partook of this passion, as indeed some of them venture to maintain, then, inasmuch as it originated with Logos,[1] but flowed onwards to Sophia, they will thus be convicted of tracing back the passion to Logos, who is the [2] Nous of this Propator, and so acknowledging the Nous of the Propator and the Father Himself to have experienced passion. For the Father of all is not to be regarded as a kind of compound Being, who can be separated from his Nous (mind), as I have already shown; but Nous is the Father, and the Father Nous. It necessarily follows, therefore, both that he who springs from Him as Logos, or rather that Nous himself, since he is Logos, must be perfect and impassible, and that those productions which proceed from him, seeing that they are of the same substance with himself, should be perfect and impassible, and should ever remain similar to him who produced them.

8. It cannot therefore longer be held, as these men teach, that Logos, as occupying the third place in generation, was ignorant of the Father. Such a thing might indeed perhaps be deemed probable in the case of the generation of human beings, inasmuch as these frequently know nothing of their parents; but it is altogether impossible in the case of the Logos of the Father. For if, existing in the Father, he knows Him in whom he exists — that is, is not ignorant of himself — then those productions which issue from him being his powers (faculties), and always present with him, will not be ignorant of him who emitted them, any more than rays [may be supposed to be] of the sun. It is impossible, therefore, that the Sophia (wisdom) of God, she who is within the Pleroma, inasmuch as she has been produced in such a manner, should have fallen under the influence of passion, and conceived such ignorance. But it *is* possible that that Sophia (wisdom) who pertains to [the scheme] of Valentinus, inasmuch as she is a production of the devil, should fall into every kind of passion, and exhibit the profoundest ignorance. For when they themselves bear testimony concerning their mother, to the effect that she was the offspring of an erring Æon, we need no longer search for a reason why the sons of such a mother should be ever swimming in the depths of ignorance.

9. I am not aware that, besides these productions [which have been mentioned], they are able to speak of any other; indeed, they have not been known to me (although I have had very frequent discussions with them concerning forms of this kind) as ever setting forth any other peculiar kind of being as produced [in the manner under consideration]. This only they maintain, that each one of these *was so produced* as to know merely that one who produced him, while he was ignorant of the one who immediately preceded. But they do not in this matter go forward [in their account] with any kind of demonstration as to the manner in which these were produced, or how such a thing could take place among spiritual beings. For, in whatsoever way they may choose to go forward, they will feel themselves bound (while, as regards the truth, they depart [3] entirely from right reason) to proceed so far as to maintain that their Word, who springs from the Nous of the Propator, — to maintain, I say, that he was produced in a state of degeneracy. For [they hold] that perfect Nous, previously begotten by the perfect Bythus, was not capable of rendering that production which issued from him perfect, but [could only bring it forth] utterly blind to the knowledge and greatness of the Father. They also maintain that the Saviour exhibited an emblem of this mystery in the case of that man who was blind from his birth,[4] since the Æon was in this manner produced by Monogenes blind, that is, in ignorance, thus falsely ascribing ignorance and blindness to the Word of God, who, according to their own theory, holds the second [place of] production from the Propator. Admirable sophists, and explorers of the sublimities of the unknown Father, and rehearsers of those super-celestial mysteries " which the angels desire to look into !"[5] — that they may learn that from the Nous of that Father who is above all, the Word was produced *blind*, that is, ignorant of the Father who produced him !

---

[1] Comp. i. 2, 2.
[2] It seems needless to insert an "et" before this word, as Harvey suggests, or, as an alternative, to strike out the first "Nun Propatoris."
[3] Some read "cæcutientes" instead of "circumeuntes," as above.
[4] John ix. 1, etc.
[5] 1 Pet. i. 12.

10. But, ye miserable sophists, how could the Nous of the Father, or rather the very Father Himself, since He is Nous and perfect in all things, have produced his own Logos as an imperfect and blind Æon, when He was able also to produce along with him the knowledge of the Father? As ye affirm that Christ was generated[1] after the rest, and yet declare that he was produced perfect, much more then should Logos, who is anterior to him in age, be produced by the same Nous, unquestionably perfect, and not blind; nor could he, again, have produced Æons still blinder than himself, until at last your Sophia, always utterly blinded, gave birth to so vast a body of evils. And your Father is the cause of all this mischief; for ye declare the magnitude and power of your Father to be the causes of ignorance, assimilating Him to Bythus, and assigning this as a name to Him who is the unnameable Father. But if ignorance is an evil, and ye declare all evils to have derived their strength from it, while ye maintain that the greatness and power of the Father is the cause of this ignorance, ye do thus set Him forth as the author of [all] evils. For ye state as the cause of evil this fact, that [no one] could contemplate His greatness. But if it was really impossible for the Father to make Himself known from the beginning to those [beings] that were formed by Him, He must in that case be held free from blame, inasmuch as He *could not* remove the ignorance of those who came after Him. But if, at a subsequent period, when He so willed it, He *could* take away that ignorance which had increased with the successive productions as they followed each other, and thus become deeply seated in the Æons, much more, had He so willed it might He formerly have prevented that ignorance, which as yet was not, from coming into existence.

11. Since therefore, as soon as He so pleased, He did become known not only to the Æons, but also to these men who lived in these latter times; but, as He did not so please to be known from the beginning, He remained unknown — the cause of ignorance is, according to you, the will of the Father. For if He foreknew that these things would in future happen in such a manner, why then did He not guard against the ignorance of these beings before it had obtained a place among them, rather than afterwards, as if under the influence of repentance, deal with it through the production of Christ? For the knowledge which through Christ He conveyed to all, He might long before have imparted through Logos, who was also the first-begotten of Monogenes. Or if, knowing them beforehand, He willed that these things should happen [as they have done], then the works of ignorance must endure for ever, and never pass away. For the things which have been made in accordance with the will of your Propator must continue along with the will of Him who willed them; or if they pass away, the will of Him also who decreed that they should have a being will pass away along with them. And why did the Æons find rest and attain perfect knowledge through learning [at last] that the Father is altogether[2] incomprehensible? They might surely have possessed this knowledge before they became involved in passion; for the greatness of the Father did not suffer diminution from the beginning, so that these might[3] know that He was altogether incomprehensible. For if, on account of His infinite greatness, He remained unknown, He ought also on account of His infinite love to have preserved those impassible who were produced by Him, since nothing hindered, and expediency rather required, that they should have known from the beginning that the Father was altogether incomprehensible.

CHAP. XVIII. — SOPHIA WAS NEVER REALLY IN IGNORANCE OR PASSION; HER ENTHYMESIS COULD NOT HAVE BEEN SEPARATED FROM HERSELF, OR EXHIBITED SPECIAL TENDENCIES OF ITS OWN.

1. How can it be regarded as otherwise than absurd, that they also affirm this Sophia (wisdom) to have been involved in ignorance, and degeneracy, and passion? For these things are alien and contrary to wisdom, nor can they ever be qualities belonging to it. For wherever there is a want of foresight, and an ignorance of the course of utility, there wisdom does not exist. Let them therefore no longer call this suffering Æon, Sophia, but let them give up either her name or her sufferings. And let them, moreover, not call their entire Pleroma spiritual, if this Æon had a place within it when she was involved in such a tumult of passion. For even a vigorous soul, not to say a spiritual substance, would not pass through any such experience.

2. And, again, how could her Enthymesis, going forth [from her] along with the passion, have become a separate existence? For Enthymesis (thought) is understood in connection with some person, and can never have an isolated existence by itself. For a bad Enthymesis is destroyed and absorbed by a good one, even as a state of disease is by health. What, then, was the sort of Enthymesis which preceded that of passion? [It was this]: to investigate the [nature of] the Father, and to consider His

---

[1] " Postgenitum quidem reliquis," the representative, according to Grabe, of ἀπόγονον μὲν λοιποῖς in the Greek. Harvey remarks that τῶν λοιπῶν would have been better, and proposes to read " progenitum " in the Latin; but we do not see any necessity for change.

[2] " Incapabilis et incomprehensibilis," corresponding to ἀχώρητος καὶ ἀκατάληπτος in the Greek.
[3] Literally, " to these knowing," " his scientibus."

greatness. But what did she afterwards become persuaded of, and so was restored to health? [This, viz.], that the Father is incomprehensible, and that He is past finding out. It was not, then, a proper feeling that she wished to know the Father, and on this account she became passible; but when she became persuaded that He is unsearchable, she was restored to health. And even Nous himself, who was inquiring into the [nature of] the Father, ceased, according to them, to continue his researches, on learning that the Father is incomprehensible.

3. How then could the Enthymesis separately conceive passions, which themselves also were her affections? For affection is necessarily connected with an individual: it cannot come into being or exist apart by itself. This opinion [of theirs], however, is not only untenable, but also opposed to that which was spoken by our Lord: "Seek, and ye shall find."[1] For the Lord renders His disciples perfect by their seeking after and finding the Father; but that Christ of theirs, who is above, has rendered them perfect, by the fact that He has commanded the Æons not to seek after the Father, persuading them that, though they should labour hard, they would not find Him. And they[2] declare that they themselves are perfect, by the fact that they maintain they have found their Bythus; while the Æons [have been made perfect] through means of this, that *He* is unsearchable who was inquired after by them.

4. Since, therefore, the Enthymesis herself could not exist separately, apart from the Æon, [it is obvious that] they bring forward still greater falsehood concerning her passion, when they further proceed to divide and separate it from her, while they declare that it was the substance of matter. As if God were not light, and as if no Word existed who could convict them, and overthrow their wickedness. For it is certainly true, that whatsoever the Æon thought, that she also suffered; and what she suffered, that she also thought. And her Enthymesis was, according to them, nothing else than the passion of one thinking how she might comprehend the incomprehensible. And thus Enthymesis (thought) was the passion; for she was thinking of things impossible. How then could affection and passion be separated and set apart from the Enthymesis, so as to become the substance of so vast a material creation, when Enthymesis herself was the passion, and the passion Enthymesis? Neither, therefore, can Enthymesis apart from the Æon, nor the affections apart from Enthymesis, separately possess substance; and thus once more their system breaks down and is destroyed.

5. But how did it come to pass that the Æon was both dissolved [into her component parts], and became subject to passion? She was undoubtedly of the same substance as the Pleroma; but the entire Pleroma was of the Father. Now, any substance, when brought in contact with what is of a similar nature, will not be dissolved into nothing, nor will be in danger of perishing, but will rather continue and increase, such as fire in fire, spirit in spirit, and water in water; but those which are of a contrary nature to each other do, [when they meet,] suffer and are changed and destroyed. And, in like manner, if there had been a production of light, it would not suffer passion, or incur any danger in light like itself, but would rather glow with the greater brightness, and increase, as the day does from [the increasing brilliance of] the sun; for they maintain that Bythus [himself] was the image of their father[3] (Sophia). Whatever animals are alien [in habits] and strange to each other, or are mutually opposed in nature, fall into danger [on meeting together], and are destroyed; whereas, on the other hand, those who are accustomed to each other, and of a harmonious disposition, suffer no peril from being together in the same place, but rather secure both safety and life by such a fact. If, therefore, this Æon was produced by the Pleroma of the same substance as the whole of it, she could never have undergone change, since she was consorting with beings similar to and familiar with herself, a spiritual essence among those that were spiritual. For fear, terror, passion, dissolution, and such like, may perhaps occur through the struggle of contraries among such beings as we are, who are possessed of bodies; but among spiritual beings, and those that have the light diffused among them, no such calamities can possibly happen. But these men appear to me to have endowed their Æon with the [same sort of] passion as belongs to that character in the comic poet Menander,[4] who was himself deeply in love, but an object of hatred [to his beloved]. For those who have invented such opinions have rather had an idea and mental conception of some unhappy lover among men, than of a spiritual and divine substance.

6. Moreover, to meditate how to search into [the nature of] the perfect Father, and to have a desire to exist within Him, and to have a comprehension of His [greatness], could not entail the stain of ignorance or passion, and that upon a spiritual Æon; but would rather [give rise to] perfection, and impassibility, and truth. For they do not say that even they, though they be but men, by meditating on Him who was before

---

[1] Matt. vii. 7.
[2] It seems necessary to read "se quidem" instead of "si quidem," as in the MSS.
[3] Although Sophia was a feminine Æon, she was regarded as being the father of Enthymesis, who again was the *mother* of the Valentinians.
[4] Stieren refers for this allusion to Meineke's edition of the *Reliquiæ Menan. et Philem.*, p. 116.

them, — and while now, as it were, comprehending the perfect, and being placed within the knowledge of Him, — are thus involved in a passion of perplexity, but rather attain to the knowledge and apprehension of truth. For they affirm that the Saviour said, "Seek, and ye shall find," to His disciples with this view, that they should seek after Him who, by means of imagination, has been conceived of by them as being above the Maker of all — the ineffable Bythus; and they desire themselves to be regarded as "the perfect," because they have sought and found the perfect One, while they are still on earth. Yet they declare that that Æon who was within the Pleroma, a wholly spiritual being, by seeking after the Propator, and endeavouring to find a place within His greatness, and desiring to have a comprehension of the truth of the Father, fell down into [the endurance of] passion, and such a passion that, unless she had met with that Power who upholds all things, she would have been dissolved into the general substance [of the Æons], and thus come to an end of her [personal] existence.

7. Absurd is such presumption, and truly an opinion of men totally destitute of the truth. For, that this Æon is superior to themselves, and of greater antiquity, they themselves acknowledge, according to their own system, when they affirm that they are the fruit of the Enthymesis of that Æon who suffered passion, so that this Æon is the father of their mother, that is, their own grandfather. And to them, the later grandchildren, the search after the Father brings, as they maintain, truth, and perfection, and establishment, and deliverance from unstable matter, and reconciliation to the Father; but on their grandfather this same search entailed ignorance, and passion, and terror, and perplexity, from which [disturbances] they also declare that the substance of matter was formed. To say, therefore, that the search after and investigation of the perfect Father, and the desire for communion and union with Him, were things quite beneficial to them, but to an Æon, from whom also they derive their origin, these things were the cause of dissolution and destruction, how can such assertions be otherwise viewed than as totally inconsistent, foolish, and irrational? Those, too, who listen to these teachers, truly blind themselves, while they possess blind guides, justly [are left to] fall along with them into the gulf of ignorance which lies below them.

CHAP. XIX. — ABSURDITIES OF THE HERETICS AS TO THEIR OWN ORIGIN : THEIR OPINIONS RESPECTING THE DEMIURGE SHOWN TO BE EQUALLY UNTENABLE AND RIDICULOUS.

1. But what sort of talk also is this concerning their seed — that it was conceived by the mother according to the configuration of those angels who wait upon the Saviour, — shapeless, without form, and imperfect; and that it was deposited in the Demiurge without his knowledge, in order that through his instrumentality it might attain to perfection and form in that soul which he had, [so to speak,] filled with seed? This is to affirm, in the first place, that those angels who wait upon their Saviour are imperfect, and without figure or form; if indeed that which was conceived according to their appearance was generated any such kind of being [as has been described].

2. Then, in the next place, as to their saying that the Creator was ignorant of that deposit of seed which took place into him, and again, of that impartation of seed which was made by him to man, their words are futile and vain, and are in no way susceptible of proof. For how could he have been ignorant of it, if that seed had possessed any substance and peculiar properties? If, on the other hand, it was without substance and without quality, and so was really nothing, then, as a matter of course, he was ignorant of it. For those things which have a certain motion of their own, and quality, either of heat, or swiftness, or sweetness, or which differ from others in brilliance, do not escape the notice even of men, since they mingle in the sphere of human action : far less can they [be hidden from] God, the Maker of this universe. With reason, however, [is it said, that] their seed was not known to Him, since it is without any quality of general utility, and without the substance requisite for any action, and is, in fact, a pure nonentity. It really seems to me, that, with a view to such opinions, the Lord expressed Himself thus : "For every idle word that men speak, they shall give account on the day of judgment."[1] For all teachers of a like character to these, who fill men's ears with idle talk, shall, when they stand at the throne of judgment, render an account for those things which they have vainly imagined and falsely uttered against the Lord, proceeding, as they have done, to such a height of audacity as to declare of themselves that, on account of the substance of their seed, they are acquainted with the spiritual Pleroma, because that man who dwells within reveals to them the true Father; for the animal nature required[2] to be disciplined by means of the senses. But [they hold that] the Demiurge, while receiving into himself the whole of this seed, through its being deposited in him by the Mother, still remained utterly ignorant of all things, and had no understanding of anything connected with the Pleroma.

---

[1] Matt. xii. 36. [The serious spirit of this remark lends force to it as exposition.]
[2] Comp. i. 6, 1.

3. And that they are the truly "spiritual," inasmuch as a certain particle of the Father of the universe has been deposited in their souls, since, according to their assertions, they have souls formed of the same substance as the Demiurge himself, yet that he, although he received from the Mother, once for all, the whole [of the divine] seed, and possessed it in himself, still remained of an animal nature, and had not the slightest understanding of those things which are above, which things they boast that they themselves understand, while they are still on earth; — does not this crown all possible absurdity? For to imagine that the very same seed conveyed knowledge and perfection to the souls of these men, while it only gave rise to ignorance in the God who made them, is an opinion that can be held only by those utterly frantic, and totally destitute of common sense.

4. Further, it is also a most absurd and groundless thing for them to say that the seed was, by being thus deposited, reduced to form and increased, and so was prepared for all the reception of perfect rationality. For there will be in it an admixture of matter — that substance which they hold to have been derived from ignorance and defect; [and this will prove itself] more apt and useful than was the light of their Father, if indeed, when born, according to the contemplation of that [light], it was without form or figure, but derived from this [matter], form, and appearance, and increase, and perfection. For if that light which proceeds from the Pleroma was the cause to a spiritual being that it possessed neither form, nor appearance, nor its own special magnitude, while its descent to this world added all these things to it, and brought it to perfection, then a sojourn here (which they also term darkness) would seem much more efficacious and useful than was the light of their Father. But how can it be regarded as other than ridiculous, to affirm that their mother ran the risk of being almost extinguished in matter, and was almost on the point of being destroyed by it, had she not then with difficulty stretched herself outwards, and leaped, [as it were,] out of herself, receiving assistance from the Father; but that her seed increased in this same matter, and received a form, and was made fit for the reception of perfect rationality; and this, too, while "bubbling up" among substances dissimilar and unfamiliar to itself, according to their own declaration that the earthly is opposed to the spiritual, and the spiritual to the earthly? How, then, could "a little particle,"[1] as they say, increase, and receive shape, and reach perfection, in the midst of substances contrary to and unfamiliar to itself?

5. But further, and in addition to what has been said, the question occurs, Did their mother, when she beheld the angels, bring forth the seed all at once, or only one by one [in succession]? If she brought forth the whole simultaneously and at once, that which was thus produced cannot now be of an infantile character: its descent, therefore, into those men who now exist must be superfluous.[2] But if one by one, then she did not form her conception according to the figure of those angels whom she beheld; for, contemplating them all together, and once for all, so as to conceive by them, she ought to have brought forth once for all the offspring of those from whose forms she had once for all conceived.

6. Why was it, too, that, beholding the angels along with the Saviour, she did indeed conceive *their* images, but not that of the *Saviour*, who is far more beautiful than they? Did He not please her; and did she not, on that account, conceive after His likeness?[3] How was it, too, that the Demiurge, whom they can call an animal being, having, as they maintain, his own special magnitude and figure, was produced perfect as respects his substance; while that which is spiritual, which also ought to be more effective than that which is animal, was sent forth imperfect, and he required to descend into a soul, that in it he might obtain form, and thus becoming perfect, might be rendered fit for the reception of perfect reason? If, then, he obtains form in mere earthly and animal men, he can no longer be said to be after the likeness of angels whom they call lights, but [after the likeness] of those men who are here below. For he will not possess in that case the likeness and appearance of angels, but of those souls in whom also he receives shape; just as water when poured into a vessel takes the form of that vessel, and if on any occasion it happens to congeal in it, it will acquire the form of the vessel in which it has thus been frozen, since souls themselves possess the figure[4] of the body [in which they dwell]; for they themselves have been adapted to the vessel [in which they exist], as I have said before. If, then, that seed [referred to] is here solidified and formed into a definite shape, it will possess the figure of a man, and not the form of the angels. How is it possible, therefore, that that seed should be after images of the angels, seeing it has obtained a form after the likeness of men? Why, again, since it was of a spiritual nature, had it any need of descending into flesh? For what is carnal stands in need of that which is spiritual, if indeed

---

[1] "Parvum emissum"— *a small emission.*

[2] That is, there could be no need for its descending into them that it might increase, receive form, and thus be prepared for the reception of perfect reason.

[3] Or, "on beholding Him."

[4] As Massuet here remarks, we may infer from this passage that Irenæus believed souls to be corporeal, as being possessed of a definite form, — an opinion entertained by not a few of the ancients. [And, before we censure them, let us reflect whether their perceptions of "the carnal mind" as differing from the spirit of a man, may not account for it. 1 Thess. v. 23.]

it is to be saved, that in it it may be sanctified and cleared from all impurity, and that what is mortal may be swallowed up by immortality;[1] but that which is spiritual has no need whatever of those things which are here below. For it is not we who benefit it, but it that improves us.

7. Still more manifestly is that talk of theirs concerning their seed proved to be false, and that in a way which must be evident to every one, by the fact that they declare those souls which have received seed from the Mother to be superior to all others; wherefore also they have been honoured by the Demiurge, and constituted princes, and kings, and priests. For if this were true, the high priest Caiaphas, and Annas, and the rest of the chief priests, and doctors of the law, and rulers of the people, would have been the first to believe in the Lord, agreeing as they did with respect[2] to that relationship; and even before them should have been Herod the king. But since neither he, nor the chief priests, nor the rulers, nor the eminent of the people, turned to Him [in faith], but, on the contrary, those who sat begging by the highway, the deaf, and the blind, while He was rejected and despised by others, according to what Paul declares, "For ye see your calling, brethren, that there are not many wise men among you, not many noble, not many mighty; but those things of the world which were despised hath God chosen."[3] Such souls, therefore, were not superior to others on account of the seed deposited in them, nor on this account were they honoured by the Demiurge.

8. As to the point, then, that their system is weak and untenable as well as utterly chimerical, enough has been said. For it is not needful, to use a common proverb, that one should drink up the ocean who wishes to learn that its water is salt. But, just as in the case of a statue which is made of clay, but coloured on the outside that it may be thought to be of gold, while it really is of clay, any one who takes out of it a small particle, and thus laying it open reveals the clay, will set free those who seek the truth from a false opinion; in the same way have I (by exposing not a small part only, but the several heads of their system which are of the greatest importance) shown to as many as do not wish wittingly to be led astray, what is wicked, deceitful, seductive, and pernicious, connected with the school of the Valentinians, and all those other heretics who promulgate[4] wicked opinions respecting the Demiurge, that is, the Fashioner and Former of this universe, and who is in fact the only true God — exhibiting, [as I have done,] how easily their views are overthrown.

9. For who that has any intelligence, and possesses only a small proportion of truth, can tolerate them, when they affirm that there is another god above the Creator; and that there is another Monogenes as well as another Word of God, whom also they describe as having been produced in [a state of] degeneracy; and another Christ, whom they assert to have been formed, along with the Holy Spirit, later than the rest of the Æons; and another Saviour, who, they say, did not proceed from the Father of all, but was a kind of joint production of those Æons who were formed in [a state of] degeneracy, and that He was produced of necessity on account of this very degeneracy? It is thus their opinion that, unless the Æons had been in a state of ignorance and degeneracy, neither Christ, nor the Holy Spirit, nor Horos, nor the Saviour, nor the angels, nor their Mother, nor her seed, nor the rest of the fabric of the world, would have been produced at all; but the universe would have been a desert, and destitute of the many good things which exist in it. They are therefore not only chargeable with impiety against the Creator, declaring Him the fruit of a defect, but also against Christ and the Holy Spirit, affirming that they were produced on account of that defect; and, in like manner, that the Saviour [was produced] subsequently to [the existence of] that defect. And who will tolerate the remainder of their vain talk, which they cunningly endeavour to accommodate to the parables, and have in this way plunged both themselves, and those who give credit to them, in the profoundest depths of impiety?

CHAP. XX. — FUTILITY OF THE ARGUMENTS ADDUCED TO DEMONSTRATE THE SUFFERINGS OF THE TWELFTH ÆON, FROM THE PARABLES, THE TREACHERY OF JUDAS, AND THE PASSION OF OUR SAVIOUR.

1. That they improperly and illogically apply both the parables and the actions of the Lord to their falsely-devised system, I prove as follows: They endeavour, for instance, to demonstrate that passion which, they say, happened in the case of the twelfth Æon, from this fact, that the passion of the Saviour was brought about by the twelfth apostle, and happened in the twelfth month. For they hold that He preached [only] for one year after His baptism. They maintain also that the same thing was clearly set forth in the case of her who suffered from the issue of blood. For the woman suffered during twelve years, and

---

[1] Comp. 1 Cor. xv. 44; 2 Cor. v. 4. [As a Catholic I cannot accept everything contained in the *Biblical Psychology* of Dr. Delitzsch, but may I entreat the reader who has not studied it to do so before dismissing the ideas of Irenæus on such topics. A translation has been provided for English readers, by the Messrs. T. & T. Clark of Edinburgh, 1867.]

[2] The meaning apparently is, that by the high position which all these in common occupied, they proved themselves, on the principles of the heretics, to belong to the favoured "seed," and should therefore have eagerly have welcomed the Lord. Or the meaning may be, " hurrying together to that relationship," that is, to the relationship secured by faith in Christ.

[3] 1 Cor. i. 26, 28, somewhat loosely quoted.

[4] " Male tractant;" literally, *handle badly*.

through touching the hem of the Saviour's garment she was made whole by that power which went forth from the Saviour, and which, they affirm, had a previous existence. For that Power who suffered was stretching herself outwards and flowing into immensity, so that she was in danger of being dissolved into the general substance [of the Æons]; but then, touching the primary Tetrad, which is typified by the hem of the garment, she was arrested, and ceased from her passion.

2. Then, again, as to their assertion that the passion of the twelfth Æon was proved through the conduct of Judas, how is it possible that Judas can be compared [with this Æon] as being an emblem of her — he who was expelled from the number of the twelve,[1] and never restored to his place? For that Æon, whose type they declare Judas to be, after being separated from her Enthymesis, was restored or recalled [to her former position]; but Judas was deprived [of his office], and cast out, while Matthias was ordained in his place, according to what is written, "And his bishopric let another take."[2] They ought therefore to maintain that the twelfth Æon was cast out of the Pleroma, and that another was produced, or sent forth to fill her place; if, that is to say, she is pointed at in Judas. Moreover, they tell us that it was the Æon herself who suffered, but Judas was the betrayer, [and not the sufferer.] Even they themselves acknowledge that it was the suffering Christ, and not Judas, who came to [the endurance of] passion. How, then, could Judas, the betrayer of Him who had to suffer for our salvation, be the type and image of that Æon who suffered?

3. But, in truth, the passion of Christ was neither similar to the passion of the Æon, nor did it take place in similar circumstances. For the Æon underwent a passion of dissolution and destruction, so that she who suffered was in danger also of being destroyed. But the Lord, our Christ, underwent a valid, and not a merely[3] accidental passion; not only was He Himself not in danger of being destroyed, but He also established fallen man[4] by His own strength, and recalled him to incorruption. The Æon, again, underwent passion while she was seeking after the Father, and was not able to find Him; but the Lord suffered that He might bring those who have wandered from the Father, back to knowledge and to His fellowship. The search into the greatness of the Father became to her a passion leading to destruction; but the Lord, having suffered, and bestowing the knowledge of the Father, conferred on us salvation. Her passion, as they declare, gave origin to a female offspring, weak, infirm, unformed, and ineffective; but His passion gave rise to strength and power. For the Lord, through means of suffering, "ascending into the lofty place, led captivity captive, gave gifts to men,"[5] and conferred on those that believe in Him the power "to tread upon serpents and scorpions, and on all the power of the enemy,"[6] that is, of the leader of apostasy. Our Lord also by His passion destroyed death, and dispersed error, and put an end to corruption, and destroyed ignorance, while He manifested life and revealed truth, and bestowed the gift of incorruption. But their Æon, when she had suffered, established[7] ignorance, and brought forth a substance without shape, out of which all material works have been produced — death, corruption, error, and such like.

4. Judas, then, the twelfth in order of the disciples, was not a type of the suffering Æon, nor, again, was the passion of the Lord; for these two things have been shown to be in every respect mutually dissimilar and inharmonious. This is the case not only as respects the points which I have already mentioned, but with regard to the very number. For that Judas the traitor is the twelfth in order, is agreed upon by all, there being twelve apostles mentioned by name in the Gospel. But this Æon is not the *twelfth*, but the *thirtieth;* for, according to the views under consideration, there were not twelve Æons only produced by the will of the Father, nor was she sent forth the twelfth in order: they reckon her, [on the contrary,] as having been produced in the thirtieth place. How, then, can Judas, the twelfth in order, be the type and image of that Æon who occupies the thirtieth place?

5. But if they say that Judas in perishing was the image of her Enthymesis, neither in this way will the image bear any analogy to that truth which [by hypothesis] corresponds to it. For the Enthymesis having been separated fromt he Æon, and itself afterwards receiving a shape from Christ,[8] then being made a partaker of intelligence by the Saviour, and having formed all things which are outside of the Pleroma, after the image of those which are within the Pleroma, is said at last to have been received by them into the Pleroma, and, according to [the principle of] conjunction, to have been united to that Saviour who was formed out of all. But Judas having been once for all cast away, never returns

---

[1] Or, "from the twelfth number" — the twelfth position among the apostles.
[2] Acts i. 20, from Ps. cix. 8.
[3] The text is here uncertain. Most editions read "et quæ non cederet," but Harvey prefers "quæ non accederet" (for "accideret"), and remarks that the corresponding Greek would be καὶ οὐ τυχόν, which we have translated as above.
[4] "Corruptum hominem."

[5] Ps. lxviii. 18; Eph. iv. 8.
[6] Luke x. 19; [Mark xvi. 17, 18.]
[7] Though the reading "substituit" is found in all the MSS. and editions, it has been deemed corrupt, and "sustinuit" has been proposed instead of it. Harvey supposes it the equivalent of ὑπεστην, and then somewhat strangely adds "for ἀπέστησε." There seems to us no difficulty in the word, and consequently no necessity for change.
[8] Compare, in illustration of this sentence, book i. 4, 1, and i. 4, 5.

into the number of the disciples; otherwise a different person would not have been chosen to fill his place. Besides, the Lord also declared regarding him, "Woe to the man by whom the Son of man shall be betrayed;"[1] and, "It were better for him if he had never been born;"[2] and he was called the "son of perdition"[3] by Him. If, however, they say that Judas was a type of the Enthymesis, not as separated from the Æon, but of the passion entwined with her, neither in this way can the number twelve be regarded as a [fitting] type of the number three. For in the one case Judas was cast away, and Matthias was ordained instead of him; but in the other case, the Æon is said to have been in danger of dissolution and destruction, and [there are also] her Enthymesis and passion: for they markedly distinguish Enthymesis from the passion; and they represent the Æon as being restored, and Enthymesis as acquiring form, but the passion, when separated from these, as becoming matter. Since, therefore, there are thus these three, the Æon, her Enthymesis, and her passion, Judas and Matthias, being only two, cannot be the types of them.

CHAP. XXI.—THE TWELVE APOSTLES WERE NOT A TYPE OF THE ÆONS.

1. If, again, they maintain that the twelve apostles were a type only of that group of twelve Æons which Anthropos in conjunction with Ecclesia produced, then let them produce ten other apostles as a type of those ten remaining Æons, who, as they declare, were produced by Logos and Zoe. For it is unreasonable to suppose that the junior, and for that reason inferior Æons, were set forth by the Saviour through the election of the apostles, while their seniors, and on this account their superiors, were not thus foreshown; since the Saviour (if, that is to say, He chose the apostles with this view, that by means of them He might show forth the Æons who are in the Pleroma) might have chosen other ten apostles also, and likewise other eight before these, that thus He might set forth the original and primary Ogdoad. He could not,[4] in regard to the second [Duo] Decad, show forth [any emblem of it] through the number of the apostles being [already] constituted a type. For [He made choice of no such other number of disciples; but] after the twelve apostles, our Lord is found to have sent seventy others before Him.[5] Now *seventy* cannot possibly be the type either of an Ogdoad, a Decad, or a Triacontad. What is the reason, then, that the inferior Æons are, as I have said, represented by means of the apostles; but the superior, from whom, too, the former derived their being, are not prefigured at all? But if[6] the twelve apostles were chosen with this object, that the number of the twelve Æons might be indicated by means of them, then the seventy also ought to have been chosen to be the type of seventy Æons; and in that case, they must affirm that the Æons are no longer thirty, but eighty-two in number. For He who made choice of the apostles, that they might be a type of those Æons existing in the Pleroma, would never have constituted them types of some and not of others; but by means of the apostles He would have tried to preserve an image and to exhibit a type of those Æons that exist in the Pleroma.

2. Moreover, we must not keep silence respecting Paul, but demand from them after the type of what Æon that apostle has been handed down to us, unless perchance [they affirm that he is a representative] of the Saviour compounded of them [all], who derived his being from the collected gifts of the whole, and whom they term *All Things*, as having been formed out of them all. Respecting this being the poet Hesiod has strikingly expressed himself, styling him Pandora—that is, "The gift of all"—for this reason, that the best gift in the possession of all was centred in him. In describing these gifts the following account is given: Hermes (so[7] he is called in the Greek language), Αἰμυλίους[8] τε λόγους καὶ ἐπίκλοπον ἦθος αὐτοὺς Κάτθετο (or to express this in the English[9] language), "implanted words of fraud and deceit in their minds, and thievish habits," for the purpose of leading foolish men astray, that such should believe their falsehoods. For their Mother—that is, Leto[10]—secretly stirred them up (whence also she is called Leto,[11] according to the meaning of the Greek word, because she *secretly* stirred up men), without the knowledge of the Demiurge, to give forth profound and unspeakable mysteries to itching ears.[12] And not only did their Mother bring it about that this mystery should be declared by Hesiod; but very skilfully also by means of the lyric poet Pindar, when he describes to the Demiurge[13] the

---

[1] Matt. xxvi. 24.
[2] Mark xiv. 21.
[3] John xvii. 12.
[4] This passage is hopelessly corrupt. The editors have twisted it in every direction, but with no satisfactory result. Our version is quite as far from being certainly trustworthy as any other that has been proposed, but it seems something like the meaning of the words as they stand. Both the text and punctuation of the Latin are in utter confusion.
[5] Luke x. 1.
[6] "Si" is wanting in the MSS. and early editions, and Harvey pleads for its exclusion, but the sense becomes clearer through inserting it.
[7] This clause is, of course, an interpolation by the Latin translator.
[8] The words are loosely quoted *memoriter*, as is the custom with Irenæus. See Hesiod, *Works and Days*, i. 77, etc.
[9] *Latin*, of course, in the text.
[10] There is here a play upon the words Λητώ and ληθεῖν, the former being supposed to be derived from the latter, so as to denote *secrecy*.
[11] This clause is probably an interpolation by the translator.
[12] 2 Tim. iv. 3.
[13] "Cœlet Demiurgo," such is the reading in all the MSS. and editions. Harvey, however, proposes to read "celet Demiurgum;" but the change which he suggests, besides being without authority, does not clear away the obscurity which hangs upon the sentence.

case of Pelops, whose flesh was cut in pieces by the Father, and then collected and brought together, and compacted anew by all the gods,[1] did she in this way indicate Pandora; and these men having their consciences seared[2] by her, declaring, as they maintain, the very same things, are [proved] of the same family and spirit as the others.

CHAP. XXII. — THE THIRTY ÆONS ARE NOT TYPIFIED BY THE FACT THAT CHRIST WAS BAPTIZED IN HIS THIRTIETH YEAR: HE DID NOT SUFFER IN THE TWELFTH MONTH AFTER HIS BAPTISM, BUT WAS MORE THAN FIFTY YEARS OLD WHEN HE DIED.

1. I have shown that the number *thirty* fails them in every respect; too few Æons, as they represent them, being at one time found within the Pleroma, and then again too many [to correspond with that number]. There are not, therefore, thirty Æons, nor did the Saviour come to be baptized when He was thirty years old, for this reason, that He might show forth the thirty silent[3] Æons of their system, otherwise they must first of all separate and eject [the Saviour] Himself from the Pleroma of all. Moreover, they affirm that He suffered in the twelfth month, so that He continued to preach for one year after His baptism; and they endeavour to establish this point out of the prophet (for it is written, "To proclaim the acceptable year of the Lord, and the day of retribution"[4]), being truly blind, inasmuch as they affirm they have found out the mysteries of Bythus, yet not understanding that which is called by Isaiah the acceptable year of the Lord, nor the day of retribution. For the prophet neither speaks concerning a day which includes the space of twelve hours, nor of a year the length of which is twelve months. For even they themselves acknowledge that the prophets have very often expressed themselves in parables and allegories, and [are] not [to be understood] according to the mere sound of the words.

2. That, then, was called the day of retribution on which the Lord will render to every one according to his works — that is, the judgment. The acceptable year of the Lord, again, is this present time, in which those who believe Him are called by Him, and become acceptable to God — that is, the whole time from His advent onwards to the consummation [of all things], during which He acquires to Himself as fruits [of the scheme of mercy] those who are saved. For, according to the phraseology of the prophet, the day of retribution follows the [acceptable] year; and the prophet will be proved guilty of falsehood if the Lord preached only for a year, and if he speaks of it. For where is the day of retribution? For the year has passed, and the day of retribution has not yet come; but He still "makes His sun to rise upon the good and upon the evil, and sends rain upon the just and unjust."[5] And the righteous suffer persecution, are afflicted, and are slain, while sinners are possessed of abundance, and "drink with the sound of the harp and psaltery, but do not regard the works of the Lord."[6] But, according to the language [used by the prophet], they ought to be combined, and the day of retribution to follow the [acceptable] year. For the words are, "to proclaim the acceptable year of the Lord, and the day of retribution." This present time, therefore, in which men are called and saved by the Lord, is properly understood to be denoted by "the acceptable year of the Lord;" and there follows on this "the day of retribution," that is, the judgment. And the time thus referred to is not called "a year" only, but is also named "a day" both by the prophet and by Paul, of whom the apostle, calling to mind the Scripture, says in the Epistle addressed to the Romans, "As it is written, for thy sake we are killed all the day long, we are counted as sheep for the slaughter."[7] But here the expression "all the day long" is put for all this time during which we suffer persecution, and are killed as sheep. As then this *day* does not signify one which consists of twelve hours, but the whole time during which believers in Christ suffer and are put to death for His sake, so also the *year* there mentioned does not denote one which consists of twelve months, but the whole time of faith during which men hear and believe the preaching of the Gospel, and those become acceptable to God who unite themselves to Him.

3. But it is greatly to be wondered at, how it has come to pass that, while affirming that they have found out the mysteries of God, they have not examined the Gospels to ascertain how often after His baptism the Lord went up, at the time of the passover, to Jerusalem, in accordance with what was the practice of the Jews from every land, and every year, that they should assemble at this period in Jerusalem, and there celebrate the feast of the passover. First of all, after He had made the water wine at Cana of Galilee, He went up to the festival day of the passover, on which occasion it is written, "For many believed in Him, when they saw the signs which He did,"[8]

---

[1] Comp. Pindar, *Olymp.*, i. 38, etc.
[2] "Compuncti," supposed to correspond to κεκαυτηριασμένοι: see 1 Tim. iv. 2. The whole passage is difficult and obscure.
[3] Harvey wishes, without any authority, to substitute "tacitus" for "tacitos," but there is no necessity for alteration. Irenæus is here playing upon the word, according to a practice in which he delights, and quietly scoffs at the *Sigè* (Silence) of the heretics by styling those Æons *silent* who were derived from her.
[4] Isa. lxi. 2.
[5] Matt. v. 45.
[6] Isa. v. 12.
[7] Rom. viii. 36.
[8] John ii. 23.

as John the disciple of the Lord records. Then, again, withdrawing Himself [from Judæa], He is found in Samaria; on which occasion, too, He conversed with the Samaritan woman, and while at a distance, cured the son of the centurion by a word, saying, "Go thy way, thy son liveth."[1] Afterwards He went up, the second time, to observe the festival day of the passover[2] in Jerusalem; on which occasion He cured the paralytic man, who had lain beside the pool thirty-eight years, bidding him rise, take up his couch, and depart. Again, withdrawing from thence to the other side of the sea of Tiberias,[3] He there, seeing a great crowd had followed Him, fed all that multitude with five loaves of bread, and twelve baskets of fragments remained over and above. Then, when He had raised Lazarus from the dead, and plots were formed against Him by the Pharisees, He withdrew to a city called Ephraim; and from that place, as it is written, "He came to Bethany six days before the passover,"[4] and going up from Bethany to Jerusalem, He there ate the passover, and suffered on the day following. Now, that these three occasions of the passover are not included within one year, every person whatever must acknowledge. And that the special month in which the passover was celebrated, and in which also the Lord suffered, was not the twelfth, but the first, those men who boast that they know all things, if they know not this, may learn it from Moses. Their explanation, therefore, both of the year and of the twelfth month has been proved false, and they ought to reject either their explanation or the Gospel; otherwise [this unanswerable question forces itself upon them], How is it possible that the Lord preached for one year only?

4. Being thirty years old when He came to be baptized, and then possessing the full age of a Master,[5] He came to Jerusalem, so that He might be properly acknowledged[6] by all as a Master. For He did not seem one thing while He was another, as those affirm who describe Him as being man only in appearance; but what He was, that He also appeared to be. Being a Master, therefore, He also possessed the age of a Master, not despising or evading any condition of humanity, nor setting aside in Himself that law which He had[7] appointed for the human race, but sanctifying every age, by that period corresponding to it which belonged to Himself. For He came to save all through means of Himself—all, I say, who through Him are born again to God[8]—infants,[9] and children, and boys, and youths, and old men. He therefore passed through every age, becoming an infant for infants, thus sanctifying infants; a child for children, thus sanctifying those who are of this age, being at the same time made to them an example of piety, righteousness, and submission; a youth for youths, becoming an example to youths, and thus sanctifying them for the Lord. So likewise He was an old man for old men, that He might be a perfect Master for all, not merely as respects the setting forth of the truth, but also as regards age, sanctifying at the same time the aged also, and becoming an example to them likewise. Then, at last, He came on to death itself, that He might be "the first-born from the dead, that in all things He might have the pre-eminence,"[10] the Prince of life,[11] existing before all, and going before all.[12]

5. They, however, that they may establish their false opinion regarding that which is written, "to proclaim the acceptable year of the Lord," maintain that He preached for one year only, and then suffered in the twelfth month. [In speaking thus], they are forgetful to their own disadvantage, destroying His whole work, and robbing Him of that age which is both more necessary and more honourable than any other; that more advanced age, I mean, during which also as a teacher He excelled all others. For how could He have had disciples, if He did not teach? And how could He have taught, unless He had reached the age of a Master? For when He came to be baptized, He had not yet completed His thirtieth year, but was beginning to be about thirty years of age (for thus Luke, who has mentioned His years, has expressed it: "Now Jesus was, as it were, beginning to be thirty years old,"[13] when He came to receive baptism); and, [according to these men,] He preached only one year reckoning from His baptism. On completing His thirtieth year He suffered, being in fact still a young man, and who had by no means attained to advanced age. Now, that the first

---

[1] John iv. 50.
[2] John v. 1, etc. It is well known that, to fix what is meant by the ἑορτή, referred to in this passage of St. John, is one of the most difficult points in New Testament criticism. Some modern scholars think that the feast of Purim is intended by the Evangelist; but, upon the whole, the current of opinion that has always prevailed in the Church has been in favour of the statement here made by Irenæus. Christ would therefore be present at four passovers after His baptism: (1) John ii. 13; (2) John v. 1; (3) John vi. 4; (4) John xiii. 1.
[3] John vi. 1, etc.
[4] John xi. 54, xii. 1.
[5] Or, "teacher," *magistri*.
[6] Harvey strangely remarks here, that "the reading *audiret*, followed by Massuet, makes no sense." He gives *audiretur* in his text, but proposes to read *ordiretur*. The passage may, however, be translated as above, without departing from the Benedictine reading *audiret*.

[7] "Neque solvens suam legem in se humani generis." Massuet would expunge "suam;" but, as Harvey well observes, "it has a peculiar significance, *nor abrogating his own law*."
[8] "Renascuntur in Deum." The reference in these words is doubtless to baptism, as clearly appears from comparing book iii. 17, 1.
[9] It has been remarked by Wall and others, that we have here the statement of a valuable fact as to the baptism of infants in the primitive Church.
[10] Col. i. 18.
[11] Acts iii. 15.
[12] [That our Lord was *prematurely* old may be inferred from the text which Irenæus regards as proof that he literally lived to be old. St. John viii. 56, 57; comp. Is. liii. 2.]
[13] Luke iii. 23.

stage of early life embraces thirty years,[1] and that this extends onwards to the fortieth year, every one will admit; but from the fortieth and fiftieth year a man begins to decline towards old age, which our Lord possessed while He still fulfilled the office of a Teacher, even as the Gospel and all the elders testify; those who were conversant in Asia with John, the disciple of the Lord, [affirming] that John conveyed to them that information.[2] And he remained among them up to the times of Trajan.[3] Some of them, moreover, saw not only John, but the other apostles also, and heard the very same account from them, and bear testimony as to the [validity of] the statement. Whom then should we rather believe? Whether such men as these, or Ptolemæus, who never saw the apostles, and who never even in his dreams attained to the slightest trace of an apostle?

6. But, besides this, those very Jews who then disputed with the Lord Jesus Christ have most clearly indicated the same thing. For when the Lord said to them, "Your father Abraham rejoiced to see My day; and he saw it, and was glad," they answered Him, "Thou art not yet fifty years old, and hast Thou seen Abraham?"[4] Now, such language is fittingly applied to one who has already passed the age of forty, without having as yet reached his fiftieth year, yet is not far from this latter period. But to one who is only thirty years old it would unquestionably be said, "Thou art not yet forty years old." For those who wished to convict Him of falsehood would certainly not extend the number of His years far beyond the age which they saw He had attained; but they mentioned a period near His real age, whether they had truly ascertained this out of the entry in the public register, or simply made a conjecture from what they observed that He was above forty years old, and that He certainly was not one of only thirty years of age. For it is altogether unreasonable to suppose that they were mistaken by twenty years, when they wished to prove Him younger than the times of Abraham. For what they saw, that they also expressed; and He whom they beheld was not a mere phantasm, but an actual being[5] of flesh and blood. He did not then want much of being fifty years old;[6] and, in accordance with that fact, they said to Him, "Thou art not yet fifty years old, and hast Thou seen Abraham?" He did not therefore preach only for one year, nor did He suffer in the twelfth month of the year. For the period included between the thirtieth and the fiftieth year can never be regarded as *one* year, unless indeed, among their Æons, there be so long years assigned to those who sit in their ranks with Bythus in the Pleroma; of which beings Homer the poet, too, has spoken, doubtless being inspired by the Mother of their [system of] error: —

Οἱ δὲ θεοὶ πὰρ Ζηνὶ καθήμενοι ἠγορόωντο
Χρυσέῳ ἐν δαπέδῳ·[7]

which we may thus render into English:[8] —

"The gods sat round, while Jove presided o'er,
And converse held upon the golden floor."

CHAP. XXIII. — THE WOMAN WHO SUFFERED FROM AN ISSUE OF BLOOD WAS NO TYPE OF THE SUFFERING ÆON.

1. Moreover, their ignorance comes out in a clear light with respect to the case of that woman who, suffering from an issue of blood, touched the hem of the Lord's garment, and so was made whole; for they maintain that through her was shown forth that twelfth power who suffered passion, and flowed out towards immensity, that is, the twelfth Æon. [This ignorance of theirs appears] first, because, as I have shown, according to their own system, that was not the twelfth Æon. But even granting them this point [in the meantime], there being twelve Æons, eleven of these are said to have continued impassible, while the twelfth suffered passion; but the woman, on the other hand, being healed in the twelfth year, it is manifest that she had continued to suffer during eleven years, and was healed in the twelfth. If indeed they were to say that eleven Æons were involved in passion, but the twelfth one was healed, it would then be a plausible thing to say that the woman was a type of these. But since she suffered during eleven years, and [all that time] obtained no cure, but was healed in the twelfth year, in what way can she be a type of the twelfth of the Æons, eleven of whom, [according to hypothesis,] did not suffer at all, but the twelfth alone participated in suffering? For a type and emblem is, no doubt, sometimes diverse from the truth [signified] as to matter and substance; but it ought, as to the general form and features, to maintain

---

[1] The Latin text of this clause is, "Quia autem triginta annorum ætas prima indolis est juvenis" — words which it seems almost impossible to translate. Grabe regarded "indolis" as being in the nominative, while Massuet contends it is in the genitive case; and so regarding it, we might translate, "Now that the age of thirty is the first age of the mind of youth," etc. But Harvey re-translates the clause into Greek as follows: ῞Οτι δὲ ἡ τῶν τριάκοντα ἐτῶν ἡλικία ἡ πρώτη τῆς διαθέσεώς ἐστι νέας — words which we have endeavoured to render as above. The meaning clearly is, that the age of thirty marked the transition point from youth to maturity.
[2] With respect to this extraordinary assertion of Irenæus, Harvey remarks: "The reader may here perceive the unsatisfactory character of tradition, where a mere fact is concerned. From reasonings founded upon the evangelical history, as well as from a preponderance of external testimony, it is most certain that our Lord's ministry extended but little over three years; yet here Irenæus states that it included more than ten years, and appeals to a tradition derived, as he says, from those who had conversed with an apostle.
[3] Trajan's reign commenced A.D. 98, and St. John is said to have lived to the age of a hundred years.
[4] John viii. 56, 57.
[5] Sed veritas" — literally, "the truth."
[6] [This statement is simply astounding, and might seem a providential illustration of the worthlessness of *mere* tradition unsustained by the written Word. No mere tradition could be more creditably authorized than this.]
[7] *Iliad*, iv. 1.
[8] *Latin*, of course, in the text.

a likeness [to what is typified], and in this way to shadow forth by means of things present those which are yet to come.

2. And not only in the case of this woman have the years of her infirmity (which they affirm to fit in with their figment) been mentioned, but, lo! another woman was also healed, after suffering in like manner for eighteen years; concerning whom the Lord said, "And ought not this daughter of Abraham, whom Satan has bound during eighteen years, to be set free on the Sabbath-day?"[1] If, then, the former was a type of the twelfth Æon that suffered, the latter should also be a type of the eighteenth Æon in suffering. But they cannot maintain this; otherwise their primary and original Ogdoad will be included in the number of Æons who suffered together. Moreover, there was also a certain other person[2] healed by the Lord, after he had suffered for eight-and-thirty years: they ought therefore to affirm that the Æon who occupies the thirty-eighth place suffered. For if they assert that the things which were done by the Lord were types of what took place in the Pleroma, the type ought to be preserved throughout. But they can neither adapt to their fictitious system the case of her who was cured after eighteen years, nor of him who was cured after thirty-eight years. Now, it is in every way absurd and inconsistent to declare that the Saviour preserved the type in certain cases, while He did not do so in others. The type of the woman, therefore, [with the issue of blood] is shown to have no analogy to their system of Æons.[3]

CHAP. XXIV. — FOLLY OF THE ARGUMENTS DERIVED BY THE HERETICS FROM NUMBERS, LETTERS, AND SYLLABLES.

1. This very thing, too, still further demonstrates their opinion false, and their fictitious system untenable, that they endeavour to bring forward proofs of it, sometimes through means of numbers and the syllables of names, sometimes also through the letter of syllables, and yet again through those numbers which are, according to the practice followed by the Greeks, contained in [different] letters; — [this, I say,] demonstrates in the clearest manner their overthrow or confusion,[4] as well as the untenable and perverse character of their [professed] knowledge. For, transferring the name *Jesus*, which belongs to another language, to the numeration of the Greeks, they sometimes call it "Episemon,"[5] as having six letters, and at other times "the Plenitude of the Ogdoads," as containing the number eight hundred and eighty-eight. But His [corresponding] Greek name, which is "Soter," that is, *Saviour*, because it does not fit in with their system, either with respect to numerical value or as regards its letters, they pass over in silence. Yet surely, if they regard the names of the Lord, as, in accordance with the preconceived purpose of the Father, by means of their numerical value and letters, indicating number in the Pleroma, *Soter*, as being a Greek name, ought by means of its letters and the numbers [expressed by these], in virtue of its being Greek, to show forth the mystery of the Pleroma. But the case is not so, because it is a word of five letters, and its numerical value is one thousand four hundred and eight.[6] But these things do not in any way correspond with their Pleroma: the account, therefore, which they give of transactions in the Pleroma cannot be true.

2. Moreover, *Jesus*, which is a word belonging to the proper tongue of the Hebrews, contains, as the learned among them declare, two letters and a half,[7] and signifies that Lord who contains heaven and earth;[8] for *Jesus* in the ancient Hebrew language means "heaven," while again "earth" is expressed by the words *sura usser*.[9] The word, therefore, which contains heaven and earth is just *Jesus*. Their explanation, then, of the *Episemon* is false, and their numerical calculation is also manifestly overthrown. For, in their own language, *Soter* is a Greek word of five letters; but, on the other hand, in the Hebrew tongue, *Jesus* contains only two letters and a half. The total which they reckon up, viz., eight hundred and eighty-eight, therefore falls to the ground. And throughout, the Hebrew letters do not correspond in number with the Greek, although these especially, as being the more ancient and unchanging, ought to uphold the reckoning connected with the names. For these ancient, original, and generally called *sacred* letters [10] of the Hebrews are ten in number (but they are written by means of fifteen [11]), the last letter

---

[1] Luke xiii. 16.
[2] John v. 5.
[3] The text of this sentence is very uncertain. We follow Massuet's reading, " negotio Æonum," in preference to that suggested by Harvey.
[4] " Sive confusionem " is very probably a marginal gloss which has found its way into the text. The whole clause is difficult and obscure.
[5] Comp. i. 14, 4.

[6] Thus: Σωτήρ (σ = 200, ω = 800, τ = 300, η = 8, ρ = 100) = 1408.
[7] Being written thus, יש׳, and the small ׳ being apparently regarded as only half a letter. Harvey proposes a different solution which seems less probable.
[8] This is one of the most obscure passages in the whole work of Irenæus, and the editors have succeeded in throwing very little light upon it. We may merely state that יש׳ seems to be regarded as containing in itself the initials of the three words יְהֹוָה, *Jehovah;* שָׁמַיִם, *heaven;* and אֶרֶץ, *and earth.*
[9] Nothing can be made of these words: they have probably been corrupted by ignorant transcribers, and are now wholly unintelligible.
[10] " Literæ sacerdotales," — another enigma which no man can solve. Massuet supposes the reference to be to the archaic Hebrew characters, still used by the *priests* after the square Chaldaic letters had been generally adopted. Harvey thinks that *sacerdotales* represents the Greek λειτουργικά, " meaning letters as popularly used in common computation."
[11] The editors have again long notes on this most obscure passage. Massuet expunges " quæque," and gives a lengthened explanation of the clause, to which we can only refer the curious reader.

being joined to the first. And thus they write some of these letters according to their natural sequence, just as we do, but others in a reverse direction, from the right hand towards the left, thus tracing the letters backwards. The name *Christ*, too, ought to be capable of being reckoned up in harmony with the Æons of their Pleroma, inasmuch as, according to their statements, He was produced for the establishment and rectification of their Pleroma. The Father, too, in the same way, ought, both by means of letters and numerical value, to contain the number of those Æons who were produced by Him; Bythus, in like manner, and not less Monogenes; but pre-eminently the name which is above all others, by which God is called, and which in the Hebrew tongue is expressed by *Baruch*,[1] [a word] which also contains two and a half letters. From this fact, therefore, that the more important names, both in the Hebrew and Greek languages, do not conform to their system, either as respects the number of letters or the reckoning brought out of them, the forced character of their calculations respecting the rest becomes clearly manifest.

3. For, choosing out of the law whatever things agree with the number adopted in their system, they thus violently strive to obtain proofs of its validity. But if it was really the purpose of their Mother, or the Saviour, to set forth, by means of the Demiurge, types of those things which are in the Pleroma, they should have taken care that the types were found in things more exactly correspondent and more holy; and, above all, in the case of the Ark of the Covenant, on account of which the whole tabernacle of witness was formed. Now it was constructed thus: its length[2] was two cubits and a half, its breadth one cubit and a half, its height one cubit and a half; but such a number of cubits in no respect corresponds with their system, yet by it the type ought to have been, beyond everything else, clearly set forth. The mercy-seat[3] also does in like manner not at all harmonize with their expositions. Moreover, the table of shew-bread[4] was two cubits in length, while its height was a cubit and a half. These stood before the holy of holies, and yet in them not a single number is of such an amount as contains an indication of the Tetrad, or the Ogdoad, or of the rest of their Pleroma. What of the candlestick,[5] too, which had seven[6] branches and seven lamps? while, if these had been made according to the type, it ought to have had eight branches and a like number of lamps, after the type of the primary Ogdoad, which shines pre-eminently among the Æons, and illuminates the whole Pleroma. They have carefully enumerated the curtains[7] as being ten, declaring these a type of the ten Æons; but they have forgotten to count the coverings of skin, which were eleven[8] in number. Nor, again, have they measured the size of these very curtains, each curtain[9] being eight-and-twenty cubits in length. And they set forth the length of the pillars as being ten cubits, with a reference to the Decad of Æons. "But the breadth of each pillar was a cubit and a half;"[10] and this they do not explain, any more than they do the entire number of the pillars or of their bars, because that does not suit the argument. But what of the anointing oil,[11] which sanctified the whole tabernacle? Perhaps it escaped the notice of the Saviour, or, while their Mother was sleeping, the Demiurge of himself gave instructions as to its weight; and on this account it is out of harmony with their Pleroma, consisting,[12] as it did, of five hundred shekels of myrrh, five hundred of cassia, two hundred and fifty of cinnamon, two hundred and fifty of calamus, and oil in addition, so that it was composed of five ingredients. The incense[13] also, in like manner, [was compounded] of stacte, onycha, galbanum, mint, and frankincense, all which do in no respect, either as to their mixture or weight, harmonize with their argument. It is therefore unreasonable and altogether absurd [to maintain] that the types were not preserved in the sublime and more imposing enactments of the law; but in other points, when any number coincides with their assertions, to affirm that it was a type of the things in the Pleroma; while [the truth is, that] every number occurs with the utmost variety in the Scriptures, so that, should any one desire it, he might form not only an Ogdoad, and a Decad, and a Duodecad, but any sort of number from the Scriptures, and then maintain that this was a type of the system of error devised by himself.

4. But that this point is true, that that number which is called *five*, which agrees in no respect with their argument, and does not harmonize with their system, nor is suitable for a typical manifestation of the things in the Pleroma, [yet has a wide prevalence,[14]] will be proved as follows from the Scriptures. Soter is a name of

---

[1] בָּרוּךְ, Baruch, *blessed*, one of the commonest titles of the Almighty. The final ך seems to be reckoned only a half-letter, as being different in form from what it is when accompanied by a vowel at the beginning or in the middle of a word.
[2] Ex. xxv. 10.
[3] Ex. xxv. 17.
[4] Ex. xxv. 23.
[5] Ex. xxv. 31, etc.
[6] Only *six* branches are mentioned in Ex. xxv. 32.
[7] Ex. xxvi. 1.
[8] Ex. xxvi. 7.
[9] Ex. xxvi. 2.
[10] Ex. xxvi. 16.
[11] Ex. xxvi. 26.
[12] Ex. xxx. 23, etc.
[13] Ex. xxx. 34.
[14] Some such supplement as this seems requisite, but the syntax in the Latin text is very confused.

five letters; Pater, too, contains five letters; Agape (love), too, consists of five letters; and our Lord, after[1] blessing the five loaves, fed with them five thousand men. Five virgins[2] were called wise by the Lord; and, in like manner, five were styled foolish. Again, five men are said to have been with the Lord when He obtained testimony[3] from the Father,—namely, Peter, and James, and John, and Moses, and Elias. The Lord also, as the fifth person, entered into the apartment of the dead maiden, and raised her up again; for, says [the Scripture], "He suffered no man to go in, save Peter and James,[4] and the father and mother of the maiden."[5] The rich man in hell[6] declared that he had five brothers, to whom he desired that one rising from the dead should go. The pool from which the Lord commanded the paralytic man to go into his house, had five porches. The very form of the cross, too, has five extremities,[7] two in length, two in breadth, and one in the middle, on which [last] the person rests who is fixed by the nails. Each of our hands has five fingers; we have also five senses; our internal organs may also be reckoned as five, viz., the heart, the liver, the lungs, the spleen, and the kidneys. Moreover, even the whole person may be divided into this number [of parts],—the head, the breast, the belly, the thighs, and the feet. The human race passes through five ages: first infancy, then boyhood, then youth, then maturity,[8] and then old age. Moses delivered the law to the people in five books. Each table which he received from God contained five[9] commandments. The veil covering[10] the holy of holies had five pillars. The altar of burnt-offering also was five cubits in breadth.[11] Five priests were chosen in the wilderness,—namely, Aaron,[12] Nadab, Abiud, Eleazar, Ithamar. The ephod and the breastplate, and other sacerdotal vestments, were formed out of five[13] materials; for they combined in themselves gold, and blue, and purple, and scarlet, and fine linen. And there were five[14] kings of the Amorites, whom Joshua the son of Nun shut up in a cave, and directed the people to trample upon their heads. Any one, in fact, might collect many thousand other things of the same kind, both with respect to this number and any other he chose to fix upon, either from the Scriptures, or from the works of nature lying under his observation.[15] But although such is the case, we do not therefore affirm that there are five Æons above the Demiurge; nor do we consecrate the Pentad, as if it were some divine thing; nor do we strive to establish things that are untenable, nor ravings [such as they indulge in], by means of that vain kind of labour; nor do we perversely force a creation well adapted by God [for the ends intended to be served], to change itself into types of things which have no real existence; nor do we seek to bring forward impious and abominable doctrines, the detection and overthrow of which are easy to all possessed of intelligence.

5. For who can concede to them that the year has three hundred and sixty-five days only, in order that there may be twelve months of thirty days each, after the type of the twelve Æons, when the type is in fact altogether out of harmony [with the antitype]? For, in the one case, each of the Æons is a thirtieth part of the entire Pleroma, while in the other they declare that a month is the twelfth part of a year. If, indeed, the year were divided into thirty parts, and the month into twelve, then a fitting type might be regarded as having been found for their fictitious system. But, on the contrary, as the case really stands, their Pleroma is divided into thirty parts, and a portion of it into twelve; while again the whole year is divided into twelve parts, and a certain portion of it into thirty. The Saviour therefore acted unwisely in constituting the month a type of the entire Pleroma, but the year a type only of that Duodecad which exists in the Pleroma; for it was more fitting to divide the year into thirty parts, even as the whole Pleroma is divided, but the month into twelve, just as the Æons are in their Pleroma. Moreover, they divide the entire Pleroma into three portions,—namely, into an Ogdoad, a Decad, and a Duodecad. But our year is divided into four parts,—namely, spring, summer, autumn, and winter. And again, not even do the months, which they maintain to be a type of the Triacontad, consist precisely of thirty days, but some have more and some less, inasmuch as five days remain to them as an overplus.[16] The day, too, does not always consist precisely of twelve hours, but rises from nine[17] to fifteen, and then falls again from fifteen to nine. It cannot therefore be held that months of thirty days each were so formed for the sake of [typifying]

---

[1] Matt. xiv. 19, 21; Mark vi. 41, 44; Luke ix. 13, 14; John vi. 9, 10, 11.
[2] Matt. xxv. 2, etc.
[3] Matt. xvii. 1.
[4] St. John is here strangely overlooked.
[5] Luke viii. 51.
[6] Luke xvi. 28.
[7] "Fines et summitates;" comp. Justin Mart., *Dial. c. Tryph.*, 91.
[8] "Juvenis," *one in the prime of life.*
[9] It has been usual in the Christian Church to reckon four commandments in the first table, and six in the second; but the above was the ancient Jewish division. See Joseph., *Antiq.*, iii. 6.
[10] Ex. xxvi. 37.
[11] Ex. xxvii. 1; "altitudo" in the text must be exchanged for "latitudo."
[12] Ex. xxviii. 1.
[13] Ex. xxviii. 5.
[14] Josh. x. 17.
[15] [Note the manly contempt with which our author dismisses a class of similitudes, which seem, even in our day, to have great attractions for some minds not otherwise narrow.]
[16] 365 (the days of the year) = 12 × 30 + 5.
[17] These hours of daylight, at the winter and summer solstice respectively, correspond to the latitude of Lyons, 45° 45′ N., where Irenæus resided.

the Æons; for, in that case, they would have consisted precisely of thirty days: nor, again, the days of these months, that by means of twelve hours they might symbolize the twelve Æons; for, in that case, they would always have consisted precisely of twelve hours.

6. But further, as to their calling material substances "on the left hand," and maintaining that those things which are thus on the left hand of necessity fall into corruption, while they also affirm that the Saviour came to the lost sheep, in order to transfer it to the right hand, that is, to the ninety and nine sheep which were in safety, and perished not, but continued within the fold, yet were of the left hand,[1] it follows that they must acknowledge that the enjoyment[2] of rest did not imply salvation. And that which has not in like manner the same number, they will be compelled to acknowledge as belonging to the left hand, that is, to corruption. This Greek word *Agape* (love), then, according to the letters of the Greeks, by means of which reckoning is carried on among them, having a numerical value of *ninety-three*,[3] is in like manner assigned to the place of rest on the left hand. Aletheia (truth), too, having in like manner, according to the principle indicated above, a numerical value of sixty-four,[4] exists among material substances. And thus, in fine, they will be compelled to acknowledge that all those sacred names which do not reach a numerical value of one hundred, but only contain the numbers summed by the left hand, are corruptible and material.

CHAP. XXV. — GOD IS NOT TO BE SOUGHT AFTER BY MEANS OF LETTERS, SYLLABLES, AND NUMBERS; NECESSITY OF HUMILITY IN SUCH INVESTIGATIONS.

1. If any one, however, say in reply to these things, What then? Is it a meaningless and accidental thing, that the positions of names, and the election of the apostles, and the working of the Lord, and the arrangement of created things, are what they are? — we answer them: Certainly not; but with great wisdom and diligence, all things have clearly been made by God, fitted and prepared [for their special purposes]; and His word formed both things ancient and those belonging to the latest times; and men ought not to connect those things with the number *thirty*,[5] but to harmonize them with what actually exists, or with right reason. Nor should they seek to prosecute inquiries respecting God by means of numbers, syllables, and letters. For this is an uncertain mode of proceeding, on account of their varied and diverse systems, and because every sort of hypothesis may at the present day be, in like manner, devised[6] by any one; so that[7] they can derive arguments against the truth from these very theories, inasmuch as they may be turned in many different directions. But, on the contrary, they ought to adapt the numbers themselves, and those things which have been formed, to the true theory lying before them. For system[8] does not spring out of numbers, but numbers from a system; nor does God derive His being from things made, but things made from God. For all things originate from one and the same God.

2. But since created things are various and numerous, they are indeed well fitted and adapted to the whole creation; yet, when viewed individually, are mutually opposite and inharmonious, just as the sound of the lyre, which consists of many and opposite notes, gives rise to one unbroken melody, through means of the interval which separates each one from the others. The lover of truth therefore ought not to be deceived by the interval between each note, nor should he imagine that one was due to one artist and author, and another to another, nor that one person fitted the treble, another the bass, and yet another the tenor strings; but he should hold that one and the same person [formed the whole], so as to prove the judgment, goodness, and skill exhibited in the whole work and [specimen of] wisdom. Those, too, who listen to the melody, ought to praise and extol the artist, to admire the tension of some notes, to attend to the softness of others, to catch the sound of others between both these extremes, and to consider the special character of others, so as to inquire at what each one aims, and what is the cause of their variety, never failing to apply our rule, neither giving up the [one[9]] artist, nor casting off faith in the one God who formed all things, nor blaspheming our Creator.

3. If, however, any one do not discover the cause of all those things which become objects of investigation, let him reflect that man is infinitely inferior to God; that he has received grace only in part, and is not yet equal or similar to his Maker; and, moreover, that he cannot have experience or form a conception of all things

---

[1] "Alluding," says Harvey, "to a custom among the ancients, of summing the numbers below 100 by various positions of the left hand and its fingers; 100 and upwards being reckoned by corresponding gestures of the right hand. The ninety and nine sheep, therefore, that remained quietly in the fold were summed upon the left hand, and Gnostics professed that they were typical of the true spiritual seed; but Scripture always places the workers of iniquity on the left hand, and in the Gnostic theory the evil principle of matter was sinistral, therefore," etc., as above.
[2] "Levamen," corresponding probably to the Greek ἀνάπαυσιν.
[3] Ἀγάπη (α = 1, γ = 3, α = 1, π = 80, η = 8) = 93.
[4] Ἀλήθεια (α = 1, λ = 30, η = 8, θ = 9, ε = 5, ι = 10, α = 1) = 64.

[5] Some read xx., but xxx. is probably correct.
[6] Harvey proposes "commentitum" instead of "commentatum," but the alteration seems unnecessary.
[7] The syntax is in confusion, and the meaning obscure.
[8] "Regula."
[9] "Errantes ab artifice." The whole sentence is most obscure.

like God; but in the same proportion as he who was formed but to-day, and received the beginning of his creation, is inferior to Him who is uncreated, and who is always the same, in that proportion is he, as respects knowledge and the faculty of investigating the causes of all things, inferior to Him who made him. For thou, O man, art not an uncreated being, nor didst thou always co-exist[1] with God, as did His own Word; but now, through His pre-eminent goodness, receiving the beginning of thy creation, thou dost gradually learn from the Word the dispensations of God who made thee.

4. Preserve therefore the proper order of thy knowledge, and do not, as being ignorant of things really good, seek to rise above God Himself, for He cannot be surpassed; nor do thou seek after any one above the Creator, for thou wilt not discover such. For thy Former cannot be contained within limits; nor, although thou shouldst measure all this [universe], and pass through all His creation, and consider it in all its depth, and height, and length, wouldst thou be able to conceive of any other above the Father Himself. For thou wilt not be able to think Him fully out, but, indulging in trains of reflection opposed to thy nature, thou wilt prove thyself foolish; and if thou persevere in such a course, thou wilt fall into utter madness, whilst thou deemest thyself loftier and greater than thy Creator, and imaginest that thou canst penetrate beyond His dominions.

CHAP. XXVI. — "KNOWLEDGE PUFFETH UP, BUT LOVE EDIFIETH."

1. It is therefore better and more profitable to belong to the simple and unlettered class, and by means of love to attain to nearness to God, than, by imagining ourselves learned and skilful, to be found [among those who are] blasphemous against their own God, inasmuch as they conjure up another God as the Father. And for this reason Paul exclaimed, " Knowledge puffeth up, but love edifieth: "[2] not that he meant to inveigh against a true knowledge of God, for in that case he would have accused himself; but, because he knew that some, puffed up by the pretence of knowledge, fall away from the love of God, and imagine that they themselves are perfect, for this reason that they set forth an imperfect Creator, with the view of putting an end to the pride which they feel on account of knowledge of this kind, he says, " Knowledge puffeth up, but love edifieth." Now there can be no greater conceit than this, that any one should imagine he is better and more perfect than He who made and fashioned him, and imparted to him the breath of life, and commanded this very thing into existence. It is therefore better, as I have said, that one should have no knowledge whatever of any one reason why a single thing in creation has been made, but should believe in God, and continue in His love, than[3] that, puffed up through knowledge of this kind, he should fall away from that love which is the life of man; and that he should search after no other knowledge except [the knowledge of] Jesus Christ the Son of God, who was crucified for us, than that by subtle questions and hair-splitting expressions he should fall into impiety.[4]

2. For how would it be, if any one, gradually elated by attempts of the kind referred to, should, because the Lord said that " even the hairs of your head are all numbered,"[5] set about inquiring into the number of hairs on each one's head, and endeavour to search out the reason on account of which one man has so many, and another so many, since all have not an equal number, but many thousands upon thousands are to be found with still varying numbers, on this account that some have larger and others smaller heads, some have bushy heads of hair, others thin, and others scarcely any hair at all, — and then those who imagine that they have discovered the number of the hairs, should endeavour to apply that for the commendation of their own sect which they have conceived? Or again, if any one should, because of this expression which occurs in the Gospel, " Are not two sparrows sold for a farthing? and not one of them falls to the ground without the will of your Father,"[6] take occasion to reckon up the number of sparrows caught daily, whether over all the world or in some particular district, and to make inquiry as to the reason of so many having been captured yesterday, so many the day before, and so many again on this day, and should then join on the number of sparrows to his [particular] hypothesis, would he not in that case mislead himself altogether, and drive into absolute insanity those that agreed with him, since men are always eager in such matters to be thought to have discovered something more extraordinary than their masters?[7]

3. But if any one should ask us whether every number of all the things which have been made, and which are made, is known to God, and whether every one of these [numbers] has, according to His providence, received that special amount which it contains; and on our agreeing

---

[1] Alluding to the imaginary Æon *Anthropos*, who existed from eternity.
[2] 1 Cor. viii. 1.
[3] " Aut; " ἤ having been thus mistakenly rendered instead of " quam."
[4] [This seems anticipatory of the dialectics of scholasticism, and of its immense influence in Western Christendom, after St. Bernard's feeble adhesion to the Biblical system of the ancients.]
[5] Matt. x. 30.
[6] Matt. x. 29.
[7] [Illustrated by the history of modern thought in Germany. See the meritorious work of Professor Kahnis, on *German Protestantism*," (translated). Edinburgh, T. & T. Clark, 1856.]

that such is the case, and acknowledging that not one of the things which have been, or are, or shall be made, escapes the knowledge of God, but that through His providence every one of them has obtained its nature, and rank, and number, and special quantity, and that nothing whatever either has been or is produced in vain or accidentally, but with exceeding suitability [to the purpose intended], and in the exercise of transcendent knowledge, and that it was an admirable and truly divine intellect [1] which could both distinguish and bring forth the proper causes of such a system: if, [I say,] any one, on obtaining our adherence and consent to this, should proceed to reckon up the sand and pebbles of the earth, yea also the waves of the sea and the stars of heaven, and should endeavour to think out the causes of the number which he imagines himself to have discovered, would not his labour be in vain, and would not such a man be justly declared mad, and destitute of reason, by all possessed of common sense? And the more he occupied himself beyond others in questions of this kind, and the more he imagines himself to find out beyond others, styling them unskilful, ignorant, and animal beings, because they do not enter into his so useless labour, the more is he [in reality] insane, foolish, struck as it were with a thunderbolt, since indeed he does in no one point own himself inferior to God; but, by the knowledge which he imagines himself to have discovered, he changes God Himself, and exalts his own opinion above the greatness of the Creator.

CHAP. XXVII. — PROPER MODE OF INTERPRETING PARABLES AND OBSCURE PASSAGES OF SCRIPTURE.

1. A sound mind, and one which does not expose its possessor to danger, and is devoted to piety and the love of truth, will eagerly meditate upon those things which God has placed within the power of mankind, and has subjected to our knowledge, and will make advancement in [acquaintance with] them, rendering the knowledge of them easy to him by means of daily study. These things are such as fall [plainly] under our observation, and are clearly and unambiguously in express terms set forth in the Sacred Scriptures. And therefore the parables ought not to be adapted to ambiguous expressions. For, if this be not done, both he who explains them will do so without danger, and the parables will receive a like interpretation from all, and the body [2] of truth remains entire, with a harmonious adaptation of its members, and without any collision [of its several parts]. But to apply expressions which are not clear or evident to interpretations of the parables, such as every one discovers for himself as inclination leads him, [is absurd.[3]] For in this way no one will possess the rule of truth; but in accordance with the number of persons who explain the parables will be found the various systems of truth, in mutual opposition to each other, and setting forth antagonistic doctrines, like the questions current among the Gentile philosophers.

2. According to this course of procedure, therefore, man would always be inquiring but never finding, because he has rejected the very method of discovery. And when the Bridegroom [4] comes, he who has his lamp untrimmed, and not burning with the brightness of a steady light, is classed among those who obscure the interpretations of the parables, forsaking Him who by His plain announcements freely imparts gifts to all who come to Him, and is excluded from His marriage-chamber. Since, therefore, the entire Scriptures, the prophets, and the Gospels, can be clearly, unambiguously, and harmoniously understood by all, although all do not believe them; and [5] since they proclaim that one only God, to the exclusion of all others, formed all things by His word, whether visible or invisible, heavenly or earthly, in the water or under the earth, as I have shown [6] from the very words of Scripture; and since the very system of creation to which we belong testifies, by what falls under our notice, that one Being made and governs it, — those persons will seem truly foolish who blind their eyes to such a clear demonstration, and will not behold the light of the announcement [made to them]; but they put fetters upon themselves, and every one of them imagines, by means of their obscure interpretations of the parables, that he has found out a God of his own. For that there is nothing whatever openly, expressly, and without controversy said in any part of Scripture respecting the Father conceived of by those who hold a contrary opinion, they themselves testify, when they maintain that the Saviour privately taught these same things not to all, but to certain only of His disciples who could comprehend them, and who understood what was intended by Him through means of arguments, enigmas, and parables. They come, [in fine,] to this, that they maintain there is one Being who is proclaimed as God, and another as Father, He who is set forth as such through means of parables and enigmas.

---

[1] "Rationem."
[2] We read "veritatis corpus" for "a veritate corpus" in the text.
[3] Some such expression of disapproval must evidently be supplied, though wanting in the Latin text.
[4] Matt. xxv. 5, etc.
[5] The text is here elliptical, and we have supplied what seems necessary to complete the sense.
[6] It is doubtful whether "demonstravimus" or "demonstrabimus" be the proper reading: if the former, the reference will be to book i. 22, or ii. 2; if the latter, to book iii. 8.

3. But since parables admit of many interpretations, what lover of truth will not acknowledge, that for them to assert God is to be searched out from these, while they desert what is certain, indubitable, and true, is the part of men who eagerly throw themselves into danger, and act as if destitute of reason? And is not such a course of conduct not to build one's house upon a rock[1] which is firm, strong, and placed in an open position, but upon the shifting sand? Hence the overthrow of such a building is a matter of ease.

CHAP. XXVIII.—PERFECT KNOWLEDGE CANNOT BE ATTAINED IN THE PRESENT LIFE: MANY QUESTIONS MUST BE SUBMISSIVELY LEFT IN THE HANDS OF GOD.

1. Having therefore the truth itself as our rule, and the testimony concerning God set clearly before us, we ought not, by running after numerous and diverse answers to questions, to cast away the firm and true knowledge of God. But it is much more suitable that we, directing our inquiries after this fashion, should exercise ourselves in the investigation of the mystery and administration of the living God, and should increase in the love of Him who has done, and still does, so great things for us; but never should fall from the belief by which it is most clearly proclaimed that this Being alone is truly God and Father, who both formed this world, fashioned man, and bestowed the faculty of increase on His own creation, and called him upwards from lesser things to those greater ones which are in His own presence, just as He brings an infant which has been conceived in the womb into the light of the sun, and lays up wheat in the barn after He has given it full strength on the stalk. But it is one and the same Creator who both fashioned the womb and created the sun; and one and the same Lord who both reared the stalk of corn, increased and multiplied the wheat, and prepared the barn.

2. If, however, we cannot discover explanations of all those things in Scripture which are made the subject of investigation, yet let us not on that account seek after any other God besides Him who really exists. For this is the very greatest impiety. We should leave things of that nature to God who created us, being most properly assured that the Scriptures are indeed perfect, since they were spoken by the Word of God and His Spirit; but we, inasmuch as we are inferior to, and later in existence than, the Word of God and His Spirit, are on that very account[2] destitute of the knowledge of His mysteries. And there is no cause for wonder if this is the case with us as respects things spiritual and heavenly, and such as require to be made known to us by revelation, since many even of those things which lie at our very feet (I mean such as belong to this world, which we handle, and see, and are in close contact with) transcend our knowledge, so that even these we must leave to God. For it is fitting that He should excel all [in knowledge]. For how stands the case, for instance, if we endeavour to explain the cause of the rising of the Nile? We may say a great deal, plausible or otherwise, on the subject; but what is true, sure, and incontrovertible regarding it, belongs only to God. Then, again, the dwelling-place of birds—of those, I mean, which come to us in spring, but fly away again on the approach of autumn—though it is a matter connected with this world, escapes our knowledge. What explanation, again, can we give of the flow and ebb of the ocean, although every one admits there must be a certain cause [for these phenomena]? Or what can we say as to the nature of those things which lie beyond it?[3] What, moreover, can we say as to the formation of rain, lightning, thunder, gatherings of clouds, vapours, the bursting forth of winds, and such like things; or tell as to the storehouses of snow, hail, and other like things? [What do we know respecting] the conditions requisite for the preparation of clouds, or what is the real nature of the vapours in the sky? What as to the reason why the moon waxes and wanes, or what as to the cause of the difference of nature among various waters, metals, stones, and such like things? On all these points we may indeed say a great deal while we search into their causes, but God alone who made them can declare the truth regarding them.

3. If, therefore, even with respect to creation, there are some things [the knowledge of] which belongs only to God, and others which come within the range of our own knowledge, what ground is there for complaint, if, in regard to those things which we investigate in the Scriptures (which are throughout spiritual), we are able by the grace of God to explain some of them, while we must leave others in the hands of God, and that not only in the present world, but also in that which is to come, so that God should for ever teach, and man should for ever learn the things taught him by God? As the apostle has said on this point, that, when other things have been done away, then these three, "faith, hope, and charity, shall endure."[4] For faith, which has respect to our Master, endures[5] unchangeably,

---

[1] Matt. vii. 25.
[2] Or, "to that degree."
[3] Comp. Clem. Rom., *Ep. to Cor.*, c. xx.; and August., *De Civit Dei*, xvi. 9.
[4] 1 Cor. xiii. 13.
[5] "Permanet firma,"—no doubt corresponding to the μένει of the apostle, 1 Cor. xiii. 13. Harvey here remarks, that "the author seems to misapprehend the apostle's meaning. . . . There will be no longer room for hope, when the substance of things hoped for shall have become a matter of fruition; neither will there be any room for faith, when the soul shall be admitted to see God as He is." But the best modern interpreters take the same view of the passage as Irenæus. They regard the νυνὶ δέ of St. Paul as not being *temporal*, but *logical*, and conclude therefore the meaning to be, that *faith* and *hope*, as well as *love*, will, in a sense, endure for ever. Comp., e.g., Alford, *in loc.*

assuring us that there is but one true God, and that we should truly love Him for ever, seeing that He alone is our Father; while we hope ever to be receiving more and more from God, and to learn from Him, because He is good, and possesses boundless riches, a kingdom without end, and instruction that can never be exhausted. If, therefore, according to the rule which I have stated, we leave some questions in the hands of God, we shall both preserve our faith uninjured, and shall continue without danger; and all Scripture, which has been given to us by God, shall be found by us perfectly consistent; and the parables shall harmonize with those passages which are perfectly plain; and those statements the meaning of which is clear, shall serve to explain the parables; and through the many diversified utterances [of Scripture] there shall be heard [1] one harmonious melody in us, praising in hymns that God who created all things. If, for instance, any one asks, "What was God doing before He made the world?" we reply that the answer to such a question lies with God Himself. For that this world was formed perfect [2] by God, receiving a beginning in time, the Scriptures teach us; but no Scripture reveals to us what God was employed about before this event. The answer therefore to that question remains with God, and it is not proper [3] for us to aim at bringing forward foolish, rash, and blasphemous suppositions [in reply to it]; so, as by one's imagining that he has discovered the origin of matter, he should in reality set aside God Himself who made all things.

4. For consider, all ye who invent such opinions, since the Father Himself is alone called God, who has a real existence, but whom ye style the Demiurge; since, moreover, the Scriptures acknowledge Him alone as God; and yet again, since the Lord confesses Him alone as His own Father, and knows no other, as I shall show from His very words, — when ye style this very Being the fruit of defect, and the offspring of ignorance, and describe Him as being ignorant of those things which are above Him, with the various other allegations which you make regarding Him, — consider the terrible blasphemy [ye are thus guilty of] against Him who truly is God. Ye seem to affirm gravely and honestly enough that ye believe in God; but then, as ye are utterly unable to reveal any other God, ye declare this very Being in whom ye profess to believe, the fruit of defect and the offspring of ignorance. Now this blindness and foolish talking flow to you from the fact that ye reserve nothing for God, but ye wish to proclaim the nativity and production both of God Himself, of His Ennœa, of His Logos, and Life, and Christ; and ye form the idea of these from no other than a mere human experience; not understanding, as I said before, that it is possible, in the case of man, who is a compound being, to speak in this way of the mind of man and the thought of man; and to say that thought (ennœa) springs from mind (sensus), intention (enthymesis) again from thought, and word (logos) from intention (but which logos? [4] for there is among the Greeks one logos which is the principle that thinks, and another which is the instrument by means of which thought is expressed); and [to say] that a man sometimes is at rest and silent, while at other times he speaks and is active. But since God is [5] all mind, all reason, all active spirit, all light, and always exists one and the same, as it is both beneficial for us to think of God, and as we learn regarding Him from the Scriptures, such feelings and divisions [of operation] cannot fittingly be ascribed to Him. For our tongue, as being carnal, is not sufficient to minister to the rapidity of the human mind, inasmuch as that is of a spiritual nature, for which reason our word is restrained [6] within us, and is not at once expressed as it has been conceived by the mind, but is uttered by successive efforts, just as the tongue is able to serve it.

5. But God being all Mind, and all Logos, both speaks exactly what He thinks, and thinks exactly what He speaks. For His thought is Logos, and Logos is Mind, and Mind comprehending all things is the Father Himself. He, therefore, who speaks of the mind of God, and ascribes to it a special origin of its own, declares Him a compound Being, as if God were one thing, and the original Mind another. So, again, with respect to Logos, when one attributes to him the third [7] place of production from the Father; on which supposition he is ignorant of His greatness; and thus Logos has been far separated from God. As for the prophet, he declares respecting Him, "Who shall describe His generation?" [8] But ye pretend to set forth His generation from the Father, and ye transfer the production of the word of men which takes place by means of a tongue to the Word of God, and thus are righteously exposed by your own

---

[1] The Latin text is here untranslateable. Grabe proposes to read, "*una consonans melodia in nobis sentietur;*" while Stieren and others prefer to exchange αἰσθήσεται for ἀσθήσεται.
[2] "Apotelesticos." This word, says Harvey, "may also refer to the vital energy of nature, whereby its effects are for ever reproduced in unceasing succession." Comp. Hippol., *Philos.*, vii. 24.
[3] We here follow Grabe, who understands *decet*. Harvey less simply explains the very obscure Latin text.
[4] The Greek term λόγος, as is well known, denotes both *ratio* (reason) and *sermo* (speech). Some deem the above parenthesis an interpolation.
[5] Comp. i. 12, 2.
[6] "Suffugatur:" some read "suffocatur;" and Harvey proposes "suffragatur," as the representative of the Greek ψηφίζεται. The meaning in any case is, that while ideas are instantaneously formed in the human mind, they can be expressed through means of words only fractionally, and by successive utterances.
[7] Thus: *Bythus, Nous, Logos.*
[8] Isa. liii. 8.

selves as knowing neither things human nor divine.

6. But, beyond reason inflated [with your own wisdom], ye presumptuously maintain that ye are acquainted with the unspeakable mysteries of God; while even the Lord, the very Son of God, allowed that the Father alone knows the very day and hour of judgment, when He plainly declares, "But of that day and that hour knoweth no man, neither the Son, but the Father only."[1] If, then, the Son was not ashamed to ascribe the knowledge of that day to the Father only, but declared what was true regarding the matter, neither let us be ashamed to reserve for God those greater questions which may occur to us. For no man is superior to his master.[2] If any one, therefore, says to us, "How then was the Son produced by the Father?" we reply to him, that no man understands that production, or generation, or calling, or revelation, or by whatever name one may describe His generation, which is in fact altogether indescribable. Neither Valentinus, nor Marcion, nor Saturninus, nor Basilides, nor angels, nor archangels, nor principalities, nor powers [possess this knowledge], but the Father only who begat, and the Son who was begotten. Since therefore His generation is unspeakable, those who strive to set forth generations and productions cannot be in their right mind, inasmuch as they undertake to describe things which are indescribable. For that a word is uttered at the bidding of thought and mind, all men indeed well understand. Those, therefore, who have excogitated [the theory of] emissions have not discovered anything great, or revealed any abstruse mystery, when they have simply transferred what all understand to the only-begotten Word of God; and while they style Him unspeakable and unnameable, they nevertheless set forth the production and formation of His first generation, as if they themselves had assisted at His birth, thus assimilating Him to the word of mankind formed by emissions.

7. But we shall not be wrong if we affirm the same thing also concerning the substance of matter, that God produced it. For we have learned from the Scriptures that God holds the supremacy over all things. But whence or in what way He produced it, neither has Scripture anywhere declared; nor does it become us to conjecture, so as, in accordance with our own opinions, to form endless conjectures concerning God, but we should leave such knowledge in the hands of God Himself. In like manner, also, we must leave the cause why, while all things were made by God, certain of His creatures sinned and revolted from a state of submission to God, and others, indeed the great majority, persevered, and do still persevere, in [willing] subjection to Him who formed them, and also of what nature those are who sinned, and of what nature those who persevere, — [we must, I say, leave the cause of these things] to God and His Word, to whom alone He said, "Sit at my right hand, until I make Thine enemies Thy footstool."[3] But as for us, we still dwell upon the earth, and have not yet sat down upon His throne. For although the Spirit of the Saviour that is in Him "searcheth all things, even the deep things of God,"[4] yet as to us "there are diversities of gifts, differences of administrations, and diversities of operations;"[5] and we, while upon the earth, as Paul also declares, "know in part, and prophesy in part."[6] Since, therefore, we know but in part, we ought to leave all sorts of [difficult] questions in the hands of Him who in some measure, [and that only,] bestows grace on us. That eternal fire, [for instance,] is prepared for sinners, both the Lord has plainly declared, and the rest of the Scriptures demonstrate. And that God foreknew that this would happen, the Scriptures do in like manner demonstrate, since He prepared eternal fire from the beginning for those who were [afterwards] to transgress [His commandments]; but the cause itself of the nature of such transgressors neither has any Scripture informed us, nor has an apostle told us, nor has the Lord taught us. It becomes us, therefore, to leave the knowledge of this matter to God, even as the Lord does of the day and hour [of judgment], and not to rush to such an extreme of danger, that we will leave nothing in the hands of God, even though we have received only a measure of grace [from Him in this world]. But when we investigate points which are above us, and with respect to which we cannot reach satisfaction, [it is absurd[7]] that we should display such an extreme of presumption as to lay open God, and things which are not yet discovered,[8] as if already we had found out, by the vain talk about emissions, God Himself, the Creator of all things, and to assert that He derived His substance from apostasy and ignorance, so as to frame an impious hypothesis in opposition to God.

8. Moreover, they possess no proof of their system, which has but recently been invented by them, sometimes resting upon certain numbers, sometimes on syllables, and sometimes, again, on names; and there are occasions, too, when,

---

[1] Mark xiii. 32. The words, "neither the angels which are in heaven," are here omitted, probably because, as usual, the writer quotes from memory.
[2] Comp. Matt. x. 24; Luke xi. 40.
[3] Ps. cx. 1.
[4] 1 Cor. ii. 10.
[5] 1 Cor. xii. 4, 5, 6.
[6] 1 Cor. xiii. 9.
[7] Massuet proposes to insert these words, and some such supplement seems clearly necessary to complete the sense. But the sentence still remains confused and doubtful.
[8] [Gen. xl. 8; Deut. xxix. 29; Ps. cxxxi.]

by means of those letters which are contained in letters, by parables not properly interpreted, or by certain [baseless] conjectures, they strive to establish that fabulous account which they have devised. For if any one should inquire the reason why the Father, who has fellowship with the Son in all things, has been declared by the Lord alone to know the hour and the day [of judgment], he will find at present no more suitable, or becoming, or safe reason than this (since, indeed, the Lord is the only true Master), that we may learn through Him that the Father is above all things. For "the Father," says He, "is greater than I."[1] The Father, therefore, has been declared by our Lord to excel with respect to knowledge; for this reason, that we, too, as long as we are connected with the scheme of things in this world, should leave perfect knowledge, and such questions [as have been mentioned], to God, and should not by any chance, while we seek to investigate the sublime nature of the Father, fall into the danger of starting the question whether there is another God above God.[2]

9. But if any lover of strife contradict what I have said, and also what the apostle affirms, that "we know in part, and prophesy in part,"[3] and imagine that he has acquired not a partial, but a universal, knowledge of all that exists, — being such an one as Valentinus, or Ptolemæus, or Basilides, or any other of those who maintain that they have searched out the deep[4] things of God, — let him not (arraying himself in vainglory) boast that he has acquired greater knowledge than others with respect to those things which are invisible, or cannot be placed under our observation; but let him, by making diligent inquiry, and obtaining information from the Father, tell us the reasons (which we know not) of those things which are in this world, — as, for instance, the number of hairs on his own head, and the sparrows which are captured day by day, and such other points with which we are not previously acquainted, — so that we may credit him also with respect to more important points. But if those who are *perfect* do not yet understand the very things in their hands, and at their feet, and before their eyes, and on the earth, and especially the rule followed with respect to the hairs of their head, how can we believe them regarding things spiritual, and super-celestial,[5] and those which, with a vain confidence, they assert to be above God? So much, then, I have said concerning numbers, and names, and syllables, and questions respecting such things as are above our comprehension, and concerning their improper expositions of the parables: [I add no more on these points,] since thou thyself mayest enlarge upon them.

CHAP. XXIX. — REFUTATION OF THE VIEWS OF THE HERETICS AS TO THE FUTURE DESTINY OF THE SOUL AND BODY.

1. Let us return, however, to the remaining points of their system. For when they declare[6] that, at the consummation of all things, their mother shall re-enter the Pleroma, and receive the Saviour as her consort; that they themselves, as being spiritual, when they have got rid of their animal souls, and become intellectual spirits, will be the consorts of the spiritual angels; but that the Demiurge, since they call him animal, will pass into the place of the Mother; that the souls of the righteous shall psychically repose in the intermediate place; — when they declare that like will be gathered to like, spiritual things to spiritual, while material things continue among those that are material, they do in fact contradict themselves, inasmuch as they no longer maintain that souls pass, on account of their nature, into the intermediate place to those substances which are similar to themselves, but [that they do so] on account of the deeds done [in the body], since they affirm that those of the righteous do pass [into that abode], but those of the impious continue in the fire. For if it is on account of their nature that all souls attain to the place of enjoyment,[7] and all belong to the intermediate place simply because they are souls, as being thus of the same nature with it, then it follows that faith is altogether superfluous, as was also the descent[8] of the Saviour [to this world]. If, on the other hand, it is on account of their righteousness [that they attain to such a place of rest], then it is no longer because they are *souls* but because they are *righteous*. But if souls would have[9] perished unless they had been righteous, then righteousness must have power to save the bodies also [which these souls inhabited]; for why should it not save them, since they, too, participated in righteousness? For if nature and substance are the means of salvation, then all souls shall be saved; but if righteousness and faith, why should these not save those bodies which, equally with the souls, will enter[10] into

---

[1] John xiv. 28.
[2] [On the great matter of the περιχώρησις, the subordination of the Son, etc., Bull has explored Patristic doctrine, and may well be consulted here. *Defens. Fid. Nicænæ*, sect. iv.; see also vol. v. 363.]
[3] 1. Cor. xiii. 9.
[4] "Altitudines," literally, *heights*.
[5] [Wisdom, ix. 13, 17. A passage of marvellous beauty.]

[6] Comp. i. 7, 1.
[7] "Refrigerium," *place of refreshment*.
[8] Billius, with great apparent reason, proposes to read "descensio" for the unintelligible "discessio" of the Latin text.
[9] Grabe and Massuet read, "Si autem animæ perire inciperent, nisi justæ fuissent," for "Si autem animæ quæ perituræ essent inciperent nisi justæ fuissent," — words which defy all translation.
[10] The text is here uncertain and confused; but, as Harvey remarks, "the argument is this, That if souls are saved *qua* intellectual substance, then all are saved alike; but if by reason of any moral qualities, then the bodies that have executed the moral purposes of the soul, must also be considered to be heirs of salvation."

immortality? For righteousness will appear, in matters of this kind, either impotent or unjust, if indeed it saves some substances through participating in it, but not others.

2. For it is manifest that those acts which are deemed righteous are performed in bodies. Either, therefore, all souls will of necessity pass into the intermediate place, and there will never be a judgment; or bodies, too, which have participated in righteousness, will attain to the place of enjoyment, along with the souls which have in like manner participated, if indeed righteousness is powerful enough to bring thither those substances which have participated in it. And then the doctrine concerning the resurrection of bodies which we believe, will emerge true and certain [from their system]; since, [as we hold,] God, when He resuscitates our mortal bodies which preserved righteousness, will render them incorruptible and immortal. For God is superior to nature, and has in Himself the disposition [to show kindness], because He is good; and the ability to do so, because He is mighty; and the faculty of fully carrying out His purpose, because He is rich and perfect.

3. But these men are in all points inconsistent with themselves, when they decide that all souls do not enter into the intermediate place, but those of the righteous only. For they maintain that, according to nature and substance, three sorts [of being] were produced by the Mother: the first, which proceeded from perplexity, and weariness, and fear — that is material substance; the second from impetuosity [1] — that is animal substance; but that which she brought forth after the vision of those angels who wait upon Christ, is spiritual substance. If, then, that substance [2] which she brought forth will by all means enter into the Pleroma because it is spiritual, while that which is material will remain below because it is material, and shall be totally consumed by the fire which burns within it, why should not the whole animal substance go into the intermediate place, into which also they send the Demiurge? But what is it which shall enter within their Pleroma? For they maintain that souls shall continue in the intermediate place, while bodies, because they possess material substance, when they have been resolved into matter, shall be consumed by that fire which exists in it; but their body being thus destroyed, and their soul remaining in the intermediate place, no part of man will any longer be left to enter in within the Pleroma. For the intellect of man — his mind, thought, mental intention, and such like — is nothing else than his soul; but the emotions and operations of the soul itself have no substance apart from the soul. What part of them, then, will still remain to enter into the Pleroma? For they themselves, in as far as they are souls, remain in the intermediate place; while, in as far as they are body, they will be consumed with the rest of matter.

CHAP. XXX. — ABSURDITY OF THEIR STYLING THEMSELVES SPIRITUAL, WHILE THE DEMIURGE IS DECLARED TO BE ANIMAL.

1. Such being the state of the case, these infatuated men declare that they rise above the Creator (Demiurge); and, inasmuch as they proclaim themselves superior to that God who made and adorned the heavens, and the earth, and all things that are in them, and maintain that they themselves are spiritual, while they are in fact shamefully carnal on account of their so great impiety, — affirming that He, who has made His angels [3] spirits, and is clothed with light as with a garment, and holds the circle [4] of the earth, as it were, in His hand, in whose sight its inhabitants are counted as grasshoppers, and who is the Creator and Lord of all spiritual substance, is of an animal nature, — they do beyond doubt and verily betray their own madness; and, as if truly struck with thunder, even more than those giants who are spoken of in [heathen] fables, they lift up their opinions against God, inflated by a vain presumption and unstable glory, — men for whose purgation all the hellebore [5] on earth would not suffice, so that they should get rid of their intense folly.

2. The superior person is to be proved by his deeds. In what way, then, can they show themselves superior to the Creator (that I too, through the necessity of the argument in hand, may come down to the level of their impiety, instituting a comparison between God and foolish men, and, by descending to their argument, may often refute them by their own doctrines; but in thus acting may God be merciful to me, for I venture on these statements, not with the view of comparing Him to them, but of convicting and overthrowing their insane opinions) — they, for whom many foolish persons entertain so great an admiration, as if, forsooth, they could learn from them something more precious than the truth itself! That expression of Scripture, "Seek, and ye shall find," [6] they interpret as spoken with this view, that they should discover themselves to be above the Creator, styling themselves greater and better than God, and calling themselves spiritual, but the Creator animal; and [affirming] that for this reason they rise upwards above God, for that

---

[1] "De impetu:" it is generally supposed that these words correspond to ἐκ τῆς ἐπιστροφῆς (comp. i. 5, 1), but Harvey thinks ἐξ ὁρμῆς preferable (i. 4, 1).
[2] The syntax of this sentence is in utter confusion, but the meaning is doubtless that given above.
[3] Ps. civ. 2, 4.
[4] Isa. xl. 12, 22.
[5] Irenæus was evidently familiar with Horace; comp. *Ars Poet.*, 300.
[6] Matt. vii. 7.

they enter in within the Pleroma, while He remains in the intermediate place. Let them, then, prove themselves by their deeds superior to the Creator; for the superior person ought to be proved not by what is said, but by what has a real existence.

3. What work, then, will they point to as having been accomplished through themselves by the Saviour, or by their Mother, either greater, or more glorious, or more adorned with wisdom, than those which have been produced by Him who was the disposer of all around us? What heavens have they established? what earth have they founded? what stars have they called into existence? or what lights of heaven have they caused to shine? within what circles, moreover, have they confined them? or, what rains, or frosts, or snows, each suited to the season, and to every special climate, have they brought upon the earth? And again, in opposition to these, what heat or dryness have they set over against them? or, what rivers have they made to flow? what fountains have they brought forth? with what flowers and trees have they adorned this sublunary world? or, what multitude of animals have they formed, some rational, and others irrational, but all adorned with beauty? And who can enumerate one by one all the remaining objects which have been constituted by the power of God, and are governed by His wisdom? or who can search out the greatness of that God who made them? And what can be told of those existences which are above heaven, and which do not pass away, such as Angels, Archangels, Thrones, Dominions, and Powers innumerable? Against what one of these works, then, do they set themselves in opposition? What have they similar to show, as having been made through themselves, or by themselves, since even they too are the workmanship and creatures of this [Creator]? For whether the Saviour or their Mother (to use their own expressions, proving them false by means of the very terms they themselves employ) used this Being, as they maintain, to make an image of those things which are within the Pleroma, and of all those beings which she saw waiting upon the Saviour, she used him (the Demiurge) as being [in a sense] superior to herself, and better fitted to accomplish her purpose through his instrumentality; for she would by no means form the images of such important beings through means of an inferior, but by a superior, agent.

4. For, [be it observed,] they themselves, according to their own declarations, were then existing, as a spiritual conception, in consequence of the contemplation of those beings who were arranged as satellites around Pandora. And they indeed continued useless, the Mother accomplishing nothing through their instrumentality,[1] — an idle conception, owing their being to the Saviour, and fit for nothing, for not a thing appears to have been done by them. But the God who, according to them, was produced, while, as they argue, inferior to themselves (for they maintain that he is of an animal nature), was nevertheless the active agent in all things, efficient, and fit for the work to be done, so that by him the images of all things were made; and not only were these things which are seen formed by him, but also all things invisible, Angels, Archangels, Dominations, Powers, and Virtues, — [by him, I say,] as being the superior, and capable of ministering to her desire. But it seems that the Mother made nothing whatever through their instrumentality, as indeed they themselves acknowledge; so that one may justly reckon them as having been an abortion produced by the painful travail of their Mother. For no accoucheurs performed their office upon her, and therefore they were cast forth as an abortion, useful for nothing, and formed to accomplish no work of the Mother. And yet they describe themselves as being superior to Him by whom so vast and admirable works have been accomplished and arranged, although by their own reasoning they are found to be so wretchedly inferior!

5. It is as if there were two iron tools, or instruments, the one of which was continually in the workman's hands and in constant use, and by the use of which he made whatever he pleased, and displayed his art and skill, but the other of which remained idle and useless, never being called into operation, the workman never appearing to make anything by it, and making no use of it in any of his labours; and then one should maintain that this useless, and idle, and unemployed tool was superior in nature and value to that which the artisan employed in his work, and by means of which he acquired his reputation. Such a man, if any such were found, would justly be regarded as imbecile, and not in his right mind. And so should those be judged of who speak of themselves as being spiritual and superior, and of the Creator as possessed of an animal nature, and maintain that for this reason they will ascend on high, and penetrate within the Pleroma to their own husbands (for, according to their own statements, they are themselves feminine), but that God [the Creator] is of an inferior nature, and therefore remains in the intermediate place, while all the time they bring forward no proofs of these assertions: for the better man is shown by his works, and all works have been accomplished by the Creator; but they, having nothing worthy of reason to point to as having been produced by themselves, are

---

[1] The punctuation is here doubtful. With Massuet and Stieren we expunge "vel" from the text.

labouring under the greatest and most incurable madness.

6. If, however, they labour to maintain that, while all material things, such as the heaven, and the whole world which exists below it, were indeed formed by the Demiurge, yet all things of a more spiritual nature than these, — those, namely, which are above the heavens, such as Principalities, Powers, Angels, Archangels, Dominations, Virtues, — were produced by a spiritual process of birth (which they declare themselves to be), then, in the first place, we prove from the authoritative Scriptures[1] that all the things which have been mentioned, visible and invisible, have been made by one God. For these men are not more to be depended on than the Scriptures; nor ought we to give up the declarations of the Lord, Moses, and the rest of the prophets, who have proclaimed the truth, and give credit to them, who do indeed utter nothing of a sensible nature, but rave about untenable opinions. And, in the next place, if those things which are above the heavens were really made through their instrumentality, then let them inform us what is the nature of things invisible, recount the number of the Angels, and the ranks of the Archangels, reveal the mysteries of the Thrones, and teach us the differences between the Dominations, Principalities, Powers, and Virtues. But they can say nothing respecting them; therefore these beings were not made by them. If, on the other hand, these were made by the Creator, as was really the case, and are of a spiritual and holy character, then it follows that He who produced spiritual beings is not Himself of an animal nature, and thus their fearful system of blasphemy is overthrown.

7. For that there are spiritual creatures in the heavens, all the Scriptures loudly proclaim; and Paul expressly testifies that there are spiritual things when he declares that he was caught up into the third heaven,[2] and again, that he was carried away to paradise, and heard unspeakable words which it is not lawful for a man to utter. But what did that profit him, either his entrance into paradise or his assumption into the third heaven, since all these things are still but under the power of the Demiurge, if, as some venture to maintain, he had already begun[3] to be a spectator and a hearer of those mysteries which are affirmed to be above the Demiurge? For if it is true that he was becoming acquainted with that order of things which is above the Demiurge, he would by no means have remained in the regions of the Demiurge, and that so as not even thoroughly to explore even these (for, according to their manner of speaking, there still lay before him four heavens,[4] if he were to approach the Demiurge, and thus behold the whole seven lying beneath him); but he might have been admitted, perhaps, into the intermediate place, that is, into the presence of the Mother, that he might receive instruction from her as to the things within the Pleroma. For that inner man which was in him, and spoke in him, as they say, though invisible, could have attained not only to the third heaven, but even as far as the presence of their Mother. For if they maintain that they themselves, that is, their [inner] man, at once ascends above the Demiurge, and departs to the Mother, much more must this have occurred to the [inner] man of the apostle; for the Demiurge would not have hindered him, being, as they assert, himself already subject to the Saviour. But if he had tried to hinder him, the effort would have gone for nothing. For it is not possible that he should prove stronger than the providence of the Father, and that when the inner man is said to be invisible even to the Demiurge. But since he (Paul) has described that assumption of himself up to the third heaven as something great and pre-eminent, it cannot be that these men ascend above the seventh heaven, for they are certainly not superior to the apostle. If they do maintain that they are more excellent than he, let them prove themselves so by their works, for they have never pretended to anything like [what he describes as occurring to himself]. And for this reason he added, "Whether in the body, or whether out of the body, God knoweth,"[5] that the body might neither be thought to be a partaker in that vision,[6] as if it could have participated in those things which it had seen and heard; nor, again, that any one should say that he was not carried higher on account of the weight of the body; but it is therefore thus far permitted even without the body to behold spiritual mysteries which are the operations of God, who made the heavens and the earth, and formed man, and placed him in paradise, so that those should be spectators of them who, like the apostle, have reached a high degree of perfection in the love of God.

8. This Being, therefore, also made spiritual things, of which, as far as to the third heaven, the apostle was made a spectator, and heard un-

---

[1] Or, "the Scriptures of the Lord;" but the words "dominicis scripturis" probably here represent the Greek κυρίων γραφῶν, and are to be rendered as above.
[2] 2 Cor. xii. 2, 3, 4.
[3] "Inciperet fieri;" perhaps for "futurus esset," *was to be.*
[4] "Quartum cœlum;" there still being, according to their theory of seven heavens, a *fourth* beyond that to which St. Paul had penetrated.
[5] 2 Cor. xii. 3, defectively quoted.
[6] This is an exceedingly obscure and difficult sentence. Grabe and some of the later editors read, "uti neque *non* corpus," thus making Irenæus affirm that the body *did* participate in the vision. But Massuet contends strenuously that this is contrary to the author's purpose, as wishing to maintain, against a possible exception of the Valentinians, that Paul then witnessed *spiritual* realities, and by omitting this "non" before "corpus," makes Irenæus deny that the body was a partaker in the vision. The point can only be doubtfully decided, but Massuet's ingenious note inclines us to his side of the question.

speakable words which it is not possible for a man to utter, inasmuch as they are spiritual; and He Himself bestows[1] [gifts] on the worthy as inclination prompts Him, for paradise is His; and He is truly the Spirit of God, and not an animal Demiurge, otherwise He should never have created spiritual things. But if He really is of an animal nature, then let them inform us by whom spiritual things were made. They have no proof which they can give that this was done by means of the travail of their Mother, which they declare themselves to be. For, not to speak of spiritual things, these men cannot create even a fly, or a gnat, or any other small and insignificant animal, without observing that law by which from the beginning animals have been and are naturally produced by God — through the deposition of seed in those that are of the same species. Nor was anything formed by the Mother alone; [for] they say that this Demiurge was produced by her, and that *he* was the Lord (the author) of all creation. And they maintain that he who is the Creator and Lord of all that has been made is of an animal nature, while they assert that they themselves are spiritual, — they who are neither the authors nor lords of any one work, not only of those things which are extraneous to them, but not even of their own bodies! Moreover, these men, who call themselves spiritual, and superior to the Creator, do often suffer much bodily pain, sorely against their will.

9. Justly, therefore, do we convict them of having departed far and wide from the truth. For if the Saviour formed the things which have been made, by means of him (the Demiurge), he is proved in that case not to be inferior but superior to them, since he is found to have been the former even of themselves; for they, too, have a place among created things. How, then, can it be argued that these men indeed are spiritual, but that he by whom they were created is of an animal nature? Or, again, if (which is indeed the only true supposition, as I have shown by numerous arguments of the very clearest nature) He (the Creator) made all things freely, and by His own power, and arranged and finished them, and His will is the substance[2] of all things, then He is discovered to be the one only God who created all things, who alone is Omnipotent, and who is the only Father founding and forming all things, visible and invisible, such as may be perceived by our senses and such as cannot, heavenly and earthly, "by the word of His power;"[3] and He has fitted and arranged all things by His wisdom, while He contains all things, but He Himself can be contained by no one:

He is the Former, He the Builder, He the Discoverer, He the Creator, He the Lord of all; and there is no one besides Him, or above Him, neither has He any mother, as they falsely ascribe to Him; nor is there a second God, as Marcion has imagined; nor is there a Pleroma of thirty Æons, which has been shown a vain supposition; nor is there any such being as Bythus or Proarche; nor are there a series of heavens; nor is there a virginal light,[4] nor an unnameable Æon, nor, in fact, any one of those things which are madly dreamt of by these, and by all the heretics. But there is one only God, the Creator — He who is above every Principality, and Power, and Dominion, and Virtue: He is Father, He is God, He the Founder, He the Maker, He the Creator, who made those things by Himself, that is, through His Word and His Wisdom — heaven and earth, and the seas, and all things that are in them: He is just; He is good; He it is who formed man, who planted paradise, who made the world, who gave rise to the flood, who saved Noah; He is the God of Abraham, and the God of Isaac, and the God of Jacob, the God of the living: He it is whom the law proclaims, whom the prophets preach, whom Christ reveals, whom the apostles make known[5] to us, and in whom the Church believes. He is the Father of our Lord Jesus Christ: through His Word, who is His Son, through Him He is revealed and manifested to all to whom He *is* revealed; for those [only] know Him to whom the Son has revealed Him. But the Son, eternally co-existing with the Father, from of old, yea, from the beginning, always reveals the Father to Angels, Archangels, Powers, Virtues, and all to whom He wills that God should be revealed.

CHAP. XXXI. — RECAPITULATION AND APPLICATION OF THE FOREGOING ARGUMENTS.

1. Those, then, who are of the school of Valentinus being overthrown, the whole multitude of heretics are, in fact, also subverted. For all the arguments I have advanced against their Pleroma, and with respect to those things which are beyond it, showing how the Father of all is shut up and circumscribed by that which is beyond Him (if, indeed, there be anything beyond Him), and how there is an absolute necessity [on their theory] to conceive of many Fathers, and many Pleromas, and many creations of worlds, beginning with one set and ending with another, as existing on every side; and that all [the beings referred to] continue in their own domains, and do not curiously intermeddle with others, since, indeed, no common interest nor any fellowship exists between them; and that there is no other

---

[1] "Præstat dignis:" here a very ambiguous expression.
[2] That is, as Massuet notes, all things derive not only their *existence*, but their *qualities*, from His will. Harvey proposes to read *causa* instead of *substantia*, but the change seems needless.
[3] Heb. i. 3.
[4] That is, *Barbelos:* comp. i. 29, 1.
[5] "Tradunt;" literally, **hand down.**

God of all, but that that name belongs only to the Almighty; — [all these arguments, I say,] will in like manner apply against those who are of the school of Marcion, and Simon, and Menander, or whatever others there may be who, like them, cut off that creation with which we are connected from the Father. The arguments, again, which I have employed against those who maintain that the Father of all no doubt contains all things, but that the creation to which we belong was not formed by Him, but by a certain other power, or by angels having no knowledge of the Propator, who is surrounded as a centre by the immense extent of the universe, just as a stain is by the [surrounding] cloak; when I showed that it is not a probable supposition that any other being than the Father of all formed that creation to which we belong, — these same arguments will apply against the followers of Saturninus, Basilides, Carpocrates, and the rest of the Gnostics, who express similar opinions. Those statements, again, which have been made with respect to the emanations, and the Æons, and the [supposed state of] degeneracy, and the inconstant character of their Mother, equally overthrow Basilides, and all who are falsely styled Gnostics, who do, in fact, just repeat the same views under different names, but do, to a greater extent than the former,[1] transfer those things which lie outside[2] of the truth to the system of their own doctrine. And the remarks I have made respecting numbers will also apply against all those who misappropriate things belonging to the truth for the support of a system of this kind. And all that has been said respecting the Creator (Demiurge) to show that he alone is God and Father of all, and whatever remarks may yet be made in the following books, I apply against the heretics at large. The more moderate and reasonable among them thou wilt convert and convince, so as to lead them no longer to blaspheme their Creator, and Maker, and Sustainer, and Lord, nor to ascribe His origin to defect and ignorance; but the fierce, and terrible, and irrational [among them] thou wilt drive far from thee, that you may no longer have to endure their idle loquaciousness.

2. Moreover, those also will be thus confuted who belong to Simon and Carpocrates, and if there be any others who are said to perform miracles — who do not perform what they do either through the power of God, or in connection with the truth, nor for the well-being of men, but for the sake of destroying and misleading mankind, by means of magical deceptions, and with universal deceit, thus entailing greater harm than good on those who believe them, with respect to the point on which they lead them astray. For they can neither confer sight on the blind, nor hearing on the deaf, nor chase away all sorts of demons — [none, indeed,] except those that are sent into others by themselves, if they can even do so much as this. Nor can they cure the weak, or the lame, or the paralytic, or those who are distressed in any other part of the body, as has often been done in regard to bodily infirmity. Nor can they furnish effective remedies for those external accidents which may occur. And so far are they from being able to raise the dead, as the Lord raised them, and the apostles did by means of prayer, and as has been frequently done in the brotherhood on account of some necessity — the entire Church in that particular locality entreating [the boon] with much fasting and prayer, the spirit of the dead man has returned, and he has been bestowed in answer to the prayers of the saints — that they do not even believe this can be possibly be done, [and hold] that the resurrection from the dead[3] is simply an acquaintance with that truth which they proclaim.

3. Since, therefore, there exist among them error and misleading influences, and magical illusions are impiously wrought in the sight of men; but in the Church, sympathy, and compassion, and stedfastness, and truth, for the aid and encouragement of mankind, are not only displayed[4] without fee or reward, but we ourselves lay out for the benefit of others our own means; and inasmuch as those who are cured very frequently do not possess the things which they require, they receive them from us; — [since such is the case,] these men are in this way undoubtedly proved to be utter aliens from the divine nature, the beneficence of God, and all spiritual excellence. But they are altogether full of deceit of every kind, apostate inspiration, demoniacal working, and the phantasms of idolatry, and are in reality the predecessors of that dragon[5] who, by means of a deception of the same kind, will with his tail cause a third part of the stars to fall from their place, and will cast them down to the earth. It behoves us to flee from them as we would from him; and the greater the display with which they are said to perform [their marvels], the more carefully should we watch them, as having been endowed with a greater spirit of wickedness. If any one will consider the prophecy referred to, and the daily practices of these men, he will find that

---

[1] *Qui*, though here found in all the MSS., seems to have been rightly expunged by the editors.
[2] The reference probably is to opinions and theories of the heathen.
[3] Comp. 2 Tim. ii. 17, 18. [On the sub-apostolic age and this subject of miracles, Newman, in spite of his sophistical argumentation, may well be consulted for his references, etc. *Translation of the Abbé Fleury*, p. xi. Oxford, 1842.]
[4] "Perficiatur:" it is difficult here to give a fitting translation of this word. Some prefer to read "impertiatur."
[5] Rev. xii. 14.

their manner of acting is one and the same with the demons.

CHAP. XXXII. — FURTHER EXPOSURE OF THE WICKED AND BLASPHEMOUS DOCTRINES OF THE HERETICS.

1. Moreover, this impious opinion of theirs with respect to actions — namely, that it is incumbent on them to have experience of all kinds of deeds, even the most abominable — is refuted by the teaching of the Lord, with whom not only is the adulterer rejected, but also the man who desires to commit adultery;[1] and not only is the actual murderer held guilty of having killed another to his own damnation, but the man also who is angry with his brother without a cause: who commanded [His disciples] not only not to hate men, but also to love their enemies; and enjoined them not only not to swear falsely, but not even to swear at all; and not only not to speak evil of their neighbours, but not even to style any one "Raca" and "fool;" [declaring] that otherwise they were in danger of hell-fire; and not only not to strike, but even, when themselves struck, to present the other cheek [to those that maltreated them]; and not only not to refuse to give up the property of others, but even if their own were taken away, not to demand it back again from those that took it; and not only not to injure their neighbours, nor to do them any evil, but also, when themselves wickedly dealt with, to be long-suffering, and to show kindness towards those [that injured them], and to pray for them, that by means of repentance they might be saved — so that we should in no respect imitate the arrogance, lust, and pride of others. Since, therefore, He whom these men boast of as their Master, and of whom they affirm that He had a soul greatly better and more highly toned than others, did indeed, with much earnestness, command certain things to be done as being good and excellent, and certain things to be abstained from not only in their actual perpetration, but even in the thoughts which lead to their performance, as being wicked, pernicious, and abominable, — how then can they escape being put to confusion, when they affirm that such a Master was more highly toned [in spirit] and better than others, and yet manifestly give instruction of a kind utterly opposed to His teaching? And, again, if there were really no such thing as good and evil, but certain things were deemed righteous, and certain others unrighteous, in human opinion only, He never would have expressed Himself thus in His teaching: "The righteous shall shine forth as the sun in the kingdom of their Father;"[2] but He shall send the unrighteous, and those who do not the works of righteousness, "into everlasting fire, where their worm shall not die, and the fire shall not be quenched."[3]

2. When they further maintain that it is incumbent on them to have experience of every kind[4] of work and conduct, so that, if it be possible, accomplishing all during one manifestation in this life, they may [at once] pass over to the state of perfection, they are, by no chance, found striving to do those things which wait upon virtue, and are laborious, glorious, and skilful,[5] which also are approved universally as being good. For if it be necessary to go through every work and every kind of operation, they ought, in the first place, to learn all the arts: all of them, [I say,] whether referring to theory or practice, whether they be acquired by self-denial, or are mastered through means of labour, exercise, and perseverance; as, for example, every kind of music, arithmetic, geometry, astronomy, and all such as are occupied with intellectual pursuits: then, again, the whole study of medicine, and the knowledge of plants, so as to become acquainted with those which are prepared for the health of man; the art of painting and sculpture, brass and marble work, and the kindred arts: moreover, [they have to study] every kind of country labour, the veterinary art, pastoral occupations, the various kinds of skilled labour, which are said to pervade the whole circle of [human] exertion; those, again, connected with a maritime life, gymnastic exercises, hunting, military and kingly pursuits, and as many others as may exist, of which, with the utmost labour, they could not learn the tenth, or even the thousandth part, in the whole course of their lives. The fact indeed is, that they endeavour to learn none of these, although they maintain that it is incumbent on them to have experience of every kind of work; but, turning aside to voluptuousness, and lust, and abominable actions, they stand self-condemned when they are tried by their own doctrine. For, since they are destitute of all those [virtues] which have been mentioned, they will [of necessity] pass into the destruction of fire. These men, while they boast of Jesus as being their Master, do in fact emulate the philosophy of Epicurus and the indifference of the Cynics, [calling Jesus their Master,] who not only turned His disciples away from evil deeds, but even from [wicked] words and thoughts, as I have already shown.

3. Again, while they assert that they possess souls from the same sphere as Jesus, and that they are like to Him, sometimes even maintaining that they are superior; while [they affirm that they were] produced, like Him, for the

---

[1] Matt. v. 21, etc.
[2] Matt. xiii. 43.
[3] Matt. xxv. 41; Mark ix. 44.
[4] Comp. i. 25, 4.
[5] "Artificialia."

performance of works tending to the benefit and establishment of mankind, they are found doing nothing of the same or a like kind [with His actions], nor what can in any respect be brought into comparison with them. And if they have in truth accomplished anything [remarkable] by means of magic, they strive [in this way] deceitfully to lead foolish people astray, since they confer no real benefit or blessing on those over whom they declare that they exert] supernatural] power; but, bringing forward mere boys[1] [as the subjects on whom they practise], and deceiving their sight, while they exhibit phantasms that instantly cease, and do not endure even a moment of time,[2] they are proved to be like, not Jesus our Lord, but Simon the magician. It is certain,[3] too, from the fact that the Lord rose from the dead on the third day, and manifested Himself to His disciples, and was in their sight received up into heaven, that, inasmuch as these men die, and do not rise again, nor manifest themselves to any, they are proved as possessing souls in no respect similar to that of Jesus.

4. If, however, they maintain that the Lord, too, performed such works simply in appearance, we shall refer them to the prophetical writings, and prove from these both that all things were thus[4] predicted regarding Him, and did take place undoubtedly, and that He is the only Son of God. Wherefore, also, those who are in truth His disciples, receiving grace from Him, do in His name perform [miracles], so as to promote the welfare of other men, according to the gift which each one has received from Him. For some do certainly and truly drive out devils, so that those who have thus been cleansed from evil spirits frequently both believe [in Christ], and join themselves to the Church. Others have foreknowledge of things to come: they see visions, and utter prophetic expressions. Others still, heal the sick by laying their hands upon them, and they are made whole. Yea, moreover, as I have said, the dead even have been raised up, and remained[5] among us for many years. And what shall I more say? It is not possible to name the number of the gifts which the Church, [scattered] throughout the whole world, has received from God, in the name of Jesus Christ, who was crucified under Pontius Pilate, and which she exerts day by day for the benefit of the Gentiles, neither practising deception upon any, nor taking any reward[6] from them [on account of such miraculous interpositions]. For as she has received freely[7] from God, freely also does she minister [to others].

5. Nor does she perform anything by means of angelic invocations,[8] or by incantations, or by any other wicked curious art; but, directing her prayers to the Lord, who made all things, in a pure, sincere, and straightforward spirit, and calling upon the name of our Lord Jesus Christ, she has been accustomed to work[9] miracles for the advantage of mankind, and not to lead them into error. If, therefore, the name of our Lord Jesus Christ even now confers benefits [upon men], and cures thoroughly and effectively all who anywhere believe on Him, but not that of Simon, or Menander, or Carpocrates, or of any other man whatever, it is manifest that, when He was made man, He held fellowship with His own creation, and[10] did all things truly through the power of God, according to the will of the Father of all, as the prophets had foretold. But what these things were, shall be described in dealing with the proofs to be found in the prophetical writings.

CHAP. XXXIII. — ABSURDITY OF THE DOCTRINE OF THE TRANSMIGRATION OF SOULS.

1. We may subvert their doctrine as to transmigration from body to body by this fact, that souls remember nothing whatever of the events which took place in their previous states of existence. For if they were sent forth with this object, that they should have experience of every kind of action, they must of necessity retain a remembrance of those things which have been previously accomplished, that they might fill up those in which they were still deficient, and not by always hovering, without intermission, round the same pursuits, spend their labour wretchedly in vain (for the mere union of a body [with a soul] could not altogether extinguish the memory and contemplation of those things which had formerly been experienced[11]), and especially as they came [into the world] for this very purpose. For as, when the body is asleep and at rest, whatever things the soul sees by herself, and does in a vision, recollecting

---

[1] "Pureos investes," boys that have not yet reached the age of puberty.
[2] The text has "stillicidio temporis," literally "a *drop* of time (σταγμῇ χρόνου); but the original text was perhaps στιγμῇ χρόνου, "a *moment* of time." With either reading the meaning is the same.
[3] Some have deemed the words "firmum esse" an interpolation.
[4] That is, as being done *in reality*, and not in appearance.
[5] Harvey here notes: "The reader will not fail to remark this highly interesting testimony, that the divine χαρίσματα bestowed upon the infant Church were not wholly extinct in the days of Irenæus. Possibly the venerable Father is speaking from his own personal recollection of some who had been raised from the dead, and had continued for a time living witnesses of the efficacy of Christian faith." [See cap. xxxi., *supra*.]
[6] Comp. Acts viii. 9, 18.
[7] Matt. x. 8.
[8] Grabe contends that these words imply that no invocations of angels, good or bad, were practised in the primitive Church. Massuet, on the other hand, maintains that the words of Irenæus are plainly to be restricted to evil spirits, and have no bearing on the general question of angelic invocation.
[9] We follow the common reading, "perfecit;" but one MS. has "perficit," *works*, which suits the context better.
[10] We insert "et," in accordance with Grabe's suggestion.
[11] Harvey thinks that this parenthesis has fallen out of its proper place, and would insert it immediately after the opening period of the chapter.

many of these, she also communicates them to the body; and as it happens that, when one awakes, perhaps after a long time, he relates what he saw in a dream, so also would he undoubtedly remember those things which he did before he came into this particular body. For if that which is seen only for a very brief space of time, or has been conceived of simply in a phantasm, and by the soul alone, through means of a dream, is remembered after she has mingled again with the body, and been dispersed through all the members, much more would she remember those things in connection with which she stayed during so long a time, even throughout the whole period of a bypast life.

2. With reference to these objections, Plato, that ancient Athenian, who also was the first[1] to introduce this opinion, when he could not set them aside, invented the [notion of] a cup of oblivion, imagining that in this way he would escape this sort of difficulty. He attempted no kind of proof [of his supposition], but simply replied dogmatically [to the objection in question], that when souls enter into this life, they are caused to drink of oblivion by that demon who watches their entrance [into the world], before they effect an entrance into the bodies [assigned them]. It escaped him, that [by speaking thus] he fell into another greater perplexity. For if the cup of oblivion, after it has been drunk, can obliterate the memory of all the deeds that have been done, how, O Plato, dost thou obtain the knowledge of this fact (since thy soul is now in the body), that, before it entered into the body, it was made to drink by the demon a drug which caused oblivion? For if thou hast a remembrance of the demon, and the cup, and the entrance [into life], thou oughtest also to be acquainted with other things; but if, on the other hand, thou art ignorant of them, then there is no truth in the story of the demon, nor in the cup of oblivion prepared with art.

3. In opposition, again, to those who affirm that the body itself is the drug of oblivion, this observation may be made: How, then, does it come to pass, that whatsoever the soul sees by her own instrumentality, both in dreams and by reflection or earnest mental exertion, while the body is passive, she remembers, and reports to her neighbours? But, again, if the body itself were [the cause of] oblivion, then the soul, as existing in the body, could not remember even those things which were perceived long ago either by means of the eyes or the ears; but, as soon as the eye was turned from the things looked at, the memory of them also would undoubtedly be destroyed. For the soul, as existing in the very [cause of] oblivion, could have no knowledge of anything else than that only which it saw at the present moment. How, too, could it become acquainted with divine things, and retain a remembrance of them while existing in the body, since, as they maintain, the body itself is [the cause of] oblivion? But the prophets also, when they were upon the earth, remembered likewise, on their returning to their ordinary state of mind,[2] whatever things they spiritually saw or heard in visions of heavenly objects, and related them to others. The body, therefore, does not cause the soul to forget those things which have been spiritually witnessed; but the soul teaches the body, and shares with it the spiritual vision which it has enjoyed.

4. For the body is not possessed of greater power than the soul, since indeed the former is inspired, and vivified, and increased, and held together by the latter; but the soul possesses[3] and rules over the body. It is doubtless retarded in its velocity, just in the exact proportion in which the body shares in its motion; but it never loses the knowledge which properly belongs to it. For the body may be compared to an instrument; but the soul is possessed of the reason of an artist. As, therefore, the artist finds the idea of a work to spring up rapidly in his mind, but can only carry it out slowly by means of an instrument, owing to the want of perfect pliability in the matter acted upon, and thus the rapidity of his mental operation, being blended with the slow action of the instrument, gives rise to a moderate kind of movement [towards the end contemplated]; so also the soul, by being mixed up with the body belonging to it, is in a certain measure impeded, its rapidity being blended with the body's slowness. Yet it does not lose altogether its own peculiar powers; but while, as it were, sharing life with the body, it does not itself cease to live. Thus, too, while communicating other things to the body, it neither loses the knowledge of them, nor the memory of those things which have been witnessed.

5. If, therefore, the soul remembers nothing[4] of what took place in a former state of existence, but has a perception of those things which are here, it follows that she never existed in other bodies, nor did things of which she has no knowledge, nor [once] knew things which she cannot [now mentally] contemplate. But, as each one of us receives his body through the skilful

---

[1] It is a mistake of Irenæus to say that the doctrine of metempsychosis originated with Plato: it was first publicly taught by Pythagoras, who learned it from the Egyptians. Comp. Clem. Alex., *Strom.*, i. 15: Herodot., ii. 123.

[2] "In hominem conversi," literally, "returning into man."
[3] "Possidet." Massuet supposes this word to represent κυριεύει, "rules over," and Stieren κρατύνει, *governs;* while Harvey thinks the whole clause corresponds to κρατεῖ καὶ κυριεύει τοῦ σώματος, which we have rendered as above.
[4] Literally, *none of things past.*

working of God, so does he also possess his soul. For God is not so poor or destitute in resources, that He cannot confer its own proper soul on each individual body, even as He gives it also its special character. And therefore, when the number [fixed upon] is completed, [that number] which He had predetermined in His own counsel, all those who have been enrolled for life [eternal] shall rise again, having their own bodies, and having also their own souls, and their own spirits, in which they had pleased God. Those, on the other hand, who are worthy of punishment, shall go away into it, they too having their own souls, and their own bodies, in which they stood apart from the grace of God. Both classes shall then cease from any longer begetting and being begotten, from marrying and being given in marriage; so that the number of mankind, corresponding to the fore-ordination of God, being completed, may fully realize the scheme formed by the Father.[1]

CHAP. XXXIV. — SOULS CAN BE RECOGNISED IN THE SEPARATE STATE, AND ARE IMMORTAL ALTHOUGH THEY ONCE HAD A BEGINNING.

1. The Lord has taught with very great fulness, that souls not only continue to exist, not by passing from body to body, but that they preserve the same form [2] [in their separate state] as the body had to which they were adapted, and that they remember the deeds which they did in this state of existence, and from which they have now ceased, — in that narrative which is recorded respecting the rich man and that Lazarus who found repose in the bosom of Abraham. In this account He states [3] that Dives knew Lazarus after death, and Abraham in like manner, and that each one of these persons continued in his own proper position, and that [Dives] requested Lazarus to be sent to relieve him — [Lazarus], on whom he did not [formerly] bestow even the crumbs [which fell] from his table. [He tells us] also of the answer given by Abraham, who was acquainted not only with what respected himself, but Dives also, and who enjoined those who did not wish to come into that place of torment to believe Moses and the prophets, and to receive [4] the preaching of Him who was [5] to rise again from the dead. By these things, then, it is plainly declared that souls continue to exist, that they do not pass from body to body, that they possess the form of a man, so that they may be recognised, and retain the memory of things in this world; moreover, that the gift of prophecy was possessed by Abraham, and that each class [of souls] receives a habitation such as it has deserved, even before the judgment.

2. But if any persons at this point maintain that those souls, which only began a little while ago to exist, cannot endure for any length of time; but that they must, on the one hand, either be unborn, in order that they may be immortal, or if they have had a beginning in the way of generation, that they should die with the body itself — let them learn that God alone, who is Lord of all, is without beginning and without end, being truly and for ever the same, and always remaining the same unchangeable Being. But all things which proceed from Him, whatsoever have been made, and are made, do indeed receive their own beginning of generation, and on this account are inferior to Him who formed them, inasmuch as they are not unbegotten. Nevertheless they endure, and extend their existence into a long series of ages in accordance with the will of God their Creator; so that He grants them that they should be thus formed at the beginning, and that they should so exist afterwards.

3. For as the heaven which is above us, the firmament, the sun, the moon, the rest of the stars, and all their grandeur, although they had no previous existence, were called into being, and continue throughout a long course of time according to the will of God, so also any one who thinks thus respecting souls and spirits, and, in fact, respecting all created things, will not by any means go far astray, inasmuch as all things that have been made had a beginning when they were formed, but endure as long as God wills that they should have an existence and continuance. The prophetic Spirit bears testimony to these opinions, when He declares, " For He spake, and they were made; He commanded, and they were created: He hath established them for ever, yea, for ever and ever." [6] And again, He thus speaks respecting the salvation of man: "He asked life of Thee, and Thou gavest him length of days for ever and ever;" [7] indicating that it is the Father of all who imparts continuance for ever and ever on those who are saved. For life does not arise from us, nor from our own nature; but it is bestowed according to the grace of God. And therefore he who shall preserve the life bestowed upon him, and give thanks to Him who imparted it, shall receive also length of days for ever and ever. But he who shall reject it, and prove himself ungrateful to his Maker, inasmuch as he has been created, and has not recognised Him who

---

[1] The Latin text is here very confused, but the Greek original of the greater part of this section has happily been preserved. [This Father here anticipates in outline many ideas which St. Augustine afterwards corrected and elaborated.]
[2] Grabe refers to Tertullian, *De Anima*, ch. vii., as making a similiar statement. Massuet, on the other hand, denies that Irenæus here expresses an opinion like that of Tertullian in the passage referred to, and thinks that the special form (*character*) mentioned is to be understood as simply denoting individual *spiritual* properties. But his remarks are not satisfactory.
[3] Luke xvi. 19, etc.
[4] With Massuet and Stieren, we here supply *esse*.
[5] Some read *resurgeret*, and others *resurrexerit;* we deem the former reading preferable.
[6] Ps. cxlviii. 5, 6.
[7] Ps. xxi. 4.

bestowed [the gift upon him], deprives himself of [the privilege of] continuance for ever and ever.[1] And, for this reason, the Lord declared to those who showed themselves ungrateful towards Him: "If ye have not been faithful in that which is little, who will give you that which is great?"[2] indicating that those who, in this brief temporal life, have shown themselves ungrateful to Him who bestowed it, shall justly not receive from Him length of days for ever and ever.

4. But as the animal body is certainly not itself the soul, yet has fellowship with the soul as long as God pleases; so the soul herself is not life,[3] but partakes in that life bestowed upon her by God. Wherefore also the prophetic word declares of the first-formed man, "He became a living soul,"[4] teaching us that by the participation of life the soul became alive; so that the soul, and the life which it possesses, must be understood as being separate existences. When God therefore bestows life and perpetual duration, it comes to pass that even souls which did not previously exist should henceforth endure [for ever], since God has both willed that they should exist, and should continue in existence. For the will of God ought to govern and rule in all things, while all other things give way to Him, are in subjection, and devoted to His service. Thus far, then, let me speak concerning the creation and the continued duration of the soul.

CHAP. XXXV. — REFUTATION OF BASILIDES, AND OF THE OPINION THAT THE PROPHETS UTTERED THEIR PREDICTIONS UNDER THE INSPIRATION OF DIFFERENT GODS.

1. Moreover, in addition to what has been said, Basilides himself will, according to his own principles, find it necessary to maintain not only that there are three hundred and sixty-five heavens made in succession by one another, but that an immense and innumerable multitude of heavens have always been in the process of being made, and are being made, and will continue to be made, so that the formation of heavens of this kind can never cease. For if from the efflux[5] of the first heaven the second was made after its likeness, and the third after the likeness of the second, and so on with all the remaining subsequent ones, then it follows, as a matter of necessity, that from the efflux of our heaven, which he indeed terms the last, another be formed like to it, and from that again a third; and thus there can never cease, either the process of efflux from those heavens which have been already made, or the manufacture of [new] heavens, but the operation must go on *ad infinitum*, and give rise to a number of heavens which will be altogether indefinite.

2. The remainder of those who are falsely termed Gnostics, and who maintain that the prophets uttered their prophecies under the inspiration of different gods, will be easily overthrown by this fact, that all the prophets proclaimed one God and Lord, and that the very Maker of heaven and earth, and of all things which are therein; while they moreover announced the advent of His Son, as I shall demonstrate from the Scriptures themselves, in the books which follow.

3. If, however, any object that, in the Hebrew language, diverse expressions [to represent God] occur in the Scriptures, such as Sabaoth, Eloë, Adonai, and all other such terms, striving to prove from these that there are different powers and gods, let them learn that all expressions of this kind are but announcements and appellations of one and the same Being. For the term *Eloë* in the Jewish language denotes *God*, while *Elōeim*[6] and *Elōeuth* in the Hebrew language signify "*that which contains all.*" As to the appellation *Adonai*, sometimes it denotes what is *nameable*[7] and *admirable;* but at other times, when the letter *Daleth* in it is doubled, and the word receives an initial[8] guttural sound — thus Addonai — [it signifies], "One who bounds and separates the land from the water," so that the water should not subsequently[9] submerge the land. In like manner also, *Sabaoth*,[10] when it is spelled by a Greek Omega in the last syllable [Sabaōth], denotes "*a voluntary agent;*" but when it is spelled with a Greek Omicron — as, for instance, Sabaŏth — it expresses "*the first heaven.*" In the same way, too, the word *Jaōth*,[11] when the last syllable is made long and aspirated,

---

[1] As Massuet observes, this statement is to be understood in harmony with the repeated assertion of Irenæus that the wicked will exist in misery for ever. It refers not to annihilation, but to deprivation of happiness.
[2] Luke xvi. 11, quoted loosely from memory. Grabe, however, thinks they are cited from the apocryphal Gospel according to the Egyptians.
[3] Comp. Justin Martyr, *Dial. c. Tryph.*, ch. vi.
[4] Gen. ii. 7.
[5] *Ex defluxu*, corresponding to ἐξ ἀπορροίας in the Greek.

[6] *Eloæ* here occurs in the Latin text, but Harvey supposes that the Greek had been Ἐλωείμ. He also remarks that *Eloeuth* (אֱלֹהוּת) is the rabbinical abstract term, *Godhead*.
[7] All that can be remarked on this is, that the Jews substituted the term *Adonai* (אֲדֹנָי) for the name *Jehovah*, as often as the latter occurred in the sacred text. The former might therefore be styled *nameable*.
[8] The Latin text is, "aliquando autem duplicata litera delta cum aspiratione," and Harvey supposes that the doubling of the Daleth would give "to the scarcely articulate א a more decidedly guttural character;" but the sense is extremely doubtful.
[9] Instead of "nec posteaquam insurgere," Feuardent and Massuet read "ne possit insurgere," and include the clause in the definition of *Addonai*.
[10] The author is here utterly mistaken, and, notwithstanding Harvey's earnest claim for him of a knowledge of Hebrew, seems clearly to betray his ignorance of that language. The term *Sabaoth* is never written with an Omicron, either in the LXX. or by the Greek Fathers, but always with an Omega (Σαβαώθ). Although Harvey remarks in his preface, that "it is hoped the Hebrew attainments of Irenæus will no longer be denied," there appears enough, in the etymologies and explanations of Hebrew terms given in this chapter by the venerable Father, to prevent such a conclusion; and Massuet's observation on the passage seems not improbable, when he says, "Sciolus quispiam Irenæo nostro, in Hebraicis haud satis perito, hic fucum ecisse videtur."
[11] Probably corresponding to the Hebrew term *Jehovah* (יְהֹוָה).

denotes "*a predetermined measure;*" but when it is written shortly by the Greek letter Omicron, namely *Jaŏth*, it signifies "*one who puts evils to flight.*" All the other expressions likewise bring out[1] the title of one and the same Being; as, for example (in English[2]), *The Lord of Powers, The Father of all, God Almighty, The Most High, The Creator, The Maker,* and such like. These are not the names and titles of a succession of different beings, but of one and the same, by means of which the one God and Father is revealed, He who contains all things, and grants to all the boon of existence.

4. Now, that the preaching of the apostles, the authoritative teaching of the Lord, the announcements of the prophets, the dictated utterances of the apostles,[3] and the ministration of the law — all of which praise one and the same Being, the God and Father of all, and not many diverse beings, nor one deriving his substance from different gods or powers, but [declare] that all things [were formed] by one and the same Father (who nevertheless adapts [His works] to the natures and tendencies of the materials dealt with), things visible and invisible, and, in short, all things that have been made [were created] neither by angels, nor by any other power, but by God alone, the Father — are all in harmony with our statements, has, I think, been sufficiently proved, while by these weighty arguments it has been shown that there is but one God, the Maker of all things. But that I may not be thought to avoid that series of proofs which may be derived from the Scriptures of the Lord (since, indeed, these Scriptures do much more evidently and clearly proclaim this very point), I shall, for the benefit of those at least who do not bring a depraved mind to bear upon them, devote a special book to the Scriptures referred to, which shall fairly follow them out [and explain them], and I shall plainly set forth from these divine Scriptures proofs to [satisfy] all the lovers of truth.[4]

---

[1] Literally, "belong to one and the same name."
[2] "Secundum *Latinitatem*" in the text.
[3] The words are "apostolorum dictatio," probably referring to the *letters* of the apostles, as distinguished from their *preaching* already mentioned.

[4] This last sentence is very confused and ambiguous, and the editors throw but little light upon it. We have endeavoured to translate it according to the ordinary text and punctuation, but strongly suspect interpolation and corruption. If we might venture to strike out "has Scripturas," and connect "his tamen" with "prædicantibus," a better sense would be yielded, as follows: "But that I may not be thought to avoid that series of proofs which may be derived from the Scriptures of the Lord (since, indeed, these Scriptures do much more evidently and clearly set forth this very point, to those at least who do not bring a depraved mind to their consideration), I shall devote the particular book which follows to them, and shall," etc.

IRENÆUS AGAINST HERESIES

BOOK III.

PREFACE.

Thou hast indeed enjoined upon me, my very dear friend, that I should bring to light the Valentinian doctrines, concealed, as their votaries imagine; that I should exhibit their diversity, and compose a treatise in refutation of them. I therefore have undertaken — showing that they spring from Simon, the father of all heretics — to exhibit both their doctrines and successions, and to set forth arguments against them all. Wherefore, since the conviction of these men and their exposure is in many points but one work, I have sent unto thee [certain] books, of which the first comprises the opinions of all these men, and exhibits their customs, and the character of their behaviour. In the second, again, their perverse teachings are cast down and overthrown, and, such as they really are, laid bare and open to view. But in this, the third book, I shall adduce proofs from the Scriptures, so that I may come behind in nothing of what thou hast enjoined; yea, that over and above what thou didst reckon upon, thou mayest receive from me the means of combating and vanquishing those who, in whatever manner, are propagating falsehood. For the love of God, being rich and ungrudging, confers upon the suppliant more than he can ask from it. Call to mind, then, the things which I have stated in the two preceding books, and, taking these in connection with them, thou shalt have from me a very copious refutation of all the heretics; and faithfully and strenuously shalt thou resist them in defence of the only true and life-giving faith, which the Church has received from the apostles and imparted to her sons. For the Lord of all gave to His apostles the power of the Gospel, through whom also we have known the truth, that is, the doctrine of the Son of God; to whom also did the Lord declare: "He that heareth you, heareth Me; and he that despiseth you, despiseth Me, and Him that sent Me."[1]

---

[1] Luke x. 16.

CHAP. I. — THE APOSTLES DID NOT COMMENCE TO PREACH THE GOSPEL, OR TO PLACE ANYTHING ON RECORD, UNTIL THEY WERE ENDOWED WITH THE GIFTS AND POWER OF THE HOLY SPIRIT. THEY PREACHED ONE GOD ALONE, MAKER OF HEAVEN AND EARTH.

1. We have learned from none others the plan of our salvation, than from those through whom the Gospel has come down to us, which they did at one time proclaim in public, and, at a later period, by the will of God, handed down to us in the Scriptures, to be the ground and pillar of our faith.[2] For it is unlawful to assert that they preached before they possessed "perfect knowledge," as some do even venture to say, boasting themselves as improvers of the apostles. For, after our Lord rose from the dead, [the apostles] were invested with power from on high when the Holy Spirit came down [upon them], were filled from all [His gifts], and had perfect knowledge: they departed to the ends of the earth, preaching the glad tidings of the good things [sent] from God to us, and proclaiming the peace of heaven to men, who indeed do all equally and individually possess the Gospel of God. Matthew also issued a written Gospel among the Hebrews[3] in their own dialect, while Peter and Paul were preaching at Rome, and laying the foundations of the Church. After their departure, Mark, the disciple and interpreter of Peter, did also hand down to us in writing what had been preached by Peter. Luke also, the companion of Paul, recorded in a book the Gospel preached by him. Afterwards, John, the disciple of the Lord, who also had leaned upon His breast, did himself publish a Gospel during his residence at Ephesus in Asia.

2. These have all declared to us that there is one God, Creator of heaven and earth, announced

---

[2] See 1 Tim. iii. 15, where these terms are used in reference to the Church.
[3] On this and similar statements in the Fathers, the reader may consult Dr. Roberts's *Discussions on the Gospels*, in which they are fully criticised, and the Greek original of St. Matthew's Gospel maintained.

by the law and the prophets; and one Christ, the Son of God. If any one do not agree to these truths, he despises the companions of the Lord; nay more, he despises Christ Himself the Lord; yea, he despises the Father also, and stands self-condemned, resisting and opposing his own salvation, as is the case with all heretics.

CHAP. II.—THE HERETICS FOLLOW NEITHER SCRIPTURE NOR TRADITION.

1. When, however, they are confuted from the Scriptures, they turn round and accuse these same Scriptures, as if they were not correct, nor of authority, and [assert] that they are ambiguous, and that the truth cannot be extracted from them by those who are ignorant of tradition. For [they allege] that the truth was not delivered by means of written documents, but *vivâ voce:* wherefore also Paul declared, "But we speak wisdom among those that are perfect, but not the wisdom of this world."[1] And this wisdom each one of them alleges to be the fiction of his own inventing, forsooth; so that, according to their idea, the truth properly resides at one time in Valentinus, at another in Marcion, at another in Cerinthus, then afterwards in Basilides, or has even been indifferently in any other opponent,[2] who could speak nothing pertaining to salvation. For every one of these men, being altogether of a perverse disposition, depraving the system of truth, is not ashamed to preach himself.

2. But, again, when we refer them to that tradition which originates from the apostles, [and] which is preserved by means of the successions of presbyters in the Churches, they object to tradition, saying that they themselves are wiser not merely than the presbyters, but even than the apostles, because they have discovered the unadulterated truth. For [they maintain] that the apostles intermingled the things of the law with the words of the Saviour; and that not the apostles alone, but even the Lord Himself, spoke as at one time from the Demiurge, at another from the intermediate place, and yet again from the Pleroma, but that they themselves, indubitably, unsulliedly, and purely, have knowledge of the hidden mystery: this is, indeed, to blaspheme their Creator after a most impudent manner! It comes to this, therefore, that these men do now consent neither to Scripture nor to tradition.

3. Such are the adversaries with whom we have to deal, my very dear friend, endeavouring like slippery serpents to escape at all points. Wherefore they must be opposed at all points, if perchance, by cutting off their retreat, we may succeed in turning them back to the truth. For, though it is not an easy thing for a soul under the influence of error to repent, yet, on the other hand, it is not altogether impossible to escape from error when the truth is brought alongside it.

CHAP. III.—A REFUTATION OF THE HERETICS, FROM THE FACT THAT, IN THE VARIOUS CHURCHES, A PERPETUAL SUCCESSION OF BISHOPS WAS KEPT UP.

1. It is within the power of all, therefore, in every Church, who may wish to see the truth, to contemplate clearly the tradition of the apostles manifested throughout the whole world; and we are in a position to reckon up those who were by the apostles instituted bishops in the Churches, and [to demonstrate] the succession of these men to our own times; those who neither taught nor knew of anything like what these [heretics] rave about. For if the apostles had known hidden mysteries, which they were in the habit of imparting to "the perfect" apart and privily from the rest, they would have delivered them especially to those to whom they were also committing the Churches themselves. For they were desirous that these men should be very perfect and blameless in all things, whom also they were leaving behind as their successors, delivering up their own place of government to these men; which men, if they discharged their functions honestly, would be a great boon [to the Church], but if they should fall away, the direst calamity.

2. Since, however, it would be very tedious, in such a volume as this, to reckon up the successions of all the Churches, we do put to confusion all those who, in whatever manner, whether by an evil self-pleasing, by vainglory, or by blindness and perverse opinion, assemble in unauthorized meetings; [we do this, I say,] by indicating that tradition derived from the apostles, of the very great, the very ancient, and universally known Church founded and organized at Rome by the two most glorious apostles, Peter and Paul; as also [by pointing out] the faith preached to men, which comes down to our time by means of the successions of the bishops. For it is a matter of necessity that every Church should agree with this Church, on account of its preeminent authority,[3] that is, the faithful every-

---
[1] 1 Cor. ii. 6.
[2] This is Harvey's rendering of the old Latin, *in illo qui contra disputat.*
[3] The Latin text of this difficult but important clause is, "Ad hanc enim ecclesiam propter potiorem principalitatem necesse est omnem convenire ecclesiam." Both the text and meaning have here given rise to much discussion. It is impossible to say with certainty of what words in the Greek original "potiorem principalitatem" may be the translation. We are far from sure that the rendering given above is correct, but we have been unable to think of anything better. [A most extraordinary confession. It would be hard to find a worse; but take the following from a candid Roman Catholic, which is better and more literal: "For to this Church, on account of more potent principality, it is necessary that every Church (that is, those who are on every side faithful) *resort;* in which Church ever, *by those who are on every side,* has been preserved that tradition which is from the apostles." (Berington and Kirk, vol. i. p. 252.) ›Here it is obvious that the faith was kept at Rome, by *those who resort there* from all quarters. She was a mirror of the Catholic World, owing her orthodoxy to them; not the Sun, dispensing her own light to others, but the glass bringing their rays into a focus. See note at end of book iii.] A discussion of the subject may be seen in chap. xii. of Dr. Wordsworth's *St. Hippolytus and the Church of Rome.*

where, inasmuch as the apostolical tradition has been preserved continuously by those [faithful men] who exist everywhere.

3. The blessed apostles, then, having founded and built up the Church, committed into the hands of Linus the office of the episcopate. Of this Linus, Paul makes mention in the Epistles to Timothy. To him succeeded Anacletus; and after him, in the third place from the apostles, Clement was allotted the bishopric. This man, as he had seen the blessed apostles, and had been conversant with them, might be said to have the preaching of the apostles still echoing [in his ears], and their traditions before his eyes. Nor was he alone [in this], for there were many still remaining who had received instructions from the apostles. In the time of this Clement, no small dissension having occurred among the brethren at Corinth, the Church in Rome despatched a most powerful letter to the Corinthians, exhorting them to peace, renewing their faith, and declaring the tradition which it had lately received from the apostles, proclaiming the one God, omnipotent, the Maker of heaven and earth, the Creator of man, who brought on the deluge, and called Abraham, who led the people from the land of Egypt, spake with Moses, set forth the law, sent the prophets, and who has prepared fire for the devil and his angels. From this document, whosoever chooses to do so, may learn that He, the Father of our Lord Jesus Christ, was preached by the Churches, and may also understand the apostolical tradition of the Church, since this Epistle is of older date than these men who are now propagating falsehood, and who conjure into existence another god beyond the Creator and the Maker of all existing things. To this Clement there succeeded Evaristus. Alexander followed Evaristus; then, sixth from the apostles, Sixtus was appointed; after him, Telephorus, who was gloriously martyred; then Hyginus; after him, Pius; then after him, Anicetus. Soter having succeeded Anicetus, Eleutherius does now, in the twelfth place from the apostles, hold the inheritance of the episcopate. In this order, and by this succession, the ecclesiastical tradition from the apostles, and the preaching of the truth, have come down to us. And this is most abundant proof that there is one and the same vivifying faith, which has been preserved in the Church from the apostles until now, and handed down in truth.

4. But Polycarp also was not only instructed by apostles, and conversed with many who had seen Christ, but was also, by apostles in Asia, appointed bishop of the Church in Smyrna, whom I also saw in my early youth, for he tarried [on earth] a very long time, and, when a very old man, gloriously and most nobly suffering martyrdom,[1] departed this life, having always taught the things which he had learned from the apostles, and which the Church has handed down, and which alone are true. To these things all the Asiatic Churches testify, as do also those men who have succeeded Polycarp down to the present time, — a man who was of much greater weight, and a more stedfast witness of truth, than Valentinus, and Marcion, and the rest of the heretics. He it was who, coming to Rome in the time of Anicetus caused many to turn away from the aforesaid heretics to the Church of God, proclaiming that he had received this one and sole truth from the apostles, — that, namely, which is handed down by the Church.[2] There are also those who heard from him that John, the disciple of the Lord, going to bathe at Ephesus, and perceiving Cerinthus within, rushed out of the bath-house without bathing, exclaiming, "Let us fly, lest even the bath-house fall down, because Cerinthus, the enemy of the truth, is within." And Polycarp himself replied to Marcion, who met him on one occasion, and said, "Dost thou know me?" "I do know thee, the first-born of Satan." Such was the horror which the apostles and their disciples had against holding even verbal communication with any corrupters of the truth; as Paul also says, "A man that is an heretic, after the first and second admonition, reject; knowing that he that is such is subverted, and sinneth, being condemned of himself."[3] There is also a very powerful[4] Epistle of Polycarp written to the Philippians, from which those who choose to do so, and are anxious about their salvation, can learn the character of his faith, and the preaching of the truth. Then, again, the Church in Ephesus, founded by Paul, and having John remaining among them permanently until the times of Trajan, is a true witness of the tradition of the apostles.

CHAP. IV. — THE TRUTH IS TO BE FOUND NOWHERE ELSE BUT IN THE CATHOLIC CHURCH, THE SOLE DEPOSITORY OF APOSTOLICAL DOCTRINE. HERESIES ARE OF RECENT FORMATION, AND CANNOT TRACE THEIR ORIGIN UP TO THE APOSTLES.

1. Since therefore we have such proofs, it is not necessary to seek the truth among others which it is easy to obtain from the Church; since the apostles, like a rich man [depositing his money] in a bank, lodged in her hands most copiously all things pertaining to the truth: so that every man, whosoever will, can draw from her the

---

[1] Polycarp suffered about the year 167, in the reign of Marcus Aurelius. His great age of eighty-six years implies that he was contemporary with St. John for nearly twenty years.
[2] So the Greek. The Latin reads: "which he also handed down to the Church."
[3] Tit. iii. 10.
[4] ἱκανωτάτη. Harvey translates this *all-sufficient*, and thus paraphrases: *But his Epistle is all-sufficient, to teach those that are desirous to learn.*

water of life.[1] For she is the entrance to life; all others are thieves and robbers. On this account are we bound to avoid *them*, but to make choice of the things pertaining to the Church with the utmost diligence, and to lay hold of the tradition of the truth. For how stands the case? Suppose there arise a dispute relative to some important question[2] among us, should we not have recourse to the most ancient Churches with which the apostles held constant intercourse, and learn from them what is certain and clear in regard to the present question? For how should it be if the apostles themselves had not left us writings? Would it not be necessary, [in that case,] to follow the course of the tradition which they handed down to those to whom they did commit the Churches?

2. To which course many nations of those barbarians who believe in Christ do assent, having salvation written in their hearts by the Spirit, without paper or ink, and, carefully preserving the ancient tradition,[3] believing in one God, the Creator of heaven and earth, and all things therein, by means of Christ Jesus, the Son of God; who, because of His surpassing love towards His creation, condescended to be born of the virgin, He Himself uniting man through Himself to God, and having suffered under Pontius Pilate, and rising again, and having been received up in splendour, shall come in glory, the Saviour of those who are saved, and the Judge of those who are judged, and sending into eternal fire those who transform the truth, and despise His Father and His advent. Those who, in the absence of written documents,[4] have believed this faith, are barbarians, so far as regards our language; but as regards doctrine, manner, and tenor of life, they are, because of faith, very wise indeed; and they do please God, ordering their conversation in all righteousness, chastity, and wisdom. If any one were to preach to these men the inventions of the heretics, speaking to them in their own language, they would at once stop their ears, and flee as far off as possible, not enduring even to listen to the blasphemous address. Thus, by means of that ancient tradition of the apostles, they do not suffer their mind to conceive anything of the [doctrines suggested by the] portentous language of these teachers, among whom neither Church nor doctrine has ever been established.

3. For, prior to Valentinus, those who follow Valentinus had no existence; nor did those from Marcion exist before Marcion; nor, in short, had any of those malignant-minded people, whom I have above enumerated, any being previous to the initiators and inventors of their perversity. For Valentinus came to Rome in the time of Hyginus, flourished under Pius, and remained until Anicetus. Cerdon, too, Marcion's predecessor, himself arrived in the time of Hyginus, who was the ninth bishop.[5] Coming frequently into the Church, and making public confession, he thus remained, one time teaching in secret, and then again making public confession; but at last, having been denounced for corrupt teaching, he was excommunicated[6] from the assembly of the brethren. Marcion, then, succeeding him, flourished under Anicetus, who held the tenth place of the episcopate. But the rest, who are called Gnostics, take rise from Menander, Simon's disciple, as I have shown; and each one of them appeared to be both the father and the high priest of that doctrine into which he has been initiated. But all these (the Marcosians) broke out into their apostasy much later, even during the intermediate period of the Church.

CHAP. V. — CHRIST AND HIS APOSTLES, WITHOUT ANY FRAUD, DECEPTION, OR HYPOCRISY, PREACHED THAT ONE GOD, THE FATHER, WAS THE FOUNDER OF ALL THINGS. THEY DID NOT ACCOMMODATE THEIR DOCTRINE TO THE PREPOSSESSIONS OF THEIR HEARERS.

1. Since, therefore, the tradition from the apostles does thus exist in the Church, and is permanent among us, let us revert to the Scriptural proof furnished by those apostles who did also write the Gospel, in which they recorded the doctrine regarding God, pointing out that our Lord Jesus Christ is the truth,[7] and that no lie is in Him. As also David says, prophesying His birth from a virgin, and the resurrection from the dead, "Truth has sprung out of the earth."[8] The apostles, likewise, being disciples of the truth, are above all falsehood; for a lie has no fellowship with the truth, just as darkness has none with light, but the presence of the one shuts out that of the other. Our Lord, therefore, being the truth, did not speak lies; and whom He knew to have taken origin from a defect, He never would have acknowledged as God, even the God of all, the Supreme King, too, and His own Father, an imperfect being as a perfect one, an animal one as a spiritual, Him who was without the Pleroma as Him who was within it.

---

[1] Rev. xxii. 17.
[2] Latin, "modica quæstione."
[3] [The uneducated barbarians must receive the Gospel on testimony. Irenæus puts *apostolic* traditions, genuine and uncorrupt, in this relation to the primary authority of the written word. 2 Thess. ii. 15, iii. 6.]
[4] Literally, "without letters;" equivalent to, "without paper and ink," a few lines previously.
[5] The old Latin translation says the *eighth bishop;* but there is no discrepancy. Eusebius, who has preserved the Greek of this passage, probably counted the apostles as the *first step* in the episcopal succession. As Irenæus tells us in the preceding chapter, Linus is to be counted as the first bishop.
[6] It is thought that this does not mean excommunication properly so called, but a species of *self-excommunication*, i.e., anticipating the sentence of the Church, by quitting it altogether. See Valesius's note in his edition of Eusebius.
[7] John xiv. 6.
[8] Ps. lxxxv. 11.

Neither did His disciples make mention of any other God, or term any other Lord, except Him, who was truly the God and Lord of all, as these most vain sophists affirm that the apostles did with hypocrisy frame their doctrine according to the capacity of their hearers, and gave answers after the opinions of their questioners, — fabling blind things for the blind, according to their blindness; for the dull according to their dulness; for those in error according to their error. And to those who imagined that the Demiurge alone was God, they preached him; but to those who are capable of comprehending the unnameable Father, they did declare the unspeakable mystery through parables and enigmas: so that the Lord and the apostles exercised the office of teacher not to further the cause of truth, but even in hypocrisy, and as each individual was able to receive it!

2. Such [a line of conduct] belongs not to those who heal, or who give life: it is rather that of those bringing on diseases, and increasing ignorance; and much more true than these men shall the law be found, which pronounces every one accursed who sends the blind man astray in the way. For the apostles, who were commissioned to find out the wanderers, and to be for sight to those who saw not, and medicine to the weak, certainly did not address them in accordance with their opinion at the time, but according to revealed truth. For no persons of any kind would act properly, if they should advise blind men, just about to fall over a precipice, to continue their most dangerous path, as if it were the right one, and as if they might go on in safety. Or what medical man, anxious to heal a sick person, would prescribe in accordance with the patient's whims, and not according to the requisite medicine? But that the Lord came as the physician of the sick, He does Himself declare, saying, "They that are whole need not a physician, but they that are sick; I came not to call the righteous, but sinners to repentance."[1] How then shall the sick be strengthened, or how shall sinners come to repentance? Is it by persevering in the very same courses? or, on the contrary, is it by undergoing a great change and reversal of their former mode of living, by which they have brought upon themselves no slight amount of sickness, and many sins? But ignorance, the mother of all these, is driven out by knowledge. Wherefore the Lord used to impart knowledge to His disciples, by which also it was His practice to heal those who were suffering, and to keep back sinners from sin. He therefore did not address them in accordance with their pristine notions, nor did He reply to them in harmony with the opinion of His questioners, but according to the doctrine leading to salvation, without hypocrisy or respect of person.

3. This is also made clear from the words of the Lord, who did truly reveal the Son of God to those of the circumcision — Him who had been foretold as Christ by the prophets; that is, He set Himself forth, who had restored liberty to men, and bestowed on them the inheritance of incorruption. And again, the apostles taught the Gentiles that they should leave vain stocks and stones, which they imagined to be gods, and worship the true God, who had created and made all the human family, and, by means of His creation, did nourish, increase, strengthen, and preserve them in being; and that they might look for His Son Jesus Christ, who redeemed us from apostasy with His own blood, so that we should also be a sanctified people, — who shall also descend from heaven in His Father's power, and pass judgment upon all, and who shall freely give the good things of God to those who shall have kept His commandments. He, appearing in these last times, the chief cornerstone, has gathered into one, and united those that were far off and those that were near;[2] that is, the circumcision and the uncircumcision, enlarging Japhet, and placing him in the dwelling of Shem.[3]

CHAP. VI. — THE HOLY GHOST, THROUGHOUT THE OLD TESTAMENT SCRIPTURES, MADE MENTION OF NO OTHER GOD OR LORD, SAVE HIM WHO IS THE TRUE GOD.

1. Therefore neither would the Lord, nor the Holy Spirit, nor the apostles, have ever named as God, definitely and absolutely, him who was not God, unless he were truly God; nor would they have named any one in his own person Lord, except God the Father ruling over all, and His Son who has received dominion from His Father over all creation, as this passage has it: "The LORD said unto my Lord, Sit Thou at my right hand, until I make Thine enemies Thy footstool."[4] Here the [Scripture] represents to us the Father addressing the Son; He who gave Him the inheritance of the heathen, and subjected to Him all His enemies. Since, therefore, the Father is truly Lord, and the Son truly Lord, the Holy Spirit has fitly designated them by the title of Lord. And again, referring to the destruction of the Sodomites, the Scripture says, "Then the LORD rained upon Sodom and upon Gomorrah fire and brimstone from the LORD out of heaven."[5] For it here points out that the Son, who had also been talking with Abraham, had received power to judge the Sodomites

---

[1] Luke v. 31, 32.
[2] Eph. ii. 17.
[3] Gen. ix. 27.
[4] Ps. cx. 1.
[5] Gen. xix. 24.

for their wickedness. And this [text following] does declare the same truth: "Thy throne, O God, is for ever and ever; the sceptre of Thy kingdom is a right sceptre. Thou hast loved righteousness, and hated iniquity: therefore God, Thy God, hath anointed Thee."[1] For the Spirit designates both [of them] by the name of God — both Him who is anointed as Son, and Him who does anoint, that is, the Father. And again: "God stood in the congregation of the gods, He judges among the gods."[2] He [here] refers to the Father and the Son, and those who have received the adoption; but these are the Church. For she is the synagogue of God, which God — that is, the Son Himself — has gathered by Himself. Of whom He again speaks: "The God of gods, the Lord hath spoken, and hath called the earth."[3] Who is meant by God? He of whom He has said, "God shall come openly, our God, and shall not keep silence;"[4] that is, the Son, who came manifested to men, who said, "I have openly appeared to those who seek Me not."[5] But of what gods [does he speak]? [Of those] to whom He says, "I have said, Ye are gods, and all sons of the Most High."[6] To those, no doubt, who have received the grace of the "adoption, by which we cry, Abba Father."[7]

2. Wherefore, as I have already stated, no other is named as God, or is called Lord, except Him who is God and Lord of all, who also said to Moses, "I AM THAT I AM. And thus shalt thou say to the children of Israel: He who is, hath sent me unto you;"[8] and His Son Jesus Christ our Lord, who makes those that believe in His name the sons of God. And again, when the Son speaks to Moses, He says, "I am come down to deliver this people."[9] For it is He who descended and ascended for the salvation of men. Therefore God has been declared through the Son, who is in the Father, and has the Father in Himself — He WHO IS, the Father bearing witness to the Son, and the Son announcing the Father. — As also Esaias says, "I too am witness," he declares, "saith the LORD God, and the Son whom I have chosen, that ye may know, and believe, and understand that I AM."[10]

3. When, however, the Scripture terms them [gods] which are no gods, it does not, as I have already remarked, declare them as gods in every sense, but with a certain addition and signification, by which they are shown to be no gods at all. As with David: "The gods of the heathen are idols of demons;"[11] and, "Ye shall not follow other gods."[12] For in that he says "the gods of the heathen" — but the heathen are ignorant of the true God — and calls them "other gods," he bars their claim [to be looked upon] as gods at all. But as to what they are in their own person, he speaks concerning them; "for they are," he says, "the idols of demons." And Esaias: "Let them be confounded, all who blaspheme God, and carve useless things;[13] even I am witness, saith God."[14] He removes them from [the category of] gods, but he makes use of the word alone, for this [purpose], that we may know of whom he speaks. Jeremiah also says the same: "The gods that have not made the heavens and earth, let them perish from the earth which is under the heaven."[15] For, from the fact of his having subjoined their destruction, he shows them to be no gods at all. Elias, too, when all Israel was assembled at Mount Carmel, wishing to turn them from idolatry, says to them, "How long halt ye between two opinions?[16] If the LORD be God,[17] follow Him."[18] And again, at the burnt-offering, he thus addresses the idolatrous priests: "Ye shall call upon the name of your gods, and I will call on the name of the LORD my God; and the Lord that will hearken by fire,[19] He is God." Now, from the fact of the prophet having said these words, he proves that these gods which were reputed so among those men, are no gods at all. He directed them to that God upon whom he believed, and who was truly God; whom invoking, he exclaimed, "LORD God of Abraham, God of Isaac, and God of Jacob, hear me to-day, and let all this people know that Thou art the God of Israel."[20]

4. Wherefore I do also call upon thee, LORD God of Abraham, and God of Isaac, and God of Jacob and Israel, who art the Father of our Lord Jesus Christ, the God who, through the abundance of Thy mercy, hast had a favour towards us, that we should know Thee, who hast made heaven and earth, who rulest over all, who art the only and the true God, above whom there is none other God; grant, by our Lord Jesus Christ, the governing power of the Holy Spirit; give to every reader of this book to know Thee, that Thou art God alone, to be strengthened in Thee, and to avoid every heretical, and godless, and impious doctrine.

---

[1] Ps. xlv. 6.
[2] Ps. lxxxii. 1.
[3] Ps. l. 1.
[4] Ps. l. 3.
[5] Isa. lxv. 1.
[6] Ps. lxxxii. 6.
[7] Rom. viii. 15.
[8] Ex. iii. 14.
[9] Ex. iii. 8.
[10] Isa. xliii. 10.
[11] Ps. xcvi. 5.
[12] Ps. lxxxi. 9.
[13] These words are an interpolation: it is supposed they have been carelessly repeated from the preceding quotation of Isaiah.
[14] Isa. xliv. 9.
[15] Jer. x. 11.
[16] Literally, "In both houghs," *in ambabus suffraginibus*.
[17] The old Latin translation has, "Si *unus* est Dominus Deus" — *If the Lord God is one;* which is supposed by the critics to have occurred through carelessness of the translator.
[18] 1 Kings xviii. 21, etc.
[19] The Latin version has, "that answereth to-day" (*hodie*), — an evident error for *igne*.
[20] 1 Kings xviii. 36.

5. And the Apostle Paul also, saying, "For though ye have served them which are no gods; ye now know God, or rather, are known of God,"[1] has made a separation between those that were not [gods] and Him who is God. And again, speaking of Antichrist, he says, "who opposeth and exalteth himself above all that is called God, or that is worshipped."[2] He points out here those who are called gods, by such as know not God, that is, idols. For the Father of all is called God, and is so; and Antichrist shall be lifted up, not above Him, but above those which are indeed called gods, but are not. And Paul himself says that this is true: "We know that an idol is nothing, and that there is none other God but one. For though there be that are called gods, whether in heaven or in earth; yet to us there is but one God, the Father, of whom are all things, and we through Him; and one Lord Jesus Christ, by whom are all things, and we by Him."[3] For he has made a distinction, and separated those which are indeed called gods, but which are none, from the one God the Father, from whom are all things, and, he has confessed in the most decided manner in his own person, one Lord Jesus Christ. But in this [clause], "whether in heaven or in earth," he does not speak of the formers of the world, as these [teachers] expound it; but his meaning is similar to that of Moses, when it is said, "Thou shalt not make to thyself any image for God, of whatsoever things are in heaven above, whatsoever in the earth beneath, and whatsoever in the waters under the earth."[4] And he does thus explain what are meant by the things in heaven: "Lest when," he says, "looking towards heaven, and observing the sun, and the moon, and the stars, and all the ornament of heaven, falling into error, thou shouldest adore and serve them."[5] And Moses himself, being a man of God, was indeed given as a god before Pharaoh;[6] but he is not properly termed Lord, nor is called God by the prophets, but is spoken of by the Spirit as "Moses, the faithful minister and servant of God,"[7] which also he was.

CHAP. VII. — REPLY TO AN OBJECTION FOUNDED ON THE WORDS OF ST. PAUL (2 COR. IV. 5). ST. PAUL OCCASIONALLY USES WORDS NOT IN THEIR GRAMMATICAL SEQUENCE.

1. As to their affirming that Paul said plainly in the Second [Epistle] to the Corinthians, "In whom the god of this world hath blinded the minds of them that believe not,"[8] and maintaining that there is indeed one god of this world, but another who is beyond all principality, and beginning, and power, we are not to blame if they, who give out that they do themselves know mysteries beyond God, know not how to read Paul. For if any one read the passage thus — according to Paul's custom, as I show elsewhere, and by many examples, that he uses transposition of words — "In whom God," then pointing it off, and making a slight interval, and at the same time read also the rest [of the sentence] in one [clause], "hath blinded the minds of them of this world that believe not," he shall find out the true [sense]; that it is contained in the expression, "God hath blinded the minds of the unbelievers of this world." And this is shown by means of the little interval [between the clause]. For Paul does not say, "the God of this world," as if recognising any other beyond Him; but he confessed God as indeed God. And he says, "the unbelievers of this world," because they shall not inherit the future age of incorruption. I shall show from Paul himself, how it is that God has blinded the minds of them that believe not, in the course of this work, that we may not just at present distract our mind from the matter in hand, [by wandering] at large.

2. From many other instances also, we may discover that the apostle frequently uses a transposed order in his sentences, due to the rapidity of his discourses, and the impetus of the Spirit which is in him. An example occurs in the [Epistle] to the Galatians, where he expresses himself as follows: "Wherefore then the law of works?[9] It was added, until the seed should come to whom the promise was made; [and it was] ordained by angels in the hand of a Mediator."[10] For the order of the words runs thus: "Wherefore then the law of works? Ordained by angels in the hand of a Mediator, it was added until the seed should come to whom the promise was made," — man thus asking the question, and the Spirit making answer. And again, in the Second to the Thessalonians, speaking of Antichrist, he says, "And then shall that wicked be revealed, whom the Lord Jesus Christ[11] shall slay with the Spirit of His mouth, and shall destroy him[11] with the presence of his coming; [even him] whose coming is after the working of Satan, with all power, and signs, and lying wonders."[12] Now in these [sentences] the order of the words is this: "And then shall be revealed that wicked, whose coming is after the working of Satan, with all power, and signs, and lying wonders, whom

---

[1] Gal. iv. 8, 9.
[2] 2 Thess. ii. 4.
[3] 1 Cor. viii. 4, etc.
[4] Deut. v. 8.
[5] Deut. iv. 19.
[6] Ex. vii. 1.
[7] Heb. iii. 5; Num. xii. 7.
[8] 2 Cor. iv. 4.

[9] This is according to the reading of the old Italic version, for it is not so read in any of our existing manuscripts of the Greek New Testament.
[10] Gal. iii. 19.
[11] This word is not found in the second quotation of this passage immediately following.
[12] 2 Thess. ii. 8.

the Lord Jesus shall slay with the Spirit of His mouth, and shall destroy with the presence of His coming." For he does not mean that the coming of the Lord is after the working of Satan; but the coming of the wicked one, whom we also call Antichrist. If, then, one does not attend to the [proper] reading [of the passage], and if he do not exhibit the intervals of breathing as they occur, there shall be not only incongruities, but also, when reading, he will utter blasphemy, as if the advent of the Lord could take place according to the working of Satan. So therefore, in such passages, the *hyperbaton* must be exhibited by the reading, and the apostle's meaning following on, preserved; and thus we do not read in that passage, " the god of this world," but, " God," whom we do truly call God; and we hear [it declared of] the unbelieving and the blinded of this world, that they shall not inherit the world of life which is to come.

CHAP. VIII. — ANSWER TO AN OBJECTION, ARISING FROM THE WORDS OF CHRIST (MATT. VI. 24). GOD ALONE IS TO BE REALLY CALLED GOD AND LORD, FOR HE IS WITHOUT BEGINNING AND END.

1. This calumny, then, of these men, having been quashed, it is clearly proved that neither the prophets nor the apostles did ever name another God, or call [him] Lord, except the true and only God. Much more [would this be the case with regard to] the Lord Himself, who did also direct us to " render unto Cæsar the things that are Cæsar's, and to God the things that are God's;"[1] naming indeed Cæsar as Cæsar, but confessing God as God. In like manner also, that [text] which says, " Ye cannot serve two masters,"[2] He does Himself interpret, saying, " Ye cannot serve God and mammon;" acknowledging God indeed as God, but mentioning mammon, a thing having also an existence. He does not call mammon Lord when He says, " Ye cannot serve two masters;" but He teaches His disciples who serve God, not to be subject to mammon, nor to be ruled by it. For He says, " He that committeth sin is the slave of sin."[3] Inasmuch, then, as He terms those " the slaves of sin" who serve sin, but does not certainly call sin itself God, thus also He terms those who serve mammon " the slaves of mammon," not calling mammon God. For mammon is, according to the Jewish language, which the Samaritans do also use, a *covetous* man, and one who wishes to have more than he ought to have. But according to the Hebrew, it is by the addition of a syllable (*adjunctive*) called Mamuel,[4] and signifies *gulosum*, that is, one whose gullet is insatiable. Therefore, according to both these things which are indicated, we cannot serve God and mammon.

2. But also, when He spoke of the devil as strong, not absolutely so, but as in comparison with us, the Lord showed Himself under every aspect and truly to be the strong man, saying that one can in no other way " spoil the goods of a strong man, if he do not first bind the strong man himself, and then he will spoil his house."[5] Now we were the vessels and the house of this [strong man] when we were in a state of apostasy; for he put us to whatever use he pleased, and the unclean spirit dwelt within us. For he was not strong, as opposed to Him who bound him, and spoiled his house; but as against those persons who were his tools, inasmuch as he caused their thought to wander away from God: these did the Lord snatch from his grasp. As also Jeremiah declares, " The LORD hath redeemed Jacob, and has snatched him from the hand of him that was stronger than he."[6] If, then, he had not pointed out Him who binds and spoils his goods, but had merely spoken of him as being strong, the strong man should have been unconquered. But he also subjoined Him who obtains and retains possession; for *he* holds who binds, but *he is* held who is bound. And this he did without any comparison, so that, apostate slave as he was, he might not be compared to the Lord: for not he alone, but not one of created and subject things, shall ever be compared to the Word of God, by whom all things were made, who is our Lord Jesus Christ.

3. For that all things, whether Angels, or Archangels, or Thrones, or Dominions, were both established and created by Him who is God over all, through His Word, John has thus pointed out. For when he had spoken of the Word of God as having been in the Father, he added, " All things were made by Him, and without Him was not anything made."[7] David also, when he had enumerated [His] praises, subjoins by name all things whatsoever I have mentioned, both the heavens and all the powers therein : " For He commanded, and they were created; He spake, and they were made." Whom, therefore, did He command? The Word, no doubt, " by whom," he says, " the heavens were established, and all their power by the breath of His mouth."[8] But that He did Him-

---

[1] Matt. xxii. 21.
[2] Matt. vi. 24.
[3] John viii. 34.
[4] A word of which many explanations have been proposed, but none are quite satisfactory. Harvey seems inclined to suspect the reading to be corrupt, through the ignorance and carelessness of the copyist. [Irenæus undoubtedly relied for Hebrew criticisms on some incompetent retailer of rabbinical refinements.]
[5] Matt. xii. 29.
[6] Jer. xxxi. 11.
[7] John i. 3.
[8] Ps. xxxiii. 6.

self make all things freely, and as He pleased, again David says, "But our God is in the heavens above, and in the earth; He hath made all things whatsoever He pleased."[1] But the things established are distinct from Him who has established them, and what have been made from Him who has made them. For He is Himself uncreated, both without beginning and end, and lacking nothing. He is Himself sufficient for Himself; and still further, He grants to all others this very thing, existence; but the things which have been made by Him have received a beginning. But whatever things had a beginning, and are liable to dissolution, and are subject to and stand in need of Him who made them, must necessarily in all respects have a different term [applied to them], even by those who have but a moderate capacity for discerning such things; so that He indeed who made all things can alone, together with His Word, properly be termed God and Lord: but the things which have been made cannot have this term applied to them, neither should they justly assume that appellation which belongs to the Creator.

CHAP. IX. — ONE AND THE SAME GOD, THE CREATOR OF HEAVEN AND EARTH, IS HE WHOM THE PROPHETS FORETOLD, AND WHO WAS DECLARED BY THE GOSPEL. PROOF OF THIS, AT THE OUTSET, FROM ST. MATTHEW'S GOSPEL.

1. This, therefore, having been clearly demonstrated here (and it shall yet be so still more clearly), that neither the prophets, nor the apostles, nor the Lord Christ in His own person, did acknowledge any other Lord or God, but the God and Lord supreme: the prophets and the apostles confessing the Father and the Son; but naming no other as God, and confessing no other as Lord: and the Lord Himself handing down to His disciples, that He, the Father, is the only God and Lord, who alone is God and ruler of all; — it is incumbent on us to follow, if we are their disciples indeed, their testimonies to this effect. For Matthew the apostle — knowing, as one and the same God, Him who had given promise to Abraham, that He would make his seed as the stars of heaven,[2] and Him who, by His Son Christ Jesus, has called us to the knowledge of Himself, from the worship of stones, so that those who were not a people were made a people, and she beloved who was not beloved[3] — declares that John, when preparing the way for Christ, said to those who were boasting of their relationship [to Abraham] according to the flesh, but who had their mind tinged and stuffed with all manner of evil, preaching that repentance which should call them back from their evil doings, said, "O generation of vipers, who hath shown you to flee from the wrath to come? Bring forth therefore fruit meet for repentance. And think not to say within yourselves, We have Abraham [to our] father: for I say unto you, that God is able of these stones to raise up children unto Abraham."[4] He preached to them, therefore, the repentance from wickedness, but he did not declare to them another God, besides Him who made the promise to Abraham; he, the forerunner of Christ, of whom Matthew again says, and Luke likewise, "For this is he that was spoken of from the Lord by the prophet, The voice of one crying in the wilderness, Prepare ye the way of the Lord, make straight the paths of our God. Every valley shall be filled, and every mountain and hill brought low; and the crooked shall be made straight, and the rough into smooth ways; and all flesh shall see the salvation of God."[5] There is therefore one and the same God, the Father of our Lord, who also promised, through the prophets, that He would send His forerunner; and His salvation — that is, His Word — He caused to be made visible to all flesh, [the Word] Himself being made incarnate, that in all things their King might become manifest. For it is necessary that those [beings] which are judged do see the judge, and know Him from whom they receive judgment; and it is also proper, that those which follow on to glory should know Him who bestows upon them the gift of glory.

2. Then again Matthew, when speaking of the angel, says, "The angel of the Lord appeared to Joseph in sleep."[6] Of what Lord he does himself interpret: "That it may be fulfilled which was spoken of the Lord by the prophet, Out of Egypt have I called my son."[7] "Behold, a virgin shall conceive, and shall bring forth a son, and they shall call his name Emmanuel; which is, being interpreted, God with us."[8] David likewise speaks of Him who, from the virgin, is Emmanuel: "Turn not away the face of Thine anointed. The LORD hath sworn a truth to David, and will not turn from him. Of the fruit of thy body will I set upon thy seat."[9] And again: "In Judea is God known; His place has been made in peace, and His dwelling in Zion."[10] Therefore there is one and the same God, who was proclaimed by the prophets and announced by the Gospel; and His Son, who was of the fruit of David's body, that is, of the virgin of [the house of] David, and Emmanuel; whose star also Balaam thus prophesied: "There shall come a star out of Jacob, and a

---

[1] Ps. cxv. 3.
[2] Gen. xv. 5.
[3] Rom. ix. 25.
[4] Matt. iii. 7.
[5] Matt. iii. 3.
[6] Matt. i. 20.
[7] Matt. ii. 15.
[8] Matt. i. 23.
[9] Ps. cxxxii. 11.
[10] Ps. lxxvi. 1.

leader shall rise in Israel." [1] But Matthew says, that the Magi, coming from the east, exclaimed, "For we have seen His star in the east, and are come to worship Him;" [2] and that, having been led by the star into the house of Jacob to Emmanuel, they showed, by these gifts which they offered, who it was that was worshipped; *myrrh*, because it was He who should die and be buried for the mortal human race; *gold*, because He was a King, "of whose kingdom is no end;" [3] and *frankincense*, because He was God, who also "was made known in Judea," [4] and was "declared to those who sought Him not." [5]

3. And then, [speaking of His] baptism, Matthew says, "The heavens were opened, and He saw the Spirit of God, as a dove, coming upon Him: and lo a voice from heaven, saying, This is my beloved Son, in whom I am well pleased." [6] For Christ did not at that time descend upon Jesus, neither was Christ one and Jesus another: but the Word of God—who is the Saviour of all, and the ruler of heaven and earth, who is Jesus, as I have already pointed out, who did also take upon Him flesh, and was anointed by the Spirit from the Father—was made Jesus Christ, as Esaias also says, "There shall come forth a rod from the root of Jesse, and a flower shall rise from his root; and the Spirit of God shall rest upon Him: the spirit of wisdom and understanding, the spirit of counsel and might, the spirit of knowledge and piety, and the spirit of the fear of God, shall fill Him. He shall not judge according to glory,[7] nor reprove after the manner of speech; but He shall dispense judgment to the humble man, and reprove the haughty ones of the earth." [8] And again Esaias, pointing out beforehand His unction, and the reason why he was anointed, does himself say, "The Spirit of God is upon Me, because He hath anointed Me: He hath sent Me to preach the Gospel to the lowly, to heal the broken up in heart, to proclaim liberty to the captives, and sight to the blind; to announce the acceptable year of the Lord, and the day of vengeance; to comfort all that mourn." [9] For inasmuch as the Word of God was man from the root of Jesse, and son of Abraham, in this respect did the Spirit of God rest upon Him, and anoint Him to preach the Gospel to the lowly. But inasmuch as He was God, He did not judge according to glory, nor reprove after the manner of speech. For "He needed not that any should testify to Him of man,[10] for He Himself knew what was in man." [11] For He called all men that mourn; and granting forgiveness to those who had been led into captivity by their sins, He loosed them from their chains, of whom Solomon says, "Every one shall be holden with the cords of his own sins." [12] Therefore did the Spirit of God descend upon Him, [the Spirit] of Him who had promised by the prophets that He would anoint Him, so that we, receiving from the abundance of His unction, might be saved. Such, then, [is the witness] of Matthew.

CHAP. X.—PROOFS OF THE FOREGOING, DRAWN FROM THE GOSPELS OF MARK AND LUKE.

1. Luke also, the follower and disciple of the apostles, referring to Zacharias and Elisabeth, from whom, according to promise, John was born, says: "And they were both righteous before God, walking in all the commandments and ordinances of the Lord blameless." [13] And again, speaking of Zacharias: "And it came to pass, that while he executed the priest's office before God in the order of his course, according to the custom of the priest's office, his lot was to burn incense;" [14] and he came to sacrifice, "entering into the temple of the Lord." [15] Whose angel Gabriel, also, who stands prominently in the presence of the Lord, simply, absolutely, and decidedly confessed in his own person as God and Lord, Him who had chosen Jerusalem, and had instituted the sacerdotal office. For he knew of none other above Him; since, if he had been in possession of the knowledge of any other more perfect God and Lord besides Him, he surely would never—as I have already shown—have confessed Him, whom he knew to be the fruit of a defect, as absolutely and altogether God and Lord. And then, speaking of John, he thus says: "For he shall be great in the sight of the Lord, and many of the children of Israel shall he turn to the Lord their God. And he shall go before Him in the spirit and power of Elias, to make ready a people prepared for the Lord." [16] For whom, then, did he prepare the people, and in the sight of what Lord was he made great? Truly of Him who said that John had something even "more than a prophet," [17] and that "among those born of women none is greater than John the Baptist;" who did also make the people ready for the Lord's advent, warning his fellow-servants, and preaching to them repentance, that

---

[1] Num. xxiv. 17.
[2] Matt. ii. 2.
[3] Luke i. 33.
[4] Ps. lxxvi. 1.
[5] Isa. lxv. 1. [A beautiful idea for poets and orators, but not to be pressed dogmatically.]
[6] Matt. iii. 16.
[7] This is after the version of the Septuagint, οὐ κατὰ τὴν δόξαν: but the word δόξα may have the meaning *opinio* as well as *gloria*. If this be admitted here, the passage would bear much the same sense as it does in the authorized version, "He shall not judge after the sight of His eyes."
[8] Isa. xi. 1, etc.
[9] Isa. lxi. 1.

[10] This is according to the Syriac Peschito version.
[11] John ii. 25.
[12] Prov. v. 22.
[13] Luke i. 6.
[14] Literally, "that he should place the incense." The next clause is most likely an interpolation for the sake of explanation.
[15] Luke i. 8, etc.
[16] Luke i. 15, etc.
[17] Matt. xi. 9, 11.

they might receive remission from the Lord when He should be present, having been converted to Him, from whom they had been alienated because of sins and transgressions. As also David says, "The alienated are sinners from the womb: they go astray as soon as they are born."[1] And it was on account of this that he, turning them to their Lord, prepared, in the spirit and power of Elias, a perfect people for the Lord.

2. And again, speaking in reference to the angel, he says: "But at that time the angel Gabriel was sent from God, who did also say to the virgin, Fear not, Mary; for thou hast found favour with God."[2] And he says concerning the Lord: "He shall be great, and shall be called the Son of the Highest: and the Lord God shall give unto Him the throne of His father David: and He shall reign over the house of Jacob for ever; and of His kingdom there shall be no end."[3] For who else is there who can reign uninterruptedly over the house of Jacob for ever, except Jesus Christ our Lord, the Son of the Most High God, who promised by the law and the prophets that He would make His salvation visible to all flesh; so that He would become the Son of man for this purpose, that man also might become the son of God? And Mary, exulting because of this, cried out, prophesying on behalf of the Church, "My soul doth magnify the Lord, and my spirit hath rejoiced in God my Saviour. For He hath taken up His child Israel, in remembrance of His mercy, as He spake to our fathers, Abraham, and his seed for ever."[4] By these and such like [passages] the Gospel points out that it was God who spake to the fathers; that it was He who, by Moses, instituted the legal dispensation, by which giving of the law we know that He spake to the fathers. This same God, after His great goodness, poured His compassion upon us, through which compassion "the Dayspring from on high hath looked upon us, and appeared to those who sat in darkness and the shadow of death, and has guided our feet into the way of peace;"[5] as Zacharias also, recovering from the state of dumbness which he had suffered on account of unbelief, having been filled with a new spirit, did bless God in a new manner. For all things had entered upon a new phase, the Word arranging after a new manner the advent in the flesh, that He might win back[6] to God that human nature (*hominem*) which had departed from God; and therefore men were taught to worship God after a new fashion, but not another god, because in truth there is but "one God, who justifieth the circumcision by faith, and the uncircumcision through faith."[7] But Zacharias prophesying, exclaimed, "Blessed be the Lord God of Israel; for He hath visited and redeemed His people, and hath raised up an horn of salvation for us in the house of His servant David; as He spake by the mouth of His holy prophets, which have been since the world begun; salvation from our enemies, and from the hand of all that hate us; to perform the mercy [promised] to our fathers, and to remember His holy covenant, the oath which He sware to our father Abraham, that He would grant unto us, that we, being delivered out of the hand of our enemies, might serve Him without fear, in holiness and righteousness before Him, all our days."[8] Then he says to John: "And thou, child, shalt be called the prophet of the Highest: for thou shalt go before the face of the Lord to prepare His ways; to give knowledge of salvation to His people, for the remission of their sins."[9] For this is the knowledge of salvation which was wanting to them, that of the Son of God, which John made known, saying, "Behold the Lamb of God, who taketh away the sin of the world. This is He of whom I said, After me cometh a man who was made before me;[10] because He was prior to me: and of His fulness have all we received."[11] This, therefore, was the knowledge of salvation; but [it did not consist in] another God, nor another Father, nor Bythus, nor the Pleroma of thirty Æons, nor the Mother of the (lower) Ogdoad: but the knowledge of salvation was the knowledge of the Son of God, who is both called and actually is, salvation, and Saviour, and salutary. Salvation, indeed, as follows: "I have waited for Thy salvation, O Lord."[12] And then again, Saviour: "Behold my God, my Saviour, I will put my trust in Him."[13] But as bringing salvation, thus: "God hath made known His salvation (*salutare*) in the sight of the heathen."[14] For He is indeed Saviour, as being the Son and Word of God; but salutary, since [He is] Spirit; for he says: "The Spirit of our countenance, Christ the Lord."[15] But salvation, as being flesh: for "the Word was made flesh, and dwelt among us."[16] This knowledge of salvation, therefore, John did impart to those repenting, and believing in the Lamb of God, who taketh away the sin of the world.

3. And the angel of the Lord, he says,

---

[1] Ps. lviii. 3.
[2] Luke i. 26, etc.
[3] Luke i. 32.
[4] Luke i. 46.
[5] Luke i. 78.
[6] "Ascriberet Deo"—make the property of God.
[7] Rom. iii. 30.
[8] Luke i. 68, etc.
[9] Luke i. 76.
[10] Harvey observes that the Syriac, agreeing with the Latin here, expresses priority in point of time; but our translation, without reason, makes it the precedence of honour, viz., *was preferred before me*. The Greek is, πρῶτός μου.
[11] John i. 29, 15, 16.
[12] Gen. xlix. 18.
[13] Isa. xii. 2.
[14] Ps. xcviii. 2.
[15] Lam. iv. 20, after LXX.
[16] John i. 14.

appeared to the shepherds, proclaiming joy to them: "For[1] there is born in the house of David, a Saviour, which is Christ the Lord. Then [appeared] a multitude of the heavenly host, praising God, and saying, Glory in the highest to God, and on earth peace, to men of good will."[2] The falsely-called Gnostics say that these angels came from the Ogdoad, and made manifest the descent of the superior Christ. But they are again in error, when saying that the Christ and Saviour from above was not born, but that also, after the baptism of the dispensational Jesus, he, [the Christ of the Pleroma,] descended upon him as a dove. Therefore, according to these men, the angels of the Ogdoad lied, when they said, "For unto you is born this day a Saviour, who is Christ the Lord, in the city of David." For neither was Christ nor the Saviour born at that time, by their account; but it was he, the dispensational Jesus, who is of the framer of the world, the [Demiurge], and upon whom, after his baptism, that is, after [the lapse of] thirty years, they maintain the Saviour from above descended. But why did [the angels] add, "in the city of David," if they did not proclaim the glad tidings of the fulfilment of God's promise made to David, that from the fruit of his body there should be an eternal King? For the Framer [Demiurge] of the entire universe made promise to David, as David himself declares: "My help is from God, who made heaven and earth;"[3] and again: "In His hand are the ends of the earth, and the heights of the mountains are His. For the sea is His, and He did Himself make it; and His hands founded the dry land. Come ye, let us worship and fall down before Him, and weep in the presence of the Lord who made us; for He is the Lord our God."[4] The Holy Spirit evidently thus declares by David to those hearing him, that there shall be those who despise Him who formed us, and who is God alone. Wherefore he also uttered the foregoing words, meaning to say: See that ye do not err; besides or above Him there is no other God, to whom ye should rather stretch out [your hands], thus rendering us pious and grateful towards Him who made, established, and [still] nourishes us. What, then, shall happen to those who have been the authors of so much blasphemy against their Creator? This identical truth was also what the angels [proclaimed]. For when they exclaim, "Glory to God in the highest, and in earth peace," they have glorified with these words Him who is the Creator of the highest, that is, of super-celestial things, and the Founder of everything on earth: who has sent to His own handiwork, that is, to men, the blessing of His salvation from heaven. Wherefore he adds: "The shepherds returned, glorifying God for all which they had heard and seen, as it was told unto them."[5] For the Israelitish shepherds did not glorify another god, but Him who had been announced by the law and the prophets, the Maker of all things, whom also the angels glorified. But if the angels who were from the Ogdoad were accustomed to glorify any other, different from Him whom the shepherds [adored], these angels from the Ogdoad brought to them error and not truth.

4. And still further does Luke say in reference to the Lord: "When the days of purification were accomplished, they brought Him up to Jerusalem, to present Him before the Lord, as it is written in the law of the Lord, That every male opening the womb shall be called holy to the Lord; and that they should offer a sacrifice, as it is said in the law of the Lord, a pair of turtle-doves, or two young pigeons:"[6] in his own person most clearly calling Him Lord, who appointed the legal dispensation. But "Simeon," he also says, "blessed God, and said, Lord, now lettest Thou Thy servant depart in peace; for mine eyes have seen Thy salvation, which Thou hast prepared before the face of all people; a light for the revelation of the Gentiles, and the glory of Thy people Israel."[7] And "Anna"[8] also, "the prophetess," he says, in like manner glorified God when she saw Christ, "and spake of Him to all them who were looking for the redemption of Jerusalem."[9] Now by all these one God is shown forth, revealing to men the new dispensation of liberty, the covenant, through the new advent of His Son.

5. Wherefore also Mark, the interpreter and follower of Peter, does thus commence his Gospel narrative: "The beginning of the Gospel of Jesus Christ, the Son of God; as it is written in the prophets, Behold, I send My messenger before Thy face, which shall prepare Thy way.[10] The voice of one crying in the wilderness, Prepare ye the way of the Lord, make the paths

---

[1] Luke ii. 11, etc.
[2] Thus found also in the Vulgate. Harvey supposes that the original of Irenæus read according to our *textus receptus*, and that the Vulgate rendering was adopted in this passage by the transcribers of the Latin version of our author. [No doubt a just remark.] There can be no doubt, however, that the reading εὐδοκίας is supported by many and weighty ancient authorities. [But on this point see the facts as given by Burgon, in his refutation of the rendering adopted by late revisers, *Revision Revised*, p. 41. London, Murray, 1883.]
[3] Ps. cxxiv. 8.
[4] Ps. xcv. 4.
[5] Luke ii. 20.
[6] Luke ii. 22.
[7] Luke ii. 29, etc.
[8] Luke ii. 38.
[9] The text seems to be corrupt in the old Latin translation. The rendering here follows Harvey's conjectural restoration of the original Greek of the passage.
[10] The Greek of this passage in St. Mark [i. 2] reads, τὰς τρίβους αὐτοῦ, i.e., *His paths*, which varies from the Hebrew original, to which the text of Irenæus seems to revert, unless indeed his copy of the Gospels contained the reading of the Codex Bezæ. [See book iii. cap. xii. 3, 14, below; also, xiv. 2 and xxiii. 3. On this Codex, see Burgon, *Revision Revised*, p. 12, etc., and references.]

straight before our God." Plainly does the commencement of the Gospel quote the words of the holy prophets, and point out Him at once, whom they confessed as God and Lord; Him, the Father of our Lord Jesus Christ, who had also made promise to Him, that He would send His messenger before His face, who was John, crying in the wilderness, in "the spirit and power of Elias,"[1] "Prepare ye the way of the Lord, make straight paths before our God." For the prophets did not announce one and another God, but one and the same; under various aspects, however, and many titles. For varied and rich in attribute is the Father, as I have already shown in the book preceding[2] this; and I shall show [the same truth] from the prophets themselves in the further course of this work. Also, towards the conclusion of his Gospel, Mark says: "So then, after the Lord Jesus had spoken to them, He was received up into heaven, and sitteth on the right hand of God;"[3] confirming what had been spoken by the prophet: "The LORD said to my Lord, Sit Thou on My right hand, until I make Thy foes Thy footstool."[4] Thus God and the Father are truly one and the same; He who was announced by the prophets, and handed down by the true Gospel; whom we Christians worship and love with the whole heart, as the Maker of heaven and earth, and of all things therein.

CHAP. XI.—PROOFS IN CONTINUATION, EXTRACTED FROM ST. JOHN'S GOSPEL. THE GOSPELS ARE FOUR IN NUMBER, NEITHER MORE NOR LESS. MYSTIC REASONS FOR THIS.

1. John, the disciple of the Lord, preaches this faith, and seeks, by the proclamation of the Gospel, to remove that error which by Cerinthus had been disseminated among men, and a long time previously by those termed Nicolaitans, who are an offset of that "knowledge" falsely so called, that he might confound them, and persuade them that there is but one God, who made all things by His Word; and not, as they allege, that the Creator was one, but the Father of the Lord another; and that the Son of the Creator was, forsooth, one, but the Christ from above another, who also continued impassible, descending upon Jesus, the Son of the Creator, and flew back again into His Pleroma; and that Monogenes was the beginning, but Logos was the true son of Monogenes; and that this creation to which we belong was not made by the primary God, but by some power lying far below Him, and shut off from communion with the things invisible and ineffable. The disciple of the Lord therefore desiring to put an end to all such doctrines, and to establish the rule of truth in the Church, that there is one Almighty God, who made all things by His Word, both visible and invisible; showing at the same time, that by the Word, through whom God made the creation, He also bestowed salvation on the men included in the creation; thus commenced His teaching in the Gospel: "In the beginning was the Word, and the Word was with God, and the Word was God. The same was in the beginning with God. All things were made by Him, and without Him was nothing made.[5] What was made was life in Him, and the life was the light of men. And the light shineth in darkness, and the darkness comprehended it not."[6] "All things," he says, "were made by Him;" therefore in "all things" this creation of ours is [included], for we cannot concede to these men that [the words] "all things" are spoken in reference to those within their Pleroma. For if their Pleroma do indeed contain these, this creation, as being such, is not outside, as I have demonstrated in the preceding book;[7] but if they are outside the Pleroma, which indeed appeared impossible, it follows, in that case, that their Pleroma cannot be "all things:" therefore this vast creation is not outside [the Pleroma].

2. John, however, does himself put this matter beyond all controversy on our part, when he says, "He was in this world, and the world was made by Him, and the world knew Him not. He came unto His own [things], and His own [people] received Him not."[8] But according to Marcion, and those like him, neither was the world made by Him; nor did He come to His own things, but to those of another. And, according to certain of the Gnostics, this world was made by angels, and not by the Word of God. But according to the followers of Valentinus, the world was not made by Him, but by the Demiurge. For he (Soter) caused such similitudes to be made, after the pattern of things above, as they allege; but the Demiurge accomplished the work of creation. For they say that he, the Lord and Creator of the plan of creation, by whom they hold that this world was made, was produced from the Mother; while the Gospel affirms plainly, that by the Word, which was in the beginning with God, all things were made, which Word, he says, "was made flesh, and dwelt among us."[9]

3. But, according to these men, neither was the Word made flesh, nor Christ, nor the Saviour (Soter), who was produced from [the joint con-

---

[1] Luke i. 17.
[2] See ii. 35, 3.
[3] Mark xvi. 19
[4] Ps. cx. 1.
[5] Irenæus frequently quotes this text, and always uses the punctuation here adopted. Tertullian and many others of the Fathers follow his example.
[6] John i. 1, etc.
[7] See ii. 1, etc.
[8] John i. 10, 11.
[9] John i. 14.

tributions of] all [the Æons]. For they will have it, that the Word and Christ never came into this world; that the Saviour, too, never became incarnate, nor suffered, but that He descended like a dove upon the dispensational Jesus; and that, as soon as He had declared the unknown Father, He did again ascend into the Pleroma. Some, however, make the assertion, that this dispensational Jesus did become incarnate, and suffered, whom they represent as having passed through Mary just as water through a tube; but others allege him to be the Son of the Demiurge, upon whom the dispensational Jesus descended; while others, again, say that Jesus was born from Joseph and Mary, and that the Christ from above descended upon him, being without flesh, and impassible. But according to the opinion of no one of the heretics was the Word of God made flesh. For if any one carefully examines the systems of them all, he will find that the Word of God is brought in by all of them as not having become incarnate (*sine carne*) and impassible, as is also the Christ from above. Others consider Him to have been manifested as a transfigured man; but they maintain Him to have been neither born nor to have become incarnate; whilst others [hold] that He did not assume a human form at all, but that, as a dove, He did descend upon that Jesus who was born from Mary. Therefore the Lord's disciple, pointing them all out as false witnesses, says, "And the Word was made flesh, and dwelt among us."[1]

4. And that we may not have to ask, Of what God was the Word made flesh? he does himself previously teach us, saying, "There was a man sent from God, whose name was John. The same came as a witness, that he might bear witness of that Light. He was not that Light, but [came] that he might testify of the Light."[2] By what God, then, was John, the forerunner, who testifies of the Light, sent [into the world]? Truly it was by Him, of whom Gabriel is the angel, who also announced the glad tidings of his birth: [that God] who also had promised by the prophets that He would send His messenger before the face of His Son,[3] who should prepare His way, that is, that he should bear witness of that Light in the spirit and power of Elias.[4] But, again, of what God was Elias the servant and the prophet? Of Him who made heaven and earth,[5] as he does himself confess. John, therefore, having been sent by the founder and maker of this world, how could he testify of that Light, which came down from things unspeakable and invisible? For all the heretics have decided that the Demiurge was ignorant of that Power above him, whose witness and herald John is found to be. Wherefore the Lord said that He deemed him "more than a prophet."[6] For all the other prophets preached the advent of the paternal Light, and desired to be worthy of seeing Him whom they preached; but John did both announce [the advent] beforehand, in a like manner as did the others, and actually saw Him when He came, and pointed Him out, and persuaded many to believe on Him, so that he did himself hold the place of both prophet and apostle. For this is to be more than a prophet, because, "first apostles, secondarily prophets;"[7] but all things from one and the same God Himself.

5. That wine,[8] which was produced by God in a vineyard, and which was first consumed, was good. None[9] of those who drank of it found fault with it; and the Lord partook of it also. But that wine was better which the Word made from water, on the moment, and simply for the use of those who had been called to the marriage. For although the Lord had the power to supply wine to those feasting, independently of any created substance, and to fill with food those who were hungry, He did not adopt this course; but, taking the loaves which the earth had produced, and giving thanks,[10] and on the other occasion making water wine, He satisfied those who were reclining [at table], and gave drink to those who had been invited to the marriage; showing that the God who made the earth, and commanded it to bring forth fruit, who established the waters, and brought forth the fountains, was He who in these last times bestowed upon mankind, by His Son, the blessing of food and the favour of drink: the Incomprehensible [acting thus] by means of the comprehensible, and the Invisible by the visible; since there is none beyond Him, but He exists in the bosom of the Father.

6. For "no man," he says, "hath seen God at any time," unless "the only-begotten Son of God, which is in the bosom of the Father, He hath declared [Him]."[11] For He, the Son who is in His bosom, declares to all the Father who is invisible. Wherefore *they* know Him to whom the Son reveals Him; and again, the Father, by means of the Son, gives knowledge of His Son to those who love Him. By whom also Nathanael, being taught, recognised [Him], he to whom also the Lord bare witness, that he was "an Israelite indeed, in whom was no guile."[12] The

---

[1] John i. 14.
[2] John i. 6.
[3] Mal. iii. 1.
[4] Luke i. 17.
[5] This evidently refers to 1 Kings xviii. 36, where Elijah invokes God as the God of Abraham, Isaac, and Jacob, etc.
[6] Matt. xi. 9; Luke vii. 26.
[7] 1. Cor. xii. 28.
[8] The transition here is so abrupt, that some critics suspect the loss of part of the text before these words.
[9] John ii. 3.
[10] John vi. 11.
[11] John i. 18.
[12] John i. 47.

Israelite recognised his King, therefore did he cry out to Him, "Rabbi, Thou art the Son of God, Thou art the King of Israel." By whom also Peter, having been taught, recognised Christ as the Son of the living God, when [God] said, "Behold My dearly beloved Son, in whom I am well pleased: I will put my Spirit upon Him, and He shall show judgment to the Gentiles. He shall not strive, nor cry; neither shall any man hear His voice in the streets. A bruised reed shall He not break, and smoking flax shall He not quench, until He send forth judgment into contention;[1] and in His name shall the Gentiles trust."[2]

7. Such, then, are the first principles of the Gospel: that there is one God, the Maker of this universe; He who was also announced by the prophets, and who by Moses set forth the dispensation of the law,—[principles] which proclaim the Father of our Lord Jesus Christ, and ignore any other God or Father except Him. So firm is the ground upon which these Gospels rest, that the very heretics themselves bear witness to them, and, starting from these [documents], each one of them endeavours to establish his own peculiar doctrine. For the Ebionites, who use Matthew's Gospel[3] only, are confuted out of this very same, making false suppositions with regard to the Lord. But Marcion, mutilating that according to Luke, is proved to be a blasphemer of the only existing God, from those [passages] which he still retains. Those, again, who separate Jesus from Christ, alleging that Christ remained impassible, but that it was Jesus who suffered, preferring the Gospel by Mark, if they read it with a love of truth, may have their errors rectified. Those, moreover, who follow Valentinus, making copious use of that according to John, to illustrate their conjunctions, shall be proved to be totally in error by means of this very Gospel, as I have shown in the first book. Since, then, our opponents do bear testimony to us, and make use of these [documents], our proof derived from them is firm and true.

8. It is not possible that the Gospels can be either more or fewer in number than they are. For, since there are four zones of the world in which we live, and four principal winds,[4] while the Church is scattered throughout all the world, and the "pillar and ground"[5] of the Church is the Gospel and the spirit of life; it is fitting that she should have four pillars, breathing out immortality on every side, and vivifying men afresh. From which fact, it is evident that the Word, the Artificer of all, He that sitteth upon the cherubim, and contains all things, He who was manifested to men, has given us the Gospel under four aspects, but bound together by one Spirit. As also David says, when entreating His manifestation, "Thou that sittest between the cherubim, shine forth."[6] For the cherubim, too, were four-faced, and their faces were images of the dispensation of the Son of God. For, [as the Scripture] says, "The first living creature was like a lion,"[7] symbolizing His effectual working, His leadership, and royal power; the second [living creature] was like a calf, signifying [His] sacrificial and sacerdotal order; but "the third had, as it were, the face as of a man,"—an evident description of His advent as a human being; "the fourth was like a flying eagle," pointing out the gift of the Spirit hovering with His wings over the Church. And therefore the Gospels are in accord with these things, among which Christ Jesus is seated. For that according to John relates His original, effectual, and glorious generation from the Father, thus declaring, "In the beginning was the Word, and the Word was with God, and the Word was God."[8] Also, "all things were made by Him, and without Him was nothing made." For this reason, too, is that Gospel full of all confidence, for such is His person.[9] But that according to Luke, taking up [His] priestly character, commenced with Zacharias the priest offering sacrifice to God. For now was made ready the fatted calf, about to be immolated for[10] the finding again of the younger son. Matthew, again, relates His generation as a man, saying, "The book of the generation of Jesus Christ, the son of David, the son of Abraham;"[11] and also, "The birth of Jesus Christ was on this wise." This, then, is the Gospel of His humanity;[12] for which reason it is, too, that [the character of] a humble and meek man is kept up through the whole Gospel. Mark, on the other hand, commences with [a reference to] the prophetical spirit coming down from on high to men, saying, "The beginning of the Gospel of Jesus Christ, as it is written in Esaias the prophet,"—pointing to the winged aspect of the Gospel; and on this account he made a compendious and cursory narrative, for such is the prophetical character. And the Word of God Himself used to converse with the ante-Mosaic patriarchs, in accordance with His di-

---

[1] The reading νεῖκος having been followed instead of νῖκος, victory.
[2] John i. 49, vi. 69; Matt. xii. 18
[3] Harvey thinks that this is the Hebrew Gospel of which Irenæus speaks in the opening of this book; but comp. Dr. Roberts's *Discussions on the Gospels*, part ii. chap. iv.
[4] Literally, "four catholic spirits;" Greek, τέσσαρα καθολικὰ πνεύματα: Latin, "quatuor principales spiritus."
[5] 1 Tim. iii. 15.
[6] Ps. lxxx. 1.
[7] Rev. iv. 7.
[8] John i. 1.
[9] The above is the literal rendering of this very obscure sentence; it is not at all represented in the Greek here preserved.
[10] The Greek is ὑπέρ: the Latin, "pro."
[11] Matt. i. 1, 18.
[12] The Greek text of this clause, literally rendered, is, "This Gospel, then, is anthropomorphic."

vinity and glory; but for those under the law he instituted a sacerdotal and liturgical service.[1] Afterwards, being made man for us, He sent the gift of the celestial Spirit over all the earth, protecting us with His wings. Such, then, as was the course followed by the Son of God, so was also the form of the living creatures; and such as was the form of the living creatures, so was also the character of the Gospel.[2] For the living creatures are quadriform, and the Gospel is quadriform, as is also the course followed by the Lord. For this reason were four principal (καθολικαί) covenants given to the human race:[3] one, prior to the deluge, under Adam; the second, that after the deluge, under Noah; the third, the giving of the law, under Moses; the fourth, that which renovates man, and sums up all things in itself by means of the Gospel, raising and bearing men upon its wings into the heavenly kingdom.

9. These things being so, all who destroy the form of the Gospel are vain, unlearned, and also audacious; those, [I mean,] who represent the aspects of the Gospel as being either more in number than as aforesaid, or, on the other hand, fewer. The former class [do so], that they may seem to have discovered more than is of the truth; the latter, that they may set the dispensations of God aside. For Marcion, rejecting the entire Gospel, yea rather, cutting himself off from the Gospel, boasts that he has part in the [blessings of] the Gospel.[4] Others, again (the Montanists), that they may set at nought the gift of the Spirit, which in the latter times has been, by the good pleasure of the Father, poured out upon the human race, do not admit that *aspect* [of the evangelical dispensation] presented by John's Gospel, in which the Lord promised that He would send the Paraclete;[5] but set aside at once both the Gospel and the prophetic Spirit. Wretched men indeed! who wish to be pseudo-prophets, forsooth, but who set aside the gift of prophecy from the Church; acting like those (the Encratitæ)[6] who, on account of such as come in hypocrisy, hold themselves aloof from the communion of the brethren. We must conclude, moreover, that these men (the Montanists) cannot admit the Apostle Paul either. For, in his Epistle to the Corinthians,[7] he speaks expressly of prophetical gifts, and recognises men and women prophesying in the Church. Sinning, therefore, in all these particulars, against the Spirit of God,[8] they fall into the irremissible sin. But those who are from Valentinus, being, on the other hand, altogether reckless, while they put forth their own compositions, boast that they possess more Gospels than there really are. Indeed, they have arrived at such a pitch of audacity, as to entitle their comparatively recent writing "the Gospel of Truth," though it agrees in nothing with the Gospels of the Apostles, so that they have really no Gospel which is not full of blasphemy. For if what they have published is the Gospel of truth, and yet is totally unlike those which have been handed down to us from the apostles, any who please may learn, as is shown from the Scriptures themselves, that that which has been handed down from the apostles can no longer be reckoned the Gospel of truth. But that these Gospels alone are true and reliable, and admit neither an increase nor diminution of the aforesaid number, I have proved by so many and such [arguments]. For, since God made all things in due proportion and adaptation, it was fit also that the outward aspect of the Gospel should be well arranged and harmonized. The opinion of those men, therefore, who handed the Gospel down to us, having been investigated, from their very fountainheads, let us proceed also to the remaining apostles, and inquire into their doctrine with regard to God; then, in due course we shall listen to the very words of the Lord.

CHAP. XII. — THE DOCTRINE OF THE REST OF THE APOSTLES.

1. The Apostle Peter, therefore, after the resurrection of the Lord, and His assumption into the heavens, being desirous of filling up the number of the twelve apostles, and in electing into the place of Judas any substitute who should be chosen by God, thus addressed those who were present: "Men [and] brethren, this Scripture must needs have been fulfilled, which the Holy Ghost, by the mouth of David, spake before concerning Judas, which was made guide to them that took Jesus. For he was numbered with us:[9] . . . Let his habitation be desolate,

---

[1] Or, "a sacerdotal and liturgical order," following the fragment of the Greek text recovered here. Harvey thinks that the old Latin "actum" indicates the true reading of the original πρᾶξιν, and that τάξιν is an error. The earlier editors, however, are of a contrary opinion.
[2] That is, the appearance of the Gospel taken as a whole; it being presented under a fourfold aspect.
[3] A portion of the Greek has been preserved here, but it differs materially from the old Latin version, which seems to represent the original with greater exactness, and has therefore been followed. The Greek represents the first covenant as having been given to Noah, at the deluge, under the sign of the rainbow; the second as that given to Abraham, under the sign of circumcision; the third, as being the giving of the law, under Moses; and the fourth, as that of the Gospel, through our Lord Jesus Christ. [Paradise with the *tree of life*, Adam with the *Shechinah* (Gen. iii. 24, iv. 16), Noah with the *rainbow*, Abraham with *circumcision*, Moses with *the ark*, Messiah with *the sacraments*, and heaven with the *river of life*, seem the complete system.]
[4] The old Latin reads, "partem gloriatur se habere Evangelii." Massuet changed *partem* into *pariter*, thinking that *partem* gave a sense inconsistent with the Marcionite curtailment of St. Luke. Harvey, however, observes: "But the *Gospel* here means the *blessings of the Gospel*, in which Marcion certainly claimed a share."
[5] John xiv. 16, etc.
[6] Slighting, as did some later heretics, the Pauline Epistles.
[7] 1 Cor. xi. 4, 5.
[8] Matt. xii. 31.
[9] Acts i. 16, etc.

and let no man dwell therein;[1] and, His bishoprick let another take;"[2] — thus leading to the completion of the apostles, according to the words spoken by David. Again, when the Holy Ghost had descended upon the disciples, that they all might prophesy and speak with tongues, and some mocked them, as if drunken with new wine, Peter said that they were not drunken, for it was the third hour of the day; but that this was what had been spoken by the prophet: "It shall come to pass in the last days, saith God, I will pour out of my Spirit upon all flesh, and they shall prophesy."[3] The God, therefore, who did promise by the prophet, that He would send His Spirit upon the whole human race, was He who did send; and God Himself is announced by Peter as having fulfilled His own promise.

2. For Peter said, "Ye men of Israel, hear my words; Jesus of Nazareth, a man approved by God among you by powers, and wonders, and signs, which God did by Him in the midst of you, as ye yourselves also know: Him, being delivered by the determined counsel and foreknowledge of God, by the hands of wicked men ye have slain, affixing [to the cross]: whom God hath raised up, having loosed the pains of death; because it was not possible that he should be holden of them. For David speaketh concerning Him,[4] I foresaw the Lord always before my face; for He is on my right hand, lest I should be moved: therefore did my heart rejoice, and my tongue was glad; moreover also, my flesh shall rest in hope: because Thou wilt not leave my soul in hell, neither wilt Thou give Thy Holy One to see corruption."[5] Then he proceeds to speak confidently to them concerning the patriarch David, that he was dead and buried, and that his sepulchre is with them to this day. He said, "But since he was a prophet, and knew that God had sworn with an oath to him, that of the fruit of his body one should sit in his throne; foreseeing this, he spake of the resurrection of Christ, that He was not left in hell, neither did His flesh see corruption. This Jesus," he said, "hath God raised up, of which we all are witnesses: who, being exalted by the right hand of God, receiving from the Father the promise of the Holy Ghost, hath shed forth this gift[6] which ye now see and hear. For David has not ascended into the heavens; but he saith himself, The LORD said unto my Lord, Sit Thou on My right hand, until I make Thy foes Thy footstool. Therefore let all the house of Israel know assuredly, that God hath made that same Jesus, whom ye have crucified, both Lord and Christ."[7] And when the multitudes exclaimed, "What shall we do then?" Peter says to them, "Repent, and be baptized every one of you in the name of Jesus for the remission of sins, and ye shall receive the gift of the Holy Ghost."[8] Thus the apostles did not preach another God, or another Fulness; nor, that the Christ who suffered and rose again was one, while he who flew off on high was another, and remained impassible; but that there was one and the same God the Father, and Christ Jesus who rose from the dead; and they preached faith in Him, to those who did not believe on the Son of God, and exhorted them out of the prophets, that the Christ whom God promised to send, He sent in Jesus, whom they crucified and God raised up.

3. Again, when Peter, accompanied by John, had looked upon the man lame from his birth, before that gate of the temple which is called Beautiful, sitting and seeking alms, he said to him, "Silver and gold I have none; but such as I have give I thee: In the name of Jesus Christ of Nazareth, rise up and walk. And immediately his legs and his feet received strength; and he walked, and entered with them into the temple, walking, and leaping, and praising God."[9] Then, when a multitude had gathered around them from all quarters because of this unexpected deed, Peter addressed them: "Ye men of Israel, why marvel ye at this; or why look ye so earnestly on us, as though by our own power we had made this man to walk? The God of Abraham, the God of Isaac, and the God of Jacob, the God of our fathers, hath glorified His Son, whom ye delivered up for judgment,[10] and denied in the presence of Pilate, when he wished to let Him go. But ye were bitterly set against[10] the Holy One and the Just, and desired a murderer to be granted unto you; but ye killed the Prince of life, whom God hath raised from the dead, whereof we are witnesses. And in the faith of His name, him, whom ye see and know, hath His name made strong; yea, the faith which is by Him, hath given him this perfect soundness in the presence of you all. And now, brethren, I wot that through ignorance ye did this wickedness.[10] . . . But those things which God before had showed by the mouth of all the prophets, that His Christ should suffer, He hath so fulfilled. Repent ye therefore, and be converted, that your sins may be blotted out, and that[11] the times of refresh-

---

[1] Ps. lxix. 25.
[2] Ps. cix. 8.
[3] Joel ii. 28.
[4] Ps. xv. 8.
[5] Acts ii. 22-27.
[6] The word δῶρον or δώρημα is supposed by some to have existed in the earliest Greek texts, although not found in any extant now. It is thus quoted by others besides Irenæus.

[7] Acts ii. 30-37.
[8] Acts ii. 37, 38.
[9] Acts iii. 6, etc.
[10] These interpolations are also found in the Codex Bezæ.
[11] "Et veniant" in Latin text: ὅπως ἂν ἔλθωσιν in Greek. The translation of these Greek words by "when . . . come," is one of the most glaring errors in the authorized English version.

ing may come to you from the presence of the Lord; and He shall send Jesus Christ, prepared for you beforehand,[1] whom the heaven must indeed receive until the times of the arrangement[2] of all things, of which God hath spoken by His holy prophets. For Moses truly said unto our fathers, Your Lord God shall raise up to you a Prophet from your brethren, like unto me; Him shall ye hear in all things whatsoever He shall say unto you. And it shall come to pass, that every soul, whosoever will not hear that Prophet, shall be destroyed from among the people. And all [the prophets] from Samuel, and henceforth, as many as have spoken, have likewise foretold of these days. Ye are the children of the prophets, and of the covenant which God made with our fathers, saying unto Abraham, And in thy seed shall all the kindreds of the earth be blessed. Unto you first, God, having raised up His Son, sent Him blessing you, that each may turn himself from his iniquities."[3] Peter, together with John, preached to them this plain message of glad tidings, that the promise which God made to the fathers had been fulfilled by Jesus; not certainly proclaiming another god, but the Son of God, who also was made man, and suffered; thus leading Israel into knowledge, and through Jesus preaching the resurrection of the dead,[4] and showing, that whatever the prophets had proclaimed as to the suffering of Christ, these had God fulfilled.

4. For this reason, too, when the chief priests were assembled, Peter, full of boldness, said to them, "Ye rulers of the people, and elders of Israel, if we this day be examined by you of the good deed done to the impotent man, by what means he has been made whole; be it known to you all, and to all the people of Israel, that by the name of Jesus Christ of Nazareth, whom ye crucified, whom God raised from the dead, even by Him doth this man stand here before you whole. This is the stone which was set at nought of you builders, which is become the head-stone of the corner. [Neither is there salvation in any other: for] there is none other name under heaven, which is given to men, whereby we must be saved."[5] Thus the apostles did not change God, but preached to the people that Christ was Jesus the crucified One, whom the same God that had sent the prophets, being God Himself, raised up, and gave in Him salvation to men.

5. They were confounded, therefore, both by this instance of healing ("for the man was above forty years old on whom this miracle of healing took place "[6]), and by the doctrine of the apostles, and by the exposition of the prophets, when the chief priests had sent away Peter and John. [These latter] returned to the rest of their fellow-apostles and disciples of the Lord, that is, to the Church, and related what had occurred, and how courageously they had acted in the name of Jesus. The whole Church, it is then said, "when they had heard that, lifted up the voice to God with one accord, and said, Lord, Thou art God, which hast made heaven, and earth, and the sea, and all that in them is; who, through the Holy Ghost,[7] by the mouth of our father David, Thy servant, hast said, Why did the heathen rage, and the people imagine vain things? The kings of the earth stood up, and the rulers were gathered together against the Lord, and against His Christ. For of a truth, in this city,[8] against Thy holy Son Jesus, whom Thou hast anointed, both Herod and Pontius Pilate, with the Gentiles, and the people of Israel, were gathered together, to do whatsoever Thy hand and Thy counsel determined before to be done."[9] These [are the] voices of the Church from which every Church had its origin; these are the voices of the metropolis of the citizens of the new covenant; these are the voices of the apostles; these are voices of the disciples of the Lord, the truly perfect, who, after the assumption of the Lord, were perfected by the Spirit, and called upon the God who made heaven, and earth, and the sea, — who was announced by the prophets, — and Jesus Christ His Son, whom God anointed, and who knew no other [God]. For at that time and place there was neither Valentinus, nor Marcion, nor the rest of these subverters [of the truth], and their adherents. Wherefore God, the Maker of all things, heard them. For it is said, "The place was shaken where they were assembled together; and they were all filled with the Holy Ghost, and they spake the word of God with boldness "[10] to every one that was willing to believe.[11] "And with great power," it is added, "gave the apostles witness of the resurrection of the Lord Jesus,"[12] saying to them, "The God of our fathers raised up Jesus, whom ye seized and slew, hanging [Him] upon a beam of wood: Him hath God raised up by His right hand [13] to be a Prince and Saviour, to give repentance to Israel, and

---

[1] Irenæus, like the majority of the early authorities, manifestly read προκεχειρισμένον instead of προκεκηρυγμένον, as in *textus receptus*.
[2] Dispositionis.
[3] Acts iii. 12, etc.
[4] Acts iv. 2.
[5] Acts iv. 8, etc.
[6] Acts iv. 22.
[7] These words, though not in *textus receptus*, are found in some ancient mss. and versions; but not the words "our father," which follow.
[8] "In hac civitate" are words not represented in the *textus receptus*, but have a place in all modern critical editions of the New Testament.
[9] Acts iv. 24, etc.
[10] Acts iv. 31.
[11] The Latin is, "ut convertat se unusquisque."
[12] Acts iv. 33.
[13] This is following Grabe's emendation of the text. The old Latin reads "gloria sua," the translator having evidently mistaken δεξιᾷ for δόξῃ.

forgiveness of sins. And we are in this witnesses of these words; as also is the Holy Ghost, whom God hath given to them that believe in Him."[1] "And daily," it is said, "in the temple, and from house to house, they ceased not to teach and preach Christ Jesus,"[2] the Son of God. For this was the knowledge of salvation, which renders those who acknowledge His Son's advent perfect towards God.

6. But as some of these men impudently assert that the apostles, when preaching among the Jews, could not declare to them another god besides Him in whom they (their hearers[3]) believed, we say to them, that if the apostles used to speak to people in accordance with the opinion instilled into them of old, no one learned the truth from them, nor, at a much earlier date, from the Lord; for they say that He did Himself speak after the same fashion. Wherefore neither do these men themselves know the truth; but since such was their opinion regarding God, they had just received doctrine as they were able to hear it. According to this manner of speaking, therefore, the rule of truth can be with nobody; but all learners will ascribe this practice to all [teachers], that just as every person thought, and as far as his capability extended, so was also the language addressed to him. But the advent of the Lord will appear superfluous and useless, if He did indeed come intending to tolerate and to preserve each man's idea regarding God rooted in him from of old. Besides this, also, it was a much heavier task, that He whom the Jews had seen as a man, and had fastened to the cross, should be preached as Christ the Son of God, their eternal King. Since this, however, was so, they certainly did not speak to them in accordance with their old belief. For they, who told them to their face that they were the slayers of the Lord, would themselves also much more boldly preach that Father who is above the Demiurge, and not what each individual bid himself believe [respecting God]; and the sin was much less, if indeed they had not fastened to the cross the superior Saviour (to whom it behoved them to ascend), since He was impassible. For, as they did not speak to the Gentiles in compliance with their notions, but told them with boldness that their gods were no gods, but the idols of demons; so would they in like manner have preached to the Jews, if they had known another greater or more perfect Father, not nourishing nor strengthening the untrue opinion of these men regarding God. Moreover, while destroying the error of the Gentiles, and bearing them away from their gods, they did not certainly induce another error upon them; but, removing those which were no gods, they pointed out Him who alone was God and the true Father.

7. From the words of Peter, therefore, which he addressed in Cæsarea to Cornelius the centurion, and those Gentiles with him, to whom the word of God was first preached, we can understand what the apostles used to preach, the nature of their preaching, and their idea with regard to God. Eor this Cornelius was, it is said, "a devout man, and one who feared God with all his house, giving much alms to the people, and praying to God always. He saw therefore, about the ninth hour of the day, an angel of God coming in to him, and saying, Thine alms are come up for a memorial before God. Wherefore send to Simon, who is called Peter."[4] But when Peter saw the vision, in which the voice from heaven said to him, "What God hath cleansed, that call not thou common,"[5] this happened [to teach him] that the God who had, through the law, distinguished between clean and unclean, was He who had purified the Gentiles through the blood of His Son — He whom also Cornelius worshipped; to whom Peter, coming in, said, "Of a truth I perceive that God is no respecter of persons: but in every nation, he that feareth Him, and worketh righteousness, is acceptable to Him."[6] He thus clearly indicates, that He whom Cornelius had previously feared as God, of whom he had heard through the law and the prophets, for whose sake also he used to give alms, is, in truth, God. the knowledge of the Son was, however, wanting to him; therefore did [Peter] add, "The word, ye know, which was published throughout all Judea, beginning from Galilee, after the baptism which John preached, Jesus of Nazareth, how God anointed Him with the Holy Ghost, and with power; who went about doing good, and healing all that were oppressed of the devil; for God was with Him. And we are witnesses of all those things which He did both in the land of the Jews and in Jerusalem; whom they slew, hanging Him on a beam of wood: Him God raised up the third day, and showed Him openly; not to all the people, but unto us, witnesses chosen before of God, who did eat and drink with Him after the resurrection from the dead. And He commanded us to preach unto the people, and to testify that it is He which was ordained of God to be the Judge of quick and dead. To Him give all the prophets witness, that, through His name, every one that believeth in Him does receive remission of sins."[7] The apostles, therefore, did preach the Son of God, of whom men were ignorant; and His advent, to those

---

[1] Acts v. 30.
[2] Acts v. 42.
[3] These words have apparently been omitted through inadvertence.
[4] Acts x. 1-5.
[5] Acts x. 15.
[6] Acts x. 34, 35.
[7] Acts x. 37-44.

who had been already instructed as to God; but they did not bring in another god. For if Peter had known any such thing, he would have preached freely to the Gentiles, that the God of the Jews was indeed one, but the God of the Christians another; and all of them, doubtless, being awe-struck because of the vision of the angel, would have believed whatever he told them. But it is evident from Peter's words that he did indeed still retain the God who was already known to them; but he also bare witness to them that Jesus Christ was the Son of God, the Judge of quick and dead, into whom he did also command them to be baptized for the remission of sins; and not this alone, but he witnessed that Jesus was Himself the Son of God, who also, having been anointed with the Holy Spirit, is called Jesus Christ. And He is the same being that was born of Mary, as the testimony of Peter implies. Can it really be, that Peter was not at that time as yet in possession of the perfect knowledge which these men discovered afterwards? According to them, therefore, Peter was imperfect, and the rest of the apostles were imperfect; and so it would be fitting that they, coming to life again, should become disciples of these men, in order that they too might be made perfect. But this is truly ridiculous. These men, in fact, are proved to be not disciples of the apostles, but of their own wicked notions. To this cause also are due the various opinions which exist among them, inasmuch as each one adopted error just as he was capable [1] [of embracing it]. But the Church throughout all the world, having its origin firm from the apostles, perseveres in one and the same opinion with regard to God and His Son.

8. But again: Whom did Philip preach to the eunuch of the queen of the Ethiopians, returning from Jerusalem, and reading Esaias the prophet, when he and this man were alone together? Was it not He of whom the prophet spoke: "He was led as a sheep to the slaughter, and as a lamb dumb before the shearer, so He opened not the mouth?" "But who shall declare His nativity? for His life shall be taken away from the earth." [2] [Philip declared] that this was Jesus, and that the Scripture was fulfilled in Him; as did also the believing eunuch himself: and, immediately requesting to be baptized, he said, "I believe Jesus Christ to be the Son of God." [3] This man was also sent into the regions of Ethiopia, to preach what he had himself believed, that there was one God preached by the prophets, but that the Son of this [God] had already made [His] appearance in human nature (*secundum hominem*), and had been led as a sheep to the slaughter; and all the other statements which the prophets made regarding Him.

9. Paul himself also — after that the Lord spoke to him out of heaven, and showed him that, in persecuting His disciples, he persecuted his own Lord, and sent Ananias to him that he might recover his sight, and be baptized — "preached," it is said, "Jesus in the synagogues at Damascus, with all freedom of speech, that this is the Son of God, the Christ." [4] This is the mystery which he says was made known to him by revelation, that He who suffered under Pontius Pilate, the same is Lord of all, and King, and God, and Judge, receiving power from Him who is the God of all, because He became "obedient unto death, even the death of the cross." [5] And inasmuch as this is true, when preaching to the Athenians on the Areopagus — where, no Jews being present, he had it in his power to preach God with freedom of speech — he said to them: "God, who made the world, and all things therein, He, being Lord of heaven and earth, dwelleth not in temples made with hands; neither is He touched [6] by men's hands, as though He needed anything, seeing He giveth to all life, and breath, and all things; who hath made from one blood the whole race of men to dwell upon the face of the whole earth,[7] predetermining the times according to the boundary of their habitation, to seek the Deity, if by any means they might be able to track Him out, or find Him, although He be not far from each of us. For in Him we live, and move, and have our being, as certain men of your own have said, For we are also His offspring. Inasmuch, then, as we are the offspring of God, we ought not to think that the Deity is like unto gold or silver, or stone graven by art or man's device. Therefore God, winking at the times of ignorance, does now command all men everywhere to turn to Him with repentance; because He hath appointed a day, on which the world shall be judged in righteousness by the man Jesus; whereof He hath given assurance by raising Him from the dead." [8] Now in this passage he does not only declare to them God as the Creator of the world, no Jews being present, but that He did also make one race of men to dwell upon all the earth; as also Moses declared: "When the Most High divided the nations, as He scattered the sons of Adam, He set the bounds of the nations after the number of the angels of God;" [9] but

---

[1] *Quemadmodum capiebat;* perhaps, "just as it presented itself to him."
[2] Acts viii. 32; Isa. liii. 7, 8.
[3] Acts viii. 37.
[4] Acts ix. 20.
[5] Phil. ii. 8.
[6] Latin translation, *tractatur;* which Harvey thinks affords a conclusive proof that Irenæus occasionally quotes Scripture by retranslating from the Syriac.
[7] It will be observed that Scripture is here very loosely quoted.
[8] Acts xvii. 24, etc.
[9] Deut. xxxii. 8 [LXX.].

that people which believes in God is not now under the power of angels, but under the Lord's [rule]. "For His people Jacob was made the portion of the Lord, Israel the cord of His inheritance."[1] And again, at Lystra of Lycia (Lycaonia), when Paul was with Barnabas, and in the name of our Lord Jesus Christ had made a man to walk who had been lame from his birth, and when the crowd wished to honour them as gods because of the astonishing deed, he said to them: "We are men like unto you, preaching to you God, that ye may be turned away from these vain idols to [serve] the living God, who made heaven, and earth, and the sea, and all things that are therein; who in times past suffered all nations to walk in their own ways, although He left not Himself without witness, performing acts of goodness, giving you rain from heaven, and fruitful seasons, filling your hearts with food and gladness."[2] But that all his Epistles are consonant to these declarations, I shall, when expounding the apostle, show from the Epistles themselves, in the right place. But while I bring out by these proofs the truths of Scripture, and set forth briefly and compendiously things which are stated in various ways, do thou also attend to them with patience, and not deem them prolix; taking this into account, that proofs [of the things which are] contained in the Scriptures cannot be shown except from the Scriptures themselves.

10. And still further, Stephen, who was chosen the first deacon by the apostles, and who, of all men, was the first to follow the footsteps of the martyrdom of the Lord, being the first that was slain for confessing Christ, speaking boldly among the people, and teaching them, says: "The God of glory appeared to our father Abraham, . . . and said to him, Get thee out of thy country, and from thy kindred, and come into the land which I shall show thee; . . . and He removed him into this land, wherein ye now dwell. And He gave him none inheritance in it, no, not so much as to set his foot on; yet He promised that He would give it to him for a possession, and to his seed after him. . . . And God spake on this wise, That his seed should sojourn in a strange land, and should be brought into bondage, and should be evil-entreated four hundred years; and the nation whom they shall serve will I judge, says the Lord. And after that shall they come forth, and serve me in this place. And He gave him the covenant of circumcision: and so [Abraham] begat Isaac."[3] And the rest of his words announce the same God, who was with Joseph and with the patriarchs, and who spake with Moses.

11. And that the whole range of the doctrine of the apostles proclaimed one and the same God, who removed Abraham, who made to him the promise of inheritance, who in due season gave to him the covenant of circumcision, who called his descendants out of Egypt, preserved outwardly by circumcision — for he gave it as a sign, that they might not be like the Egyptians — that He was the Maker of all things, that He was the Father of our Lord Jesus Christ, that He was the God of glory, — they who wish may learn from the very words and acts of the apostles, and may contemplate the fact that this God is one, above whom is no other. But even if there were another god above Him, we should say, upon [instituting] a comparison of the quantity [of the work done by each], that the latter is superior to the former. For by deeds the better man appears, as I have already remarked;[4] and, inasmuch as these men have no works of their father to adduce, the latter is shown to be God alone. But if any one, "doting about questions,"[5] do imagine that what the apostles have declared about God should be allegorized, let him consider my previous statements, in which I set forth one God as the Founder and Maker of all things, and destroyed and laid bare their allegations; and he shall find them agreeable to the doctrine of the apostles, and so to maintain what they used to teach, and were persuaded of, that there is one God, the Maker of all things. And when he shall have divested his mind of such error, and of that blasphemy against God which it implies, he will of himself find reason to acknowledge that both the Mosaic law and the grace of the new covenant, as both fitted for the times [at which they were given], were bestowed by one and the same God for the benefit of the human race.

12. For all those who are of a perverse mind, having been set against the Mosaic legislation, judging it to be dissimilar and contrary to the doctrine of the Gospel, have not applied themselves to investigate the causes of the difference of each covenant. Since, therefore, they have been deserted by the paternal love, and puffed up by Satan, being brought over to the doctrine of Simon Magus, they have apostatized in their opinions from Him who is God, and imagined that they have themselves discovered more than the apostles, by finding out another god; and [maintained] that the apostles preached the Gospel still somewhat under the influence of Jewish opinions, but that they themselves are purer [in doctrine], and more intelligent, than the apostles. Wherefore also Marcion and his followers have betaken themselves to mutilating the Scriptures, not acknowledging some books

---

[1] Deut. xxxii. 9.
[2] Acts xiv. 15-17.
[3] Acts vii. 2-8.
[4] Book ii. ch. xxx. 2.
[5] 1 Tim. vi. 4.

at all; and, curtailing the Gospel according to Luke and the Epistles of Paul, they assert that these are alone authentic, which they have themselves thus shortened. In another work,[1] however, I shall, God granting [me strength], refute them out of these which they still retain. But all the rest, inflated with the false name of "knowledge," do certainly recognise the Scriptures; but they pervert the interpretations, as I have shown in the first book. And, indeed, the followers of Marcion do directly blaspheme the Creator, alleging him to be the creator of evils, [but] holding a more tolerable[2] theory as to his origin, [and] maintaining that there are two beings, gods by nature, differing from each other,—the one being good, but the other evil. Those from Valentinus, however, while they employ names of a more honourable kind, and set forth that He who is Creator is both Father, and Lord, and God, do [nevertheless] render their theory or sect more plasphemous, by maintaining that He was not produced from any one of those Æons within the Pleroma, but from that defect which had been expelled beyond the Pleroma. Ignorance of the Scriptures and of the dispensation of God has brought all these things upon them. And in the course of this work I shall touch upon the cause of the difference of the covenants on the one hand, and, on the other hand, of their unity and harmony.

13. But that both the apostles and their disciples thus taught as the Church preaches, and thus teaching were perfected, wherefore also they were called away to that which is perfect—Stephen, teaching these truths, when he was yet on earth, saw the glory of God, and Jesus on His right hand, and exclaimed, "Behold, I see the heavens opened, and the Son of man standing on the right hand of God."[3] These words he said, and was stoned; and thus did he fulfil the perfect doctrine, copying in every respect the Leader of martyrdom, and praying for those who were slaying him, in these words: "Lord, lay not this sin to their charge." Thus were they perfected who knew one and the same God, who from beginning to end was present with mankind in the various dispensations; as the prophet Hosea declares: "I have filled up visions, and used similitudes by the hands of the prophets."[4] Those, therefore, who delivered up their souls to death for Christ's Gospel—how could they have spoken to men in accordance with old-established opinion? If this had been the course adopted by them, they should not have suffered; but inasmuch as they did preach things contrary to those persons who did not assent to the truth, for that reason they suffered. It is evident, therefore, that they did not relinquish the truth, but with all boldness preached to the Jews and Greeks. To the Jews, indeed, [they proclaimed] that the Jesus who was crucified by them was the Son of God, the Judge of quick and dead, and that He has received from His Father an eternal kingdom in Israel, as I have pointed out; but to the Greeks they preached one God, who made all things, and Jesus Christ His Son.

14. This is shown in a still clearer light from the letter of the apostles, which they forwarded neither to the Jews nor to the Greeks, but to those who from the Gentiles believed in Christ, confirming their faith. For when certain men had come down from Judea to Antioch—where also, first of all, the Lord's disciples were called Christians, because of their faith in Christ—and sought to persuade those who had believed on the Lord to be circumcised, and to perform other things after the observance of the law; and when Paul and Barnabas had gone up to Jerusalem to the apostles on account of this question, and the whole Church had convened together, Peter thus addressed them: "Men, brethren, ye know how that from the days of old God made choice among you, that the Gentiles by my mouth should hear the word of the Gospel, and believe. And God, the Searcher of the heart, bare them witness, giving them the Holy Ghost, even as to us; and put no difference between us and them, purifying their hearts by faith. Now therefore why tempt ye God, to impose a yoke upon the neck of the disciples, which neither our fathers nor we were able to bear? But we believe that, through the grace of our Lord Jesus Christ, we are to be saved, even as they."[5] After him James spoke as follows: "Men, brethren, Simon hath declared how God did purpose to take from among the Gentiles a people for His name. And thus[6] do the words of the prophets agree, as it is written, After this I will return, and will build again the tabernacle of David, which is fallen down; and I will build the ruins thereof, and I will set it up: that the residue of men may seek after the Lord, and all the Gentiles, among whom my name has been invoked, saith the Lord, doing these things.[7] Known from eternity is His work to God. Wherefore I for my part give judgment, that we trouble not them who from among the Gentiles are turned to God: but that it be enjoined them, that they

---

[1] No reference is made to this promised work in the writings of his successors. Probably it never was undertaken.
[2] Most of the MSS. read "intolerabiliorem," but one reads as above, and is followed by all the editors.
[3] Acts vii. 56.
[4] Hos. xii. 10.
[5] Acts xv. 15, etc.
[6] Irenæus manifestly read οὕτως for τούτῳ, and in this he agrees with Codex Bezæ. We may remark, once for all, that in the variations from the received text of the New Testament which occur in our author, his quotations are very often in accordance with the readings of the Cambridge MS.
[7] Amos ix. 11, 12.

do abstain from the vanities of idols, and from fornication, and from blood; and whatsoever[1] they wish not to be done to themselves, let them not do to others."[2] And when these things had been said, and all had given their consent, they wrote to them after this manner: "The apostles, and the presbyters, [and] the brethren, unto those brethren from among the Gentiles who are in Antioch, and Syria, and Cilicia, greeting: Forasmuch as we have heard that certain persons going out from us have troubled you with words, subverting your souls, saying, Ye must be circumcised, and keep the law; to whom we gave no such commandment: it seemed good unto us, being assembled with one accord, to send chosen men unto you with our beloved Barnabas and Paul; men who have delivered up their soul for the name of our Lord Jesus Christ. We have sent therefore Judas and Silas, that they may declare our opinion by word of mouth. For it seemed good to the Holy Ghost, and to us, to lay upon you no greater burden than these necessary things; that ye abstain from meats offered to idols, and from blood, and from fornication; and whatsoever ye do not wish to be done to you, do not ye to others: from which preserving yourselves, ye shall do well, walking[3] in the Holy Spirit." From all these passages, then, it is evident that they did not teach the existence of another Father, but gave the new covenant of liberty to those who had lately believed in God by the Holy Spirit. But they clearly indicated, from the nature of the point debated by them, as to whether or not it were still necessary to circumcise the disciples, that they had no idea of another god.

15. Neither [in that case] would they have had such a terror with regard to the first covenant, as not even to have been willing to eat with the Gentiles. For even Peter, although he had been sent to instruct them, and had been constrained by a vision to that effect, spake nevertheless with not a little hesitation, saying to them: "Ye know how it is an unlawful thing for a man that is a Jew to keep company with, or to come unto, one of another nation; but God hath shown me that I should not call any man common or unclean. Therefore came I without gainsaying;"[4] indicating by these words, that he would not have come to them unless he had been commanded. Neither, for a like reason, would he have given them baptism so readily, had he not heard them prophesying when the Holy Ghost rested upon them. And therefore did he exclaim, "Can any man forbid water, that these should not be baptized, who have received the Holy Ghost as well as we?"[5] He persuaded, at the same time, those that were with him, and pointed out that, unless the Holy Ghost had rested upon them, there might have been some one who would have raised objections to their baptism. And the apostles who were with James allowed the Gentiles to act freely, yielding us up to the Spirit of God. But they themselves, while knowing the same God, continued in the ancient observances; so that even Peter, fearing also lest he might incur their reproof, although formerly eating with the Gentiles, because of the vision, and of the Spirit who had rested upon them, yet, when certain persons came from James, withdrew himself, and did not eat with them. And Paul said that Barnabas likewise did the same thing.[6] Thus did the apostles, whom the Lord made witnesses of every action and of every doctrine — for upon all occasions do we find Peter, and James, and John present with Him — scrupulously act according to the dispensation of the Mosaic law, showing that it was from one and the same God; which they certainly never would have done, as I have already said, if they had learned from the Lord [that there existed] another Father besides Him who appointed the dispensation of the law.

CHAP. XIII — REFUTATION OF THE OPINION, THAT PAUL WAS THE ONLY APOSTLE WHO HAD KNOWLEDGE OF THE TRUTH.

1. With regard to those (the Marcionites) who allege that Paul alone knew the truth, and that to him the mystery was manifested by revelation, let Paul himself convict them, when he says, that one and the same God wrought in Peter for the apostolate of the circumcision, and in himself for the Gentiles.[7] Peter, therefore, was an apostle of that very God whose was also Paul; and Him whom Peter preached as God among those of the circumcision, and likewise the Son of God, did Paul [declare] also among the Gentiles. For our Lord never came to save Paul alone, nor is God so limited in means, that He should have but one apostle who knew the dispensation of His Son. And again, when Paul says, "How beautiful are the feet of those bringing glad tidings of good things, and preaching the Gospel of peace,"[8] he shows clearly that it was not merely one, but there were many who used to preach the truth. And again, in the Epistle to the Corinthians, when he had recounted all those who had seen God[9] after the resurrection, he

---

[1] This addition is also found in Codex Bezæ, and in Cyprian and others.
[2] Acts xv. 14, etc.
[3] Another addition, also found in the Codex Bezæ, and in Tertullian.
[4] Acts x. 28, 29.
[5] Acts x. 47.
[6] Gal. ii. 12, 13.
[7] Gal. ii. 8.
[8] Rom. x. 15; Isa. lii. 7.
[9] All the previous editors accept the reading *Deum* without remark, but Harvey argues that it must be regarded as a mistake for *Dominum*. He scarcely seems, however, to give sufficient weight to the quotation which immediately follows.

says in continuation, "But whether it were I or they, so we preach, and so ye believed,"[1] acknowledging as one and the same, the preaching of all those who saw God[2] after the resurrection from the dead.

2. And again, the Lord replied to Philip, who wished to behold the Father, "Have I been so long a time with you, and yet thou hast not known Me, Philip? He that sees Me, sees also the Father; and how sayest thou then, Show us the Father? For I am in the Father, and the Father in Me; and henceforth ye know Him, and have seen Him."[3] To these men, therefore, did the Lord bear witness, that in Himself they had both known and seen the Father (and the Father is truth). To allege, then, that these men did not know the truth, is to act the part of false witnesses, and of those who have been alienated from the doctrine of Christ. For why did the Lord send the twelve apostles to the lost sheep of the house of Israel,[4] if these men did not know the truth? How also did the seventy preach, unless they had themselves previously known the truth of what was preached? Or how could Peter have been in ignorance, to whom the Lord gave testimony, that flesh and blood had not revealed to him, but the Father, who is in heaven?[5] Just, then, as "Paul [was] an apostle, not of men, neither by man, but by Jesus Christ, and God the Father,"[6] [so with the rest;][7] the Son indeed leading them to the Father, but the Father revealing to them the Son.

3. But that Paul acceded to [the request of] those who summoned him to the apostles, on account of the question [which had been raised], and went up to them, with Barnabas, to Jerusalem, not without reason, but that the liberty of the Gentiles might be confirmed by them, he does himself say, in the Epistle to the Galatians: "Then, fourteen years after, I went up again to Jerusalem with Barnabas, taking also Titus. But I went up by revelation, and communicated to them that Gospel which I preached among the Gentiles."[8] And again he says, "For an hour we did give place to subjection,[9] that the truth of the gospel might continue with you." If, then, any one shall, from the Acts of the Apostles, carefully scrutinize the time concerning which it is written that he went up to Jerusalem on account of the forementioned question, he will find those years mentioned by Paul coinciding with it. Thus the statement of Paul harmonizes with, and is, as it were, identical with, the testimony of Luke regarding the apostles.

CHAP. XIV. — IF PAUL HAD KNOWN ANY MYSTERIES UNREVEALED TO THE OTHER APOSTLES, LUKE, HIS CONSTANT COMPANION AND FELLOW-TRAVELLER, COULD NOT HAVE BEEN IGNORANT OF THEM; NEITHER COULD THE TRUTH HAVE POSSIBLY LAIN HID FROM HIM, THROUGH WHOM ALONE WE LEARN MANY AND MOST IMPORTANT PARTICULARS OF THE GOSPEL HISTORY.

1. But that this Luke was inseparable from Paul, and his fellow-labourer in the Gospel, he himself clearly evinces, not as a matter of boasting, but as bound to do so by the truth itself. For he says that when Barnabas, and John who was called Mark, had parted company from Paul, and sailed to Cyprus, "we came to Troas;"[10] and when Paul had beheld in a dream a man of Macedonia, saying, "Come into Macedonia, Paul, and help us," "immediately," he says, "we endeavoured to go into Macedonia, understanding that the Lord had called us to preach the Gospel unto them. Therefore, sailing from Troas, we directed our ship's course towards Samothracia." And then he carefully indicates all the rest of their journey as far as Philippi, and how they delivered their first address: "for, sitting down," he says, "we spake unto the women who had assembled;"[11] and certain believed, even a great many. And again does he say, "But we sailed from Philippi after the days of unleavened bread, and came to Troas, where we abode seven days."[12] And all the remaining [details] of his course with Paul he recounts, indicating with all diligence both places, and cities, and number of days, until they went up to Jerusalem; and what befell Paul there,[13] how he was sent to Rome in bonds; the name of the centurion who took him in charge;[14] and the signs of the ships, and how they made shipwreck;[15] and the island upon which they escaped, and how they received kindness there, Paul healing the chief man of that island; and how they sailed from thence to Puteoli, and from that arrived at Rome; and for what period they sojourned at Rome. As Luke was present at all these occurrences, he carefully noted them down in writing, so that he cannot be convicted of falsehood or boastfulness, because all these [particulars] proved both that he was senior to all those who now teach otherwise, and that he was not ignorant of the truth. That he

---

[1] 1 Cor. xv. 11.
[2] See note 9, p. 436.
[3] John xiv. 7, 9, 10.
[4] Matt. x. 6.
[5] Matt. xvi. 17.
[6] Gal. i. 1.
[7] Some such supplement seems necessary, as Grabe suggests, though Harvey contends that no apodosis is requisite.
[8] Gal. ii. 1, 2.
[9] Latin, "Ad horam cessimus subjectioni" (Gal. ii. 5). Irenæus gives it an altogether different meaning from that which it has in the received text. Jerome says that there was as much variation in the copies of Scripture in his day with regard to the passage, — some retaining, others rejecting the negative. Tertullian argues for the removal of the negative (*Adv. Marc.* v. 3).
[10] Acts xvi. 8, etc.
[11] Acts xvi. 13.
[12] Acts xx. 5, 6.
[13] Acts xxi.
[14] Acts xxvii.
[15] Acts xxviii. 11.

was not merely a follower, but also a fellow-labourer of the apostles, but especially of Paul, Paul has himself declared also in the Epistles, saying: "Demas hath forsaken me, . . . and is departed unto Thessalonica; Crescens to Galatia, Titus to Dalmatia. Only Luke is with me."[1] From this he shows that he was always attached to and inseparable from him. And again he says, in the Epistle to the Colossians: "Luke, the beloved physician, greets you."[2] But surely if Luke, who always preached in company with Paul, and is called by him "the beloved," and with him performed the work of an evangelist, and was entrusted to hand down to us a Gospel, learned nothing different from him (Paul), as has been pointed out from his words, how can these men, who were never attached to Paul, boast that they have learned hidden and unspeakable mysteries?

2. But that Paul taught with simplicity what he knew, not only to those who were [employed] with him, but to those that heard him, he does himself make manifest. For when the bishops and presbyters who came from Ephesus and the other cities adjoining had assembled in Miletus, since he was himself hastening to Jerusalem to observe Pentecost, after testifying many things to them, and declaring what must happen to him at Jerusalem, he added: "I know that ye shall see my face no more. Therefore I take you to record this day, that I am pure from the blood of all. For I have not shunned to declare unto you all the counsel of God. Take heed, therefore, both to yourselves, and to all the flock over which the Holy Ghost has placed you as bishops, to rule the Church of the Lord,[3] which He has acquired for Himself through His own blood."[4] Then, referring to the evil teachers who should arise, he said: "I know that after my departure shall grievous wolves come to you, not sparing the flock. Also of your own selves shall men arise, speaking perverse things, to draw away disciples after them." "I have not shunned," he says, "to declare unto you all the counsel of God." Thus did the apostles simply, and without respect of persons, deliver to all what they had themselves learned from the Lord. Thus also does Luke, without respect of persons, deliver to us what he had learned from them, as he has himself testified, saying, "Even as they delivered them unto us, who from the beginning were eye-witnesses and ministers of the Word."[5]

3. Now if any man set Luke aside, as one who did not know the truth, he will, [by so acting,] manifestly reject that Gospel of which he claims to be a disciple. For through him we have become acquainted with very many and important parts of the Gospel; for instance, the generation of John, the history of Zacharias, the coming of the angel to Mary, the exclamation of Elisabeth, the descent of the angels to the shepherds, the words spoken by them, the testimony of Anna and of Simeon with regard to Christ, and that at twelve years of age He was left behind at Jerusalem; also the baptism of John, the number of the Lord's years when He was baptized, and that this occurred in the fifteenth year of Tiberius Cæsar. And in His office of teacher this is what He has said to the rich: "Woe unto you that are rich, for ye have received your consolation;"[6] and, "Woe unto you that are full, for ye shall hunger; and ye who laugh now, for ye shall weep;" and, "Woe unto you when all men shall speak well of you: for so did your fathers to the false prophets." All things of the following kind we have known through Luke alone (and numerous actions of the Lord we have learned through him, which also all [the Evangelists] notice): the multitude of fishes which Peter's companions enclosed, when at the Lord's command they cast the nets;[7] the woman who had suffered for eighteen years, and was healed on the Sabbath-day;[8] the man who had the dropsy, whom the Lord made whole on the Sabbath, and how He did defend Himself for having performed an act of healing on that day; how He taught His disciples not to aspire to the uppermost rooms; how we should invite the poor and feeble, who cannot recompense us; the man who knocked during the night to obtain loaves, and did obtain them, because of the urgency of his importunity;[9] how, when [our Lord] was sitting at meat with a Pharisee, a woman that was a sinner kissed His feet, and anointed them with ointment, with what the Lord said to Simon on her behalf concerning the two debtors;[10] also about the parable of that rich man who stored up the goods which had accrued to him, to whom it was also said, "In this night they shall demand thy soul from thee; whose then shall those things be which thou hast prepared?"[11] and similar to this, that of the rich man, who was clothed in purple and who fared sumptuously, and the indigent Lazarus;[12] also the answer which He gave to His disciples when they said, "Increase our faith;"[13] also His conversation with Zaccheus the publican;[14] also about

---

[1] 2 Tim. iv. 10, 11.
[2] Col. iv. 14.
[3] In this very important passage of Scripture, Irenæus manifestly read Κυρίου instead of Θεοῦ, which is found in *text. rec.* The Codex Bezæ has the same reading; but all the other most ancient MSS. agree with the received text.
[4] Acts xx. 25, etc.
[5] Luke i. 2.
[6] Luke vi. 24, etc.
[7] Luke v.
[8] Luke xiii.
[9] Luke xi.
[10] Luke vii.
[11] Luke xii. 20.
[12] Luke xvi.
[13] Luke xvii. 5.
[14] Luke xix.

the Pharisee and the publican, who were praying in the temple at the same time;[1] also the ten lepers, whom He cleansed in the way simultaneously;[2] also how He ordered the lame and the blind to be gathered to the wedding from the lanes and streets;[3] also the parable of the judge who feared not God, whom the widow's importunity led to avenge her cause;[4] and about the fig-tree in the vineyard which produced no fruit. There are also many other particulars to be found mentioned by Luke alone, which are made use of by both Marcion and Valentinus. And besides all these, [he records] what [Christ] said to His disciples in the way, after* the resurrection, and how they recognised Him in the breaking of bread.[5]

4. It follows then, as of course, that these men must either receive the rest of his narrative, or else reject these parts also. For no persons of common sense can permit them to receive some things recounted by Luke as being true, and to set others aside, as if he had not known the truth. And if indeed Marcion's followers reject these, they will then possess no Gospel; for, curtailing that according to Luke, as I have said already, they boast in having the Gospel [in what remains]. But the followers of Valentinus must give up their utterly vain talk; for they have taken from that [Gospel] many occasions for their own speculations, to put an evil interpretation upon what he has well said. If, on the other hand, they feel compelled to receive the remaining portions also, then, by studying the perfect Gospel, and the doctrine of the apostles, they will find it necessary to repent, that they may be saved from the danger [to which they are exposed].

CHAP. XV.—REFUTATION OF THE EBIONITES, WHO DISPARAGED THE AUTHORITY OF ST. PAUL, FROM THE WRITINGS OF ST. LUKE, WHICH MUST BE RECEIVED AS A WHOLE. EXPOSURE OF THE HYPOCRISY, DECEIT, AND PRIDE OF THE GNOSTICS. THE APOSTLES AND THEIR DISCIPLES KNEW AND PREACHED ONE GOD, THE CREATOR OF THE WORLD.

1. But again, we allege the same against those who do not recognise Paul as an apostle: that they should either reject the other words of the Gospel which we have come to know through Luke alone, and not make use of them; or else, if they do receive all these, they must necessarily admit also that testimony concerning Paul, when he (Luke) tells us that the Lord spoke at first to him from heaven: "Saul, Saul, why persecutest thou Me? I am Jesus Christ, whom thou persecutest;"[6] and then to Ananias, saying regarding him: "Go thy way; for he is a chosen vessel unto Me, to bear My name among the Gentiles, and kings, and the children of Israel. For I will show him, from this time, how great things he must suffer for My name's sake."[7] Those, therefore, who do not accept of him [as a teacher], who was chosen by God for this purpose, being that he might boldly bear His name, as being sent to the forementioned nations, do despise the election of God, and separate themselves from the company of the apostles. For neither can they contend that Paul was no apostle, when he was chosen for this purpose; nor can they prove Luke guilty of falsehood, when he proclaims the truth to us with all diligence. It may be, indeed, that it was with this view that God set forth very many Gospel truths, through Luke's instrumentality, which all should esteem it necessary to use, in order that all persons, following his subsequent testimony, which treats upon the acts and the doctrine of the apostles, and holding the unadulterated rule of truth, may be saved. His testimony, therefore, is true, and the doctrine of the apostles is open and stedfast, holding nothing in reserve; nor did they teach one set of doctrines in private, and another in public.

2. For this is the subterfuge of false persons, evil seducers, and hypocrites, as they act who are from Valentinus. These men discourse to the multitude about those who belong to the Church, whom they do themselves term "vulgar," and "ecclesiastic."[8] By these words they entrap the more simple, and entice them, imitating our phraseology, that these [dupes] may listen to them the oftener; and then these are asked[9] regarding us, how it is, that when they hold doctrines similar to ours, we, without cause, keep ourselves aloof from their company; and [how it is, that] when they say the same things, and hold the same doctrine, we call them heretics? When they have thus, by means of questions, overthrown the faith of any, and rendered them uncontradicting hearers of their own, they describe to them in private the unspeakable mystery of their Pleroma. But they are altogether deceived, who imagine that they may learn from the Scriptural texts adduced by heretics, that [doctrine] which their words plausibly teach.[10] For error is plausible, and bears a re-

---

[1] Luke xviii.
[2] Luke xvii.
[3] Luke xviii.
[4] Luke xiii.
[5] Luke xxiv.
[6] Acts xxii. 8, xxvi. 15.
[7] Acts ix. 15, 16.
[8] Latin, "communes et ecclesiasticos:" καθολικούς is translated here "communes," as for some time after the word *catholicus* had not been added to the Latin language in its ecclesiastical sense. [The Roman Creed was remarkable for its omission of the word *Catholic*. See Bingham, *Antiquities*, book x. cap. iv. sect. 11.]
[9] We here follow the text of Harvey, who prints, without remark, *quæruntur*, instead of *queruntur*, as in Migne's edition.
[10] Such is the sense educed by Harvey from the old Latin version, which thus runs: "Decipiuntur autem omnes, qui quod est in verbis verisimile, se putant posse discere a veritate." For "omnes" he would read "omnino," and he discards the emendation proposed by the former editors, viz., "discernere" for "discere."

semblance to the truth, but requires to be disguised; while truth is without disguise, and therefore has been entrusted to children. And if any one of their auditors do indeed demand explanations, or start objections to them, they affirm that he is one not capable of receiving the truth, and not having from above the seed [derived] from their Mother; and thus really give him no reply, but simply declare that he is of the intermediate regions, that is, belongs to animal natures. But if any one do yield himself up to them like a little sheep, and follows out their practice, and their "redemption," such an one is puffed up to such an extent, that he thinks he is neither in heaven nor on earth, but that he has passed within the Pleroma; and having already embraced his angel, he walks with a strutting gait and a supercilious countenance, possessing all the pompous air of a cock. There are those among them who assert that that man who comes from above ought to follow a good course of conduct; wherefore they do also pretend a gravity [of demeanour] with a certain superciliousness. The majority, however, having become scoffers also, as if already perfect, and living without regard [to appearances], yea, in contempt [of that which is good], call themselves "the spiritual," and allege that they have already become acquainted with that place of refreshing which is within their Pleroma.

3. But let us revert to the same line of argument [hitherto pursued]. For when it has been manifestly declared, that they who were the preachers of the truth and the apostles of liberty termed no one else God, or named him Lord, except the only true God the Father, and His Word, who has the pre-eminence in all things; it shall then be clearly proved, that they (the apostles) confessed as the Lord God Him who was the Creator of heaven and earth, who also spoke with Moses, gave to him the dispensation of the law, and who called the fathers; and that they knew no other. The opinion of the apostles, therefore, and of those (Mark and Luke) who learned from their words, concerning God, has been made manifest.

CHAP. XVI. — PROOFS FROM THE APOSTOLIC WRITINGS, THAT JESUS CHRIST WAS ONE AND THE SAME, THE ONLY BEGOTTEN SON OF GOD, PERFECT GOD AND PERFECT MAN.

1. But[1] there are some who say that Jesus was merely a receptacle of Christ, upon whom the Christ, as a dove, descended from above, and that when He had declared the unnameable Father He entered into the Pleroma in an incomprehensible and invisible manner: for that He was not comprehended, not only by men, but not even by those powers and virtues which are in heaven, and that Jesus was the Son, but that[2] Christ was the Father, and the Father of Christ, God; while others say that He merely suffered in outward appearance, being naturally impassible. The Valentinians, again, maintain that the dispensational Jesus was the same who passed through Mary, upon whom that Saviour from the more exalted [region] descended, who was also termed *Pan*,[3] because He possessed the names (*vocabula*) of all those who had produced Him; but that [this latter] shared with Him, the dispensational one, His power and His name; so that by His means death was abolished, but the Father was made known by that Saviour who had descended from above, whom they do also allege to be Himself the receptacle of Christ and of the entire Pleroma; confessing, indeed, in tongue one Christ Jesus, but being divided in [actual] opinion: for, as I have already observed, it is the practice of these men to say that there was one Christ, who was produced by Monogenes, for the confirmation of the Pleroma; but that another, the Saviour, was sent [forth] for the glorification of the Father; and yet another, the dispensational one, and whom they represent as having suffered, who also bore [in himself] Christ, that Saviour who returned into the Pleroma. I judge it necessary therefore to take into account the entire mind of the apostles regarding our Lord Jesus Christ, and to show that not only did they never hold any such opinions regarding Him; but, still further, that they announced through the Holy Spirit, that those who should teach such doctrines were agents of Satan, sent forth for the purpose of overturning the faith of some, and drawing them away from life.

2. That John knew the one and the same Word of God, and that He was the only begotten, and that He became incarnate for our salvation, Jesus Christ our Lord, I have sufficiently proved from the word of John himself. And Matthew, too, recognising one and the same Jesus Christ, exhibiting his generation as a man from the Virgin,[4] even as God did promise David that He would raise up from the fruit of his body an eternal King, having made the same promise to Abraham a long time previously, says: "The book of the generation of Jesus Christ, the son of David, the son of Abraham."[5] Then, that he might free our mind from suspicion regarding Joseph, he says: "But the birth of Christ[6] was on this

---

[1] We here omit *since*, and insert *therefore* afterwards, to avoid the extreme length of the sentence as it stands in the Latin version. The apodosis does not occur till the words, "I judge it necessary," are reached.

[2] See book i. 12, 4.
[3] The Latin text has "Christum," which is supposed to be an erroneous reading. See also book ii. c. xii. s. 6.
[4] Ps. cxxxii. 11.
[5] Matt. i. 1.
[6] Matt. i. 18. It is to be observed that Irenæus here reads *Christ* instead of *Jesus Christ*, as in *text. rec.*, thus agreeing with the reading of the Vulgate in the passage.

wise. When His mother was espoused to Joseph, before they came together, she was found with child of the Holy Ghost." Then, when Joseph had it in contemplation to put Mary away, since she proved with child, [Matthew tells us of] the angel of God standing by him, and saying: "Fear not to take unto thee Mary thy wife: for that which is conceived in her is of the Holy Ghost. And she shall bring forth a son, and thou shalt call His name Jesus; for He shall save His people from their sins. Now this was done, that it might be fulfilled which was spoken of the Lord by the prophet: Behold, a virgin shall conceive, and bring forth a son, and they shall call His name Emmanuel, which is, God with us;" clearly signifying that both the promise made to the fathers had been accomplished, that the Son of God was born of a virgin, and that He Himself was Christ the Saviour whom the prophets had foretold; not, as these men assert, that Jesus was He who was born of Mary, but that Christ was He who descended from above. Matthew might certainly have said, "Now the birth of *Jesus* was on this wise;" but the Holy Ghost, foreseeing the corrupters [of the truth], and guarding by anticipation against their deceit, says by Matthew, "But the birth of *Christ* was on this wise;" and that He is Emmanuel, lest perchance we might consider Him as a mere man: for "not by the will of the flesh, nor by the will of man, but by the will of God, was the Word made flesh;"[1] and that we should not imagine that Jesus was one, and Christ another, but should know them to be one and the same.

3. Paul, when writing to the Romans, has explained this very point: "Paul, an apostle of Jesus Christ, predestinated unto the Gospel of God, which He had promised by His prophets in the holy Scriptures, concerning His Son, who was made to Him of the seed of David according to the flesh, who was predestinated the Son of God with power through the Spirit of holiness, by the resurrection from the dead of our Lord Jesus Christ."[2] And again, writing to the Romans about Israel, he says: "Whose are the fathers, and from whom is Christ according to the flesh, who is God over all, blessed for ever."[3] And again, in his Epistle to the Galatians, he says: "But when the fulness of time had come, God sent forth His Son, made of a woman, made under the law, to redeem them that were under the law, that we might receive the adoption;"[4] plainly indicating one God, who did by the prophets make promise of the Son, and one Jesus Christ our Lord, who was of the seed of David according to His birth from Mary; and that Jesus Christ was appointed the Son of God with power, according to the Spirit of holiness, by the resurrection from the dead, as being the first begotten in all the creation;[5] the Son of God being made the Son of man, that through Him we may receive the adoption, — humanity[6] sustaining, and receiving, and embracing the Son of God. Wherefore Mark also says: "The beginning of the Gospel of Jesus Christ, the Son of God; as it is written in the prophets."[7] Knowing one and the same Son of God, Jesus Christ, who was announced by the prophets, who from the fruit of David's body was Emmanuel, "the messenger of great counsel of the Father;"[8] through whom God caused the day-spring and the Just One to arise to the house of David, and raised up for him an horn of salvation, "and established a testimony in Jacob;"[9] as David says when discoursing on the causes of His birth: "And He appointed a law in Israel, that another generation might know [Him,] the children which should be born from these, and they arising shall themselves declare to their children, so that they might set their hope in God, and seek after His commandments."[10] And again, the angel said, when bringing good tidings to Mary: "He shall be great, and shall be called the Son of the Highest; and the Lord shall give unto Him the throne of His father David;"[11] acknowledging that He who is the Son of the Highest, the same is Himself also the Son of David. And David, knowing by the Spirit the dispensation of the advent of this Person, by which He is supreme over all the living and dead, confessed Him as Lord, sitting on the right hand of the Most High Father.[12]

4. But Simeon also — he who had received an intimation from the Holy Ghost that he should not see death, until first he had beheld Christ Jesus — taking Him, the first-begotten of the Virgin, into his hands, blessed God, and said, "Lord, now lettest Thou Thy servant depart in peace, according to Thy word: because mine eyes have seen Thy salvation, which Thou hast prepared before the face of all people; a light to lighten the Gentiles, and the glory of Thy people Israel;"[13] confessing thus, that the infant whom he was holding in his hands, Jesus, born of Mary, was Christ Himself, the Son of God, the light of all, the glory of Israel itself,

---

[1] John i. 13, 14. From this, and also a quotation of the same passage in chap. xix. of this book, it appears that Irenæus must have read ὅς . . . ἐγεννήθη here, and not οἳ . . . ἐγεννήθησαν. Tertullian quotes the verse to the same effect (*Lib. de Carne Christi*, cap. 19 and 24).
[2] Rom. i. 1–4.
[3] Rom. ix. 5.
[4] Gal. iv. 4, 5.
[5] Col. i. 14, 15.
[6] "Homine."
[7] Mark i. 1.
[8] Isa. ix. 6 (LXX.).
[9] Luke i. 69.
[10] Ps. lxxviii. 5.
[11] Luke i. 32.
[12] Ps. cx. 1.
[13] Luke ii. 29.

and the peace and refreshing of those who had fallen asleep. For He was already despoiling men, by removing their ignorance, conferring upon them His own knowledge, and scattering abroad those who recognised Him, as Esaias says: "Call His name, Quickly spoil, Rapidly divide."[1] Now these are the works of Christ. He therefore was Himself Christ, whom Simeon carrying [in his arms] blessed the Most High; on beholding whom the shepherds glorified God; whom John, while yet in his mother's womb, and He (Christ) in that of Mary, recognising as the Lord, saluted with leaping; whom the Magi, when they had seen, adored, and offered their gifts [to Him], as I have already stated, and prostrated themselves to the eternal King, departed by another way, not now returning by the way of the Assyrians. "For before the child shall have knowledge to cry, Father or mother, He shall receive the power of Damascus, and the spoils of Samaria, against the king of the Assyrians;"[2] declaring, in a mysterious manner indeed, but emphatically, that the Lord did fight with a hidden hand against Amalek.[3] For this cause, too, He suddenly removed those children belonging to the house of David, whose happy lot it was to have been born at that time, that He might send them on before into His kingdom; He, since He was Himself an infant, so arranging it that human infants should be martyrs, slain, according to the Scriptures, for the sake of Christ, who was born in Bethlehem of Judah, in the city of David.[4]

5. Therefore did the Lord also say to His disciples after the resurrection, "O thoughtless ones, and slow of heart to believe all that the prophets have spoken! Ought not Christ to have suffered these things, and to enter into His glory?"[5] And again does He say to them: "These are the words which I spake unto you while I was yet with you, that all things must be fulfilled which were written in the law of Moses, and in the prophets, and in the Psalms, concerning Me. Then opened He their understanding, that they should understand the Scriptures, and said unto them, Thus it is written, and thus it behoved Christ to suffer, and to rise again from the dead, and that repentance for the remission of sins be preached in His name among all nations."[6] Now this is He who was born of Mary; for He says: "The Son of man must suffer many things, and be rejected, and crucified, and on the third day rise again."[7] The Gospel, therefore, knew no other son of man but Him who was of Mary, who also suffered; and no Christ who flew away from Jesus before the passion; but Him who was born it knew as Jesus Christ the Son of God, and that this same suffered and rose again, as John, the disciple of the Lord, verifies, saying: "But these are written, that ye might believe that Jesus is the Christ, the Son of God, and that believing ye might have eternal life in His name,"[8] — foreseeing these blasphemous systems which divide the Lord, as far as lies in their power, saying that He was formed of two different substances. For this reason also he has thus testified to us in his Epistle: "Little children, it is the last time; and as ye have heard that Antichrist doth come, now have many antichrists appeared; whereby we know that it is the last time. They went out from us, but they were not of us; for if they had been of us, they would have continued with us: but [they departed], that they might be made manifest that they are not of us. Know ye therefore, that every lie is from without, and is not of the truth. Who is a liar, but he that denieth that Jesus is the Christ? This is Antichrist."[9]

6. But inasmuch as all those before mentioned, although they certainly do with their tongue confess one Jesus Christ, make fools of themselves, thinking one thing and saying another;[10] for their hypotheses vary, as I have already shown, alleging, [as they do,] that one Being suffered and was born, and that this was Jesus; but that there was another who descended upon Him, and that this was Christ, who also ascended again; and they argue, that he who proceeded from the Demiurge, or he who was dispensational, or he who sprang from Joseph, was the Being subject to suffering; but upon the latter there descended from the invisible and ineffable [places] the former, whom they assert to be incomprehensible, invisible, and impassible: they thus wander from the truth, because their doctrine departs from Him who is truly God, being ignorant that His only-begotten Word, who is always present with the human race, united to and mingled with His own creation, according to the Father's pleasure, and who became flesh, is Himself Jesus Christ our Lord, who did also suffer for us, and rose again on our behalf, and who will come again in the glory of His Father, to raise up all flesh, and for the manifestation of salvation, and to apply the rule of just judgment to all who were made by Him. There is therefore, as I have pointed out, one God the Father, and one Christ Jesus, who came by means of the whole dispensational arrangements [connected with Him], and gath-

---

[1] Isa. viii. 3.
[2] Isa. viii. 4.
[3] Ex. xvii. 16 (LXX.).
[4] Matt. ii. 16.
[5] Luke xxiv. 25.
[6] Luke xxiv. 44, etc.
[7] Mark viii. 31 and Luke ix. 22.
[8] John xx. 31.
[9] 1 John ii. 18, etc., loosely quoted.
[10] The text here followed is that of two Syriac MSS., which prove the loss of several consecutive words in the old Latin version, and clear up the meaning of a confused sentence, showing that the word "autem" is here, as it probably is elsewhere, merely a contraction for "aut eum."

ered together all things in Himself.[1] But in every respect, too, He is man, the formation of God; and thus He took up man into Himself, the invisible becoming visible, the incomprehensible being made comprehensible, the impassible becoming capable of suffering, and the Word being made man, thus summing up all things in Himself: so that as in super-celestial, spiritual, and invisible things, the Word of God is supreme, so also in things visible and corporeal He might possess the supremacy, and, taking to Himself the pre-eminence, as well as constituting Himself Head of the Church, He might draw all things to Himself at the proper time.

7. With Him is nothing incomplete or out of due season, just as with the Father there is nothing incongruous. For all these things were foreknown by the Father; but the Son works them out at the proper time in perfect order and sequence. This was the reason why, when Mary was urging [Him] on to [perform] the wonderful miracle of the wine, and was desirous before the time to partake[2] of the cup of emblematic significance, the Lord, checking her untimely haste, said, "Woman, what have I to do with thee? mine hour is not yet come"[3]—waiting for that hour which was foreknown by the Father. This is also the reason why, when men were often desirous to take Him, it is said, "No man laid hands upon Him, for the hour of His being taken was not yet come;"[4] nor the time of His passion, which had been foreknown by the Father; as also says the prophet Habakkuk, "By this Thou shalt be known when the years have drawn nigh; Thou shalt be set forth when the time comes; because my soul is disturbed by anger, Thou shalt remember Thy mercy."[5] Paul also says: "But when the fulness of time came, God sent forth His Son."[6] By which is made manifest, that all things which had been foreknown of the Father, our Lord did accomplish in their order, season, and hour, foreknown and fitting, being indeed one and the same, but rich and great. For He fulfils the bountiful and comprehensive will of His Father, inasmuch as He is Himself the Saviour of those who are saved, and the Lord of those who are under authority, and the God of all those things which have been formed, the only-begotten of the Father, Christ who was announced, and the Word of God, who became incarnate when the fulness of time had come, at which the Son of God had to become the Son of man.

8. All, therefore, are outside of the [Christian] dispensation, who, under pretext of knowledge, understand that Jesus was one, and Christ another, and the Only-begotten another, from whom again is the Word, and that the Saviour is another, whom these disciples of error allege to be a production of those who were made Æons in a state of degeneracy. Such men are to outward appearance sheep; for they appear to be like us, by what they say in public, repeating the same words as we do; but inwardly they are wolves. Their doctrine is homicidal, conjuring up, as it does, a number of gods, and simulating many Fathers, but lowering and dividing the Son of God in many ways. These are they against whom the Lord has cautioned us beforehand; and His disciple, in his Epistle already mentioned, commands us to avoid them, when he says: "For many deceivers are entered into the world, who confess not that Jesus Christ is come in the flesh. This is a deceiver and an antichrist. Take heed to them, that ye lose not what ye have wrought."[7] And again does he say in the Epistle: "Many false prophets are gone out into the world. Hereby know ye the Spirit of God: Every spirit that confesseth that Jesus Christ is come in the flesh is of God; and every spirit which separates Jesus Christ is not of God, but is of antichrist."[8] These words agree with what was said in the Gospel, that "the Word was made flesh, and dwelt among us." Wherefore he again exclaims in his Epistle, "Every one that believeth that Jesus is the Christ, has been born of God;"[9] knowing Jesus Christ to be one and the same, to whom the gates of heaven were opened, because of His taking upon Him flesh: who shall also come in the same flesh in which He suffered, revealing the glory of the Father.

9. Concurring with these statements, Paul, speaking to the Romans, declares: "Much more they who receive abundance of grace and righteousness for [eternal] life, shall reign by one, Christ Jesus."[10] It follows from this, that he knew nothing of that Christ who flew away from Jesus; nor did he of the Saviour above, whom they hold to be impassible. For if, in

---

[1] Eph. i. 10.
[2] "Participare compendii poculo," i.e., the cup which *recapitulates* the suffering of Christ, and which, as Harvey thinks, refers to the symbolical character of the cup of the Eucharist, as setting forth the passion of Christ.
[3] John ii. 4.
[4] John vii. 30.
[5] Hab. iii. 2.
[6] Gal. iv. 4.

[7] 2 John, 7, 8. Irenæus seems to have read αὐτούς instead of ἑαυτούς, as in the received text.
[8] 1 John iv. 1, 2. This is a material difference from the received text of the passage: "Every spirit that confesseth not that Jesus Christ is come in the flesh." The Vulgate translation and Origen agree with Irenæus, and Tertullian seems to recognise both readings (*Adv. Marc.*, v. 16). Socrates tells us (vii. 32, p. 381) that the passage had been corrupted by those who wished to separate the humanity of Christ from His divinity, and that the old copies read, πᾶν πνεῦμα ὃ λύει τὸν Ἰησοῦν ἀπὸ τοῦ Θεοῦ οὐκ ἔστι, which exactly agrees with Origen's quotation, and very nearly with that of Irenæus, now before us. Polycarp (*Ep.*, c. vii.) seems to allude to the passage as we have it now, and so does Ignatius (*Ep. Smyr.*, c. v.) See the question discussed by Burton, in his *Ante-Nicene Testimonies* [to the *Div. of Christ*. Another work of Burton has a similar name. See British Critic, vol. ii. (of 1827), p. 265].
[9] 1 John v. 1.
[10] Rom. v. 17.

truth, the one suffered, and the other remained incapable of suffering, and the one was born, but the other descended upon him who was born, and left him again, it is not one, but two, that are shown forth. But that the apostle did know Him as one, both who was born and who suffered, namely Christ Jesus, he again says in the same Epistle: "Know ye not, that so many of us as were baptized in Christ Jesus were baptized in His death? that like as Christ rose from the dead, so should we also walk in newness of life."[1] But again, showing that Christ did suffer, and was Himself the Son of God, who died for us, and redeemed us with His blood at the time appointed beforehand, he says: "For how is it, that Christ, when we were yet without strength, in due time died for the ungodly? But God commendeth His love towards us, in that, while we were yet sinners, Christ died for us. Much more, then, being now justified by His blood, we shall be saved from wrath through Him. For if, when we were enemies, we were reconciled to God by the death of His Son; much more, being reconciled, we shall be saved by His life."[2] He declares in the plainest manner, that the same Being who was laid hold of, and underwent suffering, and shed His blood for us, was both Christ and the Son of God, who did also rise again, and was taken up into heaven, as he himself [Paul] says: "But at the same time, [it is] Christ [that] died, yea rather, that is risen again, who is even at the right hand of God."[3] And again, "Knowing that Christ, rising from the dead, dieth no more: "[4] for, as himself foreseeing, through the Spirit, the subdivisions of evil teachers [with regard to the Lord's person], and being desirous of cutting away from them all occasion of cavil, he says what has been already stated, [and also declares:] "But if the Spirit of Him that raised up Jesus from the dead dwell in you, He that raised up Christ from the dead shall also quicken your mortal bodies."[5] This he does not utter to those alone who wish to hear: Do not err, [he says to all:] Jesus Christ, the Son of God, is one and the same, who did by suffering reconcile us to God, and rose from the dead; who is at the right hand of the Father, and perfect in all things; "who, when He was buffeted, struck not in return; who, when He suffered, threatened not;"[6] and when He underwent tyranny, He prayed His Father that He would forgive those who had crucified Him. For He did Himself truly bring in salvation: since He is Himself the Word of God, Himself the Only-begotten of the Father, Christ Jesus our Lord.

CHAP. XVII. — THE APOSTLES TEACH THAT IT WAS NEITHER CHRIST NOR THE SAVIOUR, BUT THE HOLY SPIRIT, WHO DID DESCEND UPON JESUS. THE REASON FOR THIS DESCENT.

1. It certainly was in the power of the apostles to declare that Christ descended upon Jesus, or that the so-called superior Saviour [came down] upon the dispensational one, or he who is from the invisible places upon him from the Demiurge; but they neither knew nor said anything of the kind: for, had they known it, they would have also certainly stated it. But what really was the case, that did they record, [namely,] that the Spirit of God as a dove descended upon Him; this Spirit, of whom it was declared by Isaiah, "And the Spirit of God shall rest upon Him,"[7] as I have already said. And again: "The Spirit of the Lord is upon Me, because He hath anointed Me."[8] That is the Spirit of whom the Lord declares, "For it is not ye that speak, but the Spirit of your Father which speaketh in you."[9] And again, giving to the disciples the power of regeneration into God,[10] He said to them, "Go and teach all nations, baptizing them in the name of the Father, and of the Son, and of the Holy Ghost."[11] For [God] promised, that in the last times He would pour Him [the Spirit] upon [His] servants and handmaids, that they might prophesy; wherefore He did also descend upon the Son of God, made the Son of man, becoming accustomed in fellowship with Him to dwell in the human race, to rest with human beings, and to dwell in the workmanship of God, working the will of the Father in them, and renewing them from their old habits into the newness of Christ.

2. This Spirit did David ask for the human race, saying, "And stablish me with Thine all-governing Spirit;"[12] who also, as Luke says, descended at the day of Pentecost upon the disciples after the Lord's ascension, having power to admit all nations to the entrance of life, and to the opening of the new covenant; from whence also, with one accord in all languages, they uttered praise to God, the Spirit bringing distant tribes to unity, and offering to the Father the first-fruits of all nations. Wherefore also the Lord promised to send the Comforter,[13] who should join us to God. For as a compacted lump of dough cannot be formed of dry wheat

---

[1] Rom. vi. 3, 4.
[2] Rom. v. 6-10. Irenæus appears to have read, as does the Vulgate, εἰς τί γάρ, for ἔτι γάρ in *text. rec.*
[3] Rom. viii. 34.
[4] Rom. vi. 9.
[5] Rom. viii. 11.
[6] 1 Pet. ii. 23.
[7] Isa. xi 2.
[8] Isa. lxi. 1.
[9] Matt. x. 20.
[10] Harvey remarks on this: "The sacrament of baptism is therefore ἡ δύναμις τῆς ἀναγεννήσεως εἰς Θεόν." [Comp. book i. cap. xxi.]
[11] Matt. xxviii. 19.
[12] Ps. li. 12.
[13] John xvi. 7.

without fluid matter, nor can a loaf possess unity, so, in like manner, neither could we, being many, be made one in Christ Jesus without the water from heaven. And as dry earth does not bring forth unless it receive moisture, in like manner we also, being originally a dry tree, could never have brought forth fruit unto life without the voluntary rain from above. For our bodies have received unity among themselves by means of that laver which leads to incorruption; but our souls, by means of the Spirit. Wherefore both are necessary, since both contribute towards the life of God, our Lord compassionating that erring Samaritan woman[1] — who did not remain with one husband, but committed fornication by [contracting] many marriages — by pointing out, and promising to her living water, so that she should thirst no more, nor occupy herself in acquiring the refreshing water obtained by labour, having in herself water springing up to eternal life. The Lord, receiving this as a gift from His Father, does Himself also confer it upon those who are partakers of Himself, sending the Holy Spirit upon all the earth.

3. Gideon,[2] that Israelite whom God chose, that he might save the people of Israel from the power of foreigners, foreseeing this gracious gift, changed his request, and prophesied that there would be dryness upon the fleece of wool (a type of the people), on which alone at first there had been dew; thus indicating that they should no longer have the Holy Spirit from God, as saith Esaias, "I will also command the clouds, that they rain no rain upon it,"[3] but that the dew, which is the Spirit of God, who descended upon the Lord, should be diffused throughout all the earth, "the spirit of wisdom and understanding, the spirit of counsel and might, the spirit of knowledge and piety, the spirit of the fear of God."[4] This Spirit, again, He did confer upon the Church, sending throughout all the world the Comforter from heaven, from whence also the Lord tells us that the devil, like lightning, was cast down.[5] Wherefore we have need of the dew of God, that we be not consumed by fire, nor be rendered unfruitful, and that where we have an accuser there we may have also an Advocate,[6] the Lord commending to the Holy Spirit His own man,[7] who had fallen among thieves,[8] whom He Himself compassionated, and bound up his wounds, giving two royal *denaria*; so that we, receiving by the Spirit the image and superscription of the Father and the Son, might cause the *denarium* entrusted to us to be fruitful, counting out the increase [thereof] to the Lord.[9]

4. The Spirit, therefore, descending under the predestined dispensation, and the Son of God, the Only-begotten, who is also the Word of the Father, coming in the fulness of time, having become incarnate in man for the sake of man, and fulfilling all the conditions of human nature, our Lord Jesus Christ being one and the same, as He Himself the Lord doth testify, as the apostles confess, and as the prophets announce, — all the doctrines of these men who have invented putative Ogdoads and Tetrads, and imagined subdivisions [of the Lord's person], have been proved falsehoods. These[10] men do, in fact, set the Spirit aside altogether; they understand that Christ was one and Jesus another; and they teach that there was not one Christ, but many. And if they speak of them as united, they do again separate them: for they show that one did indeed undergo sufferings, but that the other remained impassible; that the one truly did ascend to the Pleroma, but the other remained in the intermediate place; that the one does truly feast and revel in places invisible and above all name, but that the other is seated with the Demiurge, emptying him of power. It will therefore be incumbent upon thee, and all others who give their attention to this writing, and are anxious about their own salvation, not readily to express acquiescence when they hear abroad the speeches of these men: for, speaking things resembling the [doctrine of the] faithful, as I have already observed, not only do they hold opinions which are different, but absolutely contrary, and in all points full of blasphemies, by which they destroy those persons who, by reason of the resemblance of the words, imbibe a poison which disagrees with their constitution, just as if one, giving lime mixed with water for milk, should mislead by the similitude of the colour; as a man[11] superior to me has said, concerning all that in any way corrupt the things of God and adulterate the truth, "Lime is wickedly mixed with the milk of God."

CHAP. XVIII. — CONTINUATION OF THE FOREGOING ARGUMENT. PROOFS FROM THE WRITINGS OF ST. PAUL, AND FROM THE WORDS OF OUR LORD, THAT CHRIST AND JESUS CANNOT BE CONSIDERED AS DISTINCT BEINGS; NEITHER CAN IT BE ALLEGED THAT THE SON OF GOD BECAME MAN MERELY IN APPEARANCE, BUT THAT HE DID SO TRULY AND ACTUALLY.

1.[12] As it has been clearly demonstrated that

---

[1] Irenæus refers to this woman as a type of the heathen world: for, among the Jews, Samaritan and Idolater were convertible terms.
[2] Judg. vi. 37, etc.
[3] Isa. v. 6.
[4] Isa. xi. 2.
[5] Luke x. 18.
[6] 1 John ii.1.
[7] "Suum hominem," i.e., the human race.
[8] Luke x. 35.
[9] Matt. xxv. 14.
[10] The following period is translated from a Syriac fragment (see Harvey's *Irenæus*, vol. ii. p. 439), as it supplies some words inconveniently omitted in the old Latin version.
[11] Comp. book i. pref. note 2.
[12] Again a Syriac fragment supplies some important words. See Harvey, vol. ii. p. 440.

the Word, who existed in the beginning with God, by whom all things were made, who was also always present with mankind, was in these last days, according to the time appointed by the Father, united to His own workmanship, inasmuch as He became a man liable to suffering, [it follows] that every objection is set aside of those who say, "If our Lord was born at that time, Christ had therefore no previous existence." For I have shown that the Son of God did not then begin to exist, being with the Father from the beginning; but when He became incarnate, and was made man, He commenced afresh[1] the long line of human beings, and furnished us, in a brief, comprehensive manner, with salvation; so that what we had lost in Adam — namely, to be according to the image and likeness of God — that we might recover in Christ Jesus.

2. For as it was not possible that the man who had once for all been conquered, and who had been destroyed through disobedience, could reform himself, and obtain the prize of victory; and as it was also impossible that he could attain to salvation who had fallen under the power of sin, — the Son effected both these things, being the Word of God, descending from the Father, becoming incarnate, stooping low, even to death, and consummating the arranged plan of our salvation, upon whom [Paul], exhorting us unhesitatingly to believe, again says, "Who shall ascend into heaven? that is, to bring down Christ; or who shall descend into the deep? that is, to liberate Christ again from the dead."[2] Then he continues, "If thou shalt confess with thy mouth the Lord Jesus, and shalt believe in thine heart that God hath raised Him from the dead, thou shalt be saved."[3] And he renders the reason why the Son of God did these things, saying, "For to this end Christ both lived, and died, and revived, that He might rule over the living and the dead."[4] And again, writing to the Corinthians, he declares, "But we preach Christ Jesus crucified;"[5] and adds, "The cup of blessing which we bless, is it not the communion of the blood of Christ?"[6]

3. But who is it that has had fellowship with us in the matter of food? Whether is it he who is conceived of by them as the Christ above, who extended himself through Horos, and imparted a form to their mother; or is it He who is from the Virgin, Emmanuel, who did eat butter and honey,[7] of whom the prophet declared, "He is also a man, and who shall know him?"[8] He was likewise preached by Paul: "For I delivered," he says, "unto you first of all, that Christ died for our sins, according to the Scriptures; and that He was buried, and rose again the third day, according to the Scriptures."[9] It is plain, then, that Paul knew no other Christ besides Him alone, who both suffered, and was buried, and rose again, who was also born, and whom he speaks of as man. For after remarking, "But if Christ be preached, that He rose from the dead,"[10] he continues, rendering the reason of His incarnation, "For since by man came death, by man [came] also the resurrection of the dead." And everywhere, when [referring to] the passion of our Lord, and to His human nature, and His subjection to death, he employs the name of Christ, as in that passage: "Destroy not him with thy meat for whom Christ died."[11] And again: "But now, in Christ, ye who sometimes were far off are made nigh by the blood of Christ."[12] And again: "Christ has redeemed us from the curse of the law, being made a curse for us: for it is written, Cursed is every one that hangeth upon a tree."[13] And again: "And through thy knowledge shall the weak brother perish, for whom Christ died;"[14] indicating that the impassible Christ did not descend upon Jesus, but that He Himself, because He was Jesus Christ, suffered for us; He, who lay in the tomb, and rose again, who descended and ascended, — the Son of God having been made the Son of man, as the very name itself doth declare. For in the name of Christ is implied, He that anoints, He that is anointed, and the unction itself with which He is anointed. And it is the Father who anoints, but the Son who is anointed by the Spirit, who is the unction, as the Word declares by Isaiah, "The Spirit of the Lord is upon me, because He hath anointed me,"[15] — pointing out both the anointing Father, the anointed Son, and the unction, which is the Spirit.

4. The Lord Himself, too, makes it evident who it was that suffered; for when He asked the disciples, "Who do men say that I, the Son of man, am?"[16] and when Peter had replied, "Thou art the Christ, the Son of the living God;" and when he had been commended by Him [in these words], "That flesh and blood had not revealed it to him, but the Father who is in heaven," He made it clear that He, the Son of man, is Christ the Son of the living God. "For from that time forth," it is said, "He began to show to His disciples, how that He must go unto Jerusalem,

---

[1] So the Syriac. The Latin has, "in seipso recapitulavit," *He summed up in Himself*. [As the Second Adam, 1 Cor. xv. 47.]
[2] Rom. x. 6, 7.
[3] Rom. x. 9.
[4] Rom. xiv. 9.
[5] 1 Cor. i. 23.
[6] 1 Cor. x. 16.
[7] Isa. viii. 14.
[8] Jer. xvii. 9.
[9] 1 Cor. xv. 3, 4.
[10] 1 Cor. xv. 12.
[11] Rom. xiv. 15.
[12] Eph. ii. 13.
[13] Gal. iii. 13; Deut. xxi. 23.
[14] 1 Cor. viii. 11.
[15] Isa. lxi. 1.
[16] Matt. xvi. 13.

and suffer many things of the priests, and be rejected, and crucified, and rise again the third day."[1] He who was acknowledged by Peter as Christ, who pronounced him blessed because the Father had revealed the Son of the living God to him, said that He must Himself suffer many things, and be crucified; and then He rebuked Peter, who imagined that He was the Christ as the generality of men supposed[2] [that the Christ should be], and was averse to the idea of His suffering, [and] said to the disciples, "If any man will come after Me, let him deny himself, and take up his cross, and follow Me. For whosoever will save his life, shall lose it; and whosoever will lose it for My sake shall save it."[3] For these things Christ spoke openly, He being Himself the Saviour of those who should be delivered over to death for their confession of Him, and lose their lives.

5. If, however, He was Himself not to suffer, but should fly away from Jesus, why did He exhort His disciples to take up the cross and follow Him, — that cross which these men represent Him as not having taken up, but [speak of Him] as having relinquished the dispensation of suffering? For that He did not say this with reference to the acknowledging of the *Stauros* (cross) above, as some among them venture to expound, but with respect to the suffering which He should Himself undergo, and that His disciples should endure, He implies when He says, "For whosoever will save his life, shall lose it; and whosoever will lose, shall find it. And that His disciples must suffer for His sake, He [implied when He] said to the Jews, "Behold, I send you prophets, and wise men, and scribes: and some of them ye shall kill and crucify."[4] And to the disciples He was wont to say, "And ye shall stand before governors and kings for My sake; and they shall scourge some of you, and slay you, and persecute you from city to city."[5] He knew, therefore, both those who should suffer persecution, and He knew those who should have to be scourged and slain because of Him; and He did not speak of any other cross, but of the suffering which He should Himself undergo first, and His disciples afterwards. For this purpose did He give them this exhortation: "Fear not them which kill the body, but are not able to kill the soul; but rather fear Him who is able to send both soul and body into hell;"[6] [thus exhorting them] to hold fast those professions of faith which they had made in reference to Him. For He promised to confess before His Father those who should confess His name before men; but declared that He would deny those who should deny Him, and would be ashamed of those who should be ashamed to confess Him. And although these things are so, some of these men have proceeded to such a degree of temerity, that they even pour contempt upon the martyrs, and vituperate those who are slain on account of the confession of the Lord, and who suffer all things predicted by the Lord, and who in this respect strive to follow the footprints of the Lord's passion, having become martyrs of the suffering One; these we do also enrol with the martyrs themselves. For, when inquisition shall be made for their blood,[7] and they shall attain to glory, then all shall be confounded by Christ, who have cast a slur upon their martyrdom. And from this fact, that He exclaimed upon the cross, "Father, forgive them, for they know not what they do,"[8] the long-suffering, patience, compassion, and goodness of Christ are exhibited, since He both suffered, and did Himself exculpate those who had maltreated Him. For the Word of God, who said to us, "Love your enemies, and pray for those that hate you,"[9] Himself did this very thing upon the cross; loving the human race to such a degree, that He even prayed for those putting Him to death. If, however, any one, going upon the supposition that there are two[Christs], forms a judgment in regard to them, that [Christ] shall be found much the better one, and more patient, and the truly good one, who, in the midst of His own wounds and stripes, and the other [cruelties] inflicted upon Him, was beneficent, and unmindful of the wrongs perpetrated upon Him, than he who flew away, and sustained neither injury nor insult.

6. This also does likewise meet [the case] of those who maintain that He suffered only in appearance. For if He did not truly suffer, no thanks to Him, since there was no suffering at all; and when we shall actually begin to suffer, He will seem as leading us astray, exhorting us to endure buffeting, and to turn the other[10] cheek, if He did not Himself before us in reality suffer the same; and as He misled them by seeming to them what He was not, so does He also mislead us, by exhorting us to endure what He did not endure Himself. [In that case] we shall be even above the Master, because we suffer and sustain what our Master never bore or endured. But as our Lord is alone truly Master, so the Son of God is truly good and patient, the Word of God the Father having been made the Son of man. For He fought and conquered; for He was man contending for the fathers,[11] and

---

[1] Matt. xvi. 21.
[2] Literally, " supposing Him to be Christ according to the idea of men."
[3] Matt. xvi. 24, 25.
[4] Matt. xxiii. 24.
[5] Matt. x. 17, 18.
[6] Matt. x. 28.
[7] Ps. ix. 12.
[8] Luke xxiii. 34.
[9] Matt. v. 44.
[10] Matt. v. 39.
[11] "*Pro patribus*, ἀντὶ τῶν πατρῶν. The reader will here observe the clear statement of the doctrine of the atonement, whereby alone sin is done away."—HARVEY.

through obedience doing away with disobedience completely: for He bound the strong man,[1] and set free the weak, and endowed His own handiwork with salvation, by destroying sin. For He is a most holy and merciful Lord, and loves the human race.

7. Therefore, as I have already said, He caused man (human nature) to cleave to and to become one with God. For unless man had overcome the enemy of man, the enemy would not have been legitimately vanquished. And again: unless it had been God who had freely given salvation, we could never have possessed it securely. And unless man had been joined to God, he could never have become a partaker of incorruptibility. For it was incumbent upon the Mediator between God and men, by His relationship to both, to bring both to friendship and concord, and present man to God, while He revealed God to man.[2] For, in what way could we be partakers of the adoption of sons, unless we had received from Him through the Son that fellowship which refers to Himself, unless His Word, having been made flesh, had entered into communion with us? Wherefore also He passed through every stage of life, restoring to all communion with God. Those, therefore, who assert that He appeared putatively, and was neither born in the flesh nor truly made man, are as yet under the old condemnation, holding out patronage to sin; for, by their showing, death has not been vanquished, which "reigned from Adam to Moses, even over them that had not sinned after the similitude of Adam's transgression."[3] But the law coming, which was given by Moses, and testifying of sin that it is a sinner, did truly take away his (death's) kingdom, showing that he was no king, but a robber; and it revealed him as a murderer. It laid, however, a weighty burden upon man, who had sin in himself, showing that he was liable to death. For as the law was spiritual, it merely made sin to stand out in relief, but did not destroy it. For sin had no dominion over the spirit, but over man. For it behoved Him who was to destroy sin, and redeem man under the power of death, that He should Himself be made that very same thing which he was, that is, man; who had been drawn by sin into bondage, but was held by death, so that sin should be destroyed by man, and man should go forth from death. For as by the disobedience of the one man who was originally moulded from virgin soil, the many were made sinners,[4] and forfeited life; so was it necessary that, by the obedience of one man, who was originally born from a virgin, many should be justified and receive salvation. Thus, then, was the Word of God made man, as also Moses says: "God, true are His works."[5] But if, not having been made flesh, He did appear as if flesh, His work was not a true one. But what He did appear, that He also was: God recapitulated in Himself the ancient formation of man, that He might kill sin, deprive death of its power, and vivify man; and therefore His works are true.

CHAP. XIX.—JESUS CHRIST WAS NOT A MERE MAN, BEGOTTEN FROM JOSEPH IN THE ORDINARY COURSE OF NATURE, BUT WAS VERY GOD, BEGOTTEN OF THE FATHER MOST HIGH, AND VERY MAN, BORN OF THE VIRGIN.

1. But again, those who assert that He was simply a mere man, begotten by Joseph, remaining in the bondage of the old disobedience, are in a state of death; having been not as yet joined to the Word of God the Father, nor receiving liberty through the Son, as He does Himself declare: "If the Son shall make you free, ye shall be free indeed."[6] But, being ignorant of Him who from the Virgin is Emmanuel, they are deprived of His gift, which is eternal life;[7] and not receiving the incorruptible Word, they remain in mortal flesh, and are debtors to death, not obtaining the antidote of life. To whom the Word says, mentioning His own gift of grace: "I said, Ye are all the sons of the Highest, and gods; but ye shall die like men."[8] He speaks undoubtedly these words to those who have not received the gift of adoption, but who despise the incarnation of the pure generation of the Word of God,[9] defraud human nature of promotion into God, and prove themselves ungrateful to the Word of God, who became flesh for them. For it was for this end that the Word of God was made man, and He who was the Son of God became the Son of man, that man, having been taken into the Word, and receiving the adoption, might become the son of God. For by no other means could we have attained to incorruptibility and immortality, unless we had been united to incorruptibility and immortality. But how could we be joined to incorruptibility and immortality, unless, first, incorruptibility and immortality had

---

[1] Matt. xii. 29.
[2] The Latin text, "et facere, ut et Deus assumeret hominem, et homo se dederet Deo," here differs widely from the Greek preserved by Theodoret. We have followed the latter, which is preferred by all the editors.
[3] Rom. v. 14.
[4] Rom. v. 19.
[5] Deut. xxxii. 4.
[6] John viii. 36.
[7] Rom. vi. 23.
[8] Ps. lxxxii. 6, 7.
[9] The original Greek is preserved here by Theodoret, differing in some respects from the old Latin version: καὶ ἀποστεροῦντας τὸν ἄνθρωπον τῆς εἰς Θεὸν ἀνόδου καὶ ἀχαριστοῦντας τῷ ὑπὲρ αὐτῶν σαρκωθέντι λόγῳ τοῦ Θεοῦ. Εἰς τοῦτο γὰρ ὁ λόγος ἄνθρωπος . . . ἵνα ὁ ἄνθρωπος τὸν λόγον χωρήσας, καὶ τὴν υἱοθεσίαν λαβὼν, υἱὸς γένηται Θεοῦ. The old Latin runs thus: "fraudantes hominem ab ea ascensione quæ est ad Dominum, et ingrate existentes Verbo Dei, qui incarnatus est propter ipsos. Propter hoc enim Verbum Dei homo, et qui Filius Dei est, Filius Hominis factus est . . . commixtus Verbo Dei, et adoptionem percipiens fiat filius Dei." [A specimen of the liberties taken by the Latin translators with the original of Irenæus. Others are much less innocent.]

become that which we also are, so that the corruptible might be swallowed up by incorruptibility, and the mortal by immortality, that we might receive the adoption of sons?

2. For this reason [it is said], "Who shall declare His generation?"[1] since "He is a man, and who shall recognise Him?"[2] But he to whom the Father which is in heaven has revealed Him,[3] knows Him, so that he understands that He who "was not born either by the will of the flesh, or by the will of man,"[4] is the Son of man, this is Christ, the Son of the living God. For I have shown from the Scriptures,[5] that no one of the sons of Adam is as to everything, and absolutely, called God, or named Lord. But that He is Himself in His own right, beyond all men who ever lived, God, and Lord, and King Eternal, and the Incarnate Word, proclaimed by all the prophets, the apostles, and by the Spirit Himself, may be seen by all who have attained to even a small portion of the truth. Now, the Scriptures would not have testified these things of Him, if, like others, He had been a mere man. But that He had, beyond all others, in Himself that pre-eminent birth which is from the Most High Father, and also experienced that pre-eminent generation which is from the Virgin,[6] the divine Scriptures do in both respects testify of Him: also, that He was a man without comeliness, and liable to suffering;[7] that He sat upon the foal of an ass;[8] that He received for drink, vinegar and gall;[9] that He was despised among the people, and humbled Himself even to death; and that He is the holy Lord, the Wonderful, the Counsellor, the Beautiful in appearance, and the Mighty God,[10] coming on the clouds as the Judge of all men;[11] — all these things did the Scriptures prophesy of Him.

3. For as He became man in order to undergo temptation, so also was He the Word that He might be glorified; the Word remaining quiescent, that He might be capable of being tempted, dishonoured, crucified, and of suffering death, but the human nature being swallowed up in it (the divine), when it conquered, and endured [without yielding], and performed acts of kindness, and rose again, and was received up [into heaven]. He therefore, the Son of God, our Lord, being the Word of the Father, and the Son of man, since He had a generation as to His human nature from Mary — who was descended from mankind, and who was herself a human being — was made the Son of man.[12] Wherefore also the Lord Himself gave us a sign, in the depth below, and in the height above, which man did not ask for, because he never expected that a virgin could conceive, or that it was possible that one remaining a virgin could bring forth a son, and that what was thus born should be "*God with us*," and descend to those things which are of the earth beneath, seeking the sheep which had perished, which was indeed His own peculiar handiwork, and ascend to the height above, offering and commending to His Father that human nature (*hominem*) which had been found, making in His own person the first-fruits of the resurrection of man; that, as the Head rose from the dead, so also the remaining part of the body — [namely, the body] of every man who is found in life — when the time is fulfilled of that condemnation which existed by reason of disobedience, may arise, blended together and strengthened through means of joints and bands[13] by the increase of God, each of the members having its own proper and fit position in the body. For there are many mansions in the Father's house,[14] inasmuch as there are also many members in the body.

CHAP. XX. — GOD SHOWED HIMSELF, BY THE FALL OF MAN, AS PATIENT, BENIGN, MERCIFUL, MIGHTY TO SAVE. MAN IS THEREFORE MOST UNGRATEFUL, IF, UNMINDFUL OF HIS OWN LOT, AND OF THE BENEFITS HELD OUT TO HIM, HE DO NOT ACKNOWLEDGE DIVINE GRACE.

1. Long-suffering therefore was God, when man became a defaulter, as foreseeing that victory which should be granted to him through the Word. For, when strength was made perfect in weakness,[15] it showed the kindness and transcendent power of God. For as He patiently suffered Jonah to be swallowed by the whale, not that he should be swallowed up and perish altogether, but that, having been cast out again, he might be the more subject to God, and might glorify Him the more who had conferred upon him such an unhoped-for deliverance, and might bring the Ninevites to a lasting repentance, so that they should be converted to the Lord, who would deliver them from death, having been struck with awe by that portent which had been wrought in Jonah's case, as the Scripture says of them, "And they returned each from his evil way, and the unrighteousness which was in their hands, saying, Who knoweth if God will repent, and turn away His anger from us, and we shall not perish?"[16] — so also, from the beginning, did God permit man to be

---

[1] Isa. liii. 8.
[2] Jer. xvii. 9.
[3] Matt. xvi. 16.
[4] John i. 13.
[5] See above, iii. 6.
[6] Isa. vii. 14.
[7] Isa liii. 2.
[8] Zech. ix. 9.
[9] Ps. lxix. 21.
[10] Isa. ix. 6.
[11] Dan. vii. 13.
[12] Isa. vii. 13
[13] Eph. iv. 16.
[14] John xiv. 2.
[15] 2 Cor. xii. 9.
[16] Jonah iii. 8, 9.

swallowed up by the great whale, who was the author of transgression, not that he should perish altogether when so engulphed; but, arranging and preparing the plan of salvation, which was accomplished by the Word, through the sign of Jonah, for those who held the same opinion as Jonah regarding the Lord, and who confessed, and said, "I am a servant of the Lord, and I worship the Lord God of heaven, who hath made the sea and the dry land."[1] [This was done] that man, receiving an unhoped-for salvation from God, might rise from the dead, and glorify God, and repeat that word which was uttered in prophecy by Jonah: "I cried by reason of mine affliction to the Lord my God, and He heard me out of the belly of hell;"[2] and that he might always continue glorifying God, and giving thanks without ceasing, for that salvation which he has derived from Him, "that no flesh should glory in the Lord's presence;"[3] and that man should never adopt an opposite opinion with regard to God, supposing that the incorruptibility which belongs to him is his own naturally, and by thus not holding the truth, should boast with empty superciliousness, as if he were naturally like to God. For he (Satan) thus rendered him (man) more ungrateful towards his Creator, obscured the love which God had towards man, and blinded his mind not to perceive what is worthy of God, comparing himself with, and judging himself equal to, God.

2. This, therefore, was the [object of the] long-suffering of God, that man, passing through all things, and acquiring the knowledge of moral discipline, then attaining to the resurrection from the dead, and learning by experience what is the source of his deliverance, may always live in a state of gratitude to the Lord, having obtained from Him the gift of incorruptibility, that he might love Him the more; for "he to whom more is forgiven, loveth more:"[4] and that he may know himself, how mortal and weak he is; while he also understands respecting God, that He is immortal and powerful to such a degree as to confer immortality upon what is mortal, and eternity upon what is temporal; and may understand also the other attributes of God displayed towards himself, by means of which being instructed he may think of God in accordance with the divine greatness. For the glory of man [is] God, but [His] works [are the glory] of God; and the receptacle of all His wisdom and power [is] man. Just as the physician is proved by his patients, so is God also revealed through men. And therefore Paul declares, "For God hath concluded all in unbelief, that He may have mercy upon all;"[5] not saying this in reference to spiritual Æons, but to man, who had been disobedient to God, and being cast off from immortality, then obtained mercy, receiving through the Son of God that adoption which is [accomplished] by Himself. For he who holds, without pride and boasting, the true glory (opinion) regarding created things and the Creator, who is the Almighty God of all, and who has granted existence to all; [such an one,] continuing in His love [6] and subjection, and giving of thanks, shall also receive from Him the greater glory of promotion,[7] looking forward to the time when he shall become like Him who died for him, for He, too, "was made in the likeness of sinful flesh,"[8] to condemn sin, and to cast it, as now a condemned thing, away beyond the flesh, but that He might call man forth into His own likeness, assigning him as [His own] imitator to God, and imposing on him His Father's law, in order that he may see God, and granting him power to receive the Father; [being][9] the Word of God who dwelt in man, and became the Son of man, that He might accustom man to receive God, and God to dwell in man, according to the good pleasure of the Father.

3. On this account, therefore, the Lord Himself,[10] who is Emmanuel from the Virgin,[11] is the sign of our salvation, since it was the Lord Himself who saved them, because they could not be saved by their own instrumentality; and, therefore, when Paul sets forth human infirmity, he says: "For I know that there dwelleth in my flesh no good thing,"[12] showing that the "good thing" of our salvation is not from us, but from God. And again: "Wretched man that I am, who shall deliver me from the body of this death?"[13] Then he introduces the Deliverer, [saying,] "The grace of Jesus Christ our Lord." And Isaiah declares this also, [when he says:] "Be ye strengthened, ye hands that hang down, and ye feeble knees; be ye encouraged, ye feeble-minded; be comforted, fear not: behold, our God has given judgment with retribution, and shall recompense: He will come Himself, and will save us."[14] Here we see, that not by ourselves, but by the help of God, we must be saved.

4. Again, that it should not be a mere man who should save us, nor [one] without flesh — for the angels are without flesh — [the same

---

[1] Jonah i. 9.
[2] Jonah ii. 2.
[3] 1 Cor. i. 29.
[4] Luke vii. 43.
[5] Rom. xi. 32.
[6] John xv. 9.
[7] "Provectus." This word has not a little perplexed the editors. Grabe regards it as being the *participle*, Massuet the *accusative plural* of the noun, and Harvey the *genitive singular*. We have doubtfully followed the latter.
[8] Rom. viii. 3.
[9] The punctuation and exact meaning are very uncertain.
[10] The construction and sense of this passage are disputed. Grabe, Massuet, and Harvey take different views of it. We have followed the rendering proposed by Massuet.
[11] Isa. vii. 4.
[12] Rom. vii. 18.
[13] Rom. vii. 24.
[14] Isa. xxv. 3.

prophet] announced, saying: "Neither an elder,[1] nor angel, but the Lord Himself will save them, because He loves them, and will spare them: He will Himself set them free."[2] And that He should Himself become very man, visible, when He should be the Word giving salvation, Isaiah again says: "Behold, city of Zion: thine eyes shall see our salvation."[3] And that it was not a mere man who died for us, Isaiah says: "And the holy Lord remembered His dead Israel, who had slept in the land of sepulture; and He came down to preach His salvation to them, that He might save them."[4] And Amos (Micah) the prophet declares the same: "He will turn again, and will have compassion upon us: He will destroy our iniquities, and will cast our sins into the depths of the sea."[5] And again, specifying the place of His advent, he says: "The Lord hath spoken from Zion, and He has uttered His voice from Jerusalem."[6] And that it is from that region which is towards the south of the inheritance of Judah that the Son of God shall come, who is God, and who was from Bethlehem, where the Lord was born, [and] will send out His praise through all the earth, thus[7] says the prophet Habakkuk: "God shall come from the south, and the Holy One from Mount Effrem. His power covered the heavens over, and the earth is full of His praise. Before His face shall go forth the Word, and His feet shall advance in the plains."[8] Thus he indicates in clear terms that He is God, and that His advent was [to take place] in Bethlehem, and from Mount Effrem, which is towards the south of the inheritance, and that [He is] man. For he says, "His feet shall advance in the plains:" and this is an indication proper to man.[9]

CHAP. XXI. — A VINDICATION OF THE PROPHECY IN ISAIAH (VII. 14) AGAINST THE MISINTERPRETATIONS OF THEODOTION, AQUILA, THE EBIONITES, AND THE JEWS. AUTHORITY OF THE SEPTUAGINT VERSION. ARGUMENTS IN PROOF THAT CHRIST WAS BORN OF A VIRGIN.

1. God, then, was made man, and the Lord did Himself save us, giving us the token of the Virgin. But not as some allege, among those now presuming to expound the Scripture, [thus:] "Behold, a young woman shall conceive, and bring forth a son,"[10] as Theodotion the Ephesian has interpreted, and Aquila of Pontus,[11] both Jewish proselytes. The Ebionites, following these, assert that He was begotten by Joseph; thus destroying, as far as in them lies, such a marvellous dispensation of God, and setting aside the testimony of the prophets which proceeded from God. For truly this prediction was uttered before the removal of the people to Babylon; that is, anterior to the supremacy acquired by the Medes and Persians. But it was interpreted into Greek by the Jews themselves, much before the period of our Lord's advent, that there might remain no suspicion that perchance the Jews, complying with our humour, did put this interpretation upon these words. They indeed, had they been cognizant of our future existence, and that we should use these proofs from the Scriptures, would themselves never have hesitated to burn their own Scriptures, which do declare that all other nations partake of [eternal] life, and show that they who boast themselves as being the house of Jacob and the people of Israel, are disinherited from the grace of God.

2. For before the Romans possessed their kingdom,[12] while as yet the Macedonians held Asia, Ptolemy the son of Lagus, being anxious to adorn the library which he had founded in Alexandria, with a collection of the writings of all men, which were [works] of merit, made request to the people of Jerusalem, that they should have their Scriptures translated into the Greek language. And they — for at that time they were still subject to the Macedonians — sent to Ptolemy seventy of their elders, who were thoroughly skilled in the Scriptures and in both the languages, to carry out what he had desired.[13] But he, wishing to test them individually, and fearing lest they might perchance, by taking counsel together, conceal the truth in the Scriptures, by their interpretation, separated them from each other, and commanded them all to write the same translation. He did this with respect to all the books. But when they came together in the same place before Ptolemy, and

---

[1] Grabe remarks that the word πρέσβυς, here translated "senior," seems rather to denote a *mediator* or *messenger*.
[2] Isa. lxiii. 9.
[3] Isa. xxxiii. 20.
[4] Irenæus quotes this as from Isaiah on the present occasion; but in book iv. 22, 1, we find him referring the same passage to Jeremiah. It is somewhat remarkable that it is to be found in neither prophet, although Justin Martyr, in his dialogue with Trypho, [chap. lxxii. and notes, Dial. with Trypho, in this volume], brings it forward as an argument against him, and directly accuses the Jews of having fraudulently removed it from the sacred text. It is, however, to be found in no ancient version or Jewish Targum, which fact may be regarded as a decisive proof of its spuriousness.
[5] Mic. vii. 9.
[6] Joel iii. 16; Amos i. 2.
[7] As Massuet observes, we must either expunge "sicut" altogether, or read "sic" as above.
[8] Hab. iii. 3, 5.
[9] This quotation from Habakkuk, here commented on by Irenæus, differs both from the Hebrew and the LXX., and comes nearest to the old Italic version of the passage.

[10] Isa. vii. 14.
[11] Epiphanius, in his *De Mensuris*, gives an account of these two men. The former published his version of the Old Testament in the year 181. The latter put forth his translation half a century earlier, about 129 A.D. This reference to the version of Theodotion furnishes a note of date as to the time when Irenæus published his work: it must have been subsequently to A.D. 181.
[12] The Greek text here is, κρατῦναι τὴν ἀρχὴν αὐτῶν, translated into Latin by "possiderent regnum suum," — words which are somewhat ambiguous in both languages. Massuet remarks, that "regnum *eorum*" would have been a better rendering, referring the words to the *Jews*.
[13] The Greek text of this narrative has been preserved by Eusebius (*Hist. Eccl.*, v. 8). The Latin translation has been adopted here. Eusebius has ποιήσαντος τοῦ Θεοῦ ὅπερ ἐβούλετο — *God having accomplished what He intended*.

each of them compared his own interpretation with that of every other, God was indeed glorified, and the Scriptures were acknowledged as truly divine. For all of them read out the common translation [which they had prepared] in the very same words and the very same names, from beginning to end, so that even the Gentiles present perceived that the Scriptures had been interpreted by the inspiration of God.[1] And there was nothing astonishing in God having done this, — He who, when, during the captivity of the people under Nebuchadnezzar, the Scriptures had been corrupted, and when, after seventy years, the Jews had returned to their own land, then, in the times of Artaxerxes king of the Persians, inspired Esdras the priest, of the tribe of Levi, to recast[2] all the words of the former prophets, and to re-establish with the people the Mosaic legislation.

3. Since, therefore, the Scriptures have been interpreted with such fidelity, and by the grace of God, and since from these God has prepared and formed again our faith towards His Son, and has preserved to us the unadulterated Scriptures in Egypt, where the house of Jacob flourished, fleeing from the famine in Canaan; where also our Lord was preserved when He fled from the persecution set on foot by Herod; and [since] this interpretation of these Scriptures was made prior to our Lord's descent [to earth], and came into being before the Christians appeared — for our Lord was born about the forty-first year of the reign of Augustus; but Ptolemy was much earlier, under whom the Scriptures were interpreted; — [since these things are so, I say,] truly these men are proved to be impudent and presumptuous, who would now show a desire to make different translations, when we refute them out of these Scriptures, and shut them up to a belief in the advent of the Son of God. But *our* faith is stedfast, unfeigned, and the only true one, having clear proof from these Scriptures, which were interpreted in the way I have related; and the preaching of the Church is without interpolation. For the apostles, since they are of more ancient date than all these [heretics], agree with this aforesaid translation; and the translation harmonizes with the tradition of the apostles. For Peter, and John, and Matthew, and Paul, and the rest successively, as well as their followers, did set forth all prophetical [announcements], just as[3] the interpretation of the elders contains them.

4. For the one and the same Spirit of God, who proclaimed by the prophets what and of what sort the advent of the Lord should be, did by these elders give a just interpretation of what had been truly prophesied; and He did Himself, by the apostles, announce that the fulness of the times of the adoption had arrived, that the kingdom of heaven had drawn nigh, and that *He* was dwelling within those that believe on Him who was born Emmanuel of the Virgin. To this effect they testify, [saying,] that before Joseph had come together with Mary, while she therefore remained in virginity, "she was found with child of the Holy Ghost;"[4] and that the angel Gabriel said unto her, "The Holy Ghost shall come upon thee, and the power of the Highest shall overshadow thee; therefore also that holy thing which shall be born of thee shall be called the Son of God;"[5] andt hat the angel said to Joseph in a dream, "Now this was done, that it might be fulfilled which was spoken by Isaiah the prophet, Behold, a virgin shall be with child."[6] But the elders have thus interpreted what Esaias said: "And the Lord, moreover, said unto Ahaz, Ask for thyself a sign from the Lord thy God out of the depth below, or from the height above. And Ahaz said, I will not ask, and I will not tempt the Lord. And he said, It is not a small thing[7] for you to weary men; and how does the Lord weary them? Therefore the Lord himself shall give you a sign; Behold, a virgin shall conceive, and bear a son; and ye shall call His name Emmanuel. Butter and honey shall He eat: before He knows or chooses out things that are evil, He shall exchange them for what is good; for before the child knows good or evil, He shall not consent to evil, that He may choose that which is good."[8] Carefully, then, has the Holy Ghost pointed out, by what has been said, His birth from a virgin, and His essence, that He is God (for the name Emmanuel indicates this). And He shows that He is a man, when He says, "Butter and honey shall He eat;" and in that He terms Him a child also, [in saying,] "before He knows good and evil;" for these are all the tokens of a human infant. But that He "will not consent to evil, that He may choose that which is good," — this is proper to God; that by the fact, that He shall eat butter and honey, we should not understand that He is a mere man only, nor, on the other hand, from the name Emmanuel, should suspect Him to be God without flesh.

5. And when He says, "Hear, O house of David,"[9] He performed the part of one indi-

---

[1] [See Justin Martyr, *To the Greeks*, cap. xiii. The testimony of Justin naturalized this Jewish legend among Christians.]
[2] The Greek term is ἀνατάξασθαι, which the Latin renders "re memorare," but Massuet prefers "digerere."
[3] This is a very interesting passage, as bearing on the question, From what source are the quotations made by the writers of the New Testament derived? Massuet, indeed, argues that it is of little or no weight in the controversy; but the passage speaks for itself. Comp. Dr. Roberts's *Discussions on the Gospels*, part i. ch. iv. and vii.
[4] Matt. i. 18.
[5] Luke i. 35.
[6] Matt. i. 23.
[7] We here read "non pusillum" for "num pusillum," as in some texts Cyprian and Tertullian confirm the former reading.
[8] Isa. vii. 10–17.
[9] Isa. vii. 13.

cating that He whom God promised David that He would raise up from the fruit of his belly (*ventris*) an eternal King, is the same who was born of the Virgin, herself of the lineage of David. For on this account also, He promised that the King should be "of the fruit of his *belly*," which was the appropriate [term to use with respect] to a virgin conceiving, and not "of the fruit of his *loins*," nor "of the fruit of his *reins*," which expression is appropriate to a generating man, and a woman conceiving by a man. In this promise, therefore, the Scripture excluded all virile influence; yet it certainly is not mentioned that He who was born was not from the will of man. But it has fixed and established "the fruit of the *belly*," that it might declare the generation of Him who should be [born] from the Virgin, as Elisabeth testified when filled with the Holy Ghost, saying to Mary, "Blessed art thou among women, and blessed is the fruit of thy belly;"[1] the Holy Ghost pointing out to those willing to hear, that the promise which God had made, of raising up a King from the fruit of [David's] belly, was fulfilled in the birth from the Virgin, that is, from Mary. Let those, therefore, who alter the passage of Isaiah thus, "Behold, a young woman shall conceive," and who will have Him to be Joseph's son, also alter the form of the promise which was given to David, when God promised him to raise up, from the fruit of his belly, the horn of Christ the King. But they did not understand, otherwise they would have presumed to alter even this passage also.

6. But what Isaiah said, "From the height above, or from the depth beneath,"[2] was meant to indicate, that "He who descended was the same also who ascended."[3] But in this that he said, "The Lord Himself shall give you a sign," he declared an unlooked-for thing with regard to His generation, which could have been accomplished in no other way than by God the Lord of all, God Himself giving a sign in the house of David. For what great thing or what sign should have been in this, that a young woman conceiving by a man should bring forth, — a thing which happens to all women that produce offspring? But since an unlooked-for salvation was to be provided for men through the help of God, so also was the unlooked-for birth from a virgin accomplished; God giving this sign, but man not working it out.

7. On this account also, Daniel,[4] foreseeing His advent, said that a stone, cut out without hands, came into this world. For this is what "without hands" means, that His coming into this world was not by the operation of human hands, that is, of those men who are accustomed to stone-cutting; that is, Joseph taking no part with regard to it, but Mary alone co-operating with the pre-arranged plan. For this stone from the earth derives existence from both the power and the wisdom of God. Wherefore also Isaiah says: "Thus saith the Lord, Behold, I deposit in the foundations of Zion a stone, precious, elect, the chief, the corner-one, to be had in honour."[5] So, then, we understand that His advent in human nature was not by the will of a man, but by the will of God.

8. Wherefore also Moses giving a type, cast his rod upon the earth,[6] in order that it, by becoming flesh, might expose and swallow up all the opposition of the Egyptians, which was lifting itself up against the pre-arranged plan of God;[7] that the Egyptians themselves might testify that it is the finger of God which works salvation for the people, and not the son of Joseph. For if He were the son of Joseph, how could He be greater than Solomon, or greater than Jonah,[8] or greater than David,[9] when He was generated from the same seed, and was a descendant of these men? And how was it that He also pronounced Peter blessed, because he acknowledged Him to be the Son of the living God?[10]

9. But besides, if indeed He had been the son of Joseph, He could not, according to Jeremiah, be either king or heir. For Joseph is shown to be the son of Joachim and Jechoniah, as also Matthew sets forth in his pedigree.[11] But Jechoniah, and all his posterity, were disinherited from the kingdom; Jeremiah thus declaring, "As I live, saith the Lord, if Jechoniah the son of Joachim king of Judah had been made the signet of my right hand, I would pluck him thence, and deliver him into the hand of those seeking thy life."[12] And again: "Jechoniah is dishonoured as a useless vessel, for he has been cast into a land which he knew not. Earth, hear the word of the Lord: Write this man a disinherited person; for none of his seed, sitting on the throne of David, shall prosper, or be a prince in Judah."[13] And again, God speaks of Joachim his father: "Therefore thus saith the Lord concerning Joachim his father, king of Judea, There shall be from him none sitting upon the throne of David: and his dead body shall be cast out in the heat of day, and in the frost of night. And I will look upon him, and upon

---

[1] Luke i. 42.
[2] Isa. vii. 11.
[3] Eph. iv. 10.
[4] Dan. ii. 34.
[5] Isa. xxviii. 16.
[6] Ex. vii. 9.
[7] Ex. viii. 19.
[8] Matt. xii. 41, 42.
[9] Matt. xxii. 43.
[10] Matt. xvi. 17.
[11] Matt. i. 12-16.
[12] Jer. xxii. 24, 25.
[13] Jer. xxii. 28, etc.

his sons, and will bring upon them, and upon the inhabitants of Jerusalem, upon the land of Judah, all the evils that I have pronounced against them." [1] Those, therefore, who say that He was begotten of Joseph, and that they have hope in Him, do cause themselves to be disinherited from the kingdom, falling under the curse and rebuke directed against Jechoniah and his seed. Because for this reason have these things been spoken concerning Jechoniah, the [Holy] Spirit foreknowing the doctrines of the evil teachers; that they may learn that from his seed — that is, from Joseph — He was not to be born, but that, according to the promise of God, from David's belly the King eternal is raised up, who sums up all things in Himself, and has gathered into Himself the ancient formation [of man]. [2]

10. For as by one man's disobedience sin entered, and death obtained [a place] through sin; so also by the obedience of one man, righteousness having been introduced, shall cause life to fructify in those persons who in times past were dead. [3] And as the protoplast himself, Adam, had his substance from untilled and as yet virgin soil ("for God had not yet sent rain, and man had not tilled the ground" [4]), and was formed by the hand of God, that is, by the Word of God, for "all things were made by Him," [5] and the Lord took dust from the earth and formed man; so did He who is the Word, recapitulating Adam in Himself, rightly receive a birth, enabling Him to gather up Adam [into Himself], from Mary, who was as yet a virgin. If, then, the first Adam had a man for his father, and was born of human seed, it were reasonable to say that the second Adam was begotten of Joseph. But if the former was taken from the dust, and God was his Maker, it was incumbent that the latter also, making a recapitulation in Himself, should be formed as man by God, to have an analogy with the former as respects His origin. Why, then, did not God again take dust, but wrought so that the formation should be made of Mary? It was that there might not be another formation called into being, nor any other which should [require to] be saved, but that the very same formation should be summed up [in Christ as had existed in Adam], the analogy having been preserved.

CHAP. XXII. — CHRIST ASSUMED ACTUAL FLESH, CONCEIVED AND BORN OF THE VIRGIN.

1. Those, therefore, who allege that He took nothing from the Virgin do greatly err, [since,] in order that they may cast away the inheritance of the flesh, they also reject the analogy [between Him and Adam]. For if the one [who sprang] from the earth had indeed formation and substance from both the hand and workmanship of God, but the other not from the hand and workmanship of God, then He who was made after the image and likeness of the former did not, in that case, preserve the analogy of man, and He must seem an inconsistent piece of work, not having wherewith He may show His wisdom. But this is to say, that He also appeared putatively as man when He was not man, and that He was made man while taking nothing from man. For if He did not receive the substance of flesh from a human being, He neither was made man nor the Son of man; and if He was not made what we were, He did no great thing in what He suffered and endured. But every one will allow that we are [composed of] a body taken from the earth, and a soul receiving spirit from God. This, therefore, the Word of God was made, recapitulating in Himself His own handiwork; and on this account does He confess Himself the Son of man, and blesses "the meek, because they shall inherit the earth." [6] The Apostle Paul, moreover, in the Epistle to the Galatians, declares plainly, "God sent His Son, made of a woman." [7] And again, in that to the Romans, he says, "Concerning His Son, who was made of the seed of David according to the flesh, who was predestinated as the Son of God with power, according to the spirit of holiness, by the resurrection from the dead, Jesus Christ our Lord." [8]

2.[9] Superfluous, too, in that case is His descent into Mary; for why did He come down into her if He were to take nothing of her? Still further, if He had taken nothing of Mary, He would never have availed Himself of those kinds of food which are derived from the earth, by which that body which has been taken from the earth is nourished; nor would He have hungered, fasting those forty days, like Moses and Elias, unless His body was craving after its own proper nourishment; nor, again, would John His disciple have said, when writing of Him, "But Jesus, being wearied with the journey, was sitting [to rest];" [10] nor would David have proclaimed of Him beforehand, "They have added to the grief of my wounds;" [11] nor would He have wept over Lazarus, nor have sweated great drops of blood; nor have declared, "My soul is exceeding sorrowful;" [12] nor, when His side was pierced, would there

---

[1] Jer. xxxvi. 30, 31.
[2] Harvey prefixes this last clause to the following section.
[3] Rom. v. 19.
[4] Gen. ii. 5.
[5] John i. 3.
[6] Matt. v. 5.
[7] Gal. iv. 4.
[8] Rom. i. 3, 4.
[9] In addition to the Greek text preserved by Theodoret in this place, we have for some way a *Syriac* translation, differing slightly from both Greek and Latin. It seems, however, to run smoother than either, and has therefore been followed by us.
[10] John iv. 6.
[11] Ps. lxix. 27.
[12] Matt. xxvi. 38.

have come forth blood and water. For all these are tokens of the flesh which had been derived from the earth, which He had recapitulated in Himself, bearing salvation to His own handiwork.

3. Wherefore Luke points out that the pedigree which traces the generation of our Lord back to Adam contains seventy-two generations, connecting the end with the beginning, and implying that it is He who has summed up in Himself all nations dispersed from Adam downwards, and all languages and generations of men, together with Adam himself. Hence also was Adam himself termed by Paul "the figure of Him that was to come,"[1] because the Word, the Maker of all things, had formed beforehand for Himself the future dispensation of the human race, connected with the Son of God; God having predestined that the first man should be of an animal nature, with this view, that he might be saved by the spiritual One. For inasmuch as He had a pre-existence as a saving Being, it was necessary that what might be saved should also be called into existence, in order that the Being who saves should not exist in vain.

4. In accordance with this design, Mary the Virgin is found obedient, saying, "Behold the handmaid of the Lord; be it unto me according to thy word."[2] But Eve was disobedient; for she did not obey when as yet she was a virgin. And even as she, having indeed a husband, Adam, but being nevertheless as yet a virgin (for in Paradise "they were both naked, and were not ashamed,"[3] inasmuch as they, having been created a short time previously, had no understanding of the procreation of children: for it was necessary that they should first come to adult age,[4] and then multiply from that time onward), having become disobedient, was made the cause of death, both to herself and to the entire human race; so also did Mary, having a man betrothed [to her], and being nevertheless a virgin, by yielding obedience, become the cause of salvation, both to herself and the whole human race. And on this account does the law term a woman betrothed to a man, the wife of him who had betrothed her, although she was as yet a virgin; thus indicating the back-reference from Mary to Eve, because what is joined together could not otherwise be put asunder than by inversion of the process by which these bonds of union had arisen;[5] so that the former ties be cancelled by the latter, that the latter may set the former again at liberty. And it has, in fact, happened that the first compact looses from the second tie, but that the second tie takes the position of the first which has been cancelled.[6] For this reason did the Lord declare that the first should in truth be last, and the last first.[7] And the prophet, too, indicates the same, saying, "Instead of fathers, children have been born unto thee."[8] For the Lord, having been born "the First-begotten of the dead,"[9] and receiving into His bosom the ancient fathers, has regenerated them into the life of God, He having been made Himself the beginning of those that live, as Adam became the beginning of those who die.[10] Wherefore also Luke, commencing the genealogy with the Lord, carried it back to Adam, indicating that it was He who regenerated them into the Gospel of life, and not they Him. And thus also it was that the knot of Eve's disobedience was loosed by the obedience of Mary. For what the virgin Eve had bound fast through unbelief, this did the virgin Mary set free through faith.

CHAP. XXIII. — ARGUMENTS IN OPPOSITION TO TATIAN, SHOWING THAT IT WAS CONSONANT TO DIVINE JUSTICE AND MERCY THAT THE FIRST ADAM SHOULD FIRST PARTAKE IN THAT SALVATION OFFERED TO ALL BY CHRIST.

1. It was necessary, therefore, that the Lord, coming to the lost sheep, and making recapitulation of so comprehensive a dispensation, and seeking after His own handiwork, should save that very man who had been created after His image and likeness, that is, Adam, filling up the times of His condemnation, which had been incurred through disobedience, — [times] "which the Father had placed in His own power."[11] [This was necessary,] too, inasmuch as the whole economy of salvation regarding man came to pass according to the good pleasure of the Father, in order that God might not be conquered, nor His wisdom lessened, [in the estimation of His creatures.] For if man, who had been created by God that he might live, after losing life, through being injured by the serpent that had corrupted him, should not any more return to life, but should be utterly [and for ever] abandoned to death, God would [in that case] have been conquered, and the wickedness of the serpent would have prevailed over the will of God. But inasmuch as God is invincible and long-suffering, He did indeed show Himself to be long-suffering in the matter of the correction of man and the probation of all, as I have already

---

[1] Rom. v. 14.
[2] Luke i. 38.
[3] Gen. ii. 25.
[4] This seems quite a peculiar opinion of Irenæus, that our first parents, when created, were not of the age of maturity.
[5] Literally, "unless these bonds of union be turned backwards."
[6] It is very difficult to follow the reasoning of Irenæus in this passage. Massuet has a long note upon it, in which he sets forth the various points of comparison and contrast here indicated between Eve and Mary; but he ends with the remark, "hæc certe et quæ sequuntur, paulo subtiliora."
[7] Matt. xix. 30, xx. 16.
[8] Ps. xlv. 17.
[9] Rev. i. 5.
[10] Comp. 1 Cor. xv. 20-22.
[11] Acts i. 7.

observed; and by means of the second man did He bind the strong man, and spoiled his goods,[1] and abolished death, vivifying that man who had been in a state of death. For at the first Adam became a vessel in his (Satan's) possession, whom he did also hold under his power, that is, by bringing sin on him iniquitously, and under colour of immortality entailing death upon him. For, while promising that they should be as gods, which was in no way possible for him to be, he wrought death in them: wherefore he who had led man captive, was justly captured in his turn by God; but man, who had been led captive, was loosed from the bonds of condemnation.

2. But this is Adam, if the truth should be told, the first formed man, of whom the Scripture says that the Lord spake, "Let Us make man after Our own image and likeness;"[2] and we are all from him: and as we are from him, therefore have we all inherited his title. But inasmuch as man is saved, it is fitting that he who was created the original man should be saved. For it is too absurd to maintain, that he who was so deeply injured by the enemy, and was the first to suffer captivity, was not rescued by Him who conquered the enemy, but that his children were,—those whom he had begotten in the same captivity. Neither would the enemy appear to be as yet conquered, if the old spoils remained with him. To give an illustration: If a hostile force had overcome certain [enemies], had bound them, and led them away captive, and held them for a long time in servitude, so that they begat children among them; and somebody, compassionating those who had been made slaves, should overcome this same hostile force; he certainly would not act equitably, were he to liberate the children of those who had been led captive, from the sway of those who had enslaved their fathers, but should leave these latter, who had suffered the act of capture, subject to their enemies,—those, too, on whose very account he had proceeded to this retaliation,—the children succeeding to liberty through the avenging of their fathers' cause, but not[3] so that their fathers, who suffered the act of capture itself, should be left [in bondage]. For God is neither devoid of power nor of justice, who has afforded help to man, and restored him to His own liberty.

3. It was for this reason, too, that immediately after Adam had transgressed, as the Scripture relates, He pronounced no curse against Adam personally, but against the ground, in reference to his works, as a certain person among the ancients has observed: "God did indeed transfer the curse to the earth, that it might not remain in man."[4] But man received, as the punishment of his transgression, the toilsome task of tilling the earth, and to eat bread in the sweat of his face, and to return to the dust from whence he was taken. Similarly also did the woman [receive] toil, and labour, and groans, and the pangs of parturition, and a state of subjection, that is, that she should serve her husband; so that they should neither perish altogether when cursed by God, nor, by remaining unreprimanded, should be led to despise God. But the curse in all its fulness fell upon the serpent, which had beguiled them. "And God," it is declared, "said to the serpent: Because thou hast done this, cursed art thou above all cattle, and above all the beasts of the earth."[5] And this same thing does the Lord also say in the Gospel, to those who are found upon the left hand: "Depart from me, ye cursed, into everlasting fire, which my Father hath prepared for the devil and his angels;"[6] indicating that eternal fire was not originally prepared for man, but for him who beguiled man, and caused him to offend—for him, I say, who is chief of the apostasy, and for those angels who became apostates along with him; which [fire], indeed, they too shall justly feel, who, like him, persevere in works of wickedness, without repentance, and without retracing their steps.

4. [These act][7] as Cain [did, who], when he was counselled by God to keep quiet, because he had not made an equitable division of that share to which his brother was entitled, but with envy and malice thought that he could domineer over him, not only did not acquiesce, but even added sin to sin, indicating his state of mind by his action. For what he had planned, that did he also put in practice: he tyrannized over and slew him; God subjecting the just to the unjust, that the former might be proved as the just one by the things which he suffered, and the latter detected as the unjust by those which he perpetrated. And he was not softened even by this, nor did he stop short with that evil deed; but being asked where his brother was, he said, "I know not; am I my brother's keeper?" extending and aggravating [his] wickedness by his answer. For if it is wicked to slay a brother, much worse is it thus insolently and irreverently to reply to the omniscient God as if he could baffle Him. And for this he did himself bear a curse about with him, because he gratuitously brought

---

[1] Matt. xii. 29.
[2] Gen. i. 26.
[3] The old Latin translation is: "Sed non relictis ipsis patribus." Grabe would cancel *non*, while Massuet pleads for retaining it. Harvey conjectures that the translator perhaps mistook οὐκ ἀνειλημμένων for οὐκ ἀναλελειμένων. We have followed Massuet, though we should prefer deleting *non*, were it not found in all the MSS.

[4] Gen. iii. 16, etc.
[5] Gen. iii. 14.
[6] Matt. xxv. 41. This reading of Irenæus agrees with that of the Codex Bezæ, at Cambridge.
[7] Gen. iv. 7, after LXX. version.

an offering of sin, having had no reverence for God, nor being put to confusion by the act of fratricide.[1]

5. The case of Adam, however, had no analogy with this, but was altogether different. For, having been beguiled by another under the pretext of immortality, he is immediately seized with terror, and hides himself; not as if he were able to escape from God; but, in a state of confusion at having transgressed His command, he feels unworthy to appear before and to hold converse with God. Now, "the fear of the Lord is the beginning of wisdom;"[2] the sense of sin leads to repentance, and God bestows His compassion upon those who are penitent. For [Adam] showed his repentance by his conduct, through means of the girdle [which he used], covering himself with fig-leaves, while there were many other leaves, which would have irritated his body in a less degree. He, however, adopted a dress conformable to his disobedience, being awed by the fear of God; and resisting the erring, the lustful propensity of his flesh (since he had lost his natural disposition and child-like mind, and had come to the knowledge of evil things), he girded a bridle of continence upon himself and his wife, fearing God, and waiting for His coming, and indicating, as it were, some such thing [as follows]: Inasmuch as, he says, I have by disobedience lost that robe of sanctity which I had from the Spirit, I do now also acknowledge that I am deserving of a covering of this nature, which affords no gratification, but which gnaws and frets the body. And he would no doubt have retained this clothing for ever, thus humbling himself, if God, who is merciful, had not clothed them with tunics of skins instead of fig-leaves. For this purpose, too, He interrogates them, that the blame might light upon the woman; and again, He interrogates her, that she might convey the blame to the serpent. For she related what had occurred. "The serpent," says she, "beguiled me, and I did eat."[3] But He put no question to the serpent; for He knew that he had been the prime mover in the guilty deed; but He pronounced the curse upon him in the first instance, that it might fall upon man with a mitigated rebuke. For God detested him who had led man astray, but by degrees, and little by little, He showed compassion to him who had been beguiled.

6. Wherefore also He drove him out of Paradise, and removed him far from the tree of life, not because He envied him the tree of life, as some venture to assert, but because He pitied him, [and did not desire] that he should continue a sinner for ever, nor that the sin which surrounded him should be immortal, and evil interminable and irremediable. But He set a bound to his [state of] sin, by interposing death, and thus causing sin to cease,[4] putting an end to it by the dissolution of the flesh, which should take place in the earth, so that man, ceasing at length to live to sin, and dying to it, might begin to live to God.

7. For this end did He put enmity between the serpent and the woman and her seed, they keeping it up mutually: He, the sole of whose foot should be bitten, having power also to tread upon the enemy's head; but the other biting, killing, and impeding the steps of man, until the seed did come appointed to tread down his head, — which was born of Mary, of whom the prophet speaks: "Thou shalt tread upon the asp and the basilisk; thou shalt trample down the lion and the dragon;"[5] — indicating that sin, which was set up and spread out against man, and which rendered him subject to death, should be deprived of its power, along with death, which rules [over men]; and that the lion, that is, antichrist, rampant against mankind in the latter days, should be trampled down by Him; and that He should bind "the dragon, that old serpent,"[6] and subject him to the power of man, who had been conquered,[7] so that all his might should be trodden down. Now Adam had been conquered, all life having been taken away from him: wherefore, when the foe was conquered in his turn, Adam received new life; and the last enemy, death, is destroyed,[8] which at the first had taken possession of man. Therefore, when man has been liberated, "what is written shall come to pass, Death is swallowed up in victory. O death, where is thy victory? O death, where is thy sting?"[9] This could not be said with justice, if that man, over whom death did first obtain dominion, were not set free. For his salvation is death's destruction. When therefore the Lord vivifies man, that is, Adam, death is at the same time destroyed.

8. All therefore speak falsely who disallow his (Adam's) salvation, shutting themselves out from life for ever, in that they do not believe that the sheep which had perished has been found.[10] For if it has not been found, the whole human race is still held in a state of perdition. False, therefore, is that man who first started this idea, or rather, this ignorance and blindness — Tatian.[11]

---

[1] The old Latin reads "parricidio." The crime of parricide was alone known to the Roman law; but it was a *generic* term, including the murder of all near relations. All the editors have supposed that the original word was ἀδελφοκτονία, which has here been adopted.
[2] Prov. i. 7, ix. 10.
[3] Gen. iii. 13.
[4] Rom. vi. 7.
[5] Ps. xci. 13.
[6] Rev. xx. 2.
[7] Luke x. 19.
[8] 1 Cor. xv. 26.
[9] 1 Cor. xv. 54, 55.
[10] Luke xv. 4.
[11] An account of Tatian will be given in a future volume with his only extant work.

As I have already indicated, this man entangled himself with all the heretics.[1] This dogma, however, has been invented by himself, in order that, by introducing something new, independently of the rest, and by speaking vanity, he might acquire for himself hearers void of faith, affecting to be esteemed a teacher, and endeavouring from time to time to employ sayings of this kind often [made use of] by Paul: "In Adam we all die;"[2] ignorant, however, that "where sin abounded, grace did much more abound."[3] Since this, then, has been clearly shown, let all his disciples be put to shame, and let them wrangle[4] about Adam, as if some great gain were to accrue to them if he be not saved; when they profit nothing more [by that], even as the serpent also did not profit when persuading man [to sin], except to this effect, that he proved him a transgressor, obtaining man as the first-fruits of his own apostasy.[5] But he did not know God's power.[6] Thus also do those who disallow Adam's salvation gain nothing, except this, that they render themselves heretics and apostates from the truth, and show themselves patrons of the serpent and of death.

CHAP. XXIV. — RECAPITULATION OF THE VARIOUS ARGUMENTS ADDUCED AGAINST GNOSTIC IMPIETY UNDER ALL ITS ASPECTS. THE HERETICS, TOSSED ABOUT BY EVERY BLAST OF DOCTRINE, ARE OPPOSED BY THE UNIFORM TEACHING OF THE CHURCH, WHICH REMAINS SO ALWAYS, AND IS CONSISTENT WITH ITSELF.

1. Thus, then, have all these men been exposed, who bring in impious doctrines regarding our Maker and Framer, who also formed this world, and above whom there is no other God; and those have been overthrown by their own arguments who teach falsehoods regarding the substance of our Lord, and the dispensation which He fulfilled for the sake of His own creature man. But [it has, on the other hand, been shown], that the preaching of the Church is everywhere consistent, and continues in an even course, and receives testimony from the prophets, the apostles, and all the disciples — as I have proved — through [those in] the beginning, the middle, and the end,[7] and through the entire dispensation of God, and that well-grounded system which tends[8] to man's salvation, namely, our faith; which, having been received from the Church, we do preserve, and which always, by the Spirit of God, renewing its youth, as if it were some precious deposit in an excellent vessel, causes the vessel itself containing it to renew its youth also. For this gift of God has been entrusted to the Church, as breath was to the first created man,[9] for this purpose, that all the members receiving it may be vivified; and the [means of] communion with Christ has been distributed throughout it, that is, the Holy Spirit, the earnest of incorruption, the means of confirming our faith, and the ladder of ascent to God. "For in the Church," it is said, "God hath set apostles, prophets, teachers,"[10] and all the other means through which the Spirit works; of which all those are not partakers who do not join themselves to the Church, but defraud themselves of life through their perverse opinions and infamous behaviour. For where the Church is, there is the Spirit of God; and where the Spirit of God is, there is the Church, and every kind of grace; but the Spirit is truth. Those, therefore, who do not partake of Him, are neither nourished into life from the mother's breasts, nor do they enjoy that most limpid fountain which issues from the body of Christ; but they dig for themselves broken cisterns[11] out of earthly trenches, and drink putrid water out of the mire, fleeing from the faith of the Church lest they be convicted; and rejecting the Spirit, that they may not be instructed.

2. Alienated thus from the truth, they do deservedly wallow in all error, tossed to and fro by it, thinking differently in regard to the same things at different times, and never attaining to a well-grounded knowledge, being more anxious to be sophists of words than disciples of the truth. For they have not been founded upon the one rock, but upon the sand, which has in itself a multitude of stones. Wherefore they also imagine many gods, and they always have the excuse of searching [after truth] (for they are blind), but never succeed in finding it. For they blaspheme the Creator, Him who is truly God, who also furnishes power to find [the truth]; imagining that they have discovered another god beyond God, or another Pleroma, or another dispensation. Wherefore also the light which is from God does not illumine them, because they have dishonoured and despised God, holding Him of small account, because, through His love and infinite benignity, He has come within reach of human knowledge (knowledge, however, not with regard to His greatness, or with regard to His essence — for that has no

---

[1] His heresy being just a mixture of the opinions of the various Gnostic sects.
[2] 1 Cor. xv. 22.
[3] Rom. v. 20.
[4] Though unnoticed by the editors, there seems a difficulty in the different moods of the two verbs, *erubescant* and *concertant*.
[5] "Initium et materiam apostasiæ suæ habens hominem:" the meaning is very obscure, and the editors throw no light upon it.
[6] Literally, "but he did not *see* God." The translator is supposed to have read οἶδεν, *knew*, for εἶδεν, *saw*.
[7] Literally, "through the beginnings, the means, and the end." These three terms refer to the Prophets, the Apostles, and the Church Catholic.
[8] The Latin is "solidam operationem," which we know not how to translate, in accordance with the context, except as above.

[9] This seems to be the meaning conveyed by the old Latin, "quemadmodum aspiratio plasmationi."
[10] 1 Cor. xii. 28.
[11] Jer. ii. 13.

man measured or handled — but after this sort: that we should know that He who made, and formed, and breathed in them the breath of life, and nourishes us by means of the creation, establishing all things by His Word, and binding them together by His Wisdom [1] — this is He who is the only true God); but they dream of a non-existent being above Him, that they may be regarded as having found out the great God, whom nobody, [they hold,] can recognise as holding communication with the human race, or as directing mundane matters: that is to say, they find out the god of Epicurus, who does nothing either for himself or others; that is, he exercises no providence at all.

CHAP. XXV. — THIS WORLD IS RULED BY THE PROVIDENCE OF ONE GOD, WHO IS BOTH ENDOWED WITH INFINITE JUSTICE TO PUNISH THE WICKED, AND WITH INFINITE GOODNESS TO BLESS THE PIOUS, AND IMPART TO THEM SALVATION.

1. God does, however, exercise a providence over all things, and therefore He also gives counsel; and when giving counsel, He is present with those who attend to moral discipline.[2] It follows then of course, that the things which are watched over and governed should be acquainted with their ruler; which things are not irrational or vain, but they have understanding derived from the providence of God. And, for this reason, certain of the Gentiles, who were less addicted to [sensual] allurements and voluptuousness, and were not led away to such a degree of superstition with regard to idols, being moved, though but slightly, by His providence, were nevertheless convinced that they should call the Maker of this universe the Father, who exercises a providence over all things, and arranges the affairs of our world.

2. Again, that they might remove the rebuking and judicial power from the Father, reckoning that as unworthy of God, and thinking that they had found out a God both without anger and [merely] good, they have alleged that one [God] judges, but that another saves, unconsciously taking away the intelligence and justice of both deities. For if the judicial one is not also good, to bestow favours upon the deserving, and to direct reproofs against those requiring them, he will appear neither a just nor a wise judge. On the other hand, the good God, if he is merely good, and not one who tests those upon whom he shall send his goodness, will be out of the range of justice and goodness; and his goodness will seem imperfect, as not saving all; [for it should do so,] if it be not accompanied with judgment.

3. Marcion, therefore, himself, by dividing God into two, maintaining one to be good and the other judicial, does in fact, on both sides, put an end to deity. For he that is the judicial one, if he be not good, is not God, because he from whom goodness is absent is no God at all; and again, he who is good, if he has no judicial power, suffers the same [loss] as the former, by being deprived of his character of deity. And how can they call the Father of all wise, if they do not assign to Him a judicial faculty? For if He is wise, He is also one who tests [others]; but the judicial power belongs to him who tests, and justice follows the judicial faculty, that it may reach a just conclusion; justice calls forth judgment, and judgment, when it is executed with justice, will pass on to wisdom. Therefore the Father will excel in wisdom all human and angelic wisdom, because He is Lord, and Judge, and the Just One, and Ruler over all. For He is good, and merciful, and patient, and saves whom He ought: nor does goodness desert Him in the exercise of justice,[3] nor is His wisdom lessened; for He saves those whom He should save, and judges those worthy of judgment. Neither does He show Himself unmercifully just; for His goodness, no doubt, goes on before, and takes precedency.

4. The God, therefore, who does benevolently cause His sun to rise upon all,[4] and sends rain upon the just and unjust, shall judge those who, enjoying His equally distributed kindness, have led lives not corresponding to the dignity of His bounty; but who have spent their days in wantonness and luxury, in opposition to His benevolence, and have, moreover, even blasphemed Him who has conferred so great benefits upon them.

5. Plato is proved to be more religious than these men, for he allowed that the same God was both just and good, having power over all things, and Himself executing judgment, expressing himself thus, "And God indeed, as He is also the ancient Word, possessing the beginning, the end, and the mean of all existing things, does everything rightly, moving round about them according to their nature; but retributive justice always follows Him against those who depart from the divine law."[5] Then, again, he points out that the Maker and Framer of the universe is good. "And to the good," he says, "no envy ever springs up with regard to anything;"[6] thus establishing the goodness of God, as the beginning and the cause of the creation of the world, but not ignorance, nor an erring Æon, nor the

---

[1] i. e., the Spirit.
[2] Literally, "who have a foresight of morals"—*qui morum providentiam habent.* The meaning is very obscure. [Prov. xxii. 3, xxvii. 12.]
[3] The text is here very uncertain, but the above seems the probable meaning.
[4] Matt. v. 45.
[5] Plato, *de Leg.*, iv. and p. 715, 16.
[6] In *Timæo,* vi. p. 29.

consequence of a defect, nor the Mother weeping and lamenting, nor another God or Father.

6. Well may their Mother bewail them, as capable of conceiving and inventing such things; for they have worthily uttered this falsehood against themselves, that their Mother is beyond the Pleroma, that is, beyond the knowledge of God, and that their entire multitude became [1] a shapeless and crude abortion: for it apprehends nothing of the truth; it falls into void and darkness: for their wisdom (*Sophia*) was void, and wrapped up in darkness; and Horos did not permit her to enter the Pleroma: for the Spirit (Achamoth) did not receive them into the place of refreshment. For their father, by begetting ignorance, wrought in them the sufferings of death. We do not misrepresent [their opinions on] these points; but they do themselves confirm, they do themselves teach, they do glory in them, they imagine a lofty [mystery] about their Mother, whom they represent as having been begotten without a father, that is, without God, a female from a female,[2] that is, corruption from error.

[1] The Latin is "collectio eorum;" but what *collectio* here means, it is not easy to determine. Grabe, with much probability, deems it the representative of σύστασις. Harvey prefers ἐνθύμημα: but it is difficult to perceive the relevancy of his references to the rhetorical syllogism.
[2] See book i. cap. xvi. note.

7. We do indeed pray that these men may not remain in the pit which they themselves have dug, but separate themselves from a Mother of this nature, and depart from Bythus, and stand away from the void, and relinquish the shadow; and that they, being converted to the Church of God, may be lawfully begotten, and that Christ may be formed in them, and that they may know the Framer and Maker of this universe, the only true God and Lord of all. We pray for these things on their behalf, loving them better than they seem to love themselves. For our love, inasmuch as it is true, is salutary to them, if they will but receive it. It may be compared to a severe remedy, extirpating the proud and sloughing flesh of a wound; for it puts an end to their pride and haughtiness. Wherefore it shall not weary us, to endeavour with all our might to stretch out the hand unto them. Over and above what has been already stated, I have deferred to the following book, to adduce the words of the Lord; if, by convincing some among them, through means of the very instruction of Christ, I may succeed in persuading them to abandon such error, and to cease from blaspheming their Creator, who is both God alone, and the Father of our Lord Jesus Christ. Amen.

ELUCIDATION

The editor of this American Series confines himself in general to such occasional and *very* brief annotations as may suggest to students and others the practical views which are requisite to a clear comprehension of authors who wrote for past ages; for a sort and condition of men no longer existing, whose extinction as a class is, indeed, largely due to these writings. But he reserved to himself the privilege of correcting palpable mistakes, especially in points which bear upon questions of our own times.

That our learned translators have unaccountably admitted a very inaccurate translation of the crucial paragraph in book iii. cap. iii. sect. 2, I have shown in the footnote at that place. It is evident, (1) because they themselves are not satisfied with it, and (2) because I have set it side by side with the more literal rendering of a writer who would have preferred their reading if it could have borne the test of criticism.

Now, the authors of the Latin translation [1] may have designed the ambiguity which gives the Ultramontane party an apparent advantage; but it is an advantage which disappears as soon as it is examined, and hence I am content to take it as it stands. Various conjectures have been made as to the original Greek of Irenæus; but the Latin answers every purpose of the author's argument, and is fatal to the claims of the Papacy. Let me recur to the translation given, *in loco*, from a Roman Catholic, and this will be seen at once.

For he thus renders it:—

1. In this Church, "ever, *by those who are on every side*, has been preserved that tradition

[1] One of the Antiochian Canons probably reflects the current language of an earlier antiquity thus: διὰ τὸ ἐν τῇ μητροπόλει πανταχόθεν συντρέχειν πάντας τοὺς τὰ πράγματα ἔχοντας; and, if so, this συντρέχειν gives the meaning of *convenire*.

which is from apostles." How would such a proposition have sounded to Pius IX. in the Vatican Council? The faith is preserved *by those who come to Rome*, not by the Bishop who presides there.

2. "For to this Church, on account of more potent principality,[1] it is necessary that *every Church* (that is, those who are, on every side, faithful) resort." The greatness of Rome, that is, as the capital of the Empire, imparts to the local Church a superior dignity, even as compared with Lyons, or any other metropolitical Church. Everybody visits Rome: hence you find there faithful witnesses from every side (from all the Churches); and *their united testimony* it is which preserves in Rome the pure apostolic traditions.

The Latin, thus translated by a candid Roman Catholic, reverses the whole system of the Papacy. Pius IX. informed his Bishops, at the late Council, that they were not called to bear their testimony, but to hear his infallible decree; "reducing us," said the Archbishop of Paris, "to a council of sacristans."

Sustaining these views by a few footnotes, I add (1) a literal rendering of my own, and then (2) a metaphrase of the same, bringing out the argument from the crabbed obstructions of the Latin text. This, then, is what Irenæus says: (*a*) "For it is necessary for every Church (that is to say, the faithful from all parts) to meet in this Church, on account of the superior magistracy; in which Church, by those who are from all places, the tradition of the apostles has been preserved." Or, more freely rendered: (*b*) "On account of the chief magistracy[2] [of the empire], the faithful from all parts, representing every Church, are obliged to resort to Rome, and there to come together; so that [it is the distinction of this Church that], in it, the tradition of the apostles has been preserved by Christians gathered together out of all the Churches." Taking the entire argument of our author with the context, then, it amounts to this: "We must ask, not for local, but universal, testimony. Now, in every Church founded by the apostles has been handed down their traditions; but, as it would be a tedious thing to collect them all, let this suffice. Take that Church (nearest at hand, and which is the only Apostolic Church of the West), the great and glorious Church at Rome, which was there founded by the two apostles Peter and Paul. In her have been preserved the traditions *of all the Churches*, because everybody is forced to go to the seat of empire: and therefore, by these representatives of the whole Catholic Church, the apostolic traditions have been all collected in Rome:[3] and you have a synoptical view of all Churches in what is there preserved." Had the views of the modern Papacy ever entered the head of Irenæus, what an absurdity would be this whole argument. He would have said, "It is no matter what may be gathered elsewhere; for the Bishop of Rome is the infallible oracle of all Catholic truth, and you will always find it by his mouth." It should be noted that Orthodoxy was indeed preserved there, just so long as Rome permitted other Churches to contribute their testimony on the principle of Irenæus, and thus to make her the depository of all Catholic tradition, as witnessed "by *all, everywhere,* and from the beginning." But all this is turned upside down by modern Romanism. No other Church is to be heard or considered; but Rome takes all into her own power, and may dictate to all Churches what they are to believe, however novel, or contrary to the torrent of antiquity in the teachings of their own founders and great doctors in all past time.

---

[1] "*Its* more potent," etc., is not a strict rendering: "*the* more potent," rather; which leaves the *principalitas* to the city, not the Church.

[2] Bishop Wordsworth inclines to the idea that the original Greek was ἱκανωτέραν ἀρχαιότητα, thus conceding that Irenæus was speaking of the *greater antiquity* of Rome as compared with other (Western) Churches. Even so, he shows that the argument of Irenæus is fatal to Roman pretensions, which admit of no such ideas as he advances, and no such freedom as that of his dealings with Rome.

[3] Nobody has more forcibly stated the argument of Irenæus than the Abbé Guettée, in his exhaustive work on the Papacy. I published a translation of this valuable historical epitome in New York (Carleton), 1867; but it is out of print. The original may be had in Paris (Fischbacher), No. 33 Rue de Seine.

IRENÆUS AGAINST HERESIES

BOOK IV.

PREFACE.

1. By transmitting to thee, my very dear friend, this fourth book of the work which is [entitled] *The Detection and Refutation of False Knowledge,* I shall, as I have promised, add weight, by means of the words of the Lord, to what I have already advanced; so that thou also, as thou hast requested, mayest obtain from me the means of confuting all the heretics everywhere, and not permit them, beaten back at all points, to launch out further into the deep of error, nor to be drowned in the sea of ignorance; but that thou, turning them into the haven of the truth, mayest cause them to attain their salvation.

2. The man, however, who would undertake their conversion, must possess an accurate knowledge of their systems or schemes of doctrine. For it is impossible for any one to heal the sick, if he has no knowledge of the disease of the patients. This was the reason that my predecessors — much superior men to myself, too — were unable, notwithstanding, to refute the Valentinians satisfactorily, because they were ignorant of these men's system;[1] which I have with all care delivered to thee in the first book, in which I have also shown that their doctrine is a recapitulation of all the heretics. For which reason also, in the second, we have had, as in a mirror, a sight of their entire discomfiture. For they who oppose these men (the Valentinians) by the right method, do [thereby] oppose all who are of an evil mind; and they who overthrow them, do in fact overthrow every kind of heresy.

3. For their system is blasphemous above all [others], since they represent that the Maker and Framer, who is one God, as I have shown, was produced from a defect or apostasy. They utter blasphemy, also, against our Lord, by cutting off and dividing Jesus from Christ, and Christ from the Saviour, and again the Saviour from the Word, and the Word from the Onlybegotten. And since they allege that the Creator originated from a defect or apostasy, so have they also taught that Christ and the Holy Spirit were emitted on account of this defect, and that the Saviour was a product of those Æons who were produced from a defect; so that there is nothing but blasphemy to be found among them. In the preceding book, then, the ideas of the apostles as to all these points have been set forth, [to the effect] that not only did they, "who from the beginning were eye-witnesses and ministers of the word"[2] of truth, hold no such opinions, but that they did also preach to us to shun these doctrines,[3] foreseeing by the Spirit those weak-minded persons who should be led astray.[4]

4. For as the serpent beguiled Eve, by promising her what he had not himself,[5] so also do these men, by pretending [to possess] superior knowledge, and [to be acquainted with] ineffable mysteries; and, by promising that admittance which they speak of as taking place within the Pleroma, plunge those that believe them into death, rendering them apostates from Him who made them. And at that time, indeed, the apostate angel, having effected the disobedience of mankind by means of the serpent, imagined that he escaped the notice of the Lord; wherefore God assigned him the form[6] and name [of a serpent]. But now, since the last times are [come upon us], evil is spread abroad among men, which not only renders them apostates, but by many machinations does [the devil] raise up blasphemers against the

---

[1] [The reader who marvels at the tedious recitals must note this (1) as proof of the author's practical wisdom, and (2) as evidence of his fidelity in what he exhibits.]

[2] Luke i. 2.
[3] 2 Tim. ii. 23.
[4] [The solemnity of the apostolic testimonies against the crop of tares that was to spring up receives great illustration from Irenæus. 1 John ii. 18.]
[5] [2 Pet. ii. 19.]
[6] [Rev. xii. 9. A little essay, *Messias and Anti-Messias,* by the Rev. C. I. Black, London (Masters, 1847), is commended to those who need light on this very mysterious subject.]

Creator, namely, by means of all the heretics already mentioned. For all these, although they issue forth from diverse regions, and promulgate different [opinions], do nevertheless concur in the same blasphemous design, wounding [men] unto death, by teaching blasphemy against God our Maker and Supporter, and derogating from the salvation of man. Now man is a mixed organization of soul and flesh, who was formed after the likeness of God, and moulded by His hands, that is, by the Son and Holy Spirit, to whom also He said, "Let Us make man."[1] This, then, is the aim of him who envies our life, to render men disbelievers in their own salvation, and blasphemous against God the Creator. For whatsoever all the heretics may have advanced with the utmost solemnity, they come to this at last, that they blaspheme the Creator, and disallow the salvation of God's workmanship, which the flesh truly is; on behalf of which I have proved, in a variety of ways, that the Son of God accomplished the whole dispensation [of mercy], and have shown that there is none other called God by the Scriptures except the Father of all, and the Son, and those who possess the adoption.

CHAP. I. — THE LORD ACKNOWLEDGED BUT ONE GOD AND FATHER.

1. Since, therefore, this is sure and stedfast, that no other God or Lord was announced by the Spirit, except Him who, as God, rules over all, together with His Word, and those who receive the Spirit of adoption,[2] that is, those who believe in the one and true God, and in Jesus Christ the Son of God; and likewise that the apostles did of themselves term no one else as God, or name [no other] as Lord; and, what is much more important, [since it is true] that our Lord [acted likewise], who did also command us to confess no one as Father, except Him who is in the heavens, who is the one God and the one Father; — those things are clearly shown to be false which these deceivers and most perverse sophists advance, maintaining that the being whom they have themselves invented is by nature both God and Father; but that the Demiurge is naturally neither God nor Father, but is so termed merely by courtesy (*verbo tenus*), because of his ruling the creation, as these perverse mythologists state, setting their thoughts against God; and, putting aside the doctrine of Christ, and of themselves divining falsehoods, they dispute against the entire dispensation of God. For they maintain that their Æons, and gods, and fathers, and lords, are also still further termed heavens, together with their Mother, whom they do also call "the Earth," and "Jerusalem," while they also style her many other names.

2. Now to whom is it not clear, that if the Lord had known many fathers and gods, He would not have taught His disciples to know [only] one God,[3] and to call Him alone Father? But He did the rather distinguish those who by word merely (*verbo tenus*) are termed gods, from Him who is truly God, that they should not err as to His doctrine, nor understand one [in mistake] for another. And if He did indeed teach us to call one Being Father and God, while He does from time to time Himself confess other fathers and gods in the same sense, then He will appear to enjoin a different course upon His disciples from what He follows Himself. Such conduct, however, does not bespeak the good teacher, but a misleading and invidious one. The apostles, too, according to these men's showing, are proved to be transgressors of the commandment, since they confess the Creator as God, and Lord, and Father, as I have shown — if He is not alone God and Father. Jesus, therefore, will be to them the author and teacher of such transgression, inasmuch as He commanded that one Being should be called Father,[4] thus imposing upon them the necessity of confessing the Creator as their Father, as has been pointed out.

CHAP. II. — PROOFS FROM THE PLAIN TESTIMONY OF MOSES, AND OF THE OTHER PROPHETS, WHOSE WORDS ARE THE WORDS OF CHRIST, THAT THERE IS BUT ONE GOD, THE FOUNDER OF THE WORLD, WHOM OUR LORD PREACHED, AND WHOM HE CALLED HIS FATHER.

1. Moses, therefore, making a recapitulation of the whole law, which he had received from the Creator (Demiurge), thus speaks in Deuteronomy: "Give ear, O ye heavens, and I will speak; and hear, O earth, the words of my mouth."[5] Again, David saying that his help came from the Lord, asserts: "My help is from the LORD, who made heaven and earth."[6] And Esaias confesses that words were uttered by God, who made heaven and earth, and governs them. He says: "Hear, O heavens; and give ear, O earth: for the LORD hath spoken."[7] And again: "Thus saith the LORD God, who made the heaven, and stretched it out; who established the earth, and the things in it; and who giveth breath to the people upon it, and spirit to them who walk therein."[8]

2. Again, our Lord Jesus Christ confesses this same Being as His Father, where He says: "I

---
[1] Gen. i. 26.
[2] See iii. 6, 1.
[3] [St. John xvii. 3.]
[4] Matt. xxiii. 9.
[5] Deut. xxxii. 1.
[6] Ps. cxxiv. 8.
[7] Isa. i. 2.
[8] Isa. xlii. 5.

confess to thee, O Father, Lord of heaven and earth." [1] What Father will those men have us to understand [by these words], those who are most perverse sophists of Pandora? Whether shall it be Bythus, whom they have fabled of themselves; or their Mother; or the Only-begotten? Or shall it be he whom the Marcionites or the others have invented as god (whom I indeed have amply demonstrated to be no god at all); or shall it be (what is really the case) the Maker of heaven and earth, whom also the prophets proclaimed, — whom Christ, too, confesses as His Father, — whom also the law announces, saying: "Hear, O Israel; The Lord thy God is one God?" [2]

3. But since the writings (*literæ*) of Moses are the words of Christ, He does Himself declare to the Jews, as John has recorded in the Gospel: "If ye had believed Moses, ye would have believed Me: for he wrote of Me. But if ye believe not his writings, neither will ye believe My words." [3] He thus indicates in the clearest manner that the writings of Moses are His words. If, then, [this be the case with regard] to Moses, so also, beyond a doubt, the words of the other prophets are His [words], as I have pointed out. And again, the Lord Himself exhibits Abraham as having said to the rich man, with reference to all those who were still alive: "If they do not obey Moses and the prophets, neither, if any one were to rise from the dead and go to them, will they believe him." [4]

4. Now, He has not merely related to us a story respecting a poor man and a rich one; but He has taught us, in the first place, that no one should lead a luxurious life, nor, living in worldly pleasures and perpetual feastings, should be the slave of his lusts, and forget God. "For there was," He says, "a rich man, who was clothed in purple and fine linen, and delighted himself with splendid feasts." [5]

Of such persons, too, the Spirit has spoken by Esaias: "They drink wine with [the accompaniment of] harps, and tablets, and psalteries, and flutes; but they regard not the works of God, neither do they consider the work of His hands." [6] Lest, therefore, we should incur the same punishment as these men, the Lord reveals [to us] their end; showing at the same time, that if they obeyed Moses and the prophets, they would believe in Him whom these had preached, the Son of God, who rose from the dead, and bestows life upon us; and He shows that all are from one essence, that is, Abraham, and Moses, and the prophets, and also the Lord Himself, who rose from the dead, in whom many believe who are of the circumcision, who do also hear Moses and the prophets announcing the coming of the Son of God. But those who scoff [at the truth] assert that these men were from another essence, and they do not know the first-begotten from the dead; understanding Christ as a distinct being, who continued as if He were impassible, and Jesus, who suffered, as being altogether separate [from Him].

5. For they do not receive from the Father the knowledge of the Son; neither do they learn who the Father is from the Son, who teaches clearly and without parables Him who truly is God. He says: "Swear not at all; neither by heaven, for it is God's throne; nor by the earth, for it is His footstool; neither by Jerusalem, for it is the city of the great King." [7] For these words are evidently spoken with reference to the Creator, as also Esaias says: "Heaven is my throne, the earth is my footstool." [8] And besides this Being there is no other God; otherwise He would not be termed by the Lord either "God" or "the great King;" for a Being who can be so described admits neither of any other being compared with nor set above Him. For he who has any superior over him, and is under the power of another, this being never can be called either "God" or "the great King."

6. But neither will these men be able to maintain that such words were uttered in an ironical manner, since it is proved to them by the words themselves that they were in earnest. For He who uttered them was Truth, and did truly vindicate His own house, by driving out of it the changers of money, who were buying and selling, saying unto them: "It is written, My house shall be called the house of prayer; but ye have made it a den of thieves." [9] And what reason had He for thus doing and saying, and vindicating His house, if He did preach another God? But [He did so], that He might point out the transgressors of His Father's law; for neither did He bring any accusation against the house, nor did He blame the law, which He had come to fulfil; but He reproved those who were putting His house to an improper use, and those who were transgressing the law. And therefore the scribes and Pharisees, too, who from the times of the law had begun to despise God, did not receive His Word, that is, they did not believe on Christ. Of these Esaias says: "Thy princes are rebellious, companions of thieves, loving gifts, following after rewards, not judging the fatherless, and negligent of the cause of the widows." [10] And Jeremiah, in like manner:

---

[1] Matt. xi. 25; Luke x. 21.
[2] Deut. vi. 4.
[3] John v. 46, 47.
[4] Luke xvi. 31.
[5] Luke xvi. 19.
[6] Isa. v. 12.
[7] Matt. v. 34.
[8] Isa. lxvi. 1.
[9] Matt. xxi. 13.
[10] Isa. i. 23.

"They," he says, "who rule my people did not know me; they are senseless and imprudent children; they are wise to do evil, but to do well they have no knowledge."[1]

7. But as many as feared God, and were anxious about His law, these ran to Christ, and were all saved. For He said to His disciples: "Go ye to the sheep of the house of Israel,[2] which have perished." And many more Samaritans, it is said, when the Lord had tarried among them two days, "believed because of His words, and said to the woman, Now we believe, not because of thy saying, for we ourselves have heard [Him], and know that this man is truly the Saviour of the world."[3] And Paul likewise declares, "And so all Israel shall be saved;"[4] but he has also said, that the law was our pedagogue [to bring us] to Christ Jesus.[5] Let them not therefore ascribe to the law the unbelief of certain [among them]. For the law never hindered them from believing in the Son of God; nay, but it even exhorted them[6] so to do, saying[7] that men can be saved in no other way from the old wound of the serpent than by believing in Him who, in the likeness of sinful flesh, is lifted up from the earth upon the tree of martyrdom, and draws all things to Himself,[8] and vivifies the dead.

CHAP. III. — ANSWER TO THE CAVILS OF THE GNOSTICS. WE ARE NOT TO SUPPOSE THAT THE TRUE GOD CAN BE CHANGED, OR COME TO AN END, BECAUSE THE HEAVENS, WHICH ARE HIS THRONE, AND THE EARTH, HIS FOOTSTOOL, SHALL PASS AWAY.

1. Again, as to their malignantly asserting that if heaven is indeed the throne of God, and earth His footstool, and if it is declared that the heaven and earth shall pass away, then when these pass away the God who sitteth above must also pass away, and therefore He cannot be the God who is over all; in the first place, they are ignorant what the expression means, that heaven is [His] throne and earth [His] footstool. For they do not know what God is, but they imagine that He sits after the fashion of a man, and is contained within bounds, but does not contain. And they are also unacquainted with [the meaning of] the passing away of the heaven and earth; but Paul was not ignorant of it when he declared, "For the figure of this world passeth away."[9] In the next place, David explains their question, for he says that when the fashion of this world passes away, not only shall God remain, but His servants also, expressing himself thus in the 101st Psalm: "In the beginning, Thou, O LORD, hast founded the earth, and the heavens are the works of Thy hands. They shall perish, but Thou shalt endure, and all shall wax old as a garment; and as a vesture Thou shalt change them, and they shall be changed: but Thou art the same, and Thy years shall not fail. The children of Thy servants shall continue, and their seed shall be established for ever;"[10] pointing out plainly what things they are that pass away, and who it is that doth endure for ever — God, together with His servants. And in like manner Esaias says: "Lift up your eyes to the heavens, and look upon the earth beneath; for the heaven has been set together as smoke, and the earth shall wax old like a garment, and they who dwell therein shall die in like manner. But my salvation shall be for ever, and my righteousness shall not pass away."[11]

CHAP. IV. — ANSWER TO ANOTHER OBJECTION, SHOWING THAT THE DESTRUCTION OF JERUSALEM, WHICH WAS THE CITY OF THE GREAT KING, DIMINISHED NOTHING FROM THE SUPREME MAJESTY AND POWER OF GOD, FOR THAT THIS DESTRUCTION WAS PUT IN EXECUTION BY THE MOST WISE COUNSEL OF THE SAME GOD.

1. Further, also, concerning Jerusalem and the Lord, they venture to assert that, if it had been "the city of the great King,"[12] it would not have been deserted.[13] This is just as if any one should say, that if straw were a creation of God, it would never part company with the wheat; and that the vine twigs, if made by God, never would be lopped away and deprived of the clusters. But as these [vine twigs] have not been originally made for their own sake, but for that of the fruit growing upon them, which being come to maturity and taken away, they are left behind, and those which do not conduce to fructification are lopped off altogether; so also [was it with] Jerusalem, which had in herself borne the yoke of bondage (under which man was reduced, who in former times was not subject to God when death was reigning, and being subdued, became a fit subject for liberty), when the fruit of liberty had come, and reached maturity, and been reaped and stored in the barn, and when those which had the power to produce fruit had been carried away from her [i.e., from Jerusalem], and scattered throughout all the world. Even as Esaias saith, "The children of

---

[1] Jer. iv. 22.
[2] Matt. x. 6.
[3] John iv. 41.
[4] Rom. xi. 26.
[5] Gal. iii. 24.
[6] Num. xxi. 8.
[7] This passage is quoted by Augustine, in his treatise on original sin, written to oppose Pelagius (lib. i. c. ii.), about 400 A.D.
[8] John xii. 32, iii. 14.
[9] 1 Cor. vii. 31.
[10] Ps. cii. 25-28. The cause of the difference in the numbering of the Psalms is that the Septuagint embraces in one psalm — the ninth — the two which form the ninth and tenth in the Hebrew text.
[11] Isa. li. 6.
[12] Matt. v. 35.
[13] [Jer. vii. 4. One of the most powerful arguments in all Scripture is contained in the first twelve verses of this chapter, and it rebukes an inveterate superstition of the human heart. Comp. Rev. ii. 5, and the message to Rome, Rom. xi. 21.]

Jacob shall strike root, and Israel shall flourish, and the whole world shall be filled with his fruit."[1] The fruit, therefore, having been sown throughout all the world, she (Jerusalem) was deservedly forsaken, and those things which had formerly brought forth fruit abundantly were taken away; for from these, according to the flesh, were Christ and the apostles enabled to bring forth fruit. But now these are no longer useful for bringing forth fruit. For all things which have a beginning in time must of course have an end in time also.

2. Since, then, the law originated with Moses, it terminated with John as a necessary consequence. Christ had come to fulfil it: wherefore "the law and the prophets were" with them "until John."[2] And therefore Jerusalem, taking its commencement from David,[3] and fulfilling its own times, must have an end of legislation[4] when the new covenant was revealed. For God does all things by measure and in order; nothing is unmeasured with Him, because nothing is out of order. Well spake he, who said that the unmeasurable Father was Himself subjected to measure in the Son; for the Son is the measure of the Father, since He also comprehends Him. But that the administration of them (the Jews) was temporary, Esaias says: "And the daughter of Zion shall be left as a cottage in a vineyard, and as a lodge in a garden of cucumbers."[5] And when shall these things be left behind? Is it not when the fruit shall be taken away, and the leaves alone shall be left, which now have no power of producing fruit?

3. But why do we speak of Jerusalem, since, indeed, the fashion of the whole world must also pass away, when the time of its disappearance has come, in order that the fruit indeed may be gathered into the garner, but the chaff, left behind, may be consumed by fire? "For the day of the Lord cometh as a burning furnace, and all sinners shall be stubble, they who do evil things, and the day shall burn them up."[6] Now, who this Lord is that brings such a day about, John the Baptist points out, when he says of Christ, "He shall baptize you with the Holy Ghost and with fire, having His fan in His hand to cleanse His floor; and He will gather His fruit into the garner, but the chaff He will burn up with unquenchable fire."[7] For He who makes the chaff and He who makes the wheat are not different persons, but one and the same, who judges them, that is, separates them. But the wheat and the chaff, being inanimate and irrational, have been made such by nature. But man, being endowed with reason, and in this respect like to God, having been made free in his will, and with power over himself, is himself the cause to himself, that sometimes he becomes wheat, and sometimes chaff. Wherefore also he shall be justly condemned, because, having been created a rational being, he lost the true rationality, and living irrationally, opposed the righteousness of God, giving himself over to every earthly spirit, and serving all lusts; as says the prophet, "Man, being in honour, did not understand: he was assimilated to senseless beasts, and made like to them."[8]

CHAP. V.—THE AUTHOR RETURNS TO HIS FORMER ARGUMENT, AND SHOWS THAT THERE WAS BUT ONE GOD ANNOUNCED BY THE LAW AND PROPHETS, WHOM CHRIST CONFESSES AS HIS FATHER, AND WHO, THROUGH HIS WORD, ONE LIVING GOD WITH HIM, MADE HIMSELF KNOWN TO MEN IN BOTH COVENANTS.

1. God, therefore, is one and the same, who rolls up the heaven as a book, and renews the face of the earth; who made the things of time for man, so that coming to maturity in them, he may produce the fruit of immortality; and who, through His kindness, also bestows [upon him] eternal things, "that in the ages to come He may show the exceeding riches of His grace;"[9] who was announced by the law and the prophets, whom Christ confessed as His Father. Now He is the Creator, and He it is who is God over all, as Esaias says, "I am witness, saith the LORD God, and my servant whom I have chosen, that ye may know, and believe, and understand that I AM. Before me there was no other God, neither shall be after me. I am God, and besides me there is no Saviour. I have proclaimed, and I have saved."[10] And again: "I myself am the first God, and I am above things to come."[11] For neither in an ambiguous, nor arrogant, nor boastful manner, does He say these things; but since it was impossible, without God, to come to a knowledge of God, He teaches men, through His Word, to know God. To those, therefore, who are ignorant of these matters, and on this account imagine that they have discovered another Father, justly does one say, "Ye do err, not knowing the Scriptures, nor the power of God."[12]

2. For our Lord and Master, in the answer which He gave to the Sadducees, who say that there is no resurrection, and who do therefore

---

[1] Isa. xxvii. 6.
[2] Luke xvi. 16.
[3] 2 Sam. v. 7, where David is described as taking the stronghold of Zion from the Jebusites.
[4] The text fluctuates between "legis dationem" and "legis dationis." We have followed the latter.
[5] Isa. i. 8.
[6] Mal. iv. 1.
[7] Matt. iii. 11, etc.
[8] Ps. xlix. 12.
[9] Eph. ii. 7.
[10] Isa. xliii. 10, etc.
[11] Isa. xii. 4.
[12] Matt. xxii. 29.

dishonour God, and lower the credit of the law, did both indicate a resurrection, and reveal God, saying to them, "Ye do err, not knowing the Scriptures, nor the power of God." "For, touching the resurrection of the dead," He says, "have ye not read that which was spoken by God, saying, I am the God of Abraham, the God of Isaac, and the God of Jacob?"[1] And He added, "He is not the God of the dead, but of the living; for all live to Him." By these arguments He unquestionably made it clear, that He who spake to Moses out of the bush, and declared Himself to be the God of the fathers, He is the God of the living. For who is the God of the living unless He who is God, and above whom there is no other God? Whom also Daniel the prophet, when Cyrus king of the Persians said to him, "Why dost thou not worship Bel?"[2] did proclaim, saying, "Because I do not worship idols made with hands, but the living God, who established the heaven and the earth, and has dominion over all flesh." Again did he say, "I will adore the Lord my God, because He is the living God." He, then, who was adored by the prophets as the living God, He is the God of the living; and His Word is He who also spake to Moses, who also put the Sadducees to silence, who also bestowed the gift of resurrection, thus revealing [both] truths to those who are blind, that is, the resurrection and God [in His true character]. For if He be not the God of the dead, but of the living, yet was called the God of the fathers who were sleeping, they do indubitably live to God, and have not passed out of existence, since they are children of the resurrection. But our Lord is Himself the resurrection, as He does Himself declare, "I am the resurrection and the life."[3] But the fathers are His children; for it is said by the prophet: "Instead of thy fathers, thy children have been made to thee."[4] Christ Himself, therefore, together with the Father, is the God of the living, who spake to Moses, and who was also manifested to the fathers.

3. And teaching this very thing, He said to the Jews: "Your father Abraham rejoiced that he should see my day; and he saw it, and was glad."[5] What is intended? "Abraham believed God, and it was imputed unto him for righteousness."[6] In the first place, [he believed] that He was the maker of heaven and earth, the only God; and in the next place, that He would make his seed as the stars of heaven. This is what is meant by Paul, [when he says,] "as lights in the world."[7] Righteously, therefore, having left his earthly kindred, he followed the Word of God, walking as a pilgrim with the Word, that he might [afterwards] have his abode with the Word.

4. Righteously also the apostles, being of the race of Abraham, left the ship and their father, and followed the Word. Righteously also do we, possessing the same faith as Abraham, and taking up the cross as Isaac did the wood,[8] follow Him. For in Abraham man had learned beforehand, and had been accustomed to follow the Word of God. For Abraham, according to his faith, followed the command of the Word of God, and with a ready mind delivered up, as a sacrifice to God, his only-begotten and beloved son, in order that God also might be pleased to offer up for all his seed His own beloved and only-begotten Son, as a sacrifice for our redemption.

5. Since, therefore, Abraham was a prophet and saw in the Spirit the day of the Lord's coming, and the dispensation of His suffering, through whom both he himself and all who, following the example of his faith, trust in God, should be saved, he rejoiced exceedingly. The Lord, therefore, was not unknown to Abraham, whose day he desired to see;[9] nor, again, was the Lord's Father, for he had learned from the Word of the Lord, and believed Him; wherefore it was accounted to him by the Lord for righteousness. For faith towards God justifies a man; and therefore he said, "I will stretch forth my hand to the most high God, who made the heaven and the earth."[10] All these truths, however, do those holding perverse opinions endeavour to overthrow, because of one passage, which they certainly do not understand correctly.

CHAP. VI. — EXPLANATION OF THE WORDS OF CHRIST, "NO MAN KNOWETH THE FATHER, BUT THE SON," ETC.; WHICH WORDS THE HERETICS MISINTERPRET. PROOF THAT, BY THE FATHER REVEALING THE SON, AND BY THE SON BEING REVEALED, THE FATHER WAS NEVER UNKNOWN.

1. For the Lord, revealing Himself to His disciples, that He Himself is the Word, who imparts knowledge of the Father, and reproving the Jews, who imagined that they had [the knowledge of] God, while they nevertheless rejected His Word, through whom God is made known, declared, "No man knoweth the Son, but the Father; neither knoweth any man the Father, save the Son, and he to whom the Son has willed to reveal [Him]."[11] Thus hath Matthew set it

---

[1] Matt. xxii. 29, etc.; Ex. iii. 6.
[2] In the Septuagint and Vulgate versions, this story constitutes the fourteenth chapter of the book of Daniel. It is not extant in Hebrew, and has therefore been removed to the Apocrypha, in the Anglican canon [the Greek and St. Jerome's] of Scripture, under the title of "Bel and the Dragon."
[3] John xi. 25.
[4] Ps. xlv. 17.
[5] John viii. 56.
[6] Rom. iv. 3.
[7] Phil. ii. 15.
[8] Gen. xxii. 6.
[9] John viii. 56.
[10] Gen. xiv. 22.
[11] Matt. xi. 27; Luke x. 22.

down, and Luke in like manner, and Mark[1] the very same; for John omits this passage. They, however, who would be wiser than the apostles, write [the verse] in the following manner: "No man *knew* the Father, but the Son; nor the Son, but the Father, and he to whom the Son has willed to reveal [Him];" and they explain it as if the true God were known to none prior to our Lord's advent; and that God who was announced by the prophets, they allege not to be the Father of Christ.

2. But if Christ did then [only] begin to have existence when He came [into the world] as man, and [if] the Father did remember [only] in the times of Tiberius Cæsar to provide for [the wants of] men, and His Word was shown to have not always coexisted with His creatures; [it may be remarked that] neither then was it necessary that another God should be proclaimed, but [rather] that the reasons for so great carelessness and neglect on His part should be made the subject of investigation. For it is fitting that no such question should arise, and gather such strength, that it would indeed both change God, and destroy our faith in that Creator who supports us by means of His creation. For as we do direct our faith towards the Son, so also should we possess a firm and immoveable love towards the Father. In his book against Marcion, Justin[2] does well say: "I would not have believed the Lord Himself, if He had announced any other than He who is our framer, maker, and nourisher. But because the only-begotten Son came to us from the one God, who both made this world and formed us, and contains and administers all things, summing up His own handiwork in Himself, my faith towards Him is stedfast, and my love to the Father immoveable, God bestowing both upon us."

3. For no one can know the Father, unless through the Word of God, that is, unless by the Son revealing [Him]; neither can he have knowledge of the Son, unless through the good pleasure of the Father. But the Son performs the good pleasure of the Father; for the Father sends, and the Son is sent, and comes. And His Word knows that His Father is, as far as regards us, invisible and infinite; and since He cannot be declared [by any one else], He does Himself declare Him to us; and, on the other hand, it is the Father alone who knows His own Word. And both these truths has our Lord declared. Wherefore the Son reveals the knowledge of the Father through His own manifestation. For the manifestation of the Son is the knowledge of the Father; for all things are manifested through the Word. In order, therefore, that we might know that the Son who came is He who imparts to those believing on Him a knowledge of the Father, He said to His disciples:[3] "No man knoweth the Son but the Father, nor the Father but the Son, and those to whomsoever the Son shall reveal Him;" thus setting Himself forth and the Father as He [really] is, that we may not receive any other Father, except Him who is revealed by the Son.

4. But this [Father] is the Maker of heaven and earth, as is shown from His words; and not he, the false father, who has been invented by Marcion, or by Valentinus, or by Basilides, or by Carpocrates, or by Simon, or by the rest of the "Gnostics," falsely so called. For none of these was the Son of God; but Christ Jesus our Lord [was], against whom they set their teaching in opposition, and have the daring to preach an unknown God. But they ought to hear [this] against themselves: How is it that He is unknown, who is known by them? for, whatever is known even by a few, is not unknown. But the Lord did not say that both the Father and the Son could not be known at all (*in totum*), for in that case His advent would have been superfluous. For why did He come hither? Was it that He should say to us, "Never mind seeking after God; for He is unknown, and ye shall not find Him;" as also the disciples of Valentinus falsely declare that Christ said to their Æons? But this is indeed vain. For the Lord taught us that no man is capable of knowing God, unless he be taught of God; that is, that God cannot be known without God: but that this is the express will of the Father, that God should be known. For they shall know[4] Him to whomsoever the Son has revealed Him.

5. And for this purpose did the Father reveal the Son, that through His instrumentality He might be manifested to all, and might receive those righteous ones who believe in Him into incorruption and everlasting enjoyment (now, to believe in Him is to do His will); but He shall righteously shut out into the darkness which they have chosen for themselves, those who do not believe, and who do consequently avoid His light. The Father therefore has revealed Himself to all, by making His Word visible to all; and, conversely, the Word has declared to all the Father and the Son, since He has become visible to all. And therefore the righteous judgment of God [shall fall] upon all who, like

---

[1] Not now to be found in Mark's Gospel.
[2] Photius, 125, makes mention of Justin Martyr's work, λόγοι κατὰ Μαρκίωνος. See also Eusebius's *Ecclesiastical History*, book iv. c. 18, where this passage of Irenæus is quoted. [The vast importance of Justin's startling remark is that it hinges on the words of Christ Himself, concerning His antecedents and notes as set forth in the Scriptures, St. John v. 30–39.]
[3] [A most emphatic and pregnant text which Irenæus here expounds with great beauty. The reference (St. Matt. xi. 27) seems to have been inadvertently omitted in this place where the repetition is desirable.]
[4] The ordinary text reads *cognoscunt*, i.e., do know; but Harvey thinks it should be the future — *cognoscent*.

others, have seen, but have not, like others, believed.

6. For by means of the creation itself, the Word reveals God the Creator; and by means of the world [does He declare] the Lord the Maker of the world; and by means of the formation [of man] the Artificer who formed him; and by the Son that Father who begat the Son: and these things do indeed address all men in the same manner, but all do not in the same way believe them. But by the law and the prophets did the Word preach both Himself and the Father alike [to all]; and all the people heard Him alike, but all did not alike believe. And through the Word Himself who had been made visible and palpable, was the Father shown forth, although all did not equally believe in Him; but all saw the Father in the Son: for the Father is the invisible of the Son, but the Son the visible of the Father. And for this reason all spake with Christ when He was present [upon earth], and they named Him God. Yea, even the demons exclaimed, on beholding the Son: "We know Thee who Thou art, the Holy One of God."[1] And the devil looking at Him, and tempting Him, said: "If Thou art the Son of God;"[2] — all thus indeed seeing and speaking of the Son and the Father, but all not believing [in them].

7. For it was fitting that the truth should receive testimony from all, and should become [a means of] judgment for the salvation indeed of those who believe, but for the condemnation of those who believe not; that all should be fairly judged, and that the faith in the Father and Son should be approved by all, that is, that it should be established by all [as the one means of salvation], receiving testimony from all, both from those belonging to it, since they are its friends, and by those having no connection with it, though they are its enemies. For that evidence is true, and cannot be gainsaid, which elicits even from its adversaries striking[3] testimonies in its behalf; they being convinced with respect to the matter in hand by their own plain contemplation of it, and bearing testimony to it, as well as declaring it.[4] But after a while they break forth into enmity, and become accusers [of what they had approved], and are desirous that their own testimony should not be [regarded as] true. He, therefore, who was known, was not a different being from Him who declared, "No man knoweth the Father," but one and the same, the Father making all things subject to Him; while He received testimony from all that He was very man, and that He was very God, from the Father, from the Spirit, from angels, from the creation itself, from men, from apostate spirits and demons, from the enemy, and last of all, from death itself. But the Son, administering all things for the Father, works from the beginning even to the end, and without Him no man can attain the knowledge of God. For the Son is the knowledge of the Father; but the knowledge of the Son is in the Father, and has been revealed through the Son; and this was the reason why the Lord declared: "No man knoweth the Son, but the Father; nor the Father, save the Son, and those to whomsoever the Son shall reveal [Him]."[5] For "shall reveal" was said not with reference to the future alone, as if then [only] the Word had begun to manifest the Father when He was born of Mary, but it applies indifferently throughout all time. For the Son, being present with His own handiwork from the beginning, reveals the Father to all; to whom He wills, and when He wills, and as the Father wills. Wherefore, then, in all things, and through all things, there is one God, the Father, and one Word, and one Son, and one Spirit, and one salvation to all who believe in Him.

CHAP. VII. — RECAPITULATION OF THE FOREGOING ARGUMENT, SHOWING THAT ABRAHAM, THROUGH THE REVELATION OF THE WORD, KNEW THE FATHER, AND THE COMING OF THE SON OF GOD. FOR THIS CAUSE, HE REJOICED TO SEE THE DAY OF CHRIST, WHEN THE PROMISES MADE TO HIM SHOULD BE FULFILLED. THE FRUIT OF THIS REJOICING HAS FLOWED TO POSTERITY, VIZ., TO THOSE WHO ARE PARTAKERS IN THE FAITH OF ABRAHAM, BUT NOT TO THE JEWS WHO REJECT THE WORD OF GOD.

1. Therefore Abraham also, knowing the Father through the Word, who made heaven and earth, confessed Him to be God; and having learned, by an announcement [made to him], that the Son of God would be a man among men, by whose advent his seed should be as the stars of heaven, he desired to see that day, so that he might himself also embrace Christ; and, seeing it through the spirit of prophecy, he rejoiced.[6] Wherefore Simeon also, one of his descendants, carried fully out the rejoicing of the patriarch, and said: "Lord, now lettest Thou Thy servant depart in peace. For mine eyes have seen Thy salvation, which Thou hast pre-

---

[1] Mark i. 24.
[2] Matt. iv. 3; Luke iv. 3.
[3] *Singula*, which with Massuet we here understand in the sense of *singularia*.
[4] Some, instead of *significantibus*, read *signantibus*, "stamping it as true."
[5] Matt. xi. 27; Luke x. 22. Harvey observes here, that "it is remarkable that this text, having been correctly quoted a short time previously in accordance with the received Greek text, ᾧ ἐὰν βούληται ὁ υἱὸς ἀποκαλύψαι, the translator now not only uses the single verb *revelaverit*, but says pointedly that it was so written by the venerable author. It is probable, therefore, that the previous passage has been made to harmonize with the received text by a later hand; with which, however, the Syriac form agrees.
[6] Gen. xvii. 17.

pared before the face of all people: a light for the revelation of the Gentiles,[1] and the glory of the people Israel."[2] And the angels, in like manner, announced tidings of great joy to the shepherds who were keeping watch by night.[3] Moreover, Mary said, "My soul doth magnify the Lord, and my spirit hath rejoiced in God my salvation;"[4] — the rejoicing of Abraham descending upon those who sprang from him, — those, namely, who were watching, and who beheld Christ, and believed in Him; while, on the other hand, there was a reciprocal rejoicing which passed backwards from the children to Abraham, who did also desire to see the day of Christ's coming. Rightly, then, did our Lord bear witness to him, saying, "Your father Abraham rejoiced to see my day; and he saw it, and was glad."

2. For not alone upon Abraham's account did He say these things, but also that He might point out how all who have known God from the beginning, and have foretold the advent of Christ, have received the revelation from the Son Himself; who also in the last times was made visible and passable, and spake with the human race, that He might from the stones raise up children unto Abraham, and fulfil the promise which God had given him, and that He might make his seed as the stars of heaven,[5] as John the Baptist says: "For God is able from these stones to raise up children unto Abraham."[6] Now, this Jesus did by drawing us off from the religion of stones, and bringing us over from hard and fruitless cogitations, and establishing in us a faith like to Abraham. As Paul does also testify, saying that we are children of Abraham because of the similarity of our faith, and the promise of inheritance.[7]

3. He is therefore one and the same God, who called Abraham and gave him the promise. But He is the Creator, who does also through Christ prepare lights in the world, [namely] those who believe from among the Gentiles. And He says, "Ye are the light of the world;"[8] that is, as the stars of heaven. Him, therefore, I have rightly shown to be known by no man, unless by the Son, and to whomsoever the Son shall reveal Him. But the Son reveals the Father to all to whom He wills that He should be known; and neither without the goodwill of the Father, nor without the agency of the Son, can any man know God. Wherefore did the Lord say to His disciples, "I am the way, the truth, and the life: and no man cometh unto the Father but by Me. If ye had known Me, ye would have known My Father also: and from henceforth ye have both known Him, and have seen Him."[9] From these words it is evident, that He is known by the Son, that is, by the Word.

4. Therefore have the Jews departed from God, in not receiving His Word, but imagining that they could know the Father [apart] by Himself, without the Word, that is, without the Son; they being ignorant of that God who spake in human shape to Abraham,[10] and again to Moses, saying, "I have surely seen the affliction of My people in Egypt, and I have come down to deliver them."[11] For the Son, who is the Word of God, arranged these things beforehand from the beginning, the Father being in no want of angels, in order that He might call the creation into being, and form man, for whom also the creation was made; nor, again, standing in need of any instrumentality for the framing of created things, or for the ordering of those things which had reference to man; while, [at the same time,] He has a vast and unspeakable number of servants. For His *offspring* and His *similitude*[12] do minister to Him in every respect; that is, the Son and the Holy Spirit, the Word and Wisdom; whom all the angels serve, and to whom they are subject. Vain, therefore, are those who, because of that declaration, "No man knoweth the Father, but the Son,"[13] do introduce another unknown Father.

CHAP. VIII. — VAIN ATTEMPTS OF MARCION AND HIS FOLLOWERS, WHO EXCLUDE ABRAHAM FROM THE SALVATION BESTOWED BY CHRIST, WHO LIBERATED NOT ONLY ABRAHAM, BUT THE SEED OF ABRAHAM, BY FULFILLING AND NOT DESTROYING THE LAW WHEN HE HEALED ON THE SABBATH-DAY.

1. Vain, too, is [the effort of] Marcion and his followers when they [seek to] exclude Abraham from the inheritance, to whom the Spirit through many men, and now by Paul, bears witness, that "he believed God, and it was imputed unto him for righteousness."[14] And the Lord [also bears witness to him,] in the first place, indeed, by raising up children to him from the stones, and making his seed as the stars of heaven, saying, "They shall come from the east and from the west, from the north and from the south, and shall recline with Abraham, and Isaac, and Jacob in the kingdom of heaven;"[15] and then again by saying to the Jews, "When ye shall see Abraham, and Isaac, and Jacob, and all the prophets in the kingdom of heaven, but you

---

[1] The text has *oculorum*, probably by mistake for *populorum*.
[2] Luke ii. 29, etc.
[3] Luke ii. 8.
[4] Luke i. 46.
[5] Gen. xv. 5.
[6] Matt. iii. 9.
[7] Rom. iv. 12; Gal. iv. 28.
[8] Matt. v. 14.
[9] John xiv. 6, 7.
[10] Gen. xviii. 1.
[11] Ex. iii. 7, 8.
[12] Massuet here observes, that the fathers called the Holy Spirit the similitude of the Son.
[13] Matt. xi. 27; Luke x. 22.
[14] Rom. iv. 3.
[15] Matt. viii. 11.

yourselves cast out."[1] This, then, is a clear point, that those who disallow his salvation, and frame the idea of another God besides Him who made the promise to Abraham, are outside the kingdom of God, and are disinherited from [the gift of] incorruption, setting at naught and blaspheming God, who introduces, through Jesus Christ, Abraham to the kingdom of heaven, and his seed, that is, the Church, upon which also is conferred the adoption and the inheritance promised to Abraham.

2. For the Lord vindicated Abraham's posterity by loosing them from bondage and calling them to salvation, as He did in the case of the woman whom He healed, saying openly to those who had not faith like Abraham, "Ye hypocrites,[2] doth not each one of you on the Sabbath-days loose his ox or his ass, and lead him away to watering? And ought not this woman, being a daughter of Abraham, whom Satan hath bound these eighteen years, be loosed from this bond on the Sabbath-days?"[3] It is clear, therefore, that He loosed and vivified those who believe in Him as Abraham did, doing nothing contrary to the law when He healed upon the Sabbath-day. For the law did not prohibit men from being healed upon the Sabbaths; [on the contrary,] it even circumcised them upon that day, and gave command that the offices should be performed by the priests for the people; yea, it did not disallow the healing even of dumb animals. Both at Siloam and on frequent subsequent[4] occasions, did He perform cures upon the Sabbath; and for this reason many used to resort to Him on the Sabbath-days. For the law commanded them to abstain from every servile work, that is, from all grasping after wealth which is procured by trading and by other worldly business; but it exhorted them to attend to the exercises of the soul, which consist in reflection, and to addresses of a beneficial kind for their neighbours' benefit. And therefore the Lord reproved those who unjustly blamed Him for having healed upon the Sabbath-days. For He did not make void, but fulfilled the law, by performing the offices of the high priest, propitiating God for men, and cleansing the lepers, healing the sick, and Himself suffering death, that exiled man might go forth from condemnation, and might return without fear to his own inheritance.

3. And again, the law did not forbid those who were hungry on the Sabbath-days to take food lying ready at hand: it did, however, forbid them to reap and to gather into the barn. And therefore did the Lord say to those who were blaming His disciples because they plucked and ate the ears of corn, rubbing them in their hands, "Have ye not read this, what David did, when himself was an hungered; how he went into the house of God, and ate the shew-bread, and gave to those who were with him; which it is not lawful to eat, but for the priests alone?"[5] justifying His disciples by the words of the law, and pointing out that it was lawful for the priests to act freely. For David had been appointed a priest by God, although Saul persecuted him. For all the righteous possess the sacerdotal rank.[6] And all the apostles of the Lord are priests, who do inherit here neither lands nor houses, but serve God and the altar continually. Of whom Moses also says in Deuteronomy, when blessing Levi, "Who said unto his father and to his mother, I have not known thee; neither did he acknowledge his brethren, and he disinherited his own sons: he kept Thy commandments, and observed Thy covenant."[7] But who are they that have left father and mother, and have said adieu to all their neighbours, on account of the word of God and His covenant, unless the disciples of the Lord? Of whom again Moses says, "They shall have no inheritance, for the Lord Himself is their inheritance."[8] And again, "The priests the Levites shall have no part in the whole tribe of Levi, nor substance with Israel; their substance is the offerings (*fructifications*) of the Lord: these shall they eat."[9] Wherefore also Paul says, "I do not seek after a gift, but I seek after fruit."[10] To His disciples He said, who had a priesthood of the Lord,[11] to whom it was lawful when hungry to eat the ears of corn,[12] "For the workman is worthy of his meat."[13] And the priests in the temple profaned the Sabbath, and were blameless. Wherefore, then, were they blameless? Because when in the temple they were not engaged in secular affairs, but in the service of the Lord, fulfilling the law, but not going beyond it, as that man did, who of his own accord carried dry wood into the camp of God, and was justly stoned to death.[14] "For every tree that bringeth not forth good fruit shall be hewn down, and cast into the fire;"[15] and "whosoever shall defile the temple of God, him shall God defile."[16]

---

[1] Luke xiii. 28.
[2] Harvey prefers the singular—"*hypocrite*."
[3] Luke xiii. 15, 16.
[4] The text here is rather uncertain. Harvey's conjectural reading of *et jam* for *etiam* has been followed.
[5] Luke vi. 3, 4.
[6] This clause is differently quoted by Antonius Melissa and John Damascenus, thus: Πᾶς βασιλεὺς δίκαιος ἱερατικὴν ἔχει τάξιν, i.e., *Every righteous king possesses a priestly order.* Comp. 1 Pet. ii. 5, 9. [And with St. Peter's testimony to the priesthood of the laity, compare the same under the law. Ex. xix. 6. The Western Church has recognised the "Episcopate *ab extra*" of sovereigns; while, in the East, it has grown into *Cæsaropapism.*]
[7] Deut. xxxiii. 9.
[8] Num. xviii. 20.
[9] Deut. xviii. 1.
[10] Phil. iv. 17.
[11] Literally, "the Lord's Levitical substance"—*Domini Leviticam substantiam.*
[12] Literally, "to take food from seeds."
[13] Matt. x. 10.
[14] Num. xv. 32, etc.
[15] Matt. iii. 10.
[16] 1 Cor. iii. 17.

CHAP. IX.—THERE IS BUT ONE AUTHOR, AND ONE END TO BOTH COVENANTS.

1. All things therefore are of one and the same substance, that is, from one and the same God; as also the Lord says to the disciples: "Therefore every scribe, which is instructed unto the kingdom of heaven, is like unto a man that is an householder, which bringeth forth out of his treasure things new and old."[1] He did not teach that he who brought forth the old was one, and he that brought forth the new, another; but that they were one and the same. For the Lord is the good man of the house, who rules the entire house of His Father; and who delivers a law suited both for slaves and those who are as yet undisciplined; and gives fitting precepts to those that are free, and have been justified by faith, as well as throws His own inheritance open to those that are sons. And He called His disciples "scribes" and "teachers of the kingdom of heaven;" of whom also He elsewhere says to the Jews: "Behold, I send unto you wise men, and scribes, and teachers; and some of them ye shall kill, and persecute from city to city."[2] Now, without contradiction, He means by those things which are brought forth from the treasure new and old, the two covenants; the old, that giving of the law which took place formerly; and He points out as the new, that manner of life required by the Gospel, of which David says, "Sing unto the LORD a new song;"[3] and Esaias, "Sing unto the LORD a new hymn. His beginning (*initium*), His name is glorified from the height of the earth: they declare His powers in the isles."[4] And Jeremiah says: "Behold, I will make a new covenant, not as I made with your fathers"[5] in Mount Horeb. But one and the same householder produced both covenants, the Word of God, our Lord Jesus Christ, who spake with both Abraham and Moses, and who has restored us anew to liberty, and has multiplied that grace which is from Himself.

2. He declares: "For in this place is One greater than the temple."[6] But [the words] *greater* and *less* are not applied to those things which have nothing in common between themselves, and are of an opposite nature, and mutually repugnant; but are used in the case of those of the same substance, and which possess properties in common, but merely differ in number and size; such as water from water, and light from light, and grace from grace. Greater, therefore, is that legislation which has been given in order to liberty than that given in order to bondage; and therefore it has also been diffused, not throughout one nation [only], but over the whole world. For one and the same Lord, who is greater than the temple, greater than Solomon, and greater than Jonah, confers gifts upon men, that is, His own presence, and the resurrection from the dead; but He does not change God, nor proclaim another Father, but that very same one, who always has more to measure out to those of His household. And as their love towards God increases, He bestows more and greater [gifts]; as also the Lord said to His disciples: "Ye shall see greater things than these."[7] And Paul declares: "Not that I have already attained, or that I am justified, or already have been made perfect. For we know in part, and we prophesy in part; but when that which is perfect has come, the things which are in part shall be done away."[8] As, therefore, when that which is perfect is come, we shall not see another Father, but Him whom we now desire to see (for "blessed are the pure in heart: for they shall see God"[9]); neither shall we look for another Christ and Son of God, but Him who [was born] of the Virgin Mary, who also suffered, in whom too we trust, and whom we love; as Esaias says: "And they shall say in that day, Behold our LORD God, in whom we have trusted, and we have rejoiced in our salvation;"[10] and Peter says in his Epistle: "Whom, not seeing, ye love; in whom, though now ye see Him not, ye have believed, ye shall rejoice with joy unspeakable;"[11] neither do we receive another Holy Spirit, besides Him who is with us, and who cries, "Abba, Father;"[12] and we shall make increase in the very same things [as now], and shall make progress, so that no longer through a glass, or by means of enigmas, but face to face, we shall enjoy the gifts of God;—so also now, receiving more than the temple, and more than Solomon, that is, the advent of the Son of God, we have not been taught another God besides the Framer and the Maker of all, who has been pointed out to us from the beginning; nor another Christ, the Son of God, besides Him who was foretold by the prophets.

3. For the new covenant having been known and preached by the prophets, He who was to carry it out according to the good pleasure of the Father was also preached, having been revealed to men as God pleased; that they might always make progress through believing in Him, and by means of the [successive] covenants,

---

[1] Matt. xiii. 52.
[2] Matt. xxiii. 34.
[3] Ps. xcvi. 1.
[4] Isa. xlii. 10, quoted from memory.
[5] Jer. xxxi. 31.
[6] Matt. xii. 6.
[7] John i. 50.
[8] These words of Scripture are quoted by memory from Phil. iii. 12, 1 Cor. iv. 4, and xiii. 9, 10. It is remarkable that the second is incorporated with the preceding in a similar way, in the ancient Italic version known as the St. Germain copy.
[9] Matt. v. 8.
[10] Isa. xxv. 9.
[11] 1 Pet. i. 8.
[12] Rom. viii. 15.

should gradually attain to perfect salvation.¹ For there is one salvation and one God; but the precepts which form the man are numerous, and the steps which lead man to God are not a few. It is allowable for an earthly and temporal king, though he is [but] a man, to grant to his subjects greater advantages at times: shall not this then be lawful for God, since He is [ever] the same, and is always willing to confer a greater [degree of] grace upon the human race, and to honour continually with many gifts those who please Him? But if this be to make progress, [namely,] to find out another Father besides Him who was preached from the beginning; and again, besides him who is imagined to have been discovered in the second place, to find out a third other,—then the progress of this man will consist in his also proceeding from a third to a fourth; and from this, again, to another and another: and thus he who thinks that he is always making progress of such a kind, will never rest in one God. For, being driven away from Him who truly is [God], and being turned backwards, he shall be for ever seeking, yet shall never find out God;² but shall continually swim in an abyss without limits, unless, being converted by repentance, he return to the place from which he had been cast out, confessing one God, the Father, the Creator, and believing [in Him] who was declared by the law and the prophets, who was borne witness to by Christ, as He did Himself declare to those who were accusing His disciples of not observing the tradition of the elders: "Why do ye make void the law of God by reason of your tradition? For God said, Honour thy father and mother; and, Whosoever curseth father or mother, let him die the death."³ And again, He says to them a second time: "And ye have made void the word of God⁴ by reason of your tradition;" Christ confessing in the plainest manner Him to be Father and God, who said in the law, "Honour thy father and mother; that it may be well with thee."⁵ For the true God did confess the commandment of the law as the word of God, and called no one else God besides His own Father.

CHAP. X.—THE OLD TESTAMENT SCRIPTURES, AND THOSE WRITTEN BY MOSES IN PARTICULAR, DO EVERYWHERE MAKE MENTION OF THE SON OF GOD, AND FORETELL HIS ADVENT AND PASSION. FROM THIS FACT IT FOLLOWS THAT THEY WERE INSPIRED BY ONE AND THE SAME GOD.

1. Wherefore also John does appropriately relate that the Lord said to the Jews: "Ye search the Scriptures, in which ye think ye have eternal life; these are they which testify of me. And ye are not willing to come unto Me, that ye may have life."⁶ How therefore did the Scriptures testify of Him, unless they were from one and the same Father, instructing men beforehand as to the advent of His Son, and foretelling the salvation brought in by Him? "For if ye had believed Moses, ye would also have believed Me; for he wrote of Me;"⁷ [saying this,] no doubt, because the Son of God is implanted everywhere throughout his writings: at one time, indeed, speaking with Abraham, when about to eat with him; at another time with Noah, giving to him the dimensions [of the ark]; at another, inquiring after Adam; at another, bringing down judgment upon the Sodomites; and again, when He becomes visible,⁸ and directs Jacob on his journey, and speaks with Moses from the bush.⁹ And it would be endless to recount [the occasions] upon which the Son of God is shown forth by Moses. Of the day of His passion, too, he was not ignorant; but foretold Him, after a figurative manner, by the name given to the passover;¹⁰ and at that very festival, which had been proclaimed such a long time previously by Moses, did our Lord suffer, thus fulfilling the passover. And he did not describe the day only, but the place also, and the time of day at which the sufferings ceased,¹¹ and the sign of the setting of the sun, saying: "Thou mayest not sacrifice the passover within any other of thy cities which the LORD God gives thee; but in the place which the LORD thy God shall choose that His name be called on there, thou shalt sacrifice the passover at even, towards the setting of the sun."¹²

2. And already he had also declared His advent, saying, "There shall not fail a chief in Judah, nor a leader from his loins, until He come for whom it is laid up, and He is the hope of the nations; binding His foal to the vine, and His ass's colt to the creeping ivy. He shall wash His stole in wine, and His upper garment

---

¹ This is in accordance with Harvey's text—"Maturescere profectum salutis." Grabe, however, reads, "Maturescere prefectum salutis;" making this equivalent to "ad prefectam salutem." In most MSS "profectum" and "prefectum" would be written alike. The same word ("profectus") occurs again almost immediately, with an evident reference to and comparison with this clause.
² 2 Tim. iii. 7.
³ Matt. xv. 3, 4.
⁴ Another variation from the *textus receptus* borne out by the Codex Bezæ, and some ancient versions.
⁵ Ex. xx. 12, LXX.

⁶ John v. 39, 40.
⁷ John v. 46.
⁸ See Gen. xviii. 13 and xxxi. 11, etc. There is an allusion here to a favourite notion among the Fathers, derived from Philo the Jew, that the name *Israel* was compounded from the three Hebrew words איש ראה אל, i.e., "the man seeing God."
⁹ Ex. iii. 4, etc.
¹⁰ Feuardent infers with great probability from this passage, that Irenæus, like Tertullian and others of the Fathers, connected the word *Pascha* with πάσχειν, *to suffer*. [The LXX. constantly giving colour to early Christian ideas in this manner, they concluded, perhaps, that such coincidences were designed. The LXX. were credited with a sort of inspiration, as we learn from our author.]
¹¹ Latin, "et extremitatem temporum."
¹² Deut. xvi. 5, 6.

in the blood of the grape; His eyes shall be more joyous than wine,[1] and His teeth whiter than milk."[2] For, let those who have the reputation of investigating everything, inquire at what time a prince and leader failed out of Judah, and who is the hope of the nations, who also is the vine, what was the ass's colt [referred to as] His, what the clothing, and what the eyes, what the teeth, and what the wine, and thus let them investigate every one of the points mentioned; and they shall find that there was none other announced than our Lord, Christ Jesus. Wherefore Moses, when chiding the ingratitude of the people, said, "Ye infatuated people, and unwise, do ye thus requite the LORD?"[3] And again, he indicates that He who from the beginning founded and created them, the Word, who also redeems and vivifies us in the last times, is shown as hanging on the tree, and they will not believe on Him. For he says, "And thy life shall be hanging before thine eyes, and thou wilt not believe thy life."[4] And again, "Has not this same one thy Father owned thee, and made thee, and created thee?"[5]

CHAP. XI. — THE OLD PROPHETS AND RIGHTEOUS MEN KNEW BEFOREHAND OF THE ADVENT OF CHRIST, AND EARNESTLY DESIRED TO SEE AND HEAR HIM, HE REVEALING HIMSELF IN THE SCRIPTURES BY THE HOLY GHOST, AND WITHOUT ANY CHANGE IN HIMSELF, ENRICHING MEN DAY BY DAY WITH BENEFITS, BUT CONFERRING THEM IN GREATER ABUNDANCE ON LATER THAN ON FORMER GENERATIONS.

1. But that it was not only the prophets and many righteous men, who, foreseeing through the Holy Spirit His advent, prayed that they might attain to that period in which they should see their Lord face to face, and hear His words, the Lord has made manifest, when He says to His disciples, "Many prophets and righteous men have desired to see those things which ye see, and have not seen them; and to hear those things which ye hear, and have not heard them."[6] In what way, then, did they desire both to hear and to see, unless they had foreknowledge of His future advent? But how could they have foreknown it, unless they had previously received foreknowledge from Himself? And how do the Scriptures testify of Him, unless all things had ever been revealed and shown to believers by one and the same God through the Word; He at one time conferring with His creature, and at another propounding His law; at one time, again, reproving, at another exhorting, and then setting free His servant, and adopting him as a son (*in filium*); and, at the proper time, bestowing an incorruptible inheritance, for the purpose of bringing man to perfection? For He formed him for growth and increase, as the Scripture says: "Increase and multiply."[7]

2. And in this respect God differs from man, that God indeed makes, but man is made; and truly, He who makes is always the same; but that which is made must receive both beginning, and middle, and addition, and increase. And God does indeed create after a skilful manner, while, [as regards] man, he *is* created skilfully. God also is truly perfect in all things, Himself equal and similar to Himself, as He is all light, and all mind, and all substance, and the fount of all good; but man receives advancement and increase towards God. For as God is always the same, so also man, when found in God, shall always go on towards God. For neither does God at any time cease to confer benefits upon, or to enrich man; nor does man ever cease from receiving the benefits, and being enriched by God. For the receptacle of His goodness, and the instrument of His glorification, is the man who is grateful to Him that made him; and again, the receptacle of His just judgment is the ungrateful man, who both despises his Maker and is not subject to His Word; who has promised that He will give very much to those always bringing forth fruit, and more [and more] to those who have the Lord's money. "Well done," He says, "good and faithful servant: because thou hast been faithful in little, I will appoint thee over many things; enter thou into the joy of thy Lord."[8] The Lord Himself thus promises very much.

3. As, therefore, He has promised to give very much to those who do now bring forth fruit, according to the gift of His grace, but not according to the changeableness of "knowledge;" for the Lord remains the same, and the same Father is revealed; thus, therefore, has the one and the same Lord granted, by means of His advent, a greater gift of grace to those of a later period, than what He had granted to those under the Old Testament dispensation. For they indeed used to hear, by means of [His] servants, that the King would come, and they rejoiced to a certain extent, inasmuch as they hoped for His coming; but those who have beheld Him actually present, and have obtained liberty, and been made partakers of His gifts, do possess a greater amount of grace, and a higher degree of exultation, rejoicing because of the King's arrival: as

---

[1] The Latin is, "lætifici oculi ejus a vino," the Hebrew method of indicating comparison being evidently imitated.
[2] Gen. xlix. 10–12, LXX.
[3] Deut. xxxii. 6.
[4] Deut. xxviii. 66. Tertullian, Cyprian, and other early Fathers, agree with Irenæus in his exposition of this text.
[5] Deut. xxxii. 6. "Owned thee," i.e., following the meaning of the Hebrew, "owned thee by generation."
[6] Matt. xiii. 17.
[7] Gen. i. 28.
[8] Matt. xxv. 21, etc.

also David says, "My soul shall rejoice in the Lord; it shall be glad in His salvation."¹ And for this cause, upon His entrance into Jerusalem, all those who were in the way² recognised David their king in His sorrow of soul, and spread their garments for Him, and ornamented the way with green boughs, crying out with great joy and gladness, "Hosanna to the Son of David; blessed is He that cometh in the name of the Lord: hosanna in the highest."³ But to the envious wicked stewards, who circumvented those under them, and ruled over those that had no great intelligence,⁴ and for this reason were unwilling that the king should come, and who said to Him, "Hearest thou what these say?" did the Lord reply, "Have ye never read, Out of the mouths of babes and sucklings hast Thou perfected praise?"⁵ — thus pointing out that what had been declared by David concerning the Son of God, was accomplished in His own person; and indicating that they were indeed ignorant of the meaning of the Scripture and the dispensation of God; but declaring that it was Himself who was announced by the prophets as Christ, whose name is praised in all the earth, and who perfects praise to His Father from the mouth of babes and sucklings; wherefore also His glory has been raised above the heavens.

4. If, therefore, the self-same person is present who was announced by the prophets, our Lord Jesus Christ, and if His advent has brought in a fuller [measure of] grace and greater gifts to those who have received Him, it is plain that the Father also is Himself the same who was proclaimed by the prophets, and that the Son, on His coming, did not spread the knowledge of another Father, but of the same who was preached from the beginning; from whom also He has brought down liberty to those who, in a lawful manner, and with a willing mind, and with all the heart, do Him service; whereas to scoffers, and to those not subject to God, but who follow outward purifications for the praise of men (which observances had been given as a type of future things, — the law typifying, as it were, certain things in a shadow, and delineating eternal things by temporal, celestial by terrestrial), and to those who pretend that they do themselves observe more than what has been prescribed, as if preferring their own zeal to God Himself, while within they are full of hypocrisy, and covetousness, and all wickedness, — [to such] has He assigned everlasting perdition by cutting them off from life.

¹ Ps. xxxv. 9.
² Or, "all those who were in the *way of David*"—*omnes qui erant in via David, in dolore animæ cognoverunt suum regem.*
³ Matt. xxi. 8.
⁴ The Latin text is ambiguous: "dominabantur eorum, quibus ratio non constabat." The rendering may be, "and ruled over those things with respect to which it was not right that they should do so."
⁵ Matt. xxi. 16; Ps. viii. 3.

CHAP. XII. — IT CLEARLY APPEARS THAT THERE WAS BUT ONE AUTHOR OF BOTH THE OLD AND THE NEW LAW, FROM THE FACT THAT CHRIST CONDEMNED TRADITIONS AND CUSTOMS REPUGNANT TO THE FORMER, WHILE HE CONFIRMED ITS MOST IMPORTANT PRECEPTS, AND TAUGHT THAT HE WAS HIMSELF THE END OF THE MOSAIC LAW.

1. For the tradition of the elders themselves, which they pretended to observe from the law, was contrary to the law given by Moses. Wherefore also Esaias declares: "Thy dealers mix the wine with water,"⁶ showing that the elders were in the habit of mingling a watered tradition with the simple command of God; that is, they set up a spurious law, and one contrary to the [true] law; as also the Lord made plain, when He said to them, "Why do ye transgress the commandment of God, for the sake of your tradition?"⁷ For not only by actual transgression did they set the law of God at nought, mingling the wine with water; but they also set up their own law in opposition to it, which is termed, even to the present day, the pharisaical. In this [law] they suppress certain things, add others, and interpret others, again, as they think proper, which their teachers use, each one in particular; and desiring to uphold these traditions, they were unwilling to be subject to the law of God, which prepares them for the coming of Christ. But they did even blame the Lord for healing on the Sabbath-days, which, as I have already observed, the law did not prohibit. For they did themselves, in one sense, perform acts of healing upon the Sabbath-day, when they circumcised a man [on that day]; but they did not blame themselves for transgressing the command of God through tradition and the aforesaid pharisaical law, and for not keeping the commandment of the law, which is the love of God.

2. But that this is the first and greatest commandment, and that the next [has respect to love] towards our neighbour, the Lord has taught, when He says that the entire law and the prophets hang upon these two commandments. Moreover, He did not Himself bring down [from heaven] any other commandment greater than this one, but renewed this very same one to His disciples, when He enjoined them to love God with all their heart, and others as themselves. But if He had descended from another Father, He never would have made use of the first and greatest commandment of the law; but He would undoubtedly have endeavoured by all means to bring down a greater one than this from the perfect Father, so as not to make use of that which had been given by the

⁶ Isa. i. 22.
⁷ Matt. xv. 3.

God of the law. And Paul in like manner declares, "Love is the fulfilling of the law:"[1] and [he declares] that when all other things have been destroyed, there shall remain "faith, hope, and love; but the greatest of all is love;"[2] and that apart from the love of God, neither knowledge avails anything,[3] nor the understanding of mysteries, nor faith, nor prophecy, but that without love all are hollow and vain; moreover, that love makes man perfect; and that he who loves God is perfect, both in this world and in that which is to come. For we do never cease from loving God; but in proportion as we continue to contemplate Him, so much the more do we love Him.

3. As in the law, therefore, and in the Gospel [likewise], the first and greatest commandment is, to love the Lord God with the whole heart, and then there follows a commandment like to it, to love one's neighbour as one's self; the author of the law and the Gospel is shown to be one and the same. For the precepts of an absolutely perfect life, since they are the same in each Testament, have pointed out [to us] the same God, who certainly has promulgated particular laws adapted for each; but the more prominent and the greatest [commandments], without which salvation cannot [be attained], He has exhorted [us to observe] the same in both.

4. The Lord, too, does not do away with this [God], when He shows that the law was not derived from another God, expressing Himself as follows to those who were being instructed by Him, to the multitude and to His disciples: "The scribes and Pharisees sit in Moses' seat. All, therefore, whatsoever they bid you observe, that observe and do; but do not ye after their works: for they say, and do not. For they bind heavy burdens, and lay them upon men's shoulders; but they themselves will not so much as move them with a finger."[4] He therefore did not throw blame upon that law which was given by Moses, when He exhorted it to be observed, Jerusalem being as yet in safety; but He *did* throw blame upon those persons, because they repeated indeed the words of the law, yet were without love. And for this reason were they held as being unrighteous as respects God, and as respects their neighbours. As also Isaiah says: "This people honoureth Me with their lips, but their heart is far from Me: howbeit in vain do they worship Me, teaching the doctrines and the commandments of men."[5] He does not call the law given by Moses commandments of men, but the traditions of the elders themselves which they had invented, and in upholding which they made the law of God of none effect, and were on this account also not subject to His Word. For this is what Paul says concerning these men: "For they, being ignorant of God's righteousness, and going about to establish their own righteousness, have not submitted themselves to the righteousness of God. For Christ is the end of the law for righteousness to every one that believeth."[6] And how is Christ the end of the law, if He be not also the final cause of it? For He who has brought in the end has Himself also wrought the beginning; and it is He who does Himself say to Moses, "I have surely seen the affliction of my people which is in Egypt, and I have come down to deliver them;"[7] it being customary from the beginning with the Word of God to ascend and descend for the purpose of saving those who were in affliction.

5. Now, that the law did beforehand teach mankind the necessity of following Christ, He does Himself make manifest, when He replied as follows to him who asked Him what he should do that he might inherit eternal life: "If thou wilt enter into life, keep the commandments."[8] But upon the other asking "Which?" again the Lord replies: "Do not commit adultery, do not kill, do not steal, do not bear false witness, honour father and mother, and thou shalt love thy neighbour as thyself,"—setting as an ascending series (*velut gradus*) before those who wished to follow Him, the precepts of the law, as the entrance into life; and what He then said to one He said to all. But when the former said, "All these have I done" (and most likely he had not kept them, for in that case the Lord would not have said to him, "Keep the commandments"), the Lord, exposing his covetousness, said to him, "If thou wilt be perfect, go, sell all that thou hast, and distribute to the poor; and come, follow me;" promising to those who would act thus, the portion belonging to the apostles (*apostolorum partem*). And He did not preach to His followers another God the Father, besides Him who was proclaimed by the law from the beginning; nor another Son; nor the Mother, the enthymesis of the Æon, who existed in suffering and apostasy; nor the Pleroma of the thirty Æons, which has been proved vain, and incapable of being believed in; nor that fable invented by the other heretics. But He taught that they should obey the commandments which God enjoined from the beginning, and do away with their former covetousness by good works,[9] and follow after Christ. But that

---

[1] Rom. xiii. 10.
[2] 1 Cor. xiii. 13.
[3] 1 Cor. xiii. 2.
[4] Matt. xxiii. 2-4.
[5] Isa. xxix. 13.
[6] Rom. x. 3, 4.
[7] Ex. iii. 7, 8.
[8] Matt. xix. 17, 18, etc.
[9] Harvey here remarks: "In a theological point of view, it should be observed, that no saving merit is ascribed to almsgiving: it is spoken of here as the negation of the vice of covetousness, which is wholly inconsistent with the state of salvation to which we are called."

possessions distributed to the poor do annul former covetousness, Zaccheus made evident, when he said, "Behold, the half of my goods I give to the poor; and if I have defrauded any one, I restore fourfold."[1]

CHAP. XIII. — CHRIST DID NOT ABROGATE THE NATURAL PRECEPTS OF THE LAW, BUT RATHER FULFILLED AND EXTENDED THEM. HE REMOVED THE YOKE AND BONDAGE OF THE OLD LAW, SO THAT MANKIND, BEING NOW SET FREE, MIGHT SERVE GOD WITH THAT TRUSTFUL PIETY WHICH BECOMETH SONS.

1. And that the Lord did not abrogate the natural [precepts] of the law, by which man[2] is justified, which also those who were justified by faith, and who pleased God, did observe previous to the giving of the law, but that He extended and fulfilled them, is shown from His words. "For," He remarks, "it has been said to them of old time, Do not commit adultery. But I say unto you, That every one who hath looked upon a woman to lust after her, hath committed adultery with her already in his heart."[3] And again: "It has been said, Thou shalt not kill. But I say unto you, Every one who is angry with his brother without a cause, shall be in danger of the judgment."[4] And, "It hath been said, Thou shalt not forswear thyself. But I say unto you, Swear not at all; but let your conversation be, Yea, yea, and Nay, nay."[5] And other statements of a like nature. For all these do not contain or imply an opposition to and an overturning of the [precepts] of the past, as Marcion's followers do strenuously maintain; but [they exhibit] a fulfilling and an extension of them, as He does Himself declare: "Unless your righteousness shall exceed that of the scribes and Pharisees, ye shall not enter into the kingdom of heaven."[6] For what meant the excess referred to? In the first place, [we must] believe not only in the Father, but also in His Son now revealed; for He it is who leads man into fellowship and unity with God. In the next place, [we must] not only say, but we must do; for they said, but did not. And [we must] not only abstain from evil deeds, but even from the desires after them. Now He did not teach us these things as being opposed to the law, but as fulfilling the law, and implanting in us the varied righteousness of the law. That would have been contrary to the law, if He had commanded His disciples to do anything which the law had prohibited. But this which He did command — namely, not only to abstain from things forbidden by the law, but even from longing after them — is not contrary to [the law], as I have remarked, neither is it the utterance of one destroying the law, but of one fulfilling, extending, and affording greater scope to it.

2. For the law, since it was laid down for those in bondage, used to instruct the soul by means of those corporeal objects which were of an external nature, drawing it, as by a bond, to obey its commandments, that man might learn to serve God. But the Word set free the soul, and taught that through it the body should be willingly purified. Which having been accomplished, it followed as of course, that the bonds of slavery should be removed, to which man had now become accustomed, and that he should follow God without fetters: moreover, that the laws of liberty should be extended, and subjection to the king increased, so that no one who is converted should appear unworthy to Him who set him free, but that the piety and obedience due to the Master of the household should be equally rendered both by servants and children; while the children possess greater confidence [than the servants], inasmuch as the working of liberty is greater and more glorious than that obedience which is rendered in [a state of] slavery.

3. And for this reason did the Lord, instead of that [commandment], "Thou shalt not commit adultery," forbid even concupiscence; and instead of that which runs thus, "Thou shalt not kill," He prohibited anger; and instead of the law enjoining the giving of tithes, [He told us] to share[7] all our possessions with the poor; and not to love our neighbours only, but even our enemies; and not merely to be liberal givers and bestowers, but even that we should present a gratuitous gift to those who take away our goods. For "to him that taketh away thy coat," He says, "give to him thy cloak also; and from him that taketh away thy goods, ask them not again; and as ye would that men should do unto you, do ye unto them:"[8] so that we may not grieve as those who are unwilling to be defrauded, but may rejoice as those who have given willingly, and as rather conferring a favour upon our neighbours than yielding to necessity. "And if any one," He says, "shall compel thee [to go] a mile, go with him twain;"[9] so that thou mayest not follow him as a slave, but may as a free man go before him, showing thyself in all things kindly disposed and useful to thy neighbour, not regarding their evil intentions, but performing thy kind offices, assimilating thyself to the Father, "who maketh His sun to rise upon the evil and the good, and sendeth

---

[1] Luke xix. 8.
[2] That is, as Harvey observes, *the natural man*, as described in Rom. ii. 27.
[3] Matt. v. 27, 28.
[4] Matt. v. 21, 22.
[5] Matt. v. 33, etc.
[6] Matt. v. 20.

[7] Matt. xix. 21.
[8] Luke vi. 29–31.
[9] Matt. v. 41.

rain upon the just and unjust."[1] Now all these [precepts], as I have already observed, were not [the injunctions] of one doing away with the law, but of one fulfilling, extending, and widening it among us; just as if one should say, that the more extensive operation of liberty implies that a more complete subjection and affection towards our Liberator had been implanted within us. For He did not set us free for this purpose, that we should depart from Him (no one, indeed, while placed out of reach of the Lord's benefits, has power to procure for himself the means of salvation), but that the more we receive His grace, the more we should love Him. Now the more we have loved Him, the more glory shall we receive from Him, when we are continually in the presence of the Father.

4. Inasmuch, then, as all natural precepts are common to us and to them (the Jews), they had in them indeed the beginning and origin; but in us they have received growth and completion. For to yield assent to God, and to follow His Word, and to love Him above all, and one's neighbour as one's self (now man is neighbour to man), and to abstain from every evil deed, and all other things of a like nature which are common to both [covenants], do reveal one and the same God. But this is our Lord, the Word of God, who in the first instance certainly drew slaves to God, but afterwards He set those free who were subject to Him, as He does Himself declare to His disciples: "I will not now call you servants, for the servant knoweth not what his lord doeth; but I have called you friends, for all things which I have heard from My Father I have made known."[2] For in that which He says, "I will not now call you servants," He indicates in the most marked manner that it was Himself who did originally appoint for men that bondage with respect to God through the law, and then afterwards conferred upon them freedom. And in that He says, "For the servant knoweth not what his lord doeth," He points out, by means of His own advent, the ignorance of a people in a servile condition. But when He terms His disciples "the friends of God," He plainly declares Himself to be the Word of God, whom Abraham also followed voluntarily and under no compulsion (*sine vinculis*), because of the noble nature of his faith, and so became "the friend of God."[3] But the Word of God did not accept of the friendship of Abraham, as though He stood in need of it, for He was perfect from the beginning ("Before Abraham was," He says, "I am"[4]), but that He in His goodness might bestow eternal life upon Abraham himself, inasmuch as the friendship of God imparts immortality to those who embrace it.

CHAP. XIV.— IF GOD DEMANDS OBEDIENCE FROM MAN, IF HE FORMED MAN, CALLED HIM AND PLACED HIM UNDER LAWS, IT WAS MERELY FOR MAN'S WELFARE; NOT THAT GOD STOOD IN NEED OF MAN, BUT THAT HE GRACIOUSLY CONFERRED UPON MAN HIS FAVOURS IN EVERY POSSIBLE MANNER.

1. In the beginning, therefore, did God form Adam, not as if He stood in need of man, but that He might have [some one] upon whom to confer His benefits. For not alone antecedently to Adam, but also before all creation, the Word glorified His Father, remaining in Him; and was Himself glorified by the Father, as He did Himself declare, "Father, glorify Thou Me with the glory which I had with Thee before the world was."[5] Nor did He stand in need of our service when He ordered us to follow Him; but He thus bestowed salvation upon ourselves. For to follow the Saviour is to be a partaker of salvation, and to follow light is to receive light. But those who are in light do not themselves illumine the light, but are illumined and revealed by it: they do certainly contribute nothing to it, but, receiving the benefit, they are illumined by the light. Thus, also, service [rendered] to God does indeed profit God nothing, nor has God need of human obedience; but He grants to those who follow and serve Him life and incorruption and eternal glory, bestowing benefit upon those who serve [Him], because they do serve Him, and on His followers, because they do follow Him; but does not receive any benefit from them: for He is rich, perfect, and in need of nothing. But for this reason does God demand service from men, in order that, since He is good and merciful, He may benefit those who continue in His service. For, as much as God is in want of nothing, so much does man stand in need of fellowship with God. For this is the glory of man, to continue and remain permanently in God's service. Wherefore also did the Lord say to His disciples, "Ye have not chosen Me, but I have chosen you;"[6] indicating that they did not glorify Him when they followed Him; but that, in following the Son of God, they were glorified by Him. And again, "I will, that where I am, there they also may be, that they may behold My glory;"[7] not vainly boasting because of this, but desiring that His disciples should share in His glory: of whom Esaias also says, "I will bring thy seed from the east, and will gather thee from the

---

[1] Matt. v. 45.
[2] John xv. 15.
[3] Jas. ii. 23.
[4] John viii. 58.
[5] John xvii. 5.
[6] John xv. 16.
[7] John xvii. 24.

west; and I will say to the north, Give up; and to the south, Keep not back: bring My sons from far, and My daughters from the ends of the earth; all, as many as have been called in My name: for in My glory I have prepared, and formed, and made him."[1] Inasmuch as, then, "wheresoever the carcase is, there shall also the eagles be gathered together,"[2] we do participate in the glory of the Lord, who has both formed us, and prepared us for this, that, when we are with Him, we may partake of His glory.

2. Thus it was, too, that God formed man at the first, because of His munificence; but chose the patriarchs for the sake of their salvation; and prepared a people beforehand, teaching the headstrong to follow God; and raised up prophets upon earth, accustoming man to bear His Spirit [within him], and to hold communion with God: He Himself, indeed, having need of nothing, but granting communion with Himself to those who stood in need of it, and sketching out, like an architect, the plan of salvation to those that pleased Him. And He did Himself furnish guidance to those who beheld Him not in Egypt, while to those who became unruly in the desert He promulgated a law very suitable [to their condition]. Then, on the people who entered into the good land He bestowed a noble inheritance; and He killed the fatted calf for those converted to the Father, and presented them with the finest robe.[3] Thus, in a variety of ways, He adjusted the human race to an agreement with salvation. On this account also does John declare in the Apocalypse, "And His voice as the sound of many waters."[4] For the Spirit [of God] is truly [like] many waters, since the Father is both rich and great. And the Word, passing through all those [men], did liberally confer benefits upon His subjects, by drawing up in writing a law adapted and applicable to every class [among them].

3. Thus, too, He imposed upon the [Jewish] people the construction of the tabernacle, the building of the temple, the election of the Levites, sacrifices also, and oblations, legal monitions, and all the other service of the law. He does Himself truly want none of these things, for He is always full of all good, and had in Himself all the odour of kindness, and every perfume of sweet-smelling savours, even before Moses existed. Moreover, He instructed the people, who were prone to turn to idols, instructing them by repeated appeals to persevere and to serve God, calling them to the things of primary importance by means of those which were secondary; that is, to things that are real, by means of those that are typical; and by things temporal, to eternal; and by the carnal to the spiritual; and by the earthly to the heavenly; as was also said to Moses, "Thou shalt make all things after the pattern of those things which thou sawest in the mount."[5] For during forty days He was learning to keep [in his memory] the words of God, and the celestial patterns, and the spiritual images, and the types of things to come; as also Paul says: "For they drank of the rock which followed them: and the rock was Christ."[6] And again, having first mentioned what are contained in the law, he goes on to say: "Now all these things happened to them in a figure; but they were written for our admonition, upon whom the end of the ages is come." For by means of types they learned to fear God, and to continue devoted to His service.

CHAP. XV. — AT FIRST GOD DEEMED IT SUFFICIENT TO INSCRIBE THE NATURAL LAW, OR THE DECALOGUE, UPON THE HEARTS OF MEN; BUT AFTERWARDS HE FOUND IT NECESSARY TO BRIDLE, WITH THE YOKE OF THE MOSAIC LAW, THE DESIRES OF THE JEWS, WHO WERE ABUSING THEIR LIBERTY; AND EVEN TO ADD SOME SPECIAL COMMANDS, BECAUSE OF THE HARDNESS OF THEIR HEARTS.

1. They (the Jews) had therefore a law, a course of discipline, and a prophecy of future things. For God at the first, indeed, warning them by means of natural precepts, which from the beginning He had implanted in mankind, that is, by means of the Decalogue (which, if any one does not observe, he has no salvation), did then demand nothing more of them. As Moses says in Deuteronomy, "These are all the words which the Lord spake to the whole assembly of the sons of Israel on the mount, and He added no more; and He wrote them on two tables of stone, and gave them to me."[7] For this reason [He did so], that they who are willing to follow Him might keep these commandments. But when they turned themselves to make a calf, and had gone back in their minds to Egypt, desiring to be slaves instead of freemen, they were placed for the future in a state of servitude suited to their wish, — [a slavery] which did not indeed cut them off from God, but subjected them to the yoke of bondage; as Ezekiel the prophet, when stating the reasons for the giving of such a law, declares: "And their eyes were after the desire of their heart; and I gave them statutes that were not good, and judgments in which they shall not live."[8]

---

[1] Isa. xliii. 5.
[2] Matt. xxiv. 28.
[3] Luke xv. 22, 23.
[4] Rev. i. 15.
[5] Ex. xxv. 40.
[6] 1 Cor. x. 11.
[7] Deut. v. 22.
[8] Ezek. xx. 24.

Luke also has recorded that Stephen, who was the first elected into the diaconate by the apostles,[1] and who was the first slain for the testimony of Christ, spoke regarding Moses as follows: "This man did indeed receive the commandments of the living God to give to us, whom your fathers would not obey, but thrust [Him from them], and in their hearts turned back again into Egypt, saying unto Aaron, Make us gods to go before us; for we do not know what has happened to [this] Moses, who led us from the land of Egypt. And they made a calf in those days, and offered sacrifices to the idol, and were rejoicing in the works of their own hands. But God turned, and gave them up to worship the hosts of heaven; as it is written in the book of the prophets:[2] O ye house of Israel, have ye offered to Me sacrifices and oblations for forty years in the wilderness? And ye took up the tabernacle of Moloch, and the star of the god Remphan,[3] figures which ye made to worship them;"[4] pointing out plainly, that the law being such, was not given to them by another God, but that, adapted to their condition of servitude, [it originated] from the very same [God as we worship]. Wherefore also He says to Moses in Exodus: "I will send forth My angel before thee; for I will not go up with thee, because thou art a stiff-necked people."[5]

2. And not only so, but the Lord also showed that certain precepts were enacted for them by Moses, on account of their hardness [of heart], and because of their unwillingness to be obedient, when, on their saying to Him, "Why then did Moses command to give a writing of divorcement, and to send away a wife?" He said to them, "Because of the hardness of your hearts he permitted these things to you; but from the beginning it was not so;"[6] thus exculpating Moses as a faithful servant, but acknowledging one God, who from the beginning made male and female, and reproving them as hard-hearted and disobedient. And therefore it was that they received from Moses this law of divorcement, adapted to their hard nature. But why say I these things concerning the Old Testament? For in the New also are the apostles found doing this very thing, on the ground which has been mentioned, Paul plainly declaring, But these things I say, not the Lord."[7] And again: "But this I speak by permission, not by commandment."[8] And again: "Now, as concerning virgins, I have no commandment from the Lord; yet I give my judgment, as one that hath obtained mercy of the Lord to be faithful."[9] But further, in another place he says: "That Satan tempt you not for your incontinence."[10] If, therefore, even in the New Testament, the apostles are found granting certain precepts in consideration of human infirmity, because of the incontinence of some, lest such persons, having grown obdurate, and despairing altogether of their salvation, should become apostates from God, — it ought not to be wondered at, if also in the Old Testament the same God permitted similar indulgences for the benefit of His people, drawing them on by means of the ordinances already mentioned, so that they might obtain the gift of salvation through them, while they obeyed the Decalogue, and being restrained by Him, should not revert to idolatry, nor apostatize from God, but learn to love Him with the whole heart. And if certain persons, because of the disobedient and ruined Israelites, do assert that the giver (*doctor*) of the law was limited in power, they will find in our dispensation, that "many are called, but few chosen;"[11] and that there are those who inwardly are wolves, yet wear sheep's clothing in the eyes of the world (*foris*); and that God has always preserved freedom, and the power of self-government in man,[12] while at the same time He issued His own exhortations, in order that those who do not obey Him should be righteously judged (condemned) because they have not obeyed Him; and that those who have obeyed and believed on Him should be honoured with immortality.

CHAP. XVI. — PERFECT RIGHTEOUSNESS WAS CONFERRED NEITHER BY CIRCUMCISION NOR BY ANY OTHER LEGAL CEREMONIES. THE DECALOGUE, HOWEVER, WAS NOT CANCELLED BY CHRIST, BUT IS ALWAYS IN FORCE: MEN WERE NEVER RELEASED FROM ITS COMMANDMENTS.

1. Moreover, we learn from the Scripture itself, that God gave circumcision, not as the completer of righteousness, but as a sign, that the race of Abraham might continue recognisable. For it declares: "God said unto Abraham, Every male among you shall be circumcised; and ye shall circumcise the flesh of your foreskins, as a token of the covenant between Me and you."[13] This same does Ezekiel the prophet say with regard to the Sabbaths: "Also I gave them My Sabbaths, to be a sign between Me and them, that they might know that I am the Lord, that sanctify them."[14] And in Exodus, God says to

---

[1] [Acts vi. 3-7. It is evident that the laity *elected*, and the apostles ordained.]
[2] Amos v 25, 26.
[3] In accordance with the Codex Bezæ.
[4] Acts vii 38, etc.
[5] Ex. xxxiii. 2, 3.
[6] Matt. xix. 7, 8.
[7] 1 Cor. vii. 12.
[8] 1 Cor. vii. 6.
[9] 1 Cor. vii. 25.
[10] 1 Cor. vii. 5.
[11] Matt. xx. 16.
[12] [Note this stout assertion of the freedom of human actions.]
[13] Gen. xvii. 9-11.
[14] Ezek. xx. 12.

Moses: "And ye shall observe My Sabbaths; for it shall be a sign between Me and you for your generations."[1] These things, then, were given for a sign; but the signs were not unsymbolical, that is, neither unmeaning nor to no purpose, inasmuch as they were given by a wise Artist; but the circumcision after the flesh typified that after the Spirit. For "we," says the apostle, "have been circumcised with the circumcision made without hands."[2] And the prophet declares, "Circumcise the hardness of your heart."[3] But the Sabbaths taught that we should continue day by day in God's service.[4] "For we have been counted," says the Apostle Paul, "all the day long as sheep for the slaughter;"[5] that is, consecrated [to God], and ministering continually to our faith, and persevering in it, and abstaining from all avarice, and not acquiring or possessing treasures upon earth.[6] Moreover, the Sabbath of God (*requietio Dei*), that is, the kingdom, was, as it were, indicated by created things; in which [kingdom], the man who shall have persevered in serving God (*Deo assistere*) shall, in a state of rest, partake of God's table.

2. And that man was not justified by these things, but that they were given as a sign to the people, this fact shows, — that Abraham himself, without circumcision and without observance of Sabbaths, "believed God, and it was imputed unto him for righteousness; and he was called the friend of God."[7] Then, again, Lot, without circumcision, was brought out from Sodom, receiving salvation from God. So also did Noah, pleasing God, although he was uncircumcised, receive the dimensions [of the ark], of the world of the second race [of men]. Enoch, too, pleasing God, without circumcision, discharged the office of God's legate to the angels although he was a man, and was translated, and is preserved until now as a witness of the just judgment of God, because the angels when they had transgressed fell to the earth for judgment, but the man who pleased [God] was translated for salvation.[8] Moreover, all the rest of the multitude of those righteous men who lived before Abraham, and of those patriarchs who preceded Moses, were justified independently of the things above mentioned, and without the law of Moses. As also Moses himself says to the people in Deuteronomy: "The LORD thy God formed a covenant in Horeb. The LORD formed not this covenant with your fathers, but for you."[9]

3. Why, then, did the Lord not form the covenant for the fathers? Because "the law was not established for righteous men."[10] But the righteous fathers had the meaning of the Decalogue written in their hearts and souls,[11] that is, they loved the God who made them, and did no injury to their neighbour. There was therefore no occasion that they should be cautioned by prohibitory mandates (*correptoriis literis*),[12] because they had the righteousness of the law in themselves. But when this righteousness and love to God had passed into oblivion, and became extinct in Egypt, God did necessarily, because of His great goodwill to men, reveal Himself by a voice, and led the people with power out of Egypt, in order that man might again become the disciple and follower of God; and He afflicted those who were disobedient, that they should not contemn their Creator; and He fed them with manna, that they might receive food for their souls (*uti rationalem acciperent escam*); as also Moses says in Deuteronomy: "And fed thee with manna, which thy fathers did not know, that thou mightest know that man doth not live by bread alone; but by every word of God proceeding out of His mouth doth man live."[13] And it enjoined love to God, and taught just dealing towards our neighbour, that we should neither be unjust nor unworthy of God, who prepares man for His friendship through the medium of the Decalogue, and likewise for agreement with his neighbour, — matters which did certainly profit man himself; God, however, standing in no need of anything from man.

4. And therefore does the Scripture say, "These words the Lord spake to all the assembly of the children of Israel in the mount, and He added no more;"[14] for, as I have already observed, He stood in need of nothing from them. And again Moses says: "And now Israel, what doth the LORD thy God require of thee, but to fear the LORD thy God, to walk in all His ways, and to love Him, and to serve the LORD thy God with all thy heart, and with all thy soul?"[15] Now these things did indeed make man glorious, by supplying what was wanting to him, namely, the friendship of God; but they profited God nothing, for God did not at all

---

[1] Ex. xxi. 13.
[2] Col. ii. 11.
[3] Deut. x. 16, LXX. version.
[4] The Latin text here is: "Sabbata autem perseverantiam totius diei erga Deum deservitionis edocebant;" which might be rendered, "The Sabbaths taught that we should continue the whole day in the service of God;" but Harvey conceives the original Greek to have been, τὴν καθημερινὴν διαμονὴν τῆς περὶ τὸν Θεὸν λατρείας.
[5] Rom. viii. 36.
[6] Matt. vi. 19.
[7] Jas. ii. 23.
[8] Massuet remarks here that Irenæus makes a reference to the apocryphal book of Enoch, in which this history is contained. It was the belief of the later Jews, followed by the Christian fathers, that "the sons of God" (Gen. vi. 2) who took wives of the daughters of men, were the apostate angels. The LXX. translation of that passage accords with this view. See the articles "Enoch," "Enoch, Book of," in Smith's *Dictionary of the Bible*. [See Paradise Lost, b. i. 323-431.]

[9] Deut. v. 2.
[10] 1 Tim. i. 9.
[11] [Hearts and souls; i.e., moral and mental natures. For a correct view of the patristic conceptions of the Gentiles before the law, this is valuable.]
[12] i.e., the *letters* of the Decalogue on the two tables of stone.
[13] Deut. viii. 3.
[14] Deut. v. 22.
[15] Deut. x. 12.

stand in need of man's love. For the glory of God was wanting to man, which he could obtain in no other way than by serving God. And therefore Moses says to them again: "Choose life, that thou mayest live, and thy seed, to love the Lord thy God, to hear His voice, to cleave unto Him; for this is thy life, and the length of thy days."[1] Preparing man for this life, the Lord Himself did speak in His own person to all alike the words of the Decalogue; and therefore, in like manner, do they remain permanently with us,[2] receiving by means of His advent in the flesh, extension and increase, but not abrogation.

5. The laws of bondage, however, were one by one promulgated to the people by Moses, suited for their instruction or for their punishment, as Moses himself declared: "And the Lord commanded me at that time to teach you statutes and judgments."[3] These things, therefore, which were given for bondage, and for a sign to them, He cancelled by the new covenant of liberty. But He has increased and widened those laws which are natural, and noble, and common to all, granting to men largely and without grudging, by means of adoption, to know God the Father, and to love Him with the whole heart, and to follow His word unswervingly, while they abstain not only from evil deeds, but even from the desire after them. But He has also increased the feeling of reverence; for sons should have more veneration than slaves, and greater love for their father. And therefore the Lord says, "As to every idle word that men have spoken, they shall render an account for it in the day of judgment."[4] And, "he who has looked upon a woman to lust after her, hath committed adultery with her already in his heart;"[5] and, "he that is angry with his brother without a cause, shall be in danger of the judgment."[6] [All this is declared,] that we may know that we shall give account to God not of deeds only, as slaves, but even of words and thoughts, as those who have truly received the power of liberty, in which [condition] a man is more severely tested, whether he will reverence, and fear, and love the Lord. And for this reason Peter says "that we have not liberty as a cloak of maliciousness,"[7] but as the means of testing and evidencing faith.

CHAP. XVII.—PROOF THAT GOD DID NOT APPOINT THE LEVITICAL DISPENSATION FOR HIS OWN SAKE, OR AS REQUIRING SUCH SERVICE; FOR HE DOES, IN FACT, NEED NOTHING FROM MEN.

1. Moreover, the prophets indicate in the fullest manner that God stood in no need of their slavish obedience, but that it was upon their own account that He enjoined certain observances in the law. And again, that God needed not their oblation, but [merely demanded it], on account of man himself who offers it, the Lord taught distinctly, as I have pointed out. For when He perceived them neglecting righteousness, and abstaining from the love of God, and imagining that God was to be propitiated by sacrifices and the other typical observances, Samuel did even thus speak to them: "God does not desire whole burnt-offerings and sacrifices, but He will have His voice to be hearkened to. Behold, a ready obedience is better than sacrifice, and to hearken than the fat of rams."[8] David also says: "Sacrifice and oblation Thou didst not desire, but mine ears hast Thou perfected;[9] burnt-offerings also for sin Thou hast not required."[10] He thus teaches them that God desires obedience, which renders them secure, rather than sacrifices and holocausts, which avail them nothing towards righteousness; and [by this declaration] he prophesies the new covenant at the same time. Still clearer, too, does he speak of these things in the fiftieth Psalm: "For if Thou hadst desired sacrifice, then would I have given it: Thou wilt not delight in burnt-offerings. The sacrifice of God is a broken spirit; a broken and contrite heart the Lord will not despise."[11] Because, therefore, God stands in need of nothing, He declares in the preceding Psalm: "I will take no calves out of thine house, nor he-goats out of thy fold. For Mine are all the beasts of the earth, the herds and the oxen on the mountains: I know all the fowls of heaven, and the various tribes[12] of the field are Mine. If I were hungry, I would not tell thee: for the world is Mine, and the fulness thereof. Shall I eat the flesh of bulls, or drink the blood of goats?"[13] Then, lest it might be supposed that He refused these things in His anger, He continues, giving him (man) counsel: "Offer unto God the sacrifice of praise, and pay thy vows to the Most High; and call upon Me in the day of thy trouble, and I will deliver thee, and thou shalt glorify Me;"[14] rejecting, indeed, those things by which sinners imagined they could propitiate God, and showing that He does Himself stand in need of nothing; but He exhorts and advises them to those

---

[1] Deut. xxx. 19, 20.
[2] [Most noteworthy among primitive testimonies to the catholic reception of the Decalogue.]
[3] Deut. iv. 14.
[4] Matt. xii. 36.
[5] Matt. v. 28.
[6] Matt. v. 22.
[7] 1 Pet. ii. 16.
[8] 1 Sam. xv. 22.
[9] Latin, "aures autem perfecisti mihi;" a reading agreeable to neither the Hebrew nor Septuagint version, as quoted by St. Paul in Heb. x. 9. Harvey, however, is of opinion that the text of the old Latin translation was originally "perforasti;" indicating thus an entire concurrence with the Hebrew, as now read in this passage. [Both readings illustrated by their apparent reference to Ex. xxi. 6, compared with Heb. v. 7, 8, 9.]
[10] Ps. xl. 6.
[11] Ps. li. 17.
[12] Or, "the beauty," *species*.
[13] Ps. l. 9.
[14] Ps. l. 14, 15.

things by which man is justified and draws nigh to God. This same declaration does Esaias make: "To what purpose is the multitude of your sacrifices unto Me? saith the Lord. I am full."[1] And when He had repudiated holocausts, and sacrifices, and oblations, as likewise the new moons, and the sabbaths, and the festivals, and all the rest of the services accompanying these, He continues, exhorting them to what pertained to salvation: "Wash you, make you clean, take away wickedness from your hearts from before mine eyes: cease from your evil ways, learn to do well, seek judgment, relieve the oppressed, judge the fatherless, plead for the widow; and come, let us reason together, saith the LORD."

2. For it was not because He was angry, like a man, as many venture to say, that He rejected their sacrifices; but out of compassion to their blindness, and with the view of suggesting to them the true sacrifice, by offering which they shall appease God, that they may receive life from Him. As He elsewhere declares: "The sacrifice to God is an afflicted heart: a sweet savour to God is a heart glorifying Him who formed it."[2] For if, when angry, He had repudiated these sacrifices of theirs, as if they were persons unworthy to obtain His compassion, He would not certainly have urged these same things upon them as those by which they might be saved. But inasmuch as God is merciful, He did not cut them off from good counsel. For after He had said by Jeremiah, "To what purpose bring ye Me incense from Saba, and cinnamon from a far country? Your whole burnt-offerings and sacrifices are not acceptable to Me;"[3] He proceeds: "Hear the word of the Lord, all Judah. These things saith the LORD, the God of Israel, Make straight your ways and your doings, and I will establish you in this place. Put not your trust in lying words, for they will not at all profit you, saying, The temple of the LORD, The temple of the LORD, it is [here]."[4]

3. And again, when He points out that it was not for this that He led them out of Egypt, that they might offer sacrifice to Him, but that, forgetting the idolatry of the Egyptians, they should be able to hear the voice of the Lord, which was to them salvation and glory, He declares by this same Jeremiah: "Thus saith the LORD; Collect together your burnt-offerings with your sacrifices, and eat flesh. For I spake not unto your fathers, nor commanded them in the day that I brought them out of Egypt, concerning burnt-offerings or sacrifices: but this word I commanded them, saying, Hear My voice, and I will be your God, and ye shall be My people; and walk in all My ways whatsoever I have commanded you, that it may be well with you. But they obeyed not, nor hearkened; but walked in the imaginations of their own evil heart, and went backwards, and not forwards."[5] And again, when He declares by the same man, "But let him that glorieth, glory in this, to understand and know that I am the LORD, who doth exercise loving-kindness, and righteousness, and judgment in the earth;"[6] He adds, "For in these things I delight, says the LORD," but not in sacrifices, nor in holocausts, nor in oblations. For the people did not receive these precepts as of primary importance (*principaliter*), but as secondary, and for the reason already alleged, as Isaiah again says: "Thou hast not [brought to] Me the sheep of thy holocaust, nor in thy sacrifices hast thou glorified Me: thou hast not served Me in sacrifices, nor in [the matter of] frankincense hast thou done anything laboriously; neither hast thou bought for Me incense with money, nor have I desired the fat of thy sacrifices; but thou hast stood before Me in thy sins and in thine iniquities."[7] He says, therefore, "Upon this man will I look, even upon him that is humble, and meek, and who trembles at My words."[8] "For the fat and the fat flesh shall not take away from thee thine unrighteousness."[9] "This is the fast which I have chosen, saith the LORD. Loose every band of wickedness, dissolve the connections of violent agreements, give rest to those that are shaken, and cancel every unjust document. Deal thy bread to the hungry willingly, and lead into thy house the roofless stranger. If thou hast seen the naked, cover him, and thou shalt not despise those of thine own flesh and blood (*domesticos seminis tui*). Then shall thy morning light break forth, and thy health shall spring forth more speedily; and righteousness shall go before thee, and the glory of the LORD shall surround thee: and whilst thou art yet speaking, I will say, Behold, here I am."[10] And Zechariah also, among the twelve prophets, pointing out to the people the will of God, says: "These things does the LORD Omnipotent declare: Execute true judgment, and show mercy and compassion each one to his brother. And oppress not the widow, and the orphan, and the proselyte, and the poor; and let none imagine evil against your brother in his heart."[11] And again, he says: "These are the words which ye

---

[1] Isa. i. 11.
[2] This passage is not now found in holy Scripture. Harvey conjectures that it may have been taken from the apocryphal Gospel according to the Egyptians. It is remarkable that we find the same words quoted also by Clement of Alexandria. [But he (possibly with this place in view) merely quotes it as a *saying*, in close connection with Ps. li. 19, which is here partially cited. See Clement, *Pædagogue*, b. iii. cap. xii.]
[3] Jer. vi. 20.
[4] Jer. vii. 2, 3.
[5] Jer. vii. 21.
[6] Jer. ix. 24.
[7] Isa. xliii. 23, 24.
[8] Isa. xlvi. 2.
[9] Jer. xi. 15.
[10] Isa. lviii. 6, etc.
[11] Zech. vii. 9, 10.

shall utter. Speak ye the truth every man to his neighbour, and execute peaceful judgment in your gates, and let none of you imagine evil in his heart against his brother, and ye shall not love false swearing: for all these things I hate, saith the LORD Almighty."[1] Moreover, David also says in like manner: "What man is there who desireth life, and would fain see good days? Keep thy tongue from evil, and thy lips that they speak no guile. Shun evil, and do good: seek peace, and pursue it."[2]

4. From all these it is evident that God did not seek sacrifices and holocausts from them, but faith, and obedience, and righteousness, because of their salvation. As God, when teaching them His will in Hosea the prophet, said, "I desire mercy rather than sacrifice, and the knowledge of God more than burnt-offerings."[3] Besides, our Lord also exhorted them to the same effect, when He said, "But if ye had known what [this] meaneth, I will have mercy, and not sacrifice, ye would not have condemned the guiltless."[4] Thus does He bear witness to the prophets, that they preached the truth; but accuses these men (His hearers) of being foolish through their own fault.

5. Again, giving directions to His disciples to offer to God the first-fruits[5] of His own created things — not as if He stood in need of them, but that they might be themselves neither unfruitful nor ungrateful — He took that created thing, bread, and gave thanks, and said, "This is My body."[6] And the cup likewise, which is part of that creation to which we belong, He confessed to be His blood, and taught the new oblation of the new covenant; which the Church receiving from the apostles, offers to God throughout all the world, to Him who gives us as the means of subsistence the first-fruits of His own gifts in the New Testament, concerning which Malachi, among the twelve prophets, thus spoke beforehand: "I have no pleasure in you, saith the LORD Omnipotent, and I will not accept sacrifice at your hands. For from the rising of the sun, unto the going down [of the same], My name is glorified among the Gentiles, and in every place incense is offered to My name, and a pure sacrifice; for great is My name among the Gentiles, saith the LORD Omnipotent;"[7] — indicating in the plainest manner, by these words, that the former people [the Jews] shall indeed cease to make offerings to God, but that in every place sacrifice shall be offered to Him, and that a pure one; and His name is glorified among the Gentiles.[8]

6. But what other name is there which is glorified among the Gentiles than that of our Lord, by whom the Father is glorified, and man also? And because it is [the name] of His own Son, who was made man by Him, He calls it His own. Just as a king, if he himself paints a likeness of his son, is right in calling this likeness his own, for both these reasons, because it is [the likeness] of his son, and because it is his own production; so also does the Father confess the name of Jesus Christ, which is throughout all the world glorified in the Church, to be His own, both because it is that of His Son, and because He who thus describes it gave Him for the salvation of men. Since, therefore, the name of the Son belongs to the Father, and since in the omnipotent God the Church makes offerings through Jesus Christ, He says well on both these grounds, "And in every place incense is offered to My name, and a pure sacrifice." Now John, in the Apocalypse, declares that the "incense" is "the prayers of the saints."[9]

CHAP. XVIII. — CONCERNING SACRIFICES AND OBLATIONS, AND THOSE WHO TRULY OFFER THEM.

1. The oblation of the Church, therefore, which the Lord gave instructions to be offered throughout all the world, is accounted with God a pure sacrifice, and is acceptable to Him; not that He stands in need of a sacrifice from us, but that he who offers is himself glorified in what he does offer, if his gift be accepted. For by the gift both honour and affection are shown forth towards the King; and the Lord, wishing us to offer it in all simplicity and innocence, did express Himself thus: "Therefore, when thou offerest thy gift upon the altar, and shalt remember that thy brother hath ought against thee, leave thy gift before the altar, and go thy way; first be reconciled to thy brother, and then return and offer thy gift."[10] We are bound, therefore, to offer to God the first-fruits of His creation, as Moses also says, "Thou shalt not appear in the presence of the Lord thy God empty;"[11] so that man, being accounted as grateful, by those things in which he has shown his gratitude, may receive that honour which flows from Him.[12]

2. And the class of oblations in general has not been set aside; for there were both oblations

---

[1] Zech. viii. 16, 17.
[2] Ps. xxxiv. 13, 14.
[3] Hos. vi. 6.
[4] Matt. xii. 7.
[5] Grabe has a long and important note on this passage and what follows, which may be seen in Harvey, *in loc*. See, on the other side, and in connection with the whole of the following chapter, Massuet's third dissertation on the doctrine of Irenæus, art. vii., reprinted in Migne's edition.
[6] Matt. xxvi. 26, etc.
[7] Mal. i. 10, 11.
[8] [One marvels that there should be any critical difficulty here as to our author's teaching. Creatures of bread and wine are the body and blood; materially one thing, mystically another. See cap. xviii. 5 below.]
[9] Rev. v. 8. [Material incense seems to be always disclaimed by the primitive writers.]
[10] Matt. v. 23, 24.
[11] Deut. xvi. 16.
[12] The text of this passage is doubtful in some words.

there [among the Jews], and there are oblations here [among the Christians]. Sacrifices there were among the people; sacrifices there are, too, in the Church: but the species alone has been changed, inasmuch as the offering is now made, not by slaves, but by freemen. For the Lord is [ever] one and the same; but the character of a servile oblation is peculiar [to itself], as is also that of freemen, in order that, by the very oblations, the indication of liberty may be set forth. For with Him there is nothing purposeless, nor without signification, nor without design. And for this reason they (the Jews) had indeed the tithes of their goods consecrated to Him, but those who have received liberty set aside all their possessions for the Lord's purposes, bestowing joyfully and freely not the less valuable portions of their property, since they have the hope of better things [hereafter]; as that poor widow acted who cast all her living into the treasury of God.[1]

3. For at the beginning God had respect to the gifts of Abel, because he offered with single-mindedness and righteousness; but He had no respect unto the offering of Cain, because his heart was divided with envy and malice, which he cherished against his brother, as God says when reproving his hidden [thoughts], "Though thou offerest rightly, yet, if thou dost not divide rightly, hast thou not sinned? Be at rest;"[2] since God is not appeased by sacrifice. For if any one shall endeavour to offer a sacrifice merely to outward appearance, unexceptionably, in due order, and according to appointment, while in his soul he does not assign to his neighbour that fellowship with him which is right and proper, nor is under the fear of God;—he who thus cherishes secret sin does not deceive God by that sacrifice which is offered correctly as to outward appearance; nor will such an oblation profit him anything, but [only] the giving up of that evil which has been conceived within him, so that sin may not the more, by means of the hypocritical action, render him the destroyer of himself.[3] Wherefore did the Lord also declare: "Woe unto you, scribes and Pharisees, hypocrites, for ye are like whited sepulchres. For the sepulchre appears beautiful outside, but within it is full of dead men's bones, and all uncleanness; even so ye also outwardly appear righteous unto men, but within ye are full of wickedness and hypocrisy."[4] For while they were thought to offer correctly so far as outward appearance went, they had in themselves jealousy like to Cain; therefore they slew the Just One, slighting the counsel of the Word, as did also Cain. For [God] said to him, "Be at rest;" but he did not assent. Now what else is it to "be at rest" than to forego purposed violence? And saying similar things to these men, He declares: "Thou blind Pharisee, cleanse that which is within the cup, that the outside may be clean also."[5] And they did not listen to Him. For Jeremiah says, "Behold, neither thine eyes nor thy heart are good; but [they are turned] to thy covetousness, and to shed innocent blood, and for injustice, and for man-slaying, that thou mayest do it."[6] And again Isaiah saith, "Ye have taken counsel, but not of Me; and made covenants, [but] not by My Spirit."[7] In order, therefore, that their inner wish and thought, being brought to light, may show that God is without blame, and worketh no evil — that God who reveals what is hidden [in the heart], but who worketh not evil — when Cain was by no means at rest, He saith to him: "To thee shall be his desire, and thou shalt rule over him."[8] Thus did He in like manner speak to Pilate: "Thou shouldest have no power at all against Me, unless it were given thee from above;"[9] God always giving up the righteous one [in this life to suffering], that he, having been tested by what he suffered and endured, may [at last] be accepted; but that the evil-doer, being judged by the actions he has performed, may be rejected. Sacrifices, therefore, do not sanctify a man, for God stands in no need of sacrifice; but it is the conscience of the offerer that sanctifies the sacrifice when it is pure, and thus moves God to accept [the offering] as from a friend. "But the sinner," says He, "who kills a calf [in sacrifice] to Me, is as if he slew a dog."[10]

4. Inasmuch, then, as the Church offers with single-mindedness, her gift is justly reckoned a pure sacrifice with God. As Paul also says to the Philippians, "I am full, having received from Epaphroditus the things that were sent from you, the odour of a sweet smell, a sacrifice acceptable, pleasing to God."[11] For it behoves us to make an oblation to God, and in all things to be found grateful to God our Maker, in a pure mind, and in faith without hypocrisy, in well-grounded hope, in fervent love, offering the first-fruits of His own created things. And the Church alone offers this pure oblation to the Creator, offering to Him, with giving of thanks, [the things taken] from His creation. But the Jews do not offer thus: for their hands are full of blood; for they have not received the Word,

---

[1] Luke xxi. 4. [The law of tithes abrogated; the law of Acts ii. 44, 45, morally binding. This seems to be our author's view.]
[2] Gen. iv. 7, LXX.
[3] The Latin text is: "ne per assimulatam operationem, magis autem peccatum, ipsum sibi homicidam faciat hominem."
[4] Matt. xxiii. 27, 28.
[5] Matt. xxiii. 26.
[6] Jer. xxii. 17.
[7] Isa. xxx. 1.
[8] Gen. iv. 7.
[9] John xix. 11.
[10] Isa. lxvi. 3.
[11] Phil. iv. 18.

through whom it is offered to God.[1] Nor, again, do any of the conventicles (*synagogæ*) of the heretics [offer this]. For some, by maintaining that the Father is different from the Creator, do, when they offer to Him what belongs to this creation of ours, set Him forth as being covetous of another's property, and desirous of what is not His own. Those, again, who maintain that the things around us originated from apostasy, ignorance, and passion, do, while offering unto Him the fruits of ignorance, passion, and apostasy, sin against their Father, rather subjecting Him to insult than giving Him thanks. But how can they be consistent with themselves, [when they say] that the bread over which thanks have been given is the body of their Lord,[2] and the cup His blood, if they do not call Himself the Son of the Creator of the world, that is, His Word, through whom the wood fructifies, and the fountains gush forth, and the earth gives "first the blade, then the ear, then the full corn in the ear."[3]

5. Then, again, how can they say that the flesh, which is nourished with the body of the Lord and with His blood, goes to corruption, and does not partake of life? Let them, therefore, either alter their opinion, or cease from offering the things just mentioned.[4] But our opinion is in accordance with the Eucharist, and the Eucharist in turn establishes our opinion. For we offer to Him His own, announcing consistently the fellowship and union of the flesh and Spirit.[5] For as the bread, which is produced from the earth, when it receives the invocation of God, is no longer common bread,[6] but the Eucharist, consisting of two realities, earthly and heavenly; so also our bodies, when they receive the Eucharist, are no longer corruptible, having the hope of the resurrection to eternity.

6. Now we make offering to Him, not as though He stood in need of it, but rendering thanks for His gift,[7] and thus sanctifying what has been created. For even as God does not need our possessions, so do we need to offer something to God; as Solomon says: "He that hath pity upon the poor, lendeth unto the Lord."[8] For God, who stands in need of nothing, takes our good works to Himself for this purpose, that He may grant us a recompense of His own good things, as our Lord says: "Come, ye blessed of My Father, receive the kingdom prepared for you. For I was an hungered, and ye gave Me to eat: I was thirsty, and ye gave Me drink: I was a stranger, and ye took Me in: naked, and ye clothed Me; sick, and ye visited Me; in prison, and ye came to Me."[9] As, therefore, He does not stand in need of these [services], yet does desire that we should render them for our own benefit, lest we be unfruitful; so did the Word give to the people that very precept as to the making of oblations, although He stood in no need of them, that they might learn to serve God: thus is it, therefore, also His will that we, too, should offer a gift at the altar, frequently and without intermission. The altar, then, is in heaven[10] (for towards that place are our prayers and oblations directed); the temple likewise [is there], as John says in the Apocalypse, "And the temple of God was opened:"[11] the tabernacle also: "For, behold," He says, "the tabernacle of God, in which He will dwell with men."

CHAP. XIX. — EARTHLY THINGS MAY BE THE TYPE OF HEAVENLY, BUT THE LATTER CANNOT BE THE TYPES OF OTHERS STILL SUPERIOR AND UNKNOWN; NOR CAN WE, WITHOUT ABSOLUTE MADNESS, MAINTAIN THAT GOD IS KNOWN TO US ONLY AS THE TYPE OF A STILL UNKNOWN AND SUPERIOR BEING.

1. Now the gifts, oblations, and all the sacrifices, did the people receive in a figure, as was shown to Moses in the mount, from one and the same God, whose name is now glorified in the Church among all nations. But it is congruous that those earthly things, indeed, which are spread all around us, should be types of the celestial, being [both], however, created by the same God. For in no other way could He assimilate an image of spiritual things [to suit our comprehension]. But to allege that those things which are super-celestial and spiritual, and, as far as we are concerned, invisible and ineffable, are in their turn the types of celestial

---

[1] The text here fluctuates between *quod offertur Deo*, and *per quod offertur Deo*. Massuet adopts the former, and Harvey the latter. If the first reading be chosen, the translation will be, "the Word who is offered to God," implying, according to Massuet, that the body of Christ is really offered as a sacrifice in the Eucharist; if the second reading be followed, the translation will be as above. [Massuet's idea is no more to be found, even in his text, than Luther's or Calvin's. The crucial point is, *how* offered? One may answer "figuratively," "corporally," "mystically," or otherwise. Irenæus gives no answer in this place. But see below.]
[2] Comp. Massuet and Harvey respectively for the meaning to be attached to these words.
[3] Mark iv. 28.
[4] "Either let them acknowledge that *the earth is the Lord's, and the fulness thereof*, or let them cease to offer to God those elements that they deny to be vouchsafed by Him." — HARVEY.
[5] That is, according to Harvey, " while we offer to Him His own creatures of bread and wine, we tell forth the fellowship of flesh with spirit; i.e., that the flesh of every child of man is receptive of the Spirit." The words, καὶ ὁμολογοῦντες . . . ἐγερσιν, which here occur in the Greek text, are rejected as an interpolation by Grabe and Harvey, but defended as genuine by Massuet.
[6] See Harvey's long note on this passage, and what immediately follows. [But, note, we are only asking what Irenæus teaches. Could words be plainer, — "*two* realities," — (i.) bread, (ii.) spiritual food? Bread — but not "common bread;" matter and grace, flesh and Spirit. In the Eucharist, an earthly and a heavenly part.]

[7] The text fluctuates between *dominationi* and *donationi*.
[8] Prov. xix. 17.
[9] Matt. xxv. 34, etc.
[10] [The *Sursum Corda* seems here in mind. The object of Eucharistic adoration is the Creator, our "great High Priest, passed into the heavens," and in bodily substance there enthroned, according to our author.]
[11] Rev. xi. 19.

things and of another Pleroma, and [to say] that God is the image of another Father, is to play the part both of wanderers from the truth, and of absolutely foolish and stupid persons. For, as I have repeatedly shown, such persons will find it necessary to be continually finding out types of types, and images of images, and will never [be able to] fix their minds on one and the true God. For their imaginations range beyond God, they having in their hearts surpassed the Master Himself, being indeed in idea elated and exalted above [Him], but in reality turning away from the true God.

2. To these persons one may with justice say (as Scripture itself suggests), To what distance above God do ye lift up your imaginations, O ye rashly elated men? Ye have heard "that the heavens are meted out in the palm of [His] hand:"[1] tell me the measure, and recount the endless multitude of cubits, explain to me the fulness, the breadth, the length, the height, the beginning and end of the measurement, — things which the heart of man understands not, neither does it comprehend them. For the heavenly treasuries are indeed great: God cannot be measured in the heart, and incomprehensible is He in the mind; He who holds the earth in the hollow of His hand. Who perceives the measure of His right hand? Who knoweth His finger? Or who doth understand His hand, — that hand which measures immensity; that hand which, by its own measure, spreads out the measure of the heavens, and which comprises in its hollow the earth with the abysses; which contains in itself the breadth, and length, and the deep below, and the height above of the whole creation; which is seen, which is heard and understood, and which is invisible? And for this reason God is "above all principality, and power, and dominion, and every name that is named,"[2] of all things which have been created and established. He it is who fills the heavens, and views the abysses, who is also present with every one of us. For he says, "Am I a God at hand, and not a God afar off? If any man is hid in secret places, shall I not see him?"[3] For His hand lays hold of all things, and that it is which illumines the heavens, and lightens also the things which are under the heavens, and trieth the reins and the hearts, is also present in hidden things, and in our secret [thoughts], and does openly nourish and preserve us.

3. But if man comprehends not the fulness and the greatness of His hand, how shall any one be able to understand or know in his heart so great a God? Yet, as if they had now measured and thoroughly investigated Him, and explored Him on every side,[4] they feign that beyond Him there exists another Pleroma of Æons, and another Father; certainly not looking up to celestial things, but truly descending into a profound abyss (Bythus) of madness; maintaining that their Father extends only to the border of those things which are beyond the Pleroma, but that, on the other hand, the Demiurge does not reach so far as the Pleroma; and thus they represent neither of them as being perfect and comprehending all things. For the former will be defective in regard to the whole world formed outside of the Pleroma, and the latter in respect of that [ideal] world which was formed within the Pleroma; and [therefore] neither of these can be the God of all. But that no one can fully declare the goodness of God from the things made by Him, is a point evident to all. And that His greatness is not defective, but contains all things, and extends even to us, and is with us, every one will confess who entertains worthy conceptions of God.

CHAP. XX. — THAT ONE GOD FORMED ALL THINGS IN THE WORLD, BY MEANS OF THE WORD AND THE HOLY SPIRIT: AND THAT ALTHOUGH HE IS TO US IN THIS LIFE INVISIBLE AND INCOMPREHENSIBLE, NEVERTHELESS HE IS NOT UNKNOWN; INASMUCH AS HIS WORKS DO DECLARE HIM, AND HIS WORD HAS SHOWN THAT IN MANY MODES HE MAY BE SEEN AND KNOWN.

1. As regards His greatness, therefore, it is not possible to know God, for it is impossible that the Father can be measured; but as regards His love (for this it is which leads us to God by His Word), when we obey Him, we do always learn that there is so great a God, and that it is He who by Himself has established, and selected, and adorned, and contains all things; and among the all things, both ourselves and this our world. We also then were made, along with those things which are contained by Him. And this is He of whom the Scripture says, "And God formed man, taking clay of the earth, and breathed into his face the breath of life."[5] It was not angels, therefore, who made us, nor who formed us, neither had angels power to make an image of God, nor any one else, except the Word of the Lord, nor any Power remotely distant from the Father of all things. For God did not stand in need of these [beings], in order to the accomplishing of what He had Himself determined with Himself beforehand should be done, as if He did not possess His own hands. For with Him were always present the Word and Wisdom, the Son and the Spirit, by whom and in whom,

---

[1] Isa. xl. 12.
[2] Eph. i. 21.
[3] Jer. xxiii. 23.
[4] The Latin is, "et universum eum decurrerint." Harvey imagines that this last word corresponds to κατατρέχωσι, but it is difficult to fit such a meaning into the context.
[5] Gen. ii. 7.

freely and spontaneously, He made all things, to whom also He speaks, saying, "Let Us make man after Our image and likeness;"[1] He taking from Himself the substance of the creatures [formed], and the pattern of things made, and the type of all the adornments in the world.

2. Truly, then, the Scripture declared, which says, "First[2] of all believe that there is one God, who has established all things, and completed them, and having caused that from what had no being, all things should come into existence:" He who contains all things, and is Himself contained by no one. Rightly also has Malachi said among the prophets: "Is it not one God who hath established us? Have we not all one Father?"[3] In accordance with this, too, does the apostle say, "There is one God, the Father, who is above all, and in us all."[4] Likewise does the Lord also say: "All things are delivered to Me by My Father;"[5] manifestly by Him who made all things; for He did not deliver to Him the things of another, but His own. But in *all things* [it is implied that] nothing has been kept back [from Him], and for this reason the same person is the Judge of the living and the dead; "having the key of David: He shall open, and no man shall shut: He shall shut, and no man shall open."[6] For no one was able, either in heaven or in earth, or under the earth, to open the book of the Father, or to behold Him, with the exception of the Lamb who was slain, and who redeemed us with His own blood, receiving power over all things from the same God who made all things by the Word, and adorned them by [His] Wisdom, when "the Word was made flesh;" that even as the Word of God had the sovereignty in the heavens, so also might He have the sovereignty in earth, inasmuch as [He was] a righteous man, "who did no sin, neither was there found guile in His mouth;"[7] and that He might have the pre-eminence over those things which are under the earth, He Himself being made "the first-begotten of the dead;"[8] and that all things, as I have already said, might behold their King; and that the paternal light might meet with and rest upon the flesh of our Lord, and come to us from His resplendent flesh, and that thus man might attain to immortality, having been invested with the paternal light.

3. I have also largely demonstrated, that the Word, namely the Son, was always with the Father; and that Wisdom also, which is the Spirit, was present with Him, anterior to all creation, He declares by Solomon: "God by Wisdom founded the earth, and by understanding hath He established the heaven. By His knowledge the depths burst forth, and the clouds dropped down the dew."[9] And again: "The Lord created me the beginning of His ways in His work: He set me up from everlasting, in the beginning, before He made the earth, before He established the depths, and before the fountains of waters gushed forth; before the mountains were made strong, and before all the hills, He brought me forth."[10] And again: "When He prepared the heaven, I was with Him, and when He established the fountains of the deep; when He made the foundations of the earth strong, I was with Him preparing [them]. I was He in whom He rejoiced, and throughout all time I was daily glad before His face, when He rejoiced at the completion of the world, and was delighted in the sons of men."[11]

4. There is therefore one God, who by the Word and Wisdom created and arranged all things; but this is the Creator (Demiurge) who has granted this world to the human race, and who, as regards His greatness, is indeed unknown to all who have been made by Him (for no man has searched out His height, either among the ancients who have gone to their rest, or any of those who are now alive); but as regards His love, He is always known through Him by whose means He ordained all things. Now this is His Word, our Lord Jesus Christ, who in the last times was made a man among men, that He might join the end to the beginning, that is, man to God. Wherefore the prophets, receiving the prophetic gift from the same Word, announced His advent according to the flesh, by which the blending and communion of God and man took place according to the good pleasure of the Father, the Word of God foretelling from the beginning that God should be seen by men, and hold converse with them upon earth, should confer with them, and should be present with His own creation, saving it, and becoming capable of being perceived by it, and freeing us from the hands of all that hate us, that is, from every spirit of wickedness; and causing us to serve Him in holiness and righteousness all our days,[12] in order that man, having embraced the Spirit of God, might pass into the glory of the Father.

5. These things did the prophets set forth in a prophetical manner; but they did not, as some allege, [proclaim] that He who was seen by the prophets was a different [God], the Father of

---

[1] Gen. i. 26.
[2] This quotation is taken from the *Shepherd of Hermas*, book ii. sim. 1.
[3] Mal. ii. 10.
[4] Eph. iv. 6.
[5] Matt. xi. 27.
[6] Rev. iii. 7.
[7] 1 Pet. ii. 23.
[8] Col. i. 18.
[9] Prov. iii. 19, 20.
[10] Prov. viii. 22-25. [This is one of the favourite Messianic quotations of the Fathers, and is considered as the base of the first chapter of St. John's Gospel.]
[11] Prov. viii. 27-31.
[12] Luke i. 71, 75.

all being invisible. Yet this is what those [heretics] declare, who are altogether ignorant of the nature of prophecy. For prophecy is a prediction of things future, that is, a setting forth beforehand of those things which shall be afterwards. The prophets, then, indicated beforehand that God should be seen by men; as the Lord also says, "Blessed are the pure in heart, for they shall see God."[1] But in respect to His greatness, and His wonderful glory, "no man shall see God and live,"[2] for the Father is incomprehensible; but in regard to His love, and kindness, and as to His infinite power, even this He grants to those who love Him, that is, to see God, which thing the prophets did also predict. "For those things that are impossible with men, are possible with God."[3] For man does not see God by his own powers; but when He pleases He is seen by men, by whom He wills, and when He wills, and as He wills. For God is powerful in all things, having been seen at that time indeed, prophetically through the Spirit, and seen, too, adoptively through the Son; and He shall also be seen paternally in the kingdom of heaven, the Spirit truly preparing man in the Son[4] of God, and the Son leading him to the Father, while the Father, too, confers [upon him] incorruption for eternal life, which comes to every one from the fact of his seeing God. For as those who see the light are within the light, and partake of its brilliancy; even so, those who see God are in God, and receive of His splendour. But [His] splendour vivifies them; those, therefore, who see God, do receive life. And for this reason, He, [although] beyond comprehension, and boundless and invisible, rendered Himself visible, and comprehensible, and within the capacity of those who believe, that He might vivify those who receive and behold Him through faith.[5] For as His greatness is past finding out, so also His goodness is beyond expression; by which having been seen, He bestows life upon those who see Him. It is not possible to live apart from life, and the means of life is found in fellowship with God; but fellowship with God is to know God, and to enjoy His goodness.

6. Men therefore shall see God, that they may live, being made immortal by that sight, and attaining even unto God; which, as I have already said, was declared figuratively by the prophets, that God should be seen by men who bear His Spirit [in them], and do always wait patiently for His coming. As also Moses says in Deuteronomy, "We shall see in that day that God will talk to man, and he shall live."[6] For certain of these men used to see the prophetic Spirit and His active influences poured forth for all kinds of gifts; others, again, [beheld] the advent of the Lord, and that dispensation which obtained from the beginning, by which He accomplished the will of the Father with regard to things both celestial and terrestrial; and others [beheld] paternal glories adapted to the times, and to those who saw and who heard them then, and to all who were subsequently to hear them. Thus, therefore, was God revealed; for God the Father is shown forth through all these [operations], the Spirit indeed working, and the Son ministering, while the Father was approving, and man's salvation being accomplished. As He also declares through Hosea the prophet: "I," He says, "have multiplied visions, and have used similitudes by the ministry (*in manibus*) of the prophets."[7] But the apostle expounded this very passage, when he said, "Now there are diversities of gifts, but the same Spirit; and there are differences of ministrations, but the same Lord; and there are diversities of operations, but it is the same God which worketh all in all. But the manifestation of the Spirit is given to every man to profit withal."[8] But as He who worketh all things in all is God, [as to the points] of what nature and how great He is, [God] is invisible and indescribable to all things which have been made by Him, but He is by no means unknown: for all things learn through His Word that there is one God the Father, who contains all things, and who grants existence to all, as is written in the Gospel: "No man hath seen God at any time, except the only-begotten Son, who is in the bosom of the Father; He has declared [Him.]"[9]

7. Therefore the Son of the Father declares [Him] from the beginning, inasmuch as He was with the Father from the beginning, who did also show to the human race prophetic visions, and diversities of gifts, and His own ministrations, and the glory of the Father, in regular order and connection, at the fitting time for the benefit [of mankind]. For where there is a regular succession, there is also fixedness; and where fixedness, there suitability to the period; and where suitability, there also utility. And for this reason did the Word become the dispenser of the paternal grace for the benefit of men, for whom He made such great dispensations, revealing God indeed to men, but presenting man to God, and preserving at the same time the invisibility of the Father, lest man should at any time become a despiser of God, and that he should

---

[1] Matt. v. 8.
[2] Ex. xxxiii. 20.
[3] Luke xviii. 27.
[4] Some read "in filium" instead of "in filio," as above.
[5] A part of the original Greek text is preserved here, and has been followed, as it makes the better sense.
[6] Deut. v. 24.
[7] Hos. xii. 10.
[8] 1 Cor. xii. 4-7.
[9] John i. 18.

always possess something towards which he might advance; but, on the other hand, revealing God to men through many dispensations, lest man, falling away from God altogether, should cease to exist. For the glory of God is a living man; and the life of man consists in beholding God. For if the manifestation of God which is made by means of the creation, affords life to all living in the earth, much more does that revelation of the Father which comes through the Word, give life to those who see God.

8. Inasmuch, then, as the Spirit of God pointed out by the prophets things to come, forming and adapting us beforehand for the purpose of our being made subject to God, but it was still a future thing that man, through the good pleasure of the Holy Spirit, should see [God], it necessarily behoved those through whose instrumentality future things were announced, to see God, whom they intimated as to be seen by men; in order that God, and the Son of God, and the Son, and the Father, should not only be prophetically announced, but that He should also be seen by all His members who are sanctified and instructed in the things of God, that man might be disciplined beforehand and previously exercised for a reception into that glory which shall afterwards be revealed in those who love God. For the prophets used not to prophesy in word alone, but in visions also, and in their mode of life, and in the actions which they performed, according to the suggestions of the Spirit. After this invisible manner, therefore, did they see God, as also Esaias says, "I have seen with mine eyes the King, the LORD of hosts,"[1] pointing out that man should behold God with his eyes, and hear His voice. In this manner, therefore, did they also see the Son of God as a man conversant with men, while they prophesied what was to happen, saying that He who was not come as yet was present; proclaiming also the impassible as subject to suffering, and declaring that He who was then in heaven had descended into the dust of death.[2] Moreover, [with regard to] the other arrangements concerning the summing up that He should make, some of these they beheld through visions, others they proclaimed by word, while others they indicated typically by means of [outward] action, seeing visibly those things which were to be seen; heralding by word of mouth those which should be heard; and performing by actual operation what should take place by action; but [at the same time] announcing all prophetically. Wherefore also Moses declared that God was indeed a consuming fire[3] (*igneum*) to the people that transgressed the law, and threatened that God would bring upon them a day of fire; but to those who had the fear of God he said, "The LORD God is merciful and gracious, and long-suffering, and of great commiseration, and true, and keeps justice and mercy for thousands, forgiving unrighteousness, and transgressions, and sins."[4]

9. And the Word spake to Moses, appearing before him, "just as any one might speak to his friend."[5] But Moses desired to see Him openly who was speaking with him, and was thus addressed: "Stand in the deep place of the rock, and with My hand I will cover thee. But when My splendour shall pass by, then thou shalt see My back parts, but My face thou shalt not see: for no man sees My face, and shall live."[6] Two facts are thus signified: that it is impossible for man to see God; and that, through the wisdom of God, man shall see Him in the last times, in the depth of a rock, that is, in His coming as a man. And for this reason did He [the Lord] confer with him face to face on the top of a mountain, Elias being also present, as the Gospel relates,[7] He thus making good in the end the ancient promise.

10. The prophets, therefore, did not openly behold the actual face of God, but [they saw] the dispensations and the mysteries through which man should afterwards see God. As was also said to Elias: "Thou shalt go forth to-morrow, and stand in the presence of the LORD; and, behold, a wind great and strong, which shall rend the mountains, and break the rocks in pieces before the LORD. And the LORD [was] not in the wind; and after the wind an earthquake, but the LORD [was] not in the earthquake; and after the earthquake a fire, but the Lord [was] not in the fire; and after the fire a scarcely audible voice" (*vox auræ tenuis*).[8] For by such means was the prophet — very indignant, because of the transgression of the people and the slaughter of the prophets — both taught to act in a more gentle manner; and the Lord's advent as a man was pointed out, that it should be subsequent to that law which was given by Moses, mild and tranquil, in which He would neither break the bruised reed, nor quench the smoking flax.[9] The mild and peaceful repose of His kingdom was indicated likewise. For, after the wind which rends the mountains, and after the earthquake, and after the fire, come the tranquil and peaceful times of His kingdom, in which the Spirit of God does, in the most gentle manner, vivify and increase mankind. This, too, was made still clearer by Ezekiel, that the proph-

---

[1] Isa. vi. 5.
[2] Ps. xxii. 15.
[3] Deut. iv. 24.
[4] Ex. xxxiv. 6, 7.
[5] Num. xii. 8.
[6] Ex. xxxiii. 20–22.
[7] Matt. xvii. 3, etc.
[8] 1 Kings xix. 11, 12.
[9] Isa. xlii. 3.

ets saw the dispensations of God in part, but not actually God Himself. For when this man had seen the vision[1] of God, and the cherubim, and their wheels, and when he had recounted the mystery of the whole of that progression, and had beheld the likeness of a throne above them, and upon the throne a likeness as of the figure of a man, and the things which were upon his loins as the figure of amber, and what was below like the sight of fire, and when he set forth all the rest of the vision of the thrones, lest any one might happen to think that in those [visions] he had actually seen God, he added: "This was the appearance of the likeness of the glory of God."[2]

11. If, then, neither Moses, nor Elias, nor Ezekiel, who had all many celestial visions, did see God; but if what they did see were similitudes of the splendour of the Lord, ánd prophecies of things to come; it is manifest that the Father is indeed invisible, of whom also the Lord said, "No man hath seen God at any time."[3] But His Word, as He Himself willed it, and for the benefit of those who beheld, did show the Father's brightness, and explained His purposes (as also the Lord said: "The only-begotten God,[4] which is in the bosom of the Father, He hath declared [Him];" and He does Himself also interpret the Word of the Father as being rich and great); not, in one figure, nor in one character, did He appear to those seeing Him, but according to the reasons and effects aimed at in His dispensations, as it is written in Daniel. For at one time He was seen with those who were around Ananias, Azarias, Misael, as present with them in the furnace of fire, in the burning, and preserving them from [the effects of] fire: "And the appearance of the fourth," it is said, "was like to the Son of God."[5] At another time [He is represented as] "a stone cut out of the mountain without hands,"[6] and as smiting all temporal kingdoms, and as blowing them away (*ventilans ea*), and as Himself filling all the earth. Then, too, is this same individual beheld as the Son of man coming in the clouds of heaven, and drawing near to the Ancient of Days, and receiving from Him all power and glory, and a kingdom. "His dominion," it is said, "is an everlasting dominion, and His kingdom shall not perish."[7] John also, the Lord's disciple, when beholding the sacerdotal and glorious advent of His kingdom, says in the Apocalypse: "I turned to see the voice that spake with me. And, being turned, I saw seven golden candlesticks; and in the midst of the candlesticks One like unto the Son of man, clothed with a garment reaching to the feet, and girt about the paps with a golden girdle; and His head and His hairs were white, as white as wool, and as snow; and His eyes were as a flame of fire; and His feet like unto fine brass, as if He burned in a furnace. And His voice [was] as the voice of waters; and He had in His right hand seven stars; and out of His mouth went a sharp two-edged sword; and His countenance was as the sun shining in his strength."[8] For in these words He sets forth something of the glory [which He has received] from His Father, as [where He makes mention of] the head; something in reference to the priestly office also, as in the case of the long garment reaching to the feet. And this was the reason why Moses vested the high priest after this fashion. Something also alludes to the end [of all things], as [where He speaks of] the fine brass burning in the fire, which denotes the power of faith, and the continuing instant in prayer, because of the consuming fire which is to come at the end of time. But when John could not endure the sight (for he says, "I fell at his feet as dead;"[9] that what was written might come to pass: "No man sees God, and shall live"[10]), and the Word reviving him, and reminding him that it was He upon whose bosom he had leaned at supper, when he put the question as to who should betray Him, declared: "I am the first and the last, and He who liveth, and was dead, and behold I am alive for evermore, and have the keys of death and of hell." And after these things, seeing the same Lord in a second vision, he says: "For I saw in the midst of the throne, and of the four living creatures, and in the midst of the elders, a Lamb standing as it had been slain, having seven horns, and seven eyes, which are the seven spirits of God, sent forth into all the earth."[11] And again, he says, speaking of this very same Lamb: "And behold a white horse; and He that sat upon him was called Faithful and True; and in righteousness doth He judge and make war. And His eyes were as a flame of fire, and on His head were many crowns; having a name written, that no man knoweth but Himself: and He was girded around with a vesture sprinkled with blood: and His name is called The Word of God. And the armies of heaven followed Him upon white horses, clothed in pure white linen. And out of His mouth goeth a sharp sword, that with it He may smite the nations; and He shall

---

[1] Ezek. i. 1.
[2] Ezek. ii. 1.
[3] John i. 18.
[4] "This text, as quoted a short time ago, indicated 'the only-begotten Son;' but the agreement of the Syriac version induces the belief that the present reading was that expressed by Irenæus, and that the previous quotation has been corrected to suit the Vulgate. The former reading, however, occurs in book iii. c. xi. 5."—HARVEY.
[5] Dan. iii. 26.
[6] Dan. vii. 13, 14.
[7] Dan. vii. 4.
[8] Rev. i. 12.
[9] Rev. i. 17.
[10] Ex. xxxiii. 20.
[11] Rev. v. 6.

rule (*pascet*) them with a rod of iron: and He treadeth the wine-press of the fierceness of the wrath of God Almighty. And He hath upon His vesture and upon His thigh a name written, KING OF KINGS AND LORD OF LORDS."[1] Thus does the Word of God always preserve the outlines, as it were, of things to come, and points out to men the various forms (*species*), as it were, of the dispensations of the Father, teaching us the things pertaining to God.

12. However, it was not by means of visions alone which were seen, and words which were proclaimed, but also in actual works, that He was beheld by the prophets, in order that through them He might prefigure and show forth future events beforehand. For this reason did Hosea the prophet take "a wife of whoredoms," prophesying by means of the action, "that in committing fornication the earth should fornicate from the LORD,"[2] that is, the men who are upon the earth; and from men of this stamp it will be God's good pleasure to take out[3] a Church which shall be sanctified by fellowship with His Son, just as that woman was sanctified by intercourse with the prophet. And for this reason, Paul declares that the "unbelieving wife is sanctified by the believing husband."[4] Then again, the prophet names his children, "Not having obtained mercy," and "Not a people,"[5] in order that, as says the apostle, "what was not a people may become a people; and she who did not obtain mercy may obtain mercy. And it shall come to pass, that in the place where it was said, This is not a people, there shall they be called the children of the living God."[6] That which had been done typically through his actions by the prophet, the apostle proves to have been done truly by Christ in the Church. Thus, too, did Moses also take to wife an Ethiopian woman, whom he thus made an Israelitish one, showing by anticipation that the wild olive tree is grafted into the cultivated olive, and made to partake of its fatness. For as He who was born Christ according to the flesh, had indeed to be sought after by the people in order to be slain, but was to be set free in Egypt, that is, among the Gentiles, to sanctify those who were there in a state of infancy, from whom also He perfected His Church in that place (for Egypt was Gentile from the beginning, as was Ethiopia also); for this reason, by means of the marriage of Moses, was shown forth the marriage of the Word;[7] and by means of the Ethiopian bride, the Church taken from among the Gentiles was made manifest; and those who do detract from, accuse, and deride it, shall not be pure. For they shall be full of leprosy, and expelled from the camp of the righteous. Thus also did Rahab the harlot, while condemning herself, inasmuch as she was a Gentile, guilty of all sins, nevertheless receive the three spies,[8] who were spying out all the land, and hid them at her home; [which three were] doubtless [a type of] the Father and the Son, together with the Holy Spirit. And when the entire city in which she lived fell to ruins at the sounding of the seven trumpets, Rahab the harlot was preserved, when all was over [*in ultimis*], together with all her house, through faith of the scarlet sign; as the Lord also declared to those who did not receive His advent,—the Pharisees, no doubt, nullify the sign of the scarlet thread, which meant the passover, and the redemption and exodus of the people from Egypt,—when He said, "The publicans and the harlots go into the kingdom of heaven before you."[9]

CHAP. XXI.—ABRAHAM'S FAITH WAS IDENTICAL WITH OURS; THIS FAITH WAS PREFIGURED BY THE WORDS AND ACTIONS OF THE OLD PATRIARCHS.

1. But that our faith was also prefigured in Abraham, and that he was the patriarch of our faith, and, as it were, the prophet of it, the apostle has very fully taught, when he says in the Epistle to the Galatians: "He therefore that ministereth to you the Spirit, and worketh miracles among you, [doeth he it] by the works of the law, or by the hearing of faith? Even as Abraham believed God, and it was accounted unto him for righteousness. Know ye therefore, that they which are of faith, the same are the children of Abraham. But the Scripture, foreseeing that God would justify the heathen through faith, announced beforehand unto Abraham, that in him all nations should be blessed. So then they which be of faith shall be blessed with faithful Abraham."[10] For which [reasons the apostle] declared that this man was not only the prophet of faith, but also the father of those who from among the Gentiles believe in Jesus Christ, because his faith and ours are one and the same: for he believed in things future, as if they were already accomplished, because of the promise of God; and in like manner do we also, because of the promise of God, behold through faith that inheritance [laid up for us] in the [future] kingdom.

2. The history of Isaac, too, is not without a

---

[1] Rev. xix. 11-17.
[2] Hos. i. 2, 3.
[3] Acts xv. 14.
[4] 1 Cor. vii. 14. [But Hosea himself says (xii. 10), "I have used similitudes;" and this history may be fairly referred to prophetic vision. Dr. Pusey, in his *Minor Prophets, in loc.*, argues against this view, however; and his reasons deserve consideration.]
[5] Hos. i. 6-9.
[6] Rom. ix. 25, 26.
[7] The text is here uncertain; and while the general meaning of the sentence is plain, its syntax is confused and obscure.
[8] Irenæus seems here to have written "three" for "two" from a lapse of memory.
[9] Matt. xxi. 31.
[10] Gal. iii. 5-9; Gen. xii. 3.

symbolical character. For in the Epistle to the Romans, the apostle declares: "Moreover, when Rebecca had conceived by one, even by our father Isaac," she received answer[1] from the Word, "that the purpose of God according to election might stand, not of works, but of Him that calleth, it was said unto her, Two nations are in thy womb, and two manner of people are in thy body; and the one people shall overcome the other, and the elder shall serve the younger."[2] From which it is evident, that not only [were there] prophecies of the patriarchs, but also that the children brought forth by Rebecca were a prediction of the two nations; and that the one should be indeed the greater, but the other the less; that the one also should be under bondage, but the other free; but [that both should be] of one and the same father. Our God, one and the same, is also their God, who knows hidden things, who knoweth all things before they can come to pass; and for this reason has He said, "Jacob have I loved, but Esau have I hated."[3]

3. If any one, again, will look into Jacob's actions, he shall find them not destitute of meaning, but full of import with regard to the dispensations. Thus, in the first place, at his birth, since he laid hold on his brother's heel,[4] he was called Jacob, that is, *the supplanter*— one who holds, but is not held; binding the feet, but not being bound; striving and conquering; grasping in his hand his adversary's heel, that is, victory. For to this end was the Lord born, the type of whose birth he set forth beforehand, of whom also John says in the Apocalypse: "He went forth conquering, that He should conquer."[5] In the next place, [Jacob] received the rights of the first-born, when his brother looked on them with contempt; even as also the younger nation received Him, Christ, the first-begotten, when the elder nation rejected Him, saying, "We have no king but Cæsar."[6] But in Christ every blessing [is summed up], and therefore the latter people has snatched away the blessings of the former from the Father, just as Jacob took away the blessing of this Esau. For which cause his brother suffered the plots and persecutions of a brother, just as the Church suffers this self-same thing from the Jews. In a foreign country were the twelve tribes born, the race of Israel, inasmuch as Christ was also, in a strange country, to generate the twelve-pillared foundation of the Church. Various coloured sheep were allotted to this Jacob as his wages; and the wages of Christ are human beings, who from various and diverse nations come together into one cohort of faith, as the Father promised Him, saying, "Ask of Me, and I will give Thee the heathen for Thine inheritance, the uttermost parts of the earth for Thy possession."[7] And as from the multitude of his sons the prophets of the Lord [afterwards] arose, there was every necessity that Jacob should beget sons from the two sisters, even as Christ did from the two laws of one and the same Father; and in like manner also from the handmaids, indicating that Christ should raise up sons of God, both from freemen and from slaves after the flesh, bestowing upon all, in the same manner, the gift of the Spirit, who vivifies us.[8] But he (Jacob) did all things for the sake of the younger, she who had the handsome eyes,[9] Rachel, who prefigured the Church, for which Christ endured patiently; who at that time, indeed, by means of His patriarchs and prophets, was prefiguring and declaring beforehand future things, fulfilling His part·by anticipation in the dispensations of God, and accustoming His inheritance to obey God, and to pass through the world as in a state of pilgrimage, to follow His word, and to indicate beforehand things to come. For with God there is nothing without purpose or due signification.

CHAP. XXII.— CHRIST DID NOT COME FOR THE SAKE OF THE MEN OF ONE AGE ONLY, BUT FOR ALL WHO, LIVING RIGHTEOUSLY AND PIOUSLY, HAD BELIEVED UPON HIM; AND FOR THOSE, TOO, WHO SHALL BELIEVE.

1. Now in the last days, when the fulness of the time of liberty had arrived, the Word Himself did by Himself "wash away the filth of the daughters of Zion,"[10] when He washed the disciples' feet with His own hands.[11] For this is the end of the human race inheriting God; that as in the beginning, by means of our first [parents], we were all brought into bondage, by being made subject to death; so at last, by means of the New Man, all who from the beginning [were His] disciples, having been cleansed and washed from things pertaining to death, should come to the life of God. For He who washed the feet of the disciples sanctified the entire body, and rendered it clean. For this reason, too, He administered food to them in a recumbent posture, indicating that those who were lying in the earth were they to whom He came to impart life. As Jeremiah declares, "The holy Lord remembered His dead Israel, who slept in the land of sepulture; and He descended to them to make known to them His

---

[1] Massuet would cancel these words.
[2] Rom. ix. 10–13; Gen. xxv. 23.
[3] Rom. ix. 13; Mal. i. 2.
[4] Gen. xxv. 26.
[5] Rev. vi. 2.
[6] John xix. 15.
[7] Ps. ii. 8.
[8] The text of this sentence is in great confusion, and we can give only a doubtful translation.
[9] [Leah's eyes were *weak*, according to the LXX.; and Irenæus infers that Rachel's were "beautiful exceedingly." Canticles, i. 15.]
[10] Isa. iv. 4.
[11] John xiii. 5.

salvation, that they might be saved."[1] For this reason also were the eyes of the disciples weighed down when Christ's passion was approaching; and when, in the first instance, the Lord found them sleeping, He let it pass,— thus indicating the patience of God in regard to the state of slumber in which men lay; but coming the second time, He aroused them, and made them stand up, in token that His passion is the arousing of His sleeping disciples, on whose account "He also descended into the lower parts of the earth,"[2] to behold with His eyes the state of those who were resting from their labours,[3] in reference to whom He did also declare to the disciples: "Many prophets and righteous men have desired to see and hear what ye do see and hear."[4]

2. For it was not merely for those who believed on Him in the time of Tiberius Cæsar that Christ came, nor did the Father exercise His providence for the men only who are now alive, but for all men altogether, who from the beginning, according to their capacity, in their generation have both feared and loved God, and practised justice and piety towards their neighbours, and have earnestly desired to see Christ, and to hear His voice. Wherefore He shall, at His second coming, first rouse from their sleep all persons of this description, and shall raise them up, as well as the rest who shall be judged, and give them a place in His kingdom. For it is truly "one God who" directed the patriarchs towards His dispensations, and "has justified the circumcision by faith, and the uncircumcision through faith."[5] For as in the first we were prefigured, so, on the other hand, are they represented in us, that is, in the Church, and receive the recompense for those things which they accomplished.

CHAP. XXIII. — THE PATRIARCHS AND PROPHETS, BY POINTING OUT THE ADVENT OF CHRIST, FORTIFIED THEREBY, AS IT WERE, THE WAY OF POSTERITY TO THE FAITH OF CHRIST; AND SO THE LABOURS OF THE APOSTLES WERE LESSENED, INASMUCH AS THEY GATHERED IN THE FRUITS OF THE LABOURS OF OTHERS.

1. For which reason the Lord declared to the disciples: "Behold, I say unto you, Lift up your eyes, and look upon the districts (*regiones*), for they are white [already] to harvest. For the harvest-man receiveth wages, and gathereth fruit unto life eternal, that both he that soweth and he that reapeth may rejoice together. For in this is the saying true, that one soweth and another reapeth. For I have sent you forward to reap that whereon ye bestowed no labour; other men have laboured, and ye have entered into their labours."[6] Who, then, are they that have laboured, and have helped forward the dispensations of God? It is clear that they are the patriarchs and prophets, who even prefigured our faith, and disseminated through the earth the advent of the Son of God, who and what He should be: so that posterity, possessing the fear of God, might easily accept the advent of Christ, having been instructed by the prophets. And for this reason it was, that when Joseph became aware that Mary was with child, and was minded to put her away privily, the angel said to him in sleep: "Fear not to take to thee Mary thy wife; for that which is conceived in her is of the Holy Ghost. For she shall bring forth a son, and thou shalt call His name Jesus; for He shall save His people from their sins."[7] And exhorting him [to this], he added: "Now all this has been done, that it might be fulfilled which was spoken from the Lord by the prophet, saying, Behold, a virgin shall be with child, and shall bring forth a son, and His name shall be called Emmanuel;" thus influencing him by the words of the prophet, and warding off blame from Mary, pointing out that it was she who was the virgin mentioned by Isaiah beforehand, who should give birth to Emmanuel. Wherefore, when Joseph was convinced beyond all doubt, he both did take Mary, and joyfully yielded obedience in regard to all the rest of the education of Christ, undertaking a journey into Egypt and back again, and then a removal to Nazareth. [For this reason,] those who knew not the Scriptures nor the promise of God, nor the dispensation of Christ, at last called him the father of the child. For this reason, too, did the Lord Himself read at Capernaum the prophecies of Isaiah:[8] "The Spirit of the Lord is upon Me, because He hath anointed Me; to preach the Gospel to the poor hath He sent Me, to heal the broken-hearted, to preach deliverance to the captives, and sight to the blind."[9] At the same time, showing that it was He Himself who had been foretold by Esaias the prophet, He said to them: "This day is this Scripture fulfilled in your ears."

2. For this reason, also, Philip, when he had discovered the eunuch of the Ethiopians' queen reading these words which had been written: "He was led as a sheep to the slaughter; and as a lamb is dumb before the shearer, so He opened not His mouth: in His humiliation His judgment was taken away;"[10] and all the rest which the prophet proceeded to relate in regard

---

[1] This spurious quotation has been introduced before. See book iii. 20, 4.
[2] Eph. iv. 9.
[3] So Harvey understands the obscure Latin text, "id quod erat inoperatum conditionis."
[4] Matt. xiii. 17.
[5] Rom. iii. 30.
[6] John iv. 35, etc.
[7] Matt. i. 20, etc.
[8] Luke iv. 18.
[9] Isa. lxi. 1.
[10] Acts viii. 27; Isa. liii. 7.

to His passion and His coming in the flesh, and how He was dishonoured by those who did not believe Him; easily persuaded him to believe on Him, that He was Christ Jesus, who was crucified under Pontius Pilate, and suffered whatsoever the prophet had predicted, and that He was the Son of God, who gives eternal life to men. And immediately when [Philip] had baptized him, he departed from him. For nothing else [but baptism] was wanting to him who had been already instructed by the prophets: he was not ignorant of God the Father, nor of the rules as to the [proper] manner of life, but was merely ignorant of the advent of the Son of God, which, when he had become acquainted with, in a short space of time, he went on his way rejoicing, to be the herald in Ethiopia of Christ's advent. Therefore Philip had no great labour to go through with regard to this man, because he was already prepared in the fear of God by the prophets. For this reason, too, did the apostles, collecting the sheep which had perished of the house of Israel, and discoursing to them from the Scriptures, prove that this crucified Jesus was the Christ, the Son of the living God; and they persuaded a great multitude, who, however, [already] possessed the fear of God. And there were, in one day, baptized three, and four, and five thousand men.[1]

CHAP. XXIV. — THE CONVERSION OF THE GENTILES WAS MORE DIFFICULT THAN THAT OF THE JEWS; THE LABOURS OF THOSE APOSTLES, THEREFORE, WHO ENGAGED IN THE FORMER TASK, WERE GREATER THAN THOSE WHO UNDERTOOK THE LATTER.

1. Wherefore also Paul, since he was the apostle of the Gentiles, says, "I laboured more than they all."[2] For the instruction of the former, [viz., the Jews,] was an easy task, because they could allege proofs from the Scriptures, and because they, who were in the habit of hearing Moses and the prophets, did also readily receive the First-begotten of the dead, and the Prince of the life of God, — Him who, by the spreading forth of hands, did destroy Amalek, and vivify man from the wound of the serpent, by means of faith which was [exercised] towards Him. As I have pointed out in the preceding book, the apostle did, in the first place, instruct the Gentiles to depart from the superstition of idols, and to worship one God, the Creator of heaven and earth, and the Framer of the whole creation; and that His Son was His Word, by whom He founded all things; and that He, in the last times, was made a man among men; that He re-formed the human race, but destroyed and conquered the enemy of man, and gave to His handiwork victory against the adversary. But although they who were of the circumcision still did not obey the words of God, for they were despisers, yet they were previously instructed not to commit adultery, nor fornication, nor theft, nor fraud; and that whatsoever things are done to our neighbours' prejudice, were evil, and detested by God. Wherefore also they did readily agree to abstain from these things, because they had been thus instructed.

2. But they were bound to teach the Gentiles also this very thing, that works of such a nature were wicked, prejudicial, and useless, and destructive to those who engaged in them. Wherefore he who had received the apostolate to the Gentiles,[3] did labour more than those who preached the Son of God among them of the circumcision. For they were assisted by the Scriptures, which the Lord confirmed and fulfilled, in coming such as He had been announced; but here, [in the case of the Gentiles,] there was a certain foreign erudition, and a new doctrine [to be received, namely], that the gods of the nations not only were no gods at all, but even the idols of demons; and that there is one God, who is "above all principality, and dominion, and power, and every name which is named;"[4] and that His Word, invisible by nature, was made palpable and visible among men, and did descend "to death, even the death of the cross;"[5] also, that they who believe in Him shall be incorruptible and not subject to suffering, and shall receive the kingdom of heaven. These things, too, were preached to the Gentiles by word, without [the aid of] the Scriptures: wherefore, also, they who preached among the Gentiles underwent greater labour. But, on the other hand, the faith of the Gentiles is proved to be of a more noble description, since they followed the word of God without the instruction [derived] from the [sacred] writings (*sine instructione literarum*).

CHAP. XXV. — BOTH COVENANTS WERE PREFIGURED IN ABRAHAM, AND IN THE LABOUR OF TAMAR; THERE WAS, HOWEVER, BUT ONE AND THE SAME GOD TO EACH COVENANT.

1. For thus it had behoved the sons of Abraham [to be], whom God has raised up to him from the stones,[6] and caused to take a place beside him who was made the chief and the forerunner of our faith (who did also receive the covenant of circumcision, after that justification by faith which had pertained to him, when he was yet in uncircumcision, so that in him both covenants might be prefigured, that he might be

---

[1] Acts ii. 41, iv. 4.
[2] 1 Cor. xv. 10.
[3] [A clear note of recognition on the part of our author, that St. Paul's mission was world-wide, while St. Peter's was limited.]
[4] Eph. i. 21.
[5] Phil. ii. 8.
[6] Matt. iii. 9.

the father of all who follow the Word of God, and who sustain a life of pilgrimage in this world, that is, of those who from among the circumcision and of those from among the uncircumcision are faithful, even as also "Christ[1] is the chief corner-stone," sustaining all things); and He gathered into the one faith of Abraham those who, from either covenant, are eligible for God's building. But this faith which is in uncircumcision, as connecting the end with the beginning, has been made [both] the first and the last. For, as I have shown, it existed in Abraham antecedently to circumcision, as it also did in the rest of the righteous who pleased God : and in these last times, it again sprang up among mankind through the coming of the Lord. But circumcision and the law of works occupied the intervening period.[2]

2. This fact is indeed set forth by many other [occurrences], but typically by [the history of] Thamar, Judah's daughter-in-law.[3] For when she had conceived twins, one of them put forth his hand first ; and as the midwife supposed that he was the first-born, she bound a scarlet token on his hand. But after this had been done, and he had drawn back his hand, his brother Phares came forth the first ; then, after him, Zara, upon whom was the scarlet line, [was born] the second: the Scripture clearly pointing out that people which possessed the scarlet sign, that is, faith in a state of circumcision, which was shown beforehand, indeed, in the patriarchs first ; but after that withdrawn, that his brother might be born ; and also, in like manner, him who was the elder, as being born in the second place, [him] who was distinguished by the scarlet token, which was [fastened] on him, that is, the passion of the Just One, which was prefigured from the beginning in Abel, and described by the prophets, but perfected in the last times in the Son of God.

3. For it was requisite that certain facts should be announced beforehand by the fathers in a paternal manner, and others prefigured by the prophets in a legal one, but others, described after the form of Christ, by those who have received the adoption ; while in one God are all things shown forth. For although Abraham was one, he did in himself prefigure the two covenants, in which some indeed have sown, while others have reaped ; for it is said, " In this is the saying true, that it is one 'people' who sows, but another who shall reap ; "[4] but it is one God who bestows things suitable upon both — seed to the sower, but bread for the reaper to eat. Just as it is one that planteth, and another who watereth, but one God who giveth the increase.[5] For the patriarchs and prophets sowed the word [concerning] Christ, but the Church reaped, that is, received the fruit. For this reason, too, do these very men (the prophets) also pray to have a dwelling-place in it, as Jeremiah says, " Who will give me in the desert the last dwelling-place ? "[6] in order that both the sower and the reaper may rejoice together in the kingdom of Christ, who is present with all those who were from the beginning approved by God, who granted them His Word to be present with them.[7]

CHAP. XXVI. — THE TREASURE HID IN THE SCRIPTURES IS CHRIST ; THE TRUE EXPOSITION OF THE SCRIPTURES IS TO BE FOUND IN THE CHURCH ALONE.

1. If any one, therefore, reads the Scriptures with attention, he will find in them an account of Christ, and a foreshadowing of the new calling (*vocationis*). For Christ is the treasure which was hid in the field,[8] that is, in this world (for "the field is the world"[9]); but the treasure hid in the Scriptures is Christ, since He was pointed out by means of types and parables. Hence His human nature could not [10] be understood, prior to the consummation of those things which had been predicted, that is, the advent of Christ. And therefore it was said to Daniel the prophet: " Shut up the words, and seal the book even to the time of consummation, until many learn, and knowledge be completed. For at that time, when the dispersion shall be accomplished, they shall know all these things." [11] But Jeremiah also says, " In the last days they shall understand these things." [12] For every prophecy, before its fulfilment, is to men [full of] enigmas and ambiguities. But when the time has arrived, and the prediction has come to pass, then the prophecies have a clear and certain exposition. And for this reason, indeed, when at this present time the law is read to the Jews, it is like a fable ; for they do not possess the explanation of all things pertaining to the advent of the Son of God, which took place in human nature ; but when it is read by the Christians, it is a treasure, hid indeed in a field, but brought to light by the cross of Christ, and

---

[1] Eph. ii. 20.
[2] [Note, the Gentile Church was the old religion and was Catholic; in Christ it became Catholic again: the Mosaic system was a parenthetical thing of fifteen hundred years only. Such is the *luminous* and clarifying scheme of Irenæus, expounding St. Paul (Gal. iii. 14-20). Inferences: (1) They who speak as if the Mosaic system covered the whole *Old Testament* darken the divine counsels. (2) The God of Scripture was never the God of the Jews only.]
[3] Gen. xxxviii. 28, etc.
[4] John iv. 37.
[5] 1 Cor. iii. 7.
[6] Jer. ix. 2. [A "*remote* dwelling-place" rather (σταθμὸν ἔσχατον according to LXX.) to square with the argument.]
[7] [The touching words which conclude the former paragraph are illustrated by the noble sentence which begins this paragraph. The childlike spirit of these Fathers recognises Christ everywhere, in the *Old Testament*, prefigured by countless images and tokens in *paternal* and legal (ceremonial) forms.]
[8] Matt. xiii. 44.
[9] Matt. xiii. 38.
[10] Harvey cancels " non," and reads the sentence interrogatively.
[11] Dan. xii. 4, 7.
[12] Jer. xxiii. 20.

explained, both enriching the understanding of men, and showing forth the wisdom of God, and declaring His dispensations with regard to man, and forming the kingdom of Christ beforehand, and preaching by anticipation the inheritance of the holy Jerusalem, and proclaiming beforehand that the man who loves God shall arrive at such excellency as even to see God, and hear His word, and from the hearing of His discourse be glorified to such an extent, that others cannot behold the glory of his countenance, as was said by Daniel: "Those who do understand, shall shine as the brightness of the firmament, and many of the righteous [1] as the stars for ever and ever." [2] Thus, then, I have shown it to be,[3] if any one read the Scriptures. For thus it was that the Lord discoursed with the disciples after His resurrection from the dead, proving to them from the Scriptures themselves "that Christ must suffer, and enter into His glory, and that remission of sins should be preached in His name throughout all the world." [4] And the disciple will be perfected, and [rendered] like the householder, "who bringeth forth from his treasure things new and old." [5]

2. Wherefore it is incumbent to obey the presbyters who are in the Church, — those who, as I have shown, possess the succession from the apostles; those who, together with the succession of the episcopate, have received the certain gift of truth, according to the good pleasure of the Father. But [it is also incumbent] to hold in suspicion others who depart from the primitive succession, and assemble themselves together in any place whatsoever, [looking upon them] either as heretics of perverse minds, or as schismatics puffed up and self-pleasing, or again as hypocrites, acting thus for the sake of lucre and vainglory. For all these have fallen from the truth. And the heretics, indeed, who bring strange fire to the altar of God — namely, strange doctrines — shall be burned up by the fire from heaven, as were Nadab and Abiud.[6] But such as rise up in opposition to the truth, and exhort others against the Church of God, [shall] remain among those in hell (*apud inferos*), being swallowed up by an earthquake, even as those who were with Chore, Dathan, and Abiron.[7]

But those who cleave asunder, and separate the unity of the Church, [shall] receive from God the same punishment as Jeroboam did.[8]

3. Those, however, who are believed to be presbyters by many, but serve their own lusts, and do not place the fear of God supreme in their hearts, but conduct themselves with contempt towards others, and are puffed up with the pride of holding the chief seat, and work evil deeds in secret, saying, "No man sees us," shall be convicted by the Word, who does not judge after outward appearance (*secundum gloriam*), nor looks upon the countenance, but the heart; and they shall hear those words, to be found in Daniel the prophet: "O thou seed of Canaan, and not of Judah, beauty hath deceived thee, and lust perverted thy heart.[9] Thou that art waxen old in wicked days, now thy sins which thou hast committed aforetime are come to light; for thou hast pronounced false judgments, and hast been accustomed to condemn the innocent, and to let the guilty go free, albeit the Lord saith, The innocent and the righteous shalt thou not slay." [10] Of whom also did the Lord say: "But if the evil servant shall say in his heart, My lord delayeth his coming, and shall begin to smite the man-servants and maidens, and to eat and drink and be drunken; the lord of that servant shall come in a day that he looketh not for him, and in an hour that he is not aware of, and shall cut him asunder, and appoint him his portion with the unbelievers." [11]

4. From all such persons, therefore, it behoves us to keep aloof, but to adhere to those who, as I have already observed, do hold the doctrine of the apostles, and who, together with the order of priesthood (*presbyterii ordine*), display sound speech and blameless conduct for the confirmation and correction of others.[12] In this way, Moses, to whom such a leadership was entrusted, relying on a good conscience, cleared himself before God, saying, "I have not in covetousness taken anything belonging to one of these men, nor have I done evil to one of them." [13] In this way, too, Samuel, who judged the people so many years, and bore rule over Israel without any pride, in the end cleared himself, saying, "I have walked before you from my childhood even unto this day: answer me in the sight of God, and before His anointed (*Christi ejus*); whose ox or whose ass of yours have I taken, or over whom have I tyrannized, or whom have I oppressed? or if I have received from the hand of any a bribe or [so much as] a shoe, speak out

---

[1] The Latin is "a multis justis," corresponding to the Greek version of the Hebrew text. If the translation be supposed as corresponding to the Hebrew comparative, the English equivalent will be, "and above (more than) many righteous."
[2] Dan. xii. 3.
[3] The text and punctuation are here in great uncertainty, and very different views of both are taken by the editors.
[4] Luke xxiv. 26, 47. [The walk to Emmaus is the fountain-head of Scriptural exposition, and the forty days (Acts i. 3) is the river that came forth like that which went out of Eden. Ecclesiasticus iv. 31.]
[5] Matt. xiii. 52. [I must express my delight in the great principle of exposition here unfolded. The Old Scriptures are a night-bound wilderness, till Christ rises and illuminates them, glorifying alike hill and dale, and, as this author supposes, every shrub and flower, also, making the smallest leaf with its dewdrops glitter like the rainbow.]
[6] Lev. x. 1, 2.
[7] Num. xvi. 33.

[8] 1 Kings xiv. 10.
[9] Hist. Sus. ver. 56.
[10] *Ibid.* ver. 52, etc.; Ex. xxiii. 7.
[11] Matt. xxiv. 48, etc.; Luke xii. 45.
[12] [Contrast this spirit of a primitive Father, with the state of things which Wiclif rose up to purify, five hundred years ago.]
[13] Num. xvi. 15.

against me, and I will restore it to you."¹ And when the people had said to him, "Thou hast not tyrannized, neither hast thou oppressed us, neither hast thou taken ought of any man's hand," he called the Lord to witness, saying, "The LORD is witness, and His Anointed is witness this day, that ye have not found ought in my hand. And they said to him, He is witness." In this strain also the Apostle Paul, inasmuch as he had a good conscience, said to the Corinthians: "For we are not as many, who corrupt the Word of God: but as of sincerity, but as of God, in the sight of God speak we in Christ;"² "We have injured no man, corrupted no man, circumvented no man."³

5. Such presbyters does the Church nourish, of whom also the prophet says: "I will give thy rulers in peace, and thy bishops in righteousness."⁴ Of whom also did the Lord declare, "Who then shall be a faithful steward (*actor*), good and wise, whom the Lord sets over His household, to give them their meat in due season? Blessed is that servant whom his Lord, when He cometh, shall find so doing."⁵ Paul then, teaching us where one may find such, says, "God hath placed in the Church, first, apostles; secondly, prophets; thirdly, teachers."⁶ Where, therefore, the gifts of the Lord have been placed, there it behoves us to learn the truth, [namely,] from those who possess that succession of the Church which is from the apostles,⁷ and among whom exists that which is sound and blameless in conduct, as well as that which is unadulterated and incorrupt in speech. For these also preserve this faith of ours in one God who created all things; and they increase that love [which we have] for the Son of God, who accomplished such marvellous dispensations for our sake: and they expound the Scriptures to us without danger, neither blaspheming God, nor dishonouring the patriarchs, nor despising the prophets.

CHAP. XXVII. — THE SINS OF THE MEN OF OLD TIME, WHICH INCURRED THE DISPLEASURE OF GOD, WERE, BY HIS PROVIDENCE, COMMITTED TO WRITING, THAT WE MIGHT DERIVE INSTRUCTION THEREBY, AND NOT BE FILLED WITH PRIDE. WE MUST NOT, THEREFORE, INFER THAT THERE WAS ANOTHER GOD THAN HE WHOM CHRIST PREACHED; WE SHOULD RATHER FEAR, LEST THE ONE AND THE SAME GOD WHO INFLICTED PUNISHMENT ON THE ANCIENTS, SHOULD BRING DOWN HEAVIER UPON US.

1. As I have heard from a certain presbyter,⁸ who had heard it from those who had seen the apostles, and from those who had been their disciples, the punishment [declared] in Scripture was sufficient for the ancients in regard to what they did without the Spirit's guidance. For as God is no respecter of persons, He inflicted a proper punishment on deeds displeasing to Him. As in the case of David,⁹ when he suffered persecution from Saul for righteousness' sake, and fled from King Saul, and would not avenge himself of his enemy, he both sung the advent of Christ, and instructed the nations in wisdom, and did everything after the Spirit's guidance, and pleased God. But when his lust prompted him to take Bathsheba, the wife of Uriah, the Scripture said concerning him, "Now, the thing (*sermo*) which David had done appeared wicked in the eyes of the LORD;"¹⁰ and Nathan the prophet is sent to him, pointing out to him his crime, in order that he, passing sentence upon and condemning himself, might obtain mercy and forgiveness from Christ: "And [Nathan] said to him, There were two men in one city; the one rich, and the other poor. The rich man had exceeding many flocks and herds; but the poor man had nothing, save one little ewe-lamb, which he possessed, and nourished up; and it had been with him and with his children together: it did eat of his own bread, and drank of his cup, and was to him as a daughter. And there came a guest unto the rich man; and he spared to take of the flock of his own ewe-lambs, and from the herds of his own oxen, to entertain the guest; but he took the ewe-lamb of the poor man, and set it before the man that had come unto him. And David's anger was greatly kindled against the man; and he said to Nathan, As the LORD liveth, the man that hath done this thing shall surely die (*filius mortis est*): and he shall restore the lamb fourfold, because he hath done this thing, and because he had no pity for the poor man. And Nathan said unto him, Thou art the man who hast done this."¹¹ And then he proceeds with the rest [of the narrative], upbraiding him, and recounting God's benefits towards him, and [showing him] how much his conduct had displeased the Lord. For [he declared] that works of this nature were not pleasing to God, but that great wrath was suspended over his house. David, however, was struck with remorse on hearing this, and exclaimed, "I have sinned against the LORD;" and he sung a penitential psalm, waiting for the coming of the Lord, who washes and makes clean the man who had

---

¹ 1 Sam. xii. 3.
² 2 Cor. ii. 17.
³ 2 Cor. vii. 2.
⁴ Isa. lx. 17.
⁵ Matt. xxiv. 45, 46.
⁶ 1 Cor. xii. 28.
⁷ [Note the limitation; not the succession only, but with it (1) pure morality and holiness and (2) unadulterated testimony. No catholicity apart from these.]

⁸ Polycarp, Papias, Pothinus, and others, have been suggested as probably here referred to, but the point is involved in utter uncertainty. [Surely this testimony is a precious intimation of the apostle's meaning (Rom. ii. 12-16), and the whole chapter is radiant with the purity of the Gospel.]
⁹ 1 Sam. xviii.
¹⁰ 2 Sam. xi. 27.
¹¹ 2 Sam. xii. 1, etc.

been fast bound with [the chain of] sin. In like manner it was with regard to Solomon, while he continued to judge uprightly, and to declare the wisdom of God, and built the temple as the type of truth, and set forth the glories of God, and announced the peace about to come upon the nations, and prefigured the kingdom of Christ, and spake three thousand parables about the Lord's advent, and five thousand songs, singing praise to God, and expounded the wisdom of God in creation, [discoursing] as to the nature of every tree, every herb, and of all fowls, quadrupeds, and fishes; and he said, "Will God, whom the heavens cannot contain, really dwell with men upon the earth?"[1] And he pleased God, and was the admiration of all; and all kings of the earth sought an interview with him (*quærebant faciem ejus*) that they might hear the wisdom which God had conferred upon him.[2] The queen of the south, too, came to him from the ends of the earth, to ascertain the wisdom that was in him:[3] she whom the Lord also referred to as one who should rise up in the judgment with the nations of those men who do hear His words, and do not believe in Him, and should condemn them, inasmuch as she submitted herself to the wisdom announced by the servant of God, while these men despised that wisdom which proceeded directly from the Son of God. For Solomon was a servant, but Christ is indeed the Son of God, and the Lord of Solomon. While, therefore, he served God without blame, and ministered to His dispensations, then was he glorified: but when he took wives from all nations, and permitted them to set up idols in Israel, the Scripture spake thus concerning him: "And King Solomon was a lover of women, and he took to himself foreign women; and it came to pass, when Solomon was old, his heart was not perfect with the LORD his God. And the foreign women turned away his heart after strange gods. And Solomon did evil in the sight of the LORD: he did not walk after the LORD, as did David his father. And the LORD was angry with Solomon; for his heart was not perfect with the LORD, as was the heart of David his father."[4] The Scripture has thus sufficiently reproved him, as the presbyter remarked, in order that no flesh may glory in the sight of the Lord.

2. It was for this reason, too, that the Lord descended into the regions beneath the earth, preaching His advent there also, and [declaring] the remission of sins received by those who believe in Him.[5] Now all those believed in Him who had hope towards Him, that is, those who proclaimed His advent, and submitted to His dispensations, the righteous men, the prophets, and the patriarchs, to whom He remitted sins in the same way as He did to us, which sins we should not lay to their charge, if we would not despise the grace of God. For as these men did not impute unto us (the Gentiles) our transgressions, which we wrought before Christ was manifested among us, so also it is not right that *we* should lay blame upon those who sinned before Christ's coming. For "all men come short of the glory of God,"[6] and are not justified of themselves, but by the advent of the Lord,— they who earnestly direct their eyes towards His light. And it is for our instruction that their actions have been committed to writing, that we might know, in the first place, that our God and theirs is one, and that sins do not please Him although committed by men of renown; and in the second place, that we should keep from wickedness. For if these men of old time, who preceded us in the gifts [bestowed upon them], and for whom the Son of God had not yet suffered, when they committed any sin and served fleshly lusts, were rendered objects of such disgrace, what shall the men of the present day suffer, who have despised the Lord's coming, and become the slaves of their own lusts? And truly the death of the Lord became [the means of] healing and remission of sins to the former, but Christ shall not die again in behalf of those who now commit sin, for death shall no more have dominion over Him; but the Son shall come in the glory of the Father, requiring from His stewards and dispensers the money which He had entrusted to them, with usury; and from those to whom He had given most shall He demand most. We ought not, therefore, as that presbyter remarks, to be puffed up, nor be severe upon those of old time, but ought ourselves to fear, lest perchance, after [we have come to] the knowledge of Christ, if we do things displeasing to God, we obtain no further forgiveness of sins, but be shut out from His kingdom.[6] And therefore it was that Paul said, "For if [God] spared not the natural branches, [take heed] lest He also spare not thee, who, when thou wert a wild olive tree, wert grafted into the fatness of the olive tree, and wert made a partaker of its fatness."[7]

3. Thou wilt notice, too, that the transgressions of the common people have been described in like manner, not for the sake of those who did then transgress, but as a means of instruction unto us, and that we should understand that it is one and the same God against whom these

---

[1] 1 Kings viii. 27.
[2] 1 Kings iv. 34.
[3] 1 Kings x. 1.
[4] 1 Kings xi. 1.
[5] [1 Pet. iii. 19, 20.]
[6] Rom. iii. 23. [Another testimony to the mercy of God in the judgment of the unevangelized. There must have been some reason for the secrecy with which "that presbyter's" name is guarded. Irenæus may have scrupled to draw the wrath of the Gnostics upon any name but his own.]
[7] Rom. xi. 21, 17.

men sinned, and against whom certain persons do now transgress from among those who profess to have believed in Him. But this also, [as the presbyter states,] has Paul declared most plainly in the Epistle to the Corinthians, when he says, "Brethren, I would not that ye should be ignorant, how that all our fathers were under the cloud, and were all baptized unto Moses in the sea, and did all eat the same spiritual meat, and did all drink the same spiritual drink: for they drank of that spiritual rock that followed them; and the rock was Christ. But with many of them God was not well pleased, for they were overthrown in the wilderness. These things were for our example (*in figuram nostri*), to the intent that we should not lust after evil things, as they also lusted; neither be ye idolaters, as were some of them, as it is written:[1] The people sat down to eat and drink, and rose up to play. Neither let us commit fornication, as some of them also did, and fell in one day three and twenty thousand. Neither let us tempt Christ, as some of them also tempted, and were destroyed of serpents. Neither murmur ye, as some of them murmured, and were destroyed of the destroyer. But all these things happened to them in a figure, and were written for our admonition, upon whom the end of the world (*sæculorum*) is come. Wherefore let him that thinketh he standeth, take heed lest he fall."[2]

4. Since therefore, beyond all doubt and contradiction, the apostle shows that there is one and the same God, who did both enter into judgment with these former things, and who does inquire into those of the present time, and points out why these things have been committed to writing; all these men are found to be unlearned and presumptuous, nay, even destitute of common sense, who, because of the transgressions of them of old time, and because of the disobedience of a vast number of them, do allege that there was indeed one God of these men, and that He was the maker of the world, and existed in a state of degeneracy; but that there was another Father declared by Christ, and that this Being is He who has been conceived by the mind of each of them; not understanding that as, in the former case, God showed Himself not well pleased in many instances towards those who sinned, so also in the latter, "many are called, but few are chosen."[3] As then the unrighteous, the idolaters, and fornicators perished, so also is it now: for both the Lord declares, that such persons are sent into eternal fire;[4] and the apostle says, "Know ye not that the unrighteous shall not inherit the kingdom of God? Be not deceived: neither fornicators, nor idolaters, nor adulterers, nor effeminate, nor abusers of themselves with mankind, nor thieves, nor covetous, nor drunkards, nor revilers, nor extortioners, shall inherit the kingdom of God."[5] And as it was not to those who are without that he said these things, but to us, lest we should be cast forth from the kingdom of God, by doing any such thing, he proceeds to say, "And such indeed were ye; but ye are washed, but ye are sanctified in the name of the Lord Jesus Christ, and by the Spirit of our God." And just as then, those who led vicious lives, and put other people astray, were condemned and cast out, so also even now the offending eye is plucked out, and the foot and the hand, lest the rest of the body perish in like manner.[6] And we have the precept: "If any man that is called a brother be a fornicator, or covetous, or an idolater, or a railer, or a drunkard, or an extortioner, with such an one no not to eat."[7] And again does the apostle say, "Let no man deceive you with vain words; for because of these things cometh the wrath of God upon the sons of mistrust. Be not ye therefore partakers with them."[8] And as then the condemnation of sinners extended to others who approved of them, and joined in their society; so also is it the case at present, that "a little leaven leaveneth the whole lump."[9] And as the wrath of God did then descend upon the unrighteous, here also does the apostle likewise say: "For the wrath of God shall be revealed from heaven against all ungodliness and unrighteousness of those men who hold back the truth in unrighteousness."[10] And as, in those times, vengeance came from God upon the Egyptians who were subjecting Israel to unjust punishment, so is it now, the Lord truly declaring, "And shall not God avenge His own elect, which cry day and night unto Him? I tell you, that He will avenge them speedily."[11] So says the apostle, in like manner, in the Epistle to the Thessalonians: "Seeing it is a righteous thing with God to recompense tribulation to them that trouble you; and to you who are troubled rest with us, at the revealing of our Lord Jesus Christ from heaven with His mighty angels, and in a flame of fire, to take vengeance upon those who know not God, and upon those that obey not the Gospel of our Lord Jesus Christ: who shall also be punished with everlasting destruction from the presence of the Lord, and from the glory of His power; when He shall come to be glorified in

---

[1] Ex. xxxii. 6.
[2] 1 Cor. x. 1, etc.
[3] Matt. xx. 16.
[4] Matt. xxv. 41.
[5] 1 Cor. vi. 9, 10.
[6] Matt. xviii. 8, 9.
[7] 1 Cor. v. 11.
[8] Eph. v. 6, 7.
[9] 1 Cor. v. 6.
[10] Rom. i. 18.
[11] Luke xviii. 7, 8.

His saints, and to be admired in all them who have believed in Him."[1]

CHAP. XXVIII.—THOSE PERSONS PROVE THEMSELVES SENSELESS WHO EXAGGERATE THE MERCY OF CHRIST, BUT ARE SILENT AS TO THE JUDGMENT, AND LOOK ONLY AT THE MORE ABUNDANT GRACE OF THE NEW TESTAMENT; BUT, FORGETFUL OF THE GREATER DEGREE OF PERFECTION WHICH IT DEMANDS FROM US, THEY ENDEAVOUR TO SHOW THAT THERE IS ANOTHER GOD BEYOND HIM WHO CREATED THE WORLD.

1. Inasmuch, then, as in both Testaments there is the same righteousness of God [displayed] when God takes vengeance, in the one case indeed typically, temporarily, and more moderately; but in the other, really, enduringly, and more rigidly: for the fire is eternal, and the wrath of God which shall be revealed from heaven from the face of our Lord (as David also says, "But the face of the Lord is against them that do evil, to cut off the remembrance of them from the earth"[2]), entails a heavier punishment on those who incur it,—the elders pointed out that those men are devoid of sense, who, [arguing] from what happened to those who formerly did not obey God, do endeavour to bring in another Father, setting over against [these punishments] what great things the Lord had done at His coming to save those who received Him, taking compassion upon them; while they keep silence with regard to His judgment, and all those things which shall come upon such as have heard His words, but done them not, and that it were better for them if they had not been born,[3] and that it shall be more tolerable for Sodom and Gomorrha in the judgment than for that city which did not receive the word of His disciples.[4]

2. For as, in the New Testament, that faith of men [to be placed] in God has been increased, receiving in addition [to what was already revealed] the Son of God, that man too might be a partaker of God; so is also our walk in life required to be more circumspect, when we are directed not merely to abstain from evil actions, but even from evil thoughts, and from idle words, and empty talk, and scurrilous language:[5] thus also the punishment of those who do not believe the Word of God, and despise His advent, and are turned away backwards, is increased; being not merely temporal, but rendered also eternal. For to whomsoever the Lord shall say, "Depart from me, ye cursed, into everlasting fire,"[6] these shall be damned for ever; and to whomsoever He shall say, "Come, ye blessed of my Father, inherit the kingdom prepared for you for eternity,"[7] these do receive the kingdom for ever, and make constant advance in it; since there is one and the same God the Father, and His Word, who has been always present with the human race, by means indeed of various dispensations, and has wrought out many things, and saved from the beginning those who are saved, (for these are they who love God, and follow the Word of God according to the class to which they belong,) and has judged those who are judged, that is, those who forget God, and are blasphemous, and transgressors of His word.

3. For the same heretics already mentioned by us have fallen away from themselves, by accusing the Lord, in whom they say that they believe. For those points to which they call attention with regard to the God who then awarded temporal punishments to the unbelieving, and smote the Egyptians, while He saved those that were obedient; these same [facts, I say,] shall nevertheless repeat themselves in the Lord, who judges for eternity those whom He doth judge, and lets go free for eternity those whom He does let go free: and He shall [thus] be discovered, according to the language used by these men, as having been the cause of their most heinous sin to those who laid hands upon Him, and pierced Him. For if He had not so come, it follows that these men could not have become the slayers of their Lord; and if He had not sent prophets to them, they certainly could not have killed them, nor the apostles either. To those, therefore, who assail us, and say, If the Egyptians had not been afflicted with plagues, and, when pursuing after Israel, been choked in the sea, God could not have saved His people, this answer may be given;—Unless, then, the Jews had become the slayers of the Lord (which did, indeed, take eternal life away from them), and, by killing the apostles and persecuting the Church, had fallen into an abyss of wrath, we could not have been saved. For as they were saved by means of the blindness of the Egyptians, so are we, too, by that of the Jews; if, indeed, the death of the Lord is the condemnation of those who fastened Him to the cross, and who did not believe His advent, but the salvation of those who believe in Him. For the apostle does also say in the Second [Epistle] to the Corinthians: "For we are unto God a sweet savour of Christ, in them which are saved, and in them which perish: to the one indeed the savour of death unto death,

---

[1] 2 Thess. i. 6–10.
[2] Ps. xxxiv. 16.
[3] Matt. xxvi. 24.
[4] Matt. x. 15.
[5] [Eph. v. 4. Even from the εὐτραπελία which might signify a *bon-mot*, literally, and which certainly is not "scurrility," unless the apostle was ironical, reflecting on jokes which heathen considered "good."]
[6] Matt. xxv. 41.
[7] Matt. xxv. 34.

but to the other the savour of life unto life."[1] To whom, then, is there the savour of death unto death, unless to those who believe not, neither are subject to the Word of God? And who are they that did even then give themselves over to death? Those men, doubtless, who do not believe, nor submit themselves to God. And again, who are they that have been saved, and received the inheritance? Those, doubtless, who do believe God, and who have continued in His love; as did Caleb [the son] of Jephunneh and Joshua [the son] of Nun,[2] and innocent children,[3] who have had no sense of evil. But who are they that are saved now, and receive life eternal? Is it not those who love God, and who believe His promises, and who "in malice have become as little children?"[4]

CHAP. XXIX. — REFUTATION OF THE ARGUMENTS OF THE MARCIONITES, WHO ATTEMPTED TO SHOW THAT GOD WAS THE AUTHOR OF SIN, BECAUSE HE BLINDED PHARAOH AND HIS SERVANTS.

1. "But," say they, "God hardened the heart of Pharaoh and of his servants."[5] Those, then, who allege such difficulties, do not read in the Gospel that passage where the Lord replied to the disciples, when they asked Him, "Why speakest Thou unto them in parables?" — "Because it is given unto you to know the mystery of the kingdom of heaven; but to them I speak in parables, that seeing they may not see, and hearing they may not hear, understanding they may not understand; in order that the prophecy of Isaiah regarding them may be fulfilled, saying, Make the heart of this people gross, and make their ears dull, and blind their eyes. But blessed are your eyes, which see the things that ye see; and your ears, which hear what ye do hear."[6] For one and the same God [that blesses others] inflicts blindness upon those who do not believe, but who set Him at naught; just as the sun, which is a creature of His, [acts with regard] to those who, by reason of any weakness of the eyes, cannot behold his light; but to those who believe in Him and follow Him, He grants a fuller and greater illumination of mind. In accordance with this word, therefore, does the apostle say, in the Second [Epistle] to the Corinthians: "In whom the god of this world hath blinded the minds of them that believe not, lest the light of the glorious Gospel of Christ should shine [unto them]."[7] And again, in that to the Romans: "And as they did not think fit to have God in their knowledge, God gave them up to a reprobate mind, to do those things that are not convenient."[8] Speaking of antichrist, too, he says clearly in the Second to the Thessalonians: "And for this cause God shall send them the working of error, that they should believe a lie; that they all might be judged who believed not the truth, but consented to iniquity."[9]

2. If, therefore, in the present time also, God, knowing the number of those who will not believe, since He foreknows all things, has given them over to unbelief, and turned away His face from men of this stamp, leaving them in the darkness which they have themselves chosen for themselves, what is there wonderful if He did also at that time give over to their unbelief, Pharaoh, who never would have believed, along with those who were with him? As the Word spake to Moses from the bush: "And I am sure that the king of Egypt will not let you go, unless by a mighty hand."[10] And for the reason that the Lord spake in parables, and brought blindness upon Israel, that seeing they might not see, since He knew the [spirit of] unbelief in them, for the same reason did He harden Pharaoh's heart; in order that, while seeing that it was the finger of God which led forth the people, he might not believe, but be precipitated into a sea of unbelief, resting in the notion that the exit of these [Israelites] was accomplished by magical power, and that it was not by the operation of God that the Red Sea afforded a passage to the people, but that this occurred by merely natural causes (*sed naturaliter sic se habere*).

CHAP. XXX. — REFUTATION OF ANOTHER ARGUMENT ADDUCED BY THE MARCIONITES, THAT GOD DIRECTED THE HEBREWS TO SPOIL THE EGYPTIANS.

1. Those, again, who cavil and find fault because the people did, by God's command, upon the eve of their departure, take vessels of all kinds and raiment from the Egyptians,[11] and so went away, from which [spoils], too, the tabernacle was constructed in the wilderness, prove themselves ignorant of the righteous dealings of God, and of His dispensations; as also the presbyter remarked: For if God had not accorded this in the typical exodus, no one could now be saved in our true exodus; that is, in the faith in which we have been established, and by which we have been brought forth from among the number of the Gentiles. For in some cases there follows us a small, and in others a large

---

[1] 2 Cor. ii. 15, 16.
[2] Num. xiv. 30.
[3] [Jonah iv. 11. The tenderness of our author constantly asserts itself, as in this reference to children.]
[4] 1 Cor. xiv. 20.
[5] Ex. ix. 35.
[6] Matt. xiii. 11-16; Isa. vi. 10.
[7] 2 Cor. iv. 4.
[8] Rom. i. 28.
[9] 2 Thess. ii. 11.
[10] Ex. iii. 19.
[11] Ex. iii. 22, xi. 2. [Our English translation "borrow" is a gratuitous injury to the text. As "King of kings" the Lord enjoins a just tax, which any earthly sovereign might have imposed uprightly. Our author argues well.]

amount of property, which we have acquired from the mammon of unrighteousness. For from what source do we derive the houses in which we dwell, the garments in which we are clothed, the vessels which we use, and everything else ministering to our every-day life, unless it be from those things which, when we were Gentiles, we acquired by avarice, or received them from our heathen parents, relations, or friends who unrighteously obtained them? — not to mention that even now we acquire such things when we are in the faith. For who is there that sells, and does not wish to make a profit from him who buys? Or who purchases anything, and does not wish to obtain good value from the seller? Or who is there that carries on a trade, and does not do so that he may obtain a livelihood thereby? And as to those believing ones who are in the royal palace, do they not derive the utensils they employ from the property which belongs to Cæsar; and to those who have not, does not each one of these [Christians] give according to his ability? The Egyptians were debtors to the [Jewish] people, not alone as to property, but as to their very lives, because of the kindness of the patriarch Joseph in former times; but in what way are the heathen debtors to us, from whom we receive both gain and profit? Whatsoever they amass with labour, these things do we make use of without labour, although we are in the faith.

2. Up to that time the people served the Egyptians in the most abject slavery, as saith the Scripture: "And the Egyptians exercised their power rigorously upon the children of Israel; and they made life bitter to them by severe labours, in mortar and in brick, and in all manner of service in the field which they did, by all the works in which they oppressed them with rigour."[1] And with immense labour they built for them fenced cities, increasing the substance of these men throughout a long course of years, and by means of every species of slavery; while these [masters] were not only ungrateful towards them, but had in contemplation their utter annihilation. In what way, then, did [the Israelites] act unjustly, if out of many things they took a few, they who might have possessed much property had they not served them, and might have gone forth wealthy, while, in fact, by receiving only a very insignificant recompense for their heavy servitude, they went away poor? It is just as if any free man, being forcibly carried away by another, and serving him for many years, and increasing his substance, should be thought, when he ultimately obtains some support, to possess some small portion of his [master's] property, but should in reality depart, having obtained only a little as the result of his own great labours, and out of vast possessions which have been acquired, and this should be made by any one a subject of accusation against him, as if he had not acted properly.[2] He (the accuser) will rather appear as an unjust judge against him who had been forcibly carried away into slavery. Of this kind, then, are these men also, who charge the people with blame, because they appropriated a few things out of many, but who bring no charge against those who did not render them the recompense due to their fathers' services; nay, but even reducing them to the most irksome slavery, obtained the highest profit from them. And [these objectors] allege that [the Israelites] acted dishonestly, because, forsooth, they took away for the recompense of their labours, as I have observed, unstamped gold and silver in a few vessels; while they say that they themselves (for let truth be spoken, although to some it may seem ridiculous) do act honestly, when they carry away in their girdles from the labours of others, coined gold, and silver, and brass, with Cæsar's inscription and image upon it.

3. If, however, a comparison be instituted between us and them, [I would ask] which party shall seem to have received [their worldly goods] in the fairer manner? Will it be the [Jewish] people, [who took] from the Egyptians, who were at all points their debtors; or we, [who receive property] from the Romans and other nations, who are under no similar obligation to us? Yea, moreover, through their instrumentality the world is at peace, and we walk on the highways without fear, and sail where we will.[3] Therefore, against men of this kind (namely, the heretics) the word of the Lord applies, which says: "Thou hypocrite, first cast the beam out of thine eye, and then shalt thou see clearly to pull out the mote out of thy brother's eye."[4] For if he who lays these things to thy charge, and glories in his own wisdom, has been separated from the company of the Gentiles, and possesses nothing [derived from] other people's goods, but is literally naked, and barefoot, and dwells homeless among the mountains, as any of those animals do which feed on grass, he will stand excused [in using such language], as being ignorant of the necessities of our mode of life. But if he do partake of what, in the opinion of men, is the property of others, and if [at the same time] he runs down their type,[5] he proves him-

---

[1] Ex. i. 13, 14.

[2] This perplexed sentence is pointed by Harvey interrogatively, but we prefer the above.
[3] [A touching tribute to the imperial law, at a moment when Christians were "dying daily" and "as sheep for the slaughter." So powerfully worked the divine command, Luke vi. 29.]
[4] Matt. vii. 5.
[5] This is, if he inveighs against the Israelites for spoiling the Egyptians; the former being a type of the Christian Church in relation to the Gentiles.

self most unjust, turning this kind of accusation against himself. For he will be found carrying about property not belonging to him, and coveting goods which are not his. And therefore has the Lord said: "Judge not, that ye be not judged: for with what judgment ye shall judge, ye shall be judged."[1] [The meaning is] not certainly that we should not find fault with sinners, nor that we should consent to those who act wickedly; but that we should not pronounce an unfair judgment on the dispensations of God, inasmuch as He has Himself made provision that all things shall turn out for good, in a way consistent with justice. For, because He knew that we would make a good use of our substance, which we should possess by receiving it from another, He says, "He that hath two coats, let him impart to him that hath none; and he that hath meat, let him do likewise."[2] And, "For I was an hungered, and ye gave Me meat; I was thirsty, and ye gave Me drink; I was naked, and ye clothed Me."[3] And, "When thou doest thine alms, let not thy left hand know what thy right hand doeth."[4] And we are proved to be righteous by whatsoever else we do well, redeeming, as it were, our property from strange hands. But thus do I say, "from strange hands," not as if the world were not God's possession, but that we have gifts of this sort, and receive them from others, in the same way as these men had them from the Egyptians who knew not God; and by means of these same do we erect in ourselves the tabernacle of God: for God dwells in those who act uprightly, as the Lord says: "Make to yourselves friends of the mammon of unrighteousness, that they, when ye shall be put to flight,"[5] may receive you into eternal tabernacles."[6] For whatsoever we acquired from unrighteousness when we were heathen, we are proved righteous, when we have become believers, by applying it to the Lord's advantage.

4. As a matter of course, therefore, these things were done beforehand in a type, and from them was the tabernacle of God constructed; those persons justly receiving them, as I have shown, while we were pointed out beforehand in them, — [we] who should afterwards serve God by the things of others. For the whole exodus of the people out of Egypt, which took place under divine guidance,[7] was a type and image of the exodus of the Church which should take place from among the Gentiles;[8] and for this cause He leads it out at last from this world into His own inheritance, which Moses the servant of God did not [bestow], but which Jesus the Son of God shall give for an inheritance. And if any one will devote a close attention to those things which are stated by the prophets with regard to the [time of the] end, and those which John the disciple of the Lord saw in the Apocalypse,[9] he will find that the nations [are to] receive the same plagues universally, as Egypt then did particularly.

CHAP. XXXI. — WE SHOULD NOT HASTILY IMPUTE AS CRIMES TO THE MEN OF OLD TIME THOSE ACTIONS WHICH THE SCRIPTURE HAS NOT CONDEMNED, BUT SHOULD RATHER SEEK IN THEM TYPES OF THINGS TO COME: AN EXAMPLE OF THIS IN THE INCEST COMMITTED BY LOT.

1. WHEN recounting certain matters of this kind respecting them of old time, the presbyter [before mentioned] was in the habit of instructing us, and saying: "With respect to those misdeeds for which the Scriptures themselves blame the patriarchs and prophets, we ought not to inveigh against them, nor become like Ham, who ridiculed the shame of his father, and so fell under a curse; but we should [rather] give thanks to God in their behalf, inasmuch as their sins have been forgiven them through the advent of our Lord; for He said that they gave thanks [for us], and gloried in our salvation.[10] With respect to those actions, again, on which the Scriptures pass no censure, but which are simply set down [as having occurred], we ought not to become the accusers [of those who committed them], for we are not more exact than God, nor can we be superior to our Master; but we should search for a type [in them]. For not one of those things which have been set down in Scripture without being condemned is without significance." An example is found in the case of Lot, who led forth his daughters from Sodom, and these then conceived by their own father; and who left behind him within the confines [of the land] his wife, [who remains] a pillar of salt unto this day. For Lot, not acting under the impulse of his own will, nor at the prompting of carnal concupiscence, nor having any knowledge or thought of anything of the kind, did [in fact] work out a type [of future events]. As says the Scripture: "And that night the elder went in

---

[1] Matt. vii. 1, 2.
[2] Luke iii. 11.
[3] Matt. xxv. 35, 36.
[4] Matt. vi. 3.
[5] As Harvey remarks, this is "a strange translation for ἐκλίπητε" of the *text. rec.*, and he adds that "possibly the translator read ἐκτράπητε."
[6] Luke xvi. 9.
[7] We here follow the punctuation of Massuet in preference to that of Harvey.

[8] [The Fathers regarded the whole Mosaic system, and the history of the faithful under it, as one great allegory. In everything they saw "similitudes," as we do in the *Faery Queen* of Spenser, or the *Pilgrim's Progress*. The ancients may have carried this principle too far, but as a principle it receives countenance from our Lord Himself and His apostles. To us there is often a barren bush, where the Fathers saw a bush that burned with fire.]
[9] See Rev. xv., xvi.
[10] [Thus far we have a most edifying instruction. The reader will be less edified with what follows, but it is a very striking example of what is written: "to the pure all things are pure." Tit. i. 15.]

and lay with her father; and Lot knew not when she lay down, nor when she arose."[1] And the same thing took place in the case of the younger: "And he knew not," it is said, "when she slept with him, nor when she arose."[2] Since, therefore, Lot knew not [what he did], nor was a slave to lust [in his actions], the arrangement [designed by God] was carried out, by which the two daughters (that is, the two churches[3]), who gave birth to children begotten of one and the same father, were pointed out, apart from [the influence of] the lust of the flesh. For there was no other person, [as they supposed], who could impart to them quickening seed, and the means of their giving birth to children, as it is written: "And the elder said unto the younger, And there is not a man on the earth to enter in unto us after the manner of all the earth: come, let us make our father drunk with wine, and let us lie with him, and raise up seed from our father."[4]

2. Thus, after their simplicity and innocence, did these daughters [of Lot] so speak, imagining that all mankind had perished, even as the Sodomites had done, and that the anger of God had come down upon the whole earth. Wherefore also they are to be held excusable, since they supposed that they only, along with their father, were left for the preservation of the human race; and for this reason it was that they deceived their father. Moreover, by the words they used this fact was pointed out — that there is no other one who can confer upon the elder and younger church the [power of] giving birth to children, besides our Father. Now the father of the human race is the Word of God, as Moses points out when he says, "Is not He thy father who hath obtained thee [by generation], and formed thee, and created thee?"[5] At what time, then, did He pour out upon the human race the life-giving seed — that is, the Spirit of the remission of sins, through means of whom we are quickened? Was it not then, when He was eating with men, and drinking wine upon the earth? For it is said, "The Son of man came eating and drinking;"[6] and when He had lain down, He fell asleep, and took repose. As He does Himself say in David, "I slept, and took repose."[7] And because He used thus to act while He dwelt and lived among us, He says again, "And my sleep became sweet unto me."[8]

Now this whole matter was indicated through Lot, that the seed of the Father of all — that is, of the Spirit of God, by whom all things were made — was commingled and united with flesh — that is, with His own workmanship; by which commixture and unity the two synagogues — that is, the two churches — produced from their own father living sons to the living God.

3. And while these things were taking place, his wife remained in [the territory of] Sodom, no longer corruptible flesh, but a pillar of salt which endures for ever;[9] and by those natural processes[10] which appertain to the human race, indicating that the Church also, which is the salt of the earth,[11] has been left behind within the confines of the earth, and subject to human sufferings; and while entire members are often taken away from it, the pillar of salt still endures,[12] thus typifying the foundation of the faith which maketh strong, and sends forward, children to their Father.

CHAP. XXXII. — THAT ONE GOD WAS THE AUTHOR OF BOTH TESTAMENTS, IS CONFIRMED BY THE AUTHORITY OF A PRESBYTER WHO HAD BEEN TAUGHT BY THE APOSTLES.

1. After this fashion also did a presbyter,[13] a disciple of the apostles, reason with respect to the two testaments, proving that both were truly from one and the same God. For [he maintained] that there was no other God besides Him who made and fashioned us, and that the discourse of those men has no foundation who affirm that this world of ours was made either by angels, or by any other power whatsoever, or by another God. For if a man be once moved away from the Creator of all things, and if he grant that this creation to which we belong was formed by any other or through any other [than the one God], he must of necessity fall into much inconsistency, and many contradictions of this sort; to which he will [be able to] furnish

---

[1] Gen. xix. 33.
[2] Gen. xix. 35.
[3] "Id est duæ synagogæ," referring to the Jews and Gentiles. Some regard the words as a marginal gloss which has crept into the text.
[4] Gen. xix. 31, 32.
[5] Deut. xxxii. 6, LXX. [Let us reflect that this effort to spiritualize this awful passage in the history of Lot is an innocent but unsuccessful attempt to imitate St. Paul's allegory, Gal. iv. 24.]
[6] Matt. xi. 19.
[7] Ps. iii. 6.
[8] Jer. xxxi. 26.

[9] Comp. Clem. Rom., chap. xi. Josephus (*Antiq.*, i. 11, 4) testifies that he had himself seen this pillar.
[10] The Latin is "per naturalia," which words, according to Harvey, correspond to δἰ ἐμμηνορροίας. There is a poem entitled *Sodoma* preserved among the works of Tertullian and Cyprian which contains the following lines: —

"Dicitur et vivens, alio jam corpore, sexus
Munificos solito dispungere sanguine menses."

[11] Matt. v. 13.
[12] The poem just referred to also says in reference to this pillar: —

"Ipsaque imago sibi formam sine corpore servans
Durat adhuc, et enim nuda statione sub æthram
Nec pluviis dilapsa situ, nec diruta ventis.
Quin etiam si quis mutilaverit advena formam,
Protinus ex sese suggestu vulnera complet."

[That a pillar of salt is still to be seen in this vicinity, is now confirmed by many modern travellers (report of Lieut. Lynch, United States Navy), which accounts for the natural inference of Josephus and others on whom our author relied. The coincidence is noteworthy.]
[13] Harvey remarks here, that this can hardly be the same presbyter mentioned before, "who was only a hearer of those who had heard the apostles. Irenæus may here mean the venerable martyr Polycarp, bishop of Smyrna."

no explanations which can be regarded as either probable or true. And, for this reason, those who introduce other doctrines conceal from us the opinion which they themselves hold respecting God, because they are aware of the untenable[1] and absurd nature of their doctrine, and are afraid lest, should they be vanquished, they should have some difficulty in making good their escape. But if any one believes in [only] one God, who also made all things by the Word, as Moses likewise says, "God said, Let there be light: and there was light;"[2] and as we read in the Gospel, "All things were made by Him; and without Him was nothing made;"[3] and the Apostle Paul [says] in like manner, "There is one Lord, one faith, one baptism, one God and Father, who is above all, and through all, and in us all"[4] — this man will first of all "hold the head, from which the whole body is compacted and bound together, and, through means of every joint according to the measure of the ministration of each several part, maketh increase of the body to the edification of itself in love."[5] And then shall every word also seem consistent to him,[6] if he for his part diligently read the Scriptures in company with those who are presbyters in the Church, among whom is the apostolic doctrine, as I have pointed out.

2. For all the apostles taught that there were indeed two testaments among the two peoples; but that it was one and the same God who appointed both for the advantage of those men (for whose[7] sakes the testaments were given) who were to believe in God, I have proved in the third book from the very teaching of the apostles; and that the first testament was not given without reason, or to no purpose, or in an accidental sort of manner; but that it subdued[8] those to whom it was given to the service of God, for their benefit (for God needs no service from men), and exhibited a type of heavenly things, inasmuch as man was not yet able to see the things of God through means of immediate vision;[9] and foreshadowed the images of those things which [now actually] exist in the Church, in order that our faith might be firmly established;[10] and contained a prophecy of things to come, in order that man might learn that God has foreknowledge of all things.

CHAP. XXXIII. — WHOSOEVER CONFESSES THAT ONE GOD IS THE AUTHOR OF BOTH TESTAMENTS, AND DILIGENTLY READS THE SCRIPTURES IN COMPANY WITH THE PRESBYTERS OF THE CHURCH, IS A TRUE SPIRITUAL DISCIPLE; AND HE WILL RIGHTLY UNDERSTAND AND INTERPRET ALL THAT THE PROPHETS HAVE DECLARED RESPECTING CHRIST AND THE LIBERTY OF THE NEW TESTAMENT.

1. A spiritual disciple of this sort truly receiving the Spirit of God, who was from the beginning, in all the dispensations of God, present with mankind, and announced things future, revealed things present, and narrated things past — [such a man] does indeed "judge all men, but is himself judged by no man."[11] For he judges the Gentiles, "who serve the creature more than the Creator,"[12] and with a reprobate mind spend all their labour on vanity. And he also judges the Jews, who do not accept of the word of liberty, nor are willing to go forth free, although they have a Deliverer present [with them]; but they pretend, at a time unsuitable [for such conduct], to serve, [with observances] beyond [those required by] the law, God who stands in need of nothing, and do not recognise the advent of Christ, which He accomplished for the salvation of men, nor are willing to understand that all the prophets announced His two advents: the one, indeed, in which He became a man subject to stripes, and knowing what it is to bear infirmity,[13] and sat upon the foal of an ass,[14] and was a stone rejected by the builders,[15] and was led as a sheep to the slaughter,[16] and by the stretching forth of His hands destroyed Amalek;[17] while He gathered from the ends of the earth into His Father's fold the children who were scattered abroad,[18] and remembered His own dead ones who had formerly fallen asleep,[19] and came down to them that He might deliver them: but the second in which He will come on the clouds,[20] bringing on the day which burns as a furnace,[21] and smiting the earth with the word of His mouth,[22] and slaying the impious with the breath of His lips, and having a fan in His hands, and cleansing His floor, and gathering the wheat indeed into His barn, but burning the chaff with unquenchable fire.[23]

2. Moreover, he shall also examine the doc-

---

[1] "Quassum et futile." The text varies much in the MSS.
[2] Gen. i. 3.
[3] John i. 3.
[4] Eph. iv. 5, 6.
[5] Eph iv. 16; Col. ii. 19.
[6] "Constabit ei."
[7] We here read "secundum *quos*" with Massuet, instead of the usual "secundum *quod*."
[8] "Concurvans," corresponding to συγκάμπτων, which, says Harvey, "would be expressive of those who were brought under the law, as the neck of the steer is bent to the yoke."
[9] The Latin is, "per proprium visum."
[10] [If this and the former chapter seem to us superfluous, we must reflect that such testimony, from the beginning, has established the unity of Holy Scripture, and preserved to us — THE BIBLE.]

[11] 1 Cor. ii. 15. [The argument of this chapter hinges on Ps. xxv. 14, and expounds a difficult text of St. Paul. A man who has the mind of God's Spirit is the only judge of spiritual things. Worldly men are incompetent critics of Scripture and of Christian exposition.]
[12] Rom. i. 21.
[13] Isa. liii. 3.
[14] Zech. ix. 9.
[15] Ps. cxviii. 22.
[16] Isa. liii. 7.
[17] Ex. xvii. 11.
[18] Isa. xi. 12.
[19] Comp. book iii. 20, 4.
[20] Dan. vii. 13.
[21] Mal. iv. 1.
[22] Isa. xi. 4.
[23] Matt. iii. 12; Luke iii. 17.

trine of Marcion, [inquiring] how he holds that there are two gods, separated from each other by an infinite distance.[1] Or how can *he* be good who draws away men that do not belong to him from him who made them, and calls them into his own kingdom? And why is his goodness, which does not save all [thus], defective? Also, why does he, indeed, seem to be good as respects men, but most unjust with regard to him who made men, inasmuch as he deprives him of his possessions? Moreover, how could the Lord, with any justice, if He belonged to another father, have acknowledged the bread to be His body, while He took it from that creation to which we belong, and affirmed the mixed cup to be His blood?[2] And why did He acknowledge Himself to be the Son of man, if He had not gone through that birth which belongs to a human being? How, too, could He forgive us those sins for which we are answerable to our Maker and God? And how, again, supposing that He was not flesh, but was a man merely in appearance, could He have been crucified, and could blood and water have issued from His pierced side?[3] What body, moreover, was it that those who buried Him consigned to the tomb? And what was that which rose again from the dead?

3. [This spiritual man] shall also judge all the followers of Valentinus, because they do indeed confess with the tongue one God the Father, and that all things derive their existence from Him, but do at the same time maintain that He who formed all things is the fruit of an apostasy or defect. [He shall judge them, too, because] they do in like manner confess with the tongue one Lord Jesus Christ, the Son of God, but assign in their [system of] doctrine a production of his own to the Only-begotten, one of his own also to the Word, another to Christ, and yet another to the Saviour; so that, according to them, all these beings are indeed said [in Scripture to be], as it were, one; [while they maintain], notwithstanding, that each one of them should be understood [to exist] separately [from the rest], and to have [had] his own special origin, according to his peculiar conjunction. [It appears], then,[4] that their tongues alone, forsooth, have conceded the unity [of God], while their [real] opinion and their understanding (by their habit of investigating profundities) have fallen away from [this doctrine of] unity, and taken up the notion of manifold deities, — [this, I say, must appear] when they shall be examined by Christ as to the points [of doctrine] which they have invented. Him, too, they affirm to have been born at a later period than the Pleroma of the Æons, and that His production took place after [the occurrence of] a degeneracy or apostasy; and they maintain that, on account of the passion which was experienced by Sophia, they themselves were brought to the birth. But their own special prophet Homer, listening to whom they have invented such doctrines, shall himself reprove them, when he expresses himself as follows: —

"Hateful to me that man as Hades' gates,
Who one thing thinks, while he another states."[5]

[This spiritual man] shall also judge the vain speeches of the perverse Gnostics, by showing that they are the disciples of Simon Magus.

4. He will judge also the Ebionites; [for] how can they be saved unless it was God who wrought out their salvation upon earth? Or how shall man pass into God, unless God has [first] passed into man? And how shall he (man) escape from the generation subject to death, if not by means[6] of a new generation, given in a wonderful and unexpected manner (but as a sign of salvation) by God — [I mean] that regeneration which flows from the virgin through faith?[7] Or how shall they receive adoption from God if they remain in this [kind of] generation, which is naturally possessed by man in this world? And how could He (Christ) have been greater than Solomon,[8] or greater than Jonah, or have been the Lord of David,[9] who was of the same substance as they were? How, too, could He have subdued[10] him who was stronger than men,[11] who had not only overcome man, but also retained him under his power, and conquered him who had conquered, while he set free mankind who had been conquered, unless He had been greater than man who had thus been vanquished? But who else is superior to, and more eminent than, that man who was formed after the likeness of God, except the Son of God, after whose image man was created? And for this reason He did in these last days[12] exhibit the similitude; [for] the Son of God was made man, assuming the ancient production [of His hands] into His own nature,[13] as I have shown in the immediately preceding book.

---

[1] Harvey points this sentence interrogatively.
[2] "Temperamentum calicis:" on which Harvey remarks that "the mixture of water with the wine in the holy Eucharist was the universal practice of antiquity . . . the wine signifying the mystical Head of the Church, the water the body." [Whatever the significance, it harmonizes with the Paschal chalice, and with 1 John v. 6, and St John's Gospel, xix. 34, 35.]
[3] John xix. 34.
[4] This sentence is very obscure in the Latin text.
[5] *Iliad*, ix. 312, 313.
[6] The text is obscure, and the construction doubtful.
[7] The Latin here is, "quæ est ex virgine per fidem regenerationem." According to Massuet, "virgine" here refers not to Mary, but to the Church. Grabe suspects that some words have been lost.
[8] Matt. xii. 41, 42.
[9] Matt. xxii. 43.
[10] Matt. xxii. 29; Luke xi. 21, 22.
[11] Literally, "who was strong against men."
[12] In fine; lit. "in the end."
[13] In semetipsum: lit. "unto Himself."

5. He shall also judge those who describe Christ as [having become man] only in [human] opinion. For how can they imagine that they do themselves carry on a real discussion, when their Master was a mere imaginary being? Or how can they receive anything stedfast from Him, if He was a merely imagined being, and not a verity? And how can these men really be partakers of salvation, if He in whom they profess to believe, manifested Himself as a merely imaginary being? Everything, therefore, connected with these men is unreal, and nothing [possessed of the character of] truth; and, in these circumstances, it may be made a question whether (since, perchance, they themselves in like manner are not men, but mere dumb animals) they do not present,[1] in most cases, simply a shadow of humanity.

6. He shall also judge false prophets, who, without having received the gift of prophecy from God, and not possessed of the fear of God, but either for the sake of vainglory, or with a view to some personal advantage, or acting in some other way under the influence of a wicked spirit, pretend to utter prophecies, while all the time they lie against God.

7. He shall also judge those who give rise to schisms, who are destitute of the love of God, and who look to their own special advantage rather than to the unity of the Church; and who for trifling reasons, or any kind of reason which occurs to them, cut in pieces and divide the great and glorious body of Christ, and so far as in them lies, [positively] destroy it, — men who prate of peace while they give rise to war, and do in truth strain out a gnat, but swallow a camel.[2] For no reformation of so great importance can be effected by them, as will compensate for the mischief arising from their schism. He shall also judge all those who are beyond the pale of the truth, that is, who are outside the Church; but he himself shall be judged by no one. For to him all things are consistent: he has a full faith in one God Almighty, of whom are all things; and in the Son of God, Jesus Christ our Lord, by whom are all things, and in the dispensations connected with Him, by means of which the Son of God became man; and a firm belief in the Spirit of God, who furnishes us with a knowledge of the truth, and has set forth the dispensations of the Father and the Son, in virtue of which He dwells with every generation of men,[3] according to the will of the Father.

8. True knowledge[4] is [that which consists in] the doctrine of the apostles, and the ancient constitution[5] of the Church throughout all the world, and the distinctive manifestation of the body[6] of Christ according to the successions of the bishops, by which they have handed down that Church which exists in every place, and has come even unto us, being guarded and preserved,[7] without any forging of Scriptures, by a very complete system[8] of doctrine, and neither receiving addition nor [suffering] curtailment [in the truths which she believes]; and [it consists in] reading [the word of God] without falsification, and a lawful and diligent exposition in harmony with the Scriptures, both without danger and without blasphemy; and [above all, it consists in] the pre-eminent gift of love,[9] which is more precious than knowledge, more glorious than prophecy, and which excels all the other gifts [of God].

9. Wherefore the Church does in every place, because of that love which she cherishes towards God, send forward, throughout all time, a multitude of martyrs to the Father; while all others[10] not only have nothing of this kind to point to among themselves, but even maintain that such witness-bearing is not at all necessary, for that their system of doctrines is the true witness [for Christ], with the exception, perhaps, that one or two among them, during the whole time which has elapsed since the Lord appeared on earth, have occasionally, along with our martyrs, borne the reproach of the name (as if he too [the heretic] had obtained mercy), and have been led forth with them [to death], being, as it were, a sort of retinue granted unto them. For the Church alone sustains with purity the reproach of those who suffer persecution for righteousness' sake, and endure all sorts of punishments, and are put to death because of the love which they bear to God, and their confession of His Son; often weakened indeed, yet immediately increasing her members, and becoming whole again, after the same manner as her type,[11] Lot's wife, who became a pillar of salt. Thus, too, [she passes through an experience] similar to that of the ancient prophets, as the Lord declares, "For so persecuted they

---

[1] We here follow the reading "proferant:" the passage is difficult and obscure, but the meaning is as above.
[2] Matt. xxiii. 24.
[3] The Greek text here is σκηνοβατοῦν (lit. "to tabernacle:" comp. ἐσκήνωσεν, John i. 14) καθ' ἑκάστην γενεὰν ἐν τοῖς ἀνθρώποις: the Latin is, "Secundum quas (dispositiones) aderat generi humano." We have endeavoured to express the meaning of both.
[4] The following section is an important one, but very difficult to translate with undoubted accuracy. The editors differ considerably both as to the construction and the interpretation. We have done our best to represent the meaning in English, but may not have been altogether successful.
[5] The Greek is σύστημα: the Latin text has "status."
[6] The Latin is, "character corporis."
[7] The text here is, "custodita sine fictione scripturarum;" some prefer joining "scripturarum" to the following words.
[8] We follow Harvey's text, "tractatione;" others read "tractatio." According to Harvey, the creed of the Church is denoted by "tractatione;" but Massuet renders the clause thus: ["True knowledge consists in] a very complete *tractatio* of the Scriptures, which has come down to us by being preserved ('custoditione' being read instead of 'custodita') without falsification."
[9] Comp. 2 Cor. viii. 1; 1 Cor. xiii.
[10] i.e., the heretics.
[11] Comp. above, xxxi. 2.

the prophets who were before you;"[1] inasmuch as she does indeed, in a new fashion, suffer persecution from those who do not receive the word of God, while the self-same spirit rests upon her[2] [as upon these ancient prophets].

10. And indeed the prophets, along with other things which they predicted, also foretold this, that all those on whom the Spirit of God should rest, and who would obey the word of the Father, and serve Him according to their ability, should suffer persecution, and be stoned and slain. For the prophets prefigured in themselves all these things, because of their love to God, and on account of His word. For since they themselves were members of Christ, each one of them in his place as a member did, in accordance with this, set forth the prophecy [assigned him]; all of them, although many, prefiguring only one, and proclaiming the things which pertain to one. For just as the working of the whole body is exhibited through means of our members, while the figure of a complete man is not displayed by one member, but through means of all taken together, so also did all the prophets prefigure the one [Christ]; while every one of them, in his special place as a member, did, in accordance with this, fill up the [established] dispensation, and shadowed forth beforehand that particular working of Christ which was connected with that member.

11. For some of them, beholding Him in glory, saw His glorious life (*conversationem*) at the Father's right hand;[3] others beheld Him coming on the clouds as the Son of man;[4] and those who declared regarding Him, "They shall look on Him whom they have pierced,"[5] indicated His [second] advent, concerning which He Himself says, "Thinkest thou that when the Son of man cometh, He shall find faith on the earth?"[6] Paul also refers to this event when he says, "If, however, it is a righteous thing with God to recompense tribulation to them that trouble you, and to you that are troubled rest with us, at the revelation of the Lord Jesus from heaven, with His mighty angels, and in a flame of fire."[7] Others again, speaking of Him as a judge, and [referring], as if it were a burning furnace, [to] the day of the Lord, who "gathers the wheat into His barn, but will burn up the chaff with unquenchable fire,"[8] were accustomed to threaten those who were unbelieving, concerning whom also the Lord Himself declares, "Depart from me, ye cursed, into everlasting fire, which my Father has prepared for the devil and his angels."[9] And the apostle in like manner says [of them], "Who shall be punished with everlasting death from the face of the Lord, and from the glory of His power, when He shall come to be glorified in His saints, and to be admired in those who believe in Him."[10] There are also some [of them] who declare, "Thou art fairer than the children of men;"[11] and, "God, Thy God, hath anointed Thee with the oil of gladness above Thy fellows;"[12] and, "Gird Thy sword upon Thy thigh, O Most Mighty, with Thy beauty and Thy fairness, and go forward and proceed prosperously; and rule Thou because of truth, and meekness, and righteousness."[13] And whatever other things of a like nature are spoken regarding Him, these indicated that beauty and splendour which exist in His kingdom, along with the transcendent and pre-eminent exaltation [belonging] to all who are under His sway, that those who hear might desire to be found there, doing such things as are pleasing to God. Again, there are those who say, "He is a man, and who shall know him?"[14] and, "I came unto the prophetess, and she bare a son, and His name is called Wonderful, Counsellor, the Mighty God;"[15] and those [of them] who proclaimed Him as Immanuel, [born] of the Virgin, exhibited the union of the Word of God with His own workmanship, [declaring] that the Word should become flesh, and the Son of God the Son of man (the pure One opening purely that pure womb which regenerates men unto God, and which He Himself made pure); and having become this which we also are, He [nevertheless] is the Mighty God, and possesses a generation which cannot be declared. And there are also some of them who say, "The Lord hath spoken in Zion, and uttered His voice from Jerusalem;"[16] and, "In Judah is God known;"[17] — these indicated His advent which took place in Judea. Those, again, who declare that "God comes from the south, and from a mountain thick with foliage,"[18] announced His advent at Bethlehem, as I have pointed out in the preceding book.[19] From that place, also, He who rules, and who feeds the people of His Father, has come. Those, again, who declare that at His coming "the lame man shall leap as an hart, and the tongue of the dumb shall

---

[1] Matt. v. 12.
[2] Comp. 1 Pet. iv. 14.
[3] Isa. vi. 1; Ps. cx. 1.
[4] Dan. vii. 13.
[5] Zech. xii. 10.
[6] Luke xviii. 8. There is nothing to correspond with "putas" in the received text.
[7] 2 Thess. i. 6-8.
[8] Matt. iii. 12.
[9] Matt. xxv. 41.
[10] 2 Thess. i. 9, 10.
[11] Ps. xlv. 2.
[12] Ps. xlv. 7.
[13] Ps. xlv. 3, 4.
[14] Jer. xvii. 9 (Sept.). Harvey here remarks: "The LXX. read אנוֹשׁ instead of אנשׁ. Thus, from a text that teaches us that *the heart is deceitful above all things*, the Fathers extract a proof of the manhood of Christ."
[15] Isa. viii. 3, ix. 6, vii. 14. [A confusion of texts.]
[16] Joel iii. 16.
[17] Ps. lxxvi. 1.
[18] Hab. iii. 3.
[19] See III. xx. 4.

[speak] plainly, and the eyes of the blind shall be opened, and the ears of the deaf shall hear,"[1] and that "the hands which hang down, and the feeble knees, shall be strengthened,"[2] and that "the dead which are in the grave shall arise,"[3] and that He Himself "shall take [upon Him] our weaknesses, and bear our sorrows,"[4] — [all these] proclaimed those works of healing which were accomplished by Him.

12. Some of them, moreover — [when they predicted that] as a weak and inglorious man, and as one who knew what it was to bear infirmity,[5] and sitting upon the foal of an ass,[6] He should come to Jerusalem; and that He should give His back to stripes,[7] and His cheeks to palms [which struck Him]; and that He should be led as a sheep to the slaughter;[8] and that He should have vinegar and gall given Him to drink;[9] and that He should be forsaken by His friends and those nearest to Him;[10] and that He should stretch forth His hands the whole day long;[11] and that He should be mocked and maligned by those who looked upon Him;[12] and that His garments should be parted, and lots cast upon His raiment;[13] and that He should be brought down to the dust of death,[14] with all [the other] things of a like nature — prophesied His coming in the character of a man as He entered Jerusalem, in which by His passion and crucifixion He endured all the things which have been mentioned. Others, again, when they said, "The holy Lord remembered His own dead ones who slept in the dust, and came down to them to raise them up, that He might save them,"[15] furnished us with the reason on account of which He suffered all these things. Those, moreover, who said, "In that day, saith the Lord, the sun shall go down at noon, and there shall be darkness over the earth in the clear day; and I will turn your feast days into mourning, and all your songs into lamentation,"[16] plainly announced that obscuration of the sun which at the time of His crucifixion took place from the sixth hour onwards, and that after this event, those days which were their festivals according to the law, and their songs, should be changed into grief and lamentation when they were handed over to the Gentiles. Jeremiah, too, makes this point still clearer, when he thus speaks concerning Jerusalem: "She that hath born [seven] languisheth; her soul hath become weary; her sun hath gone down while it was yet noon; she hath been confounded, and suffered reproach: the remainder of them will I give to the sword in the sight of their enemies."[17]

13. Those of them, again, who spoke of His having slumbered and taken sleep, and of His having risen again because the Lord sustained Him,[18] and who enjoined the principalities of heaven to set open the everlasting doors, that the King of glory might go in,[19] proclaimed beforehand His resurrection from the dead through the Father's power, and His reception into heaven. And when they expressed themselves thus, "His going forth is from the height of heaven, and His returning even to the highest heaven; and there is no one who can hide himself from His heat,"[20] they announced that very truth of His being taken up again to the place from which He came down, and that there is no one who can escape His righteous judgment. And those who said, "The LORD hath reigned; let the people be enraged: [even] He who sitteth upon the cherubim; let the earth be moved,"[21] were thus predicting partly that wrath from all nations which after His ascension came upon those who believed in Him, with the movement of the whole earth against the Church; and partly the fact that, when He comes from heaven with His mighty angels, the whole earth shall be shaken, as He Himself declares, "There shall be a great earthquake, such as has not been from the beginning."[22] And again, when one says, "Whosoever is judged, let him stand opposite; and whosoever is justified, let him draw near to the servant[23] of God;"[24] and, "Woe unto you, for ye shall wax old as doth a garment, and the moth shall eat you up;" and, "All flesh shall be humbled, and the LORD alone shall be exalted in the highest,"[25] — it is thus indicated that, after His passion and ascension, God shall cast down under His feet all who were opposed to Him, and He shall be exalted above all, and there shall be no one who can be justified or compared to Him.

14. And those of them who declare that God would make a new covenant[26] with men, not such as that which He made with the fathers at Mount Horeb, and would give to men a new heart and a new spirit;[27] and again, "And remember ye not the things of old: behold, I

---

[1] Isa. xxxv. 5, 6.
[2] Isa. xxxv. 3.
[3] Isa. xxvi. 19.
[4] Isa. liii. 4.
[5] Isa. liii. 3.
[6] Zech. ix. 9.
[7] Isa. l. 6.
[8] Isa. liii. 7.
[9] Ps. lxix. 21.
[10] Ps. xxxviii. 11.
[11] Isa. lxv. 2.
[12] Ps xxii. 7.
[13] Ps. xxii. 18.
[14] Ps. xxii. 15.
[15] Comp. book iii. cap. xx. 4 and book iv. cap. xxii. 1.
[16] Amos viii. 9, 10.
[17] Jer. xv. 9.
[18] Ps. iii. 5.
[19] Ps. xxiv. 7.
[20] Ps. xix. 6.
[21] Ps. xcix. 1.
[22] Matt. xxiv. 21.
[23] Or "son."
[24] Isa. l. 8, 9 (loosely quoted).
[25] Isa. ii. 17.
[26] Jer. xxxi. 31, 32.
[27] Ezek. xxxvi. 26.

make new things which shall now arise, and ye shall know it; and I will make a way in the desert, and rivers in a dry land, to give drink to my chosen people, my people whom I have acquired, that they may show forth my praise,"[1] — plainly announced that liberty which distinguishes the new covenant, and the new wine which is put into new bottles,[2] [that is], the faith which is in Christ, by which He has proclaimed the way of righteousness sprung up in the desert, and the streams of the Holy Spirit in a dry land, to give water to the elect people of God, whom He has acquired, that they might show forth His praise, but not that they might blaspheme Him who made these things, that is, God.

15. And all those other points which I have shown the prophets to have uttered by means of so long a series of Scriptures, he who is truly spiritual will interpret by pointing out, in regard to every one of the things which have been spoken, to what special point in the dispensation of the Lord is referred, and [by thus exhibiting] the entire system of the work of the Son of God, knowing always the same God; and always acknowledging the same Word of God, although He has [but] now been manifested to us; acknowledging also at all times the same Spirit of God, although He has been poured out upon us after a new fashion in these last times, [knowing that He descends] even from the creation of the world to its end upon the human race simply as such, from whom those who believe God and follow His word receive that salvation which flows from Him. Those, on the other hand, who depart from Him, and despise His precepts, and by their deeds bring dishonour on Him who made them, and by their opinions blaspheme Him who nourishes them, heap up against themselves most righteous judgment.[3] He therefore (i.e., the spiritual man) sifts and tries them all, but he himself is tried by no man:[4] he neither blasphemes his Father, nor sets aside His dispensations, nor inveighs against the fathers, nor dishonours the prophets, by maintaining that they were [sent] from another God [than he worships], or again, that their prophecies were derived from different sources.[5]

CHAP. XXXIV. — PROOF AGAINST THE MARCIONITES, THAT THE PROPHETS REFERRED IN ALL THEIR PREDICTIONS TO OUR CHRIST.

1. Now I shall simply say, in opposition to all the heretics, and principally against the followers of Marcion, and against those who are like to these, in maintaining that the prophets were from another God [than He who is announced in the Gospel], read with earnest care that Gospel which has been conveyed to us by the apostles, and read with earnest care the prophets, and you will find that the whole conduct, and all the doctrine, and all the sufferings of our Lord, were predicted through them. But if a thought of this kind should then suggest itself to you, to say, What then did the Lord bring to us by His advent? — know ye that He brought all [possible] novelty, by bringing Himself who had been announced. For this very thing was proclaimed beforehand, that a novelty should come to renew and quicken mankind. For the advent of the King is previously announced by those servants who are sent [before Him], in order to the preparation and equipment of those men who are to entertain their Lord. But when the King has actually come, and those who are His subjects have been filled with that joy which was proclaimed beforehand, and have attained to that liberty which He bestows, and share in the sight of Him, and have listened to His words, and have enjoyed the gifts which He confers, the question will not then be asked by any that are possessed of sense what new thing the King has brought beyond [that proclaimed by] those who announced His coming. For He has brought Himself, and has bestowed on men those good things which were announced beforehand, which things the angels desired to look into.[6]

2. But the servants would then have been proved false, and not sent by the Lord, if Christ on His advent, by being found exactly such as He was previously announced, had not fulfilled their words. Wherefore He said, "Think not that I have come to destroy the law or the prophets; I came not to destroy, but to fulfil. For verily I say unto you, Until heaven and earth pass away, one jot or one tittle shall not pass from the law and the prophets till all come to pass."[7] For by His advent He Himself fulfilled all things, and does still fulfil in the Church the new covenant foretold by the law, onwards to the consummation [of all things]. To this effect also Paul, His apostle, says in the Epistle to the Romans, "But now,[8] without the law, has the righteousness of God been manifested, being witnessed by the law and the prophets; for the just shall live by faith."[9] But this fact, that the just shall live by faith, had been previously announced[10] by the prophets.

3. But whence could the prophets have had power to predict the advent of the King, and to preach beforehand that liberty which was be-

---

[1] Isa. xliii. 19-21.
[2] Matt. ix. 17.
[3] Rom. ii. 5.
[4] 1 Cor. ii 15.
[5] "Ex alia et alia substantia fuisse prophetias."
[6] 1 Pet. i. 12.
[7] Rom. iii. 21.
[8] Matt. v. 17, 18.
[9] Rom. i. 17.
[10] Hab. ii. 4.

stowed by Him, and previously to announce all things which were done by Christ, His words, His works, and His sufferings, and to predict the new covenant, if they had received prophetical inspiration from another God [than He who is revealed in the Gospel], they being ignorant, as ye allege, of the ineffable Father, of His kingdom, and His dispensations, which the Son of God fulfilled when He came upon earth in these last times? Neither are ye in a position to say that these things came to pass by a certain kind of chance, as if they were spoken by the prophets in regard to some other person, while like events happened to the Lord. For all the prophets prophesied these same things, but they never came to pass in the case of any one of the ancients. For if these things had happened to any man among them of old time, those [prophets] who lived subsequently would certainly not have prophesied that these events should come to pass in the last times. Moreover, there is in fact none among the fathers, nor the prophets, nor the ancient kings, in whose case any one of these things properly and specifically took place. For all indeed prophesied as to the sufferings of Christ, but they themselves were far from enduring sufferings similar to what was predicted. And the points connected with the passion of the Lord, which were foretold, were realized in no other case. For neither did it happen at the death of any man among the ancients that the sun set at mid-day, nor was the veil of the temple rent, nor did the earth quake, nor were the rocks rent, nor did the dead rise up, nor was any one of these men [of old] raised up on the third day, nor received into heaven, nor at his assumption were the heavens opened, nor did the nations believe in the name of any other; nor did any from among them, having been dead and rising again, lay open the new covenant of liberty. Therefore the prophets spake not of any one else but of the Lord, in whom all these aforesaid tokens concurred.

4. If any one, however, advocating the cause of the Jews, do maintain that this new covenant consisted in the rearing of that temple which was built under Zerubbabel after the emigration to Babylon, and in the departure of the people from thence after the lapse of seventy years, let him know that the temple constructed of stones was indeed then rebuilt (for as yet that law was observed which had been made upon tables of stone), yet no new covenant was given, but they used the Mosaic law until the coming of the Lord; but from the Lord's advent, the new covenant which brings back peace, and the law which gives life, has gone forth over the whole earth, as the prophets said: "For out of Zion shall go forth the law, and the word of the Lord from Jerusalem; and He shall rebuke many people; and they shall break down their swords into ploughshares, and their spears into pruning-hooks, and they shall no longer learn to fight."[1] If therefore another law and word, going forth from Jerusalem, brought in such a [reign of] peace among the Gentiles which received it (the word), and convinced, through them, many a nation of its folly, then [only] it appears that the prophets spake of some other person. But if the law of liberty, that is, the word of God, preached by the apostles (who went forth from Jerusalem) throughout all the earth, caused such a change in the state of things, that these [nations] did form the swords and war-lances into ploughshares, and changed them into pruning-hooks for reaping the corn, [that is], into instruments used for peaceful purposes, and that they are now unaccustomed to fighting, but when smitten, offer also the other cheek,[2] then the prophets have not spoken these things of any other person, but of Him who effected them. This person is our Lord, and in Him is that declaration borne out; since it is He Himself who has made the plough, and introduced the pruning-hook, that is, the first semination of man, which was the creation exhibited in Adam,[3] and the gathering in of the produce in the last times by the Word; and, for this reason, since He joined the beginning to the end, and is the Lord of both, He has finally displayed the plough, in that the wood has been joined on to the iron, and has thus cleansed His land; because the Word, having been firmly united to flesh, and in its mechanism fixed with pins,[4] has reclaimed the savage earth. In the beginning, He figured forth the pruning-hook by means of Abel, pointing out that there should be a gathering in of a righteous race of men. He says, "For behold how the just man perishes, and no man considers it; and righteous men are taken away, and no man layeth it to heart."[5] These things were acted beforehand in Abel, were also previously declared by the prophets, but were accomplished in the Lord's person; and the same [is still true] with regard to us, the body following the example of the Head.

5. Such are the arguments proper[6] [to be used] in opposition to those who maintain that the prophets [were inspired] by a different God, and that our Lord [came] from another Father, if perchance [these heretics] may at length de-

---

[1] Isa. ii. 3, 4; Mic. iv. 2, 3.
[2] Matt. v. 39.
[3] Book 1. p. 327, this volume.
[4] This is following Harvey's conjectural emendation of the text, viz., " taleis " for " talis." He considers the *pius* here as symbolical of the *nails* by which our Lord was fastened to the cross. The whole passage is almost hopelessly obscure, though the general meaning maybe guessed.
[5] Isa. lvii. 1.
[6] [If it be remembered that we know Irenæus here, only through a most obscure Latin rendering, we shall be slow to censure this conclusion.]

sist from such extreme folly. This is my earnest object in adducing these Scriptural proofs, that confuting them, as far as in me lies, by these very passages, I may restrain them from such great blasphemy, and from insanely fabricating a multitude of gods.

CHAP. XXXV. — A REFUTATION OF THOSE WHO ALLEGE THAT THE PROPHETS UTTERED SOME PREDICTIONS UNDER THE INSPIRATION OF THE HIGHEST, OTHERS FROM THE DEMIURGE. DISAGREEMENTS OF THE VALENTINIANS AMONG THEMSELVES WITH REGARD TO THESE SAME PREDICTIONS.

1. Then again, in opposition to the Valentinians, and the other Gnostics, falsely so called, who maintain that some parts of Scripture were spoken at one time from the Pleroma (*a summitate*) through means of the seed [derived] from that place, but at another time from the intermediate abode through means of the audacious mother Prunica, but that many are due to the Creator of the world, from whom also the prophets had their mission, we say that it is altogether irrational to bring down the Father of the universe to such straits, as that He should not be possessed of His own proper instruments, by which the things in the Pleroma might be perfectly proclaimed. For of whom was He afraid, so that He should not reveal His will after His own way and independently, freely, and without being involved with that spirit which came into being in a state of degeneracy and ignorance? Was it that He feared that very many would be saved, when more should have listened to the unadulterated truth? Or, on the other hand, was He incapable of preparing for Himself those who should announce the Saviour's advent?

2. But if, when the Saviour came to this earth, He sent His apostles into the world to proclaim with accuracy His advent, and to teach the Father's will, having nothing in common with the doctrine of the Gentiles or of the Jews, much more, while yet existing in the Pleroma, would He have appointed His own heralds to proclaim His future advent into this world, and having nothing in common with those prophecies originating from the Demiurge. But if, when within the Pleroma, He availed Himself of those prophets who were under the law, and declared His own matters through their instrumentality; much more would He, upon His arrival hither, have made use of these same teachers, and have preached the Gospel to us by their means. Therefore let them not any longer assert that Peter and Paul and the other apostles proclaimed the truth, but that it was the scribes and Pharisees, and the others, through whom the law was propounded. But if, at His advent, He sent forth His own apostles in the spirit of truth, and not in that of error, He did the very same also in the case of the prophets; for the Word of God was always the self-same: and if the Spirit from the Pleroma was, according to these men's system, the Spirit of light, the Spirit of truth, the Spirit of perfection, and the Spirit of knowledge, while that from the Demiurge was the spirit of ignorance, degeneracy, and error, and the offspring of obscurity; how can it be, that in one and the same being there exists perfection and defect, knowledge and ignorance, error and truth, light and darkness? But if it was impossible that such should happen in the case of the prophets, for they preached the word of the Lord from one God, and proclaimed the advent of His Son, much more would the Lord Himself never have uttered words, on one occasion from above, but on another from degeneracy below, thus becoming the teacher at once of knowledge and of ignorance; nor would He have ever glorified as Father at one time the Founder of the world, and at another Him who is above this one, as He does Himself declare: "No man putteth a piece of a new garment upon an old one, nor do they put new wine into old bottles."[1] Let these men, therefore, either have nothing whatever to do with the prophets, as with those that are ancients, and allege no longer that these men, being sent beforehand by the Demiurge, spake certain things under that new influence which pertains to the Pleroma; or, on the other hand, let them be convinced by our Lord, when He declares that new wine cannot be put into old bottles.

3. But from what source could the offspring of their mother derive his knowledge of the mysteries within the Pleroma, and power to discourse regarding them? Suppose that the mother, while beyond the Pleroma, did bring forth this very offspring; but what is beyond the Pleroma they represent as being beyond the pale of knowledge, that is, ignorance. How, then, could that seed, which was conceived in ignorance, possess the power of declaring knowledge? Or how did the mother herself, a shapeless and undefined being, one cast out of doors as an abortion, obtain knowledge of the mysteries within the Pleroma, she who was organized outside it and given a form there, and prohibited by Horos from entering within, and who remains outside the Pleroma till the consummation [of all things], that is, beyond the pale of knowledge? Then, again, when they say that the Lord's passion is a type of the extension of the Christ above, which he effected through Horos, and so imparted a form to their mother, they are refuted in the other particulars [of the Lord's passion], for they have no semblance of a type to show with regard

---

[1] Luke v. 36, 37.

to them. For when did the Christ above have vinegar and gall given him to drink? Or when was his raiment parted? Or when was he pierced, and blood and water came forth? Or when did he sweat great drops of blood? And [the same may be demanded] as to the other particulars which happened to the Lord, of which the prophets have spoken. From whence, then, did the mother or her offspring divine the things which had not yet taken place, but which should occur afterwards?

4. They affirm that certain things still, besides these, were spoken from the Pleroma, but are confuted by those which are referred to in the Scriptures as bearing on the advent of Christ. But what these are [that are spoken from the Pleroma] they are not agreed, but give different answers regarding them. For if any one, wishing to test them, do question one by one with regard to any passage those who are their leading men, he shall find one of them referring the passage in question to the Propator — that is, to Bythus; another attributing it to Arche — that is, to the Only-begotten; another to the Father of all — that is, to the Word; while another, again, will say that it was spoken of that one Æon who was [formed from the joint contributions] of the Æons in the Pleroma;[1] others [will regard the passage] as referring to Christ, while another [will refer it] to the Saviour. One, again, more skilled than these,[2] after a long protracted silence, declares that it was spoken of Horos; another that it signifies the Sophia which is within the Pleroma; another that it announces the mother outside the Pleroma; while another will mention the God who made the world (the Demiurge). Such are the variations existing among them with regard to one [passage], holding discordant opinions as to the same Scriptures; and when the same identical passage is read out, they all begin to purse up their eyebrows, and to shake their heads, and they say that they might indeed utter a discourse transcendently lofty, but that all cannot comprehend the greatness of that thought which is implied in it; and that, therefore, among the wise the chief thing is silence. For that Sige (*silence*) which is above must be typified by that silence which they preserve. Thus do they, as many as they are, all depart [from each other], holding so many opinions as to one thing, and bearing about their clever notions in secret within themselves. When, therefore, they shall have agreed among themselves as to the things predicted in the Scriptures, then also shall they be confuted by us. For, though holding wrong opinions, they do in the meanwhile, however, convict themselves, since they are not of one mind with regard to the same words. But as we follow for our teacher the one and only true God, and possess His words as the rule of truth, we do all speak alike with regard to the same things, knowing but one God, the Creator of this universe, who sent the prophets, who led forth the people from the land of Egypt, who in these last times manifested His own Son, that He might put the unbelievers to confusion, and search out the fruit of righteousness.

CHAP. XXXVI. — THE PROPHETS WERE SENT FROM ONE AND THE SAME FATHER FROM WHOM THE SON WAS SENT.

1. Which [God] the Lord does not reject, nor does He say that the prophets [spake] from another god than His Father; nor from any other essence, but from one and the same Father; nor that any other being made the things in the world, except His own Father, when He speaks as follows in His teaching: "There was a certain householder, and he planted a vineyard, and hedged it round about, and digged in it a winepress, and built a tower, and let it out to husbandmen, and went into a far country: And when the time of the fruit drew near, he sent his servants unto the husbandmen, that they might receive the fruits of it. And the husbandmen took his servants: they cut one to pieces, stoned another, and killed another. Again he sent other servants more than the first: and they did unto them likewise. But last of all he sent unto them his only son, saying, Perchance they will reverence my son. But when the husbandmen saw the son, they said among themselves, This is the heir; come, let us kill him, and we shall possess his inheritance. And they caught him, and cast him out of the vineyard, and slew him. When, therefore, the lord of the vineyard shall come, what will he do unto these husbandmen? They say unto him, He will miserably destroy these wicked men, and will let out his vineyard to other husbandmen, who shall render him the fruits in their season."[3] Again does the Lord say: "Have ye never read, The stone which the builders rejected, the same is become the head of the corner: this is the Lord's doing, and it is marvellous in our eyes? Therefore I say unto you, That the kingdom of God shall be taken from you, and given to a nation bringing forth the fruits thereof."[4] By these words He clearly points out to His disciples one and the same Householder — that is, one God the Father, who made all things by Himself; while [He shows] that there are various husbandmen, some obstinate, and proud, and worthless, and slayers of the Lord, but others who render Him, with all obedience, the fruits

---

[1] Book i. p. 334, this volume.
[2] Illorum; following the Greek form of the comparative degree.
[3] Matt. xxi. 33-41.
[4] Matt. xxi. 42-44.

in their seasons; and that it is the same Householder who sends at one time His servants, at another His Son. From that Father, therefore, from whom the Son was sent to those husbandmen who slew Him, from Him also were the servants [sent]. But the Son, as coming from the Father with supreme authority (*principali auctoritate*), used to express Himself thus: "But I say unto you."[1] The servants, again, [who came] as from their Lord, spake after the manner of servants, [delivering a message]; and they therefore used to say, "Thus saith the Lord."

2. Whom these men did therefore preach to the unbelievers as Lord, Him did Christ teach to those who obey Him; and the God who had called those of the former dispensation, is the same as He who has received those of the latter. In other words, He who at first used that law which entails bondage, is also He who did in after times [call His people] by means of adoption. For God planted the vineyard of the human race when at the first He formed Adam and chose the fathers; then He let it out to husbandmen when He established the Mosaic dispensation: He hedged it round about, that is, He gave particular instructions with regard to their worship: He built a tower, [that is], He chose Jerusalem: He digged a winepress, that is, He prepared a receptacle of the prophetic Spirit. And thus did He send prophets prior to the transmigration to Babylon, and after that event others again in greater number than the former, to seek the fruits, saying thus to them (the Jews): "Thus saith the LORD, Cleanse your ways and your doings, execute just judgment, and look each one with pity and compassion on his brother: oppress not the widow nor the orphan, the proselyte nor the poor, and let none of you treasure up evil against his brother in your hearts, and love not false swearing. Wash you, make you clean, put away evil from your hearts, learn to do well, seek judgment, protect the oppressed, judge the fatherless (*pupillo*), plead for the widow; and come, let us reason together, saith the LORD."[2] And again: "Keep thy tongue from evil, and thy lips that they speak no guile; depart from evil, and do good; seek peace, and pursue it."[3] In preaching these things, the prophets sought the fruits of righteousness. But last of all He sent to those unbelievers His own Son, our Lord Jesus Christ, whom the wicked husbandmen cast out of the vineyard when they had slain Him. Wherefore the Lord God did even give it up (no longer hedged around, but thrown open throughout all the world) to other husbandmen, who render the fruits in their seasons, — the beautiful elect tower being also raised everywhere. For the illustrious Church is [now] everywhere, and everywhere is the winepress digged: because those who do receive the Spirit are everywhere. For inasmuch as the former have rejected the Son of God, and cast Him out of the vineyard when they slew Him, God has justly rejected them, and given to the Gentiles outside the vineyard the fruits of its cultivation. This is in accordance with what Jeremiah says, "The LORD hath rejected and cast off the nation which does these things; for the children of Judah have done evil in my sight, saith the LORD."[4] And again in like manner does Jeremiah speak: "I set watchmen over you; hearken to the sound of the trumpet; and they said, We will not hearken. Therefore have the Gentiles heard, and they who feed the flocks in them."[5] It is therefore one and the same Father who planted the vineyard, who led forth the people, who sent the prophets, who sent His own Son, and who gave the vineyard to those other husbandmen that render the fruits in their season.

3. And therefore did the Lord say to His disciples, to make us become good workmen: "Take heed to yourselves, and watch continually upon every occasion, lest at any time your hearts be overcharged with surfeiting and drunkenness, and cares of this life, and that day shall come upon you unawares; for as a snare shall it come upon all dwelling upon the face of the earth."[6] "Let your loins, therefore, be girded about, and your lights burning, and ye like to men who wait for their lord, when he shall return from the wedding."[7] "For as it was in the days of Noe, they did eat and drink, they bought and sold, they married and were given in marriage, and they knew not, until Noe entered into the ark, and the flood came and destroyed them all; as also it was in the days of Lot, they did eat and drink, they bought and sold, they planted and builded, until the time that Lot went out of Sodom; it rained fire from heaven, and destroyed them all: so shall it also be at the coming of the Son of man."[8] "Watch ye therefore, for ye know not in what day your Lord shall come."[9] [In these passages] He declares one and the same Lord, who in the times of Noah brought the deluge because of men's disobedience, and who also in the days of Lot rained fire from heaven because of the multitude of sinners among the Sodomites, and who, on account of this same disobedience and similar sins, will bring on the day of judgment at the end of

---

[1] Matt. v. 22.
[2] Jer. vii. 3; Zech. vii. 9, 10, viii. 17; Isa. i. 17-19.
[3] Ps. xxxiv. 13, 14.
[4] Jer. vii. 29, 30.
[5] Jer. vi. 17, 18.
[6] Luke xxi. 34, 35.
[7] Luke xii. 35, 36.
[8] Luke xvii. 26, etc.
[9] Matt. xxiv. 42.

time (*in novissimo*); on which day He declares that it shall be more tolerable for Sodom and Gomorrah than for that city and house which shall not receive the word of His apostles. "And thou, Capernaum," He said, "is it that thou shalt be exalted to heaven?[1] Thou shalt go down to hell. For if the mighty works which have been done in thee had been done in Sodom, it would have remained unto this day. Verily I say unto you, that it shall be more tolerable for Sodom in the day of judgment than for you."[2]

4. Since the Son of God is always one and the same, He gives to those who believe on Him a well of water[3] [springing up] to eternal life, but He causes the unfruitful fig-tree immediately to dry up; and in the days of Noah He justly brought on the deluge for the purpose of extinguishing that most infamous race of men then existent, who could not bring forth fruit to God, since the angels that sinned had commingled with them, and [acted as He did] in order that He might put a check upon the sins of these men, but [that at the same time] He might preserve the archetype,[4] the formation of Adam. And it was He who rained fire and brimstone from heaven, in the days of Lot, upon Sodom and Gomorrah, "an example of the righteous judgment of God,"[5] that all may know, "that every tree that bringeth not forth good fruit shall be cut down, and cast into the fire."[6] And it is He who uses [the words], that it will be more tolerable for Sodom in the general judgment than for those who beheld His wonders, and did not believe on Him, nor receive His doctrine.[7] For as He gave by His advent a greater privilege to those who believed on Him, and who do His will, so also did He point out that those who did not believe on Him should have a more severe punishment in the judgment; thus extending equal justice to all, and being to exact more from those to whom He gives the more; the more, however, not because He reveals the knowledge of another Father, as I have shown so fully and so repeatedly, but because He has, by means of His advent, poured upon the human race the greater gift of paternal grace.

5. If, however, what I have stated be insufficient to convince any one that the prophets were sent from one and the same Father, from whom also our Lord was sent, let such a one, opening the mouth of his heart, and calling upon the Master, Christ Jesus the Lord, listen to Him when He says, "The kingdom of heaven is like unto a king who made a marriage for his son, and he sent forth his servants to call them who were bidden to the marriage." And when they would not obey, He goes on to say, "Again he sent other servants, saying, Tell them that are bidden, Come ye, I have prepared my dinner; my oxen and all the fatlings are killed, and everything is ready; come unto the wedding. But they made light of it, and went their way, some to their farm, and others to their merchandize; but the remnant took his servants, and some they treated despitefully, while others they slew. But when the king heard this, he was wroth, and sent his armies and destroyed these murderers, and burned up their city, and said to his servants, The wedding is indeed ready, but they which were bidden were not worthy. Go out therefore into the highways, and as many as ye shall find, gather in to the marriage. So the servants went out, and collected together as many as they found, bad and good, and the wedding was furnished with guests. But when the king came in to see the guests, he saw there a man not having on a wedding garment; and he said unto him, Friend, how camest thou hither, not having on a wedding garment? But he was speechless. Then said the king to his servants, Take him away, hand and foot, and cast him into outer darkness: there shall be weeping and gnashing of teeth. For many are called, but few are chosen."[8] Now, by these words of His, does the Lord clearly show all [these points, viz.,] that there is one King and Lord, the Father of all, of whom He had previously said, "Neither shalt thou swear by Jerusalem, for it is the city of the great King;"[9] and that He had from the beginning prepared the marriage for His Son, and used, with the utmost kindness, to call, by the instrumentality of His servants, the men of the former dispensation to the wedding feast; and when they would not obey, He still invited them by sending out other servants, yet that even then they did not obey Him, but even stoned and slew those who brought them the message of invitation. He accordingly sent forth His armies and destroyed them, and burned down their city; but He called together from all the highways, that is, from all nations, [guests] to the marriage feast of His Son, as also He says by Jeremiah: "I have sent also unto you my servants the prophets to say, Return ye now, every man, from

---

[1] No other of the Greek Fathers quotes this text as above; from which fact Grabe infers that the old Latin translator, or his transcribers, altered the words of Irenæus [N.B. — From one example infer the rest] to suit the Latin versions.
[2] Matt. xi. 23, 24.
[3] John iv. 14.
[4] This is Massuet's conjectural emendation of the text, viz., *archetypum* for *arcœtypum*. Grabe would insert *per* before *arcœ*, and he thinks the passage to have a reference to 1 Pet. iii. 20. Irenæus, in common with the other ancient Fathers, believed that the fallen angels were the "sons of God" who commingled with "the daughters of men," and thus produced a race of spurious men. [Gen. vi. 1, 2, 3, and Josephus.]
[5] Jude 7. [And note "strange flesh" (Gr. σαρκὸς ἑτέρας) as to the angels. Gen. xix. 4, 5.]
[6] Matt. iii. 10.
[7] Matt. xi. 24; Luke x. 12.
[8] Matt. xxii. 1, etc.
[9] Matt. v. 35. Instead of placing a period here, as the editors do, it seems to us preferable to carry on the construction.

his very evil way, and amend your doings."[1] And again He says by the same prophet: "I have also sent unto you my servants the prophets throughout the day and before the light; yet they did not obey me, nor incline their ears unto me. And thou shalt speak this word to them: This is a people that obeyeth not the voice of the Lord, nor receiveth correction; faith has perished from their mouth."[2] The Lord, therefore, who has called us everywhere by the apostles, is He who called those of old by the prophets, as appears by the words of the Lord; and although they preached to various nations, the prophets were not from one God, and the apostles from another; but, [proceeding] from one and the same, some of them announced the Lord, others preached the Father, and others again foretold the advent of the Son of God, while yet others declared Him as already present to those who then were afar off.

6. Still further did He also make it manifest, that we ought, after our calling, to be also adorned with works of righteousness, so that the Spirit of God may rest upon us; for this is the wedding garment, of which also the apostle speaks, "Not for that we would be unclothed, but clothed upon, that mortality might be swallowed up by immortality."[3] But those who have indeed been called to God's supper, yet have not received the Holy Spirit, because of their wicked conduct "shall be," He declares, "cast into outer darkness."[4] He thus clearly shows that the very same King who gathered from all quarters the faithful to the marriage of His Son, and who grants them the incorruptible banquet, [also] orders that man to be cast into outer darkness who has not on a wedding garment, that is, one who despises it. For as in the former covenant, "with many of them was He not well pleased;"[5] so also is it the case here, that "many are called, but few chosen."[6] It is not, then, one God who judges, and another Father who calls us together to salvation; nor one, forsooth, who confers eternal light, but another who orders those who have not on the wedding garment to be sent into outer darkness. But it is one and the same God, the Father of our Lord, from whom also the prophets had their mission, who does indeed, through His infinite kindness, call the unworthy; but He examines those who are called, [to ascertain] if they have on the garment fit and proper for the marriage of His Son, because nothing unbecoming or evil pleases Him. This is in accordance with what the Lord said to the man who had been healed: "Behold, thou art made whole; sin no more, lest a worse thing come unto thee."[7] For he who is good, and righteous, and pure, and spotless, will endure nothing evil, nor unjust, nor detestable in His wedding chamber. This is the Father of our Lord, by whose providence all things consist, and all are administered by His command; and He confers His free gifts upon those who should [receive them]; but the most righteous Retributor metes out [punishment] according to their deserts, most deservedly, to the ungrateful and to those that are insensible of His kindness; and therefore does He say, "He sent His armies, and destroyed those murderers, and burned up their city."[8] He says here, "His armies," because all men are the property of God. For "the earth is the Lord's, and the fulness thereof; the world, and all that dwell therein."[9] Wherefore also the Apostle Paul says in the Epistle to the Romans, "For there is no power but of God; the powers that be are ordained of God. Whosoever resisteth the power, resisteth the ordinance of God; and they that resist shall receive unto themselves condemnation. For rulers are not for a terror to a good work, but to an evil. Wilt thou then not be afraid of the power? Do that which is good, and thou shalt have praise of the same; for he is the minister of God to thee for good. But if thou do that which is evil, be afraid; for he beareth not the sword in vain: for he is the minister of God, the avenger for wrath upon him that doeth evil. Wherefore ye must needs be subject, not only for wrath, but also for conscience sake. For this cause pay ye tribute also; for they are God's ministers, attending continually upon this very thing."[10] Both the Lord, then, and the apostles announce as the one only God the Father, Him who gave the law, who sent the prophets, who made all things; and therefore does He say, "He sent His armies," because every man, inasmuch as he is a man, is His workmanship, although he may be ignorant of his God. For He gives existence to all; He, "who maketh His sun to rise upon the evil and the good, and sendeth rain upon the just and unjust."[11]

7. And not alone by what has been stated, but also by the parable of the two sons, the younger of whom consumed his substance by living luxuriously with harlots, did the Lord teach one and the same Father, who did not even allow a kid to his elder son; but for him who had been lost, [namely] his younger son, he ordered the fatted calf to be killed, and he gave him the best robe.[12]

---

[1] Jer. xxxv. 15.
[2] Jer. vii. 25, etc.
[3] 2 Cor. v. 4.
[4] Matt. xxii. 13.
[5] 1 Cor. x. 5.
[6] Matt. xxii. 14.
[7] John v. 14.
[8] Matt. xxii. 7.
[9] Ps. xxiv. 1.
[10] Rom. xiii. 1-7.
[11] Matt. v. 45.
[12] Luke xv. 11.

Also by the parable of the workmen who were sent into the vineyard at different periods of the day, one and the same God is declared[1] as having called some in the beginning, when the world was first created; but others afterwards, and others during the intermediate period, others after a long lapse of time, and others again in the end of time; so that there are many workmen in their generations, but only one householder who calls them together. For there is but one vineyard, since there is also but one righteousness, and one dispensator, for there is one Spirit of God who arranges all things; and in like manner is there one hire, for they all received a penny each man, having [stamped upon it] the royal image and superscription, the knowledge of the Son of God, which is immortality. And therefore He began by giving the hire to those [who were engaged] last, because in the last times, when the Lord was revealed, He presented Himself to all [as their reward].

8. Then, in the case of the publican, who excelled the Pharisee in prayer, [we find] that it was not because he worshipped another Father that he received testimony from the Lord that he was justified rather [than the other]; but because with great humility, apart from all boasting and pride, he made confession to the same God.[2] The parable of the two sons also: those who are sent into the vineyard, of whom one indeed opposed his father, but afterwards repented, when repentance profited him nothing; the other, however, promised to go, at once assuring his father, but he did not go (for " every man is a liar;"[3] "to will is present with him, but he finds not means to perform"[4]),—[this parable, I say], points out one and the same Father. Then, again, this truth was clearly shown forth by the parable of the fig-tree, of which the Lord says, " Behold, now these three years I come seeking fruit on this fig-tree, but I find none "[5] (pointing onwards, by the prophets, to His advent, by whom He came from time to time, seeking the fruit of righteousness from them, which he did not find), and also by the circumstance that, for the reason already mentioned, the fig-tree should be hewn down. And, without using a parable, the Lord said to Jerusalem, ' O Jerusalem, Jerusalem, thou that killest the prophets, and stonest those that are sent unto thee; how often would I have gathered thy children together, as a hen gathereth her chickens under her wings, and ye would not! Behold, your house shall be left unto you desolate."[6] For that which had been said in the parable, " Behold, for three years I come seeking fruit," and in clear terms, again, [where He says], " How often would I have gathered thy children together," shall be [found] a falsehood, if we do not understand His advent, which is [announced] by the prophets — if, in fact, He came to them but once, and then for the first time. But since He who chose the patriarchs and those [who lived under the first covenant], is the same Word of God who did both visit them through the prophetic Spirit, and us also who have been called together from all quarters by His advent; in addition to what has been already said, He truly declared, " Many shall come from the east and from the west, and shall recline with Abraham, and Isaac, and Jacob, in the kingdom of heaven. But the children of the kingdom shall go into outer darkness; there shall be weeping and gnashing of teeth."[7] If, then, those who do believe in Him through the preaching of His apostles throughout the east and west shall recline with Abraham, Isaac, and Jacob, in the kingdom of heaven, partaking with them of the [heavenly] banquet, one and the same God is set forth as He who did indeed choose the patriarchs, visited also the people, and called the Gentiles.

CHAP. XXXVII. — MEN ARE POSSESSED OF FREE WILL, AND ENDOWED WITH THE FACULTY OF MAKING A CHOICE. IT IS NOT TRUE, THEREFORE, THAT SOME ARE BY NATURE GOOD, AND OTHERS BAD.

1. This expression [of our Lord], " How often would I have gathered thy children together, and thou wouldest not,"[8] set forth the ancient law of human liberty, because God made man a free [agent] from the beginning, possessing his own power, even as he does his own soul, to obey the behests (*ad utendum sententia*) of God voluntarily, and not by compulsion of God. For there is no coercion with God, but a good will [towards us] is present with Him continually. And therefore does He give good counsel to all. And in man, as well as in angels, He has placed the power of choice (for angels are rational beings), so that those who had yielded obedience might justly possess what is good, given indeed by God, but preserved by themselves. On the other hand, they who have not obeyed shall, with justice, be not found in possession of the good, and shall receive condign punishment: for God did kindly bestow on them what was good; but they themselves did not diligently keep it, nor deem it something precious, but poured contempt upon His super-eminent goodness. Rejecting therefore the good, and as it were spuing it out, they shall all deservedly incur

---

[1] Matt. xx. 1, etc.
[2] Luke xviii. 10.
[3] Ps. cxvi. 2.
[4] Rom. vii. 18.
[5] Luke xiii. 6.
[6] Luke xiii. 34; Matt. xxiii. 37.
[7] Matt. viii. 11, 12.
[8] Matt. xxiii. 37.

the just judgment of God, which also the Apostle Paul testifies in his Epistle to the Romans, where he says, "But dost thou despise the riches of His goodness, and patience, and long-suffering, being ignorant that the goodness of God leadeth thee to repentance? But according to thy hardness and impenitent heart, thou treasurest to thyself wrath against the day of wrath, and the revelation of the righteous judgment of God." "But glory and honour," he says, "to every one that doeth good."[1] God therefore has given that which is good, as the apostle tells us in this Epistle, and they who work it shall receive glory and honour, because they have done that which is good when they had it in their power not to do it; but those who do it not shall receive the just judgment of God, because they did not work good when they had it in their power so to do.

2. But if some had been made by nature bad, and others good, these latter would not be deserving of praise for being good, for such were they created; nor would the former be reprehensible, for thus they were made [originally]. But since all men are of the same nature, able both to hold fast and to do what is good; and, on the other hand, having also the power to cast it from them and not to do it, — some do justly receive praise even among men who are under the control of good laws (and much more from God), and obtain deserved testimony of their choice of good in general, and of persevering therein; but the others are blamed, and receive a just condemnation, because of their rejection of what is fair and good. And therefore the prophets used to exhort men to what was good, to act justly and to work righteousness, as I have so largely demonstrated, because it is in our power so to do, and because by excessive negligence we might become forgetful, and thus stand in need of that good counsel which the good God has given us to know by means of the prophets.

3. For this reason the Lord also said, "Let your light so shine before men, that they may see your good deeds, and glorify your Father who is in heaven."[2] And, "Take heed to yourselves, lest perchance your hearts be overcharged with surfeiting, and drunkenness, and worldly cares."[3] And, "Let your loins be girded about, and your lamps burning, and ye like unto men that wait for their Lord, when He returns from the wedding, that when He cometh and knocketh, they may open to Him. Blessed is that servant whom his Lord, when He cometh, shall find so doing."[4] And again, "The servant who knows his Lord's will, and does it not, shall be beaten with many stripes."[5] And, "Why call ye me, Lord, Lord, and do not the things which I say?"[6] And again, "But if the servant say in his heart, The Lord delayeth, and begin to beat his fellow-servants, and to eat, and drink, and to be drunken, his Lord will come in a day on which he does not expect Him, and shall cut him in sunder, and appoint his portion with the hypocrites."[7] All such passages demonstrate the independent will[8] of man, and at the same time the counsel which God conveys to him, by which He exhorts us to submit ourselves to Him, and seeks to turn us away from [the sin of] unbelief against Him, without, however, in any way coercing us.

4. No doubt, if any one is unwilling to follow the Gospel itself, it is in his power [to reject it], but it is not expedient. For it is in man's power to disobey God, and to forfeit what is good; but [such conduct] brings no small amount of injury and mischief. And on this account Paul says, "All things are lawful to me, but all things are not expedient;"[9] referring both to the liberty of man, in which respect "all things are lawful," God exercising no compulsion in regard to him; and [by the expression] "not expedient" pointing out that we "should not use our liberty as a cloak of maliciousness,"[10] for this is not expedient. And again he says, "Speak ye every man truth with his neighbour."[11] And, "Let no corrupt communication proceed out of your mouth, neither filthiness, nor foolish talking, nor scurrility, which are not convenient, but rather giving of thanks."[12] And, "For ye were sometimes darkness, but now are ye light in the Lord; walk honestly as children of the light, not in rioting and drunkenness, not in chambering and wantonness, not in anger and jealousy. And such were some of you; but ye have been washed, but ye have been sanctified in the name of our Lord."[13] If then it were not in our power to do or not to do these things, what reason had the apostle, and much more the Lord Himself, to give us counsel to do some things, and to abstain from others? But because man is possessed of free will from the beginning, and God is possessed of free will, in whose likeness man was created, advice is always given to him to keep fast the good, which thing is done by means of obedience to God.

5. And not merely in works, but also in faith, has God preserved the will of man free and under his own control, saying, "According to thy faith

---

[1] Rom. ii. 4, 5, 7.
[2] Matt. v. 16.
[3] Luke xxi. 34.
[4] Luke xii. 35, 36.
[5] Luke xii. 47.
[6] Luke vi. 46.
[7] Luke xii. 45 46; Matt. xxiv. 48 51.
[8] τὸ αὐτεξούσιον.
[9] 1 Cor. vi. 12.
[10] 1 Pet. ii. 16.
[11] Eph. iv. 25.
[12] Eph. iv. 29.
[13] 1 Cor. vi. 11.

be it unto thee;"[1] thus showing that there is a faith specially belonging to man, since he has an opinion specially his own. And again, "All things are possible to him that believeth;"[2] and, "Go thy way; and as thou hast believed, so be it done unto thee."[3] Now all such expressions demonstrate that man is in his own power with respect to faith. And for this reason, "he that believeth in Him has eternal life; while he who believeth not the Son hath not eternal life, but the wrath of God shall remain upon him."[4] In the same manner therefore the Lord, both showing His own goodness, and indicating that man is in his own free will and his own power, said to Jerusalem, "How often have I wished to gather thy children together, as a hen [gathereth] her chickens under her wings, and ye would not! Wherefore your house shall be left unto you desolate."[5]

6. Those, again, who maintain the opposite to these [conclusions], do themselves present the Lord as destitute of power, as if, forsooth, He were unable to accomplish what He willed; or, on the other hand, as being ignorant that they were by nature "material," as these men express it, and such as cannot receive His immortality. "But He should not," say they, "have created angels of such a nature that they were capable of transgression, nor men who immediately proved ungrateful towards Him; for they were made rational beings, endowed with the power of examining and judging, and were not [formed] as things irrational or of a [merely] animal nature, which can do nothing of their own will, but are drawn by necessity and compulsion to what is good, in which things there is one mind and one usage, working mechanically in one groove (*inflexibiles et sine judicio*), who are incapable of being anything else except just what they had been created." But upon this supposition, neither would what is good be grateful to them, nor communion with God be precious, nor would the good be very much to be sought after, which would present itself without their own proper endeavour, care, or study, but would be implanted of its own accord and without their concern. Thus it would come to pass, that their being good would be of no consequence, because they were so by nature rather than by will, and are possessors of good spontaneously, not by choice; and for this reason they would not understand this fact, that good is a comely thing, nor would they take pleasure in it. For how can those who are ignorant of good enjoy it? Or what credit is it to those who have not aimed at it? And what crown is it to those who have not followed in pursuit of it, like those victorious in the contest?

7. On this account, too, did the Lord assert that the kingdom of heaven was the portion of "the violent;" and He says, "The violent take it by force;"[6] that is, those who by strength and earnest striving are on the watch to snatch it away on the moment. On this account also Paul the Apostle says to the Corinthians, "Know ye not, that they who run in a racecourse, do all indeed run, but one receiveth the prize? So run, that ye may obtain. Every one also who engages in the contest is temperate in all things: now these men [do it] that they may obtain a corruptible crown, but we an incorruptible. But I so run, not as uncertainty; I fight, not as one beating the air; but I make my body livid, and bring it into subjection, lest by any means, when preaching to others, I may myself be rendered a castaway."[7] This able wrestler, therefore, exhorts us to the struggle for immortality, that we may be crowned, and may deem the crown precious, namely, that which is acquired by our struggle, but which does not encircle us of its own accord (*sed non ultro coalitam*). And the harder we strive, so much is it the more valuable; while so much the more valuable it is, so much the more should we esteem it. And indeed those things are not esteemed so highly which come spontaneously, as those which are reached by much anxious care. Since, then, this power has been conferred upon us, both the Lord has taught and the apostle has enjoined us the more to love God, that we may reach this [prize] for ourselves by striving after it. For otherwise, no doubt, this our good would be [virtually] irrational, because not the result of trial. Moreover, the faculty of seeing would not appear to be so desirable, unless we had known what a loss it were to be devoid of sight; and health, too, is rendered all the more estimable by an acquaintance with disease; light, also, by contrasting it with darkness; and life with death. Just in the same way is the heavenly kingdom honourable to those who have known the earthly one. But in proportion as it is more honourable, so much the more do we prize it; and if we have prized it more, we shall be the more glorious in the presence of God. The Lord has therefore endured all these things on our behalf, in order that we, having been instructed by means of them all, may be in all respects circumspect for the time to come, and that, having been rationally taught to love God, we may continue in His perfect love: for God has displayed long-suffering in the case of man's apostasy; while man has been instructed by means of it, as also the prophet says, "Thine own apostasy shall heal thee;"[8] God thus determining all things beforehand for the

---

[1] Matt. ix. 29.
[2] Mark ix. 23.
[3] Matt. viii. 13.
[4] John iii. 36.
[5] Matt. xxiii. 37, 38.
[6] Matt. xi. 12.
[7] 1 Cor. ix. 24–27.
[8] Jer. ii. 19.

bringing of man to perfection, for his edification, and for the revelation of His dispensations, that goodness may both be made apparent, and righteousness perfected, and that the Church may be fashioned after the image of His Son, and that man may finally be brought to maturity at some future time, becoming ripe through such privileges to see and comprehend God.[1]

CHAP. XXXVIII. — WHY MAN WAS NOT MADE PERFECT FROM THE BEGINNING.

1. If, however, any one say, "What then? Could not God have exhibited man as perfect from the beginning?" let him know that, inasmuch as God is indeed always the same and unbegotten as respects Himself, all things are possible to Him. But created things must be inferior to Him who created them, from the very fact of their later origin; for it was not possible for things recently created to have been uncreated. But inasmuch as they are not uncreated, for this very reason do they come short of the perfect. Because, as these things are of later date, so are they infantile; so are they unaccustomed to, and unexercised in, perfect discipline. For as it certainly is in the power of a mother to give strong food to her infant, [but she does not do so], as the child is not yet able to receive more substantial nourishment; so also it was possible for God Himself to have made man perfect from the first, but man could not receive this [perfection], being as yet an infant. And for this cause our Lord, in these last times, when He had summed up all things into Himself, came to us, not as He might have come, but as we were capable of beholding Him. He might easily have come to us in His immortal glory, but in that case we could never have endured the greatness of the glory; and therefore it was that He, who was the perfect bread of the Father, offered Himself to us as milk, [because we were] as infants. He did this when He appeared as a man, that we, being nourished, as it were, from the breast of His flesh, and having, by such a course of milk-nourishment, become accustomed to eat and drink the Word of God, may be able also to contain in ourselves the Bread of immortality, which is the Spirit of the Father.

2. And on this account does Paul declare to the Corinthians, "I have fed you with milk, not with meat, for hitherto ye were not able to bear it."[2] That is, ye have indeed learned the advent of our Lord as a man; nevertheless, because of your infirmity, the Spirit of the Father has not as yet rested upon you. "For when envying and strife," he says, "and dissensions are among you, are ye not carnal, and walk as men?"[3] That is, that the Spirit of the Father was not yet with them, on account of their imperfection and shortcomings of their walk in life. As, therefore, the apostle had the power to give them strong meat — for those upon whom the apostles laid hands received the Holy Spirit, who is the food of life [eternal] — but they were not capable of receiving it, because they had the sentient faculties of the soul still feeble and undisciplined in the practice of things pertaining to God; so, in like manner, God had power at the beginning to grant perfection to man; but as the latter was only recently created, he could not possibly have received it, or even if he had received it, could he have contained it, or containing it, could he have retained it. It was for this reason that the Son of God, although He was perfect, passed through the state of infancy in common with the rest of mankind, partaking of it thus not for His own benefit, but for that of the infantile stage of man's existence, in order that man might be able to receive Him. There was nothing, therefore, impossible to and deficient in God, [implied in the fact] that man was not an uncreated being; but this merely applied to him who was lately created, [namely] man.

3. With God there are simultaneously exhibited power, wisdom, and goodness. His power and goodness [appear] in this, that of His own will He called into being and fashioned things having no previous existence; His wisdom [is shown] in His having made created things parts of one harmonious and consistent whole; and those things which, through His super-eminent kindness, receive growth and a long period of existence, do reflect the glory of the uncreated One, of that God who bestows what is good ungrudgingly. For from the very fact of these things having been created, [it follows] that they are not uncreated; but by their continuing in being throughout a long course of ages, they shall receive a faculty of the Uncreated, through the gratuitous bestowal of eternal existence upon them by God. And thus in all things God has the pre-eminence, who alone is uncreated, the first of all things, and the primary cause of the existence of all, while all other things remain under God's subjection. But being in subjection to God is continuance in immortality, and immortality is the glory of the uncreated One. By this arrangement, therefore, and these harmonies, and a sequence of this nature, man, a created and organized being, is rendered after the image and likeness of the uncreated God, — the Father planning everything well and giving His commands, the Son carrying these into exe-

---

[1] [If we but had the original, this would doubtless be found in all respects a noble specimen of primitive theology.]
[2] 1 Cor. iii. 2.
[3] 1 Cor. iii. 3.

cution and performing the work of creating, and the Spirit nourishing and increasing [what is made], but man making progress day by day, and ascending towards the perfect, that is, approximating to the uncreated One. For the Uncreated is perfect, that is, God. Now it was necessary that man should in the first instance be created; and having been created, should receive growth; and having received growth, should be strengthened; and having been strengthened, should abound; and having abounded, should recover [from the disease of sin]; and having recovered, should be glorified; and being glorified, should see his Lord. For God is He who is yet to be seen, and the beholding of God is productive of immortality, but immortality renders one nigh unto God.

4. Irrational, therefore, in every respect, are they who await not the time of increase, but ascribe to God the infirmity of their nature. Such persons know neither God nor themselves, being insatiable and ungrateful, unwilling to be at the outset what they have also been created — men subject to passions; but go beyond the law of the human race, and before that they become men, they wish to be even now like God their Creator, and they who are more destitute of reason than dumb animals [insist] that there is no distinction between the uncreated God and man, a creature of to-day. For these, [the dumb animals], bring no charge against God for not having made them men; but each one, just as he has been created, gives thanks that he has been created. For we cast blame upon Him, because we have not been made gods from the beginning, but at first merely men, then at length gods; although God has adopted this course out of His pure benevolence, that no one may impute to Him invidiousness or grudgingness. He declares, "I have said, Ye are gods; and ye are all sons of the Highest." [1] But since we could not sustain the power of divinity, He adds, "But ye shall die like men," setting forth both truths — the kindness of His free gift, and our weakness, and also that we were possessed of power over ourselves. For after His great kindness He graciously conferred good [upon us], and made men like to Himself, [that is] in their own power; while at the same time by His prescience He knew the infirmity of human beings, and the consequences which would flow from it; but through [His] love and [His] power, He shall overcome the substance of created nature.[2] For it was necessary, at first, that nature should be exhibited; then, after that, that what was mortal should be conquered and swallowed up by immortality, and the corruptible by incorruptibility, and that man should be made after the image and likeness of God, having received the knowledge of good and evil.

CHAP. XXXIX. — MAN IS ENDOWED WITH THE FACULTY OF DISTINGUISHING GOOD AND EVIL; SO THAT, WITHOUT COMPULSION, HE HAS THE POWER, BY HIS OWN WILL AND CHOICE, TO PERFORM GOD'S COMMANDMENTS, BY DOING WHICH HE AVOIDS THE EVILS PREPARED FOR THE REBELLIOUS.

1. Man has received the knowledge of good and evil. It is good to obey God, and to believe in Him, and to keep His commandment, and this is the life of man; as not to obey God is evil, and this is his death. Since God, therefore, gave [to man] such mental power (*magnanimitatem*) man knew both the good of obedience and the evil of disobedience, that the eye of the mind, receiving experience of both, may with judgment make choice of the better things; and that he may never become indolent or neglectful of God's command; and learning by experience that it is an evil thing which deprives him of life, that is, disobedience to God, may never attempt it at all, but that, knowing that what preserves his life, namely, obedience to God, is good, he may diligently keep it with all earnestness. Wherefore he has also had a twofold experience, possessing knowledge of both kinds, that with dicipline he may make choice of the better things. But how, if he had no knowledge of the contrary, could he have had instruction in that which is good? For there is thus a surer and an undoubted comprehension of matters submitted to us than the mere surmise arising from an opinion regarding them. For just as the tongue receives experience of sweet and bitter by means of tasting, and the eye discriminates between black and white by means of vision, and the ear recognises the distinctions of sounds by hearing; so also does the mind, receiving through the experience of both the knowledge of what is good, become more tenacious of its preservation, by acting in obedience to God: in the first place, casting away, by means of repentance, disobedience, as being something disagreeable and nauseous; and afterwards coming to understand what it really is, that it is contrary to goodness and sweetness, so that the mind may never even attempt to taste disobedience to God. But if any one do shun the knowledge of both these kinds of things, and the twofold perception of knowledge, he unawares divests himself of the character of a human being.

2. How, then, shall he be a God, who has not as yet been made a man? Or how can he be perfect who was but lately created? How, again, can he be immortal, who in his mortal nature

---

[1] Ps. lxxxii. 6, 7.
[2] That is, that man's human nature should not prevent him from becoming a partaker of the divine.

did not obey his Maker? For it must be that thou, at the outset, shouldest hold the rank of a man, and then afterwards partake of the glory of God. For thou dost not make God, but God thee. If, then, thou art God's workmanship, await the hand of thy Maker which creates everything in due time; in due time as far as thou art concerned, whose creation is being carried out.[1] Offer to Him thy heart in a soft and tractable state, and preserve the form in which the Creator has fashioned thee, having moisture in thyself, lest, by becoming hardened, thou lose the impressions of His fingers. But by preserving the framework thou shalt ascend to that which is perfect, for the moist clay which is in thee is hidden [there] by the workmanship of God. His hand fashioned thy substance; He will cover thee over [too] within and without with pure gold and silver, and He will adorn thee to such a degree, that even "the King Himself shall have pleasure in thy beauty."[2] But if thou, being obstinately hardened, dost reject the operation of His skill, and show thyself ungrateful towards Him, because thou wert created a [mere] man, by becoming thus ungrateful to God, thou hast at once lost both His workmanship and life. For creation is an attribute of the goodness of God; but to be created is that of human nature. If, then, thou shalt deliver up to Him what is thine, that is, faith towards Him and subjection, thou shalt receive His handiwork, and shalt be a perfect work of God.

3. If, however, thou wilt not believe in Him, and wilt flee from His hands, the cause of imperfection shall be in thee who didst not obey, but not in Him who called [thee]. For He commissioned [messengers] to call people to the marriage, but they who did not obey Him deprived themselves of the royal supper.[3] The skill of God, therefore, is not defective, for He has power of the stones to raise up children to Abraham;[4] but the man who does not obtain it, is the cause to himself of his own imperfection. Nor, [in like manner], does the light fail because of those who have blinded themselves; but while it remains the same as ever, those who are [thus] blinded are involved in darkness through their own fault. The light does never enslave any one by necessity; nor, again, does God exercise compulsion upon any one unwilling to accept the exercise of His skill. Those persons, therefore, who have apostatized from the light given by the Father, and transgressed the law of liberty, have done so through their own fault, since they have been created free agents, and possessed of power over themselves.

4. But God, foreknowing all things, prepared fit habitations for both, kindly conferring that light which they desire on those who seek after the light of incorruption, and resort to it; but for the despisers and mockers who avoid and turn themselves away from this light, and who do, as it were, blind themselves, He has prepared darkness suitable to persons who oppose the light, and He has inflicted an appropriate punishment upon those who try to avoid being subject to Him. Submission to God is eternal rest, so that they who shun the light have a place worthy of their flight; and those who fly from eternal rest, have a habitation in accordance with their fleeing. Now, since all good things are with God, they who by their own determination fly from God, do defraud themselves of all good things; and having been [thus] defrauded of all good things with respect to God, they shall consequently fall under the just judgment of God. For those persons who shun rest shall justly incur punishment, and those who avoid the light shall justly dwell in darkness. For as in the case of this temporal light, those who shun it do deliver themselves over to darkness, so that they do themselves become the cause to themselves that they are destitute of light, and do inhabit darkness; and, as I have already observed, the light is not the cause of such an [unhappy] condition of existence to them; so those who fly from the eternal light of God, which contains in itself all good things, are themselves the cause to themselves of their inhabiting eternal darkness, destitute of all good things, having become to themselves the cause of [their consignment to] an abode of that nature.

CHAP. XL.—ONE AND THE SAME GOD THE FATHER INFLICTS PUNISHMENT ON THE REPROBATE, AND BESTOWS REWARDS ON THE ELECT.

1. It is therefore one and the same God the Father who has prepared good things with Himself for those who desire His fellowship, and who remain in subjection to Him; and who has prepared the eternal fire for the ringleader of the apostasy, the devil, and those who revolted with him, into which [fire] the Lord[5] has declared those men shall be sent who have been set apart by themselves on His left hand. And this is what has been spoken by the prophet, "I am a jealous God, making peace, and creating evil things;"[6] thus making peace and friendship with those who repent and turn to Him, and bringing [them to] unity, but preparing for the impenitent, those who shun the light, eternal fire and outer darkness, which are evils indeed to those persons who fall into them.

---

[1] Efficeris.
[2] Ps. xlv. 11.
[3] Matt. xxii. 3, etc.
[4] Matt. iii. 9.
[5] Matt. xxv. 41.
[6] Isa. xlv. 7.

2. If, however, it were truly one Father who confers rest, and another God who has prepared the fire, their sons would have been equally different [one from the other]; one, indeed, sending [men] into the Father's kingdom, but the other into eternal fire. But inasmuch as one and the same Lord has pointed out that the whole human race shall be divided at the judgment, "as a shepherd divideth the sheep from the goats,"[1] and that to some He will say, "Come, ye blessed of My Father, receive the kingdom which has been prepared for you,"[2] but to others, "Depart from me, ye cursed, into everlasting fire, which My Father has prepared for the devil and his angels,"[3] one and the same Father is manifestly declared [in this passage], "making peace and creating evil things," preparing fit things for both; as also there is one Judge sending both into a fit place, as the Lord sets forth in the parable of the tares and the wheat, where He says, "As therefore the tares are gathered together, and burned in the fire, so shall it be at the end of the world. The Son of man shall send His angels, and they shall gather from His kingdom everything that offendeth, and those who work iniquity, and shall send them into a furnace of fire: there shall be weeping and gnashing of teeth. Then shall the just shine forth as the sun in the kingdom of their Father."[4] The Father, therefore, who has prepared the kingdom for the righteous, into which the Son has received those worthy of it, is He who has also prepared the furnace of fire, into which these angels commissioned by the Son of man shall send those persons who deserve it, according to God's command.

3. The Lord, indeed, sowed good seed in His own field;[5] and He says, "The field is the world." But while men slept, the enemy came, and "sowed tares in the midst of the wheat, and went his way."[6] Hence we learn that this was the apostate angel and the enemy, because he was envious of God's workmanship, and took in hand to render this [workmanship] an enmity with God. For this cause also God has banished from His presence him who did of his own accord stealthily sow the tares, that is, him who brought about the transgression;[7] but He took compassion upon man, who, through want of care no doubt, but still wickedly [on the part of another], became involved in disobedience; and He turned the enmity by which [the devil] had designed to make [man] the enemy of God, against the author of it, by removing His own anger from man, turning it in another direction, and sending it instead upon the serpent. As also the Scripture tells us that God said to the serpent, "And I will place enmity between thee and the woman, and between thy seed and her seed. He[8] shall bruise thy head, and thou shalt bruise his heel."[9] And the Lord summed up in Himself this enmity, when He was made man from a woman, and trod upon his [the serpent's] head, as I have pointed out in the preceding book.

CHAP. XLI. — THOSE PERSONS WHO DO NOT BELIEVE IN GOD, BUT WHO ARE DISOBEDIENT, ARE ANGELS AND SONS OF THE DEVIL, NOT INDEED BY NATURE, BUT BY IMITATION. CLOSE OF THIS BOOK, AND SCOPE OF THE SUCCEEDING ONE.

1. Inasmuch as the Lord has said that there are certain angels, [viz., those] of the devil, for whom eternal fire is prepared; and as, again, He declares with regard to the tares, "The tares are the children of the wicked one,"[10] it must be affirmed that He has ascribed all who are of the apostasy to him who is the ringleader of this transgression. But He made neither angels nor men so by nature. For we do not find that the devil created anything whatsoever, since indeed he is himself a creature of God, like the other angels. For God made all things, as also David says with regard to all things of the kind: "For He spake the word, and they were made; He commanded, and they were created."[11]

2. Since, therefore, all things were made by God, and since the devil has become the cause of apostasy to himself and others, justly does the Scripture always term those who remain in a state of apostasy "sons of the devil" and "angels of the wicked one" (*maligni*). For [the word] "son," as one before me has observed, has a twofold meaning: one [is a son] in the order of nature, because he was born a son; the other, in that he was made so, is reputed a son, although there be a difference between being born so and being made so. For the first is indeed born from the person referred to; but the second is made so by him, whether as respects his creation or by the teaching of his doctrine. For when any person has been taught from the mouth of another, he is termed the son of him who instructs him, and the latter [is called] his father. According to nature, then — that is, according to creation, so to speak — we are all sons of God, because we have all been created by God. But with respect to obedience

---

[1] Matt. xxv. 32.
[2] Matt. xxv. 34.
[3] Matt. xxv. 41.
[4] Matt. xiii. 40–43.
[5] Matt. xiii. 34. [Applicable to the origin of heresies.]
[6] Matt. xiii. 28.
[7] The old Latin translator varies from this (the Greek of which was recovered by Grabe from two ancient *Catenæ Patrum*), making the clause run thus, *that is, the transgression which he had himself introduced*, making the explanatory words to refer to the *tares*, and not, as in the Greek, to the *sower of the tares*.

[8] Following the reading of the LXX., αὐτός σου τηρήσει κεφαλήν.
[9] Gen. iii. 15.
[10] Matt. xiii. 38.
[11] Ps. cxlix. 5.

and doctrine we are not all the sons of God: those only are so who believe in Him and do His will. And those who do not believe, and do not obey His will, are sons and angels of the devil, because they do the works of the devil. And that such is the case He has declared in Isaiah: "I have begotten and brought up children, but they have rebelled against Me."[1] And again, where He says that these children are aliens: "Strange children have lied unto Me."[2] According to nature, then, they are [His] children, because they have been so created; but with regard to their works, they are not His children.

3. For as, among men, those sons who disobey their fathers, being disinherited, are still their sons in the course of nature, but by law are disinherited, for they do not become the heirs of their natural parents; so in the same way is it with God, — those who do not obey Him being disinherited by Him, have ceased to be His sons. Wherefore they cannot receive His inheritance: as David says, "Sinners are alienated from the womb; their anger is after the likeness of a serpent."[3] And therefore did the Lord term those whom He knew to be the offspring of men "a generation of vipers;"[4] because after the manner of these animals they go about in subtilty, and injure others. For He said, "Beware of the leaven of the Pharisees and of the Sadducees."[5] Speaking of Herod, too, He says, "Go ye and tell that fox,"[6] aiming at his wicked cunning and deceit. Wherefore the prophet David says, "Man, being placed in honour, is made like unto cattle."[7] And again Jeremiah says, "They are become like horses, furious about females; each one neighed after his neighbour's wife."[8] And Isaiah, when preaching in Judea, and reasoning with Israel, termed them "rulers of Sodom" and "people of Gomorrah;"[9] intimating that they were like the Sodomites in wickedness, and that the same description of sins was rife among them, calling them by the same name, because of the similarity of their conduct. And inasmuch as they were not by nature so created by God, but had power also to act rightly, the same person said to them, giving them good counsel, "Wash ye, make you clean; take away iniquity from your souls before mine eyes; cease from your iniquities."[10] Thus, no doubt, since they had transgressed and sinned in the same manner, so did they receive the same reproof as did the Sodomites. But when they should be converted and come to repentance, and cease from evil, they should have power to become the sons of God, and to receive the inheritance of immortality which is given by Him. For this reason, therefore, He has termed those "angels of the devil," and "children of the wicked one,"[11] who give heed to the devil, and do his works. But these are, at the same time, all created by the one and the same God. When, however, they believe and are subject to God, and go on and keep His doctrine, they are the sons of God; but when they have apostatized and fallen into transgression, they are ascribed to their chief, the devil — to him who first became the cause of apostasy to himself, and afterwards to others.

4. Inasmuch as the words of the Lord are numerous, while they all proclaim one and the same Father, the Creator of this world, it was incumbent also upon me, for their own sake, to refute by many [arguments] those who are involved in many errors, if by any means, when they are confuted by many [proofs], they may be converted to the truth and saved. But it is necessary to subjoin to this composition, in what follows, also the doctrine of Paul after the words of the Lord, to examine the opinion of this man, and expound the apostle, and to explain whatsoever [passages] have received other interpretations from the heretics, who have altogether misunderstood what Paul has spoken, and to point out the folly of their mad opinions; and to demonstrate from that same Paul, from whose [writings] they press questions upon us, that they are indeed utterers of falsehood, but that the apostle was a preacher of the truth, and that he taught all things agreeable to the preaching of the truth; [to the effect that] it was one God the Father who spake with Abraham, who gave the law, who sent the prophets beforehand, who in the last times sent His Son, and conferred salvation upon His own handiwork — that is, the substance of flesh. Arranging, then, in another book, the rest of the words of the Lord, which He taught concerning the Father not by parables, but by expressions taken in their obvious meaning (*sed simpliciter ipsis dictionibus*), and the exposition of the Epistles of the blessed apostle, I shall, with God's aid, furnish thee with the complete work of the exposure and refutation of knowledge, falsely so called; thus practising myself and thee in [these] five books for presenting opposition to all heretics.

---

[1] Isa. i. 2.
[2] Ps. xviii. 45.
[3] Ps. lviii. 3, 4.
[4] Matt. xxiii. 33.
[5] Matt. xvi. 6.
[6] Luke xiii. 32.
[7] Ps. xlix. 21.
[8] Jer. v. 8.
[9] Isa. i. 10.
[10] Isa. i. 16.
[11] Matt. xxv. 41, xiii. 38.

IRENÆUS AGAINST HERESIES

BOOK V.

PREFACE.

IN the four preceding books, my very dear friend, which I put forth to thee, all the heretics have been exposed, and their doctrines brought to light, and these men refuted who have devised irreligious opinions. [I have accomplished this by adducing] something from the doctrine peculiar to each of these men, which they have left in their writings, as well as by using arguments of a more general nature, and applicable to them all.[1] Then I have pointed out the truth, and shown the preaching of the Church, which the prophets proclaimed (as I have already demonstrated), but which Christ brought to perfection, and the apostles have handed down, from whom the Church, receiving [these truths], and throughout all the world alone preserving them in their integrity (*bene*), has transmitted them to her sons. Then also — having disposed of all questions which the heretics propose to us, and having explained the doctrine of the apostles, and clearly set forth many of those things which were said and done by the Lord in parables — I shall endeavour, in this the fifth book of the entire work which treats of the exposure and refutation of knowledge falsely so called, to exhibit proofs from the rest of the Lord's doctrine and the apostolical epistles: [thus] complying with thy demand, as thou didst request of me (since indeed I have been assigned a place in the ministry of the word); and, labouring by every means in my power to furnish thee with large assistance against the contradictions of the heretics, as also to reclaim the wanderers and convert them to the Church of God, to confirm at the same time the minds of the neophytes, that they may preserve stedfast the faith which they have received, guarded by the Church in its integrity, in order that they be in no way perverted by those who endeavour to teach them false doctrines, and lead them away from the truth. It will be incumbent upon thee, however, and all who may happen to read this writing, to peruse with great attention what I have already said, that thou mayest obtain a knowledge of the subjects against which I am contending. For it is thus that thou wilt both controvert them in a legitimate manner, and wilt be prepared to receive the proofs brought forward against them, casting away their doctrines as filth by means of the celestial faith; but following the only true and stedfast Teacher, the Word of God, our Lord Jesus Christ, who did, through His transcendent love, become what we are, that He might bring us to be even what He is Himself.

CHAP. I. — CHRIST ALONE IS ABLE TO TEACH DIVINE THINGS, AND TO REDEEM US: HE, THE SAME, TOOK FLESH OF THE VIRGIN MARY, NOT MERELY IN APPEARANCE, BUT ACTUALLY, BY THE OPERATION OF THE HOLY SPIRIT, IN ORDER TO RENOVATE US. STRICTURES ON THE CONCEITS OF VALENTINUS AND EBION.

1. FOR in no other way could we have learned the things of God, unless our Master, existing as the Word, had become man. For no other being had the power of revealing to us the things of the Father, except His own proper Word. For what other person "knew the mind of the Lord," or who else "has become His counsellor?"[2] Again, we could have learned in no other way than by seeing our Teacher, and hearing His voice with our own ears, that, having become imitators of His works as well as doers of His words, we may have communion with Him, receiving increase from the perfect One, and from Him who is prior to all creation. We — who were but lately created by the only best and good Being, by Him also who has the gift of immortality, having been formed after

---

[1] Ex ratione universis ostensionibus procedente. The words are very obscure.

[2] Rom. xi. 34.

His likeness (predestinated, according to the prescience of the Father, that we, who had as yet no existence, might come into being), and made the first-fruits of creation[1] — have received, in the times known beforehand, [the blessings of salvation] according to the ministration of the Word, who is perfect in all things, as the mighty Word, and very man, who, redeeming us by His own blood in a manner consonant to reason, gave Himself as a redemption for those who had been led into captivity. And since the apostasy tyrannized over us unjustly, and, though we were by nature the property of the omnipotent God, alienated us contrary to nature, rendering us its own disciples, the Word of God, powerful in all things, and not defective with regard to His own justice, did righteously turn against that apostasy, and redeem from it His own property, not by violent means, as the [apostasy] had obtained dominion over us at the beginning, when it insatiably snatched away what was not its own, but by means of persuasion, as became a God of counsel, who does not use violent means to obtain what He desires; so that neither should justice be infringed upon, nor the ancient handiwork of God go to destruction. Since the Lord thus has redeemed us through His own blood, giving His soul for our souls, and His flesh for our flesh,[2] and has also poured out the Spirit of the Father for the union and communion of God and man, imparting indeed God to men by means of the Spirit, and, on the other hand, attaching man to God by His own incarnation, and bestowing upon us at His coming immortality durably and truly, by means of communion with God, — all the doctrines of the heretics fall to ruin.

2. Vain indeed are those who allege that He appeared in mere seeming. For these things were not done in appearance only, but in actual reality. But if He did appear as a man, when He was not a man, neither could the Holy Spirit have rested upon Him, — an occurrence which did actually take place — as the Spirit is invisible; nor, [in that case], was there any degree of truth in Him, for He was not that which He seemed to be. But I have already remarked that Abraham and the other prophets beheld Him after a prophetical manner, foretelling in vision what should come to pass. If, then, such a being has now appeared in outward semblance different from what he was in reality, there has been a certain prophetical vision made to men; and another advent of His must be looked forward to, in which He shall be such as He has now been seen in a prophetic manner. And I have proved already, that it is the same thing to say that He appeared merely to outward seeming, and [to affirm] that He received nothing from Mary. For He would not have been one truly possessing flesh and blood, by which He redeemed us, unless He had summed up in Himself the ancient formation of Adam. Vain therefore are the disciples of Valentinus who put forth this opinion, in order that they may exclude the flesh from salvation, and cast aside what God has fashioned.

3. Vain also are the Ebionites, who do not receive by faith into their soul the union of God and man, but who remain in the old leaven of [the natural] birth, and who do not choose to understand that the Holy Ghost came upon Mary, and the power of the Most High did overshadow her:[3] wherefore also what was generated is a holy thing, and the Son of the Most High God the Father of all, who effected the incarnation of this being, and showed forth a new [kind of] generation; that as by the former generation we inherited death, so by this new generation we might inherit life. Therefore do these men reject the commixture of the heavenly wine,[4] and wish it to be water of the world only, not receiving God so as to have union with Him, but they remain in that Adam who had been conquered and was expelled from Paradise: not considering that as, at the beginning of our formation in Adam, that breath of life which proceeded from God, having been united to what had been fashioned, animated the man, and manifested him as a being endowed with reason; so also, in [the times of] the end, the Word of the Father and the Spirit of God, having become united with the ancient substance of Adam's formation, rendered man living and perfect, receptive of the perfect Father, in order that as in the natural [Adam] we all were dead, so in the spiritual we may all be made alive.[5] For never at any time did Adam escape the hands[6] of God, to whom the Father speaking, said, "Let Us make man in Our image, after Our likeness." And for this reason in the last times (*fine*), not by the will of the flesh, nor by the will of man, but by the good pleasure of the Father,[7] His hands formed a living man, in order that Adam might be created [again] after the image and likeness of God.

CHAP. II. — WHEN CHRIST VISITED US IN HIS GRACE, HE DID NOT COME TO WHAT DID NOT BELONG TO HIM: ALSO, BY SHEDDING HIS TRUE BLOOD FOR US, AND EXHIBITING TO US HIS TRUE FLESH IN THE EUCHARIST, HE CONFERRED UPON OUR FLESH THE CAPACITY OF SALVATION.

1. And vain likewise are those who say that

---

[1] "Initium facturæ," which Grabe thinks should be thus translated with reference to Jas. i. 18.
[2] [Compare Clement, cap. 49, p.18, this volume.]
[3] Luke i. 35.
[4] In allusion to the mixture of water in the eucharistic cup, as practised in these primitive times. The Ebionites and others used to consecrate the element of water alone.
[5] 1 Cor. xv. 22.
[6] Viz., the Son and the Spirit.
[7] John i. 13.

God came to those things which did not belong to Him, as if covetous of another's property; in order that He might deliver up that man who had been created by another, to that God who had neither made nor formed anything, but who also was deprived from the beginning of His own proper formation of men. The advent, therefore, of Him whom these men represent as coming to the things of others, was not righteous; nor did He truly redeem us by His own blood, if He did not really become man, restoring to His own handiwork what was said [of it] in the beginning, that man was made after the image and likeness of God; not snatching away by stratagem the property of another, but taking possession of His own in a righteous and gracious manner. As far as concerned the apostasy, indeed, He redeems us righteously from it by His own blood; but as regards us who have been redeemed, [He does this] graciously. For we have given nothing to Him previously, nor does He desire anything from us, as if He stood in need of it; but we do stand in need of fellowship with Him. And for this reason it was that He graciously poured Himself out, that He might gather us into the bosom of the Father.

2. But vain in every respect are they who despise the entire dispensation of God, and disallow the salvation of the flesh, and treat with contempt its regeneration, maintaining that it is not capable of incorruption. But if this indeed do not attain salvation, then neither did the Lord redeem us with His blood, nor is the cup of the Eucharist the communion of His blood, nor the bread which we break the communion of His body.[1] For blood can only come from veins and flesh, and whatsoever else makes up the substance of man, such as the Word of God was actually made. By His own blood he redeemed us, as also His apostle declares, "In whom we have redemption through His blood, even the remission of sins."[2] And as we are His members, we are also nourished by means of the creation (and He Himself grants the creation to us, for He causes His sun to rise, and sends rain when He wills[3]). He has acknowledged the cup (which is a part of the creation) as His own blood, from which He bedews our blood; and the bread (also a part of the creation) He has established as His own body, from which He gives increase to our bodies.[4]

3. When, therefore, the mingled cup and the manufactured bread receives the Word of God, and the Eucharist of the blood and the body of Christ is made,[5] from which things the substance of our flesh is increased and supported, how can they affirm that the flesh is incapable of receiving the gift of God, which is life eternal, which [flesh] is nourished from the body and blood of the Lord, and is a member of Him? — even as the blessed Paul declares in his Epistle to the Ephesians, that "we are members of His body, of His flesh, and of His bones."[6] He does not speak these words of some spiritual and invisible man, for a spirit has not bones nor flesh;[7] but [he refers to] that dispensation [by which the Lord became] an actual man, consisting of flesh, and nerves, and bones, — that [flesh] which is nourished by the cup which is His blood, and receives increase from the bread which is His body. And just as a cutting from the vine planted in the ground fructifies in its season, or as a corn of wheat falling into the earth and becoming decomposed, rises with manifold increase by the Spirit of God, who contains all things, and then, through the wisdom of God, serves for the use of men, and having received the Word of God, becomes the Eucharist, which is the body and blood of Christ; so also our bodies, being nourished by it, and deposited in the earth, and suffering decomposition there, shall rise at their appointed time, the Word of God granting them resurrection to the glory of God, even the Father, who freely gives to this mortal immortality, and to this corruptible incorruption,[8] because the strength of God is made perfect in weakness,[9] in order that we may never become puffed up, as if we had life from ourselves, and exalted against God, our minds becoming ungrateful; but learning by experience that we possess eternal duration from the excelling power of this Being, not from our own nature, we may neither undervalue that glory which surrounds God as He is, nor be ignorant of our own nature, but that we may know what God can effect, and what benefits man receives, and thus never wander from the true comprehension of things as they are, that is, both with regard to God and with regard to man. And might it not be the case, perhaps, as I have already observed, that for this purpose God permitted our resolution into the common dust of mortality,[10] that we, being instructed by every mode, may be accurate in all things for the future, being ignorant neither of God nor of ourselves?

---

[1] 1 Cor. x. 16.
[2] Col i. 14.
[3] Matt. v. 45.
[4] [Again, he carefully asserts that the *bread* is the *body*, and the *wine* (cup) is the *blood*. The elements are sanctified, not changed materially.]
[5] The Greek text, of which a considerable portion remains here, would give, "and the Eucharist becomes the body of Christ."
[6] Eph. v. 30.
[7] Luke xxiv. 39.
[8] 1 Cor. xv. 53.
[9] 2 Cor. xii. 3.
[10] This is Harvey's free rendering of the passage, which is in the Greek (as preserved in the Catena of John of Damascus): καὶ διὰ τοῦτο ἠνέσχετο ὁ Θεὸς τὴν εἰς τὴν γῆν ἡμῶν ἀνάλυσιν. In the Latin: Propter hoc passus est Deus fieri in nobis resolutionem. See Book iii. cap. xx. 2.

CHAP. III. — THE POWER AND GLORY OF GOD SHINE FORTH IN THE WEAKNESS OF HUMAN FLESH, AS HE WILL RENDER OUR BODY A PARTICIPATOR OF THE RESURRECTION AND OF IMMORTALITY, ALTHOUGH HE HAS FORMED IT FROM THE DUST OF THE EARTH; HE WILL ALSO BESTOW UPON IT THE ENJOYMENT OF IMMORTALITY, JUST AS HE GRANTS IT THIS SHORT LIFE IN COMMON WITH THE SOUL.

1. The Apostle Paul has, moreover, in the most lucid manner, pointed out that man has been delivered over to his own infirmity, lest, being uplifted, he might fall away from the truth. Thus he says in the second [Epistle] to the Corinthians: "And lest I should be lifted up by the sublimity of the revelations, there was given unto me a thorn in the flesh, the messenger of Satan to buffet me. And upon this I besought the Lord three times, that it might depart from me. But he said unto me, My grace is sufficient for thee; for strength is made perfect in weakness. Gladly therefore shall I rather glory in infirmities, that the power of Christ may dwell in me."[1] What, therefore? (as some may exclaim:) did the Lord wish, in that case, that His apostles should thus undergo buffeting, and that he should endure such infirmity? Even so it was; the word says it. For strength is made perfect in weakness, rendering him a better man who by means of his infirmity becomes acquainted with the power of God. For how could a man have learned that he is himself an infirm being, and mortal by nature, but that God is immortal and powerful, unless he had learned by experience what is in both? For there is nothing evil in learning one's infirmities by endurance; yea, rather, it has even the beneficial effect of preventing him from forming an undue opinion of his own nature (*non aberrare in natura sua*). But the being lifted up against God, and taking His glory to one's self, rendering man ungrateful, has brought much evil upon him. [And thus, I say, man must learn both things by experience], that he may not be destitute of truth and love either towards himself or his Creator.[2] But the experience of both confers upon him the true knowledge as to God and man, and increases his love towards God. Now, where there exists an increase of love, there a greater glory is wrought out by the power of God for those who love Him.

2. Those men, therefore, set aside the power of God, and do not consider what the word declares, when they dwell upon the infirmity of the flesh, but do not take into consideration the power of Him who raises it up from the dead. For if He does not vivify what is mortal, and does not bring back the corruptible to incorruption, He is not a God of power. But that He is powerful in all these respects, we ought to perceive from our origin, inasmuch as God, taking dust from the earth, formed man. And surely it is much more difficult and incredible, from non-existent bones, and nerves, and veins, and the rest of man's organization, to bring it about that all this should be, and to make man an animated and rational creature, than to re-integrate again that which had been created and then afterwards decomposed into earth (for the reasons already mentioned), having thus passed into those [elements] from which man, who had no previous existence, was formed. For He who in the beginning caused him to have being who as yet was not, just when He pleased, shall much more reinstate again those who had a former existence, when it is His will [that they should inherit] the life granted by Him. And that flesh shall also be found fit for and capable of receiving the power of God, which at the beginning received the skilful touches of God; so that one part became the eye for seeing; another, the ear for hearing; another, the hand for feeling and working; another, the sinews stretched out everywhere, and holding the limbs together; another, arteries and veins, passages for the blood and the air;[3] another, the various internal organs; another, the blood, which is the bond of union between soul and body. But why go [on in this strain]? Numbers would fail to express the multiplicity of parts in the human frame, which was made in no other way than by the great wisdom of God. But those things which partake of the skill and wisdom of God, do also partake of His power.

3. The flesh, therefore, is not destitute [of participation] in the constructive wisdom and power of God. But if the power of Him who is the bestower of life is made perfect in weakness — that is, in the flesh — let them inform us, when they maintain the incapacity of flesh to receive the life granted by God, whether they do say these things as being living men at present, and partakers of life, or acknowledge that, having no part in life whatever, they are at the present moment dead men. And if they really are dead men, how is it that they move about, and speak, and perform those other functions which are not the actions of the dead, but of the living? But if they are now alive, and if their whole body partakes of life, how can they venture the assertion that the flesh is not quali-

---

[1] 2 Cor. xii. 7-9.
[2] We have adopted here the explanation of Massuet, who considers the preceding period as merely parenthetical. Both Grabe and Harvey, however, would make conjectural emendations in the text, which seem to us to be inadmissible.

[3] The ancients erroneously supposed that the arteries were *air-vessels*, from the fact that these organs, after death, appear quite empty, from all the blood stagnating in the veins when death supervenes.

fied to be a partaker of life, when they do confess that they have life at the present moment? It is just as if anybody were to take up a sponge full of water, or a torch on fire, and to declare that the sponge could not possibly partake of the water, or the torch of the fire. In this very manner do those men, by alleging that they are alive and bear life about in their members, contradict themselves afterwards, when they represent these members as not being capable of [receiving] life. But if the present temporal life, which is of such an inferior nature to eternal life, can nevertheless effect so much as to quicken our mortal members, why should not eternal life, being much more powerful than this, vivify the flesh, which has already held converse with, and been accustomed to sustain, life? For that the flesh can really partake of life, is shown from the fact of its being alive; for it lives on, as long as it is God's purpose that it should do so. It is manifest, too, that God has the power to confer life upon it, inasmuch as He grants life to us who are in existence. And, therefore, since the Lord has power to infuse life into what He has fashioned, and since the flesh is capable of being quickened, what remains to prevent its participating in incorruption, which is a blissful and never-ending life granted by God?

CHAP. IV. — THOSE PERSONS ARE DECEIVED WHO FEIGN ANOTHER GOD THE FATHER BESIDES THE CREATOR OF THE WORLD; FOR HE MUST HAVE BEEN FEEBLE AND USELESS, OR ELSE MALIGNANT AND FULL OF ENVY, IF HE BE EITHER UNABLE OR UNWILLING TO EXTEND EXTERNAL LIFE TO OUR BODIES.

1. Those persons who feign the existence of another Father beyond the Creator, and who term him the good God, do deceive themselves; for they introduce him as a feeble, worthless, and negligent being, not to say malign and full of envy, inasmuch as they affirm that our bodies are not quickened by him. For when they say of things which it is manifest to all do remain immortal, such as the spirit and the soul, and such other things, that they are quickened by the Father, but that another thing [viz. the body] which is quickened in no different manner than by God granting [life] to it, is abandoned by life, — [they must either confess] that this proves their Father to be weak and powerless, or else envious and malignant. For since the Creator does even here quicken our mortal bodies, and promises them resurrection by the prophets, as I have pointed out; who [in that case] is shown to be more powerful, stronger, or truly good? Whether is it the Creator who vivifies the whole man, or is it their Father, falsely so called? He feigns to be the quickener of those things which are immortal by nature, to which things life is always present by their very nature; but he does not benevolently quicken those things which required his assistance, that they might live, but leaves them carelessly to fall under the power of death. Whether is it the case, then, that their Father does not bestow life upon them when he has the power of so doing, or is it that he does not possess the power? If, on the one hand, it is because he cannot, he is, upon that supposition, not a powerful being, nor is he more perfect than the Creator; for the Creator grants, as we must perceive, what *He* is unable to afford. But if, on the other hand, [it be that he does not grant this] when he has the power of so doing, then he is proved to be not a good, but an envious and malignant Father.

2. If, again, they refer to any cause on account of which their Father does not impart life to bodies, then that cause must necessarily appear superior to the Father, since it restrains Him from the exercise of His benevolence; and His benevolence will thus be proved weak, on account of that cause which they bring forward. Now every one must perceive that bodies are capable of receiving life. For they live to the extent that God pleases that they should live; and that being so, the [heretics] cannot maintain that [these bodies] are utterly incapable of receiving life. If, therefore, on account of necessity and any other cause, those [bodies] which are capable of participating in life are not vivified, their Father shall be the slave of necessity and that cause, and not therefore a free agent, having His will under His own control.

CHAP. V. — THE PROLONGED LIFE OF THE ANCIENTS, THE TRANSLATION OF ELIJAH AND OF ENOCH IN THEIR OWN BODIES, AS WELL AS THE PRESERVATION OF JONAH, OF SHADRACH, MESHACH, AND ABEDNEGO, IN THE MIDST OF EXTREME PERIL, ARE CLEAR DEMONSTRATIONS THAT GOD CAN RAISE UP OUR BODIES TO LIFE ETERNAL.

1. [In order to learn] that bodies did continue in existence for a lengthened period, as long as it was God's good pleasure that they should flourish, let [these heretics] read the Scriptures, and they will find that our predecessors advanced beyond seven hundred, eight hundred, and nine hundred years of age; and that their bodies kept pace with the protracted length of their days, and participated in life as long as God willed that they should live. But why do I refer to these men? For Enoch, when he pleased God, was translated in the same body in which he did please Him, thus pointing out by anticipation the translation of the just. Elijah, too, was caught up [when he was yet] in the substance of the [natural] form; thus exhibiting in prophecy the

assumption of those who are spiritual, and that nothing stood in the way of their body being translated and caught up. For by means of the very same hands through which they were moulded at the beginning, did they receive this translation and assumption. For in Adam the hands of God had become accustomed to set in order, to rule, and to sustain His own workmanship, and to bring it and place it where they pleased. Where, then, was the first man placed? In paradise certainly, as the Scripture declares: "And God planted a garden [*paradisum*] eastward in Eden, and there He placed the man whom He had formed."[1] And then afterwards, when [man] proved disobedient, he was cast out thence into this world. Wherefore also the elders who were disciples of the apostles tell us that those who were translated were transferred to that place (for paradise has been prepared for righteous men, such as have the Spirit; in which place also Paul the apostle, when he was caught up, heard words which are unspeakable as regards us in our present condition[2]), and that there shall they who have been translated remain until the consummation [of all things], as a prelude to immortality.

2. If, however, any one imagine it impossible that men should survive for such a length of time, and that Elias was not caught up in the flesh, but that his flesh was consumed in the fiery chariot, let him consider that Jonah, when he had been cast into the deep, and swallowed down into the whale's belly, was by the command of God again thrown out safe upon the land.[3] And then, again, when Ananias, Azarias, and Misaël were cast into the furnace of fire seven fold heated, they sustained no harm whatever, neither was the smell of fire perceived upon them. As, therefore, the hand of God was present with them, working out marvellous things in their case — [things] impossible [to be accomplished] by man's nature — what wonder was it, if also in the case of those who were translated it performed something wonderful, working in obedience to the will of God, even the Father? Now this is the Son of God, as the Scripture represents Nebuchadnezzar the king as having said, "Did not we cast three men bound into the furnace? and, lo, I do see four walking in the midst of the fire, and the fourth is like the Son of God."[4] Neither the nature of any created thing, therefore, nor the weakness of the flesh, can prevail against the will of God. For God is not subject to created things, but created things to God; and all things yield obedience to His will. Wherefore also the Lord declares, "The things which are impossible with men, are possible with God."[5] As, therefore, it might seem to the men of the present day, who are ignorant of God's appointment, to be a thing incredible and impossible that any man could live for such a number of years, yet those who were before us did live [to such an age], and those who were translated do live as an earnest of the future length of days; and [as it might also appear impossible] that from the whale's belly and from the fiery furnace men issued forth unhurt, yet they nevertheless did so, led forth as it were by the hand of God, for the purpose of declaring His power: so also now, although some, not knowing the power and promise of God, may oppose their own salvation, deeming it impossible for God, who raises up the dead, to have power to confer upon them eternal duration, yet the scepticism of men of this stamp shall not render the faithfulness of God of none effect.

CHAP. VI. — GOD WILL BESTOW SALVATION UPON THE WHOLE NATURE OF MAN, CONSISTING OF BODY AND SOUL IN CLOSE UNION, SINCE THE WORD TOOK IT UPON HIM, AND ADORNED IT WITH THE GIFTS OF THE HOLY SPIRIT, OF WHOM OUR BODIES ARE, AND ARE TERMED, THE TEMPLES.

1. Now God shall be glorified in His handiwork, fitting it so as to be conformable to, and modelled after, His own Son. For by the hands of the Father, that is, by the Son and the Holy Spirit, man, and not [merely] a part of man, was made in the likeness of God. Now the soul and the spirit are certainly a *part* of the man, but certainly not *the* man; for the perfect man consists in the commingling and the union of the soul receiving the spirit of the Father, and the admixture of that fleshly nature which was moulded after the image of God. For this reason does the apostle declare, "We speak wisdom among them that are perfect,"[6] terming those persons "perfect" who have received the Spirit of God, and who through the Spirit of God do speak in all languages, as he used Himself also to speak. In like manner we do also hear[7] many brethren in the Church, who possess prophetic gifts, and who through the Spirit speak all kinds of languages, and bring to light for the general benefit the hidden things of men, and declare the mysteries of God, whom also the apostle terms "spiritual," they being spiritual because they partake of the Spirit, and not because their flesh has been stripped off and taken away, and because they have become purely spiritual. For if any one take away the sub-

---

[1] Gen. ii. 8.
[2] 2 Cor. xii. 4.
[3] Jon. ii. 11.
[4] Dan. iii. 19-25.
[5] Luke xviii. 27.
[6] 1 Cor. ii. 6.
[7] The old Latin has "audivimus," *have heard*.

stance of flesh, that is, of the handiwork [of God], and understand that which is purely spiritual, such then would not be a spiritual man, but would be the spirit of a man, or the Spirit of God. But when the spirit here blended with the soul is united to [God's] handiwork, the man is rendered spiritual and perfect because of the outpouring of the Spirit, and this is he who was made in the image and likeness of God. But if the Spirit be wanting to the soul, he who is such is indeed of an animal nature, and being left carnal, shall be an imperfect being, possessing indeed the image [of God] in his formation (*in plasmate*), but not receiving the similitude through the Spirit; and thus is this being imperfect. Thus also, if any one take away the image and set aside the handiwork, he cannot then understand this as being a man, but as either some part of a man, as I have already said, or as something else than a man. For that flesh which has been moulded is not a perfect man in itself, but the body of a man, and part of a man. Neither is the soul itself, considered apart by itself, the man; but it is the soul of a man, and part of a man. Neither is the spirit a man, for it is called the spirit, and not a man; but the commingling and union of all these constitutes the perfect man. And for this cause does the apostle, explaining himself, make it clear that the saved man is a complete man as well as a spiritual man; saying thus in the first Epistle to the Thessalonians, "Now the God of peace sanctify you perfect (*perfectos*); and may your spirit, and soul, and body be preserved whole without complaint to the coming of the Lord Jesus Christ."[1] Now what was his object in praying that these three — that is, soul, body, and spirit — might be preserved to the coming of the Lord, unless he was aware of the [future] reintegration and union of the three, and [that they should be heirs of] one and the same salvation? For this cause also he declares that those are "the perfect" who present unto the Lord the three [component parts] without offence. Those, then, are the perfect who have had the Spirit of God remaining in them, and have preserved their souls and bodies blameless, holding fast the faith of God, that is, that faith which is [directed] towards God, and maintaining righteous dealings with respect to their neighbours.

2. Whence also he says, that this handiwork is "the temple of God," thus declaring: "Know ye not that ye are the temple of God, and that the Spirit of God dwelleth in you? If any man, therefore, will defile the temple of God, him will God destroy: for the temple of God is holy, which [temple] ye are."[2] Here he manifestly declares the body to be the temple in which the Spirit dwells. As also the Lord speaks in reference to Himself, "Destroy this temple, and in three days I will raise it up. He spake this, however," it is said, "of the temple of His body."[3] And not only does he (the apostle) acknowledge our bodies to be a temple, but even the temple of Christ, saying thus to the Corinthians, "Know ye not that your bodies are members of Christ? Shall I then take the members of Christ, and make them the members of an harlot?"[4] He speaks these things, not in reference to some other spiritual man; for a being of such a nature could have nothing to do with an harlot: but he declares "our body," that is, the flesh which continues in sanctity and purity, to be "the members of Christ;" but that when it becomes one with an harlot, it becomes the members of an harlot. And for this reason he said, "If any man defile the temple of God, him will God destroy." How then is it not the utmost blasphemy to allege, that the temple of God, in which the Spirit of the Father dwells, and the members of Christ, do not partake of salvation, but are reduced to perdition? Also, that our bodies are raised not from their own substance, but by the power of God, he says to the Corinthians, "Now the body is not for fornication, but for the Lord, and the Lord for the body. But God hath both raised up the Lord, and shall raise us up by His own power."[5]

CHAP. VII. — INASMUCH AS CHRIST DID RISE IN OUR FLESH, IT FOLLOWS THAT WE SHALL BE ALSO RAISED IN THE SAME; SINCE THE RESURRECTION PROMISED TO US SHOULD NOT BE REFERRED TO SPIRITS NATURALLY IMMORTAL, BUT TO BODIES IN THEMSELVES MORTAL.

1. In the same manner, therefore, as Christ did rise in the substance of flesh, and pointed out to His disciples the mark of the nails and the opening in His side[6] (now these are the tokens of that flesh which rose from the dead), so "shall He also," it is said, "raise us up by His own power."[7] And again to the Romans. he says, "But if the Spirit of Him that raised up Jesus from the dead dwell in you, He that raised up Christ from the dead shall also quicken your mortal bodies."[8] What, then, are mortal bodies? Can they be souls? Nay, for souls are incorporeal when put in comparison with mortal bodies; for God "breathed into the face of man the breath of life, and man became a living soul." Now the breath of life is an incorporeal

---

[1] 1 Thess. v. 23. [I have before referred the student to the "Biblical Psychology" of Prof. Delitzsch (translation), T. & T. Clark, Edinburgh, 1868.]
[2] 1 Cor. iii. 16.
[3] John ii. 19-21.
[4] 1 Cor. iii. 17.
[5] 1 Cor. vi. 13, 14.
[6] John xx. 20, 25, 27.
[7] 1 Cor. vi. 14.
[8] Rom. viii. 11.

thing. And certainly they cannot maintain that the very breath of life is mortal. Therefore David says, "My soul also shall live to Him,"[1] just as if its substance were immortal. Neither, on the other hand, can they say that the spirit is the mortal body. What therefore is there left to which we may apply the term "mortal body," unless it be the thing that was moulded, that is, the flesh, of which it is also said that God will vivify it? For this it is which dies and is decomposed, but not the soul or the spirit. For to die is to lose vital power, and to become henceforth breathless, inanimate, and devoid of motion, and to melt away into those [component parts] from which also it derived the commencement of [its] substance. But this event happens neither to the soul, for it is the breath of life; nor to the spirit, for the spirit is simple and not composite, so that it cannot be decomposed, and is itself the life of those who receive it. We must therefore conclude that it is in reference to the flesh that death is mentioned; which [flesh], after the soul's departure, becomes breathless and inanimate, and is decomposed gradually into the earth from which it was taken. This, then, is what is mortal. And it is this of which he also says, "He shall also quicken your mortal bodies." And therefore in reference to it he says, in the first [Epistle] to the Corinthians: "So also is the resurrection of the dead: it is sown in corruption, it rises in incorruption."[2] For he declares, "That which thou sowest cannot be quickened, unless first it die."[3]

2. But what is that which, like a grain of wheat, is sown in the earth and decays, unless it be the bodies which are laid in the earth, into which seeds are also cast? And for this reason he said, "It is sown in dishonour, it rises in glory."[4] For what is more ignoble than dead flesh? Or, on the other hand, what is more glorious than the same when it arises and partakes of incorruption? "It is sown in weakness, it is raised in power:"[5] in its own weakness certainly, because since it is earth it goes to earth; but [it is quickened] by the power of God, who raises it from the dead. "It is sown an animal body, it rises a spiritual body."[6] He has taught, beyond all doubt, that such language was not used by him, either with reference to the soul or to the spirit, but to bodies that have become corpses. For these are animal bodies, that is, [bodies] which partake of life, which when they have lost, they succumb to death; then, rising through the Spirit's instrumentality, they become spiritual bodies, so that by the Spirit they possess a perpetual life. "For now," he says, "we know in part, and we prophesy in part, but then face to face."[7] And this it is which has been said also by Peter: "Whom having not seen, ye love; in whom now also, not seeing, ye believe; and believing, ye shall rejoice with joy unspeakable."[8] For our face shall see the face of the Lord,[9] and shall rejoice with joy unspeakable, — that is to say, when it shall behold its own Delight.

CHAP. VIII. — THE GIFTS OF THE HOLY SPIRIT WHICH WE RECEIVE PREPARE US FOR INCORRUPTION, RENDER US SPIRITUAL, AND SEPARATE US FROM CARNAL MEN. THESE TWO CLASSES ARE SIGNIFIED BY THE CLEAN AND UNCLEAN ANIMALS IN THE LEGAL DISPENSATION.

1. But we do now receive a certain portion of His Spirit, tending towards perfection, and preparing us for incorruption, being little by little accustomed to receive and bear God; which also the apostle terms "an earnest," that is, a part of the honour which has been promised us by God, where he says in the Epistle to the Ephesians, "In which ye also, having heard the word of truth, the Gospel of your salvation, believing in which ye have been sealed with the Holy Spirit of promise, which is the earnest of our inheritance."[10] This earnest, therefore, thus dwelling in us, renders us spiritual even now, and the mortal is swallowed up by immortality.[11] "For ye," he declares, "are not in the flesh, but in the Spirit, if so be that the Spirit of God dwell in you."[12] This, however, does not take place by a casting away of the flesh, but by the impartation of the Spirit. For those to whom he was writing were not without flesh, but they were those who had received the Spirit of God, "by which we cry, Abba, Father."[13] If therefore, at the present time, having the earnest, we do cry, "Abba, Father," what shall it be when, on rising again, we behold Him face to face; when all the members shall burst out into a continuous hymn of triumph, glorifying Him who raised them from the dead, and gave the gift of eternal life? For if the earnest, gathering man into itself, does even now cause him to cry, "Abba, Father," what shall the complete grace of the Spirit effect, which shall be given to men by God? It will render us like unto Him, and accomplish the will[14] of the Father; for it shall make man after the image and likeness of God.

---

[1] Ps. xxii. 31, LXX.
[2] 1 Cor. xv. 42.
[3] 1 Cor. xv. 36.
[4] 1 Cor. xv. 43.
[5] 1 Cor. xv. 43.
[6] 1 Cor. xv. 44.
[7] 1 Cor. xiii. 9, 12.
[8] 1 Pet. i. 8.
[9] Grabe, Massuet, and Stieren prefer to read, "the face of the living God;" while Harvey adopts the above, reading merely "Domini," and not "Dei vivi."
[10] Eph. i. 13, etc.
[11] 2 Cor. v. 4.
[12] Rom. viii. 9.
[13] Rom. viii. 15.
[14] This is adopting Harvey's emendation of "voluntatem" for "voluntate."

2. Those persons, then, who possess the earnest of the Spirit, and who are not enslaved by the lusts of the flesh, but are subject to the Spirit, and who in all things walk according to the light of reason, does the apostle properly term "spiritual," because the Spirit of God dwells in them. Now, spiritual men shall not be incorporeal spirits; but our substance, that is, the union of flesh and spirit, receiving the Spirit of God, makes up the spiritual man. But those who do indeed reject the Spirit's counsel, and are the slaves of fleshly lusts, and lead lives contrary to reason, and who, without restraint, plunge headlong into their own desires, having no longing after the Divine Spirit, do live after the manner of swine and of dogs; these men, [I say], does the apostle very properly term "carnal," because they have no thought of anything else except carnal things.

3. For the same reason, too, do the prophets compare them to irrational animals, on account of the irrationality of their conduct, saying, "They have become as horses raging for the females; each one of them neighing after his neighbour's wife."[1] And again, "Man, when he was in honour, was made like unto cattle."[2] This denotes that, for his own fault, he is likened to cattle, by rivalling their irrational life. And we also, as the custom is, do designate men of this stamp as cattle and irrational beasts.

4. Now the law has figuratively predicted all these, delineating man by the [various] animals:[3] whatsoever of these, says [the Scripture], have a double hoof and ruminate, it proclaims as clean; but whatsoever of them do not possess one or other of these [properties], it sets aside by themselves as unclean. Who then are the clean? Those who make their way by faith steadily towards the Father and the Son; for this is denoted by the steadiness of those which divide the hoof; and they meditate day and night upon the words of God,[4] that they may be adorned with good works: for this is the meaning of the ruminants. The unclean, however, are those which do neither divide the hoof nor ruminate; that is, those persons who have neither faith in God, nor do meditate on His words: and such is the abomination of the Gentiles. But as to those animals which do indeed chew the cud, but have not the double hoof, and are themselves unclean, we have in them a figurative description of the Jews, who certainly have the words of God in their mouth, but who do not fix their rooted stedfastness in the Father and in the Son; wherefore they are an unstable generation. For those animals which have the hoof all in one piece easily slip; but those which have it divided are more sure-footed, their cleft hoofs succeeding each other as they advance, and the one hoof supporting the other. In like manner, too, those are unclean which have the double hoof but do not ruminate: this is plainly an indication of all heretics, and of those who do not meditate on the words of God, neither are adorned with works of righteousness; to whom also the Lord says, "Why call ye Me Lord, Lord, and do not the things which I say to you?"[5] For men of this stamp do indeed say that they believe in the Father and the Son, but they never meditate as they should upon the things of God, neither are they adorned with works of righteousness; but, as I have already observed, they have adopted the lives of swine and of dogs, giving themselves over to filthiness, to gluttony, and recklessness of all sorts. Justly, therefore, did the apostle call all such "carnal" and "animal,"[6] — [all those, namely], who through their own unbelief and luxury do not receive the Divine Spirit, and in their various phases cast out from themselves the life-giving Word, and walk stupidly after their own lusts: the prophets, too, spake of them as beasts of burden and wild beasts; custom likewise has viewed them in the light of cattle and irrational creatures; and the law has pronounced them unclean.

CHAP. IX. — SHOWING HOW THAT PASSAGE OF THE APOSTLE WHICH THE HERETICS PERVERT, SHOULD BE UNDERSTOOD; VIZ., "FLESH AND BLOOD SHALL NOT POSSESS THE KINGDOM OF GOD."

1. Among the other [truths] proclaimed by the apostle, there is also this one, "That flesh and blood cannot inherit the kingdom of God."[7] This is [the passage] which is adduced by all the heretics in support of their folly, with an attempt to annoy us, and to point out that the handiwork of God is not saved. They do not take this fact into consideration, that there are three things out of which, as I have shown, the complete man is composed — flesh, soul, and spirit. One of these does indeed preserve and fashion [the man] — this is the spirit; while as to another it is united and formed — that is the flesh; then [comes] that which is between these two — that is the soul, which sometimes indeed, when it follows the spirit, is raised up by it, but sometimes it sympathizes with the flesh, and falls into carnal lusts. Those then, as many as they be, who have not that which saves and forms [us] into life [eternal], shall be, and shall be called, [mere] flesh and blood; for these are they

---

[1] Jer. v. 3.
[2] Ps. xlix. 20.
[3] Lev. xi. 2; Deut. xiv. 3, etc.
[4] Ps. i. 2.

[5] Luke vi. 46.
[6] 1 Cor. ii. 14, iii. 1, etc.
[7] 1 Cor. xv. 50.

who have not the Spirit of God in themselves. Wherefore men of this stamp are spoken of by the Lord as "dead;" for, says He, "Let the dead bury their dead,"[1] because they have not the Spirit which quickens man.

2. On the other hand, as many as fear God and trust in His Son's advent, and who through faith do establish the Spirit of God in their hearts, — such men as these shall be properly called both "pure," and "spiritual,", and "those living to God," because they possess the Spirit of the Father, who purifies man, and raises him up to the life of God. For as the Lord has testified that "the flesh is weak," so [does He also say] that "the spirit is willing."[2] For this latter is capable of working out its own suggestions. If, therefore, any one admix the ready inclination of the Spirit to be, as it were, a stimulus to the infirmity of the flesh, it inevitably follows that what is strong will prevail over the weak, so that the weakness of the flesh will be absorbed by the strength of the Spirit; and that the man in whom this takes place cannot in that case be carnal, but spiritual, because of the fellowship of the Spirit. Thus it is, therefore, that the martyrs bear their witness, and despise death, not after the infirmity of the flesh, but because of the readiness of the Spirit. For when the infirmity of the flesh is absorbed, it exhibits the Spirit as powerful; and again, when the Spirit absorbs the weakness [of the flesh], it possesses the flesh as an inheritance in itself, and from both of these is formed a living man, — living, indeed, because he partakes of the Spirit, but man, because of the substance of flesh.

3. The flesh, therefore, when destitute of the Spirit of God, is dead, not having life, and cannot possess the kingdom of God: [it is as] irrational blood, like water poured out upon the ground. And therefore he says, "As is the earthy, such are they that are earthy."[3] But where the Spirit of the Father is, there is a living man; [there is] the rational blood preserved by God for the avenging [of those that shed it]; [there is] the flesh possessed by the Spirit, forgetful indeed of what belongs to it, and adopting the quality of the Spirit, being made conformable to the Word of God. And on this account he (the apostle) declares, "As we have borne the image of him who is of the earth, we shall also bear the image of Him who is from heaven."[4] What, therefore, is the earthly? That which was fashioned. And what is the heavenly? The Spirit. As therefore he says, when we were destitute of the celestial Spirit, we walked in former times in the oldness of the flesh, not obeying God; so now let us, receiving the Spirit, walk in newness of life, obeying God. Inasmuch, therefore, as without the Spirit of God we cannot be saved, the apostle exhorts us through faith and chaste conversation to preserve the Spirit of God, lest, having become non-participators of the Divine Spirit, we lose the kingdom of heaven; and he exclaims, that flesh in itself, and blood, cannot possess the kingdom of God.

4. If, however, we must speak strictly, [we would say that] the flesh *does not* inherit, but *is* inherited; as also the Lord declares, "Blessed are the meek, for they shall possess the earth by inheritance;"[5] as if in the [future] kingdom, the earth, from whence exists the substance of our flesh, is to be possessed by inheritance. This is the reason for His wishing the temple (i.e., the flesh) to be clean, that the Spirit of God may take delight therein, as a bridegroom with a bride. As, therefore, the bride cannot [be said] to wed, but to be wedded, when the bridegroom comes and takes her, so also the flesh cannot by itself possess the kingdom of God by inheritance; but it can be taken *for* an inheritance into the kingdom of God. For a living person inherits the goods of the deceased; and it is one thing to inherit, another to be inherited. The former rules, and exercises power over, and orders the things inherited at his will; but the latter things are in a state of subjection, are under order, and are ruled over by him who has obtained the inheritance. What, therefore, is it that lives? The Spirit of God, doubtless. What, again, are the possessions of the deceased? The various parts of the man, surely, which rot in the earth. But these are inherited by the Spirit when they are translated into the kingdom of heaven. For this cause, too, did Christ die, that the Gospel covenant being manifested and known to the whole world, might in the first place set free His slaves; and then afterwards, as I have already shown, might constitute them heirs of His property, when the Spirit possesses them by inheritance. For he who lives inherits, but the flesh is inherited. In order that we may not lose life by losing that Spirit which possesses us, the apostle, exhorting us to the communion of the Spirit, has said, according to reason, in those words already quoted, "That flesh and blood cannot inherit the kingdom of God." Just as if he were to say, "Do not err; for unless the Word of God dwell with, and the Spirit of the Father be in you, and if ye shall live frivolously and carelessly as if ye were this only, viz., mere flesh and blood, ye cannot inherit the kingdom of God."

---

[1] Luke x. 60.
[2] Matt. xxvi. 41.
[3] 1 Cor. xv. 48.
[4] 1 Cor. xv. 49.

[5] Matt. v. 5.

CHAP. X. — BY A COMPARISON DRAWN FROM THE WILD OLIVE-TREE, WHOSE QUALITY BUT NOT WHOSE NATURE IS CHANGED BY GRAFTING, HE PROVES MORE IMPORTANT THINGS; HE POINTS OUT ALSO THAT MAN WITHOUT THE SPIRIT IS NOT CAPABLE OF BRINGING FORTH FRUIT, OR OF INHERITING THE KINGDOM OF GOD.

1. This truth, therefore, [he declares], in order that we may not reject the engrafting of the Spirit while pampering the flesh. "But thou, being a wild olive-tree," he says, "hast been grafted into the good olive-tree, and been made a partaker of the fatness of the olive-tree."[1] As, therefore, when the wild olive has been engrafted, if it remain in its former condition, viz., a wild olive, it is "cut off, and cast into the fire;"[2] but if it takes kindly to the graft, and is changed into the good olive-tree, it becomes a fruit-bearing olive, planted, as it were, in a king's park (*paradiso*) : so likewise men, if they do truly progress by faith towards better things, and receive the Spirit of God, and bring forth the fruit thereof, shall be spiritual, as being planted in the paradise of God. But if they cast out the Spirit, and remain in their former condition, desirous of being of the flesh rather than of the Spirit, then it is very justly said with regard to men of this stamp, "That flesh and blood shall not inherit the kingdom of God;"[3] just as if any one were to say that the wild olive is not received into the paradise of God. Admirably therefore does the apostle exhibit our nature, and God's universal appointment, in his discourse about flesh and blood and the wild olive. For as the good olive, if neglected for a certain time, if left to grow wild and to run to wood, does itself become a wild olive; or again, if the wild olive be carefully tended and grafted, it naturally reverts to its former fruit-bearing condition : so men also, when they become careless, and bring forth for fruit the lusts of the flesh like woody produce, are rendered, by their own fault, unfruitful in righteousness. For when men sleep, the enemy sows the material of tares;[4] and for this cause did the Lord command His disciples to be on the watch.[5] And again, those persons who are not bringing forth the fruits of righteousness, and are, as it were, covered over and lost among brambles, if they use diligence, and receive the word of God as a graft,[6] arrive at the pristine nature of man — that which was created after the image and likeness of God.

2. But as the engrafted wild olive does not certainly lose the substance of its wood, but changes the quality of its fruit, and receives another name, being now not a wild olive, but a fruit-bearing olive, and is called so; so also, when man is grafted in by faith and receives the Spirit of God, he certainly does not lose the substance of flesh, but changes the quality of the fruit [brought forth, i.e.,] of his works, and receives another name,[7] showing that he has become changed for the better, being now not [mere] flesh and blood, but a spiritual man, and is called such. Then, again, as the wild olive, if it be not grafted in, remains useless to its lord because of its woody quality, and is cut down as a tree bearing no fruit, and cast into the fire; so also man, if he does not receive through faith the engrafting of the Spirit, remains in his old condition, and being [mere] flesh and blood, he cannot inherit the kingdom of God. Rightly therefore does the apostle declare, "Flesh and blood cannot inherit the kingdom of God;"[8] and, "Those who are in the flesh cannot please God:"[9] not repudiating [by these words] the substance of flesh, but showing that into it the Spirit must be infused.[10] And for this reason, he says, "This mortal must put on immortality, and this corruptible must put on incorruption."[11] And again he declares, "But ye are not in the flesh, but in the Spirit, if so be that the Spirit of God dwell in you."[12] He sets this forth still more plainly, where he says, "The body indeed is dead, because of sin; but the Spirit is life, because of righteousness. But if the Spirit of Him who raised up Jesus from the dead dwell in you, He that raised up Christ from the dead shall also quicken your mortal bodies, because of His Spirit dwelling in you."[13] And again he says, in the Epistle to the Romans, "For if ye live after the flesh, ye shall die."[14] [Now by these words] he does not prohibit them from living their lives in the flesh, for he was himself in the flesh when he wrote to them; but he cuts away the lusts of the flesh, those which bring death upon a man. And for this reason he says in continuation, "But if ye through the Spirit do mortify the works of the flesh, ye shall live. For whosoever are led by the Spirit of God, these are the sons of God."

CHAP. XI. — TREATS UPON THE ACTIONS OF CARNAL AND OF SPIRITUAL PERSONS; ALSO, THAT THE SPIRITUAL CLEANSING IS NOT TO BE REFERRED TO THE SUBSTANCE OF OUR BODIES, BUT TO THE MANNER OF OUR FORMER LIFE.

1. [The apostle], foreseeing the wicked speeches of unbelievers, has particularized the

---

[1] Rom. xi. 17.
[2] Matt. vii. 19.
[3] 1 Cor. xv. 50.
[4] Matt. xiii. 25.
[5] Matt. xxiv. 42, xxv. 13; Mark xiii. 33.
[6] Jas. i. 21.
[7] Rev. ii. 17.
[8] 1 Cor. xv. 50.
[9] Rom. viii. 8.
[10] The Latin has, "sed infusionem Spiritus attrahens."
[11] 1 Cor. xv. 53.
[12] Rom. viii. 9.
[13] Rom. viii. 10, etc.
[14] Rom. viii. 13.

works which he terms carnal; and he explains himself, lest any room for doubt be left to those who do dishonestly pervert his meaning, thus saying in the Epistle to the Galatians: "Now the works of the flesh are manifest, which are: adulteries, fornications, uncleanness, luxuriousness, idolatries, witchcrafts,[1] hatreds, contentions, jealousies, wraths, emulations, animosities, irritable speeches, dissensions, heresies, envyings, drunkenness, carousings, and such like; of which I warn you, as also I have warned you, that they who do such things shall not inherit the kingdom of God."[2] Thus does he point out to his hearers in a more explicit manner what it is [he means when he declares], "Flesh and blood shall not inherit the kingdom of God." For they who do these things, since they do indeed walk after the flesh, have not the power of living unto God. And then, again, he proceeds to tell us the spiritual actions which vivify a man, that is, the engrafting of the Spirit; thus saying, "But the fruit of the Spirit is love, joy, peace, long-suffering, goodness, benignity, faith, meekness, continence, chastity: against these there is no law."[3] As, therefore, he who has gone forward to the better things, and has brought forth the fruit of the Spirit, is saved altogether because of the communion of the Spirit; so also he who has continued in the aforesaid works of the flesh, being truly reckoned as carnal, because he did not receive the Spirit of God, shall not have power to inherit the kingdom of heaven. As, again, the same apostle testifies, saying to the Corinthians, "Know ye not that the unrighteous shall not inherit the kingdom of God? Do not err," he says: "neither fornicators, nor idolaters, nor adulterers, nor effeminate, nor abusers of themselves with mankind, nor thieves, nor covetous, nor revilers, nor rapacious persons, shall inherit the kingdom of God. And these ye indeed have been; but ye have been washed, but ye have been sanctified, but ye have been justified in the name of the Lord Jesus Christ, and in the Spirit of our God."[4] He shows in the clearest manner through what things it is that man goes to destruction, if he has continued to live after the flesh; and then, on the other hand, [he points out] through what things he is saved. Now he says that the things which save are the name of our Lord Jesus Christ, and the Spirit of our God.

2. Since, therefore, in that passage he recounts those works of the flesh which are without the Spirit, which bring death [upon their doers], he exclaimed at the end of his Epistle, in accordance with what he had already declared, "And as we have borne the image of him who is of the earth, we shall also bear the image of Him who is from heaven. For this I say, brethren, that flesh and blood cannot inherit the kingdom of God."[5] Now this which he says, "as we have borne the image of him who is of the earth," is analogous to what has been declared, "And such indeed ye were; but ye have been washed, but ye have been sanctified, but ye have been justified in the name of our Lord Jesus Christ, and in the Spirit of our God." When, therefore, did we bear the image of him who is of the earth? Doubtless it was when those actions spoken of as "works of the flesh" used to be wrought in us. And then, again, when [do we bear] the image of the heavenly? Doubtless when he says, "Ye have been washed," believing in the name of the Lord, and receiving His Spirit. Now we have washed away, not the substance of our body, nor the image of our [primary] formation, but the former vain conversation. In these members, therefore, in which we were going to destruction by working the works of corruption, in these very members are we made alive by working the works of the Spirit.

CHAP. XII. — OF THE DIFFERENCE BETWEEN LIFE AND DEATH; OF THE BREATH OF LIFE AND THE VIVIFYING SPIRIT: ALSO HOW IT IS THAT THE SUBSTANCE OF FLESH REVIVES WHICH ONCE WAS DEAD.

1. For as the flesh is capable of corruption, so is it also of incorruption; and as it is of death, so is it also of life. These two do mutually give way to each other; and both cannot remain in the same place, but one is driven out by the other, and the presence of the one destroys that of the other. If, then, when death takes possession of a man, it drives life away from him, and proves him to be dead, much more does life, when it has obtained power over the man, drive out death, and restore him as living unto God. For if death brings mortality, why should not life, when it comes, vivify man? Just as Esaias the prophet says, "Death devoured when it had prevailed."[6] And again, "God has wiped away every tear from every face." Thus that former life is expelled, because it was not given by the Spirit, but by the breath.

2. For the breath of life, which also rendered man an animated being, is one thing, and the vivifying Spirit another, which also caused him to become spiritual. And for this reason Isaiah said, "Thus saith the LORD, who made heaven and established it, who founded the earth and the things therein, and gave breath to the people

---

[1] Or, "poisonings."
[2] Gal. v. 19, etc.
[3] Gal. v. 22.
[4] 1 Cor. vi. 9-11.
[5] 1 Cor. xv. 49, etc.
[6] Isa. xxv. 8, LXX.

upon it, and Spirit to those walking upon it;"[1] thus telling us that breath is indeed given in common to all people upon earth, but that the Spirit is theirs alone who tread down earthly desires. And therefore Isaiah himself, distinguishing the things already mentioned, again exclaims, "For the Spirit shall go forth from Me, and I have made every breath."[2] Thus does he attribute the Spirit as peculiar to God, which in the last times He pours forth upon the human race by the adoption of sons; but [he shows] that breath was common throughout the creation, and points it out as something created. Now what has been made is a different thing from him who makes it. The breath, then, is temporal, but the Spirit eternal. The breath, too, increases [in strength] for a short period, and continues for a certain time; after that it takes its departure, leaving its former abode destitute of breath. But when the Spirit pervades the man within and without, inasmuch as it continues there, it never leaves him. "But that is not first which is spiritual," says the apostle, speaking this as if with reference to us human beings; "but that is first which is animal, afterwards that which is spiritual,"[3] in accordance with reason. For there had been a necessity that, in the first place, a human being should be fashioned, and that what was fashioned should receive the soul; afterwards that it should thus receive the communion of the Spirit. Wherefore also "the first Adam was made" by the Lord "a living soul, the second Adam a quickening spirit."[4] As, then, he who was made a living soul forfeited life when he turned aside to what was evil, so, on the other hand, the same individual, when he reverts to what is good, and receives the quickening Spirit, shall find life.

3. For it is not one thing which dies and another which is quickened, as neither is it one thing which is lost and another which is found, but the Lord came seeking for that same sheep which had been lost. What was it, then, which was dead? Undoubtedly it was the substance of the flesh; the same, too, which had lost the breath of life, and had become breathless and dead. This same, therefore, was what the Lord came to quicken, that as in Adam we do all die, as being of an animal nature, in Christ we may all live, as being spiritual, not laying aside God's handiwork, but the lusts of the flesh, and receiving the Holy Spirit; as the apostle says in the Epistle to the Colossians: "Mortify, therefore, your members which are upon the earth." And what these are he himself explains: "Fornication, uncleanness, inordinate affection, evil concupiscence, and covetousness, which is idolatry."[5] The laying aside of these is what the apostle preaches; and he declares that those who do such things, as being merely flesh and blood, cannot inherit the kingdom of heaven. For their soul, tending towards what is worse, and descending to earthly lusts, has become a partaker in the same designation which belongs to these [lusts, viz., "earthly"], which, when the apostle commands us to lay aside, he says in the same Epistle, "Cast ye off the old man with his deeds."[6] But when he said this, he does not remove away the ancient formation [of man]; for in that case it would be incumbent on us to rid ourselves of its company by committing suicide.

4. But the apostle himself also, being one who had been formed in a womb, and had issued thence, wrote to us, and confessed in his Epistle to the Philippians that "to live in the flesh was the fruit of [his] work;"[7] thus expressing himself. Now the final result of the work of the Spirit is the salvation of the flesh.[8] For what other visible fruit is there of the invisible Spirit, than the rendering of the flesh mature and capable of incorruption? If then [he says], "To live in the flesh, this is the result of labour to me," he did not surely contemn the substance of flesh in that passage where he said, "Put ye off the old man with his works;"[9] but he points out that we should lay aside our former conversation, that which waxes old and becomes corrupt; and for this reason he goes on to say, "And put ye on the new man, that which is renewed in knowledge, after the image of Him who created him." In this, therefore, that he says, "which is renewed in knowledge," he demonstrates that he, the selfsame man who was in ignorance in times past, that is, in ignorance of God, is renewed by that knowledge which has respect to Him. For the knowledge of God renews man. And when he says, "after the image of the Creator," he sets forth the recapitulation of the same man, who was at the beginning made after the likeness of God.

5. And that he, the apostle, was the very same person who had been born from the womb, that is, of the ancient substance of flesh, he does himself declare in the Epistle to the Galatians: "But when it pleased God, who separated me from my mother's womb, and called me by His grace, to reveal His Son in me, that I might preach Him among the Gentiles,"[10] it was not, as I have already observed, one person who had

---

[1] Isa. xlii. 5.
[2] Isa. lvii. 16.
[3] 1 Cor. xv. 46.
[4] 1 Cor. xv. 45.
[5] Col. iii. 5.
[6] Col. iii. 9.
[7] 1 Phil. i. 22.
[8] Following Harvey's explanation of a somewhat obscure passage.
[9] Col. iii. 10.
[10] Gal. i. 15, 16.

been born from the womb, and another who preached the Gospel of the Son of God; but that same individual who formerly was ignorant, and used to persecute the Church, when the revelation was made to him from heaven, and the Lord conferred with him, as I have pointed out in the third book,[1] preached the Gospel of Jesus Christ the Son of God, who was crucified under Pontius Pilate, his former ignorance being driven out by his subsequent knowledge: just as the blind men whom the Lord healed did certainly lose their blindness, but received the substance of their eyes perfect, and obtained the power of vision in the very same eyes with which they formerly did not see; the darkness being merely driven away by the power of vision, while the substance of the eyes was retained, in order that, by means of those eyes through which they had not seen, exercising again the visual power, they might give thanks to Him who had restored them again to sight. And thus, also, he whose withered hand was healed, and all who were healed generally, did not change those parts of their bodies which had at their birth come forth from the womb, but simply obtained these anew in a healthy condition.

6. For the Maker of all things, the Word of God, who did also from the beginning form man, when He found His handiwork impaired by wickedness, performed upon it all kinds of healing. At one time [He did so], as regards each separate member, as it is found in His own handiwork; and at another time He did once for all restore man sound and whole in all points, preparing him perfect for Himself unto the resurrection. For what was His object in healing [different] portions of the flesh, and restoring them to their original condition, if those parts which had been healed by Him were not in a position to obtain salvation? For if it was [merely] a temporary benefit which He conferred, He granted nothing of importance to those who were the subjects of His healing. Or how can they maintain that the flesh is incapable of receiving the life which flows from Him, when it received healing from Him? For life is brought about through healing, and incorruption through life. He, therefore, who confers healing, the same does also confer life; and He [who gives] life, also surrounds His own handiwork with incorruption.

CHAP. XIII. — IN THE DEAD WHO WERE RAISED BY CHRIST WE POSSESS THE HIGHEST PROOF OF THE RESURRECTION; AND OUR HEARTS ARE SHOWN TO BE CAPABLE OF LIFE ETERNAL, BECAUSE THEY CAN NOW RECEIVE THE SPIRIT OF GOD.

1. Let our opponents — that is, they who speak against their own salvation — inform us [as to this point] : The deceased daughter of the high priest;[2] the widow's dead son, who was being carried out [to burial] near the gate [of the city];[3] and Lazarus, who had lain four days in the tomb,[4] — in what bodies did they rise again? In those same, no doubt, in which they had also died. For if it were not in the very same, then certainly those same individuals who had died did not rise again. For [the Scripture] says, "The Lord took the hand of the dead man, and said to him, Young man, I say unto thee, Arise. And the dead man sat up, and He commanded that something should be given him to eat; and He delivered him to his mother."[5] Again, He called Lazarus "with a loud voice, saying, Lazarus, come forth; and he that was dead came forth bound with bandages, feet and hands." This was symbolical of that man who had been bound in sins. And therefore the Lord said, "Loose him, and let him depart." As, therefore, those who were healed were made whole in those members which had in times past been afflicted; and the dead rose in the identical bodies, their limbs and bodies receiving health, and that life which was granted by the Lord, who prefigures eternal things by temporal, and shows that it is He who is Himself able to extend both healing and life to His handiwork, that His words concerning its [future] resurrection may also be believed; so also at the end, when the Lord utters His voice "by the last trumpet,"[6] the dead shall be raised, as He Himself declares: "The hour shall come, in which all the dead which are in the tombs shall hear the voice of the Son of man, and shall come forth; those that have done good to the resurrection of life, and those that have done evil to the resurrection of judgment."[7]

2. Vain, therefore, and truly miserable, are those who do not choose to see what is so manifest and clear, but shun the light of truth, blinding themselves like the tragic Œdipus. And as those who are not practised in wrestling, when they contend with others, laying hold with a determined grasp of some part of [their opponent's] body, really fall by means of that which they grasp, yet when they fall, imagine that they are gaining the victory, because they have obstinately kept their hold upon that part which they seized at the outset, and besides falling, become

---

[1] Vol. i. pp. 306, 321.
[2] Mark v. 22. Irenæus confounds the ruler of the synagogue with the high priest. [Let not those who possess printed Bibles and concordances and commentaries, and all manner of helps to memory, blame the Fathers for such mistakes, until they at least equal them in their marvellous and minute familiarity with the inspired writers.]
[3] Luke vii. 12.
[4] John ix. 30.
[5] The two miracles of raising the widow's son and the rabbi's daughter are here amalgamated.
[6] 1 Cor. xv. 52.
[7] John v. 28.

subjects of ridicule; so is it with respect to that [favourite] expression of the heretics: "Flesh and blood cannot inherit the kingdom of God;" while taking two expressions of Paul's, without having perceived the apostle's meaning, or examined critically the force of the terms, but keeping fast hold of the mere expressions by themselves, they die in consequence of their influence (περὶ αὐτάς), overturning as far as in them lies the entire dispensation of God.

3. For thus they will allege that this passage refers to the flesh strictly so called, and not to fleshly works, as I have pointed out, so representing the apostle as contradicting himself. For immediately following, in the same Epistle, he says conclusively, speaking thus in reference to the flesh: "For this corruptible must put on incorruption, and this mortal must put on immortality. So, when this mortal shall have put on immortality, then shall be brought to pass the saying which is written, Death is swallowed up in victory. O death, where is thy sting? O death, where is thy victory?"[1] Now these words shall be appropriately said at the time when this mortal and corruptible flesh, which is subject to death, which also is pressed down by a certain dominion of death, rising up into life, shall put on incorruption and immortality. For then, indeed, shall death be truly vanquished, when that flesh which is held down by it shall go forth from under its dominion. And again, to the Philippians he says: "But our conversation is in heaven, from whence also we look for the Saviour, the Lord Jesus, who shall transfigure the body of our humiliation conformable to the body of His glory, even as He is able (*ita ut possit*) according to the working of His own power."[2] What, then, is this "body of humiliation" which the Lord shall transfigure, [so as to be] conformed to "the body of His glory?" Plainly it is this body composed of flesh, which is indeed humbled when it falls into the earth. Now its transformation [takes place thus], that while it is mortal and corruptible, it becomes immortal and incorruptible, not after its own proper substance, but after the mighty working of the Lord, who is able to invest the mortal with immortality, and the corruptible with incorruption. And therefore he says,[3] "that mortality may be swallowed up of life. He who has perfected us for this very thing is God, who also has given unto us the earnest of the Spirit."[4] He uses these words most manifestly in reference to the flesh; for the soul is not mortal, neither is the spirit. Now, what is mortal shall be swallowed up of life, when the flesh is dead no longer, but remains living and incorruptible, hymning the praises of God, who has perfected us for this very thing. In order, therefore, that we may be perfected for this, aptly does he say to the Corinthians, "Glorify God in your body."[5] Now God is He who gives rise to immortality.

4. That he uses these words with respect to the body of flesh, and to none other, he declares to the Corinthians manifestly, indubitably, and free from all ambiguity: "Always bearing about in our body the dying of Jesus,[6] that also the life of Jesus Christ might be manifested in our body. For if we who live are delivered unto death for Jesus' sake, it is that the life of Jesus may also be manifested in our mortal flesh."[7] And that the Spirit lays hold on the flesh, he says in the same Epistle, "That ye are the epistle of Christ, ministered by us, inscribed not with ink, but with the Spirit of the living God, not in tables of stone, but in the fleshly tables of the heart."[8] If, therefore, in the present time, fleshly hearts are made partakers of the Spirit, what is there astonishing if, in the resurrection, they receive that life which is granted by the Spirit? Of which resurrection the apostle speaks in the Epistle to the Philippians: "Having been made conformable to His death, if by any means I might attain to the resurrection which is from the dead."[9] In what other mortal flesh, therefore, can life be understood as being manifested, unless in that substance which is also put to death on account of that confession which is made of God? — as he has himself declared, "If, as a man, I have fought with beasts[10] at Ephesus, what advantageth it me if the dead rise not? For if the dead rise not, neither has Christ risen. Now, if Christ has not risen, our preaching is vain, and your faith is vain. In that case, too, we are found false witnesses for God, since we have testified that He raised up Christ, whom [upon that supposition] He did not raise up.[11] For if the dead rise not, neither has Christ risen. But if Christ be not risen, your faith is vain, since ye are yet in your sins. Therefore those who have fallen asleep in Christ have perished. If in this life only we have hope in Christ, we are more miserable than all men. But now Christ has

---

[1] 1 Cor. xv. 53.
[2] Phil. iii. 29, etc.
[3] The original Greek text is preserved here, as above; the Latin translator inserts, "in secunda ad Corinthios." Harvey observes: "The interpolation of the Scriptural reference by the translator suggests the suspicion that the greater number of such references have come in from the margin."
[4] 2 Cor. v. 4.
[5] 1 Cor. vi. 20.
[6] Agreeing with the Syriac version in omitting "the Lord" before the word "Jesus," and in reading ἀεί as εἰ, which Harvey considers the true text.
[7] 2 Cor. iv. 10, etc.
[8] 2 Cor. iii. 3.
[9] Phil. iii. 11.
[10] The Syriac translation seems to take a literal meaning out of this passage: "If, as one of the sons of men, I have been cast forth to the wild beasts at Ephesus."
[11] This is in accordance with the Syriac, which omits the clause, εἴπερ ἄρα νεκροὶ οὐκ ἐγείρονται.

risen from the dead, the first-fruits of those that sleep; for as by man [came] death, by man also [came] the resurrection of the dead."[1]

5. In all these passages, therefore, as I have already said, these men must either allege that the apostle expresses opinions contradicting himself, with respect to that statement, "Flesh and blood cannot inherit the kingdom of God;" or, on the other hand, they will be forced to make perverse and crooked interpretations of all the passages, so as to overturn and alter the sense of the words. For what sensible thing can they say, if they endeavour to interpret otherwise this which he writes: "For this corruptible must put on incorruption, and this mortal put on immortality;"[2] and, "That the life of Jesus may be made manifest in our mortal flesh;"[3] and all the other passages in which the apostle does manifestly and clearly declare the resurrection and incorruption of the flesh? And thus shall they be compelled to put a false interpretation upon passages such as these, they who do not choose to understand one correctly.

CHAP. XIV. — UNLESS THE FLESH WERE TO BE SAVED, THE WORD WOULD NOT HAVE TAKEN UPON HIM FLESH OF THE SAME SUBSTANCE AS OURS: FROM THIS IT WOULD FOLLOW THAT NEITHER SHOULD WE HAVE BEEN RECONCILED BY HIM.

1. And inasmuch as the apostle has not pronounced against the very substance of flesh and blood, that it cannot inherit the kingdom of God, the same apostle has everywhere adopted the term "flesh and blood" with regard to the Lord Jesus Christ, partly indeed to establish His human nature (for He did Himself speak of Himself as the Son of man), and partly that He might confirm the salvation of our flesh. For if the flesh were not in a position to be saved, the Word of God would in no wise have become flesh. And if the blood of the righteous were not to be inquired after, the Lord would certainly not have had blood [in His composition]. But inasmuch as blood cries out (*vocalis est*) from the beginning [of the world], God said to Cain, when he had slain his brother, "The voice of thy brother's blood crieth to Me."[4] And as their blood will be inquired after, He said to those with Noah, "For your blood of your souls will I require, [even] from the hand of all beasts;"[5] and again, "Whosoever will shed man's blood,[6] it shall be shed for his blood." In like manner, too, did the Lord say to those who should afterwards shed His blood, "All righteous blood shall be required which is shed upon the earth, from the blood of righteous Abel to the blood of Zacharias the son of Barachias, whom ye slew between the temple and the altar. Verily I say unto you, All these things shall come upon this generation."[7] He thus points out the recapitulation that should take place in his own person of the effusion of blood from the beginning, of all the righteous men and of the prophets, and that by means of Himself there should be a requisition of their blood. Now this [blood] could not be required unless it also had the capability of being saved; nor would the Lord have summed up these things in Himself, unless He had Himself been made flesh and blood after the way of the original formation [of man], saving in his own person at the end that which had in the beginning perished in Adam.

2. But if the Lord became incarnate for any other order of things, and took flesh of any other substance, He has not then summed up human nature in His own person, nor in that case can He be termed flesh. For flesh has been truly made [to consist in] a transmission of that thing moulded originally from the dust. But if it had been necessary for Him to draw the material [of His body] from another substance, the Father would at the beginning have moulded the material [of flesh] from a different substance [than from what He actually did]. But now the case stands thus, that the Word has saved that which really was [created, viz.,] humanity which had perished, effecting by means of Himself that communion which should be held with it, and seeking out its salvation. But the thing which had perished possessed flesh and blood. For the Lord, taking dust from the earth, moulded man; and it was upon his behalf that all the dispensation of the Lord's advent took place. He had Himself, therefore, flesh and blood, recapitulating in Himself not a certain other, but that original handiwork of the Father, seeking out that thing which had perished. And for this cause the apostle, in the Epistle to the Colossians, says, "And though ye were formerly alienated, and enemies to His knowledge by evil works, yet now ye have been reconciled in the body of His flesh, through His death, to present yourselves holy and chaste, and without fault in His sight."[8] He says, "Ye have been reconciled in the body of His flesh," because the righteous flesh has reconciled that flesh which was being kept under bondage in sin, and brought it into friendship with God.

3. If, then, any one allege that in this respect the flesh of the Lord was different from ours, because it indeed did not commit sin, neither

---
[1] 1 Cor. xv. 13, etc.
[2] 1 Cor. xv. 53.
[3] 2 Cor. iv. 11.
[4] Gen. iv. 10.
[5] Gen. ix. 5, 6, LXX.
[6] One of the MSS. reads here: Sanguis pro sanguine ejus effundetur.
[7] Matt. xxiii. 35, etc.; Luke xi. 50.
[8] Col. i. 21, etc.

was deceit found in His soul, while we, on the other hand, are sinners, he says what is the fact. But if he pretends that the Lord possessed another substance of flesh, the sayings respecting reconciliation will not agree with that man. For that thing is reconciled which had formerly been in enmity. Now, if the Lord had taken flesh from another substance, He would not, by so doing, have reconciled that one to God which had become inimical through transgression. But now, by means of communion with Himself, the Lord has reconciled man to God the Father, in reconciling us to Himself by the body of His own flesh, and redeeming us by His own blood, as the apostle says to the Ephesians, "In whom we have redemption through His blood, the remission of sins;"[1] and again to the same he says, "Ye who formerly were far off have been brought near in the blood of Christ;"[2] and again, "Abolishing in His flesh the enmities, [even] the law of commandments [contained] in ordinances."[3] And in every Epistle the apostle plainly testifies, that through the flesh of our Lord, and through His blood, we have been saved.

4. If, therefore, flesh and blood are the things which procure for us life, it has not been declared of flesh and blood, in the literal meaning (*proprie*) of the terms, that they cannot inherit the kingdom of God; but [these words apply] to those carnal deeds already mentioned, which, perverting man to sin, deprive him of life. And for this reason he says, in the Epistle to the Romans: "Let not sin, therefore, reign in your mortal body, to be under its control: neither yield ye your members instruments of unrighteousness unto sin; but yield yourselves to God, as being alive from the dead, and your members as instruments of righteousness unto God."[4] In these same members, therefore, in which we used to serve sin, and bring forth fruit unto death, does He wish us to [be obedient] unto righteousness, that we may bring forth fruit unto life. Remember, therefore, my beloved friend, that thou hast been redeemed by the flesh of our Lord, re-established[5] by His blood; and "holding the Head, from which the whole body of the Church, having been fitted together, takes increase"[6] — that is, acknowledging the advent in the flesh of the Son of God, and [His] divinity (*deum*), and looking forward with constancy to His human nature[7] (*hominem*), availing thyself also of these proofs drawn from Scripture — thou dost easily overthrow, as I have pointed out, all those notions of the heretics which were concocted afterwards.

CHAP. XV. — PROOFS OF THE RESURRECTION FROM ISAIAH AND EZEKIEL; THE SAME GOD WHO CREATED US WILL ALSO RAISE US UP.

1. Now, that He who at the beginning created man, did promise him a second birth after his dissolution into earth, Esaias thus declares: "The dead shall rise again, and they who are in the tombs shall arise, and they who are in the earth shall rejoice. For the dew which is from Thee is health to them."[8] And again: "I will comfort you, and ye shall be comforted in Jerusalem: and ye shall see, and your heart shall rejoice, and your bones shall flourish as the grass; and the hand of the Lord shall be known to those who worship Him."[9] And Ezekiel speaks as follows: "And the hand of the LORD came upon me, and the LORD led me forth in the Spirit, and set me down in the midst of the plain, and this place was full of bones. And He caused me to pass by them round about: and, behold, there were many upon the surface of the plain very dry. And He said unto me, Son of man, can these bones live? And I said, Lord, Thou who hast made them dost know. And He said unto me, Prophesy upon these bones, and thou shalt say to them, Ye dry bones, hear the word of the LORD. Thus saith the LORD to these bones, Behold, I will cause the spirit of life to come upon you, and I will lay sinews upon you, and bring up flesh again upon you, and I will stretch skin upon you, and will put my Spirit into you, and ye shall live; and ye shall know that I am the LORD. And I prophesied as the Lord had commanded me. And it came to pass, when I was prophesying, that, behold, an earthquake, and the bones were drawn together, each one to its own articulation: and I beheld, and, lo, the sinews and flesh were produced upon them, and the skins rose upon them round about, but there was no breath in them. And He said unto me, Prophesy to the breath, son of man, and say to the breath, These things saith the LORD, Come from the four winds (*spiritibus*), and breathe upon these dead, that they may live. So I prophesied as the Lord had commanded me, and the breath entered into them; and they did live, and stood upon their feet, an exceeding great gathering."[10] And again he says, "Thus saith the LORD, Behold, I will set your graves open, and cause you to come out of your graves, and bring you into the land of Israel; and ye shall know that I am the LORD,

---

[1] Eph. i. 7.
[2] Eph. ii. 13.
[3] Eph. ii. 15.
[4] Rom. vi. 12, etc.
[5] "Et sanguine ejus redhibitus," corresponding to the Greek term ἀποκατασταθείς. "Redhibere" is properly a *forensic* term, meaning to cause any article to be restored to the vendor.
[6] Col. ii. 19.
[7] Harvey restores the Greek thus, καὶ τὸν αὐτοῦ ἄνθρωπον βεβαίως ἐκδεχόμενος, which he thinks has a reference to the patient waiting for "Christ's second advent to judge the world." The phrase might also be translated, and "receiving stedfastly His human nature."

[8] Isa. xxvi. 19.
[9] Isa. lxvi. 13.
[10] Ezek. xxxvii. 1, etc.

when I shall open your sepulchres, that I may bring my people again out of the sepulchres: and I will put my Spirit into you, and ye shall live; and I will place you in your land, and ye shall know that I am the LORD. I have said, and I will do, saith the LORD."[1] As we at once perceive that the Creator (*Demiurgo*) is in this passage represented as vivifying our dead bodies, and promising resurrection to them, and resuscitation from their sepulchres and tombs, conferring upon them immortality also (He says, "For as the tree of life, so shall their days be"[2]), He is shown to be the only God who accomplishes these things, and as Himself the good Father, benevolently conferring life upon those who have not life from themselves.

2. And for this reason did the Lord most plainly manifest Himself and the Father to His disciples, lest, forsooth, they might seek after another God besides Him who formed man, and who gave him the breath of life; and that men might not rise to such a pitch of madness as to feign another Father above the Creator. And thus also He healed by a word all the others who were in a weakly condition because of sin; to whom also He said, "Behold, thou art made whole, sin no more, lest a worse thing come upon thee:"[3] pointing out by this, that, because of the sin of disobedience, infirmities have come upon men. To that man, however, who had been blind from his birth, He gave sight, not by means of a word, but by an outward action; doing this not without a purpose, or because it so happened, but that He might show forth the hand of God, that which at the beginning had moulded man. And therefore, when His disciples asked Him for what cause the man had been born blind, whether for his own or his parents' fault, He replied, "Neither hath this man sinned, nor his parents, but that the works of God should be made manifest in him."[4] Now the work of God is the fashioning of man. For, as the Scripture says, He made [man] by a kind of process: "And the Lord took clay from the earth, and formed man."[5] Wherefore also the Lord spat on the ground and made clay, and smeared it upon the eyes, pointing out the original fashioning [of man], how it was effected, and manifesting the hand of God to those who can understand by what [hand] man was formed out of the dust. For that which the artificer, the Word, had omitted to form in the womb, [viz., the blind man's eyes], He then supplied in public, that the works of God might be manifested in him, in order that we might not be seeking out another hand by which man was fashioned, nor another Father; knowing that this hand of God which formed us at the beginning, and which does form us in the womb, has in the last times sought us out who were lost, winning back His own, and taking up the lost sheep upon His shoulders, and with joy restoring it to the fold of life.

3. Now, that the Word of God forms us in the womb, He says to Jeremiah, "Before I formed thee in the womb, I knew thee; and before thou wentest forth from the belly, I sanctified thee, and appointed thee a prophet among the nations."[6] And Paul, too, says in like manner, "But when it pleased God, who separated me from my mother's womb, that I might declare Him among the nations."[7] As, therefore, we are by the Word formed in the womb, this very same Word formed the visual power in him who had been blind from his birth; showing openly who it is that fashions us in secret, since the Word Himself had been made manifest to men: and declaring the original formation of Adam, and the manner in which he was created, and by what hand he was fashioned, indicating the whole from a part. For the Lord who formed the visual powers is He who made the whole man, carrying out the will of the Father. And inasmuch as man, with respect to that formation which was after Adam, having fallen into transgression, needed the laver of regeneration, [the Lord] said to him [upon whom He had conferred sight], after He had smeared his eyes with the clay, " Go to Siloam, and wash ;"[8] thus restoring to him both [his perfect] confirmation, and that regeneration which takes place by means of the laver. And for this reason when he was washed he came seeing, that he might both know Him who had fashioned him, and that man might learn [to know] Him who has conferred upon him life.

4. All the followers of Valentinus, therefore, lose their case, when they say that man was not fashioned out of this earth, but from a fluid and diffused substance. For, from the earth out of which the Lord formed eyes for that man, from the same earth it is evident that man was also fashioned at the beginning. For it were incompatible that the eyes should indeed be formed from one source and the rest of the body from another; as neither would it be compatible that one [being] fashioned the body, and another the eyes. But He, the very same who formed Adam at the beginning, with whom also the Father spake, [saying], " Let Us make man after Our image and likeness,"[9] revealing Himself in these last times to men, formed visual organs (*visionem*) for him who had been blind [in

---

[1] Ezek. xxxvii. 12, etc.
[2] Isa. lxv. 22.
[3] John v. 14.
[4] John ix. 3.
[5] Gen. ii. 7.
[6] Jer. i. 5.
[7] Gal. i. 15.
[8] John ix. 7.
[9] Gen. i. 25.

that body which he had derived] from Adam. Wherefore also the Scripture, pointing out what should come to pass, says, that when Adam had hid himself because of his disobedience, the Lord came to him at eventide, called him forth, and said, "Where art thou?"[1] That means that in the last times the very same Word of God came to call man, reminding him of his doings, living in which he had been hidden from the Lord. For just as at that time God spake to Adam at eventide, searching him out; so in the last times, by means of the same voice, searching out his posterity, He has visited them.

CHAP. XVI. — SINCE OUR BODIES RETURN TO THE EARTH, IT FOLLOWS THAT THEY HAVE THEIR SUBSTANCE FROM IT; ALSO, BY THE ADVENT OF THE WORD, THE IMAGE OF GOD IN US APPEARED IN A CLEARER LIGHT.

1. And since Adam was moulded from this earth to which we belong, the Scripture tells us that God said to him, "In the sweat of thy face shalt thou eat thy bread, until thou turnest again to the dust from whence thou wert taken."[2] If then, after death, our bodies return to any other substance, it follows that from it also they have their substance. But if it be into this very [earth], it is manifest that it was also from it that man's frame was created; as also the Lord clearly showed, when from this very substance He formed eyes for the man [to whom He gave sight]. And thus was the hand of God plainly shown forth, by which Adam was fashioned, and we too have been formed; and since there is one and the same Father, whose voice from the beginning even to the end is present with His handiwork, and the substance from which we were formed is plainly declared through the Gospel, we should therefore not seek after another Father besides Him, nor [look for] another substance from which we have been formed, besides what was mentioned beforehand, and shown forth by the Lord; nor another hand of God besides that which, from the beginning even to the end, forms us and prepares us for life, and is present with His handiwork, and perfects it after the image and likeness of God.

2. And then, again, this Word was manifested when the Word of God was made man, assimilating Himself to man, and man to Himself, so that by means of his resemblance to the Son, man might become precious to the Father. For in times long past, it was *said* that man was created after the image of God, but it was not [actually] *shown;* for the Word was as yet invisible, after whose image man was created. Wherefore also he did easily lose the similitude. When, however, the Word of God became flesh, He confirmed both these: for He both showed forth the image truly, since He became Himself what was His image; and He re-established the similitude after a sure manner, by assimilating man to the invisible Father through means of the visible Word.

3. And not by the aforesaid things alone has the Lord manifested Himself, but [He has done this] also by means of His passion. For doing away with [the effects of] that disobedience of man which had taken place at the beginning by the occasion of a tree, "He became obedient unto death, even the death of the cross;"[3] rectifying that disobedience which had occurred by reason of a tree, through that obedience which was [wrought out] upon the tree [of the cross]. Now He would not have come to do away, by means of that same [image], the disobedience which had been incurred towards our Maker if He proclaimed another Father. But inasmuch as it was by these things that we disobeyed God, and did not give credit to His word, so was it also by these same that He brought in obedience and consent as respects His Word; by which things He clearly shows forth God Himself, whom indeed we had offended in the first Adam, when he did not perform His commandment. In the second Adam, however, we are reconciled, being made obedient even unto death. For we were debtors to none other but to Him whose commandment we had transgressed at the beginning.

CHAP. XVII. — THERE IS BUT ONE LORD AND ONE GOD, THE FATHER AND CREATOR OF ALL THINGS, WHO HAS LOVED US IN CHRIST, GIVEN US COMMANDMENTS, AND REMITTED OUR SINS; WHOSE SON AND WORD CHRIST PROVED HIMSELF TO BE, WHEN HE FORGAVE OUR SINS.

1. Now this being is the Creator (*Demiurgus*), who is, in respect of His love, the Father; but in respect of His power, He is Lord; and in respect of His wisdom, our Maker and Fashioner; by transgressing whose commandment we became His enemies. And therefore in the last times the Lord has restored us into friendship through His incarnation, having become "the Mediator between God and men;"[4] propitiating indeed for us the Father against whom we had sinned, and cancelling (*consolatus*) our disobedience by His own obedience; conferring also upon us the gift of communion with, and subjection to, our Maker. For this reason also He has taught us to say in prayer, "And forgive us our debts;"[5] since indeed He is our Father, whose debtors we were, having transgressed His commandments. But who is this Being? Is He some unknown one, and a Father who gives no com-

---

[1] Gen. iii. 9.
[2] Gen. iii. 19.
[3] Phil. ii. 8.
[4] 1 Tim. ii. 5.
[5] Matt. vi. 12.

mandment to any one? Or is He the God who is proclaimed in the Scriptures, to whom we were debtors, having transgressed His commandment? Now the commandment was given to man by the Word. For Adam, it is said, "heard the voice of the LORD God."[1] Rightly then does His Word say to man, "Thy sins are forgiven thee;"[2] He, the same against whom we had sinned in the beginning, grants forgiveness of sins in the end. But if indeed we had disobeyed the command of any other, while it was a different being who said, "Thy sins are forgiven thee;"[2] such an one is neither good, nor true, nor just. For how can he be good, who does not give from what belongs to himself? Or how can he be just, who snatches away the goods of another? And in what way can sins be truly remitted, unless that He against whom we have sinned has Himself granted remission "through the bowels of mercy of our God," in which "He has visited us"[3] through His Son?

2. And therefore, when He had healed the man sick of the palsy, [the evangelist] says: "The people upon seeing it glorified God, who gave such power unto men."[4] What God, then, did the bystanders glorify? Was it indeed that unknown Father invented by the heretics? And how could they glorify him who was altogether unknown to them? It is evident, therefore, that the Israelites glorified Him who has been proclaimed as God by the law and the prophets, who is also the Father of our Lord; and therefore He taught men, by the evidence of their senses through those signs which He accomplished, to give glory to God. If, however, He Himself had come from another Father, and men glorified a different Father when they beheld His miracles, He [in that case] rendered the mungrateful to that Father who had sent the gift of healing. But as the only-begotten Son had come for man's salvation from Him who is God, He did both stir up the incredulous by the miracles which He was in the habit of working, to give glory to the Father; and to the Pharisees, who did not admit the advent of His Son, and who consequently did not believe in the remission [of sins] which was conferred by Him, He said, "That ye may know that the Son of man hath power to forgive sins."[5] And when He had said this, He commanded the paralytic man to take up the pallet upon which he was lying, and go into his house. By this work of His He confounded the unbelievers, and showed that He is Himself the voice of God, by which man received commandments, which he broke, and became a sinner; for the paralysis followed as a consequence of sins.

3. Therefore, by remitting sins, He did indeed heal man, while He also manifested Himself who He was. For if no one can forgive sins but God alone, while the Lord remitted them and healed men, it is plain that He was Himself the Word of God made the Son of man, receiving from the Father the power of remission of sins; since He was man, and since He was God, in order that since as man He suffered for us, so as God He might have compassion on us, and forgive us our debts, in which we were made debtors to God our Creator. And therefore David said beforehand, "Blessed are they whose iniquities are forgiven, and whose sins are covered. Blessed is the man to whom the LORD has not imputed sin;"[6] pointing out thus that remission of sins which follows upon His advent, by which "He has destroyed the handwriting" of our debt, and "fastened it to the cross;"[7] so that as by means of a tree we were made debtors to God, [so also] by means of a tree we may obtain the remission of our debt.

3. This fact has been strikingly set forth by many others, and especially through means of Elisha the prophet. For when his fellow-prophets were hewing wood for the construction of a tabernacle, and when the iron [head], shaken loose from the axe, had fallen into the Jordan and could not be found by them, upon Elisha's coming to the place, and learning what had happened, he threw some wood into the water. Then, when he had done this, the iron part of the axe floated up, and they took up from the surface of the water what they had previously lost.[8] By this action the prophet pointed out that the sure word of God, which we had negligently lost by means of a tree, and were not in the way of finding again, we should receive anew by the dispensation of a tree, [viz., the cross of Christ]. For that the word of God is likened to an axe, John the Baptist declares [when he says] in reference to it, "But now also is the axe laid to the root of the trees."[9] Jeremiah also says to the same purport: "The word of God cleaveth the rock as an axe."[10] This word, then, what was hidden from us, did the dispensation of the tree make manifest, as I have already remarked. For as we lost it by means of a tree, by means of a tree again was it made manifest to all, showing the height, the length, the breadth, the depth in itself; and, as a certain man among our predecessors observed, "Through the extension of the hands of a divine person,"[11] gathering together the two peoples to one God."

---

[1] Gen. iii. 8.
[2] Matt. ix. 2; Luke v. 20.
[3] Luke i. 78.
[4] Matt. ix. 8.
[5] Matt. ix. 6.
[6] Ps. xxxii. 1, 2.
[7] Col. ii. 14.
[8] 2 Kings vi. 6.
[9] Matt. iii. 10.
[10] Jer. xxiii. 29.
[11] The Greek is preserved here, and reads, διὰ τῆς θείας ἐκτάσεως τῶν χειρῶν — literally, "through the divine extension of hands." The old Latin merely reads, "per extensionem manuum."

For these were two hands, because there were two peoples scattered to the ends of the earth; but there was one head in the middle, as there is but one God, who is above all, and through all, and in us all.

CHAP. XVIII.—GOD THE FATHER AND HIS WORD HAVE FORMED ALL CREATED THINGS (WHICH THEY USE) BY THEIR OWN POWER AND WISDOM, NOT OUT OF DEFECT OR IGNORANCE. THE SON OF GOD, WHO RECEIVED ALL POWER FROM THE FATHER, WOULD OTHERWISE NEVER HAVE TAKEN FLESH UPON HIM.

1. And such or so important a dispensation He did not bring about by means of the creations of others, but by His own; neither by those things which were created out of ignorance and defect, but by those which had their substance from the wisdom and power of His Father. For He was neither unrighteous, so that He should covet the property of another; nor needy, that He could not by His own means impart life to His own, and make use of His own creation for the salvation of man. For indeed the creation could not have sustained Him [on the cross], if He had sent forth [simply by commission] what was the fruit of ignorance and defect. Now we have repeatedly shown that the incarnate Word of God was suspended upon a tree, and even the very heretics do acknowledge that He was crucified. How, then, could the fruit of ignorance and defect sustain Him who contains the knowledge of all things, and is true and perfect? Or how could that creation which was concealed from the Father, and far removed from Him, have sustained His Word? And if this world were made by the angels (it matters not whether we suppose their ignorance or their cognizance of the Supreme God), when the Lord declared, "For I am in the Father, and the Father in Me,"[1] how could this workmanship of the angels have borne to be burdened at once with the Father and the Son? How, again, could that creation which is beyond the Pleroma have contained Him who contains the entire Pleroma? Inasmuch, then, as all these things are impossible and incapable of proof, that preaching of the Church is alone true [which proclaims] that His own creation bare Him, which subsists by the power, the skill, and the wisdom of God; which is sustained, indeed, after an invisible manner by the Father, but, on the contrary, after a visible manner it bore His Word: and this is the true [Word].

2. For the Father bears the creation and His own Word simultaneously, and the Word borne by the Father grants the Spirit to all as the Father wills.[2] To some He gives after the manner of creation what is made;[3] but to others [He gives] after the manner of adoption, that is, what is from God, namely generation. And thus one God the Father is declared, who is above all, and through all, and in all. The Father is indeed above all, and He is the Head of Christ; but the Word is through all things, and is Himself the Head of the Church; while the Spirit is in us all, and He is the living water,[4] which the Lord grants to those who rightly believe in Him, and love Him, and who know that "there is one Father, who is above all, and through all, and in us all."[5] And to these things does John also, the disciple of the Lord, bear witness, when he speaks thus in the Gospel: "In the beginning was the Word, and the Word was with God, and the Word was God. This was in the beginning with God. All things were made by Him, and without Him was nothing made."[6] And then he said of the Word Himself: "He was in the world, and the world was made by Him, and the world knew Him not. To His own things He came, and His own people received Him not. However, as many as did receive Him, to these gave He power to become the sons of God, to those that believe in His name."[7] And again, showing the dispensation with regard to His human nature, John said: "And the Word was made flesh, and dwelt among us."[8] And in continuation he says, "And we beheld His glory, the glory as of the Only-begotten by the Father, full of grace and truth." He thus plainly points out to those willing to hear, that is, to those having ears, that there is one God, the Father over all, and one Word of God, who is through all, by whom all things have been made; and that this world belongs to Him, and was made by Him, according to the Father's will, and not by angels; nor by apostasy, defect, and ignorance; nor by any power of Prunicus, whom certain of them also call "the Mother;" nor by any other maker of the world ignorant of the Father.

3. For the Creator of the world is truly the Word of God: and this is our Lord, who in the last times was made man, existing in this world, and who in an invisible manner contains all things created, and is inherent in the entire creation, since the Word of God governs and arranges all

---

[1] John xiv. 11.

[2] From this passage Harvey infers that Irenæus held the procession of the Holy Spirit from the Father and the Son,—a doctrine denied by the Oriental Church in after times. [Here is nothing about the "procession:" only the "mission" of the Spirit is here concerned. And the Easterns object to the double procession itself olny in so far as any one means thereby to deny "quod solus Pater est divinarum personarum, Principium et Fons,"— ρίζα καὶ πηγή. See Procopowicz, *De Processione*, Gothæ, 1772].

[3] Grabe and Harvey insert the words, "quod est conditionis," but on slender authority.

[4] John vii. 39.

[5] Eph. iv. 6.

[6] John i. 1, etc.

[7] John i. 10, etc.

[8] John i. 14.

things; and therefore He came to His own in a visible[1] manner, and was made flesh, and hung upon the tree, that He might sum up all things in Himself. "And His own peculiar people did not receive Him," as Moses declared this very thing among the people: "And thy life shall be hanging before thine eyes, and thou wilt not believe thy life."[2] Those therefore who did not receive Him did not receive life. "But to as many as received Him, to them gave He power to become the sons of God."[3] For it is He who has power from the Father over all things, since He is the Word of God, and very man, communicating with invisible beings after the manner of the intellect, and appointing a law observable to the outward senses, that all things should continue each in its own order; and He reigns manifestly over things visible and pertaining to men; and brings in just judgment and worthy upon all; as David also, clearly pointing to this, says, "Our God shall openly come, and will not keep silence."[4] Then he shows also the judgment which is brought in by Him, saying, "A fire shall burn in His sight, and a strong tempest shall rage round about Him. He shall call upon the heaven from above, and the earth, to judge His people."

CHAP. XIX. — A COMPARISON IS INSTITUTED BETWEEN THE DISOBEDIENT AND SINNING EVE AND THE VIRGIN MARY, HER PATRONESS. VARIOUS AND DISCORDANT HERESIES ARE MENTIONED.

1. That the Lord then was manifestly coming to His own things, and was sustaining them by means of that creation which is supported by Himself, and was making a recapitulation of that disobedience which had occurred in connection with a tree, through the obedience which was [exhibited by Himself when He hung] upon a tree, [the effects] also of that deception being done away with, by which that virgin Eve, who was already espoused to a man, was unhappily misled, — was happily announced, through means of the truth [spoken] by the angel to the Virgin Mary, who was [also espoused] to a man.[5] For just as the former was led astray by the word of an angel, so that she fled from God when she had transgressed His word; so did the latter, by an angelic communication, receive the glad tidings that she should sustain (*portaret*) God, being obedient to His word. And if the former did disobey God, yet the latter was persuaded to be obedient to God, in order that the Virgin Mary might become the patroness[6] (*advocata*) of the virgin Eve. And thus, as the human race fell into bondage to death by means of a virgin, so is it rescued by a virgin; virginal disobedience having been balanced in the opposite scale by virginal obedience. For in the same way the sin of the first created man (*protoplasti*) receives amendment by the correction of the First-begotten, and the coming of the serpent is conquered by the harmlessness of the dove, those bonds being unloosed by which we had been fast bound to death.

2. The heretics being all unlearned and ignorant of God's arrangements, and not acquainted with that dispensation by which He took upon Him human nature (*inscii ejus quæ est secundum hominem dispensationis*), inasmuch as they blind themselves with regard to the truth, do in fact speak against their own salvation. Some of them introduce another Father besides the Creator; some, again, say that the world and its substance was made by certain angels; certain others [maintain] that it was widely separated by Horos[7] from him whom they represent as being the Father — that it sprang forth (*floruisse*) of itself, and from itself was born. Then, again, others [of them assert] that it obtained substance in those things which are contained by the Father, from defect and ignorance; others still, despise the advent of the Lord manifest [to the senses], for they do not admit His incarnation; while others, ignoring the arrangement [that He should be born] of a virgin, maintain that He was begotten by Joseph. And still further, some affirm that neither their soul nor their body can receive eternal life, but merely the inner man. Moreover, they will have it that this [inner man] is that which is the understanding (*sensum*) in them, and which they decree as being the only thing to ascend to "the perfect." Others [maintain], as I have said in the first book, that while the soul is saved, their body does not participate in the salvation which comes from God; in which [book] I have also set forward the hypotheses of all these men, and in the second have pointed out their weakness and inconsistency.

CHAP. XX. — THOSE PASTORS ARE TO BE HEARD TO WHOM THE APOSTLES COMMITTED THE CHURCHES, POSSESSING ONE AND THE SAME DOCTRINE OF SALVATION; THE HERETICS, ON THE OTHER HAND, ARE TO BE AVOIDED. WE MUST THINK SOBERLY WITH REGARD TO THE MYSTERIES OF THE FAITH.

1. Now all these [heretics] are of much later date than the bishops to whom the apostles committed the Churches; which fact I have in the third book taken all pains to demonstrate. It follows, then, as a matter of course, that these

---

[1] The text reads "invisibiliter," which seems clearly an error.
[2] Deut. xxviii. 66.
[3] John i. 13.
[4] Ps. l. 3, 4.
[5] The text is here most uncertain and obscure.
[6] [This word *patroness* is ambiguous. The Latin may stand for Gr. ἀντίληψις, — a person called in to help, or to take hold of the other end of a burden. The argument implies that Mary was thus the counterpart or balance of Eve.]
[7] The text reads "porro," which makes no sense; so that Harvey looks upon it as a corruption of the reading "per Horum."

heretics aforementioned, since they are blind to the truth, and deviate from the [right] way, will walk in various roads; and therefore the footsteps of their doctrine are scattered here and there without agreement or connection. But the path of those belonging to the Church circumscribes the whole world, as possessing the sure tradition from the apostles, and gives unto us to see that the faith of all is one and the same, since all receive one and the same God the Father, and believe in the same dispensation regarding the incarnation of the Son of God, and are cognizant of the same gift of the Spirit, and are conversant with the same commandments, and preserve the same form of ecclesiastical constitution,[1] and expect the same advent of the Lord, and await the same salvation of the complete man, that is, of the soul and body. And undoubtedly the preaching of the Church is true and stedfast, in which one and the same way of salvation is shown throughout the whole world. For to her is entrusted the light of God; and therefore the "wisdom" of God, by means of which she saves all men, " is declared in [its] going forth; it uttereth [its voice] faithfully in the streets, is preached on the tops of the walls, and speaks continually in the gates of the city."[3] For the Church preaches the truth everywhere, and she is the seven-branched candlestick which bears the light of Christ.

2. Those, therefore, who desert the preaching of the Church, call in question the knowledge of the holy presbyters, not taking into consideration of how much greater consequence is a religious man, even in a private station, than a blasphemous and impudent sophist.[4] Now, such are all the heretics, and those who imagine that they have hit upon something more beyond the truth, so that by following those things already mentioned, proceeding on their way variously, inharmoniously, and foolishly, not keeping always to the same opinions with regard to the same things, as blind men are led by the blind, they shall deservedly fall into the ditch of ignorance lying in their path, ever seeking and never finding out the truth.[5] It behoves us, therefore, to avoid their doctrines, and to take careful heed lest we suffer any injury from them; but to flee to the Church, and be brought up in her bosom, and be nourished with the Lord's Scriptures. For the Church has been planted as a garden (*paradisus*) in this world; therefore says the Spirit of God, "Thou mayest freely eat from every tree of the garden,"[6] that is, Eat ye from every Scripture of the Lord; but ye shall not eat with an uplifted mind, nor touch any heretical discord. For these men do profess that they have themselves the knowledge of good and evil; and they set their own impious minds above the God who made them. They therefore form opinions on what is beyond the limits of the understanding. For this cause also the apostle says, "Be not wise beyond what it is fitting to be wise, but be wise prudently,"[7] that we be not cast forth by eating of the "knowledge" of these men (that knowledge which knows more than it should do) from the paradise of life. Into this paradise the Lord has introduced those who obey His call, "summing up in Himself all things which are in heaven, and which are on earth;"[8] but the things in heaven are spiritual, while those on earth constitute the dispensation in human nature (*secundum hominem est dispositio*). These things, therefore, He recapitulated in Himself: by uniting man to the Spirit, and causing the Spirit to dwell in man, He is Himself made the head of the Spirit, and gives the Spirit to be the head of man: for through Him (the Spirit) we see, and hear, and speak.

CHAP. XXI.—CHRIST IS THE HEAD OF ALL THINGS ALREADY MENTIONED. IT WAS FITTING THAT HE SHOULD BE SENT BY THE FATHER, THE CREATOR OF ALL THINGS, TO ASSUME HUMAN NATURE, AND SHOULD BE TEMPTED BY SATAN, THAT HE MIGHT FULFIL THE PROMISES, AND CARRY OFF A GLORIOUS AND PERFECT VICTORY.

1. He has therefore, in His work of recapitulation, summed up all things, both waging war against our enemy, and crushing him who had at the beginning led us away captives in Adam, and trampled upon his head, as thou canst perceive in Genesis that God said to the serpent, "And I will put enmity between thee and the woman, and between thy seed and her seed; He shall be on the watch for (*observabit*[9]) thy head, and thou on the watch for His heel."[10] For from that time, He who should be born of a woman, [namely] from the Virgin, after the likeness of Adam, was preached as keeping watch for the head of the serpent. This is the seed of which the apostle says in the Epistle to the Galatians, "that the law of works was established until the seed should come to whom the promise was made."[11] This fact is exhibited in a still clearer light in the same Epistle, where he thus speaks: "But when the fulness of time was come, God

---

[1] "Et eandem figuram ejus quæ est erga ecclesiam ordinationis custodientibus." Grabe supposes this refers to the ordained ministry of the Church, but Harvey thinks it refers more probably to its general constitution.
[2] [He thus outlines the creed, and epitomizes "the faith once delivered to the saints," as all that is requisite to salvation.]
[3] Prov. i. 20, 21.
[4] That is, the private Christian as contrasted with the sophist of the schools.
[5] 2 Tim. iii. 7.
[6] Gen. ii. 16.
[7] Rom. xii. 3.
[8] Eph. i. 10.
[9] τηρήσει and τερέσει have probably been confounded.
[10] Gen. iii. 15.
[11] Gal. iii. 19.

sent forth His Son, made of a woman."¹ For indeed the enemy would not have been fairly vanquished, unless it had been a man [born] of a woman who conquered him. For it was by means of a woman that he got the advantage over man at first, setting himself up as man's opponent. And therefore does the Lord profess Himself to be the Son of man, comprising in Himself that original man out of whom the woman was fashioned (*ex quo ea quæ secundum mulierem est plasmatio facta est*), in order that, as our species went down to death through a vanquished man, so we may ascend to life again through a victorious one; and as through a man death received the palm [of victory] against us, so again by a man we may receive the palm against death.

2. Now the Lord would not have recapitulated in Himself that ancient and primary enmity against the serpent, fulfilling the promise of the Creator (*Demiurgi*), and performing His command, if He had come from another Father. But as He is one and the same, who formed us at the beginning, and sent His Son at the end, the Lord did perform His command, being made of a woman, by both destroying our adversary, and perfecting man after the image and likeness of God. And for this reason He did not draw the means of confounding him from any other source than from the words of the law, and made use of the Father's commandment as a help towards the destruction and confusion of the apostate angel. Fasting forty days, like Moses and Elias, He afterwards hungered, first, in order that we may perceive that He was a real and substantial man — for it belongs to a man to suffer hunger when fasting; and secondly, that His opponent might have an opportunity of attacking Him. For as at the beginning it was by means of food that [the enemy] persuaded man, although not suffering hunger, to transgress God's commandments, so in the end he did not succeed in persuading Him that was an hungered to take that food which proceeded from God. For, when tempting Him, he said, "If thou be the Son of God, command that these stones be made bread."² But the Lord repulsed him by the commandment of the law, saying, "It is written, Man doth not live by bread alone."³ As to those words [of His enemy,] "If thou be the Son of God," [the Lord] made no remark; but by thus acknowledging His human nature He baffled His adversary, and exhausted the force of his first attack by means of His Father's word. The corruption of man, therefore, which occurred in paradise by both [of our first parents] eating, was done away with by [the Lord's] want of food in this world.⁴ But he, being thus vanquished by the law, endeavoured again to make an assault by himself quoting a commandment of the law. For, bringing Him to the highest pinnacle of the temple, he said to Him, "If thou art the Son of God, cast thyself down. For it is written, That God shall give His angels charge concerning thee, and in their hands they shall bear thee up, lest perchance thou dash thy foot against a stone;"⁵ thus concealing a falsehood under the guise of Scripture, as is done by all the heretics. For that was indeed written, [namely], "That He hath given His angels charge concerning Him;" but "cast thyself down from hence" no Scripture said in reference to Him: this kind of persuasion the devil produced from himself. The Lord therefore confuted him out of the law, when He said, "It is written again, Thou shalt not tempt the LORD thy God;"⁶ pointing out by the word contained in the law that which is the duty of man, that he should not tempt God; and in regard to Himself, since He appeared in human form, [declaring] that He would not tempt the LORD his God.⁷ The pride of reason, therefore, which was in the serpent, was put to nought by the humility found in the man [Christ], and now twice was the devil conquered from Scripture, when he was detected as advising things contrary to God's commandment, and was shown to be the enemy of God by [the expression of] his thoughts. He then, having been thus signally defeated, and then, as it were, concentrating his forces, drawing up in order all his available power for falsehood, in the third place "showed Him all the kingdoms of the world, and the glory of them,"⁸ saying, as Luke relates, "All these will I give thee, — for they are delivered to me; and to whom I will, I give them, — if thou wilt fall down and worship me." The Lord then, exposing him in his true character, says, " Depart, Satan; for it is written, Thou shalt worship the Lord thy God, and Him only shalt thou serve."⁹ He both revealed him by this name, and showed [at the same time] who He Himself was. For the Hebrew word "Satan" signifies an apostate. And thus, vanquishing him for the third time, He spurned him from Him finally as being conquered out of the law; and there was done away with that infringement of God's commandment which had occurred in Adam, by means of the precept of the law, which the Son of man ob-

---

⁴ The Latin of this obscure sentence is: Quæ ergo fuit in Paradiso repletio hominis per duplicem gustationem, dissoluta est per eam, quæ fuit in hoc mundo, indigentiam. Harvey thinks that *repletio* is an error of the translation reading ἀναπλήρωσις for ἀναπήρωσις. This conjecture is adopted above.
⁵ Ps. lxxxix. 11.
⁶ Deut. vi. 16.
⁷ This sentence is one of great obscurity.
⁸ Luke iv. 6, 7.
⁹ Matt. iv. 10.

¹ Gal. iv. 4.
² Matt. iv. 3.
³ Deut. viii. 3.

served, who did not transgress the commandment of God.

3. Who, then, is this Lord God to whom Christ bears witness, whom no man shall tempt, whom all should worship, and serve Him alone? It is, beyond all manner of doubt, that God who also gave the law. For these things had been predicted in the law, and by the words (*sententiam*) of the law the Lord showed that the law does indeed declare the Word of God from the Father ; and the apostate angel of God is destroyed by its voice, being exposed in his true colours, and vanquished by the Son of man keeping the commandment of God. For as in the beginning he enticed man to transgress his Maker's law, and thereby got him into his power; yet his power consists in transgression and apostasy, and with these he bound man [to himself] ; so again, on the other hand, it was necessary that through man himself he should, when conquered, be bound with the same chains with which he had bound man, in order that man, being set free, might return to his Lord, leaving to him (Satan) those bonds by which he himself had been fettered, that is, sin. For when Satan is bound, man is set free; since "none can enter a strong man's house and spoil his goods, unless he first bind the strong man himself."[1] The Lord therefore exposes him as speaking contrary to the word of that God who made all things, and subdues him by means of the commandment. Now the law is the commandment of God. The Man proves him to be a fugitive from and a transgressor of the law, an apostate also from God. After [the Man had done this], the Word bound him securely as a fugitive from Himself, and made spoil of his goods, — namely, those men whom he held in bondage, and whom he unjustly used for his own purposes. And justly indeed is he led captive, who had led men unjustly into bondage ; while man, who had been led captive in times past, was rescued from the grasp of his possessor, according to the tender mercy of God the Father, who had compassion on His own handiwork, and gave to it salvation, restoring it by means of the Word — that is, by Christ — in order that men might learn by actual proof that he receives incorruptibility not of himself, but by the free gift of God.

CHAP. XXII. — THE TRUE LORD AND THE ONE GOD IS DECLARED BY THE LAW, AND MANIFESTED BY CHRIST HIS SON IN THE GOSPEL ; WHOM ALONE WE SHOULD ADORE, AND FROM HIM WE MUST LOOK FOR ALL GOOD THINGS, NOT FROM SATAN.

1. Thus then does the Lord plainly show that it was the true Lord and the one God who had been set forth by the law; for Him whom the law proclaimed as God, the same did Christ point out as the Father, whom also it behoves the disciples of Christ alone to serve. By means of the statements of the law, He put our adversary to utter confusion ; and the law directs us to praise God the Creator (*Demiurgum*), and to serve Him alone. Since this is the case, we must not seek for another Father besides Him, or above Him, since there is one God who justifies the circumcision by faith, and the uncircumcision through faith.[2] For if there were any other perfect Father above Him, He (Christ) would by no means have overthrown Satan by means of His words and commandments. For one ignorance cannot be done away with by means of another ignorance, any more than one defect by another defect. If, therefore, the law is due to ignorance and defect, how could the statements contained therein bring to nought the ignorance of the devil, and conquer the strong man? For a strong man can be conquered neither by an inferior nor by an equal, but by one possessed of greater power. But the Word of God is the superior above all, He who is loudly proclaimed in the law: "Hear, O Israel, the LORD thy God is one God;" and, "Thou shalt love the LORD thy God with all thy heart;" and, "Him shalt thou adore, and Him alone shalt thou serve."[3] Then in the Gospel, casting down the apostasy by means of these expressions, He did both overcome the strong man by His Father's voice, and He acknowledges the commandment of the law to express His own sentiments, when He says, "Thou shalt not tempt the LORD thy God."[4] For He did not confound the adversary by the saying of any other, but by that belonging to His own Father, and thus overcame the strong man.

2. He taught by His commandment that we who have been set free should, when hungry, take that food which is given by God ; and that, when placed in the exalted position of every grace [that can be received], we should not, either by trusting to works of righteousness, or when adorned with super-eminent [gifts of] ministration, by any means be lifted up with pride, nor should we tempt God, but should feel humility in all things, and have ready to hand [this saying], "Thou shalt not tempt the LORD thy God."[5] As also the apostle taught, saying, "Minding not high things, but consenting to things of low estate;"[6] that we should neither be ensnared with riches, nor mundane glory, nor present fancy, but should know that we must "worship the LORD thy God, and serve Him alone," and

---

[1] Matt. xii. 29 and Mark iii. 27.
[2] Rom. iii. 30.
[3] Deut. vi. 4, 5, 13.
[4] Matt. iv. 7.
[5] Deut. vi. 16.
[6] Rom. xii. 16.

give no heed to him who falsely promised things not his own, when he said, "All these will I give thee, if, falling down, thou wilt worship me." For he himself confesses that to adore him, and to do his will, is to fall from the glory of God. And in what thing either pleasant or good can that man who has fallen participate? Or what else can such a person hope for or expect, except death? For death is next neighbour to him who has fallen. Hence also it follows that he will not give what he has promised. For how can he make grants to him who has fallen? Moreover, since God rules over men and him too, and without the will of our Father in heaven not even a sparrow falls to the ground,[1] it follows that his declaration, "All these things are delivered unto me, and to whomsoever I will I give them," proceeds from him when puffed up with pride. For the creation is not subjected to his power, since indeed he is himself but one among created things. Nor shall he give away the rule over men to men; but both all other things, and all human affairs, are arranged according to God the Father's disposal. Besides, the Lord declares that "the devil is a liar from the beginning, and the truth is not in him."[2] If then he be a liar, and the truth be not in him, he certainly did not speak truth, but a lie, when he said, "For all these things are delivered to me, and to whomsoever I will I give them."[3]

CHAP. XXIII. — THE DEVIL IS WELL PRACTISED IN FALSEHOOD, BY WHICH ADAM HAVING BEEN LED ASTRAY, SINNED ON THE SIXTH DAY OF THE CREATION, IN WHICH DAY ALSO HE HAS BEEN RENEWED BY CHRIST.

1. He had indeed been already accustomed to lie against God, for the purpose of leading men astray. For at the beginning, when God had given to man a variety of things for food, while He commanded him not to eat of one tree only, as the Scripture tells us that God said to Adam: "From every tree which is in the garden thou shalt eat food; but from the tree of knowledge of good and evil, from this ye shall not eat: for in the day that ye shall eat of it, ye shall die by death;"[4] he then, lying against the Lord, tempted man, as the Scripture says that the serpent said to the woman: "Has God indeed said this, Ye shall not eat from every tree of the garden?"[5] And when she had exposed the falsehood, and simply related the command, as He had said, "From every tree of the garden we shall eat; but of the fruit of the tree which is in the midst of the garden, God hath said, Ye shall not eat of it, neither shall ye touch it, lest ye die:"[6] when he had [thus] learned from the woman the command of God, having brought his cunning into play, he finally deceived her by a falsehood, saying, "Ye shall not die by death; for God knew that in the day ye shall eat of it your eyes shall be opened, and ye shall be as gods, knowing good and evil."[7] In the first place, then, in the garden of God he disputed about God, as if God was not there, for he was ignorant of the greatness of God; and then, in the next place, after he had learned from the woman that God had said that they should die if they tasted the aforesaid tree, opening his mouth, he uttered the third falsehood, "Ye shall not die by death." But that God was true, and the serpent a liar, was proved by the result, death having passed upon them who had eaten. For along with the fruit they did also fall under the power of death, because they did eat in disobedience; and disobedience to God entails death. Wherefore, as they became forfeit to death, from that [moment] they were handed over to it.

2. Thus, then, in the day that they did eat, in the same did they die, and became death's debtors, since it was one day of the creation. For it is said, "There was made in the evening, and there was made in the morning, one day." Now in this same day that they did eat, in that also did they die. But according to the cycle and progress of the days, after which one is termed first, another second, and another third, if anybody seeks diligently to learn upon what day out of the seven it was that Adam died, he will find it by examining the dispensation of the Lord. For by summing up in Himself the whole human race from the beginning to the end, He has also summed up its death. From this it is clear that the Lord suffered death, in obedience to His Father, upon that day on which Adam died while he disobeyed God. Now he died on the same day in which he did eat. For God said, "In that day on which ye shall eat of it, ye shall die by death." The Lord, therefore, recapitulating in Himself this day, underwent His sufferings upon the day preceding the Sabbath, that is, the sixth day of the creation, on which day man was created; thus granting him a second creation by means of His passion, which is that [creation] out of death. And there are some, again, who relegate the death of Adam to the thousandth year; for since "a day of the Lord is as a thousand years,"[8] he did not overstep the thousand years, but died within them, thus bearing out the sentence of his sin. Whether, therefore, with respect to disobedience, which is death; whether

---

[1] Matt. x. 29.
[2] John viii. 44.
[3] Luke iv. 6.
[4] Gen. ii. 16, 17.
[5] Gen. iii. 1.
[6] Gen. iii. 2, 3.
[7] Gen. iii. 4.
[8] 2 Pet. iii. 8.

[we consider] that, on account of that, they were delivered over to death, and made debtors to it; whether with respect to [the fact that on] one and the same day on which they ate they also died (for it is one day of the creation); whether [we regard this point], that, with respect to this cycle of days, they died on the day in which they did also eat, that is, the day of the preparation, which is termed "the pure supper," that is, the sixth day of the feast, which the Lord also exhibited when He suffered on that day; or whether [we reflect] that he (Adam) did not overstep the thousand years, but died within their limit, — it follows that, in regard to all these significations, God is indeed true. For they died who tasted of the tree; and the serpent is proved a liar and a murderer, as the Lord said of him: "For he is a murderer from the beginning, and the truth is not in him."[1]

CHAP. XXIV. — OF THE CONSTANT FALSEHOOD OF THE DEVIL, AND OF THE POWERS AND GOVERNMENTS OF THE WORLD, WHICH WE OUGHT TO OBEY, INASMUCH AS THEY ARE APPOINTED OF GOD, NOT OF THE DEVIL.

1. As therefore the devil lied at the beginning, so did he also in the end, when he said, "All these are delivered unto me, and to whomsoever I will I give them."[2] For it is not he who has appointed the kingdoms of this world, but God; for "the heart of the king is in the hand of God."[3] And the Word also says by Solomon, "By me kings do reign, and princes administer justice. By me chiefs are raised up, and by me kings rule the earth."[4] Paul the apostle also says upon this same subject: "Be ye subject to all the higher powers; for there is no power but of God: now those which are have been ordained of God."[5] And again, in reference to them he says, "For he beareth not the sword in vain; for he is the minister of God, the avenger for wrath to him who does evil."[6] Now, that he spake these words, not in regard to angelical powers, nor of invisible rulers — as some venture to expound the passage — but of those of actual human authorities, [he shows when] he says, "For this cause pay ye tribute also: for they are God's ministers, doing service for this very thing."[7] This also the Lord confirmed, when He did not do what He was tempted to by the devil; but He gave directions that tribute should be paid to the tax-gatherers for Himself and Peter;[8] because "they are the ministers of God, serving for this very thing."

2. For since man, by departing from God, reached such a pitch of fury as even to look upon his brother as his enemy, and engaged without fear in every kind of restless conduct, and murder, and avarice; God imposed upon mankind the fear of man, as they did not acknowledge the fear of God, in order that, being subjected to the authority of men, and kept under restraint by their laws, they might attain to some degree of justice, and exercise mutual forbearance through dread of the sword suspended full in their view, as the apostle says: "For he beareth not the sword in vain; for he is the minister of God, the avenger for wrath upon him who does evil." And for this reason too, magistrates themselves, having laws as a clothing of righteousness whenever they act in a just and legitimate manner, shall not be called in question for their conduct, nor be liable to punishment. But whatsoever they do to the subversion of justice, iniquitously, and impiously, and illegally, and tyrannically, in these things shall they also perish; for the just judgment of God comes equally upon all, and in no case is defective. Earthly rule, therefore, has been appointed by God for the benefit of nations,[9] and not by the devil, who is never at rest at all, nay, who does not love to see even nations conducting themselves after a quiet manner, so that under the fear of human rule, men may not eat each other up like fishes; but that, by means of the establishment of laws, they may keep down an excess of wickedness among the nations. And considered from this point of view, those who exact tribute from us are "God's ministers, serving for this very purpose."

3. As, then, "the powers that be are ordained of God," it is clear that the devil lied when he said, "These are delivered unto me; and to whomsoever I will, I give them." For by the law of the same Being as calls men into existence are kings also appointed, adapted for those men who are at the time placed under their government. Some of these [rulers] are given for the correction and the benefit of their subjects, and for the preservation of justice; but others, for the purposes of fear and punishment and rebuke: others, as [the subjects] deserve it, are for deception, disgrace, and pride; while the just judgment of God, as I have observed already, passes equally upon all. The devil, however, as he is the apostate angel, can only go to this length, as he did at the beginning, [namely] to deceive and lead astray the mind of man into disobeying the commandments of God, and grad-

---

[1] John viii. 44.
[2] Matt. iv. 9; Luke iv. 6.
[3] Prov. xxi. 1.
[4] Prov. viii. 15.
[5] Rom. xiii. 1.
[6] Rom. xiii. 4.
[7] Rom. xiii. 6.
[8] Matt. xvii. 27.

[9] [Well says Benjamin Franklin: "He who shall introduce into public affairs the principles of primitive Christianity will change the face of the world." See Bancroft, *Hist. U.S.*, vol. ix. p. 492.]

ually to darken the hearts of those who would endeavour to serve him, to the forgetting of the true God, but to the adoration of himself as God.

4. Just as if any one, being an apostate, and seizing in a hostile manner another man's territory, should harass the inhabitants of it, in order that he might claim for himself the glory of a king among those ignorant of his apostasy and robbery; so likewise also the devil, being one among those angels who are placed over the spirit of the air, as the Apostle Paul has declared in his Epistle to the Ephesians,[1] becoming envious of man, was rendered an apostate from the divine law: for envy is a thing foreign to God. And as his apostasy was exposed by man, and man became the [means of] searching out his thoughts (*et examinatio sententiæ ejus, homo factus est*), he has set himself to this with greater and greater determination, in opposition to man, envying his life, and wishing to involve him in his own apostate power. The Word of God, however, the Maker of all things, conquering him by means of human nature, and showing him to be an apostate, has, on the contrary, put him under the power of man. For He says, "Behold, I confer upon you the power of treading upon serpents and scorpions, and upon all the power of the enemy,"[2] in order that, as he obtained dominion over man by apostasy, so again his apostasy might be deprived of power by means of man turning back again to God.

CHAP. XXV. — THE FRAUD, PRIDE, AND TYRANNICAL KINGDOM OF ANTICHRIST, AS DESCRIBED BY DANIEL AND PAUL.

1. And not only by the particulars already mentioned, but also by means of the events which shall occur in the time of Antichrist is it shown that he, being an apostate and a robber, is anxious to be adored as God; and that, although a mere slave, he wishes himself to be proclaimed as a king. For he (Antichrist) being endued with all the power of the devil, shall come, not as a righteous king, nor as a legitimate king, [i.e., one] in subjection to God, but an impious, unjust, and lawless one; as an apostate, iniquitous and murderous; as a robber, concentrating in himself [all] satanic apostasy, and setting aside idols to persuade [men] that he himself is God, raising up himself as the only idol, having in himself the multifarious errors of the other idols. This he does, in order that they who do [now] worship the devil by means of many abominations, may serve himself by this one idol, of whom the apostle thus speaks in the second Epistle to the Thessalonians: "Unless there shall come a falling away first, and the man of sin shall be revealed, the son of perdition, who opposeth and exalteth himself above all that is called God, or that is worshipped; so that he sitteth in the temple of God, showing himself as if he were God." The apostle therefore clearly points out his apostasy, and that he is lifted up above all that is called God, or that is worshipped — that is, above every idol — for these are indeed so called by men, but are not [really] gods; and that he will endeavour in a tyrannical manner to set himself forth as God.

2. Moreover, he (the apostle) has also pointed out this which I have shown in many ways, that the temple in Jerusalem was made by the direction of the true God. For the apostle himself, speaking in his own person, distinctly called it the temple of God. Now I have shown in the third book, that no one is termed God by the apostles when speaking for themselves, except Him who truly is God, the Father of our Lord, by whose directions the temple which is at Jerusalem was constructed for those purposes which I have already mentioned; in which [temple] the enemy shall sit, endeavouring to show himself as Christ, as the Lord also declares: "But when ye shall see the abomination of desolation, which has been spoken of by Daniel the prophet, standing in the holy place (let him that readeth understand), then let those who are in Judea flee into the mountains; and he who is upon the house-top, let him not come down to take anything out of his house: for there shall then be great hardship, such as has not been from the beginning of the world until now, nor ever shall be."[3]

3. Daniel too, looking forward to the end of the last kingdom, i.e., the ten last kings, amongst whom the kingdom of those men shall be partitioned, and upon whom the son of perdition shall come, declares that ten horns shall spring from the beast, and that another little horn shall arise in the midst of them, and that three of the former shall be rooted up before his face. He says: "And, behold, eyes were in this horn as the eyes of a man, and a mouth speaking great things, and his look was more stout than his fellows. I was looking, and this horn made war against the saints, and prevailed against them, until the Ancient of days came and gave judgment to the saints of the most high God, and the time came, and the saints obtained the kingdom."[4] Then, further on, in the interpretation of the vision, there was said to him: "The fourth beast shall be the fourth kingdom upon earth, which shall excel all other kingdoms, and devour the whole earth, and tread it down, and cut it in pieces. And its ten horns are ten kings which shall arise; and after them shall arise another, who shall surpass in evil deeds all that were be-

---

[1] Eph. ii. 2.
[2] Luke x. 19.
[3] Matt. xxiv. 15, 21.
[4] Dan. vii. 8, etc.

fore him, and shall overthrow three kings; and he shall speak words against the most high God, and wear out the saints of the most high God, and shall purpose to change times and laws; and [everything] shall be given into his hand until a time of times and a half time,"[1] that is, for three years and six months, during which time, when he comes, he shall reign over the earth. Of whom also the Apostle Paul again, speaking in the second [Epistle] to the Thessalonians, and at the same time proclaiming the cause of his advent, thus says: "And then shall the wicked one be revealed, whom the Lord Jesus shall slay with the spirit of His mouth, and destroy by the presence of His coming; whose coming [i.e., the wicked one's] is after the working of Satan, in all power, and signs, and portents of lies, and with all deceivableness of wickedness for those who perish; because they did not receive the love of the truth, that they might be saved. And therefore God will send them the working of error, that they may believe a lie; that they all may be judged who did not believe the truth, but gave consent to iniquity."[2]

4. The Lord also spoke as follows to those who did not believe in Him: "I have come in my Father's name, and ye have not received Me: when another shall come in his own name, him ye will receive,"[3] calling Antichrist "the other," because he is alienated from the Lord. This is also the unjust judge, whom the Lord mentioned as one "who feared not God, neither regarded man,"[4] to whom the widow fled in her forgetfulness of God, — that is, the earthly Jerusalem, — to be avenged of her adversary. Which also he shall do in the time of his kingdom: he shall remove his kingdom into that [city], and shall sit in the temple of God, leading astray those who worship him, as if he were Christ. To this purpose Daniel says again: "And he shall desolate the holy place; and sin has been given for a sacrifice,[5] and righteousness been cast away in the earth, and he has been active (*fecit*), and gone on prosperously."[6] And the angel Gabriel, when explaining his vision, states with regard to this person: "And towards the end of their kingdom a king of a most fierce countenance shall arise, one understanding [dark] questions, and exceedingly powerful, full of wonders; and he shall corrupt, direct, influence (*faciet*), and put strong men down, the holy people likewise; and his yoke shall be directed as a wreath [round their neck]; deceit shall be in his hand, and he shall be lifted up in his heart: he shall also ruin many by deceit, and lead many to perdition, bruising them in his hand like eggs."[7] And then he points out the time that his tyranny shall last, during which the saints shall be put to flight, they who offer a pure sacrifice unto God: "And in the midst of the week," he says, "the sacrifice and the libation shall be taken away, and the abomination of desolation [shall be brought] into the temple: even unto the consummation of the time shall the desolation be complete."[8] Now three years and six months constitute the half-week.

5. From all these passages are revealed to us, not merely the particulars of the apostasy, and [the doings] of him who concentrates in himself every satanic error, but also, that there is one and the same God the Father, who was declared by the prophets, but made manifest by Christ. For if what Daniel prophesied concerning the end has been confirmed by the Lord, when He said, "When ye shall see the abomination of desolation, which has been spoken of by Daniel the prophet"[9] (and the angel Gabriel gave the interpretation of the visions to Daniel, and he is the archangel of the Creator (*Demiurgi*), who also proclaimed to Mary the visible coming and the incarnation of Christ), then one and the same God is most manifestly pointed out, who sent the prophets, and made promise[10] of the Son, and called us into His knowledge.

CHAP. XXVI. — JOHN AND DANIEL HAVE PREDICTED THE DISSOLUTION AND DESOLATION OF THE ROMAN EMPIRE, WHICH SHALL PRECEDE THE END OF THE WORLD AND THE ETERNAL KINGDOM OF CHRIST. THE GNOSTICS ARE REFUTED, THOSE TOOLS OF SATAN, WHO INVENT ANOTHER FATHER DIFFERENT FROM THE CREATOR.

1. In a still clearer light has John, in the Apocalypse, indicated to the Lord's disciples what shall happen in the last times, and concerning the ten kings who shall then arise, among whom the empire which now rules [the earth] shall be partitioned. He teaches us what the ten horns shall be which were seen by Daniel, telling us that thus it had been said to him: "And the ten horns which thou sawest are ten kings, who have received no kingdom as yet, but shall receive power as if kings one hour with the beast. These have one mind, and give their strength and power to the beast. These shall make war with the Lamb, and the Lamb shall overcome them, because He is the Lord of lords and the King of kings."[11] It is manifest, therefore, that

---

[1] Dan. vii. 23, etc.
[2] 2 Thess. ii. 8.
[3] John v. 43.
[4] Luke xviii. 2, etc.
[5] This may refer to Antiochus Epiphanes, Antichrist's prototype, who offered swine upon the altar in the temple at Jerusalem. The LXX. version has, ἐδόθη ἐπὶ τὴν θυσίαν ἁμαρτία, i.e., sin has been given against (or, *upon*) the sacrifice.
[6] Dan. viii. 12.
[7] Dan. viii. 23, etc.
[8] Dan. ix. 27.
[9] Matt. xxiv. 15.
[10] The MSS. have "præmisit," but Harvey suggests "promisit," which we have adopted.
[11] Rev. xvii. 12, etc.

of these [potentates], he who is to come shall slay three, and subject the remainder to his power, and that he shall be himself the eighth among them. And they shall lay Babylon waste, and burn her with fire, and shall give their kingdom to the beast, and put the Church to flight. After that they shall be destroyed by the coming of our Lord. For that the kingdom must be divided, and thus come to ruin, the Lord [declares when He] says: "Every kingdom divided against itself is brought to desolation, and every city or house divided against itself shall not stand."[1] It must be, therefore, that the kingdom, the city, and the house be divided into ten; and for this reason He has already foreshadowed the partition and division [which shall take place]. Daniel also says particularly, that the end of the fourth kingdom consists in the toes of the image seen by Nebuchadnezzar, upon which came the stone cut out without hands; and as he does himself say: "The feet were indeed the one part iron, the other part clay, until the stone was cut out without hands, and struck the image upon the iron and clay feet, and dashed them into pieces, even to the end."[2] Then afterwards, when interpreting this, he says: "And as thou sawest the feet and the toes, partly indeed of clay, and partly of iron, the kingdom shall be divided, and there shall be in it a root of iron, as thou sawest iron mixed with baked clay. And the toes were indeed the one part iron, but the other part clay."[3] The ten toes, therefore, are these ten kings, among whom the kingdom shall be partitioned, of whom some indeed shall be strong and active, or energetic; others, again, shall be sluggish and useless, and shall not agree; as also Daniel says: "Some part of the kingdom shall be strong, and part shall be broken from it. As thou sawest the iron mixed with the baked clay, there shall be minglings among the human race, but no cohesion one with the other, just as iron cannot be welded on to pottery ware."[4] And since an end shall take place, he says: "And in the days of these kings shall the God of heaven raise up a kingdom which shall never decay, and His kingdom shall not be left to another people. It shall break in pieces and shatter all kingdoms, and shall itself be exalted for ever. As thou sawest that the stone was cut without hands from the mountain, and brake in pieces the baked clay, the iron, the brass, the silver, and the gold, God has pointed out to the king what shall come to pass after these things; and the dream is true, and the interpretation trustworthy."[5]

2. If therefore the great God showed future things by Daniel, and confirmed them by His Son; and if Christ is the stone which is cut out without hands, who shall destroy temporal kingdoms, and introduce an eternal one, which is the resurrection of the just; as he declares, "The God of heaven shall raise up a kingdom which shall never be destroyed,"—let those thus confuted come to their senses, who reject the Creator (*Demiurgum*), and do not agree that the prophets were sent beforehand from the same Father from whom also the Lord came, but who assert that prophecies originated from diverse powers. For those things which have been predicted by the Creator alike through all the prophets has Christ fulfilled in the end, ministering to His Father's will, and completing His dispensations with regard to the human race. Let those persons, therefore, who blaspheme the Creator, either by openly expressed words, such as the disciples of Marcion, or by a perversion of the sense [of Scripture], as those of Valentinus and all the Gnostics falsely so called, be recognised as agents of Satan by all those who worship God; through whose agency Satan now, and not before, has been seen to speak against God, even Him who has prepared eternal fire for every kind of apostasy. For he did not venture to blaspheme his Lord openly of himself; as also in the beginning he led man astray through the instrumentality of the serpent, concealing himself as it were from God. Truly has Justin remarked:[6] That before the Lord's appearance Satan never dared to blaspheme God, inasmuch as he did not yet know his own sentence, because it was contained in parables and allegories; but that after the Lord's appearance, when he had clearly ascertained from the words of Christ and His apostles that eternal fire has been prepared for him as he apostatized from God of his own free-will, and likewise for all who unrepentant continue in the apostasy, he now blasphemes, by means of such men, the Lord who brings judgment [upon him] as being already condemned, and imputes the guilt of his apostasy to his Maker, not to his own voluntary disposition. Just as it is with those who break the laws, when punishment overtakes them: they throw the blame upon those who frame the laws, but not upon themselves. In like manner do those men, filled with a satanic spirit, bring innumerable accusations against our Creator, who has both given to us the spirit of life, and established a law adapted for all; and they will not admit that the judgment of God is just. Wherefore also they set about imagining some other Father who neither cares about nor exercises a providence

---

[1] Matt. xii. 25.
[2] Dan. ii. 33, 34.
[3] Dan. ii. 41, 42.
[4] Dan. ii. 42, 43.
[5] Dan. ii. 44, 45.

[6] The Greek text is here preserved by Eusebius, *Hist. Eccl.*, iv. 18; but we are not told from what work of Justin Martyr it is extracted. The work is now lost. An ancient catena continues the Greek for several lines further.

over our affairs, nay, one who even approves of all sins.

CHAP. XXVII.—THE FUTURE JUDGMENT BY CHRIST. COMMUNION WITH AND SEPARATION FROM THE DIVINE BEING. THE ETERNAL PUNISHMENT OF UNBELIEVERS.

1. If the Father, then, does not exercise judgment, [it follows] that judgment does not belong to Him, or that He consents to all those actions which take place; and if He does not judge, all persons will be equal, and accounted in the same condition. The advent of Christ will therefore be without an object, yea, absurd, inasmuch as [in that case] He exercises no judicial power. For " He came to divide a man against his father, and the daughter against the mother, and the daughter-in-law against the mother-in-law;"[1] and when two are in one bed, to take the one, and to leave the other; and of two women grinding at the mill, to take one and leave the other:[2] [also] at the time of the end, to order the reapers to collect first the tares together, and bind them in bundles, and burn them with unquenchable fire, but to gather up the wheat into the barn;[3] and to call the lambs into the kingdom prepared for them, but to send the goats into everlasting fire, which has been prepared by His Father for the devil and his angels.[4] And why is this? Has the Word come for the ruin and for the resurrection of many? For the ruin, certainly, of those who do not believe Him, to whom also He has threatened a greater damnation in the judgment-day than that of Sodom and Gomorrah;[5] but for the resurrection of believers, and those who do the will of His Father in heaven. If then the advent of the Son comes indeed alike to all, but is for the purpose of judging, and separating the believing from the unbelieving, since, as those who believe do His will agreeably to their own choice, and as, [also] agreeably to their own choice, the disobedient do not consent to His doctrine; it is manifest that His Father has made all in a like condition, each person having a choice of his own, and a free understanding; and that He has regard to all things, and exercises a providence over all, " making His sun to rise upon the evil and on the good, and sending rain upon the just and unjust."[6]

2. And to as many as continue in their love towards God, does He grant communion with Him. But communion with God is life and light, and the enjoyment of all the benefits which He has in store. But on as many as, according to their own choice, depart from God. He inflicts that separation from Himself which they have chosen of their own accord. But separation from God is death, and separation from light is darkness; and separation from God consists in the loss of all the benefits which He has in store. Those, therefore, who cast away by apostasy these forementioned things, being in fact destitute of all good, do experience every kind of punishment. God, however, does not punish them immediately of Himself, but that punishment falls upon them because they are destitute of all that is good. Now, good things are eternal and without end with God, and therefore the loss of these is also eternal and never-ending. It is in this matter just as occurs in the case of a flood of light: those who have blinded themselves, or have been blinded by others, are for ever deprived of the enjoyment of light. It is not, [however], that the light has inflicted upon them the penalty of blindness, but it is that the blindness itself has brought calamity upon them: and therefore the Lord declared, " He that believeth in Me is not condemned,"[7] that is, is not separated from God, for he is united to God through faith. On the other hand, He says, " He that believeth not is condemned already, because he has not believed in the name of the only-begotten Son of God;" that is, he separated himself from God of his own accord. " For this is the condemnation, that light is come into this world, and men have loved darkness rather than light. For every one who doeth evil hateth the light, and cometh not to the light, lest his deeds should be reproved. But he that doeth truth cometh to the light, that his deeds may be made manifest, that he has wrought them in God."

CHAP. XXVIII. — THE DISTINCTION TO BE MADE BETWEEN THE RIGHTEOUS AND THE WICKED. THE FUTURE APOSTASY IN THE TIME OF ANTI-CHRIST, AND THE END OF THE WORLD.

1. Inasmuch, then, as in this world ($αἰῶνι$) some persons betake themselves to the light, and by faith unite themselves with God, but others shun the light, and separate themselves from God, the Word of God comes preparing a fit habitation for both. For those indeed who are in the light, that they may derive enjoyment from it, and from the good things contained in it; but for those in darkness, that they may partake in its calamities. And on this account He says, that those upon the right hand are called into the kingdom of heaven, but that those on the left He will send into eternal fire; for they have deprived themselves of all good.

2. And for this reason the apostle says: " Be-

---

[1] Matt. x. 25.
[2] Luke xvii. 34.
[3] Matt. xiii. 30.
[4] Matt. xxv. 33, etc.
[5] Luke x. 12.
[6] Matt. v. 45.

[7] John iii. 18, 21.

cause they received not the love of God, that they might be saved, therefore God shall also send them the operation of error, that they may believe a lie, that they all may be judged who have not believed the truth, but consented to unrighteousness."[1] For when he (Antichrist) is come, and of his own accord concentrates in his own person the apostasy, and accomplishes whatever he shall do according to his own will and choice, sitting also in the temple of God, so that his dupes may adore him as the Christ; wherefore also shall he deservedly "be cast into the lake of fire:"[2] [this will happen according to divine appointment], God by His prescience foreseeing all this, and at the proper time sending such a man, "that they may believe a lie, that they all may be judged who did not believe the truth, but consented to unrighteousness;" whose coming John has thus described in the Apocalypse: "And the beast which I had seen was like unto a leopard, and his feet as of a bear, and his mouth as the mouth of a lion; and the dragon conferred his own power upon him, and his throne, and great might. And one of his heads was as it were slain unto death; and his deadly wound was healed, and all the world wondered after the beast. And they worshipped the dragon because he gave power to the beast; and they worshipped the beast, saying, Who is like unto this beast, and who is able to make war with him? And there was given unto him a mouth speaking great things, and blasphemy and power was given to him during forty and two months. And he opened his mouth for blasphemy against God, to blaspheme His name and His tabernacle, and those who dwell in heaven. And power was given him over every tribe, and people, and tongue, and nation. And all who dwell upon the earth worshipped him, [every one] whose name was not written in the book of the Lamb slain from the foundation of the world. If any one have ears, let him hear. If any one shall lead into captivity, he shall go into captivity. If any shall slay with the sword, he must be slain with the sword. Here is the endurance and the faith of the saints."[3] After this he likewise describes his armour-bearer, whom he also terms a false prophet: "He spake as a dragon, and exercised all the power of the first beast in his sight, and caused the earth, and those that dwell therein, to adore the first beast, whose deadly wound was healed. And he shall perform great wonders, so that he can even cause fire to descend from heaven upon the earth in the sight of men, and he shall lead the inhabitants of the earth astray."[4] Let no one imagine that he performs these wonders by divine power, but by the working of magic. And we must not be surprised if, since the demons and apostate spirits are at his service, he through their means performs wonders, by which he leads the inhabitants of the earth astray. John says further: "And he shall order an image of the beast to be made, and he shall give breath to the image, so that the image shall speak; and he shall cause those to be slain who will not adore it." He says also: "And he will cause a mark [to be put] in the forehead and in the right hand, that no one may be able to buy or sell, unless he who has the mark of the name of the beast or the number of his name; and the number is six hundred and sixty-six,"[5] that is, six times a hundred, six times ten, and six units. [He gives this] as a summing up of the whole of that apostasy which has taken place during six thousand years.

3. For in as many days as this world was made, in so many thousand years shall it be concluded. And for this reason the Scripture says: "Thus the heaven and the earth were finished, and all their adornment. And God brought to a conclusion upon the sixth day the works that He had made; and God rested upon the seventh day from all His works."[6] This is an account of the things formerly created, as also it is a prophecy of what is to come. For the day of the Lord is as a thousand years;[7] and in six days created things were completed: it is evident, therefore, that they will come to an end at the sixth thousand year.

4. And therefore throughout all time, man, having been moulded at the beginning by the hands of God, that is, of the Son and of the Spirit, is made after the image and likeness of God: the chaff, indeed, which is the apostasy, being cast away; but the wheat, that is, those who bring forth fruit to God in faith, being gathered into the barn. And for this cause tribulation is necessary for those who are saved, that having been after a manner broken up, and rendered fine, and sprinkled over by the patience of the Word of God, and set on fire [for purification], they may be fitted for the royal banquet. As a certain man of ours said, when he was condemned to the wild beasts because of his testimony with respect to God: "I am the wheat of Christ, and am ground by the teeth of the wild beasts, that I may be found the pure bread of God."[8]

---

[1] 2 Thess. ii. 10-12.
[2] Rev. xix. 20.
[3] Rev. xiii. 2, etc.
[4] Rev. xiii. 11, etc.
[5] Rev. xiii. 14, etc.
[6] Gen. ii. 2.
[7] 2 Pet. iii. 8.
[8] This is quoted from the Epistle of Ignatius to the Romans, ch. iv. It is found in the two Greek recensions of his works, and also in the Syriac. See pp. 75 and 103 of this volume. The Latin translation is here followed: the Greek of Ignatius would give "the wheat of God," and omits "of God" towards the end, as quoted by Eusebius.

CHAP. XXIX.— ALL THINGS HAVE BEEN CREATED FOR THE SERVICE OF MAN. THE DECEITS, WICKEDNESS, AND APOSTATE POWER OF ANTICHRIST. THIS WAS PREFIGURED AT THE DELUGE, AS AFTERWARDS BY THE PERSECUTION OF SHADRACH, MESHACH, AND ABEDNEGO.

1. In the previous books I have set forth the causes for which God permitted these things to be made, and have pointed out that all such have been created for the benefit of that human nature which is saved, ripening for immortality that which is [possessed] of its own free will and its own power, and preparing and rendering it more adapted for eternal subjection to God. And therefore the creation is suited to [the wants of] man; for man was not made for its sake, but creation for the sake of man. Those nations, however, who did not of themselves raise up their eyes unto heaven, nor returned thanks to their Maker, nor wished to behold the light of truth, but who were like blind mice concealed in the depths of ignorance, the word justly reckons "as waste water from a sink, and as the turning-weight of a balance — in fact, as nothing;"[1] so far useful and serviceable to the just, as stubble conduces towards the growth of the wheat, and its straw, by means of combustion, serves for working gold. And therefore, when in the end the Church shall be suddenly caught up from this, it is said, "There shall be tribulation such as has not been since the beginning, neither shall be."[2] For this is the last contest of the righteous, in which, when they overcome, they are crowned with incorruption.

2. And there is therefore in this beast, when he comes, a recapitulation made of all sorts of iniquity and of every deceit, in order that all apostate power, flowing into and being shut up in him, may be sent into the furnace of fire. Fittingly, therefore, shall his name possess the number six hundred and sixty-six, since he sums up in his own person all the commixture of wickedness which took place previous to the deluge, due to the apostasy of the angels. For Noah was six hundred years old when the deluge came upon the earth, sweeping away the rebellious world, for the sake of that most infamous generation which lived in the times of Noah. And [Antichrist] also sums up every error of devised idols since the flood, together with the slaying of the prophets and the cutting off of the just. For that image which was set up by Nebuchadnezzar had indeed a height of sixty cubits, while the breadth was six cubits; on account of which Ananias, Azarias, and Misaël, when they did not worship it, were cast into a furnace of fire, pointing out prophetically, by what happened to them, the wrath against the righteous which shall arise towards the [time of the] end. For that image, taken as a whole, was a prefiguring of this man's coming, decreeing that he should undoubtedly himself alone be worshipped by all men. Thus, then, the six hundred years of Noah, in whose time the deluge occurred because of the apostasy, and the number of the cubits of the image for which these just men were sent into the fiery furnace, do indicate the number of the name of that man in whom is concentrated the whole apostasy of six thousand years, and unrighteousness, and wickedness, and false prophecy, and deception; for which things' sake a cataclysm of fire shall also come [upon the earth].

CHAP. XXX.— ALTHOUGH CERTAIN AS TO THE NUMBER OF THE NAME OF ANTICHRIST, YET WE SHOULD COME TO NO RASH CONCLUSIONS AS TO THE NAME ITSELF, BECAUSE THIS NUMBER IS CAPABLE OF BEING FITTED TO MANY NAMES. REASONS FOR THIS POINT BEING RESERVED BY THE HOLY SPIRIT. ANTICHRIST'S REIGN AND DEATH.

1. Such, then, being the state of the case, and this number being found in all the most approved and ancient copies[3] [of the Apocalypse], and those men who saw John face to face bearing their testimony [to it]; while reason also leads us to conclude that the number of the name of the beast, [if reckoned] according to the Greek mode of calculation by the [value of] the letters contained in it, will amount to six hundred and sixty and six; that is, the number of tens shall be equal to that of the hundreds, and the number of hundreds equal to that of the units (for that number which [expresses] the digit six being adhered to throughout, indicates the recapitulations of that apostasy, taken in its full extent, which occurred at the beginning, during the intermediate periods, and which shall take place at the end), — I do not know how it is that some have erred following the ordinary mode of speech, and have vitiated the middle number in the name, deducting the amount of fifty from it, so that instead of six decades they will have it that there is but one. [I am inclined to think that this occurred through the fault of the copyists, as is wont to happen, since numbers also are expressed by letters; so that the Greek letter which expresses the number sixty was easily expanded into the letter Iota of the Greeks.][4] Others then received this read-

---

[1] Isa. xl. 15.
[2] Matt. xxiv. 21.
[3] ἐν πᾶσι τοῖς σπουδαίοις καὶ ἀρχαίοις ἀντιγράφοις. This passage is interesting, as showing how very soon the autographs of the New Testament must have perished, and various readings crept into the MSS. of the canonical books.
[4] That is, Ξ into ΕΙ, according to Harvey, who considers the whole of this clause as an evident interpolation. It does not occur in the Greek here preserved by Eusebius (*Hist. Eccl.*, v. 8).

ing without examination; some in their simplicity, and upon their own responsibility, making use of this number expressing one decad; while some, in their inexperience, have ventured to seek out a name which should contain the erroneous and spurious number. Now, as regards those who have done this in simplicity, and without evil intent, we are at liberty to assume that pardon will be granted them by God. But as for those who, for the sake of vainglory, lay it down for certain that names containing the spurious number are to be accepted, and affirm that this name, hit upon by themselves, is that of him who is to come; such persons shall not come forth without loss, because they have led into error both themselves and those who confided in them. Now, in the first place, it is loss to wander from the truth, and to imagine that as being the case which is not; then again, as there shall be no light punishment [inflicted] upon him who either adds or subtracts anything from the Scripture,[1] under that such a person must necessarily fall. Moreover, another danger, by no means trifling, shall overtake those who falsely presume that they know the name of Antichrist. For if these men assume one [number], when this [Antichrist] shall come having another, they will be easily led away by him, as supposing him not to be the expected one, who must be guarded against.

2. These men, therefore, ought to learn [what really is the state of the case], and go back to the true number of the name, that they be not reckoned among false prophets. But, knowing the sure number declared by Scripture, that is, six hundred sixty and six, let them await, in the first place, the division of the kingdom into ten; then, in the next place, when these kings are reigning, and beginning to set their affairs in order, and advance their kingdom, [let them learn] to acknowledge that he who shall come claiming the kingdom for himself, and shall terrify those men of whom we have been speaking, having a name containing the aforesaid number, is truly the abomination of desolation. This, too, the apostle affirms: "When they shall say, Peace and safety, then sudden destruction shall come upon them."[2] And Jeremiah does not merely point out his sudden coming, but he even indicates the tribe from which he shall come, where he says, "We shall hear the voice of his swift horses from Dan; the whole earth shall be moved by the voice of the neighing of his galloping horses: he shall also come and devour the earth, and the fulness thereof, the city also, and they that dwell therein."[3] This, too, is the reason that this tribe is not reckoned in the Apocalypse along with those which are saved.[4]

3. It is therefore more certain, and less hazardous, to await the fulfilment of the prophecy, than to be making surmises, and casting about for any names that may present themselves, inasmuch as many names can be found possessing the number mentioned; and the same question will, after all, remain unsolved. For if there are many names found possessing this number, it will be asked which among them shall the coming man bear. It is not through a want of names containing the number of that name that I say this, but on account of the fear of God, and zeal for the truth: for the name *Evanthas* (ΕΥΑΝΘΑΣ) contains the required number, but I make no allegation regarding it. Then also *Lateinos* (ΛΑΤΕΙΝΟΣ) has the number six hundred and sixty-six; and it is a very probable [solution], this being the name of the last kingdom [of the four seen by Daniel]. For the Latins are they who at present bear rule:[5] I will not, however, make any boast over this [coincidence]. *Teitan* too, (ΤΕΙΤΑΝ, the first syllable being written with the two Greek vowels ε and ι), among all the names which are found among us, is rather worthy of credit. For it has in itself the predicted number, and is composed of six letters, each syllable containing three letters; and [the word itself] is ancient, and removed from ordinary use; for among our kings we find none bearing this name Titan, nor have any of the idols which are worshipped in public among the Greeks and barbarians this appellation. Among many persons, too, this name is accounted divine, so that even the sun is termed "Titan" by those who do now possess [the rule]. This word, too, contains a certain outward appearance of vengeance, and of one inflicting merited punishment because he (Antichrist) pretends that he vindicates the oppressed.[6] And besides this, it is an ancient name, one worthy of credit, of royal dignity, and still further, a name belonging to a tyrant. Inasmuch, then, as this name "Titan" has so much to recommend it, there is a strong degree of probability, that from among the many [names suggested], we infer, that perchance he who is to come shall be called "Titan." We will not, however, incur the risk of pronouncing positively as to the name of Antichrist; for if it were necessary that his name should be distinctly revealed in this present time, it would have been announced by him who beheld the apocalyptic vision. For that was seen no very long time

---

[1] Rev. xxii. 19.
[2] 1 Thess. v. 3.
[3] Jer. viii. 16.

[4] Rev. vii. 5–7. [The Danites (though not all) corrupted the Hebrew church and the Levitical priesthood, by image-worship, (Judg. xviii.), and forfeited the blessings of the old covenant.]
[5] [A very pregnant passage, as has often been noted. But let us imitate the pious reticence with which this section concludes.]
[6] Massuet here quotes Cicero and Ovid in proof of the sun being termed *Titan*. The Titans waged war against the gods, to avenge themselves upon Saturn.

since, but almost in our day, towards the end of Domitian's reign.

4. But he indicates the number of the name now, that when this man comes we may avoid him, being aware who he is: the name, however, is suppressed, because it is not worthy of being proclaimed by the Holy Spirit. For if it had been declared by Him, he (Antichrist) might perhaps continue for a long period. But now as "he was, and is not, and shall ascend out of the abyss, and goes into perdition,"[1] as one who has no existence; so neither has his name been declared, for the name of that which does not exist is not proclaimed. But when this Antichrist shall have devastated all things in this world, he will reign for three years and six months, and sit in the temple at Jerusalem; and then the Lord will come from heaven in the clouds, in the glory of the Father, sending this man and those who follow him into the lake of fire; but bringing in for the righteous the times of the kingdom, that is, the rest, the hallowed seventh day; and restoring to Abraham the promised inheritance, in which kingdom the Lord declared, that "many coming from the east and from the west should sit down with Abraham, Isaac, and Jacob."[2]

CHAP. XXXI. — THE PRESERVATION OF OUR BODIES IS CONFIRMED BY THE RESURRECTION AND ASCENSION OF CHRIST: THE SOULS OF THE SAINTS DURING THE INTERMEDIATE PERIOD ARE IN A STATE OF EXPECTATION OF THAT TIME WHEN THEY SHALL RECEIVE THEIR PERFECT AND CONSUMMATED GLORY.

1. Since, again, some who are reckoned among the orthodox go beyond the pre-arranged plan for the exaltation of the just, and are ignorant of the methods by which they are disciplined beforehand for incorruption, they thus entertain heretical opinions. For the heretics, despising the handiwork of God, and not admitting the salvation of their flesh, while they also treat the promise of God contemptuously, and pass beyond God altogether in the sentiments they form, affirm that immediately upon their death they shall pass above the heavens and the Demiurge, and go to the Mother (Achamoth) or to that Father whom they have feigned. Those persons, therefore, who disallow a resurrection affecting the whole man (*universam reprobant resurrectionem*), and as far as in them lies remove it from the midst [of the Christian scheme], how can they be wondered at, if again they know nothing as to the plan of the resurrection? For they do not choose to understand, that if these things are as they say, the Lord Himself, in whom they profess to believe, did not rise again upon the third day; but immediately upon His expiring on the cross, undoubtedly departed on high, leaving His body to the earth. But the case was, that for three days He dwelt in the place where the dead were, as the prophet says concerning Him: "And the Lord remembered His dead saints who slept formerly in the land of sepulture; and He descended to them, to rescue and save them."[3] And the Lord Himself says, "As Jonas remained three days and three nights in the whale's belly, so shall the Son of man be in the heart of the earth."[4] Then also the apostle says, "But when He ascended, what is it but that He also descended into the lower parts of the earth?"[5] This, too, David says when prophesying of Him, "And thou hast delivered my soul from the nethermost hell;"[6] and on His rising again the third day, He said to Mary, who was the first to see and to worship Him, "Touch Me not, for I have not yet ascended to the Father; but go to the disciples, and say unto them, I ascend unto My Father, and unto your Father."[7]

2. If, then, the Lord observed the law of the dead, that He might become the first-begotten from the dead, and tarried until the third day "in the lower parts of the earth;"[8] then afterwards rising in the flesh, so that He even showed the print of the nails to His disciples,[9] He thus ascended to the Father; — [if all these things occurred, I say], how must these men not be put to confusion, who allege that "the lower parts" refer to this world of ours, but that their inner man, leaving the body here, ascends into the super-celestial place? For as the Lord "went away in the midst of the shadow of death,"[10] where the souls of the dead were, yet afterwards arose in the body, and after the resurrection was taken up [into heaven], it is manifest that the souls of His disciples also, upon whose account the Lord underwent these things, shall go away into the invisible place allotted to them by God, and there remain until the resurrection, awaiting that event; then receiving their bodies, and rising in their entirety, that is bodily, just as the Lord arose, they shall come thus into the presence of God. "For no disciple is above the Master, but every one that is perfect shall be as his Master."[11] As our Master, therefore, did not at once depart, taking flight [to heaven], but awaited the time of His resurrection prescribed by the Father, which had been also shown forth through Jonas, and rising again after three days was taken up [to heaven];

---

[1] Rev. xvii. 8.
[2] Matt. viii. 11.
[3] See the note, book iii. xx. 4.
[4] Matt. xi. 40.
[5] Eph. iv. 9.
[6] Ps. lxxxvi. 23.
[7] John xx. 17.
[8] Eph. iv. 9.
[9] John xx. 20, 27.
[10] Ps. xxiii. 4.
[11] Luke vi. 40.

so ought we also to await the time of our resurrection prescribed by God and foretold by the prophets, and so, rising, be taken up, as many as the Lord shall account worthy of this [privilege].[1]

CHAP. XXXII.—IN THAT FLESH IN WHICH THE SAINTS HAVE SUFFERED SO MANY AFFLICTIONS, THEY SHALL RECEIVE THE FRUITS OF THEIR LABOURS; ESPECIALLY SINCE ALL CREATION WAITS FOR THIS, AND GOD PROMISES IT TO ABRAHAM AND HIS SEED.

1. Inasmuch, therefore, as the opinions of certain [orthodox persons] are derived from heretical discourses, they are both ignorant of God's dispensations, and of the mystery of the resurrection of the just, and of the [earthly] kingdom which is the commencement of incorruption, by means of which kingdom those who shall be worthy are accustomed gradually to partake of the divine nature (*capere Deum*[2]); and it is necessary to tell them respecting those things, that it behoves the righteous first to receive the promise of the inheritance which God promised to the fathers, and to reign in it, when they rise again to behold God in this creation which is renovated, and that the judgment should take place afterwards. For it is just that in that very creation in which they toiled or were afflicted, being proved in every way by suffering, they should receive the reward of their suffering; and that in the creation in which they were slain because of their love to God, in that they should be revived again; and that in the creation in which they endured servitude, in that they should reign. For God is rich in all things, and all things are His. It is fitting, therefore, that the creation itself, being restored to its primeval condition, should without restraint be under the dominion of the righteous; and the apostle has made this plain in the Epistle to the Romans, when he thus speaks: "For the expectation of the creature waiteth for the manifestation of the sons of God. For the creature has been subjected to vanity, not willingly, but by reason of him who hath subjected the same in hope; since the creature itself shall also be delivered from the bondage of corruption into the glorious liberty of the sons of God."[3]

2. Thus, then, the promise of God, which He gave to Abraham, remains stedfast. For thus He said: "Lift up thine eyes, and look from this place where now thou art, towards the north and south, and east and west. For all the earth which thou seest, I will give to thee and to thy seed, even for ever."[4] And again He says, "Arise, and go through the length and breadth of the land, since I will give it unto thee;"[5] and [yet] he did not receive an inheritance in it, not even a footstep, but was always a stranger and a pilgrim therein.[6] And upon the death of Sarah his wife, when the Hittites were willing to bestow upon him a place where he might bury her, he declined it as a gift, but bought the burying-place (giving for it four hundred talents of silver) from Ephron the son of Zohar the Hittite.[7] Thus did he await patiently the promise of God, and was unwilling to appear to receive from men, what God had promised to give him, when He said again to him as follows: "I will give this land to thy seed, from the river of Egypt even unto the great river Euphrates."[8] If, then, God promised him the inheritance of the land, yet he did not receive it during all the time of his sojourn there, it must be, that together with his seed, that is, those who fear God and believe in Him, he shall receive it at the resurrection of the just. For his seed is the Church, which receives the adoption to God through the Lord, as John the Baptist said: "For God is able from the stones to raise up children to Abraham."[9] Thus also the apostle says in the Epistle to the Galatians: "But ye, brethren, as Isaac was, are the children of the promise."[10] And again, in the same Epistle, he plainly declares that they who have believed in Christ do receive Christ, the promise to Abraham thus saying, "The promises were spoken to Abraham, and to his seed. Now He does not say, And of seeds, as if [He spake] of many, but as of one, And to thy seed, which is Christ."[11] And again, confirming his former words, he says, "Even as Abraham believed God, and it was accounted to him for righteousness. Know ye therefore, that they which are of faith are the children of Abraham. But the Scripture, foreseeing that God would justify the heathen through faith, declared to Abraham beforehand, That in thee shall all nations be blessed. So then they which are of faith shall be blessed with faithful Abraham."[12] Thus, then, they who are of faith shall be blessed with faithful Abraham, and these are the children of Abraham. Now God made promise of the earth to Abraham and his seed; yet neither Abraham nor his seed, that is, those who are justified by faith, do now receive any

---

[1] The five following chapters were omitted in the earlier editions, but added by Feuardentius. Most MSS., too, did not contain them. It is probable that the scribes of the middle ages rejected them on account of their inculcating millenarian notions, which had been long extinct in the Church. Quotations from these five chapters have been collected by Harvey from Syriac and Armenian MSS. lately come to light.
[2] Or, "gradually to comprehend God."
[3] Rom. viii. 19, etc.
[4] Gen. xiii. 13, 14.
[5] Gen. xiii. 17.
[6] Acts vii. 5; Heb. xi. 13.
[7] Gen. xxiii. 11.
[8] Gen. xv. 13.
[9] Luke iii. 8.
[10] Gal. iv. 28.
[11] Gal. iii. 16.
[12] Gal. iii. 6, etc.

inheritance in it; but they shall receive it at the resurrection of the just. For God is true and faithful; and on this account He said, "Blessed are the meek, for they shall inherit the earth."[1]

CHAP. XXXIII. — FURTHER PROOFS OF THE SAME PROPOSITION, DRAWN FROM THE PROMISES MADE BY CHRIST, WHEN HE DECLARED THAT HE WOULD DRINK OF THE FRUIT OF THE VINE WITH HIS DISCIPLES IN HIS FATHER'S KINGDOM, WHILE AT THE SAME TIME HE PROMISED TO REWARD THEM AN HUNDRED-FOLD, AND TO MAKE THEM PARTAKE OF BANQUETS. THE BLESSING PRONOUNCED BY JACOB HAD POINTED OUT THIS ALREADY, AS PAPIAS AND THE ELDERS HAVE INTERPRETED IT.

1. For this reason, when about to undergo His sufferings, that He might declare to Abraham and those with him the glad tidings of the inheritance being thrown open, [Christ], after He had given thanks while holding the cup, and had drunk of it, and given it to the disciples, said to them: "Drink ye all of it: this is My blood of the new covenant, which shall be shed for many for the remission of sins. But I say unto you, I will not drink henceforth of the fruit of this vine, until that day when I will drink it new with you in my Father's kingdom."[2] Thus, then, He will Himself renew the inheritance of the earth, and will re-organize the mystery of the glory of [His] sons; as David says, "He who hath renewed the face of the earth."[3] He promised to drink of the fruit of the vine with His disciples, thus indicating both these points: the inheritance of the earth in which the new fruit of the vine is drunk, and the resurrection of His disciples in the flesh. For the new flesh which rises again is the same which also received the new cup. And He cannot by any means be understood as drinking of the fruit of the vine when settled down with his [disciples] above in a super-celestial place; nor, again, are they who drink it devoid of flesh, for to drink of that which flows from the vine pertains to flesh, and not spirit.

2. And for this reason the Lord declared, "When thou makest a dinner or a supper, do not call thy friends, nor thy neighbours, nor thy kinsfolk, lest they ask thee in return, and so repay thee. But call the lame, the blind, and the poor, and thou shalt be blessed, since they cannot recompense thee, but a recompense shall be made thee at the resurrection of the just."[4] And again He says, "Whosoever shall have left lands, or houses, or parents, or brethren, or children because of Me, he shall receive in this world an hundred-fold, and in that to come he shall inherit eternal life."[5] For what are the hundred-fold [rewards] in this world, the entertainments given to the poor, and the suppers for which a return is made? These are [to take place] in the times of the kingdom, that is, upon the seventh day, which has been sanctified, in which God rested from all the works which He created, which is the true Sabbath of the righteous, which they shall not be engaged in any earthly occupation; but shall have a table at hand prepared for them by God, supplying them with all sorts of dishes.

3. The blessing of Isaac with which he blessed his younger son Jacob has the same meaning, when he says, "Behold, the smell of my son is as the smell of a full field which the Lord has blessed."[6] But "the field is the world."[7] And therefore he added, "God give to thee of the dew of heaven, and of the fatness of the earth, plenty of corn and wine. And let the nations serve thee, and kings bow down to thee; and be thou lord over thy brother, and thy father's sons shall bow down to thee: cursed shall be he who shall curse thee, and blessed shall be he who shall bless thee."[8] If any one, then, does not accept these things as referring to the appointed kingdom, he must fall into much contradiction and contrariety, as is the case with the Jews, who are involved in absolute perplexity. For not only did not the nations in this life serve this Jacob; but even after he had received the blessing, he himself going forth [from his home], served his uncle Laban the Syrian for twenty years;[9] and not only was he not made lord of his brother, but he did himself bow down before his brother Esau, upon his return from Mesopotamia to his father, and offered many gifts to him.[10] Moreover, in what way did he inherit much corn and wine here, he who emigrated to Egypt because of the famine which possessed the land in which he was dwelling, and became subject to Pharaoh, who was then ruling over Egypt? The predicted blessing, therefore, belongs unquestionably to the times of the kingdom, when the righteous shall bear rule upon their rising from the dead;[11] when also the creation, having been renovated and set free, shall fructify with an abundance of all kinds of food, from the dew of heaven, and from the fertility of the earth: as the elders who saw John, the disciple of the Lord, related that they had heard

---

[1] Matt. v. 5.
[2] Matt. xxvi. 27.
[3] Ps. civ. 30.
[4] Luke xiv. 12, 13.
[5] Matt. xix. 29; Luke xviii. 29, 30.
[6] Gen. xxvii. 27, etc.
[7] Matt. xiii. 38.
[8] Gen. xxvii. 28, 29.
[9] Gen. xxxi. 41.
[10] Gen. xxxiii. 3.
[11] From this to the end of the section there is an Armenian version extant, to be found in the *Spicil. Solesm.* i. p. 1, edited by M. Pitra, Paris 1852, and which was taken by him from an Armenian MS. in the Mechitarist Library at Venice, described as being of the twelfth century.

from him how the Lord used to teach in regard to these times, and say: The days will come, in which vines shall grow, each having ten thousand branches, and in each branch ten thousand twigs, and in each true[1] twig ten thousand shoots, and in each one of the shoots ten thousand clusters, and on every one of the clusters ten thousand grapes, and every grape when pressed will give five and twenty metretes of wine. And when any one of the saints shall lay hold of a cluster,[2] another shall cry out, "I am a better cluster, take me; bless the Lord through me." In like manner [the Lord declared] that a grain of wheat would produce ten thousand ears, and that every ear should have ten thousand grains, and every grain would yield ten pounds (*quinque bilibres*) of clear, pure, fine flour; and that all other fruit-bearing trees,[3] and seeds and grass, would produce in similar proportions (*secundum congruentiam iis consequentem*); and that all animals feeding [only] on the productions of the earth, should [in those days] become peaceful and harmonious among each other, and be in perfect subjection to man.

4. And these things are borne witness to in writing by Papias, the hearer of John, and a companion of Polycarp, in his fourth book; for there were five books compiled (συντεταγμένα) by him.[4] And he says in addition, "Now these things are credible to believers." And he says that, "when the traitor Judas did not give credit to them, and put the question, 'How then can things about to bring forth so abundantly be wrought by the Lord?' the Lord declared, 'They who shall come to these [times] shall see.'" When prophesying of these times, therefore, Esaias says: "The wolf also shall feed with the lamb, and the leopard shall take his rest with the kid; the calf also, and the bull, and the lion shall eat together; and a little boy shall lead them. The ox and the bear shall feed together, and their young ones shall agree together; and the lion shall eat straw as well as the ox. And the infant boy shall thrust his hand into the asp's den, into the nest also of the adder's brood; and they shall do no harm, nor have power to hurt anything in my holy mountain." And again he says, in recapitulation, "Wolves and lambs shall then browse together, and the lion shall eat straw like the ox, and the serpent earth as if it were bread; and they shall neither hurt nor annoy anything in my holy mountain, saith the Lord."[5] I am quite aware that some persons endeavour to refer these words to the case of savage men, both of different nations and various habits, who come to believe, and when they have believed, act in harmony with the righteous. But although this is [true] now with regard to some men coming from various nations to the harmony of the faith, nevertheless in the resurrection of the just [the words shall also apply] to those animals mentioned. For God is rich in all things. And it is right that when the creation is restored, all the animals should obey and be in subjection to man, and revert to the food originally given by God (for they had been originally subjected in obedience to Adam), that is, the productions of the earth. But some other occasion, and not the present, is [to be sought] for showing that the lion shall [then] feed on straw. And this indicates the large size and rich quality of the fruits. For if that animal, the lion, feeds upon straw [at that period], of what a quality must the wheat itself be whose straw shall serve as suitable food for lions?

CHAP. XXXIV. — HE FORTIFIES HIS OPINIONS WITH REGARD TO THE TEMPORAL AND EARTHLY KINGDOM OF THE SAINTS AFTER THEIR RESURRECTION, BY THE VARIOUS TESTIMONIES OF ISAIAH, EZEKIEL, JEREMIAH, AND DANIEL; ALSO BY THE PARABLE OF THE SERVANTS WATCHING, TO WHOM THE LORD PROMISED THAT HE WOULD MINISTER.

1. Then, too, Isaiah himself has plainly declared that there shall be joy of this nature at the resurrection of the just, when he says: "The dead shall rise again; those, too, who are in the tombs shall arise, and those who are in the earth shall rejoice. For the dew from Thee is health to them."[6] And this again Ezekiel also says: "Behold, I will open your tombs, and will bring you forth out of your graves; when I will draw my people from the sepulchres, and I will put breath in you, and ye shall live; and I will place you on your own land, and ye shall know that I am the Lord."[7] And again the same speaks thus: "These things saith the Lord, I will gather Israel from all nations whither they have been driven, and I shall be sanctified in them in the sight of the sons of the nations: and they shall dwell in their own land, which I gave to my servant Jacob. And they shall dwell in it in peace; and they shall build houses, and plant vineyards, and dwell in hope, when I shall cause judgment to fall among all who have dishonoured them, among those who encircle them round about; and they shall know that I am the Lord their God, and the God of their fathers."[8] Now I have shown a short time ago that the church is the seed of Abraham; and for this reason, that we may know that He who in the New Testament "raises up from the stones children unto

---

[1] This word "true" is not found in the Armenian.
[2] Or, following Arm. vers., "But if any one shall lay hold of an holy cluster."
[3] The Arm. vers. is here followed; the old Latin reads, "Et reliqua autem poma."
[4] [See pp. 151-154, this volume.]
[5] Isa. xl. 6, etc.
[6] Isa. xxvi. 19.
[7] Ezek. xxxvii. 12, etc.
[8] Ezek. xxviii. 25, 26.

Abraham,"[1] is He who will gather, according to the Old Testament, those that shall be saved from all the nations, Jeremiah says: "Behold, the days come, saith the LORD, that they shall no more say, The LORD liveth, who led the children of Israel from the north, and from every region whither they had been driven; He will restore them to their own land which He gave to their fathers."[2]

2. That the whole creation shall, according to God's will, obtain a vast increase, that it may bring forth and sustain fruits such [as we have mentioned], Isaiah declares: "And there shall be upon every high mountain, and upon every prominent hill, water running everywhere in that day, when many shall perish, when walls shall fall. And the light of the moon shall be as the light of the sun, seven times that of the day, when He shall heal the anguish of His people, and do away with the pain of His stroke."[3] Now "the pain of the stroke" means that inflicted at the beginning upon disobedient man in Adam, that is, death; which [stroke] the Lord will heal when He raises us from the dead, and restores the inheritance of the fathers, as Isaiah again says: "And thou shalt be confident in the LORD, and He will cause thee to pass over the whole earth, and feed thee with the inheritance of Jacob thy father."[4] This is what the Lord declared: "Happy are those servants whom the Lord when He cometh shall find watching. Verily I say unto you, that He shall gird Himself, and make them to sit down [to meat], and will come forth and serve them. And if He shall come in the evening watch, and find them so, blessed are they, because He shall make them sit down, and minister to them; or if this be in the second, or it be in the third, blessed are they."[5] Again John also says the very same in the Apocalypse: "Blessed and holy is he who has part in the first resurrection."[6] Then, too, Isaiah has declared the time when these events shall occur; he says: "And I said, Lord, how long? Until the cities be wasted without inhabitant, and the houses be without men, and the earth be left a desert. And after these things the LORD shall remove us men far away (*longe nos faciet Deus homines*), and those who shall remain shall multiply upon the earth."[7] Then Daniel also says this very thing: "And the kingdom and dominion, and the greatness of those under the heaven, is given to the saints of the Most High God, whose kingdom is everlasting, and all dominions shall serve and obey Him."[8] And lest the promise named should be understood as referring to this time, it was declared to the prophet: "And come thou, and stand in thy lot at the consummation of the days."[9]

3. Now, that the promises were not announced to the prophets and the fathers alone, but to the Churches united to these from the nations, whom also the Spirit terms "the islands" (both because they are established in the midst of turbulence, suffer the storm of blasphemies, exist as a harbour of safety to those in peril, and are the refuge of those who love the height [of heaven], and strive to avoid Bythus, that is, the depth of error), Jeremiah thus declares: "Hear the word of the LORD, ye nations, and declare it to the isles afar off; say ye, that the LORD will scatter Israel, He will gather him, and keep him, as one feeding his flock of sheep. For the Lord hath redeemed Jacob, and rescued him from the hand of one stronger than he. And they shall come and rejoice in Mount Zion, and shall come to what is good, and into a land of wheat, and wine, and fruits, of animals and of sheep; and their soul shall be as a tree bearing fruit, and they shall hunger no more. At that time also shall the virgins rejoice in the company of the young men: the old men, too, shall be glad, and I will turn their sorrow into joy; and I will make them exult, and will magnify them, and satiate the souls of the priests the sons of Levi; and my people shall be satiated with my goodness."[10] Now, in the preceding book[11] I have shown that all the disciples of the Lord are Levites and priests, they who used in the temple to profane the Sabbath, but are blameless.[12] Promises of such a nature, therefore, do indicate in the clearest manner the feasting of that creation in the kingdom of the righteous, which God promises that He will Himself serve.

4. Then again, speaking of Jerusalem, and of Him reigning there, Isaiah declares, "Thus saith the LORD, Happy is he who hath seed in Zion, and servants in Jerusalem. Behold, a righteous king shall reign, and princes shall rule with judgment."[13] And with regard to the foundation on which it shall be rebuilt, he says: "Behold, I will lay in order for thee a carbuncle stone, and sapphire for thy foundations; and I will lay thy ramparts with jasper, and thy gates with crystal, and thy wall with choice stones: and all thy children shall be taught of God, and great shall be the peace of thy children; and in righteousness shalt thou be built up."[14] And yet again

---

[1] Matt. iii. 9.
[2] Jer. xxiii. 7, 6.
[3] Isa. xxx. 25, 26.
[4] Isa. lviii. 14.
[5] Luke xii. 37, 38.
[6] Rev. xx. 6.
[7] Isa. vi. 11.
[8] Dan. vii. 27.
[9] Dan. xii. 13.
[10] Jer. xxxi. 10, etc.
[11] See iv. 8, 3.
[12] Matt. xii. 5.
[13] Isa. xxxi. 9, xxxii. 1.
[14] Isa. liv. 11-14.

does he say the same thing: "Behold, I make Jerusalem a rejoicing, and my people [a joy]; for the voice of weeping shall be no more heard in her, nor the voice of crying. Also there shall not be there any immature [one], nor an old man who does not fulfil his time: for the youth shall be of a hundred years; and the sinner shall die a hundred years old, yet shall be accursed. And they shall build houses, and inhabit them themselves; and shall plant vineyards, and eat the fruit of them themselves, and shall drink wine. And they shall not build, and others inhabit; neither shall they prepare the vineyard, and others eat. For as the days of the tree of life shall be the days of the people in thee; for the works of their hands shall endure."[1]

CHAP. XXXV. — HE CONTENDS THAT THESE TESTIMONIES ALREADY ALLEGED CANNOT BE UNDERSTOOD ALLEGORICALLY OF CELESTIAL BLESSINGS, BUT THAT THEY SHALL HAVE THEIR FULFILMENT AFTER THE COMING OF ANTICHRIST, AND THE RESURRECTION, IN THE TERRESTRIAL JERUSALEM. TO THE FORMER PROPHECIES HE SUBJOINS OTHERS DRAWN FROM ISAIAH, JEREMIAH, AND THE APOCALYPSE OF JOHN.

1. If, however, any shall endeavour to allegorize [prophecies] of this kind, they shall not be found consistent with themselves in all points, and shall be confuted by the teaching of the very expressions [in question]. For example: "When the cities" of the Gentiles "shall be desolate, so that they be not inhabited, and the houses so that there shall be no men in them, and the land shall be left desolate."[2] "For, behold," says Isaiah, "the day of the LORD cometh past remedy, full of fury and wrath, to lay waste the city of the earth, and to root sinners out of it."[3] And again he says, "Let him be taken away, that he behold not the glory of God."[4] And when these things are done, he says, "God will remove men far away, and those that are left shall multiply in the earth."[5] "And they shall build houses, and shall inhabit them themselves: and plant vineyards, and eat of them themselves."[6] For all these and other words were unquestionably spoken in reference to the resurrection of the just, which takes place after the coming of Antichrist, and the destruction of all nations under his rule; in [the times of] which [resurrection] the righteous shall reign in the earth, waxing stronger by the sight of the Lord: and through Him they shall become accustomed to partake in the glory of God the Father, and shall enjoy in the kingdom intercourse and communion with the holy angels, and union with spiritual beings; and [with respect to] those whom the Lord shall find in the flesh, awaiting Him from heaven, and who have suffered tribulation, as well as escaped the hands of the Wicked one. For it is in reference to them that the prophet says: "And those that are left shall multiply upon the earth." And Jeremiah[7] the prophet has pointed out, that as many believers as God has prepared for this purpose, to multiply those left upon earth, should both be under the rule of the saints to minister to this Jerusalem, and that [His] kingdom shall be in it, saying, "Look around Jerusalem towards the east, and behold the joy which comes to thee from God Himself. Behold, thy sons shall come whom thou hast sent forth: they shall come in a band from the east even unto the west, by the word of that Holy One, rejoicing in that splendour which is from thy God. O Jerusalem, put off thy robe of mourning and of affliction, and put on that beauty of eternal splendour from thy God. Gird thyself with the double garment of that righteousness proceeding from thy God; place the mitre of eternal glory upon thine head. For God will show thy glory to the whole earth under heaven. For thy name shall for ever be called by God Himself, the peace of righteousness and glory to him that worships God. Arise, Jerusalem, stand on high, and look towards the east, and behold thy sons from the rising of the sun, even to the west, by the word of that Holy One, rejoicing in the very remembrance of God. For the footmen have gone forth from thee, while they were drawn away by the enemy. God shall bring them in to thee, being borne with glory as the throne of a kingdom. For God has decreed that every high mountain shall be brought low, and the eternal hills, and that the valleys be filled, so that the surface of the earth be rendered smooth, that Israel, the glory of God, may walk in safety. The woods, too, shall make shady places, and every sweet-smelling tree shall be for Israel itself by the command of God. For God shall go before with joy in the light of His splendour, with the pity and righteousness which proceeds from Him."

2. Now all these things being such as they are, cannot be understood in reference to supercelestial matters; "for God," it is said, "will show to the whole earth that is under heaven thy glory." But in the times of the kingdom, the earth has been called again by Christ [to its pristine condition], and Jerusalem rebuilt after the pattern of the Jerusalem above, of which the prophet Isaiah says, "Behold, I have depicted thy walls upon my hands, and thou art always in

---

[1] Isa. lxv. 18.
[2] Isa. vi. 11.
[3] Isa. xiii. 9.
[4] Isa. xxvi. 10.
[5] Isa. vi. 12.
[6] Isa. lxv. 21.

[7] The long quotation following is not found in Jeremiah, but in the apocryphal book of Baruch, chap. iv. 36, etc., and the whole of chap. v.

my sight."¹ And the apostle, too, writing to the Galatians, says in like manner, "But the Jerusalem which is above is free, which is the mother of us all."² He does not say this with any thought of an erratic Æon, or of any other power which departed from the Pleroma, or of Prunicus, but of the Jerusalem which has been delineated on [God's] hands. And in the Apocalypse John saw this new [Jerusalem] descending upon the new earth.³ For after the times of the kingdom, he says, "I saw a great white throne, and Him who sat upon it, from whose face the earth fled away, and the heavens; and there was no more place for them."⁴ And he sets forth, too, the things connected with the general resurrection and the judgment, mentioning "the dead, great and small." "The sea," he says, "gave up the dead which it had in it, and death and hell delivered up the dead that they contained; and the books were opened. Moreover," he says, "the book of life was opened, and the dead were judged out of those things that were written in the books, according to their works; and death and hell were sent into the lake of fire, the second death."⁵ Now this is what is called Gehenna, which the Lord styled eternal fire.⁶ "And if any one," it is said, "was not found written in the book of life, he was sent into the lake of fire."⁷ And after this, he says, "I saw a new heaven and a new earth, for the first heaven and earth have passed away; also there was no more sea. And I saw the holy city, new Jerusalem, coming down from heaven, as a bride adorned for her husband." "And I heard," it is said, "a great voice from the throne, saying, Behold, the tabernacle of God is with men, and He will dwell with them; and they shall be His people, and God Himself shall be with them as their God. And He will wipe away every tear from their eyes; and death shall be no more, neither sorrow, nor crying, neither shall there be any more pain, because the former things have passed away."⁸ Isaiah also declares the very same: "For there shall be a new heaven and a new earth; and there shall be no remembrance of the former, neither shall the heart think about them, but they shall find in it joy and exultation."⁹ Now this is what has been said by the apostle: "For the fashion of this world passeth away."¹⁰ To the same purpose did the Lord also declare, "Heaven and earth shall pass away."¹¹ When these things, therefore, pass away above the earth, John, the Lord's disciple, says that the new Jerusalem above shall [then] descend, as a bride adorned for her husband; and that this is the tabernacle of God, in which God will dwell with men. Of this Jerusalem the former one is an image — that Jerusalem of the former earth in which the righteous are disciplined beforehand for incorruption and prepared for salvation. And of this tabernacle Moses received the pattern in the mount;¹² and nothing is capable of being allegorized, but all things are stedfast, and true, and substantial, having been made by God for righteous men's enjoyment. For as it is God truly who raises up man, so also does man truly rise from the dead, and not allegorically, as I have shown repeatedly. And as he rises actually, so also shall he be actually disciplined beforehand for incorruption, and shall go forwards and flourish in the times of the kingdom, in order that he may be capable of receiving the glory of the Father. Then, when all things are made new, he shall truly dwell in the city of God. For it is said, "He that sitteth on the throne said, Behold, I make all things new. And the Lord says, Write all this; for these words are faithful and true. And He said to me, They are done."¹³ And this is the truth of the matter.

CHAP. XXXVI. — MEN SHALL BE ACTUALLY RAISED; THE WORLD SHALL NOT BE ANNIHILATED; BUT THERE SHALL BE VARIOUS MANSIONS FOR THE SAINTS, ACCORDING TO THE RANK ALLOTTED TO EACH INDIVIDUAL. ALL THINGS SHALL BE SUBJECT TO GOD THE FATHER, AND SO SHALL HE BE ALL IN ALL.

1. For since there are real men, so must there also be a real establishment (*plantationem*), that they vanish not away among non-existent things, but progress among those which have an actual existence. For neither is the substance nor the essence of the creation annihilated (for faithful and true is He who has established it), but "the *fashion* of the world passeth away;"¹⁴ that is, those things among which transgression has occurred, since man has grown old in them. And therefore this [present] fashion has been formed temporary, God foreknowing all things; as I have pointed out in the preceding book,¹⁵ and have also shown, as far as was possible, the cause of the creation of this world of temporal things. But when this [present] fashion [of things] passes away, and man has been renewed, and flourishes in an incorruptible state, so as to preclude the possibility of becoming old, [then] there shall be the new heaven and the new earth, in which the new man shall remain [con-

---

¹ Isa. xlix. 16.
² Gal. iv. 26.
³ Rev. xxi. 2.
⁴ Rev. xx. 11.
⁵ Rev. xx. 12–14.
⁶ Matt. xxv. 41.
⁷ Rev. xx. 15.
⁸ Rev. xxi. 1–4.
⁹ Isa lxv. 17, 18.
¹⁰ 1 Cor. vii. 31.
¹¹ Matt. xxvi. 35.

¹² Ex. xxv. 40.
¹³ Rev. xxi. 5, 6.
¹⁴ 1 Cor. vii. 31.
¹⁵ Lib. iv. 5, 6.

tinually], always holding fresh converse with God. And since (*or*, that) these things shall ever continue without end, Isaiah declares, "For as the new heavens and the new earth which I do make, continue in my sight, saith the LORD, so shall your seed and your name remain."[1] And as the presbyters say, Then those who are deemed worthy of an abode in heaven shall go there, others shall enjoy the delights of paradise, and others shall possess the splendour of the city; for everywhere the Saviour[2] shall be seen according as they who see Him shall be worthy.

2. [They say, moreover], that there is this distinction between the habitation of those who produce an hundred-fold, and that of those who produce sixty-fold, and that of those who produce thirty-fold: for the first will be taken up into the heavens, the second will dwell in paradise, the last will inhabit the city; and that it was on this account the Lord declared, "In My Father's house are many mansions."[3] For all things belong to God, who supplies all with a suitable dwelling-place; even as His Word says, that a share is allotted to all by the Father, according as each person is or shall be worthy. And this is the couch on which the guests shall recline, having been invited to the wedding.[4] The presbyters, the disciples of the apostles, affirm that this is the gradation and arrangement of those who are saved, and that they advance through steps of this nature; also that they ascend through the Spirit to the Son, and through the Son to the Father, and that in due time the Son will yield up His work to the Father, even as it is said by the apostle, "For He must reign till He hath put all enemies under His feet. The last enemy that shall be destroyed is death."[5] For in the times of the kingdom, the righteous man who is upon the earth shall then forget to die. "But when He saith, All things shall be subdued unto Him, it is manifest that He is excepted who did put all things under Him. And when all things shall be subdued unto Him, then shall the Son also Himself be subject unto Him who put all things under Him, that God may be all in all."[6]

3. John, therefore, did distinctly foresee the first "resurrection of the just,"[7] and the inheritance in the kingdom of the earth; and what the prophets have prophesied concerning it harmonize [with his vision]. For the Lord also taught these things, when He promised that He would have the mixed cup new with His disciples in the kingdom. The apostle, too, has confessed that the creation shall be free from the bondage of corruption, [so as to pass] into the liberty of the sons of God.[8] And in all these things, and by them all, the same God the Father is manifested, who fashioned man, and gave promise of the inheritance of the earth to the fathers, who brought it (the creature) forth [from bondage] at the resurrection of the just, and fulfils the promises for the kingdom of His Son; subsequently bestowing in a paternal manner those things which neither the eye has seen, nor the ear has heard, nor has [thought concerning them] arisen within the heart of man,[9] For there is the one Son, who accomplished His Father's will; and one human race also in which the mysteries of God are wrought, "which the angels desire to look into;"[10] and they are not able to search out the wisdom of God, by means of which His handiwork, confirmed and incorporated with His Son, is brought to perfection; that His offspring, the First-begotten Word, should descend to the creature (*facturam*), that is, to what had been moulded (*plasma*), and that it should be contained by Him; and, on the other hand, the creature should contain the Word, and ascend to Him, passing beyond the angels, and be made after the image and likeness of God.[11]

---

[1] Isa. lxvi. 22.
[2] Thus in a Greek fragment; in the Old Latin, *Deus*.
[3] John xiv. 2.
[4] Matt. xxii. 10.
[5] 1 Cor. xx. 25, 26.
[6] 1 Cor. xv. 27, 28.
[7] Luke xiv. 14.
[8] Rom. viii. 21.
[9] 1 Cor. ii. 9; Isa. lxiv. 4.
[10] 1 Pet. i. 12.
[11] Grabe and others suppose that some part of the work has been lost, so that the above was not its original conclusion.

FRAGMENTS FROM THE LOST WRITINGS OF IRENÆUS

I.

I ADJURE thee, who shalt transcribe this book,[1] by our Lord Jesus Christ, and by His glorious appearing, when He comes to judge the living and the dead, that thou compare what thou hast transcribed, and be careful to set it right according to this copy from which thou hast transcribed; also, that thou in like manner copy down this adjuration, and insert it in the transcript.

II.

These[2] opinions, Florinus, that I may speak in mild terms, are not of sound doctrine; these opinions are not consonant to the Church, and involve their votaries in the utmost impiety; these opinions, even the heretics beyond the Church's pale have never ventured to broach; these opinions, those presbyters who preceded us, and who were conversant with the apostles, did not hand down to thee. For, while I was yet a boy, I saw thee in Lower Asia with Polycarp, distinguishing thyself in the royal court,[3] and endeavouring to gain his approbation. For I have a more vivid recollection of what occurred at that time than of recent events (inasmuch as the experiences of childhood, keeping pace with the growth of the soul, become incorporated with it); so that I can even describe the place where the blessed Polycarp used to sit and discourse — his going out, too, and his coming in — his general mode of life and personal appearance, together with the discourses which he delivered to the people; also how he would speak of his familiar intercourse with John, and with the rest of those who had seen the Lord; and how he would call their words to remembrance. Whatsoever things he had heard from them respecting the Lord, both with regard to His miracles and His teaching, Polycarp having thus received [information] from the eye-witnesses of the Word of life, would recount them all in harmony with the Scriptures. These things, through God's mercy which was upon me, I then listened to attentively, and treasured them up not on paper, but in my heart; and I am continually, by God's grace, revolving these things accurately in my mind. And I can bear witness before God, that if that blessed and apostolical presbyter had heard any such thing, he would have cried out, and stopped his ears, exclaiming as he was wont to do: "O good God, for what times hast Thou reserved me, that I should endure these things?" And he would have fled from the very spot where, sitting or standing, he had heard such words. This fact, too, can be made clear, from his Epistles which he despatched, whether to the neighbouring Churches to confirm them, or to certain of the brethren, admonishing and exhorting them.

III.

For[4] the controversy is not merely as regards the day, but also as regards the form itself of the fast.[5] For some consider themselves bound to fast one day, others two days, others still more, while others [do so during] forty: the diurnal and the nocturnal hours they measure out together as their [fasting] day.[6] And this variety among the observers [of the fasts] had not its origin in our time, but long before in that of our predecessors, some of whom probably, being not very accurate in their observance of it,

---

[1] This fragment is quoted by Eusebius, *Hist. Eccl.*, v. 20. It occurred at the close of the lost treatise of Irenæus entitled *De Ogdoade*.

[2] This interesting extract we also owe to Eusebius, who (*ut sup.*) took it from the work *De Ogdoade*, written after this former friend of Irenæus had lapsed to Valentinianism. Florinus had previously held that God was the author of evil, which sentiment Irenæus opposed in a treatise, now lost, called περὶ μοναρχίας.

[3] Comp. p. 32, this volume, and Phil. iv. 22.

[4] See pp. 31 and 312, of this volume. We are indebted again to Eusebius for this valuable fragment from the Epistle of Irenæus to Victor Bishop of Rome (*Hist. Eccl.*, v. 24; copied also by Nicephorus, iv. 39). It appears to have been a synodical epistle to the head of the Roman Church, the historian saying that it was written by Irenæus, "in the name of (ἐκ προσώπου) those brethren over whom he ruled throughout Gaul." Neither are these expressions to be limited to the Church at Lyons, for the same authority records (v. 23) that it was the testimony "of the dioceses throughout Gaul, which Irenæus superintended" (Harvey).

[5] According to Harvey, the early paschal controversy resolved itself into two particulars: (*a*) as regards the precise day on which our Lord's resurrection should be celebrated; (*b*) as regards the custom of the fast preceding it.

[6] Both reading and punctuation are here subjects of controversy. We have followed Massuet and Harvey.

handed down to posterity the custom as it had, through simplicity or private fancy, been [introduced among them]. And yet nevertheless all these lived in peace one with another, and we also keep peace together. Thus, in fact, the difference [in observing] the fast establishes the harmony of [our common] faith.[1] And the presbyters preceding Soter in the government of the Church which thou dost now rule — I mean, Anicetus and Pius, Hyginus and Telesphorus, and Sixtus — did neither themselves observe it [after that fashion], nor permit those with them[2] to do so. Notwithstanding this, those who did not keep [the feast in this way] were peacefully disposed towards those who came to them from other dioceses in which it was [so] observed, although such observance was [felt] in more decided contrariety [as presented] to those who did not fall in with it; and none were ever cast out [of the Church] for this matter. On the contrary, those presbyters who preceded thee, and who did not observe [this custom], sent the Eucharist to those of other dioceses who did observe it.[3] And when the blessed Polycarp was sojourning in Rome in the time of Anicetus, although a slight controversy had arisen among them as to certain other points, they were at once well inclined towards each other [with regard to the matter in hand], not willing that any quarrel should arise between them upon this head. For neither could Anicetus persuade Polycarp to forego the observance [in his own way], inasmuch as these things had been always [so] observed by John the disciple of our Lord, and by other apostles with whom he had been conversant; nor, on the other hand, could Polycarp succeed in persuading Anicetus to keep [the observance in his way], for he maintained that he was bound to adhere to the usage of the presbyters who preceded him. And in this state of affairs they held fellowship with each other; and Anicetus conceded to Polycarp in the Church the celebration of the Eucharist, by way of showing him respect; so that they parted in peace one from the other, maintaining peace with the whole Church, both those who did observe [this custom] and those who did not.[4]

IV.

As[5] long as any one has the means of doing good to his neighbours, and does not do so, he shall be reckoned a stranger to the love of the Lord.[6]

V.

The[7] will and the energy of God is the effective and foreseeing cause of every time and place and age, and of every nature. The will is the reason (λόγος) of the intellectual soul, which [reason] is within us, inasmuch as it is the faculty belonging to it which is endowed with freedom of action. The will is the mind desiring [some object], and an appetite possessed of intelligence, yearning after that thing which is desired.

VI.

Since[8] God is vast, and the Architect of the world, and omnipotent, He created things that reach to immensity both by the Architect of the world and by an omnipotent will, and with a new effect, potently and efficaciously, in order that the entire fulness of those things which have been produced might come into being, although they had no previous existence — that is, whatever does not fall under [our] observation, and also what lies before our eyes. And so does He contain all things in particular, and leads them on to their own proper result, on account of which they were called into being and produced, in no way changed into anything else than what it (the end) had originally been by nature. For this is the property of the working of God, not merely to proceed to the infinitude of the understanding, or even to overpass [our] powers of mind, reason and speech, time and place, and every age; but also to go beyond substance, and fulness or perfection.

VII.

This[9] [custom], of not bending the knee upon Sunday, is a symbol of the resurrection, through which we have been set free, by the grace of Christ, from sins, and from death, which has been put to death under Him. Now this custom took its rise from apostolic times, as the blessed Irenæus, the martyr and bishop of Lyons, declares in his treatise *On Easter*, in which he makes mention of Pentecost also; upon which [feast] we do not bend the knee, because it is

---

[1] "The observance of *a* day, though not everywhere the same, showed unity, so far as faith in the Lord's resurrection was concerned." — HARVEY.
[2] Following the reading of Rufinus, the ordinary text has μετ' αὐτούς, i.e., after them.
[3] This practice was afterwards forbidden by the Council of Laodicea [held about A.D. 360].
[4] It was perhaps in reference to this pleasing episode in the annals of the Church, that the Council of Arles, A D. 314, decreed that the holy Eucharist should be consecrated by any foreign bishop present at its celebration.
[5] Quoted by Maximus Bishop of Turin, A.D. 422, *Serm.* vii. *de Eleemos.*, as from the Epistle to Pope Victor. It is also found in some other ancient writers.
[6] One of the MSS. reads here τοῦ Θεοῦ, of God.
[7] Also quoted by Maximus Turinensis, *Op.* ii. 152, who refers it to Irenæus's *Sermo de Fide*, which work, not being referred to by Eusebius or Jerome, causes Massuet to doubt the authenticity of the fragment. Harvey, however, accepts it.
[8] We owe this fragment also to Maximus, who quoted it from the same work, *de Fide*, written by Irenæus to Demetrius, a deacon of Vienne. This and the last fragment were first printed by Feuardentius, who obtained them from Faber; no reference, however, being given as to the source from whence the Latin version was derived. The Greek of this Fragment vi. is not extant.
[9] Taken from a work (*Quæs. et Resp. ad Othod.*) ascribed to Justin Martyr, but certainly written after the Nicene Council. It is evident that this is not an exact quotation from Irenæus, but a summary of his words. The "Sunday" here referred to must be Easter Sunday. Massuet's emendation of the text has been adopted, ἐπ' αὐτοῦ for ἐπ' αὐτῶν.

of equal significance with the Lord's day, for the reason already alleged concerning it.

VIII.

For[1] as the ark [of the covenant] was gilded within and without with pure gold, so was also the body of Christ pure and resplendent; for it was adorned within by the Word, and shielded without by the Spirit, in order that from both [materials] the splendour of the natures might be clearly shown forth.

IX.

Ever[2], indeed, speaking well of the deserving, but never ill of the undeserving, we also shall attain to the glory and kingdom of God.

X.

It is indeed proper to God, and befitting His character, to show mercy and pity, and to bring salvation to His creatures, even though they be brought under danger of destruction. "For with Him," says the Scripture, "is propitiation."[3]

XI.

The business of the Christian is nothing else than to be ever preparing for death (μελετᾶν ἀποθνήσκειν).

XII.

We therefore have formed the belief that [our] bodies also do rise again. For although they go to corruption, yet they do not perish; for the earth, receiving the remains, preserves them, even like fertile seed mixed with more fertile ground. Again, as a bare grain is sown, and, germinating by the command of God its Creator, rises again, clothed upon and glorious, but not before it has died and suffered decomposition, and become mingled with the earth; so [it is seen from this, that] we have not entertained a vain belief in the resurrection of the body. But although it is dissolved at the appointed time, because of the primeval disobedience, it is placed, as it were, in the crucible of the earth, to be recast again; not then as this corruptible [body], but pure, and no longer subject to decay: so that to each body its own soul shall be restored; and when it is clothed upon with this, it shall not experience sorrow, but shall rejoice, continuing permanently in a state of purity, having for its companion a just consort, not an insidious one, possessing in every respect the things pertaining to it, it shall receive these with perfect accuracy;[4] it shall not receive bodies diverse from what they had been, nor delivered from suffering or disease, nor as [rendered] glorious, but as they departed this life, in sins or in righteous actions: and such as they were, such shall they be clothed with upon resuming life; and such as they were in unbelief, such shall they be faithfully judged.

XIII.

For[5] when the Greeks, having arrested the slaves of Christian catechumens, then used force against them, in order to learn from them some secret thing [practised] among Christians, these slaves, having nothing to say that would meet the wishes of their tormentors, except that they had heard from their masters that the divine communion was the body and blood of Christ, and imagining that it was actually flesh and blood, gave their inquisitors answer to that effect. Then these latter, assuming such to be the case with regard to the practices of Christians, gave information regarding it to other Greeks, and sought to compel the martyrs Sanctus and Blandina to confess, under the influence of torture, [that the allegation was correct]. To these men Blandina replied very admirably in these words: "How should those persons endure such [accusations], who, for the sake of the practice [of piety], did not avail themselves even of the flesh that was permitted [them to eat]?"

XVI.

How[6] is it possible to say that the serpent, created by God dumb and irrational, was endowed with reason and speech? For if it had the power of itself to speak, to discern, to understand, and to reply to what was spoken by the woman, there would have been nothing to prevent every serpent from doing this also. If, however, they say again that it was according to the divine will and dispensation that this [serpent] spake with a human voice to Eve, they render God the author of sin. Neither was it possible for the evil demon to impart speech to a speechless nature, and thus from that which is not to produce that which is; for if that were the case, he never would have ceased (with the view of leading men astray) from conferring with and deceiving them by means of serpents, and beasts, and birds. From what quarter, too, did it, being a beast, obtain information regarding the injunc-

---

[1] Cited by Leontius of Byzantium, who flourished about the year A.D. 600; but he does not mention the writing of Irenæus from which it is extracted. Massuet conjectures that it is from the *De Ogdoade*, addressed to the apostate Florinus.
[2] This fragment and the next three are from the *Parallela* of John of Damascus. Frag. ix. x. xii. seem to be quotations from the treatise of Irenæus on the resurrection. No. xi. is extracted from his *Miscellaneous Dissertations*, a work mentioned by Eusebius, βιβλίον τι διαλεξέων διαφόρων.
[3] Ps. cxxx. 7.
[4] This sentence in the original seems incomplete; we have followed the conjectural restoration of Harvey.
[5] "This extract is found in Œcumenius upon 1 Pet. c. iii. p. 198; and the words used by him indicate, as Grabe has justly observed, that he only condensed a longer passage." — HARVEY.
[6] From the *Contemplations* of Anastasius Sinaita, who flourished A.D. 685. Harvey doubts as to this fragment being a genuine production of Irenæus; and its whole style of reasoning confirms the suspicion.

tion of God to the man given to him alone, and in secret, not even the woman herself being aware of it? Why also did it not prefer to make its attack upon the man instead of the woman? And if thou sayest that it attacked her as being the weaker of the two, [I reply that], on the contrary, she was the stronger, since she appears to have been the helper of the man in the transgression of the commandment. For she did by herself alone resist the serpent, and it was after holding out for a while and making opposition that she ate of the tree, being circumvented by craft; whereas Adam, making no fight whatever, nor refusal, partook of the fruit handed to him by the woman, which is an indication of the utmost imbecility and effeminacy of mind. And the woman indeed, having been vanquished in the contest by a demon, is deserving of pardon; but Adam shall deserve none, for he was worsted by a woman, — he who, in his own person, had received the command from God. But the woman, having heard of the command from Adam, treated it with contempt, either because she deemed it unworthy of God to speak by means of it, or because she had her doubts, perhaps even held the opinion that the command was given to her by Adam of his own accord. The serpent found her working alone, so that he was enabled to confer with her apart. Observing her then either eating or not eating from the trees, he put before her the fruit of the [forbidden] tree. And if he saw her eating, it is manifest that she was partaker of a body subject to corruption. "For everything going in at the mouth, is cast out into the draught."[1] If then corruptible, it is obvious that she was also mortal. But if mortal, then there was certainly no curse; nor was that a [condemnatory] sentence, when the voice of God spake to the man, " For earth thou art, and unto earth shalt thou return,"[2] as the true course of things proceeds [now and always]. Then again, if the serpent observed the woman not eating, how did he induce her to eat who never had eaten? And who pointed out to this accursed man-slaying serpent that the sentence of death pronounced against them by God would not take [immediate] effect, when He said, " For in the day that ye eat thereof, ye shall surely die?" And not this merely, but that along with the impunity[3] [attending their sin] the eyes of those should be opened who had not seen until then? But with the opening [of their eyes] referred to, they made entrance upon the path of death.

---

[1] Matt. xv. 17.
[2] Gen. iii. 19.
[3] The Greek reads the barbarous word ἀθριξία, which Massuet thinks is a corruption of ἀθανασία, immortality. We have, however, followed the conjecture of Harvey, who would substitute ἀπληξίᾳ, which seems to agree better with the context.

XV.

When,[4] in times of old, Balaam spake these things in parables, he was not acknowledged; and now, when Christ has appeared and fulfilled them, He was not believed. Wherefore [Balaam], foreseeing this, and wondering at it, exclaimed, " Alas! alas! who shall live when God brings these things to pass?"[5]

XVI.

Expounding again the law to that generation which followed those who were slain in the wilderness, he published Deuteronomy; not as giving to them a different law from that which had been appointed for their fathers, but as recapitulating this latter, in order that they, by hearing what had happened to their fathers, might fear God with their whole heart.

XVII.

By these Christ was typified, and acknowledged, and brought into the world; for He was prefigured in Joseph: then from Levi and Judah He was descended according to the flesh, as King and Priest; and He was acknowledged by Simeon in the temple: through Zebulon He was believed in among the Gentiles, as says the prophet, "the land of Zabulon;"[6] and through Benjamin [that is, Paul] He was glorified, by being preached throughout all the world.[7]

XVIII.

And this was not without meaning; but that by means of the number of the ten men,[8] he (Gideon) might appear as having Jesus for a helper, as [is indicated] by the compact entered into with them. And when he did not choose to partake with them in their idol-worship, they threw the blame upon him: for "Jerubbaal" signifies the judgment-seat of Baal.

XIX.

"Take unto thee Joshua (Ἰησοῦν) the son of Nun."[9] For it was proper that Moses should lead the people out of Egypt, but that Jesus (Joshua) should lead them into the inheritance. Also that Moses, as was the case with the law, should cease to be, but that Joshua (Ἰησοῦν), as the word, and no untrue type of the Word made

---

[4] This and the eight following fragments may be referred to the *Miscellaneous Dissertations* of our author; see note on Frag. ix. They are found in three MSS. in the Imperial Collection at Paris, on the Pentateuch, Joshua, Judges, and Ruth.
[5] Num. xxiv. 23.
[6] Isa. ix. 1.
[7] Compare the statement of Clemens Romanus (page 6 of this volume), where, speaking of St. Paul, he says: " After preaching both in the east and west . . . . having taught righteousness to the whole world, and come to the extreme limit of the west."
[8] See Judg. vi. 27. It is not very clear how Irenæus makes out this allegory, but it is thought that he refers to the initial letter in the name Ἰησοῦς, which stands for *ten* in the Greek enumeration. Compare the *Epistle of Barnabas*, cap. ix. p. 143, of this volume.
[9] Num. xxvii. 18.

flesh (ἐνυποστάτου), should be a preacher to the people. Then again, [it was fit] that Moses should give manna as food to the fathers, but Joshua wheat;[1] as the first-fruits of life, a type of the body of Christ, as also the Scripture declares that the manna of the Lord ceased when the people had eaten wheat from the land.[2]

XX.

"And[3] he laid his hands upon him."[4] The countenance of Joshua was also glorified by the imposition of the hands of Moses, but not to the same degree [as that of Moses]. Inasmuch, then, as he had obtained a certain degree of grace, [the Lord] said, "And thou shalt confer upon him of thy glory."[5] For [in this case] the thing given does not cease to belong to the giver.

XXI.

But he does not give, as Christ did, by means of breathing, because he is not the fount of the Spirit.

XXII.

"Thou shalt not go with them, neither shalt thou curse the people."[6] He does not hint at anything with regard to the people, for they all lay before his view, but [he refers] to the mystery of Christ pointed out beforehand. For as He was to be born of the fathers according to the flesh, the Spirit gives instructions to the man (Balaam) beforehand, lest, going forth in ignorance, he might pronounce a curse upon the people.[7] Not, indeed, that [his curse] could take any effect contrary to the will of God; but [this was done] as an exhibition of the providence of God which He exercised towards them on account of their forefathers.

XXIII.

"And he mounted upon his ass."[8] The ass was the type of the body of Christ, upon whom all men, resting from their labours, are borne as in a chariot. For the Saviour has taken up the burden of our sins.[9] Now the angel who appeared to Balaam was the Word Himself; and in His hand He held a sword, to indicate the power which He had from above.

XXIV.

"God is not as a man."[10] He thus shows that all men are indeed guilty of falsehood, inasmuch as they change from one thing to another (μεταφερόμενοι); but such is not the case with God, for He always continues true, perfecting whatever He wishes.

XXV.

"To inflict vengeance from the Lord on Midian."[11] For this man (Balaam), when he speaks no longer in the Spirit of God, but contrary to God's law, by setting up a different law with regard to fornication,[12] is certainly not then to be counted as a prophet, but as a soothsayer. For he who did not keep to the commandment of God, received the just recompense of his own evil devices.[13]

XXVI.

Know[14] thou that every man is either empty or full. For if he has not the Holy Spirit, he has no knowledge of the Creator; he has not received Jesus Christ the Life; he knows not the Father who is in heaven; if he does not live after the dictates of reason, after the heavenly law, he is not a sober-minded person, nor does he act uprightly: such an one is empty. If, on the other hand, he receives God, who says, "I will dwell with them, and walk in them, and I will be their God,"[15] such an one is not empty, but full.

XXVII.

The little boy, therefore, who guided Samson by the hand,[16] pre-typified John the Baptist, who showed to the people the faith in Christ. And the house in which they were assembled signifies the world, in which dwell the various heathen and unbelieving nations, offering sacrifice to their idols. Moreover, the two pillars are the two covenants. The fact, then, of Samson leaning himself upon the pillars, [indicates] this, that the people, when instructed, recognized the mystery of Christ.

XXVIII.

"And the man of God said, Where did it fall? And he showed him the place. And he cut down a tree, and cast it in there, and the iron floated."[17] This was a sign that souls should be borne aloft (ἀναγωγῆς ψυχῶν) through the instrumentality of wood, upon which He suffered who can lead those souls aloft that follow His ascension. This event was also an indication of

---

[1] Harvey conceives the reading here (which is doubtful) to have been τὸν νέον σῖτον, the new wheat; and sees an allusion to the wave-sheaf of the new corn offered in the temple on the morning of our Lord's resurrection.
[2] Josh. v. 12.
[3] Massuet seems to more than doubt the genuineness of this fragment and the next, and would ascribe them to the pen of Apollinaris, bishop of Hierapolis in Phrygia, a contemporary of Irenæus. Harvey passes over these two fragments.
[4] Num. xxvii. 23.
[5] Num. xxvii. 20.
[6] Num. xxii. 12.
[7] The conjectural emendation of Harvey has been adopted here, but the text is very corrupt and uncertain.
[8] Num. xxii. 22, 23
[9] From one of the MSS. Stieren would insert ἐν τῷ ἰδίῳ σώματι, in His own body; see 1 Pet. ii. 24.

[10] Num. xxiii. 19.
[11] Num. xxxi. 3.
[12] Num. xxxi. 16.
[13] Num. xxxi. 8.
[14] It is not certain from what work of Irenæus this extract is derived; Harvey thinks it to be from his work περὶ ἐπιστήμης, i.e., concerning Knowledge.
[15] Lev. xxvi. 12.
[16] Judg. xvi. 26.
[17] 2 Kings vi. 6. Comp. book v. chap. xvii. 4.

the fact, that when the holy soul of Christ descended [to Hades], many souls ascended and were seen in their bodies.[1] For just as the wood, which is the lighter body, was submerged in the water; but the iron, the heavier one, floated: so, when the Word of God became one with flesh, by a physical and hypostatic union, the heavy and terrestrial [part], having been rendered immortal, was borne up into heaven, by the divine nature, after the resurrection.

XXIX.

The [2] Gospel according to Matthew was written to the Jews. For they laid particular stress upon the fact that Christ [should be] of the seed of David. Matthew also, who had a still greater desire [to establish this point], took particular pains to afford them convincing proof that Christ is of the seed of David; and therefore he commences with [an account of] His genealogy.

XXX.[3]

"The axe unto the root,"[4] he says, urging us to the knowledge of the truth, and purifying us by means of fear, as well as preparing [us] to bring forth fruit in due season.

XXXI.

Observe[5] that, by means of the grain of mustard seed in the parable, the heavenly doctrine is denoted which is sown like seed in the world, as in a field, [seed] which has an inherent force, fiery and powerful. For the Judge of the whole world is thus proclaimed, who, having been hidden in the heart of the earth in a tomb for three days, and having become a great tree, has stretched forth His branches to the ends of the earth. Sprouting out from Him, the twelve apostles, having become fair and fruitful boughs, were made a shelter for the nations as for the fowls of heaven, under which boughs, all having taken refuge, as birds flocking to a nest, have been made partakers of that wholesome and celestial food which is derived from them.

XXXII.[6]

Josephus says, that when Moses had been brought up in the royal palaces, he was chosen as general against the Ethiopians; and having proved victorious, obtained in marriage the daughter of that king, since indeed, out of her affection for him, she delivered the city up to him.[7]

Why was it, that when these two (Aaron and Miriam) had both acted with despite towards him (Moses), the latter alone was adjudged punishment?[8] First, because the woman was the more culpable, since both nature and the law place the woman in a subordinate condition to the man. Or perhaps it was that Aaron was to a certain degree excusable, in consideration of his being the elder [brother], and adorned with the dignity of high priest. Then again, inasmuch as the leper was accounted by the law unclean, while at the same time the origin and foundation of the priesthood lay in Aaron, [the Lord] did not award a similar punishment to him, lest this stigma should attach itself to the entire [sacerdotal] race; but by means of his sister's [example] He awoke his fears, and taught him the same lesson. For Miriam's punishment affected him to such an extent, that no sooner did she experience it, than he entreated [Moses], who had been injured, that he would by his intercession do away with the affliction. And he did not neglect to do so, but at once poured forth his supplication. Upon this the Lord, who loves mankind, made him understand how He had not chastened her as a judge, but as a father; for He said, "If her father had spit in her face, should she not be ashamed? Let her be shut out from the camp seven days, and after that let her come in again."[9]

XXXIII.

Inasmuch[10] as certain men, impelled by what considerations I know not, remove from God the half of His creative power, by asserting that He is merely the cause of quality resident in matter, and by maintaining that matter itself is uncreated, come now let us put the question, What is at any time . . . is immutable. Matter, then, is immutable. But if matter be immutable, and the immutable suffers no change in regard to quality, it does not form the substance of the world. For which reason it seems to them superfluous, that God has annexed qualities to matter, since indeed matter admits of no possible alteration, it being in itself an uncreated thing. But further, if matter be uncreated, it has been made altogether according to a certain

---

[1] Matt. xxvii. 52.
[2] Edited by P. Possin, in a *Catena Patrum* on St. Matthew. See book iii. chap. xi. 8.
[3] From the same *Catena*. Compare book v. chap. xvii. 4.
[4] Matt. iii. 10.
[5] First edited in Latin by Corderius, afterwards in Greek by Grabe, and also by Dr. Cramer in his *Catena* on St. Luke.
[6] Massuet's Fragment xxxii. is here passed over; it is found in book iii. chap. xviii. 7.
[7] See Josephus' *Antiquities*, book ii. chap. x., where we read that this king's daughter was called Tharbis. Immediately upon the surrender of this city (Saba, afterwards called Meroë) Moses married her, and returned to Egypt. Whiston, in the notes to his translation of Josephus, says, "Nor, perhaps, did St. Stephen refer to anything else when he said of Moses, before he was sent by God to the Israelites, that he was not only learned in all the wisdom of the Egyptians, but was also mighty in words and in deeds" (Acts vii. 22).
[8] Num. xii. 1, etc.
[9] Num. xii. 14.
[10] Harvey considers this fragment to be a part of the work of Irenæus referred to by Photius under the title *De Universo*, or *de Substantiâ Mundi*. It is to be found in Codex 3011 of the Bodleian Library, Oxford.

quality, and this immutable, so that it cannot be receptive of more qualities, nor can it be the thing of which the world is made. But if the world be not made from it, [this theory] entirely excludes God from exercising power on the creation [of the world].

XXXIV.

"And [1] dipped himself," says [the Scripture], "seven times in Jordan."[2] It was not for nothing that Naaman of old, when suffering from leprosy, was purified upon his being baptized, but [it served] as an indication to us. For as we are lepers in sin, we are made clean, by means of the sacred water and the invocation of the Lord, from our old transgressions; being spiritually regenerated as new-born babes, even as the Lord has declared: "Except a man be born again through water and the Spirit, he shall not enter into the kingdom of heaven."[3]

XXXV.

If the corpse of Elisha raised a dead man,[4] how much more shall God, when He has quickened men's dead bodies, bring them up for judgment?

XXXVI.

True[5] knowledge, then, consists in the understanding of Christ, which Paul terms the wisdom of God hidden in a mystery, which "the natural man receiveth not,"[6] the doctrine of the cross; of which if any man "taste,"[7] he will not accede to the disputations and quibbles of proud and puffed-up men,[8] who go into matters of which they have no perception.[9] For the truth is unsophisticated ($\dot{a}\sigma\chi\eta\mu\dot{a}\tau\iota\sigma\tau\sigma$); and "the word is nigh thee, in thy mouth and in thy heart,"[10] as the same apostle declares, being easy of comprehension to those who are obedient. For it renders us like to Christ, if we experience "the power of his resurrection and the fellowship of His sufferings."[11] For this is the affinity[12] of the apostolical teaching and the most holy "faith delivered unto us,"[13] which the unlearned receive, and those of slender knowledge have taught, not "giving heed to endless genealogies,"[14] but studying rather [to observe] a straightforward course of life; lest, having been deprived of the Divine Spirit, they fail to attain to the kingdom of heaven. For truly the first thing is to deny one's self and to follow Christ; and those who do this are borne onward to perfection, having fulfilled all their Teacher's will, becoming sons of God by spiritual regeneration, and heirs of the kingdom of heaven; those who seek which first shall not be forsaken.

XXXVII.

Those who have become acquainted with the secondary (i.e., under Christ) constitutions of the apostles,[15] are aware that the Lord instituted a new oblation in the new covenant, according to [the declaration of] Malachi the prophet. For, "from the rising of the sun even to the setting my name has been glorified among the Gentiles, and in every place incense is offered to my name, and a pure sacrifice;"[16] as John also declares in the Apocalypse: "The incense is the prayers of the saints."[17] Then again, Paul exhorts us "to present our bodies a living sacrifice, holy, acceptable unto God, which is your reasonable service."[18] And again, "Let us offer the sacrifice of praise, that is, the fruit of the lips."[19] Now those oblations are not according to the law, the handwriting of which the Lord took away from the midst by cancelling it;[20] but they are according to the Spirit, for we must worship God "in spirit and in truth."[21] And therefore the oblation of the Eucharist is not a carnal one, but a spiritual; and in this respect it is pure. For we make an oblation to God of the bread and the cup of blessing, giving Him thanks in that He has commanded the earth to bring forth these fruits for our nourishment. And then, when we have perfected the oblation, we invoke the Holy Spirit, that He may exhibit this sacrifice, both the bread the body of Christ, and the cup the blood of Christ, in order that the receivers of these antitypes[22] may obtain remission of sins and life eternal. Those persons, then, who perform these oblations in remem-

---

[1] This and the next fragment first appeared in the Benedictine edition reprinted at Venice, 1734. They were taken from a MS. *Catena* on the book of Kings in the Coislin Collection.
[2] 2 Kings v. 14.
[3] John iii. 5.
[4] 2 Kings xiii. 21.
[5] This extract and the next three were discovered in the year 1715 by [Christopher Matthew] Pfaff, a learned Lutheran, in the Royal Library at Turin. The MSS. from which they were taken were neither catalogued nor classified, and have now disappeared from the collection. It is impossible to say with any degree of probability from what treatises of our author these four fragments have been culled. For a full account of their history, see Stieren's edition of Irenæus, vol. ii. p. 381. [But, in all candor, let Pfaff himself be heard. His little work is full of learning, and I have long possessed it as a treasure to which I often recur. Pfaff's *Irenæi Fragmenta* was published at The Hague, 1715.]
[6] 1 Cor. ii. 14.
[7] 1 Pet. ii. 3.
[8] 1 Tim. vi. 4, 5.
[9] Col. ii. 18.
[10] Rom. x. 8; Deut. xxx. 14.
[11] Phil. iii. 10.
[12] Harvey's conjectural emendation, ἐπιπλοκὴ for ἐπιλογὴ, has been adopted here.
[13] Jude 3.
[14] 1 Tim. i. 4.
[15] ταῖς δευτέραις τῶν ἀποστόλων διατάξεσι. Harvey thinks that these words imply, "the formal constitution, which the apostles, acting under the impulse of the Spirit, though still in a secondary capacity, gave to the Church."
[16] Mal. i. 11.
[17] Rev. v. 8. The same view of the eucharistic oblation, etc., is found in book iv. chap. xvii.: as also in Justin Martyr; see *Trypho*, cap. xli. *supra* in this volume.
[18] Rom. xii. 1.
[19] Heb. xiii. 15.
[20] Col. ii. 14.
[21] John iv. 24.
[22] Harvey explains this word ἀντιτύπων as meaning an "exact counterpart." He refers to the word where it occurs in *Contra Hæreses*, lib. i. chap. xxiv. (p. 349, this vol.) as confirmatory of his view.

brance of the Lord, do not fall in with Jewish views, but, performing the service after a spiritual manner, they shall be called sons of wisdom.

XXXVIII.

The [1] apostles ordained, that "we should not judge any one in respect to meat or drink, or in regard to a feast day, or the new moons, or the sabbaths." [2] Whence then these contentions? whence these schisms? We keep the feast, but in the leaven of malice and wickedness, cutting in pieces the Church of God; and we preserve what belongs to its exterior, that we may cast away these better things, faith and love. We have heard from the prophetic words that these feasts and fasts are displeasing to the Lord.[3]

XXXIX.

Christ,[4] who was called the Son of God before the ages, was manifested in the fulness of time, in order that He might cleanse us through His blood, who were under the power of sin, presenting us as pure sons to His Father, if we yield ourselves obediently to the chastisement of the Spirit. And in the end of time He shall come to do away with all evil, and to reconcile all things, in order that there may be an end of all impurities.

XL.

"And [5] he found the jaw-bone of an ass." [6] It is to be observed that, after [Samson had committed] fornication, the holy Scripture no longer speaks of the things happily accomplished by him in connection with the formula, "The Spirit of the Lord came upon him." [7] For thus, according to the holy apostle, the sin of fornication is perpetrated against the body, as involving also sin against the temple of God.[8]

XLI.

This [9] indicates the persecution against the Church set on foot by the nations who still continue in unbelief. But he (Samson) who suffered those things, trusted that there would be a retaliation against those waging this war. But retaliation through what means? First of all, by his betaking himself to the Rock [10] not cognizable to the senses; [11] secondly, by the finding of the jaw-bone of an ass. Now the type of the jaw-bone is the body of Christ.

XLII.

Speaking always well of the worthy, but never ill of the unworthy, we also shall attain to the glory and kingdom of God.

XLIII.

In [12] these things there was signified by prophecy that the people, having become transgressors, shall be bound by the chains of their own sins. But the breaking of the bonds of their own accord indicates that, upon repentance, they shall be again loosed from the shackles of sin.

XLIV.

It [13] is not an easy thing for a soul, under the influence of error, to be persuaded of the contrary opinion.

XLV.

"And [14] Balaam the son of Beor they slew with the sword." [15] For, speaking no longer by the Spirit of God, but setting up another law of fornication contrary to the law of God,[16] this man shall no longer be reckoned as a prophet, but as a soothsayer. For, as he did not continue in the commandment of God, he received the just reward of his evil devices.

XLVI.

"The [17] god of the world;" [18] that is, Satan, who was designated God to those who believe not.

XLVII.

The [19] birth of John [the Baptist] brought the dumbness of Zacharias to an end. For he did not burden his father, when the voice issued forth from silence; but as when not believed it rendered him tongue-tied, so did the voice sounding out clearly set his father free, to whom he had both been announced and born. Now the voice and the burning light [20] were a precursor of the Word and the Light.

---

[1] Taken apparently from the *Epistle to Blastus, de Schismate*. Compare a similar passage, lib. iv. chap. xxxiii. 7.
[2] Col. ii. 16.
[3] Isa. i. 14.
[4] "From the same collection at Turin. The passage seems to be of cognate matter with the treatise *De Resurrec.* Pfaff referred it either to the διαλέξεις διάφοροι or to the ἐπίδειξις ἀποστολικοῦ κηρύγματος." — HARVEY.
[5] This and the four following fragments are taken from MSS. in the Vatican Library at Rome. They are apparently quoted from the homiletical expositions of the historical books already referred to.
[6] Judg. xv. 15.
[7] Judg. xiv. 6-19.
[8] 1 Cor. iii. 16, 17.
[9] These words were evidently written during a season of persecution in Gaul; but what that persecution was, it is useless to conjecture.
[10] Judg. xv. 11.
[11] That is, when he fled to the rock Etam, he typified the true believer taking refuge in the spiritual Rock, Christ.
[12] Most probably from a homily upon the third and fourth chapters of Ezekiel. It is found repeated in Stieren's and Migne's edition as Fragment xlviii. extracted from a *Catena* on the Book of Judges.
[13] We give this brief fragment as it appears in the editions of Stieren, Migne, and Harvey, who speculate as to its origin. They seem to have overlooked the fact that it is the Greek original of the old Latin, *non facile est ab errore apprehensam resipiscere animam*, — a sentence found towards the end of book iii. chap. ii.
[14] With the exception of the initial text, this fragment is almost identical with No. xxv.
[15] Num. xxxi. 8.
[16] Rev. ii. 14.
[17] From the *Catena* on St. Paul's Epistles to the Corinthians, edited by Dr. Cramer, and reprinted by Stieren.
[18] 2 Cor. iv. 4.
[19] Extracted from a MS. of Greek theology in the Palatine Library at Vienna. The succeeding fragment in the editions of Harvey, Migne, and Stieren, is omitted, as it is merely a transcript of book iii. ch. x. 4.
[20] John v. 35.

XLVIII.

As[1] therefore seventy tongues are indicated by number, and from[2] dispersion the tongues are gathered into one by means of their interpretation; so is that ark declared a type of the body of Christ, which is both pure and immaculate. For[3] as that ark was gilded with pure gold both within and without, so also is the body of Christ pure and resplendent, being adorned within by the Word, and shielded on the outside by the Spirit, in order that from both [materials] the splendour of the natures might be exhibited together.

XLIX.

Now[4] therefore, by means of this which has been already brought forth a long time since, the Word has assigned an interpretation. We are convinced that there exist [so to speak] two men in each one of us. The one is confessedly a hidden thing, while the other stands apparent; one is corporeal, the other spiritual; although the generation of both may be compared to that of twins. For both are revealed to the world as but one, for the soul was not anterior to the body in its essence; nor, in regard to its formation, did the body precede the soul: but both these were produced at one time; and their nourishment consists in purity and sweetness.

L.

For[5] then there shall in truth be a common joy consummated to all those who believe unto life, and in each individual shall be confirmed the mystery of the Resurrection, and the hope of incorruption, and the commencement of the eternal kingdom, when God shall have destroyed death and the devil. For that human nature and flesh which has risen again from the dead shall die no more; but after it had been changed to incorruption, and made like to spirit, when the heaven was opened, [our Lord] full of glory offered it (the flesh) to the Father.

LI.

Now,[6] however, inasmuch as the books of these men may possibly have escaped your observation, but have come under our notice, I call your attention to them, that for the sake of your reputation you may expel these writings from among you, as bringing disgrace upon you, since their author boasts himself as being one of your company. For they constitute a stumbling-block to many, who simply and unreservedly receive, as coming from a presbyter, the blasphemy which they utter against God. Just [consider] the writer of these things, how by means of them he does not injure assistants [in divine service] only, who happen to be prepared in mind for blasphemies against God, but also damages those among us, since by his books he imbues their minds with false doctrines concerning God.

LII.

The[7] sacred books acknowledge with regard to Christ, that as He is the Son of man, so is the same Being not a [mere] man; and as He is flesh, so is He also spirit, and the Word of God, and God. And as He was born of Mary in the last times, so did He also proceed from God as the First-begotten of every creature; and as He hungered, so did He satisfy [others]; and as He thirsted, so did He of old cause the Jews to drink, for the "Rock was Christ"[8] Himself: thus does Jesus now give to His believing people power to drink spiritual waters, which spring up to life eternal.[9] And as He was the son of David, so was He also the Lord of David. And as He was from Abraham, so did He also exist before Abraham.[10] And as He was the servant of God, so is He the Son of God, and Lord of the universe. And as He was spit upon ignominiously, so also did He breathe the Holy Spirit into His disciples.[11] And as He was saddened, so also did He give joy to His people. And as He was capable of being handled and touched, so again did He, in a non-apprehensible form, pass through the midst of those who sought to injure Him,[12] and entered without impediment through closed doors.[13] And as He slept, so did He also rule the sea, the winds, and the storms. And as He suffered, so also is He alive, and life-giving, and healing all our infirmity. And as He died, so is He also the Resurrection of the dead. He suffered shame on earth, while He is higher than all glory and praise in heaven; who, "though He was crucified through weakness, yet He liveth by divine power;"[14] who "descended into the lower parts of the earth," and who "ascended up above the heavens;"[15] for whom a manger

---

[1] This fragment commences a series derived from the Nitrian Collection of Syriac MSS. in the British Museum.
[2] The Syriac text is here corrupt and obscure.
[3] See No. viii., which is the same as the remainder of this fragment.
[4] The Syriac MS. introduces this quotation as follows: "From the holy Irenæus Bp. of Lyons, from the first section of his interpretation of the Song of Songs."
[5] This extract is introduced as follows: "For Irenæus Bishop of Lyons, who was a contemporary of the disciple of the apostle, Polycarp Bishop of Smyrna, and martyr, and for this reason is held in just estimation, wrote to an Alexandrian to the effect that it is right, with respect to the feast of the Resurrection, that we should celebrate it upon the first day of the week." This shows us that the extract must have been taken from the work *Against Schism* addressed to Blastus.
[6] From the same MS. as the preceding fragment It is thus introduced: "And Irenæus Bp. of Lyons, to Victor Bp. of Rome, concerning Florinus, a presbyter, who was a partisan of the error of Valentinus, and published an abominable book, thus wrote."
[7] This extract had already been printed by M. Pitra in his *Spicilegium Solesmense*, p. 6.
[8] 1 Cor. x. 4.
[9] John iv. 14.
[10] John viii. 58.
[11] John xx. 22.
[12] John viii. 59.
[13] John xx. 26.
[14] 2 Cor. xiii. 4.
[15] Eph. iv. 9, 10.

sufficed, yet who filled all things; who was dead, yet who liveth for ever and ever. Amen.

LIII.

With [1] regard to Christ, the law and the prophets and the evangelists have proclaimed that He was born of a virgin, that He suffered upon a beam of wood, and that He appeared from the dead; that He also ascended to the heavens, and was glorified by the Father, and is the Eternal King; that He is the perfect Intelligence, the Word of God, who was begotten before the light; that He was the Founder of the universe, along with it (light), and the Maker of man; that He is All in all: Patriarch among the patriarchs; Law in the laws; Chief Priest among priests; Ruler among kings; the Prophet among prophets; the Angel among angels; the Man among men; Son in the Father; God in God; King to all eternity. For it is He who sailed [in the ark] along with Noah, and who guided Abraham; who was bound along with Isaac, and was a Wanderer with Jacob; the Shepherd of those who are saved, and the Bridegroom of the Church; the Chief also of the cherubim, the Prince of the angelic powers; God of God; Son of the Father; Jesus Christ; King for ever and ever. Amen.

LIV.

The [2] law and the prophets and evangelists have declared that Christ was born of a virgin, and suffered on the cross; was raised also from the dead, and taken up to heaven; that He was glorified, and reigns for ever. He is Himself termed the Perfect Intellect, the Word of God. He is the First-begotten,[3] after a transcendent manner, the Creator of man; All in all; Patriarch among the patriarchs; Law in the law; the Priest among priests; among kings Prime Leader; the Prophet among the prophets; the Angel among angels; the Man among men; Son in the Father; God in God; King to all eternity. He was sold with Joseph, and He guided Abraham; was bound along with Isaac, and wandered with Jacob; with Moses He was Leader, and, respecting the people, Legislator. He preached in the prophets; was incarnate of a virgin; born in Bethlehem; received by John, and baptized in Jordan; was tempted in the desert, and proved to be the Lord. He gathered the apostles together, and preached the kingdom of heaven; gave light to the blind, and raised the dead; was seen in the temple, but was not held by the people as worthy of credit; was arrested by the priests, conducted before Herod, and condemned in the presence of Pilate; He manifested Himself in the body, was suspended upon a beam of wood, and raised from the dead; shown to the apostles, and, having been carried up to heaven, sitteth on the right hand of the Father, and has been glorified by Him as the Resurrection of the dead. Moreover, He is the Salvation of the lost, the Light to those dwelling in darkness, and Redemption to those who have been born; the Shepherd of the saved, and the Bridegroom of the Church; the Charioteer of the cherubim, the Leader of the angelic host; God of God; Jesus Christ our Saviour.

LV.

"Then [4] drew near unto Him the mother of Zebedee's children, with her sons, worshipping, and seeking a certain thing from Him."[5] These people are certainly not void of understanding, nor are the words set forth in that passage of no signification: being stated beforehand like a preface, they have some agreement with those points formerly expounded.

"Then drew near." Sometimes virtue excites our admiration, not merely on account of the display which is given of it, but also of the occasion when it was manifested. I may refer, for example, to the premature fruit of the grape, or of the fig, or to any fruit whatsoever, from which, during its process [of growth], no man expects maturity or full development; yet, although any one may perceive that it is still somewhat imperfect, he does not for that reason despise as useless the immature grape when plucked, but he gathers it with pleasure as appearing early in the season; nor does he consider whether the grape is possessed of perfect sweetness; nay, he at once experiences satisfaction from the thought that this one has appeared before the rest. Just in the same way does God also, when He perceives the faithful possessing wisdom though still imperfect, and but a small degree of faith, overlook their defect in this respect, and therefore does not reject them; nay, but on the contrary, He kindly welcomes and accepts them as premature fruits, and honours the mind, whatsoever it may be, which is stamped with virtue, although not yet perfect. He makes allowance for it, as being among the harbingers of the vintage,[6] and esteems it highly, inasmuch as, being of a readier disposition than the rest, it has forestalled, as it were, the blessing to itself.

---

[1] This extract from the Syriac is a shorter form of the next fragment, which seems to be interpolated in some places. The latter is from an Armenian MS. in the Mechitarist Library at Venice.

[2] This fragment is thus introduced in the Armenian copy: "From St. Irenæus, bishop, follower of the apostles, on the Lord's resurrection."

[3] The Armenian text is confused here; we have adopted the conjectural emendation of Quatremere.

[4] From an Armenian MS. in the Library of the Mechitarist Convent at Vienna, edited by M. Pitra, who considers this fragment as of very doubtful authority. It commences with this heading: "From the second series of Homilies of Saint Irenæus, follower of the Apostles; a Homily upon the Sons of Zebedee."

[5] Matt. xx. 20.

[6] That is, the wine which flows from the grapes before they are trodden out.

Abraham therefore, Isaac, and Jacob, our fathers, are to be esteemed before all, since they did indeed afford us such early examples of virtue. How many martyrs can be compared to Daniel? How many martyrs, I ask, can rival the three youths in Babylon, although the memory of the former has not been brought before us so conspicuously as that of the latter? These were truly first-fruits, and indications of the [succeeding] fructification. Hence God has directed their life to be recorded, as a model for those who should come after.

And that their virtue was thus accepted by God, as the first-fruits of the produce, hear what He has Himself declared: "As a grape," He says, "I have found Israel in the wilderness, and as first-ripe figs your fathers."[1] Call not therefore the faith of Abraham merely blessed because he believed. Do you wish to look upon Abraham with admiration? Then behold how that one man alone professed piety when in the world six hundred had been contaminated with error. Dost thou wish Daniel to carry thee away to amazement? Behold that [city] Babylon, haughty in the flower and pride of impiousness, and its inhabitants completely given over to sin of every description. But he, emerging from the depth, spat out the brine of sins, and rejoiced to plunge into the sweet waters of piety. And now, in like manner, with regard to that mother of Zebedee's children, do not admire merely what she said, but also the time at which she uttered these words. For when was it that she drew near to the Redeemer? Not after the resurrection, nor after the preaching of His name, nor after the establishment of His kingdom; but it was when the Lord said, "Behold, we go up to Jerusalem, and the Son of man shall be delivered to the chief priests and the scribes; and they shall kill Him, and on the third day He shall rise again."[2]

[1] Hos. ix. 10.
[2] Matt. xx. 18.

These things the Saviour told in reference to His sufferings and cross; to these persons He predicted His passion. Nor did He conceal the fact that it should be of a most ignominious kind, at the hands of the chief priests. This woman, however, had attached another meaning to the dispensation of His sufferings. The Saviour was foretelling death; and she asked for the glory of immortality. The Lord was asserting that He must stand arraigned before impious judges; but she, taking no note of that judgment, requested as of the judge: "Grant," she said, "that these my two sons may sit, one on the right hand, and the other on the left, in Thy glory." In the one case the passion is referred to, in the other the kingdom is understood. The Saviour was speaking of the cross, while she had in view the glory which admits no suffering. This woman, therefore, as I have already said, is worthy of our admiration, not merely for what she sought, but also for the occasion of her making the request.

She did indeed suffer, not merely as a pious person, but also as a woman. For, having been instructed by His words, she considered and believed that it would come to pass, that the kingdom of Christ should flourish in glory, and walk in its vastness throughout the world, and be increased by the preaching of piety. She understood, as was [in fact] the case, that He who appeared in a lowly guise had delivered and received every promise. I will inquire upon another occasion, when I come to treat upon this humility, whether the Lord rejected her petition concerning His kingdom. But she thought that the same confidence would not be possessed by her, when, at the appearance of the angels, He should be ministered to by the angels, and receive service from the entire heavenly host. Taking the Saviour, therefore, apart in a retired place, she earnestly desired of Him those things which transcend every human nature.

POSTSCRIPT.

THE American editor omitted in the proper place (p. 315, note 4, after what is said by the translator) to insert this important note: viz.,—

[On this matter of quotations from anonymous authors of the apostolic times, not infrequently made by Irenæus, consult the important tractate of Dr. Routh, in his *Reliquiæ Sacræ*, vol. i. pp. 45-68.]

INDEXES

THE APOSTOLIC FATHERS.

INDEX OF SUBJECTS

Abel, 6, 55, 89.
Abraham, 7, 9, 13, 142.
Adultery, 35, 108, 143.
Afflictions of Christ, 139.
Alms-giving, 16, 148.
Angels, 68, 88, 118, 148.
Anger, 17, 35, 54.
Animals, cloven-footed, 144.
    ruminant, 143.
    forbidden or allowed as food to Israel, spiritual significance of, 143.
Antichrist, 34, 138.
Antioch, church at, 48, 85, 91, 96, 100, 129.
Antiochians, supposed Epistle of Ignatius to them, wherein he speaks of his bonds, of the true doctrine concerning Christ against the views of the early heretics, and exhorts them to certain duties, 110, 112.
Apostates, 68, 71, 82–83.
Apostles, ordinances as to the ministry, 16, 17, 18, 66, 84.

Baptism prefigured in Old Testament, 144.
Barnabas, who he was, 133.
    his Epistle, wherein he warns his readers against Judaism, and seeks to explain some Jewish customs, 137–149.
Believers, a spiritual temple, 147; what Christ is to them, 11, 14, 15, 18, 33.
Benediction, forms of, 15, 21, 30, 43, 58, 72, 85, 92, 96.
Birds, allowed as food to Israel, 143.
Bishop, subjection to him, 17, 50–96.
    though youthful, to be obeyed, 60.
Bishop to be consulted in all things, 50, 62, 79, 89.
    to be honoured, 90, 95.
    duties of, 69, 85, 90, 94, 96.
Blessings, divine, how obtained, 13, 14, 21, 28, 29.
    to be sought, 28, 149.
Brazen serpent, 145.
Burrhus of Ephesus, 50.

Cain, 6.
Catholic, 39, 40, 42, 90.

Chastisement, 47.
Christ, *His person*, 9, 52, 55, 57, 61–62, 64, 70, 71, 76, 81, 84, 86, 87, 88, 94, 145.
    His sufferings, 9, 64, 66, 70, 71, 83, 84, 86, 88, 89, 139, 140, 142, 145.
    His resurrection, 11, 33, 71, 87.
    His second coming, 11, 33, 64, 87.
    the source of blessings, 14, 84.
Chastity, 34, 148.
Christians, heirs of the covenant, 145.
    true and false, 55, 61.
    manners of, 26; their relation to the world, 27.
    called children, 153.
Church, order in the, 16, 17, 90; order of ministers in, 16; the regard Moses had for order in, 17; the regard the apostles had for order in, 18; this order disturbed by the wicked, 17–20.
Circumcision, spiritual meaning of, 142–143.
Clement, introductory notice of, 1–3.
    his first epistle, 5–21.
Commandments, of God, 33, 148.
Confession of sin, 19.
    of Christ, 41, 55, 83, 129.
Conformity to Christ, 50.
Corinthians, Epistle of Clement to, wherein he commends them, 5; shows the effects of envy among them, 5, 6, 18; exhorts them to repentance, 7; to humility, 9, 11, 15; to peace, 16; to good works, 14; to Church order, 16–17; to brotherly love, 18, 19.
Covenant, the, lost by the Jews, 139; who are heirs of, 145.
Covetousness, 35.
Crocus of Ephesus, 50.
Cross, the, of Christ prefigured in Old Testament, 144.
    the glory of, 56.

Damas, bishop of Magnesia, 59, 60.
Danaids, martyrdom of, 6.
Daniel, 60, 61.
Darkness, the way of, 149.
David, his humility, 10.
Deacons, 34, 61, 69, 72, 85, 89, 95.
Devil, snares of the, 30, 55, 69, 83, 117–119, 148.

Diognetus, Epistle to, wherein the writer shows why he wrote it, 25; the vanity of idols, 25; the superstitions of the Jews, 26; the manifestation of Christ, 27; the state of the world before Christ came, 28; why Christ came so late, 28; the blessings He brings, 29; the importance of divine knowledge, 29.
Dircæ, martyrdom of, 6.
Doctrines, false, 34, 53, 56, 62, 68, 71, 83, 88, 146.
    profound, 68.
Duties, Christian, 9, 20, 54, 62, 81, 95, 148.
    of deacons, etc., 34, 81.
    of presbyters, etc., 34, 90.
    relative, 81, 90.
Duties of husbands and wives, 34, 35, 81, 95.
    of the Christian flock, 35, 95.

Ebionite, 83.
Enoch, 7.
Envy, 67; its effects on Corinthian Church, 6, 17, 18; on the Church in all ages, 6, 17.
Ephesians, Epistle of Ignatius to, 49–58; he commends them, 49, 52; exhorts them to unity, 50; to various duties, 55, 57; warns against false teachers and doctrines, 52; Syriac version of Epistle, 101–102.
Esther, her example, 20.
Eucharist, 16, 17, 55, 76–77, 81, 89, 90.
Evil deeds, 6.
    desires, 35.
    speaking, 17.
Example of Christ, 9, 35, 54.
Examples of love, 19, 20.

Faith, 8, 13, 14, 29, 53, 55, 64, 66, 84, 86, 89.
Falsehood, 56.
Fasting, 34; the acceptable, 138; a type of Christ, 141.
Fathers exhorted, 81.
Fear of God, 54, 69.
Fish, Israel may not eat, spiritual significance of, 143.

581

Goat, the, sent away, 141.
God, His character, 10, 11–12, 13, 16, 80.
 how to draw near and serve Him, 12, 14, 20, 34.
 imitators of, 13; of faith in, 35.
Good deeds, 13, 95.
Gospel superior to law, 63, 146, 147.
Grace, 63, 92.
Graces, Christian, 35, 81.
Grief, 35.

Happiness, 28.
Harmony in the Church, 61; in the universe, 10.
Heretics, views of early, 34, 56, 62, 63, 68, 71, 80, 81, 88, 89, 138, 149.
Hero, deacon of Antioch, Epistle of Ignatius to him, wherein he is exhorted to earnestness and moderation, cautioned against false teachers, instructed as to certain duties, and pointed out as the future bishop of Antioch, 114–115.
Holy Spirit, 5, 17, 43, 52, 53, 56, 57, 83, 85, 92, 101, 140, 146.
Holiness, 13, 42, 43, 53, 67, 108.
Humility enjoined, 9, 11, 15, 53; of Christ, 9; of saints, 9, 10, 20.
Husbands, duty of, 26, 35, 95, 111, 148.
Hyssop, 142.

Idols, vanity of, 25, 56, 129.
Ignatius, mentioned by Polycarp, 35, 36; introductory note to his Epistles, 45, 48.
 Epistle to the Ephesians, 49, 58.
 Epistle to the Magnesians, 59, 65.
 Epistle to the Trallians, 66, 72.
 Epistle to the Romans, 73, 78.
 Epistle to the Philadelphians, 79, 85.
 Epistle to the Smyrnæans, 86, 92.
 Epistle to Polycarp, 93, 96.
 In them he speaks of his bonds, 50, 58, 59, 70, 72, 75, 91; his desire for martyrdom, 49, 74, 75, 76, 96; seeks the prayers of the Churches, 53, 54, 77; speaks of his need of humility, 67; of his knowledge, 64, 68.
 Syriac versions of his Epistles to Polycarp, Ephesians, Romans, 98, 104.
 Account of his martyrdom, 129–131; condemned by Trajan, 48; sails to Smyrna, 130; writes to the Churches, 130; is brought to Rome, 130; is devoured by wild beasts at Rome, 131; appears in a vision after death, 131.
 Spurious Epistles of, 105–126; Introductory note, 105–106; to the Tarsians, 107; to the Antiochians, 110; to Hero, a deacon of Antioch, 114; to the Philippians, 116; from Maria the Proselyte, 120; to Mary at Neapolis, 122; to John the Apostle, 124; a second Epistle to John, 125; to the Virgin Mary, 126.
Imitators of the Creator, 10, 28; of Christ, 50, 69, 76.

Impure thoughts, 111, 149.
Isaac, 13.

Jacob, 12, 13.
James the Just, 69, 155.
Jews not heirs of covenant, 138–139.
 superstitions of, 26.
 observances of, 62, 82.
Jewish sacrifices abolished, 137.
John the Apostle, Epistles of Ignatius to him, 124–125.
Jonah, 7, 70.
Josiah, 60.
Judaizing teachers, 63, 71, 82.
Judas, 40, 117, 153-154.
Judith, 20.
Judged in the flesh, 85, 108.
Justification, 13, 63, 64.

Kingdom of God looked for, 43, 76, 154.
Knowledge, 29, 64, 68, 137.

Law of Christ, 138.
Life, 29, 76, 89.
Light, way of, 148.
Lot, his example, 8.
Lord's day, 63.
Love commended, 19, 55.
 brotherly, 18, 19, 55.
 Moses an example of, 19.
 other examples of, 19.
 to God, 18, 89, 137.
Luxury abjured, 13, 27, 63, 82.

Magnesians, Epistle of Ignatius to, 59–65; wherein he shows the honour and submission due by them to their bishop, 61–64; warns against Judaism, 63, and false doctrine, 62.
Magus, Simon, 72.
Marriage, 26, 81, 95.
Martyrdom of Polycarp, 37, 44.
 of Ignatius, 129, 130.
Martyrs, 6, 39, 74.
Maries, the, in the Gospels, 155.
Mary at Neapolis, spurious Epistle, 122.
Maria the Proselyte, her spurious letter to Ignatius, 120.
Mary, the Virgin, spurious letter of Ignatius, and her reply, 126.
Mathetes, his Epistle to Diognetus, 23, 30.
Matthew's and Mark's Gospels according to Papias, 154–155.
Messengers of Magnesian Church, 59.
 to be sent to Antioch, 96.
Millennium, questionable traditions of, 153.
Ministers, order of, in Church, 16, 17, 50, 61, 64.
Moses, 6, 10, 144–146; quelling strife, 16; his love for Israel, 19.
Mystery of circumcision, 142–143.
Mysteries, three, hid from Satan, 57, 102.

Noah, 7.
Nicolaitans, 71, 83.

Obedience to God, 8, 11, 12, 50, 61.
 to Christ, 15, 51.

Office-bearers of Church at Ephesus, 50; at Magnesia, 59; at Philadelphia, 85.
Onesimus, bishop of Ephesus, 49.
Order in the Church, 16, 17, 90.

Papias, fragments of, 151.
Patience, 35.
Paul and Peter, martyrdom of, 11.
Peace, 10; of universe, 10; of Church, 19.
Philadelphians, Epistle of Ignatius to them, consisting chiefly of exhortations to unity, 79, 85.
Philippians, Epistle of Polycarp to them, consisting of commendations of them, and exhortations to Christian duties, 33–36.
 Spurious Epistle of Ignatius to them, wherein he declares the unity of the Godhead, also facts in the history of Christ; shows the malignity, folly, inconsistency, and ignorance of Satan, and concludes with exhortations, 116–119.
Phœnix, the, 12.
Polybius, bishop of Tralles, 66, 67.
Polycarp. Introductory notice, 31; his Epistle, 33; his humility, 33; his praise of Paul, 35; he is betrayed, 40; he refuses to revile Christ, 41; confesses Christ, 41; his last prayer, 42; in the fire, 42; his body burned, 43.
 mentioned by Ignatius, 58, 92; Epistle of Ignatius to him, consisting of counsels as to his work, 93–96; Syriac version of the same, 99.
Prayer, 34, 53, 82.
Prayers requested, 58, 65, 82.
Presbyters, duties of, 17, 34, 72.
Presbytery, submission to, 50, 51, 67, 89; its function, 69.
Priestly office, contention regarding, 16, 17, 18.
Prophets, the, speak of Christ, 140; to be esteemed, 82.
Purification, 138, 142.
Purity of heart, 12.
 of conduct, 95.

Quintus the apostate, 40.

Rahab, her example, 8.
Red heifer, 142.
Repentance, 7, 53, 147.
Reprobate men, various classes of, 149.
Resurrection, Christ's, 11, 12, 33, 70, 87.
 our, 11, 12, 34.
Revelation, inspiration of the, 155.
Righteous, the, their sufferings, 17, 18; we should cleave to them, 40.
Romans, Epistle of Ignatius to, wherein he expresses his desire for martyrdom, and his reasons for the same, 73, 78.
 Syriac version of the same, 103-104.
Sabbath, the true, 146; how to be kept, 63.
Sacrifices, Jewish, abolished, 137.
Sadness, 20.

THE APOSTOLIC FATHERS: INDEX OF SUBJECTS. 583

Saints, examples of, 7, 9, 10.
  their reward, 8, 14.
Salutations to Churches, etc., 5, 33, 39, 65, 72, 73, 77, 85, 91, 96, 104, 109, 112, 114, 119, 123, 137, 149.
Salvation, 14, 28, 55, 59, 82, 139.
Samuel, 60, 121.
Satan, his malignity, folly, inconsistency, ignorance, 57, 102, 117, 118, 138, 148.
Schismatics, how to be dealt with, 20, 80.
Sedition in Church of Corinth, 8, 20.
  to be avoided, 11.
Self-conceit condemned, 15.
Self-restraint enjoined, 94.
Sheep and shepherd, 6, 80, 84, 110, 120, 140, 147.
Silence (*Sige*), 62.
Sinners, 149.
Sins confessed, 19, 55, 149.
Slaves, duty of, 94, 95, 99, 114.
Smyrnæans, Epistle of Ignatius to, 86–92; wherein he states incidents in the history of Christ, 87; gives views of early heretics, 88, and enjoins submission to their bishop, 89, 90.
Strife, its effects, 5, 6, 17.
Submission to Christ, 90.
  to one another, 15.

of authors of sedition, 11.
Sufferings of Christ, 76. See Christ.
  of men, 6, 39, 129.
Superstitions, of Jews, 26.
Swine not allowed as food to Israel, 143.
Tarsians, spurious Epistle of Ignatius to, wherein he speaks of his sufferings, the true doctrine concerning Christ as against prevailing errors, and exhorts to duties, 108–109.
Teachers, false, 11, 52, 53, 56, 89.
  fate of such, 56.
Temple, Jewish view of, 147.
  the true, 147.
Temptation, 34, 55.
Testament given to Moses and to us, 84, 146.
Thoughts, silent, 55.
Tower, Jewish Church compared to, 147.
Traditions, Jewish, 15.
Trallians, Epistle of Ignatius to, 66–72; wherein he commends them, and exhorts them to be subject to their spiritual rulers, 67; warns them against heretics, 68 –71; shows the reality of the history given us of Christ, 70, 71.

Trees, the similitude of, 30, 144.
Tribulation, patience in, 35.

Unbelievers, 88.
Unity, exhortations to, 50, 51, 57, 62, 64, 72, 80, 81, 90.
Unity of Godhead, 116.

Valens the presbyter, 35.
Vice forsaken and virtue followed, 34, 35, 148.
Vine, 153.
Virgins exhorted, 34, 81, 100.
Virgin Mary, 57, 71; spurious letter of Ignatius to her, and her reply, 126.
Vision seen by Polycarp, 40.

Water of baptism prefigured in Old Testament, 144.
Way, the, of light, 148.
  of darkness, 149.
Widows, 34, 82, 94.
Wives, duties of, 34, 81, 95, 100.
Works, good, 13, 14, 95.
  evil, 149.
World, relations of Christians to, 27.
  its state before Christ's coming, 28.
Worship of God, 55, 62, 81.

Youthful piety, 60.

THE APOSTOLIC FATHERS

INDEX OF TEXTS

	PAGE
Gen. i. 26	14, 140
i. 26, 27	14, 110, 140
i. 28	14, 140, 141
ii. 2	146
ii. 23	6
iii. 19	62
iv. 3–8	6
v. 1	110
v. 24	7
vii.	7
ix. 6	110
xii. 1–3	7
xiii. 14–16	7
xiv. 14	143
xv. 5, 6	7
xv. 6	146
xvii. 5	146
xvii. 26, 27	143
xviii. 27	9, 64
xix. 24	8, 110
xxi. 22	8
xxii. 17	13
xxv. 21, 23	145
xxvii. 41	6
xxviii. 4	13
xxviii. 14	63
xxxvii.	6
xlviii. 11	145
xlviii. 18, 19	145
xlix. 10	85
Ex. ii. 14	6
iii. 11	10
iv. 10	10, 64
xiv.	19
xvi. 8	60
xvii. 14	145
xx. 8	146
xxiv. 18	146
xxxi. 18	139, 146
xxxii. 7, 9	19, 139, 146
xxxii. 7	146
xxxii. 32	19
xxxiii. 1	140
xxxiv. 28	139
Lev. xi.	143
xx. 24	140
Num. xii. 3	54, 64
xii. 7	10
xii. 10	16
xii. 14, 15	6
xvi.	19

	PAGE
Num. xvi. 1, 31	60
xvi. 33	6
xvii.	16
xviii. 27	13
xxi. 6–9	87, 145
Deut. iv. 1	143
v. 12	146
vi. 5	89
ix. 12	19, 139, 146
x. 16	142
xiii. 6, 8	80
xiv.	143
xxvii. 15	145
xxxii. 8, 9	13
xxxii. 15	5, 56
Josh. ii.	8
1 Sam. iii. 1	60
viii. 7	60
xiii. 11	60
xviii. 18	82
2 Sam. vii. 18	82
xviii. 14	60
xx. 22	60
1 Kings iii. 16	60
xviii. 8	6
2 Kings xxii., xxiii.	60
1 Chron. xvii. 16	64
2 Chron. xx. 7	7
xxvi. 20	60
xxxi. 14	13
Esther vii., viii.	20
Job i. 1	9
iv. 16–21	15
v. 1–5	15
v. 17–26	20
xi. 2, 3	13
xiv. 4, 5	10
xv. 15	15
xix. 25, 26	12
xxx. 19	64
xxxi. 13, 15	81
xxxii. 8, 9	60
xxxviii. 11	10
Ps. i. 1	143
i. 3–6	144
ii. 7, 8	15
ii. 11	33
iii. 6	12
iv. 5	35
vi. 5	90
vi. 12	63

	PAGE
Ps. vii. 4	54
xii. 3–5	9, 63
xviii. 25, 26	17
xviii. 44	142
xix. 1–3	12
xxii. 6–8	9
xxii. 17, 19	140
xxii. 21	140
xxii. 23	141
xxiv. 1	19
xxviii. 7	12
xxxi. 18	9
xxxii. 1, 2	19
xxxii. 10	11
xxxiv. 11–13	142
xxxiv. 11–17	11
xxxvii. 35–37	8
xli. 10	71
xlii. 2	141
l. 14, 15	19
l. 16–23	14
li. 1–17	10
li. 12	82
li. 17	19
li. 19	138
lxii. 4	9
lxix. 31, 32	19
lxxviii. 36, 37	9
lxxxii. 8	71
lxxxv. 9	69
lxxxix. 21	10
xc. 4	146
civ. 4	15
cx. 1	15, 145
cxvi. 12	77
cxviii. 12	140
cxviii. 18	20
cxviii. 19, 20	18
cxviii. 22, 24	140
cxix. 1	53
cxix. 21	80
cxix. 83	10
cxix. 120	140
cxxx. 3	63
cxxxi. 2	54
cxxxix. 7–10	12
cxxxix. 15	15
cxli. 5	20
Prov. i. 6	140
i. 17	139
i. 23, 31	20

	PAGE
Prov. ii. 21, 22	8
iii. 12	20
iii. 34	13, 51
vii. 3	5
ix. 1	87
x. 25	52
xi. 3	52
xviii. 9	69
xviii. 17	64
xx. 27	11
xxii. 29	52
xxiii. 24	81
xxiv. 21	90
xxvii. 2	15
Song of Sol. i. 3, 4	56
ii. 15	80
Isa. i. 2, 10	142
i. 6–9	140
i. 11–14	138
i. 13	147
i. 16, 18, 20	7
iii. 9	140
v.	147
v. 21	139
v. 26	86
vi. 3	14
vii. 14	57
viii. 14	140
xvi. 1, 2	144
xxvi. 20	18
xxviii. 16	140
xxix. 13	9
xxxiii. 13	142
xxxiii. 16–18	144
xxxv. 4	62
xl. 10	14
xl. 12	147
xl. 13	140
xli. 8	7, 63
xlii. 6, 7	146
xliii. 26	64
xlv. 1	145
xlv. 2, 3	144
xlix. 6	146
xlix. 17	147
xlix. 22	86
l. 6–9	140
lii. 5	35
liii. 5, 7	139
liii. 8	140
lvi. 10	52

THE APOSTOLIC FATHERS: INDEX OF TEXTS.

	PAGE
Isa. lviii. 4, 5	138
lviii. 6	84
lviii. 6–10	138
lx. 17	16
lxi. 1, 2	146
lxii. 2, 12	63
lxii. 11	14, 90
lxiv. 1	147
lxv. 2	145
lxvi. 1	147
lxvi. 2	8, 69, 148
Jer. i. 7	60
ii. 12, 13	144
iv. 3	142
iv. 4	142
vii. 2	142
vii. 22	138
viii. 4	54
ix. 23, 24	8
ix. 25, 26	142
xv. 19	54
xvii. 24, 25	146
xxiii. 15	80
xxv.	147
Ezek. xi. 19	141
xviii. 23, 32	85
xviii. 30	7
xxxiii. 11	7, 85
xxxvi. 26	141
xlvii. 12	144
Dan. ii. 44	61
iii. 20	17
vi. 16	17
vii. 7, 8	138
vii. 10	14
vii. 14, 27	61
vii. 24	138
ix. 24–27	138, 147
xiii. 52	60
Hos. v. 1	196
Jon. iii.	7
Habak. ii. 3	11
ii. 11	144
Zeph. iii. 19	144
Hag. ii. 10	147
Zech. iii. 1	89
viii. 17	138
xii. 10	70, 87
xiii. 7	140
Mal. iii. 1, 2	11, 27
Matt. i. 23	57
iii. 9	63
iii. 15	86
v. 3, 10	33
v. 4	54
v. 19	55
v. 21	139
v. 42	148
v. 44	36
v. 45, 48	80
vi. 10	40
vi. 12, 14	33, 34
vi. 12–15	8
vi. 13	35
vi. 14	69
vi. 25	28
vii. 1, 2	33
vii. 2	8, 33
vii. 15	51, 80
vii. 25	79
viii. 11	93
ix. 13	139
x. 16	94
x. 23	40
x. 41	90

	PAGE
Matt. xii. 33	55
xii. 40	70
xv. 8	9
xv. 13	71
xvi. 26	76
xviii. 6	18
xviii. 19	51
xix. 12	89
xix. 17	28
xx. 16	139, 140
xx. 22	42
xx. 28	34
xxii. 14	139
xxii. 40	89
xxii. 43–45	145
xxiii. 35	55
xxiv. 25	51
xxiv. 35	12
xxvi. 24	18
xxvi. 39	42
xxvi. 41	35
xxvi. 55	40
xxvii. 52	62, 70
xxviii. 19	85
Mark ii. 17	139
vii. 6	9
ix. 42	18
x. 38	42
xiv. 38	35
Luke i. 6	79
v. 32	139
vi. 20, 36, 37, 38	33
vi. 30	148
vi. 36–38	8, 33
vi. 46	61
viii. 5	12
x. 27	55
xvi. 15	64
xvii. 2	18
xvii. 10	64
xviii. 13	64
xxii. 31	89
xxii. 32	89
xxiii. 34	54
xxiv. 39	87
John i. 14	52, 70, 87
i. 18	82
ii. 19	87
iii. 8	83
iii. 14	87
iii. 14–18	145
iii. 36	51
iv. 14	76
v. 30	62
v. 46	62
vii. 38	77
viii. 29	50
viii. 44	82
viii. 46	70
viii. 56, 58	62
x. 9, 11	84
xi. 25, 26, 42	71
xii. 7	56
xii. 32	53, 87
xiii. 34	89
xiv. 6	53, 84
xiv. 24	53
xv. 19	74
xvi. 13, 14	53
xvii. 4, 6	53
xvii. 11, 12	51
xvii. 11, 14, 16	27
xvii. 31	89
xx. 27, 28	87
i. 11	87

	PAGE
Acts ii. 24	33
v. 41	35
ix. 15	55
xi. 26	63
xiii. 48	63
xiv. 22	142
xvii. 30	28
xvii. 31	33
xx. 35	5
xxi. 14	40
xxvi. 14	84
Rom. i. 3	86
i. 32	14
ii. 4	54
ii. 6	64
iii. 21–26	28
iv. 3	7, 146
v. 18	137
v. 20	28
viii. 11	33
viii. 17	88
viii. 29, 30	148
viii. 32	69
ix. 5	13
x. 10	55
xii. 5	17
xii. 17	34
xiii. 1–7	41
xiv. 10–12	34
xv. 15, 16	16
xvi. 3, 4	20
1 Cor. i. 10	50, 68
i. 18, 20, 25	56
i. 31	8, 67
ii. 8	71
ii. 9	14, 39
iii. 13	18
iii. 16	84
iv. 4	75
iv. 13	52, 56
iv. 18	56
iv. 20	55
v. 7	63
vi. 2	35
vi. 9, 10	34, 56
vi. 14	33
vi. 19	56, 84
vii. 22	81
viii. 1	30
x. 4	84
x. 13	59
x. 26, 28	19
x. 31	95
xi. 1	50
xii. 12	15
xii. 26	35
xiii. 4	18
xv. 8, 9	77
xv. 20	11
xv. 32	75
xvi. 1, 2	16
xvi. 18	50
2 Cor. i. 21	6
ii. 17	68
iv. 12	27
iv. 14	33
iv. 18	74
v. 10	34
v. 17	62, 140
vi. 9, 10	27
vi. 14, 16	56
viii. 18	56
viii. 31	34
x. 3	27

	PAGE
2 Cor. x. 17	8
xii. 7	148
Gal. i. 1	36, 80
ii. 2	35
ii. 20	77
iii. 28	81
iv. 4	28
iv. 9	59
iv. 10	26
iv. 26	33
vi. 7	34
Eph. i. 1	53
ii. 2	83, 89
ii. 4	69
ii. 8, 9	33
ii. 21	141
iv. 4	52
iv. 4–6	17, 52
iv. 5	81
iv. 20	6
iv. 26	35
v. 1, 2	49
v. 21	5
v. 22	81
v. 25	95
vi. 4	81
vi. 9	148
vi. 11	34
vi. 12	55
vi. 14	33
vi. 16	55
Phil. i. 4	101
i. 5	33, 35
i. 27	34
ii. 2	83
ii. 3	84
ii. 10	33
ii. 16	35
ii. 25	82
ii. 30	20
iii. 10	54
iii. 18	71
iii. 18, 19	63
iii. 20	27
iv. 13	88
iv. 15	18
Col. i. 15	57, 87
i. 16	145
i. 18	11
i. 23	54
i. 25	57
1 Thess. iv. 5	80
v. 12, 13	11
v. 17	34, 93
v. 22	35
2 Thess. iii. 10	62
iii. 15	35
1 Tim. i. 1	64
i. 3	94
i. 4	57, 62
i. 5	55
i. 14	55
ii. 2	36
ii. 4	80
ii. 6	69
iii. 8	34
iii. 16	29
iv. 10	52, 59
iv. 12	60
v. 21	11
vi. 1	69
vi. 3	94
vi. 7, 10	34
2 Tim. i. 6	49
i. 10	84

	PAGE		PAGE		PAGE		PAGE
2 Tim. i. 16	50	Heb. iii. 2	10	Jas. iv. 6	13, 51	2 Pet. ii. 6–9	8
i. 18	91	iii. 5	16, 146	v. 20	18	iii. 3, 4	11
ii. 12	34	vi. 18	12	1 Pet. i. 8	33	iii. 8	146
ii. 24, 25	54	x. 12, 13	70	i. 13, 21	33	iii. 9	85
ii. 26	80	x. 29	90	ii. 5	53	iii. 15	33
iii. 4	63	x. 37	11	ii. 9	53, 81	1 John iii. 7	55
iii. 6	80	xi. 5	7	ii. 11	34, 27	iv. 3	34
iv. 1	64	xi. 17	8	ii. 12	35	iv. 9	35
iv. 21	21	xi. 31	8	ii. 17, 21, 24	5, 35	Jude 3	34
Tit. i. 2	12	xi. 37	9	ii. 23	54	Rev. i. 7	87
i. 10	68	xii. 1	10	iii. 9, 22	33	v. 9	30
ii. 5	69	xii. 6	20	iii. 18	43	xix. 7	30
ii. 14	20, 81	xiii. 17	11, 66	iii. 20	7	xx. 5	30
iii. 1	5, 41	Jas. i. 8	11, 148	iv. 7	34, 54	xxii. 12	14
iii. 13	77	i. 16	56	iv. 8	18		
Philem. 8, 9	50	ii. 21	13	iv. 16	35		
Heb. i. 3, 4, 5, 7, 13	15	ii. 23	7, 63	v. 5	5, 13, 35, 51		
ii. 12	141	iv. 1	17	ii. 5	7		

JUSTIN MARTYR.

INDEX OF SUBJECTS.

Adrian, Emperor, his Epistle in behalf of the Christians, 186.
Advents of Christ, 210, 221, 253–254.
Æschylus on the unity of God, 290.
Amen, 186.
Analogies, heathen, to Christ's doctrine, 169.
   to Christ's history, 170.
   to the Sonship of Christ, 170.
Anaximander and Anaximenes, 274.
Angels, how they transgressed, 190, 238; their freedom, 250, 269, 301; who taught them, 164.
Antoninus, Emperor, Epistle in behalf of the Christians, 186.
Apostles, 175, 179.
Archelaus, the Athenian, 274.
Argument, the, of Justin's Apology stated, 170.
Aristotle, opinions of, 275.
Atheism, 164.
Aurelius, 187.

Baptism, Christian, 183, 201, 216.
   its imitation by demons, 183.
Birds, the two, in Lev. xiv., 301.

Chariton, examination of, by the Prefect Rusticus, 305.
Chastity, 167.
Children, exposed, 172.
Christ Jesus, 170, 177, 190, 219, 236–238, 253, 265, 301.
   shown to be God, from His appearances to Abraham, 222–225; objection met, that He ate, 225; from visions to Jacob, 225; from His interviews with Moses, 226; from the testimony of Proverbs, 228.
   called the Lord of Hosts, 212, 241, 301.
   distinguished from the Father, 264.
   called the Word, 164, 166, 170, 174, 192, 263–264.
   the Son of God, 164, 166, 170, 178, 182, 190, 216, 219, 250, 257, 258, 263.
   His humanity, 170, 174, 179, 193, 216, 219, 228, 231, 241, 301.
   His early history, 237–238, 250.

Christ Jesus, crucified, 166, 173, 174, 179, 222, 247–251.
   His work, 179.
   blood of, 173, 200, 222, 228.
   His cross, symbols of, 181, 242–244, 247.
   the curse He endured, 246–248.
   His advent foretold, 173, 175, 260.
   His appearances before His coming in the flesh, 262–263.
   His titles in Scripture, 190, 262.
   His first and second coming, 209, 210, 221, 253–254.
   testimony of Scripture regarding Him: of Moses, 173, 221, 223, 236; of David, 175, 176, 211, 212, 213, 229, 235, 240, 241, 248, 252; of Isaiah, 174, 179, 200, 236–237, 241; of Micah, 174; of Zephaniah, 175; of Zechariah, 221.
   His teaching, 167, 168, 246.
   the Holy Spirit received by Him, 243.
   figures of: Joshua, 255–258, 265; Noah, 268–269; Mosaic laws, 214–216.
   called Jacob, Israel, and Son of man, 248, 262.
   His reign and majesty, 176, 178, 179, 209, 236, 267.
   not a magician, 172.
   compared to Socrates, 191.
   His resurrection 252–253, 298.
   His rejection by the Jews, 175, 179, 253, 267.
   of faith in, 191, 199, 257, 260.
   salvation alone in, 207, 216–217.
Christians, Apologies for, by Justin Martyr, 164–193.
   their treatment at the hands of the heathen world, 170, 182, 188, 191, 253–254.
   testimonies of Roman emperors as to, 186–187.
   accused of atheism, 164.
   inquiry into charges against them demanded, 163–165.
   charges refuted; shown they do not worship idols, 169, 171.
   worship God, 164, 165.

Christians, their moral life, 165–166, 172, 189, 192.
   their worship, 185.
   their treatment at the hands of the Jews, 203, 214, 246–247, 256.
   blamed for not observing the law, 199, 203; for not submitting to be circumcised, 206, 208, 256.
   have the true righteousness, 209.
   shown to be called like Abraham, 258; promised as seed to the patriarchs, 259; are the true Israel 261, 267; are the sons of God, 261
Church, Jacob's marriage a figure of, 266–267.
Circumcision, 202, 203, 206, 208, 245, 256.
Continence of Christians, 172.
Corruption, 301.
Crescens, his prejudices, 189.
Cross, symbols of the, 181, 242, 244, 247.
Curse, the, 246–248.

Death, 165, 192.
Deeds, evil, their punishment, 165; their detection, 166.
Demons, 167, 190, 192; their imitation of divine things, 181, 182, 183–184; cause persecution, 182.
Devil as a roaring lion against Christ, 251.
   why plots against us, 300.
Devils, 181, 182, 184, 185, 238.
   distort the truth, 233, 234.
Dialogue of Justyn Martyr with Trypho the Jew, 194–270.
Divinations, 168–169.
Dream-senders, 168–169.

Elijah, 219.
Emperors, Roman, testimony to Christians, 186–187.
Epicurus, opinions of, 192–193, 274–275.
Eucharist, 185.
Euripides, on future judgment, 291; on false gods, 292, 293.

Fables, heathen, 233.

587

JUSTIN MARTYR: INDEX OF SUBJECTS.

Faith in Christ, 191, 199, 257, 260.
Fasting, 202.
Fate, 177–178.
Forgiveness of sin, 200, 217.
Foreknowledge of God, 178.
Forerunner of Christ, 220–221.
Free-will in man and angels, 249–250, 270, 301.

Gentiles, 180; conversion of, 253, 260, 264, 265.
Goats, 301.
God, 164–166, 172, 177–178, 190, 197, 198, 199, 200, 300.
His care for men, 172.
how He appeared to Moses, 184.
how known, 246–247.
not give His glory to another, 230.
His righteousness, 245–246.
what He decreed concerning Christ, 250.
His namelessness, 281.
rejected by the Jews, 262–263.
His unity and sole government, treatise by Justin Martyr on, 290–293.
testimonies to unity from Greek poets: Æschylus, 290; Sophocles, 290; Philemon and Orpheus, 290.
opinions of Greek philosophers as to, 274–275.
Gods, false, 171, 181, 283.
Greeks, Justin's Discourse to, 271–274; wherein he justifies his departure from Greek customs, 271–272; exposes the Greek theogony, 271; follies of Greek mythology, 272; the shameless practices of the Greeks, 274; calls upon them to study the divine word, 272.
Justin's Hortatory Address to, 273–289; wherein he shows that their poets are unfit to be religious teachers, 273–274.
opinions of their philosophers, as Thales, 274; of Pythagoras and Epicurus, 274–275; of Plato and Aristotle, 275–276.
what their philosophers and poets learned from Moses' writings, 276, 277, 278.

Happiness, 196.
Hell, 170.
Heraclitus and Hippasus, 274.
Hercules, 192.
Human doctrine, 182, 219.
Homer, passages from, showing his views as to his gods, 273–274; his testimony to monotheism, 280; his obligations to the sacred writer, 282–283; his knowledge of man's origin, 286.
Hystaspes, 169.

Idols, 165, 171.
Images, 287.
Immorality of the heathen, 171, 272.
Israel applied to Christ, 264; He is King of, 267.

Jacob, Leah and Rachel figures of the Church, 266.

Jews, their treatment of Christ, 175–179, 253.
treatment of Christians, 175, 203, 214, 247.
blame the Christians for not observing the law, 199.
they violate the eternal, and interpret that of Moses, 200.
why circumcision was given, 202.
why the law was given them, 203.
why the choice of meats, 204.
the Sabbaths instituted, and sacrifices and oblations, 205.
the injury to God from their opinion of the law, 206.
they boast in vain that they are the sons of Abraham, 206, 269.
in disputations, 256.
how they treat Scriptures, 176, 232.
their interpretations, 261.
their circumcision differs from the Christian, 256.
their hardheartedness, 266.
salvation for them only in Christ, 207, 216–217.
rejecting Christ, they reject God, 267–268.
exhorted to repent and be converted, 258, 268.
John the Baptist, 220–221.
Jonah, the sign of, 252.
Joshua, a figure of Christ, 255, 265–266.
Judea, its desolations foretold, 178.
Judge, the, 180.
Judgment, future, testimonies of Greek writers to, 291.
Jupiter, 164, 170, 192.
Justice demanded for Christians, 163–164.
Justin Martyr, introductory notice of, 159–161.
his First Apology for Christians, 163–187.
his Second Apology, 188-193.
his Dialogue with Trypho a Jew, 194–270; he studies philosophy, 195; his conversion, 195; his arguments in favor of Christianity as against Judaism, 194–270.
his Discourse to the Greeks, 271–272.
his Hortatory Address to the Greeks, 273–289; spurious, 289.
on the Sole Government of God, 290–293.
on the Resurrection, 294–299.
fragments from his lost writings, 301–302.
he is examined and condemned by the Prefect Rusticus, 305.

Kingdom, Christians look for, 166.
Knowledge, 196.

Lamb, a type of Christ, 214.
Law, the, 199, 200, 203, 214–216.
Life, 198.
Lord's Day, 186.
Lucius, the philosopher, 163.

Magi, 237–238.
Man, his creation, 165, 228, 250; corruption of, 301.
origin of Homer's opinion of, 286.

Marcion, 171, 182.
Marcus Aurelius, the emperor, his testimony of the Christians, 187.
Marriages, impure, 167.
Martyrdom of holy martyrs at Rome, 305–306.
Meats, choice of, why prescribed to Israel, 204.
Menander, 171; his views of God, 292.
Millennium, 236–240.
Mithras, mysteries of, 234.
Monotheism, testimonies to: of Orpheus, 279; of the Sibyl, 280; of Homer, 280, 282; of Pythagoras, 280; of Plato, 281, 282, 283.
Moses predicts Christ's coming, 173.
God appears to, 184–185, 223–226.
foretells Christ's cross, 224.
his antiquity proved by Greek writers, 277–278.
heathen oracles testify of, 278.
training and inspiration of, 278.
Plato indebted to, 182, 283, 284, 286.
Homer indebted to, 284.
Mosaic laws, figures of things which pertain to Christ, 214–215, 216.
Mythology, heathen, its origin, 181.
Greek, the follies of, 272.

Names of God and Christ, 190, 262.
Necromancy, 168–169.
Noah, a figure of Christ, 268, 269.

Obedience, civil, 168.
Oracles, heathen, 169; testify of Moses, 278.
Orpheus, his testimony to Monotheism, 279, 290.

Patience, 168.
Peripatetics, 195.
Philemon, testifies to a future judgment, 291; shows how God is appeased, 291.
Philosophers, 164–165, 177.
have not true knowledge, 288.
Greek, their opinions of God, 274, 275.
opinions as to resurrection, 296.
their indebtedness to Moses, 182, 278–280, 288–289.
Philosophy, 195.
Phylactery, 218.
Plato, 165, 169, 177, 183, 275, 276, 281; ambiguity of, 282; self-contradictory, 282; his agreement with Homer, 282–283; his knowledge of God's eternity, 283; indebted to Moses, 182, 183, 284, 285, 286; to the prophets, 283–284; his knowledge of judgment, 284; his doctrine of form, 285–286; of the heavenly gift, 286–287; of the beginning of time, 287; of the universe, 296.
Platonists, 195.
Polytheism, 181, 190, 192.
Prayers, 186, 257.
Prophecy, different modes of, 175.
certainly fulfilled, 180.
concerning Christ, 173–175, 210–216, 220, 221–225, 235–238, 240–242.

Prophets, Hebrew, 173; use the past tense, 176–177; truth learned from them, 198.
Psalms that speak of Christ, 176, 211, 212–213, 228, 235, 240, 241, 248–252.
Punishment, everlasting, 165, 166, 169, 172, 191, 300.
Pythagoras, opinions of, 274–275, 280–281.
Pythagorean, 195.

Repentance, 167, 258.
Responsibility, human, 177, 190.
Resurrection, treatise of Justin on, 294–299.
   objections to, 294, 295; not impossible, 295.
   arguments for; Christ has risen, 298.
   Christ's, 178, 298.
Righteousness, 201, 208, 209, 217, 245–246.
Rusticus, the prefect, examines Christians, 305–306.

Sabbath, why instituted, 204, 207, 301–302.
Sacraments, the, 185.
Sacrifices, why instituted, 205.

Salvation, 207, 216–217.
Satan, 172; blasphemes, 300.
Saturn, 192.
Scriptures, 198, 199, 232, 234–235, 245; searched, 232.
Semo, the inscription, 171, 187.
Septuagint, history of, 278–279.
   treatment of, by Jews, 234.
Sibyl, the, 169, 280, 288–289.
Simon, the Samaritan, 171–172, 182, 193.
Sins, forgiven, 200.
Six, the number, 301–302.
Socrates, 191.
Sophocles, on unity of God, 290; on future judgment, 291.
Souls, 196–197.
Spirit, Holy, 164, 167, 177, 243.
Stoics, the, 169, 190, 191, 192.
Sunday, 185–186.
Swearing, 168.

Teachers, Christian, their antiquity, inspiration, and harmony, 268–269.
Teaching of Christ, 164, 167, 168.
Thales, his views as to God, 274.
Theogony, Greek, exposed, 271.
Titus, the emperor, 163.
Traditional opinions, 163.

Trinity, the, 164, 185.
Truth, the, 166; known from the prophets, 198, 289.
   misrepresented, 183, 184–185.
   its power, 272, 294.
Types of Christ, 214–216, 255, 265–266, 268.

Unity of God, 290–293.
Urbicus condemns the Christians to death, 188.

Verissimus the philosopher, 163.
Vice and virtue, 192.

Wicked, their punishment, 164–165, 166, 168.
Wine, in the Eucharist, unchanged but not common, 185.
Wisdom, Christ the, 227–228.
Word, the, is Christ, 164, 166, 170, 178, 190, 191, 192–193, 263, 272.
World preserved for sake of Christians, 190.
Worship, weekly, of Christians, 185–186.
   who is worthy, 232.
   heathen, 171.

Xenophon, 192.

JUSTIN MARTYR

INDEX OF TEXTS

	PAGE		PAGE		PAGE		PAGE
Gen. i. 1	285	Ex. xxv. 9	285, 286	Ps. xix. 4	215	Isa. iii. 9–15	266
i. 26	297	xxv. 40	286	xix. 5	181, 233	iii. 16	208
i. 26, 28	228	xxviii. 33	215	xxii.	248–252	v. 18, 20	203
ii. 3	204	xxxii. 6	204	xxii. 7, 18	175	v. 18–25	266
ii. 7	286, 297	Lev. xiv. 49–53	301	xxii. 16	174	v. 20	179
iii. 15	250	xxvi. 40, 41	202	xxii. 16–18	247	v. 21	214
iii. 19	286	Num. xi. 17	220	xxiv.	213	vi. 8	236
iii. 22	228, 264	xi. 23	263	xxiv. 7	180, 241, 263	vi. 10	200
vii. 16	263	xiii. 16	236	xxxii. 2	270	vii. 10–17	216, 231
viii. 10, 12	204	xv. 38	218	xlv.	213	vii. 14	174
ix. 24–27	269	xxi. 8	183	xlv. 6, 7	224	viii. 4	216, 231
xi. 5	263	xxiv. 17	252	xlv. 6–11	229	ix. 6	174, 236
xi. 6	250	xxvii. 18	220	xlv. 7	242	xi. 1 ff.	174, 243
xv. 6	245	Deut. iv. 19	222, 260	xlvii. 5–9	213	xiv. 1	260, 261
xviii. 1, 2	223	vi. 6	218	l.	206	xviii. 6	175
xviii. 2	263	x. 16 f.	202	lxviii. 18	243	xix. 24 f.	261
xviii. 10	223	xxi. 23	247	lxviii. 19	214	xxvi. 2, 3	206
xviii. 13 f.	263	xxvii. 26	247	lxxii.	211	xxvii. 1	255
xviii. 13, 14	224	xxx. 15, 19	177	lxxii. 1, etc.	230	xxix. 13	219, 269
xviii. 16, 17	224, 263	xxxi. 2 f.	263	lxxii. 17	260	xxix. 13, 14	238
xviii. 20–23, 33	224	xxxi. 16–18	236	lxxxii.	262	xxix. 14	210, 261
xviii. 22	263	xxxii. 6, 20	204	xc. 4	240	xxx. 1–5	238
xix. 1, 10	224	xxxii. 7 ff.	265	xcvi. 1, etc.	176, 235	xxxiii. 13–19	234
xix. 16–25	225	xxxii. 15	204	xcvi. 5	222, 238, 296	xxxv. 1–7	233
xix. 23	224	xxxii. 16–23	258	xcviii.	213	xxxv. 5	295
xix. 24	263	xxxii. 20	261	xcix.	213	xxxv. 6	179
xix. 27, 28	223	xxxii. 22	182, 183	xcix. 1–7	229	xxxix. 8	220
xxi. 9–12	223	xxxii. 43	264	cx.	210, 240	xl. 1–17	220
xxii.	226	xxxiii. 13–17	245	cx. 1	178, 224, 263	xlii. 1–4	261, 267
xxvi. 4	259	xxxiv. 9	220	cx. 3	237	xlii. 5–13	231
xxviii. 10–19	226	Josh. i. 13–15	227	cx. 3, 4	229	xlii. 6, 16	260
xxviii. 14	259	v. 2	206	cx. 4	258	xlii. 6, 7	207
xxxi. 10–13	226	v. 13, *ad fin.*	228	cxv. 5	296	xlii. 8	230
xxxii. 22–30	226	vi. 1, 2	228	cxv. 16	286	xlii. 19 f.	261
xxxii. 24, 30	263	1 Sam. v.	266	cxviii. 24	249	xliii. 10	260
xxxv. 6–10	226	vi. 14	266	cxxviii. 3	254	xliii. 15	267
xxxv. 7	227	xxviii. 12, 13	252	cxlviii. 1, 2	242	xliv.	183
xlix. 5, 8, 9, 10, 11, 18, 24	221	2 Sam. vii. 14 f.	258	Prov. viii. 21 ff.	228	xliv. 6	281
xlix. 8–12	221	1 Kings xix. 11, 12	286	viii. 22 ff.	264	xliv. 9–20	165
xlix. 10	173, 181, 259	xix. 14, 18	214	viii. 27	237	xlv. 24	180
xlix. 24	242	Job i. 6	238	Isa. i. 3	184	xlix. 6, 8	260
Ex. ii. 23	226	Ps. i. 2	176	i. 3, 14	175	l. 4	250
iii. 2–4	227	i. 3	242	i. 7	178	l. 6	175
iii. 6	184	ii. 7	244, 251, 261 f.	i. 9	181, 269	li. 4, 5	200
iii. 16	226	iii. 4, 5	247	i. 16, etc.	177	lii. 5	203
vi. 2 ff.	263	iii. 5	175	i. 16–20	183	lii. 10 ff.	201
vi. 29	263	viii. 3	256	i. 23	240	lii. 13–15	179
xii. 19	260	xviii. 43	208	i. 27	244	lii. 15	258
xv. 27	242	xix.	209	ii. 3	175	liii. 1–8	179
xxiii. 20, 21	236	xix. 1–6	230	ii. 5 f.	267	liii. 1, 2	215, 256, 258
		xix. 2, etc.	176	iii. 9 ff.	203, 268	liii. 7	254, 256

JUSTIN MARTYR: INDEX OF TEXTS.

	PAGE		PAGE		PAGE		PAGE
Isa. liii. 8	216, 229, 258	Jer. xxxi. 27	261	Matt. iv 9, 10	251, 262	Mark xii. 30	168
liii. 8–12	180	xxxi. 31, 32	200	v. 20	252	Luke i. 32	174
liii. 9	247	Lam. iv. 20	181	v. 28, 29 32	167	i. 35, 38	249
liv. 1	180	Ezek. iii. 17–19	240	v. 34, 37	168	i. 78	249
liv. 9	268	xi. 22	286	v. 44, 45, 46	167, 168	vi. 28, 30, 34	167
lv. 3 ff.	200, 202	xiv. 18, 20	269	vi. 1	168	vi. 29, 36	168
lvii. 1	179, 254	xiv. 20	217	vi. 16, 22, 41	168	vi. 35	247
lvii. 1–4	203	xvi. 3	237	vi. 19, 20	167	ix. 22	237
lviii. 1–12	202	xviii. 20	269	vi. 21, 25, 26, 33,	168	x. 16	184
lviii. 2	174	xx. 12	204	vii. 15	212	x. 19	236
lviii. 13, 14	207	xx. 19–26	205	vii. 15, 16, 19	168	xi.	203
lxii. 10, to end	207	xxxiii. 11–20	219	vii. 21	168	xii. 48	168
lxii. 12	259	xxxvi. 12	261	vii. 22	236	xiii. 26	168
lxiii. 1–6	207	xxxvii. 7, 8	180	viii. 11	236, 259, 269	xviii. 18 f.	249
lxiii. 15, to end	207	xliv. 3	258	ix. 13	167	xx. 34, 35	295
lxiii. 17	180	Dan. vii. 9–28	210	x. 28	169	xx. 35 f.	240
lxiv.	207	vii. 13	180	xi. 12–15	221	xxii. 19	185
lxiv. 10–12	178	Hos. i., ii.	204	xi. 27	184, 249	xxii. 42, 44	251
lxiv. 11	180	x. 6	251	xii. 38 f.	252	xxiii. 46	252
lxv. 1	259	Joel ii. 28 f.	243	xiii. 3	262	xxiv. 32	298
lxv. 1–3	179, 206	Amos v. 18, to end	205	xiii. 42	168	John iii. 5	183
lxv. 2	174, 175, 247, 256	vi. 1–7	205	xv. 22–28	269	iii. 14	245
lxv. 8 f. 9–12	267	Jon. iv. 10 f.	253	xvi. 21	249	x. 33–35	222
lxv. 17, to end	239	Mic. iv. 1 ff.	253	xvi. 26	167	xii. 40	200
lxvi. 1	175, 206	v. 2	174, 237	xvii. 12	220	xii. 47, 48	219
lxvi. 5–11	242	Zech. ii. 8	268	xix. 6, 17	168	Acts i. 9	298
lxvi. 21	257	ii. 10–13	256	xix. 12	167	xvii. 11	224
lxvi. 24	180, 217, 264, 269	ii. 11	258	xix. 26	169	Rom. i. 28	260
		iii. 1	238	xix. 28	255	iii. 10 ff.	208
Jer. ii. 13	256, 269	iii. 1, 2	256	xxi. 13	203	x. 21	247
ii. 19	301	iii. 8	249	xxii. 17, 19–21	168	xv. 15, 16, 17	257
iv. 3	208	vi. 12	252, 260	xxii. 37	246	1 Cor. x. 4	200
vii. 21 f.	205	ix. 9	175, 222	xxiii.	203	x. 20	164
vii. 24, 26	200	xii. 3–14	180	xxiii. 15	260	xi. 19	212
ix. 25 f.	208	xii. 12	260	xxiii. 23, 24, 27	255	Gal. iii. 13	247
ix. 26	181	xiii. 7	222	xxiv. 11	212	iv. 12	272
x. 3	165	Mal. i. 10, etc.	208	xxv. 41	236	2 Thess. ii. 3	253
xi. 8	200	i. 10–12	215, 257	xxvi. 27	185	ii. 6, 7	178
xi. 19	234	iv. 5	219	xxvi. 39	248	Heb. iv.	8
xvii. 23	200	Matt. i. 21	174	xxvii. 39	175	1 Pet. ii. 9	257
xxxi. 15	238	iii. 11, 12	219	Mark ii. 17	297	2 Pet. iii. 8	240
		iii. 17	251	xii. 25	294	Rev. xx. 4, 5	240

IRENÆUS

INDEX OF SUBJECTS

Aaron and Miriam, their sin against Moses, and its punishment, 573.
Abel and Cain, the offerings of, 485.
Abominations, the, practised by the Valentinians, 324, etc.
Abraham, saw the day of Christ, 467, 469, etc.; vain attempt of Marcion to exclude him from Christ's salvation, 470, etc.; had faith identical with ours, 492; both covenants prefigured in, 495, 496; waited for the promises of God, 561.
Abraxas, Basilides' doctrine of, 350.
Acceptable year of the Lord, the, 390.
Achamoth, an account of, 320; origin of the visible world from, 321, etc.; shall at last enter the Pleroma, 325; asserted to be referred to in Scripture, 326-328.
Adam and Eve, the story of, according to the Ophites, 356.
Adam, the first, made a partaker of salvation, 455; his repentance signified by the girdle which he made, 457; why driven out of Paradise, 457; in Paradise, 531; sinned on the sixth day of creation, 551; death of, 552.
— analogy between the first and the second, 454.
Æon, the twelfth, the sufferings of, not to be deduced from Scripture, 387; nor typified by the woman with the issue of blood, 392.
Æons, the thirty, of Valentinus, 316, etc.; English equivalents of the Greek names of, 316, note; how the thirty are said to be indicated in Scripture, 319; the production of, 373, 8, etc., 379, etc.; further inquiry into and refutation of the speculations respecting, 380, 381; the theory of, further exposed, 382, 383, etc.; the twelve apostles not types of the twelve, 389; the thirty, not typified by the baptism of Jesus in His thirtieth year, 390.
Agape, 396.
Αἰών, meaning of the term, 316.

Aletheia, the Æon so called, 317; how her passion is said to be indicated in Scripture, 319; of Ptolemy, 333; revealed by Tetrad, 337, etc.
— the numerical value of, does not square with Valentinianism, 396.
Anaxagoras, 376.
Anaximander, 376.
Angels, the world not made by, 361; could not be ignorant of the Supreme God, 365.
— of the devil, 524, etc.
Animal men, the, of the Valentinians, 323, 327.
Animals, clean and unclean, 534.
Anthropos and Ecclesia, the Æons so named, 317, 333, 355.
Antichrist, the fraud, pride, and tyranny of the kingdom of, 553, 554; concentrates in himself the apostasy, 557; the number of the name of, 558.
Antiphanes, the theogony of, 376.
Apator, 322.
Apocryphal Scriptures, the, of the Marcosians, 394, 395.
Apostles, the twelve, not types of the twelve Æons, 389.
— the, did not begin to preach till endued with the Holy Spirit, 414; preached one God, 414; the doctrine of, 429-436; the labours of, lessened by their predecessors, 494, 495.
Aquila and Theodotion, their interpretation of Isa. vii. 14 referred to, 451.
Ark of the covenant, 394, 570.
Autogenes, 353.
Axe, the, made to float by means of wood, 572.
— the, laid at the root, 573.

Balaam, 571; forbidden to curse Israel, 572; his ass a type, 572; slain, 572.
Baptism of Jesus in His thirtieth year not a type of the thirty Æons, 390.
Barbeliotes or Borborians, the, 353.
Basilides, the doctrines of, 348, etc.;

absurd notion of, as to the death of Jesus, 349; this notion of, refuted, 412.
Beast, the, 557, 558, etc.
Bel and the dragon, 467.
Bishops, a succession of, in various churches, 415, etc.; first, of Rome, 416.
Blandina, the martyr, 570.
Blood, the, of Christ, redeems, 527, 528.
— the Christians accused of eating, how the calumny originated, 570.
Bodies, the, of men, temples of the Holy Ghost, 532; from the earth, 544.
Body and soul, the views of heretics respecting the future destiny of, refuted, 402.
Bread and wine in the Eucharist, 528.
Breath of life, the, 537.
Bythus, 316, 333; absurdity of, 362, 363.

Cain, 456; and Abel, the respective offerings of, 485.
Cainites, the doctrines of the, 358.
Carnal and spiritual, 536, 537.
Carpocrates, the doctrines of, 350; the followers of, practised magic and incantations, 350; immorality of the system of, 350, 351; his views of the devil, 351; his followers branded with external marks, and have images of Jesus, etc., 351.
Centurion, the, of the Gospels, asserted by the Valentinians to be the Demiurge, 326.
Cerdo, the doctrines of, 352.
Cerinthus, the doctrines of, 351, 352.
Christ, Valentinus's views of, 319, 323, 325, 332, 334; the origin of, according to the Ophites, 354; the descent of, upon Jesus, according to the Ophites, 357; the apostles of, their preaching, 417; and Jesus, the same, the only-begotten Son of God, 440-444; not, but the Holy Spirit, descended upon Jesus, 444; and Jesus of Nazareth proved from

593

the writings of Paul to be one and the same, 445, etc.; did not flee away from Jesus at the cross, 446; did not suffer in appearance merely, 446; assumed actual flesh, conceived and born of the Virgin, 454, etc.; the advent of, foretold, 473; the advent of, foreknown and desired by righteous men, 474; did not abolish the law, 475; is the end of the law, 476; did not abrogate the natural precepts of the law, but removed the bondage, 477; came for the sake of men of all ages, 485, etc.; is the treasure hid in the field, 496; descended into regions beneath the earth, 499; foreseen and foretold by the prophets, 509; the prophets referred all their predictions to, 511, etc.; alone able to redeem us, 526, etc.; took flesh, not seemingly, but really, 527; conferred on our flesh the capacity of salvation, 527, 528; his resurrection a proof of ours, 532, etc.; the dead raised by, a proof of the resurrection, 539; fitting that He should take human nature, and be tempted by the devil, 548, etc.; His victory over Satan, 549; temptation of, 549, etc.; His kingdom eternal, 554, 555; the resurrection of, 560; how prefigured, 571; testimony of the sacred books to, 576, 577.

Christians, calumnies against the, 570.

Church, the, her gifts, 409; performs nothing by incantations or curious arts, 409; of Rome, founded by Peter and Paul, 415; the catholic, the depository of truth, 416, etc.

Clean and unclean, 534.

Colorbasus, the doctrines of, 333.

Commandment, the first and greatest, 476.

Communion with God, 556.

Cosmocrator, the, 323.

Covenant, the new, 512.

Covenants, one author and one end to both, 472, etc.; the oneness of both proved by Jesus' reproof of customs repugnant to the former, 475.

Created things, made after the image of invisible things, according to the Marcosians, 342, etc.
not images of Æons within the Pleroma, 366–368; not a shadow of the Pleroma, 368, 369.

Creation, the, of all things out of nothing by God, 369, 370.

Creator, but one, of the world, 369.
the, made all things, spiritual and material, 405, 406; is the Word of God, 546.
the, could not be ignorant of the Supreme God, 365.

Day, the, does not square with the theory of Valentinus, 395.

Day of retribution, the, 390.

Dead, the, raised by Christ, a proof of the resurrection, 539.

Death, the, and life, 537.

Decalogue, the, at first inscribed on the hearts of men, 479; not cancelled by Christ, 481, 482.

Demiurge, the, the formation of, according to Valentinus, 322; the creator of all things outside the Pleroma, 322; ignorant of what he created, 322; ignorant of the offspring of his mother Achamoth, 323; passes into the intermediate habitation, 325; instructed by the Saviour, 326; is the centurion of the Gospels, 326; views of the heretics respecting, exposed and confuted, 385, etc.; declared by the heretics to be animal, 403; if animal, how could he make things spiritual? 405, 406.

Devil, views of the Carpocratians respecting, 350.
practised in falsehoods, he tempted man, 551; his lie in regard to the government of the world, 552, 553.
the sons of the, 525.

Deuteronomy, 571.

Diatheses, the, of Ptolemy, 333.

Disciples, the true spiritual, 506, etc.

Discriminating faculty, the, in man, 522.

Disobedient, the, are the angels of the devil, 524.

Duodecad, the, of Valentinus, how said to be indicated in Scripture, 319.

Dyad, the, of Valentinus, 332.

Earthly things, types of heavenly, 486.

Ebionites, the, 351, 352; refutation of, who disparaged the writings of Paul, 439, etc.; strictures on, 527.

Ecclesia, the, of the Valentinians, 323; of Ptolemy, 333.

Egyptians, the Israelites commanded to spoil the goods of, an exposition and vindication, 502–504.

Elements, the twenty-four, of Marcus, 329, etc.

Elijah, 530.

Elisha, 545.

Elucidation, by the American editor, end of book iii., 460, 461.

Emanations, the, of Valentinus and others, an account of, 316–328, 332, 333, etc., 339, etc.; ridicule poured on, 332, 333.

Encratites, the, 353.

Enmity, the, put between Eve and the serpent, 457.

Ennoæ, 316, 333, etc., 353, 354.

Enoch, the translation of, 530.

Enthymesis, the, of Sophia or Achamoth, 318, 322; the absurdity of, 383, etc.; the treachery of Judas not a type of, 387, 388.

Error, how often set off, 315.

Eucharist, the, 485, 527, 528.

Evanthas, 559.

Eve and the Virgin Mary compared, 547, etc.

Eve, the story of, according to the Ophites, 356.

Faith, the unity of the, in the universal Church, 330.

Faith of Abraham, the, the same as ours, 332.

Father, the, the world made by, through the Word, 361.
the, how no one knows, but the Son, 467; reveals the Son, 468.

Fear produces (according to Valentinus) animal substances, 323.

Five, the number, the frequent use of, in Scripture, 394, 395.

Flesh, the, as nourished by the body of the Lord, incorruptible, 485; made capable of salvation, 527, 528; quickened, 537, etc.; saved by the Word taking flesh, 541; the saints having suffered in, shall receive their rewards in, 561, 562, etc.
and blood, 534, 535.
the works of the, 536, etc.

Florinus, 568.

Free-will, man endowed with, 518, 519.

Fruit of the belly and of the loins, 453.

Gentiles, the conversion of, more difficult than that of the Jews, 495.

Gideon, a type, 445, 571.

Gifts, the, of the Holy Spirit, 533.

Gnostics, the hypocrisy and pride of, 439.

God, but one, proved against Marcion and others, 359, 360; the world made by, 361, 362; created all things out of nothing, 369, 370; not to be sought after by means of syllables and letters, 396, etc.; many things, the knowledge of which must be left in His hands, 399, 400; alone knows all things, 400; all things made by, 405; different names of, in the Hebrew Scriptures, 412, 413; one, proclaimed by Christ and the apostles, 417; the Holy Ghost throughout the Old Testament mentions but one, 418; objection to the doctrine of one, deduced from 2 Cor. iv. 5, answered, 420; objection from Matt. vi. 24 answered, 421; proved to be one and the same the Creator, from the Gospel of Matthew, 422; from Mark and Luke, 423; from John, 426, 428, etc.; showed Himself to be merciful and mighty to save after the fall of man, 449, etc.; His providential rule over the world, 459; just to punish and good to save, 459; but one, who is the Father, 463; the unity of proved from Moses, the prophets and Christ, 463, 464; immutable and eternal, 465; the destruction of Jerusalem derogates nothing from His majesty, 465; but one announced by the law and the prophets, whom Christ confesses as His Father, 466, etc.; has placed man under law for man's own benefit, 478, etc.; needs

nothing from man, 482, 483; formed all things by the Word and Spirit, 487–489; declared by the Son, 489; seen by men, yet invisible, 490; not the author of sin, 502; the author of both testaments, 505; attributes of, 521; the misery of departure from, 523; one and the same, inflicts punishments and bestows rewards, 523, etc.; His power and glory will shine forth in the resurrection, 529, etc.; those deceived who feign another, 530, etc.; the image of, in which man was made, 544; unity of, re-affirmed, 544; pardons our sins, 544, 545, etc.; and the Word, formed all things by their own power, 546, etc.; declared by the law and manifested in Christ, 550, etc.; communion with, 556; His infinitude, 569; always true and faithful, 572.
God of this world, the, 420.
Gods, the so-called, in the Old Testament, 419.
Good works not necessary for Valentinian heretics, 324.
Gospels, the four, there can be neither more nor fewer, 428; symbolized by the four living creatures, 428; respective characteristics of, 428, 429; those who destroy the form of, vain and unlearned, 429.
Government, civil, of God, and to be obeyed, 552, etc.
Grain of mustard seed, the, 573.
Greater and less, application of the phrase, 472, 473.
Grief, evil spirits said by Valentinus to derive their origin from, 373.

Heaven, the, of Valentinus, 322.
Heavens, the new, different abodes in, 566, 567.
Helena and Simon Magus, 348.
Henotes, 332.
Heresies, of recent origin, 416, 417.
Heretics, the, resort to Scripture to support their opinions, 319, 343, 344; modes of initiation practised by, 346–349; deviation of, from the truth, 347, etc.; their perverse interpretations of Scripture, 369; have fallen into an abyss of error, 370, etc.; the first order of productions maintained by (viz., Æons), indefensible, 373, etc.; borrow their systems from the heathen, 376–379; miracles claimed to be wrought by, 407, etc.; blasphemous doctrines of, further exposed, 408, etc.; follow neither Scripture nor tradition, 415; refutation of, from the orderly succession of bishops in the churches, 415; tossed about by every wind of doctrine, 418, 419; unlearned, ignorant, and divided in opinion, 547; to be avoided, 547, etc.
Holy Spirit, the, descended on Jesus at His baptism, not Christ nor the Saviour, 444.
Holy Spirit, gifts of the, 533.
Homer, laid under contribution by the Valentinians, curious instances of, 330.
Hope, 399, 476.
Horos and Stauros, 318, 319.

Ialdabaoth, 355.
I AM THAT I AM, 419.
Iao, 321.
Ignorance, human, of divine things, 399–402.
Image of God, the, in which man was created, 544.
Immorality, the, of the Valentinian heretics, 324.
Initiation, modes of, practised by the heretics, 346.
Intermediate state, the, 560.
Isaac, the history of, symbolical, 492, 493; the blessing of, 562.
Isaiah, his prophecy respecting the virgin conceiving, vindicated against Theodotion, Aquila, and the Ebionites, 451, etc.

Jacob, the actions of, typical, 493.
Jerusalem, the destruction of, derogates nothing from the majesty of God, 465, etc.
Jesus, the significance of the letters of the name, 339–393.
how certain Æons are said to be indicated by the name of, 319; meaning of the letters of the name of, 339; the generation of, according to Marcus, 339, 340; according to Basilides, was not crucified, but Simon of Cyrene in His stead, 349; descent of the Christ upon, according to the Ophites, 357; His baptism when thirty years old, not a type of the thirty Æons, 390; passed through every stage of life, to sanctify all, 391; the ministry of, extended over ten years, 392; lived at least till near fifty years old, 392; His teaching, 408; the baptism of, 423; the same with Christ, the only-begotten Son of God, perfect God and perfect man, 440; with Him nothing incomplete — His time, 443; neither Christ nor Saviour, but the Holy Spirit descended upon Him at His baptism, 444, etc.; and Christ, proved from the writings of Paul to be one and the same, 445, etc.; not a mere man, but very God, 448; became man so as to be capable of being tempted and crucified, 449; His birth foretold by Isaiah, 452; His reply to the Sadducees, 466, 467. [See Christ.]
John, and Cerinthus, a curious story relating to, 416.
Joshua, 571.
Judas not an emblem of the twelfth Æon, 388.
Judgment, the future, by Jesus Christ, 523, 556, etc.
Justin quoted against Marcion, 468.

Keltæ, the, 316.
Kingdom, the, of Christ, eternal, 556. the earthly, of the saints after their resurrection, 563, 564; the prophecies respecting, not allegorical, 564, 565, etc.
Knee, bending the, a symbol of the resurrection, 569.
Knowledge, puffs up, 397; perfect, not attainable in this life, 399–402.
the true, 508, 574.

Lateinos, 559.
Law, the old and the new, has but one author, 472, etc.; Christ did not abrogate the natural precepts of, but removed the bondage of, 477, etc.; man was placed under, for his own benefit, 478; originally inscribed on the hearts of men, but afterwards, as the Mosaic, made by God to bridle the desires of the Jews, 479–480; perfect righteousness not obtained by, 480–482.
Letters and syllables, the absurd theories of Marcion respecting, 339–341; absurdity of arguments derived from, 393; God not to be sought after by means of, 396, etc.
Levitical dispensation, the, not appointed by God for His own sake, 482, etc.
Life and death, 537, etc.
Linus, bishop of Rome, 416.
Living creatures, the symbolic import of the four, 428.
Logos, the Æon so-called, and Sige, 372; absurdity of the Valentinian account of the generation of, 381, etc., 401.
Lord, the, is one God, the Father, 463; testimony of Moses to, 463, etc.
Lot and his daughters, the typical import of the story of, 504, 505; the wife of, turned into a pillar of salt, 504.
Luke, and Paul, 437; refutation of the Ebionites who tried to disparage the authority of Paul from the writings of, 439.

Magic, our Lord's miracles not performed by, 409.
Magical practices, the, of Marcus, 334.
Man, the first, according to the Ophites, 354.
God's mercy to, after the fall, 449; the object of God's long-suffering, 450; needs a greater than man to save, 450, 451; why not at first made perfect, 521, etc.; endowed with the faculty of distinguishing good and evil, 522; the whole nature of, has salvation conferred on it, 531, etc.; unfruitful, without the Holy Spirit, 536, etc.; all things created for the service of, 558; every, either empty or full, 572. the threefold kind, feigned by the heretics, 323; the respective des-

tinations of the threefold kind of, 325, 326.
Mansions, the many, 567.
Marcion, the doctrines of, 352; mutilates the Gospels, 352; vain attempt of, to exclude Abraham from Christ's salvation, 470, etc.
Marcionites, the, refuted, in relation to prophecy, 511, etc.
Marcosians, the, absurd interpretations of, 341, 342; absurd theories of, respecting things created, 342, 343; appeal of, to Moses, 343, 344; cite Scripture to prove that the Father was unknown before the coming of Christ, 344; the apocryphal Scriptures of, 344; pervert the Gospels, 345; views of, respecting redemption, 345-347; departure of, from the truth, 347.
Marcus, the deceitful arts and nefarious practices of, 334; pretends to confer the gift of prophecy, 334; corrupts women, 334; hypothesis of, respecting letters and syllables, 336-338; pretended revelations of Sige to, 339, 340.
Mary, would hasten on Jesus, but is checked by Him, 443; and Eve, compared, 547.
Matter, 573.
Men possessed of free-will, 518; not true that some are by nature good, and some bad, 519.
spiritual, 506, etc.; 533-536, etc.
the three kinds of, feigned by the heretics, 323, 324.
Menander, successor to Simon Magus, 348.
Mercy, not to be exaggerated at the expense of justice, 501.
Metropator, 322.
Miracles claimed to be performed by heretics, 407, 408; performed by Christ and His disciples, 409.
Moral faculty, the, in man, 522.
Monogenes, the, of Valentinus, 318; of Ptolemy, 333.
Monotes, 332.
Months, the, do not fall in with the Valentinian theories of Æons, 394.
Moses, 573; Aaron and Miriam sin against, 573.
Mother, the, of the Valentinian heresy, 386.

Naaman, cleansed of his leprosy, 574.
Names of God, different, in the Hebrew Scriptures, 413.
of our Lord, 393, 394.
New covenant, the, 512.
Nicolaitanes, the, 351.
Nous, or Monogenes, 317, 333, 355.
Number of the beast, the, 558, 559.
Numbers and letters, the folly of deriving arguments from, 393-396.

Oblation, the new, instituted by Christ, 535.
Oblations and sacrifices, 484, etc.

Ogdoad, the first, of Valentinus, 316, 322; John asserted to have set forth, 328.
Old Testament, the, everywhere mentions and predicts the advent of Christ, 473.
Olive, the wild, the symbolical significance of, 536, etc.
Ophites, the, 354.

Papias, quoted, 563.
Parables, 517, 518.
the proper mode of interpreting, 398.
Paschal solemnities, differences in the observance of, 568.
Passion of the twelfth Æon, how said to be indicated in Scripture, 323; not to be proved from Scripture, 387, 388.
Passions, animal, produce, according to Valentinus, material substances, 323.
Pastors, the, to whom the apostles committed the churches, to be heard, 547, etc.
Patriarchs and prophets foretold the advent of Christ, 494.
Paul, caught up into the third heavens, 405; and Peter, founders of the Church of Rome, 415; sometimes uses words not in their grammatical sequence, 420; knew no mysteries unrevealed to the other apostles, 437; refutation of the Ebionites who disparaged the writings of, 439, etc.
Perfect, why man was not made, 521.
Persecution foretold, 509.
Pharaoh's heart hardened, how, 502.
Plato, quoted, 459.
Pleroma, the, of Valentinus, 316, 320; shown to be absurd, 362, 379, 380.
Polycarp, conversed with the apostles, 416; his reply to Marcion, 416; the epistle of, 416; Irenæus' testimony respecting, 416.
Predictions of the prophets, the, 507, 508, etc.; all uttered under the same inspiration, 513.
Presbyters, the, ought to be obeyed, 497; false, 497; faithful, 497, 498.
Proarche, the, of Valentinus, 333.
Production, the first order of, maintained by heretics proved to be indefensible, 373, etc.; and absurd 379, 383.
Prophets, the, refutation of the notion that they uttered their predictions under the inspiration of different gods, 412, 413, 513; their predictions, 507, etc.; referred all their predictions to Christ, 509, etc.; sent by the same Father who sent the Son, 514, etc.
Propator, the, of Valentinus, 316; of Ptolemy, 333.
Protarchontes, 353.
Providence of God, the world ruled by, 459.
Prunicus, 354, 356.

Ptolemy the heresiarch, the doctrines of, 333, etc.
Ptolemy, the son of Lagus, procures a translation of the Jewish Scriptures to be made, 452.
Pythagoras, the heretics borrow from, 377.

Redemption, the views of, entertained by heretics, 345, etc.
Resurrection, the, of the dead, asserted by Jesus against the Sadducees, 466; of the flesh asserted, 529, etc.; of the body, 530, etc.; various proofs of, from the Old Testament, 530, etc.; proved by the resurrection of Christ, 532, etc., 539, etc.; proofs of, from Isaiah and Ezekiel, 542; an actual, 565, etc.; illustrated, 570.
Retribution, the day of, 390.
Ridicule, poured upon the emanations and nomenclature of Valentinus, 332, 333, etc.
Righteous, the, and the wicked, 553.
Righteousness, perfect, not conferred by the law, 480.
Rod, the, of Moses, 453.
Roman Empire, the dissolution of the, predicted, 534.
Rome, the Church of, founded and organized by Peter and Paul, 415; the first bishops of, 416.

Sabaoth, 412 and note.
Sabbath-day, the law did not prohibit the hungry eating food ready to hand on the, 471.
Sacrifices, not required by God for their own sake, 482, 483; further remarks on, 484.
Sadducees, the reply of Jesus to the question asked by the, 466, 467.
Samson, and the boy who guided him, types, 572; further reference to, 575.
Satan, 549; blasphemes God, 555.
Saturninus, the doctrines of, 348.
Saviour, the, asserted by the Valentinians to be derived from all the Æons, 321, 323; various opinions of, among the heretics, 333.
Scriptures, the, appealed to by the heretics, 319; how perverted by the heretics, 326, etc.; refutation of false interpretations of, 329, etc.; perverted by the Marcosians to support their absurdities, 343-345; perverse interpretations of the heretics, 369; proper method of interpreting the obscure passages of, 398, 399; translation of the Hebrew, into Greek, 451; interpreted with fidelity by the LXX. translators, 452.
Seed, Valentinian absurdities respecting, exposed, 385.
Seeing God, 489-492.
Separatists, to be shunned, 497.
Septuagint, the story of the origin of, 451.
Serpent, the, cursed, 456; speculations respecting, 570, 571.

Sethians, the doctrines of the, 354.
Shadrach, etc., in the fiery furnace, 531.
Sige, 316 and note, 317; pretended revelation made by, to Marcus, 339; and Logos, mutually contradictory and repugnant, 372.
Simeon and Jesus, 441.
Simon of Cyrene, curious opinion of Basilides respecting, 349.
Simon Magus, 347; the pretensions of, 347; honoured with a statue, 348; and Helena, 348; the priests of, 348; succeeded by Menander, 348.
Sin, God not the author of, refutation of the Marcionites, 502, etc. the pardon of, 544.
Sins of former times, recorded in Scripture for a warning to us, 498.
Son, meaning of the term, 524.
of God, the, not made man in appearance only, 447–448; everywhere set forth in the Old Testament, 473, etc.
the, reveals the Father, 468; revealed by the Father, 468.
Sons of the devil, 525.
Soul and body, views of the heretics relating to the future destruction of, refuted, 402, etc.
Souls, absurdity of the doctrine of the transmigration of, 409; existence of, after death, 410; immortal, although they had a beginning, 411.
Soter, 393.
Sophia, the Æon, so called, 317; her passion, 317; another name of Achamoth, 320, 353; could have produced nothing apart from her consort, 372; exposure of the absurdity of the whole Valentinian theory respecting, 383, etc.
Spirit, the Holy, gifts of the, 533.
Spiritual, the absurdity of heretics claiming to be, while they declare the Demiurge to be animal, 403.

Spiritual men, 506, 533; and animal, 536, etc.
Spoiling the Egyptians, the act examined and vindicated, 502.
Stauros and Horos, 318, 319.
Stesichorus, the story of, 348.
Stone, the, cut out without hands, 453.
Tatian, the doctrines of, 353; refuted in his denial of the salvation of Adam, 457.
Teaching, the, of Jesus, opposed to the opinions of heretics, 408.
Teitan, 559.
Temptation, the, of Christ, 549.
Testaments, the two, God the author of both, 505.
Tetrad, the first, 316; of Marcus reveals Aletheia, 337.
Thamar, her labour typical, 495.
Thelesis, 333.
Theodotion and Aquila, their interpretation of Isa. vii. 14 refuted, 451.
Translation, the, of Enoch and Elijah, 530.
Transmigration of souls, the, the absurdity of the doctrine of, 409, 410.
Treasure hid in a field, the, 496.
Triacontad, the, of the heretics, 371.
Truth, the, to be found in the Catholic Church, 426.
Types, earthly, of heavenly things, 486, 487, etc.
Unity, the, of the faith of the universal Church, 330.
of God, 418, etc., 544, 550.
Utter emptiness, the, of Valentinus, 332, 333.
Vacuum, the absurdity of the, of the heretics, 362.
Valentinian views of Jesus refuted from the apostolic writings, 440.
Valentinians, the, their immoral opinions and practices, 324; how they pervert Scripture to support their own opinions, 326,

etc.; refutation of their false interpretations of Scripture, 329, etc.; quote Homer to support their views, 330; the inconsistent and contradictory opinions of, 332, etc.
Valentinus, the absurd ideas held by, 316; his system derived from the heathen, with only a change of terms, 376–379; recapitulation of arguments against the views of, 406, etc.
Virgin, Jesus born of a, 446, 454, 455; prophecy of Isaiah relating to, 451, etc.
Virgin Mary, the, and Eve, a comparison between, 547.
Visions of God, 489, 490.
Will, the freedom of the, in man, 518, etc.
Wine, and water, the mixture of, 527; and bread, in the Eucharist, 528.
Woman, the, with the issue of blood, not a type of the suffering Æon, 392.
Word, the, the world made through, 362; reveals the Father, 467, 468; always with the Father, 487; all things created by, 487, 488; declares God, 489; takes flesh to save the flesh, 541; the image of God, 544; the creator, 546.
Works of the flesh, the, 536.
World, the, not made by angels, but by God through the Word, 361, 362; not formed by any other beings within the territory contained by the Father, 364, etc.; the Creator of, one, 369; ruled by the providence of God, 459; to be annihilated, 536.

Year, the divisions of, do not really suit the Valentinian theory of Æons, 395.
Year of the Lord, the acceptable, 391.

Zoe, 316.

IRENÆUS

INDEX OF TEXTS

	PAGE		PAGE		PAGE		PAGE
Gen. i. 1	343, 363	Gen. xxxiii. 3	562	Num. xiv. 30	502	2 Sam. v. 7	466
i. 2	343	xxxv. 22	344	xv. 32	471	xi. 27	498
i. 3	506	xxxviii. 28	496	xvi. 15, 33	497	xii. 1	498
i. 25	543	xl. 8	401	xviii. 1, 20	471	1 Kings iv. 34	499
i. 26	349, 355, 456, 463, 488	xlii. 3	344	xxi. 8	465	viii. 27	499
		xlix. 10–12	474	xxii. 12, 22, 23	572	x. 1	499
i. 28	474	xlix. 18	424	xxiii. 19	572	xi. 1	499
ii. 2	557	xlix. 28	344	xxiv. 17	423	xi. 31	344
ii. 5	454	Ex. i. 13, 14	503	xxiv. 23	571	xiv. 10	497
ii. 7	412, 487	iii. 4	473	xxvii. 18, 20, 23	571, 572	xviii. 21, 36	419
ii. 8	531	iii. 6	467			xviii. 27	333
ii. 16, 17	546, 551	iii. 7, 8	419, 476	xxxi. 3, 8, 13	572, 575	xix. 11, 12	490
ii. 25	455	iii. 14	419	Deut. iv. 14	482	2 Kings v. 14	574
iii. 1	551	iii. 19	502	iv. 19	420	vi. 6	545
iii. 2, 3, 4	551	vii. 1	420	iv. 24	490	xiii. 21	574
iii. 8, 9	544, 545	vii. 9	453	v. 2, 22	481	Ps. i. 2	534
iii. 13	456	viii. 19	453	v. 8	420	ii. 8	493
iii. 14	456	ix. 35	502	v. 24	489	iii. 5	510
iii. 15	548	xi. 2	502	vi. 4, 5, 13	464, 550	iii. 6	505
iii. 16	456	xiii. 2	319	vi. 16	549	viii. 1	338
iii. 19	544, 571	xvii. 11	506	viii. 3	481	viii. 3	475
iv. 7	456, 485	xvii. 16	442	x. 12, 16	549	ix. 12	447
iv. 10	541	xix. 6	471	xiv. 3, etc.	534	xiv. 3	344
vi. 2	484	xx. 5	354	xvi. 5, 6	473	xv. 8	430
vi. 15	344	xx. 12	473, 480	xvi. 16	484	xviii. 45	525
vi. 18	343	xxi. 6, 13	481, 482	xviii. 1	471	xix. 1	538
ix. 5, 6	541	xxiii. 7	497	xxi. 23	446	xix. 6	510
ix. 27	418	xxiv. 4	344	xxviii. 66	474	xxi. 4	411
xii. 3	492	xxv. 10, 17	394	xxix. 20	401	xxii. 7, 15, 18	490, 510
xiii. 13, 14, 15, 17	561	xxv. 23, 31, 32	394	xxx. 14	574	xxii. 31, LXX.	533
xiv. 22	467	xxv. 40	479, 566	xxx. 19, 20	482	xxiii. 4	560
xv. 5	422, 470	xxvi. 1, 2	343, 344, 394	xxxii. 1, 20	463	xxiv. 1	517
xv. 13	561			xxxii. 4	448	xxiv. 7	510
xv. 19	343	xxvi. 7, 8	344, 394	xxxii. 6	474, 505	xxv. 14	506
xvi. 2	343	xxvi. 16, 26	394	xxxii. 8, LXX.,	433	xxxii. 1, 2	545
xvii. 9–11	480	xxvi. 37	395	xxxii. 9	434	xxxiii. 6	347, 421
xvii. 12	343	xxvii. 1	395	xxxiii. 9	471	xxxiii. 9	362
xvii. 17	469	xxviii. 1, 5	395	Josh. iii. 12	344	xxxiv. 13, 14	484
xviii. 1	470	xxviii. 2	344	iv. 3	344	xxxiv. 16	501
xviii. 13	473	xxviii. 17	343	v. 12	572	xxxv. 9	475
xix. 22	467	xxx. 23	394	x. 17	395	xxxviii. 11	510
xix. 24	418	xxx. 34	394	Judg. vi. 27	571	xl. 6	482
xix. 31, 32, 33	135, 505	xxxii. 6	500	vi. 37	445	xlv. 2, 3, 4, 7	509, 523
		xxxiii. 2, 3	480	xiv. 6–19	575	xlv. 6	419
xxi. 11	473	xxxiii. 20	344, 490	xv. 11	575	xlv. 11	523
xxii. 6	467	xxxiii. 20–22	491	xv. 15	575	xlv. 17	455
xxiii. 11	561	xxxiv. 6, 7	490	xvi. 26	572	xlix. 12	466
xxiv. 22, 25	344	xxxvi. 2, 8, 21	344	1 Sam. ix. 22	344	xlix. 20	534
xxv. 23, 26	493	Lev. x. 1, 2	497	xii. 3	498	xlix. 21	525
xxvii. 27, 28, 29	562	xi. 2	534	xv. 22	482	l. 1, 3	419
xxxi. 2	340	xxvi. 12	572	xvi. 10	343	l. 3, 4	547
xxxi. 11	473	Num. xii. 1, 14	573	xviii.	498	l. 9	482
xxxi. 41	562	xii. 7	420	xx. 5	344	l. 14, 15	482

IRENÆUS: INDEX OF TEXTS.

	PAGE		PAGE		PAGE		PAGE
Ps. li. 12	444	Isa. vii. 10–17	452	Jer. ii. 13	458	Jonah ii. 2	450
li. 17	482	vii. 11	453	ii. 19	520	ii. 11	531
li. 19	483	vii. 13	449, 452	iv. 22	465	iii. 8, 9	449
lviii. 3	424	vii. 14	449, 451, 509	v. 3	534	Mic. iv. 2, 3	512
lviii. 3, 4	525	viii. 3, 4	442, 509	v. 8	525	vii. 9	451
lxviii. 18	388	viii. 14	446	vi. 17, 18	515	Hab. ii. 4	511
lxix. 21	510	ix. 1	571	vi. 20	483	iii. 2	443
lxix. 25	430	ix. 6	441, 449, 509	vii. 2, 3	483	iii. 3	509
lxix. 27	454	xi. 1	423	vii. 3	515	iii. 3, 5	451
lxxviii. 1	422, 423, 509	xi. 2	445	vii. 21	483	Zech. vii. 9, 10	483
lxxviii. 5	441	xi. 4, 12	506	vii. 25	517	viii. 16, 17	484, 515
lxxx. 1	428	xii. 2	424	vii. 29, 30	515	ix. 9	449, 506
lxxxi. 9	419	xii. 4	466	viii. 16	559	Zech. xii. 10	509
lxxxii. 1, 6	419	xiii. 9	565	ix. 2	496	Mal. i. 2	493
lxxxii. 6, 7	522	xxv. 3	450	ix. 24	483	i. 10, 11	484
lxxxv. 11	417	xxv. 8	537	x. 11	419	i. 11	574
lxxxvi. 23	560	xxv. 9	472	xi. 15	483	ii. 10	488
lxxxix. 11	549	xxvi. 10	565	xv. 9	510	iii. 1	427
xci. 13	457	xxvi. 19	510, 542, 563	xvii. 9	446, 449, 509	iv. 1	506
xcv. 4	425	xxvii. 6	466	xxii. 17	485	Ecclesiasticus iv. 31	497
xcvi. 1	472	xxviii. 16	453	xxii. 24, 25	453	Hist. of Susanna, 56	497
xcvi. 5	419	xxix. 13	476	xxii. 28, etc.	453	Wisdom ix. 13, 17	402
xcviii. 2	424	xxx. 1	485	xxiii. 6, 7	564	Matt. i. 1	440
xcix. 1	510	xxx. 25, 26	564	xxiii. 17	485	i. 1, 18	428
cii. 25–27	465	xxxi. 9	564	xxiii. 20	496	i. 12–16	453
civ. 2, 4	403	xxxii. 1	564	xxiii. 23	487	i. 18	440, 452
civ. 30	562	xxxiii. 20	451	xxiii. 29	545	i. 20	422
cix. 8	388, 430	xxxv. 3, 5, 6	510	xxxi. 10	564	i. 20, etc.	494
cx. 1	401, 418, 426, 441, 509	xl. 6	563	xxxi. 11	421	i. 23	422, 452
cxv. 3	422	xl. 12	487	xxxi. 26	505	ii. 2	423
cxvi. 2	518	xl. 12, 22	403	xxxi. 31	472	ii. 15	422
cxviii. 22	506	xl. 15	558	xxxi. 31, 32	510	ii. 16	442
cxxiv. 8	425, 463	xlii. 3	490	xxxv. 15	517	iii. 3	422
cxxx. 7	570	xlii. 5	538	xxxvi. 30, 31	454	iii. 7	422
cxxxi.	401	xlii. 10	472	Lam. iv. 20	424	iii. 9	470, 495, 523
cxxxii. 11	422, 440	xliii. 5	475	Ezek. i. 1	491	iii. 10	471, 516, 545, 573
cxlviii. 5	362	xliii. 10	472	ii. 1	491	iii. 11	466
cxlviii. 5, 6	411	xliii. 19, 21	511	xx. 12	480	iii. 12	506, 509
cxlix. 5	524	xliii. 23, 24	483	xx. 24	479	iii. 16	423
Prov. i. 7	457	xliv. 9	419	xxviii. 25, 26	563	iv. 3	469, 549
i. 20, 21	548	xlv. 5, 6	323, 354	xxxvi. 26	510	iv. 7	550
iii. 19, 20	488	xlv. 7	523	xxxvii. 1	542	iv. 9	552
v. 22	423	xlvi. 2	483	xxxvii. 12	543, 563	iv. 10	549
viii. 15	552	xlvi. 9	323, 367	Dan. ii. 33, 34	555	v. 5	454, 535
viii. 22–25	488	xlviii. 32	342	ii. 34	453	v. 8	472, 489
viii. 27–31	488	xlix. 16	566	ii. 41, 42, 43	555	v. 12	506, 509
ix. 10	457	l. 6, 8, 9	510	ii. 44, 45	555	v. 13	505
xix. 17	486	li. 6	465	iii. 19, 25	521	v. 13, 14	324
xxi. 1	552	lii. 7	436	iii. 26	491	v. 14	470
xxii. 3	459	liii. 2	391, 449	vii. 4	491	v. 16	316, 519
xxvii. 12	459	liii. 3, 4	506, 510	vii. 8, 23	553, 554	v. 17, 18	511
Canticles (Song of Solomon) i. 15	358	liii. 7	494, 506	vii. 10	367	v. 18	319
		liii. 7, 8	433	vii. 13	449, 506, 509	v. 20	477
Isa. i. 2	525	liii. 8	400, 449	vii. 13, 14	491	v. 21	408, 477
i. 3	344	liv. 1	323	vii. 27	564	v. 22	482, 516
i. 8	466	liv. 11–14	564	viii. 12, 23	554	v. 23, 24	484
i. 10, 16	525	lvii. 1	512	ix. 27	554	v. 25, 26	351
i. 11	483	lvii. 16	538	xii. 3	497	v. 27, 28	477
i. 14	575	lviii. 6	483	xii. 4, 7	496	v. 28	482
i. 17–19	515	lviii. 8	374	xii. 9, 10	344	v. 33	477
i. 22	475	lviii. 14	564	xii. 13	564	v. 34	464
i. 23	464	lix. 17	498	Hos. i. 2, 3	492	v. 35	465, 516
ii. 3, 4	512	lxi. 1	423, 444, 446	i. 6–9	492	v. 39	447, 512
ii. 17	510	lxi. 2	390	ii. 23	331	v. 41	477
iv. 4	493	lxiii. 9	451	iv. 1	344	v. 44	477
iv. 8	374	lxiv. 4	564	vi. 6	484	v. 45	369, 390, 459, 477, 517, 528, 556
v. 6	445	lxv. 1	419, 423	ix. 10	578		
v. 12	390	lxv. 2	510	xii. 10	435, 489	vi. 3	504
v. 20	351	lxv. 17, 18	565, 566	Joel ii. 28	430	vi. 9	369
vi. 1	509	lxv. 22	543	iii. 16	451, 509	vi. 12	544
vi. 5	490	lxvi. 1	464	Amos i. 2	451	vi. 19	481
vi. 10	502	lxvi. 3	485	v. 25, 26	480	vi. 24	421
vi. 11	564, 565	lxvi. 13	542	viii. 9, 10	510	vii. 1, 2	504
vii. 4	450	lxvi. 22	567	ix. 11, 12	435	vii. 5	503
		Jer. i. 5	543	Jonah i. 9	450		

	PAGE		PAGE		PAGE		PAGE
Matt. vii. 7	376, 384, 403	Matt. xviii. 12	348	Mark xvi. 17, 18	388	Luke xii. 35, 36	519
vii. 15	315	xix. 7, 8	480	xvi. 19	426	xii. 37, 38	564
vii. 19	536	xix. 17, 18	476	Luke i. 2	438, 362	xii. 45, 46	497, 515, 519
vii. 25	399	xix. 21	477	i. 6, 8	423	xii. 47	519
viii. 9	326	xix. 29	562	i. 15	423	xii. 50	345
viii. 11	470	xix. 30	455	i. 17	426, 427	xii. 58	358
viii. 11, 12	518	xx. 1	518	i. 26	424	xiii.	438, 439
viii. 13	520	xx. 1–16	317	i. 32	432, 441	xiii. 6	518
ix. 2	545	xx. 16	455, 480, 500	i. 33	423	xiii. 15, 16	471
ix. 6	545	xx. 20	577	i. 35	452, 527	xiii. 16	393
ix. 8	545	xxi. 8	475	i. 38	455	xiii. 28	471
ix. 17	511	xxi. 13	464	i. 42	453	xiii. 32	525
ix. 29	520	xxi. 16	475	i. 46	470	xiii. 34	518
x. 6	437, 465	xxi. 23	345	i. 68	424	xiv. 12, 13	562
x. 8	321, 409	xxi. 31	492	i. 69	442	xiv. 14	564
x. 10	471	xxi. 33–41	514	i. 71, 75	488	xiv. 27	320
x. 15	501	xxi. 42–44	514	i. 76	424	xv. 4	341
x. 17, 18	447	xxii. 1, etc.	516	i. 78	424, 545	xv. 4, 8	327
x. 20	444	xxii. 3	523	ii. 8	470	xv. 8	341
x. 21	320	xxii. 7	517	ii. 11	425	xv. 11	517
x. 24	401	xxii. 10, 11	578	ii. 20	425	xv. 22, 23	479
x. 25	556	xxii. 13, 14	517	ii. 22	425	xvi.	438
x. 26	316	xxii. 21	421	ii. 23	319	xvi. 9	504
x. 28	447	xxii. 29	466, 507	ii. 28	328	xvi. 11	412
x. 29	397, 551	xxii. 43	453, 507	ii. 29	425, 441, 470	xvi. 16	466
x. 30	397	xxiii. 2–4	476	ii. 36	328	xvi. 19	411, 464
x. 34	320	xxiii. 9	463	ii. 38	425	xvi. 28	395
xi. 9	423	xxiii. 24	447	ii. 42	319	xvi. 31	464
xi. 11	427	xxiii. 26	485	ii. 49	345	xvii.	439
xi. 12	520	xxiii. 27, 28	485	iii. 8	561	xvii. 5	438
xi. 19	505	xxiii. 33	525	iii. 11	504	xvii. 26	515
xi. 23, 24	516	xxiii. 34	472	iii. 17	320	xvii. 34	556
xi. 25	464	xxiii. 35	541	iii. 23	317, 391	xviii.	439
xi. 25–27	345	xxiii. 37	518, 520	iv. 3	469	xviii. 2	554
xi. 27	365, 469	xxiv. 15, 21	553, 554	iv. 6	551, 552	xviii. 7, 8	500
xi. 28	345	xxiv. 21	510	iv. 6, 7	549, 551, 553	xviii. 10	518
xi. 40	560	xxiv. 28	479	iv. 18	492	xviii. 18	345
xii. 5	564	xxiv. 42	515, 536	v.	434	xviii. 27	370, 489, 531
xii. 6	472	xxiv. 45, 46	498	v. 20	548		
xii. 7	484	xxiv. 48, 51	497, 519	v. 31, 32	415	xviii. 29, 30	562
xii. 18	428	xxv. 2	395	v. 36, 37	518	xix.	438
xii. 25	555	xxv. 5	398	vi. 3, 4	473	xix. 5	327
xii. 29	421, 448, 456, 550	xxv. 13	536	vi. 13	311	xix. 8	477
		xxv. 14	445	vi. 24	439	xix. 26	324
xii. 31	429	xxv. 21	474	vi. 29–31	477, 508	xix. 42	345
xii. 36	385, 482	xxv. 32, 34	524	vi. 40	560	xxi. 4	485
xii. 41	507	xxv. 34	486, 501	vi. 46	519, 534	xxi. 34	519
xii. 41, 42	453	xxv. 35, 36	504	vii.	438	xxi. 34, 35	515, 519
xii. 43	342	xxv. 41	367, 408, 500, 525	vii. 8	326	xxiii. 34	447
xiii. 11–16	502			vii. 12	539	xxiv.	439
xiii. 17	474, 494	xxvi. 24	389, 501	vii. 26	427	xxiv. 25	442
xiii. 25	536	xxvi. 26	484	vii. 35	328	xxiv. 39	528
xiii. 28	524	xxvi. 27	562	vii. 43	450	xxiv. 44	442
xiii. 30	556	xxvi. 35	566	viii. 41	327	John i. 1	428, 546
xiii. 34	524	xxvi. 38, 39	327, 454	viii. 51	395	i. 1, 2, 3, 4	328
xiii. 38	496, 524, 562	xxvi. 41	535	ix. 13, 14	395	i. 3	347, 362, 421, 454, 506
xiii. 40–43	524	xxvii. 46	327	ix. 22	442		
xiii. 43	408	xxvii. 52	573	ix. 57, 58	327	i. 5	328
xiii. 44	496	xxviii. 19	444	ix. 60	327	i. 6	427
xiii. 52	472, 497	Mark i. 1	441	ix. 61, 62	327	i. 10, 11	426, 546
xiv. 19, 21	395	i. 2	425	x. 1	389	i. 13	441, 449, 527
xv. 3	473	i. 24	469	x. 12	516, 556	i. 13, 14	441
xv. 3, 4	473	iii. 27	550	x. 13	553	i. 14	328, 424, 426, 508, 546
xvi. 6	449	iv. 28	486	x. 16	414		
xvi. 13	446	v. 22	539	x. 18	445	i. 15, 16	424
xvi. 16	449	v. 31	319	x. 19	388, 457, 553	i. 18	427, 489, 491
xvi. 17	437, 453, 571	vi. 41, 44	395	x. 21	464	i. 29	424
xvi. 21, 24, 25	447	viii. 31	482	x. 22	469, 470	i. 47	427
xvii. 1, etc.	395	ix. 2	338	x. 35	445	i. 49	428
xvii. 3, etc.	490	ix. 23	520	x. 60	535	i. 50	472
xvii. 7	338	x. 17	345	xi.	438	ii. 3	427
xvii. 27	552	x. 38	345	xi. 21, 22	507	ii. 4	443
xviii. 8, 9	500	xiii. 32	401	xi. 40	401	ii. 19–21	532
xviii. 10	336	xiii. 33	536	xi. 50	541	ii. 23	390
		xiv. 21	389	xii. 20	438	ii. 25	423

	PAGE		PAGE		PAGE		PAGE
John iii. 5	574	Acts ii. 41	495	Rom. viii. 21	567	1 Cor. xiii. 9	401, 402
iii. 14	465	ii. 44, 45	485	viii. 34	444	xiii. 9, 10	472
iii. 18–21	556	iii. 6	430	viii. 36	390, 481	xiii.	508
iv. 6	454	iii. 12	431	ix. 5	441	xiii. 13	399, 476
iv. 14	516, 576	iii. 15	391	ix. 10–13	493	xiv. 16	336
iv. 24	574	iv. 2. 8	431	ix. 13	493	xiv. 20	502
iv. 35	494	iv. 4	495	ix. 25	331, 422	xv. 3, 4	446
iv. 37	496	iv. 22, 24	431	ix. 25, 26	492	xv. 8	327
iv. 41	465	iv. 31, 33	431	x. 3, 4	476	xv. 10	495
iv. 50	391	v. 30	432	x. 6, 7	446	xv. 11	437
v. 1	391	v. 42	432	x. 8	574	xv. 12	446
v. 5	393	vii. 2–8	434	x. 9	446	xv. 13	541
v. 14	516, 543	vii. 5, 6	561	x. 15	436	xv. 20–22	455
v. 28	539	vii. 38	480	xi. 16	327	xv. 22	458, 527
v. 35	575	vii. 56	435	xi. 17	536	xv. 25, 26	567
v. 30–39	468	xiii. 9–11	347	xi. 21, 17	499	xv. 26	457
v. 39, 40, 46	473	viii. 9, 18	409	xi. 26	465	xv. 27, 28	567
v. 43	554	viii. 20, 21, 23	347	xi. 32	331, 450	xv. 36	533
v. 46, 47	464	viii. 27	494	xi. 33	331	xv. 41	381
vi. 1	391	viii. 32, 37	433	xi. 34	526	xv. 42	533
vi. 4	391	ix. 15, 16	439	xi. 36	320	xv. 43	533
vi. 9, 10, 11	395	ix. 20	433	xii. 1	574	xv. 44	387, 533
vi. 11	427	x. 1–5	432	xii. 3	548	xv. 45, 46	538
vi. 69	428	x. 15	432	xii. 16	550	xv. 48	327, 535
vii. 30	443	x. 28, 29	436	xiii. 1	552	xv. 49	535, 537
vii. 39	546	x. 34, 35	432	xiii. 1–7	517	xv. 50	357, 534, 536
viii. 34	421	x. 37–44	432	xiii. 4	552	xv. 52	539
viii. 36	448	x. 47	436	xiii. 6	552	xv. 53	528, 536, 540
viii. 44	551, 552	xiv. 15–17	434	xiii. 10	476		541
viii. 56	467	xv. 14	436, 492	xiv. 9	446	xv. 54	331
viii. 56, 57	392	xv. 15	435	xiv. 15	446	xv. 54, 55	457
viii. 58	478, 576	xvi. 8, 13	437	1 Cor. i. 18	320	2 Cor. ii. 15, 16	502
viii. 59	576	xvii. 24	433	i. 23	446	ii. 17	498
ix. 1	382	xx. 5, 6	437	i. 26–28	387	iii. 3	540
ix. 3	543	xx. 25	438	i. 29	450	iv. 4	420, 502, 575
ix. 7	543	xxi.	437	ii. 6	328, 415, 531	iv. 10	540
ix. 30	539	xxii. 8	439	ii. 9	567	iv. 11	541
xi. 25	467	xxvi. 15	439	ii. 10	401	v. 4	517, 533, 540
xi. 54	391	xxvii.	437	ii. 14	327, 534, 574	vii. 2	498
xii. 1	391	xxviii. 11	437	ii. 15	327, 506, 511	viii. 1	508
xii. 27	327	Rom. i. 1–4	441	iii. 1	534	x. 5	517
xii. 32	465	i. 3, 4	454	iii. 2	521	xii. 2, 3, 4	405, 531
xiii. 2	391	i. 17	511	iii. 3	521	xii. 4	531
xiii. 5	493	i. 18	500	iii. 7	496	xii. 7–9	528
xiv. 2	449, 567	i. 21	506	iii. 16	532	xii. 9	449
xiv. 6	417	i. 25	369	iii. 16, 17	575	xiii. 4	576
xiv. 6, 7	470	i. 28	502	iii. 17	471, 532	Gal. i. 1	437
xiv. 7, 9, 10	437	ii. 4, 5, 7	519	iv. 4	472	i. 15, 16	538, 543
xiv. 11	546	ii. 5	511	v. 6, 11	500	ii. 1, 2	437
xiv. 16	429	ii. 27	477	vi. 9, 10	500	ii. 5	437
xiv. 28	402	iii. 8	351	vi. 9–11	537	ii. 8	436
xv. 9	450	iii. 11	344	vi. 11	519	ii. 12, 13	436
xv. 15, 16	478	iii. 21	511	vi. 12	519	iii. 5–9	492
xvi. 7	444	iii. 23	499	vi. 13	532	iii. 6	561
xvii. 3	463	iii. 30	494, 550	vi. 20	540	iii. 13	446
xvii. 5, 24	478	iv. 3	467	vii. 5, 6	480	iii. 16	561
xvii. 12	389	iv. 3, 12	470	vii. 12	480	iii. 19	420, 465
xvii. 16	325	v. 14	448, 455	vii. 14	492	iii. 24	465
xix. 11	485	v. 17	443	vii. 25	480	iv. 4, 5	441, 443, 454, 549
xix. 15	493	v. 19	448, 454	vii. 31	465, 566	iv. 8	369
xix. 34, 35	507	v. 20	458	viii. 1	397	iv. 8, 9	420
xx. 17, 20, 27	560	vi. 3, 4	444	viii. 4, etc.	420	iv. 26	566
xx. 20, 26	576	vi. 7	457	viii. 11	446	iv. 27	331
xx. 22	576	vi. 9	444	ix. 24, 27	520	iv. 28	470, 561
xx. 24	344	vi. 12, 13	542	x. 1, etc.	500	v. 19, 22	537
xx. 25–27	532	vii. 18	450, 518	x. 4	576	v. 21	324
xx. 26	576	vii. 24	450	x. 5	517	vi. 14	320
xx. 31	442	viii. 3	450	x. 11	479	Eph. i. 7	542
Acts i. 3	319	viii. 8	536	x. 16	446, 528	i. 10	320, 330, 443, 548
i. 7	455	viii. 9	533, 536	xi. 4, 5	429	i. 13	533
i. 16	429	viii. 10	536	xi. 10	327	i. 21	487, 495
i. 20	388	viii. 11	444, 532	xi. 19	310	ii. 2	553
ii. 22–27	430	viii. 13	536	xii. 4, 5, 6	401	ii. 7	466
ii. 30–37	430	viii. 15	419, 472, 533	xii. 28	427, 498	ii. 13, 15	446, 542
ii. 37, 38	430	viii. 19	561	xiii. 2	476		

	PAGE		PAGE		PAGE		PAGE
Eph. ii. 17	418	Phil. ii. 10, 11	330	Tit. i. 15	504	Rev. i. 12	491
ii. 20	496	ii. 15	417, 467	iii. 10	341, 416	i. 15	479
iii. 21	319	iii. 6	417	Heb. i. 3	406	i. 17	491
iv. 5, 6	506	iii. 10	574	iii. 5	420	ii. 5	465
iv. 6	362, 488	iii. 11	540	v. 7–9	482	ii. 6	352
iv. 8	388	iii. 29	540	x. 9	482	ii. 17	536
iv. 9	494, 560	iv. 17	471	xi. 13	561	iii. 7	488
iv. 9, 10	576	iv. 18	485	xiii. 15	574	iv. 7	428
iv. 25, 29	519	1 Thess. ii. 10–12	532	Jas. i. 18	527	v. 6	491
v. 6, 7	500	v. 3	559	i. 21	536	v. 8	484, 574
v. 13	328	v. 23	386	ii. 23	478, 481	vi. 2	493
v. 30	528	2 Thess. i. 6–10	501	1 Pet. i. 8	472, 533	vii. 5–7	559
v. 32	328	i. 9, 10	509	i. 12	382, 511, 567	xi. 19	486
vi. 12	330	ii. 4	420	ii. 3	574	xii. 14	407
Col. i. 14	528	ii. 8	420, 554	ii. 5–9	471	xiii. 2	557
i. 14, 15	441	ii. 11	502	ii. 16	482, 519	xiii. 11, 14	557
i. 16	321	1 Tim. i. 4	315, 574	ii. 23	444, 488	xv., xvi.	504
i. 18	391, 488	i. 9	481	ii. 24	572	xvii. 8	560
i. 21	541	ii. 5	544	iii. 19, 20	499	xvii. 12	554
ii. 9	320	iii. 15	414	iii. 20	343	xix. 11–17	492
ii. 11	481	iv. 2	390	iv. 14	509	xix. 20	557
ii. 14	545, 574	iv. 3	348, 359	2 Pet. iii. 8	550, 556	xx. 2	457
ii. 16	575	vi. 4	434	1 John ii. 1	445	xx. 6	564
ii. 18	574	vi. 4, 5	574	ii. 18	442, 462	xx. 11, 15	566
ii. 19	506, 542	vi. 20	348, 378	iv. 1, 2	443	xx. 12–14	566
iii. 5	538	2 Tim. ii. 17, 18	407	v. 1	443	xx. 15	566
iii. 9	538	ii. 23	462	v. 6	507	xxi. 1–4	566
iii. 10	538	ii. 24–26	310	2 John 7, 8	443	xxi. 2	566
iii. 11	320	iii. 6	336	10, 11	342	xxi. 5, 6	566
iv. 14	438	iii. 7	473, 548	Jude 3	574	xxii. 17	417
Phil. i. 22	538	iv. 3	389	7	516	xxii. 19	559
ii. 8	433, 495, 544	iv. 10, 11	438	Rev. i. 5	455		

www.ingramcontent.com/pod-product-compliance
Lightning Source LLC
Chambersburg PA
CBHW081828170426
43199CB00017B/2674